Dictionary
of Americanisms,
Briticisms, Canadianisms
and Australianisms

The Dictionary of Americanisms, Canadianisms, Briticisms and Australianisms is a complete, modern, and comprehensive dictionary featuring a large word list of more than 20000 entries. The purpose of this dictionary is to provide a generous sampling of words and expressions characteristic of the various spheres of life in the USA, Great Britain, Australia and Canada during the last centuries. The dictionary also features a collection of slang and colloquial expressions in frequent use in these four countries in the twentieth century.

It has a clear, easy-to-use format and is ideal for students, schools, libraries, tourists and for anyone who is interested in the varieties of English spoken in major English-speaking countries.

Dictionary of Americanisms, Briticisms, Canadianisms and Australianisms

An exhaustive selection of words and phrases specific to American, British, Canadian and Australian speech and writing. A valuable tool for teachers, students and readers of English language.

V.S. Matyushenkov

Copyright © 2010 by V.S. Matyushenkov.

ISBN: Softcover   978-1-4500-3245-2
           Ebook   978-1-4500-3246-9

All rights reserved. No part of this book may be reproduced or transmitted in any form or by any means, electronic or mechanical, including photocopying, recording, or by any information storage and retrieval system, without permission in writing from the copyright owner.

This book was printed in the United States of America.

To order additional copies of this book, contact:
Xlibris Corporation
1-888-795-4274
www.Xlibris.com
Orders@Xlibris.com
75478

To my wife Ludmilla and daughter Olga without whom this book wouldn't be possible
V.S. Matyushenkov.

Bibliography

Advanced Learner's Dictionary of Current English. Hornby A.S., Gatenby E.V., Wakefield H. London, Oxford University Press, 1988.
American-British Dictionary and Helpful Hints to Travellers. De Funiak W.Q. 3rd edition, San Francisco, Orbit graphic arts, 1967.
The American Heritage Dictionary. Second College edition, Boston, Houghton Mifflin, 1985.
American Slang. ed. by Chapman R.L., Harper and Row, 1987.
The American Language. Mencken H.L. 4th edition, A.A. Knopf. N.Y. 1938.
A British / American Dictionary Moss N., Harper and Row, 1973.
British English, A to Z. Schur N.W., Oxford. Facts on file, 1987.
Business Colloquialese. B. Hoshovskaya., Wiedza Powszechna, 1976.
Cambridge International Dictionary of English. Cambridge University Press. 1998.
Cambridge International Dictionary of Idioms. Cambridge University Press. 1988.
21st Century Dictionary of Slang. ed. by The Princeton Language Institute. K. Watts, compiler. Laurel Book. 1994.
Collins Cobuild English Dictionary. Harper Collins Publishers. London. 1998.
Collind Cobuild Dictionary of Idioms. Harper Collins. 1998.
A Concise Dictionary of Canadianisms. ed. by Avis W.S., Crate C., et al. Toronto, Gage, 1972.
A Concise Dictionary of English Slang. Phythian B.A., London, Hodder and Stoughton, 1984.
Dictionary of American Idioms. 2nd edition ed. by Makkai A. based on earlier edition by Boatner M.T., Gates J.E., and Makkai A., Barron's, 1987.
A Dictionary of American Slang. Wentworth H. and Flexner S.B., N.Y., 1960.
A Dictionary of American Slang and Colloquial Expressions. Spears R.A., Lincolnwood, Illinois, USA, 1991.
A Dictionary of Historical Slang. Partridge E., Penguin, 1972.
A Dictionary of Modern American and British English on a Contrastive Basis. Zvidadze G.D., Tbilisi State University publishers, 1973.
An A to Z of British Life. Dictionary of Britain. Adrian Room. Oxford University Press. 1995.
Dictionary of Afro-American Slang. C. Major. International Publishers. NY. 1971
Dictionary of Banking and Finance. Peter Collin Publishing.1977.
Dictionary of Law. Peter Collin Publishing. 1977.
Dictionary of Modern Slang. Thorne T., Bloomsbury, 1990.
English Idioms. Sayings and Slang. Magnuson W., Prairie House Books, Calgary, 1995.
Glossary and Handbook of Canadian-British Words. Davies D.L., Vancouver, Pauline's books, 1967.
Handbook of American Idioms and Idiomatic Usage. Whiteford H.C. and Dixon R.J., N.Y., Regents, 1973.
How to Talk American. Jim Crotty. Houghton Mifflin. 1997.
Listening to America. Flexner S.B., N.Y., Simon and Schuster, 1982.
Longman Dictionary of Contemporary English V1-2. 2nd edition, Longman, 1987.
Longman Dictionary of Contemporary English. New Edition. Longman, 1995.
Longman Dictionary of Idioms. Longman. 1998.
Longman Dictionary of Phrasal Verbs. Courtney R., Longman, 1983.
Longman Register of New Words. Ayto J., Longman, 1989.
Macquarie Book of Slang. Australian slang in the '90s., Macquarie Library Pty Ltd., 1996.
The New Oxford Dictionary of English. Oxford University Press, 1999.
Oxford-American Dictionary. Ehrlich E., Flexner S.B. et al., Oxford University Press, 1980.
Oxford Dictionary of Modern Slang. John Ayto, John Simpson. Oxford University Press. 1996.
The Oxford Dictionary of New Words. Ed. by E. Knowles with J. Elliott. Oxford university Press, 1998.
Oxford-Duden Pictorial English. Oxford University Press, 1982.
The Shorter Oxford English Dictionary on Historical Principles. 3rd ed. rev. with addenda., Oxford, 1994.
The Slang Thesaurus. Green J. Penguin. 1988.
Webster's Seventh Collegiate Dictionary. Springfield., Mass., Merriam, 1972.
Webster's Third New International Dictionary of the English language. Springfield, Mass., Merriam-Webster, 1981.
The World Book Dictionary ed. by Barnhart C.L. and Barnhart R.K. V1-2., Chicago, World Book, 1984.

Abbreviations

abbr.	abbreviation.
adj.	adjective.
adv.	adverb.
Am.	Americanism.
Aus.	Australianism.
bl.	black use
Br.	Briticism.
Can.	Canadianism.
col.	colloquial.
comb.	combination.
derog.	derogatory.
dial.	dialectism.
esp.	especially.
euph.	euphemism.
excl.	exclamation.
fml.	formal.
humor.	humorous.
impers.	impersonal
Ir. Eng.	Irish English.
joc.	jocular use.
law	legal term.
mil.	military.
n.	noun.
nonst.	non-standard.
NZ.	New Zealand English.
obs.	obsolete.
opp.	opposite.
pass.	passive.
phr.	phrase.
pomp.	pompous.
print.	printing term.
radio.	radio use.
rare.	passing out of use.
sb.	somebody.
sl.	slang.
smth.	something.
taboo.	very offensive word.
tdmk.	trademark.
tech.	technical term.
usu.	usually.
v.	verb.

The books, newspapers and magazines cited in the dictionary

K. Ablow	Projection. St. Martin's Paperbacks. 1999.
E. Acosta	The Healing. Ma Cuny Copy center. Baltimore, 1990,
Alcoholics Anonymous	AA World Services, Inc. NY City 1976.
J. Aldridge	One Last Glimpse. Penguin books.
Anonymous	The Pretty Women of Paris. Wordsworth Classics, 1996
J. Austen	Pride and Prejudice. Penguin books. 1996.
D. Bann	The Print Production Handbook. Little, Brown and Company. 1994.
J. Baez	And a Voice to Sing With. N.Y. Summit books, 1987.
B.R. Barber	Jihad vs McWorld. Ballintine books, N.Y., 1996.
D.L. Barlett and J.B. Steele	America: What Went Wrong? Andrews and McMeal. 1992.
R.N. Bellah and others	The Good Society. Vintage books, 1992.
S. Bellow	Herzog. Penguin, 1981.
P.L. Berger and others	The Homeless Mind. Pelican books, 1974.
K. Blair	No Other Haven. Toronto, Harlequin books, 1975.
A. Bloom	The Closing of the American Mind. Simon and Schuster, 1987.
R. Borchgrave, R. Moss	The Spike. Avon books, 1980.
A. De Botton	Essays in Love. Picador, 1994.
R. Bradbury	Dandelion Wine. Bantam, 1946.
R. Brautigan	Trout Fishing in America. Vintage, 1997.
D. Brenner	Soft Pretzels with Mustard. N.Y. A Berkely book, 1984.
V.W. Brooks	The Writer in America. An Avon book. 1964.
B. Bryson	Notes from a Small Island. Black Swan. 1997.
A. Buchwald	USA. Inside View. Moscow, Voenizdat, 1971.
A. Burgess	A Clockwork Orange. Penguin, 1984.
A. Burgess	Honey for the Bears. Ballantine, 1965.
L. Burkett	Investing for the Future. Victor books, 1992.
E. Caldwell	Georgia Boy. A Sygnet book. 1957.
E. Caldwell	God's Little Acre. Sygnet book. 1983.
E. Caldwell	Tobacco Road. Sygnet book. 1932.
T. Caldwell	Testimony of Two Men. Fawcett Crest, 1968.
T. Capote	The Grass Harp. Breakfast at Tiffany's. Moscow. Progress, 1974.
D. Carnegie	How to Stop Worrying and Start Living. Pocket books, 1985.
I. Carr, D. Fairweather, B. Priestley	Jazz. The Rough Guide. Rough Guide. London. 2000.
J.D. Carr	The Witch of the Low Tide. Bantam, 1968.
P. Case, J. Migliore	Total Recall. PaperJacks Ltd., 1987.
R. Chandler	Farewell, My Lovely. Short Stories. Moscow. Raduga, 1983.
J. Cheever	Falconer. Penguin, 1977.
K. Chopin	At Fault. Penguin, 2002.
A. Christie	Cards on the Table, Berkely book, 1984.
A. Christie	Third Girl. Pocket books, 1976
A. Christie	13 for Luck. Dell.
E. Cleaver	Post-prison Writings+Speeches. Ramparts book, 1967.
E. Cleaver	Soul on Ice. Ramparts, 1971.
J. Conrad	Heart of Darkness. Secret sharer. NAL, 1980.
R. Cook	Coma. NAL, 1978.
R. Cox	The Botticelli Madonna. N.Y. Ballantine, 1979.
R. Crais	Free Fall. Bantam Books. 1993.
C.R. Cross	Room Full of Mirrors. Hyperion, 2005

M. Daly	My Favorite Mystery Stories. Bantam Books, 1968.
K. Davis	Labrador. An Anchor Book. N.Y. 1988.
J. DeFelice	Coyote Bird. St.Martin's, 1993.
D. Divoky	How Old Will You Be in 1984? Disco / Avon, 1974.
J.P. Donleavy	The Onion Eaters. Penguin, 1977.
E.L. Doctorow	Ragtime. Pan, 1977.
F. Edwards	Flying Saucers – Serious Business. Bantam, 1966.
H. Fast	The Dinner Party. Hodder and Stoughton, 1987.
H. Fast	The Legacy. Dell, 1981.
H. Fast	The Immigrants. Dell. 1979.
J. Fischer	Why They Behave Like Russians. Harper and brothers, 1947.
F.S. Fitzgerald	Pat Hobby Stories. Penguin, 1979.
I. Fleming	From Russia with Love. Pan, 1973.
E.M. Forster	A Passage to India. Penguin, 1984.
J. Fowles	Daniel Martin. NEL, 1977.
D. Francis	For Kicks. Pan, 1965.
C.M. Fraser	Blue Above the Chimneys. Fontana/Collins, 1985.
J. Fraser	The Chinese. Fontana, 1982.
A. Frommer	Guide to New York. Frommer/Pasmantur, 1977.
J.W. Fullbright	The Arrogance of Power. N.Y. Random House, 1966.
J. Gabree	The World of Rock. Fawcett, 1968.
J. Galswarthy	The Man of Property. Interlude. Progress, 1964.
W. Grady	The Penguin Book of Canadian Short Stories ed. by W. Grady. Penguin, 1984.
S. Grafton	"I" is for Innocent. Fawcett Crest. 1993.
G. Greene	A Burnt-out Case. Penguin. 1977.
G. Greene	Doctor Fisher of Geneva or the Bomb Party. Penguin. 1981.
G. Greene	Journey Without Maps. Penguin. 1981.
G. Greene	Loser Takes All. Penguin. 1980.
G. Greene	The Heart of the Matter. Penguin. 1975.
G. Greene	The Man Within. Penguin. 1981.
G. Greene	The Ministry of Fear. Penguin. 1982.
G. Greene	The Power and the Glory. Penguin. 1971.
Alex Haley, Malcolm X.	The Autobiography of Malcolm X. N.Y.Grove press, inc. 1966.
Arthur Hailey	Hotel. A Bantam book. 1965.
C. Handy	The Age of Reason. Century Business. 1993.
D. Hammet	Selected Detective Prose. Moscow. Raduga. 1985.
J. O'Hara	Elizabeth Appleton. Bantam. 1963.
J. O'Hara	Great Short Storiesof John O'Hara. Bantam books. 1965.
J. O'Hara	Ten North Frederick. Bantam. 1970.
T. Hardy	The Woodlanders. Macmillan. 1974.
J. Harmer, R. Rossner	More than words. Book 2. Longman. 1997.
T.A. Harris	I'm O.K.-You're O.K. Avon. 1969.
E. Hautzig	The Endless Steppe. Harper. 1968.
T. de Haven	The Last Human. Bantam Books. 1992.
E. Heller	Kafka. Fontana/Collins, 1979.
E. Hemingway	Fiesta. Moscow International relations. 1981.
E. Hemingway	The Short Stories of Ernest Hemingway. C. Scribner's Sons. 1966.
N. Hentoff	Speaking Freely. Alfred A. Knopf, Inc. 1997.
J. Herriot	It shouldn't Happen to a Vet. Pan. 1972.
G.V. Higgins	Cogan's Trade. Hodder and Stoughton. 1974.
J. Higgins	A Season in Hell. A Pocket Book. 1990.
K.F. Hird	Offset Lithographic Technology. Goodheart-Willcox Company, inc. 1992.

J.P. Hogan	The Multiplex Man. Bantam Books. 1992.
B. Holliday, W. Duffy	Lady Sings the Blues. Lancer Books, Inc. N.Y. 1972.
V. Holt	The Legend of the Seventh Virgin. Collins/Fontana. 1977.
C. Hoover	How to Write an Uncommonly Good Novel. Ariadna press. Washington D.C. 1990
J. Hopkins	Elvis – The Final Years. Berkely Books, NJ. 1986.
Houghton Mifflin	English. H.M.C. 1983.
A.E. Hotchner	Her Own Story. Doris Day. Bantam, 1976.
J.W. Houston, J.D. Houston.	A Farewell to Manzanar. Bantam. 1973.
P. Howard	The State of the Language. Oxford University Press. 1984.
A. Huxley	Brave New World. Harper and Row. 1948.
A. Huxley	Brief Candles. Panther. 1972.
A. Huxley	Point Counter Point. Penguin. 1975.
J. Hyams	Bogie. Mayflower. 1973.
W. Jack, B. Laursen	Have Mercy. Warner books. 1995.
E. James, D. Ritz	Rage to Survive. Villard Books. New York. 1995.
M. Jones, J. Chilton.	Louis Armstrong. Mayflower. 1975.
J. Joyce	Dubliners. The Portrait of the Artist as a Young Man. Moscow. Progress, 1982.
B. Kaufman	Up the Down Staircase. Avon. 1964.
M.M. Kaye	Death in Zanzibar. Penguin.1983.
B.C. Keane	The Family Circus. Fawcett. 1964.
J. Kellerman	Devil's Waltz. Bantam Books. 1993.
J. Kerouac	Lonesome Traveler. Ballantine Books, N.Y. 1973.
J. Kerouac	On the Road. Signet book. 1957.
W. Kerr	The Secret of Stalingrad. Playboy. 1979.
J. Kessel	Belle de Jour. Dell. 1962.
R.G. Kaiser	Russia: The People and the Power. Pocket Book. 1976.
E. Kazan	America America. Stein and Day. 1974.
D.H. Lawrence	Rainbow. Penguin.1983.
S. Lawrence	Jimi Hendrix. Harper, 2006.
L. Lee	As I Walked Out One Midsummer Morning. Andre Deutch. 1969.
D. Lessing	Martha Quest. Panther books. 1978.
K. Lipper	Wall Street. Beverly Books, 1988.
Living in the USA	Youth For Understanding International Exchange, 1995
D. Lodge	Nice Work. Penguin Books. 1988.
J. London	Martin Eden. Airmont.1970.
N. Mailer	Marilyn. Warner Books. 1975
Captain Marryat	Peter Simple. Leipzig. Bernard Tauchnitz. 1842.
D. Marsh	Trapped. Bantam.1985.
W.S. Maugham	Theatre. Moscow. International relations. 1979.
E. McBain	Doll. Pan. 1976.
R.E. McConnel	Our Own Voice. Gage. 1978.
C. McCullers	The Mortgaged Heart. Penguin. 1981.
"M"	The Sensuous Man. Dell, 1972.
McGraw-Hill	English. Mark. E. Gibson. 1986.
McGraw-Hill	English. McGraw-Hill School Division. 1990.
A. McLean	Force 10 from Navarone. Collins/Fontana. 1970.
A. McLean	Night Without End. Collins/Fontana. 1971.
A. McLean	The Last Frontier. Collins/Fontana. 1975.
R.McRum, W.Cran, R.McNeil	The Story of English. Faber and Faber. BBC books. 1987.
D.H. Meadows and others	The Limits to Growth. A Signet book, 1975.
J.A. Michener	Hawaii. Fawcett crest. 1959.
J.A. Michener	Iberia. Random House. 1968.

A. Miller	The Death of a Salesman. Penguin. 1949.
G. Mikes and Bentley	How to Be an Alien. Andre Deutch. 1962.
R. Moore	French Connection. Bantam. 1970.
A. Moorehead	The Russian Revolution. Perennial library. Time,inc. 1965.
D. Mortman	True Colors. IVY books. N.Y. 1996.
F. Mowatt	The Siberians. Penguin. 1973.
I. Murdoch	The Bell. Triad Panther. 1978.
Pierre La Mure	Moulin Rouge. Signet Book. 1958.
T. Murphy	Auction. Signet. 1980.
W. Murphy	The Destroyer. L.A. A Pinnacle book. 1981.
R.K. Mussle	Nicholas and Alexandra. Dell. 1969.
G. O'Neill, D. Lehr	The Underboss. St.Martin's Press. N.Y. 1989.
S. Nichols	Sislby. Popular Library. 1977.
C. Nordhoff, J.N. Hall	Mutiny on the Bounty. Cardinal. 1965.
P. Norman	Shout. London. Corgi. 1981.
S. North	Rascal. Avon Flare book. 1963.
S.B. Oates	Let the Trumpets Sound. NAL Mentor book. 1982.
F. O'Brien	At Swim-Two-Birds. NAL. 1976.
S. Orman	Ask Suze...about Love and Money. Riverhead Books. 2007.
S. Orman	Ask Suze...about Wills and Trusts. Riverhead Books, 2007.
G. Orwell	Animal Farm. Penguin.1975.
G. Otis	Eldridge Cleaver: Ice and Fire. Bible Voice, 1977.
R. Palley	Unlikely Passages. Seven Seas Press, inc. Newport. R.I. 1984.
F. Pascal	No Means No. Bantam Books, 1995.
F. Pascal	The Truth about Ryan. Bantam Books, 1997.
J. Dos Passos	1919. NAL. 1079.
J. Dos Passos	The Big Money. NAL. 1979.
J. Dos Passos	The 42 Parallel. NAL. 1979.
J. Dos Passos	Three Soldiers. Houghton Mifflin. 1971.
J. Patterson	Season of Machete. Time Warner, 1995.
A. Peterson	Words, Words, Words. The Fairfax library. 1986.
E.A. Poe	Tales of Mystery and Imagination. J.M. Dent and sons, ltd. 1959.
E.A. Poe	Prose and Poetry. Moscow. Raduga.
L. van der Post.	Journey into Russia. Penguin. 1973.
M. Puzo	The Godfather. Fawcett Crest, 1970.
R.J Randisi, M. Wallace	Deadly Allies. Doubleday. 1992.
T. Rattigan	The Winslow Boy. Moscow. Progress. 1978.
D.J. Reese	A New World Emerges. Arnold Publishing Ltd. 1994.
D. Reeman	Rendez-vous-South Atlantic. London. Arrow. 1984.
H.H. Richardson	Australia Felix. Heineman. 1962.
Y. Richmond	From Nyet to Da. Intercultural Press, Inc. 1992.
J. Riffkin, T. Howard	Entropy. A New World View. Bantam. 1981.
P. Robertson	The New World Order. Word Publishing. 1991.
B. Robinson	The Best Christmas Pageant Ever. Avon. 1979.
P. Roth	Letting go. Transworld Publishers. London. 1964.
L. Roxon	Rock Encyclopedia. N.Y. Grosset and Dunlop. 1975.
J. Ruppeldtova	British Life and Institutions. SPN. Bratislava. 1967.
J.A. Salinger	9 Stories. Franny and Zooey. Raise High the Roof Beam, Carpenters. Progress. Moscow. 1982.
J.D. Salinger	The Catcher in the Rye. Moscow. Progress. 1979.
A. Scaduto	Bob Dylan. NAL. 1973.
E. Segal	Man, Woman and Child. Panther. 1981.
I. Shaw	Evening in Byzantium. NEL Times/Mirror. 1973.
I. Shaw	God Was Here but He Left Early. Pan. 1973.

I. Shaw	Mixed Company NEL. 1978.
S. Sheldon	The Naked Face. Pan. 1973.
H. Smith	The New Russians. Random House. 1990.
G. Stein	Three Lives. Vintage Books. 1936.
J. Steinbeck	Sweet Thursday. Pan.1958.
J.Steinbeck	Tortilla Flat. Pan.1978.
J. Steinbeck	Travels with Charlie. Bantam. 1977.
R.L. Stine	Beach House. Scholastic Inc. 1992.
R.L. Stine	Beach Party. Scholastic Inc. 1990.
R.L. Stine	Blind Date. Scholastic Inc. 1986.
R.L. Stine	The Boyfriend. Scholastic Inc. 1990.
R.L. Stine	Broken Hearts. Archway Paperback. 1993.
R.L. Stine	Call Waiting. Scholastic Inc. 1994.
R.L. Stine	College weekend. Archway Paperback. 1995.
R.L. Stine	Hit and Run. Scholastic Inc. 1992.
R.L. Stine	Runaway. Archway. 1997.
R.L. Stine	The Dare. Archway Paperback. 1994.
R.L. Stine	The Dead Fire. Archway Paperback. 1995.
R.L. Stine	The Dead Girlfriend. Archway Paperback. 1993.
R.L. Stine	The Dead Lifeguard. Archway Paperback. 1994.
R.L. Stine	First Date. Archway Paperback. 1992.
R.L. Stine	Goodnight Kiss. Archway Paperback. 1992.
R.L. Stine	Lights Out. Archway Paperback. 1991.
R.L. Stine	The Betrayal. Archway Paperback. 1993.
R.L. Stine	The Confession. Archway Paperback. 1996.
R.L. Stine	The New Boy. Archway Paperback. 1994.
R.L. Stine	The New Evil. Archway Paperback. 1994.
R.L. Stine	The New Year's Party. Archway Paperback. 1995.
R.L. Stine	Night Games. Archway Paperback. 1996.
R.L Stine	The Perfect Date. Archway Paperback. 1996.
R.L. Stine	The Prom Queen. Archway Paperback. 1992.
R.L. Sine	The Secret Room. Archway Paperback. 1991.
R.L. Stine	Ski Weekend. Archway Paperback. 1991.
R.L. Stine	The Sleepwalker. Archway Paperback. 1990.
R.L. Stine	The Stepsister. Archway Paperback. 1990.
R.L. Stine	Sunburn. Archway Paperback. 1993.
R.L. Stine	Twisted. Scholastic Inc. 1987.
R.L. Stine	What Holly Heard. Archway. 1996.
I. Stone	Jack London. Sailor on Horseback. Signet. 1969.
I Stone	Lust for Life. Transworld publishers. London, 1962.
R. Stout	Before Midnight. Penguin. 1982.
W. Strunk Jr., E.B. Strunk	The Elements of Style. Collier Macmillan. 1979.
A. Summers, R. Swan	Sinatra. The Life. Alfred A. Knoff. New York, 2005.
E. Taylor	Elizabeth Takes Off. Pan. 1989.
J. Tesh	Intelligence for your Life. Thomas Nelson, Inc., 2008.
T. Thompson	Blood and Money. Dell.1978.
B. Tillman	Dauntless. Bantam. 1992.
A. Toffler	The Third Wave. Pan. 1989.
M. Torgov	A Good Place to Come From. Toronto. Totem. 1976.
S. Townsend	The Secret Diary of Adrian Mole Aged 13 ¾. Methuen, 1984.
H. Troyat	Catherine the Great. N.Y. Berkely books. 1980.
H.S. Truman	Memoirs by Harry S. Truman. V1., V2. Sygnet Book, 1965.
M. Twain	Pudd'nhead Wilson. N.Y. Airmont. 1966.
M. Twain	The Adventures of Huckleberry Finn. Moscow. Progress. 1984.

J. Updike	Rabbit, Run. Penguin, 1977.
L. Uris	Exodus. Bantam. 1958.
L. Uris	QB 8. Bantam. 1970.
K. Vonnegut,Jr.	Cat's Cradle. Dell. 1976.
K. Vonnegut, Jr.	God Blesss You, Dr. Kevorkian. Seven Sories Press, New York, 1999.
K. Vonnegut, Jr.	God Bless You, Mr. Rosewater. Granada, 1978.
K. Vonnegut, Jr.	Happy Birthday, Wanda June. Granada, 1979.
K. Vonnegut, Jr.	Jaildird. A Dell book, 1982.
K. Vonnegut, Jr.	Mother Night. Triad Panther, 1979.
K. Vonnegut, Jr.	Palm Sunday. Granada, 1982.
K. Vonnegut, Jr.	Slapstick or Lonesome No More. Panther, 1977.
K. Vonnegut, Jr.	Slaughterhouse 5. Granada. 1970.
K. Vonnegut, Jr.	The Sirens of Titan. Dell. 1970.
K. Vonnegut, Jr.	Welcome to the Monkey House. Panther, 1979.
L. Waller	The Banker. Granada. 1963.
R.P. Warren	All the King's Men. Moscow. Progress. 1979.
R. Westall	The Promise. Scholastic Inc. 1990.
S. Whang	Guide to Happy Home Buying. Meredith Books. 2006.
T. Wilder	The Cabala. Heaven's My Destination. Our Town. Moscow. Raduga. 1988.
E. Williams	Arbeits Kommando. Hodder and Stoughton. 1975.
C. Woolrich	Rendezvous in black. Ace Books, Inc. 1948.
Zacherlay's Midnight Snacks. A. Hitchcock Mystery Magazine	N.Y. Ballantine. 1960.
America under Siege	1996 Aug., May.
	2001 Sept.
Arcansas Times	1997 May 23.
Atlantic Monthly	1971 July, September.
Award Journal	1991 Autumn.
BigO	1997 Apr., May.
The Bulletin	1988. Nov. 15.
Cheshire Life	1984. June.
Daily News	1996 May 5.
Downbeat	1993. July.
Ebony	1995 Oct. 15.
The Economist	1989. June 17, May 13; 1990 Oct. 20, June 9.
Esquire	1991. March.; 1992 Oct.
Evening Standard	1977 May 8.
Forbes	1990 Feb. 5.
Fortune	1999 June 7
The Gloucester Citizen	1991. Nov. 2.
Guideposts	1992 Jan., Nov., 1993 July, Aug., 1996 March. 1997 Jan., Feb., March, Apr.
Harper's Magazine	1971 Sept, 2003 July.
Kansas City Star	1996 July 24.
Life	1991 Apr.
Los Angeles Times	1996 May 19.
M	2001 July
Marie Claire	2009 April
McLean's	1990 Dec.,1988. Jan. 25., 1996 Feb. 5.
National Geographic	1978 July., 1989 July., 1993 July, Aug.
National Post	2008 May 28
Nation's Restaurant News	1995 Nov.6., 1995. Dec. 4.
New Idea	1991 Sept.14, Sept.28.; 1992. Feb.15, Feb. 29, March 7, 21, 28,

	Apr. 4, 11, 18, May 2, 5, 9, 30, June 4, Sept 14, 28.
Newsweek	1969 May 26; 1979. Nov.26; 1982. Nov.; 1988. Nov.15, Nov. 26.; 1990 June 4, Jan. 1.; 1991 Feb. 4. 1996 Aug. 5.
New York	1992 Oct., 1996 Apr. 15, May., Apr. 29., May 6.
New Yorker	1990 Feb.26; 1993. Aug.23, Aug.30.
Observer	1982. Nov.14.
Omni	1989 Oct; 1990 Jan., Apr., Dec.
Outdoor Life	1996 Feb.
Pasadena City College Courier	2007 May 31.
People	2001 Sept. 11.
Playboy	1975 May.
Premiere	1990 Jan.
Reader's Digest	1977 July; 1982. March, Aug.; 1988. Oct.; 1992 Apr, June, July, Aug., Sept; 1994 Jan., May; 1996 Apr., Feb.,Sept.;1997 Jan., Apr.; 1998 Oct.; 2001 July.; 2002 July., Oct., Nov., 2004 March, July, Aug.,
Sept., Dec.	
Rolling Stone	1985 May 9.
Signs of the Times	1997 May.
Star	2001 Oct. 2.
Sydney Calendar Magazine	1986.
Teen People	2001 Oct.
Tiger Beat	1999, Feb.
Time	1977 June 27.; 1988. June 20.; 1981. Jan 4.; 1989. Jan. 5, Apr. 10, 17, May 22, 29, June 19, Aug. 7, 14, 21, Sept. 28, 11, Oct. 1, 23, 30, July 10, Nov. 6, 13, Dec. 11, 18, 25.; 1990 Jan. 1, May 1, Nov. 12, Dec. 3, Oct. 22.; 1995 Sept. 4; 1996 March 25, Apr. 29, May 13, Aug. 5, Summer 1996 special edition., 2001 Oct. 15, 2003 June 30.
USA Today	1990 Nov.28, 29., Dec. 1, 5., 1995 Sept. 27., 1996 Feb. 12., July 24, July 31, Aug. 6.
US News and World Report	2001 Sept. 14.
Vanity Fair	Apr. 1991, Sept. 1992.
Washington Post	July 19, 1998.
Woman's Own	July 7. 1992.
World Monitor	March 1991.
Young Citizen's Passport	Citizenship Foundation 199/2000.
You	June 2. 1985

Preface

Differences within a language arise mainly from separation. Groups of speakers of a language become separated either regionally or socially. The varieties of the language they speak then evolve in their own ways. If the separation continues, the varieties may change enough to become different languages. For example, French, Spanish, Portuguese, and Italian were all at one time varieties of Latin, but they are now discrete languages. If, however, the differences are not great enough to prevent mutual intelligibility, the varieties may be called dialects of the same language.

The English language today, which is spoken as a first language by over three hundred million people, has hundreds of varieties within it. The four major varieties of English are British, American, Australian and Canadian English. Each of these major varieties of English has within it features of vocabulary, grammar, and sound that set it apart from the other varieties; yet each also contains sub-varieties, the special usages of smaller regional and social groups. Strictly speaking, if a variety of language has recognizable features that set it apart, it may be called a dialect. But for clarification we shall use the term dialect for the sub-varieties only. The methods of studying these differences within a language apply to all varieties, both large and small.

The specific variety of English is best illustrated by the vocabulary, for there are hundreds of words that are native to the country, where this variety of English is spoken, or which have meanings peculiar to it. As might be expected, many of these words refer to topographical features, plants, trees, fish, animals and birds; and many others to social, economic and political institutions and activities.

The purpose of this dictionary is to provide a generous sampling of words and expressions characteristic of the various spheres of life in the USA, Great Britain, Australia and Canada during the last centuries. The dictionary also features a collection of slang and colloquial expressions in frequent use in these four countries in the twentieth century.

An Americanism, Briticism, Australianism or Canadianism is a word, expression, or meaning which is native to the USA, Great Britain, Australia or Canada or which is distinctly characteristic of their usage in these countries though not necessarily exclusive to them.

Many indeed are the processes of change by which the vocabulary has grown - by borrowing, by compounding, by shortening, by blending, by the generalization of proper names, and by new coinages; moreover the range of meaning of terms has been altered and expanded by extension, transference, deterioration and amelioration, and by folk etymology. Thus this dictionary offers compelling evidence of the inventiveness of people living in these four countries in the past and present in the realm of word creation.

For the purpose of this volume, I have taken the most popular English dictionaries as generally handy guides to English language, and have included most of the words which are recorded there as belonging to one of the four major varieties of English. In struggling to reduce the remaining body of language I have been guided by three criteria: firstly, standard words have been emphasised at the expense of colloquialisms and slang; secondly, I have tried to confine myself largely to current usage; thirdly, I paid special attention to the frequency of occurrences of the words in Modern English, especially their use in books, newspapers and magazines. Over 300 of them were used as sources of evidence in compiling this collection

The compiler of this dictionary will be thankful for all the critical remarks that will help to improve this book in future editions. All remarks and suggestions should be sent to the publishing house.

How to Use This Dictionary

The headwords are entered in alphabetical (in bold face), together with any variant spellings or alternative forms.

Next each word is given a regional label (in italics). This indicates the country of origin, or the country in which the term is most prevalent.

If a particular term has more than one quite separate meaning, these meanings are numbered.

If one overall sense of a term is commonly subdivided into several slightly different meanings, these are indicated by letters (a., b., c., etc.).

The headword, regional label and some other marks are followed by a definition.

Phrases, word combinations, word-building elements are also mentioned in the dictionary along with common words.

Some grammar information is also given when it is necessary to specify what part of speech a particular word is and which specific phrases it is often used in.

Special terms have their own abbreviations (tech., print., etc.).

Colloquial words, slang are marked with abbreviations (col., sl.).

Many definitions are followed by an illustrative phrase or sentence (in italics). If this example is an actual citation, its source follows the example.

At the end of some word entries other words forming different parts of speech but which are derived from the main word, are also given (in bold face).

A

AA *Am.* /*Br.* **AC**/ abbr. print. *Am.* Author's Alterations, *Br.* Author's Corrections.
AB 1. *Br.* able-bodied seaman. 2. *Am.* /*Br.* **BA**/ Bachelor of Arts: *A.B. Math, Poughkeepsie Coll.* - J. Kellerman, *I'm still getting my BA.* – P. Roth.
abattoir *esp. Br.* slaughterhouse.
abbreviated piece of nothing *Am.* sl. worthless person or thing.
ABCs *Am.* the letters of the alphabet.
Abdul *Am.* derog. an Arab.
abjuration/ **oath of abjuration** *Am.* oath of resigning one's former citizenship.
abjure allegiance *Am.* resign citizenship.
ablutions *Br.* mil. public washroom.
abo *Aus.* taboo. sl. Australian Aborigine.
aboiteau *Can.* the sluice-gate, or valve, arrangement in the dike.
abolitionist *Am.* antislavery fighter in pre-Civil War America: *The most alienated view of America was preached by the Abolitionists* - E. Cleaver. /**abolition, abolitionary, abolitionism, abolitionize**/.
Aboriginal *Aus.* n. adj. native of Australia.
abortion mill *esp. Am., Can.* derog. abortion clinic.
about 1. /*Am., Aus.* usu. **around**/ *esp. Br.* prep. surrounding, around. 2. *Br.* somewhere near the place, e.g. *Is Patric about?*
about and about *Am.* very like, similar.
about/ **be nervous about** smth. *Am.* /*Br.* **be nervous of** smth./ be excited about smth.
about/ **About time too!** *Br.* col. It should have happened earlier.
about/ **not about to** *esp. Am.* very unwilling to.
about-turn *esp. Br., Aus.* /*esp. Am., Can. Aus.* **about-face**/ 1. reversal of opinion or attitude: *he doesn't want his antagonist to do a complete about-face.* - J.W. Fulbright., *His mood did a complete about-face.* - D. Mortman. 2. mil. order to turn around and face the opposite direction.
above-ground *Am.* honest and straightforward.
abovestairs *Br.* living quarters above.
above the salt *Br.* /*Br.* humour. obs., **above**/ in a position of distinction (**sit above** one's **salt**).
abseil *Br.* /*Am.* **rappel**/ (of mountain climbers) go down a cliff or rock by clinging in a controlled way down the rope with their feet against the cliff or rock.
absent *Am., Can.* prep. without.
absent/ **absent one thing, another will happen** *Am., Can.* if the first thing doesn't happen, the second thing will.
absentee/ **vote by absentee ballot** *Am., Can.* /*Br.* **vote by postal vote, postal vote**/ vote in advance because one will be away on the day of an election.
absentee interview *Am.* one taken to find out the cause why the person was absent.
absolute majority 1. *esp. Br.* /*esp. Am.* **majority**/ the number of votes cast in any election above the total of all other voices cast. 2. *esp. Am.* majority of all the registered voters.
absquatulate *esp. Am., Can.* sl. flee, run away.
abuilding *esp. Am.* in a state of building.
AC 1. *Br.* aircraftsmen. 2. *Am.* Air Corps /before World War One/. 3. *Am., Can.* acre.
academicals *Br.* /*Am.* **academic costume**/ cap and gown, the formal university dress worn on special occasions.
academic rank *Am., Can.* university teacher rank.
academic teacher; instructor *Am.* /*Br.* **university teacher; lecturer**/.
academic year *esp. Br.* time when there are courses at school or university.
Academy Award *Am.* Academy of Motion Pictures, Arts and Sciences Award /"Oscar"/: *The People versus Larrry Flynt goes all the way and wins the Academy award.* - BigO.
Acadia *Can.* former French colony of Eastern Canada that included Nova Scotia and New Brunswick; **Acadian** is a descendant of this colony.
Acadian *Am.* a descendant of the Acadians deported to Louisiana in the 18th century, a Cajun.
acceleration *Am., Can.* advancement of superior pupils or students.
accelerator *Br.* /*Am.* **gas pedal**/: *He instinctively pressed his foot hard on the deck as on an accelerator.* - A. Burgess.
acceptance/ **speech of acceptance** *Am.* speech expressing agreement to run for the office of President or Governor.
access course *Br.* a set of classes taken by sb. to get qualifications to enter university or college.
accession *Am.* sudden fit or outburst.
accessorize *Am.* supplement with accessories.
access road, ramp *Am.* /*Br.* **slip road**/: *There is an access route off the highway now* - Harper's Magazine.
accident /frequency/ rate *Am.* occupational injuries factor.
acclaim *Can.* elect without any opposition with standing ovation.
acclimate *esp. Am., Can.* acclimatize /**acclimatation:** *it was important for Kevin to get "acclimated to his new home base."* – R.L. Stine.
accommodation *Br., Aus.* furnished room: *I have had to put up with inferiour accommodation* – S. Townsend.

accommodation address *Br.* /*Am.* **mail drop**/ temporary mailing address.

accommodation collar *Am.* sl. arrest made by police to fill up the needed quota.

accommodationist *Am.* (black) person who adopts the behaviour of the (white) majority.

accommodations *Am., Can.* 1. lodging, food and services: *the missionaries offered me no accomodations* - B.E. Olson., *conversion of single-room-occupancy hotels into upscale tourist accomodations* - R.N. Bellah and others. 2. seat or place, esp. on a boat or train.

accommodation train *Am.* train that stops at all the stations.

accommodator *Am.* part-time domestic help.

accomplishment *esp. Am.* /*esp. Br.* **achievement**/ attainment, skill, esp. in combinations: **accomplishment age, quotient, test**: *cramming for her SATs and achievement tests.* - D. Mortman., *academic-achievement tests are only one measure of what schools offer* - Time.

accord/ **with one accord** *Br.* with every one agreeing to do smth. at the same time.

accordance/ **in accordance to** *esp. Am.* in agreement.

according as *Br.* conj. depending on whether.

According to Cocker *Br.* /*Am., Can.* **according to Hoyle**/ correctly: *It's not according to Hoyle to hit a man when he's down.* – A. Makkai.

accordion fold *Am.* /*Br.* **concertina fold**/ print. a series of parallel folds in which the paper is "pleated" by making each fold in the opposite direction.

accouche *Am.* col. rare. help to produce, create.

account/ *Br., Aus.* **pay the cheque into** /*Am., Aus.* **deposit check in**/ in one's account.

accounting *Am.* /*esp. Br.* **accountancy**/ the work or job of an accountant.

accounts/ **hand in** one's **accounts** *Am.* die.

accumulator 1. *esp. Br., Aus.* /*Am., Aus.* **storage battery**/ storage cell: *Mr. Harcourt wanted his accumulator.* - A. Hitchcock Mystery Magazine. 2. *Br.* set of bets on four or more horse races.

ace *Am.* sl. 1. a dollar: *Give me an ace. I have to get some telephone change.* - R.A. Spears. 2. one-year prison term. 3. also *Can., Aus.* get a high mark, succeed: *I was impressed by the way he managed to... ace his classes* - Guideposts. 4. *Aus.* sl. also **freckle, date** the buttocks.

ace/ **ace** sb. **out** *Am., Can.* outdo sb. in a contest.

ace/ **have the ace in** one's **hand** *Br.* have a hidden advantage.

ace-high *Am.* col. excellent: *His reputation is ace-high.* - R.L. Stine.

ace-in-the-hole *Am.* col. 1. also *Can.* /*Br.* **ace in the pack**/ hidden reserve or advantage: *I always kept an ace in the hole.* - D. Carnegie. 2. true friend.

achievement *esp. Br.* /*esp. Am.* **accomplishment**/.

achoo *Am.* /*Br.* **attishoo**/ sounds produced while sneezing.

acid/ **put the acid on** sb. *Aus., NZ.* sl. 1. borrow money from sb. 2. accost a woman in a rude way.

acid/ **come the old acid** *Br.* sl. speak sarcastically.

acid/ **put on the acid** *Aus.* sl. steal smth.

acid drop *Br.* lollipop made of sugar and ice with a sharp taste.

ackers *Br.* sl. money.

acorn shell *Br.* rock barnacle.

across/ **be**/**get across** smth. *Aus.* become fully aware of the details or complexity of the matter.

across (from) *esp. Am.* the opposite of.

across the board *Am.* (in horse racing) a bet in which equal amounts are staked on the same horse to win, place or show in a race.

across the lines *Can.* in the USA.

act/ **Organic Act** *Am.* law about transforming the territory into state.

act wise *Am., Can.* act with discretion.

action/ **a piece (slice) of the action** *esp. Br.* an exciting activity.

action replay or **repeat** *Br., Aus.* /*Am., Aus.* **(instant) replay**/ replay of an important moment at a sports event on TV.

action stations *esp. Br.* (often a command) the positions taken by military personnel in preparation for action.

activate *Am.* set up a military unit with the necessary personnel and equipment: *When Austin's unit was thrown into combat, Gerald asked to be activated and sent to Korea.* - Reader's Digest. /**activation, activation area**/.

active citizen *Am.* sl. louse.

active duty /or **service**/ *esp. Am.* full time service: *National Guard and active duty military personnel are on Olympics duty* - Time., *young men with higher degrees usually avoid active duty.* - R.G. Kaiser.

active service/ **on active service** *Br.* actually fighting in the armed forces: *my husband and his regiments were on active service somewhere* - M.M. Kaye.

actress/ **as the actress said to the bishop** *Br.* col. humor. smth. just said can have a sexual meaning.

actually /In conversation in *Br.* **actually** can be used to make what you say softer, esp. if you are correcting sb., disagreeing or complaining, but it can also be used with opposite effect.

actual bodily harm, grievous bodily harm (GBH) *Br.* a crime where violence is actually used.

adaptor, adapter *Br.* a special plug for joining electrical equipment to power supply.

A-day *Am.* a day for doing smth. important.

ADC *Br.* time and charges for a long distance call. / abbr. for Advice for Duration and Charges.

add up; total *esp. Am.* /*esp. Br.* **do sums**/.

adder *Am.* col. non-venomous snake.

adder/ have death adders in one's **pockets** *Aus.* sl. be stingy.

addition *Am.* a part added to the building: *the school too would get an addition within the year.* - W. Grady.

add-up *Am.* col. the sum total, gist.

adhesive tape *esp. Am.* /*esp. Br.* **sticking plaster**/.

adios *esp. Am.* col. excl. goodbye.

adjie *Aus.* aide-de-camp.

adjunct-professor *Am.* university teacher rank.

adjustable spanner *esp. Br.* /*esp. Am.* **monkey wrench, adjustable wrench**/ adjustable tool for holding or turning things.

adjuster/ loss adjuster *Br.* /*Am.* **claims adjuster**/ an insurance company officer deciding how much money to pay to a person involved in an accident for loss or injury: *He conferred with Larry Coats, an Allstate claims adjuster* – Reader's Digest.

adless *Am.* without presenting any advertising.

admass *Br.* derog. col. rare. 1. mass advertising: *the equally menacing development of admass* - J. Ruppeldtova. 2. people influenced by it.

admin *esp. Br.* col. administration.

administration *esp. Am., Can.* /period of/ government esp. of a particular president or ruling party.

administrate *Am.* administer.

administrative *esp. Am.* executive.

Admiral *esp. Br.* head of the fishing fleet.

Admiralty *Br.* the government department in charge of the Navy.

admit to the Bar *Am.* /*Br.* **call to the Bar**/ allow to act as a lawyer.

adolesce *esp. Am.* 1. be or become adolescent. 2. behave like adolescent.

adopt *Br.* officially choose sb. to represent a political party in an election; n. **adoption**.

adrift *esp. Br.* col. 1. not working or reasoning properly. 2. unattested; failing to reach a target, esp. in sports. 3. no longer fixed in a position.

advance *Am.* /*Br.* **sub**/.

advance *Am.* v. n. /organise/ pre-election campaign., **advance agent**.

advanced class/course *Am.* a school class doing work at a higher standard than is usual for students at that stage in their education: *These classes are called* **advanced placement** *("AP") courses.* – Living in the USA.

advance man *esp. Am., Can.* a person who visits a location before the arrival of an important person to make all the proper arrangements.

advantage/ play the advantage over sb. *Am.* cheat sb.

advantage/ You have the advantage of me *Br.* You know smth. that I don't.

adventure playground *Br.* one containing ropes, slides, tunnels and other objects and structures for children to play in.

adventuresome *esp. Am.* adventurous.

advert *Br.* col. advertisement: *it was about as realistic as an advert for Pear's soap.* – R. Westall.

advertisement/ be a/an (good) advertisement *Br.* be a good example for smth.

advertising manager / director *Am.* /*Br.* **advertisement manager**/ person encouraging people to buy goods or use services: *Offered the job of advertising manager for an eastern automotive company, I moved to Philadelphia* - Alcoholics Anonymous., *The Advertisement Manager has a counterpart in the Publicity Manager* - J. Ruppeldtova.

advise with *Am.* consult with: *Before making any decision, the President usually advises with leading members of his special information committee.* - Longman.

advisee *esp. Am.* student assigned to an advisor.

advisement *Am., Can.* or. obs. careful consideration / **under advisement**.

advisor *Am.* tutor of students.

advisory *Am., Can.* information bulletin, esp. weather report.

adwoman *Am.* woman engaged in advertising business.

advocacy group or **organisation** *Am.* one that tries to influence the decisions of a government or other authority.

advocate (for a particular group) *esp. Am.* one who works for the interests of that group.

aerial *esp. Br.* /*esp. Am., Aus.* **antenna**/ radio (car) antenna.

aerialist *esp. Am.* springboard acrobat: *forego foolhardy ventures unless you're trained aerialist.* - "M"

aerial ladder *Am.* motor turntable ladder.
aerodrome *esp. Br.* obs. /*Am.* **airdrome**/ airfield.
aeroengine *esp. Br.* aircraft engine: *My father tried to join the RAF, as an aero-engine fitter.* – R. Westall.
aeroplane *esp. Br., Aus.* /*Am.* **airplane**/ flying vehicle, plane: *Many years ago there was an airplane crash in Uzbekistan.* - R.G. Kaiser.
aeroquay *Can.* airport building.
affair *Am.* col. party or other social occasion.
affiant *Am.* law. a person who makes an affidavit.
affiliated, sectarian school *Am.* /*Br.* **denominational, nonsecular school**/.
affiliation order *Br.* law. obs. order by a law court for a man who is not married to the mother of his child to pay certain amount of money to the mother to support his child.
affinity group *esp. Am.* a group of people linked by a common interest or purpose.
affirmative action *esp. Am.* /*Br.* **positive discrimination**/ making sure that members of disadvantaged groups, such as racial minorities or women get an appropriate share of the opportunities available, esp. in employment and education.
afghan *Am.* knitted or crocheted wool cover: *I picked up one of the hundreds of afghans with which mama had filled our houses* - K. Davis.
Afro-American, also **African-American** *esp. Am.* n. adj. black American: *Hilary is an African American.* – R.L. Stine.
after *Am.* past / in defining time e.g. *15 after 5 p.m., He was in bed at half after midnight.* - I. Stone.
aftermarket *esp. Am.* market for spare parts, accessories and components, esp. for motor vehicles.
afternoons *esp. Am.* during any afternoon.
afternoon tea *Br.* a drink of tea and sometimes a light meal taken at about 4 o'clock in the afternoon.
afters *Br.* col. dessert, sweet course after the main dish: *An orange each for afters* - A. Burgess.
after the break *Br.* /*Am.* **after the messages**/ after advertisements.
afterward *esp. Am.* afterwards.
Aga (cooker) *Br.* tdmk. a large iron cooker which keeps heat.
agate line *Am.* space one column wide and 1/14 inch deep used in advertising as measurement: *Mr. Harrisburg's press the following morning did not total more than forty agate lines* – J. O'Hara.
agate type *Am.* /*Br.* **ruby type**/ size of type of 5.05 points.
agency 1. *esp. Am.* department of government or international body. 2. *Br.* service station where fuel is billed directly to the company.

agency shop *Am.* enterprise where every worker is a member of a trade union.
agent 1. *Am.* member of the state enterprise, esp. FBI man: *Agent Buckley was working the graveyard shift* - G. O'Neill, D. Lehr. 2. *Am.* mil. war gas: *a biological agent - 130 grams of ricin* - Reader's Digest. 3. *Am.* mil. messenger, orderly.
agent/ (road) agent *Am.* highway man.
agent/ advance agent *Am.* person who makes contracts for the performing band, etc.
agent/ station agent *esp. Am.* /*esp. Br.* **booking clerk, booking office cashier, station manager**/ person who sells tickets, esp. at a railway station.
agent/ traveling agent *Am.* travelling salesman.
aggro *Br., Aus.* col. fighting, esp. between street gangs, or any trouble or difficulty: *I guess I was a bit aggro last night.* - T. Thorne.
aggro *Am.* sl. wonderful.
agony/ pile on the agony *Br., Aus.* col. try to get sympathy from other people by making your problems seem worse than they really are.
agony aunt / uncle *Br.* col. /*Am.* **advice columnist**/ woman /or man/ who gives advice on readers' personal problems.
agony column *Br.* col. /*esp. Am.* **advice column**/ part of newspaper, magazine, etc. devoted to readers' personal problems: *Streetwise's agony column, Advice Special, gets hundreds of letters from young people.* - Streetwise.
agree (smth.) *esp. Br.* /*Am., Aus.* **agree to**/ accept an idea, opinion, etc.: *The workers have agreed the company's pay offer.* - Longman.
ahead of the game *Am., Can* sl. being early, in a winning or advantageous position: *The time you spend studying when you are in school will put you ahead of the game in college.* - A. Makkai.
ahead of time *esp. Am.* in advance.
ahold/ get ahold of sb. or smth. *esp. Am.* manage to contract, find, or get sb. or smth.: *hero the tourist board hadn't yet got ahold of.* - W. Grady.
ahold/ get ahold of oneself *esp. Am.* manage to stay calm after a shock or difficult situation.
aid *Am.* aide, assistant.
aid/ What...in aid of? *Br., Aus.* col. What...for?: *What's all this in aid of?* - A. McLean.
aim/ take aim at *esp. Am.* criticise sb. strongly.
ain't/ it ain't all that (sb. **ain't all that**) *Am.* sl. sb. is doing it much better.
air *esp. Am.* broadcast on the radio or television: *The program airs Sundays at 7:30 p.m.* - Ebony., *We will air our show.* - H. Smith.
air/ come up for air *Aus.* col. have a rest, make a break.
air/ get the air *Am.* sl. be discharged, be fired.

air/ give the air *Am.* sl. discharge, fire: *Give him the air, baby.* - J. O'Hara.
air alert/ also **aircraft warning** *Am.* air-ride warning.
airball *Am.* sl. stupid person.
air bed *Br., Aus. /Am.* **air mattress/** a rubber or plastic bag filled with air to lie on in water or use as a bed.
airbrained *Am.* sl. silly: *She's not just some airbrained bimbo, you know.* - T. Thorne.
airbrick *Br., Aus.* a brick with holes in it which allow air go through a wall.
air bridge *Br.* a movable covered passage by which passengers can go from an airport building to a plane.
airdrome *Am. /esp. Br.* obs. **aerodrome/** airport.
airer *Br.* a frame or stand for airing and drying.
airgun *Br. /Am.* **BB gun/** rifle from which a projectile is propelled by compresed air.
airhole *Am.* air current that causes an airplane to drop suddenly.
airhop *Am.* take frequent short rides by plane.
air hostess *Br.* and *Aus.* obs. flight attendant, stewardess.
airing cupboard *Br.* closet around a hot-water pipe to dry clothes: *I have seen them shoved down the side of the airing cupboard.* – S. Townsend.
airline *esp. Am., Can.* shortest route between two points.
airline hostess or **stewardess** *Am.* airhostess, stewardess.
airmiss *Br.* an instance of two or more planes on different routes being less than prescribed distance apart.
airmobile *Am.* mil. adj. carried by air.
airplane *Am. /Br.* **aeroplane/** flying vehicle, plane.
airplane carrier *Am.* aircraft carrier.
airscape *Am.* bird's eye view.
airs-screw *Br. /Am.* **propeller/** aircraft propeller.
airship *Am.* carry luggage by air.
airsome *Can.* cold.
airway *Am.* 1. special radio frequency. 2. col. TV channel.
airy *Am.* col. 1. arrogant. 2. affected.
airy-fairy *esp. Br.* col. (of ideas) not clear or practical.
aisle *Am.* cutting in a forest.
ait *esp. Br.* island.
aitch/ drop one's **aitches** *esp. Br., Aus.* not pronounce h at the beginning of words
aitch-bone *Br.* 1. large bone at the back end / rump/ of a cow. 2. a piece of meat cut from over this bone.

Aladin cave *esp. Br.* a treasure trove.
Aladin's cave *Br.* a store with a lot of interesting and unusual objects.
a la mode *Am., Can.* adj. adv. /used after nouns/ served with ice cream.
Albany doctor, also **Freemantle doctor** *Aus.* fresh wind/ in Pert.
albert *Br.* watch chain with the bar at one end for attaching to a buttonhole.
album *Am.* visitors book/ in a hotel, etc.
alcometer *Am.* col. drunkometer.
alderman, alderwoman *Am., Can., Aus.* an elected male or female member of a city council.
ale 1. *esp. Br.* any beer other than lager, stout or porter. 2. *Am., Can.* beer brewed by top fermentation.
alec *Aus.* col. a silly or stupid person.
aled, aled-up *Br.* sl. drunk.
alf, also **ocher** *Aus.* col. stupid person.
alfalfa *esp. Am. /Br* **lucerne/**: *Then we stood in the high entrance of the great bar and smelled the sweetness of alfalfa* - J. Steinbeck.
Alf Garnet *Br. /Am.* sl. **Archie Bunker/**.
Alibi Ike *Am.* sl. person who always finds excuses for his/her failures: *The unofficial trainer, rubber, water-boy, pep-talker, Alibi Ike, booster and pigskin patron-in-chief to the Trojan Eleven?* – M. Daly.
Alice band *esp. Br.* wide coloured headband.
alienist *esp. Am.* psychiatrist who assesses the competence of a defendant in a law court: *Oddly the alienists interpreted his brooding lethargy as an improvement.* – Pierre La Mure.
alimony, child support *Am. /Br.* **maintenance/** money to be paid towards the living costs of the children of the divorced couple by one of the parents: *He had doubled the alimony she was granted.* – K. Chopin.
alkili flat *Am.* arid plane.
all *Br.* /used in combinations/ absolute nothing, e.g. *damn-all, bugger-all*.
all American speakers use **all year around, all of the year,** British speakers more often use **all the year round,** etc. Americans also say **all of the dishes,** etc. instead of all the dishes.
all over the shop *Br.* col. /Am.* col. **all over the lot,** *Am., Can.* **all over the map/** 1. scattered everywhere: *they were always in the loop on all things Hendrix* – S. Lawrence. 2. confused and badly-organized.
all/ it's all gone pear-shaped *Br.* col. it's gone completely wrong.
all/ it's all one to me *Aus.* it's all the same to me.

all/ that's all she wrote *Am.* col. there's nothing more to say.

all-American *Am.* (of a sports player) honoured as one of the best amateur competitors in the US.

all-around *Am.* adj. /*Br., Aus.* **all-round**/.

all-arounder *Am.* /*Br., Aus.* **all-rounder**/ person competent in many fields.

all-comers *Br.* contest open for all participants.

alley/ (right) up / down one's **alley** *esp. Am., Can.* /*esp. Br.* **(just) right up** one's **street**/ in one's power, according to one's taste: *It wasn't up his alley at all.* - J.D. Salinger., *It's right up your alley.* - J. Updike.

alley apple *Am.* sl. a piece of horse manure: *Harry is collecting alley apples for his garden.* - R.A. Spears.

alley cat *esp. Am.* stray cat.

all get out *esp. Am., Can., Aus.* col. the extreme case of what is indicated, esp. in **as all get-out**: *They were maneuverable as hell and went like all-get-out for their time.* - J. DeFelice.

alligator clip *Am., Can.* crocodile clip.

The Alligator State *Am.* Florida.

all-in *Br.* 1. (esp. of prices) inclusive of all. 2. anything goes, no holds barred.

all-in-one *Br.* a piece of clothing covering the whole body without separate top and bottoms.

allophone *Can.* a person living in French Canada who speaks a language other than French or English; non-native Canadian.

allotment *Am.* obs. a plot of land made over by the government to an American Indian.

all-outer *Am.* 1. resolute man. 2. extremist.

allow *Am., Can.* col. assert, be of the opinion that.

allowable *Am.* amount of oil permitted to produce by state or federal authority.

allowance *esp. Am.* /*esp. Br.* **pocket money**/ money given weekly to a child by his/her parents: *he lives on allowance* - USA Today., *Two dollars a week allowance you get* - J. O'Hara., *he went over his allowance on flowers and gifts* - L. Uris.

allowance/ (tax) allowance *Br.* /*Am.* **exemption**/ amount of money that you're allowed to earn before you have to start paying income tax.

all party *Br.* involving all political parties.

all-points bulletin (APB) *Am.* a radio message given to all police officers giving details of suspected criminal or stolen vehicle.

all-purpose flour *Am.* /*Br., Aus.* **plain flour**/.

all right/ it's all right for sb. *Br.* col. some people get all the luck.

allrightnik *Am.* sl. complacent philistine.

all-rounder *Br.* versatile person, good at different skills, academic subjects, or sports.

allseater *Br.* (of a stadium) having enough seats for all spectators and no standing places.

all singing or **all dancing** *esp. Br.* very modern and advanced.

all Sir Garnet *Br.* all correct.

all sorts *esp. Br.* assorted candies.

all the fun of the fair *Br.* sl. great fun.

all-up weight *esp. Br.* the total weight of an aircraft with passengers, cargo and fuel or some other vehicle.

all wet *Am., Can.* sl. entirely wrong or confused: *If you think I like baseball, you're all wet.* - A. Makkai.

all-wheel drive *Am., Can.* four-wheel drive.

Alma Mater *Am.* the song of a school or university: *He sang his Alma Mater so beautifully* - T. Wilder.

almond green *Am.* yellowish green colour.

almond paste *Br.* marzipan.

almoner *Br.* obs. a social worker who works in a hospital.

alms box *Br.* church box for alms.

The Aloha State *Am.* Hawaii.

along *Am.* col. somewhere near, around, e.g. along about 4 o'clock.

along/ right along *Am.* constantly.

alongside of *Am., Can.* prep. alongside.

alpha *Am.* radio. letter A.

alphabet *Am.* alphabetize.

alpha beta gamma *Br.* A. B. C. /university marks for quality of students' work/.

alphabetical agency *Am.* departmental agency/ its name often used as acronym.

alphabet soup *esp. Am.* joc. abbreviations of government institutions: *difficult probe conducted by an alphabet soup of state and federal agencies.* - Newsweek.

already *esp. Am., Can.* col. (intensifier) right now, without further ado.

Alsatian *esp. Br.* /*esp. Am., Aus.* **German shepherd**/ wolflike dog used by police or to guard property: *a picture of an alsatian on the front.* – S. Townsend.

alter *esp. Am., Aus.* euph. castrate /an animal/.

alternate *esp. Am.* 1. substitute, deputy: *These alternates made a careful study of all points* - H. Truman. 2. adj. alternative: *he gave her an alternate assignment* - E. Cleaver.

altho *Am.* col. although.

atogether/ in the altogether *Br.* without any clothes on.

aluminium *Br., Can., Aus.* /*Am.* **aluminum**/ light easily shaped white metal.

alumnus *esp. Am.* /*esp. Br.* **graduate, school-leaver**/ former student of a school, college, or university: *From phone booth I called the college's alumni office.* - Reader's Digest., *Open any alumni magazine, turn to the class notes* - W. Strunk., *MIT is also for allowing its alumni to work for foreign firms.* - Newsweek.

AM *Am.* Master of Arts.

ambassador-at-large *Am., Can.* one with special duties, not appointed to a particular country.

amber fluid/liquid *esp. Aus.* col. beer.

amber gambler *Br.* col. a reckless driver passing the traffic lights when they are about to tell them to stop.

the amber nectar *Br.* beer.

Ambitious City *Can.* nickname for the city of Hamilton, Ontario.

ambulance-chaser *esp. Am., Can.* derog. lawyer specializing in cases seeking damages for personal injury: *But ambulance-chasing lawyers are getting rich off frivolous suits.* – Reader's Digest.

ambulanceman *Br., Aus.* an ambulance driver who also helps or gives treatment to people carried in it.

ambulator *Am.* range finder.

amen corner *Am.* col. part of a church occupied by fervent worshippers: *a viewpoint on the public front of leading citizens and "amen-corner-praying" churchmen.* - H. Truman.

amendatory *Am.* corrective.

amenity bed *Br.* bed in a private room in a National Health Service hospital available for a payment to a patient receiving free treatment.

America *Can.* North America, esp. Canada and US.

American cloth *Br.* plastic furniture cloth.

American football *Br., Aus.* /*Am.* **football**/ American game, related to Rugby.

American organ *esp. Br.* melodeon.

amidships/ **rudder amidships** *Am.* helm amidships.

amicus brief *Am.* legal submission by a person who is not a party to a case but has an interest in its outcome: *he was considering filing an amicus brief in support of Paula Jones' right to see the President.* - Time.

amigo *esp. Am., Can.* col. form of address, esp. in a Spanish-speaking area.

amiss/it wouldn't come amiss *Br., Aus.* col. it would be useful.

amp *Am.* sl. electric guitar.

ampster *Aus.* col. the accomplice of a sideshow operator.

AMT *Am.* alternative minimum tax, used to prevent people and companies from trying to avoid paying taxes by using deductions and credits.

amtrack *Am.* amphibious tracked vehicle used for landing assault troops on a shore.

amusement arcade *Br.* a place where children can play games on machines by putting coins in them: *There are no age restrictions on who can play fruit and slot machines in amusement arcades and fairs.* - Young Citizen's Passport.

amusement park, carnival *esp. Am., Can., Aus.* /*esp. Br.* (**fun**)**fair**/ recreation park: *Joan noticed an amusement park with pony rides.* - T. Thompson., *The amusement park was still open.* - J. Cheever.

anabranch *Am.* a branch of the river.

analyst *Am.* 1. commentator: *Other analysts think Assad's worried* - Time. 2. psychoanalyst.

anchor(person) /also **anchorman, anchorwoman, anchorette**/ *esp. Am.* /*esp. Br.* **newsreader**/ television news broadcaster who has the principal and coordinating role in the programme., v. **anchor**: *Anchor Judy Woodruff was rushed on the air at 2:42 a.m.* - Newsweek.

anchors *Br.* col. the brakes of a car.

ancient lights *Br.* law. windows whose light must not be overshadowed by new buildings.

and 1. *esp. Br.* /used instead of to after come, go, try, etc./ e.g. *Come and see me.* 2. *esp. Am.* and is often left out by Americans after the word hundred before one to ninety-nine.

angel *Br.* col. nurse.

angel food cake *Am., Can.* angel cake, cake made with eggs, flour but no fat, usu. in the form of a ring and covered with icing: *They made angel cake white and devils's food cake chocolate.*- Reader's Digest.

Angelino *Am.* citizen of Los Angeles: *almost every Angelino gets stopped sooner or later for a traffic violation.* - New York., *Angelinos wanted to live near their work* - R. Crais.

angels/ angels on horseback *Br.* oysters wrapped in bacon, served on toast.

angels/ join the angels *Am.* die.

angle *Am.* sl. selfish motive: *I knew he had to have an angle* - S. Sheldon., *What's your angle?* - D. Brenner.

anglepoise lamp *esp. Br.* tdmk. adjustable table lamp.

Anglo 1. *esp. Am., Aus.* sl. person of Anglo-Saxon ethnic origin: *They're mainly anglos out on Long*

Island these days. - T. Thorne. 2. *Br.* an English club player selected for a Scottish, Irish or Welsh National sports team.

angry white man *esp. Am.* a right-wing or anti-liberal white man, esp. from the working class.

animateur *Br.* person who uses energetic and exciting methods to teach performing arts such as dance and theatre.

ankle *esp. Am.* col. v. 1. walk. 2. leave, quit: *I didn't fire her. I told her she could ankle if she wanted.* - R.A. Spears.

ankle-biter *esp. Am., Can., Aus., NZ.* humor. a child.

anklet *esp. Am., Can.* ankle sock.

Annie /Oakley/ *Am.* sl. free ticket to a game or entertainment.

announce /for/ *Am.* declare one's candidate/ for a political office.

annual general meeting (AGM) *Br.* a meeting held once every year in which a company or an organisation discusses past year's activity and elects new officers.

annualize *Am.* compute /income, etc./ for a year.

anode *Br. /Am.* **plate/** part of electric instrument which collects electrons.

A. No. 1. *Am.* col. excellent.

anorak 1. *esp. Br., Can. /Am., Aus.* **parka/** light waterproof jacket, parka: *The wind whipped our anoraks* - B. Bryson. 2. *Br.* col. derog. a person who pursues an interest with obsessive dedication.

A.N.Other. *Br.* (used when listing sports teams) a player who has not been named or whose election hasn't been confirmed.

another pair of shoes / boots *Br.* horse of a different colour, smth. completely different.

another place *Br.* the other House of Parliament.

anothery *Aus.* another one.

answer/ Good answer! *Am.* sl. excl. of approval or agreement with sb.

answer back *Br. /Am.* **talk back/** speak rudely when answering sb. in authority.

answering machine *esp. Am. /esp. Br.* **answerphone/** a device connected to a telephone which answers calls automatically and records messages for callers.

antagonize *Am.* struggle, fight: *she'd practically gone out of her way to antagonize and alienate her best friend from high school.* - F. Pascal.

ante *esp. Am.* col. amount paid, price: *Bleckner knows how to up the ante with each attack* - New York.

ante/ up/raise the ante *esp. Am.* increase the risks that you take with the aim of gaining more from the current situation later.

ante (up) *esp. Am. Can.* col. /*Br.* **cough up/** pay /an amount/, esp. reluctantly and in advance, put down one's stake: *So Billings didn't ante up the hundred grand.* - P. Case, J. Migliore.

ante-bellum *Am.* adj. pre-Civil War in America: *How could one understand the ante-bellum southern writers if one knew nothing of the "Cottom Kingdom"* – V.W. Brooks.

antenatal *esp. Br.* tech. /*esp. Am., Aus.* **prenatal/** antenatal medical examination.

antenatal adj. *Br.* /*Am.* **prenatal/** pertaining to the time before a birth: *It's best to talk to someone about this, such as your doctor or someone at the antenatal clinic* - Young Citizen's Passport.

antenna *esp. Am., Can., Aus.* or tech. /*esp. Br.* **aerial/** radio or TV (car) antenna: *Radio signals from them get through the cloud to Fred's antenna.* - K. Vonnegut, Jr.

ante-post *Br.* (of a bet in a horse race) placed at odds fixed at the time and before the runners are known, on a horse likely to be entered.

anticlockwise *Br., Aus. /Am.* **counterclockwise/** in the opposite direction to the hands of a clock: *The plane was flying in an anticlockwise direction* - A. McLean., *I told you before - not anti-clockwise.* - G. Greene.

antiunion *Am.* antitradeunion.

antsy *Am.* col. easily irritated or slightly angry about smth.: *he occasionally gets antsy.* Time.

anvil chorus *Am.* mass of angry people.

anxious seat/ on anxious seat *Am.* in trouble.

any *Am.* col. adv. /used at the end of a sentence/ in the least, at all: *The jerky swing of a plane as it started to roll didn't help any.* - J. DeFelice., *I don't help the pain any by shouting, do I?* - P. Case, J. Migliore.

any/ get any *Am.* sl. have sexual intercourse/ esp. in the phr. *Getting any?*

anyplace *Am.* col. adv. anywhere: *He never went anyplace without it.* - I. Shaw., *a burning desire to go, to move, to get under way any place away from here* - J. Steinbeck., *But he couldn't buy any paper anyplace* - E. Houtzig.

AOB *Br.* any other business (used at the end of subjects to be discussed at a meeting).

A-OK *Am.* adv., adj. completely right and acceptable.

The Apache State, Copper State *Am.* Arizona.

apart from *Br.* a. except for. b. in addition to.

apartment 1. *esp. Am., Can. /Br., Aus.* **flat/** private flat or service flat, they are usu. rented.

2. *esp. Br.* a large and expensive flat. / in Britain **apartment** is a room, in plural - a set of rooms used with no kitchen: *But this so far is a nice and very expensive group of flats. - Why do they call "the apartments" flats? I've been in one. Lavish, surrounded by gardens.* - T. Caldwell.

apartment block *esp. Am., Can. /Br.* **flat block, block of flats/** residential block divided up into perfectly self-contained suites: *a fresh clean city of glass and modern flat-blocks.* - A. Burgess.

apartment hotel *Am., Can. /Br.* **(block of) service flats/** hotel with furnished apartments to let for permanent residents: *Elizabethan apartment-hotels called "Tudor City" near the East River* - K. Vonnegut, Jr.

apartment house /also **apartment building** or **unit, complex**/ *esp. Am. /Br.* **block of flats, dwelling house/** a large building with many apartments: *the cab pulled up in front of Selena's apartment house.* - J.D. Salinger.

apartment house, also **high rise apartment house** *Am. /Br.* **tower block (of flats)/** very high apartment building: *the high-rise apartment houses going up all around Baku were "beautiful"* - R.G. Kaiser., *they reached the big block of flats* - D. Lessing.

ape/ go ape *esp. Am., Can.* sl. go crazy: *Then Frank went ape.* – A. Summers, R. Swan.

apparel *esp. Am.* /in combinations/ clothes, clothing, etc., e.g. *ladies ready-to-wear apparel.*

appeal against smth. *Br. /Am.* **appeal** smth./ ask formally to change smth.

appearance/ from all appearance *Am.* judging from what can be seen.

appearing *Am.* /in combinations/ looking e.g. *youthful appearing.*

appendicectomy *Br.* appendectomy.

appetizer(s) *esp. Am. /esp. Br.* **hors d'oeuvres/** small snacks before the main course.

applause line *Am.* a statement in a political speech calculated to win applause from an audience.

Apple Island *Aus.* Tasmania.

applejack *esp. Am., Can.* home-brewed apple brandy: *I buy myself a little pint of something, applejack usually* - I. Shaw., *He sipped the applejack with deep appreciation.* - J. Steinback., *I will make cider and applejack.* - C. McCullers.

appleknocker *Am.* 1. derog. sl. rustic person, esp. a farmer. 2. col. a peson who picks or sells apples.

apple pendowdy *Am.* dessert of sliced apples.

apple-pie *Am., Can.* 1. typically American, esp. in **as American as apple pie/** e.g. **apple-pie virtues,** etc. 2. used to represent a cherished idea of homeliness.

apple-pie bed *Br.* trick done to sb.'s bed when the sheets are folded in a particular way so that a person can't get into bed.

apple-pie order/ in apple-pie order *Am.* col. very tidy and correctly arranged.

apple-polish *esp. Am., Can.* col. seek favour by toadying. n. **-er**: *Harry Kagan is a politician and apple-polisher.* - B. Kaufman.

apples *Aus.* col. fine, perfect; **she'll be apples** *Aus.* col. everything will be all right.

How do you like them apples! - *Am., Aus.* col. 1. something that one says to show one's superiority. 2. exclamation of surprise or disappointment.

apples and oranges *esp. Am., Can.* two completely different things or people.

applesauce *Am.* sl. 1. insincere flattery. 2. nonsense: *A lot of those campaign promises to lower taxes were just so much applesauce.* - J.C. Whitford., R.J. Dixson.

appliance *Br.* the action or process of bringing smth. into operation.

applianced *Am.* (of a kitchen) having or fitted wth appliances.

appointive *Am., Can.* related to or subject to appointment: *key appointive positions receive the same scrutiny* - P. Robertson.

appointments column *Br.* part of the newspaper where jobs are advertised.

appraiser *Am.* person estimating the cost or value of smth. such as property: *professional appraisers charge up to $300 an hour for a consultation* – Reader's Digest.

appro/ on appro *Br.* col. on approval.

approach road *Br.* one leading up to a certain place or feature.

approbate *esp. Am.* rare. approve, sanction.

approved school *Br.* boarding school for young criminals in Great Britain abolished in 1971.

apres-skis *Br.* adj. /of clothes/ worn on skiing holiday.

apron *Am.* print. extra space left at the edge of a page for a fold-out.

aquaplane *esp. Br. /Am.* **hydroplane/** (of cars) slide forwards without control on a wet road: *cars aquaplaned daringly through these temporary lakes* - B. Bryson.

Arabian *Am.* a type of fast gracefull horse.

Arbor Day *esp. Am., Can., Aus.* day set apart for planting trees.

(shopping) arcade *esp. Br.* covered walk with shops along one or both sides.

Archer, Jeffrey *Br.* sl. the sum of 2,000 pounds: *The usual two Archers in a plain envelope.* - T. Thorne.

Archie Bunker *Am.* sl. /*Br.* **Alf Garnet/** a bigoted lower middle-class American /British: *He has the support of the traditional Republican establishment, and is adding the Archie Bunker vote* - R.L. Chapman.

arctics *Am., Can.* galoshes: *Marie Leslie waved to a police sergeant, a tall stout policeman in uniform, arctics and airmuffs* - J. O'Hara.

area code *esp. Am., Can., Aus.* /*Br.* **dialling code, prefix, STD code/** telephone service area dialling code / a 3-digit number used in making long distance calls: *A phone number with an 818 area code.* - J. Kellerman.

area school *Am.* school serving several districts.

areaway 1. *Am., Can.* /*esp. Br.* **area/** sunken area or court at the entrance to a cellar or basement: *I...stepped down into the areaway, from where I could see our stoop.* - J. Riffkin, T. Howard. 2. *Am.* passage between buildings.

argue down *esp. Am.* defeat /an opponent/ in a speaking competition: *The speakers were well-informed, but I was able to argue them down.* - Longman.

argy-bargy *esp. Br.* 1. col. empty talk. 2. col. n. v. squabble: *she couldn't face all the argy-bargy at home.* - J. Fowles.

aristo *Br.* col. aristocrat: *He wouldn't be the first well-heeled aristo to go back on his class* - M.M. Kaye.

ark *Am.* 1. large flat boat for carrying freight. 2. any large clumsy building. 3. sl. old car: *Why don't you get rid of that old ark?* - R.A. Spears. 4. large hot-house under polythene cover.

ark / be/go out of the Ark *Br., Aus.* obs. be very old-fashioned; **went/had gone out with the Ark** *Br., Aus.* humor. or obs. not in use anymore.

Arkie *Am.* sl. 1. migratory worker, esp. from Arkansas: *the Arkie drawl of the CB user* - R.L. Chapman. 2. any poor Southern farmer.

arm *Br.* 1. /*Am.* **stem/** an arm of glasses. 2. sl. power, influence.

arm/ an arm and a leg *esp. Am., Can.* sl. very exorbitant price: *It costs me an arm and a leg.* - New Idea.

arm/ chance one's **arm/luck** *Br., Aus.* col. take a risk in obtaining smth. or doing smth. new.

arm/ on the arm *Am.* sl. 1. on credit. 2. free of charge.

arm/ put the arm on sb. *Am., Can.* col. try to force sb. to do smth.: *you are trying to put the arm on me for dough* – J. O'Hara.

armfull *Am.* col. plump girl.

armoury *Am., Can.* drill hall.

armpit/ the armpit of *Am.* col. very undesirable place: *The town should be called the armpit of the nation.* - R.A. Spears.

armpit/ be in debt up to the armpits *Am.* be heavily in debt.

Army Day *Am.* Army Day in the USA /formerly April 6/ replaced by Armed Forces Day.

army list *Br.* /*Am.* **army register/** official list of officers within the army commission.

army-navy (store) *Am., Can.* /*Aus.* **army disposal store/** army surplus store which usu. sells clothes and equipment not needed by the army.

A-road *Br.* a trunk road usu. running between major towns and cities.

around *esp. Am.* /*esp. Br.* **round/** adv. 1. from one place to another. 2. in various places. 3. on all sides. 4. so as to face opposite direction. 5. measured in a circle.

around *esp. Am.* prep. on all sides of, surrounding.

around/ up and around *esp. Am.* out of bed after illness.

arrestee *Am.* person who has been arrested.

arroyo *Am.* watercourse in an arid region, the bed of a stream: *we might find water in one of those arroyos.* - A. Hitchcock Mystery Magazine.

arse *Br., Aus.* taboo. sl. /*Am., Can.* **ass/**. 1. buttocks. 2. fool.

arse about /or **around/** *Br., Aus.* taboo. sl. waste time.

arse/ can't/ couldn't be arsed *Br.* not to do smth. feeling too lazy.

arse over tit/tip or **arse about face** *Br.* /*Am.* **ass over teakettle, ass backwards/** upside down with one's feet above the head; done in the wrong order.

arse bandit *Br.* taboo. sl. a male homosexual.

art *Am.* print. abbr. for artwork or more usually a Mechanical.

artichoke *Aus.* sl. quarrelsome woman, old hag.

article *Am.* sl. clever person.

article/ be doing/in articles *Br., Aus.* be working in a law office where people are training to be a lawyer.

articled *Br.* (to a firm of lawyers or accountants) employed by the firm and training to be qualified; **articled clerk** *Br.* a trainee solicitor.

articles *Br.* agreement by which sb. finishes their education, esp. as a lawyer, by working for a company.

articles of incorporation *Am.* joint stock company registration certificate: *The articles of incorporation of the Lester Corporation, were* *among the first documents bound in the Lester Corp files.* - R. Crais.

articulated *esp. Br.* /of transport vehicles/ having parts joined in a way that allows easy movement: *the pickets argued with the driver of an articulated wagon* - D. Lodge.

articulated lorry, also col. **artic** *Br.* /*Am.* **tractor-trailer**/ truck with a trailer: *In Britain an American cookie is biscuit, a tractor-trailer is an articulated lorry* - Newsweek.

artificials *Am.* artificial flowers.

artillery *Am.* sl. 1. weapons, esp. a handgun: *This isn't the time to pull the artillery* - R. Chandler. 2. equipment used to inject drugs: *Have you got the artillery ready, man?* - T. Thorne.

artiste *esp. Br.* professional entertainer, e.g. singer or dancer.

artmobile *Am.* mobile exhibition on a truck.

art paper *Br.* high-quality paper with a smooth surface.

art theatre *Am.* theatre showing experimental or foreign films.

art union *Aus.* lottery, raffle.

artwork *Br.* print. material (other than text only) for reproduction: *he hasn't got the artwork he needed* - R. Carter, M. McCarthy. Finished artwork or **mechanicals** /*Am.*/ are usu. completely camera ready and include any type matter in position, as well as halftones in the form of pre-screened prints.

arty *Br.* /*esp. Am., Can.* **artsy**/ with an affected, insincere interest in art: *You're one of them artsy-fartsy creative types.* - J. Kellerman; also *Br.* col. **arty-farty** /*Am.* col. **artsy-fartsy**/ making or enjoying decorative objects.

arty-crafty *esp. Br.* col. involved in making decorative and artistc objects.

arvo *Aus., NZ.* col. (this) afternoon: *There's no excuse for being in that state in the middle of the arvo!* - T. Thorne.

as and when *Br.* /*Am., Aus.* **if and when**/ at the time or in the way that.

as...as *Am.* though, e.g. *as improbable as it seems it's true.*

as of *Am.* as for, as to: *As of now we don't know much about Mars.* - A. Makkai.

ascot *Br.* /*Am.* **cravat**/ tie with wide square ends made of silk or wool: *He was wearing a wing collar and an ascot.* - E.L. Doctorow.

asdic (**equipment**) *esp. Br.* /*Am.* **sonar** (**system**)/ an apparatus using sound waves for finding the position of underwater objects.

ASEP (**after school enrichment program**) *Am.* extra-curricular activities at school.

ash-can, garbage can, trash can *esp. Am., Can.* /*esp. Br.* **dust-bin**/ a can for garbage: *I saw the cage on a sidewalk ash-can, waiting for the garbage collector.* - T. Capote., *This is hardly the way to drop me in the ash-can.* - J. Fowles.

ash key *Br.* the winged fruit of an ash tree.

ashman *Am.* man employed to remove waste from ash-cans.

aside from *esp. Am.* adv. 1. as well: *Our gravest problem at present, aside from the country's economic distress, is to forestall Yugoslav occupation* - H. Truman. 2. except for: *Aside from his meager savings, he has no resources to fall back on.* - H.C. Whitford., R.J. Dixson.

ask around *Am.* inquire here and there.

asleep at the switch *Am., Can.* col. not attentive or alert, inactive.

as long as *Am.* /usu. at the beginning of the sentence and used with be or -ing form/ since, it being true that.

as of right *Br.* by right, according to law.

ASPIC *Br.* print. Authors' Symbolic Pre-press Interfacing Codes.

ass *Am.* taboo. sl. 1. arse: *You can take it and shove it up your ass.* - R.L. Chapman. 2. (**a bit of**) **ass** *Am.* a. girl. b. sexual act with a woman.

ass/ sb.'s **ass is in a sling** *Am.* taboo. sl. that person is in trouble.

ass/ be ass out *Am.* sl. be in trouble.

ass/ be up sb.'s **arse** *Br.* /*Am.* **be on** sb.'s **ass**/ annoy sb. by refusing to leave them.

ass/ get your ass over here *Am.* derog. come here quickly.

assault and battery 1. *Br.* a threat to attack sb. followed either by a violent physical act or by unfriendly touching. 2. *Am.* a violent physical attack on sb.: *Frank was accused of assault and battery, and settled out of court.* – A. Summers, R. Swan.

assault course *Br.* /*Am.* **obstacle course**/ an area of land for fitness and strength exercises for soldiers.

ascent/ Royal ascent *Br.* an official signature received from the monarch so that an Act of Parliament could become law.

assemblyman /**assemblywoman**/ *Am.* member of an assembly of lawmakers: *He owes Vic his job as assemblyman* - L. Waller.

assembly room *esp. Br.* public room or hall, in which meetings or social functions are held.

assessable income *Br.* the amount of money which is considered when calculating tax payments.

assessor/ legal assessor *Br. /Am.* **expert witness/** a specialist who gives advice on a technical subject to a law school.

(home) assignment *esp. Am., Aus. /esp. Br.* **homework,** col. prep/ student's homework / do one's **assignment**: *She got books, test dates, assignments* - Reader's Digest.

assist *esp. Am., Can.* col. act of assistance: *The Russians, however, with a good assist from the French, defeated these efforts.* - H. Truman.

assist the police with/in their inquiries *Br.* be taken to the police station about a crime for questioning.

assistant *Br.* a shop assistant.

assistant-principal, vice-prinipal *Am. /Br.* **the head of the teaching (curriculum) department/** deputy of head teacher taking care of academic studies at school.

assistant professor *Am., Can. /Br.* **senior lecturer/** university teacher rank/ one below associate professor but higher than instructor: *She soon had become an assistant professor of anatomy.* - McGraw-Hill.

assistantship *Am., Can.* position of assistant professor held by American student usu. on a part-time base.

assisted area *Br.* a region of high unemployment where the government encourages industrial development (there are two types of them **development areas** and **intermediate areas**.

associate *Am.* a student holding an associate degree (qualification given to a student by a junior college on successful completion of two years of study).

associate editor *Am.* editor assistant.

associate professor *Am. /Br.* **reader/** one above assistant professor and below a full one: *I made love in the apartment of an associate professor of anthropology* - K. Vonnegut, Jr.

Association football *Br.* football, soccer.

assurance *esp. Br.* tech. */Am.* **insurance/** insurance against events that are certain rather than possible.

assure *esp. Br.* insure against a particular event, esp. death, in return for small regular payments.

assured *Br.* insured against loss.

assurer *esp. Br.* 1. person who insures. 2. person who insures one's life.

Athens of the New World / of America *Am.* Boston.

athletics *Br. /Am.* **track and field/**.

Atlantic *Am.* Eastern/ about states, etc.

Atlantic Provinces *Can.* Nova Scotia, New Brunswick, Prince Edward Island /PEI/ and Newfoundland.

ATM (automatic teller machine) *Am. /Br.* **cashpoint, cash dispenser** or **machine/** machine that you get money from: *The best I can do is bleed all the branch ATMs.* - R.J. Randisi, M. Wallace.

ATM card *Am. /Br.* **cash card/** plasic bank card for getting money at ATM.

atop *esp. Am.* on top of: *the flashlight was atop a black-and-white police car* – R.L. Stine.

ATP *Br.* abbr. **automatic train protection** (a system stopping the train automatically if the driver doesn't observe signal warnings or speed restrictions).

attachment *Br.* temporary secondment to an organisation.

attack *Br. /Am.* **offence/** players who usu. score goals in a ball game.

attention deficit disorder (ADD) *esp. Am., Can. /esp. Br.* **hyperactivity/** a behavioural disorder with such symptoms as poor concentration, hyperactivity, and learning difficulties.

attested *Br. /Am.* **certified/** tested and shown to be free from disease / of cows and milk.

attitude *Am., Aus.* sl. antisocial behaviour, esp. in **have attitude**: *You've got an attitude problem.* - T. Thorne., *The kid was giving attitude* - R. Crais.

attorney *esp. Am. /Br.* **barrister, solicitor/** lawyer: *Kindly engage an attorney when you appear before me in this court.* - I. Shaw., *I familiarised myself with his rating as a attorney* - D. Carnegie., *He assigned the newly hired, first female attorney* - G. O'Neill, D. Lehr.

attrit *Am.* col. wear down (an opponent or enemy) by sustained effort.

attrition *esp. Am., Can., Aus., NZ.* reduction of work force by not taking any new workers when some of the old ones leave rather than by redundancy.

aubergine *esp. Br. /esp. Am., Aus.* **eggplant/**: *She gets to grips with it - squeezing aubergines, sniffing tomatoes* - J. Harmer, R. Rossner.

auction/ by auction *Br.* at auction.

audiotypist *Br.* person typing letters that have been recorded.

audit *Am., Can.* attend (a class) informally without working for a credit or taking any exams.

(school) auditorium *esp. Am., Can. /Br.* **assembly hall/** a large room, hall or building

which is used for events such as meetings and concerts.
aunt *Am.* sl. madam of a brothel.
aunt/ my sainted Aunt *esp. Br.* col. excl. of surprise and disbelief.
Aunt Jane /or **Jemima**/ *Am.* female "Uncle Tom": *that's the secret of Aunt Jemima's bandanna.* - E. Cleaver.
Aunt Sally *Br.* 1. game played at a fair. 2. scapegoat.
Aunt Tabby *Am.* derog. sl. woman of conservative views.
Auntie/ Since Auntie had her accident *Aus.* sl. very long ago.
Aussie (land) also **The Land of the Wattle, Kangaroo land** *Aus.* col. Australia.
Australia Day *Aus.* a national holiday in Australia observed in commemoration of the landing of the British at Sydney Cove in 1788 and observed on Jan. 26 if a Monday and otherwise on the next Monday.
Australian /Rules/ Football *Aus.* Australian game like Rugby.
Autralian grip *Aus.* strong friendly handshake.
Australian policy *Aus.* politics that bans immigration from Asian countries.
Authorized Version *esp. Br.* an English translation of Bible made in 1661, also known as King James Bible.
auto *esp. Am., Can.* col. /*Br.* **car**/ n. adj. motor car: *I'll go down the hill and seize up an auto* - L. Uris., *Inside the auto, he changed into his invisible clothing* - W. Murphy.
auto *Am.* col. drive a car.
The Auto State *Am.* Michigan.
autobus *Am.* bus.
autocade *Am.* motorcade.
autocide *Am.* rare. suicide in a car crash.
auto court *Am., Can.* motel: *I found a pleasant auto court* - J. Steinbeck.
autocross 1. *Br.* form of motor racing which includes driving on rough terrain or unmade roads. 2. *Am., Can.* a form of motor racing in which cars are driven around an obstacle course on an empty car park.
Autocue *esp. Br.* tdmk. /*Am., Aus.* tdmk. **TelePrompter**/ a device which makes it possible for broadcasters to read text while looking directly at the cinema camera.
autodom *Am.* world of car builders and car dealers.
autoloader *Am.* rare. fork-lift truck.
automaker *Am.* car builder; company that makes cars.

automarket *Am.* self-service shop.
Automat *Am.* tdmk. a restaurant where food is obtained from enclosed boxes whose doors open when money is put in.
automobile *esp. Am., Can.* /*Br.* **motorcar,** *Br., Can.* **car**/ car: *Automobiles, handguns and silverware can be registered, traced and recorded more easily than children.* - Reader's Digest., *he started out to invent a self-starter for automobiles.* - D. Carnegie., *you can't own an automobile* - J. Riffkin, T. Howard.
automobile tire *Am.* car tyre.
automobilist /also *Am.* **autoist**/ *esp. Am.* motorist.
autopsy *esp. Am.* /*Br.* **postmortem**/ examination of a dead body to discover the cause of death.
autostop *esp. Br.* hitchhike.
autotrain *Am.* train carrying cars with their passengers.
autotruck *Am.* motor driven truck for carrying goods.
autumn *esp. Br., Can.* /*esp. Am., Can.* **fall**/ one of the four seasons of the year.
auxiliary nurses, nursing auxiliaries *Br.* /*Am.* **nurses' aides,** *Aus.* **nursing aids**/ persons who help nurses to take care of people.
avails *Am.* profits or proceeds, esp. from a business or the sales of property.
avenue *Br.* a wide countryside path or road with trees on both sides, esp. one which leads to a large house.
aviation spirit *Br.* /*Am.* **aviation gasoline**/ aviation fuel: *Pilot wrestling hopelessly with controls, tons of bombs, hundreds of gallons of aviation spirit* – R. Westall.
avigation *Am.* navigation of airplanes.
avoirdupois *Am.* sl. weight, fatness: *too much avoirdupois, so I'm dieting* - R.L. Chapman., *a resistance of some one hundred and seventy-five pounds of solid avoirduois.* – K. Chopin.
Aw *esp. Am., Can.* speech sound signifying disapproval, disappointment, disbelief, etc.: *Aw, heck, John that's not fair.* - R. Bradbury.
award wage *Aus.* minimum pay rate.
away, out *Br.* /*Am.* **missing**/ absent at the lesson.
away off *Am.* far away.
awesome *esp. Am., Can., Aus.* very good: *He wasn't awesome, but he did the best he could.* - Guideposts.
awful *esp. Am., Can.* col. very.
awfullize *Am.* imagine that things are much worse than they really are.
awfully *Am.* very.
awhile *Am.* /*Br.* **a while**/ for a short time.

(the) awkward squad *esp. Br.* col. 1. untrained recruits. 2. uncooperative people.
aw-shucks *Am., Can.* col. adj. shy or modest in behaviour, self-deprecating.

B

B/ not to know B from a broomstick *Am.* not to know the basics.
B.A./ hang a B.A. *Am.* sl. /*Br.* **throw a moon**/ bend over and show one's bare buttocks.
babe *esp. Am., Can., Aus.* girl: *lying in the sun, poolside at a classy hotel, picking up exquisite little babes.* - H. Fast., *He was scoring two babes a day.* - Vanity Fair., *See you at the airport, babe.* - M.M. Kaye.
babe in arms *esp. Br.* very young person.
babe in the woods *Am.* easy victim.
babu, baboo *Br.* Indian clerk or government official of low rank.
babushka *Am., Can.* a headscarf tied under the chin, traditionally worn by Russian women.
baby in the woods *Am., Aus.* inexperienced person.
baby *esp. Am., Aus.* sl. 1. person, esp. a girl or woman. 2. girlfriend: *What's your bag, baby?* - S. Sheldon., *Baby, you're almost late.* - L. Waller., *Some guy next to me was snowing hell out of the baby he was with*, - J.D. Salinger., *Shoot the works, baby.* - Reader's Digest.
baby basket *Am.* (also *Am.* tdmk. **portacrib**, *esp. Br.* **carrycot**) boxlike container in which a baby can be carried.
baby bonus *Can.* sl. monthly allowance paid by the state to the parents or trustees of children under 16 years of age.
baby bottle *Am.* /*Br.* **baby's bottle**/ one used to feed a little child with milk.
baby bouncer *Br.* a special harness for baby used to exercise its legs.
baby buggy or **carriage** *esp. Am., Can.* /*esp. Br., Aus.* **pram**/ a 4-wheeled carriage, pushed by hand, in which a baby can sleep or be taken about: *They joined hands consciously and walked without talking among the baby carriages.* - I. Shaw., *You push a baby buggy.* - McGraw-Hill English, 1986.
baby bust *esp. Am., Can.* col. a temporary marked decrease in the birth rate.
Babygro *Br.* tdmk. piece of clothing for a baby, that covers their whole body.

(the) Babylon *Br.* sl. 1. (used mostly by Rastafarians) a racist white society, Britain. 2. the police force.
baby milk *Br.* /*Am.* **formula**/.
baby-minder or **baby-watcher** *Br.* /also *esp. Br.* **child-minder**, *esp. Am.* **baby-sitter**/ person who takes care of babies while their parents are away working and is paid for it., v. **baby-mind, baby-watch.**
The Baby /or **Valentine**/ **State** *Am.* Arizona.
baby-snatcher *Br.* cradle-snatcher.
baby tooth *Am.* milk tooth.
baccalaureate sermon *Am.* graduation speech.
bachelor apartment 1. *Am., Can.* one occupied by a bachelor. 2. *Can.* apartment consisting of a single large room serving as a bedroom and living room with a separate bathroom.
bachelorette 1. *Am., Can.* a young unmarried woman. 2. *Can.* a very small bachelor apartment.
bachelor party *Am., Can.* /*Br.* **stag night**/ a party given to a man who is about to get married, usu. attended by men only; opp. **bachelorette party**.
back *Am., Can.* losing by specified margin, e.g. *be 5 points back.*
back/ be glad to see the back of sb. *esp. Br.* be glad that sb. has gone or a bad situation has ended.
back/ get one's **own back on** sb. *esp. Br.* take revenge on sb.
back/ have a broad back *Br.* be tough and good enough to deal with difficulties.
back/ in back *Am.* in the rear part of smth. esp. a car or building: *Ahmad from the base addresses the crowd in back.* – Harper's Magazine.
back/ in the back, out back *Am.* behind a house or other building.
back/ off the back of a lorry *Br.* /*Am.* **truck**/ humor. stolen.
back/ put one's **back into it** *Br.* col. work very hard to achieve smth.
back/ put/get sb.'s **back up** *Br.* col. annoy sb.
back/ round the back, out the back *Br., Aus.* behind smth. such as house or other building.
back/ talk out of the back of one's **head** *Br., Aus.* col. talk nonsense.
back and fill *Am.* col. be undecided, shilly-shally. n. **back and filling**: *After weeks of backing and ffilling, Henry accepted the offer of a job.* - H.C. Whitford, R.J. Dixson., *I saw her backing and filling and fluttering after her manner.* - I. Stone.

back /or **in back**/ of *esp. Am., Can.* prep. adv. 1. at the back of, behind: *the fire back of her dark deep-set eyes was shining in her excitement.* - R. Stout., *Back of her was the court.* - E. Hemingway. 2. being a cause or reason of. 3. helping, in support of.

back down (the drive) *Am.* /*Br.* **reverse down (the drive)**/ reverse the movement of a car.

back off *esp. Am.* 1. back down, yield; stop annoying: *the government backed off.* - Time., *Quinn had his agents back off for a while* - G. O'Neill, D. Lehr. 2. move backwards, away from smth. 3. gradually stop taking part in smth. or supporting smth.

back to front *Br.* /*Am.* **backwards**/ with the back at the front, e.g. *John's shirt is on back to front.*

back up 1. *esp. Am.* /usu. of liquids/ block a narrow place: *toilets back up just as in-laws arrive* - Reader's Digest. 2. *Am.* /*esp. Br., Aus.* **reverse**/ reverse the movement of a motor vehicle: *a van had stalled in the center lane backing up traffic for blocks and blocks.* – R.L. Stine.

back bar *esp. Am.* a structure behind bar counter, with shelves for holding bottles, other supplies and equipment.

Back Bay *Am.* fashionable part of Boston or any other big city.

backblocks *Aus., NZ.* 1. country remote from settled areas or from a river-front. 2. adj. experienced. 3. slums: *In the backblocks of Florida that sort of stuff was dynamite.* - Bulletin.

back chat *esp. Br., Aus.* /*Am., Can.* **back talk**/ col. rude reply: *Double talk and back chat abounded.* - C.M. Fraser., *there was a little barbed backchat between him and Barney* - J. Fowles.

backcloth *esp. Br.* backdrop: *Flanking them were pack upon pack of mountains steep as a backcloth for melodrama* - L. Van Der Post., *he hadn't been spotted against that vast backcloth of white.* - A. McLean., *whole family can spend the day against a backcloth of luxurious design* - Cheshire Life.

backcomb *esp. Br.* /*Am., Aus.* **(back)tease**/ comb hair against the direction of growth, in order to make it look thicker.

back concession *Can.* any rural region: *They... scrabbled around in back-concession attics* - W. Grady.

back country *esp. Am., Can., Aus.* /also **back district** or **settlement**/ remote (rural) region (in America it is usu. in the mountains away from roads and towns): *The back country roads were narrow and tortuous.* - Reader's Digest.., **back country man** or **back settler.**

background *Am., Can.* col. provide documentation, briefing, etc. for a story., n. **backgrounder.**

backhander *Br.* col. a bribe offered to get smth. done.

backhoe *Am., Can.* machine for digging trenches: *he brought over an enormous dump truck and backhoe* - Reader's Digest.

backlash *Am.* 1. strike back. 2. cause negative reaction.

backmarker *Br.* 1. one who starts with the worst handicap in a race. 2. a competitor who is among the last in a river.

backmatter *Am.* /*Br.* **endmatter**/ print. the final pages of a book, such as the index.

back of beyond *esp. Br., Aus.* col., also *Aus.* **back of Bourke, middle of nowhere** almost inaccessible faraway region.

back-out *Am.* going back on one's promise, position, etc.

backpack *esp. Am., Aus.* /*Br.* **rucksack**/ n. v. / carry/ a rucksack on one's back. n. **-er, -ing**: *She...casually slid the glass into her backpack.* - New York., *the backpack was visible near the base of one of the speaker towers.* - Newsweek.

back passage *Br.* euph. rectum.

backroom boys *esp. Br.* col. workers whose efforts, though vital, receive no publicity or general recognition: *The backroom boys have decided too many things in the past.* - R.S. Spears.

back saw *Am.* /*Br.* **tenon saw**/a small tool with a sharp thin blade and a strong metal back.

backseat driver *esp. Am.* businessman or politician who tries to control things that they are not responsible for.

backside *esp. Am., Can.* the reverse or rearward side of a thing.

backside/ a boot up the backside *Br.* col. used to show disapproval with sb. and encouragement to stop being lazy and start working.

backside/ get off your backside *Br., Aus.* col. taboo. start doing smth.

backside/ sit (around) on one's **backside** *Br., Aus.* col. taboo. do nothing.

back space *Br.* /*Am.* **backspace key**/ key of a typewriter that one presses to make the movable part move one or more spaces towards the beginning of the line.

backstop *Am.* col. catcher.

back-straight *Br.* /*Am., Can.* **back stretch**/ back stretch of a race track.

back-street abortion *Br., Aus.* /*Am.* **back-alley abortion**/ illegal and dangerous operation to end pregnancy done by sb. who is not medically qualified.

back talk *Am., Can. /Br.* **back chat/** rude reply: *No more cross talk and back talk.* - M. Torgov.

back-to-back *esp. Br.* a house in a row built with its back against the back of a house in a parallel row.

back-to-basics *Am.* coming back to major principles.

back to front *Br., Aus. /esp. Am.* **backwards/** (of clothes) put on the other way around.

backup *Am., Aus.* backing music or singing which is played to support a song or a tune, esp. a popular one; **backup singer**.

back-up 1. *Am. /Br.* **tailback/** a traffic jam. 2. *Am.* a substitute player.

back-up light *Am., Can. /Br.* **reversing light/** warning light at the rear of a motor vehicle.

backward *esp. Am.* backwards.

backward/ not backward in coming forward *Br.* col. be very direct and bold about asking what they want.

backwards *Am. /Br.* **back to front/**.

backwards/ know smth. **backwards** *esp. Br., Aus. /esp. Am.* **backwards and forwards/** know very well.

backwards/ pull over backwards *Aus.* try very hard to do smth., esp. to help or please sb. else.

backwoods *esp. Am., Can.* remote unlaboured forest land; **bacwoodsman** *esp. Am., Can.* a rural citizen, esp. uncouth or backward.

backwoodsman *Br.* col. peer who rarely if ever attends the House of Lords.

backyard 1. *Br.* a paved court behind a house. 2. *esp. Am., Can., Aus. /Br.* **back garden/** kitchen or cottage garden: *Mother grew sweet peas in our backyard* - J. Baez., *Fresh produce from their own backyard* - M. Torgov., *small onions that our fathers grew in their back gardens.* – R. Westall. 3. *Am.* col. familiar dear places.

bacon/ bring home the bacon *Br.* journalism. win or do very well in sports.

bacon/ save sb.'s **bacon** *esp. Br.* col. save sb. from failure or difficulties.

bacon-and-eggs *Aus.* eggs and bacon.

baconer *esp. Br.* pig raised for bacon.

bacony *Br.* fatty.

bad 1. *esp. Am.* col. very bad. 2. adv. *Am., Can.* badly.

bad/ be taken bed *esp. Br.* col. become ill.

bad/ my bad *Am.* sl. I'm sorry, it's my fault.

badass *esp. Am., Can.* col. aggressive, tough or uncooperative person.

bad books/ in sb.'s **bad books** *esp. Br., Can.* sl. regarded as hostile, hated and menaced: *I put myself in Dad's bad books* – R. Westall; opp. is **in** sb.'s **good books**.

baddie, baddy *Br.* col. */Am.* col. **bad guy/** bad character, esp. in a book or film.

bad egg *esp. Am.* col. a bad or dishonest person.

bad form *esp. Br.* obs. bad manners: *It's supposed to be bad form to ask us not to talk though.* - E. Hemingway., *then suddenly the war was a bad form.* - D. Lessing.

bad hair day *esp. Am.* col. a day when everything goes wrong.

bad way/ be in a bad way *Br., Aus.* be ill, unhappy or in a bad shape.

badge *Br. /Am.* **button/** a piece of metal, plastic, etc. with a writing or a picture on it.

badger game *Am.* sl. blackmail: *she did six months on a badger game charge* - D. Hammet.

The Badger State *Am.* Wisconsin / **Badger** *Am.* col. inhabitant of Wisconsin.

badman *Am.* sl. villain, esp. a killer in a cowboy movie.

badminton *esp. Br.* drink of dry wine, sugar or water.

bad-mouth *esp. Am., Aus., Can.* sl. disparage, denigrate: *He didn't want to bad-mouth his former landlady* - D. Brenner, *For years I've been hearing you bad-mouth your cousin Henry* - J. Cheever., *he had badmouthed her to the press.* - D. Mortman.

bad news *esp. Am.* disagreeable, dull or unpleasant person: *But his colleagues were bad news.* - J. O'Brien, A. Kurins.

bad-off *Am.* not having much money; poor.

bafflegab *esp. Am., Can.* derog. confusing jargon, esp. bureaucratic: *There was a lot of bafflegab in the speech, a lot of nonsense.* - W. Magnuson.

bag 1. *Am.* sl. conceal or suppress: *May be we should bag it now and get out of town.* – R.L. Stine. 2. *Aus., NZ.* col. criticize or laugh; n. **bagging**. 3. *Br.* also **handbag** a bag used by women to carry money and personal things.

bag (smth) *Br.* col. get smth. before others.

bag/ a bag of fruit *Aus.* sl. suit.

bag/ in the bag *Am.* drunk: *Dwayne had done this, supposedly, by being half in the bag* – K. Vonnegut, Jr.

bag/ set one's **bag for** smth. *Am.* try to grab smth.

bag and baggage/ go/leave bag and baggage *Br.* take all one's possessions not intending to return.

baggage *esp. Am.* /*esp. Br.* **luggage**/ traveller's bags and personal belongings: *Teddy is carrying some heavy personal baggage into the campaign* - Newsweek.

baggage-car *Am.* /*Br., Aus.* **luggage van**/ railroad car for carrying luggage, mailbags and light freight: *The coffin was loaded into the baggage-car of the train.* - E. Hemingway.

baggage check *Am.* baggage receipt.

baggage man /also **baggage master**, col. **baggage smasher**/ *Am.* porter at a railroad station, airport, etc.

baggage room *Am., Aus.* /also **checkroom**/ *Am.* / *Br.* **left luggage office**/ cloakroom, place where one can leave one's bags for some time to be collected later: *Later they put her trunk in the baggage room* - K. Blair.

baggage ticket *Am.* /*Br.* **luggage ticket**/ ticket for the freight.

baggage train *Am., Can.* /*Br.* **luggage train**/ freight train.

baggie *Am., Can.* tdmk. plastic bag, esp. for storing food.

bag job *Am.* sl. illegal search of suspect's residency to obtain incriminating evidence.

bag lunch *Am.* /*Br.* **packed lunch**/ one that person takes to school, work, etc. to be eaten at lunch time.

bag man 1. *Br.* derog. obs. /also *Br.* obs. **commercial traveller**, *Br.* col. **commercial**, *Am.* **(travelling) salesman**, *Am.* col. **drummer**/ travelling salesman. 2. *Aus.* a tramp. 3. *Can.* a political fund-raiser. 4. *Am., Aus., NZ.* an agent who collects or distributes the proceeds of illegal activities.

bags 1. *esp. Br., Aus.* col. **bags of** lots, plenty: *He's got bags of money* - R.L. Chapman. 2. *Br.* obs. loose fitting trousers. 3. *Br., Aus.* col. excl. / used by children when staking a claim, esp. in the phr. **Bags I.** 4. *Am.* sl. breasts.

bags/ rough as bags *Aus.* very rough.

bag trousers *Br.* obs. loose fitting trousers.

baidarka *Can.* kayaklike skin boat.

bail *Am.* /*Br., Aus.* **bale out**/ escape from an aircraft by parachute: *The pilot was able to bail out of the burning plane.* - Longman.

bail *esp. Br.* pole or bar used to confine or separate animals.

bail/ post bail *Am.* pay bail for sb.

bail/ bail bandit *Br.* col. person who commits crime while still on bail.

bail/ straw bail *Am.* unsafe guarantee.

bail (up) *Aus., NZ.* 1. tie a cow, when milking. 2. detain sb. for a conversation.

bailiff 1. *Br.* a. person who supervises a farm or land for the owner. b. person who takes people's property when they owe money: *I expect to find the bailiffs in the hall when I go home.* - J. Joyce. 2. *Am.* person whose job is to guard the prisoners in a court of law: *the bailiff led in the aged black maid* - T. Thompson. 3. *Br.* col. a law officer who makes sure that the decisions of a court are obeyed.

bait *Br.* sl. a fit of rage.

bak choy *Am.* /*Br.* **Chinese leaves**/.

bake 1. *Am.* social gathering at which baked food is served, esp. a sea shore picnic. 2. *Br.* a vegetable or fish bake is a dish that is made by chopping up and mixing together a number of ingredients and cooking them in the oven so that they form a fairly dry solid mass. 3. *Can.* also **white nose** new inexperienced person.

bake apple *Can.* the fruit of the cloudberry.

baked custard *Br.* /*esp. Am.* **cup custard**/ solid custard sauce.

bakehouse *Br.* bakery.

baker *Am.* small portable oven.

baker-legged *Br.* knock-kneed.

baker's *Br.* /*Am.* **baker**/ a shop that sells bread, cakes, etc.

bakeshop *Am., Can.* bakery.

baking tray *Br.* /*Am.* **cookie sheet, cupcake tin**/.

balance of payments, balance of trade *esp. Br.* the amount of money that a country earns from export of its goods compared to the amount it spends: *the Tories had a 800 million pound deficit in the balance of payments.* - J. Ruppeldtova.

bald patch *Br., Aus.* /*Am.* **bald spot**/ area of head without hair.

balk, baulk *Br.* thick rough wooden beam.

balky *Am.* refusing to do what you're asked or expected to do.

ball *Br.* (of a flower) fail to open properly.

ball *Am.* sl. 1. also *Can.* have sex: *She may not be able to judge thirteen crises and ball you at the same time* - "M." 2. have a good time: *Martha loves to ball.* - B. Holiday, W. Duffy.

ball *Am., Can.* baseball/ **play ball** *Am.* play baseball: *They can't play ball.* - T. de Haven. **ball-player** n.: *the ballplayer in a fury at something she said slammed a suitcase shut* – N. Mailer.

ball/ carry the ball *Am.* take the active part in smth.: *But you'll have to carry the ball yourself.* - Guideposts.

ball/ drop the ball *Am.* col. make a (careless) mistake.

ball/ pick up/take the ball and run with it *esp. Am.* take an idea and develop it further.

ball/ run with the ball *Am.* get smth. before the other contestants.

ball/ be no ball of fire *Am., Aus.* col. lack energy and interest: *he's no whiz, no spectacular ball of fire.* – P. Roth.

ball-breaker 1. *Br., Aus.* sl. taboo. a female man-hater. 2. *Am.* sl. also **ball-buster** a. difficult problem. b. derog. bossy woman.

ball-carrier *Am.* (American football) a player with a ball attempting to advance it.

ballgame *Am.* 1. a game of baseball or football. 2. *Am., Can.* a baseball match: *he listened to the ball game* – P. Roth.

ball game *Br.* any game with a ball.

ballhawk *Am., Can.* col. a player who is good at getting possession of or catching the ball in a game.

balloon *Br.* send the ball high in the air.

balloon/ go over like dead balloon *Br.* col. (of a speech, performance, etc.) be poorly received.

the balloon goes up *Br.* the situation has become very serious.

balloon payment *Am.* money borrowed that must be paid back in one large sum after several smaller payments have been made.

ballot *Br.* find out what people think by letting them vote.

ballot-box/ stuff the ballot-box *Am.* falsify the results of voting.

ballot paper *Br.* a paper used for voting.

ball/ the whole ball of wax *Am., Can.* col. the whole of smth.

ballpark *esp. Am., Can.* 1. a field for playing baseball with seats for people to watch the game: *you are playing in a different ballpark.* - C. Hoover. 2. col. a certain area or range. 3. col. (of a price or cost) approximate.

ballpark/ in the ballpark *Am.* approximately right.

ballpark/ in the same ballpark as another *Am.* both things are compatible.

ballpark figure or **estimate** *esp. Am.* approximate figure.

ball-player *Am.* baseball player: *My son, who is now 16, is much more interested in meeting ballplayers* – Reader's Digest.

ballpark-playfield *Am. /Br.* **park/** football field.

ballpoint pen *Am. /Br.* tdmk. **Biro/**.

balls *Br.* taboo. sl. nonsense.

balls up *Br., Aus. / Am.* **ball up** / taboo. sl. spoil smth.: *That's how Frank got balled up in all that.* - K. Vonnegut, Jr.

balls-up *Br., Aus.* taboo. sl. a terrible mess.

ballsy *esp. Am., Aus.* taboo. sl. courageous: *The Americans would call it ballsy.* - L. Uris., *I'm ballsy and clever and tenacious.* - D. Mortman.

ball-tearing *Aus.* col. 1. very demanding or exhausting. 2. spectacular; n. **ball-tearer.**

bally *Br.* obs. euph. adv., adv. bloody: *Don't make such a bally racket!* - J. Joyce., *Well, it's a bally nuisance all the time.* - M.M. Kaye.

ballyhoo *esp. Am., Can.* praise or publicize extravagantly.

balm/ heart balm *Am.* financial compensation for one's former love or bride.

balmy *esp. Am. /esp. Br.* col. **barmy/** crazy: *I was balmy.* – N. Hentoff.

Balt *Aus.* sl. an immigrant to Australia.

banana/ make like a banana/atom and split *Am.* sl. humor. leave a place.

banana/ top (second) banana *esp. Am., Can.* col. the most (second) important person in an organisation or activity.

banana belt *Am.* col. winter resorts with warm climate.

banana-bender *Aus.* col. a Queenslander.

Banana City *Aus.* Brisbane/ also **Brissie.**

Bananaland *Aus.* col. Queensland.

banana skin *Br.* col. an event or situation likely to cause difficulty or make one look foolish; **slip on a banana skin/peel** *esp. Br.* do smth. stupid.

banana truck *Am.* sl. crazy person.

Banbury cake *Br.* a kind of mince pie.

band *Am., Can.* tech. /*Br.* **ring,** *Am.* **tag/** put a ring of metal round a bird's leg to identify it.

band *Aus.* sl. prostitute.

band *Can.* obs. social unit of Indians, smaller than a tribe.

bandage 1. *esp. Br. /Am.* **gauze (bandage)/** piece of material used to bind up a wound, sore, etc.: *then you can put on a stable bandage* - J. Herriot. 2. *Am. /Br.* also **(sticking) plaster/** material that can be stuck to the skin to protect small wounds: *Wong wrapped the arm in bandages.* - Reader's Digest.

Band-Aid, bandage 1. *Am.* tdmk. /*Br.* **Elastoplast, Plaster/** a kind of sticking plaster: *Jean has washed out the cut and put a Band-Aid on it.* - H. Fast., *Mrs. Brandel was slapping Band-Aids on everyone* - B. Robinson. 2. *Am.* a temporary solution to a problem.

band aid *Am. /Br.* **patch/** print. corrections added to a program to make it work better (or at all).

b and b *Br.* abbr. for **bed and breakfast** as offered in small hotels and private houses: *something I* *had never thought to ask for in a B and B.* - B. Bryson.

bandicoot/ poor (miserable) as bandicoot *Aus.* very poor., / **be flying like a bandicoot before a bushfire** *Aus.* panic very much. / **balmy as a bandicoot** *Aus.* crazy. / **bald as a bandicoot** *Aus.* completely bald. / **bandy as a bandicoot** *Aus.* bandy-legged.

bandicoot *Aus.* steal /esp. potatoes.

bandit/ make out like a bandit *Am.* col. receive a lot of money and presents.

bandito *Am., Can.* a Mexican bandit, as they are shown in films.

bandshell *esp. Am., Can.* outdoor platform for musical concerts: *The band shell was decorated with patriotic bunting.* - E.L. Doctorow.

bang *Am.* col. a lot of excitement, thrill, kick: *They got a bang out of things.* - J.D. Salinger.

bang(s) *esp. Am., Can.* /*Br.* **fringe**/ bang of hair.

bang *esp. Am., Can.* cut (hair) in a fringe.

bang/ bang goes smth. *esp. Br.* col. it's obvious that it can't be achieved.

bang/ bang the drum (for) *Br.* support or advertise smth. publicly.

bang/ get a bang out of *esp. Am.* col. get excitement and pleasure from smth.

bang/ go over with a bang *Am.* /*Br.* **go off with a bang,** *esp. Br., Aus.* col. **go with a bang/** be very successful: *The new movie went over with a bang.* - H.C. Whitford., R.J. Dixson.

bang on *Br.* col. make repeated insistent references to smth.: *It's no use my banging on to the man about all pulling together.* - D. Lodge.

bang up *Am.* col. 1. also *Can.* damage, ruin / smth./: *A driver veers a banged-up Fiat sharply left* - Reader's Digest. 2. make (a woman) pregnant: *Some people think it's OK to sleep with a girl so long as you don't bang her up.* - Longman.

bang up *Br.* col. imprison: *Being banged up's no joke, even in an open prison.* - T. Thorne. adj. **banged-up.**

banger *esp. Br.* col. 1. also /*Aus.* **snags,** *Am.* **sausages**/ sausage: *smoked pigeon on radicchio has replaced banger and mash* - Time. 2. old ramshackle car: *The Jaguar seemed almost obscenely opulent alongside the bangers parked in this street* - D. Lodge. 3. also *Aus.* noisy fireworks.

bang for the buck *esp. Am., Can.* sl. value for the money spent: *There is a lot of bang for the buck in this unique volume of business literacy* - Omni., *Now they're looking for the biggest bang for the buck.* – Downbeat; also **give/offer/ provide more/bigger bang(s) for the/**(one's) **buck(s).**

bangin' *Br.* col. (of dance music) having a loud, relentless beat.

bang-on, bang on *Br.* col. exactly right.

bangs *Am.* /*Br.* **fringe**/ hair that is cut straight across your forehead: *You ran your hand over my forehead, smoothing the bangs away from my eyes.* - K. Davis.

bangtail muster *Aus.* a count of cattle on a station.

bang-up *Am., Can.* col. excellent.

bang-up job *Am.* col. a very successful piece of work.

bang-zone *Am.* zone of sonic boom/ from airplanes.

banjaxed *Am.* sl. demolished, ruined.

banjo *Aus., NZ.* shovel.

bank 1. *Br.* (of a locomotive) providing additional power for a train in ascending an incline. 2. *Am., Can.* (in a pool) play (a ball) so that it rebounds off a surface, such as backboard or cushion. 3. *Can.* water tank where live lobsters are kept.

bank up *Br.* arrange smth. into a pile or into rows.

bank/ in the bank *Br.* col. in deficit, in the red.

bank/ give sb. **down the banks** *Am.* col. berate sb.

bank/ You can't put it in the bank *Am.* col. It won't help much.

bank barn *esp. Am., Can.* barn with two floors built on the side of the hill so that both floors have entrances at a ground floor.

bank bill 1. *Br.* a bill of exchange drawn by one bank on another. 2. *esp. Am.* /*Br.* **banknote**/.

bank call *Am.* periodic demand by the state or federal government for sworn statements, giving the financial conditions of banks.

bank card 1. *Am.* credit card. 2. *Br.* cheque card.

banker *Br.* a supposedly certain bet.

banker *Aus.* col. overflowing river/ **run a banker** *Aus.* run flush with the banks.

banker's card *Br.* cheque card: *he couldn't find his banker's card* – S. Townsend.

banker's hours *Am., Can.* short working hours.

banker's orders, standing order *Br.* an order to a bank to pay a fixed amount from an account to a named person or organisation regularly.

bank holiday 1. *Br.* legal holiday on which banks and most businesses are closed: *Me, I don't even walk to the corner shop on bank holidays.* - B. Bryson. 2. *Am.* a period when banks are closed, usu. by government offer, to prevent money difficulties.

banking account *Br.* bank account.

bank night *Am.* lottery held in a motion picture theatre.
banknote *esp. Br. /Am.* **bill/** a piece of paper money.
bannock *Can.* a type of pancake.
bankroll *esp. Am., Can.* 1. n. supply of money: *So they had expected to find a huge bankroll.* - G. O'Neill, D. Lehr., *she carried a bankroll in her bosom.* - S. Bellow. 2. put up money for some purpose: *Chrysler bankrolls Lamborgnini in an uphill race with Ferrari.* - Time., *by selling off small parcels he's been able to bankroll his film.* - Reader's Digest.
bank swallow *Am., Can.* sand martin.
banner *Am., Can.* very good, excellent.
banner/ carry the banner *Am.* col. walk all night without a sleep (of unemployed).
bannock *Can.* thin oatmeal cake.
banqueting hall, banquet room *Am.* large room in which banquet takes place.
banting *Br.* rare. dieting, slimming.
bap *Br.* a round soft bread roll.
Bar 1. *Br., Aus.* (the members of) the profession of barrister. 2. *Am.* (the members of) the profession of lawyer: *After he passed the bar exams, Frost was called to the bar.* - H.C. Whitford., R.J. Dixson.
Bar / be called/go to the Bar 1. *Br., Aus.* become a barrister. 2. *Am. /also Am.* **be admitted to the Bar/** become a lawyer.
Bar/ be called within the Bar *Br.* be appointed a Queen's counsel.
bar *Br.* 1. one of the rooms or counter inside a pub or hotel for the sale and consumption of alcoholic drinks. 2. a heating element in electric heaters. 3. metal strip below the clasp of a medal, awarded as additional distinction. 4. a rail marking the end of each chamber of the Houses of Parliament.
bar 1. *Br. /Am.* **measure/** one of the small equal parts into which a piece of music is divided, containing a fixed number of beats. 2. *esp. Am., Can. /Br., Aus.* **bar line/** music notation mark. 3. *Am.* stripe of material worn onto the arm of a military uniform to show the rank. 4. *esp. Br.* prep. except for, apart from. 5. *Br.* (horse racing) except the horses indicated (when stating the odds).
bar/ all over bar the shooting *Br.* said when the result of the activity is known but it is not officially completed.
bar-and-grill *Am.* restaurant serving both alcoholic drinks and food.

barb(ed) wire *Am.* wire with short, sharp points on.
barbell *Am.* metal bar with weights at each end used for lifting to get stronger.
barber *Am.* 1. cut the hair, shave or trim the beard: *barbered face contorted with a grimace* - M. Puzo. 2. sl. chatter: *What the hell am I doing barbering with a lousy dick?* - D. Hammet.
barber's *Br. /esp. Am., Can.* **barber shop/** a shop where barber (men's hairdresser) works.
barbershop quartet *Am.* male quartet which sings improvised arrangements of popular songs and ballads: *he'd order tickets for the two of us to an annual barbershop-quartet show.* - Reader's Digest.
barbie *esp. Aus., Br.* col. barbecue: *spent the day drinking Fosters and putting a shrimp on the barbie.* - T. Thorne.
bar car *Am.* passenger railway car where alcoholic drinks and light food are served.
bar chart *Br. /esp. Am.* **bar graph/**.
Barcoo rot *Aus.* scurvy.
bardie *Aus.* the edible larva or pupa of certain insects.
bare-assed *Am.* sl. naked.
bare-bones *Am.* col. having only the most basic things that are needed: *a bare-bones prose style* - R.L. Chapman.
barebum *Aus.* sl. /*Br.* sl. **bumfreezer/** short jacket.
barf *esp. Am., Can., Aus.* col. v., n. /*Aus.* sl. **bark/** vomit: *If I eat another hotdog, I'll barf. I'll be sick.* - W. Magnuson.
barf(bag) *Am.* sl. a waterproof paper bag provided for each passenger on an aircraft in case they need to vomit: *you need the barf bag* – Reader's Digest.
bar-fly *Am.* col. person who frequents bars: *And now run along back to your Mediterranean bar-fly* - M.M. Kaye.
bargain *Br.* an agreement to buy or sell shares on the stock market.
bargain/ into the bargain *esp. Br, Aus. /Am., Can.* **in the bargain/** as well as everything else.
bargain on *esp. Am.* expect to find: *When John bought a car, he hadn't bargained on the cost of gasoline and garage rent.* - H.C. Whitford., R.J. Dixson.
bargaining counter *Br.* bargaining chip; smth. which sb. else wants that you are willing to lose in order to reach an agreement.
barge *esp. Br.* houseboat.
bargee *esp. Br. /Am.* **bargeman/** barge operator: *that would have shocked a Victorian bargee.* - P. Howard.

barge pole/ I wouldn't touch it (him, her), etc. with a /*Br., Aus.* **barge pole/** or /*Am.* **ten-foot pole/** I would never come close to him/her.

bar girl *Am., Can.* an attractive woman employed to encourage customers to buy drinks at a bar.

bar graph *esp. Am.* /*Br.* **bar chart/**: *pie charts, bar graphs, and linear analyses on the omnipresent computer screens* - K. Lipper.

bar hop *Am.* 1. v. n. (work as) a waiter or waitress who carries food or drinks from a bar to customers outside: *he went out bar hopping.* - Vanity Fair. 2. col. /*Br.* **pub-crawl/**.

barium meal *Br., Aus.* /*Am.* **barium sulphate/** a chemical that is swallowed by a person just before an X-ray is taken of their stomach and bowels, so that their organs can be seen clearly.

bar line *Br., Aus.* /*esp. Am., Can.* **bar/** the vertical line that divides one bar from another in a written piece of music.

bark 1. *esp. Am.* col. call out in order to sell or advertise smth., esp. at the entrance to the place of entertainment to draw customers: *He was a carny barker once* – J. Hopkins. 2. *Aus.* sl. /*Am., Can., Aus.* **barf/** vomit.

bark at the moon *Am.* col. worry about smth. you can't change.

bark/ with a bark on *Am.* col. rough man.

barking *Br.* col. obs. demented.

barking mad *Br., Aus.* obs. crazy.

barkeeper *esp. Am., Can.* /*Am.* **barkeep/** barkeeper: *Both of the barkeeps were thin, dark, and bearded* - J. Kellerman.

barley beef *Br.* beef of a cow fattened on barley.

barley sugar *Br.* a kind of sweet formerly made with barley.

barley water 1. *Br.* drink made from pearl barley. 2. *Am., Aus.* a drink made from barley and water boiled together for making ill person feel better.

barley wine *esp. Br.* a kind of very strong beer.

barlow (knife) *Am.* small jackknife with one blade.

barmaid 1. *esp. Br.* /*Am.* **bartender/** a woman who serves drinks in a pub or in a bar in a hotel: *they are served by the bar-maid* - J. Ruppeldtova. 2. *Am., Can.* a waitress who serves drinks in a bar.

barman *esp. Br.* /*Am.* **bartender/** a man who serves drinks in a pub or in a bar in a hotel.

barmy *esp. Br.* col. /*esp. Am.* **balmy/** slightly crazy: *I wouldn't be where I am if I was barmy.* - I. Flemming.

barn *Am.* large building for housing subway cars and buses and also doing light maintenance on them, garage depot/ **car barn** or **trolley barn** *Am.* tram park: *we walked to the trolley barn on Pine Street.* - D. Brenner.

barn/ born in a barn *Am.* ill-bred.

barnacle *Am.* man holding tight to his place of work.

barn burner *Am., Can.* an exciting event, esp. a sports contest.

barn dance *esp. Br.* country dance performed at a social gathering.

barnet *Br.* col. a person's hair.

barney *esp. Br., Aus.* col. noisy quarrel.

barn raising *Am.* gathering of neighbours to build a barn: *Her thick, flushed face would have looked right at a barn raising.* - J. Kellerman.

barnstorm *esp. Am., Can.* travel round rural areas with speeches, shows or sports matches.

barnstorming *Br.* (of show, performance, etc.) full of energy and exciting to watch.

barnyard *esp. Am.* farmyard.

barnyard humor *Am.* humor that is slightly rude.

baron of beef *Br.* a joint of beef consisting of two sirloins joined at the backbone.

barrack 1. *Br.* interrupt by shouting, heckle. 2. (for) *Aus.* cheer in support (of).

barrack room lawyer *Br.* one pretending to have authoritative opinions on subjects on which they are not qualified.

barrack square *Br.* a drill ground near barrack.

barranca *Am.* deep gully with steep sides: *Ben held the horses in a barranca.* - A. Hitchcock Mystery Magazine.

barrel *esp. Am., Can.* col. drive very fast, almost losing control of a vehicle: *male pro-lifers barrelled their way to the microphone, and seized it.* – N. Hentoff.

barrel/ be as funny as a barrel of monkeys, be more fun than a barrel of monkeys *Am.* be very funny.

barrel/ on the barrel(head) *Am.* /*Br.* **on the nail/** immediately and in cash.

barrel/ with both barrels *esp. Am.* col. with unrestrained force or emotion.

barrel in *esp. Am.* (of a storm) arrive with force: *Another storm system is barrelling in and should reach Eastern areas by tomorrow.* - Longman.

barrel chair *Am.* /*Br.* **tub chair/** upholstered chair with a high rounded back.

barrelhouse *Am., Can.* a cheap disreputable bar.

barren joey *Aus.* sl. prostitute.

barrens *esp. Am., Can.* area of level unproductive land, poorly forested and generally having sandy soil.

barrette *Am. /Br.* **(hair) slide/** hair slide, a small often decorative fastener to keep a girl's or woman's hair in place: *her hair was held at the top by a barrette.* - S. Bellow.

barrier cream *Br.* cream that stops dirt or chemicals from getting through to the skin.

barrio *Am.* section of a large city in which population is predominantly Spanish-speaking: *Isabelle told them about the various barrios that made up the city* - D. Mortman., *Judge Torres was raised in the New York barrio* - Reader's Digest.

barrister *esp. Br. /Can.* **lawyer**, *Am.* **attorney/** person called to the Bar and entitled to practise as an advocate, esp. in the higher courts.

barroom *esp. Am., Can.* a room where alcoholic drinks are served over the counter: *the puffy look of a veteran barroom pugilist* – A. Summers, R. Swan.

barrow *Br.* a vehicle moved by a person from which esp. fruit and vegetables are sold at the side of a road.

barrow boy (or **man**) /also *Br.* **costermonger/** *esp. Br.* man or boy who sells goods from a barrow in the street: *The barrow-boy mentality, they call it. Quick wits and an appetite for non-stop dealing.* - D. Lodge.

bar snack *Br.* a light meal served in a pub.

bartender *esp. Am. /esp. Br.* **barman, barmaid/** barman: *He got the bartender and told him to bring him his check.* - J.D. Salinger., *The bartender served the drinks.* - I. Shaw, *At the best minute the hired bartender called in sick* - Reader's Digest.

barton *Br.* farmyard.

base/ be (way) off base *Am.* col. completely wrong.

base/ get to first (second) base *esp. Am.* 1. achieve the first part of smth. but no more. 2. sl. refers to a degree of sexual intimacy.

base/ touch base *Am.* col. find out the latest information about smth.

base(board), mop board, scrub board, washboard *Am. /Br.* **skirting board/** board fixed along the base of a wall where it meets the floor of a room: *He plugged a cord from the box into an electric outlet in the baseboard* - K. Vonnegut, Jr., *The bouncer...smacked into the baseboard with a crash* - R. Chandler.

base/ change one's **base** *Am.* col. get away, run away.

base/ not get to first base (**with**) *Am.* sl. not even to begin to succeed (with): *I knew she wouldn't let him get to first base with her.* - J.D. Salinger.

base/ off base *Am., Aus.* sl. 1. completely or foolishly mistaken: *People's risky perceptions are so off base* - R.N. Bellah and others. 2. unprepared: *I don't want to draw you off base, Woody.* - L. Waller., *Consistently, the one area most of them are off base is that of stock speculation.* - L. Burkett.

base / cover all the bases *Am., Aus. /Am.* **touch all the bases/** solve every problem: *Between us, Tex and I, had all the bases covered.* - W. Jack, B. Lawrsen.

baseball boot *Br. /Am.* **basketball boot/** boots used to play baseball or basketball in.

baseburner *Am.* furnace, stove or water heater fed automatically either from a hopper or a gas line as the fuel at the base is consumed: *The big base-burner with its glowing coals sent ruddy light toward the dim corners* - S. North.

basehead *Am.* col. a drug-addict taking cocaine in the form of freebase or crack.

base rate *Br.* rate of interest the banks use as a basis when they are calculating the rates that they charge on loans.

bash *esp. Br.* col. attack with words, criticize; esp. union/government, etc. **bashing** *Br.* col. strong criticism of unions, the government, etc.

bash away at *Br.* col. go on working hard at smth.

bash on *Br.* col. continue doing smth. difficult or boring and taking a long time.

bash/ have a bash (**at**) *Br., Aus.* col. make an attempt (at): *I'll just have one bash.* - J. Fowles.

basic crops *Am.* the crops the price of which is guaranteed by the government: *The reason corn was chosen as the basic crop is, of course, evident* - H. Truman.

basin 1. *esp. Br.* bowl for holding liquids or food. 2. *Br. /Am.* **washbowl, sink/** washbasin: *splashing water up onto her face out of a white basin!* - K. Davis.

basis weight *Am.* the weight (substance) of a ream (usu. 500 sheets) of a paper or board in the same size.

basket/ like a basket of chips *Am.* joc. very nice.

basketball boot *Am. /Br.* **baseball boot/**.

basket meeting *Am.* religious meeting held in the form of picnic.

bass *Am.* double bass.

bassinet *Am.* small bed looking like a basket for a young baby.

baste *esp. Am., Aus.* tack, sew with a long loose stitch.

bat *Br. /Am.* **paddle/** table tennis racket.

bat *Br., Aus.* gait / **at full bat** *B., Aus.* very fast.

bat *Am.* 1. jockey's whip. 2. sl. wild time, spree: *he'd seen Fred on a bat over in Brooklyn.* - J. Dos Passos., *Now he's on a big bat.* - F.S. Fitzgerald., *We promised each other one more big bat.* - J. Kerouac. 3. prostitute. *your husband's running around a few miles away with some bat* - J. Updike.

bat/ bat a thousand (1000) *Am.* col. be successful.

bat/ be batting a thousand *Am.* do smth. extremely well.

bat/ go to bat for *esp. Am., Can., Aus.* col. defend sb.: *Bernie Hanighan really went to bat for me.* - B. Holiday, W. Duffy.

bat/ not bat an eyelid/eye *Br.* / **not bat an eye** *Am.* col. / seem not to be upset or surprised by something that happens: *You didn't even bat an eye.* - K. Davis.

bat/ (do smth.) off one's own bat *esp. Br., Aus.* col. (do smth.) on one's own.

bat/ play a straight bat *Br.* 1. try to avoid answering difficult questions. 2. obs. do smth. in an honest and simple way.

bat/ (right) off the bat. *esp. Am., Can., Aus.* col. without delay: *He may discover what's wrong with her right off the bat.* - J. O'Hara.

bat around/about *esp. Am., Can.* col. travel widely, frequently or casually.

bat smth. **around/about** *esp. Am, Can.* col. discuss an idea or proposal casually or idly.

bat out *Am.* sl. do smth. quickly and casually.

batch *Can.* heavy snow.

bate *Br.* col. obs. rage, fury.

bat-eared *Am.* col. (of a person) having upright ears.

bath *Br.* /*Am.* **bathe**/ 1. give a bath to (a person). 2. **have a bath** (*Am.*), **take a bath** (*Br.*): *I must have a bath* - J. Fowles. 3. *esp. Br.* /*esp. Am.* **bathtub**/ tub in a bathroom.

bath *esp. Am., Can.* bathroom.

bath/ an early bath *Br.* col. sending off a sportsplayer during a match.

bath/ take a bath *Am.* col. lose money, esp.in a business deal.

Bath(bun) *Br.* sweet roll made of yeast dough.

bath cube *Br.* a cube of perfumed salts which is dissolved in bath water.

bathe 1. *esp. Br.* obs. swim in the sea, river, etc. for pleasure. 2. *Am.. Can.* have a bath: *He liked to feed and bathe her* - D. Mortman.

bathe /also **bathing**/ *Br.* an act of bathing, esp. in the sea.

bathers *Aus., NZ.* col. swimming costume.

bathinette *Am.* portable bath for babies.

bathing cap *Am.* /*Br.* **swimming cap**/ one worn to keep one's hair dry when sb. is swimming.

bathing costume *Br.* obs. /*esp. Am., Can.* **bathing suit**, *Br., Aus.* **swimming costume**, *Am.* **swimsuit**, *Br., Aus.* col. **cossie**. *Aus.* col. **swimmers**, *esp. Aus.* col. **togs**/ suit worn esp. by women and girls for swimming: *summer people filled the narrow main street of the little town, trying on bathing suits and chic summer gear* – R.L. Stine.

bathing trunks *Br.* obs. men's swimsuit.

bathrobe *esp. Am.* /*esp. Br.* **dressing gown**/ dressing gown, esp. one worn by men: *old Spencer had on this very ratty old bathrobe* - J.D. Salinger.

bathroom 1. *Br.* room containing a bath and usu. a toilet. 2. *Am., Aus.* /*esp. Br., Aus.* **toilet, lavatory, W.C.**/ toilet, e.g. *go to the bathroom.*

bathroom tissue *Am., Can.* tissue paper.

baths *esp. Br., Aus.* obs. a public building with an indoor swimming pool and/or bathrooms: *Begin your book in the baths* - R.G. Kaiser.

bathtub *esp. Am.* a bath /*esp. Br., Aus.* **bath**/ : *I slept in the bathtub.* - I. Shaw., *He had fallen in the bathtub two months earlier.* - USA Today.

bathtub gin *Am.* sl. homebrewed gin: *America's first families patronized the place, not for bathtub gin, but Scotch* - Nation's Restaurant News.

batman *Br.* an officer's personal servant.

baton *esp. Br.* short stick, truncheon.

baton charge *Br.* an attack made by a large group of policemen running forward with their batons.

bats *esp. Br., Aus.* col. mad, batty: *He was grinning like he was bats.* - R.L. Chapman.

batten *Br.* a piece of lumber, used esp. for flooring.

batter *Am.* a thick mixture of flour, eggs, milk, etc. used for making eggs.

batterboard *Am.* profile in a building (fixed on edge at the corner).

batter up *esp. Am.* damage, ruin smth.: *He battered up his car in a race.* - Longman.

battery hens *Br.* large number of hens kept on farms in very small cages; they produce **battery eggs**.

battle smth. *Am.* struggle with smth.

The Battle-born State *Am.* Nevada.

battle stations *esp. Am.* the positions taken by military personnel in preparation for battle.

batty *Br.* col. slightly crazy: *Long hair..drove him batty* – A. Summers, R. Swan.

bauble *Br.* decoration ball at a Christmas tree.

bawl out *esp. Am., Can.* col. scold, tell off, reprimand: *he pretended to bawl out Marie*

Leslie - J. O'Hara., *He was thinking about too many other things to waste his energy bawling out Angles.* - J. DeFelice.

bawn *Can., Irish Eng.* 1. an area of grassy land near a house. 2. *Can.* a flat expanse of rocks on a beach, on which fish are spread to dry.

Bay Area *Am.* San Francisco Bay area.

Bay City *Am.* sl. San Francisco.

baygall *Am.* area of swampland having dense growth of bay trees and inkberry.

The Bayou or **Mudcat State** *Am.* Mississippi.

The Bayou State *Am.* Louisiana.

bay platform *Br.* a short terminal platform at a railway station also having through lines.

The Bay or **Puritan State, Baked Bean State** *Am.* Massachusetts: *I had been cochairman of a radical weekly paper, The Bay State Progressive* - K. Vonnegut, Jr.

BB 1. *Br.* double-black (grade of pencil lead). 2. *Am., Can.* a standard size of lead pellet used in air rifles.

B battery *esp. Am.* radio. electric battery connected to the plate lead and to the filament of the electric tube.

BB gun *Am.* /*Br.* **airgun**/.

b-boy *esp. Am.* col. young man involved with hip-hop culure.

BC *Am.* Bachelor of Chemistry.

BCE 1. *Am.* Bachelor of Chemical Engineering. 2. *esp. Am.* before common era, before Christ.

Bdr. *Br.* abbr. bombardier.

be/ I'll be *Am.* sl. Goodness gracious.

be/ be all about smth. *Am.* sl. be completely involved in smth. giving it all their energy.

be/ be all dressed up with no place to go *Am.* be prepared to do smth. but not able to do it.

be/ be all over smth. *Am.* sl. feel happy, excited, or confident about doing smth.

be / be fed up/sick to the back teeth *Br., Aus.* col. be annoyed greatly.

be/ be for it *Br.* col. be in trouble for doing smth. that makes other people angry.

be/ be home *Am.* /*Br.* **be at home**/.

be / be in bad with *esp. Am.* not to get along with sb.: *I've been in bad with him since my first day.* - Longman.

be/ be in the shit *Br.* col. be in big trouble.

be/ be on sb.'s **ass/butt** *Am.* taboo. sl. criticise sb. harshly.

beachchair *Am.* /*Br.* **deckchair**/ a folding chair with a long seat of cloth used out of doors: *Three empty beach chairs lay toppled in their wake.* - F. Pascal.

beacher *Aus.* tidal wave on the crest of which the surfer rides to the shore.

beachfront *esp. Am., Can.* a strip of land along a beach.

bead/ draw/take/get a bead on sb./smth. *esp. Am., Can.* aim a gun.

beadsman *Br.* the inmate of a beadhouse (poorhouse).

beagle *Am.* sl. pry into or about smth.

beak *Br.* col. 1. also *Aus.* judge in a lower court of law, magistrate. 2. schoolmaster, esp. the headmaster of a school.

beaker *Br.* a cup with straight sides.

beam/ be (way) off (the) beam - *Br., Aus.* be wrong.

beamends/ on one's **beamends** *Br.* col. obs. having little or no money left.

beam tetrode /**beam valve**/ *Br.* beam-power tube.

beam trammel *Am.* beam compass.

bean/ know how many beans make five *Br.* obs. be intelligent.

bean/ not have a bean *Br., Aus.* obs. have no money.

bean/ old bean *Br.* obs. col. (used to address friends): *Sort of old bean who is always going to die and never does.* - A. Christie.

bean-counter *Am., Aus.* col. derog. statistician, accountant: *Those are savings no bean counter can ignore.* - Fortune.

bean-eater *Am.* resident of Boston.

bean(er), beaneater *Am.* sl. a Hispanic American, a Mexican or Chicano: *One of them was a beaner, I think.* - J. Kellerman.

beanery *Am., Can.* col. a cheap restaurant.

bean-feast *esp. Br., Aus.* col. 1. annual dinner given by employers to their workers. 2. any festive occasion.

beanie *Am.* small round hat that fits close to one's head.

beano *esp. Br.* 1. col. noisy frolic or spree: *Junior staffs shared liberally in the beano.* - P. Norman. 2. (beans and bacon), pork and beans.

beans *Am.* 1. sl. dollars: *At least we're sitting on around a hundred beans from my brilliant idea.* - T. Thorne. 2. also *Can.* a very small amount.

beans/ know how many beans make five *Br.* col. be sensible, esp. about money.

beans/ not be worth a hill of beans *Am.* col. / *Br.* **not amount to a row of beans**/ not worth anything.

beans/ not know beans about smth. *Am., Aus.* col. humor. know nothing.

Bean Town *Am.* col. Boston: *Calls him the Beantown Bookpeddler* - D. Mortman.

bean-wagon *Am.* col. cheap restaurant.

bear *esp. Am.* col. 1. difficult task. 2. highway patrol officer; a police officer.

bear/ be like a bear with a sore head *esp. Br., Aus.* humor. /*Am.* **be like a (real) bear/** col. be very angry at sb.

bear/ smth. sb. **doesn't bear thinking about** *Br.* col. very unpleasant and shocking situation.

bear/ have a bear by the tail *Am.* risk thoughtlessly.

bear/ (be) loaded for bear *Am., Can.* col. (be) ready for action, esp. a fight.

bear/ bear left or **right** *esp. Br.* keep to the left or right of the road, esp. where the road divides: *Bear left when you reach the church* - Longman.

bear up *Br.* col. cheer up: *Bear up, your troubles will soon be over.* - Longman.

bear-cat *Am.* col. passionate woman.

bear claw *Am.* fruit covered in pastry with long cuts made across the top.

beard *Am.* print. bevel. 1. the outside edges of a letterpress block, below the printing surface, by which the block is pinned to its mount. 2. the sloping surface of hot metal type running up from the shoulder of the face.

beard *Am., Can.* col. a woman who accompanies a homosexual man as an escort to a social occasion in order to conceal his homosexuality.

beardie *Br.* col. 1. a bearded man, esp. one lacking style. 2. a bearded collie.

bear-garden *Br.* rough house, fight.

bear-lead *Br.* compel to follow. **bear-leader** n.

bearoff *Am.* print. adjusting the spacing in typematter to correct justification and composition of the copy.

The Bear or **Wonder State** *Am.* Arkansas.

bear walker *Can.* sl. witch.

beast *Br.* sl. a person convicted of a sexual offence: *20 prison officers in riot uniform were observed banging their shields in unison and chanting "Beast, beast, beast!"* - Observer, T. Thorne.

beastly *Br.* col. obs. to an extreme and unpleasant degree.

beat *Am.* 1. the securing and publishing of news ahead of one's competitors: *The news scored an important beat.* - R.L. Chapman. 2. col. taken aback, awe-struck. 3. sl. loafer, drifter. 4. col. cheat, avoid paying smth.

beat/ dead beat *Br.* very tired.

beat about the bush *Br.* /*Am.* **beat around the bush/** talk about smth. indirectly and unclear.

beat off *Am.* taboo. sl. masturbate.

beat sb. **out** (in a competition) *esp. Am.* defeat sb.

beat one's **brains out** *Am.* col. think about smth. very hard.

beat/ beat sb. **hollow** *Br., Aus.* obs. 1. defeat sb. 2. be the best.

beat oneself *Am.* col. blame oneself too much for smth.

beat/ Beat it! *esp. Am.* col. Go away!

beat/ beat one's **way** *Am.* sl. ride without ticket, stroll round.

beat/ beat the bushes (brush) for *esp. Am., Can.* col. try very hard to find or get smth.: *beating the bushes for corporate sponsors.* - Arkansas Times.

beat/ beat the heat *Am.* col. make oneself cooler.

beat/ (it) beats the hell out of me *Am.* col. I can't find an answer or explain this.

beat/ beat the living daylights (bejesus) out of sb. *Am.* sl. defeat or thrash thoroughly: *Everyone in the arena who could lay a hand on the Texan beat the bejesus out of him* - J.A. Michener.

beat the rap *esp. Am.* col. escape or avoid blame or punishment: *Books and websites aimed at beating the rap abound* – Reader's Digest.

beat/ That beats all! *Am.* col. /*esp. Am., Can.* col. **beat the band/** that is unbelievable!

beaten path/ be off the beaten path *Am.* /*Br., Am.* **track/** go where not many people go.

beater *Am., Can.* col. an old and used car: *Why does he drive that old beater? He could buy a new car.* - W. Magnuson.

beater biscuit *Am.* one made of flour, milk, shortening and salt.

beat (up) on *Am., Can.* col. attack or damage, criticize: *He beat up on a woman* - Vanity Fair.

beaut, beauty, bewdie 1. *Aus., Br.* col. adj. nice, good (of things); expression of approval. 2. *esp. Aus., NZ.* col. a particular fine example of smth., esp. a beautiful person.

beat up *Am.* col. 1. exhausted: *My body was so beat up from doing drugs.* – Reader's Digest. 2. run down, dilapidated

beauty *Can.* sl. excellent, superior: *I thought the guy was beauty.* - R.L. Chapman.

(you) beauty! *Aus.* col. excl. when sb. is very pleased with sb.

beauty mark *Am.* /*Br.* **beauty spot/** small dark mark on a woman's skin.

beauty shop, beauty parlor *Am.* /*Br.* **beauty salon/** place where women are given beauty treatments: *he grew up working in beauty shops and barber shops from the time he was 11.* - Ebony.

beaver *esp. Am., Can.* taboo. sl. 1. a woman's genitals or pubic area. 2. a woman regarded in sexual terms: *I had my face buried in a beaver.* – J. Hopkins.

beaver *Br.* col. obs. a bearded man.

beaver away *esp. Br.* col. work hard, esp. at a desk job: *he beavered away with finance director.* - Observer.

beaverboard *esp. Am., Can.* a kind of fibrewood used in building.

The Beaver State *Am.* Oregon/ **Beaver** *Am.* citizen of Oregon.

beck *Br.* col. small stream.

bed/ get in bed with *Br.* journalism. derog. start working with sb. or an organisation for one's own advantage.

bed/ get up on the wrong side of the bed *Am.* /*Br.* **get out of bed (on) the wrong side**/ be angry without any obvious reason.

bed and board *esp. Br.* board and lodging

bed and breakfast *Br.* (a private house or small hotel that provides) a place to sleep for the night and breakfast the next morning: *guess...the price of bed and breakfast at a class A boarding house in Rhyl.* - D. Lodge.

bed bath /also **blanket bath**/ *Br.* sponge bath, one given to the bed-ridden.

bedboard *Br.* headboard of bed.

bedbug *Am.* sl. Pullman porter.

bedbug/ (as) crazy as a bedbug *Am.* completely mad: *crazy as a bedbug is the only description of me that will do.* - K. Vonnegut, Jr.

bed chesterfield *Can.* upholstered couch or sofa, that is convertible into a double-bed.

bedder, bed-maker *Br.* col. a servant employed to clear and tidy, esp. in Cambridge colleges.

bedel *Br.* official with largely ceremonial duties in some universities.

bed-fast *Am.* bed-ridden: *He's bedfast now* - H. Truman.

bedhead *Br.* an upright board or panel fixed at the head of a bed.

bedroll *esp. Am., Can.* a sleeping bag or other bedding rolled into a bundle.

bedroom *Am.* 1. adj. /*esp. Br.* **dormitory**/ of or belonging to bedroom suburbs: *the exodus of Italians to such bedroom communities as Medford* - G. O'Neill, D. Lehr, n. **bedroom community** *Am.* /*esp. Br.* **dormitory community**/. 2. two-seat two-berth compartment on a train.

bed-sitter /also **bed-sitting room, bed-sit** (col.) / *Br.* a single room used for both living and sleeping in (if a bathroom is included the unit becomes a studio): *Dr. Strach found a flat...in the rather dismal bedsitter region.* - P. Norman., *I would like you to see one or two of our bed-sitting rooms.* - A. Christie., *It was the best bed-sitter in the house* - J. Fowles.

bedskirt *Am., Can.* a valance for bed.

bedsock *esp. Br.* one of a pair of thick socks worn for extra warmth in bed.

bee *Am., Aus.* col. a meeting of neighbours for joint work: *I'd be invited out after a Teflon display or a quilting bee* - J. Baez.

bee/ put the bee on sb. *Am.* sl. borrow from sb.

bee/ the bee's knees *Br., Can., Aus.* col. first-class thing or period.

BEE *Am.* Bachelor of Electrical Engineering.

beeb *Br.* col. BBC, British Broadcasting Corporation.

beef/ Where is the beef? *Am.* col. Do you have enough ideas to make it right?

Beef-heads *Am.* col. people from Texas

The Beef State, also **The Jumbo State, The Lone Star State** *Am.* Texas.

beef up *esp. Br., Can., Am.* sl. make more substantial: *We need new young soldiers to beef up the army.* - Longman.

beefburger *Br.* minced meat cooked in a flat round shape, burger.

beefeater *Am.* sl. Englishman.

beef road *Aus.* a road built in a remote area for transporting beef cattle to the market.

beefsquad *Am.* sl. gang of tough men employed for any specific violent purpose.

beef (stick) tomato *esp. Am., Can.* a very large and firm tomato.

beef tea *Br.* a drink made from beef juice, used for nourishment for sick people.

The Beehive State, also **The Mormon** or **Salt Lake State** *Am.* Utah.

beeman *Am.* beekeeper, apiarist.

been *Br.* 1. (to have) arrived and left: *I see the postman hasn't been yet.* - Longman. 2. *esp. Br.* (to have) happened: *I'm sorry, sir, the meeting's already been.* - Longman. 3. been and past participle *Br.* col. (expresses surprise): *He's been there and won the first prize.* - Longman.

beep 1. *Am.* small jeep. 2. *Br.* a short, loud sound (like one made by car horn or the engaged tone of a telephone).

beep *esp. Am., Can.* summon sb. by means of a pager.

beeper *Am., Aus., Br.* /*Br.* **pager, bleeper**/ **pager,** *Can.* **pager**/ portable device that lets one know that they must telephone sb.: *He won't even answer his beeper.* - T. Thompson.

beer *Am., Can.* beer brewed by bottom fermentation.

beer/ not all beer and skittles *Br., Aus.* col. obs. not entirely pleasant.

beer bust (or **blast**) *Am.* sl. beer-drinking party: *Kelly's having a beer blast at his place, starting tonight.* - R.A. Spears.

bear engine *Br.* a pump for drawing up beer from a barrel in a cellar.

beer garden *Br.* the garden of a pub in which customers can sit in fine weather: *find refuge as a fiddler in a cheap beer garden* - I. Stone.

beerhouse *Br.* obs. a pub licensed to sell only beer.

beer parlor *Am., Can.* a pub or room in a hotel where only beer is sold: *Beside it was a new beer parlour.* - W. Grady.

beer-slinger *Am., Can.* sl. waiter or waitress in a **beer parlor**.

Beertown *Am.* sl. Milwaukee, Wisconsin: *tiny minimum-security prisons right in the midst of Beertown* - Milwaukee Journal, R.L. Chapman.

beeswax/ none of your beeswax *Am., Can., Aus.* col. it's my life: *None of your beeswax, eh?* – K. Vonnegut, Jr.

beet(s) *Am. /esp. Br, Aus.* **beetroot/** plant with a red root, cooked and eaten as vegetable, often pickled in vinegar.

beet/ go beet red, go as red as a beet *Am.* col. / *esp. Br., Aus.* **beetroot/** col. become very red.

beetle 1. *Am.* cockchafer. 2. *Br.* cockroach. 3. *esp. Br.* wooden household utensil for beating or mashing. 4. *esp. Br.* col. move off or do smth. quickly trying not to be noticed: *he had beetled off without waiting for an answer.* - Longman. / **Beetle off** *Br.* sl. Go away. 5. *Br.* a dice game in which a picture of beetle is drawn.

beetle-crusher *Br.* col. humor. clod-hopper, big heavy strong shoe.

Beeton/ Mrs. Beeton *Br.* cooker and household management book.

beetroot/ go/turn as red as beetroot or go/ turn beetroot (red) *Br.* col. /*Am., Can.* **go/ turn as red as a beat/** become very red, esp. with shame.

beezer *Br.* col. excellent.

before (or **of**) *Am.* to (in defining time). e.g. *twenty before (or of) ten.*

beggar *Br.* fellow (used when you feel sorry for sb.; feel angry with sb.).

beggar-my-neighbour *esp. Br.* children's game of cards.

beggar's purse *Br.* an appetizer of a crepe stuffed with a savoury filling, esp. caviar and crème fraiche.

begin/ not to begin to *Am.* be far from: *But even those disturbing high figures do not begin to embrace all of the homeless.* - McLean's.

behalf/ in behalf of *Am.* on behalf of: *Our activities in behalf of women who drink are on the increase* - Alcoholics Anonymous.

behavior *Am.* be very polite.

behoove *esp. Am. /Br.* **behove/**.

belabor a point *Am. /Br.* **labour a point/** try too hard to express smth. often repeating one's actions unnecessarily.

belief/ to the best of my belief *Br.* to the best of my knowledge.

Belisha beacon *Br.* a road sign in the form of a flashing light in an orange globe on a striped pole, marking a pedestrian crossing: *England was full of words I'd never heard before - streaky bacon, short back and sides, Belisha beacon* - B. Bryson.

bell *Br., Aus.* col. v. n. (make) a telephone call: *I got a bell from old Milward yesterday.* - T. Thorne.

bell/ as sound as a bell *Br.* 1. strong and healthy. 2. fair and honest.

bell/ give sb. **a bell** *Br.* col. telephone sb.

bell/ have had one's **bell rung** *Am.* col. have been hit hard in the head.

bell/ ring sb.'s **bell** *esp. Am.* be very attractive and exciting.

bell/ with bells on 1. *Br.* humor. with gimmick 2. *Am., Can., Aus.* col. humor. done with a lot of interest and energy. 3. **be waiting with bells on** *Am.* be excited about future actions.

bell captain *Am., Can.* the supervisor of a group of bellhops.

belle/ Southern belle *Am.* beautiful woman from the American South.

bellhop, bellboy *esp. Am., Can.* messenger or attendant in a hotel or club, who often carries guests' luggage: *the doorman and bellhops found my means of traveling unusual* - J. Steinbeck., *The elderly bellhop had finished clearing away dinner.* - L. Walker., *I was a bellhop who became ambitious.* - Arthur Hailey.

bell pepper *Am., Can. /Br.* **capsicum, pepper/** a hollow red, green, or yellow vegetable: *Add bell-pepper, cook four minutes.* – Reader's Digest.

bell push *Br.* a button that operates on electric bell when pushed.

bell-ringer *Am.* sl. 1. door-to-door salesman or canvasser. 2. local politician.

bell sheep *Aus.* one caught by a shearer just before the bell rings which signals the end of a shift, and which he's allowed to shear.

belly *Br.* abdomen.
belly bomber *Am.* sl. small highly-spiced burger.
belly button *Am., Aus.* col. /*Br.* col. **tummy button**/ navel.
bellyful/ have had a bellyful (of) *Br.* be fed up with smth.
bellywhop *Am.* sl. 1. ride on a sled lying on the belly. 2. strike the water with the chest and abdomen while diving.
belong (in, on, with, at, among, under) *esp. Am.* belong to: *We belong in this tree* - T. Capote., *You belong on the street* - J.A. Michener.
belt (along, down, up) 1. *esp. Br.* col. travel fast (in a certain direction): *I belted for the front door.* - F. Mowatt. 2. *Am.* sl. drink liquor /also **belt the grape/**: *We'll drop down to the lounge and belt a few with some of the Democratic leaders.* - L. Waller.
belt up *Br., Aus.* col. shut up, stop talking: *Shhhhh. Quiet. Belt up.* - A. Burgess.
belt *esp. Br.* very fast car trip.
belt/ black belt *Am.* Virginia, North and South Carolina, Georgia, Alabama, Mississippi, Louisiana and Texas.
belt/ corn belt *Am.* states where most of the corn is produced.
belt and braces *Br.* col. superfluous action to make smth. work well.
belt line *Am.* railroad or bus line that makes a circuit around a city or special area.
beltline *Am.* conveyer.
beltman *Aus.* lifeguard.
belt-tightening *esp. Am.* forced reduction of expenditures.
beltway *Am.* /*Br., Aus.* **ring road, orbital**/ ring road, road skirting an urban area: *The vast majority were within easy access of the beltway that encircles London.* - Reader's Digest.
Beltway Bandit *Am.* sl. a company or individual, hired by a corporation to assist in securing government contracts.
bench 1. *Br.* a long seat in Parliament for politicians of a political party in power or opposition. 2. *Am., Can.* withdraw (a sports player) from a game.
bench/ take the bench *Am.* 1. become a judge or magistrate. 2. (of a judge) begin a formal meeting of a law court.
benchmarking *Am.* the examination of a rival company's product in order to establish a standard which one seeks to exceed.
bench(top) *Aus.* a worktop.
benchwarmer *Am., Can.* one who doesn't get elected to play in a sports game; a substitute.

bend *esp. Br.* pervert from the right purpose, use.
bend/ above one's **bend** *Am.* above one's power.
bend/ bend one's **elbow** *Am., Can.* drink alcohol.
bend/ drive sb. **round the bend** *esp. Br.* col. annoy sb.
bend/ on the bend *Br.* sl. on a drinking spree.
bend/ round the bend *esp. Br.* strange and foolish; **be/go round the bend/twist** *Br.* go mad.
bender 1. *esp. Am.* sl. drinking spree: *He must have been on one hell of a bender.* - M.M. Kaye., *Runs off and sets his idiot wife on a bender.* - J. Updike., *a month-long bender, where I drank like a Muscovite.* – Reader's Digest. 2. *Br.* old sl. sixpence. 3. *Am.* col. a leg. 4. *Br.* a shelter made by covering a framework of bent branches with canvas or tarpaulin.
Benedict Arnold *Am.* traitor: *Is that so, you Benedict Arnold, who's just committed high treason on my person?* - R.J. Randisi, M. Wallace.
benefit 1. *Am.* /*Br.* **relief**/ money that one is allowed not to pay in taxes for some special reason. 2. *Br.* /*Am.* **welfare**/ state compensation for sick and unemployed people.
benefit/ take the benefit (of the bankruptcy laws) *Am.* announce one's bankruptcy.
benefit tourist *Br.* col. a person who travels to or within Britain in order to live off social security payments pretending to be seeking work.
benny 1. *Br.* sl. gormless or slow-witted person, esp. derog. a Falkland islander. 2. *esp. Am.* col. a tablet of Benzedrine. 3. *Am.* col. a benefit attached to employment.
bent *esp. Br.* sl. 1. also *Aus.* dishonest, perverted, corrupt: *look like a little bent...look like you were up for a little whoremongering* - R.L. Chapman. 2. completely determined, with one's mind set on smth. 3. derog. homosexual.
bent *Am.* sl. 1. fool. 2. obs. drunk: *I've never seen two guys so bent.* - R.A. Spears. 3. angry, furious: *Come on, don't get bent. I was only kidding.* - R.A. Spears.
bent/ get bent out of shape *esp. Am., Can.* col. become very angry and upset.
Berdoo *Am.* sl. San Bernadino, California.
bergen *Br.* a type of rucksack supported by a frame used by the military.
berk, burk *Br., Aus.* col. a stupid person: *Dad, fit a washer don't be a burk.* – S. Townsend.
berm *Am.* 1. bank of the canal opposite the towing path. 2. curb, the shoulder of the road: *Metal poles set in cement sprouted may be every thirty feet along the berms* - R. Crais.

berry *Am.* col. a dollar: *She's gotten a lump sum - two hundred thousand berries by God* - D. Hammet.
berry sugar *Can.* caster sugar (used in berry jams).
bespoke *Br.* obs. (esp. of clothing) made to order.
best *esp. Am., Can.* written at the end of a letter to wish a person well.
best/ be the best of a bad bunch/lot *Br., Aus.* be slightly less bad than others.
best/ one's best bib and tucker *Br.* obs. one's best clothes.
best/ give smth./sb. **best** *Br.* admit the superiority of sb./smth.
best/ make the best of a bad job *Br., Aus.* /*Am.* **make the best of a bad situation**/ make the best of smth. unpleasant.
best/ would best *Am.* had better: *I'd best be getting back.* - T. Murphy.
the best you can *Br., Aus.* /*Am.* **as best you can**/ in the best possible way.
best/ the best of British (luck) *Br.* col. 1. good luck. 2. good things that are made in Britain.
best end *Br.* the rib end of a neck of lamb or other meat.
best-looker *Am.* col. well-dressed person.
bet/a sure bet *Am.* a certain thing.
bet/ bet on the wrong horse *Am.* support sb. who is not successful.
bet the farm/ranch *Am.* sl. bet everything one has: *he wanted to "bet the farm" in one more deal before the pull-out.* - Time., *But noone's betting the farm.* - USA Today., opp. **not bet the ranch** means not to be sure about smth.
bet/ you can bet your ass *Am.* sl. /*Am.* **bet the ranch**/ you can be sure.
beta *Br.* a second-class mark given for an essay, examination paper, etc.
bethel 1. *esp. Br.* house of worship for Christian Nonconformists. 2. *esp. Am.* a place of worship for sailors.
betless *Am.* adj. without wagers, not accepting bets.
better/ you'd better believe smth./**it** *Am.* col. it is definitely true.
better / better than a kick in the tail *Aus.* it's very stimulating.
betting/ What's the betting? *Br.* col. (used to express a belief that smth. is likely).
betting shop/office *Br.* licensed establishment for off-track betting: *She passes launderettes, hairdressers, betting shops...a DIY centre* - D. Lodge.

bettor *esp. Am.* a person who bets, esp. on a regular bases.
between maid /or **between girl**/ *Br.* maid servant who assists the cook and the housemaid, tweeny.
between whiles *Br.* in between.
between you. me and the bedpost/gatepost *Br., Aus.* /*Am.* **between you, me, and the lamppost/fencepost**/ humor. col. secretly.
Bev *Br.* billion electron volts.
bevvy *Br.* col. (take) an alcoholic drink: *We had a few bevvies on the way here.* - T. Thorne; **bevvied** *Br.* col. drunk.
beyond the next turning *Br.* in the next block.
beyond/ be proved beyond /*Am.* **a**/ **reasonable doubt** *Br., Aus.* have enough proof of sb.'s guilt.
B.F. *Br.* col. bloody fool.
B-girl *Am.* bargirl /*Br.* **nightclub hostess**/ girl that drinks with customers and is paid according to how many drinks they buy.
bialy *Am.* a flat bread roll topped with chopped onions.
bias binding *Br.* /*Am.* **bias tape**/ cloth in the form of narrow bend, used when sewing edges.
bib/ stick/poke one's **bib in** *Aus., NZ.* col. interfere.
bibb lettuce *Am., Can.* a butterhead lettuce that has crisp dark-green leaves.
bible-basher *Br., Aus.* col. /esp. *Am.* **bible-thumper**/ vehement believer in God, **bible-thumping**.
bicentennial *esp. Am.* /*Br.* **bicentenniary**/ 200th anniversary.
bickie *Br., Aus.* col., *Aus.* col. also **bikkie**, a biscuit.
bicycle route *Am.* /*Br.* **cycle path**/.
bicycling *Am.* print. moving duplicate film, artwork or copy to different trade houses and printers when simultaneous production so requires.
bid *Am.* col. invitation.
bid *Am.* (sometimes used as Past Simple of bid).
bid on *Am.* offer to do (a piece of work at a certain price): *the firm would care to bid on the decoration and fireworks contract* - E.L. Doctorow.
bid fair to do smth. *Br.* be likely to do smth. good or be successful.
biddable *esp. Br.* (of a person) easily influenced or controlled.
biddy *Am.* col. woman servant (usu. of Irish descent).
biffy *esp. Can.* sl. toilet: *Is there a biffy on the bus?* - W. Magnuson., *biffy and if so number of holes* – R. Brautigan.

big *esp. Am.* very popular: *L.B. wasn't big on discussion* - E. Taylor.

big/ be big/hot on smth. *Am.* col. like smth. a lot.

big/ get too big for one's **boots** *Br. /Am.* **britches/** believe oneself more important than one really is.

Big A *Am.* sl. l. Amarillo, Texas or Atlanta. Georgia.

the Big Apple *Am.* sl. New York: *His image of the Big Apple was a relic of schooldays.* - K. Lipper.

a big ask *Aus., NZ.* col. a difficult request.

The Big Bend State *Am.* Tennessee.

Big Board *Am.* New York Stock Exchange.

big bucks *esp. Am., Can.* col. */Aus.* col. **big bickies/** a lot of money: *Those were the days before the big bucks.* - R.J. Randisi, M. Wallace.

big-city *Am.* col. adj. metropolitan.

Big D. *Am.* sl. 1. Detroit. 2. Dallas: *He introduced his shapely blonde wife around the nightspots of Big D.* - T. Thompson.

big daddy *Am., Aus.* sl. 1. you, there, man. 2. the most respected man in the field: *What are you waiting for big daddy?* - S. Sheldon., *the big daddy of corrupt cities.* - Omni.

Big Dipper 1. *esp. Am. /esp. Br.* **Plough/** group of seven bright stars of the northern part of the world: *she loved...helping us to find the Big Dipper* – Guideposts. 2. *Br., Aus. /esp. Am.* **ferris wheel/** revolving observation wheel with seats on the rim at a funfair. 3. *Br.* a railway track at a fairground which goes over beautiful scenery which people can ride for enjoyment.

big E/ give sb. **the big E** *Br.* col. reject sb., often in a dismissive way

big ears/ have big ears *Aus.* col. eavesdrop on private conversations.

big enchilada *Am.* col. humor. the boss, leader: *I'm the head lifeguard - the big enchilada* - R.L. Stine.

big end *esp. Br., Aus.* the part of a connecting rod in a car engine which joins onto the crank: *he thinks his big-end is going.* – Sue Townsend.

bigfoot *Am., Can.* yeti: *I've been looking for a bigfoot picture for the last five years.* - A. Hitchcock Mystery Magazine.

biggety, biggitty *Am.* sl. conceited, cocky.

(you) big girl's blouse *Aus., Br.* humor. a male behaving like a woman; coward.

biggie *Aus.* big one: *a real biggie, like Brazil, went to the wall* - Playboy, R.L. Chapman., *No biggie, I thought.* – Reader's Digest.

big government *esp. Am., Can.* one that is regarded as intruding in private life of its citizens too much.

big gun *Am., Aus.* sl. very important person (VIP): *I knew they would bring in the big guns at the last time.* - R.A. Spears.

big-head *Br., Aus.* a know-it-all

the big house *Am.* sl. penitentiary: *a substantial term in the bighouse.* - Arkansas Times.

big labor *Am.* major labour unions.

big-league *Am.* important, famous: *Working for the Mafia was still the big leagues for many Italian street kids* - G. O'Neill, D. Lehr.

Big Man on Campus *Am.* col. student leader.

big mo *Am.* col. (of a politician) surge of confidence and popularity after success in an election campaign.

big-note *Aus.* sl. praise or boast: *I bignoted myself.* - T. Thorne.

big one *Am.* col. a thousand dollars: *It's going to cost you ten big ones* - R.L. Chapman.

big operator *Am.* very important person.

big pot *esp. Br.* col. important person.

Big Pretzel *Am.* sl. Philadelphia / **Big Pretzelite** *Am.* sl. citizen of Philadelphia: *several reasons for Big Pretzelites to swing into the Franklin Plaza* - R.L. Chapman.

the bigs *Am., Can.* col. the major league in a professional sport.

Big Score *Am.* sl. success: *Part of the American Dream is to make Big Score by accident* - Atlantic Monthly.

big shot *esp. Am.* a very important or powerful person: *Who's the big shot here?* – J.O'Hara.

Big Smoke *Aus.* sl. Sydney.

Big T *Am.* sl. Tucson, Arizona.

big-ticket *esp. Am., Can., Aus.* col. high-priced, expensive: *a military penchant for big-ticket weapons system* - Time., *big-ticket purchases such as carpeting flooring systems.* - World Monitor.

big time *esp. Am.* col. adv. (used to emphasize smth. that has just been said): *you get hurt big-time.* - R.J. Randisi, M. Wallace; adj. **big-time.**

big tree *Am., Can.* giant redwood.

Big Wet *Aus.* an extended period of rainy weather.

big wheel *Br., Aus. /*also *esp. Am., Aus.* **Ferris wheel,** *Br.* **Big Dipper/** revolving observation wheel: *Preschool children jumping rope and riding Big Wheels.* - R. Crais.

big shot, big wheel *Am., Can., Aus.* big boss.

bi-hourly *Am.* happening once in two hours.

bike *esp. Am.* a motorbike.

bike/ get off one's **bike** *Aus., NZ.* get angry.

bike/ get on one's **bike** *Br.* col. start working hard.

bike/ On your bike! *Br., Aus.* col. Go away!; Stop fooling around!

bike shed, also **cycle shed** *esp. Br.* a small building for storing bicycles.

biker *Br., Am. /Aus.* also **bikie/** col. a member of a gang of motorcyclists.

bikeway *esp. Am., Can.* a path or lane for bicycles.

bikie *Aus.* col. motorcyclist.

bikkie *Aus.* col. biscuit.

bi-level *Am., Can.* a two-storey house with the lower part of it sunk below ground level.

bilk sb. **out of** smth. *esp. Am.* col. cheat them out of it.

Bill *Br.* (usu. as part of a name) a long narrow piece of land sticking out into the sea and shaped like a beak.

bill 1. *Am., Can.* also *esp. Br., Aus.* (**bank**)**note** a piece of paper money, banknote: *The bills were crisp and new* - J. Dos Passos. 2. *Am.* col. cap peak: *the bill blocked the sun.* - F. Pascal. 3. *Br., Can. /esp. Am.* **check,** *esp. Am.* **tab/** a piece of paper with the price of meal on it, which the customer has just eaten and which is given before he leaves. 4. *Br.* col. police

bill/ fill the bill *Am., Aus.* be perfect.

bill/ (as) phony (or queer) as a three dollar bill *Am.* sl. very strange.

bill/ sell sb. **a bill of goods** *esp. Am. /Br., Aus.* **sell** sb. **a pup/** make sb. believe smth. which is not true.

Bill/ the (Old) Bill *Br.* col. the police.

billable *Am.* adj. that can be billed for a purchase, etc.: *a discreet amount of padding clients' billable hours.* - K. Lipper.

billabong *Aus.* 1. a dead-end channel extending from the main stream of the river. 2. streambed filled with water only in the rainy season. 3. stagnant pool of backwater.

billberry *Br. /Am., Aus.* **blueberry/** blue-black fruit of a low bushy plant.

billboard *Am., Can., Aus. /Br.* **hoarding/** high fence or board on which large advertisements are stuck (In Britain **billboard** is what newsagent uses to display the contents of a newspaper).

billetee *Br.* member of the armed forces who is assigned to a billet.

billfold *Am., Can. /esp. Br.* **notecase, purse/** wallet esp. for paper money: *I got his billfold from his back pocket.* - T. Thompson., *you can lay a billfold in the middle of a sidewalk* - K. Vonnegut., *The roubles were in a large billfold* - S. Bellow.

billiard *Am.* col. carom.

billiard parlor /also **billiard saloon, poolroom/** *Am.* billiard room.

billinsgate *esp. Br.* vulgar or abusive talk.

billion *Br.* obs. one million million.

bill of costs *Br.* a solicitor's account of charges and expense incurred while carrying out client's business.

bill of goods *Am., Can.* a consignment of merchandise.

bills of mortality *Br.* periodically published official returns of deaths.

billy *Aus.* tin container used to boil tea in the bush.

billyboy *Br.* flat-bottomed barge for river navigation.

billybread *NZ.* bread cooked over an open fire.

billy(can) *Br., Aus.* billy, tin pot for cooking or boiling water.

billy cart *Aus.* a small (children's) handcart.

billy(club) *Am., Can.* obs. /*Br., Aus.* **truncheon,** *Am.* **nightstick/** policeman's club.

billy-o/ like a billy-o *Br., Aus.* obs. col. a lot: *The whole place was burning like a billyo* - F. O'Brien.

bim(bo) *esp. Am.* sl. whore: *she catches him waltzing with a bimbo.* - Premiere., *No one's born to be a bimbo.* - Time.

bimbette *Am.* col. an adolescent female singer.

bin *Br.* sl. throw away, reject.

(dust)bin *Br., Aus. /Am.* **wastebasket, garbage can/** a container for rubbish.

bin *Br.* hop sack.

bin bag/liner *Br.* /also **dust bin/liner/** rubbish bag.

(dust) bin liner (bag) *Br. /Am.* **trash-can liner, garbage/trash bag/** rubbish bag.

bin man *Br.* col. /*Am.* **garbage man/** dustman.

bind *Br.* col. unpleasant and boring thing to do.

bind off *Am., Can.* (in knitting) remove (a number of stitches) from the needle: *At the end of the row, bind off seven stitches.* - Longman.

bind out *esp. Am.* arrange for (usu. a boy) to learn a trade from a master.

bind over *Br.* law. make (sb.) promise in court to behave well in future: *we could bind you over.* - R. Crais.

binder *Am.* a written agreement or amount of money given as a pledge to carry out some obligation, esp. when buying property.

bindle *Am.* sl. a bundle of clothing, toilet articles, etc. usu. tied to a stick which hobo carries over his shoulder: *The guy had a bindle tied to a stick, just like an old-time tramp.* - R.A. Spears.

bindlestiff /also **hobo/** *Am.* col. tramp: *I was a bindlestiff.* - R.L. Chapman.

bin-end *Br.* one of the last bottles from a bin of wine, usu. sold at reduced price.
binghi *Aus.* col., esp. derog. an Aboriginal.
bingle *Aus.* col. a collision.
bingo *Can.* sl. any cheap wine.
bingy *Aus.* col. the stomach.
binliner *Br.* plastic bag placed inside a dustbin and used to collect waste.
binman *Br.* col. /*Am.* **garbageman, garbagecollector**/ dustman.
bint *Br.* derog. col. girl or woman: *I've got to keep him and that Russian bint one step ahead of the police.* - T. Thorne.
biodata, resume *Am.* /*Br.* **curriculum vitae/ CV**/.
biograph *Am.* obs. cinematograph.
bippie *Am.* sl. the buttocks: *You can bet your bippie.* - R. Palley.
Bircher /Burchist, Burchite/ *Am.* John Burch society member.
bird *Br.* 1. sl. becoming obs. or *Aus.* a young woman /usu. considered offensive to woman/: *I want to show a bird a good time.* - D. Francis. 2. also *Aus.* col. obs. a period of time spent in prison /esp. in the phr. **do bird**/: *This is worse than doing bird.* - D. Francis.
bird/ flip/give sb. **the bird** *Am., Aus.* taboo. col. give a rude gesture with a middle finger.
bird/ give/get sb. **the bird** *Br.* col. dismiss sb., shout at sb. or show disapproval of them by making rude noises.
bird/ have a bird *Am., Can.* col. be very shocked and excited.
bird/ (strictly) for the birds esp. *Am., Can., Aus.* col. worthless, silly: *This publicly financed campaign business is for the birds.* - Esquire.
bird/ dead bird *Aus.* sl. a certainty.
birdband *Am., Can.* /*Br.* **bird ring**/ v., n. (put) a band on a bird's leg to identify it for the study of its range of flight,. **-er, -ing** n.
bird course *Can.* sl. easy course in a college.
bird dog *Am., Can.* 1. gundog: *we hunt like bird-dogs after the facts* - D. Carnegie., *he froze in the manner of a bird dog coming to a point.* - S. North. 2. sl. detective. 3. sl. agent searching for the orders for his/her firm.
birddog *Am.* col. v. 1. search out for smth. 2. search for the orders for one's firm: *He birddogs around town picking up leads and gags.* - L. Waller.
birder esp. *Am., Can.* a bird watcher: *Here's to the whale savers, and wolf lovers, and all the lovely birders.* – Reader's Digest.
birdhouse *Am., Can.* a box for birds to nest in.

birdie *Am.* /*Br.* **shuttlecock**/.
birding esp. *Am., Can.* the observation of birds in their natural habitat as a hobby.
bird table *Br.* a small platform or table in a garden on which food for birds is placed.
bird watcher *Am.* sl. a newsman who spends much time near missile test centres to observe launchings.
biro esp. *Br., Aus.* tdmk. /*Am.* **ballpoint (pen)**/: *Reynolds straightened, dug out a Biro pen from his inside pocket* - A. McLean.
Birthday Honours *Br.* the titles of honour conferred by the Queen on each anniversary of her birthday.
biscuit 1. *Br., Aus.* also *Br., Aus.* col. **bickie,** *Aus.* **bikkie.** /*Am., Aus., Can.* **cookie**/ flat thin crisp cakes, sweetened and unleavened / also *Br.* **sweetened biscuit,** *Aus.* **biscuit,** *Am.* **cookie**/ or unsweetened cheese **biscuits** /*Am., Can., Aus.* **cracker**/, usu. sold in tins or packets. 2. *Am., Can.* /*Br.* roughly **scone**/ soft usu. round breadlike cake of a size for one person, sometimes containing dried fruit, which can be eaten with butter and jam/ to get **cookies** in Britain specify sweet biscuit, tea biscuit or petit-fours.
biscuit/ take the biscuit /*Am.* col. **take the cake/** *Br., Aus.* col. be the best (or worst) thing one has ever seen or heard of: *That takes a biscuit.* - J. Joyce.
biscuit/ be like/be as easy as/ taking candy from a baby *Am.* col. be very easy.
biscuit barrel *Br.* a small barrel-shaped container for biscuits.
bish *NZ.* col. v. throw.
bishop *Am.* obs. woman's bustle.
bit 1. *Br.* col. a small coin, esp. one worth three or six old pence. 2. *Am., Can.* col. 12.5 cents / **two bits** 25 cents, **six bits** 75 cents, **short bit** 10 cents, **long bit** 15 cents/. 3. *Am.* sl. prison sentence: *I did a two-year bit in Sing-Song.* - R.A. Spears. 4. *Am., Can.* sl. small part in a play / **bit part, role**: *the bit was in service of his own needs.* - New York., *I'd probably be only a bit player in it* - A. Hitchcock Mystery Magazine. 5. esp. *Br.* col. a. a little. b. very; quite a lot. 6. *Br.* col. a small amount; *play the piano a bit, speak French a bit.* 7. *Br.* col. a part or piece of smth. larger.
bit/ a bit esp. *Br.* a small part of smth.
bit/ a bit at a time esp. *Br.* in several small parts, not all at the same time.
bit/ a bit much *Br.* not fair.
bit/ a bit of smth. esp. *Br.* a small piece of it.

bit/ a bit of a bend *Br.* col. a nuisance or hindrance.

bit/ a bit of all right *Br.* col. very good thing or person, esp. a sexually attractive person: *it's nice when men think that your woman's a bit of all right.* – R. Westall.

bit/ a bit of a problem /surprise /fool, etc. *Br.* col. a problem, etc., esp. not a very great or serious one.

bit/ a (nice) bit of fluff (goods, skirt, stuff) *Br.* sl. pretty girl: *It was strangely flattering for a woman to be treated as a little bit of fluff that you just tumbled onto a bed.* - W.S. Maugham.

bit/ a good/quite a bit *esp. Br.* fairly large amount.

a bit of how's your father *Br., Aus.* humor. sexual activity.

a bit of rough *Br.* humor. of lower social class than one's sexual partner.

a bit on the side *Br., Aus.* col. often humor. having sex outside one's family.

bit/ bit by bit *esp. Br.* gradually.

bit/ for a bit/in a bit *Br.* col. for a short time.

bit/ do one's **bit** *Br.* col. do one's part of shared work.

bit/ get the bit between one's **teeth** *Br. /Am.* **take the bit between** one's **teeth/** start doing smth. determinedly.

bit/ not a bit (of it) *esp. Br.* (expression used to make a strong negative statement).

bit/ take a bit of doing/fixing, etc. *Br.* be difficult to do.

bit/ That's a bit steep! *Br., Aus. /Br.* **it's/that's a bit much/** it's not fair.

bit/ the whole bit *Am.* col. the whole of everything.

bit/ with a bit of luck *esp. Br.* fortunately.

bitch *Am.* col. smth. that causes problems.

bitchin' *Am., Aus.* sl. excellent: *This is a totally bitchin' pair of jeans!* - R.A. Spears.

bite *Am.* sl. the amount of money taken from total, usu. in one operation for one person, etc., cut: *domestic sugar policy takes a "$1.4 billion yearly bite out of U.S. consumers' pockets"* – Time; **take a bite out of** smth. *esp. Am.* take a part of it, esp. a sum of money.

bite back *Br.* stop saying smth.

bite me! *Am.* taboo. sl. used as an answer to an insult.

bite/ a bite on the cherry *Br., Aus.* a part of smth. good.

bite/ bite the big one *Am., Can.* col. die.

bite/have/get another/second bite at the cherry, two bites of a cherry *Br.* have another opportunity to do smth.

bite/ put the bite on *Am., Can., Aus.* 1. col. borrow: *He says you...tried to put the bite on him.* - R. Chandler. 2. journalism. do smth. that forces people or businesses to spend more money so that to work in a normal way.

bite/ that bites (the big one) *Am.* sl. excl. of annoyance when smth. can't be made.

the biter gets bit *Br.* a person suffers the result of one's own actions.

bits/ love sb. **to bits/pieces** *Br.* col. love sb. very much.

bits/ thrilled to bits/pieces *Br.* col. be very much pleased about smth. that has happened.

bits and bobs/bits and pieces *Br.* col. odds and ends.

bitsy *Am.* col. very small.

bitter *Br., Aus.* bitter beer, very dry dark heavily hopped ale opposite to mild beer/ the most widely consumed kind of beer in Britain and rival to tea as British national drink: *muffins or a pint of bitter* - G. Greene.

bitter and twisted *Br., Aus.* unpleasantly strange.

bitter greens *Am., Can.* mixed green leaves of a variety of salad vegetables, such as endives, chicory, or spinach.

bitter lemon *Br.* a carbonated semi-sweet soft drink flavoured with lemons.

bittersweet chocolate *Am.* bitter chocolate with an unpleasantly sharp taste.

bitty 1. *esp. Br., Aus.* col. made of little bits or connected parts. 2. *esp. Am.* col. very small, often in **a little bitty**.

bitzer *Aus.* col. a thing made from previously unrelated parts.

biweekly *Am. /Br.* **fortnightly/** (of event or publication) happening or appearing once every two weeks.

bizzy *Br.* sl. a policeman.

BL *Br.* Bachelor of Law.

black 1. *Br.* obs. (esp. of trade union) refuse to work with (goods, company, etc.). 2. *esp. Br.* adj. obs. not approved of, or not to be handled by members of a trade union during a strike.

black/ put up a black *Br.* sl. make an error.

black/ (as) black as a burnt log (also **as the inside of a cow** or **dog**). *Aus.* very dark.

black/ be not as black as sb. **is painted** *Br.* obs. be not as bad as people think they are.

black and tan 1. *esp. Br., Aus.* alcoholic drink, a mixture of bitter and a kind of stout. 2. *Am.* sl. serving both white and black people (in a cafe, bar, etc.).

black bag job *Am.* sl. burglary or robbery done by government agents: *In the FBI he'd never had*

anything to do with the famous black bag jobs - R.L. Chapman.
black beetle *Br.* col. cockroach.
blackboard rubber *Br.* /*esp. Am.* **eraser**/ smth. that is used to erase marks, esp. cloth or a piece of rubber.
black bourse *Br.* black market.
black boy *Aus.* a kind of Australian tree which has long thin leaves like grass.
black cattle *Br.* cattle raised for beef, regardless of colour/ opp. to dairy cattle.
black coat(ed) *Br.* adj. white-collar.
black diamond *Am., Can.* difficult ski slope.
black eye *Am., Can.* bad reputation: *His subversive action will give a black eye to the whole liberal movement.* - H.C. Whitford, R.J. Dixson.
black-eyed bean *Br.* /*Am.* **black-eyed pea**/ small pale bean with a black spot on it.
black face 1. *Br.* hardy kind of sheep with a dark face. 2. *Am.* white actor playing the role of a black man: *Blackface Mister Shenvair. Not real smokes.* - R. Chandler., *They did both numbers in blackface* - B. Holiday, W. Duffy.
black fellow *Aus.* derog. black Aborigene.
blackforest cake *Am.* a chocolate sponge cake having layers of morello cheese or cherry jam and whipped cream and topped with chocolate icing.
black frost *esp. Br.* hard slipping frost without any white covering.
blackgame *Br.* black grouse.
black gold *Am., Can.* col. oil.
blackgoods *Br.* pieces of house equipment of black colour, such as TV or hi-fis.
the block hole of Calcutta *Br.* a dark and very hot place too full of people or things.
black ink *Am.* profit.
blackjack, sap 1. *Am., Can.* /*Br.* **cosh**/ col. short heavy metal pipe or filled rubber tube used as a weapon: *Bugs dropped the cloth-wrapped blackjack on the grass.* - E. Hemingway. 2. *esp. Am., Can.* a gambling card game of 21.
blackleg *Br.* derog. v. n. (be) a person who takes place of a worker on strike: *I happened to be looking on at a fight between strikers and blacklegs.* - A. Huxley.
blacklung *Am.* col. lung disease of the miners caused by breathing coal dust.
Black Maria *Br.* obs. /*Am.* **patrol wagon**/ prison van.
Black or white? *Br.* Black or regular? (about coffee) white in Britain means mixed with hot milk from a jug, Americans use cold milk to mix with other drinks.

blackout *Am.* adj. secret.
black pudding *Br.* a kind of sausage made of animal blood and fat and grain.
blacksnake *Am.* long, heavy whip made of braided leather.
black spot *esp. Br.* 1. part of a road where many accidents have happened. 2. any place or area of serious trouble or difficulties, esp. an area of economic depression.
blackstrap molasses *Am.* the darkest thickest molasses.
black stuff *Br.* sl. tarmacadam.
black stump *Aus.* col. a mythical marker of distance in the outback.
black stump/ near (beyond) the other side of the black stump *Aus.* very faraway place.
blackthorn winter *Br.* a spell of cold weather at the time in early spring when the blossoms flower.
black tie *Br.* a black bow tie worn with a dinner jacket.
blacktop *esp. Am., Can.* 1. /*Br.* **tarmac**/ tar macadam, bitumen: *Soon the hum of tires on the blacktop became an eerie lullaby* - Reader's Digest., *The sun's just kissed the blacktop.* - Time. 2. road surface.
blacktown *Am.* part of the town where mostly black people live.
blacktracker *Aus.* aboriginal used by police to catch criminals in the bush: *A black tracker would horsewhip them before bringing them back.* – Reader's Digest.
blackwages *Br.* wages higher than those provided for by a labour union contract paid to attract non-union workers because of the shortage of labour.
black widow *Am.* sl. unpopular girl.
blades *Aus., NZ.* hand shears.
bladework *esp. Br.* the way oars are used in rowing.
blag *Br.* col. 1. violent robbing or raid. 2. an act of cheating using a persuasion to obtain smth. dishonestly, v.
blah 1. *Br.* col. boring remarks. 2. *Am.* col. a. (of appearance, character) uninteresting. b. sl. unwell or unhappy.
(the) blahs *Am., Can.* col. a state of mental depression: *You look like you've got the blahs.* - R.A. Spears.
blancmange *Br.* cold sweet food made from cornflour, milk, and sugar.
blank 1. *Am., Can.* sl. hold an opponent scoreless: *The hapless Tigers were blanked twice last week* - R.L. Chapman. 2. *Br.* col. deliberately ignore sb.

blank *esp. Am. /esp. Br.* **form/** official paper with spaces in which one must answer questions and give other information.
blank/ draw a blank *Am.* fail to answer a question.
blankbook *Am.* a book of blank pages or forms for accounts, memorandums, etc.
blanket/ born on the wrong side of the blanket *Br.* euph. now rare. born of unmarried parents.
blanket bath /bed bath/ *Br.* sponge bath.
blanket coat *Am., Can.* a coat made from blanket(-like material).
blanketed *Am.* (of certain animals) with a white stripe.
blanket roll *Am., Can.* a soldier's blanket and kit made into a roll for use on active service.
blanket sheet *Am.* 1. large-size newspaper sheet. 2. cotton blanket.
blankety blank *Am.* col. damned.
blarney *esp. Br.* col. pleasant but untrue things.
blast *Am.* sl. 1. a (fist) blow/ **put the blast on** sb.: *a blast in the kisser* - R.L. Chapman. 2. verbal attack, harsh criticism: *The senator leveled a blast at the administration.* - R.A. Spears. 3. dismal failure. 4. single dose of drugs. 5. also *Can.* exciting party or experience: *It was a blast.* - Esquire., *We had a blast.* - Reader's Digest.
blast *Am.* sl. 1. also *Can.* attack verbally: *She really blasted the plan in front of the board.* - R.A. Spears. 2. become a drug addict: *start blasting opium from a water pipe* - R.L. Chapman. 3. advertise.
blast *Br.* excl. (used when you are annoyed about something).
blast off *Am.* sl. leave without saying good-bye.
blasted *Am.* sl. drunk.
blat *Am.* col. blab, chatter.
blatherskite *esp. Am., Can.* a person who talks at great length without making much sense.
blaxploitation *esp. Am.* smth. concerned with blacks, esp. with regard to stereotyped roles of them in films.
blazer *Am.* 1. a small cooking apparatus. 2. col. a. vulgar thing. b. immodesty.
bleachers *esp. Am., Can.* cheap, uncovered stand at a sports stadium: *You can burn in the bleachers or pick up a poolroom tan.* - Bulletin., *concentrate on the ball and bleachers.* - C. McCullers., *Normal people sat at the bleachers quite a distance away.* - J. Baez.
bleat *Br.* col. complain in an annoying way.
bleeder *Br.* col. 1. contemptible person. 2. any person, esp. one recorded with disrespect or pity. 3. very troublesome thing. e.g. *a bleeder of a snowstorm.*

bleeding *Br.* col. (used for giving force to an expression esp. of annoyance) bloody, damned.
bleep *Br.* col. let sb. know through their **bleepers**, that you want to telephone them.
bleeper *Br.* pager.
blend /blended whiskey/ *Am.* one with 20% straight whiskey and 80% neutral spirits.
blended family *esp. Am., Can.* a couple and the children from this and all previous relationships.
blessed *Br.* col. (used to show that you are annoyed).
the blessed event *Am.* the birth of a child.
blighter *Br.* obs. col. 1. despicable person. 2. any person (sometimes used to express sympathy or mild envy, as in **lucky blighter**).
Blighty *Br.* col. 1. England, Home: *One need not even mention Blighty* - Maclean's. 2. a wound that sends a soldier home.
(cor) blimey *Br.* col. excl. (used for expressing surprise): *Blimey, exclaimed the cheerful lad* - D. Francis.
blimp *esp. Am.* an airship.
(Colonel) Blimp *esp. Br.* col. obs. pompous, reactionary establishment figure: *I was in serious danger of turning into one of the Colonel Blimp types* - B. Bryson.
blimp *Am., Can.* obese person.
blimpish *Br.* col. (esp. of an old man) having old-fashioned military principles and too much pride in his country.
(window)blind *Br. /Am., Aus.* (window) **shade/** flexible screen regulating the light or view through a window which usu. can be rolled or folded up.
blind 1. *Br.* col. curse, esp. in the phr. **effing and blinding.** 2. *Br.* sl. drinking spree. 3. *esp. Am. /Br., Aus.* **hide/** hidden place from which one can watch animals, esp. when hunting: *A ground blind finally pays off with an impressive kudu bull.* - Outdoor Life.
blind/ blind sb. **with science** *Br., Aus.* confuse sb. by using difficult and technical words to describe smth.
blind/ not make a blind bit of difference *Br.* col. not matter at all.
blind/ not to take a blind bit of notice *Br., Aus.* col. not pay any attention.
blind/ swear blind *Br. /Am.* **swear up and down/** insist on telling the truth.
blind drunk *Br.* col. euph. drunk.
blinder *Br.* col. 1. wild party with a lot of drinking/ **put, go, be on a blinder.** 2. dazzling performance (usu. of a sportsman or musician).

blinders 1. *esp. Am., Can.* /*esp. Br., Aus.* **blinkers**/ a pair of flat pieces of leather fixed beside a horse's eyes to prevent it seeing objects on either side: *like a horse in blinders, he sat in the pew.* - S. Bellow. 2. *Am.* an inability to see or understand: *She wore rose-colored blinders.* - H. Troyat., *Their field of vision narrowed by ideological blinders* - Y. Richmond.

blinding *Br.* col. excellent.

blind pig /**blind tiger**/ *Am., Can.* col. speakeasy, an illegal place for drinking alcohol: *Then he went to a blind tiger he knew* - J. Dos Passos.

blind road *Br.* dead end street.

blindside *Am., Can.* 1. hit or attack sb. on their blind side. 2. give unpleasant surprise.

blind-staggers *Am.* sl. extreme drunkenness.

blind trust *esp. Am., Can.* a trust independently administering the private business interests of a person in public office to prevent a conflict of interest.

blinger *Am.* sl. smth. remarkable, whopper. e.g. *a blinger of a headache.*

blink *Am.* /*Br.* **wink**/ flash or cause (a light) to flash on and off.

blink/do smth. **without a blink** *Br.* do smth. without any emotion.

blink/ on the blink *Br.* col. not working properly.

blinkered *Am., Aus.* unable or unwilling to understand smth.

blinkers 1. *Am.* col. /*Br.* **winkers**/ the small lights on a car which flash either on the right or left to show it will move towards that direction. 2. *esp. Br., Aus.* /*esp. Am., Can.* **blinders**/.

blinking *Br.* euph. col. bloody, damned.

bliss out *Am.* sl. become ecstatic: *I always bliss out from talk like that* - R.A. Spears.; n. **blissout**.

blitz on smth. *Br.* try to do smth. quick with a great effort.

blitzed *Am.* col. very tired or drunk.

blizzard *Am.* 1. witty answer. 2. col. sudden large amount of smth. that a person must deal with.

The Blizzard State *Am.* South Dakota.

bloat *Am.* col. wasteful or needless expansion of staff, expenditures, etc.

block 1. *esp. Am., Can.* a. an area of city or town enclosed by streets on each side: *right in the middle of the block under the Appolo Theater marquee* - J. Kerouac. b. the length of one side of a city block. 2. *Am.* /*esp. Br.* **(toy) brick**/ a small building block (esp. a child's toy): *It looks like so many children's blocks scattered at random* - R.G. Kaiser. 3. *Am.* a platform from which property is sold at auction, hence **go to the block** *Am.* sell at auction: *La Casa was about to go on the block* - D. Mortman., *more than 300 yearlings go on the block* - Daily News; **on the (auction) block** *esp. Am., Can.* /*Br.* **under the hammer**/ on sale, esp. at auction. 4. *Aus.* geodesic lot. 5. *Br.* sl. head: *That block of yours is pretty dense.* - R.A. Spears. 6. *Aus., NZ.* an urban or suburban building plant. 7. *Aus., NZ.* an area of land, esp. a tract offered to an individual settler by a government. 8. *Am.* (in Am. football) impede the progress of player with a ball with one's body. 9. *Aus. NZ.* large piece of land.

block *esp. Br.* 1. a large building with many homes or offices in it. 2. *esp. Br.* a set of sheets of paper glued along the edge, used for writing or drawing on.

block *Br.* print. 1. (in binding) to impress or /*Am.* **stamp**, *Br.* **emboss**/ a design upon the cover. 2. (in printing) a **letterpress block** /*Am.* **cut**/ is the etched copper or zink plate, mounted on wood or metal, from which an illustration or text is printed: *the process department which makes the "blocks" from which pictures are reproduced* - J. Ruppeldtova.

block/ be around the block (a few times) *Am.* col. be quite experinced in smth.

block/ do the blocks *Aus.* sl. stroll.

blockade *Am.* traffic jam.

blockage *Am.* 1. special obstruction on the road. 2. road metal.

blockboard *Br.* building material consisting of a core of wooden strips between two layers of plywood.

blockbuster *esp. Am.* a person who gets white people to sell their houses to him cheaply by telling them that the black people are going to move into the area: *What do they call these Negroes who are the first to move into a white neighborhood? Hong Kong laughed. The blockbusters?* - J.A. Michener / also v. **blockbust**, n. **blockbusting**.

block heater 1. *Br.* /*Br.* **storage heater**/. 2. *Am., Can.* a device for heating the engine block of a vehicle.

blocking *Br.* print. 1. /*Am.* **tooling**/ making an impression on paper or board from a **block**. 2. /*Am.* **engraving**/ printing of smth. on paper or cardboard.

block of flats *Br., Aus.* /*Am.* **apartment building** or **house**, *Can.* **apartment block**/ a building containing separate residential flats/apartments.

block of service flats *Br.* /*Am.* **apartment hotel**/.

block party *Am.* charity party held on the street by the residents of a block or neighbourhood to raise money for local church organisation, etc.

block release *Br.* the release of employees from their place of work for an extended period so that they can attend a college of further education or higher education with the aim of obtaining a qualification related to their work.

block training *Br.* temporary release from job for additional training: *the student spends block periods in industry sandwiched between periods at the college.* - J. Ruppeldtova.

bloke *esp. Br., Aus.* col. a man: *the bloke was looking the other way.* - P. Norman., *Nice bloke, she thought.* - D. Reeman., *These blokes work very long hours.* - You., *I'll talk slang to the bloke who understands it.* - R. McRum., W. Cran., R. McNeil.

blok(e)ish, blokey *Br.* col. humor. behaving like a typical ordinary man.

blonde/ bushfire blonde *Aus.* col. red-haired woman.

blondine *Am.* 1. v. dye (hair) blond, bleach: *But how many Sirio's blondined darlings will eat trash?* - New York. 2. preparation for doing this. 3. adj. (of hair) bleached.

blood *Am.* sl. fellow black, also **blood brother**: *and these cats...well, we was all bloods* - R.L. Chapman.

blood *Br.* give sb. their first experience of an activity, esp. a difficult or unpleasant one.

blood and guts *Am.* col. adj. full of action or violence.

blood and thunder *Br.* (of speech or performance) full of exaggerated feelings and behaviour.

blood/ be after sb.'s **blood** *Br.* be determined to punish them.

blood/ be baying for (sb.'s) **blood** *Br.* express strong criticism and demand punishment for sb.

blood/ be begging for blood *Br.* want sb. to be hurt or punished.

blood/ sb.'s **blood is up** *Br.* that person is very angry and is about to do smth. about the matter.

blood/ like getting blood out of a turnip *Am.* very difficult to get, esp. smth. like money or information.

blood/ run in one's **blood** *Br.* (about habits, etc.) come from one's parents, grandparents, etc.

blood/ scent blood *Br.* /*Am.* **smell blood/** be eager to defeat an opponent.

blood/ too rich for sb.'s **blood** *Am.* col. exceeding sb.'s capabilities, purse, desire, etc. too much.

blood group *Br.* /*Am.* **blood type/** any of the four classes of human blood.

blood sports *Br.* the hunting of wild animals such as foxes, hares and others with the aim of killing them.

bloody *esp. Br., Aus.* col. adj. adv. 1. (used as an intensive to an expression or judgement). 2. (used as an almost meaningless addition to angry speech): *not a man pays the smallest attention to me except a bloody little shop-assistant.* - W.S. Maugham., *Non o'yer bloody quod for him.* - H.H. Richardson. 3. obs. unpleasant or perverse.

bloody/ bloody/bloodied but unbowed *Am.* struggling to do smth. despite strong criticism.

bloody-minded *Br., Aus.* col. obstinate, inflexible, often unreasonably: *It's pure emotional, said Neil, just being bloody-minded.* - J. Fowles.

bloody shirt/ wave a bloody shirt *Am.* set one person against the other.

blooey *Am.* col. adj. out of order, destroyed: *wavering like a blooey television set* - J. Updike.

bloom/ the bloom is off the rose *Am., Can.* smth. is no longer new, fresh or exciting.

bloomer *Br. obs.* humor. col. /*Am* **blooper/** a silly mistake: *This dictionary, I'm afraid, is scarcely free of bloomers* - R.L. Chapman.

bloomer *Br.* a type of large loaf which has diagonal cuts on the top.

blooming *esp. Br.* col. euph. adj. adv. bloody, damned: *It's a blooming sweat shop* - D. Francis.

bloop *esp. Am., Can.* 1. (of electronic device) emit a short low-pitched noise. 2. make a mistake.

blooper /also **bloop**/ 1. *esp. Am., Can.* col. a very foolish mistake, esp. one done by an actor or TV personality: *There were some famous bloopers* - Time. 2. *Am.* generating receiver in radio.

blot on one's **escutcheon** *Br. obs.* smth. bad on one's reputation.

blotter *Am., Can.* a book where records are first written, before the information is stored elsewhere, esp. a police blotter: *The dean removed his executive reading glasses and carefully placed them on his blotter.* - R. Cook., *adsurdities have been accumulating like ink stains on a police blotter.* - New York.

blotto *esp. Br., Can., Aus.* sl. drunk: *Was I that blotto?* - B. Kaufman., *He must be blotto.* - P. Case, J. Migliore.

blouse/ big(or **great**) **girl's blouse** *Br.* col. effeminate man.

blow *Br. obs.* a walk.

blow *Am.* sl. leave, go: *I better blow town before the cops come looking for me.* - T. Thorne.

blow/ blow sb. **away** *Am.* sl. kill sb. by shooting with a gun or defeat sb. severely.
blow/ blow in *Am.* col. spend (money): *The theatre company blew in $52,000* - Longman.
blow in *esp. Am.* col. arrive unexpectedly.
blow/ blow sb. **off** *Am., Can.* col. 1. fail to keep an appointment. 2. end a romantic or sexual relationship with sb.
blow/ blow smth. **off** *Am., Can.* 1. not take it seriously. 2. fail to attend smth.
blow/ blow the doors off *Am., Can.* col. be much better than smth.
blow/ blow sb. **out** 1. *Am., Can.* col. defeat sb. thoroughly. 2. *Br.* col. disappoint sb. by not meeting them or not doing what they agreed to do.
blow/ blow smth. **out** *Am., Can.* col. render a part of body useless.
blow/ blow round *esp. Br.* col. pay a visit informally: *Why don't you blow round one evening next week?* - Longman.
blow/ blow (sb.) **up** *Br. /Am., Can.* **blow up at** sb./ be angry with sb: *If you criticize Al, he'll blow up. He's very sensitive.* - W. Magnuson.
blow/ blow a fuse *Am.* sl. /*esp. Am.* **blow** (one's) **stack/** get angry.
blow/ Blow me (down) *Br., Can.* col. obs. (an expression of surprise): *Well, blow me down, if it isn't Jack Roberts* - Longman.
blow/ blow hot *Br.* be enthusiastic.
blow/ blow hot and cold *Br.* work unevenly.
blow/ blow one's **boiler** *Aus.* col. /*Am.* **blow** one's **cool,** *esp. Am., Can.* col. **blow** one's **lid** or **stack/** get angry.
blow/ blow it/that/him, etc. *Br.* obs. excl. of annoyance with sb./smth.
blow/ blow one's **own horn** *Am. /Br.* **trumpet/** boast.
blow/ blow the gaff *Br.* col. /*Am.* **stand the gaff/** let smth. secret become known.
blow/ blow town *Am.* sl. leave town suddenly.
blower 1. *Am.* sl. braggart. 2. *Br., Aus.* sl. obs. / *Am.* **horn/** telephone: *Get me on the blower at Frank's straight off.* - G. Greene. 3. *Br.* central odds bureau (in horse-racing).
blowhard *Am., Can., Aus.* col. braggart: *the MacCabees can keep mobility and hide with a few thousand blowhards.* - L. Uris., *best known as the blowhard police chief on Hill Street Blues.* - New York.
blowie *Aus., NZ.* blowfly.
blow-in *Aus.* col. a new comer or recent arrival.
blow lamp *esp. Br.* /*esp. Am., Aus.* **blow torch,** *Br.* **brazing lamp/** lamp or gas pipe with a device which gives off a small very hot flame: *it was like a blast from a blowtorch right into his face.* – F. Edwards.
blowout 1. *esp. Am.* a sudden bursting of a tyre on a road vehicle while it is moving quickly. 2. *Br.* col. a very large meal. 3. *Am.* col. a party or social occasion. 4. *Am., Can.* col. an easy victory over sb. in a sports contest or in an election.
blowpipe *Br., Aus. /Am.* **blowgun/** a weapon in the shape of a tube with which arrows are fired by blowing through it.
blow season *Am.* col. the season of tornadoes and hurricanes.
blowy *Br.* col. windy.
BLT *esp. Am., Can.* a sandwich of bacon, lettuce and tomato.
blub *Br.* col. cry noisily.
bludge *Aus., NZ.* col. 1. avoid work. 2. cadge or scrounge or get smth. dishonestly. 3. easy job. 4. /also **bludger**/ loafer: *his neighbor called him a dole-bludger.* - New Idea.
blue 1. *Br.* person chosen to represent Oxford or Cambridge at major sport. 2. *Aus., NZ.* a fight: *They got into a blue - Kelly pushed Charlene into a gooseberry bush.* - T. Thorne. 3. *Am., Aus.* sl. adj. drunk: *You're getting a little blue.* - R.A. Spears. 4. *Br.* col. politically conservative. 5. *Aus., NZ.* a mistake. 6. *Aus., NZ.* col. a nickname for a red-headed person.
blue *Br.* col. squander money.
blue/ be in the blue *Aus.* be in debt.
blue/ full blue *Br.* cricket, crew, rugger and socccr.
blue/ half blue *Br.* tennis, lacrosse and hockey.
blue /get/ win one's **blue** *Br.* become a member of University sports team/ **Dark Blues** *Br.* Oxford or Harrow's teams, **Light Blues** *Br.* Cambridge or Eaton's teams.
blue in *Br.* spend (money) rashly, squander.
blue and white *Am.* sl. police car: *A blue and white suddenly appeared* - R.A. Spears.
blueback *esp. Am., Can.* a bird or fish, esp a trout or a sock-eyed salmon having a bluish back.
blueberry *Am., Aus. /Br.* **billberry/**.
blue blazes/ like blue blazes *Am., Aus.* col. a lot; extremely.
bluebook 1. *Am.* a. book listing the names of socially prominent people. b. any book listing the leading corporations, persons, etc. within an industry, area, etc. 2. *Am.* a. booklet used for writing answers to examinations. b. col. university exam. 3. *Am.* motorist guide-book. 4. *Br.* official report printed by the British government.

bluebottle 1. *Aus.* the Portuguese man-of-war. 2. *Br.* wild cornflower. 3. *Br.* col. obs. a police officer.

blue box 1. *esp. Am.* an electronic device used to access the long-distance telephone lines illegally. 2. *esp. Can.* a blue plastic box for collection of recyclable household materials.

blue-chipper *Am., Can.* col. a highly-valued person, esp. a sports player.

blue-collar *esp. Am., Can.* relating to manual work.

blue corn *Am., Can.* a variety of maize with bluish grains.

blue-eyed *Can.* English, Anglo-Saxon.

blue-eyed boy *esp. Br., Aus.* col. usu. derog. /*esp. Am.* **fair-haired boy**/ one's favourite male.

blue film *Br.* col. film showing sexual activity.

blue flyer *Aus.* a female kangaroo.

The Bluegrass State or **Country**, also **The Corncracker State** *Am.* Kentucky: *they could claim to be natives of the Bluegrass State.* - T. Capote.

blue hair *Am.* sl. elderly person: *Here's to Blue Hairs and Break Dancers.* – Reader's Digest.

blue heeler *Aus., NZ.* a cattle dog with a dark speckled body.

The Blue Hen State *Am.* Delaware.

blue funk/ in a blue funk *Br., Aus.* obs. /*Am.* **in a funk**/ in a state of anxiety, fear or confusion.

Blue hen chickens *Am.* col. people from Delaware.

blue jeans *esp. Am.* jeans: *Carla…was magnificent in blue jeans or nothing at all* - T. Murphy.

blue law *Am., Can.* col. /*Br.* **licensing laws**/ a. law to control sexual morals. b. statute regulating work, commerce and amusements on Sundays: *None of the Sunday games started before two P.M. because of the blue laws* - M. Puzo.

The Blue Law State, also **The Freestone** or **Nutmeg State, Constitution State** *Am.* Connecticut.

blue murder *Am.* 1. shattering defeat. 2. difficult task.

blue-nose 1. *esp. Am., Can.* any Nova Scotian: *there is a veritable Sam Slick in the flesh now selling clocks to the Bluenoses.* - W. Grady. 2. *Can.* any New Brunswicker. 3. *Am., Can.* person of very conservative views: *A few bluenoses at the office sniffed at her spendthrift manner of throwing money away* - R.J. Randisi, M. Wallace.

blue paper *Br.* government publication.

blue-plate *Am., Can.* (of a meal) a full main course ordered as a single menu item.

blueprint *Am., Can.* draw up (a plan or model).

blue prints/blues *Am.* print. a cheap proof made by contacting film in a vacuum frame with a coated paper which is then developed in ammonia vapour. Also known as **browns** or **Vandykes** /*Am.*/ or **Ozalids, diazos** or **dyelines** /*Br.*/.

blue ribbon *esp. Am.* a ribbon given to the first prize winner of a competition; adj. first-class, expert.

blue-ribbon *Am., Can.* of the highest quality.

blue-rinse brigade *Br.* humor. adj. relating to older women with traditionally right-wing values.

blue-rinsed *Am.* well-cared for and energetic (about old woman): *Hardly pestered me at all compared to my blue-rinsed friend.* - J. Fowles.

Blues and Royals *Br.* a regiment of the Household Cavalry.

Blue Shield *Am.* organisation providing surgery insurance to supplement that offered by Blue Cross.

blues/ cry the blues *Am.* col. show false modesty: *Just think a year ago you were the one crying the blues* – J. O'Hara.

blue sky *Am.* 1. not practical or concrete, done in order to test ideas. 2. col. a. (of stocks, etc.). worthless: *They dealt in real numbers, not "blue sky" projections.* - Fortune. b. (of a law) preventing the sale of worthless stock and bonds.

blue sky/ out of a clear (blue) sky *Am., Aus.* suddenly.

blue stocking *Br.* obs. very well-educated woman.

blue streak *Am., Can.* col. 1. quick, energetic person or fast moving thing. 2. rapidly/ **talk a blue streak, like a blue streak**: *He talked a blue streak all the time* - J. Dos Passos.

bluey 1. *Aus., NZ.* col. also **swag**, bushman's (esp. sundowner's or tramp's) bundle, hump. 2. *Br.* sl. a five-pound note. 3. *Aus., NZ.* col. red-headed man.

bluey *Aus.* 1. v. go tramp. 2. shirt from a coarse fabric.

bluff *Can.* a grove or clump of trees.

bluff it out *Br.* keep pretending to be confident while doing smth.

blunderbuss *Am.* awkward person.

blurb *esp. Am., Can.* col. write a blurb (a promotion or advertising description) on some goods.

blush *Am.* a powder or cream put on the cheeks to make them look pink.

blush/ save/spare sb.'s **blushes** *Br., Aus.* do smth. to prevent sb. from feeling embarrassed.

blusher *Am.* blush, cream or powder used for making one's cheeks look red or pink.

blu-tack *Br.* tdmk. blue sticky material used to attach paper to walls: *I put Blu-tack in my ears.* – S. Townsend.

BM *Am. /Br., Aus.* **MB/** Bachelor of Medecine.

BMOC *Am.* sl. Big man on campus, student leader.

bo *Am.* sl. 1. box office. 2. hobo, tramp: *From some bo on the drag I managed to learn what time a certain freight pulled out* - J. London. 3. obs. fellow: *You sure devastated me, bo* - D. Hammet.

boab *Aus.* baobab.

board *Aus.,NZ.* board on which sheep are sheared.

board out *Br.* col. pay money and arrange for an animal to stay somewhere.

board/ chopping board *Br., Aus. /Am.* **cutting board/** one to cut vegetables and fruit on.

board/ go by the boards *Am. /Br.* **go by the board/** fail.

board/ sweep the board *Br.* win all the prizes or seats in an election.

board/ take on board *Br.* understand or accept smth,. esp. an idea or task.

board and lodging *Br. /Am.* **room and board/** a room to sleep in and meals: *Seventy-five dollars a week in addition to paying her room and board* - B. Holiday, W. Duffy.

board bill *Am.* pay for the board.

boarder *Br.* a pupil who lives at school during the term.

board foot *Am., Can.* a unit of quantity for lumber equal to the volume of a board 12x12x1 inches: *she'll carry a million and a half board feet of lumber.* - H. Fast.

boarding card *Br. /Am., Aus.* **boarding pass/** a card that a passenger must have to be allowed to enter an aircraft or a ship.

Board of Education *Am., Can.* a board or committee charged with the supervision of public schools: *the Board of Education didn't care enough about it* - B. Holiday, W. Duffy.

Board of Elections *Am.* board designed to supervise elections consisting of representatives of the two major parties, appointed by local authorities.

board of estimate *Am.* city budget committee.

Board of Trade 1. *Br.* British governmental department concerned with commerce and industry. 2. *Am.* organisation of businessmen for the protection and promotion of business interests.

boards/binders *Am. /Br.* **grey board/** print. the best quality of board used for case binding and made from a solid sheet of fibre. There are different types of board like, for example: **paste** */Br./* is two or more laminations of paper, for visiting cards; **pasted** */Am./* is two or more layers of cheap board used in cased bindings.

boards *Am.* 1. entrance examinations given by an organisation. 2. low wooden wall around the area in which it is allowed to play ice-hockey.

Board shorts *Aus.* bathing trunks.

board surfing, surf-board riding *Aus.* surfing.

boardwalk *Am., Can.* footpath by the sea, often made of boards: *The next minute he'd be giving it to her under some boardwalk.* - J.D. Salinger., *A boardwalk led some 300 feet downhill to the roofed pier.* - L. Waller.

boat/ push the boat out *Br.* col. spend a lot of money while celebrating.

boat/ what(ever) floats your boat *Am.* col. whatever you like.

boatie *esp. Aus., NZ.* boating enthusiast.

The Boat Race *Br.* sports contest between Oxford and Cambridge universities / in the US between Harvard and Yale universities.

boat shell *Am., Can.* slipper limpet.

boot shoes, deck shoes *Am.* plimsolls with thick crepe soles.

bob *Am.* 1. bobsled. 2. toboggan. 3. ride on a sleigh.

bob *Br.* col. obs. shilling: *You can't come to England with fifteen bob.* - J. Kerouac., *The chairman fined him ten bob.* - Cheshire Life.

bob/ be eighteen bob in a pound *Aus.* be slightly mad.

bobble *Br. /Am.* **tassle,** *Am., Aus.* **pompom/** a small ball of material, usu. made of wool, which is used for decorating clothes and soft furnishings: *a Jimmy Carter bobble-head doll* – Reader's Digest.

bobble *Am., Can.* a mishandling of a ball.

bobble hat *Br. /Am.* **stocking cap,** *Aus.* **beanie,** *Can.* **tuque/** woollen hat with a small woollen ball on the top.

Bob's your uncle *esp. Br., Aus., Can.* col. Everything is satisfactorily completed; It's easy!: *When I asked her to give your application to the president, she said, "Bob's your uncle!"* - W. Magnuson.

bobby *Br.* col. becoming rare. policeman: *There was a great wagonload of bobbies waiting for us.* - P. Norman., *If I see a bobby, I'll hand him over.* - J. Galsworthy.

bobby calf *Br.* a calf too small to travel with the herd.
bobby-dazzler *Br., Aus.* col. obs. something special.
bobby-pin *Am., Can., Aus., NZ. /Br.* **hairgrip, Kirby grip, pin/** flat hairpin with ends pressed close together: *That and a bobby-pin beside the bed told me Lucille is a brunette.* - J. Steinbeck., *a package of bobby-pins.* - T. Capote.
bobby-sox /socks/ *Am., Can.* col. girls socks reaching above the ankle: *Some of them wore bobby-socks, too.* - J. Fischer.
bobby-soxer *Am., Can.* col. adolescent girl: *Webster's defines a boobysoxer as an "adolescent girl."* - A. Summers, R. Swan.
bobcat *Am.* lynx.
bobsled *esp. Am., Can. /Br., Aus.* **bobsleigh/** a small vehicle built for running down ice-covered tracks.
bod 1. *esp. Br., Aus.* col. person, fellow, esp. an annoying one. 2. *Am.* col. body.
bodacious *esp. Am., Can.* col. very large or important, or very enjoyable, or admiring: *the yesterday engagement between bodacious V.I.P. actress Pamela Anderson and rock rapper Kid Rock is dead.* - Time.
bodega *Am.* a small shop that mostly sells food, esp. to Spanish-speaking customers.
bodge *Br., Aus.* col. v. n. (do) a slapdash job.
bodger, bodgie *Aus.* col. 1. dandy. 2. smth. flawed or worthless.
bodgie *Aus.* sl. a boy from a street gang.
ride /sit/ bodkin *Br.* sit squeezed between two persons.
body *esp. Br. /Am.* **bodysuit, leotard/** a piece of women's clothing which fits tightly over the chest, stomach, bottom and sometimes also arms, but not the legs and which usu. has a fastening between the legs.
body blow *esp. Br.* journalism. smth. that causes a serious trouble.
body English *Am., Can.* 1. col. body motions and gestures of sports fans during a game: *He tried to help the putt fall by using body English.* - A. Makkai. 2. follow-through bodily action after throwing or hitting a ball made to improve its direction.
body shop *esp. Am., Can.* a garage where repairs to the bodywork of vehicles are carried out.
body-snatcher *Am.* sl. reporter writing about the life of famous people.
body warmer *Br. /Am.* **down vest/** a short jacket without sleeves which is made of cloth and fits closely to your body.

bodywork *Am.* making or repairing the outer shell of a vehicle.
boff 1. *Br.* sl. buttocks. 2. *Am., Can.* col. also **boffola** a successful joke or hearty laugh: *All I need is a funny hat and a boffola* - R. L. Chapman. 3. *Am., Can.* col. have sex with sb. 4. *Am., Can.* hit or strike.
boffin *esp. Br., Aus.* col. scientist; clever person: *the boffins at Minolta recognise the need for economy.* - Sydney Calendar.
boffo *Am., Can.* col. 1. loud and appreciative. 2. successful: *That was really boffo!* - R.A. Spears. 3. funny: *Bush was on guard against boffo statistics* - Time. 4. wonderful, stupendous: *religious meetings can be called boffo successes* - W. Grady.
bog *Br.* sl. a mess, disorder.
bog /bog-house/ *Br., Aus.* sl. toilet: *He was standing on top of the bog, for some reason.* - T. Thorne/ **boghouse barrister** *Br.* barrack-room lawyer.
bog (Irish) *Br., Aus.* derog. sl. person from the countryside without much experience and who is not interested in life anywhere else.
bog in *Aus., NZ.* start a task enthusiastically.
bog off *Br.* col. derog. go away.
bogan 1. *Aus.* col. a stupid person. 2. *Can.* a side stream.
bog-berry *Am.* col. small strawberry.
bog(e)y, bogie *Br.* 1. sl. policeman, cop: *The bogies aren't as smart as that.* - G. Greene. 2. col. also *Aus. /Am.* **booger/** a piece of mucus from the nose: *picking his nose and eating the bogies.* - B. Bryson.
bogie *esp. Br.* undercarriage with 4-6 wheels pivoted beneath the end of a railway vehicle.
bog roll *Br.* sl. toilet paper.
bog-standard *Br.* col. said of smth. ordinary with no exciting or interesting features.
bog-trotter *Br.* sl. an Irish person.
bogus *Am.* a drink made of rum and treacle.
bohunk *Am., Can.* derog. col. 1. immigrant from Central or Eastern Europe. 2. stupid, clumsy person. 3. unskilled worker: *I don't want this bohunk to stop me.* - E. Hemingway.
boil *Am.* whirlpool on the water surface: *He had 30 of these boils on his sections of the levee.* - Reader's Digest.
boil/ bring smth. **to the** */Br./* (or *Am.* **a) boil** heat smth. until it boils; **come to the** */Br./* (or *Am.* **a) boil** reach a climax.
boil/ go off the boil 1. *Br., Aus.* become less successful, esp. in sport 2. *Br.* become less urgent. 3. *Br.* lose interest.
boil/ on the boil *Br.* very strong or urgent.

boildown *Am.* col. summary.
boiled dinner *Am.* meat and vegetables, esp. potatoes and cabbage boiled together.
boiled shirt *Am.* person who acts grand and important.
boiled sweet(s) *Br.* /*Am.* **hard candy**/.
boiler *Br.* col. 1. a woman, esp. unattractive or unpleasant one. 2. a chicken suitable for cooking only by boiling.
boiler/ burst one's **boiler** *Am.* get into trouble, come to grief.
boilermaker *Am., Can.* a shot of whisky followed immediately by a glass of beer as a chaser.
boilerplate *esp. Am.* articles to be used as a filler, esp. any syndicated material, expressing generally accepted opinions: *The rest of the will was boilerplate.* - E. McBain., *the attorney probably has a boilerplate trust agreement that she or he will fill in with your particulars* – S. Orman.
boiler-room, also **bucket shop** *esp. Am., Can.* col. place where very dubious stocks, real estate, etc. are sold, often by telephone solicitation: *he and his brothers had a boiler-room-type system in the North End that handled dog-race betting* - G. O'Neil, D. Lehr.
boiler suit *Br., Aus.* /*Am.* **overalls**/ a single piece of clothing that combines trousers and a jacket: *my mother was wearing a boiler suit with sequins.* – S. Townsend.
boilover *Aus.* col. a surprise result.
bok choy *Am.* /*Br.* **Chinese leaves**/ a type of cabbage eaten esp. in East Asia.
bold-faced *Am.* bold in manner or conduct, esp. when knowing that what they are doing is wrong; lacking scruples.
bollard *esp. Br.* traffic post, esp. one in the middle of the street where people wait or one at the end of streets closed to the cars so that they may not enter: *a generous assortment of old-fashioned benches, bollards and lampposts.* - B. Bryson.
bollock *Br.* sl. reprimand severely: *He was all set for giving me a bollocking for parking where I shouldn't.* - Guardian, T.Thorne.
bollocking *Br.* sl. angry words, esp. in **give** sb. **a bollocking.**
bollock-naked *Br.* sl. /*Aus.* col. **bollocky**/ completely nude.
bollocks *Br., Aus.* taboo sl. excl. n. 1. /*esp. Am.* col. taboo. **nuts**/ testicles: *we are going to hang them by the bollocks.* - J.P. Donleavy. 2. nonsense: *What a load of bollocks!* – R. Westall.
bollocks up *Br., Aus.* taboo. sl. /*Am.* **bollix up**/ spoil, bungle: *I know I've bollixed things up* - P. Case, J. Migliore.

bollocks/ be a load of (old) bollocks *Br.* taboo. sl. be not true, be a nonsense.
bollocks/ be the (dog's) bollocks *Br.* taboo. sl. be very good.
bollocks to you/that/it *Br.* sl. damn it.
bolo tie *Am., Can.* a tie of a cord worn around the neck with a large ornamental fastening at the throat.
bolshie, bolshy *Br.* col. derog. stubbornly uncooperative.
bolt *Am.* v. n. break away from (political party). **-er** n.
bolt/ shoot one's **bolt** *Br.* do everything possible.
bolter *Aus.* 1. an outsider in a sporting event or contest. 2. obs. an escaped convict.
bolt-hole 1. *esp. Br.* a hole or burrow by which a rabbit or other wild animal can escape. 2. *esp. Br., Aus.* a place where you can hide, esp. from other people.
bomb 1. *Br.* col. a great success / **go like a bomb, go a bomb, go down a bomb** *Br., Aus.* go very well or very fast. 2. *Am., Can.* col. v. n. fail, flop, often in **be the bomb**: *your last film was a bomb* - E. Taylor., *the professor called on him to act out some lines before the class and he bombed.* - E. Acosta, *I was in mortal pain after the partisans bombed.* - L. Uris., *he "bombed" the next few auditions* - D. Brenner. 3. *Br.* col. a lot of money. 4. *Br.* col. move very fast. 5. *Br.* col. a lot of money.
bomb /cost/ spend a bomb *Br.* col. cost / spend a lot of money.
bomb/ go like a bomb *Br.* col. 1. go very fast, esp. of vehicle. 2. be very effective or successful.
bomb/ make a bomb *Br.* col. make a lot of money.
bomb/need/want/ought to put a bomb under *Br., Aus.* make sb. do things faster or more efficiently.
bomb along/down *Br.* col. move very quickly.
bomb disposal unit *Br.* /*Am.* **bomb squad**/ person whose job is to prevent a bomb from exploding or to remove it so no one is hurt.
bombed *esp. Am., Can.* sl. drunk: *You're bombed, Woody.* - L. Waller., *he was as bombed as you can get.* - G.V. Higgins.
bombara *Aus.* rocky reef/ **roaring like a bombara** *Aus.* very loud.
bombara *Aus.* a wave which forms over submerged offshore reefs.
bona fides/ check bona fides *Br.* check sb.'s identity.
bonanza *esp. Am.* something very profitable: *the pirates settled down, unhampered, to their*

bonanza. - P. Norman., *this could turn out to be a bonanza.* - S. Sheldon., *The bonanza sale lasted for five years.* - J. Fraser.

The Bonanza State *Am.* Montana.

bonbon *Aus.* cracker, a tube of brightly coloured paper which makes a harmless exploding sound when pulled apart.

bonce *Br.* col. head.

bonded whiskey *Am.* whiskey stored in barrels for four or five years before being bottled: *I drew the flat pint of bonded bourbon out of my pocket* - R. Chandler.

bondi *Aus.* heavy club with a knob on the end.

bonds/ Treasury bonds *Am.* state (loan) bonds.

bone *Am.* 1. sl. a dollar. 2. sl. diligent student. 3. **bone (at, on)** *Am.* study hard: *John had to bone up on several subjects* - H.C. Whitford, R.J. Dixson. 4. taboo. sl. (of a man) have sex.

bone/near to the bone *Br.* very embarrassing.

bone/ no bones about it *Am.* I'll boldly tell everyone about my actions.

bone/point the bone at *Aus.* (of an aboriginal) cast a spell on (sb.) so as to cause their sickness or death; betray or let sb. down.

bone idle *Br.* col. very lazy.

boner 1. *Am., Aus.* an embarrassing mistake. 2. *esp. Am.* taboo. sl. a penis when it is hard. 3. *NZ.* low-grade animal whose meat can only be used in sausages, pies, or processed products.

bones *Am.* dice.

boneshaker *Br.* col. humor. an old vehicle with a poor suspension.

bone-tired *Am.* col. very tired.

bonk *Br.* taboo. col. humor. (make) an act of copulating: *he had had the inestimable pleasure of bonking twin sisters* - B. Bryson.

bonkbuster *Br.* col. joc. a popular novel characterised by frequent explicit sexual encounters between the characters.

bonkers *esp. Br., Aus., Can.* sl. humor. adj. mad, often in **drive** sb. **bonkers**: *I think he just went bonkers.* - D. Francis.

bonnet *Br., Aus. /Am., Can.* **hood**/ metal lid over the front of the car: *Scott and Hemingway looked under the old bullet-nosed bonnet* - J. Aldridge.

bonus *Br.* dividend paid to insurance policy holder/ **bonus share (issue)** *Br.* stock dividend; **no-claims bonus** *Br.* reduction in the cost of motor insurance when no claims has been made during previous years.

bon viveur *esp. Br.* bon vivant.

bonzer *Aus., NZ.* col. good, nice, fine: *you could be beeping along as the winner of our bonzer Barina* - New Idea.

bonzo *Am.* sl. mad: *You are completely bonzo!* - R.A. Spears.

boo/ not say boo /*Br.* col. **say boo to a goose**, *Aus.* **say boo to a fly**/ *Am.* col. say nothing.

boob 1. *esp. Br.* /*esp. Am., Can.* **boo-boo**/ col. (make) a silly mistake: *you pulled a boo-boo tonight.* - L. Waller. 2. *Am., Can.* col. foolish person: *a constant procession of American boors and boobs.* - J.A. Michener.

booboisie *Am.* col. stupid people as a class.

booby hatch *Am.* sl. 1. an insane asylum: *I woke up in the booby-hatch.* - Alcoholics Anonymous. 2. prison.

boob tube 1. also **idiot tube** *Am., Can.* col. /*esp. Br.* humor. **goggle-box**/ TV set: *weak-minded junk on the boob tube has been of, by and for white people.* - D. Divoky., *Dr. Golden, on the boob tube, appears to be a sophisticated woman.* - Time. 2. *Br. /Am.* **tube top**/ a tight-fitting strapless top made of stretchy material and worn by women and girls.

booby hatch *Am., Can.* col. derog. mental hospital.

boodle *Am.* sl. 1. an entire lot. 2. bribe money. 3. money in general: *they'd cut GCS out of the war boodle.* - H. Fast.

boofhead *Aus.* col. a fool.

boogaloo *Am.* modern dance.

booger *Am.* sl. 1. person or thing. 2. mucus, esp. from the nose.

boogie *Am.* taboo sl. black person: *We may have to give you to the boogie man, Willie* - E.L. Doctorow.

boogey man *Am.* bogey man: *something to keep boogeyman at bay.* – E. James, D. Ritz.

boogie *Am., Can.* move or leave fast.

book 1. *esp. Br.* col. book listing the names and telephone numbers. 2. *Am.* col. bookmaker.

book 1. *Br.* arrange to have or do smth. (such as a hotel room or a ticket) at a particular time in the future: *For starters, his place was overbooked.* - Newsweek. 2. *Am.* col. arrest sb.: *The cop booked him for vagrancy.* - R.A. Spears. 3. *Br.* write the name of the player who has broken the rules in a special book (of a referee).

book/ a closed book to sb. *Br.* smth. very hard to understand.

book/ be one for the books *Am.* col. be unusual and surprising.

book/crack, /*Am., Aus.* **hit/ the book** *Am.* col. study hard.

book/ bring sb. **to book** *esp. Br., Aus.* punish sb.

book/ make book *Am.* take bets and pay out winnings on the outcome of an event.

book/ suit sb.'s **book** *Br.* be of advantage to sb.

book/ that's/there's a turn-up for the books *Br., Aus.* col. smth. strange has happened.

book in/into *esp. Br.* col. 1. (at) cause to have a place kept for one at a hotel. 2. report one's arrival, as at a hotel desk, airport, etc., usu. by signing one's name in a register /*Am.* **check in**/: *I'll just book you in and then you can have a rest.* - Longman.

book off 1. *Br.* record one's going off duty. 2. *esp. Am.* declare that one has finished a period of work: *I had to book off after eight hours of work.* - Longman. 3. *Am.* col. declare one's intention not to work on a particular day, esp. in the phr. **book off sick**.: *300 men have booked off sick at the car factory where there is still trouble with the unions.* - Longman.

book out *esp. Br.* (cause) to take formal leave of a hotel, etc.

book through *Br.* buy a ticket for the whole of divided journey: *you may be able to book through* - Longman.

bookable *Br.* (of tickets) available to be ordered.

bookie *Br.* col. book maker.

booking, advanced registration *esp. Br.* /*esp. Am.* **reservation**/ advanced reservation of a seat, hotel room, etc.

booking clerk, booking office cashier, station manager *esp. Br., Aus.* /*Am.* **ticket agent, ticket office agent**/ person who sells tickets for journeys, esp. at a railway station or airport: *she had been undercharged by the booking clerk.* - Young Citizen's Passport.

booking office, booking hall *esp. Br., Aus.* /*Am.* **ticket office, ticket agency**/ an office where tickets are sold, usu. in a theatre or railway station: *Mark and Toby went to the booking office.* - I. Murdoch.

bookmobile *Am., Can.* a vehicle that serves as a travelling library: *This noble stone-and-steel bookmobile is no bland noodle factory to us* – K. Vonnegut, Jr.

bookrest *Br.* an adjustable support for an open book on a table.

book room; media center *Am.* school library.

bookshop *esp. Br., Aus.* /*esp. Am.* **bookstore**/ shop where books are sold: *Soviet bookstores never have the great Russian classics in stock.* - R.G. Kaiser.

bookstall *esp. Br., Aus.* /*Am.* **newsstand, bookup**/ a small shop with an open front that sells books and magazines, esp. at a railway station.

bookstand/ station bookstand *Am.* station bookstall.

booksy *Br.* col. having literary or bookish pretensions.

book token *esp. Br.* gift card that can be exchanged for books at a bookshop: *Inside the card there was a book token for ten shillings.* – S. Townsend.

boom *Can.* a raft of logs for transporting by water.

boom/ lower the boom on *Am.* col. suddenly stop doing smth. that sb. doesn't approve of.

boom and bust *Am.* col. /*Br.* **boom and slump**/ upswing in the economy with the following depression.

boom box *Am.* sl. ghetto blaster, powerful portable tape recorder: *A boom box resting on an enormous Mickey Mouse beach blanket blared rap music.* - R.L. Stine., *the Sharp portable boom box she won* - Tiger Beat.

boomer 1. *Am.* sl. roving worker. 2. *Aus.* male kangaroo. 3. *Aus.* a large wave. 4. *esp. Am., Can.* a baby boomer.

boomerang/ It's a boomerang *Aus.* Yes, but give it back.

The Boomer State *Am.* Oklahoma.

boondocks, tall timber *Am., Can., Aus.* col. derog. also *Am.* col. **boonies** the backwoods, a remote rural area: *he can waste his life out in the boondocks* - H. Fast., *from the boondocks of some place like Michigan* - Newsweek., *he was an obscure figure in the boondocks of the Austro-Hungarian Empire* - Atlantic Monthly.

boondoggle *Am., Can.* v. n. col. (make) a waste of time and money.

boong *Aus.* col. derog. coloured person.

boost *esp. Am.* col. favour the interests of, esp. by speech and writing: *She is always boosting some cause.* - R.A. Spears.

boost *Am.* sl. steal, esp. by shoplifting: *that bitch had boosted everything* - B. Holiday., W. Duffy., *Farragut had boosted a mattress from the shop* - J. Cheever.

booster *esp. Am.* col. an ardent supporter /of sb. or course/: *even a conservative booster acknowledges "Atlanta's not a tourist destination..."* - Time. **boosterism** *esp. Am., Can.* the keen promotion of a person, organisation or course.

booster cushion *Br.* /*Am.* **booster seat/chair**/ special seat for a small child that lets them sit in a higher place in a car or at a table.

boot 1. *Br., Aus.* /*Am., Can.* **trunk**/ an enclosed space at the back of the car for bags and boxes. 2. *Am.* sl. a new recruit in training in the US navy, army or Marine Corps: *my son was in Marine Corps boot camp* - Reader's Digest. / also in the phrs. **boot camp, boot training**. 3. *Am.* sl. thrill: *their little games give me a real boot* - R.A. Spears. 4. *Am.* /*Br.* **clamp**/ place a wheel clamp on illegally parked car.

boot/ Boot and saddle *Am.* Saddle the horse.

boot/ boot it *Am.* col. walk on foot.

boot/ fill one's **boots** (with smth.) *Br.* 1. col. get a lot of money, often dishonestly. 2. obs. eat a lot.

boot/ put/stick the boot in(to) *esp. Br.* col. a. kick sb. hard, esp. when he is already on the ground, attack person by kicking. b. be unkind to sb. who is already upset. c. make a bad thing worse. d. criticize sb. severely.

boot/ step into sb.'s **boots** *esp. Br.* take the place and do the job of sb. who **freed** their **boots**.

boot/ the boot is on the other foot *Br.* col. the situation has changed and the power is in the other hands.

boot/ (as) tough as old boots *Br.* 1. col. very healthy and accustomed to difficult conditions. 2. calm and not upset if other people criticise them.

bootcamp *esp. Am., Can.* 1. a training camp. 2. a prison for young offenders, organised on military lines.

booth *esp. Am.* partly enclosed place in a restaurant with a table between two long seats.

bootlace tie *Br.* a very narrow tie.

bootlick *Am.* sl. flatter sb.

bootmaker *Br.* shoemaker.

boots /also **bootboy**/ *esp. Br.* becoming rare. male servant in a hotel who cleans shoes and carries bags: *there was quite probably a boots*. - G. Greene.

boots/ a bossy boots *Br., Aus.* col. a person who likes telling people what to do.

(car) boot sale, boot fair *Br.* /also *Br.* **jumble sale,** *Am.* **rummage sale**/ a sale to which people bring unwanted items for sale.

boots and all *Aus.* col. completely.

bootstrap/ to one's **bootstraps** *esp. Aus.* having all the characteristics one is expected to have.

booty *Am., Can.* col. a person's bottom.

booze/ go out on the booze *Br.* col. drink a lot of ale.

booze bus *Aus.* a police vehicle from which officers test drivers' breath to see how much alcohol they have drunk.

boozer *Br.* col. 1. tavern, pub: *My man goes tae the boozer first* - C.M. Fraser., *I went to fetch im outa the boozer for his Sunday dinner.* - J. Fowles. 2. heavy drinker: *Herridge was an untenured barroom boozer* – N. Hentoff.

booze-up *Br.* col. a party with a lot of drinking: *It was as Paul had wanted a typical Liverpool booze-up, ridiculous and noisy* - P. Norman., *A good booze-up some night when we get back.* - A. Burgess.

bop *esp. Br.* col. dance in an informal way, esp. to pop music in a disco: *I am considered quite superior on the subject of bopping.* - J. Baez.

bo-peep *Aus., NZ.* col. a quick look.

bopping gang *Am.* sl. hoodlum gang.

bordello *esp. Am., Can.* brothel.

the Border /**land, side**/ *Br.* border between Britain and Scotland.

The Border-eagle State *Am.* Mississippi.

border light *Am.* compartment batten in a theatre.

bore *esp. Br.* /*Am., Can.* **gauge**/ measurement across the widest part of a pipe or tube.

bore *esp. Br.* col. a nuisance.

bork *Am.* obstruct by systematically defaming or vilifying sb.

borough *Br.* a town with a corporation and privileges granted by a royal charter.

borouh council *esp. Br.* organisation that controls a borough.

borrow trouble *Am., Can.* col. take needless action that may have detrimental effect later.

borscht-circuit *Am.* summer resorts in the Catskills where different performers provide entertainment for the guests: *their Borscht Belt rowdiness as blissfully chomped on as a down-in-the-mouth stogie.* - New York.

borstal *Br.* obs. prison school for young offenders / also **Borstal institutions, system.**

bosh *esp. Br.* col. obs. n. excl. empty talk, nonsense: *Bosh! But I say, Dick, I wish you'd turn your peepers on 'er* - H.H. Richardson.

boss 1. *esp. Am.* usu. derog. political party chief of the local organisation: *he is a political boss.* - L. Waller. 2. *Am.* adj. col. first-class: *Jeoff's the boss driver* - R.L. Chapman, *So where did you get this boss car?* – R.L. Stine.

boss/ boss around/about *Br.* boss, tell people what to do in a way that is irritating.

boss/ make a boss shot (at) *Br.* obs. sl. make first usu. unsuccessful attempt.

boss/ You are the boss *esp. Am.* /*Br., Aus., Can.* **You are the doctor**/ You are the master (of the situation): *You're the boss do it* - J. Kerouac, *Have 'em how you like. You're the doctor.* - W. Grady.

boss-cocky *Aus.* col. a farmer who employs labour.

boss-eyed *Br.* col. cross-eyed.

bossism *Am.* a situation when a political party is controlled by party managers.

bossy *Am., Can.* col. 1. cow or calf: *A farmer in upper New York State painted the word cow in big black letters on both sides of his white bossy* - J. Steinbeck.

bossy boots *Br.* col. a domineering person.

Boston cream pie *Am.* round cake with cream custard filling.

both/ Americans use the pronoun at the end of the sentence also. e.g. *I like Bob and John both.*

botch(-up) *esp. Br.* col. smth. done badly.

bother *esp. Br.* small trouble or difficulty continuing only for a short time.

bother (it) *esp. Br.* (impers.) (used to add force to expressions of displeasure).

(a spot of) bother *Br.* col. a fighting or public disorder.

botheration *esp. Br.* excl. obs. (used for expressing slight annoyance): *"Botheration", she said.* – R. Westall.

bothered/ can't be bothered (to do smth.) *Br.* (used to say that a person doesn't have enough interest or energy to do smth.).

bothered/ not bothered *Br.* col. (used to say that something is unimportant).

(feeding) bottle, feeder *Br.* a baby's feeding bottle.

bottle *Br.* col. courage, guts, nerve, often in **have the bottle to do** smth., **need/take a lot of bottle**: *You had to have bottle - a lot of bottle.* - J. Higgins.

bottle/ bottle it/lose one's **bottle** *Br.* col. lose courage at the last moment.

bottle/ bottle out (of) *Br.* col. refuse to do smth. because one is afraid.

bottle/ bring a bottle *Br.* /*Am.* **bring your own bottle/** party to which guests bring their own bottles of alcohol.

bottle and glass *Br.* col. person's bottom.

bottle baby *Am.* sl. an alcoholic: *There is help for bottle babies.* - R.A. Spears.

bottle bank *Br.* street container for empty bottles.

bottled in bond *Am.* untaxed during government-supported storage of bottled whiskey: *the rye whiskey it served was Golden Wedding, bottled in bond.* - H. Fast.

bottled water *Am.* mineral water.

bottler *Aus., NZ.* col. remarkable person or thing.

bottle jack *NZ.* A large jack for lifting heavy vehicles.

bottle party *Br.* a party to which guests bring their own bottles of alcohol.

bottle store *esp. Aus., NZ.* /*Am.* **liquor store/** off-licence.

bottom 1. *Br.* political solidity and dependability. 2. *esp. Br.* buttocks. 3. *Aus., NZ.* excavate the earth to the level where the minerals are. 4. *Aus., NZ.* gold and other minerals found while mining.

bottom/ be bumping along the bottom *Br.* work very slowly (of economic system) or reach a low level of performance.

bottom/ the bottom falls/drops out *Am.* people stop buying smth. and the sellers lose a lot of money.

bottom out *Am.* arrange the type on a page so that there are no "widows" /short lines at the end of a paragraph left at the top of the page/.

bottom dollar/ you (can) bet your bottom dollar *esp. Am., Can.* col. you can be sure.

bottom drawer *Br.* /*Am.* **hope chest,** *Aus.* **glory box/** obs. (the place for) the clothes, sheets, etc. which a girl collects before getting married.

bottom gear *Br.* /*Am.* **low, first gear/.**

bottom land *Am., Can.* valley of the river.

bottom of the garden/road, etc. *esp. Br.* the far end of the garden/road, etc: *At the bottom of the garden she entered the shelter of the tall hedge* - T. Hardy.

bottoms up *Br.* col. (expression used by some people to each other just before drinking an alcoholic drink).

bottom-up (plan) *Br.* one in which practical details are worked out before thinking about general principles, opp. **top-down.**

booty *Br.* (used by children) buttocks.

boughten *esp. Am.* ready-made.

bouillon cube *Am.* /*Br.* **stock cube/** a small block of dried stock which is usu. dissolved in hot water before being used.

boulevard 1. *Am.* wide main road in a town or city, broad often landscaped thoroughfare. 2. *Br.* wide road in a town, usu. with trees along the sides.

bounce 1. *Am.* brightness (cinema term). 2. *Am.* a sudden upward swing in the popularity of a candidate or party.

bounce/ be bounced into (doing) smth. *Br.* esp. journalism. be forced or persuaded to make a decision quickly.

bounce/ be bouncing off the walls *Am., Can.* col. be very nervous and excited.

bound *Am.* col. having decided to do smth. (predicative use): *the man who was bound he'd marry her.* - A. Hitchcock Mystery Magazine.

bound/ be bound and determined *Am.* have a strong wish to do smth.
boundary rider *Aus., NZ.* a man taking care of the fences.
bounder *esp. Br.* old use col. unpleasant unreliable man: *Can't you see that fellow's a bounder?* - E.M. Forster., *Damned insolent little bounder.* - A. Huxley.
bourbon *Am.* derog. a conservative.
boutonniere *Am.* /*esp. Br.* **buttonhole**/.
bovver *Br.* obs. col. street fighting, esp. when hobnailed boots (**bovver boots**) are used for kicking; **bovver boy** n.: *Liberal party bovver boy Wilson Tuckey* - Bulletin.
bow *Am., Can.* 1. /also *Br.* **arm**, *Am.* **stem**/ either of two arms fastened by hinges to the outer edges of a pair of spectacles and fitting over the ears. 2. metal loop or ring forming a handle of a watch, key or scissors.
bow/ have many strings to one's **bow** *Br.* have a wide range of resources to do smth.
bow/ take a bow (before sb.) *Br.* journalism. congratulate sb. or show admiration for them.
bow-and-arrow 1. *Am.* sl. sparrow. 2. *Can.* sl. Canadian Indian.
Bow bells/ within the sound of Bow bells *Br.* within the city of London.
bower/ right bower *Aus.* VIP, boss.
bowerbird *Aus.* col. a person who collects trivial things.
bow hunting *Am., Can.* hunting when a bow is used rather than a gun.
bowie (**knife**) *Am.* strong single-edged hunting knife.
The Bowie state *Am.* Arkansas.
bowl *esp. Am.* bowl-shaped structure, esp. an athletic stadium.
bowler (**hat**) *esp. Br., Aus.* /*Am.* **derby,** *Aus.* col. **boxer**/ man's round hat: *man in a low-crowned bowler hat* - G. Orwell.
bowler-hatted *Br.* sl. demobilised.
bowling, tenpins *Am.* /*Br.* **tenpin bowling, bowls**/ an indoor game where bottle-shaped pins are knocked down by rolling a large heavy ball.
bowls *Br.* 1. /*Am.* **lawn bowling**/ an outdoor game in which you roll heavy ball towards a small ball: *the inmates play lackadaisically at bowls.* – I. Stone. 2. /*Am.* **bowling, tenpins**/ tenpin bowling or skittles.
bowser *Aus.* petrol pump.
bowyang *Aus.* a string of cord tied around the bottom of trouser legs to keep the cuffs from dangling.

box 1. *Br.* gift, present. 2. *Am.* cavity made in a tree for collecting sap. 3. *Br.* a small country house for use while hunting or fishing. 4. *Br.* a type of intersection area. 5. *Am.* col. a. phonograph: *My box is old, but still good.* - R.A. Spears. b. piano: *Man, he plays a mean box.* - R.A. Spears. 6. *Br.* col. the television. 7. *Br., Aus.* /*Am.* **cup**/ a curved piece of hard plastic worn by men to protect their outside sex organs, esp. when playing cricket. 8. *esp. Am., Can.* taboo. sl. vagina.
box/ a box of birds *Aus., NZ., Br.* col. excellent thing.
box/ box sheep up *Aus., NZ.* col. mix up different flocks.
box/ out of box *Aus., NZ.* col. unusualy good.
box/ (come first) out of the box *esp. Am.* begin an activity for the first time.
box/ out of one's **box** *Br.* col. drunk or affected by drugs.
box/ right out of the box *Am.* as soon as you start doing smth.
box/ think outside the box *Am.* col. think in an imaginative and unusual way while solving a problem.
box clever *Br.* col. act shrewdly and cunningly.
box up 1. *Am.* close with boards of wood: *you'd better box up the doorway* - Longman. 2. *Aus.* confuse /usu. an animal/: *The sheep were all boxed up, running round in circles.* - Longman.
Box and Cox *Br.* col. adj. adv. sharing something by taking turns.
box canyon *Am., Can.* a narrow canyon with vertical walls.
box-car *Am., Can.* /*Br.* **goods waggon**/ roofed freight waggon: *There were rows and rows of boxcars waiting.* - K. Vonnegut, Jr., *I was moving silently down between two strings of boxcars.* - D. Hammet., *A boxcar would hold 40 men or 8 horses.* - Life., *third-class carriages, a euphemism for boxcars* - J.A. Michener.
boxed *Am.* sl. 1. drunk. 2. in jail.
box end spanner *Am.* /*Br.* **ring spanner, (open-ended) spanner**/.
(box end) wrench *Am.* /*Br.* **box spanner**/ ring spanner.
boxer *Aus.* col. /*Br.* **bowler (hat),** *Am.* **derby**/.
box-heater *Can.* portable stove.
Boxing Day *Br.* national holiday in England and Wales, celebrated on 26 December.
box junction *Br.* /*Am.* **box**/ a crossroads with a square of yellow lines printed in the center where one can drive over only if the road in front is clear.

box lunch, bag lunch *Am.* factory made lunch in a box: *We usually bought a ten-cent box lunch* - H. Truman.

box number *Br.* address at the post office that people can use instead of their own one.

box oyster *Am.* large high grade oyster.

boxroom *Br.* /*Am.* **storage room,** *esp. Br.* **lumber room**/ storeroom, esp. for boxes, trunks, unwanted furniture and other household miscellany: *Vincent slept in the boxroom* – I. Stone.

box score *Am., Can.* the tabulated results of a sports event with statistics given for every individual player.

box seat/ in the box seat *Aus., NZ.* in an adantageous position.

box spanner *Br., Aus.* /*Am.* **box wrench**/ a metal tool with a box for fitting over and twisting nuts.

box-up *Br.* col. mix-up, confusion.

boxwagon *Am.* long open waggon.

boy *esp. Am.* col. 1. male person of any age from a particular place. 2. also *Aus., Can.* excl. (expressing excitement): *Boy, was she lousy with rocks?* - J.D. Salinger., *Boy, this is heavy* - E. Taylor., *Boy. Do I have homework?* - B. Keane.

boy *Am.* taboo. sl. way of addressing a black man.

boy/ big boy *Am.* col. a boss: *the big boys with their weapons, money, and misguided plans for social reform* - P. Robertson.

boyla *Aus.* an Aboriginal witch doctor.

boyo *Irish Eng.* a form of address to a male.

the boys in blue *Br., Aus.* the police: *He couldn't go to the boys in blue* – M. Daly.

the boys uptown *Am.* sl. the political bosses of a city.

boy toy *Am.* a sexually attractive man who has relationship with older, powerful or successful people.

boy wonder *Am.* col. whiz kid.

bozo *esp. Am., Can.* col. stupid person: *Say, that bozo looks half-starved.* - J. Dos Passos., *a manly and gallant bozo* - R. Stout.

BPE *Am.* Bachelor of Physical Education.

BR *Am., Can.* bedroom(s).

bra/ auto bra, car bra *Am., Can.* a special cover for the front bumper of a car used by a speeding motorist to avoid detection by the police radar.

braburner *Am.* sl. derog. very militant feminist: *Didn't the braburners give way to whale-savers in the seventies?* - R.A. Spears.

brace *Br.* /*Am.* **braces**/, a wire frame that some children wear to make their teeth straight: *tan and zaftig, her braces removed, her blond hair drawn back* - K. Davis.

brace/ in a brace of shakes *Br.* sl. very quickly: *We'll be back in a brace of shakes.* - J.D. Carr.

braces 1. *Br., Aus., Can.* /*Am.* **suspenders,** col. **gallusses**/ elastic cloth bands worn over the shoulders to hold up men's trousers: *I'd rather wear braces* - G. Greene., *His trousers were held up by red braces* - J. Steinbeck. 2. *Am.* /*Br., Aus.* **callipers**/ metal supports which are fastened to the legs of people who have difficulties with walking.

braces/ wear belt and braces *Br.* col. take no risks.

brackets 1. *esp. Am., Aus.* /*Br.* **square brackets**/ special signs used for enclosing a piece of information. 2. also **round brackets** *Br.* /*Am.* **parenthesis**/ pair of signs ( ) used for explaining a piece of information.

brad *Am.* /*Br.* **paper fastener**/ metal object like a button with two metal sticks that are put through several pieces of paper and folded down to hold the paper together.

bradawl *esp. Br.* small tool with a sharp point for making holes; awl.

Brahmin *Am.* a socially or culturally superior person, esp. from New England.

Brahms and Liszt *Br.* col. a drunk person.

braid *esp. Am.* /*esp. Br.* **plait**/ twist together into one string or band: *braiding through my dirty, spatulate fingers your long white ones.* - K. Davis.

braid *esp. Am.* /*esp. Br.* **plait, pigtail**/ a narrow length of braided hair: *your long braids whipped against your shoulders.* - K. Davis.

brain/ be out of one's **brain** *Br.* col. be very drunk.

brain box *Br., Aus.* col. a very smart person.

brain pan *esp. Am., Can.* a person's skull.

brain-picker *Am.* col. person who exploits the creative notions of others: *nothing but scorn for brain-pickers and imitators* - R.L. Chapman.

brain-picking *Am.* col. extraction of useful information by repeated questioning.

brainnstorm 1. *Br.* col. a sudden great disorder of the mind. 2. *esp. Am., Can.* col. /*Br.* **brainwave**/ a sudden clever idea: *I just might have a brainstorm.* - S. Sheldon., *I had a sudden brainstorm* - Reader's Digest., *Could the pilot have had a brainstorm?* - A. McLean.

brainstorm(ing) *esp. Am.* method of finding answers to problems by generating as many ideas as possible: *a brainstorming conference on national issues.* - D. Mortman.

brains trust *Br.* a group of experts answering questions on topics of general interest in TV or radio discussion.
brain trust *Am., Can.* a group of experts appointed to advise government or politician.
brain-twister *Am.* sl. a puzzle.
brake lever *Br.* /*Am., Aus.* **handbrake**/ handbrake on a bicycle.
brakeman *esp. Am., Can.* /*Br.* **brakesman**/ a railway worker responsible for a train's brakes and often working as a guard as well.
brake van *Br.* railway car on a freight train or a compartment on a passenger train where the breaks are operated.
Branch (of Government) *Am.* Authority.
branch water *Am.* col. plain water often used with whiskey to make a highball.
brand/ own brand *Br.* /*Am.* **store brand**/ made and sold by a particular store.
brandy ball *Br.* a ball of brandy-flavoured candy.
brandy butter *Br.* hard sauce of butter, castor sugar and brandy creamed together and served with plum pudding and mince pie.
brandy glass *Br.* /*Am.* **snifter**/ short-stemmed goblet with a bowl narrowing towards the top.
brannigan *Am., Can.* col. a brawl: *Republicans and Democrats alike are guilty of this brannigan* - R.L. Chapman.
brantub *Br.* tubful of bran with presents hidden in it to be drawn out at random at Christmas parties.
brash *Am.* easily broken, fragile (esp. about wood).
brass *esp. Br.* col. /also *Br.* sl. **lolly**/ obs. money: *I'll have the brass.* - A. Christie.
brass/ as old as brass *Br.* very confident and impudent.
brass/ double in brass *Am.* sl. do a second job in addition to one's primary one: *The crew doubles in brass up on the playdecks* - R. Chandler.
brass/ have the brass (neck, nerve) /*Am., Aus.* col. **brass (balls) to do** smth. *Br.* col. be very impudent.
brass/ top brass *Br.* /*Am.* col. **people in top jobs**/ people holding the most important positions.
brass-collar *Am.* adj. always supporting the official opinion of one's political party.
brassed-off, browned-off *esp. Br.* col. /*Br., Aus., Can.* sl. **cheesed-off**/ tired and irritated, fed up.
brass-hat *Am.* col. a military officer of a higher rank.
brass-knuckles *Am.* /*Br.* **knuckle-duster**/ a set of metal rings worn over the front of the doubled fist for use as a weapon: *the man with the brass-knuckles took it.* - H. Fast., *I'll bash in their heads with my brass-knuckles.* - D. Divoky.
brass-monkey *Br.* col. adj. very cold (of weather); **be cold enough to freeze the balls off the brass monkey; it's brass monkeys.**
brass neck *Br.* sl. /*Am.* sl. **brass balls**/ impudence.
(go/grab/reach for the)/get the brass ring *Am., Can.* col. (try to get) 1. big prize. 2. a chance to get rich or succeed.
bravo *Am.* radio code name for letter B.
brawn *Br., Aus.* /*Am.* **headcheese**/ (pieces of) meat from a head of a pig boiled and pressed in a pot with jelly: *cutting up the meat for pies and brawn.* - J. Herriot.
brazier *Am., Can.* barbecue.
brazing lamp *Br.* /*esp. Am., Aus.* **blowtorch, *Br.* blow lamp**/ lamp or gas-pipe used to melt metals.
breach of the piece *Br.* law. an action such as fighting that annoys people in public place.
bread-and-butter question, issue *Br.* one concerned with the most important and basic things: *the image of American labor as uncompromising on bread-and-butter issues* – D.L. Barlett, J.B. Steele.
The Bread and Butter State, also **The Wheat State** *Am.* Minnesota.
bread bin *Br., Aus.* /*Am.* **bread box**/ kitchen container for keeping bread in.
breadline 1. *Am., Can.* a line of people waiting outside a particular building to be given food. 2. *Br.* the poorest condition in which it's acceptable to live.
the breadline *Br.* the level of income sb. has when they are extremely poor.
breadline/ be/live on the breadline *Br., Aus.* be very poor.
bread roll *Br.* bun used to enclose a hamburger (*Br.* **Wimpy**).
break *Am.* 1. col. awkward social blunder, mistake: *I'll forget you made the break.* - D. Hammet. 2. sudden and abrupt decline of prices and values. 3. col. burglary.
break *esp. Br.* /*Am.* **recess**/ school break between lessons: *I bought him a Mars Bar in break today.* – S. Townsend.
break *Am.* /*Br.* **change**/ change money into notes of smaller denomination.
break/ be never given/never get an even break *esp. Am.* not get the same chance or opportunity to do smth. as other people.
break/ break one's **ass** *Am.* sl. work extremely hard.

break/ break/bust sb.'s **balls** *Am.* taboo. sl. criticise sb. angrily.

break/ break the back of smth. *Br.* succeed in dealing with the worst part of work.

break/ Give me/us a break! *esp. Am., Aus.* col. It's unbelievable!

Break a leg! *esp. Am., Can.* excl. Good luck!: *"Break a leg!" – she whispered as he walked on the stage.* – W. Magnuson.

break down *Am.* sl. explain, present in detail: *Why don't you break down* - I. Shaw.

break for *Am.* suddenly run or drive somewhere, esp. to escape from sb.

break it down *Aus.* stop talking about it.

break up 1. *Br.* (of a school or pupil) begin the holidays: *We break up next week* - Longman. 2. *Am., Aus.* amuse greatly: *I'll try to do something that will break him up.* - New Idea., *And it broke us all up.* - A. Scaduto. 3. *esp. Am., Can.* cause sb. to become very upset: *I mean, you must've been pretty broken up. About Marcy.* – R.L. Stine.

breakaway 1. *esp. Aus., NZ.* adj. n. sudden mad rush of horses or cattle. 2. *esp. Aus.* an animal that escapes from control. 3. *Am.* n. adj. an object made so that it breaks easily when hit, esp. a stage prop: *Breakaway walls and the camera traveling on its track* - A.E. Hotchner.

breakdown gang *Br.* /*Am.* **wrecking crew**/ emergency repairs crew.

breakdown van, lorry or **truck** *Br.* /*Am.* **tow truck, repair truck, crane truck, wrecking crane**/ emergency repairs crane or truck.

breaker *esp. Br.* a person who breaks up disused machinery.

breakfast food *Am.* dry cereals (used for breakfast).

breakfast television *Br.* TV programmes in the early morning.

break feeding *NZ.* a system of controlling the feeding of grazing animals by dividing their paddocks with movable electric fences.

breaking *Am.* freshly ploughed land.

breaking and entering *Br.* /*Am.* **unlawful entry**/ burglary with breaking into a house.

breakout *esp. Am.* groups which break away from a conference.

break time *Br.* /*Am.* **recess**/ pause between lessons in school.

breakwind *Aus., NZ.* a windbreak

breastpin 1. *Br.* /*Am.* **stickpin**/ a special pin for tie. 2. *Am.* /*Br.* **brooch**/.

breath/ bring a breath of fresh air to/into smth. *Br.* make smth. more interesting and exciting with new ideas.

breath/ get one's **breath back** *Br.* start breathing normally again (after doing smth. energetc).

breathalyse *Br., Aus.* test a driver's breath to see how much alcohol they have drunk.

breath test *Br.* test made with a breathalyser.

breechclout *Am., Can.* loin cloth.

breeze 1. *esp. Am.* sl. something done easily: *It was going to be a breeze.* - R. Cook., *The job would be a breeze for me* - Reader's Digest., *the birth of Daniel was a breeze.* - New Idea. 2. *Br.* col. disturbance, quarrel.

breeze/ in a breeze *esp. Am.* col. easily.

breeze/ shoot the breeze / the bull *Am.* col. have a light conversation: *I shot the breeze for a while.* - J.D. Salinger., *you seem obsessed with shooting the breeze all night* - L. Uris., *We shoot the breeze for a while.* - J. Baez.

breezeblock *Br.* /*Am.* **cinder block**/ lightweight building block of cement and cinders: *A hideous row of breeze-block pighouses had to be got rid of* - J. Fowles.

breezway *Am., Can.* a roofed passage outside a house, esp. between it and a garage.

breve *Br.* note twice as long as semibreve /*Am.* **double whole note**/.

brew up *Br.* make tea by pouring hot water over tea leaves.

brewer's/drinker's droop *Br., Aus.* humor. temporary impotence caused by drinking too much alcohol.

brewpub *esp. Am.* a public house, frequently with a restaurant, selling beer brewed on the premises.

brew-up *Br.* col. the act of making tea (or coffee).

brick *Br.* /*Am.* **block**/ a small building block as a children's toy. 2. *Br.* obs. col. or *Aus., Can.* dependable and kind person, good friend: *Oh, Julia, you are a brick.* - W.S. Maugham., *Soames is a brick.* - J. Galsworthy.

brick/ be a brick *Br.* obs. be honest and reliable person.

brick/ be bricking oneself *Br.* taboo. sl. be very worried and anxious.

brick/ drop a brick (or **clanger**) *Br.* col. behave tactlessly in a society: *The man has dropped a brick.* - J. Fowles.

brick/ drop a curtsey *Br.* make a curtsey.

brick/ hit the bricks *Am.* sl. go on a strike.

brick/ make bricks without straw *Br.* manage to do smth. without knowing the basic things that you need to do it with.

brick it *Br.* sl. be extremely nervous: *I was bricking it, when the light came on* - Evening Standard, T. Thorne.

brickfield *Br.* /*Am.* **brickyard**/ a place where bricks are made.
brickfielder *Aus.* fresh wind (in Sydney).
brickie, bricky *Br., Aus.* col. bricklayer.
brickmason *Am.* bricklayer.
brick outhouse/ built like a brick shithouse, outhouse *Am.* sl. very well-built (of a figure): *my mother would say I was built like a brick outhouse.* - Reader's Digest.
brickwall *Br.* col. stone wall.
bridal registry *esp. Am., Can.* service offered by a shop in which bridal couple's preferences are recorded for their families and friends visiting the shop.
bridal shower *Am.* party for a woman who is going to marry where relatives and friends bring gifts for her.
bridge *Am.* structure on which signals are placed over a number of parallel railroad tracks.
bridge roll *Br.* a small soft bread roll with a long, thin shape.
bridgework *esp. Am.* the bridges in a person's mouth.
bridging loan *esp. Br., Aus.* /*Am., Can.* **bridge (loan)**/ money that a bank or other company lends you for a short time to cover the period until you get money from somewhere else (often used when sb. buys a new house).
bridleway, bridlepath *Br.* a path along which horse riders have right of way.
brief 1. *esp. Br., Aus.* the instruction about someone's duties: *My brief is simply to do all sorts of stories* - New Idea., *But that was hardly in my brief.* - J. Fowles., *original brief was to promote central bank cooperation.* - Economist. 2. also **hold a brief for** *Br.* retain as a legal counsel. 3. *Am.* written summary of the facts and legal points supporting one side of a case, for presentation to a court.
brief/ hold no brief for smth. *Br.* not support it.
briefless *Br.* law. (of a barrister) having no clients.
brig *Am.* col. military prison: *some second Louie's gonna throw you in the brig.* - D. Divoky., *the Old Man gave him ten days in the brig.* - J. Hyams.
bright/ be as bright as a button *Br., Aus.* be smart and able to think quickly.
bright and breezy *Br.* cheerful and confident.
brights *Am., Can.* car headlights which are on as bright as possible: *low sports car rode our tail, belched and flashed its brights* - J. Kellerman.
bright spark *Br., Aus.* col. esp. derog. or humor. clever or cheerful person; a stupid fellow.

brill(iant) *esp. Br., Aus.* col. adj., excl. very good, brilliant: *I am having a completely utterly brill time* - T. Thorne., *it is dead brill* – S. Townsend.
brilliant *Br.* 3.5. point type known in America as **ruby.**
brilliant *Br.* excellent.
brilliantine *Am.* shiny dress fabric made of cotton and mohair (or worsted).
bring down 1. *Am.* give or leave (smth.) to people who are younger or come later: *This ring has been brought down in the family.* - Longman. 2. *esp. Am.* make a public statement about, declare officially: *The City Council will bring down the new spending plans on Monday.* - Longman.
bring forward *Br.* cause to happen earlier than usual.
bring in a law *Br.* make a new law.
bring out 1. *esp. Br.* cause (workers) to go on strike. 2. *Br.* appear at the high society for the first time: *Is Mrs. King-Brown bringing her daughter out this year?* - Longman.
bring sb. **out in** *Br.* cause to suffer the stated skin condition: *the memory of it brought me out in a cold sweat for days after.* – R. Westall.
bring up *esp. Br.* 1. also *Aus., Can.* vomit (one's food). 2. reprimand (for).
bring home the bacon *esp. Br.* provide one's family with all that is necessary: *I'm the one who brings home the bacon.* - Longman.
bring-and-buy (sale) *Br.* a (charity) sale in which people bring goods they wish to sell, and buy the goods brought by others.
bring-down *Am.* col. 1. something that depresses somebody. 2. morose person: *Don't invite John - he's a real bringdown since Sally dumped him.* - T. Thorne. 3. a cutting rebuke.
bringing-up *Am.* upbringing of children by parents.
brinkmanship *Br.* /*Am.* **brinksmanship**/.
brinny *Aus.* a stone, esp. one thrown as a missile.
briny *Br.* col. the sea.
Bristol fashion *Br.* col. in good order: *All shipshape and Bristol fashion.* - A. Christie.
bristols *Br.* col. female breasts.
britches *Am.* breeches: *Dust his britches, if he needs that* - Guideposts.
britches/ too big for one's **britches** *Am.* col. too difficult for sb.
Britisher *Am., Can.* a native of Britain.
Brixton briefcase *Br.* sl. a ghettoblaster, a large portable stereo radio-cassette recorder.
bro *esp. Am.* col. a brother (a friendly greeting and a form of address).

broach *Am.* brooch.

B-road *Br.* a secondary or minor road, often running cross-country to connect two **A-roads**.

broad *Am., Can.* derog. col. a woman: *Still a touch of piss and vinegar in the old broad.* - H. Fast., *There's the sweetest broad that ever walked God's earth.* - S. Sheldon., *she was viewed as the Limey broad with the snooty accent.* - P. Howard.

broad/ it's as broad as it's long *Br.* col. both things are equal.

broadacre *Aus.* (of farming practices and equipment) used in or suitable for large scale production.

broad arrow *Br.* mark identifying government property, formally including convict's clothing.

broad bean *Br. /Am.* **fava bean/** round pale green bean.

broad church *Br.* an organization that includes many different types of people.

broad jump *Am., Can.* long jump.

broadsheet *Br., Aus.* a newspaper that is printed on large paper or an advertisement printed on a large sheet of paper.

broadside *Am. /Br.* **broadside on/** with the longest side facing smth.: *we were hit broadside by a young man in a hot-rod* - A.E. Hotchner.

broadside *esp. Am.* crash into the side of another vehicle.

broil *esp. Am., Can. /esp. Br., Aus.* **grill/** cook (chicken, meat or fish) under or over direct fire: *It can broil, bake or smoke food.* - Newsweek.

broiler 1. *esp. Am., Can. /Br., Aus.* **grill/** a kitchen device for broiling food: *Prepare grill or broiler.* - Reader's Digest. 2. *Am.* dining car. 3. *Am.* very hot day.

broiler (pan) *Am. /Br.* **grill pan/** utensil used to cook food quickly.

broiling *esp. Am.* (of weather, sun, etc.) very hot.

broke/ flat broke *Am. /Br.* **stony broke/** having no money at all.

broken lots *Am.* job lots, a group of things of different kinds, all bought and sold together.

broken ranges *Br. /Am.* **broken sizes/** odd sizes offered in a sale.

broken reed *Br.* obs. very weak person.

broken time *Am.* time for sport chosen out of the busy schedule.

brokers' board *Am.* stock exchange.

broking *Br.* adj., n. of or having to do with brokerage, broking firm.

brolga *Aus.* fellow traveller of aboriginal descent.

brolly *Br., Aus.* col. umbrella: *You can't keep a good brolly down.* - Evening Standard.

bronc *Am., Can.* col. bronco.

bronc(h)o *Can.* sl. Englishman, esp. an English immigrant of the lower classes.

Bronx cheer *Am.* col. /*Br.* **raspberry/** a loud disapproving noise with lips and tongue: *The fans...whistled him out of the stadium - Europe's equivalent of a Bronx cheer.* - Time.

bronzewinger *Aus.* a kind of dove.

brooch *Br. /Am.* **pin/** piece of jewellery fastened to one's clothes.

broody (woman) *Br.* col. one who wants to have a baby and keeps thinking about it.

broomie, sweeper *Aus., NZ.* col. a person who sweeps the floor in a shearing shed.

brothelcreepers *Br.* col. men's suede shoes with thick crepe: *Red tiger-stripe brothel-creepers are all the rage.* - T. Thorne.

brother 1. *esp. Am., Aus.* excl. (an expression of slight annoyance and/or surprise): *"Oh, brother", Josie muttered aloud.* – R.L. Stine. 2. *esp. Am., Can.* col. a black man. 3. *Am.* member of fraternity.

brotherhood *Am., Can.* (railroad) workers trade union: *I intended also to see...George Harrison of the railroad brotherhoods* - H. Truman.

brow/ the brow of a hill *esp. Br.* the top part of a life.

brown/ be as brown as a berry *Br., Aus.* be very sun-tanned.

brown off *esp. Br.* sl. obs. cause to lose interest and/or become angry, esp. in **be/get drowned off.**

brown out *Am.* make a partial blackout. **brown-out** n.

brown/ do up brown *Am.* col. do perfectly: *He did the evening up brown by taking her to dinner, the theater, and a nightclub.* - H.C. Whitford., R.J. Dixson., *I see you've done yourself pretty brown* – M. Daly.

brown ale *Br.* common pub drink of dark, mild beer: *The car stank of brown ale.* – S. Townsend.

brown bag *Am., Can.* bag of brown colour for packed lunch: *Some students buy lunch in the school and others bring a "brown bag."* – Living in the USA.

brown-bagging *Am., Can.* col. bringing lunch food to work in a brown paper bag or bringing one's own alcohol to a restaurant which doesn't serve it.; **brown bag it** *Am., Can.* take a packed lunch to school.

brown Betty 1. *esp. Am., Can.* baked pudding of apples, bread crumbs, and spices: *Twelve apple brown bettys for thousand of workers* – Reader's

Digest. 2. *Br.* a large brown earthenware teapot.

browned-off, cheesed-off *esp. Br., Aus., Can.* col. obs. /*Br.* sl. **brassed-off**/ annoyed and discouraged, fed up: *Still a trickle of prisoners, browned-off or in the search for change or adventure continued to make the journey back.* - E. Williams.

brown goods *Br.* home electronic equipment providing entertainment such as TV and computer.

brownie 1. *esp. Am.* a chocolate cake with nuts in it: *Do you like brownies?* - J. Steinbeck. 2. *Br.* sl. a Scotch, a drink of whiskey. 3. *Aus., NZ.* a piece of sweet currant bread.

browning *Br.* darkened flour used for colouring the gravy.

brown-nose *Am., Can.* col. 1. curry favour with sb. 2. a toady.

brown-out *esp. Am., Can.* partial blackout.

brown stock *Br.* beef stock / **white stock** is chicken or fish stock.

brownstone *Am., Can.* red-brown sandstone.

brownstone *esp. Am.* adj. rich, aristocratic/ **brownstone houses (districts)**, etc.

Brownstone State *Am.* Connecticut.

Brum *Br.* col. Birmingham dialect.

brumby *Aus.* sl. unbroken horse.

brumby/ a mob of brumbies in the engine *Aus.* a very powerful engine.

brumby/ be small and wiry as a brumby *Aus.* be a short and strong person.

Brummagem *Br.* sl. Birmingham.

brummie, brummy *Br.* col. a native or inhabitant of Birmingham.

brummie *Aus.* counterfeit, showy or cheaply made.

brunch coat *Am.* short dressing gown.

brunching program *Am.* morning television programmes (for pensioners, housewives, etc.).

Brunswick stew *Am.* a stew of chicken and vegetables, including onions and tomatoes.

brush *Am.* col. a party.

brush 1. *Aus., NZ.* dense vegetation. 2. *esp. Am., Can., Aus., NZ.* small low bushes or the rough land they grow on, or brushwood. 3. *Am., Can.* cut brushwood.

brush *Aus., NZ.* col. sexually attractive women and girls.

brush *Br.* sl. 1. pubic hair. 2. sexual activity or potential sex partners.

brush oneself **down** *Br.* /*Am.* **brush** oneself **off**/ tidy oneself, esp. after a fall.

brush-fire *Am.* insignificant, local.

brush-up *Br.* an act of cleaning or smartening oneself or smth. up.

brush wolf *Am., Can.* coyote.

(brussel) sprout *Br.* brussels sprout.

brussels *Br.* col. brussels sprouts.

BS *Am.* 1. Bachelor of Science. 2. also *Can.* sl. bullshit, nonsense.

B. Th. U. *Br.* British Thermal Unit, a measure of heat: *What's its BTU rating?* - B. Bryson.

bub (bubby, bubbie) *Am., Can.* col. man, fellow, boy, guy (used when speaking to sb. you like and know well, often in a rather disrespectful way): *Don't cry, bub.* - M. Twain., *Then forget you met him, here, huh. Lerry-bubbie.* - L. Waller.

bubba *Am., Can.* col. an affectionate way of address to a brother.

bubble *Am.* burble.

bubble/ burst sb.'s **bubble, burst on the bubble** *Am., Can.* (of a sports player) occupy the last qualifying position on a team or for a contest and be liable to be replaced by another.

bubble/(be) on the bubble *Am.* journalism. (be) in a difficult situation and likely to fail, esp. if not backed financially.

bubble/ prick the bubble *Br.* do smth. that ends a happy or successful situation.

bubble/ speech bubble *Br.* circle around the words said by sb. in a cartoon.

bubble and squeak *esp. Br.* cold meat, potatoes and vegetables fried together.

bubble gum *esp. Am., Can.* insipid, simplistic, or adolescent in taste or style, esp. for children from 7 to 13 years old.

bubblehead *Am.* col. foolish, stupid person: *Here's a bubblehead who doesn't have the sense to stop* - Reader's Digest.

bubbler *Am. Aus.* /*esp. Br.* **drinking fountain**, *Am.* **water fountain**/.

buck *esp. Am., Can., Aus., NZ.* col. a dollar: *It cost him damn near 4000 bucks.* - J.D. Salinger., *Admission to the street circus costs 16 bucks* - Bulletin., *If you need a buck to blow town, come to me.* - J. Steinbeck.

buck *Am.* 1. sawhorse. 2. short thick leather covered block for gymnastic vaulting. 3. col. a young man. 4. mil. sl. lowest of a particular rank.

buck *Am.* 1. col. seek favour from people in authority: *he made some joke about bucking for promotion* - E. McBain. 2. saw logs. 3. (of a car) move with sudden stops and starts.

buck/ buck against smth. *Am.* move very suddenly against it.

buck up *Br.* col. hurry up: *Buck up, we're all waiting.* – Longman.

75

buck/ buck one's ideas up *Br.* try or think harder about one's actions to avoid trouble.
buck/ a bucks party *Aus.* a party for male friends of a man who is going to marry.
buck/ be in the bucks *Am.* col. have money.
buck/ feel/look like a million bucks *Am.* col. be very healthy, happy and beautiful.
bucked *Br.* col. obs. made more cheerful, pleased.
bucket *Br.* col. (**down**) rain very hard /synonym **rain stair-rods**/: *a heavy cloud bucketed and rolled like a ship* - D. Lessing
bucket of bolts *Am.* sl. an old car, airplane, etc.: *When are you going to get rid of that old bucket of bolts?* - A. Makkai.
bucket shop *esp. Br.* col. /*Am.* **boiler-room**/ a business, often unregistered travel agency, that obtains large quantities of tickets for air travel and sells them to the public at a low price: *what law enforcement officials call a "boiler room" operation* - Time., R.L. Chapman.
buck eye *Am.* a shrub or tree of the horse-chestnut family.
The Buckeye State *Am.* Ohio; **Buckeye** *Am.* joc. a citizen of Ohio: *Daisy was a counter girl, a Buckeye who grew up near Zanesville.* - S. Bellow.
buck fever *Am., Can.* the nervous excitement felt by inexperienced hunter when he first sights a game.
Buck House *Br.* Buckingham Palace.
buckjump *Aus.* (of a horse) do a special jump trying to unseat its rider.
buckle up *esp. Am.* fasten your seat belt.
buck-naked, butt naked *Am., Aus.* col. wearing no clothes: *Who's that buck naked?* - R.A. Spears.
Buckley's chance *Aus.* a rare chance / **two chances, mine and Buckley's, (not) have Buckley's chance** *Aus., NZ.* col. having no chance.
buckra *Am.* col. derog. a white person, esp.a man.
buck rarebit *Br.* a dish of melted cheese on toast with poached egg on top.
buckshee *Br.* col. 1. free, without payment. 2. something extra, obtained free, extra rations: *Me? A buckshee private?* - E. Williams. 3. windfall, gratuity.
Buck's fizz *Br.* a cocktail of champaigne and orange juice.
buckskin *Am., Can.* a horse of yellow-greyish colour.
buckwheat cakes *Am.* buckwheat pancakes (a popular breakfast food): *a jug of maple syrup for buckwheat cakes.* - E. Hemingway.

buckwheat plaid *Am.* man's hair braid with a ribbon in it.
bud(dy) *esp. Am., Can.* col. 1. /*Aus., Br.* col. **chum, mate**/ fellow (used as address, often in anger): *Get out of here, buddy.* - P. Norman., *That's a professional secret, buddy.* - J.D. Salinger., *Are you for real, buddy?* - R. Cook. 2. companion, partner, esp. a fellow soldier.
bud/ bud of promise *Am.* successful debutante.
buddy-buddy *Am.* col. friendly.
buddy movie *esp. Am., Can.* col. film in which close friendship between two persons is shown.
buddy system *Am.* the pairing of two persons in the same activity so that each is responsible for the other's welfare and safety: *You remember what the buddy system is, Unk?* – K. Vonnegut, Jr.
budgeree *Aus.* excellent.
budget account *Br.* account with a bank, store or public utility in which a person makes regular payments to cover bills.
budgie *Br.* a small brightly-coloured bird, often kept in a cage as a pet, budgerigar.
buff *Am., Can.* col. (of a person or body) in good physical shape with well-developed muscles.
buffalo *Am., Can.* sl. confuse, cheat: *He had all these people buffaloed* - A. Scaduto.
buff/ in the buff *Br.* obs. col. with no clothes on, naked: *Smith solves crimes in seven novels, most recently Diamond in the Buff and Death and Taxes* - R.J. Randisi., M. Wallace.
buff/ strip to the buff *esp. Br.* col. take off one's clothes.
buffalo chips (or **dungs**) *Am.* pieces of dried dung used as a fuel.
buffalo gnat *Am., Can.* blackfly.
buffalo wings *Am., Can.* deep-fried chicken wings coated in a spicy sauce and served with blue cheese dressing.
buffer *Br.* 1. col. obs. a foolish but perhaps likeable old man / esp. in the phr. **old buffer**: *Tell the buffer to take all reasonable precautions.* - D. Reeman. 2. **buffers** (two metal discs on springs that reduce the shock when a train hits them) on a train or at the end of the railroad track.
hit the buffers *Br.* journalism. fail or stop (about plan or activities).
buffet *Br.* a restaurant at a station.
buffet(-car) *Br.* dining car; railway snack bar: *a pork pie from a buffet-car.* – S. Townsend.
bug *esp. Am., Can.* any small insect: *encapsulated bugs hung in clusters.* - S. Bellow., *Bugs circled us and bit.* - B.E. Olson.

bug *esp. Am.* col. irritate or annoy: *She'll bug you to death with questions.* - H. Fast., *It bugs me when someone is watching with me.* - Reader's Digest.

bug off *Am., Can.* col. go away.

bug (out) *Am., Can.* 1. col. (of eyes) bulge out with astonishment: *My eyes bugged out* - Guideposts. 2. col. retreat, desert: *I don't relish the professional and personal embarrassment of bugging out of here at this time.* - Rolling Stone., *The chief of security implied the army had bugged out* - W. Kerr., *Bug out, she told him.* - L. Waller.

bugaboo *esp. Am., Can.* col. an imaginary cause of fear.

bug boy *Am.* sl. an apprentice jockey.

Bug-eating State, Cornhusker State *Am.* Nebraska.

bugfish *Am.* menhaden.

bugger *esp. Br., Aus.* sl. 1. taboo. an offensive or disagreeable person: *the little bugger's a vote-getter.* - H. Fast., *The bugger's been paid already.* - A. Burgess. 2. taboo. sodomite. 3. a person or animal. 4. smth. that causes a lot of trouble or difficulties: *It was a bugger, that exam* - R. Carter, M. Wallace.

bugger *Br., Aus.* 1. taboo or law. be guilty of sodomy. 2. sl. (used for adding force to expressions of displeasure): *I'm buggered if I know what the point is* - D. Lodge.

bugger about (or **around**) *Br., Aus.* taboo. sl. 1. (with) behave in a silly or foolish way: *No point buggering around with inquiries* - Bulletin. 2. **bugger** sb. **about** *Br.* sl. cause difficulties to sb.

bugger all *Br., Aus.* taboo. sl. nothing.

bugger him, bugger the cost *Br.* I don't care!

bugger me *Br.* I'm very surprised.

buggered *Br., Aus.* taboo. sl. 1. extremely tired. 2. very surprised or shocked.

buggery *Br.* taboo. and law. sodomy, anal sex.

buggery/ like buggery *Br.* col. used as a intensifier.

bugger off *Br., Aus.* taboo. sl. go away: *Fallows told Bath to "bugger off"* - B. Bryson.

bugger smth. **up** *Br.* taboo. sl. spoil, ruin.

Buggins' turn *Br.* col. a system by which appointments or awards are made in rotation rather than by merit.

buggy 1. *Am., Can. /esp. Br.* **pram/** vehicle, like small bed on wheels, for pushing babies about in: *Late April he was thrown from the buggy* - I. Stone. 2. *Am.* adj. full of small insects. 3. *Br. / Am., Aus.* **stroller/** a pushchair for baby. 4. *Am., Can.* col. mad, insane.

bug house *esp. Am.* col. 1. a mental hospital: *I thought he belonged in the bughouse for it* - K. Vonnegut, Jr. 2. crazy.

bugrake *Br.* humor. sl. a comb.

bugs(y) *Am.* sl. crazy, mad / **go bugs.**

builder *esp. Br.* a person or company that builds or repairs buildings.

builder's merchant, builders' merchant *Br.* building supply firm: *a couple of streets on a road to nowhere, with a butcher's, a builder's merchants, two pubs* - B. Bryson.

builder-upper *Am.* sl. something that increases physical stamina and moral in a person.

building-and-loan association *Am.* building society.

building society *Br., Aus. /Am.* **savings and loan association/** business organisation into which people pay money in order to save it and gain interest, and which lends money to people who want to buy houses: *building societies are having to pay more.* - J. Ruppeldtova.

building surveyer *Br.* building inspector.

building superintendent *Can.* caretaker.

bulge *Am., Can.* col. an advantage in the score line.

bulk factor *Am. /Br.* **volume/** print. the number of pages of a paper that make up a thickness of an inch.

bulk mail *Am., Can.* mail in which large numbers of identical items are sent at a reduced price.

bull *esp. Am.* sl. 1. a policeman: *Half of them're bulls.* - G.V. Higgins., *if there's bulls in the crowd I'll submit to arrest.* - J. Dos Passos. 2. n. adj. optimist(ic).

bull 1. *Br.* bull's eye, the circular centre of a target that people try to hit when shooting; or the shot or throw that hits it. 2. *Am.* a bad blunder in speech. 3. *Am.* col. nonsense.

bull *Br.* sl. 1. too great attention paid to the need for clearing, polishing and other unpleasant duties. 2. subject to intensive cleaning / **bull session.**

bull/ like a bull at a gate *Br.* move fast ignoring other people.

bull-cock *Can.* worker at a lumber camp, esp. a handyman.

bulldog *Am., Can.* wrestle (a steer) to the ground by holding its horns and twisting its neck.

bulldog 1. *Am.* gadfly. 2. *Aus.* ant.

bulldog clip *Br., Aus.* tdmk. */Am.* **clip/** a metal clip with a spring lever that is used for holding papers together.

bulldog edition *Am.* the earliest edition of a morning newspaper, esp. for distant or rural distribution.

bulldozer *Am.* sl. big revolver.
bullet *Br.* col. discharge from a job /**get**/ **give the bullet**.
bullet/ be sweating/sweat bullets *Am.* col. be very worried or frightened.
bulletin board *Am., Can.* /*Br.* **notice board**/ notice board: *It's said to be available from bulletin board* - Bulletin., *Your name's on the bulletin board.* - I. Shaw.
bullfiddle *esp. Am.* col. contrabass.
bullhorn *esp. Am., Can.* /*Br., Aus.* **loudhailer**/ (portable) megaphone: *I got on the bullhorn and asked him to exit the car* - Arkansas Times.
The Bullion State, The Butternut state *Am.* Missouri.
bullock *Aus.* work hard.
bullocky *Aus., NZ.* a driver of bullocks / also **bull puncher**.
bullpen 1. *esp. Am., Can.* an enclosure for bulls. 2. *Am.* (an exercise area for) baseball pitchers. 3. *Am.* an open-plan office area.
bull point *Br.* point served against an opponent, an advantage.
bull ring *Am.* circular stadium or arena.
bull session *Am., Can.* col. an informal group discussion.
bull's eye *Br.* large hard round sweet.
bullshot *Am.* an alcoholic drink made with vodka and bouillon.
bull trout 1. *Br.* sea trout. 2. *Am., Can.* trout found in cold rivers and lakes.
bully *esp. Am., Can.* col. excellent, first-class, esp. in **bully for you!**
bully beef *Br.* corned beef, pressed cooked beef in tins.
bully boy *Br.* col. sb. who behaves in a violent or threatening way.
bully pulpit *Am., Can.* an important job or position that sb. can use to persuade others to accept their ideas.
bullyrag *Am., Can.* col. make sb. frightened by scolding them.
bum *esp. Br., Aus.* col. the buttocks: *other people turn and stare at their bums and find them attractive.* - Bulletin., *So down with your breeches and out with your bum.* - J. Joyce.
bum/ put/get bums on seats *Br.* col. attract a lot of people.
bum *Am., Can., Aus.* derog. col. 1. wandering beggar, tramp: *I looked like a real bum* - J.A. Michener. 2. the life of a bum / **go on the bum, bum around**: *Then he came to town on the bum.* - Alcoholics Anonymous. 3. enthusiast of smth., fan: *a long-haired ski bum in Aspen,*

Colorado. - K. Lipper. 4. worthless, lazy worker or person: *Dear, it's not for me to decide if this bum is good for you* - Los Angeles Times.
bum/ (give)/get the bum's rush *esp. Am., Can.* col. dismiss sb./be dismissed.
bum/ go on the bum *Am.* sl. go wrong: *everything went on the bum there.* - E. Hemingway.
bum around *Am., Can.* col. get smth. by asking or begging.
bum out *Am.* sl. depress, discourage: *If it really bums you out we'll forget it, no hard feelings.* - D. Mortman.
bumbag *Br., Aus.* /*Am.* **fanny pack, waist pack**/ col. a small bag for money, keys and personal possessions which is fastened around one's waist.
bumble *Br.* col. bureaucrat, hence **bumbledom**.
bumf, bumph *esp. Br., Aus.* col. 1. toilet paper (from bum-fodder). 2. documentation, uninteresting written material that must be read, signed or otherwise dealt with. 3. trash, rubbish: *inundated with bumpf of one sort or another.* - T. Thorne.
bumfluff *Br.* col. derog. the first beard growth of an adolescent.
bummed out *Am.* col. disappointed: *a bummed-out little teenage boy.* - W. Jack, B. Laursen.
bummer *Am., Can.* col. 1. loafer or vagrant. 2. disagreeable person or thing: *Somebody broke a window in his car and stole his stereo. That's a bummer* - R.L. Chapman. 3. also **a real bummer** failure, bad place or situation: *Breaking up with Mike was really a bummer, you know.* – R.L. Stine.
bump *Am., Can.* force to move from a job or position, esp. in favour of sb. else.
bump *Br.* (in boat racing) overtake and touch the boat ahead.
bump/ like a bump on a log *Am.* col. not reacting adequately.
bump smth. **up** *Br.* col. increase smth.
bumper 1. *Am.* railroad buffer. 2. *Aus., NZ.* col. cigarette butt. 3. (of a vehicle) *Br.* /*Am.* **fender**/.
bumper car *Am.* /*Br., Aus.* **dodgem (car)**/ small electric cars that people try to drive skilfully in an enclosed spaces in places of amusement, so as to avoid hitting each other: *we've got to do bumper cars* – R.L. Stine.
the bumps *Br.* col. lifting a person in the air by his arms and legs on his birthday and letting him down on the ground, once for each year of his age.

bump-start *Br.* 1. start a car by getting it to roll and suddenly throwing it into gear. 2. assist in a sudden rousing to action: *We had to bump-start the bloody project by ourselves.* - T. Thorne.
bum rap *esp. Am., Can.* col. unfair blame or punishment, esp. for smth. sb. else did: *Miles Davis got a bum rap from Riley.* – N. Hentoff.
bum-rush *Am.* col. suddenly force one's way through.
bum steer *Am., Aus.* col. incorrect or false information.
bum-sucking *Br.* taboo. sl. obsequious, servile behaviour.
bun 1. *esp. Am.* a small round loaf of bread which usu. holds a piece of cooked meat. 2. *Br.* small round sweet cake.
bun/ have a bun in the oven *Br., Aus.* humor. sl. be pregnant: *The outspoken Miss Bow. who had a bun in the oven, replied* - R.L. Chapman.
bunce *Br.* col. windfall, sudden profit.
bunch *esp. Am., Can.* col. v. n. herd; large number of people or things; a large amount: *bunch of quacks who promise to help but don't come through.* - J. Kellerman., *Thanks a bunch.* _ R.L. Stine.
bunches *Br.* 1. clearance items at clothing shops. 2. girl's hair tied together in two parts with one at each side of her head.
bunch grass *Am., Can.* a grass which grows in clumps.
bunch of fives *Br.* col. 1. an act of hitting sb. with one's closed hand, punch, often used as a joke in **Do you want a bunch of fives?** 2. a hand or fist: *He ended up with a bunch of fives in the gut.* - R.A. Spears.
buncing *Br.* (in the retail trade) the practice of increasing prices to cover losses incurred through shop-lifting.
buncombe, bunk *Am.* sl. nonsense, pretentious talk. **buncomize** v.
bunco-steerer *Am.* sl. professional swindler, con man.
bundle 1. *Br.* sl. /*Am.* sl. **rumble/** teenage gang fight. 2. *Am.* sl. attractive woman: *I saw Charlie yesterday with that cute little bundle.* - R.L. Chapman.
bundle *Am.* print. two reams, 1,000 sheets.
bundle/ drop one's **bundle** *esp. Aus., NZ.* col. submit to the inevitable.
bundle/ not go a bundle on *Br.* col. not to like smth. very much; opp. **go a bundle on** *Br.* col. be very keen on.
bundle boy *Am.* a boy who helps to carry customers bags at the shop.

bun-fight *Br., Aus.* humor. col. 1. a tea party or other social occasion. 2. a heated argument or exchange.
bung 1. *esp. Br.* /*Am., Aus.* **stopper/** a round piece of rubber, wood, etc. to close the top of a container. 2. *Br.* col. a bribe.
bung *esp. Br., Aus.* col. put, push, or throw, esp. roughly: *they don't just grab things out of a deep freeze and bung them into le micro-wave.* - Cheshire Life.
bung *Aus., NZ.* col. 1. dead. 2. bankrupt, **go bung** *Aus., NZ.* a. die. b. go bankrupt.
bung/ be bunged up *Br.* col. be blocked.
bungalow 1. *esp. Br.* a house which is all on ground level. 2. *Am.* small house which is often on one level.
bungee (cord) *esp. Am.* a stretchable cord with a hook at each end which is used to hold things in place, esp. on a bicycle or car.
bungy *Br.* sl. rubber eraser: *i thro a bit of bungy at a peason* - T. Thorne.
bunk *esp. Am., Can.* sl. sleep in a narrow berth or improvised bed, esp. in shared quarters.
bunk *Am.* sl. cheat: *couldn't possibly have done a better job of bunking the American people.* - R.L. Chapman.
bunk/ do a bunk *Br.* col. run away, leave, esp. when one should not.
bunk in *Br.* sl. gatecrash.
bunk (off) *Br.* col. 1. leave in a hurry or when one should not. 2. play truant, leave school or work without permission.
bunk up (with) *Br.* sl. have sexual relationship (with).
bunker *Br.* /*Am.* (**sand**) **trap/** place dug out and filled with sand, from which it is hard to hit the ball in golf.
bunkered *Br.* (of a player) having hit the ball into a bunker.
bunkered/ be bunkered *Br.* col. face difficulties.
bunkie, also **bunkmate** *Am.* col. roommate: *My bunkie is from Iowa.* - R.A. Spears.
bunk-up *Br.* 1. col. a push up from below to help sb. climbing. 2. sl. quick sex act.
bunny 1. *Am.* squirrel. 2. *Aus.* a victim or dupe.
bunny/ be not a happy bunny *Br.* col. /*Am.* **be not a happy camper/** be not happy about a situation.
buns 1. *esp. Am., Can., Aus.* col. buttocks: *I saw his buns!* - R.L. Stine; a **bun** is one side of a person's bottom. 2. *Aus.* sl. sanitary towels or tampons. 3. *Br.* small sweet cakes, often with icing on the top.

bunt *Am.* deliberately hit the ball a short distance in baseball.

bunyip *Aus.* 1. a mythical monster inhabiting inland waterways. 2. impostor or pretender.

the burb(s) *esp. Am., Can.* col. suburb(s): *I've lived in the burbs all my life.* - R.A. Spears, *aftereffects of moving out of the city and into the burbs* – Reader's Digest.

bureau 1. (pl.) **bureaux** *Br.* a large desk or writing-table with a wooden cover which shuts or slides over the top to close it: *He sat down at his old bureau and took a pen.* - J. Galsworthy. 2. (pl.) **bureaus** *Am., Can.* chest of drawers: *Opening a bureau drawer, Palmer withdrew a shirt* - L. Waller., *She took from the top of the bureau a small black bag* - E.L. Doctorow., *her bureaus...were in wild disarray.* - E. Hautzig. 3. *Am.* a division of a large organization, esp. government department: *I'm just a clerk - with the state Economic Coordination Bureau here.* - J.P. Hogan.

burg *Am., Can.* col. a city or town: *It's a wonder you got a room and a bath in a burg like this.* - R.P. Warren., *I'm through with this burg.* - J. Dos Passos.

burglarize *Am., Can. /Br.* **burgle/** break into a building and steal from it: *He didn't even know anything about burglarising.* - Alex Hailey., *She caught him burglarizing her home.* - Daily News.

burgoo *Am., Can.* 1. hardtack and molasses cooked together. 2. a stew or thick soup of meat and vegetables.

burl *Aus., NZ.* col. a try.

burlap *Am. /Br.* **hessian/** a thick rough fabric that is used for making sacks.

burlesque *Am., Can.* a variety show, esp. one that includes striptease.

burn *Am., Can., Aus., NZ.* an act of clearing of vegetation by burning.

burn *Am.* sl. put or be put to death in the electric chair: *I'll see that you burn for this.* - R.A. Spears.

burn *Can.* forest fire.

burn/ British use burned as the past tense and past participle when the verb is intransitive.

burn/ burn rubber *Am.* col. start a car moving very quickly.

burn/ it burns me, her, etc. **that** *Am.* make sb. feel angry.

burn one's **boats** *Br., Aus.* burn one's bridges.

burn out *Am.* col. 1. make a search. 2. do smth. quickly or good.

burn up *esp. Am.* col. 1. also *Can., Aus.* cause to be very angry: *I recently met a businessman in Texas who was burned up with indignation.* - D. Carnegie., *It burned me up to be so often called "anti-Semitic"* - Alex Hailey., *I got real burned up at a young chick last month.* - S. Bellow. 2. *Am.* tell off: *The director burned Jim up for being late again.* - Longman.

burned *Am.* 1. overexposed (of film). 2. sl. disappointed, put down in a fix: *I was a little burned* - A. Scaduto.

burned/ be/get burned *esp. Am.* col. a. have one's feelings hurt. b. lose a lot of money, esp. in a business deal.

burner *Am. /Br.* **gas ring, (electric) ring/** part of the heater that produces heat or flame.

burn-up *Br.* sl. a high-speed race on a public road between young people on motorcycles.

burnoose *Am.* long loose dress worn by Arabs.

burp gun *Am.* col. a lightweight submachine gun.

burr/ a burr under sb.'s **saddle** *Am., Can.* col. a constant source of irritation.

burro *esp. Am.* (small) donkey: *He had beautiful dark eyes, like a Moroccan burro's with long lashes.* - I. Shaw., *Burros walked in the street with packs.* - J. Kerouac.

bursar *esp. Br.* financial manager of a college or university.

bursary *esp. Br.* 1. a grant. 2. the room of a bursar.

burser, also **exhibitioner** *Br.* scholarship student.

burster *Aus.* strong southern wind in Australia.

burton/ gone for a burton *Br.* col. lost, broken, soiled, or dead: *How did it go for a burton?* A. McLean, *their jobs gone for a burton very soon afterwards.* - D. Francis.

bus; Greyhound *Am. /Aus., Br.* **coach/** bus used for long-distance travel or journey: *we went on a one-nighter tour on the Crosby bus.* - A.E. Hotchner.

bus *Am., Can.* 1. work as a waiter assistant who helps to take away used dishes. 2. transport children to their schools and back on a bus: *a case that ended segregated busing.* – N. Hentoff.

bus boy, bus girl, busser *esp. Am., Can. /Br.* **commis waiter/** waiter assistant: *I became a bus boy at the Parker House in Boston.* - Alex Hailey., *This sends Filipino waiters and Indian busboys into a panic.* - Rolling Stone., *he needed a busboy at a new restaurant.* - J.A. Michener.

bush *Br.* a metal lining for a round hole, esp. one in which an axle revolves.

bush *Am.* sl. second-rate: *he's doing something bush.* - G.V. Higgins.

bush *Aus., Can.* natural vegetation, country, anywhere away from the city: *I found him,' he said, 'forty miles back in the bush.* - W. Grady.
bush/ go bush *Aus.* live a wild life, as in the bush or as a bushranger.
bush out *Am.* 1. (of a plant) grow in a spreading manner like a bush: *If you don't cut off some of the branches, that tree will bush out sideways.* - Longman., *it bushed out from her head around the ears and neck* – P. Roth. 2. trace the way on ice with green branches: *The men have gone ahead to bush out a safe way across the frozen lake* - Longman.
bush up a person *Aus.* confuse a person.
bush ape *Aus.* unskilled worker in the countryside.
bush baptist *Aus.* a man of uncertain denomination.
bush carpenter *Aus.* bad local carpenter.
bush dweller, bushman *Aus.* man living in the bush.
bushed 1. *Aus., NZ.* lost in the wild, uncultivated land. 2. *Can., Aus., NZ.* mad or bewildered.
bushel *Am.* repair, renovate, esp. men's clothes.
bushelman *Am.* tailor's assistant.
bushfire/ full of bushfire *Aus.* very energetic.
bush hospitality *Aus.* Australian hospitality.
bush hut *Aus.* a building made of local material.
bushie *Aus.* sl. a yokel: *we were "bushies"* - Southern Cross, T.Thorne.
bush lawyer *Aus., NZ.* col. unqualified person claiming legal knowledge.
bush league *Am., Can.* col. 1. a baseball minor league. 2. any subordinate apprentice or amateur enterprise. 3. adj. mediocre, second or third-rate: *my old business is bush-league stuff.* - K. Vonnegut, Jr.
bush leaguer *Am., Can.* 1. minor league player. 2. bad player or worker.
bushman *esp. Aus.* a person who lives or knows by experience how to live in the **bush** (a wild area of land).
bushman's clock *Aus.* a bird with a high piercing voice.
bushman/ Hyde Park bushman *Aus.* town dweller knowing nothing about the life in the bush.
bushman/ Picadilly bushman *Aus.* Australian living in the West End, London.
bushman/ cold and dark as a bushman's grave *Aus.* unpleasant, secretive.
bush mateship *Aus.* real, genuine friendship.
bush mile *Aus.* one mile and a bit more.

bushranger 1. *Am.* a person living far from a town or a village. 2. *Aus.* obs. (in the past) an outlaw living in the bush: *The gang of bushrangers, sure as blazes, would be waiting to stick the coach up directly it entered the bush.* - H.H. Richardson.
(the) bush telegraph *Br., Aus., Can.* humor. / *Can.* **moccasin telegraph**/ the fast spreading of information by unofficial means: *Arne gets the news through the bush telegraph. People tell him.* - W. Magnuson.
bushwa(h) *Am., Can.* col. bunk, humbug, nonsense: *Looks to me like it's all bushwa.* - J. Dos Passos.
bushwalking *esp. Aus., NZ.* the sport of walking through the bush.
bushwhack *Am., Can.* 1. live or travel in the bush. 2. ambush. 3. push or cut one's way through thick trees or bushes.
bushwhacker 1. *esp. Am.* a tramp. 2. *Aus.* person from the country, yokel. 3. *Am., Can., Aus., NZ.* a person who clears woods and bush country.
bushy *Aus., NZ.* a person who lives in the bush.
business *Am.* 1. customers, clientele, public. 2. sl. bad treatment, roughing up / **give** sb. **the business** *Am.* sl. beat sb.: *When Mrs. Brown's young son insulted her, she gave him the business.* - T. Thorne., *I expect him to give her the business.* – J. O'Hara.
business/ do the business 1. *Br., Aus.* col. achieve smth. 2. *Br.* sl. have sex.
business/ engage in business *Am.* engage in trade.
the business *Br.* col. the very best: *You should try some of this gear - it's the business.* - T. Thorne.
business day *esp. Am., Can.* working day.
business suit *Am., Can. /Br.* **lounge suit**/ a man's suit of matching coat and trousers for everyday wear: *Dean was wearing a real Western business suit* - J. Kerouac., *two men in business suits marched in* - P. Case, J. Migliore.
busk *Br., Aus.* col. play music in the street in order to earn money. **-er** n.: *It would have been no good busking or touting here* - L. Lee., *they came across a young white street singer who was busking - playing for coins of passerby* - A. Scaduto.
busman *Br.* busdriver: *The busmen and clippies were all cheering* - P. Norman.
busman's holiday *esp. Br.* spending part of a holiday as part of their normal job or everyday life.
bus pass *Br.* a special ticket entitling an old age pensioner to travel free on a bus.

buss obs. or *Am., Can.* col. kiss sb. in a friendly way, n.

bus shelter *esp. Br.* roofed structure at a bus stop where people wait for their buses.

bussy *Aus.* bus.

bust 1. *Am.* complete failure: *much of the current approach to online advertising may remain a bust.* - New York. 2. *Aus.* sl. a break-in, burglary. 3. *esp. Am., Can.* a punch or other hit.

bust *esp. Am.* col. lower (a military person) in rank, demote: *they bust you down to private* - H. Fast.

bust *esp. Am., Can.* 1. strike violently. 2. raid or search (a suspected place of a crime). 3. burst.

bust a gut, also **bust** one's **tail,** etc. *Am.* sl. exert oneself mightily: *I thought I would bust a gut* - R.P. Warren., *He busted his tail for me.* - Reader's Digest.

bust out *Am.* 1. show flowers and leaves suddenly: *June is busting all over.* - Longman. 2. col. break out, escape (from): *So I busted out.* - R.P. Warren. 3. col. start doing smth. suddenly: *So I bust out crying.* - B. Bryson.

bust (smth.) **up** *Am.* damage or spoil: *The way you're going to be killed is going to bust up the whole show.* - I. Fleming., *We are going to bust up the CIA* - R. Borchgrave, R. Ross.

buster 1. *esp. Am., Can.* col. often derog. a fellow (used as a form of address to a man): *Listen, buster, don't give me any of this give-me-a-chance business.* - D. Divoky., *You're on your own, Buster.* - B.E. Olson. 2. *Am.* person who breaks horses. 3. *Aus.* a strong wind.

bust-up *esp. Br., Aus.* col. a serious argument, esp. one which ends a relationship.

busy *esp. Am., Can.* (of telephone) in use, /*Br.* **engaged**/ (*esp. Am., Can.* **busy signal**).

busy, bizzy *Br.* col. a police officer.

busy Lizzie *Br.* an East African plant with abundant red, pink or white leaves, used as a house plant.

busywork *esp. Am., Can.* work that keeps a person busy but has little value in itself.

but/ the last/next but one / two / three *esp. Br.* one, two, three, etc. from the last / next.

but 1. *Am., Can., Aus.* sl. adv. (used to add force): *Go there but fast.* - Longman., - *the generals must have worked him over but good.* - J. DeFelice. 2. *Aus., NZ.* col. (used at the end of a sentence) though, however.

butch *esp. Br.* col. 1. adj. (of a woman) showing a lot of male tendencies: *They advise curbing flamboyant excesses and keeping drag queens and butch lesbians out of the public eye.* - Time., *butch-looking jacket* - Bulletin. 2. n. **butch woman.**

butcher *Am., Can.* col. vendor, peddler, esp. one who goes through trains or theatres selling magazines, candy, food, drinks and notions.

butcher *Am.* sl. l. cut off parts of the text while editing it.

butcherblock *Am., Can.* material used to make kitchen worktops and tables: *install butcher block in its place* – Reader's Digest.

butchers/ have or **take a butchers** *Br., Aus.* col. have a look.

butchers' meat *Br.* fresh uncured meat excluding game and poultry.

butchery 1. *esp. Br.* slaughterhouse. 2. *Br.* meat department.

butt *esp. Am., Can.* col. buttocks: *I spent more time on my butt than on my feet.* – R.L. Stine., *Get your butt out of here!* – Reader's Digest.

butt/ sb.'s **butt is on the line** *Am., Aus.* col. sb. is to blame for this.

butt/ get your **butt in/out/over** *Am.* col. derog. get in/out/over.

butt/ get one's **butt in gear** *Am.* taboo. sl. hurry up or try harder.

butt/ kick sb.'s **butt** *Am., Aus.* col. punish sb. with a lot of force.

butt in *Am.* get involved in a private situation that doesn't concern sb.

butt out *Am., Can.* col. stop interfering, leave: *We asked him to butt out so we could have a private talk.* - W. Magnuson, *I should butt out* – Reader's Digest.

butte *Am., Can.* and tech. steep, flat-topped hill standing alone: *the buttes and coulees, the cliffs and sculptured hills and ravines lost their burned and dreadful look* - J. Steinbeck.

butterball *Am., Can.* col. derog. a small plump person.

buttered eggs *Br.* scrambled eggs.

butterfly/ break a butterfly on a wheel *Br.* use more force than necessary.

butterfly cake *Br.* a small sponge cake made in the form of a butterfly.

butter muslin *Br.* cheesecloth.

buttery *Br.* a room in a college where food is kept and sold to students.

butthole *Am.* taboo. sl. 1. person's anus. 2. insulting word for a person.

buttie *Br.* sl. sandwich: *I'll trade you an autograph for a jam butty.* - P. Norman.

buttinski *Am.* an intruder, person who interrupts: *Frank is such a buttinsky.* - R.A. Spears.

buttlegging *Am.* sl. transportation of untaxed or undertaxed cigarettes across a state line: *Most of the guys at the plant do buttlegging on the way home from work.* - R.A. Spears.

butter steak *Br.* rump steak.

button *esp. Am., Can.* /*Br.* **badge**/ a small metal or plastic badge, which one wears in order to show that he/she supports a particular movement, organisation, or person, usu. fastened to one's clothes with a pin: *the button is available* - Time.

button *Am.* a bill for a small sum of money: *You could get it for buttons.* – J. O'Hara.

button/ a hot button *Am.* smth. topical and controversial.

button/ bright as a button *Br.* (esp. a child) intelligent and energetic.

button/ (right) on the button *esp. Am., Can.* col. 1. punctually. 2. exactly right: *They snatched Tom right on the button.* - M. Puzo.

button grass *esp. Aus.* a grass or sedge with rounded flowering heads.

buttonhole *esp. Br.* /*Am.* **boutonniere**/ flower to wear on one's coat and dress, esp. at a wedding.

button-through *Br.* fastened with buttons from top to bottom.

buttonwood, sycamore *Am., Can.* an American plane tree.

butty *Br.* col. sandwich (esp. regional use).

butty (boat) *Br.* unpowered freight barge intended to be towed.

buy *Am.* col. bribe sb.

buy in *Br.* buy for future use in advance.

buy the farm *Am., Can.* col. die: *Where's Henry? Oh, he bought the farm years ago - died of cancer, eh.* - W. Magnuson.

buy into *Aus., Am.* become involved into: *I bought into the rules of modern parenting* – Reader's Digest.

buy out *Br.* (in the armed forces) pay some money so that you can leave earlier than you had previously had agreed to.

buy over *Br.* bribe, buy off.

buy it *Am.* sl. be killed: *I would have bought it.* – A. Summers, R. Swan.

buyout *Am.* print. /*Br.* **outwork**/ any work that a printer does not undertake in house, such as typesetting or binding.

buzz *Am., Can.* sl. thrill, esp. in **catch a buzz (from)**: *I get a big buzz out of the fact* - New Idea., *he sometimes takes a little something, you know, to get a buzz* - A. Hitchcock Mystery Magazine.

buzz *Am.* sl. close haircut, given with clippers: *Rob wore a Marine buzz cut* – Reader's Digest.

buzzard 1. *Br.* a kind of hawk. 2. *Am.* a kind of (turkey) vulture: *Chevrolet Impala floated through buzzard-infested desert* - J. Patterson.

buzzcut *Am.* very short style of cutting hair.

buzzed *Am., Can.* sl. drunk: *she was thoroughly buzzed.* - J. Baez.

buzzer/ at the buzzer *Am., Can.* at the end of a game, esp. baseball.

buzz-saw *Am., Can.* circular saw: *We walked into a buzzsaw.* - Reader's Digest.

BVDs *Am., Can.* tdmk. col. (men's) underwear, a type of boxer shorts: *his BVDs were the most ridiculous garment ever invented.* - H. Fast.

by *esp. Am.* adv. at or to another's home: *I can stop by at your office at four o'clock.* - H. Fast.

by-blow *Br.* obs. a man's illegitimate child.

bye-bye/ go (to) bye-byes *Br.* col. (esp. used when talking to young children) go to bed.

by(e)-election *esp. Br.* special election held between regular elections to fill a position whose former holder has left or died: *If an MP dies or resigns, a by-election will take place* - Young Citizen's Passport.

bylaw 1. *Br.* special law or rule made by a local council, a railway, etc.: *Must be a by-law about there somewhere* - W. Grady. 2. *Am.* a rule made by an organisation for governing its own affairs: *That provision is still in the bylaws.* - R.G. Kaiser.

by now *esp. Am.* col. excl. goodbye.

BYO *Aus.* bring your own bottle party.

byre *Br.* obs. a farm building for cattle, cowshed: *Come into t'byre and I'll show you the cow!* - J. Herriot.

C

C *Am.* sl. $100, also **C-note**: *The C-note, as it used to be called in Raymond Chandler's novels, will never be the same.* - Time.

c/ *Aus.* care of (in addresses on envelopes).

cab *Br.* sl. 1. pilfer, steal. 2. copy smth. dishonestly from sb. 3. literal translation or crib.

cab *esp. Am., Aus.* taxi: *They drove in a yellow cab.* - P. Norman.

caballero *Am.* col. horseman.

cabana *Am., Can.* a hut, cabin or shelter at a beach or swimming pool.

cabaret *Am.* tray for glasses, cups, tumblers, etc.

cabbage 1. *Br.* col. a. derog. inactive person who takes no interest in anything: *After this shower of scientific cabbages, neither Dr. Hahn nor his* colleague Dr. Weinland, devoted any further efforts to following up what they had found. – F. Edwards. b. person who has lost the ability to think, move, etc. as a result of illness, brain damage, etc. 2. *Am.* plagiarism. 3. *Am.* sl. money: *that's a hell of a lot of cabbage!* - H. Fast.

Cabbage garden *Aus.* State of Victoria.

cabbage-looking *Br.* col. green-looking, looking foolish and inexperienced.

cabbagetown *Can.* 1. any rundown urban area, slum. 2. a district in Toronto where European immigrants live: *Restaurants in Cabbagetown serve European food.* - W. Magnuson.

cabbage worm *Am., Can.* caterpillar pest of cabbage.

cabdriver *esp. Am.* taxi driver: *On the way home I noticed a cab-driver* - T. Capote., *That's like giving your money to a cab-driver and telling him to take you for a ride.* - Time.

cabin 1. *esp. Br.* the part of a locomotive that houses the engineer and operating controls or comparable shelter on truck, tractor or crane. 2. *Br.* /*Am.* (**elevator**) **car**/ the cage of an elevator: *he went to the roundhouse and slept in an engine cab.* - I. Stone.

cabinet *Br.* a meeting of a cabinet.

cabinet reshuffle *Br.* a change in the members of the cabinet.

cabin fever *Am.* state in which a person feels bad-tempered because they haven't been outside for a long time.

cable car *Am.* a vehicle on a cable railway using cables under the road to pull passenger vehicle up steep slopes: *But he had only thrusted them rather violently to one's side in his eagerness to board the cable car that was dashing by* – K. Chopin.

(cable) conductor *Am.* /*Br.* **core**/ core of an (electric) cable.

cable ready *Am., Can.* adopted for cable TV.

cablewalk *Am.* narrow footway along a cable to the top of a suspension bridge.

caboodle/ the whole caboodle *Br.* the whole of everything.

caboose 1. *Am., Can.* /*Br.* **guard's van**/ the last waggon, esp. on goods train for people who work on it: *an old ten-wheeler pulling a baggage car, a passenger coach, and sometimes a freight car and a caboose.* - S. North. 2. *Am.* open-air cooking oven. 3. *Am., Can.* portable house.

cabover *Am., Can.* a truck with the driver's cab mounted directly above the engine.

cab rank /also **cab stand, taxi stand**/ *esp. Am.* / *Br.* **taxi rank**/ taxi stand: *we go jogging down the street to a cab stand* - J. Kerouac.

cab tout *Br.* person whose job is to fetch cabs and help with luggage.

ca-canny *Br.* col. obs. deliberate restriction of production by workers, also *Br.* **go-slow**, *Am.* **slowdown (strike).**

cack *Br.* col. excrement, dung; v. defecate.

cack-handed *Br., Aus.* col. awkward and unskilful, clumsy: *the pattern of cack-handed mimicry* - P. Norman.

cackle/ cut the cackle *Br., Aus.* col. humor. obs. be quiet, stop talking: *Oh, cut the cackle and let's have the verdict.* - E.M. Forster.

The Cactus or **Sunshine State** *Am.* New Mexico.

cad *Br.* sl. ungentlemanly person.

cadet *NZ.* a young man learning to be a sheep farmer at a sheep station.

cadge *esp. Br.* col. /*Am., Can.* **mooch**/ beg money or help, esp. food and cigarettes.

Cadillac *Am.* col. /*Br.* **Rolls Royce**/ example of the highest quality of smth.

CAF *Am., Can.* abbr. cost and freight.

café *Am., Can.* a bar or a nightclub.

caff *Br.* col. (transport) cafe, a snack bar, esp. a cheap one: *And behind Mr. Smith is the German waiter from the caff* - W. Grady.

cage *Br.* box / when filling a form one is instructed to **check** appropriate box or in Britain **tick** appropriate cage.

cagoule, kagoul(e) *Br.* a light plastic waterproof jacket with a hood worn in wet and windy weather.

Cajun *Am.* descendant of French who came to Louisiana from Acadia.

cake *Am.* pancake.

cake and ale *Br.* enjoyable time.

cake flour *Am., Can.* plain flour.

cakehole, also **gob** *Br.* col. mouth, often in **shut one's gob/cakehole**: *Any more noise from you, mate, and I'm in there to belt you in the cakehole, got it?* - A. Burgess.

cake pan, muffin tin *Am.* /*Br.* **cake tin**/ metal container for baking a cake. 2. container with a lid to keep a cake in.

cakewalk *Am.* col. smth. easy to achieve.

calabash *Am.* joc. empty head.

calaboose *Am.* /also *Am.* sl. **can, hoosegow**/ col. a small prison: *I got the twins into the common calaboose* - M. Twain.

calamity issue *Am.* controversial subject.

calamity Jane /**howler, prophet**/ *Am.* pessimist.

calculate for *esp. Am.* expect or plan for /smth. often unpleasant/: *We didn't calculate for such bad weather* - Longman.

calculate on *esp. Am.* depend on, trust in /smth. or doing smth./: *Don't calculate on going abroad this summer* - Longman.

caldron *Am.* cauldron.

calendar 1. *Am. /Br.* **diary/** book with marked separate spaces for each day of the year, in which one may write down things to be done in the future. 2. *Br. /Am.* **catalogue/** university or college catalogue including a list of lectures, examinations, and sports events or exercises.

calico 1. *Am.* printed cotton fabric, esp. multi-coloured, unbleached muslin: *She was busy feeding one of Mr. Dudley's faded old calico mother-hubbards into the wringer.* – E. Caldwell. 2. *Br.* plain white or unbleached cotton. 3. *Am., Can.* (of animals) multicoloured, piebald, esp. **calico cat**: *stuffed calico teddy bears with button eyes and ribboned necks* – Reader's Digest.

call *Am.* col. decision, esp. in **make a call, it's your call, easy/hard call**.

call *Am.* col. declare or describe in advance, predict.

call (by) *Br.* visit somewhere for a short time to see sb.

call *esp. Am. /esp. Br.* **ring up/** make a telehone call.

call about 1. *Br.* arrive at (sb.'s) home, office, etc. in connection with (a matter): *he's calling about your insurance.* - Longman. 2. *Am.* telephone (sb.) in connection with (a matter): *I tried to call you about our meeting.* - Longman.

call at/on *Br.* visit a place or person.

call back 1. *Br.* return to a house or shop that you went to earlier for a short time. 2. *Am. / Br.* **ring back/**.

call down *Am.* col. 1. express poor opinion of (smth.): *The newspapers called down Tom's latest book.* - Longman. 2. scold (sb.), reprimand: *she had called him down* - J. London. 3. *Am.* invite (sb.) to fight /*Br.* **call out/**.

call for (sb.) *Br.* go to sb.'s home before you go somewhere together.

call for *Am.* say that smth. is likely to happen, esp. when talking about vacation.

call in 1. *Am.* telephone /a message/ to a certain place, such as an office: *Kim had never before missed work without calling in.* - Reader's Digest. 2. *Br.* visit a person or place while you're on your way to somewhere else: *I called in on Grandma Mole* – S. Townsend.

call off *Am.* speak a list of (names, words, etc.): *The teacher began to call off the names on his list.* - Longman.

call out 1. *Br. /Am.* **call down/** invite (sb.) to fight: *A gentleman should call down any man who is rude to his wife.* - Longman. 2. *Am.* col. invite sb., ask sb. to a dance. 3. *Br.* order workers to go on strike.

call round *Br.* visit for a short time.

call up 1. *esp. Br.* waken (sb.). 2. *esp. Am. /Br., Aus.* **ring up/** telephone (sb.): *Somebody we never heard of called up Mother on the telephone.* - B. Robinson. 3. *esp. Br. /Am.* **draft/** order (sb.) to join the armed forces: *All the best teachers were being called up.* – R. Westall. 4. *Am.* also **call down** ask sb. to come (to some place).

call/ call a huddle *Am.* col. arrange to come together and have a meeting.

call / Your call is on the queue *Br. /Am.* **Your call is on the waiting list/** wait for your turn.

call/ call collect *Am., Can. /Br., Aus.* **reverse the charges/** make a telephone call to be paid for by the person who receives it.

call/ call one's shot *Am., Can.* sl. state exactly what one intends to do, be in charge: *how exhilarating it was to be able to call the shots* - E. Taylor., *mayors calling the shots have intimidated many local activists* - Time., *Noriega still seemed to be calling the shots.* - Newsweek.

call/ call (the meeting) to order *Am.* open the meeting: *The chair calls the meeting to order.* - McGraw-Hill English, 1990.

callanetics *Br.* tdmk. A system of physical exercises intended to make body firm and more attractive.

callback 1. *Am.* a summoning back of furloughed workers. 2. *esp. Am., Can.* an invitation to return for a second audition or interview.

call box 1. *esp. Br. /also Br., Aus.* **telephone box, phone box, telephone kiosk,** *esp. Am.* **telephone booth, phone booth/** a small hut or enclosure containing a public telephone: *a destination where help is available (a freeway callbox, an open business).* - Reader's Digest. 2. *Am.* public telephone beside a road used to telephone for help.

calldown, calling down *Am.* col. rebuke, reprimand: *His girl Lee Ann had a bad tongue and gave him a calldown every day.* - J. Kerouac.

caller 1. *Br.* person who visits your house. 2. *Aus., NZ.* a racing or sports commentator.

call-house *Am.* brothel: *It wasn't a hotel or a call-house* - J. Dos Passos.

call-in *Am. /Br.* **phone-in/** programme on radio or TV in which telephoned questions, statements, etc. from the public are broadcast: *guest on a Christian television call-in program.* - E. Cleaver.

call-in pay *Am.* the payment received by a worker who has not been notified before he reports to work that there is no work available or that he has been put on another shift.

calling card 1. *esp. Am.* visiting or business card: *the family archives show a calling card from Mr. Houdini* - E.L. Doctorow. 2. *Am., Can.* a phone card or telephone charge card.

calliope *Am.* an instrument consisting of a series of steam-whistles played by a keyboard.

callipers *Br., Aus.* /*Am.* **braces**/.

call letters *esp. Am.* /*Br.* **call sign**/ a sequence of letters used by a TV or radio station as an identified code or used by people operating communication radios.

call-on *Br.* system of hiring longshoremen in which they line up for possible call by a foreman, shape-up.

call-out charge *Br.* house call charge, repairman charge.

call-over *Br.* obs. a roll-call at school.

call-up, National service *esp. Br.* 1. /*Am.* **draft**/ an order to serve in the armed forces. 2. a period in which such orders are given out. 3. the number of people, esp. men who received such orders.

Calor gas *Br.* tdmk. gas sold in small containers to be used for cooking and heating.

caloric *esp. Am., Can.* or tech. of or relating to heat, calorific.

calorie conscious *Am.* keeping oneself slim.

calories/ watch one's **calories** *Am.* go on a diet to lose weight.

cambric tea *Am.* weak tea with milk and sugar: *eating the sick-child's supper of poached eggs on toast and cambric tea* - R.G. Kaiser.

Cambridge blue *Br.* 1. a pale-blue colour. 2. a sports player from Cambridge University.

camera boy *Am.* col. 1. photographer. 2. cameraman.

camiknickers *Br.* a piece of women's underwear, combining camisole and French knickers.

camp *Aus., NZ.* a place where livestock usu. congregate and a mastered herd is collected; v. assemble together for rest.

camp/ camp it up *Br.* deliberately perform in an exaggerated and often amusing way.

camp/ make camp *Am.* set up a camp.

camp/ take into camp *Am.* 1. take into possession. 2. win. 3. kill.

camp bed, safari bed *esp. Br., Aus.* /*Am.* **cot**/ light narrow bed which folds flat and is easily carried: *check camp beds for rust.* – S. Townsend.

camp box or **kit** *Am.* box with kitchen utensils.

camper *esp. Am., Can.* motor vehicle big enough to live in when on holiday or an enclosure put on a pick-up truck for the same purpose: *the pick-up truck on which the camper top rode.* - J. Steinbeck, **camper van** *Br., Aus. Am.* **RV**/.

campground *esp. Am., Can.* 1. /*esp. Br.* **campsite,** *Aus.* **camping ground**/ campsite: *Many National Parks' campgrounds require a visitor to obtain a permit.* - McGraw-Hill English, 1990., *we used rented ones we pick up at the campsite.* – R.L. Stine. 2. place used for outdoor religious meetings.

camping ground *Aus.* /*Am.* **campground,** *esp. Br.* **campsite**/ campsite.

camp meeting *Am.* religious meeting held in the open air.

camporee *esp. Am., Can.* meeting of boyscouts / of a district, state.

camp out (with) *esp. Br.* col. live in uncomfortable condition for a short time: *on his digs, he was always more or less camping out.* - T. Murphy.

camp site *Am.* a place for one tent at campground.

camp stove *Am.* portable stove.

campus 1. *esp. Am.* separate branch of a university: *Flack was a radical guru of the Berkely Campus.* - R. Borchgrave, R. Moss. 2. *Am., Can.* the grounds of a university or college, hospital, etc. 3. *Am.* /*Br.* **gate**/ leave sb. home as punishment.

can 1. *esp. Am.* /*Br., Aus.* **tin**/ small metal container for food or drink, esp. with a lid that can be removed. 2. *Am., Can.* col. toilet: *I went to the can and chewed the rag with him.* - J.D. Salinger. 3. *esp. Am.* buttocks: *knocked me flat on my can* - B. Holiday, W. Duffy. 4. *esp. Am., Can., Aus.* jail: *I'll ride his tail till he straightens up and flies right or winds up in the can for life.* - K. Vonnegut, Jr., *Targo's still in the can.* - R. Chandler.

can 1. *esp. Am.* /*Br., Aus.* **tin**/ preserve (esp. food) by packing it in cans: *We had canned vegetables at home* - Rolling Stone. 2. *Am., Can.* col. dismiss from a job: *He'd come here ready to can Penham* - J. DeFelice. 3. *esp. Am., Can., Aus.* col. stop, cease doing, esp. some objectionable behaviour, esp. in **can it**: *Jim, can the stuff.* - J. Dos Passos. 4. *Am.* sl. put in jail.

Canada thistle *Am., Can.* an European creeping or field thistle.

Canadian bacon *Am.* /*Br.* **bacon**/ meat from the back or sides of a pig.

canaller *Am.* person who works on canal boats or who operates a lock or other facility of a canal.

Can do *esp. Am.* Yes, I can and I will; **can-do character, approach.**
Can I Help you? is impolite in the USA, it's better to use **May I help you?**
canary pad *Am.* col. yellow paper pad.
candidature *esp. Br.* candidacy.
candies/ mixed candies *Am.* 1. assortment of sweets, bag of sweets. 2. confectionery.
candle/ the game's not worth the candle *esp. Br.* the difficulties are greater than advantages.
candlestick telephone *Br.* upright telephone.
candy 1. *esp. Am., Can.* /*Br.* **sweets**/ (a shaped piece of) various types of boiled sugar, sweets or chocolate: *I remember when a coin in a slot would get you a stick of gum or a candy bar* - J. Steinbeck. / In Britain (**sugar**) **candy** is a hard sugary fudge, e.g. toffee, mints, etc. 2. *esp. Br.* sugar crystallised by repeated boiling and slow evaparation.
candy/ like taking candy from a baby *esp. Am.* col. smth. very easy to do.
candy/ eye/mind candy *Am.* smth. good to look at.
candy/ rock (sugar) candy *Am.* lollipop.
candy apple *Am., Can.* a toffee apple.
candyass *Am., Can.* col. a cowardly person.
candy bar *Am.* a long, thin, sweet biscuit that is often covered in chocolate.
candy brake *Am., Can.* a piece of ground covered with a dense growth of canes.
candy butcher *Am.* vendor or peddler who sells candy and often other small merchandise on trains, on grandstands at sporting events and formerly in theatres.
candy cane *Am., Can.* a stick of striped sweet rock.
candy floss *Br.* 1. /*Am.* **cotton candy,** *Aus.* **fairy floss**/ fine sticky often coloured sugar threads eaten as a sweet and usu. on a stick: *He waved at the candy-floss man* - W. Grady. 2. flimsy or insubstantial ideas.
candy-man *Am., Can.* col. drug-pusher.
candy-pull *Am.* 1. a social gathering where candy is pulled, or drawn out of its semi-solid state after boiling in order to work it into desired consistency. 2. a turn at pulling and twisting taffy to make it tough and light-coloured.
candy store (shop) *Am.* /*esp. Br.* **sweetshop, confectioner's**/ a store where candy and other items, such as soft drinks, newspapers, cigarettes and stationary are sold: *he found a candy shop and bought a five pound box of chocolate.* - I. Shaw.
candy store/ like a kid in a candy store *Am.* /*Br.* **sweet shop**/ doing whatever they like.

candy-striper *Am., Can.* col. a female voluntary nurse's helper in a hospital.
cane *esp. Br.* (in newspapers) defeat completely: *American was caned at a rugby match.* - Time.
cane *Br.* sl. beat up, assault.
cane corn *Am.* col. 1. whiskey. 2. (also *esp. Am.* **moonshine**) homebrew intoxicating liquor.
Canfield *esp. Am., Can.* a card game of patience or solitaire.
canker (sore) *esp. Am.* a small ulcer of the mouth or lips.
canned *Am., Can.* sl. not fresh for the occasion, kept for easy and general use: *He was given a canned tour of Model factories* - L. Uris., *turning sports into canned sappy entertainment.* - Newsweek.
canned hunt *Am.* big-game hunt within a fenced area in which quarry is provided by the organisers.
canner *Am.* 1. the owner or worker of a cannery. 2. an old steer fit only for canning. 3. poor grade of beef obtained from such an animal.
cannon 1. a. *Br.* n. v. carom (in billiards and bagatelle). b. knock or hit against sb./smth. suddenly usu. unintentionally. 2. *Am.* sl. a firearm pistol: *Rocko pulled out his cannon and aimed it at Barlow's throat.* - R.A. Spears. 3. *Am.* sl. pickpocket: *grand larceny, when a cannon lifts a wallet from a pocket* - New York Times, R.L. Chapman.
cannot *Am.* can not.
canoe *Br.* kayak.
canoodle *Br.* obs. col. cuddle amorously (of a man and a woman).
can opener *esp. Am.* /*Br.* **tin opener**/: *But I had forgotten to pack a can opener.* - B.E. Olson.
cans *Am.* sl. earphones: *I bought a new set of cans for my new stereo.* - R.A. Spears.
cant *esp. Br.* give a sudden turn or new direction to.
can't/ can't/couldn't be arsed *Br.* taboo. sl. be too lazy or bored to do smth.
cantaloupe *Aus.* rock melon.
canteen 1. *Br., Aus.* (a case or box for) a set of knifes, forks and spoons; cutlery. 2. *esp. Br.* a place in a factory, school, military camp, etc. where meals are provided, usu. quite cheaply.
canter/ in (at) a canter *Br.* easily.
canterbury *Br.* magazine rack.
cantrail *Br.* a timber or a piece of metal supporting the roof of a railway carriage.
Canuck *esp. Am., Can.* Canadian, esp. French-Canadian / Johnny Canuck is akin to British John Bull and American Uncle Sam:

When we visited Montana, a clerk called us "Canucks" - W. Magnuson., *Henri Girard was a French Canuck* – J. O'Hara.

canvass 1. *Am.* examine (votes) officially for authenticity. n. 2. *Br., Aus.* suggest (an idea or plan) for consideration.

canvass *Am.* 1. tent. 2. travelling circus.

canvass/ under canvass *Br.* in tent.

canvasser 1. *Am.* a scrutineer of votes. 2. *Br.* person who solicits votes for a candidate or takes a poll on behalf of one.

canvass shoes *Am.* /*Br.* **sandshoes/** light cloth shoe such as a plimsoll.

cap *Br.* cap worn by a sportsman as a sign of achievement when playing for a national team.

cap *NZ.* confer a University degree on.

cap 1. *Am.* place the white cap of a nurse upon (a nursing school graduate). 2. *Br.* **rate-cap.**

cap/ (Dutch) cap *Br.* col. a circular rubber contraceptive device for women, often in **be capped.**

cap/ go cap in hand *Br.* /*Am., Can.* **go hat in hand/** ask for money or help, esp. humbly.

cap/ set one's **cap at** sb. *Br.* /*Am.* **set** one's **cap for/** obs. make sb. notice him/her because he/she wants to marry them.

cap/ to cap it all *Br.* /*Am.* **to top it all (off)/** be the last in a series of unpleasant events.

cap/ win one's **cap, be awarded a cap** *Br.* /*Am.* **win** one's **letter/** become a member of a school or university sports team.

cape/ skin the head and neck *Am., Can.* (of animals) use them to prepare a hunting trophy.

capital *Br.* obs. col. excellent, very good: *it will be a capital joke.* - G. Mikes.

capital transfer tax *Br.* tax paid when a person receive money, either as a gift or when sb. dies.

capo *esp. Am.* col. the head of one of the units or branches of the Mafia: *Pacella was reportedly a capo in the Genovese crime family* – A. Summers, R. Swan.

capote *Am., Can.* obs. a long cloak or coat with a hood.

cap peak *Br.* /*Am.* **visor/** projecting front on a cap for shading the eyes.

capper *Am., Can.* col. the climax or ending of smth.

cappish *Am.* sl. understand: *And I'm never going to get older. Capeesh?* - T. de Haven.

captain *Br.* a foreman.

captain *Am.* 1. police district chief. 2. local party boss. 3. also *Can.* supervisor of waiters or bellboys; head waiter: *the captain persuaded him to try an omelet.* - New York.

car *esp. Am., Can.* 1. /also *Br.* **carriage/** (usu. in comb.) a carriage or vehicle for use on railways or cables. 2. passenger compartment of a cable railway. 3. cage of an elevator: *Both men slumped against the back of the empty car.* - K. Lipper.

car *Br.* railway car used for a particular purpose, e.g. a dining car.

caravan 1. *Br.* /*Am., Can.* **trailer/** a vehicle which can be pulled by a car, which contains cooking and sleeping equipment and on which people live (often in **caravan sites**) or travel, usu. for holidays: *We took refuge in the caravan with cups of tea* - Award Journal. 2. *Br.* /*Am.* **wagon/** a covered horse-drawn cart in which people such as gypsies live or travel: *she was living in a borrowed caravan* - L. Lee. 3. *Am., Can.* a covered lorry.

caravanette *Br.* a motor vehicle with a rear compartment equipped for living in, used for holidays.

caravanning *Br.* /*Am.* **trailer camping/** the practice of taking holidays in a caravan. n. **caravanner.**

caravan park (site), camp(ing) site *esp. Br.* /*Am.* **trailer court, park,** *Aus.* **caravan park/** a site for parking caravans: *There are permanent caravan sites near most sea-side places* - J. Ruppeldtova.

carbarn *Am.* tramway depot.

car boot sale, boot fair *Br.* /*Am.* **swap meet,** *Aus.* **garage sale/** a (charity) sale held by car owners in order to sell second-hand or home-made goods to the public from the boot of their cars.

car bra *Am.* 1. a protective device to be fitted over the bodywork of the front of a car. 2. also *Am., Can.* **auto bra** this cover used to avoid being detected by police speeding radars.

carbuilding *Am.* building of railroad cars.

carbuncle *Br.* an architectural eyesore.

carcagou *Am., Can.* wolverine.

carcass meat *Br.* raw meat as distinct from corned or tinned meat.

carcass trade *Br.* sl. the practice of cannibalizing the framework of old but dilapidated pieces of furniture so that they can be reconstructed with new veneer and passed off as genuine antiques.

card 1. *Am.* newspaper announcement publication. 2. *Br.* thick stiff paper. 3. *Am., Can.* obs. odd or amusing person.

card *Am.* 1. place on card. 2. provide with a card. 3. list on a card: *she'd still be carded in bars when she was 30.* - R. Crais. 4. score. 5. also *Can.* ask sb. to show a document, esp. in order to find out how old they are.

card/ a card up one' **sleeve** *esp. Br.* hidden plan or asset.

card/ be carded *Can.* (of an amateur athlete) be funded by the government to pursue training.

card/ postal card *Am.* post card.

cardan joint *Br.* universal joint.

cardan shaft *Br.* a shaft with a universal joint.

cardboard city *esp. Br.* area where mostly homeless live in makeshift shelters.

card catalog *Am.* /*Br.* **card index**/ box of files containing information about smth., esp. in a library.

cardigan *Br. col.* knitted jacket or sweater fastened at the front with buttons.

cardphone *Br.* public telephone in which cards are used for making phone calls.

cardpunch *Br.* /*Am., Aus.* **keypunch**/ (esp. in the past) a machine putting information onto cards for further computer use.

cards /get/ be given one's **cards** *Br. col.* be dismissed from one's job (cards in Britain are one's insurance cards).

cards/ give cards and spades *Am. col.* give or concede a generous advantage.

cards/ on the cards *Br.* /*Am., Can.* **in the cards**/ col. probable: *Apparently it was not in the cards.* - J. Baez.

cards/ play one's **cards right** *Br.* use one's skills properly.

cards/ cards are stacked against sb. or smth. *Am.* the game is lost.

card vote *Br.* block vote, the method of voting by which the vote of each delegate is valued according to the number of his constituents.

cardy *Br. col.* cardigan.

care *Br.* guardianship or protection by local authorities, esp. in **be in care** or **put into care**.

care /have a care *Br. obs.* be more careful.

care/ I couldn't care less *Am., Can. col.* I don't care at all.

care/ in care of *Am.* at the address of: *He wants it sent to him in care of the American Embassy in Paris.* - H.C. Whitford., R.J. Dixson.

care/ Take care *Am., Can.* So long. Good-bye.

careen *esp. Am.* go forward rapidly in a zigzag way: *They careened off the road* - L. Uris.

career's officer, career's adviser *Br.* /*Am.* **career counselor**/ person who advises young people what jobs and professional training might be suited for them.

career structure *Br.* a recognised pattern of adancement within a job or profession.

Careful how you go *Br. obs.* words said when saying goodbye to sb.

caregiver, caretaker *esp. Am., Can.* a person who cares for sb., esp. a family member or paid helper who looks after a child, or sick, elderly or disabled person: *As Tom gradually lost control of his limbs, Suzanne found a caregiver* – Reader's Digest.

care package *Am.* package of food, sweets, etc. sent to sb. living away from home, esp. a student at college.

care line *Br.* a telephone service provided by the manufacturers of a product to deal with queries and complaints from customers.

carer *Br.* sb. who stays at home to look after a relative who is old, ill, etc.

caretaker 1. *esp. Am., Can.* person who provides care for people or animals, such as a parent, teacher or nurse. 2. *Br.* person who takes care /*Am.* **janitor, custodian**/ of a building. esp. a school: *the tiny grassplot that separated the caretaker's house from the road* – I. Stone.

Carey street/ in Carey street *Br.* flat broke.

carfare 1. *Am., Can.* the money that a passenger is charged for travelling in a bus, taxi, etc. within a town or city: *he couldn't afford carfare.* - I. Stone. 2. *Am. obs.* fare for trolleys in some US cities.

cargo *esp. Br.* /*esp. Am.* **freight**/ the goods carried by a ship, plane, or vehicle.

cargo boat *Br.* freighter.

carhop 1. also **curbie** *Am., Can. col.* waiter or waitress at a drive-in restaurant: *The carhops wore red and white drum majorette uniforms* - T. Thompson. 2. *Am. obs.* person who takes care of sb.'s car if that person stays in a large hotel.

carjacking *esp. Am., Can.* (an act of) stealing sb.'s car while they are in it by using physical force or threats: *He is serving a life sentence for the carjacking murder of a teenage girl* – Reader's Digest.

carjockey *Am.* person employed to take cars in and out of a parking lot or garage.

cark (it) *Aus. sl.* die: *before you know it they've carked it.* - T. Thorne.

carlot *Am., Can.* carload lot, carload shipment as defined by law.

carman *Am.* 1. person who checks and repairs railroad cars. 2. the motorman or conductor of a streetcar.

carn(e)y *Br. col.* cajole, coax, flatter.

carnival, amusement park *Am.* /*Br.* **fun fair**/ recreation park; noisy outdoor event in which people can ride special machines and play games for prizes.: *Ben, and some other guys had headed to the carnival grounds to check it out.* – R.L. Stine.

carny 1. *Am., Can.* col. a carnival: *He was a carny barker once and a good one.* – J. Hopkins. 2. also **carney** *Am.* col. carnival worker.

carollers *Am.* carol singers at Christmas.

carom *Am., Can.* (make) a shot in billiards in which the cue ball strikes each of two object balls: *caroming off people like a pinball.* - A. Hitchcock Mystery Magazine

car(r)ousal *esp. Am. /Br., Aus.* **roundabout, merry-go-round, giddy-go-round/** merry-go-round, esp. with wooden horses: *exotic carousal animals are in danger of becoming extinct.* - Reader's Digest., *Stiff as carousal horses.* - J. O'Brien, A. Kurins.

car park *esp. Br., Aus.* 1. */Am., Aus.* **parking lot/** an open area reserved for the parking of cars. 2. */Am.* **parking garage/** an enclosed building used for this purpose: *An individual style that carries right through to the carpark.* - Bulletin., *There was a fight in the car park afterwards.* - New Idea.

carpet *esp. Br.* col. blame, reprimand, esp. for a foolish behaviour.

carpet/ fitted carpet *Br. /Am.* **wall-to-wall carpet/** carpet that covers the whole floor from wall to wall: *well-travelled areas of wall-to-wall carpeting* – Reader's Digest.

carpet/ on the carpet *Br.* col. under consideration.

carpet/ be on the carpet *Br. /Am.* **be called to the carpet, call** sb. **on the carpet/** be severely criticised.

carpet/ step off the carpet *Am.* marry (sb.).

carpet/ sweep smth. **under the carpet /Am. rug/** *Br.* try to hide and forget about smth. embarrassing.

carpetbagger *esp. Am., Can.* a politician who tries to be popular in an area which is not their home, simply because they think they are more likely to succeed there: *Northern carpetbagger who had clearly come to Montgomery to defame the city and its citizens* – N. Hentoff.

car pool 1. *esp. Am., Can.* a number of cars owned by a company or other organisation for the use of its members: *Mom's office car pool gets her home a little after five.* – R.L. Stine. 2. *Am.* agreement made by a number of car owners to take turns driving each other to work, school, etc.: *only 10% travelling in car pools* – Reader's Digest.

car porter *Am. /Br.* **guard attendant/** attendant employed in a sleeping-carriage in a train.

carriage 1. *Br. /Am.* **car/** a railway passenger vehicle: *The Spaniard accompanied her to the carriage* - W.S. Maugham., *I remained alone in the bare carriage* - J. Joyce. 2. *Am.* a baby carriage. 3. *esp. Br.* (the cost of) transporting goods.

carriage bag *esp. Br. /esp. Am.* **shopping bag/** customer's bag, often given by a shop.

carriage bolt *Am., Can. /Br.* **coach bolt/**.

carriage clock *Br.* portable clock in a case with a handle on top.

carriage rug, travelling rug *Br.* lap robe, auto robe.

carriageway *Br.* one of the two sides of a motorway or dual carriageway; each carriageway may have two or more lanes: *There has been a serious accident on the southbound carriageway* - J. Harmer., R. Rossner.

carrier, also **letter carrier, mail carrier, mailman** *Am., Can. /esp. Br.* **postman/**.

carrier (bag), carriage bag *esp. Br. /esp. Am.* **shopping bag/** a cheap strong paper or plastic bag for carrying the goods away from a shop, usu. provided by it: *girl stood on the London pavement in bewilderment, clutching a carrier bag.* - P. Norman.

carrier truck *Am.* a heavy freight truck.

carrot top *Am.* sl. redhead: *Hey, carrot top, where are you going?* - R.A. Spears.

carry *Am.* 1. */Br.* **take/** (the state or area) win the election (in that state or area). 2. also *Can.* the action of keeping smth. esp a gun on one's person. 3. also *Can.* obs. route between navigable waters over which boats and supplies had to be carried.

carry on *esp. Br.* 1. continue, esp. in spite of interruption or difficulties: *his wife's brother carries on the farm for the family.* - W. Grady. 2. col. col. be in love, flirt: *chicks poured into skintight dresses, laughing and flirting and carrying on.* – E. James, D. Ritz.

carry/ carry all before one *Br.* defeat all rivals.

carry/ carry sb. **high (and dry)** *Am.* tease, laugh at sb.

carry the can *Br., Can., Aus.* col. take the blame: *he would be left carrying the can* - J. Higgins.

carry/take coals to Newcastle *Br.* do smth. superfluous.

carryall 1. *esp. Am., Can. /Br.* **holdall,** *esp. Am.* **tote bag/** a large usu. soft bag or case, holdall: *this medical school carryall is a real drag.* - M. Puzo. 2. *Am.* a car similar to an estate car, but higher usu. on a lorry chassis.

carrycot *esp. Br. /Am.* **baby basket,** tdmk. **portacrib/** portable bassinet, small boxlike container in which a baby can be carried:

Fern carrying Lisa in a pink carrycot - Woman's Own.

carrying charge 1. *esp. Am.* money added to the price of things bought by instalment plan: *There is a carrying charge of one per cent a month on those charge accounts.* - H.C. Whitford., R.J. Dixson. 2. *esp. Am., Can.* (financial term) an expense or cost arising from unproductive assets such as stored goods or unoccupied premises or sum payable for the conveying of goods.

carry-on 1. *esp. Br.* col. a piece of silly usu. annoying behaviour, fuss: *Just look at him and Darling Jill carry-on* - E. Caldwell. 2. *Br.* col. a bag or suitcase suitable for taking on to aircraft as hand luggage, **carry-on bag.**

carryout *Am.* adj. n. /also *Br.* **takeaway,** *Am.* **takeout**/ (a meal bought from) a shop from which cooked meals can be taken away to be eaten somewhere.

cart 1. also **shopping cart** *Am., Can.* /*esp. Br.* **trolley**/ a low two-wheeled or four-wheeled cart or vehicle, esp. one pushed by hand (often used in the shops): *shopping cart was loaded down with broccoli* - J. O'Brien, A. Kurins. 2. *Am.* a small motorized vehicle. 3. *Am.* /*Br.* **trolley**/ small table on wheels used to move and serve food and drinks.

cart/ in the cart *esp. Br.* col. in trouble or difficulty: *A false step now and we're all in the cart* - F. O'Brien.

carton *Am.* a large strong cardboard in which goods are packed in small containers for storage and transport.

cartoon *Am.* comic strip: *The make-believe world of cartoons can be entertaining* - McGraw-Hill English, 1986.

cartop *Am.* carry on the top of a car.

cartopper *Am.* a boat carried on the top of a car.

cart track *Br.* a narrow road with a rough surface.

cartoon strip *Br.* a short series of amusing drawings.

cartridge paper *Br.* thick strong paper used for drawing on.

carve (sb.) **up** *Br.* col. 1. (of a motorist) overtake another car and drive in front of it too soon. 2. deliberately ruin (sb.'s) chances: *We've carved up this British champ of yours* - A. McLean.

carver *Br.* the principal chair with arms in a set of dining chairs intended for carving meat.

carver/ electric carver *Br.* /*Am.* **electric knife**/ one having a blade driven by electricity, usu. used for cutting cooked meat.

carvery *Br.* a buffet or restaurant where cooked joints are displayed and carved as required in front of customers.

carve-up *Br.* col. 1. swindle (esp. perpetrated by a number of people): *Then rather tactlessly he pointed George as perennial victim of the Lennon-McCartney "carve-up".* - P. Norman. 2. ruthless division of smth. into separate areas and domains.

casaba *Am., Can.* winter melon.

case *esp. Br.* a suitcase.

case/ (just) in case *esp. Am.* if.

casebook 1. *Br.* a written record of cases dealt with, esp. one kept by doctor or investigator. 2. *Am.* a book containing a selection of source materials on certain subjects, often used as reference works or in teaching.

case knife *Am.* table knife.

cash/ cold (hard) cash *Am., Aus.* hard cash.

cash and carry *esp. Br., Can.* a large wholesale discount shop where the buyer is obliged to pay at once: *the distant sunny glints of cash and carry warehouses.* - B. Bryson.

cash in (one's) **chips** *esp. Am., Aus.* col. die: *capitulate to his problem by cashing in his chips.* - J. O'Brien, A. Kurins.

cash in hand *Br.* paid in coins and notes.

cash (smth.) **up** *Br.* /*Am.* **cash out**/ count and check takings at the end of a day's trading.

cash on the barrelhead *esp. Am., Can.* col. humor. money in coins and notes paid without delay: *a cool million dollars - "cash on the barrelhead".* - D. Carnegie., To save interest we just paid out cash on the barrelhead for the studio. - W. Jack, B. Laursen.

cash card *esp. Br.* /*Am.* **ATM card**/ a special plastic card used for obtaining money from a cash dispenser: *These cards, already in use in France, replace cash, keys, credit, debit and cash cards.* - C. Handy.

cash desk *Br.* a place in the shop or restaurant where you can pay for the things you bought.

cash dispenser *esp. Br.* /*Am.* **cashomat, ATM,** *Br.* **cashpoint,** *Aus.* **automatic teller**/ machine, esp. one placed outside a bank from which customers can obtain money at any time by putting in a cash card and pressing numbered keys to give a special number.

cashier's check *Am.* bank check.

cash point *Br.* /American signs are **Cashier** or **Pay here**/ sign for Cash register.

cashpoint *Br.* /*Am.* **ATM**/ cash dispenser, automated teller machine.

casket 1. *esp. Am., Can.* euph. /*Br.* **coffin**/: *His body rested without decoration in a simple open casket.* - H. Troyat, *I arranged for a casket* - D. Carnegie. 2. *Br.* a small wooden box for cremated ashes.

casket suit *Am.* euph. burial clothes.

cast 1. *esp. Br.* the leader of a fishing line with flies or baited hooks attached. 2. *Am.* a. forecast. b. suggestion.

cast back (to) *Am.* behave or look like a relative to the distant past: *The boy casts back to his great-great-grandfather.* - Longman.

cast off *esp. Br.* (in knitting) remove (a number of stitches) from the needle.

cast up *esp. Am.* col. be sick, bring up (food): *Jane has cast up her dinner again.* - Longman.

cast a ballot *Am.* vote in an election.

caster *Br.* /*Am.* **shaker**/ small container with holes in the top for salt, pepper, etc.

caster/castor sugar *Br., Aus.* white sugar that has been very finely ground.

castles/ build castles in Spain *Br.* have unrealistic plans.

casual 1. *esp. Br.* person who receives temporary welfare relief. 2. *Br.* a youth belonging to a subculture characterised by wearing expensive casual clothing often associated with football hooliganism.

casual labourer *Br.* transient or occasional worker, usu. applied to stevedores.

casualty (ward or **department)** *Br., Aus.* /*Am.* **emergency room**/ urgent treatment department in a hospital.

casual ward *Br.* /also *esp. Br.* **dosshouse**, *Am.* sl. **flophouse**/ cheap lodging house.

cat 1. *Br.* col. /also *Br.* **cat burgler**, *Am.* **second-story man, porch climber**/ thief who enters the house by climbing up walls, pipes, etc. 2. *esp. Am., Can.* col. a young man: *Therefore young English speakers from China to Peru call a man a "cat", a girl a "chick"* - P. Norman., *a cat can swing a lead and play a melody* - M. Jones, J. Chilton.

cat/ at night all cats are grey *Am.* it's hard to distinguish smth. at certain times and conditions.

cat/ fight like cat and dog *Br., Aus.* /*Am.* **fight like cats and dogs**/ (of two close persons) constantly keep quarelling and arguing.

cat/ have not a cat in hell's chance, not have a chance in hell *Br.* col. /*Am., Aus.* **have not a snowball's chance in hell**/ have no chance at all.

cat/ like a cat on hot bricks *esp. Br.* col. /*Am., Aus.* **like a cat on a hot tin roof**/ col. very nervous or anxious and unable to keep still or keep one's attention on one thing.

cat/ like a scalded cat *Br.* moving very fast.

cat/ like the cat that got/ate the cream *Br., Aus.* /*Am.* **like the cat that ate the canary**/ very pleased with oneself for doing smth.

cat/ no room to swing a cat *esp. Br.* very small.

cat/ put/set the cat among the pigeons *Br., Aus.* do or say smth. that causes trouble.

cat/ see which way the cat jumps *esp. Br.* delay making decision to see how situation will develop.

catalogue *Am.* /*Br.* **calendar**/ annual reference book of university or college with list of courses offered by them..

catalogue company *Br.* mail order house.

catamount *Am.* 1. cougar. 2. lynx.

cat-and-dog *Br.* adj. (of life) full of quarrels and arguments.

catapult *esp. Br.* /*Am.* **slingshot**, *Aus.* **shanghai**/ a forked stick with an elastic band attached for shooting small stones.

catastrophize *Am.* treat a trivial problem as if it were a major catastrophe.

catbird seat *Am., Can.* col. advantageous position, esp. in **be (sitting) in the catbird seat**: *Anguilo was in the catbird seat in the early sixties* - G. O'Neill, D. Lehr.

catch at *Br., Aus.* take hold of.

catch/ you'll catch it *Br.* col. you'll be punished.

catch sb. out *Br.* cause sb. to make a mistake, esp. by asking them a question they cannot answer; detect sb. doing smth. wrong, confuse sb. by sudden event.

catch (sb.) up *Br., Aus.* catch up with.

catch up *Am.* 1. col. show that sb. is wrong, find fault with (sb.): *The examiners caught him up on the third question.* - Longman. 2. prepare horses for travel.

catch the post *Br.* send a letter before the post has been collected.

catch the sun *Br.* get one's skin slightly darker, brown or red colour.

catch sb. with their trousers /*Am., Aus.* **pants**/ **down** *Br.* col. 1. catch sb. unawares. 2. make sb. feel ashamed by asking them to do smth. they can't do.

catch/bag some rays *Am.* sl. get a sun tan.

catchall *Am.* drawer, cupboard, etc., where a person puts small things.

catch crop *Br.* crop grown in the space between two main ones at a time when no main crops are being grown.

catchline *Br.* print. a short, eye-catching line of type, usu. at the top of a page such as a running head.

catch-up/ play catch-up *Am., Can.* try to equal competitor (in a sports game).

catchword *esp. Br.* entry word.

cater smth. (not cater at) *esp. Am.* provide and serve food and drinks, usu. for payment at (a public or private party rather than a restaurant): *he also caters tea parties* - S. Grafton.

cater for *esp. Br. /esp. Am.* **cater to/** 1. provide what is needed or wanted: *I mean, we cater to smokers.* - New York. 2. take into account.

cater-cornered *Am., Can.* diagonally crossed.

cat-house *esp. Am., Can.* col. brothel: *on Sunday you raped a whole cat-house.* - T. Wilder.

catkin *esp. Br.* soft flowers on trees like willow or birch.

cat-lap *Br.* col. dishwater (weak tea, etc.).

cats and dogs *Am.* sl. 1. worthless shares of stock. 2. worthless merchandise.

cat's eyes *Br., Aus.* tdmk. /*Am.* **reflectors/** glass reflectors set into rubber pads down the centre of a road to indicate traffic lanes at night.

cat's meat *Br.* col. cat food.

cat's pyjamas (whiskers), cat's meow *esp. Am., Aus.* or *Br.* obs. that's it, smth. or sb. wonderful: *Aren't you cat's pyjamas, Mr. Collin Fenwick?* - T. Capote.

catsuit *Br.* a tight fitting women's piece of clothing covering the whole body, arms and legs.

catsup *esp. Am.* /*Br.* **ketchup/** ketchup: *She'd like catsup for her French fries.* - R. Crais.

cattery *Br.* place where a person can leave cats to be looked after while he's away from home.

cat train *Am., Can.* a crawler tractor pulling a train of sleighs across snow or ice.

cattle cake *Br.* processed food for cattle in the form of cakes and blocks.

cattle call *Am., Can.* an open audition for parts in a play or film.

cattle car *Am.* horse box, cattle box.

cattle dock *Br.* /*Am.* **cattle loading pen/** cattle pen.

cattle dog *Aus., NZ.* a dog bred and trained to work cattle.

cattle-duff *Aus.* steal cattle.

cattle guard *Am.* /*Br.* **cattle grid/** grid covering a ditch allowing vehicles and pedestrians to pass over but not cattle and other animals: *we had collided with the posts of the ranch-yard cattle guard.* - Guideposts.

cattle lifter *Br.* /*Am.* **cattle rustler,** *Aus.* **cattle duffer/** cattle thief.

cattleman *Am.* cattlebreeder: *restaurant was crammed with cattlemen and ranchers in Stetsons* - National Geographic.

cattle market 1. *Br.* place where cattle is being sold. 2. *Br.* derog. beauty contest. 3. *esp. Br.* being treated in an undignified and unrespectful manner. 4. *Br.* col. /*Am., Aus.* **meat market/** a place to find sexually attractive partners.

cattle truck *Br.* vehicle or part of a train made to carry cattle.

catty-corner *Am.* kitty corner: *catty-cornered from Claude, close to him.* – Reader's Digest.

caucus *Am.* hold or meet in a caucus.

caught/ be caught *Br., Aus.* (said of a batsman when the ball hit by him is caught by the member of another team).

caught/ be caught with one's **trousers /***Am., Aus.* **pants/ down** *Br.* be caught at disadvantage.

cauli *Br.* col. cauliflower.

cauliflower cheese *Br.* a dish of cooked cauliflower in a thick sauce made with milk, flour and cheese.

caution 1. *Am.* person who provides bail. 2. *esp. Br.* a spoken warning given by a policeman when you have done something wrong; **be cautioned**.

caution money *Br.* money deposited, esp. by a college student, as security for good conduct.

cave *Br.* 1. secession or a group of seceders from a political party. 2. school sl. look out!

cavedweller *Am.* joc. tenement house dweller.

caver *Br., Aus.* /*Am.* **spelunker/** person who walks and climb in caves as a sport.

caviar to the general *Br.* smth. that only sensitive or educated can enjoy or understand.

cay *Am.* very small low island formed of coral or sand.

CC *Br.* City Council.

ceased to exist *Br.* been disconnected; **ceased line** is a disconnected line.

Ceefax *Br.* a teletext service provided by the BBC.

cellar *Am.* col. the last place in the sports competition.

cellarman *Br.* a man who works behind the scenes in a pub or one who is in charge of a wine cellar.

cell phone, mobile phone *Br.* /*Am* **cellular phone/**: *She walked across the room…and picked up the cellular phone* – R.L. Stine., And *he also sells cell phones.* _Time.

census tract *Am.* statistical area, containing an average population of 4,000 set for the study of small metropolitan sections.

cental *esp. Br.* short hundred weight.
centennial *Am., Aus.* or fml. *Br.* centenary.
The Centennial State /also **The Treasure of the Rockies**/ *Am.* Colorado.
center out *Am.* col. choose (sb.) from among others, usu. for punishment: *the child then complained that she had been centered out.* - Longman.
center lane *Am.* /*Br.* **middle lane**/.
centerpin reel *Am.* (automatic) spinning reel.
central *Am.* now rare (the people working at) a telephone exchange: *Central isn't answering.* - L. Waller., *I tried to get central to give the number.* - D. Hammet.
central casting *Am.* the casting staff department of a motion picture studio.
central reservation, centre strip *Br.* /*Am., Can., Aus.* **median (strip)**/ thin area of land running down the middle of a large road to keep traffic apart: *Wilcox made a U-turn through a gap in the road's central reservation* - D. Lodge.
centre *Br.* /*Am.* **downtown**/.
the Centre, the red centre, the dead Heat *Aus.* central dry regions of the country.
centreplate *Br.* sliding keel.
centre strip *Br.* median divider on a highway.
cents-off *Am.* having to do with a form of promotion in which the price of a product is reduced by cents when a shopper presents a coupon with a purchase. The store owner collects the cents-off coupons and returns them to the manufacturer who reimburses them.
century *Am.* sl. $100: *He had four centuries and some chicken feed.* - J. Dos Passos.
ceramic hob *Br.* a flat surface on the top of some cookers on which pans are heated.
(dead) cert *Br.* col. a certainty: *Punters put out thousands of pounds on hunches and "certs"* - Gloucester Citizen.
certifiable *esp. Am.* good enough to be officially approved.
certificated *esp. Br.* having successfully completed a course of training for a profession.
certificate of expenditure *Am.* act of writing off expenses.
certified *Br.* insane.
certified check *Am.* a check certified to be good by the bank upon which it is drawn: *Certified check, money order, or credit card info must accompany ad copy.* - New York.
certified letter *Am.* a letter that is certified by a notary as proof of authorship.
certified mail *Am., Can., Aus.* /*Br.* **recorded delivery**/ mail that is recorded and certified by the postal service for extra postage. It insures delivery to the addressee of mail that doesn't contain valuables and is cheaper than registered mail.
certified milk *Am.* /*Br.* **attested milk**/ milk produced under official medical control.
certified public accountant (CPA) *Am., Can.* /*Br.* **chartered accountant**/ one who has successfully completed his/her training: *staffed by people who had been certified public accountants* - K. Vonnegut, Jr.
cesspool, also **cesspit** *Br.* underground container or hole where wash water from a home is collected.
chaffer *Br.* exchange small talk.
chain *Br.* (when buying a house) situation when each person must complete the sale of their own house before they can buy next person's house.
chain/ pull/yank sb.'s **chain** *esp. Am.* col. tease or annoy sb. by lying deliberately.
chain-chew *Am.* chew (gum) continuously, starting a new piece once the old piece is finished.
chain of office *Br.* decoration worn by some officials at ceremonies.
chair 1. *Am.* (also **witness chair, (witness) stand,** *Br.* **witness box**) witness box. 2. *Br.* metal device to hold railroad track in place on a tie-track socket. 3. **the chair** *esp. Am.* col. the electric chair: *I don't wanna go to the chair!* - R.A. Spears. 4. *Br.* the position of being a professor at a university. 5. *Am.* the person in charge of a department in a university: *Scatelli was going to get the chair* – J. O'Hara.
chair/ pull/yank sb.'s **chair** *Am., Aus.* col. say smth. that upsets other people.
chair *esp. Br.* lift up and carry sb. as a sign of admiration.
chair-car *Am., Can.* 1. parlour-car. 2. railroad car having traditional chairs with adjustable reeling backs.
chairman *Br.* person in charge of a large company or organisation.
chairwarmer *Am.* sl. lazy person.
chaise *Am.* chaise longue.
chaise longue *Am., Can.* a sunbed with a lengthened seat for reclining on.
chairwarmer *Am.* sl. an idle person.
chalet *esp. Br.* small house, esp. in a holiday camp.
chalet party *Br.* a skiing holiday during which people stay in chalet.
chalk *Br.* charge (drinks bought in a pub or bar) to a personal account.

chalk *Br.* a point scored in a game.
chalk/ as different as chalk and/from cheese/ like chalk and cheese *Br., Aus. /esp. Am.* **(as) different as night and day/** completely different from each other.
chalk/ (not) by a long chalk *Br.* by far (used for adding emphasis for smth. one is saying).
chalkboard *esp. Am., Can., Aus.* blackboard: *Yvette wrote her name on an electronic chalkboard.* - Houghton Mifflin English.
chalkface *Br.* the ordinary working day of a teacher in a school.
chalkie *Aus., NZ.* col. a schoolteacher.
chalk (-mark) *Br.* mark with a chalk.
chalk talk *Am., Can. /Br.* **chalk and talk/** col. lecture made with the use of blackboard using traditional methods.
challenged *esp. Am.* euph. disabled, esp. in the stated way, e.g. **visually, physically, mentally,** etc. **challenged**: *new teletabloids that (in the new parlance) are reality-challenged* - B.R. Barber.
chambers *esp. Br.* (offices) used by barristers or judges.
champaigne-socialist *Br.* a supporter of socialist ideals who enjoys the life of a rich man.
champers *esp. Br., Aus.* col. champagne: *Did you cop the champers, then?* - T. Murphy.
champion *Br.* adj., adv. very good (regional use).
chance/ be in with a chance *Br.* have a possibility to do smth.
chance/ chance one's **arm/luck** *Br.* col. take the risk.
chance/ fancy one's **chances** *Br.* col. imagine how successful one could be.
chance/ not fancy/not rate sb.'s **chances** *Br.* think sb. is inlikely to succeed.
Chance would be a fine thing! *Br.* col. hope for smth. that wouldn't happen very probably.
chance-child *Br.* col. love child.
chance-come *Br.* fortuitous.
chancellery *esp. Am. /esp. Br.* **chancery/** an office attached to an embassy or consulate.
chancellor 1. *esp. Br.* the non-resident honorary head of a university. 2. *Am.* the president or chief administrator of a university. 3. *Am.* the presiding judge of a chancery court.
chance-met *Br.* met by chance.
chancer *Br.* sl. 1. incompetent person. 2. person who takes any kind of risk.
chancery *esp. Br.* government office that collects and stores official papers.
change *Br.* n. exchange.
change/ change gear, change into another gear *Br., Aus. /Am.* **shift gear/**.

change down, up *Br., Aus. /Am.* **shift down, (downshift) /up/** start using lower/higher gear.
change/ all change! *Br.* used to tell passengers to get off a train because it doesn't go any further.
change/the change of life *Br.* obs. the time in a life of a woman when she's about 50 and can't have children anymore.
change/ get no change out of *Br., Aus.* col. not to get any help from sb.
change / give change *Br. /Am.* **make change/** give money in low-value coins or notes for a coin or note of higher value.
change/ ring the changes *Br., Aus.* change the way smth. is done, usu. in a more exciting way.
change the channel *Am.* col. */esp. Am., Can., Aus.* **channel surf,** *Br.* **channel-hop/** switch to some other topic of conversation: *Let's change the channel here before there is a fight.* - R.A. Spears.
change the record *Br.* col. say smth. new.
change maker *Am.* change machine, one that gives money in exchange for money of a different type.
change purse, coin purse *Am., Can. /Br.* **purse/** a purse for both paper money and coins: *Then he takes out a change purse which holds his small money.* – E.Kazan.
Channel 1. *Br.* English Channel. 2. *esp. Br.* the bed where a natural stream of water runs.
channelize *esp. Am., Can.* cause to pass through a certain road.
channel-hopping *Br. /esp. Am., Can., Aus.* **channel-surfing/** switching quickly between different TV channels.
channel surf *Aus. /Am.* **change the channel/** change a topic of conversation.
chant *Br.* sl. tout.
chant(e)y *Am.* shanty, a song that sailors sing while working.
chap(pie) *esp. Br.* or *Aus.* col. a man or boy, fellow: *ruddy chap tried to shoot me.* - J.P. Donleavy.
chaparral *Am., Can.* tangled shrubs and thorny bushes.
chapbook *Am.* small book containing ballads, tales, or tracts.
chapel 1. *Br.* col. (of churches in England and Wales) nonconformist. 2. *esp. Am. /Br.* **chapel of rest/** undertaker's mortuary. 3. *Br.* local print or newspaper trade union.
chaperon(e) *Am.* sb., esp. an old person who is present at an event to encourage correct behaviour.
chapman *Br.* peddler.

chapess *Br.* col. a woman.

chaps *Br.* col. protective leather covers worn over person's trousers when riding a horse.

chapter *esp. Am., Can.* a local branch of a society, club, etc.: *Lopukhin...began his career as a secretary of the institute's Young Communist League chapter.*- R.G. Kaiser.

chapter/ be a chapter of accidents *Br., Aus.* col. a series of unpleasant events.

chapter 11 *Am.* a temporary protection from creditors given to a bancrupt company to help it reorganise itself.

chapter-house *Am., Can.* the house of a college fraternity or sorority.

char *Br.* obs. work as a cleaner in a house, office, public buildings, etc.: *I used to char for this lady* - Maclean's.

char 1. *Br.* col. /also **char-lady, char woman, daily cleaner**/ a woman who works as a cleaner in a house, office, or public building: *The char had been in* - G. Greene., *There was also a char-lady, who came every morning for two hours* - M.M. Kaye. 2. *esp. Br.* odd job, chore. 3. *Br.* col. tea: *Char, sir?* - D. Reeman.

charabanc *Br.* obs. excursion bus.

character *esp. Br.* obs. /*Am.* **character rating**/ a usu. written statement of a person's abilities, reference: *it was him that sacked me without a character* - M. Daly.

charbroil *Am., Can.* grill on a rack over charcoal.

charge smth. *Am.* pay with a credit card.

charge (a jury) *Am.* law. explain the details of the law to them.

charge/ be on charge *Br.* put an amount of electricity into smth., esp. put/leave the battery on charge.

charge/ get a charge out of smth. *Am.* col. think smth. is funny: *He really got a charge of scaring that couple in the car.* – R.L. Stine.

charge/ put sb. on a charge of smth. *Br.* charge sb. with a specified offence.

charge down *esp. Am.* record (smth.) to (sb.'s) debt: *Charge the goods to my account* - Longman.

charge off *Am.* 1. accept (smth.) as a total loss: *The film had to charge off the debt as hopeless.* - Longman. 2. col. defeat (opposition) completely: *the firm can charge off its success to his leadership.* - Longman.

charge (smth.) **to the public** *Am.* charge (smth.) to the state.

charge/ give (or **take**) sb. **in charge** *esp. Br.* hand sb. to the police, turn sb. in.

charge account *Am., Can.* /*Br.* **credit account**/ an account with a shop which allows one to take goods at once and pay for them later: *Fortunately we ran a charge account at the meat market* - S. North.

charge-cap *Br.* (of a government) subject (a local authority) to an upper limit on the charges it may levy on public for its services.

charge card 1. *Br.* a plastic card that you can use to buy things in one particular shop and pay for them later. 2. *Am.* a credit card.

charge hand *Br.* person in charge of workers whose position is just below that of a foreman.

charge nurse *Br., Aus.* head nurse, esp. a male one: *I found myself filling in forms and being told to present myself to the charge nurse* - B. Bryson.

charge sheet *Br.* an official document on which a police officer records the details of a crime of which the person is accused.

charity shop *Br.* /*Am.* **thrift shop**/ a shop that sells used things, esp. clothes, at a cheap price, in order to make money, for a charity, a church, etc.

Charles's Wain *esp. Br.* obs. the Plough in Ursa Major.

charley horse *Am., Can.* col. a cramp of an arm or a leg.

Charlie 1. *Am.* radio code name for letter C. 2. *Am., Aus., NZ.* sl. obs. Viet Cong soldier /also **Victor Charlie**/: *That's an American term Viet Cong Charlie, whatever.* - Rolling Stone., *he saw Charley as his enemy.*- R. Borchgave, R. Moss. 3. *Aus.* sl. girl.

charlie *Br., Aus.* col. a stupid person, esp. in **look/feel a right/proper Charlie.**

charlies *Br.* col. obs. women's breasts, tits: *"charlies" – when not applied to a pal, could do double duty and refer to a fine pair of breasts.* – A. Summers, R. Swan.

charmed life/ lead or **have a charmed life** *esp. Br.* always seem to be lucky, as if protected or helped by magic.

charm school *esp. Am.* art courses where one may learn how to dress and how to behave oneself in society, etc.: *you might need charm school* - Fortune.

charter *Br.* col. law. relating to the decision that seems to give the right to do smth. most people consider immoral.

chartered *Br.* (of a specialist) qualified as a member of a professional body that has a royal charter.

chartered accountant *Br.* /*Am.* **certified public accountant**/ an accountant who has successfully completed his/her training: *he's passed his exam and is a chartered accountant* - W.S. Maugham., *The only child of a Finchley chartered accountant, she left school at 16 with five O levels.* - Woman's Own.

chartered surveyer *Br.* licensed architect.

charter member *esp. Am., Can.* /*Br.* **foundation member**/ founder member.

chartism *Am.* the making and study of charts, esp. of stock transactions with a view of predicting future events.

charwoman /also **char lady, char**/ *esp. Br.* obs. / *Am.* **scrub woman**/ a woman who works as a cleaner in a house, office, or public building: *Half a dozen women, their hair bound like charwoman's in dusters waited in turn.* - G. Greene., *Why the hell don't you get a charwoman in?* - W.S. Maugham., *to employ an English charwoman is a compromise between having a dirty house or clearing it yourself* - G. Mikes.

chase *Br.* 1. often used in the names of important horse races, in which horses have to jump over fences, ditches or bushes. 2. (in place names) former hunting grounds.

chase/ be chased *Am.* (of a pitcher) be removed from the game because players on the opposite team are hitting the ball well.

chase/ chase around/up/down *esp. Br.* rush or hurry somewhere.

chase/ chase down *esp. Am.* run after sb. or follow them quickly and catch them.

chase/ cut to the chase *Am.* get down to business seriously.

chase/ go chase yourself *Am.* go away: *You haven't even got guts enough to tell this guy to go chase himself.* - D. Hammet.

chaser 1. *Br., Aus.* a small alcoholic drink which is drunk after a weaker alcoholic drink. 2. *Am.* a weaker alcoholic drink drunk after a stronger one: *he had a straight rye with water for a chaser.* – J.O. Hara.

chat *esp. Br.* 1. gossip, worthless and sometimes unkind talk, friendly conversation. 2. *Aus.* a bird.

chat (away) *esp. Br.* talk in a friendly way.

chat up *esp. Br., Aus.* col. /*esp. Am.* **come on to**/ charm and seduce with talk: *I'm tired of being chatted up by every lonely salesman in Britain.* - Time., *he tried to chat up a woman* - New Idea., *A uniformed man beside an ambulance chatted up a West Indian nurse in the sunlight.* - J. Fowles; n. **chat-up**.

chat-up line *Br., Aus.* /*Am.* (**come-on**) **line**/ persuasive words.

chatline *Br.* a telephone service where callers can speak to other callers or to the employees of the company.

chat show *Br.* /*Am.* **talk show**/ radio or TV show on which well-known people talk to each other and are asked questions.

chat show host *Br.* person who introduces people and asks questions on that show.

chattel mortgage *Am., Can.* a mortgage on a movable item of property.

chatterbox *Am.* sl. 1. machine gun. 2. gossip column (in a newspaper).

the chattering classes *Br.* col. humor. people who like to discuss politics and social matters.

chatty *esp. Br.* 1. liking to talk in a friendly way. 2. piece of writing that has friendly informal style.

Chautauqua *Am., Can.* assembly for education and entertainment of adults by lectures, concerts and other such activities.

chaw *esp. Am., Can.* v., n. chew.

chaw up *Am.* col. defeat (opposition) completely: *The speaker chawed up his opponent with some well-chosen words.* - Longman.

chaw-bacon *Br.* sl. derog. /*Am.* joc. **hayseed**/ (country) bumpkin: *they were all the same, the loud-mouth chaw-bacons who came here* - Arthur Hailey.

chazerai *Am., Can.* sl. odious and worthless material: *Put this chazerai in the oven* - M. Torgov.

cheap 1. *Br.* reduced in price for quick sale. 2. *esp. Am., Can.* /*Br.* **mean**/ careful with money, tight, stingy: *I didn't want to look cheap.* - S. Sheldon.

cheap and cheerful *Br.* col. costing little but attractive.

cheap and nasty *Br.* col. costing little and of bad quality.

cheap/ Cheap at half the price! *Br., Aus.* humor. That's very expensive.

cheapjack *esp. Am., Can.* col. of inferior quality.

cheaptripper *Br.* person who travels at excursion rates, tripper.

cheat on (smth. such as an agreement or taxes) *esp. Am.* not to do smth. what one should do under a set of rules.

cheater *esp. Am., Can.* a dishonest person.

cheaters *Am.* col. obs. (sun)glasses.

cheat grass *esp. Am., Can.* tough wild grass of open land.

cheat sheet *Am., Can.* col. written notes which help a person's memory, esp. when used surreptitiously in an exam.

check 1. *Am., Can. /Br.* **tick/** also *Am.* **check mark** mark or sign to show that smth. is correct: *Please check the appropriate box.* - New York. 2. *esp. Am., Can. /Br.* **bill/** a bill at a restaurant: *the other fellow is picking up the check.* - Reader's Digest. 3. *Am.* a counter used in card games (as chip in poker). 4. *Am.* a ticket or a small object which a person is given when they leave their coat or other personal possessions somewhere for a short time. 5. /*Am.* **plaid**/.

check *Am.* 1. place smth. somewhere to be looked after / **have** one's **luggage checked** *Am.* have it registered. 2. /*Br.* **tick**/ show that smth. is correct, check on. 3. write or draw a check. 4. agree with another information.

check *esp. Am., Can.* excl. used to react positively to sb. who is making certain that all the items on the list have been dealt with or included.

check smth. **in** *esp. Am.* have the return of (an article) recorded: *I'm just going to check in these books at the library.* - Longman.

check out *esp. Am., Can.* 1. examine (usu. smth. on a list) to see if it is correct: *I check out the phonebook over to the drugstore* - R.J. Randisi., M. Wallace. 2. have the removal of (a thing) recorded, esp. when borrowing books from a library: *I don't suppose you're here to check out a book.* - B. Tillman. 3. enter the price of customer's goods into a cash register in a supermarket. 4. col. die.

checkback *Am.* repeated check-up.

checkbook *Am.* /*Br.* **cheque-book**/: *I see your Grace's checkbook on the table* M. Daly.

checker 1. *Am.* /*Br.* **draught/** a small round piece used in the game of draughts. 2. *Am.* cashier in a supermarket who works at the checkout.

checkerboard *Am.* /*Br.* **chessboard, draughtsboard**/ special board used to play chess or draughts on.

checkerman *Am.* /*Br.* **draughtsman**/ person who plays draughts.

checkers *Am.* /*Br.* **draughts**/ game played with 12 round pieces on a board of 64 squares.

check-in desk *Br.* /*Am.* **check-in counter**/ place where you report your arrival.

check-in hall *Br.* an area in an airport where people go to report their arrival and obtain information about flights.

checking account *Am.* /*Br.* **current account,** *Can.* **chequing account**/ bank account which usu. doesn't earn interest and from which money can be taken at any time by cheque by using one's cheque book or cash card/: *he maintained a checking account.* - J. O'Hara., *Until recently,* there were no personal checking accounts or charge cards. - D.J. Rees.

checkoff *Am.* 1. arrangement between a union and an employer by which the employer deducts union dues from wages and turns them over to the union. 2. deductions from workers' wages made if they buy things in a company store, agree to pay their rent in this way, etc.

checkout (counter) *esp. Am.* the place in a supermarket where you pay for goods: *The fuzzy spots do not belong – not in the checkout at Star Market.* – Reader's Digest, **checkout clerk**.

checkpost *esp. Br.* checkpoint.

checkroom 1. *esp. Am., Can. /Br.* **left luggage office,** *Am.* **baggage room/** place where one can leave one's bags for a certain period to be collected later. 2. *esp. Am., Can. /Br.* **cloakroom/** place in a hotel or theatre where people leave their coats temporarily with **checkroom attendants**: *attendant he recognised from the downstairs area, near the checkroom now approached him with five slips of paper.* - L. Waller.

check-taker *Am.* 1. theatre ticket collector. 2. railway official in charge of a train.

check-till *Am.* cash register.

chedder/ hard/tough chedder *Br., Aus.* col. / *Aus.* col. **stiff cheddar/** hard luck.

cheek *Br.* a rude and annoying behaviour that shows a lack of respect, often in **have the cheek** (to do smth.)., **have a cheek, what a cheek!**

cheek *esp. Br.* /*Am.* **sass/** speak or behave disrespectfully towards.

cheek/ live/stand/work cheek by jowl (with) *Br.* be very close together (of people or things that are quite different).

cheek/ of all the cheek *Br.* an expression of indignation.

cheeky *Br.* adj. behaving rudely that often seems amusing.

cheeky monkey *Br.* an impudent person.

cheerer *Am.* person shouting words of support in an effort to help a person or team to win.

cheerio *Br.* col. excl. good-bye: *Cheerio, Toby* - I. Murdoch.

cheer leading *Am.* the act of loudly supporting an organisation, idea, etc.

cheers *Br.* 1. thank you. 2. good-bye.

cheers *Br., Aus.* col. expression used by people when they start drinking.

cheese/ hard/tough cheese *Br. /Aus.* **stiff cheese/** col. bad luck.

cheese it 1. *Am.* col. run away. 2. *Br.* obs. stop doing smth.
cheese (off) *Br., Aus.* col. tire (sb.) thoroughly, annoy sb.: *I'm cheesed off with this endless waiting for buses.* - Longman.
cheesed-off, browned-off *Br., Aus., Can.* col. / also *Br.* sl. **brassed-off**/ bored, disgruntled, fed up: *He told me he was really cheesed off with everything.* - P. Norman., *she was really cheesed off* - New Idea.
cheese head *Br.* a screw head with a slightly domed top.
cheesemonger *Br.* a person who sells diary products, esp. cheese.
cheese-paring *Br.* 1. not generous, mean. 2. stinginess.
cheesy 1. *Br.* obs. sl. swanky. 2. *Am.* col. cheap, shabby, lacking in taste, insincere: *it was an altogether hideous room - expensive but cheesy.* - J.D. Salinger., *It was real cheesy and outdated.* - W. Jack, B. Laursen.
Chelsea boot *Br.* boot or shoe with elastic sides.
Chelsea bun *Br.* a currant bun sprinkled with sugar and dried fruit inside.
chemist *Br., Aus.* /*Am.* **druggist, pharmacist**/ a skilled person who owns or runs a shop /*Br., Aus.* **chemist's (shop)**, *Am., Can.* **drugstore**/ shop where medicines are sold: *Ask the pharmacist at the chemist shop* - Woman's Own., *the same comb from the same chemist* – Alain de Botton.
chemurgy *Am., Can.* the chemical and industrial use of organic raw materials.
cheque/ **crossed cheque** *esp. Br.* cheque which must be put into a bank before being paid.
cheque book journalism. *Br.* low quality writing in newspapers that pay large amounts of money for details of private life of famous people.
cheque (guarantee) card /also **banker's card**/ *Br., Aus.* card given by a bank to those who have an account with it, which promises that the bank will pay out the money written on their cheque up to a certain amount.
cherries *Am.* sl. flashing lights on a police car.
cherry *Am.* 1. taboo. sl. virginity: *Does he still have his cherry?* - R.L. Chapman. / **lose** one's **cherry** is to lose one's virginity. 2. taboo. sl. virgin. 3. adj. in an unproved or maiden state of any sort: *He hasn't published anything yet; still cherry* - R.L. Chapman.
cherry-bomb *Am.* a type of firecracker: *his voice boomed like a cherry-bomb underneath an empty pineapple can.* - D. Brenner., *With its fuse looking like a stem it was named a Cherry Bomb.* - E.L. Doctorow.

cherry-picker *Am.* an articulated crane with a bucketlike platform: *a guy in a cherry-picker fixing the phone lines* - R.L. Chapman.
Chess Board City *Aus.* joc. Melbourne / also **Cabbage City**.
chest *Br.* financial resources of a business or organisation.
chest of drawers *Br.* /*Can.* **dresser**, *Am.* **bureau**/.
chesterfield *Can.* any large sofa or coach: *Dave took Steve's arm and sat him down beside him on the chesterfield.* - W. Grady.
chestnut *Am.* /*esp. Br.* **conker**/ seed of the horse chestnut tree, esp. as used in a children's game.
chestnut/ the/an (hoary) old chestnut *esp. Br.* smth. so often repeated that it is no longer interesting.
chest-on-chest *Am.* double chest, high chest of drawers.
chesty 1. *esp. Br.* col. suffering from disease of the chest or coughing when it's foggy. 2. *Am., Can.* conceited or arrogant.
chew *Br.* a sweet that you have to chew very hard before it becomes soft.
chew (sb.) out *esp. Am., Aus., Can.* col. tell off, reprimand, scold (sb.): *his boss chewed him out* - R. Moore., *I chew him out for it* - G.V. Higgins., *a new recruit being chewed out for not having tucked in his shirt* - J. DeFelice.
chew the cud *Br.* discuss smth. for a long time.
chew the rag 1. *Br.* col. complain. 2. *Am., Aus.* col. /*esp. Br.* **chew the fat**/ chat abot many subjects for a long time: *Let's sit down and chew the rag for a little.* - J. Dos Passos.
chewed up *Am.* sl. worried, anxious, bothered: *Don't get chewed up about the new law* - Longman.
chicane *Br.* raceway, esp. a track for automobile racing.
Chicano *Am.* a US citizen originally from Mexico.
chicharon *esp. Am.* a piece of fried pork crackling, esp. used in Mexican cooking.
chichi *Am.* col. woman's breast.
chick/ neither chick nor child *Am., Can.* no children at all.
chicadee *Am., Can.* tit.
chicken *Am.* adj. concerned with poultry raising / **chicken house (coop)**, **chicken farm(ing)**, **chicken ranch**: *my father turned the chicken farm over to me in 1948* - Reader's Digest., *our house no longer sounds like a chicken coop* - Outdoor Life.
chicken/ Blue Hen's Chicken *Am.* a citizen of Delaware.

chicken/ like a headless chicken *Br.* behaving in disorganised way.
chicken a la king *esp. Am.* chicken diced and creamed with pimento or green pepper: *eating something like chicken a la king on toast points* - R.G. Kaiser.
chicken brick *Br.* earthen container for roasting chicken in its own sauce.
chicken fixings *Am.* col. 1. chicken prepared as food as contrasted with less esteemed food. 2. anything nice or better than usual in the way of food.
chicken flesh *Br.* col. /also *Br.* **goose pimples,** *Am.* **goose bumps**/ goose flesh.
chicken-fried steak *Am.* lightly battered piece of beef fried until crisp.
chicken hawk *Am., Can.* one which often prays on domestic fowls.
chicken-hearted *Am.* not brave.
chicken ranch *Am.* sl. rural brothel.
chickenshit *esp. Am., Can.* col. derog. 1. a coward. 2. adj. worthless.
chicken thief *Am.* col. petty thief.
chicken track *Am.* sl. illegible handwriting.
chicken yard *Am.* /*Br.* **fowl run**/ poultry yard.
chicklet(te), also **chicky** *Am., Can.* sl. young woman or girl: *Teenies and chicklets came into fashion* - R.L. Chapman.
chicom *Am.* adj. n. Chinese Communist.
chicory *Br.* /*Am., Can.* **endive,** *Aus.* **witlof**/ a vegetable with bitter-tasting white leaves eaten raw in salads.
chic sale *Am.* obs. an outdoor toilet.
chief *Br.* obs. boss.
chief constable *Br.* the head of a police force of some region.
Chief Executive *Am.* 1. The President of the US. 2. State Governor. 3. corporation chief.
chief inspector *Br.* a police officer ranking above inspector and below superintendent.
(the) Chief State school officer; school superintendent *Am.* /*Br.* **the Chief of Education officer; the Director of Education**/ chief of the local board of education.
chiffon *Am.* made light, esp. by adding the clear part of eggs which have been beaten.
chifforobe *Am.* wardrobe with drawers on one side and a place to hang clothes on the other.
chigger 1. *esp. Am.* jigger, metal cup used in measuring alcoholic drinks. 2. *Am., Can.* harvest mite.
chi-ike, chi-hike, chiack 1. *Aus.* cheer loudly. 2. *esp. Aus.* jeer at, tease.

child/ like a child in a sweetshop *Br.* very pleased and behaving in a silly way.
child benefit *Br.* /*Am.* **aid to families with dependent children**/ a state payment made for all the children in a family.
childminder /also **baby-minder**/ *esp. Br.* /*esp. Am., Aus.* **baby-sitter**/ person who looks after the other people's children, usu. when both parents are at work in the daytime, often at their own house: *both took turns at child-minding* - C. Handy; v. **child-mind** *esp. Br.* /*Am., Aus.* **baby-sit**/ .
child support, alimony *Am.* /*Br.* **maintenance**/.
chili *Am.* taboo. sl. adj. Mexican / **chili food, chili boots,** etc.
chili-burger *Am.* beefsteak with chili sauce.
chili dog *Am., Can.* hot dog with chilli con carne.
chill *Am.* sl. ignore, reject / also *Am.* **put the chill** (on sb.): *leave it to them to keep the psychos chilled!* - R.J. Randisi., M. Wallace., *It will nonetheless put a chill on many of those nontraditional efforts* – Time.
chill (out) *esp. Am., Can., Aus.* col. relax, take it easy: *Chill out, girl, she warned herself.* - R.L. Stine.
chiller *Am.* sl. 1. horror show or story. 2. revolver.
chilly bin *NZ.* large container for keeping food and drinks cold.
chime with *Br.* agree with.
chimney *Br.* smokestack, esp. on a ship or locomotive.
chimney breast *esp. Br.* the wall which stands out into a room with the fire in its centre: *emphatic chimney breast and acres of trailing roses over a trim little porch.* - B. Bryson.
chimney piece *Br.* mantel piece.
chimney place *Am.* an open fireplace or hearth.
chimneystack *Br.* /*Am.* **smokestack**/ one or a group of small chimneys sticking up from a roof.
chin *Am.* sl. 1. v. talk, chat: *happily chinning in the corner* - R.L. Chapman. 2. n. also **chinfest (music)** idle chatter: *I was expected to come up and chin with you after dinner.* - J. Dos Passos.
china *Am.* sl. teeth: *If you would brush your China every day, you'd be okay.* - R.A. Spears.
chinch *Am.* (bed)bug.
chin-chin *Br.* col. obs. excl. before drinking.
Chinese *Br.* col. 1. meal of Chinese food. 2. Chinese restaurant.
Chinese fire drill *Am., Can.* col. a complete mess, confusion.

Chinese leaves *Br.* /*Am.* **bak choy**/.

Chinese whispers *Br.* passing information from one person to another, and then others when information gets slightly changed each time.

chinkie, chinky *Br.* sl. derog. 1. Chinese restaurant or takeaway food service. 2. Chinese meal: *Let's grab a chinky on the way home.* - T. Thorne. 3. Chinese person.

chinless *esp. Br.* /*Am.* **weak-chinned**/ with a small chin that slopes inwards, sometimes thought as a sign of a weak character.

chinless *Br.* col. weak and cowardly.

chinless wonder *Br.* col. foolish person, esp. an upper-class male: *What you watching that chinless wonder for?* – R. Westall.

chin music *esp. Am.* col. idle chatter.

The Chinook State *Am.* Washington State.

chintzy *Am., Can.* col. (of things) cheap and poorly made; (of people) not willing to spend money.

chin-up *esp. Am., Can.* pull-up, a physical exercise of lifting one's body up to one's chin.

chinwag *esp. Br.* col. v., n. chat.

chip 1. *esp. Br., Aus.* /*Am., Aus.* **French fry, French (fried) potato,** *Can.* **French fries, chips**/ long thin piece of potato cooked in deep fat /usu. in **chip pan** (*Br.*)/: *a carton of chips and a sachet of soy sauce.* – S. Townsend. 2. *esp. Am., Can., Aus.* /also *Br.* (**potato**) **crisp,** *esp. Am., Can., Aus.* (**potato**) **chip**/ a thin piece of potato cooked in very hot fat, dried and usu. sold in packets: *chips meaning French fries if you are American.* - World Monitor. 3. *Br.* fruit basket. 4. *Am., Aus.* very thin piece of dried potato, maize, banana and other food which is eaten cold. 5. *Br.* thin woody strips used for weaving hats and baskets.

chip 1. *esp. Br.* cut (potatoes) into small pieces ready to be cooked as chips. 2. *Br.* sl. chaff, banter. 3. *Aus.* v. harrow.

chip in *Br.* /*Am., Aus.* **butt in**/ col. interrupt (a conversation) in order to say smth.

chip heater *Aus., NZ.* a water heater in a house that burns wood chips.

chip pan *Br.* /*Am.* **deep frying kettle**/ pan for making chips.

chipped beef *Am.* smoked dried beef sliced thin.

chipper *Am., Aus.* col. pert, cheerful and healthful: *Oh, but we're in a chipper mood tonight, aren't we?* - L. Waller., *Eddie Egan looking and feeling chipper once again sat in his Corvaire* - R. Moore., *He appeared at seven next morning chipper as a woodcock* - J.A. Michener.

chipper *Am.* cheer up: *he chippered them up a good deal.* - M. Twain.

chippie 1. *Am., Aus.* sl. prostitute: *So we bring this chippie up to the studio after midnight* - L. Waller., *Some chippie tried to pick me up at the bar.* - R. Moore. 2. *Br.* sl. fish and chip shop. 3. *Br.* sl. carpenter.

chippings *esp. Br.* 1. small rough pieces of stone used when putting new surfaces on roads, railway tracks, etc.: *the path had been covered with loose chippings* - B. Bryson. 2. small fragments of stone, wood or other similar materials.

chip(p)olata *Br.* a small thin sausage.

chippy *Am., Can.* col. promiscuous woman / **chippy joint** *Am.* sl. a brothel.

chippy *Can.* sl. 1. spoiling for argument. 2. rough and bad-tempered.

chippy *Br.* col. 1. fish and chips. 2. a carpenter. 3. fish-and-chip soup.

chippy *Am., Can.* (of an ice-hockey game) rough, with a lot of penalties.

chips *Am.* manure briquettes used for heating.

chips/ be in the chips *Am.* col. get rich suddenly: *You must be in the chips* – J. O'Hara.

chip/ call in one's **chips** *Br.* decide to use one's influence to gain advantage over sb.

chips/ have had one's **chips** *Br.* col. 1. said if a person is to be punished. 2. miss an opportunity to do smth. 3. have lost one's position of importance and power.

chips/ let the chips fall where they may *Am.* do smth. without thinking about its effect.

chip shop, chippy *Br.* col. fish and chips restaurant.

chirk (up) *Am.* col. cheer up: *Tom chirked up and joined in the fun himself.* - M. Twain.

chiropodist *esp. Br.* /*Am.* **podiatrist**/ person who looks after the human feet and treats diseases of the foot.

chirpy *esp. Br.* col. happy and cheerful, light-hearted: *He is much chirpier now, more active* - New Idea.

chisel *esp. Am.* col. cheat sb. out of smth.

chisel in *esp. Am.* join other people without being invited: *Those Barzini bastards keep chiseling in on my territory.* - M. Puzo.

chisel/ full chisel *Am.* at maximum speed.

chiseling *Br.* /*Am.* **chipping**/ cutting or hewing with an axe, chisel or other edged tool.

chitlin circuit *Am.* theatres, night-clubs, etc. with Negro performers: *Many audiences on the Chitlin' Circuit expected more than music* – C.R. Cross.

Chi(town) *Am.* sl. Chicago: *I was born in Chi.* - R.A. Spears.

chitter *Am.* v. twitter, chirp.
chitterlings /also **chitlings**/ *esp. Am.* the intestines of a pig eaten as food.
chitty *Br.* col. official note allowing sb. to have smth.
choc(cy) *Br.* col. a small sweet made by covering a centre such as a nut with chocolate.
choc(y) *Br.* col. adj.,n. chocolate.
choc-ice, also **choc-bar** *Br.* ice-cream encased in chocolate.
chock *Br.* support a boat, cask, etc. on chocks.
chocka *Br.* choc-a-block, crammed.
chocker 1. *Br.* col. tired of or disgusted with smth. 2. *esp. Aus., NZ.* full.
chocolate bar *Br., Can.* /*Am.* **candy bar**/.
chocolate-box(y) *Br.* derog. pretty or sentimental.
chocolate chips *Am.* /*Br.* **polka dots, chocolate vermicelli**/ chocolate sprinkles in a dessert: *Harris went to work packing chocolate-chip cookies at Nabisco.* - Reader's Digest.
chocolate frog *Aus.* sl. 1. foreigner, immigrant. 2. informer.
choice/ of choice *esp. Am., Can.* favourite or the best.
choir/ be preaching to the choir *Am.* waste time on people who already share the same views rather than approach people who oppose them.
choirboy *Am.* innocent, naive or young male.
choir loft *Br.* place of church in which the choir sits.
choir maker *Br.* /*Am.* **choir director**/ person who trains a choir.
choirman *Br.* church or cathedral choir male singer.
choke *Am.* col. be unable to do smth. useful at an important moment under pressure, esp. in sport; n. **choker**.
choke in (or **up**) *Am.* col. 1. stop talking. 2. be unable to speak as the result of emotional stress: *When one speaker after another praised John, he choked up and couldn't thank them.* - A. Makkai.
choke (sb.) **off** *Br.* sl. discourage or reject sb.
choked (**up**) *Br.* col. disgruntled, angry or upset.
choke/ choke a horse *Am.* col. be very big or larger than usual.
choked *Br.* upset.
choke point *Am., Can.* a point of congestion.
choker *Am., Can.* a cable looped round a log to drag it.
chok(e)y *Br.* obs. col. prison.
choko *Aus., NZ.* fruit of chayote.

chook *Aus., NZ.* col. 1. chicken or fowl. 2. derog. an old woman.
choom *Aus., NZ.* col. an Englishman.
choose up *Am., Can.* col. select the opponents in a game or contest.
choosy *esp. Br.* picky.
chop *Aus.* 1. woodchoppers contest. 2. part, portion.
chop 1. *Am., Can.* crushed ground grain used as animal feed. 2. *Br.* obs. trademark, brandmark of goods.
chop/ be given the chop/be for the chop, get the chop *Br.* /*Am., Aus.* **ax,** *Br.* obs. **the chuck**/ col. 1. lose a job. 2. be stopped (of a plan or service).
chop/ not much chop *esp. Aus., NZ.* col. unsatisfactory.
chop and change *esp. Br., Aus.* col. keep changing one's opinion.
chop-chop *esp. Br., Aus.* col. adv. excl. quickly, without delay; hurry up!
chopper *Br.* large square knife used for cutting meat.
chopper *Am.* 1. ticket collector or conductor. 2. woodcutter, logger.
chopper *Br.* 1. short axe with a large blade. 2. sl. penis.
chopping board *esp. Br.* /*Am.* **cutting board**/ one for chopping vegetables on in the kitchen.
chops/ bust one's **chops** *Am., Can.* col. try to do smth. very hard.
chops/ bust sb.'s **chops** *Am., Can.* annoy or be critical of sb.
chops/ lick one's **chops** *Am.* be very excited about some future event.
Chops of the Channel *Br.* passage from Atlantic Ocean to the English Channel.
chop-shop *Am., Can., Aus.* col. 1. place where stolen cars are cut or broken up into car parts for resale: *Some of the vehicles ended up in New Jersey chop shops* - J. O'Brien, A. Kurins. 2. customising workshop for cars and motorbikes.
chopsocky *Am., Can.* col. kung fu or a similar martial art.
chopsy *Br.* sl. garrulous.
chorale *esp. Am.* a choir or choral society.
choral society *Br.* group of people who sing together.
chorine *Am.* col. a chorus girl: *Better be at liberty all summer than a chorine on the road.* - J. Dos Passos.
chorister *Am.* precentor of chorus.
chow *Am.* col. food.

chow down *Am., Can., Aus.* col. eat: *we could chow down in style.* - K. Davis.
chowderhead *Am., Can.* col. a stupid person: *Don't be such a chowderhead.* - R.A. Spears.
chow line *Am.* col. line of people waiting to be served at a cafeteria, etc.: *taking my place in the "chow lines" with my aluminum tray along with the men.* - H. Truman.
chow time *Am.* col. time for taking meal.
Chrissie *Br.* col. Christmas.
christen *esp. Br.* col. use for the first time.
Christer *Am., Can.* col. very pious christian.
Christmas box *Br.* obs. small gift of money to the postman, milkman, etc. for their services during the year.
Christmas cake *Br., Aus.* a cake containing a lot of dried fruit and nuts with icing.
Christmas club *Br.* special sort of a layaway plan at the shop at Christmas.
Christmas cracker *Br.* /*Am.* **bonbon**/ a tube of brightly coloured paper which makes a noise when pulled apart by two people and contains small presents, a paper hat and a joke.
Christmas pudding *Br., Aus.* /*Am.*, or *Br.* obs. **plum pudding**/.
Christmas tree *Am.* congressional bill to which various extraneous clauses are added, typically near the end of a session in order to facilitate their passage.
chromo/ contest (take) the chromo *Am.* sl. compete with (sb.).
chronic *Br., Aus.* col. very bad, terrible: *All sorts of queer folk, carrying on with each other something chronic.* - D. Lodge.
chrysanth *Br.* col. cultivated chrysanthemum.
chuck sb. *Br.* end a romantic relationship with sb.
chuck smth. **in** *Br.* col. stop doing a job or activity that is boring or annoying: *If I didn't have to keep the job to live, I'd have chucked it in long ago.* - R.A. Spears.
chuck up *esp. Br.* sl. vomit.
chuck-a-luck *Am., Can.* a gambling game played with dice.
chucker-out *Br.* col. bouncer.
chuckhole *Am., Can.* deep depression or hole in a street or road: *Belsen is little more than a strip of heaved tarry asphalt, pocked with the chuckholes* - R.J. Randisi., M. Wallace.
chucklehead *Am.* col. stupid person.
chuck wagon *Am., Can.* a wagon equipped with a stove and provisions for cooking: *the chuckwagon races were run around them* – J. Hopkins.

chuff *Br.* make the sound of a steam train or to move making this sound; chug.
chuffed *Br., Aus.* col. pleased or happy.
chug *Am., Can.* col. /*Am.* col. **chug-a-lug**/ drink down a whole drink without stopping.
chum *Aus.* 1. (also **old chum**) native white Australian. 2. **new chum** is an emigrant to Australia.
chum *Am., Can.* chopped fish thrown overboard to attract fish.
chum up with *Br.* make friends.
chump *Br.* obs. fool.
chump /also **chump chop/steak**/ *esp. Br., Aus.* thick piece of meat with a bone through one end.
chump/ be/go off one's **chump** *Br.* col. obs. be crazy.
chump *Am.* chew (the lollipops, etc.).
chump change *Am., Can.* col. a small amount of money.
chumpish *Am.* col. 1. silly. 2. angry.
chunder *esp. Aus.* col. vomit.
chunder circuit *Aus.* sl. pub crawl.
chunk 1. *Am., Can.* divide into chunks. 2. *Am.* col. throw (smth.): *quit chunking at this darky.* – E. Caldwell. 3. *esp. Am., Can.* move with a muffled metallic sound.
a chunk of change *Am.* a lot of money.
Chunnel *Br.* col. English Channel tunnel.
chunter *Br.* col. blab on and on or complain in a low voice: *we chuntered along between wooded hills* - B. Bryson.
church *Br.* obs. (in England and Wales) belonging to the established church.
church/ a broad church *Br.* a group or organisation that includes people with very different opinions or beliefs.
churchkey *Am.* col. bottle opener.
churchwarden 1. *Am.* church administrator. 2. *Br.* a long-stemmed clay pipe.
churinga *Aus.* amulet, charm.
churn *Br.* /*Am.* **milk can**/ milk can in which milk is stored or carried from the farm.
chute/ also **choot-the-choote, chute-the-chute**/ *Am.* steep slide in amusement park: *The dignified visitors rode the shoote-the-chutes* - E.L. Doctorow.
chute the chute *Am.* coast down the steep slide.
chutty *Aus.* chewing gum.
chutzpa(h) *esp. Am.* sl. disrespectful confidence, nerve: *Where would critics and other journalists be without chutzpah* - P. Howard., *Gallo was a man of legendary chutzpah* - G. O'Neill, D. Lehr.

cider 1. *esp. Br.* /*esp. Am., Can.* **hard cider**/ an alcoholic drink made from apple juice: *Gary drank cider* - G. Greene. 2. *esp. Am., Can.* /also **soft cider, sweet cider**/ non-alcoholic apple juice.

cider/ **all talk and no cider** *Am.* much ado about nothing.

cigarette butt *Am., Aus.* /*esp. Br.* **cigarette end**/.

cigar store *Am.* /*Br.* **tobaconist's (shop)**/.

cigarette card *Br.* a small collectible picture card, that was inside packets of cigarettes in former times.

ciggy *Br.* col. a cigarette.

cilantro *esp. Am.* /*esp. Br.* **coriander**/ a plant used to give a special taste to food: *the wonderful smells of simmering menudo and fresh-cut cilantro* - R. Crais.

cinch *esp. Am., Can.* 1. a girth for a western saddle or pack. 2. fasten a piece of clothing with a belt. 3. fix (a saddle) securely. 4. make sure that smth. will happen.

cinch up *Am., Can.* pull up: *she had to cinch up the pants to their absolute maximum before tying the cord.* - R. Cook.

cinder block *Am., Can.* /*Br.* **breeze-block**/ a large, grey-coloured brick made from coal cinders and cement used in building.

cine *esp. Br.* (in comb.) related to cinematography or film industry.

cine *esp. Br.* col. cinematography.

cinecamera *Br.* movie camera.

cinema 1. *esp. Br.* /*Am., Aus.* **movie theatre, movie house**/ a theatre in which films are shown: *she cried in cinemas* - G. Greene. 2. *Br.* /also *Br.* col. **pictures**, *esp. Am., Aus., Can.* **movies**/ a showing of film. 3. *Br.* /*esp. Am., Aus., Can.* **movies**/ the art or industry of making films.

cinema goer, film goer *esp. Br.* /*esp. Am., Aus.* **movie goer**/ person who likes watching films, esp. in the cinema.

cinematograph *esp. Br.* obs. 1. projector or camera used in cinematograph. 2. the art of making films.

cineplex *esp. Am., Can.* tdmk. multiplex, a cinema with several screens.

cinnamon toast *Am., Can.* buttered toast with cinnamon and sugar.

Cinque Ports *Br.* five ports of the south-east of Britain.

cipher *Am.* zero.

cipher out *Am.* col. think (smth.) over.

circle *Br.* /*Am.* **balcony**/ an area of seats upstairs in a theatre; balcony.

circle/ **be going round in circles** *Br.* not achieve anything because one keeps coming back to the same point or problem.

circle/ **circle the wagons** *Am., Can.* col. unite in defence of a common interest.

circle/ **square the circle** *Br.* try to solve an impossible problem.

circlip *Br.* a kind of washer in the form of a partial ring.

circs *Br.* col. circumstances.

circuit 1. *Am.* an association league of sports teams. 2. *Br.* track used for motor races, horse races or athletics.

circuit/ **be on circuit** *Br.* law. (of a judge) visit several regions for several months each year.

circuit/ **do circuits or circuit training** *Br.* col. do several exercises quickly in succession in order to make sb. do sport better.

circuit court *Am.* court session held by a court travelling from one district to another.

circuitry *Am.* the detailed plan of an electric circuit.

circular file, file 13 *Am., Can.* joc. waste basket: *I took a cab to the office, circular-filed most of the mail I found waiting for me* - R.J. Randisi., M. Wallace.

circulating notes *Am.* promissory notes.

circumstance/ **mere (remote) circumstances** *Am.* worthless person or thing.

circumstance/ **not a circumstance to** *Am.* nothing compared with.

circus 1. also **roundabout** *Br.* round open area where a number of streets join together. /*Am., Aus., Can.* **traffic hub, traffic circle, rotary**/ 2. *esp. Br.* natural amphitheatre.

cirrouse *Am.* (of hair) fluffy.

cissy *Br.* col. derog. boy who looks or behaves like a girl in some way: *boys who arrive at school with "proper" speech patterns are liable to be regarded as "cissies"* - R. McRum, W. Cran, R. McNeil.

cite *Am.* law. summon to appear in court for law violation, n. **citation, cite**.

citizen *Am.* civilian.

citizenry *Am.* or *Br.* fml. the people living in a country, state or city.

citizenship papers *Am.* US naturalisation papers.

cits *Am.* col. civvies, civilian clothes.

city/ In England the word town is used much more frequently than city; a city is created by charter and has a cathedral. In the US and Canada any town is called a city if it is incorporated.

The city *Aus.* the centre of the regional capitols of Australia such as Melbourne or Sydney.

city/ the city of Angels *Am.* Los-Angeles /LA/.
city/ the city of Magnificent Distances, The Federal city, The Capital City (of a Great Nation), The City Beautiful, The City of Lost Footsteps, The Crossroads of the World, The Grand Metropolis, The Heart of America, The Political Front, The Second Rome, The City in a Forest, The Center of History in the Making, The Great Dismal, The Mighty Capital, The Wilderness City, The Capital of Miserable Hut, The City of a Thousand Thrills, The Court City of a Nation, The Foundling Capital, The Great White City, The Nation's Headquarters, The Grand Emporium of the West *Am.* Washington.
city/ the city of Monuments *Am.* Baltimore.
city/ the city of Notions, Puritan city, Highbrowville *Am.* Boston.
city/ the city of One Hundred Hills, Golden city, the city of Golden Gate, the Queen city of the Pacific (coast). *Am.* San Francisco.
city/ the city of the Falls *Am.* Louisville.
city/ the Crescent city *Am.* New Orleans: *That long ago her knowledge of the Crescent City was of the slightest* - Arthur Hailey.
city /The Empire city, Father Knickerbocker, The Fun city, Gotham, The Bagdad on the Hudson, The City of Golden Dreams, The City of Towers, The Host of the World, The Mighty Manhattan, The Port of Many Ports, The Hub of Transport, The Big Apple, The Metropolis, The Money Town, The Wonder City, The Science City, The Big Burg, The City of Superlatives, The Frog and Toe, The Melting Pot, The Super City, The Vacation City, The World's Fair City, The Babylonian Bedlam *Am.* New York: *Fun City needs a lot more policemen and street cleaners than it has.* - H.C, Whitford., R.J. Dixson.
city/ City of Lakes *Am.* Minneapolis, Minn.
city/ City of Roses *Am.* Portland, Ore.
city/ City of Trees *Am.* Boise, Idaho.
city /the Flower of Cities All *Br.* London.
city/ the Forest city *Am.* Cleveland.
city/ the Garden city, Windy city *Am.* Chicago /Chi/.
city/ the Gate city (of the South) *Am.* Atlanta.
city/ the Quaker's city, the city of Brotherly love, Philly *Am.* Philadelphia: *this "City of Brotherly Love" which William Penn had founded* - H.S. Truman.
city/the Queen city of the Lakes *Am.* Buffalo.
city/ the Queen city of the Mississippi *Am.* Saint Louis.
city/ the Queen city of the West *Am.* Cincinnati.
city/ the Smoky city *Am.* Pittsburgh.
city/ municipal government *Am.* /*Br.* corporation/.
city article *Br.* newspaper article on economic and financial matters.
city centre *Br., Aus.* /*Am.* down town/ business centre of a city.
city desk 1. *Am.* local news column in a newspaper: *I've watched those city-desk reporters* - R.J. Randisi., M. Wallace. 2. *Br.* the department of newspaper which deals with finances.
city editor 1. *Am., Can.* one editing local news: *My city editor had made the assignment.* - Guideposts. 2. *Br.* one editing (City) financial news.
city farm *esp. Br.* experimental farm within urban area set for educational purposes.
city father *esp. Am.* pomp. member of the governing body of the city: *she had placated the city fathers* - T. Wilder.
city-folk *Am.* townspeople, townsfolk.
city gent *Br.* col. typical busunessman, like those working in the City.
city hall *esp. Am., Can.* (public building used for) a city's local government: *You can't beat city hall, in Russia as in America* - Y. Richmond.
city man *Br.* financier.
city manager *Am., Can.* official employed by an elected council to direct the administration of a city government.
city page *Br.* a section of a newspaper that deals with finances.
city planning *Am.* /*Br.* town planning/ study of the way city works in order to provide more efficient municipal services, roads, houses, etc.
city slicker *esp. Am.* col. shrewd and modish urban person, esp. as distinct from the honest and gullible provincial: *A friend told me about a farmer who sold a horse to a city slicker for three times the going price.* - Reader's Digest.
citywide *esp. Am.* involving all the areas of a city.
civics *esp. Am.* a school subject dealing with the rights and duties of citizens and the way government works: *take one course in social studies (American history, civics, or government) and one in literature or language arts* – Living in the USA.
civil block *Can.* town hall building.
civil righter (rightist) *Am.* col. advocate of civil rights.
civvy *Br.* sl. (used mostly by military) non-military person.

civvy street *Br.* col. obs. ordinary life not connected with armed forces.

clabber *esp. Am.* 1. sour milk that has thickened and curdled. 2. (of a milk) curdle.

cladding 1. *Br.* covering of any kind on a structure. 2. *Am.* metal covering on a structure.

clag *Aus.* a type of glue.

claim *Am., Aus.* a tract of land staked out.

claim *Br.* ask to be returned the value of the bought goods that happened to be of poor quality.

claim against tax *Br.* take as deduction.

claimant *Br.* person receiving money from the state because they're unemployed or unable to work because of sickness.

claiming race *Am., Can.* one in which a claim to buy at a stipulated price any of the horses running can be entered before the race.

claim jumper *Am., Can.* person who appropriates a mining claim taken by another.

clam *Am.* 1. derog. stingy person. 2. also *Can.* col. a dollar: *Otherwise three thousand clams.* - H. Fast. 3. col. person who doesn't say what they are thinking or feeling.

clam/ as happy as a clam *Am.* col. very happy.

clam/ clam, go clamming *esp. Am., Can.* gather clams, esp. by digging in the sand or mud.

clambake *esp. Am., Can.* 1. informal party by the sea, esp. one where clams, etc., are cooked and eaten: *I looked for you at the clambake at the beach.* - R.L. Stine. 2. sl. noisy, high-spirited party or political meeting: *the whole clambake was called off.* - J. O'Brien, A. Kurins.

clamp *Br. /Am.* **(Denver) boot/** fasten a piece of equipment onto the wheel of a car that has been parked illegally so that it can not be moved.

clamper *Can.* shore ice.

clanger, brick *esp. Br., Aus.* col. blunder or foolish remark / **drop a clanger, brick** also **clang** *Br., Aus.* col. make a mistake.

clap/ give sb. **a clap** *Br.* give sb. a round of applause.

clap eyes on (sb.) *Br.* col. see.

clapboard *esp. Am., Can. /Br.* **weatherboard/**, overlapping planks: *Plymouth is a red-brick and white clapboard town* - New Yorker., *The clapboard sheets were erected.* - L. Uris, *A group of clapboard houses appeared in the clearing.* - E. Acosta.

Clapham/ the man/woman on the Clapham omnibus *Br.* obs. typical British person.

clapped-out *esp. Br., Aus.* col. 1. (of a thing) old and worn out. 2. (of a person) very tired: *In the early 1980s many American businesses saw Europe as the clapped-out old world.* - Economist.

clapper *Br.* piece of equipment used by farmers that makes a noise to frighten birds away.

clapper bridge *Br.* roughly built bridge, esp. of planks and slats.

clappers/ (go/run/work) like the clappers *Br., Aus.* col. (do it) very fast.

clash *Br., Aus.* overlapping of two things, such as two subjects at school, so that they can't be done together.

class 1. *esp. Am.* group of pupils or students entering a school together and graduating in the same year: *I am glad that you're enjoying the class.* – R.L. Stine. 2. *Am. /Br.* **course/** a set of classes one attends to study a special subject: *classes typically meet once a week for four to eight sessions* – Reader's Digest. 3. *Br.* one of three levels into which university degree is divided according to the quality of work. 4. *Aus. /Am., Can.* **grade,** *Br.* **form/**.

class/ in class *Br.* during the class.

class/ take a class *Br.* teach class.

class act esp. *Am., Can.* col. high quality act: *Mechanically, this car is a class act.* - Fortune.

class action, suit *esp. Am., Can.* lawsuit set up by a group of people for their own advantages and also for that of all others with the same complaint: *a class-action lawsuit by black customers* - USA Today., *class-action suits contending they were not paid properly for their time on the job* - Nation's Restaurant News.

class book *Am.* 1. book in which a teacher records the absences and keeps the grades of students. 2. an album of the class.

class day *Am.* day on which the members of a class celebrate their graduation with special ceremonies.

classification *Am.* defining of a degree of confidentiality.

classification estimate *Am.* qualification estimate.

classified (ad) *Br. /Am.* **small ad, want ad/**.

classified directory *Br.* book that gives a list of the addresses and telephone numbers of companies under the title of their job or business.

classify *esp. Am.* officially declare secret.

class list *Br.* list dividing people who have taken university examinations into classes according to their results.

class officer; monitor *Am. /Br.* **group representative; head boy/girl; prefect/** monitor of class at school.

claw back *esp. Br.* (of a government) get back (money given to the public in tax cuts) by means of increases in other forms of tax: *we* should pay it to everyone and then claw it back progressively for those that don't need them. - C. Handy. **clawback** n.

claypan 1. *Am.* layer of clay in the soil. 2. *Aus.* shallow hole (depression) in the surface of the ground having a bottom of clay or silt.

clay pigeon shooting *Br.* /*Am.* **skeet shooting**/.

Clayton's *Aus., NZ.* col. largely illusory.

clean *esp. Br.* an act of cleaning smth.

clean *Am.* sl. penniless, broke.

clean/ (as) clean as a new pin *Br.* very clean.

clean/ clean sb.'s **clock** *Am., Can.* col. beat sb.

clean/ clean house *Am., Can.* do housework.

clean/ show sb. **a clean pair of heels** *esp. Br.* 1. obs. go faster than sb. else; win clearly and decisively. 2. journalism. show that one particular organisation is much better than others.

clean up *esp. Am.* wash (oneself): *Let's check with the doctor first and clean up* – J. Hopkins.

clean up *esp. Am.* sl. win a lot of money: *Rizzo could "clean up real good."* – A. Summers, R. Swan; n. **clean-up**.

clean up on *Am.* col. 1. make a profit on (smth.): *The company cleaned up on their recent business arrangement.* - Longman. 2. also *Can.* defeat (sb.): *The fighter cleaned up on his opponent.* - Longman.

cleaner *Am.* cleaner's: *she lived on Central Avenue and Twenty-first Street above a cleaners.* – E. James, D. Ritz.

cleaners/ take sb. **to the cleaners** *Br.* col. take a lot of sb.'s money, esp. in a business deal or in gambling.

cleanout door *Am.* ash box door in a boiler.

clean sailing *Am.* easy task.

clean sheet 1. *esp. Br.* a new shirt. 2. *Br.* no goals missed (in football).

cleansing/ the cleansing department (of the town council) *Br.* one responsible for removing household rubbish and keeping the streets clean.

cleanskin (clearskin) *Aus.* 1. unbranded animal. 2. col. person without a police record.

the clean thing *Am.* honesty, sincerity.

clean-up *esp. Am.* sl. a very large profit: *Johnson didn't care whether you were the clean-up guy or who you were* – D.L. Barlett, J.B. Steele.

clear/be a certain amount **clear of** competitor *Br.* be that amount ahead of them in a competition or race.

clear/ see clear *esp. Am.* see smth. that's a long way away clearly, e.g. *see clear to the mountains.*

clear off 1. *Am.* clear plates, knives, etc. from a table: *Please help your mother to clear off.* - Longman. 2. *Br.* col. leave a place quickly.

clear to *esp. Am., Can.* all the way through.

clearcut *Am.* area of forest that has been completely cut down.

clear-eyed *esp. Am.* seeing smth. correctly.

clearer, clearing bank *Br.* a bank which is a member of clearing house.

clear majority *Br.* majority (absolute majority or more than 50% of the votes).

clearout *esp. Br.* col. an act of clearing something out.

clearway *esp. Br.* 1. no parking thoroughfare. 2. an area by the road where cars can only stop when in difficulties. 3. a stretch of road that is of **A-road** status, on which traffic may stop only in an emergency.

cleats *Am.* football boots.

cleft stick/ in a cleft stick *esp. Br., Aus.* in a difficult position.

clerk *Am., Can.* 1. /also **salesclerk**/ person who works in a shop selling things: *Clerks in shops assume it as a fringe benefit* - R.G. Kaiser. 2. /also **desk clerk**/ a receptionist.

clerk *esp. Am., Can.* 1. col. act or work as a clerk: *Caldwell who will be clerking for a federal judge next year* - New York.

clerk of (the) works *Br.* the person in charge of building operation in a particular place: *Visitors were stunned to see the Clerk of works standing in the middle* - Reader's Digest.

clever 1. *esp. Br.* intelligent. 2. *Br.* col. healthy or well.

clever/ too clever by half *esp. Br.* col. 1. too sure of one's cleverness in a way that offends other people. 2. skilful at doing a particular thing. 3. used jokingly when sb. has done smth. silly or stupid.

clever dick, also **clever-clogs** *esp. Br., Aus.* col. humor. /*Aus.* **clever boots**/ know-it-all, wise guy: *The exhibition has all the hallmarks of a rushed and ill-considered job, knocked together by a clever-clogs rather than an art historian.* - Evening Standard, T. Thorne.

clever-clever *Br.* trying to appear to have an able mind.

cliché *esp. Br.* print. a stereotype or electrotype.

click for *Br.* col. manage to get something: *At last I've clicked for a good job in the right city.* - Longman.

clicker *esp. Am., Can.* a remote control keypad.

clicks *Br.* brief atmospherics in radio communications.

cliffdweller *Am.* joc. resident of a tall apartment house, high-rise dweller: *Joe and Nancy have become cliffdwellers - they moved up to the 30th floor.* - A. Makkai.

climate *Am.* acclimate.

climb down *Br., Aus.* admit to having made a mistake or to change an opinion in an argument; **climb-down.**

climbing frame *Br.* /*Am., Aus.* **jungle gym,** *Am.* **climber**/ large frame made of bars for children to climb on: *it was just a climbing-frame* - B. Bryson.

clingfilm *esp. Br.* tdmk. /*Am.* **Saran wrap,** *Am., Aus.* **plastic wrap**/ thin transparent plastic put round foods to keep them fresh.

clinic *esp. Br.* 1. a. building where specialised medical treatment and advice is given to outpatients: *Mary gets back from the Family Planning Clinic* – S. Townsend. b. occasion when this treatment is given. 2. occasion when medical students are taught by watching the treatment of sick people. 3. meeting held by a skilled or professional person to which people bring their problems: *He continued to be active in education and was on the faculty of several summer clinics.* – I. Carr, D. Fairweather, B. Priestley.

clinic, private hospital *esp. Am.* /*Br.* **nursing home**/ a small hospital in an area far away from large cities.

clinic 1. *esp. Am., Can.* a conference or short course on some subject: *Apparently Vitas had been in the Hamptons to play in a tennis clinic.* – Reader's Digest. 2. *Am.* a place where medical treatment is given at a low cost: *I won't be able to come down for the Wednesday clinics* – J. O'Hara. 3. *Am.* /*Br.* **practice**/ a group of doctors who work together and share the same offices.

clink *Br.* sl. money: *I'm a bit short of clink.* - T. Thorne.

clinker 1. *Br.* sl. first-rate thing. 2. *Am.* col. wrong note, mistake. 3. *Am., Can.* col. or *Br.* obs. utter failure, flop, a thing of poor quality: *Jim refused to have anything to do with this clinker* - Tattler, T. Thorne., *I could turn out clinkers too.* – N. Hentoff.

clinking *Br.* col. very good.

clip 1. *Br.* remove a piece of bus or train ticket to show that it has been used. 2. *esp. Am., Can.* swindle or rob. 3. *esp. Am.* col. travel or pass rapidly.

clip *Br.* col. v. n. (hit) a glancing blow with an open hand, smack, also clip(sb.) round the ear(hole).

clip 1. *esp. Am.* newspaper cutting: *office was faxing Linder newspaper clips about the death.* - New York. 2. *Aus., NZ.* total amount of wool from a group of sheep at one time.

clip/ **at a clip** *Am.* col. at a time, per each item, all at once.

clipper *Br.* sl. first-rate thing or person.

clippie *Br.* col. person employed to take the passengers payments on a bus: *Busmen and clippies were all cheering, they really dug us.* - P. Norman.

clipping *esp. Am.* /*Br.* **cutting**/ newspaper cutting: *And she keeps sending me clippings from Johnstown* - B. Kaufman.

clipping bureau (agency) *Am.* /*Br.* **press cutting agency**/.

cllr *Br.* councillor.

cloakroom 1. also **cloaks, public convenience** *esp. Br.* euph. /*Am.* **restroom, comfort station**/ toilet, esp. in a public building or a downstairs room in sb.'s house containing a toilet: *She slipped into a public cloakroom, changed her appearance* - A. Christie., *cloakrooms hurt her at first* - D.H. Lawrence., *I changed and shaved in the cloakroom* - D. Francis. 2. *Am.* an anteroom, a meeting place for gossip and informal exchange of views: *I turned away from that long line of serious faces and entered the Senate cloakroom* - H. Truman., hence **cloakroom talk** is *Am.* for lobby talk in political context.

clobber *esp. Br., Aus.* col. 1. the belongings that one carries around with one. 2. clothes. 3. kit, tools and equipment or clothes for the job, e.g. *fishing, swimming, football clobber.*

clobber *Br.* adorn and ornament lavishly.

clock *Br.* a downy spherical seed head, esp. of a dandelion.

clock *esp. Br.* col. 1. person's face. 2. strike; hit on the head / esp. in **clock** (sb.) **one**: *Karamzin... clocked open one of the cases.* - A. Burgess. 3. look at, see: *Villains call it clocking in Leeds* - Sunday Times, T. Thorne. 4. sl. wind back the milometer of a motor vehicle illegally; a **clocker** is a person who does it.

clock on, clock off *Br., Aus.* record the time when a person arrives at work and when they leave.

clock up *esp. Br.* win or achieve (a large number of similar things).

clock/ **clean** sb.'s **clock** *Am.* col. defeat sb. thouroughly.

clock/ **clock this/that!** *Br.* col. pay attention.

clock/ **run out** /*Am.* **kill**/ **the clock** *Am., Aus.* keep possession of the ball until the end of game to prevent the other to win any more points.

clock/ **set the clock(s) ahead** *Am.* /*Br.* **put**/ **turn the clock(s) on, forward**/ change the time shown on a clock to a time one or two hours later at the beginning of summer; opp. / *Am.* **set the clock(s) back**, *esp. Br.* **put/turn the clock(s) back/**

clock/ sleep the clock round *Br.* sleep at least 12 hours.

clocker *Am.* col. a drug dealer.

clock-house *Am.* entrance gate office, control post.

clock winder *Am.* stem of a clock

clod *Br.* 1. coarse cut of meat from the lower neck of an ox. 2. sl. penny, copper coin.

clodhopper *Am.* sl. old vehicle suitable only for short local passages.

clog *Br.* 1. sl. v. kick. 2. also **cloggy** Dutch person.

clogger *Br.* col. a footballer who often fouls when tackling sb.

clogs/ pop one's **clogs** *Br.* col. humor. die: *they pop their clogs - even Herbert Hoover* - B. Bryson.

clonk /also **clunk**/ *Am.* sl. strike: *they had clonked each other* - B. Robinson.

close *Br.* 1. road closed at one end. 2. dead-end residential area.

close *Am.* /*Br.* **bolt**/ print. any folded edge of a section other than the binding fold.

close down 1. *Am.* get closer, settle: *I pursued her at a hard walk, closing down the distance between us.* - S. Grafton. 2. *Br.* end radio or TV transmission for the day.

close out *Am.* 1. try and get rid of (goods) by selling them at reduced prices: *he decided to close out the New York operation.* - M. Puzo. 2. also *Can.* bring smth. to an end: *you close out a credit card account.* – S. Orman.

close with *Br.* 1. agree with (sb.) or to (smth.). 2. begin a fight or battle.

close/ close but no cigar *Am., Aus.* humor. not close enough; almost but not quite successful.

close/ Close the door, please *Br.* All aboard.

close/ close the stable door after the horse has bolted *Br.* /*Am.* **close the barn door after the horse has gone/** be too late to take action by a certain time.

close /near thing/close run thing *Br.* /*Am., Aus.* **close call/** smth. that has almost happened.

close-coupled *esp. Br.* (of two parts) attached or fixed close together.

closedown *esp. Br.* the end of a period of broadcasting.

closed-end *Am., Can.* (of investment trust or company) issuing a fixed number of shares.

closed season *esp. Am., Can.* /*Br.* **close season/** for hunting or fishing certain animals, birds or fish: *The 12th of August...is the end of the "close season."* - J. Ruppeldtova.

close-in *Am., Can.* near to the centre of a town or city.

close-out *Am.* /*Aus.* **sell-off**/ sale when the price of goods is reduced so that they can be sold quckly

closeout sale/price *Am.* getting rid of goods cheaply.

close season *Br.* period in summer when football teams don't play important games.

closet 1. *esp. Am., Can.* /*esp. Br.* **cupboard, wardrobe**/ cupboard built into the wall of a room and going from floor to ceiling: *We had a closet full of T- shirts* - J. Baez., *a man whose cares centred around library and book, rather than closet and wardrobe.* - M. Torgov. 2. *esp. Am.* and *Br.* obs. a very small storage room, esp. one without windows.

closing time *Br.* time when the shop or pub stop working and close for the day.

clot *esp. Br.* col. stupid person, fool: *You incredible clot.* - J.P. Donleavy., *the British are that faceless clot you don't know* - J. Steinbeck.

cloth/ cut one's **coat (according) to** one's **cloth** *esp. Br.* take account of available resources.

cloth/ cut from the same cloth *Am.* identical.

cloth/ make up smth. **out of whole cloth** *Am.* col. be not true.

clothcap *Br.* 1. a men's flat woollen cap with a peak. 2. adj. of or belonging to the working class.

cloth-eared *Br.* col. deaf; **cloth ears** *Br.* derog. or humor. a deaf man.

cloth ears/ have cloth ears *Br.* not pay attention to smth. important.

clothes/ the king's new clothes *Br.* pretending to understand and admire smth. that is not really sensible or special.

clothes/ steal sb.'s **clothes** *Br.* journalim. use other people's ideas.

clothes/ store clothes *Am.* ready-made clothes.

clothes basket *esp. Br.* large bin for dirty clothes.

clothes closet *Am.* wardrobe.

clothes hoist *Aus.* a rotary clothes drier.

clotheshorse 1. *esp. Am.* person who dresses very showily: *Her brother is the real clotheshorse.* - R.A. Spears. 2. *Br.* special frame for drying clothes.

clothespeg *Br., Aus., Can.* /*Am.* **clothespin**/ small forked instrument used for holding wet wooden clothes on a clothesline for drying: *all stuck on the line with wooden clothspins* - J. Baez., *Scaffold and builder's cranes protruded* *everywhere like clothespegs hung on the city's skyline.* - L. Van Der Post.

clothes prop *Br.* clothes pole.

clothes rack *Am.* clotheshorse / In Britain clothes rack hangs from the ceiling.

clothing store *Am.* /*Br.* **draper's**/ shop dealing in cloth, clothing: *But there was much more – including where my parents had come from in Russia, and the name of that men's clothing store.* – N. Hentoff.

clotted cream *esp. Br.* thick cream made by slowly heating milk and taking the cream from the top.

cloture *Am.* closure of session or debate in political assemblies.

cloud/ on cloud nine *esp. Am., Can.* sl. very happy: *Susan was on cloud nine.* - New Idea.

cloud-cuckooland *esp. Br.* derog. an imaginary place of unreal dreams and impossible perfection, esp. in **be (living) in cloud-cuckoo land.**

clout *esp. Br.* a hard hit: *She gave him a clout on the snoot* - R.L. Chapman.

clove *Am.* cliff /in proper names/.

cloverleaf *esp. Am., Can.* the network of curved roads intersecting at different levels formig a four-leaved clover.

club/ ball club *Am.* baseball club.

club/ go clubbing *Br.* go regularly to nightclubs: *they went clubbing.* – S. Lawrence.

club/ in the (pudding) club *esp. Br.* col. pregnant.

club/ join the club Br. /*Am., Aus.* **welcome to the club**/ col. now you know it you're in the same bad situation.

club/ club together *Br.* give money together towards the cost of smth.

clubbable *Br.* obs. sociable.

clubbie *Aus.* col. voluntary life-saving team member.

clubcar *esp. Am., Can.* car on a passenger train with swivel or movable armchairs frequently with a buffet or bar.

club class *Br.* the intermediate class of seating on an aircraft, esp. for businessmen.

club-hammer *Br.* mallet.

club-land *Br.* most popular night clubs in St. James and Piccadilli areas and people who go there.

clubman *Am.* playboy.

clubmobile *Am.* bus or truck used as a travelling canteen or club to serve soldiers, workers, firemen or disaster victims.

club sandwich *Am., Can.* three pieces of bread with layers of meat and salad between them: *I loosened my tie, sat down, and ordered a club sandwich and beer.* - J. Kellerman.

club soda *Am., Can.* /*Br.* **soda water**/ soda drink.

club subscription *Br.* dues.

cluck *esp. Am., Can.* col. 1. blockhead, fool: *Why did they send me a dumb cluck to do this work?* - R.A. Spears. 2. worthless thing: *Poor dumb cluck, Martha said.* – P. Roth.

clucky *Aus.* col. 1. (of a hen) sitting on eggs. 2. (of a woman) broody, pregnant.

clue/ have no clue *Am.* col. not know anything about the subject.

clued-in esp. *Am., Can.* col. /*Br., Aus.* **clued-up**/ (about/on smth.) knowing a lot about smth.: *How do you get clued in?* - W. Magnuson, *Could you clue me in?* – N. Hentoff; v. **clue in, up**.

clueless *esp. Br., Can., Aus.* col. 1. helpless, stupid: *a no-show for the network's best of the youth soaps, Party of Five. How clueless.* - USA Today.

clunch *Br.* soft limestone that could be easily worked.

clunk *Am.* col. 1. stupid person: *scheming maids who have been working on the poor clunks all spring* - R.L. Chapman. 2. old car or truck: *Look at that fuckin' broad in the clunk next to us* - Rolling Stone, R.L. Chapman. 3. also **clonk** v. hit.

clunker *Am., Can.* col. 1. smth. very old and almost falling apart, esp. a car. 2. a complete failure.

clunkhead *Am.* col. a fool.

clunky *Am.* 1. also *Aus.* col. rumbling, lumbering: *she's rather clunky and anxious* - New York. 2. sl. ponderous and inefficient: *The clunky plot continues to be riddled with implausibilities* - New Yorker.

clunky *esp. Am., Can.* col. solid, heavy, and old-fashioned.

cluster *Am.* small piece of metal pinned to a soldier's uniform to show a high class of honour.

clutch *Am.* 1. col. reliable. 2. sl. crucial or decisive.

clutch *Am.* clutch bag, a type of handbag.

clutch/ in the clutch/ in a clutch situation, when it comes to the clutch *Am.* in a difficult situation.

clutch release bearing *Br.* clutch throwout bearing.

C-note, Century-note *Am.* col. a hundred dollar bill: *he was depositing a C-note* - W. Jack, B. Laursen.

Co *Br., Am.* county.

coach 1. *esp. Br.* /*Am., Aus.* **bus**/ bus used for long-distance travel or touring: *the coach services are good.* - P. Howard., *11 Britons were killed on a holiday coach in France.* - Economist., *I should catch the first coach to London in the morning.* - G. Greene. 2. *Aus.* farm cow used for attracting wild cattle into a trap. 3. *Am.* house trailer. 4. *Am.* automobile body, esp. of a closed model. 5. *esp. Am.* /*esp. Br.* **sofa**/ sofa, settee. 6. *Br.* /also *Br.* **carriage,** *Am.* **car**/ one of separate sections of a train that carries passengers: *There were two third-class coaches connected to the Wagon-Lit* – M. Daly. 7. *esp. Br.* /*Am.* **tutor**/ sb. who gives special instruction to a student in a particular subject, esp. so that they can pass an exam, v.

coach/ drive a coach and horses through smth. *esp. Br.* destroy smth. or make it useless.

coach (**class**) *Am., Can.* now rare. second class on a plane or train; cheapest places there: *By 1995 the system will even be in coach sections, he says.* - USA Today.

coach bolt *Br.* /*Am.* **carriage bolt**/ a large bolt with a round head, used mainly for fixing wooden panels to masonry.

coach-built *Br.* (of a vehicle) having specially built bodywork to satisfy customer's needs made by **coach builder.**

coaching stock *Br.* passenger equipment on a train.

coachload *Br.* as much as a coach can hold.

coach park *Br.* open place where coaches may be parked, sometimes for a small payment.

coach station *Br.* /the building(s) at/ a place where coach starts and finishes its journey and where passengers can get on and off: *the coach was waiting for two hours at the coach station.* – S. Townsend.

coachwork *Br.* the body of a car, esp. its outside surface where covered with paint.

coal car *Am.* 1. an open railroad car designed for carrying coal: *He sought to hide in a coal-car* – M. Daly. 2. car for carrying coal in a mine or away from it.

coalface *esp. Br., Aus.* the place where a particular job is actually done, not just talked about, esp. at the phr. **at the coalface.**

coalhole *esp. Br.* coal bin, small usu. underground room where coal is stored.

coal oil, lamp oil *Am., esp. Can.* /*Br.* **paraffin,** *Am., Aus.* **kerosene, -ine**/.

coals *Br.* pieces of the fuel used for burning.

coals/ selling, carrying, taking, etc. **coals to Newcastle** *Br.* take smth. to a place where there is already plenty of it.

coals/ rake over the coals/the ashes *esp. Am.* /*Br.* **haul** sb. **over the coals**/ talk about smth. that happened in the past which one would rather forget or ignore.

coal whipper *Br.* person or machine that raises coal from the hold of a ship to unload it.

coarse fish *Br.* (the meat of) any fish that lives in lakes or rivers, except salmon; **coarse** relates to the sport of angling such fish.

the Coast *Am., Can.* the region lying near the Pacific ocean: *George stayed in New York for a couple of days before returning to the Coast.* - A.E. Hotchner.

coast *Am., Can.* 1. a hill or slope down which one may roll. 2. a trip down such a hill or slope.

coast *Am.* 1. col. do smth. without great effort, do smth. easily: *In that job Ellis just coasts along and hardly lifts a finger.* - H.C. Whitford., R.J. Dixson., *he could coast on* – P. Roth. 2. slide down a hill on a sledge.

coaster 1. *Am., Can.* small vehicle used for coasting down the hill or slope. 2. *Am.* roller-coaster. 3. *Aus.* col. tramp. 4. *Br.* a ship that sails along the coast taking goods to ports.

coaster brake *Am.* brake on some bicycles that works by moving the pedals backwards.

coat *Br.* obs. or *Am.* col. jacket: *a proper coat and a tie.* - W. Jack., B. Lawrsen.

coat/ be all fur and no knickers *Br.* never fulfil the promises.

coat/ trail one's **coat** *Br.* risk starting an argument.

coat check, coatroom *Am., Can.* a cloakroom with an attendant where sb. can leave their coat temporarily (**coat checker**): *Why are you pushing me into the coat room?* - R.L. Stine.

coatee 1. *Br.* short coat (of women or infants). 2. *Am.* short coat with tails.

Coat Hanger City *Aus.* Sydney.

coat peg *Br.* coat hook (on the back of the door).

coat-room *Am., Can.* cloakroom.

coattail *Am.* adj. based on another person's achievement or quality.

coattails/ on sb.'s **coattails** *esp. Am., Can.* col. with the help of another, esp. in politics: *Making a movie with Doris was a piece of cake - a sexy ride on her coattails* - A.E. Hotchner.

coat-trailing *Br.* 1. provocative conduct. 2. adj. provoking, provocative.

cob *Br.* 1. wall material (a mixture of clay, gravel, or straw). 2. a small round loaf of bread.

cob/ have/get a cob on *Br.* col. get annoyed or feel bad.

cobber *Aus., NZ.* col. friend.
cobble *esp. Br.* lump coal, the size of smallish cobblestone.
cobble *esp. Br.* mend or patch coarsely.
cobbler 1. *esp. Am.* fruit pie baked in a deep dish, usu. with a crust on top: *Yer grandma's cooking' us a big peach cobbler* - Guideposts. 2. *Aus., NZ.* the last sheared sheep.
cobblers 1. *Br., Aus.* col. foolish talk, nonsense (esp. in the phr. **a load of (old) cobblers**: *He's dismissive about awards: "A load of cobblers."* - Observer, T. Thorne. 2. *Br.* col. a man's testicles.
cobmeal *Am.* a meal of corn and corncobs ground up.
cobwebs/ blow away the cobwebs *Br., Aus.* obs. get some fresh air.
cock/ cock (smth.) **up** *Br.* sl. spoil or ruin (arrangements, plans, etc.): *Seems like I've cocked it up.* - J. Higgins.
cock/ live like fighting cocks *esp. Br.* col. live very well, esp. eating very good food.
cock 1. *Br.* col. term of address (used by men to men): *Gotcha that time, didn't, old cock?* - S. Sheldon. 2. *esp. Br.* col. bold behaviour. 3. *esp. Br. /Am., Aus.* **rooster/** a male chicken. 4. *Br.* col. nonsense, rubbish. 5. *Br.* sl. penis: *Drop your cocks and grab your socks.* - K. Vonnegut, Jr. 6. *Br.* a male lobster, crab, or salmon.
cock smth. **up** *Br.* col. spoil smth.
cock/ cock one's **snook / snoot (to/at)** *Br.* col. thumb one's nose.
the cock of the walk *Br.* obs. obs. derog. a very important person.
cock-a-hoop 1. *Am.* col. adj. n. in disorder, very untidy. 2. *Br.* col. obs. /also *Br.* **cock/** extremely pleased.
cockamamie *esp. Am., Aus.* col. 1. n. adj. absurd, crazy, ridiculous, inconceivable: *Somewhere in our cockamamie cultural history we of the West decided boredom is bad.* - R. Palley. *It's one cockamamie little amendment.* - L. Waller., *a cockamamie idea that there is this thing called Mafia* - J. O'Brien, A. Kurins. 2. (smth.) worthless.
cock and bull story *Br.* col. unbelievable story or excuse.
The Cockade State *Am.* Maryland.
cockatoo *Aus., NZ.* 1. col. the owner of a small farm. 2. sl. person posted as a look-out, esp. by criminals.
cockatoo fence *Aus.* one made of raw logs.
cocked hat *Am.* a game resembling bowling.
cocked hat/ knock smth. **into a cocked hat** *Br.* col. obs. defeat or spoil completely.

cockerel *Br.* young tough.
cockeyed *esp. Am.* col. obs. drunk.
cockeye(d) bob *Aus., NZ.* col. short storm.
cockie *Aus.* a farmer renting land.
cockle *Am.* small shell-shaped candy of sugar and flour with a motto rolled up inside.
cockling *Br.* activity of gathering cockles.
cock metal *Am.* metal used for making **faucets**.
cockpaddle *Br.* lumpfish.
cocksman *Am.* taboo. sl. macho man, esp. one who is sexually attractive.
cocksucker *esp. Am.* taboo. sl. a general term of abuse.
cocktail sausage *Am.* small thin, esp. pork sausage.
cocktail stick *Br.* a special pointed stick for serving some small items of food, like olives, cherries, etc.
cocktail waitress *Am.* waiter serving cocktails in a bar.
cock-up *Br.* taboo. sl. confused state of affairs, example of complete disorder or smth. done badly: *Made some bloody cockup, I expect.* - D. Reeman; v. **cock up**.
cocky *Aus., NZ.* col. 1. a cockatoo. 2. farmer with a small piece of farmland.
coco *Br.* sl. black or coloured person.
cocomat *Am.* /*Br.* **coconut matting/** rough material used to cover floors that is made from outer part of a coconut shell.
coconut 1. *Br.* sl. an Uncle Tom. 2. *Am.* sl. a dollar.
coconut ice *Br.* a sweet made from sugar and dessicated coconut.
coconut shy, shies *Br.* game of knocking coconuts off posts by a ball, often played at a fair.
COD *Am., Can.* collect on delivery: *I told the saleslady to send the package C.O.D.* - H.C. Whitford., R.J. Dixson.
cod *Br.* sl. 1. make a fool of (sb.): *You're not codding me* - J.P. Donleavy., *Don't you think you can cod an old trooper like me?* - W.S. Maugham. 2. n. parody: *It was only for cod.* - J. Joyce.
code/ bring smth. **up to code** *Am., Can.* renovate an old building up to the latest building regulations.
codependency *esp. Am., Can.* an emotional dependency on supporting or caring for another person or people.
codet *Am.* print. a colour control bar.
codling *Am.* hake.
cods *Br.* sl. testicles.
codswallop *Br.* or *Aus.* col. nonsense: *Equal opportunities? That's a load of old codswallop!* - T. Thorne.

coed *Am., Can.* col. female student in a college open to both sexes: *I never will forget one little blonde coed* - Alex Haley.
co-ed team *Am.* /*Br.* **mixed team**/.
C of E *Br.* Church of England.
coffee *Br.* a cup of coffee.
coffee/ wake up and smell the cofffee *esp. Am.* be more realistic and aware of the situation.
coffee and cake(s) *Am.* small salary: *I'm singing for coffee and cakes at a crib* – J. O'Hara. / **coffee and cakes job,** etc.
coffee bar *Br.* place where light meals, cakes and non-alcoholic drinks are served.
coffee break *esp. Am.* /*Br.* **elevenses** in the morning or **tea** in the afternoon/ short pause from work in the morning or afternoon for a drink, a rest, etc.: *you go for a coffee break.* - J. DeFelice., *Half hour for lunch. Two coffee breaks.* - Guideposts.
coffee cake 1. *Br., Aus.* one made with sugar, eggs, flour and butter that is flavoured with coffee. 2. *Am., Can., Aus.* a type of sweet bread which is made with nuts or fruit.
coffee cream *Am.* /*Br.* **single cream**/.
coffeeklatch *Am.* /*Br.* **coffee morning**/ social occasion when people meet each other to talk and drink coffee, often intended to collect money for charity.
coffee shop 1. *esp. Am.* small restaurant, often in a hotel that serves drinks and simple inexpensive meals: *I went back to my hotel and had a meal in the coffee shop* - R.P. Warren., *I took a job at another coffee shop* - J. Baez., *I think he's in the coffee-shoppe* - J. O'Hara. 2. *esp. Br.* place in a large shop or hotel that serves meals and non-alcoholic drinks.
coffee stall *Br.* street coffee stand.
coffee sugar, sugar crystals *Br.* large crystal sugar, usu. brown.
coffin *esp. Br., Can.* /*esp. Am.* euph. **casket**/.
cohort *esp. Am., Can.* col. often. derog. companion, associate or a group of people who support a certain leader: *Martin ignored Garcia's sneer as well as the chuckles of his two cohorts.* - D. Mortman., *Who are your cohorts, Grider?* - P. Case, J. Migliore.
coin *Br.* col. make counterfeit money. **coiner** n.
coin/ be coining it (in) *Br., Aus.* col. /*Am., Aus.* col. **be coining money**/ get rich quick.
coin/ base coin *Am.* change.
coin/ play sb. **back in their own coin** *Br.* obs. revenge them in the same manner as they did before.

coin box *Br.* a public telephone to call from which one has to use coins.
coinsure *Am.* buy or provide insurance in which the payment is split between two persons or insurance that will only pay for part of the value of smth.
cojones *esp. Am.* col. men's testicles.
coke-bottle *Am., Can.* very thick lenses for spectacles.
cold 1. *Br.* adj. (of a drink) not warm /not ice-cold/. 2. *Am.* suddenly and completely.
cold/ catch sb. **cold** *Am.* col. surprise sb.
cold/ be caught cold *Br.* journalism. be not prepared for the attack and suffer because of it.
cold/ go cold *Br.* get cold, become cold.
cold/ when sb./smth. **sneezes** sb./smth. **catches a cold** *esp. Br.* one's problem has a much worse effect on another, esp when talking about different countries.
cold bag, freezer bag *Br.* /*Am.* **cooler bag**/ bag used to transport food and drinks keeping them cold.
cold biscuit *Am.* sl. unattractive or dull girl.
cold (hard) cash *Am., Can.* hard cash.
cold cuts *esp. Am.* thinly cut pieces of various types of cold meat: *a modest lunch of cold cuts and eggplant pate.* - H. Smith.
cold deck 1. *Am.* col. stacked or marked deck of playing cards. 2. *Am., Can.* a separate pile of logs.
Cold Duck *Am.* expensive mixture of sparkling Burgundy and Champagne.
coldie *Aus.* col. a chilled can or bottle of beer.
cold table *Br.* a selection of dishes of cold food at a social occasion.
cold turkey 1. *esp. Am., Aus.* sl. a state of extreme suffering after withdrawal from drugs. 2. *esp. Am., Can.* adv. in a sudden and abrupt manner.
cold water dwelling /**pad**/ *Am.* house or flat without central heating or hot water: *Dean was staying in a cold-water pad in East Harlem* - J. Kerouac.
Coleman lantern *Am.* tdmk. gasoline lamp used by campers.
coll *Am.* abbr. collection.
collar 1. *Am.* sl. capture or arrest: *the sharp sniffing dogs are brought in to make the collar.* - Omni., *community policing, which emphasizes "problem-solving" over actual collars.* - New York. 2. *Br.* rolled up and tied piece of meat.
collar/ against the collar *Br.* with great effort, **work against the collar** *Br.* work very hard.

collar/ put one's **dog on a collar** *Br.* use a rope tied to a collar to control it.

collard(s) *Am.* stalked smooth-leaved kale: *He came to bed with the same grace a Mississippi pulpwood driver attacks a plate of collard greens* – C.R. Cross.

collarwork *Br.* very hard work.

collect 1. *Am., Can.* adj. adv. /*esp. Br., Aus.* **reverse charge**/ to be paid for by the receiver: *Call collect.* - T. Thompson., *The landlady of the apartment sent him a big parcel collect.* - R.P. Warren., *His mother and father telephoned collect from Maine* - I. Shaw. n. a **collect call** / *Br.* **reverse charge, transferred charge**/: *I have a collect call for you* – R.L. Stine. 2. *Br.* go to a particular place to bring sb. or smth. away (**collect** sb. **from**). 3. *Aus., NZ.* col. collide with. 4. *Aus., NZ.* col. a winning bet.

collection *esp. Br.* emptying of a letterbox by a postman.

collector's piece *Br.* collector's item.

colleen 1. *Am.* a girl from Ireland. 2. *Irish Eng.* a girl or a young woman.

college 1. *Br.* sl. prison. 2. *Am.* university where a student can get only a bachelor's degree: *They train doctors in six years without sending them first to an ordinary college* - R.G. Kaiser. 3. *Br.* 6th form college. 4. *Br.* (often used in the name of some British public schools) a private secondary school. 5. *esp. Br.* school for advanced education, esp. in a particular subject or skill.

college /in college *Am.* /*Br.* **at college**/.

college boards *Am.* group of tests covering several fields of aptitude and achievement given to students applying for admission to a college: *I was the first child in the history of the school to take College Boards.* - K. Vonnegut, Jr.

colleger *Am.* a student.

college try/ give (smth.) **college try** *Am., Can.* col. devote oneself to (smth.) completely: *Let's give it the old college try, boys. We can win this boat race!* - W. Magnuson.

college widow *Am.* sl. girl living in a college town who has dated students of several successive classes.

collegiate *Br.* formed of colleges.

collier *esp. Br.* 1. coal miner. 2. a ship for carrying coal.

colliery *esp. Br.* coalmine and buildings connected with it: *In the background a landscape of hills, clothed with black collieries and chimneys.* - A. Huxley.

colloquy *Am.* exchange of remarks (in Congress).

the collywobbles *Br.* uncomfortable feeling that a person gets when he is very nerous.

colonial *Am.* pertaining to the period of the first three quarters of the 18th century or the architectural style of this period in America: *his wife, Margareta, lived in a big white colonial on two wooded acres near Hartford, Connecticut.* – Reader's Digest.

the colonies *Br.* obs. all the countries that used to be British colonies.

colony/ summer colony *Am.* summer cottage settlement: *I'll live for 6 months of the year with Irene and her husband on his yacht off the summer colony of Newport, Rhode Island* - I. Shaw.

Colorado potato beetle *Am.* an insect which attacks potato plants.

color line *Am.* /*Br.* **colour bar**/ legal or social discrimination between white and non-white people: *We could not endorse a color line at home* - H. Truman.

color rotation *Am.* /*Br.* **colour sequence**/ print. the order in which the four colour process is printed.

color separator *Am.* /*Br.* **repro house**/ device for reproducing different colours on paper.

colour/ have a high colour *Br., Aus.* /*Am., Aus.* **have a lot of color**/ (of a light-skinned person) have a pink or reddish colour of their face.

colour/ nail one's **colours to the mast** *Br.* journalism. state and support one's case or other's ideas clearly and publicly.

colours *esp. Br.* items of certain colour specially worn to indentrify people as belonging to a particular group.

colour supplement *esp. Br.* a colour magazine which is one of the sections of a newspaper, esp. at weekends.

colourway *Br.* a combination of colours in which cloth or paper is printed.

Columbus day *Am.* October 12 observed as a legal holiday in many states of the US in commemoration of the landing of Columbus in the Bahamas in 1492.

combe *Br.* 1. deep narrow valley. 2. valley or basin on the flank of a hill.

combinations *Br.* /*Am.* **union suit**/ a type of underwear.

combo 1. *Aus.* white man living with an aboriginal woman. 2. *esp. Am., Can.* combination of different foods, esp. at a meal in a restaurant.

come/ as it comes *Br., Aus.* as you like it (about making a drink).

come across with (the goods) *Br.* col. provide money or information when it is needed.

come again *Br.* col. repeat the words: *Come again! I didn't hear what you said.* - Longman., *Come again? Rill said, squinting at me.* - K. Ablow.
Come along *esp. Br.* a. Make an effort. Try harder. b. Hurry up.
come apart *esp. Br.* break into pieces without anyone using force.
come at 1. *Am.* hint at. 2. *Aus.* col. start doing smth.
come around *Am.* /*Br.* **come round**/ 1. visit sb. 2. change one's opinion and agree with sb. 3. become conscious.
come away *Br.* leave.
come away (from) *Br.* become unfastened or separated from smth.
come back *esp. Am., Can.* reply to sb., esp. vigorously.
come by *esp. Am., Can.* pay an informal visit: *Why don't you come by some afternoon and have coffee with me?* - Longman.
come down (from) 1. *Br.* leave university usu. after finishing all or part of one's course: *I can't come down till I've finished my last examination.* - Longman. 2. *Aus.* (of a river) become floody.
come from *esp. Am.* have as (the background to) one's particular concern, intention, or meaning / to **know where** sb. **is coming from** is to know what sb. means: *I understand where you're coming from.* - S. Grafton.
come from Missouri *Am.* believe smth. only upon seeing it.
come in second *Am.* /*Br., Aus.* **come second**/ come second in a competition.
come in from the cold *Br.* (of unpopular people) change one's views and attitudes in order to be accepted.
come off 1. (medicine or drugs) *esp. Br.* stop using them. 2. *Am.* /*Br.* **come over**/ come across, give a specified impression: *But I probably came off like an idiot* – S. Lawrence. 3. *Br.* fall from a horse or bicycle. 4. *Br.* col. have an orgasm.
come on 1. *Am.* col. be aggressive: *He comes on kind of strong when you first see him but he's basically right.* - G.V. Higgins., *He comes on strong, but is really nice.* - McLean's. 2. *esp. Am.* col. make one's sexual interest known to sb.: *But she was definetely coming on to him.* – R.L. Stine.
come on to *Br.* begin, start: *It came on to snow.* - Longman.
come out 1. *Br.* becoming rare. (of a young lady of the upper class) be formally introduced in upper-class society, usu. at a dance: *Is Mrs. Kingbrown's daughter coming out this year?* - Longman. 2. *Am.* be offered for public viewing or sale: *The famous collection of rare old furniture is coming out next week.* - Longman. 3. *Br.* (of workers) go on strike.
come out in spots / a rash *Br.* become covered in spots because you are ill.
come out flat-footed (for) *Am.* decide strongly (for).
come out swinging *esp. Am.* defend smth. with determination.
come over *esp. Br., Aus.* col. (esp. followed by adjectives of feeling or illness) become, **come over (all) shy/nervous,** etc.: *He came over faint.* - Longman.
come through *Am.* 1. succeed, win: *every time she needed a favor I'd come through* - A. Scaduto. 2. confess, admit one's guilt.
come through *Br., Aus.* /*Am.* **come in**/ (about the results of smth.) arrive.
come up *Br.* enter a university.
come/ be coming home *Br.* col. (about one's local team) be successful in a particular sport.
come/be within an ace of doing smth. *Br.* 1. nearly succeed in doing it. 2. nearly miss doing a mistake or smth. that would be bad for you.
come/ come it (with, over) *esp. Br.* act boldly or disrespectfully.
come/ come it a bit (too) strong *esp. Br.* col. lay it on thick, go beyond the truth of smth.
come/ come the raw prawn *Aus.* sl. deceive sb.
come/ don't come it with me *Br.* col. don't argue with me.
come/ don't come the---with sb. *Br.* don't try to be the person you are not.
come rain or shine *Br.* happening in all kinds of weather.
come right/good *Br.* col. come out right.
come-along *Am., Can.* col. a hand-operated winch.
comeback *Aus., NZ.* a sheep bred for both wool and meat.
come-by-chance (child) *Br.* love child.
come-on *esp. Am.* col. an action meant to persuade sb. to do smth., esp. buy smth.: *when you bought one they gave you free records - that was the come-on* - M. Jones, J. Chilton., *they were come-ons with no payoff.* - D. Mortman.
come-on/ give sb. **the come-on** *Br.* col. clearly show that a person is sexually interested in sb.
come-outer *Am.* social or political reformer.
comer *esp. Am., Can.* col. person who appears to be very successful or likely to succeed: *In fact, he was a streamlined comer in the Mafia* - G.

O'Neill, D. Lehr., *Stankevich was a rising young comer among the Moscow radicals.* - H. Smith.

comfortable *Am.* col. drunk: *he gets comfortable with his hand on a bar.* – J. O'Hara.

comforter 1. *esp. Am.* also **comfort(able)** /*Br.* **quilt, duvet**/ a warm quilted bed cover: *We read sleepily under the soft blue comforter* - G. Hoover., *Electric blankets and comforters have replaced spreads as the favored bedcovers.* - Newsweek., *She put a comforter over him and he didn't stir* - J. O'Hara. 2. *Br.*, *Can.* /*Am.* **pacifier**/ teat of a baby's dummy.

comfort station *Am., Can.* 1. euph. /*Br.* **public convenience**/ public toilet: *Do you have a comfort station in this store?* - R.A. Spears. 2. liquor shop: *There's cops all around that comfort station. Somebody must have robbed it.* - R.A. Spears.

comfort station *Aus.* a break in a long car or bus journey to allow passengers to go to a toilet.

comic (book) 1. *esp. Am.* magazine for children containing comic strips: *take your choice of comic books* - D. Divoky. 2. *Am.* comedian.

comics *esp. Am., Can.* 1. /*esp. Br.* **comics**/ comic books: *lie in the shade, read the comics, and sleep* - I. Stone. 2. /*Br.* **strip cartoons**/ comic strips: *the comics are on top* - C. Woolrich.

command car *Am.* army car with a radio used by a commander: *General Zimmerman was still in his command car.* - A. McLean.

commence *esp. Br.* take a degree at a university.

commencement *Am.* a ceremony at which university or college students are given their degrees or diplomas: *Commencement speakers have a good deal in common with grandfather clocks* - Reader's Digest.

comment/ fair comment *Br.* col. reasonable and deserved criticism.

commercial papers *Am.* checks, bonds, etc.

commercial privilege or **concession** *Br.* special right given by the government or by a producer of goods to a person or group of people to carry on a certain type of business in a particular place, franchise.

commercial (traveller) *Br.* obs. /*Am.* **traveling salesman**, *Am.* col. **drummer**, *Br.* **doorstep salesman**/ sales representative: *Mr. Kernon was a commercial traveller of the old school* - J. Joyce.

commere *Br.* a female compere.

commie *esp. Am.* offensive word for a communist.

commish *Am., Can.* col. commissioner.

commissary 1. *esp. Am., Can.* a place where soldiers, people in prison or people employed by a firm, esp. a film company, can buy and eat food: *I walked into the MGM commissary* - E. Taylor., *He took his lunch at the Vogel-Paulson commissary.* - I. Shaw., *He saw his papa get cheated at the plantation commissary* - S.B. Oates. 2. *Am.* officer in the army who is in charge of food supplies. 3. *Am.* food store in a military camp.

commission agent *Br.* one who transacts business on commission.

commissionaire *esp. Br., Can.* /*Am.* **doorman**/ uniformed attendant at the entrance to a cinema, theatre, hotel, etc.: *Commissionaire slept on* - G. Greene.

commissioner for oaths *esp. Br.* lawyer who has the legal power to witness an oath made by sb. who is making a formal legal statement.

commis waiter *Br.* /*Am.* **busboy**/ waiter assistant / **commis chief** is an assistant chef.

commit *Am.* make a commitment.

commitment *esp. Am.* the use of money, time, people, etc. for a particular purpose.

committee 1. *Br.* law. a person entrusted with the charge of another person or other person's property. 2. *esp. Am.* a person who has been judicially committed to the charge of another because of their insanity or mental retardation.

committee stage *Br.* the third out of five readings of the law in Parliament when it still can be amended.

commode *Am., Can.* 1. euph. dial. lavatory: *But you can't see a commode from the road when you pass by.* - R.P. Warren. 2. obs. a movable washstand.

commode *Br.* piece of furniture shaped like a chair that can be used as a toilet.

common *Br.* from a low social class.

common/ as common as muck *Br., Aus.* col. from a low social class.

common fraction *esp. Am.* /*Br.* **vulgar fraction**/.

common ground *Br.* I agree with you.

commonhold *Br.* /*Am., Can.* **condominium**/ the freehold tenure of a flat within a multi-occupancy building, but with shared responsibility for common services.

common-or-garden *esp. Br.* col. /*Am.* (**common-or-)garden variety**/ ordinary: *I'm in the way of being common-or-garden pugilist.* - A. McLean., *I'm talking about ordinary common or garden facts.* - T. Rattigan.

common room *esp. Br.* room in an educational institution for use of students or staff when they are not studying or teaching.

commons *Am.* a room, esp. in a school or college where students or teachers can sit together and talk when they are not working.
commons/ be or **go on short commons** *Br.* have less food than is deserved or necessary.
common school *Am.* elementary school.
common stock *Am., Can.* ordinary shares.
Commonwealth *Aus.* Australia.
commune *esp. Am.* receive a communion.
communication cord *Br. /Am., Aus.* **emergency cord/** chain which a passenger can pull to stop in an emergency.
communistic *esp. Am.* adj. communist: *with communistic regimes you could not bank good will* - H. Truman.
community *Br.* all the people who live in the same area, town, etc.
community chest *esp. Am., Can.* amount of money collected by the people and businesses of an area to help people in need: *a man heard him sing at a community chest bazaar* - T. Wilder.
community college 1. also **junior college** *esp. Am., Can. /Br.* **vocational/technical school/** local college. 2. *Br.* a secondary school whose educational facilities are also available to adults in the local community.
community home *Br. /Am.* **reformatory/** a centre for housing young offenders or other young people in need of custodial care.
community kitchen (dining room) *Am.* public kitchen canteen.
community theatre *Am.* amateur theatre.
commutation ticket (or **book**) /also **commuter ticket/** *Am.* ticket sold at reduced price by a railway or bus company for a fixed number of trips between two places during a fixed period of time, season ticket.
commute *esp. Am.* a journey one makes when one commutes.
comp col. 1. *Br.* competition. 2. *Br.* compositor. 3. *Am., Can.* compensation. 4. *Am., Can.* give smth. free, esp. as part of a promotion, n. 5. *Br.* comprehensive school.
comp print. *Am. /Br.* **visual/** rough printed work.
compact (**car**) *Am., Can., Aus.* a small car: *the blue compact finally headed East* - R. Moore.
compadre *esp. Am.* col. (a form of address to a friend or companion).
companianable/ in a companianable silence (about sitting or walking) *Br.* enjoying being together but not talking.
companion set *Br.* a set of fireside implements on a stand.

company/ operating company *Am.* firm producing goods.
company checkers / spotters *Am.* informers working for the company.
company gunmen / thugs *Am.* col. armed guard of the company.
company secretary *Br.* member of a company who deals with money, legal matters, etc.
company union *Am.* unaffiliated labour union of the employees of a single firm.
compatriot *Am.* companion or sb. you work with.
compatriotism *esp. Br.* patriotic feeling of sympathy.
compendium *Br.* a set of different board games in one box.
compensation *esp. Am., Can.* salary or wages.
compere *Br. /Am.* col. **emcee/** v. n. (act as) a person who introduces the various acts in a TV or stage show: *everybody's friend - perhaps a frustrated talk-show host or prime-time variety compere.* - J.P. Hogan.
comping *Br.* col. the practice of entering competitions, esp. those promoting consumer products.
complected *Am., Can.* (in comb.) complexioned: *she was still little clumsy dark-complected Janice* - J. Updike.
completion *Br.* title closing. (real estate term).
compliment/ a left-handed compliment *Am. /Br.* **a back-handed compliment/** insincere compliment.
compliments slip *Br.* transmittal slip sent by tradesman.
compo *Aus., NZ.* col. (unemployment) compensation, esp. for industrial injury.
compo rations *Br.* tinned food provisions for several days.
composite photograph or **sketch** *Am. /Br., Aus.* **identity kit/**.
composite school *Br., Can.* comprehensive school.
comprehensive *Br.* (of education) (a school) teaching pupils of all abilities in the same school.
comprehensive *Am.* print. a layout of type and illustration, not to the standard of a finished rough.
compulsory purchase *Br.* officially enforced purchase of privately owned land and property for public use.
con *Am.* sl. a convict or ex-convict.
concertina *Br., Aus.* col. 1. (of a vehicle) become pressed together like a concertina as the result

of a crash. 2. bring smth. close together or fold it in a more compact way.

concertina file *Br.* /*Am.* **accordion file** or **folding file,** *Aus.* **expanding file**/ a box-shaped cardboard container used for storing documents.

concertina fold print. *Br.* /*Am.* **accordion fold**/.

concertize *esp. Am., Can.* give concert(s).

concertmaster *Am.* /*Br.* **leader**/ the first violin player of an orchestra who by custom helps the conductor: *the concertmaster of the New York Philharmonic would play it* - Guideposts.

concert party *Br.* vaudeville (music hall) show put at some place other than a regular theatre (like a park, seafront, promenade, summer camp).

concert performance *Br.* a piece of music written for an opera, ballet, etc. at a concert without the accompanying dramatic action, dance, etc.

concession 1. *Am.* a lease of a portion of premises for a particular purpose: *You count the money from the concessions* – R.J. Stine, adj. **concessionary.** 2. *Can.* a. concession road. b. remote districts (often pl.). c. subdivision of surveyed land. 3. *Br.* reduction in the price of tickets, fares, etc. for certain groups, esp. for old people or children. 4. *Am.* also **commercial privilege** a right to perform some type of business activity given by a government, owner of land, etc.: *man who ran concessions at the theatre* – A. Summers, R. Swan.

concessionaire (concessioner) *Am.* barman or kiosk minder in a cinema, theatre, etc.: *the concessionaires had to close their shutters* – K. Vonnegut, Jr.

concession road/line *Can.* rural road running East and West and separating concessions: *just at the corner of the concession line, where it meets the main road.* - W. Grady.

concessions *Am.* the things sold at a concession stand.

concession stand *Am., Can.* stand, kiosk: *fans wander among the concession stands.* - Reader's Digest.

conchie 1. *Aus.* col. n., adj. (a person who is) using a lot of effort in their work. 2. *Br.* col. derog. obs. conscientious objector.

concierge *esp. Am.* hotel worker who helps guests by giving them advice about local restaurants, etc.

conclave *Am.* meeting of men belonging to a fraternal conclave.

condemned cell *Br.* room for prisoner sentenced to death.

condition *Am.* 1. a grade in scholarship calling for re-examination or special work before the student passes to the next grade or receives credit for the course. 2. require examination or special work.

condo *Am., Can.* col. condominium: *Donald Trump tearing down his glittering condos?* - Omni.

condom *Br., Can.* /*Am.* **rubber**/.

condominium *esp. Am., Can.* /*Br.* **commonhold**/ owner-occupied flat in a block of flats or a block of flat itself: *I condominiumized. And I haven't regretted it one instant.* - R.J. Randisi., M. Wallace.

conduct disorder *esp. Am.* all types of antisocial behaviour during childhood and adolescence.

conductive education *Br.* special training for people with motor disorders, done by specially trained people (**conductors**).

conductor 1. *Am., Can.* /*esp. Br.* **guard**/ railway official in charge of a train: *Every conductor from San Jose to Los Angeles had had to wake me up to ask about my qualifications* - J. Kerouac. 2. *Br.* person collecting payments from passengers on a bus or train: *my husband has to watch pennies like a streetcar conductor.* - I. Shaw.

cone *esp. Am.* /*Br.* **cornet**/ thin pastry container for ice-cream: *they waited for cones and milkshakes.* – R.L. Stine.

cone off *esp. Br.* mark (part of a road) with cones to prevent its use by traffic: *Part of the main road was coned off after the accident.* - Longman.

confab *Am., Can.* a meeting of members of a certain group.

confection *Am.* piece of fine craftsmanship.

confectioner's sugar, powdered sugar *Am.* / *Br.* **icing sugar**/ icing sugar: *Decorate with confectioner's sugar dusted over doily.* - Reader's Digest.

conference *Am.* association (of athletic teams, universities, churches, etc.).

confidence game *Am., Can.* an act of cheating based on trust.

confinement theatre *Br.* labour ward, labour room.

conflate *esp. Am.* print. collate, check through the sections or pagination of a book after gathering to ensure that it is complete and in correct sequence for binding.

congregant *esp. Am.* member of a congregation.

conjurer *esp. Br.* magician who entertains people.

conjure woman *Am.* sorceress, esp. one who pratices voodoo.

conk 1. *Br., Aus.* humor. col. a nose. 2. *esp. Am.* hit sb. (on the head).
conk out *esp. Am.* fall asleep because sb. is tired.
conker *esp. Br.* col. /*Am.* **chestnut**/ the shiny brown nut-like seed of the horse chestnut tree often used in a children's game: *brown shoes gleaming like freshly gathered conkers.* - D. Lodge.
connect *Am.* 1. succeed in hitting sb. or smth. 2. (of people) like and understand each other: *just jotting off a birthday card or sending an e-mail with useful info can keep you connected.* – Reader's Digest.
connection rebars *Am.* projecting reinforcement (in building).
connector assembly *Am.* /*Br.* **plug-and-socket**/ electric connection with the help of socket and plug.
connexion *Br.* connection.
conniption fit *Am., Can.* col. obs. humor. a fit of rage, hysteria, esp. in **have/throw a conniption fit**: *the crackpot are having conniption fits.* - H. Truman.
con rod *Br.* col. connecting rod (in a car).
conscience/ in all conscience *esp. Br.* /*Am.* **in good conscience**/ said if one can't do smth. because he thinks it is wrong.
conscience clause *esp. Am., Can.* a clause that makes concessions to the consciences of those affected by a law.
conscription *esp. Br.* /*Am., Can.* **draft**/ enlistment in the army: *He left with barely a ruble in his pocket to avoid conscription* – Reader's Digest.
conservancy *Br.* 1. group of officials who control and protect an area of land, a river, etc. 2. nature conservation.
conservatoire *Br.* /*Aus.* **conservatorium**/ a school of music.
conservator *Am.* guardian of mentally ill persons.
conservatory 1. *esp. Am.* conservatoire: *I met a young chellist who was about to graduate from the conservatory.* - R.G. Kaiser. 2. *Br.* /*Am.* **sun porch, sun parlor**; *Aus.* **sun-room**; *Br.* **sun lounge**/.
considerable *Am.* n. a great deal, much.
consignment note *Br.* (railway) bill of lading.
consolidate *esp. Br.* combine (separate pieces of legislation) into a single legislative act.
consolidated school *Am.* public usu. elementary school formed by merging other schools.
consolidated ticket office *Am.* joint booking office.
constable *esp. Br.* /*esp. Am.* **patrolman**/.

constabulary *esp. Br.* a police force covering a certain region.
constituency 1. *Am.* col. customers, subscribers to the same newspapers, etc. 2. *esp. Br.* an area represented by a body of voters who elect their representetive to a legislative body.
constitutionalize *Am.* make subject to provisions of a country's constitution.
The Constitution State, also **The Nutmeg State** *Am.* Connecticut.
consult with *esp. Am.* ask the advice of (sb.): *I intend to consult with my tax lawyer before sending my tax reform.* - Longman.
consultant *esp. Br.* /*Am.* **specialist**/ high ranking hospital doctor who gives specialist advice in addition to that given by an ordinary doctor.
consulting room *Br.* room where doctors see patients.
consumed durables *Br.* /*Am.* **durable goods**/ large things, such as cars, TVs or furniture that people don't buy often or regularly.
consumer price index *Am., Aus.* /*Br.* **retail price index**/ list of prices for a particular period of time.
contact sb. /*Br.* **on**/ or /*Am.* **at**/ a certain number speak to sb. by telephone at a certain number.
container car *Am.* container waggon.
contest *esp. Am.* /*esp. Br.* **competition**/.
contest/ no contest *esp. Am.* Nolo contendere.
contested election 1. *Am.* challenged election result. 2. *Br.* election with opposing candidates.
contestee *Am.* candidate whose election is contested by another.
The Continent *esp. Br.* the main part of Europe.
continental 1. *Am.* of or related to or typical of North America. 2. *Br.* euph. n. immigrant from India or Pakistan. 3. *Br.* obs. adj. typical of central or southern Europe.
contingency fee *Am.* amount of money that US lawyer will be paid only if the person they are advising wins in court.
continental/ not worth a continental *Am.* col. worthless.
continental bed *Can.* bed without headboard and footboard.
continentalize *Am.* spread on the whole of a continent.
continental quilt *Br.* duvet: *Black walls and a white carpet and a racing car continental quilt.* – S. Townsend.
continuous assessment *Br.* the evaluation of a pupil's progress throughout a course as distinct from examinations.

continuous stationery *Br.* invoices and letterheads, etc. printed on a long strip of paper.

contour *Am.* the state of affairs.

contract in(to) *esp. Br.* agree or promise, esp. officially to take part.

contract out *esp. Br.* 1. (of) agree or promise not to take part: *any member may "contract out" of making such payments.* - J. Ruppeldtova. 2. (of a company, organisation, etc.) arrange by formal agreement to have (a job, services, etc.) done by another company, refuse to join in an agreement: *we contracted out everything we are not good at* - C. Handy.

contract/ award a contract *Am.* sign a contract.

contractorization *Br.* provision of service, esp. a public one by an external contractor.

contract hire *Br.* lease.

contract labor *Am.* immigrant contract workers.

contraflow *esp. Br.* arrangement by which traffic going in both directions uses only one side of the road, esp. during the time when the other side is being repaired: *8-mile-long contraflow systems erected so that some guys on a crane can change a lightbulb* - B. Bryson.

contrail *esp. Am.* vapour trail left in the sky by a plane.

contributory *Br.* law. person liable to give money towards the payments of a wound up company's debts.

contributory negligence *Br., Aus.* law. negligence of a person who is partly responsible for their injuries in an accident through not acting properly at the time of it.

contributory /*Br., Aus.* **pension scheme**/, /*Am.* **pension plan**/ one that is paid for by both employer and employee.

control/ have overall control *Br.* control a council by having more members of one's party there than the other parties have.

conurbation *Br.* a large city together with the smaller towns around it.

convener *esp. Br.* member of a committee, etc. whose job is to call meetings, esp. of trade unions.

convenience *esp. Br.* /also *Br.* **public convenience, cloakroom,** *Am.* **comfort station** (if in building)/ public toilets provided by local governments.

convenience outlet, (electric) outlet *Am.* /*Br., Aus.* **socket (outlet), power point**/.

convenience store *esp. Am., Can.* a shop that works till late at night and has a limited range of household goods and groceries: *A convenience store on a lonely highway* - D. Mortman.

convention *Am., Can.* a political party conference at which candidates are selected for an office.

conventional loan *Am.* a mortgage loan that isn't insured by a government agency.

conventioner *Am., Can.* convention's delegate.

conversant *Am.* able to hold a conversation in a foreign language, although not able to speak it perfectly.

conversation pit *Am.* sunken recessed area in or near a living room for conversation and entertaining.

conversion *Br.* house converted into separate apartments.

conversion heater *Br.* electric heater.

converted rice *Am., Can.* tdmk. white rice prepared from brown by a special technology.

conveyer *Br.* /*Am.* **conveyor**/.

convince (to do smth.) *esp. Am.* persuade (sb. to do smth.).

convo *Aus.* sl. conversation.

convocation *Am., Can.* a final ceremony for the conferment of university awards.

con(e)y *Am.* rabbit.

Coo *Br.* excl. of surprise; Gee, Gosh.

cooboo *Aus.* a child.

cooch *Am.* sl. an erotic dance: *She coquettes and wiggles her shouldres in a quick showgirl's cooch* – N. Mailer.

cooee, cooey 1. *Am.* high repeated fast call used by farmers to call hogs. 2. *Aus.* a call in the woods so as not to get lost/ **keep in touch by cooeeing**.

cooee/ within cooee *Aus., Br.* within hearing distance, near.

cook 1. *esp. Br.* falsify, tamper with: *The British government cooked press stories shamelessly in order to deceive the Argentine enemy* - Newsweek, R.L. Chapman. 2. *Aus.* col. kill (sb.). 3. *Am., Can.* col. do (smth.) well: *The Boss Brass was cookin' last night. What a band!* - W. Magnuson.

cook/ there are too many cooks in the kitchen *Am.* too many cooks spoil the broth.

cook out *Am.* cook food outdoors: *We're cooking out tonight, it's too hot indoors.* - Longman.

cookbook *esp. Am.* /*esp. Br.* **cookery book**/, recipe book /North American recipes use spoons and cupfuls not ounces/: *Do you have any cookbooks?* - I. Shaw.

cooked breakfast *Br.* a dish of fried eggs, bacon and sausages, served with toast and sometimes mushrooms and tomatoes.

cook-chill *Br.* (of food) cooked and then stored at a low temperature, but not freezed, by the manufacturer ready for reheating by the consumer.

cookee *Am.* cook assistant.

cooker *esp. Br. /esp. Am., Aus.* **stove,** *Am.* **range/** an apparatus on which food is cooked.

cooker *Br.* col. a cooking fruit, esp. apple; a sour apple which is eaten cooked.

cookery 1. *Am., Can.* delicatessen; kitchen. 2. *Br. /Am.* **cooking/** the skills and methods of preparing food cooking it.

cook general *Br.* servant whose duties include cooking and general housework.

cookie, cooky 1. *esp. Am., Can. /Br., Aus.* roughly **biscuit/** sweet biscuit: *In Britain an American cookie is a biscuit* - Newsweek., *occasionally offering cookies or fresh produce from their own backyard gardens* - M. Torgov. 2. *Am.* col. a person of a particular type: *But Larson is a different kind of cooky.* - R.P. Warren. 3. *Am.* obs. attractive young woman.

cookie-cutter *Am.* 1. an instrument that cuts cookies into special shapes before they are baked. 2. smth. similar to many others of the same type: *the Hummer, is made to appear larger than the cookie-cutter suburban houses* – Reader's Digest.

cookie jar *Am., Can.* a jar for biscuits or small cakes.

cookie jar/ caught with one's **hand in the cookie jar** *Am. /Br.* **have** one's **hand in the till/** caught stealing or doing smth. wrong.

cookie pusher *Am.* sl. 1. lover of social events at the expense of work. 2. bootlick, flatterer. 3. lazy do-nothing: *Is Martin a couch potato or a cookie pusher?* - R.A. Spears.

cookie sheet *Am., Can. /Br.* **baking tray/** flat metal pan used for baking.

cooking chocolate *Br. /Am.* **plain chocolate/** chocolate with no milk at all.

cooking stove *Br. /Am.* **cook stove/** a stove for cooking food.

cooking (with gas) *Am.* col. */Br.* col. **cooking on gas/** doing exactly right: *That's great! Now you're cooking with gas!* - R.A. Spears.

cooking/ What's cooking? *Am.* obs. What's happening?

cook-out *esp. Am., Can.* col. meal cooked and eaten outdoors, barbecue: *It's like a cook-out.* - E. Segal.

cookshop 1. *NZ.* sheep station's kitchen. 2. *Br.* shop (department) where cooking equipment is sold.

cooktop *Am., Can.* cooking unit fixed on the top of a cabinet.

cool *Am.* sl. v. kill.

cool out *Am.* col. discourage (a business opponent) by competition, etc.: *the blacks have been sold out and cooled out again.* - E. Cleaver.

coolant tank *Am. /esp. Br.* **header (tank)/**.

cool bag, cold bag, freezer bag, cool box *Br. /Am.* **cooler bag/** soft insulated container for keeping food and drinks cool.

cool box *Br.* a rigid insulated container for keeping food and drinks cool.

cooler *Am.* machine that provides air conditioning.

Coolgardie safe *Aus.* food safe cooled by strips of wetted fabric.

coon *esp. Am.* col. racoon: *I could see his nose flare open and shut like a hound sniffing a coon up a tree* – E. Caldwell.

(for/in a) coon's age *Am., Can.* (for) a long time: *We haven't been out to the coast in a coon's age. It's been years.* - W. Magnuson., *I haven't seen you for a coon's age, Fanny.* – K. Chopin.

coony *Am.* col. sly.

coop 1. *esp. Am.* sl. jail. / **fly the coop** *esp. Am.* escape from jail: *She's gone. Flew the coop.* - J. Kellerman. 2. *Br.* a basket for catching fish.

coop in *Am.* enclose, limit the freedom.

coordinate *Am.* adj. not coeducational, attending separate colleges (of men and women).

coot/ old coot *Am.* col. strange or unpleasant old man.

cootie *Am., Can.* col. 1. obs. head or body louse: *I don't have cooties!* - T. Thorne. 2. **have cooties** used by children to insult other children.

cooze *Am.* taboo sl. 1. woman: *He screams like a cooze* - R.L. Stine. 2. female sex organs.

cop, patrolman *esp. Am. /Br.* **bobby, constable/** policeman: *a couple of cops were processing a tall skinny black kid.* - R. Crais.

cop *esp. Br.* col. 1. catch or arrest (sb. doing smth. wrong). 2. **cop it, cop a load of trouble** is to be in serious trouble, esp. having a severe punishment; **cop it** *esp. Br.* be killed. 3. **cop that/**or (**a load of**) **this** also *Aus.* look at it/ that.

cop 1. *Am.* get an illegal drug: *I'd go there to cop.* – E. James, D. Ritz. 2. *Am., Can.* strike an attitude or pose.

cop 1. *Br.* col. **a fair cop** a. fair or just arrest, or admitting one's mistake. b. humor. used when sb. found out that a person has done smth. wrong and that person wants to admit it. 2. **not be much cop** *Br. /Aus.* **chop/** col. not very good: *This three or four quids a week lark isn't much cop, when you have a family to keep.* - J. Herriot. 3. *Aus.* profitable job. 4. *esp. Am.* a police officer.

cop from *Am.* col. ask for smth.: *Can I cop a cigarette from you?* - Longman.

cop off *Br.* sl. meet sb. and start a sexual relationship with them.

cop out *esp. Am.* col. admit one's guilt: *The younger of the thieves copped out* - Longman.

cop to *Am.* accept or admit to.

cop a feel *Am., Can.* col. grope (sb.) sexually: *John talks big for a 16 year old, but all he's ever done is cop a feel in a dark movie theater.* - A. Makkai.

cop a plea *Am., Can.* col. plead guilty to a lesser charge: *He'd copped a plea but had still received a tough sentence* - J. O'Brien., A. Kurins.

cop hold of smth. *Br.* col. take or hold smth.

cop (some or **a few) Z's** *Am.* sl. take a nap.

copacetic *Am., Can.* col. very good: *You stick with me and everything will be copacetic* - T. Thorne.

cope (not to be followed by anything) *esp. Br.* deal successfully: *After her illness Janet lost the ability to cope.* - Longman., *If your mother can't cope, we counsel her.* - Fortune.

coper *Br.* horse trader, usu. dishonest: *She closes directory, examines him like a coper before a doubtful horse* - J. Fowles.

copha *Aus.* a white wax-like substance made from coconut and used in cooking.

copier *Am.* /*Br.* **photocopier**/.

copper 1. *Br.* col. becoming rare. a coin of low value made of copper or bronze: *I'm trying to make a few coppers* – E. Kazan. 2. *esp. Br.* a metal vessel (as for cooking or boiling clothes). 3. *esp. Br.* col. a police officer: *I regret to inform you like a copper's nark* - P. Howard.

copper *Am.* bet against: *they offered me a chance to copper my bet at attractive odds.* - J.A. Michener.

copper-bottomed *esp. Br.* certain to be successful, very reliable.

coppering *Br.* col. the work of a police officer.

copy smth. **out** *Br.* write smth. exactly as it is written somewhere else.

copybook/ **blot** one's **copybook** *esp. Br., Aus.* col. spoil one's record or chances.

copybook *Br.* adj. very correct, proper.

copy desk *Am., Can.* desk in a newspaper office where a copy is edited before printing.

copy of verses *Br.* short composition, usu. one set at school exercise.

copyreader *Am.* 1. subeditor, one who edits copy in a newspaper and writes headlines. 2. copyholder.

copyright page *Am.* /*Br.* **imprint page**/ page holding the printer's and/or publisher's name, an ISBN, credits and British Library (GB)/ Library of Congress (US) CIP.

copy taster *Br.* person on a newspaper who looks at an incoming copy and decides what should be done with it.

Cor /**Cor blimey**/ *Br.* sl. excl. (an expression of great surprise): *Cor!, said the lads. Go on.* - D. Francis.

cor anglais *esp. Br.* /*esp. Am.* **English horn**/.

(electric) cord, extension cord *Am., Aus.* /*Br.* **flex (with plugs)**, *Am.* **wire**, *Br., Aus.* **lead**/ (electric) extension lead.

cord *Am.* specific quantity of wood cut for burning in a fire: *In summer I'd throw endless cords of wood into her basement* – R. Brautigan.

cordelle *Am., Can.* a rope for towing.

cordial 1. *Br.* sweet non-alcoholic drink made from fruit juice. 2. *Am., Can.* obs. flavoured alcoholic drink, liqueur.

cordially (yours) *Am.* sincerely yours (used at the end of the letter).

corduroy road *Am., Can.* one made of transversely laid logs to cross muddy swampy areas: *They've done fifteen miles o'mud holes an' corduroy since noon* - W. Grady.

core *Br.* /*Am.* (**cable**) **conductor**/ a wire of a cable conducting electricity.

core (curriculum) *Am., Aus.* a group of courses in various subjects which all students in a school must study.

co-respondent shoes *Br.* two-toned shoes.

core time *Br.* the period during the middle part of the day when an office or other place that operates flextime expects all its people to be working.

corinthean *Am.* an amateur yachtsman.

corkage *Br.* the charge made by a hotel or restaurant for allowing people to drink wine which they have brought with them.

corking *Br.* obs. col. very good.

cork-tipped *Br.* (of a cigarette filter) made of cork-like material.

corn 1. *esp. Br.* ./*Am.* **grain**/ (the seed of) any of various types of grain plants such as barley, oats, and esp. wheat. 2. *esp. Am., Aus., NZ, Can.* a. /*esp. Br.* **maize**/ maize: *I helped...Handsome Brown shuck the corn* – E. Caldwell. b. /*esp. Br.* **sweet corn**/ sweet corn. 3. *Am.* col. /also *Am.* sl. **corn juice, corn mule**/ corn whiskey: *He had* *come into the place in a drunken turmoil, caused partly by the swallows of corn* - C. McCullers., *Grandpaw and Paw started carrying in the bottles of corn.* - Zacherlay.

corn /earn one's **corn** *Br.* col. be successful and justify the money spent.

corn(ball) *Am., Can.* col. 1. n. adj. (smth. or sb.) sentimental, unsophisticated: *May-Ann was just too cornball for words.* - R.L. Stine. 2. (smth.) trite, banal, worthless: *the usual cornball hoke.* - L. Waller.

cornbraid *Am.* long plaits of hair: *He had long black cornbraids* - J. Patterson.

corn bread *Am.* a type of bread made from maize: *driver attacks a plate of collard greens and corn bread* – C.R. Cross.

corn cake /also **hoe cake**/ *Am.* pancake made of corn.

corn chips *Am., Aus.* thin, flat pieces of food made from crushed maize.

corn-cob pipe *Am.* a tobacco pipe with a bowl made from a dried corn-cob.

corn crib *Am., Can.* a barn or ventilated building for storing ears of maize.

corn dodger *Am.* boiled corn bread.

corn dolly *Br.* model of a human figure made of plaited straw.

corned beef 1. *Br.* pressed cooked beef sold in a tin. 2. *Am.* beef that has been covered in salt water and spices to preserve it.

corner *Br.* a triangular cut from the hind end of a side of a bacon.

the Corner *Aus.* the region of the North-eastern Australia, esp. New South Wales.

corner/ cut off a (the) corner *esp. Br.* go across a piece of grass, special area, etc.

corner/ fight one's **corner** *Br.* defend smth. vigorously.

corner/ right around the corner *Am.* just around the corner, about to happen.

corner boy 1. *esp. Irish.* street hooligan. 2. *Can.* city inhabitant.

corner-mark *Am.* mark defining private land property.

corner shop *Br., Aus.* /*Am.* **corner store**/ a small, often privately owned, general shop often near a street corner: *Me, I don't even walk to the corner shop on bank holidays.* - B. Bryson.

corner tree *Am.* one which marks the corner of a supervised track.

cornet *Br.* /*esp. Am.* **cone**/ thin pastry container for ice-cream.

corn-factor *Br.* grain broker.

corn field *Am.* maize field.

cornflake *Am.* sl. an eccentric person.

cornflour *Br., Aus.* /*Am., Can.* **cornstarch**/ fine white flour made from crushed corn, rice, or other grain, used in cooking to thicken liquids: *she fed them a bouillon of warm water and cornstarch.* - W. Grady.

The Cornhusker State *Am.* Nebraska.

cornhusking *Am.* 1. husking of corn. 2. gathering of farmers to husk corn.

Cornish cream *Br.* clotted cream.

Cornish pasty *Br.* pasty with seasoned meat and potato inside.

(corn) pone, pone bread *Am., Can.* unleavened maize bread.

corn rich *Can.* /*Am.* **corn crib**/ barn.

corn roast *Can.* a party at which green maize is roasted and eaten.

cornrow *esp. Am.* v., n. plait hair tight: *The girl wore a red polka-dot dress and had coal-black skin, cornrows and beautiful African features.* - J. Kellerman.

cornsnow *esp. Am., Can.* a snow with rough regular surface.

cornstalk 1. *Am.* stem of a corn. 2. *Aus.* obs. n. Australian, esp. from New South Wales.

The Corn State *Am.* Illinois.

corporate welfare *Am.* the compulsory funding of public welfare programmes by commercial organisations.

corporation (corp) 1. *Am.* Public Limited Company (PLC, Ltd). 2. *Br.* obs. a group of people elected to govern a town, city or borough.

corporation tax *esp. Br.* tech. tax on the profits of a company.

corpsman *Am.* A navy enlisted man trained to give first aid and apprentice medical treatment.

corral *Am., Can.* a pen for livestock on a farm or ranch; v. get livestock into a corral.

corral *esp. Am.* take possession of: *The doctor thus corraled a respected neurologist* - T. Thompson.

correctional *esp. Am., Can.* treating of offenders through a program involving penal custody, parole, and probation aimed at rectifying their behaviour.

correctional facility *esp. Am., Can.* tech. or humor. prison.

correspondence column *Br.* newspaper column devoted to the letters from readers.

corridor *Br.* passage along the side of a passenger railway carriage from which doors lead to compartments.

corroboree *Aus.* 1. aboriginal dance. 2. col. noisy gathering. 3. sl. cheap wine.

cosh 1. *Br., Aus. /Am.* **blackjack, sap/** col. short heavy metal pipe or filled rubber tube used as a weapon: *armed with coshes and bottles, they politely made way for the leaving party* - A. Burgess. 2. *esp. Br.* col. hit with a cosh or other blunt weapon: *I understand she has been-er-coshed.* - A. Christie.

cosher up *esp. Am.* treat (sb.) with kindness: *Cosher up your child, and you will come to fear him.* - Longman.

cos lettuce *Br. /esp. Am., Aus.* **romaine lettuce/** a lettuce made with long leaves.

cosmetician *Am., Can.* person whose profession is to sell or apply cosmetics

cossie, cozzie *Br., Aus.* col. a swimming costume.

cost *esp. Br., Can.* sl. be expensive to sb., esp. in the phr. **cost the earth, cost a bomb.**

cost / at cost price *Br. /Am.* **at cost/** selling smth. for the same price that one paid for it: *A local dentist has provided thousands of sets of false teeth at cost for prisoners* –Reader's Digest.

cost of living index *Am., Aus.* retail price index.

cost out *esp. Am.* (in business) guess the cost of fulfilling a contract: *We shall have to bring in professional advisers to help us to cost out his job.* - Longman.

cost clerk *Br.* cost accountant, one who keeps a record of all the costs of production in a business firm, etc.

coster(monger), barrow boy (man) *Br.* obs. / *esp. Am.* **huckster/** person who sells fruit and vegetables from a cart in the street esp. in London: *he raised his whiplash to lash the costermonger.* - J. Galsworthy., *backslang was used as a secret language by street traders and costermongers.* - R. McRum, W. Cran, R. McNeil.

costing *esp. Br.* cost accounting.

costive *Am.* col. costly.

(court) costs *Am.* money that person involved in a legal case in court has to pay to lawyers, esp. if that person is found guilty.

costume *Br.* swimming costume.

costumer *Am.* clothes tree.

cosy *Br. /Am.* **cozy/** comfortable.

cot 1. *Br., Aus. /Am., Aus.* **crib/** a small bed for a young child. 2. *Am., Can. /Br.* **camp bed/** light folding bed: *I noticed an army cot in his dressing room.* - D. Carnegie., *I slept in the cot by the window.* - J. Kerouac.

cot-case *Aus., NZ.* col. 1. bed-ridden ill person. 2. drunkard.

cot death *Br. /Am.* **crib death/** sudden death of a baby in its sleep.

cotillion *esp. Am.* formal dance party, esp. one at which young couples are introduced to society.

cottage 1. *Am.* small house for (summer) vacation, esp. at the resort area by the sea: *Someone building a cottage in the country might acquire his lumber* - R.G. Kaiser. 2. *esp. Br.* small house in the country.

cottager *Am., Can.* summer resort cottage dweller.

cottage hospital *Br., Can.* small hospital, usu. in a country area.

cottage loaf *Br.* one who has a smaller round part on top of a larger one.

cottage pie *Br.* dish of minced beef topped with brown mashed potato.

cottage roll *Can.* ham.

cottaging *Br.* sl. homosexual activity between men (**cottagers**) in public toilets.

cotton (batting, absorbent cotton, absorbent wool, *Am., Can.* 1. *Am. /Br., Aus.* **cotton wool/** soft mass of cotton used for cleansing skin, bathing wounds, etc.: *her brain feeling as numb and useless as wet cotton wool.* - M.M. Kaye. 2. *esp. Br.* thread for sewing made of cotton.

cotton on(to) *esp. Br.* col. begin to understand, realise.

cotton (up) to *esp. Am.* col. become friendly with (sb.) or become to like smth: *Charlie cottoned to her first thing* - J. Dos Passos., *I cottoned to you from the first.* - J. London.

cotton balls, cotton batting *Am.* cotton in the form of a soft mass.

cotton bud *Br., Aus. /Am.* **swab** or **Q-tip/** a short stick with a small amount of cotton on each end used usu. for cleaning ears.

cotton candy *Am., Can. /Br.* **candy floss/** fine sugar threads eaten as a sweet and usu. on a stick: *red-tinted clouds resembling pink cotton candy suspended in space.* - B. Tillman.

Cottonopolis *Br.* joc. Manchester.

cotton-picking *Am., Aus., Can.* col. (used to give force to an expression of annoyance): *just forget it and throw it out of your cotton-pickin' mind.* - M. Jones, J. Chilton.

cotton reel *Br. /Am.* **spool/** small object that cotton is wound around.

cotton socks/ bless her/his cotton socks *Br., Aus.* humor. exclamation of affection for sb.

The Cotton State *Am.* Alabama.

cottontail *Am.* small rabbit with a white tail.

cotton wool/ wrap sb. **(up) in cotton wool** *Br., Aus.* protect sb. too much.

cotton wool ball *Br.* /*Am.* **cotton ball**/.
cotton wool pads *Br., Aus.* /*Am.* **cotton pads**/ pads used along with cream for removing make-up from the face.
couch *esp. Am.* sofa: *He was staring at the fold-up valentine on the couch cushion.* – R.L. Stine.
couchette *esp. Br.* a bed in a railway carriage or on a ferry boat which is either folded against the wall or used as an ordinary seat during the day.
couch potato *esp. Am., Aus., Can.* col. lazy, inactive, unimaginative person, esp. a lazy TV watcher: *the habit he really wanted to break was that of being a couch potato.* - Reader's Digest.
cougar *esp. Am., Can.* /*Br.* **puma**, *esp. Aus., Am.* **panther**/ a large brown wild cat found in North and South America.
cough *Br.* sl. admit that one has done smth. wrong or unlawful.
cough sweets *Br.* /*Am.* **cough drops**, *Aus.* **cough lollies**/ sweets that help a coughing person get better.
cough syrup *Br.* cough mixture that helps a person to stop coughing.
could *esp. Am.* used when asking permission (also **might**) or wondering if smth. is possible.
coulee *Am., Can.* deep ravine: *the buttes and coulees, the cliffs and sculptured hills and ravines lost their burned and dreadful look* - J. Steinbeck.
council *esp. Br.* the organisation responsible for local government in a town, county, etc.
council estate *Br.* a group of council houses.
council house, flat *esp. Br.* one owned by the local council: *I wasn't a builder of council houses or factories.* - G. Greene.
council housing *Br.* /*Am.* **public housing**/ houses or flats owned by the council which people (**council tenants**) pay rent to live in.
councilman, councilwoman *esp. Am.* /*Br.* **councillor**/ a member of a local council: *Billy drove at once...taking with them two Wanaque City Councilmen* – F. Edwards.
council office, housing, worker, etc. *esp. Br.* owned, employed, etc. by local council.
council school *Br.* public county school.
counselor 1. *esp. Am.* a lawyer: *arrange an interview with a counselor.* - Arkansas Times. 2. *Am.* person who takes care of kids at a summer camp.
counselor-at-law *Am., Irish Eng.* barrister.
count/ be down for the count *Am.* 1. be in knock-down. 2. fail in smth.
count me out *Br., Am.* I won't join you.

count the cost *esp. Br.* consider the extent of damage.
counter/ hunt/run counter *Br.* run against the direction taken by a quarry.
counter/ under the counter 1. *Br.* /*Am.* **under the table**/ dishonest or illegal. 2. *Am.* buying or selling illegal goods secretly.
(kitchen) counter *Am., Can.* /*Br.* **work surface, worktop**, *Aus.* **bench(top)**/ a flat surface in the kitchen where you prepare food, worktop: *She picked up a washcloth and ran it over clean counter tiles.* - J. Kellerman.
counter *Am., Can.* a piece of a small plastic disc used in some board games.
counterclockwise *Am., Can.* /*Br.* **anticlockwise**/ in the opposite direction to the movement of the hands of a clock: *Watley made for shore, watching a dark shadow circle counterclockwise* – Reader's Digest.
counterfoil *Br.* /*esp. Am., Aus.* **stub**/ the part of a ticket, cheque, etc. which is kept as a record of payment.
counter lunch *Aus.* pub lunch.
countertop *Am., Can.* workbench: *countertop damage is significant* – Reader's Digest.
countervalue *Br.* an equivalent of value, esp. in military strategy.
count off *Am.* /*Br.* **number off**/ tech. v. number, count (things or people): *Count off the playing cards to see if you have a full set.* - Longman., *The sergeant told his squad to count off from right to left.* - H.C. Whitford., R.J. Dixson.
count out 1. *Br.* close Parliament meeting because there is not enough members: *The house was counted out.* - Longman. 2. *esp. Am.* prevent from being elected by wrong vote counting: *He wasn't voted out, he was counted out.* - Longman.
countian *esp. Am.* an inhabitant of a certain county.
counting room *Am.* counting house.
country/ appeal/go to the country *esp. Br.* (of a Prime Minister) call a general election to test public opinion after dissolving Parliament.
country house *Br.* a large house in the country which has a lot of land and has often been owned by the same family for hundreds of years.
country mile *esp. Am., Aus., Can.* col. a very long distance: *Beats Shangri-La by a country mile.* - T. de Haven.
country round *Br.* day's round of a /*Br.* **roundsman**, *esp. Am.* **delivery man**.
country seat *Br.* countryside house of sb. who is rich and owns land.

(the) county *Br.* col. adj. n. (belonging to or typical of) the gentry of a county.
county 1. *Am.* a political and administrative division of state. 2. *Br., Irish Eng.* administrative, judicial, and political division of Great Britain and Ireland.
county council *Br.* an elected group of people which forms the government of a county.
council court *Br.* a local court of law in England which deals with cases which don't involve crimes.
county fair *Am.* event that happens each year in a particular county with games and competitions for the best farm animals, cooking, etc.
county family *Br.* aristocratic family with an ancestral seat in a county.
county school *Br.* public school supported by local community.
county town *Br.* /*Am.* **county seat**/ the chief town of a county: *Alton is the county seat.* - H. Truman.
coupe *esp. Br.* car with two doors and a sloping back.
couple *Br.* col. a small number of things or people, though not exactly two.
coupon-clipper *Am., Can.* col. a person having a lot of interest bearing bonds.
courgette *Br.* /*Am., Aus.* **zuchini**/ a small green marrow eaten cooked as a vegetable.
courier *Br.* person employed by a travel company to help holiday-makers.
a course of tablets / injections / treatments, etc. *esp. Br.* medicine or medical treatment that sb. has regularly for a period of time.
course/ over the course of time *Am.* in the course of time, after time has passed.
course/ stay the course of smth *Am.* stay the course, continue to do smth. in spite of difficulties.
coursebook *Br.* textbook for a certain course of study.
Court *esp. Br.* part of the name of a short street or an apartment building.
court *esp. Br.* a block of flats.
court/ district court *Am.* court of the county.
court card *Br.* /*Am.* **face card**, *Am.* sl. **paint card**/ the king, queen or jack in a set of playing cards.
courtesy title *esp. Br.* a title of nobility having no legal status.
courthouse 1. *esp. Am.* a building in which a court of law meets: *trying to negotiate a traffic jam around the courthouse.* - A. Hitchcock Mystery Magazine. 2. *Am.* a building containing administrative offices of the county.
court of claims *Am.* federal court in which claims against the government are adjudicated.
court(s) of inquiry/enquiry *Br.* fact-finding board.
court of summary jurisdiction *Br.* magistrate's court that tries summary offences without a jury.
court shoe *Br.* /*Am.* **pump**/ plain shoe with medium sized heels and no fastenings.
court tennis *Am., Can.* real tennis.
cove *Br.* obs. col., *Aus.* sl. a man, fellow: *Now, Peter, my cove, let's all draw round the table and make oneself cosy.* - Cpt. Marryat.
Coventry/ send sb. **to Coventry** *Br.* col. refuse to speak to sb, as punishment.
cover *Br.* /*Am.* **coverage**/ protection by insurance against a liability, loss or accidents involving financial consequences.
cover/ cover (all) the bases *Am.* deal with the problem thoroughly.
cover/ cover one's **ass/butt** *Am., Can.* taboo. sl. /*Br.* **cover** one's **back**/ do smth. to protect oneself from blame if smth. goes wrong in the future.
cover the waterfront *esp. Am., Can.* col. talk or write everything about smth.: *The principal pretty well covered the waterfront on student behavior.* - A. Makkai.
coveralls *Am.* /*Br.* **overalls**/ a boiler suit: *One client in the construction business is always in coveralls and hard hat.* - Atlantic Monthly.
covered coat *Br.* short light overcoat worn for sports: *But I recognized her back – the brown hat and the blue covert coat* – M. Daly.
covered (goods) wagon *Br.* /*Am.* **boxcar**/ box-wagon.
covering letter *Br.* /*Am., Can., Aus.* **cover letter** or **note**/ a letter or note containing an explanation or additional information, sent with a parcel or another letter.
cover note *esp. Br.* short printed record proving that insurance money has been paid and giving insurance protection until a proper insurance contract (policy) is ready, esp. for a car.
cover story *Am.* magazine article illustration to which is featured on its cover: *Time's cover-story last week was about the President.* - H.C. Whitford., R.J. Dixson.
covert coat *Br.* a short light overcoat for outdoor sports, such as shooting and riding.

cow 1. *Aus., NZ.* col. disagreeable person or thing, e.g. **cow of a dog; fair cow** is a difficult situation. 2. *Br.* sl. unpleasant woman: *that was sweet revenge on the silly stuck-up cow.* - D. Lodge.
cow/ have a cow *Am., Can.* col. be very worried, upset or angry: *I know Mom would have a cow.* – R.L. Stine.
cowardy *Br.* col. a cowardly person.
cowboy *Br.* 1. col. person who is careless and dishonest in business, also **wild cowboy.** 2. col. drive recklessly.
Cowboy City *Am.* sl. Cheyenne, Wyoming.
The Cowboy State *Am.* Wyoming.
cow camp *Am., Can.* a seasonal camp used as a cattle round-up.
cowcatcher, pilot *Am.* an inclined frame on the front of a railway locomotive for throwing obstacles off the track.
cow chip, cow flop, cow pie *esp. Am., Can. /Br.* **cow pat/** round flat mass of dried solid waste from a cow.
cowcocky *Aus., NZ.* col. milk farm owner, small-scale cattle farmer.
cow college *Am.* 1. agricultural college: *Every instructor in every cow college is trying to get to be an assistant professor* - R.L. Chapman. 2. any small provincial college: *John wanted to go to a big college in New York City, not to a cow college.* - A. Makkai.
cow corn *Am.* pod corn.
cow-hide *Am.* whip made of raw hide.
cow house *Br.* a shed or shelter for cows.
cow-hunt *Am.* a search for strayed cattle.
cowlick *esp. Am.* a tuft of hair that stands up from the head: *His comb forked over on the right side of his head like a cow-lick.* – E. Caldwell.
cowly *Can.* cruel.
cowman 1. *Am.* col. a cattle owner. 2. *Br.* a male cowherd. 3. *Aus.* a person who owns a large cattle farm.
cow parsley *Br. /Am.* **Queen Anna's lace/** a wild plant with white flowers, that grows esp. in the fields and along the roads in the countryside.
cowpuncher, cow poke *Am., Can.* col. obs. cowboy.
cowtown 1. *Am., Can.* col. small town in a cattle-raising area. 2. *Can.* Calgary, Alberta: *The Calgary Stampede is the pride of Cowtown. Y'all come!* - W. Magnuson. 3. *Am.* Fort Worth, Texas.
coydog *Am., Can.* a hybrid between a coyote and a dog.
coyote *Am.* sl. person who preys on those illegally immigrating to the USA.

The Coyote State *Am.* South Dakota.
coz *Am., Can.* col. cousin.
cozy *Can.* energetic.
cozy up to *Am.* try to start a friendship with (sb.): *anxious to cozy up to Javier, she asked if he was headed inside.* - D. Mortman.
cozzie *Aus. Br.* col. a swimming costume.
CPA /*Am., Can.* **certified public accountant,** *Br.* **chartered accountant/** *Am.* one who has successfully completed his/her training: *I'm going to send my husband to school and make him a CPA.* - J. Riffkin, T. Howard., *Howie became a successful CPA.* - D. Brenner.
crab *Am.* col. person who easily becomes annoyed about unimportant things.
crabgrass *Am.* a type of weed.
(the) crack *Br.* sl. 1. also *Irish Eng.* good time; **good crack** is friendly enjoyable talk in a group: *Dad would stop and they would have a crack* – R. Westall. 2. the latest trend, news: *I tried Australia but I came back because I missed the crack.* - T. Thorne.
crack/ fall/slip through the cracks *Am., Can. /Br.* **fall/slip through the net/** not work properly.
crack/ paper over the cracks/conflict, disagreement, difference, etc. *esp. Br.* try to conceal that smth. went wrong rather than deal with it.
crack/ crack a book *Am., Can.* col. study.
crack/ crack wise *Am., Can.* col. make jokes.
crack/ slip through the net *esp. Br.* avoid being caught by a system.
crack/ take a crack at smth. *Am.* make an attempt to achieve smth.
crack on *Br.* col. go on, carry on.
crack/ a fair crack of the whip *Br., Aus.* col. a fair chance of doing smth.
crack/ crack a crib *Br.* sl. rob a house.
crack/ crack a deal *Am.* col. succeed in business after some difficulties.
crack/ crack a record *Am.* make a record, esp. in sport.
crack/ crack a smile *Am.* col. smile when. sb. has been serious, sad, or angry.
crack/ crack hardy / hearty *Aus.* pretend not to be afraid.
crack/ crack it *Br.* col. succeed in some way, esp. in seduction.
crack/ walk (a) the crack *Am.* walk straight along a floorboard.
crack/ what's the crack? *Br.* col. What's happening?
crack on *Br.* sl. talk incessantly, boast.

cracked record *Br.* person saying the same thing again and again.

cracker *esp. Am. /esp. Br.* **savoury/** small thin unsweetened biscuit.

cracker 1. *Br.* col. a very nice-looking woman. 2. *Am.* col. usu. derog. poor white person, esp. from the south-eastern US: *Haggard is no racist cracker* - Atlantic Monthly. 3. *Aus.* cattle driver's rattle. 4. *Br.* col. smth. that is very good.

cracker-barrel *Am., Can.* col. 1. unsophisticated, basic. 2. intimate, gossipy: *lawyer with a common sense voice from the cracker-barrel.* - T. Thompson.

crackerjack *esp. Am., Can.* col. very good.

crackers *esp. Br., Aus., Can.* col. (of a person) mad: *Have you gone crackers, Doc?* - A. McLean., *You're crackers.* - G. Greene.

The Cracker State *Am.* Georgia.

cracking, also **crack** *Br.* col. very good.

cracking *Br., Aus.* col. energetic / **get cracking** or **weaving** *esp. Br.* col. a. start working hard at smth.: *get cracking on that novel of yours as soon as you can.* - L. Uris. b. go or leave, esp. quickly, also **go at a cracking pace**.

crackling *Br.* 1. col. derog. attractive women regarded collectively as objects of sexual desire. 2. /*Am.* **cracklings/** hard pieces of skin of a pig cooked and easily broken.

crack-up *Am.* col. 1. nervous breakdown. 2. car accident.

cradle *Br. /Am.* **scaffold/** a frame which hangs on the side of a building, ship, etc. for people to work from.

Cradle of the Confederacy *Am.* Montgomery, Ala.

cradle-robber *Am.* humor. /*Br., Aus.* humor. **cradle-snatcher/**.

cradle snatching *Br. /Am.* **robbing the cradle/** having sexual relationship with a person of much younger age; **rob the cradle** *Am. /Br.* **cradle snatch/**.

craft *esp. Am.* make using skill, esp. by hand: *I have nothing but admiration for people who can craft their own clothes.* - Sydney Calendar., *A dining room table crafted in solid cherry costs more than a plastic table* - World Monitor.

craft beer/brew *Am.* beer with a specific flavour from a particular region.

craft knife *Br.* very sharp knife used for cutting paper, thin wood, etc.

craker *Aus.* sl. 1. whip. 2. one pound note.

cram *Br.* help sb. prepare for an exam by intensive study.

cramful *Br.* col. chockfull.

crammer *Br.* a person or institution that prepares a pupil for an examination intensively over a short period of time.

cramp severe pain from the sudden tightening of a muscle / In the US noun is countable, in Britain and Australia it is uncountable: *she won her third straight Boston Marathon despite severe cramps.* - Time.

cramps *Am., Can.* abdominal pain caused by menstruation.

crane truck, wrecking crane *Am. /Br.* **breakdown lorry/** emergency repairs crane.

crank *Am.* col. a nasty bad-tempered person: *Why are you such a crank?* - R.A. Spears.

crank (smth.) out *esp. Am., Can.* col. produce smth. in great amounts: *Media...have cranked out a plethora of feel-good features on Muslim culture.* - Reader's Digest.

crank up *Am.* col. get started: *Bennet started to crank up a new idea* - T. Thompson., *We are yakking and gossiping and hanging out and getting cranked up* - J. Baez.

cranky 1. *esp. Am., Can., Aus.* col. /*Br.* **bad-tempered/** nasty: *the members divided among themselves, cranky about their presumptive Presidential nominee* - Time. 2. *Br.* eccentric.

crap around /up/ *Am.* sl. mess around, waste time: *Why don't you stop crapping around?* – P. Roth.

crap out *Am.* col. 1. lose the game of craps: *it's the third time I've crapped out tonight.* - Longman. 2. get away.

crap/ be a load/bunch of crap *Am.* be very bad or completely untrue.

crape hair *Br.* artificial hair used by actors, esp. for beards and moustache.

crap game *Am., Can.* a game of craps.

crape hanger, crepe hanger *Am.* col. pessimist: *Instead of saying that he thought our new offices were very nice, he stood around like a crapehanger.* - H.C. Whitford., R.J. Dixson.

crapola *Am.* taboo. sl. lies and exaggeration: *He writes crapola mini-series* - Vanity Fair.

the crapper *Br.* sl. rude word for toilet.

crap(s) *Am., Can., Aus.* gambling game played with two dice / **crapshooter, crapshooting.**

crapshoot *Am., Can.* col. smth. risky or uncertain

crash *esp. Br. /esp. Am.* **wreck/** violent vehicle accident.

crash and burn *Am., Can., Aus.* col. fail suddenly and completely: *they go nuts and crash and burn* – Reader's Digest.

crash with *Am.* col. (esp. among young people) sleep or lodge in the home of (sb.) informally and often with little comfort, usu. without payment: *My parents have thrown me out, can I crash with you for tonight?* - Longman.

crash barrier *Br., Aus. /Am., Can.* **guardrail/** guard-rail on a highway at the side of a road or in the middle of it or on airport runway.

crashing bore *Br.* obs. very boring person.

crash-pad *Am.* col. a cheap lodging house esp. one for short stays: *I gotta find a crash pad for tonight.* - R.A. Spears.

crash repairs *Br.* body work, on a car.

C rations *Am., Can.* a type of tinned food formerly used by soldiers.

cravat *Br. /Am.* **ascot/** a wide piece of material loosely folded and worn round the neck by men.

craw/ stick in one's **craw** *Am.* col. be unpalatable or impossible to continue.

crawfish, crawdad esp. *Am., Can.* col. */Aus. NZ.* **cray(fish), lobster/** freshwater crayfish.

crawfish *Am.* col. retreat from a position: *Well, did he crawfish on that?* – J. O'Hara.

crawl esp. *Br.* progress from one pub to another.

crawler *Br.* col. a toady.

crawler lane *Br.* special part of a road that can be used by slow vehicles.

crazy esp. *Am.* col. 1. wonderful. 2. also *Can.* an eccentric person.

crazy/ crazy as a bedbug /Am. col. **crazy as a loon/** esp. *Am.* very illogical.

crazy bone *Am.* funny bone.

crazy golf *Br. /Am.* **miniature golf/** game like golf in which the players hit the ball through very amusing obstacles.

crazy paving esp.*Br., Aus.* irregular pieces of stone fitted together to make a path or flat place: *take down the garden wall, crazy pave the lawn.* - B. Bryson.

crazy quilt *Am.* one made of patches.

cream *Am., Can.* milk or thin cream added to coffee.

cream esp. *Am., Can., Aus.* col. defeat completely: *I think we got him cream.* - D. Brenner., *But a Jew kid and me creamed him.* – A. Summers, R. Swan

cream bun *Br.* a bun filled or topped with cream.

cream cake esp. *Br.* one with a filling of cream custard.

cream caramel *Br.* custard / British custard is a (dessert) sauce.

cream cracker *Br.* dry, unsweetened biscuit which is usually eaten with cheese.

creamed potatoes *Br. /Br.* col. **mash/** mashed potatoes.

creamer *Am.. Can., Aus.* or old use */Br.* **cream jug, milk jug/** a small vessel for holding cream.

cream pie *Am.* cream cake.

cream puff *Am., Can.* col. used car or other thing that is kept in very good condition.

cream soda *Am.* fizzy drink flavoured with vanilla.

cream tea *Br.* afternoon tea with (Devonshire) cream, scones and jam.

crease 1. (**up**) *Br.* col. (cause) to burst laughing. 2. *Am.* wound slightly, esp. by grazing.

create 1. *Br.* officially give. sb. special rank or title. 2. *Br., Aus.* obs. be noisily angry.

creature *Am.* farm animal.

creche 1. esp. *Br., Aus. /Am.* **day-care (center)/** place where babies and small children are cared for while their parents work: *Creches at the office are not the whole answer* - C. Handy. 2. *Am., Can. /Br.* **crib/** a model of the scene of Christ's birth, often placed in churches and homes at Christmas: *three dahlia bushes obscured the creche* - W. Grady.

cred *Br.* sl. respect, credibility.

credential *Am.* certificate, diploma of the university or college: *Bruce graduated from the university with B.A. degree and a teaching credential.* - K.F. Hird., *Many studenrs seek only a credential, not an education.* - Reader's Digest.

credit 1. *Am.* v. n. (give) a certificate of completion of a course by a student. 2. esp. *Am., Can.* a measure of student's work, often equal to one hour of classtime per week: *they finally gave me credits* - Alcoholics Anonymous.

credit/ in credit esp. *Br.* having money, not owing money.

credit account *Br. /*esp. *Am., Aus.* **charge account/** account with a shop which allows one to take the goods at once and pay for them later: *he'd seen it on too many a charge account* - C. Woolrich.

credit note *Br., Aus. /Am.* **credit voucher/** a piece of paper which can be given by a shop when you return smth. you don't want and allows you to buy other goods of the same value at another time.

credit slip *Br. /Am.* **deposit slip/** deposit slip in a bank.

credit squeeze *Br., Aus. /Am.* **credit crunch/** a period of economic depression when it's difficult to borrow money from banks.

credit transfer *Br.* direct payment from one bank to another.

creek 1. *Br.* long narrow body of water reaching from the sea, a lake, etc., into the land. 2. *Am., Can., Aus.* a small narrow stream.

creek/ be up sheet creek *Br.* be stupid or be misled.

creek bottom *Am.* level ground beside a stream.

creep *Br.* 1. a hole in a wall or hedge for an animal to pass through. 2. special solid food for young farm animals.

creep 1. *esp. Am.* col. very detestable person. 2. *Br.* col. insincere flatterer.

creep up to *Br.* col. flatter sb. in order to get advantage for oneself.

creepers *Am.* rompers, one-piece garment for babies combining a top and short trouser-like bottom.

creep dive /joint/ *Am.* sl. unpleasant place populated by creeps, tavern.

creepie-crawlie *Aus.* automatic vacuum cleaner for a home swimming pool.

creeping Jesus *Br.* col. hypocritically pious person.

creepy-crawly *esp. Br.* col. creeping insect: *Sleeping in the open with jungle creepy-crawlers.* - B. Tillman., *creepy crawlies that bite and sting* - National Geographic.

creole *Am.* heavy working shoe.

The Creole State, also **The Pelican State** *Am.* Louisiana.

crepe *Am.* pancake.

crescent *esp. Br.* a street or a number of houses forming an arc.

crescent wrench *Am., Can.* adjustable spanner with a crescent-like head having an adjustable screw, used for hexogonal nuts.

Crescent City *Am.* New Orleans.

crescents *Am.* croissants, crescent rolls.

crew 1. *Br.* sl. (street) gang. 2. *esp. Am.* col. a group of young people, connected with hip-hop sub-culture who spend their time together. 3. *Am., Can.* col. criminal gang.

crib 1. *esp. Am., Can., Aus.* or *Br.* obs. */Br., Aus.* **cot/** bed for a baby or young child / In Britain **crib** is used for a new-born baby only, after the that the infant sleeps in a **cot**: *a baby was wailing an unheeded lament in a crib by the nurse's station.* - R. Cook., *I'd hang over the crib and marvel at him.* - E. Taylor. 2. *Br. /Am.* **creche/** model of the scene of Christ's birth: *a photograph of his family round a Christmas crib.* - A. Burgess. 3. *Am.* a box, metal container or small building for storing grain: *the animal would unerringly find his way to the corn crib* – K. Chopin. 4. *Am., Can.* small raft of timber.

5. *esp. Am., Can.* col. an apartment or house. 6. *Aus., NZ.* a light meal 7. *Br.* sl. house one intends to rob. 8. *Am.* sl. a brothel: *some sailors from the naval yard Algiers got foolin' around in them cribs in the District.* - M. Jones, J. Chilton.

crib/ public crib *Am.* public coffers / **feast at the public crib.**

crib (notes) *esp. Am.* col. prepared notes for cheating in an examination.

crib tin *Aus.* box of food that the worker takes for his breakfast at work.

cricket/ it's/that's (just) not cricket *Br., Aus.* journalism. or obs. it's against the rules.

crikey *esp. Br.* col. excl. (an expression of surprise).

crim *esp. Aus.* col. criminal.

crime sheet *Br.* a form in which details of a reported crime are written.

crimp *Am., Can.* col. prevent smth. from developing or growing, restrict or reduce smth., n. restriction., esp. in **put a crimp on**: *But supplies have been crimped by a virus infecting pigs.* – Reader's Digest.

Crimplene *Br.* tdmk. an artificial cloth used for clothes, that doesn't easily crease.

cringe (sb.) *Br.* col. embarrass (sb.); adj. **cringe-making.**

crip *esp. Am., Can.* 1. a disabled person. 2. a member of a Los Angeles street gang.

crisp/ also **potato crisp** *Br. /Am. Aus., Can.* **(potato) chip/** thin piece of potato cooked in very hot fat, dried, and usu. sold in packets: *a packet of crisps was 5p* - B. Bryson.

crit *esp. Br.* col. (of literary or artistic work) critical review.

critical *Am.* scarce, rationed.

critical point *Am.* (in mathematics) stationary point.

critique *Am.* criticize, esp. artistic or literary work.

critter *esp. Am.* col. a living creature: *visitors hoping to spot the mysterious critter.* - Time., *Your mattress can easily harbor two million thriving little critters.* - Newsweek.

crock 1. *esp. Br.* col. an old car. 2. *Am.* col. smth. that is not true or not believable: *It's all just a crock, Mayra.* – R.L. Stine. 3. *Br.* cause an injury.

crock/ a crock of shit *esp. Am., Can.* taboo. col. smth. worthless: *But the whole thing was a crock.* – R.L. Stine.

crock/ old crock *Br.* col. an old and weak person or an old car.

crocked 1. *Am., Can.* col. drunk: *Bagged, cronked, zonked. - She sighed.* - L. Waller. 2. *Am.* sl. angry. 3. *Br.* col. obs. broken or injured.

crockery *esp. Br. /esp. Am.* **earthenware/** cups, plates, etc. made from baked clay: *smashing crockery and furniture* - J. O'Brien, A. Kurins.

Crockpot *Am., Can.* tdmk. big electric kitchen pot used for cooking meals slowly.

crocodile *Br.* col. line of people, esp. schoolchildren walking in pairs: *crocodiles of boys filed past crocodiles of girls.* – R. Westall.

crocodile clip *Br.* a special clip used for temporary electrical connections.

croft *Br.* very small farm, esp. in Scotland, **crofter** is one who lives and works on such a farm: *a brutal policy of eviction of the crofter.* - J. Ruppeldtova, n. **–ing.**

cron(e)yism *esp. Am.* nepotism.

cronk *Aus.* col. very weak.

crook *Aus.* col. adj. 1. /*Br.* **poorly/** sick. 2. (of things) nasty, bad.

crook/ go/be crook at sb. or **on** sb. *Aus., N.Z.* col. get angry or be annoyed at sb.

crooked *Aus., NZ.* col. annoyed.

crookneck *Am., Can.* a squash of club-shaped variety.

crop-dusting *Am.* crop-spraying.

cropper *esp. Am.* a sharecropper.

cropper/ come a cropper 1. *Br.* col. a. fall over. b. fall in an embarrassing way. 2. *Br.* make a mistake.

croppy *Aus.* obs. convict.

cross *Br.* a mark (x) on paper used to show where smth. is or that smth. that has been written is not correct.

cross (a cheque) *Br., Aus.* draw two lines across the middle of a cheque which means it must be paid into a bank account.

cross *Aus.* obs. profitable deal.

cross *esp. Br.* annoyed or angry.

cross/ a cross (sb.) **has to bear** *Br., Aus.* /*Am., Aus.* **carry/** one's inevitable burden.

cross/ as cross as two sticks *Br.* very annoyed.

cross/ cross sb.'s **palm with silver** *esp. Br.* give money to sb.

cross/ cross the floor *Br.* join the opposing side in Parliament.

cross/ get one's **lines crossed** *Br.* be mistaken about what sb. else means or thinks.

cross over *esp. Br.* change one's loyalty, esp. political: *The politician crossed over and joined the Opposition.* - Longman.

cross up *Am.* sl. confuse or deceive: *They are going to cross you up.* - D. Hammet.

crossbuck *Am.* warning cross (on railways).

crossbus(s)ing *Am.* cross carrying of pupils by bus from one area to another (in order to achieve integrated schooling).

cross country *Br.* race run across countryside and fields.

cross-curricular *Br.* (of education) connected with more than one subject.

cross dressing *Am.* the practice of wearing the clothes of opposite sex, esp. for sexual pleasure.

cross-hairs *Am.* cross wires (of optical device in hunting).

crossing at grade, grade crossing *Am., Can.* /*Br.* **level crossing/**.

crossing guard *Am.* /*Br.* **lollipop man, woman/** a person whose job is to stop traffic so that schoolchildren can cross the street.

cross-lots *Am.* col. adj. adv. in the shortest way possible.

crossover 1. *esp. Br.* arrangement of lines by which a train may move from one track to another. 2. *esp. Br.* /also *Br.* **flyover,** *Am.* **overpass/** road passing over another road. 3. *Am.* crossing or passage from one side, level or track to another.

crossover primary *Am.* open primary.

cross-ply *Br.* (of a tyre) with layers of fabric that have threads running diagonally to each other.

cross-pressure *Am., Can.* expose to different opinions.

crossroads *esp. Br. /esp. Am., Can.* **intersection** /a place where several roads meet.

Crossroads of the Pacific *Am.* Honolulu, Hawaii.

cross street *Am., Can.* a road crossing the main road or connecting two roads.

cross talk *Br.* rapid exchange of clever remarks, esp. between two actors: *lovely to be here together with all the cross-talk* - J. Fowles.

(cross) tie *Am.* /*Br.* **(railway) sleeper/** a piece of wood, metal, etc. supporting a railway track: *the authorities found five deep indentations in the wood of the crossties.* – F. Edwards.

crosstown *Am.* adj. running through the town. e.g. *a crosstown line.*

crosswalk *Am., Can., Aus.* /*Br.* **pedestrian crossing, zebra crossing/**: *truck caught the old fella in the crosswalk* - S. Grafton.

crotchet *Br. /esp. Am.* **quarter note/**.

croupe *Am.* col. work as a croupier.

crow/ eat crow *Am., Can.* col. be forced to admit that one was wrong: *it was a bitter experience for him to eat crow after the election results proved his predictions to be so clearly inaccurate.* - H.C. Whitford., R.J. Dixson.

crow/ stone the crows/stone me! *Br., Aus.* sl. becoming obs. (expression of surprise, disbelief, etc.).
crow bait *Am., Can.* col. derog. an old horse.
crowd 1. *Am.* col. press close to, reach a certain age. 2. *esp. Am.* make sb. angry or upset by making too many unfair demands on them.
crowd the mourners *Am.* importune sb. in an unseemly way.
crowded out *esp. Br.* col. very full, packed out.
crowd-puller *Br.., Aus.* smth. that attracts a lot of attention.
croweater *Aus.* a citizen of South Australia.
crowfoot *Am.* piece of zink on one of the poles of electrodes in batteries.
crow hop *Am., Can.* a jump made by a horse with its back arched and its legs stiffened.
crow jim(ism) *Am.* strong anti-white prejudice among blacks.
crown/ crown it all *Br., Aus.* /*Am.* **cap it all/** make good or bad luck complete.
crown estate *Br.* lands owned by the nation.
crown green *Br.* a type bowling green with a slight rise in the middle.
crown moulding *Am.* cornice, a decorative molding that crowns the walls of the room just before the ceiling.
crown prosecutor *Br.* /*Can.* **crown attorney/** official responsible for trying to prove in a law court that people accused of crimes are guilty.
crucial *Br.* sl. very good.
cruel *Aus.* col. damage, spoil.
cruel and unusual punishment *Am* one disproportionate to the crime: *recreation, diet and hygiene are required by the constitutional guarantee against cruel and unusual punishment.* - Time.
cruelty-free products *Br.* developed without being tested on animals.
cruet 1. *Br., Aus.* (a set of) containers for pepper, salt, oil, etc. for use at meals. 2. *Am.* a glass bottle for oil or vinegar for use at meals.
cruise 1. *Can.* exploratory tour through a region. 2. *Am.* sl. move through life at a comfortable pace.
cruiser 1. *Am., Can.* a police (patrol) car: *First I saw the blue-and-white police cruiser in the driveway.* – R.L. Stine. 2. *Am.* sl. a car: *The cruiser's turn signal went on* – R.L. Stine.
cruiserweight *esp. Br.* a light heavyweight boxer.
cruising for a bruising *Am., Can.* sl. looking for trouble: *Watch out - you're cruisin' for a bruisin'* - Reader's Digest.

cruller *Am., Can.* small sweet cake formed into twisted strips and fried in deep fat: *Coffee, a cruller and a Pepsy to go.* - R. Moore.
crumb *Am.* col. obs. a worthless person.
crumb (it) *Am.* sl. ruin, mess up.
crumble *Br.* a mixture of flour and fat specially prepared as topping for fruit.
crumbly *Br.* an old person.
crumbs *Br., Aus.* col. excl. (an expression of surprise).
crummy *Am., Can.* old loggers' truck used for getting to work.
crumped out *Am.* sl. drunk: *Mac crumped out, huh?* - L. Waller.
crumpet *Br.* col. 1. woman considered as sexual object (considered extremely offensive to women): *I saw a piece of crumpet dancing across the parapet.* - J.P. Donleavy. 2. a man or men considered solely from the point of view of being sexually attractive. 3. obs. head.
crumple zone *Br., Aus.* part of a car that is designed to crumple easily in an accident and to protect people inside from being hit too hard.
crunch *Am.* difficult situation caused by a lack of money; **feel the crunch** not have enough money.
crunchy *Am., Can.* col. politically liberal and environmentally aware.
crush up *Br.* col. (of people) fit into a small place moving closer to each other.
crush bar *Br.* theatre bar working only in the intervals between performances.
crush barrier *Br.* a temporary barrier for restraining a crowd.
crust *Aus.* means of existence.
crust/ earn a/one's crust *Br.* earn enough money to live on.
crustie *Br.* a member of a group of young people who have adopted a lifestyle characterised by the wearing of rough, torn clothes, and by matted, often dread-locked hair.
crutch *Br.* crotch, the part of the body between the tops of person's legs.
cry/ have a cry *esp. Br.* cry some tears.
cry/ in full cry *esp. Br.* doing smth. very actively.
cry off *Br.* say one will not fullfil a promise or agreement: *he would cry off some of these sidetrips on the cruise* - J. Fowles.
cry stinking fish *Br.* disparage one's efforts or products.
cry uncle *Am.* col. admit defeat: *the eye cried uncle.* - Time.

crying/ for crying outloud *esp. Br.* sl. (used to give strength to a demand, request, etc.) *For crying outloud shut the door!* – Longman.

crystal *Am. /Br.* **watch glass/** transparent cover over the face of a clock or watch: *The watch's crystal was gone* - D. Hammet.

CS *Br.* 1. Chartered Surveyor. 2. Civil Service. 3. Court Session.

CS gas *Br.* tear gas.

C-section *Am.* col. caesarean section.

C three or **C3** *Br. /Am.* **4F/** unfit for military duty.

cub/ the Cubs *Br.* the Cub Scout organisation.

cubby *esp. Am., Can.* cubbyhole.

cubby(hole) *Br.* glove compartment in a car.

a cuckoo in the nest *Br.* getting advantage out of situation without doing anything for the other people involved.

cuddly toys *Br., Aus.* animals which are soft and covered in fur.

cudgel/ take up the cudgels for sb./smth. *Br., Aus.* argue strongly on behalf of sb./smth.

cue in *esp. Am.* col. add (words or music) at a certain point of play: *The new song is cued in here.* - Longman.

cuff *Am., Aus. /Br.* **turn-up/** narrow band of cloth turned upwards at the bottom of a trouser leg: *Some sandfly buzzing around his trousers cuffs* - J. Patterson.

cuff/ on the cuff *Am. /esp. Br.* col. **on the slate/** on credit: *I would've done him for nothing. On the cuff.* - G.V. Higgins., *I won thirty-two dollars - on the cuff.* - D. Hammet.

cuffed pants *Am. /Br.* **turn-ups/**.

cuke *Am.* col. cucumber: *O'Brien gestured expansively over the cukes* - J. O'Brien, A. Kurins.

cull *Am.* 1. smth. rejected for inferiority or worthlessness: *The chickens my father had given me were culls, or rejects* - Reader's Digest. 2. sl. socially unacceptable person.

culture-vulture/ a bit of a culture vulture *Br.* derog. person too eager to be in the presence of cultural achievements.

cum laude *Am.* finish the university in the US and be given official praise for special achievement.

Cumberland sausage *Br.* a kind of sausage served as a spiral.

cumulative trauma disorder *Am., Can.* work related upper limb disorder.

cunning *esp. Am.* col. attractive, pretty, cute: *It was a cunning lattice of very light steel posts and beams.* - K. Vonnegut, Jr.

cunt *esp. Br.* sl. very unpleasant or stupid person: *Because I can spell Rosestreet, ye thieving cunt* - B. Bryson.

cup *Am. /Br.* **hole/** (in golf) a. hollow place in the ground into which the ball must be hit. b. area of play with such a hole at the far end.

cup 1. *esp. Am., Can.* half pint, about a quarter of a litre, unit of measure of 8 fluid ounces, much used in cooking. 2. *Br.* mixed alcoholic drink.

cup *Can.* receptacle part of a liquidiser.

cup *Am. /Br.* **box/** protective covering for male genitals used in sports.

cup/ in one's **cups** *Br.* obs. drunk.

cupboard *Br., Can. /Am.* **closet/**.

cupboard love *Br., Aus.* love shown only for the purpose of gaining a reward. e.g. by a pet hoping for food.

cupcake *Am.* sl. 1. attractive woman (often used as a form of address): *Who is that cupcake driving the beemer?* - R.A. Spears. 2. a. eccentric person. b. effeminate man. 3. also *Aus. /Br.* **fairy cake/** a small light cake with eggs, sugar and flour.

cupcake tin *Am. /Br.* **baking tray/**.

cup custard *esp. Am. /Br.* **baked custard/**.

cup final *Br.* (esp. in football) the last match to decide the winning team in a competition.

cuppa *esp. Br., Aus.* col. a cup of tea: *What about a cuppa while you're 'ere?* - D. Reeman., *there has got to be someone who has shared a cuppa with her* - New Idea., *Let's go in for a cuppa.* - C.M. Fraser.

cup-tie *Br.* (esp. in football) match between two teams competing in a competition.

cup-tied *Br.* (of a sports player) ineligible to play for one's club having played for another club in an earlier round.

curate's assistant *Br.* muffin stand.

a/the curate's egg *Br.* col. part good, part bad / usu. in **good in parts, like the curate's egg.**

curator *Aus. /esp. Br.* **groundsman/** man employed to take care of a sports field or large gardens.

curb *esp. Am. /Br., Aus.* kerb/.

curb cut *Am., Can.* a small ramp built into the curb for easier passing of bicycles and wheelchairs between pavement and the street.

curbie, also **carhop** *Am.* sl. drive-in waiter.

curd cheese *esp. Br.* cheese made from skimmed milk.

curl *Aus.* the most suitable wave for surfing.

curl up *Br.* begin to laugh uncontrollably.

curl/ curl the mo *Aus.* sl. succeed, win.

curling tongs *esp. Am. /Br.* **curling irons/** piece of equipment that a person heats and uses to put curls in their hair.

currawong *Aus.* a large black and white bird with a loud musical cry.

current account *Br. /Am.* **checking account/** bank account which usu. doesn't earn interest and from which money can be taken out at any time by cheque.

curriculum vitae, also **CV, cv** 1. *esp. Br. /Am., Aus.* **resume,** *Am.* **biodata/**. 2. *Am.* document in which university teacher writes a list of their teaching experience and articles, books, etc. they have written when they are applying for a job.

curry *esp. Am., Can.* groom (a horse) with curry-comb.

curse/ not give / care a (tinker's) curse /Am. damn/ be quite unworried (about).

curtain fire *Br. /Am.* **curtain of fire/** rapid and intense fire of artillery and/or machine-guns on a specific area.

a curtain raiser *Br.* the first thing discussed.

curtains 1. *Br. /Am.* **draperies/** window curtains. 2. *Am. /Br.* **net curtain/** very thin curtains which are hung in front of windows in order to prevent people from seeing in.

curtsey/ bob a curtsey to *Br.* make a curtsey.

curve/ throw sb. **a curve (ball), curve balls** *esp. Am., Aus.* sl. surprise or deceive sb. by smth. unpredicted: *storms during winter's end throw us a curve* - Outdoor Life.

curve ball *Am.* one that curves as it moves towards the player with the bat.

cushion 1. *Aus.* a type of surfboard. 2. *Am.* sl. money saved for the rainy day.

cushion/ on the cushion *Am.* in clover, living in comfort.

cushy number/ be on to a cushy number *Br.* find an easy job to do.

cuspidor *Am.* spittoon: *I ain't got no black marble cuspidors* - D. Hammet., *There were cuspidors in every corner.* - E.L. Doctorow.

cuss *Am.* col. or *Br.* obs. swear: *Elvis started cussing back at them.* – J. Hopkins.

cuss/ not give a (tinker's) cuss *Br. /Am.* **not give a damn/ a good, goddamn/** not to care.

cuss sb. **out** *Am.* col. swear and shout at sb. being angry at them.

cuss word *Am.* swear word.

custard *esp. Br.* yellow liquid for pouring over sweet foods made of sweetened milk thickened with eggs and flour or with a dry mixture of these sold as a custard powder / solid custard is usu. **baked custard** in Britain, **cup custard** in the US: *He ate cup custard.* - E.L. Doctorow., *She is never too busy to make real custard either.* – S. Townsend.

custard power *Br., Aus.* a yellowish powder used instead of eggs and flour to make custard.

custodian *Am. /esp. Br,* **caretaker/** caretaker of a building.

custom 1. *Am.* adj. made to order. 2. *esp. Br.* regular relations of customers with a shop or business.

cool or **tough customer** *Br.* col. phrase used to indicate person's behaviour or character.

custom-house *esp. Am.* customs house.

cut 1. *Am.* block (in printing). 2. *esp. Am.* tech. quantity of wood (timber) cut down in a particular period of time. 3. *Am.* separated part of the cattle. 4. *Aus.* corporal punishment (esp. in school). 5. *Am.* missing a class at school; usu. in **have a cut.** 6. *Br.* power cut.

cut *Am.* 1. (out) separate (cattle) from a herd. 2. vote against.

cut *esp. Am., Can.* mix other substances with a drug or alcohol.

cut a corner *Br., Aus.* fail to keep to one's side of the road when going round the corner.

cut a deal *esp. Am., Can.* make a deal: *cut special stock deals for their friends.* – D.L. Barlett, J.B. Steele.

cut (sb.) **a little slack, cut** sb. **some slack** *Am.,, Can., Aus.* col. relax regulations: *Come on, cut me a little slack* - J. Kellerman.

cut a melon *Am.* distribute profits.

cut a/the rug *esp. Am., Can.* col. dance energetically.

cut a sign *Am.* come across smth., see smth.

cut a (wide) swath / or **gash** *Am.* put on airs; attract a lot of attention.

cut class / school *Am.* col. not go to a class or to a school when you should do.

cut sb. **dead** *Br.* deliberately ignore sb. or refuse to speak.

cut high shines *Am.* sl. do smth. remarkable.

cut in line *Am. /Br.* **jump the queue/**.

cut/ cut it *esp. Am., Can.* col. meet the requirements.

cut it/ can't/couldn't cut it *Am.* can't deal with problems: *I just wasn't cutting it.* – S. Lawrence.

cut it/ this doesn't/won't cut it (with sb.**)** *Am.* it is not good enough for smth.

cut it fine *Am.* col. calculate smth. correctly: *Cut it a bit bloody fine, didn't you?* - A. McLean.

cut one's **eye** *Am.* look askance at sb.

cut loose *Am., Aus.* behave wildly.

cut sb. **off** *Am.* stop serving alcoholic drinks to sb. because they are already too drunk.

cut (quite) a dash *esp. Br.* cause people to admire sb., esp. their stylish appearance

cut the bag open *Am.* col. tell a secret.
cut the mustard *Am., Aus., Can.* col. suit in everything: *American Harp Company can cut the mustard.* - K. Vonnegut, Jr.
cut the string *Am.* suit in everything.
cut out 1. *Am.* col. go faster: *Towards evening Vincent…cut out briskly for the Loyers'house.* – I. Stone. 2. *Am., Can.* col. leave quickly: *I was really confused and embarrassed and I cut out, completely blowing my cool.* - E. Cleaver. 3. *Aus.* finish sheep shearing. 4. *Am.* leave a line of traffic when every car is going fast.
cut to the chase *Am., Can.* col. get to the essense of the matter.
cut up *Am.* 1. also *Can.* col. play the fool: *he didn't cut up that way and let his hair down only in front of Negroes* - B. Holiday., W. Duffy. 2. cut down (the stem near the ground). 3. also *Can.* col. speak ill of. 4. (of a class) behave badly: *When he gets bad marks it only discourages him more and he starts cutting up.* – B. Kaufman.
cut up sb. *Br.* /*Am.* **cut off** sb./ (of drivers) move in front of another car which was in front of you, leaving you too little place.
cut up/ be cut up about smth. *esp. Br.* col. be very upset.
cut up rough *Br.* col. become very angry.
cut up soft *Am.* be unfit for the competition.
cut and thrust *esp. Br.* the methods of arguing or behaving that are typical of any very competitive activity.
cutaway (coat or **jacket)** *Am.* /*Br.* **tailcoat**/ one which is cut diagonally from the front to the back, so that the back is longer.
cute *esp. Am., Can.* 1. confident, but in a way that seems rude, often in **get cute with.** sb.: *Don't be cute with me, you slimy pimp* - R.L. Chapman. 2. sexually attractive.
cute/ be as cute as a button *Am., Aus.* very attractive.
cutesy *Am.* adj. pretty and clever in an annoying way.
cutie *esp. Am.* col. person or thing that is charming, attractive, clever, etc.: *Your baby is a real cutie.* - R.A. Spears.
cutlery *esp. Br., Can.* /*Am.* **silverware, flatware**/.
cutlet 1. *Am.* one that is made of chopped meat. 2. *Br.* lamb or veal chop.
cut line *Am., Can.* print. caption.
cut lunch *Aus.* col. sandwiches, packed lunch.
cut marks *Am.* /*Br.* **trim marks**/ marks printed on a sheet to indicate the edge of a page to be trimmed.

cut-off *esp. Am.* by-pass, the shortest route: *They ignored both the cut-offs to the Brooklyn-battery Tunnel* - R. Moore.
cut-offs *esp. Am.* jeans cut off above the knees with frayed edges: *Just the way you looked going down Burton Street in your cutoffs this summer.* - A. Hitchcock Mystery Magazine.
cut-out 1. *Am.* a crack (esp. in the floor). 2. *Am.* cattle separated from the herd. 3. *Aus.* the end of sheep shearing.
cut-rate *esp. Am.* cut-price.
cutter *Am.* 1. horse-drawn sledge for two persons: *she always had a carriage or a cutter at her disposal.* - J. O'Hara. 2. old cow or steer.
cutthroat razor *Br.* /*Am., Can.* **straight razor**/ a folding long razor blade set in a handle.
cutting 1. *Br.* /*Am.* **clipping**/ an article, photograph, etc. that is cut from a newspaper or magazine: *The reference library…has an immense number of newspaper cuttings.* - J. Ruppeldtova. 2. *Br.* /*Am.* **cut**/ smth. produced by cutting, esp. a passage cut through a hill for a road or railway.
cutting board *Br.* /*Am.* **chopping board**/.
a/the cutting edge *Br.* the ability or the equipment one needs to be more successful than their opponents.
cutting horse *Am., Can.* one trained to separate cattle from herd.
cuttoe *Am.* couteau, knife.
cut-up *Am., Can.* col. clown, joker: *All the way to the creek she acted the cut-up.* - T. Capote., *What a cut-up the boy is!* - M.M. Kaye., *Always cheerful - a real cutup.* - B. Tillman.
CV *Br.* /*Am.* **resume, biodata**/: *Now what I need is your CV, fast as possible.* - D. Lodge.
cycle *Am.* motorcycle.
cycle *esp. Br.* ride a bicycle.
cycle path *Br.* /*Am.* **bicycle route**/.
cycler *Am.* cyclist.
cyclery *Am.* bicycle shop: *he stopped in at a cyclery on his way home* - J. London.
cycle shed, bike shed *Br.* a small building for storing bicycles.
cylinder *Br.* /*Am.* **canister**/ **vacuum cleaner** one in which dirt is collected through a long tube into a horizontal cylinder.
cylinder// be operating, playing, running, etc. **on all cylinders** *Am.* performing well using all one's energy.
czar *esp. Am.* tzar.
czar/ banking, drug, health, etc. **czar** *Am.* sb. who is very powerful in a particular job, activity, etc.

D

DA *Am.* District Attorney: *DA went to go ahead with the indictment.* - R.J. Randisi., M. Wallace.

dab hand, also **dab** *Br.* col. skilful person, expert: *I've heard you're a dab-hand at the mucking out.* - D. Francis.

dabbly *Br.* rare. wet / **dabbly summer.**

dabs *Br.* col. obs. finger prints: *He managed to lift some dabs from the wine glasses.* - T. Thorne.

Dacron *Am.* tdmk. Terelene.

dad-blamed *Am., Can.* sl. damned: *The dad-blamed fishing line is tangled! It's in knots!* - W. Magnuson.

daddy longlegs 1. *esp. Br.* crane fly, flying insect with long legs. 2. *Am.* small insect with long eight legs that is similar to a spider: *a vast leafy nest full of daddy longlegs* - S. Grafton.

Dad and Dave *Aus.* radio and TV artists showing bush life habits.

daddyism *Am.* rare. respect for one's ancestors.

daft *esp. Br.* col. silly, foolish: *You'd get daft letters from girls all over the world.* - I. Fleming., *if you are daft and a dickhead, you can snort it.* - P. Howard., *Is Abraham daft?* - L. Uris.

daft/ be daft about *Br.* col. be madly in love or be very interested in smth.

daft/ be as daft as a brush *Br.* col. be very silly.

dag *Aus.* col. 1. sheep dung. 2. unattractive person. 3. strange or stupid person.

dag *Aus., N.Z.* col. a conservative person.

dagger/ be at daggers drawn *Br., Aus.* be very angry and ready to fight.

dagger/look daggers (at sb.) *esp. Br.* look at sb. very angrily.

daggy *Aus., N.Z.* col. (of clothes) scruffy.

Dago *Am.* sl. San Diego, California.

dailies *Am.* /*Br.* **rush**/ the first prints of a film before it has been edited.

daily (**help**) *esp. Br.* col. obs. person, esp. a woman, who comes to clean a house daily but doesn't live there: *the person it affected most was the daily woman* - A. Christie.

daily (**mail**) *Br.* sl. 1. buttocks. 2 sexual activity: *Have you been getting any daily lately?* - T. Thorne.

daisy /also **daisy ham**/ *Am.* boned and smoked piece of pork from the shoulder.

daisy chain *Br.* a string of daisies used to make a necklace.

daks *Aus.* col. trousers.

dalesman *Br.* one born or living in a dale.

dallimony *Am.* allowance paid by order of a court to one partner in a former sexual relationship by the other partner whose professions of affection have been established as insincere.

Dall sheep *Am.* wild sheep.

damage *esp. Br.* the price, esp. of smth. done for you.

damage control *esp. Am., Can.* actions taken to minimize effects of an accident or error.

dame *esp. Am.* sl. obs. (esp. said by men) a woman: *it is Madrid slang for tarts, hot numbers or as I indicate, flashy dames.* - J.A. Michener., *The dames'll be climbing all over him.* - K. Vonnegut, Jr. *He's screwing every English dame he could get his hands on.* - J. O'Hara.

damnadest *esp. Am.* col. adj. the most unusual, surprising, etc.

damnadest/ do one's **damnadest** *esp. Am.* try very hard.

damn-all *Br.* col. nothing.

damn straight! *Am.* that's true!

damp *Br.* sl. ineffectual, feeble: *I always found Jenny's husband a bit damp.* - T. Thorne.

damp *Br., Aus.* light wetness on smth. or part or area that's slightly wet.

damp course /also **damp-proof course**/ *Br.* a thickness in the wall to prevent rising damp.

dampener/ put a dampener on smth. *Br.* stop it being successful or enjoyable.

damper *Aus., NZ.* unleavened bread baked in ashes.

damp squib *esp. Br., Aus.* col. smth. that fails to have its intended effect.

dance attendance on/upon sb. *Br.* do what sb. wants without asking questions, in a way that shows complete obedience.

dance/ lead sb. **a (merry) dance** *Br.* tease or annoy sb. by not telling them what will happen next.

dance-hall /also **dance house**/ *Am.* dancing hall: *an obscure spell with Binger Madison in a New York taxi dance hall.* – I. Carr, D. Fairweather, B. Priestley.

dandelion greens *Am., Can.* fresh dandelion leaves used as a salad vegetable or herb.

dandy *esp. Am.* becoming obs. very good /also **fine and dandy**/: *you fellows have done a dandy little piece of creative research.* - I. Shaw., *You Irish are real dandy haters, aren't you?* - L. Waller., *It's a dandy, well-appointed, small steam laundry.* - J. London.

dang *Am.* sl. 1. penis. 2. also *Can.* /*Am.* euph. **durn**/ damn.

danger *Br.* railway signal indicating that the line is not clear.

danger list *Br.* a list of seriously ill patients in a hospital.

danger money *esp. Br., Aus.* /*Am.* **hazardous-duty pay, danger pay**/ extra money which is paid to sb. because their job involves danger.

dangler 1. *Aus. sl.* a flasher, a male sexual exhibitionist. 2. *Br. sl.* a trailer. 3. *Am. sl.* a trapeze artist.

Danish *Am.* Danish pastry, sweet cake made of light pastry.

darb *Am. sl.* excellent person or thing: *I've got some darbs.* - E. Hemingway.

Darby and Joan *esp. Br.* humor. 1. col. happily married and quite old husband and wife. 2. **Darby and Joan-club** club for old people.

dare/ as dare *Br.* /*Br., Aus.* **for dare**, *Am.* **on dare**/ as a challenge.

daresay/ I daresay *esp. Br.* I suppose (that), perhaps.

darg *Aus., N.Z.* 1. miners' day output. 2. a fixed amount of work.

dark/ a leap in the dark *Br.* doing smth. without knowing the consequences.

dark/ keep it dark *Br.* let it be a secret among us.

Dark and Bloody Ground *Am.* Kentucky.

dark chocolate *Am.* /*Br.* **plain chocolate**/ plain or bitter chocolate not having much milk.

dark horse *Br., Aus.* humor. person who acts unexpectedly surprising everyone.

dark spell *Can.* Arctic night.

darky *Am. obs. sl.* a person with brown or black skin: *I think you'd better quit chunking at this darky.* – E. Caldwell.

Darling shower *Aus.* dust storm in central Australia.

darn(ed) *Am.* col. (used to emphasise what you are saying, esp. in **I'll be darned!**: *Well, there's darned well something up here!* – F. Edwards.

(Devil's) darning needle, darner *Am., Can.* dragon fly.

darning mushroom *Br.* darning ball.

dart *Aus.* col. scheme, plan.

darter *esp. Am.* perch-like freshwater fish.

dash 1. *esp. Am.* col. or *Br. obs.* dashboard: *She pushed her seat back, put her feet up on the dash* - J. Kellerman. 2. *Am.* a short fast race. 3. **I must/ have to dash** *Br.* col. I must leave quickly.

dash (it) (all) excl. *esp. Br.* col. euph. damn / **dashed** *Br. obs.* euph. damned: *I think I'm dashed hurt.* - J.P. Donleavy., *It's a dashed odd sort of thing* - A. Christie.

dasher 1. *Am.* fender, splashboard. 2. *Can.* the enclosing fence of a hockey rink.

data phone/set *Am.* /*esp. Br.* usu. **modem**/ device that connects computer systems to the telephone.

date *esp. Am.* col. 1. person with whom one has a planned social meeting (esp. one between a man and a woman): *we said goodnight to our dates on the sidewalk* - A.E. Hotchner. 2. also *Can.* go on or have a date: *We started dating all over again.* - P. Norman. 3. *Aus. sl.* also **freckle, ace** the buttocks.

date/ of date *Am.* of this day.

datebook *Am.* table or pocket diary of engagements.

datemate 1. *Am. sl.* a partner of the same sex to accompany one on a double date. 2. *Aus. sl.* a male homosexual partner.

dates / in the US and Canada month is written before date / e.g. 4. 10. 1995 the 10th of April; *esp. Br.* May the 24th /*esp. Am., Can.* May 24th/.

dating agency *esp. Br.* /*Am., Aus.* **dating service**/ organisation which introduces people with similar interests to each other, esp. those who want to marry: *After my divorce I turned to a computer dating service* – Reader's Digest.

dating bar *Am.* singles club, barroom.

daub up *Am.* col. paint in spots: *The children have daubed up the walls with uneven drops of paint.* - Longman.

daughter concern *Br.* subsidiary.

davenport 1. *esp. Br.* small desk, writing table. 2. *esp. Am., Can.* /*esp. Br.* **sofa**/ sofa, coach: *She would often sit in a chair or davenport* - D. Carnegie.

dawk *Am.* person who disapproves of war, but won't oppose it actively.

dawn/ a false dawn *Br.* journalim. supposed but not observed improvement in smth.

dawn chorus *esp. Br.* the singing of birds at dawn.

dawn raid *Br.* 1. sudden unexpected attempt to buy a significant proportion of a company's equity, typically at the start of a day's trading. 2. also *Aus.* a sudden entry of a building in an attempt to catch criminals.

day/ get/have one's **day in court** *Am., Aus.* explain one's actions before they have been criticised.

day/ this day week (today week, a week today) *Br.* a week from today.

day/ all day with sb. *Am.* lost cause.

day/ between two days *Am.* in the night.

day/ it's/(these are) early days (yet), it's early in the day *esp. Br.* col. it's too soon to be sure of the events in the future.

day/ some of these days *Am.* soon.

day bed *Am., Can.* a couch that can be made up into a bed.

day book *Am., Can.* diary.

day boy (or **girl**), **day pupil** *esp. Br. /Am., Aus.* **day student/** pupil who lives at home but goes to a school where some of the pupils live.

day camp *Am.* place where children can go in the day during the school holidays to do sport, art, etc.

day care *Am. /Br.* **child care/** care of young children while their parents are at work: *we don't want to put our son in day care* – Reader's Digest.

day care centre 1. *Am. /Br.* **crèche, nursery/** a place where babies are looked after while their parents are away at work: *Then I lost my job over at the day-care center.* - J. Kellerman. 2. *Br.* place where people who are old or ill can be looked after during the day.

day coach/car *Am., Can.* railway wagon with places to sit only, as opposed to sleeping car: *The day-coach went hurtling through the dusk* - C. Woolrich.

day hospital *Br.* a hospital which patients can only attend during day time.

daylight robbery *esp. Br.* col. the act of charging far too much for smth.

daylight saving time, daylight savings *Am. /Br.* **summer time**, *Aus.* **daylight saving/** time in summer when watches are put one hour ahead of standard time.

daylights/ No daylights *Am.* Fill the glasses to the brim.

day liner *Am., Can.* daily coach train travelling between two cities.

day nursery *Br.* place where small children can be left while their parents are ar work.

day of action *Br.* day when workers go on strike.

day out 1. *Br.* one day trip or excursion. 2. *esp. Br.* day spent at the beach, at the countryside, at the zoo, etc.

day pack *esp. Am., Can. /Br.* **day sack/** small rucksack.

day release (course) *Br.* educational course attended by workers who are allowed to leave their work on certain dates, usu. one day a week.

day return /also **day ticket/** *Br. /Am.* **round-trip ticket/** a ticket that one can use to go and come back on the same day, usu. cheaper than two separate single tickets.

days *Am.* adv. during any day.

day tripper *esp. Br.* often derog. person on a pleasure trip, esp. one lasting only one day: *their set-piece battle had surged back and forth, trampling day-trippers, deckchairs and children's sand castles.* - P. Norman.

dazzle *Br.* strong admiration.

deacon *Am.* 1. read (a hymn) aloud. 2. col. falsify. 3. col. pack fruit putting the best fruit on top.

deacon's bench *Am.* wooden seat for two made in colonial style.

dead *Br.* col. 1. very or extremely. 2. (of a bottle) no longer used.

dead air *Am.* unintentional time of silence during a radio or TV broadcast.

dead-and-alive, dead-alive *Br.* (of a place, person, or activity) uninteresting, dull.

dead as mackerel (or **Moses**) *Am. /Aus.* **dead as meataxe (a mutton chop)**, *Br.* **dead as a/ the dodo/** dead to the world, no longer active or popular: *Anabel Trice and Cass Mastern were long since deader than mackerel.* - R.P. Warren.

dead above the ears /also *Br.* **dead from the neck up/** *Am., Aus.* col. /*Br.* **dead from the neck upwards/** very stupid.

dead-ass *Am.* sl. adj. depressingly dreary and insignificant: *He's a real deadass.* - T. Thorne.

dead bang, also **dead to rights** *Am.* sl. /*Br.* sl. **bang to rights/** caught red-handed: *The police caught the man dead to rights.* - A. Makkai.

dead beat 1. *Am., Aus.* col. derog. a lazy person, not wanting to be a part of an ordinary society. 2. *Am., Can.* person who tries to avoid paying debts.

dead bolt *Am. /Br.* **mortice bolt/** strong lock often used on doors.

dead cert *Br., Aus.* col. sure thing.

dead duck *Am., Aus.* col. severely punished person.

dead-end kids *esp. Am.* col. children from poor areas who have to fight to stay alive: *Max was a dead-end kid from the day he was born.* - R.A. Spears.

deadfall *Am., Can.* 1. animal trap designed to kill or disable it by falling weight. 2. windfall tree(s). 3. col. disreputable bar.

deadhead 1. *Br.* remove dead flowers from a plant. 2. *Am.* (drive) a train, bus, or truck with no passengers or goods.

(the) Dead Heart *Aus.* Central Australia.

deadheat *Am.* having two joint winners.

dead horse/ beat a dead horse *Am. /Br.* **flog a dead horse/** col. waste time and effort by talking about smth. that people are not interested in any more.

deadlight *Am.* a skylight made so as not to open.

deadlock *Br.* lock requiring key to open and close it., v.

dead-man's float *Am.* way of floating in water with your body and face turned downwards.

dead man's shoes *Br.* 1. smth. that sb. is waiting to inherit. 2. no progress in one's career until sb. senior dies or retires, esp. in **be waiting for dead men's shoes.**

dead meat/ be dead meat *Am., Aus.* col. get a severe punishment: *You are dead meat!* – R.L. Stine.

dead parrot *Br.* col. smth. completely and irrevocably moribund.

dead run *Am.* one without a let-up and with full speed.

Dead slow! *Br.* Extremely slow! (a traffic sign).

dead spit/ be the dead spit of sb. *Br.* look very much alike.

dead stock *Br.* farm equipment and machinery.

dead trouble/ be in dead trouble *Br.* col. be in serious trouble.

deadwagon *Am.* a vehicle for carrying the dead.

deadwater *esp. Am., Can.* still water without any current.

deadwood/ have the deadwood on sb. *Am.* have the advantage over sb.

deaf/ be deaf as a doorknob/doornail *Aus.* be very deaf.

deaf adder *Am.* non-poisonous snake.

deaf aid *Br.* hearing aid.

deal 1. *esp. Br.* fir or pine wood, for making things from. 2. *Am.* political course, economical policy.

deal/ Let's (*esp. Am.*) **make/cut,** (*esp. Br.*) **do a deal** with each other; **make a deal on** *Br. /Am.* **make a deal for/**.

deal/ it's a done deal *esp. Am.* arrangement has been completed and can't be changed.

deal/ What's the deal (with)? *Am.* col. What has happened?

deal/ What's one's **deal?** *Am.* col. What's wrong with sb.?

dean *Am.* unofficial leader of a group of people.

deanery *Br.* number of parishes led by a rural dean.

dean's list *Am., Can.* a list of high achievers during a specific term selected by the dean of their college.

dear *esp. Br.* expensive: *It's dead expensive it's dear* - R. Carter., M. McCarthy.

dear *esp. Br.* n. a person who is loved or loveable.

Dear (me) excl. (used for expressing surprise, sorrow, slight anger, discouragement) It is more stronger expression in Britain than in the US: *Dear me! - exclaimed Mendes. – I never said that. – I. Stone.*

dear/ old dear *Br.* rude word for old woman.

dearborn *Am.* light four-wheeled carriage.

dearie *esp. Br.* col. friendly and sometimes condescending way of addressing sb.

death/ beat smth. **to death** *Am.* flog smth. to death.

death/be signing one's **own death warrant** *Br.* do smth. that will cause serious problems for them.

death/ (look/feel) like death warmed up *Br., Aus. /Am., Can.* **like death warmed over/** col. very ill.

death/ die a death *Br. /Am., Aus.* **die a natural death/** fail and end smth.

death/ flog sb./smth. **to death** *Br.* 1. make sb. work very hard. 2. discuss smth. for a very long time until everybody gets bored.

death/hanging on like grim death *esp. Br.* holding onto smth. very tightly.

death adder *Aus.* col. poisonous snake.

death duty *Br.* obs. */Am.* **death tax,** *Aus.* **probate/** inheritance tax money paid to a government on land, money and goods after the death of the owner: *he could best avoid the payment of those death-duties, which would follow his decease.* - J. Galswarthy., *other men collected pictures to escape death duties* - G. Greene.

death futures *Am.* col. life insurance policies of people who are terminally ill, bought by a third party at less than mature value as an investment redeemable on the death of the insured person.

death row *esp. Am., Can.* part of prison for prisoners to be punished by death: *he's got the role of Louisiana death-row inmate* - New York., *Ligget has spent 12 years on death row for a double murder* - Time.

death tax *Am.* inheritance tax.

de-bag *Br., Aus.* col. */Am.* sl. **depants/** take the trousers off (sb. as a joke).

debenture 1. *Br.* secured bond. 2. *Am.* a type of preferred shares.

debtor/ poor debtor *Am.* insolvent debtor (freed of paying debt by a court).

decal *esp. Am., Can.* col. */esp. Br.* **transfer/** specially prepared paper with a picture that can be transferred to other surface: *Forget the puny windshield decal.* – Reader's Digest.

decant *Br.* col. move a person or thing from one place to another.

decapitate *Am.* change leadership of government agencies (esp. after the election victory)., n. **decapitation.**

decasualisation *Br.* becoming less dependent on casual labour.

decedent *Am.* law. the dead person: *On the lips of each decedent was the blue-white of ice-nine.* - K. Vonnegut, Jr.

decedent estate *Am.* law. one left after the person's death.

decent/ be decent about smth. *esp. Br.* treat sb. fairly and sympathetically when they have done smth. wrong.

decent thing/ do the decent thing *Br.* 1. leave a job because a person has made a serious mistake that might harm the company. 2. obs. (of a man) marry a woman who is soon is going to have a baby from him.

deception *Br.* a crime of cheating people, like a credit card deception.

decidedly *esp. Br.* definitely or in a way that is easily noticed.

deck 1. *esp. Am., Can. /Br., Aus.* **pack/** a set of playing cards: *The black detectives raked in the pot and shuffled the deck.* - R.J. Randisi., M. Wallace. 2. *Am., Aus. /esp. Br.* **terrace/** roofless raised wooden entrance built out from the back or side of a house, used for relaxing on: *I stepped outside to water yellow begonias in a flower-box on our deck.* - Guideposts. 3. *Am., Can.* col. package of narcotics: *How much for a deck of dust?* - R.A. Spears. 4. *Am.* wagon roof. 5. *Am.* tipping body of a truck. 6. *Am.* sl. beat: *Vet decked by irate biker.* - Reader's Digest. 7. *Am., Can.* sun deck.

deck/ be dealt a poor deck *Am.* become a failure.

deck/ on deck 1. *esp. Am., Can., Aus.* a. ready for use: *The Higher Power was on deck to see my son through, sober.* - Alcoholics Anonymous. b. next in order. 2. *Aus.* col. alive.

deck/ all hands on deck *esp. Br.* a situation where everyone working have to carry out a task.

deck/ not playing with a full deck *Am., Can.* col. mentally retarded.

deck/ play with a stacked (or **cold**) **deck** *Am.* play with marked cards; also *esp. Am.* **stack the deck.**

deck/ sweep the deck *Am.* break the bank.

deck/ upper deck *Am.* forecastle deck.

deckchair *esp. Br. /Am.* **beachchair/** folding chair with a long seat of cloth (usu. brightly lit canvass) used out of doors: *On a deep-green lawn were several deck-chairs.* - D. Lessing.

decker *Am.* apartment: *It was an Irish neighbourhood of triple-decker apartment-houses* - G. O'Neil., G. Lehr.

deck shoes /also **boat shoes**/ *Am.* light shoes with a top made of heavy cloth with thick crepe soles: *One of my deck shoes sank full fathom five.* - Reader's Digest.

declarant (alien) *Am.* an alien who declared his intention of becoming a citizen of the US by signing his first papers.

declaration (of the poll) *Br.* official results of the votes cast for candidates in an election.

declination *Am.* formal refusal.

decompress *Am.* col. relax.

decorate *esp. Br.* 1. make the inside of a building more attractive by painting it, putting paper on walls, etc. 2. make smth. look more attractive by putting smth. pretty on it.

decoration *esp. Br.* the act or process of decorating.

Decoration Day *Am.* Memorial Day (May 30) for the victims of war.

decorator *Br.* person whose job is to decorate buildings.

decree *esp. Am.* a judgement of certain type in a court of law: *Bessie's final divorce decree had been granted.* - I. Stone.

decree absolute *Br.* law. an order by a court of law which officially ends a marriage.

decree nisi *Br.* law. an order by a court of law that a marriage will end at a particular time in the future unless there is a good reason not to end it.

dedicate *Am.* open (smth.) pompously.

deductable *Aus.* deductible.

deductible *esp. Am., Can.* the part of an insurance claim to be paid by the insured.

deed *Am.* transfer by title deed.

deed of covenant *Br.* regular payments which enable the recipient, esp. a charity to reclaim any tax paid by the donor on the amount.

deed over *Am.* make a formal gift (of smth.): *Father decided to deed the house over to his eldest son before he died* - Longman.

deep-cycle *Am., Can.* (of electrical battery) one that can be discharged fully and recharged for several times.

deep-discount *Am., Can.* having great cuts in price.

deep-dish *esp. Am., Can.* 1. (of a pie) baked in a deep dish to allow for a large filling. 2. (of pizza) having a thick dough base. 3. col. very thorough.

deep end/ go off the deep end *esp. Am.* col. go crazy.

deep frying kettle *Am.* /*Br.* **chip pan**/ one for cooking long thin pieces of potato in deep fat.

deep six *Am., Can.* col. bury, dispose of; decide not to use smth.: *As the police boat came near, the drug smugglers deep-sixed their cargo.* - A. Makkai.

deer/ like a deer caught in the headlights *Am.* very confused.

de facto *Aus.* sl. common-law spouse: *My de facto's out buying groceries.* - T. Thorne.

deferred pass *Am.* conditional transfer to a higher class.

defog, defrost *Am.* /*Br.* **demist**/.

defogger, defroster *esp. Am.* /*Br.* **demister**/.

defrost *Am.* /*Br., Aus.* **demist**/ clean steam from (the windows of a car). n. **defroster**: *Turn on your defroster.* - R.L. Stine.

degree *esp. Am., Can.* legal measure of guilt or negligence.

degree/ have a bachelor's or **master's degree in** smth. **from university** *esp. Am., Aus.* finish studies at university with getting a bachelor's or master's degree.

Degree day *Br.* /*Am.* **commencement**/ a ceremony at which university or college students are given their degrees or diplomas.

deke *Am., Can.* sl. trick, esp. by decoying; often a feint in ice hockey: *he passed and deked and shot* - Time.

dekko/ have/take a dekko (at) *Br.* col. have a look (at): *she can come and have a dekko* - J. Fowles.

delinquent (debtor or taxpayer) *Am.* one who fails to pay their debts or taxes.

delinquency *Am.* a failure to pay debts.

deliver *esp. Am.* bring (votes, influence, etc.) to the support of a political movement, a person trying to get elected, etc.: *It's a very tough assignment, but he thinks he can deliver* - R.L. Chapman.

deliver on a promise *Am.* do what sb. promised to do.

delivery man *esp. Am.* /*esp. Br.* **roundsman**/ person who delivers goods to people who have ordered them, usu. locally: *an atmosphere of controlled chaos – deliverymen calling up the stairs* – S. Lawrence.

delivery note *esp. Br.* receipt, usu. written in two copies that comes with goods that are delivered and is to be signed by the person who receives them.

delivery room, suite, unit *Br., Aus.* /*esp. Am.* **maternity ward**/ the part of a hospital where babies are born.

delivery truck *Am.* /*Br.* **float**/ motor vehicle used for delivering goods.

Delta *Am.* letter d. (in radio).

demand/ final demand *Br.* a last request for payment, esp. of utility bills, before legal actions are taken.

demarcation dispute *Br., Aus.* a disagreement between trade unions about what types of work could be done by the members of each of them.

demerge *Br.* separate (a business) from another, esp. to dissolve a previous merger.

demerit *Am., Can.* 1. a mark awarded against sb. for a fault or offence. 2. mark showing that a student has done smth. wrong at school.

demise *esp. Am.* cease to exist, die.

demisemiquaver *esp. Br.* a thirty second note.

demist *Br., Aus.* /*Am.* **defrost**/ clean steam (from windows of a car), n. **defroster/ demister.**

demo *Br.* demonstration of protest or support of smth.: *Mark's got a good demo to pitch the new song with* - R.L. Chapman.

demob *Br.* col. demobilise.

demolish *esp. Br.* col. eat all of smth. very quickly.

demolition derby *esp. Am., Can.* a contest in which cars are driven into each other until only one is left.

demon *Aus., NZ.* joc. policeman, esp. one on a motorcycle.

demon drink humor. *Br.* /*Am.* **demon alcohol**/ too much alcohol that make people behave like idiots.

den 1. *Am., Can.* a room in a house where people relax, read, watch TV, etc.: *I led the way into the den and closed the door.* – R.L. Stine. 2. *esp. Am.* a subdivision of Cub Scout pack, female leader of which is called **den leader**. 3. *Br.* obs. small work in a house where a person can work, read, etc. without being disturbed.

den up *Am.* 1. retire to a den for a winter. 2. retire to one's private room.

denarius /usu. **d.**/ *Br.* penny.

dene *Br.* 1. vale. 2. dune.

denial of export privileges *Am.* denial of the right to export goods.

denier *Br.* measure of how thin nylon or silk threads are.

dent/ put a dent in smth. *Am.* reduce the amount or level of smth.

dent up *esp. Am.* col. damage (smth.) by hitting: *John dented up the car in the accident.* - Longman.

dentist's/doctor's office *Am.* /*Br.* **surgery**/.

Denver boot *Am.* col. /*esp. Br., Aus.* **wheel clamp**/.

depants *Am.* sl. /*Br., Aus.* col. **de-bag**/ take the trousers off sb. as a joke: *We depants him.* - R.L. Stine.

department *esp. Am.* /*esp. Br.* **office, ministry**/ government department.

depasture *Br.* put animals to graze on pastures.

deplane *esp. Am., Can.* get off an aircraft.

deportment 1. *esp. Br.* the way a person, esp. a young lady stands and walks: *he drove with his eyes closed, a lifestyle of deportment alone keeping his tall and bulky form from falling askew.* - J. Galsworthy. 2. *esp. Am.* obs. the way a person, esp. a young lady behaves in the company of others: *she was a martinet concerning deportment* - S. North.

deposit (for goods) *esp. Am.* warehouse (for goods).

deposit account 1. *esp. Br.* /*Am.* **saving account**/ a bank account which earns interest and from which money can be taken out only if advance notice is given. 2. *Am.* bank account.

deposit bottle/can *Am.* a container for drinks for which a small amount of money is given back to you when you bring it back to a shop when it's empty.

deposit slip *Am.* /*Br.* **credit slip, paying-in slip**/ paying-in slip.

deposit-taking institution /also **fringe bank**/ *Br.* small bank.

depot /also **railroad depot** or **bus depot**/ *Am., Can.* small railway or bus station: *He watched it drive away in the direction of the depot.* - T. Caldwell., *there on the old farm that has since become a railroad depot.* - T. Capote., *Again we passed the skeleton of a train depot, the wrecked huts, the craters.* - J. Baez.

depot agent *Can.* station master.

depot/ freight depot, also **freight yard** *Am.* / *Br.* **goods yard, goods station**/ station where heavy articles are transported.

depot road, railroad avenue *Am.* /*Br.* **station road**/ railroad leading to railway station.

depress/ be depressed at smth. *Br.* be depressed about, by, over smth.

deputize *esp. Am.* /*Am., Can.* **deputy**/ appoint as deputy; **deputy sheriff**.

deputy *Br.* coal mine official responsible for safety.

derate *esp. Br.* relieve (industries, etc. under former rates system) from a proportion of the local taxes.

derby 1. *Am., Can.* /*esp. Br.* **bowler (hat)**, *Aus.* col. **boxer**/ a man's round hat, usu. black: *Even the derby must be the same she insisted* - T. Thompson. 2. *esp. Am.* a race which any competitor can enter. 3. *Am.* a type of horserace. 4. *Br.* sports match between two teams from the same area or city.

Derbyville *Am.* joc. Louisville, Kentucky.

derelict *Am.* n. adj. delinquent, lacking a sense of duty, negligent.

de-restricted road *Br.* road without speed limit.

derringer *Am.* short pistol: *How many television sets had he shot out with his derringer?* –J. Hoplins.

derro 1. *Aus.* homeless person or tramp. 2. *Br.* sl. unfortunate or unpleasant person: *And touching someone when you're dancing, Caris intimates, is the act of a derro* - Observer, T. Thorne.

derry *Br.* sl. derelict building.

derv *Br.* tdmk. an oil product used in diesel engines.

deselect *Br.* refuse to choose an existing MP as a candidate, at the next election.

designated driver *Am.* col. a person who agrees not to drink alcohol in order to drive other people, esp. after a party.

designated hitter *Am.* col. (from baseball) person who does the job for sb. else, esp. in politics or business.

designer drug *esp. Am., Can.* synthetic analogue of an illegal drug or fashionable artificial drug.

desk *Am.* editorial office.

desk clerk /also **front desk clerk**/ *Am.* /*Br.* **reception clerk**/ reception clerk: *From the deskclerk, Spanos got the number of the room.* - Reader's Digest., *the desk clerk coughed again behind his hand* - A. Hitchcock Mystery Magazine.

desk dictionary *esp. Am., Can.* one-volume dictionary of medium size.

desk jockey *Am.* sl. an office worker: *The desk jockeys at our place don't get paid very well.* - R.A. Spears.

desk man *Am.* one that works at a desk, esp. a newspaperman who processes news and prepares copy.

desk study *Br.* one without extensive field and laboratory investigation.

desk tidy *Br.* container for putting pens, pencils, etc. that you keep on your desk.

des res *Br.* col. humor. desirable residence, a house with many features (e.g. of design or location) attractive to prospective purchasers.

dessert 1. *esp. Am., Aus.* /*Br.* **sweets, the sweet course, the last course**/ a course of fruit, pastry, pudding, ice cream, or cheese served at the close of a meal. 2. *Br.* a fresh fruit served after a sweet course.

dessert cart *Am.* /*Br.* **dessert trolley**/ small cart on wheels from which different desserts can be served.

dessertspoon *esp. Br.* /*Am.* **tablespoon**/ 1. spoon between the sizes of a teaspoon and tablespoon, used for eating dessert. 2. also **dessert spoonful** the amount held by a dessert spoon, equal to about two teaspoons.

destock *Br.* (of a retailer) reduce the quantity of stock held.

detached *Br.* adj. (of a house) not joined to another.

detained during the Queen's / King's / pleasure *Br.* law. humor. sentenced to an indeterminate term.

detangle *esp. Am.* remove the knots in hair.

detention center *Am.* a place where people who entered the country without the necessary documents can be kept for short periods of time.

Detour *Am.* /*Br.* **Diversion**/ road sign of by-pass road.

detour/ take a detour *esp. Am., Aus.* make a detour: *The workers explained detour route to town* – Reader's Digest.

detract *Am.* divert (attention).

detruck *Am.* get down from the truck.

deuce *esp. Am.* col. 1. (throw) two of dice or playing cards. 2. two dollars: *Just let me have a deuce till tomorrow.* - T. Thorne.

development area *Br.* area of high unemployment, to which the government encourages new industries to come.

deviate, deviant *Am.* adj. (of a person or thing) different from accepted standards.

devil/ be a devil! *Br.* col. humor. do smth. that you would enjoy now, esp. have smth. nice to eat or drink.

devil/ better the devil you know (than the devil you don't) *esp. Br.* it's much better to deal with sb. you already know.

devil/ between the devil and the deep blue sea *esp. Br.* in dilemma.

devil/ the devil take the hindmost *Br.* obs. every man for himself.

devil / whip (beat) the devil round the stump *Am.* gain smth. in a roundabout way.

devil *Am., Can.* col. v. tease.

devil's food cake *Am.* chocolate cake: *Think about that angel cake white and devil's food cake chocolate.* – Reader's Digest.

devils on horseback *esp. Br.* prunes wrapped in slices of bacon, usu. served on toast.

Devonshire cream *Br.* clotted cream.

Dewar's flask *Br.* thermos bottle.

dewberry *Am., Can.* trailing brambles.

dewdrop *Br.* humor. a drop of liquid coming from the inside of sb.'s nose.

dewpond *esp. Br.* a small hollow in which dew collects.

dew worm *Am., Can.* earthworm, esp. one used as a fishing bait.

diabolic *esp. Br.* col. extremely unpleasant or of very low quality.

diagrid *Br.* supporting framework in a building made of metal or concrete.

dial 100 /*Am.* **0 (zero)**/ **for the operator** *Br.* call the operator.

dial 123 for the correct time *Br.* call for the correct time.

dialling code, STD code /also **prefix**/ *Br.* /*Am., Aus.* **area code**/ telephone code.

dialling tone *Br.* /*Am., Can., Aus.* **dial tone**/ the sound made by a telephone receiver to show that one may now dial the number that one wants: *he clicked the hook to get a dial tone.* - K. Lipper.

dialogue *esp. Am., Can.* discuss a problem in an effort to solve it.

diamond anniversary *esp. Am.* /*Br.* **diamond wedding**/.

diamond horse *Am.* the dress circle in a theatre.

diamond in the rough. *Am., Can.* col. /*esp. Br.* **rough diamond**/.

diamond jubilee 1. *Am.* 75 anniversary. 2. *Br.* 60 anniversary of some important event.

The Diamond State *Am.* Delaware.

diaper *Am., Can.* /*Br., Aus.* **nappy**/ a piece of soft cloth or paper fastened and worn between the legs and around the waist of the body of the baby: *diapers have been wet for some time.* - I. Shaw., *I must have had purple diapers.* - E. Taylor., *I changed his goddamn diapers in Nam.* - J. DeFelice.

diaper rash *Am.* /*Br., Aus.* **nappy rash**/.

diary *Br.* /*Am.* **calendar**/.

dibber *Br.* dibble, a small tool used by gardeners to make a hole in the soil where they want to put a seed or a small plant.

dibs (on) *Am.* col. claim (on smth.): *They've got dibs on the screen.* - Esquire.

dibs/ have (first) dibs on *Am.* sl. be the next person to do smth.
dice/ No dice *esp. Am., Can., Aus.* col. a. no use. b. (used to show refusal): *Today, or it's no dice.* - S. Bellow.
dice with death *Br.* take risks that endanger their life.
dicey (dicier, diciest) *esp. Br., Aus.* col. risky and uncertain: *it was after all a dicey trip for her.* - M. Jones, J. Chilton.
dick 1. *esp. Br.* a fellow. 2. *esp. Am., Aus.* col., also *Am.* col. **gumshoe** a detective: *I will not have a dick jailing me!* - S. Bellow., *The house dick would not be surprised* - Arthur Hailey. 4. *Br.* taboo. sl. a contemptible person.
dicken *Aus., NZ.* col. excl. of disgust or disbelief.
dickens *esp. Br.* col. euph. (used to add force to an expression) the devil: *Ma had a dickens of a time saving up enough to get it fixed* – E. Caldwell.
dickens/ as pretty, smart, etc. **as the dickens** *Am.* col. very pretty, clever, etc.
dicker *Am.* argue with sb., esp. about the price of goods.
dick(e)y (bow), dickie (bow) *Br.* col. bow tie.
Dickin! *Aus., NZ.* col. Don't be foolish! Stop it!
dicky *Br., Aus.* col. adj. weak, likely to break or go wrong, esp. **dicky heart/ticker**: *Blistering was a normal treatment for dicky tendons.* - D. Francis., *dicky heart after ten days in a dinghy* - A. Burgess.
dicky *esp. Br.* 1. /*Am.* **rumble seat/** small third seat at the back of an old-fashioned two-seat car. 2. obs. the driver's seat in a carriage: *Cubit sat in the dicky.* - G. Greene.
dickybird *esp. Br.* 1. (used esp. by or to children) any small bird: *He wished that he were a dickybird* - K. Vonnegut, Jr. 2. (usu. in negatives) a word, anything / e.g. *not to say a dickybird.*
dicty *Am.* (used by blacks) pretentious.
diddle 1. *Br.* sl. cheat: *Comedian Ken Dodd insisted on cash to diddle the taxman* - Daily Mirror, T. Thorne. 2. *esp. Am.* waste one's time doing nothing.
(jack) diddly (squat, shit), doodly squat *Am., Can.* col. nothing more: *For all that work, he gave me diddly squat - not even thanks.* - W. Magnuson.
diddy *Br.* col. 1. small and attractive. 2. a fool.
diddums *Br.* humor. excl. an expression which seems sympathetic but which really means the opposite, esp. used to sb. who is upset in a childish way.

dido *Am.* col. a prank / **cut up a dido, cut didoes** *Am.* col. act foolishly or mischievously.
die *Am.* singular of dice.
die *Am.* col. (of clothes) wear out.
die/ I just died *Am.* col. I was so surprised or embarrassed by smth. that happened.
die a death *Br.* (of a play, film, etc.) be a failure.
diesel *esp. Am.* col. vehicle that uses diesel fuel.
diet kitchen *Am.* 1. dietary kitchen. 2. charity canteen.
different / Teachers prefer different(ly) from, but different(ly) to (*Br.*) and differently than (*Am.*) are also commonly used.
different/ (it's) different strokes for different folks *esp. Am.* tastes differ.
differential *Br.* a difference between rates of pay for different types of work, esp. work done by people in the same industry or company.
differently-abled *esp. Am., Can.* disabled.
difficulties 1. *Am.* differences of opinion, disagreements. 2. *Br.* trouble, esp. in **be in difficulties**.
diesel *esp. Am.* col. a vehicle driven by a diesel.
dig *Am.* col. 1. diligent student. 2. work hard: *I had to dig to master even the rudiments* - R.L. Chapman.
dig down *Am.* col. pay with an effort: *just dig down a little.* - Longman.
dig for victory *Br.* grow food as part of a war effort: *we were digging for victory.* - Longman.
dig out 1. *esp. Am.* col. leave, move quickly away: *a couple fell off your roof when you dug out?* - D. Brenner. 2. *esp. Am., Can.* free oneself from being buried in snow: *Three towns in the North are digging out this morning.* - Longman.
(chocolate) digestive (biscuit) *Br., Aus.* tdmk. a type of plain slightly sweet biscuit: *have a chocolate digestive biscuit* - B. Bryson.
digger *Aus., NZ.* col. n. Australian (soldier), esp. in World War One: *Being outnumbered and unsupported drove up the Diggers temperature* - E. Williams.
digs *esp. Br., Can.* col. rooms, lodgings: *I was a landlady of digs* - Woman's Own., *nostalgic memories of the various digs she had lived in London* - I. Murdoch.
dike *esp. Br.* narrow passage dug to carry water away, ditch.
dilapidations *Br.* law. the money that one must pay for damage done to a furnished house that one has been renting.
dilate *Br.* lower the proportion of skilled workers. n. **dilation**.
Dildo *esp. Am.* a stupid man.

dill, drongo, galah, nong *Aus., NZ.* col. gullible person, idiot.

dilly *Am., Can.* col. obs. outstanding person or thing: *He's made some dillies, hasn't he?* – J. Hopkins.

dilly bag *Aus.* a bag or basket of traditional Aboriginal design made from woven grass.

dim *esp. Br.* col. stupid, slow to learn and understand: *The dim guy looks around and feels lonely.* – Reader's Digest.

dim (one's) **(head)lights** *Am.* /*Br.* **dip** (one's) **(head)lights**/ lower the angle of the front lights of a car, esp. when another car approaches.

dim bulb *Am.* sl. stupid person: *George seems to be a dim bulb* - R.A. Spears.

dime a dozen *Am., Can., Aus.* col. /*Br.* **two/ten a penny**/ not at all unusual or valuable: *in Mr. Smith's class A's are a dime a dozen.* - A. Makkai.

dime/ drop a/the dime on sb. *Am., Can.* col. inform on sb.

dime/ get off the dime *Am., Can.* col. be resolute to do smth.

dime/ not be worth dime *Am., Can.* col. not worth anything at all.

dime/ on a dime *Am., Can.* col. (of maneuvre) done within a very small area.

dime novel *Am., Can.* obs. cheap popular novel.

dime store, ten-cent store *Am., Can.* a shop that sells different kinds of cheap things: *the dime stores would not take back or exchange.* - C. McCullers.

diminished capacity *Am.* law. smth. in their mental state that has caused a person not to be in full control of their actions.

dimmer *Am.* a headlight with a low beam.

dine out on (experience or situation) *esp. Br.* entertain people by telling them about one's experience, esp. when eating a meal with them.

diner *esp. Am., Can.* 1. small restaurant beside the road with a long counter and booths: *I think there's a phone in the diner down on the left.* - R. Cook., *My dad runs a real nice diner there.* - R. Borchgrave, R. Moss. 2. dining car, restaurant car on a train: *there's a diner on a train.* - E. Hemingway.

dinero *Am.* col. money: *You got some dinero I can borrow?* - R.A. Spears.

dinette, breakfast room *Am.* /*Br.* **morning room**/a small space in or near the kitchen for eating or a set of tables and chairs for it: *the Royal Oak dinette table* - A. Hitchcock mystery magazine.

dinette set *Am.* table and matching chairs.

ding 1. *Aus.* col. a lively party or celebration. 2. *Am., Can.* col. (make) a mark or dent in a bodywork of car, boat, etc.

ding-a-ling *Am., Can.* col. crazy person: *it obviously doesn't have the ding-a-ling associations for me that it has for you.* - K. Vonnegut, Jr.

dingbat *Am.* sl. 1. gadget: *Is this the dingbat you mean?* - R.A. Spears. 2. also /*Am.* col. **ding-a-ling**/ *Can., Aus., NZ.* stupid person: *That dingbat wanted me to take off my clothes!* - W. Magnuson. 3. any undesirable person: *Look, dingbat, stop laughing!* - R.A. Spears. 4. anything suitable as a missile.

dingbat *Aus.* sl. Chinese person.

dingbats *Aus., NZ.* delusions induced by Delirium Tremens.

ding-dong 1. *esp. Br., Aus.* col. a lively quarrel or fight. 2. *Am., Can.* col. /*Am.* col. **dingleberry**/ silly, foolish person. 3. *Br.* adv. energetically.

dinge *Am.* taboo sl. Negro: *That big dinge took him by surprise.* - E. Hemingway.

dinger *esp. Am.* col. outstanding thing.

dingo *Aus.* sl. betray, esp. **in turn dingo**.

dingus *Am., Can.* sl. a thing or gadget: *the two of them had this dingus that sent a beam of green light across the board room.* - L. Waller.

dink 1. *Am.* sl. a fool: *What do I need this dink airline for?* - K. Lipper. 2. *Am., Aus.* oriental person, esp. Vietnamese.

dinkey *Am.* a small locomotive for pulling freight cars.

dinkum/dinki-di *Aus., NZ.* col. adj. honest, real, genuine.

dinkum/ fair dinkum, square dinkum *Aus.* excellent, wonderful.

dinkum Aussie *Aus.* real Australian: *A dinkum Aussie tall, blond and suntanned thrust his way through a group of civilians.* - E. Williams.

dinkum oil *Aus., NZ.* col. true information.

dinky 1. *Br.* or *Aus.* col. small and charming: *Like I was a Dinky Toy you'd been saving up your pocket money for.* – R. Westall. 2. *Am., Can.* derog. col. small and unimportant: *That dinky Junior College he teaches at pays him twenty-four thousand a year. Think you can buy a house in Watts on that* - J. Kellerman.

dinky *Br.* 1. large and impressive car. 2. (double income no kids) young couple trying to live for yourself without the children of their own.

dinner/ be done like (a) dinner (in a contest) *esp. Aus., Can.* be defeated completely, often in unfair way.

dinner/ do smth. **more than** sb. **had hot dinners** *Br.* col. have done smth. a great number of times.

dinner/ what time do you have / (*Am.*) **eat dinner.**
dinner *Br.* any meal that is eaten in the middle of the day.
dinner dance *Br.* a social event with a lot of people coming to dinner and dancing afterwards.
dinner jacket, DJ *esp. Br., Aus.* /*Am.* **tuxedo**/ special clothes worn for formal occasions in the evenings: *A middle-aged fat man in a dinner jacket came along* - W. Grady.
dinner lady *Br.* one who serves meals and supervises children at meal times in a school.
dinner pail *esp. Am.* obs. dinner pan.
dinner table *Br.* one used for dinner.
dinner theatre *Am., Can.* one in which meals are included in the price of a ticket.
dip 1. *Am.* sl. chew tobacco or take snuff orally. 2. *Am., Can.* col. also sl. **dipshit** a fool.
dip *Br., Aus.* /*Am.* **dim**/ (of the lights of a vehicle) make the beam of light point down.
dip out *Aus.* col. fail.
diploma 1. *Am.* a certificate of graduation from secondary school, college or university: *The day came when Sandra got her diploma.* - Guideposts. 2. *Br.* official certificate given after successful completion of a course of study or passing examination. 3. (**high school**) **diploma** *Am.* / *Br.* **GCE (General Certificate of Education)**/.
diplomate *esp. Am.* a person with a diploma certified as an expert, esp. a doctor.
diplomatic bag *esp. Br.* /*Am.* **diplomatic pouch**/ a container for official embassy mail, which is not subject to customs inspection.
Dipper *esp. Am.* the Plough (a group of stars).
dipshit *esp. Am., Can.* sl. contemptible person.
dipswitch *Br.* /*Am.* **dimmer**/ an instrument in a car for lowering the beam of the headlights.
dipsy *Am.* sl. 1. adj. n. alcoholic or drunk: *He was too dipsy to drive.* - R.A. Spears. 2. a foolish person.
Dip. Tech. *Br.* Diploma in Technology: *The Diploma in Technology (Dip. Tech.) is granted on the successful completion of an approved course in a technical college* - J. Ruppeldtova.
direct debit *Br.* a way of paying money that you owe to an organisation in which your bank moves money from your account into organisation's account at regular times.
direct deposit *Am.* method of paying sb.'s wages directly into their bank account.
direct dialing Am. /*Br.* **subscriber trunk dialling**/ direct long-distance telephone call.
direct discourse *esp. Am., Can.* /*Br.* **direct speech**/ exact words of a speaker.

directions *Am., Aus.* instructions how to use smth., often given in a book.
directly *Br.* conj. as soon as.
director 1. *esp. Br.* member of the governing board of a business corporation, (limited company in Britain), one who governs the company from day to day is executive director, manager. 2. *esp. Am.* one who is not continuously active in management but has a sort of superiority duty at intervals. 3. *Am.* a person in charge of a school for very young people. 4. *Am.* /*esp. Br.* **producer**/ person who directs a play or film, instructing the actors, cameramen, etc.: *the late movie director described you as an innocent.* – Reader's Digest.
director-general *esp. Br.* the chief executive of a large organisation.
The Director of Public Prosecutions *Br.* the lawyer who works for the government and decides if a person who committed a crime should be made to appear in a court of law.
directory 1. *Am.* directorate, board of directors. 2. *Br.* /*Am.* **telephone book**/: *he got the phone directory out of the desk's bottom drawer* - R.J. Randisi., M. Wallace.
directory enquiries *Br.* /*Am., Can., Aus.* **directory assistance, information**/ telephone information service: *Directory Assistance for Russian speakers is available in Moscow by dialing 09* - Y. Richmond., *I hung up and dialed long distance information.* - R.L. Stine.
dirt *esp. Am., Aus.* loose earth on the ground or soil: *A square-shaped stone jutted up right in the center of the dirt.* – R.L. Stine.
dirt/ cut dirt *Am.* col. get away.
dirt/ be digging the dirt *Br.* try to find out smth. that may cause harm to another.
dirt/ do sb. **dirt** *Am.* /*Br.* **do the dirt(y) on** sb./ betray and treat sb. very badly.
dirtbag *Am.* derog. despicable person: *All right, dirtbag, you gonna give it up* - Kansas City Star.
dirt farmer *Am., Can.* a farmer who earns his living by farming his own land, esp. without hired help: *the hardships endured by Kentucky's small dirt farmers for generations.* - A. Hitchcock Mystery Magazine.
dirt moving equipment *Am.* earth moving equipment.
dirt poor *Am.* extremely poor.
dirt track/road *Am., Can.* /also *Can.* **dirt path**, *Br., Aus.* **dirt track**/: *He grew up like any other's mother's son on the dirt roads and gully washes of a north-state farm.* - R.P. Warren., *he pulls off the highway onto a dirt road.* - Time.

dirt wagon *Am.* refuse wagon.
dirty 1. *Br., Aus.* sl. adv. extremely. 2. *Am.* sl. containing or possessing illegal drugs.
dirty/ the dirty end of the stick *esp. Br.* col. the most difficult part of smth.
dirty/ wash one's **dirty laundry/linen in public** *Br., Aus.* /*Am., Aus.* **air/do** one's **dirty laundry/ linen (in public)**/ talk about private matters.
dirty/ do the dirty on sb. *Br., Aus.* col. behave unfairly.
dirty up *Am.* col. make smth. very dirty: *You've dirtied up your dress in that mud!* - Longman.
dirty great/big *Br.* col. extremely big.
dirty money *Br.* additional pay given to stevedores for unloading foul, obnoxious, etc. cargoes.
dirty pool *Am.* col. unethical and dubious practice: *They are playing dirty pool now.* - R.A. Spears.
dirty trick(s) *esp. Am.* secret dishonest political activity.
dirty weekend *esp. Br., Aus.* amorous weekend.
dis *esp. Am.* col. act or speak disparagingly.
disbenefit *Br.* disadvantage or loss.
disc Br. /*Am.* **disk**/ computer disk.
disk drive *Br.* /*Am.* **diskette drive**/ a drive for floppy discs.
dischargee *Am.* demobilised person.
disc harrow *Br.* /*Am.* **rotary tiller**/ rotary cultivator used to till or stir the soil so that crops can be planted.
disciples *Am.* Baptists.
disco *Br.* equipment necessary for playing recorded music.
discombobulated *esp. Am., Can. Aus.* sl. confused: *Effie was but a discombobulated fly on the edge of his pin.* - T. Thompson.
discount house 1. *Am., Can.* shop selling goods at discount rates. 2. *Br.* a company that sells and buys bills of exchange.
disfellowship *Am.* expulsion (from college or religious commune).
disfranchise *esp. Am.* disenfranhise, take away from sb. their right to vote.
dish *Am.* 1. plate, flat usu. round dish with a slightly raised edge, from which food is served or eaten. 2. sl. gossip.
dish (the dirt) *Am.* sl. spread malicious gossip: *We sat around dishing the dirt until the gavel sounded* - R.L. Chapman.
dish *esp. Br., Aus.* col. cause the failure of (a person or his hopes), esp. in **dish** sb.'s **hopes/ chances**: *I don't deny that if the play is wrong, you're dished* - W.S. Maugham.

dish out *Am.* shape (a hole) like a dish: *This small desert animal dishes out a shelter for itself in the sand.* - Longman.
dish up *Br.* col. produce or serve smth., esp. a meal.
dishcloth gourd *Am., Can.* the fruit of a certain type of gourds dried and used like a sponge.
dishclout *Br.* dishcloth, a cloth for washing dishes.
dish liquid *Am.* /*Br.* **washing-up liquid**/.
dishpan *Am., Can.* /*Br.* **washing-up bowl**/ basin for washing dishes, plates, etc. after a meal: *the woman on whom dishpan hands seem out of character.* - M. Puzo.
dish rack *Am.* plate rack.
dishrag *Am.* 1. dishcloth: *The biggest culprits: sponges and dishrags, which provide warm, moist environments that cold germs thrive in.* - Reader's Digest. 2. anything wet or limp; weak person: *the very last thing he'd want would be for us to moon about like old dishrags.* - T. Murphy. 3. dishcloth gourd.
dish towel *esp. Am.* /*Br.* **washing-up cloth, wash cloth, wash rag** also *esp. Br.* **tea towel**/ a cloth for drying dishes after they have been washed: *The professor dabbed at her eyes with a dishtowel.* - A. Hitchcock Mystery Magazine.
dish (washing) liquid *Am.* /*Br.* **washing-up liquid**/.
dishy 1. *esp. Br., Aus.* col. sexually attractive: *exactly what it is to be a dishy girl bored stiff* - R.L. Chapman. 2. *Am., Can.* col. scandalous, gossipy.
disinvestment *Br.* /*Am.* **divestment**/ the act of taking one's money out of a place or business in which one invested it.
diskette *Am.* floppy disk.
disorientate *Br.* /*Am.* **disorient**/ cause to lose the sense of direction.
disorderly house *esp. Br.* law. brothel.
dispatch rider *Br.* one who travels between companies riding on a motorcycle or bicycle delivering important documents as quickly as possible.
dispensing chemist *Br., Aus.* a person who both sells medicine and is trained to dispense them or one who can make glasses and contact lenses.
dispensing optician *Br.* a person who sells glasses but who doesn't examine person's eyes.
disposable *esp. Am.* any item that is intended to be thrown away after use.
disposal *Am.* col. /*Br.* **waste disposal**/ waste disposal unit, set under kitchen's sink which breaks vegetable waste into small pieces: *dump*

the remainder of her eggs into the garbage disposal. – R.L. Stine.

diss *Am.* sl. show a strong lack of respect for sb.

dissaving *esp. Am., Can.* spending more money than a person has earned.

dissent /also **dissenting opinion**/ *esp. Am.* judge's opinion which doesn't agree with most of the other judges of a law case.

dissension among the party *Br.* dissension within the party.

dissertation fellowship *Am.* grant given to write a dissertation.

dissolution *Am.* law. divorce.

distance learning *Br.* learning through watching educational TV programmes and sending work to teachers.

distemper *esp. Br.* v. n. (paint with) a paint for walls and other surfaces that can be made thinner by mixing with water: *Moira decided to have the rather dingy hall and dining room redistempered* - A. Huxley.

distinctions *Br.* very high marks (at school).

distressed area *Br.* now rare. area of continuing high unemployment: *Scotland is drifting back once more to become a distressed area.* - J. Ruppeldtova.

district *Am., Can.* divide into areas.

The District *Am.* Washington, DC.

district council *Br.* local council of an urban or rural district.

district nurse *Br.* one who cares for ill and injured, often visiting them in their homes.

district school board *Am.* /*Br.* **LEA (Local Education Authority)**/

ditch rider *Am.* a person in charge of irrigation facilities.

ditchwater/ be dull as ditchwater *Br.* be very boring.

dithers *esp. Br.* col. dither, a state of nervous excitement and inability to make decisions / **all of a dither, be (all) in a dither.**

ditz *Am., Can.* col. silly and inane person.

ditzy, ditsy *Am., Can.* col. vapid and frivolous, silly: *Who is that ditsy old girl who just came in?* - R.A. Spears.

div *Br.* sl. eccentric person, idiot.

divan (bed) *Br.* a bed that has a thick base under the matress.

diversify *Am.* invest money in different enterprises: *you can and should diversify.* - L. Burkett.

diversion *esp. Br., Can.* /*Am., Aus., Can.* **detour**/ detour (on a highway), also a traffic sign of detour.

divest *Am.* sell (esp. a business or part of it).

divi, divvy *Br.* sl. (esp. in former times) dividend, esp. one paid by a Co-operative Society.

divide *Br.* vote in Parliament by separating into two groups expressing opposite opinions going into either of **division lobbies**.

divide *Am.* /*Br.* **watershed**/ a line of high ground between areas that are drained by different rivers.

Divide and rule *Br.* Divide and conquer.

Divide/ the Grand (Great) Divide *Am.* a. Rocky mountains / b. **go over the Great Divide** *Am.* die.

divide into constituencies *Br.* /*Am.* **(re)district**/ divide into electoral districts.

divided highway *Am., Can., Aus.* /*Br.* **dual carriageway, (divided) motorway**/ main road on which the traffic travelling in opposite directions is kept apart by a central band or separation of some sort: *windows faced the four-lane divided highway outside.* - K. Vonnegut, Jr.

dividend *Br.* the money person can win in a national competition guessing right the result of football games.

divider *Br.* central strip on a road dividing two directions of traffic.

divinity school *Am.* college where students study to become priests.

division 1. *Br.* area represented by an MP. 2. *Am.* group of several departments in the university or college. 3. *Br.* one of groups of teams that a sports competition, esp. football is divided into.

divorce *Am.* divorced male.

divot *Am.* sl. toupee.

divvy *Br.* 1. dividend. 2. col. stupid person.

divvy up *esp. Am.* col. divide smth.

Dixie (Land) *Am.* col. 1. the Southern states of the US: *She is from Dixie, as is shown by her strong Southern accent.* - H.C. Whitford., R.J. Dixson. 2. New Orleans.

Dixie/ be not whistling Dixie *esp. Am.* be honest or realistic in one's actions; **be whistling Dixie** *Am.* be happy about the situation.

DIY *esp. Br., Aus.* abbr. for Do-it-yourself: *She passes launderettes, hairdressers, betting shops...a DIY centre* - D. Lodge.

DJ *Br.* dinner jacket.

DLS *Am.* Doctor of Library Sciences.

dmu *Br.* diesel multiple unit.

DNB *Br.* Dictionary of National Biography.

D notice *Br.* government instructions to news editors not to publish specific information for reasons of national security.

do *Br.* 1. study a particular subject in a school or university. 2. punish sb., esp. in **get done for** smth.: *she will get done! –* S. Townsend.

do *esp. Br., Aus.* 1. col. (of people) cheat, punish, hurt: *Everybody around here is trying to do me. -* I. Stone. 2. serve by means of action with things: *The barber will do you next. -* Longman.

do/have do the washing-up *Br.* /*Am.* **do the wash/**; (*esp. Br.*) **have lunch, dinner, have a wash, have a shower.**

do/ How are you doing? *esp. Am.* col. (an informal greeting to a friend).

do 1. *Br., Aus.* col. /*Am.* col. **to-do/** a big party: *we were to have a special "do" with prizes for the best-dressed woman. -* New Idea., *we're going to 'ave a bit of do. -* J. Herriot. 2. *Br. Aus.* col. a swindle. 3. *Br.* a way of treating people, esp. in **Fair dos!** *Br.* sl. (used esp. when complaining of unfair treatment). 4. *Aus.* col. success. 5. *esp. Am., Can.* col. hairdo.

do/ do a deal *Br.* /*Am.* **make a deal/**: *this guy didn't come here to do a deal. -* A. Hitchcock Mystery Magazine.

do/ do a get *Aus.* leave a place quickly.

do/ do a perish *Aus.* die.

do/ do the dishes *Am.* /*esp. Br., Aus.* **wash up/** wash dishes, plates, knives, forks, etc. after a meal: *The women...are in the kitchen doing the dishes and cleaning up. –* E. Kazan.

do/ do the wash *Am.* do the washing /also *Am.* **do the washing-up/**.

DO *Am.* Doctor of Osteopathy.

do/ be done in *esp. Am.* col. be very tired.

do/ be hard done by *esp. Br., Aus.* be badly treated.

do/ do as you could be done by *Br.* British saying which means that one should treat others as one would like them to treat oneself.

do/ can't/won't be doing with *Br.* be unwilling to tolerate.

do (sb./smth.) **down** *Br.* col. 1. cheat: *we're trying to trap you or do you down. -* J.D. Carr. 2. try to make sb. seem unimportant, worthless, etc., esp. if they are not around: *There's no need to do yourself down -* Longman.

do for sb., smth. *Br.* 1. col. obs. also *Aus.* keep house for or do cleaning for: *Mrs. Whitehead has been doing for the local doctor ever since his wife died. -* Longman. 2. sl. kill, murder: *The poor fellow is done for and will die before morning. -* A. Makkai. 3. col. obs. damage or harm seriously: *I will be done for! –* S. Townsend.

do in/ be done in *esp. Am.* col. be very tired: *I'm done in and must rest here. -* Longman.

do out *esp. Br.* col. clean thoroughly.

do (smth.) **over** 1. *Am., Can.* do, make again, esp. because smth. was done wrong the first time: *She...changed her hose and shoes, did her hair over. -* C. Woolrich. 2. *esp. Br.* col. make a room better by whitewashing her: *Doesn't the bedroom look nice now that we've done it over! -* Longman.

do (a place) **over** *Br.* col. rob or steal a place and leave it untidy.

do sb. over *esp. Br., Aus.* col. hurt sb. badly, esp. by hitting or kicking them.

do up 1. *Am.* can fruit, vegetables, etc.: : *Mother is doing up some blackberries -* Longman. 2. *Br.* wash and iron clothes: *Can you do up my best shirt before tomorrow? -* Longman.

do up/ be done up *esp. Br., Aus.* col. be very tired: *You go on ahead, I'm done up and must rest here. -* Longman.

do up/ be done up/togged to the nines *Br.* be very well dressed (esp. for some occasion).

do with *Br.* col. (with negatives) allow, accept or experience willingly.

DOA *Am.* dead on arrival, said of person dead as soon as they are brought to hospital.

dob *Aus., NZ.* col. tell secretly sb. in authority that some person has done smth. wrong; n. **dobber**.

dob in *Aus.* col. suggest that sb. who is not present should be given an unpleasant job.

dobber *Am.* the float of a fishing line.

doc *Am.* col. doctor.

docent *Am.* 1. university teacher, assistant. 2. sb. who guides visitors through a museum, etc.

docer *Aus.* an eccentric person.

dock 1. *Am., Can.* wharf, pier: *The restaurant is on a riverboat tied to a dock downtown. -* R.G. Kaiser / **docking** *Am., Can.* mooring of the ship at the wharf. 2. *esp. Br.* /*Am.* **the stand/** the place in a court of law where the prisoner stands: *the accused person when brought into dock is asked by the Clerk if he is guilty -* J. Ruppeldtova. 3. *Am.* a platform for loading vehicles or trains.

dock/ in dock *Br., Aus.* (of a car, etc.) away being repaired.

docker *esp. Br.* /*Am., Can.* **longshoreman/** a dock worker.

docket 1. *esp. Br., Aus.* a certificate or ticket which shows the contents of smth. such as a parcel or cargo and proves who the goods belong to. 2. *esp. Am., Can.* law. list of cases awaiting trial in a law court or an agenda in business.

dockland(s) *Br.* the area around docks.

dockominium *Am.* a boat mooring which can be bought outright.
doctor 1. *Am.* (used when speaking to or about dentist or veterinary surgeon). 2. *Aus., NZ.* cook on a ship or in a camp or station.
doctor/ business doctor *Am.* industrial consultant.
doctor/ go for the doctor *Aus.* col. make all that is possible to do.
doctor/ under the doctor (for) *Br.* col. being treated by a doctor (for).
doctor *esp. Br., Aus.* col. euph. make (esp. an animal) unable to breed, neuter.
doctrine *Am.* a statement of official governmrnt policy, esp. foreign one.
docudrama *Am.* true story as a play shown on TV.
docutainment *Am., Can.* films and other presentations which include documentary materials.
doddle *Br.* col. smth. that is very easy, esp. in the phr. **be a doddle**.
dodgem (car) *Br.* tdmk. /*Am.* **bumper car**/ a small car used at fun fairs.
dodger 1. *Am., Aus.* small leaflet. 2. *Am.* maize pancake. 3. *Aus.* col. bread.
dodgy *esp. Br., Aus.* col. 1. not safe, risky, dangerous. 2. dishonest and unreliable. 3. not working properly.
dodo *Am.* a fool.
(hard) doer *Aus., NZ.* brave, tough, adventurous person much admired for these qualities.
dog 1. *Am.* sl. a. failure or disappointment: *a brilliant business idea that turns out to be a dog.* - J. O'Brien, A. Kurins. b. very unattractive woman: *I'm not a dog, but I could wish for some changes.* - R.A. Spears. 2. *Am.* col. smth. of not too good quality: *It's a dog.* - K. Lipper. 3. *Br.* sl. the telephone: *Get on the dog to him and find out when he's coming.* - T. Thorne. 4. *Am., Can.* col. a foot: *His left dog pained* - R.L. Chapman. 5. *Am.* sl. reject, abandon: *I'm not going to dog him out.* - Time.
dog/ the dogs *Br.* col. sports meetings where dogs, esp. greyhounds, race and people bet on them.
dog/ like a dog with a bone *Br.* go on thinking about smth. although it's unpleasant.
dog/ put on the dog *Am., Can. Aus.* col. obs. try to seem richer or more important than one really is.
dog/ Why keep a dog and bark yourself? *Br., Aus.* why do smth. that's supposed to be done by sb. else.

dog (sb.) around *Am.* sl. 1. pester. 2. behave badly.
dog it *Am., Can.* col. 1. run away: *I heard his wife yelling for kids to quit dogging it and get ready for school.* - R. Crais. 2. act lazily.
dog out *Am.* get dressed smartly.
dog-and-pony (show) *Am., Can.* col. attempt to influence by extravagant claims or high-pressure salesmanship: *I've seen that dog-and-pony show so many times* - R.A. Spears.
dogbox *Aus.* col. railway compartment without a corridor.
dogbox/ in the dogbox *NZ.* col. in disfavour.
dogcatcher *Am.* /*Br.* **dog warden**/ person who collects dogs without owners.
dog-end *Br.* sl. cigarette butt.
dogface *Am.* col. infantryman: *When they try to land they run up against the dogfaces.* - J.A. Michener.
doggery *Am.* 1. rabble, mob. 2. obs. sl. cheap saloon, dive.
doggo 1. *Am.* sl. worthless: *doggo prospects like anthropologists and landscape architects* - R.L. Chapman. 2. *Br.* sl. drugged.
doggo/ lie doggo *Br., Aus.* col. obs. hide.
doggone *Am., Can.* col. v. damn. adj. **doggoned**: *Doggone, I'd almost forgotten that.* - B. Tillman, *It's going to be so doggone exciting* - USA Today.
doggy bag, doggie bag *esp. Am., Aus.* small bag provided by a restaurant for taking home food that remains uneaten after a meal: *come with either an empty stomach or a doggie bag.* - New York.
dog(gy) paddle *Am., Aus.* a simple swimming action in which people move their arms and legs up and down in quick movements under water.
doghouse *Am., Can.* /*Br.* **kennel**/ a small building made for a dog to sleep in.
doghouse/ (be) in the doghouse *Am., Can.* col. (be) in disgrace.
dogie *Am., Can.* motherless calf in a group of cattle: *And we wouldn't dream of rustling any of you dogies off the local range* - L. Waller.
dogman *Aus., N.Z.* person giving directional signals to the operator of a crane.
dog paddle *esp. Am., Can.* elementary form of swimming with paddling arms and kicking legs.
dog-robber *esp. Am.* col. an army or navy officer's orderly.
the dogs *Br.* col. greyhound racing.
dog's age *Am., Can.* col. a very long time.
the dog's bollocks *Br.* taboo. sl. smth. outstanding.

dogsbody *Br., Aus.* col. person in a low-ranking position who has to do the least interesting job: *I just act as his dog's body, doing what he tells me.* - Observer.

dog's breakfast/dinner *Br., Aus.* derog. col. smth. badly or untidily done, esp. in **make a dog's breakfast/dinner (out) of** smth.: *I'm afraid the syllabus is a bit of a dog's breakfast.* - T. Thorne.

dog's dinner / done up/dressed (up) like a dog's dinner *Br., Aus.* col. dressed in fine clothes.

dog tag *esp. Am., Can.* col. a tag worn around the neck by a soldier with their number on it.

dog train *Can.* dog-sled.

do-hickey *Am.* sl. 1. any unspecified or unspecifiable thing: *And these little do-hickeys will hum, buzz, give off light and do everything* - L. Waller. 2. spot, pimple, etc.

doings 1. *Br.* col. any small things, esp. the name of which one forgets or doesn't know: *You've got the doings, haven't you?* - G. Greene. 2. *Am.* elaborate dishes.

dole /go/ be on the dole *Br.* col. */Am.* **be on welfare/** (start to) receive money from the government because one is unemployed /also *Am.* **be on relief/**: *After 15 months on the dole, he managed to get a job with corporation.* - P. Norman., *we live like paupers on the dole.* - L. Waller., *A man on the dole killed himself* - G. Greene.

dole-bludger *Aus.* col. 1. unemployment pay scrounger: *Newspapers are always whingeing about the dole bludgers.* - T. Thorne. 2. any idle or shiftless person.

dole queue *Br. /Am.* **unemployment line/**.

dolerite 1. *esp. Br.* diabase. 2. *Am.* any dark igneous rock.

doley, dolie *Aus.* sl. person on the dole.

doll *Am.* 1. col. a person one likes: *Oh, he was a doll!* - H. Fast., *Mary, you're a doll.* - R. Cook., *Curtie's a doll* - Arthur Hailey. 2. col. obs. a term of address to a woman or a girl by men.

dollar sale *Am.* a sale of things for one dollar each.

dollar/ (I'll bet you) dollars to donuts/ doughnuts *esp. Am., Can.* col. it's sure to happen.

dollar/have/see dollar signs (in sb.'s **eyes)** *Am., Aus.* look like sb. is thinking about money they could get.

dollars-and-cents *Am., Aus.* exact amounts of money involved.

doll corner, also **housekeeping corner** *Am.* a quiet area or corner of a school room which has dolls and small furniture arranged in it for children to play with.

doll's house *Br., Aus. /Am.* **dollhouse/** 1. child's toy house. 2. very small house.

doll's pram *Br., Aus. /Am.* **doll's carriage/** a vehicle for pushing a doll around in.

dolly in (out) *Am.* move a camera on a cart when shooting a film: *dolly out so that we get a view of the whole house.* - Longman.

dolly bag *Br.* col. Dorothy bag, small women's bag.

dolly (bird) *Br.* col. obs. usu. derog. pretty young woman, esp. one wearing fashionable clothes: *I wish you'd drop a hint to that young man that I'm not your dolly-bird.* - D. Lodge.

Dolly mixture(s) *Br.* a mixture of small sweets of various shapes and colours.

domestic *Am., Can.* a product that is not made abroad.

domestic partner *Am., Can.* person living with another in close personal and sexual relationship.

domestic science *Br.* obs. the study in school of cooking, sewing, etc.

dominie *Am., Can.* clergyman: *Theodorus had been named dominie* – I. Stone.

Dominion day *Can.* day commemorating the creation of the Dominion of Canada on July 1, 1867.

dominium *esp. Am.* law. ownership and control of property.

the Old Dominion *Am.* joc. Virginia.

don *Br.* university teacher, esp. at Oxford and Cambridge: *He hated socialists, dog-lovers and English dons.* - L. Lee., *Two university dons stayed with us for a while.* - Woman's Own. adj. **Donnish**: *I took a walk in the garden with her father, a donnish man* – Alain de Botton.

dona *Aus.* col. obs. woman or sweetheart.

done *esp. Br.* socially acceptable, esp in **it isn't done.**

done/ be done *Br.* col. be cheated.

done/ be/get done *Br.* col. be caught by police for doing smth. illegal, usu. not too serious.

done/ done and dusted *esp. Br., Aus.* finished and decided.

done in/ be all done in *Am.* 1. fail for reasons one can't control. 2. be too tired.

done deal *esp. Am.* a final decision or agreement.

dong *Aus., NZ.* col. hit or punch.

donga *Aus., NZ.* 1. dry gully formed by water. 2. makeshift or temporary shelter.

donk *Aus.* sl. 1. car engine. 2. foolish person.

donkey derby *Br.* race on donkeys done for amusement or to raise money for some cause.

donkey jacket *Br.* also **waxed jacket** thick coat, usu. dark-blue, reaching down to the top of legs, and usu. with a piece of leather or plastic across the shoulder: *man wearing a black woolen cap and navy donkey jacket sat down on the next stool.* - J.P. Hogan.

(for) donkey's years *esp. Br.* col. (for a) very long time: *Miss Ovary has done in the kitchen down there for donkey's years.* - J.P. Donleavy.

(the) donkeywork *esp. Br.* col. /*Am.* **gruntwork**/ the hard uninteresting part of a piece of work: *I don't see why large organisations, where humans do the donkeywork shouldn't be taken over by machine intelligence.* - Omni.

donnish *esp. Br.* clever, serious, more interested in ideas than real life.

don't *esp. Am.* nonst. doesn't.

donnybrook *Am., Can., Aus.* heated argument.

donut *Am., Aus.* doughnut.

doobie *Am.* sl. marihuana cigarette: *enough pot from each shipment for a doobie of my own.* - W. Jack, B. Lawrsen.

doodah *Br., Aus.* /*Am., Aus.* **doodad,** *Am.* **dohickey**/ col. unspecified or unspecifiable thing or person.

doodlebug 1. *Br.* col. a V-1 (a flying bomb). 2. *Am.* divining rod for locating oil and minerals.

doodly squat, also **diddly (squat)** *Am.* sl. nothing else: *I wouldn't tell you doodly squat* - T. Thorne., *they are not worth doodley-squat.* – K. Vonnegut, Jr.

doofus *Am., Can.* col. a foolish person.

doohickey *Am., Can.* /*Am.* **dojigger**/ col. small gadget whose precise name a speaker cannot recall.

doolally *Br.* col. adj. crazy, mad.

doomage *Am.* fine (esp. of a person who avoids paying taxes).

Doona *Aus., NZ.* tdmk. quilted eiderdown or duvet.

door/ be knocking on/at the door of smth. *Br.* be trying to join an organisation.

door/ get a leg in the door *Am.* start from a lower level in the organization trying to rise higher later.

door/ push at/against an open door *Br.* find it very easy to achieve smth.

door/ through/by the back door *esp. Br.* secretly and unofficially.

do-or-die *Am.* a situation when a person must do their best to avoid a failure.

door jamb *Am.* door post.

doorkeeper *Am.* official in charge of the building.

door knock *Aus., NZ.* a compaign of canvassing for charity or support of political candidates.

door prize *Am.* prize to sb. who has the winning number on their ticket for a show, dance, or party.

doorstep *Br.* col. humor. very thick piece of smth., esp. of bread cut from a loaf.

doorstep *Br.* col. 1. wait uninvited outside the home of famous person to get an interview or take a photograph. 2. door-to-door selling or canvassing.

doorstep salesman *Br.* door-to-door salesman.

dooryard *Am.* yard outside of the door of a house: *he walked around and around the blocks of yellow frame houses and grass dooryard* - J. Dos Passos.

dooze *Am.* sl. attractive proposition.

doozy, doozie *esp. Am., Can.* col. smth, remarkable, good or bad: *that was a doozy, wasn't it?* - K. Vonnegut, Jr.

dope *Am.* col. heroin.

dope out *Am.* col. 1. find an answer to (smth.): *Need time to think, to dope things out.* - A. Scaduto. 2. (in horse racing) make (a horse) unfit for a race by giving it a drug: *Half the runners have been doped out.* - Longman.

dope up *Am.* col. cause (sb.) to feel the full effect of (a drug): *I knew when people were doped up* – J. Hopkins.

dopester *Am., Can.* col. collector of information, esp. on sports or elections.

do-re-mi *Am.* sl. money: *It takes too much do-re-mi to live in this part of town?* - R.A. Spears.

dork 1. *esp. Am., Aus.* col. a fool, idiot; person loudly dressed and behaving awkwardly in social situations: *she looked like a total dork.* – R.L. Stine. adj. **dorkish, dorky**: *all the grown-up characters in the movie were unbelievably dorky.* - W. Jack, B. Laursen. 2. *Am., Can.* taboo. sl. penis.

dormitory /also **dorm**/ *Am., Can.* /*Br.* **hall(s) (of residence)**/ a building in a college or university, where students live and sleep: *D'Ambrosio returned to the medical school dorm* - R. Cook., *they were walking from the Vassar canteen to her dorm?* - E. Segal.

dormitory *esp. Br.* n. adj. suburbs in which commuters live.

dormitory town *Br.* /*Aus.* **dormitory suburb,** *Am.* **bedroom communities**/ suburbs where commuters live.

dormobile *Br.* tdmk. a kind of small van or bus where a person can sleep in.

Dorothy bag *Br.* a woman's bag drawn together with purse strings and carried on the wrist.

dose/ go through smth. **like a dose of salts** *Br.* col. finish dealing with smth. very quickly.

dosh *Br., Aus.* col. money.

doss *esp. Br.* col. 1. short sleep. 2. crude or makeshift bed: *Chauffer also used it as an occasional doss.* - P. Norman. 3. an easy task where a person can idle.

doss (**around, about**) *Br.* sl. do nothing in particular: *You mean they doss around here as long as they like?* - D. Lodge.

doss (**down**) *esp. Br., Aus.* col. find a (usu. humble) place to sleep; lie down: *the men dossed down in the hay* - E. Williams.

dosser *esp. Br.* col. 1. tramp, homeless person who sleeps in variety of places: *He's a queer old dosser.* - J. Joyce. 2. derog. never-do-well; a lazy person.

dosshouse, casual ward *esp. Br.* col. /*Am.* col. **flophouse**/ cheap lodging house, esp. one for short stays: *I went to a doss-house down by the docks.* - L. Lee., *he is forced to take the old man out for dinner and find him a bed in a crowded doss-house.* - L. Van Der Post.

dot *Br.* col. hit sb.

dot/ the year dot *Br. Aus.* col. often derog. a very long time ago; **in the year dot, since the year dot.**

dot one's **i's and cross** one's **t's** *esp. Br.* col. be extremely careful in a slightly annoying way.

dot for dot 1. *Br.* print. the use of pre-screened prints on artwork so that they can be reproduced without the photographs needing to be screened. 2. *Am.* print. printing colour work in perfect register.

dotted *Br.* /*Am.* **polka dot**/.

dotty *esp. Br.* col. slightly mad; **dotty about** infatuated with.

double *Br.* col. adj. n. **double** and **treble** are used in giving telephone numbers, in oral spelling double the letter not repeat it.

double/ at the double *Br., Aus.* /*Am., Aus.* **on the double**/ very quickly.

double/ double or quits *Br.* /*Am.* **double or nothing**/ the decision in the game where money is risked, as a dice, to risk winning twice the amount one has already won or losing it all.

double/ double in brass *Am.* col. hold more than one job: *he can double in brass by writing as well as printing the magazine.* - Longman.

double/ double one's **fists** *Am.* curl one's fingers tightly to make fists ready to fight.

double/ win the double *Br.* win two similar competitions.

double-bank *esp. Br.* arrange in two similar or parallel lines.

double-barrelled 1. *esp. Br.* col. (of family names) connected by hyphen. 2. *Am., Aus.* having two purposes. 3. *Am.* very strong or using a lot of force.

double-bedded *esp. Br.* with a bed big enough for two people.

double bend *Br.* s-curve on a highway.

double-bitted axe *esp. Am., Can.* double axe.

double bluff *Br.* a clever attempt to deceive sb., esp. by telling them the truth when they think you are telling lies.

double-breasting *Can.* a ploy to circumvent a trade union closed shop by which a unionised company sets up a non-unionised subsidiary and subcontracts work to it.

double-clutch *Am.* /*Br.* **double-declutch**/ step twice on the clutch when changing gears.

double cream *Br.* /*Am.* **whipping cream, heavy cream**/ very thick cream.

double date *esp. Am.* a date for two men and two women: *I had double-dated with a friend of mine at the station* - A.E. Hotchner.

double-declutch *Br.* /*Am.* **double–clutch**/ release and reengage the clutch of a vehicle twice when changing gear.

double-digit *Am.* relating to numbers 10-99, esp. as a percentage.

double-dip 1. *Am., Can.* col. v. collect more than one income at a time. n.: *Federal pensioners are "double-dippers" who also collect Social Security checks* - Time, R.L. Chapman. **double-dipping.** 2. *Aus.* receive two amounts of tax benefit for the same item in two different ways. 3. *Am.* ice-cream with two balls of ice-cream.

doubledome *Am.* sl. an intellectual, highbrow: *Not for them a double-domed debate on the op-ed page.* - Time.

double Dutch 1. *Br., Aus.* col. nonsense, gibberish. 2. *Am., Can.* jumping game where two skipping ropes are used.

double duty/ do double duty *Am.* do more than one job, use for more than one thing at the same time.

double eagle *Am.* col. 20 dollars.

double feature *Am.* double bill, cinema performance in which two films are shown one after another.

double figures *Br.* the numbers from 10 to 99.

double glass (**window**) *Am.* /*esp. Br.* **double-glazed window, double-glazing,** *Can.* **double window**/ glass on a window or door in two separate sheets with a space in between them: *She has not double-glazed the house in order to preserve its architectural integrity.* - D.

Lodge, *They had radiators and double windows.* - W. Grady.

double header *Am.* 1. two games played as a single event, esp. in baseball: *he could last throughout an entire double header without feeling tired.* - D. Carnegie. 2. train, pulled by two locomotives: *I rode...the pilots of the doubleheader.* - I. Stone.

double indemnity *Am.* law. feature of a life insurance policy that allows to double the value of the contracts to be paid in the case of death by accident.

double jeopardy *Am.* law. the act of putting sb. on trial twice for the same offence.

double jobber *Br.* person having two jobs, double-jobbing.

double play *Am.* the action of making two runners in baseball have to leave the field by throwing the ball quickly from one base to another before the runners reach each other.

double plumbing *Can.* two toilets or two washrooms or two bedrooms in a house.

double-quick *Br.* col. /*Am.* **double-time/** as quick as possible.

double ripper /or **runner**/ *Am.* sledge for two persons.

double saucepan *Br.* /*Am.* **double boiler/** a cooking utensil consisting of two saucepans fitting into each other so that the contents of the upper one can be cooked by boiling water in the lower.

double speak *esp. Am.* speak with ambiguity; also n.

double talk *esp. Am., Can.* double speak.

double time *Am.* fast military march.

double-whole note *Am.* /*Br.* **breve/**.

double-wide *Am., Can.* semi-permanent mobile home made of two separate units connected on site.

douchebag *Am., Can.* col. derog. repellent person: *And Big Gus is a douch bag.* - J. O'Brien., A. Kurins.

dough boy, dough face 1. *Am.* col. infantryman: *I washed more pans and peeled more potatoes than any other doughboy* - Alcoholics Anonymous. 2. *Br.* sl. blow, heavy punch.

doughhead *Am., Can.* col. stupid person.

doughnut/ American one is usu. in a shape of a ball, British one is in the shape of ring, and is also called a ring doughnut.

doughnuts/ do doughnuts *Am.* col. make a car spin around in cirles.

douse *Br.* n. a blow, stroke.

dove *esp. Am.* past tense of dive.

dower house *Br.* residence of a widow near the main house of her late husband's estate.

down 1. *Am.* adj. going to the centre of the town, to the capital. 2. *Br.* going from a city or place of importance to one supposed to be of less importance. 3. *Br.* going away from a university, esp. Oxford or Cambridge. 4. *Br., Aus.* non-standard. to.

down *Am., Aus.* v. defeat, esp. in sport: *the world downs me on it* - I. Stone.

down *Am.* sl. 1. (used by blacks) supporting or going along with. sb./smth. 2. following the latest fashion.

down/ be down to *Br.* /*Am., Aus.* **come down to/** some party or organisation means to be their responsibility, fault, choice or decision.

down/ down in one *Br.* col. drink smth. in one mouthful.

down/ down the road/pike/line, etc. *Am.* at some time in the future: *totally miss the things happening down the hall.* – Harper's Magazine.

down/ down tools *Br.* go on strike.

down/ have a down(er) on sb. *Br., Aus.* col. dislike sb. often unfairly.

down/ put down upon sb. *Aus.* despise sb.

down the gurgler *Aus.* col. down the drain, wasted, spoiled.

down the pan *Br.* col. wasted.

down and dirty *esp. Am., Can.* col. 1. very competitive, nasty, low, vicious and deceptive: *It came down to down-and-dirty complaining.* - Time. 2. journalism. (of performers) bold, direct, shocking.

down and out *Br., Aus.* /*Am.* **down-and-outer/** person without home, job or money.

down-at-heel *esp. Br.* /*esp. Am.* **down-at-the-heel/** (of a person) dressed in an old worn-out clothes whose condition suggests lack of money, untidy.

downeaster *Am.* citizen of New England, esp. of the State of Maine / **go down East** *Am.* go to New England: *Many people like to go down East for their summer vacation.* - A. Makkai.

downer/ be on a downer *Br.* be sad or experience a series of sad events.

downer/ have a downer on sb. *Br., Aus.* col. not like sb.

downgrade *esp. Am., Can.* (of a railway or road) downward gradient.

downgrade/ on the downgrade *esp. Am., Can.* in decline.

downhold *Am.* strict limitation.

downhome *Am., Can.* sl. simple, neighbourly, esp. characteristic of life in the rural areas in the

Southern US: *He blends favorite traditional and original tales with down-home humor.* - Arkansas Times.

downmarket *esp. Br.* concerning cheaper or less prestigious section of the market, goods and services of not very good quality.

downmost *esp. Br.* at or towards the bottom.

down-on-one's-**luck** *Am.* having no money for a long time because of bad luck.

downs *esp. Br.* low rounded grassy hills, esp. chalk hills, as in the south of England: *On the far horizon, over a countless succession of fields and hedges rose a line of downs.* - J. Galsworthy.

downscale *Am., Can.* reduce in size, scale or extent.

downshift *esp. Am., Can.* change down the speed of a vehicle, n.: *The motor then helps slow the car – not unlike downshifting* – Reader's Digest.

downsize *esp. Am.* reduce the size and weight of (a car, etc): *They call it downsizing in the USA, or de-scaling or just re-structuring.* - C. Handy.

downspout *Am., Can.* /*Br.* **drainpipe**/ rainwater pipe, drain pipe.

downstate *Am.* n. adj. adv. away from metropolitan or industrial centres usu. to the south, n. **downstater.**

down timber *Am., Can.* fallen trees brought down by wind, storm, etc.

down time *esp. Am., Can.* time when sb. is not working or active.

downtown *esp. Am., Can.* /*esp. Br.* **city centre**/ to, towards, or in the business centre of a town or city: *she had forgotten which way the man had told her to turn uptown or downtown for Smiley's Bar.* - I. Shaw., *others want to escape the high rents and downtown hassles.* - Time., *Then on the overnight layover I naturally went sightseeing in downtown Washington.* - Alex Haley.

Down Under *Aus., Br.* col. n. adj. in or towards Australia and New Zealand: *one talked to men who had still been free, in America, Down Under, and in Britain* - E. Williams.

down vest *Am.* body- warmer.

downward *Am.* downwards.

downzone *Am., Can.* (of land or property) be assigned to a zoning grade under which the permitted density of housing and development is reduced.

doze *esp. Br.* a short sleep.

dozen/ talking nineteen to the dozen *Br., Aus.* col. talking very fast without stopping.

dozy *Br.* col. stupid, slow in understanding; n. **dozyness.**

drabble *Br.* sl. puritanical person.

drack *Aus., NZ.* col. (esp. of a woman) unattractive and unwelcome.

draft, Selective Service 1. *esp. Am.* /*esp. Br.* **conscription,** *esp. Br.* **call-up, National service**/ conscription in the armed forces: *he got his 4-F classification in the draft.* - I. Shaw., *He spoke of eliminating the draft in this country* - J. Baez. 2. *esp. Am.* a group of people chosen by conscription. 3. *Am.* draught. 4. *Am., Can.* procedure of selection new players by the sports teams in a league. 5. *esp. Br.* order for money to be paid by a bank, esp. from one bank to another.

draft *esp. Am.* v. /*Br.* **conscript,** *esp. Br.* **call up**/.

draft board *Am.* committee which decides who will be drafted into the army.

draft card *Am.* conscription card: *Hugo was sorry he didn't have his draft card on him* - I. Shaw.

draft dodger *Am., Can.* col. conscription dodger: *American draft dodgers came to Canada in the 1970s.* - W. Magnuson.

draftee *esp. Am.* a man who has been conscripted into the armed forces, a conscript.

drafting room *Am.* /*Br.* **drawing office**/ room where people draw plans and sketches.

draft lift *Br.* a device which takes a skier to higher grounds.

draft pick *Am., Can.* the right of a sports team to select new players during the annual selection process.

draftsman 1. *Am., Aus.* /*esp. Br.* **draughtsman, technical drawer**/ person who makes drawings of all the parts of a new building or machine: *As a draftsman I worked for several large companies* - Alcoholics Anonymous. 2. *esp. Am.* person who draws well.

drafty *Am.* /*Br.* **draughty**/ with cold currents of air blowing through.

drag *Br.* 1. sl. a puff of cigarette. 2. col. long and boring journey.

drag *Am.* sl. 1. also *Can., Aus.* a street or road: *we went right down the main drag* - A.E. Hotchner; **the main drag** *Am.* col. biggest and longest street that goes through a town. 2. influence / **have a drag with** sb.: *We had a big drag with the waiter* - E. Hemingway, R.L. Chapman., *she never got a job that way, through a drag or anything like that.* – J. O'Hara. 3. take part in a drag race; n. *Am.* **drag-racing.**

drag up *Br., Aus.* col. bring up (a child) in a poor way, esp. without good manners.

drag/ drag sb. **into the 20th/21st century** *Br.* make people more modern in their ideas or technology.

dragger *Am., Can.* a fishing boat that uses a dragnet.

draggin' wagon *Am.* sl. tow truck.

draggy *Am.* col. slow, monotonous, sluggish: *draggy movie* - R.L. Chapman.

drag hook *Am.* 1. hasp /hook/ of the hame of a horse. 2. load hook /draw hook/.

Dragon *Aus.* a type of lizard.

drag race *Am.* race won by the car that can increase its speed fastest over a short distance: *Drag racing helped pay his way through college.* – Reader's Digest.

drain *esp. Br.* pipe that carries water or waste liquids away.

drain *esp. Am.* /*Br.* **plughole**/ a hole into which a plug is fitted, used for drainage.

drain/ laugh like a drain *Br., Aus.* col. laugh very loudly.

drainboard *Am., Can.* /*Br., Aus.* **draining board**, *Br.* **drainer**/ draining board in a kitchen: *Edith stood up and put the milk glass on the sink drain-board.* - L. Waller.

drainpipe 1. *esp. Br.* a pipe that carries rain water down from the roof of a building. 2. *Br.* /*Am.* **downspout**/ pipe that carries water or waste away from buildings.

drainpipe trousers /**drainies, drainpipes**/ *Br.* col. tight-fitting trousers with narrow legs: *There were battles too over trousers, which Jim insisted must not be "drainies" but of conventional and respectable cut.* - P. Norman.

dramatize (a situation or event) *esp. Am.* focus people's attention on the situation in a dramatic way.

dramedy *Am.* a television comedy-drama.

draper *Br.* obs. a shopkeeper who sells cloth.

draper's (shop), draper *Br.* /*Am.* **drygoods store**/.

drapery, soft goods *Br.* obs. /*Am.* **drygoods store**, *Aus., Br.* **haberdashery**/ cloth and cloth goods, esp. for making curtains: *His father kept a drapery shop* - A. Huxley

drapes, also **draperies** *Am., Aus.* heavy curtains: *Isabelle bothered by the rain went to close the drapes.* - D. Mortman., *I kept the drapes closed.* - Guideposts.

draught *Br.* /*Am.* **draft**/ flow of air (as in a fireplace/.

draught/ on draught *esp. Br.* beer on tap.

draughts *Br., Aus.* /*Am., Aus.* **checkers**/.

draw *esp. Br.* win the same number of points in the game, n.

draw *Am.* 1. a galley shallower than ravine. 2. the movable part of the bridge.

draw/ be drawn against sb. *Br.* be chosen by chance to play or compete against sb.

draw/ draw one's horns in *Br.* spend less money because sb. has financial problems.

draw a veil over (smth.) *Br.* not to speak about smth. intentionally because it is unpleasant.

draw in *Br.* (of nights, evenings or days) become dark at an earlier time in the evening, etc. because autumn or winter is approaching.

draw it mild *Br.* don't exaggerate.

drawdown *Am.* 1. reduction. 2. water level reduction.

drawgear *Br.* a coupling for railway carriage.

drawing card *Am., Aus.* a famous person.

drawing office *Br.* /*Am.* **drafting room**/.

drawing pin *Br., Aus.* /*esp. Am., Can.* **thumbtack, pushpin**/ a short pin with a broad flat head, used esp. for putting notices on boards and walls: *Bob Bosby...is having trouble digging a drawing-pin out of the notice-board* - D. Lodge.

drawing room *Am.* a private room in a railway train, in which three people can sleep: *Next day he took the Pennsylvania to Chicago, travelling in a drawing room.* - J. Dos Passos.

drawing room car *Am.* saloon carriage.

drawn butter *Am., Can.* melted butter used as sauce.

the dreaded lurgy *Br., Aus.* humor. not serious contagious illness.

dreadful *esp. Br.* 1. extremely unpleasant. 2. terrible, also adv, **dreadfully**.

dream/ Americans more often than British use dreamed for the past tense and past participle.

dreamland *esp. Br.* completely unrealistic situation.

dream ticket *Br.* two politicians who represent different opinions in their party standing for election as leader and next in charge and so getting as much support as possible.

dreary *Am.* make dull.

dreidel *Am., Can.* 1. small four-sided spinning top used by Jewish people. 2. gambling game using it.

dress (a) ship *Am.* raise state flags on the ship.

dress-down Friday *Am.* a day on which it is considered acceptable that office workers dress more casually in the workplace than on other days.

dresser 1. *esp. Br.* a place of furniture for holding dishes and other articles used in eating: *There's a toaster on the dresser* - McLean's. 2. *Am., Can.* a chest of drawers, used esp. for clothing often with a mirror on top: *There was a low Spanish dresser of dark wood with brass fittings.* - S.

Sheldon., *Sis was standing in our room before the dresser mirror.* - C. McCullers., *There was a double bed and a dresser and a hotplate.* - K. Vonnegut, Jr. /also **vanity dresser**/. 3. *Br.* person who assists a surgeon during operations.

dressing *Am., Can.* solid mixture for putting inside a chicken, etc., stuffing: *I ordered the nicoise salad with sesame dressing* - R. Crais.

dressing gown *esp. Br.* /*Am.* (**bath**)**robe**/ a robe worn esp. while dressing or resting: *Caro appeared in a dressing gown.* - J. Fowles., *There was also a bottle-green dressing gown* - M.M. Kaye.

dressing table *Br.* /*Am.* **vanity table**/ a bedroom table with a mirror on top.

dress shirt *Am., Can.* man's long-sleeved shirt, usu. worn with a tie: *there was Frank Sinatra sitting in his dress shirt and his silk socks, bow tie and his underpants.* – A. Summers, R. Swan.

dress show *Br.* fashion show.

drey *esp. Br.* squirrel's nest.

dribble *Br.* /*Am.* **drool**/ let saliva flow out of one's mouth onto one's chin.

dribble *Br.* /*Am.* **saliva**/ a flow of saliva from one's mouth.

drier *Am.* /*Br.* **tumble drier**/.

drill *Br.* col. the approved or correct way of doing smth. effectively: *They knew the drill backward and forward* - Life.

drillion *Am.* joc. a very large number.

drink *Br.* sl. small bribe, tip, etc.

drink/ **the big drink** *Am.* 1. Atlantic Ocean. 2. Mississippi river.

drink/ **a long/tall drink of water** *Am.* col. obs. a tall man.

drink-driving *Br.* /*Am.* **drunk-driving**/ the crime of driving with an excess of alcohol in the blood.

drinking fountain *esp. Br.* /*Am.* **water fountain**, *Am., Aus.* **bubbler**/ an artificial fountain in a public place to drink water from.

drinking-up time *Br.* the short time allowed in a pub for people to finish their drinks before it is closed.

drinks *Br.* social occasion on which alcoholic drinks are drunk and sometimes food is eaten.

drinks party *Br.* cocktail party.

drinks problem *Br., Aus.* /*Am., Aus.* **drinking problem**/ regular drinking too much alcohol.

drip *Br.* /*Am.* **IV**/ a dripfeed, esp. in a phr. **be put on a dripfeed**.

the drip *Br.* sl. hire purchase, usu. in **on the drip**.

drip mat *Br.* small mat placed under a glass to protect the surface of the table.

dripping *Br.* drip from roasting meat used in cooking or eaten cold as a spread.

dripping *Br.* weak, irresolute.

dripping(s) *esp. Am., Can.* the fat that has come out of meat during cooking.

drive 1. *Br.* competition of the stated type / esp. of a card game/. 2. *Am.* bargain sale. 3. *Aus., NZ.* a line of partly cut trees on hillside, felled so that the top one topples on the other (**drive system**). 4. *Br.* /*Am.* **driveway**/ small drive towards a house: *The fastest part of your commute is going down your driveway.* – Reader's Digest.

drive a coach and horses through (an argument) *Br.* destroy it completely.

drive/ **drive the porcelain bus** *Am. sl.* vomit.

drive/ **drive sb. round the bend/twist, drive sb. mad/bonkers** *Br. col.* make sb. slightly mad by bothering them too much.

drive stakes *Am.* v. camp.

drive-by *esp. Am.* (of a crime, esp. a shooting) carried out from a moving vehicle; hence figuratively of any activity; carried out in passing or on the run: *The boy had been killed in a drive-by.* – Reader's Digest.

driver *Br.* /*Am.* **engineer**/ person who drives a railway engine; **driver's seat, timetable**, etc. *Am., Aus.* /*Br.* **driving seat, timetable**, etc./.

driver's education *Am.* course that is taken at school teaching how to drive correctly.

driver's license (**certificate**) *Am., Can.* /*Br.* **driving licence**/ one allowing sb. to drive a car after passing **driver's test/driving test**: *The next two showed a driver's license* - A. Hitchcock Mystery Magazine.

drive-in *esp. Am., Can., Aus.* adj. smth. that people can use while remaining in their cars, also n.: *he saw a UFO approaching the drive-in at very low altitude* – F. Edwards.

drive-in banking *Am.* servicing a bank client in a car.

drive-through *esp. Am., Can.* relating to facility through which a person can drive and in which he can be served without leaving a car, n.: *Please get some healthier suggestions for your next visit to the drive-through.* – Reader's Digest.

drivetime *Am.* (radio term) morning or evening period when most potential listeners are driving to or from work.

driving seat *Br.* driver's seat.

driving under the influence (DUI), driving while intoxicated (DWI) *Am.* law. driving in a state of drunkenness.

driving without due care and attention *Br.* law. crime of driving a car without being careful enough.

driza-bone *Aus.* waterproof coat worn by those who live and work in the Australian bush.

drongo *esp. Aus., NZ.* col. (also **droob, dill, galah, nong**) a simple foolish person.

droob *Aus.* col. contemptible person.

drop /*esp.* **maildrop**/ *esp. Am.* a place where smth. may be dropped, esp. a letter box: *You think this is a drop?* - R. Moore., *Hawkins came and went mostly at night and rented a maildrop nearby.* - Vanity Fair.

a drop in the bucket *Am.* /*Br.* **drop in the ocean**/ a very small account.

drop a bomb *Am.* tell a bad news.

drop/ drop/land sb. in it, drop/land sb. in the shit *Br.* col. cause sb. to have problems, esp. by saying smth. that makes other people get angry with them.

drop/ drop sb./smth. like a hot brick *Br.* suddenly stop doing smth. embarrassing.

drop/ drop the ball *Am., Can.* col. make a mistake.

drop/ get the drop on sb. *Am., Can.* col. put sb. in awkward situation or do smth. before they do: *Turkeys have a way of getting a drop on a guy.* - Outdoor Life., *Andrews tried to get the drop on the circle makers* - Omni.

drop up *esp. Am.* col. arrive unexpectedly: *She said she'd drop up to tea one afternoon.* - Longman.

drop a brick / clanger *Br.* col. do or say smth. foolish and socially unacceptable.

drop one's **bundle** *Aus.* sl. panic.

drop the ball *Am.* make a mistake or fail to do smth.

drop-ball *Can.* sl. ear ring.

drop cloth *Am., Can.* /*Br.* **dustsheet**/ one for covering furniture when painting or to protect it from dust.

drop-dead *Am.* sl. sensational: *His favorite car was Zimmer - $60,000 worth of drop-dead luxury* - Rolling Stone.

drop-dead gorgeous *Br.* col. very attractive.

drophead *Br.* n. adj. convertible car: *his grandfather downshifted the sleek drophead Bentley* - T. Murphy.

drop-in centre *Br.* place where unemployed, homeless, etc. can get information, relax and talk.

drop kit *Am.* toilet bag for soap, brushes, etc. for travelling

drop letter *Am.* one delivered from the same post in which it is posted.

drop-light *Am.* desktop lamp with a movable head.

drop-off *esp. Am., Can.* a cliff: *I could see a sheer dropoff to the valley below on our right.* – R.L. Stine.

dropout slip *Am.* /*Br.* **certificate**/ document that states that a person studied at secondary school but hasn't finished it.

dropper *Aus., NZ.* vertical stave in a fence.

droppies *Br.* sl. self-employed people.

drop scone, griddle cake, Scotch pancake *Br.* / *Am.* **slapjack**/ pancake.

dross *Br.* smth. of very low quality: *The good moments...were obscured by descent into dross* - A. Summers, R. Swan.

droves/ come in one's **droves** *Br.* come in droves, come in large numbers.

droppies *Br.* sl. people who become self-employed.

drug/ be drugged up (to the eyeballs) *esp. Br.* be given a lot of drugs by a doctor.

drugged out *Am.* always taking and influenced by drugs: *there's no welcome for drugged-out rock-and-rollers here.* – S. Lawrence.

druggist *esp. Am., Can.* /*esp. Br.* **pharmacist, chemist**/ skilled person who owns or runs a pharmacy: *Nobody wants to be a druggist* - L. Waller., *she hated some of those girls with their contractors and drugggists for fathers.* - J. Updike.

druggy *esp. Am.* col. drug-addict: *Those were killers, druggies, robbers.* – Reader's Digest.

drug misuse *Br.* the practise of using drugs for pleasure rather than for medical reasons.

drugola *Am.* sl. money paid by narcotics dealers for protection, esp. to police.

drugs dealer *Am.* drug dealer, a person who sells drugs.

drugs overdose *Am.* drug overdose.

drug rehab(ilitation) *Am.* process of helping drug addicts to live without drugs.

drug squad *esp. Br.* police force department dealing with illegal drugs.

drugstore *esp. Am., Can.* /*esp. Br.* **chemist's (shop)**/ a pharmacy, esp. one which sells not only medicine, beauty products, film, etc., but also (esp. formerly) simple meals: *I worked in drugstores* - T. Caldwell.

drugstore cowboy *Am.* sl. a male who hangs around drugstores and other public places trying to impress women, loafer: *White House spokesman Marlin Fitzwater went so far as to call him a "drugstore cowboy"* - Time.

drum 1. *Br.* col. house, home or building. 2. *Irish Eng.* long narrow hill, esp. one separating two parallel lines.
(the) drum *Aus.* 1. swag, bag, belongings: *Go and turn over his drum.* - T. Thorne. 2. (give) true facts, useful advice: *I got a drum that she was in town.* - T. Thorne. 3. col. brothel.
drummer, (travelling) salesman 1. *esp. Am.* col. /*Br.* obs. **commercial traveller, bag man,** *Br.* col. **commercial**/ travelling salesman: *Come on inside, drummer boy.* - A. Miller. 2. *Aus.* tramp. 3. *Br.* col. obs. thief.
drum majorette *Am.* a woman or a girl who leads a marching musical group.
drumming *Br.* sl. 1. selling door-to-door. 2. burglary.
drum set *Am.* a drum kit.
drunk in charge *Br.* drunken driving.
drunk-driving *Br.* /*Am.* **drink-driving**/.
drunk tank *Am., Can.* col. prison cell for the detention of drunks.
(one's) druther(s) *Am., Can.* person's preference in a matter.
dry 1. *Am.* prohibition supporter: *My father... was a total abstainer and a rabid dry.* – J. O'Hara. 2. **(the) Dry** *esp. Aus.* the dry period in Central Australia. 3. *Am.* adj. made without props, equipment, etc.
dry /also **bone-dry**/ *Am.* anti-alcoholic / **dry law, town; go dry** is to stop the sale of alcohol.
dry/ **come up dry** *Am., Can.* be unsuccessful.
dry camp *Am.* a camp or halt where there is no water.
dry/ American **dry martini** is **gin and French** in Britain.
dry up *Br.* dry dishes: *I'll wash the dishes if you'll dry up for me.* - Longman.
dry goods 1. *esp. Am., Can.* /*esp. Br.* **drapery, soft goods**/ textiles and fabrics: *Mrs. County could afford the most expensive clothes at Verena's dry-goods store.* - T. Capote., *we hunted a tackle store and finally bought a rod for Bill upstairs over a dry-goods store.* - E. Hemingway., *He could rent a room over the dry-goods store in Mason City* - R.P. Warren. 2. *Aus.* hardware store.
drygoods store *Am.* /*Br.* **draper's (shop)**/.
drying line *Br.* clothes line.
dryland farming *esp. Am., Can.* farming in dry areas with the use of drout-resistant crops and conserving moisture
dry lands *esp. Am., Can.* arid area.
dry matter *NZ.* feedstuff for farm animals.
dry milk *Am.* milk in powder form.

dry run *Am., Can.* sl. a tryout, practice or rehearsal of smth. planned: *The dry run staged for the press will be good practice* - Time.
dry salter 1. *esp. Br.* a dealer in chemical products and dies. 2. *Br.* a dealer in salted and dried meats, pickles and fish.
dry sink *Am., Can.* antique kitchen cabinet with an inset sink.
drystone *Br.* (of a stonewall) built without using mortar.
drywall *Am., Can.* plasterboard: *he had once worked building an office, doing drywall and framing.* – Reader's Digest.
dry wash *Am.* 1. rough-dry wash, laundry washed and dried but not ironed. 2. the dry bed of a stream.
dual carriageway *Br.* /*Am., Aus.* **divided highway**/ a main road on which the traffic travelling in opposite directions is kept apart by a central band or separation of some sort: *driving across a dual carriageway and clambering up an embankment, I arrived breathless and late* - B. Bryson.
dual-use *Am.* applied for both civilian and military use.
dub 1. *Am.* col. awkward performer, novice: *you're a linguistic dub* - F. Mowatt. 2. *esp. Br.* make a record out of two or more different pieces of music or sound mixed together.
dub(ber) *Am.* sl. cigarette.
ducat *esp. Am.* col. a ticket or pass to a show, game, race, etc.: *Well, I've got a ducat that reads to there, anyway* - D. Hammet., *Okay, Tony, take a ducat back* - R. Chandler.
duck 1. also **ducky, duckie, ducks** *esp. Br.* col. (used for addressing) a person one likes: *There's a duck.* - G. Greene. 2. *Aus.* col. old woman.
duck *Br.* /*Am.* **dunk**/ push sb. underwater for a short time as a joke.
duckboards *esp. Br.* slatted flooring laid on a wet, muddy, or cold surfaces: *I was...shuttling to and fro across the springing duckboards* - L. Lee., *the rough streets between the duckboards that served for pavements were taken over by hens, ducks and geese, clucking and quacking.* - L. Van Der Post.
ducket *Am.* trade union membership card.
duck hunting *Br.* duck shooting, wild fowling.
duckpin *Am.* short bowling pin.
duck shoot *Am.* col. very easy task.
duck-shove *Aus., N.Z.* col. avoid smth.
duck soup *Am., Can.* col. anything done easily: *Playing a love scene with either of them is duck soup.* - A.E. Hotchner.

duck/ break one's **duck** *Br.* achieve smth. for the first time.

ducks/ get/have (all) one's **ducks in a row** *esp. Am., Can.* col. organise things well.

ducks/ play ducks and drakes (with sb.) *Br.* accuse sb. of treating oneself badly.

duck stamp *Am.* Federal stamp for hunter's license.

ducktail *Am., Can.* col. a man's hairstyle popular in 1950s.

ducky /also **duckie, duck(s)**/ 1. *esp. Br.* col. (used to address a person one likes, esp. by women): *Now sit down, duckie, I'll give you a drop of Scotch to pull you together.* - W.S. Maugham. 2. *Am.* obs. adj. perfect, satisfactory. 3. *esp. Am., Can.* col. obs. attractive in an amusing way, cute.

duct tape *Am., Can.* waterproof adheseve tape.

dude *esp. Am., Can.* col. 1. a city man, esp. an Easterner in the West. 2. a man, guy: *A dude named Bobby was supposedly holed up* - T. Thompson., *You're a lost dude this time* - G.V. Higgins., *I have found Hubert to be quite a dude.* - R.P. Warren. 3. *Am.* obs. man from a city visiting the countryside.

due *esp. Am.* / *esp. Br., Aus.* **due to**/ prep. owed or owing as a debt or right to: *Our grateful thanks are due you.* - Longman., *Lenin had been welcomed with the blazing triumph due a returning prophet* - R.K. Mussle.

due *Br., Aus.* law. necessary, e.g. *driving without due care and attention.*

due process *Am.* law. the correct process that should be followed in law and designed to protect sb.'s legal rights.

dues *Br.* fee.

duff *Am., Can.* col. rump, buttocks: *you have to get off your duffs to make a buck.* - Reader's Digest.

duff/ be up the duff *Br., Aus.* col. be pregnant.

duff 1. *Br.* col. adj. worthless, of poor quality: *You mean, it's a duff line?* - D. Lodge. 2. *Am., Can.* partly decayed organic matter under a tree.

duff 1. (**up**) *Br.* col. beat up: *Michael threatened to duff him up* - T. Thorne. 2. *Aus.* steal cattle, esp. by changing brand.

duffel *Am., Can.* transportable personal belongings, equipment and supplies: *Frank stuffed some clothes into a duffel bag* – A. Summers, R. Swan.

duffel coat *esp. Br.* a coat with a hood made of rough heavy cloth.

duffer *Aus.* 1. a mine having no minerals left in it. 2. cattle thief.

duffer *Br.* obs. col. a person very bad at doing smth.

dufus *Am.* sl. despicable person: *the self-absorbed doofuses on most of prime time.* - Time.

dugout (canoe) *Am., Aus.* a small light boat made by cutting out the middle of a tree trunk.

DUI *Am.* driving under influence of alcohol.

duke (it out) *Am., Can.* col. fight with one's fists: *What should I do, duke him or her out?* - R.L. Chapman, *combativeness – the killer instinct – to duke it out with the other newspapers in the city.* – N. Hentoff.

dull/ (as) dull as ditchwater *Br.* /*Am.* **dishwater**/ obs. col. very dull or uninteresting: *She's cute, but dull as dishwater.* - R.A. Spears.

dull *esp. Am.* not sharp (of a knife, blade, etc.).

dull up *Am.* make (smth.) dull: *This hard meat has dulled up all the knife blades.* - Longman.

dullsville *esp. Am., Can.* col. dull or boring.

dumb *esp. Am., Can.* col. stupid: *he was a dumb, a dope.* - J. Updike.

dumb down *Am., Can.* col. make simpler, esp. a text, n. **dumb-down**: *It was said that the paper was conducting a deliberate dumb-down* - New Yorker., *audience have dumbed down since then.* - New Yorker.

dumbbell *esp. Am., Can.* col. a stupid person: *Sure dumbbell, we know all that.* - C. McCullers., *She'll call him a dumbbell.* - J. O'Hara., *I know those dumbbells.* - J .Dos Passos., *some other dumbbell was out there swimming* - Atlantic Monthly.

dumb-bunny *Am.* sl. naive person: *don't think I give a damn about a dumb-bunny like you.* - C. McCullers.

dumb Dora *Am.* sl. a stupid girl: *I'm no Dumb Dora.* - R.A. Spears.

dumbhead *esp. Am., Can.* col. stupid person.

dumb show *Br.* col. hand actions and movements instead of speech.

dumbsize *esp. Am.* (of a company) reduce staff so that it harms the efficiency of its work.

dumbwaiter *esp. Br.* /*Am.* **lazy Susan**/ a small table that turns round on a fixed base put on a larger table and used for serving food.

dummy 1. *Br., Aus.* /*Am.* **pacifier**, *Can.* **soother**/ a rubber teat for sucking, put in a baby's mouth to keep it quiet: *Grandma found Maxwell's dummy in my father's bed.* – S. Townsend. 2. *esp. Am.* col. a stupid person, fool: *Willie Stark had been the dummy and the sap* - R.P. Warren., *Don't you know you've been followed, you dummy?* - I. Shaw. 3. *Am.* a drawing or pasted arrangement of words, pictures, etc., used as a guide for setting up a page in printing. 4. *Aus.* substitute, reclaimer of claims.

dummy up *Am., Can.* col. keep quiet.

dummy/ spit (out) the dummy *esp. Aus.* accuse sb. of behaving in a bad-tempered or childish way.

dummyism *Aus.* the buying of land using dummy persons.

dummy run *Br.* a trial test.

dump *Am.* 1. /also **dump car**/ railway tipper wagon with skips. 2. temporary wood storehouse. 3. sl. a low or cheap place, joint.

dump *esp. Am., Can.* an act of defecation.

(garbage) dump *esp. Am., Can. /esp.Br., Aus.* **(refuse) tip**/: *I saw people living on garbage dumps* - P. Robertson; v. **dump** *Am., Aus. /Br., Aus.* **tip**/.

dump (on) 1. *Am., Can.* col. criticise harshly, often unfairly: *I really feel dumped on.* - R.A. Spears. 2. *Aus.* pack cotton in bails. 3. *Am.* col. tell sb. all one's problems.

dump body *Am.* tipping body.

dump car *Am.* tipper wagon.

dumper 1. *esp. Aus.* a wave breaking long before reaching the shore. 2. *Am., Can.* col. a difficult situation.

dumping bucket *Am.* skip, tipping bucket.

dumping device *Am.* tipping device.

dumpster *Am.* tdmk. /*Br.* **skip**/ tdmk. a large metal container used for holding waste: *The fence ran back along the side of the building past a trash dumpster.* - R. Crais.

dump truck *Am., Can. / esp. Br.* **tipper (lorry/ truck), dumper (truck),** *Aus.* **tip truck**/ dumper, a vehicle with a large movable container on the front: *He paused at an opening in the wall to let an immense Mack dump truck grind up a sharp incline* - L. Waller., *It felt like a dump truck had unloaded on us.* - Reader's Digest.

dunce cap *Am.* dunce's cap.

Dundee cake *esp. Br.* fruit cake with almonds on top.

dune buggy *Am.* beach buggy with big wheels and no roof for driving across sands.

dungarees 1. *Br. /Am., Aus* **overalls**/ a. workmen's trousers with a bib and shoulder straps made of usu. blue denim. b. similar trousers made of any material and worn as a fashionable garment. 2. *Am.* a type of heavy jeans usu. worn for working: *Patrizzi had 84 cents in his dungarees pockets.* - G. O'Neill, D. Lehr., *Behind him dungarees begin to scuffle again.* - J. Updike.

dunk *Am. /Br.* **duck**/ drop sb. into water as a joke: *she had been dunked in the pool at the Y* – P. Roth.

dunnie, dunny *Aus.* sl. toilet, esp. outside one.

dunny/ as lonely as a country dunny *Aus.* completely alone.

duplex *Am., Can.* n. adj. 1. (a flat) having rooms on two floors of a building. 2. also *Aus.* a semi-detached house: *The Burckhardt town was a modest duplex on Central Park South* - L. Waller., *It was a ground floor duplex apartment* - D. Brenner.

durable goods *Am. /Br.* **consumer durables**/ goods of relatively long usefulness.

durex tdmk. 1. *Br.* condom: *He attached a water-filled Durex to an effigy* - P. Norman. 2. *Aus. /Br.* **sellotape,** *Am.* **scotch tape**/ sticky thin clear material used for sticking paper, mending light objects, etc.

dust 1. *Br.* household refuse, ashes. 2. *Aus.* col. flour.

dust *Am.* sl. kill: *The gang set out to dust the witness* - R.A. Spears.

dust/ kick up dust *Am.* col. make trouble.

dust/ not see sb. **for dust** *Br., Aus.* col. (of a person) be leaving the place very quickly.

dust/ shake the dust of smth. **from** one's **feet** *Br.* leave the place with the intention of never returning to it.

dust down *Br., Aus.* prepare smth. for use after it hasn't been used for a long time.

dust up *Am.* col. beat up or kill sb.

dust (it) *Am.* rush, speed along.

dustball /col. **dust bunny**/ *Am., Can.* a ball of dust: *I saw a few bust bunnies up there.* – R.L. Stine.

(dust) bin *Br. /Am., Aus.* **ashcan,** also *Can.* **garbage can,** *Am., Can.* **trash-can**/ a container with a lid for holding household refuse: *you must not put your dustbin out in front of your door before 7.30. A. M.* - G. Mikes., *she sat on a dustbin* - A. Christie., *Dustbins, cardboard boxes, black plastic sacks stood in the pavements.* - J. Fowles.

dustbin bag/liner *Br. /Am., Aus.* **garbage bag.,** *Am.* **trash can liner** or **trash bag**/ a plastic bag for refuse inside a container.

dustbin man *Br.* col. person whose job is to collect household refuse.

dustcart, dustbin lorry *Br. /Am., Aus.* **garbage truck**/ a truck which goes from house to house in a town to collect the contents of dustbins.

dust cloak *Br.* becoming rare /*Am.* **duster**/ overgarment used to protect clothing from dust.

dust cover *esp. Am. /esp. Br.* **dust jacket**/ a removable paper cover of a book: *A publisher's bland analysis of Mrs. Canby's success appears on the dust-jacket.* – K. Vonnegut, Jr.

duster 1. also **duster coat** *esp. Am., Can.* /also **linen duster**/ dust coat, a light cloak or wrap worn to keep off dust: *then a guy in a duster jumped forward* - R. Crais. 2. *Am.* col. dust storm. 3. *Br.* cloth for dusting furniture.

dust/ give the dust to sb. *Am.* leave sb. behind.

dust/ shake the dust off one's **feet** *Br.* col. go away in anger.

dust/ take the dust *Am.* get behind.

dust off *Am.* col. throw the ball very close to (the batter) in a baseball: *Watch me dust him off with this next ball.* - Longman.

dust out *Am.* make homeless (because of dust storms).

dustman, refuse collector *Br.* /*Am.* **garbage collector,** also *Aus., Can.* **garbage man, sanitation worker,** *Br.* col. **bin man**/ person employed to remove waste material from dustbins: *His job was to follow the dustman* - P. Norman., *they were council dustmen* - Economist.

dust road, unmetalled, unmade road *Br.* dirt road.

dustsheet *Br.* /*Am.* **drop cloth**/.

dust-up *Br., Can.* sl. /*Br.* **punch-up**/ a quarrel or esp. a fight: *The boys argued and had a little dust-up, no one got hurt.* - W. Magnuson.

dust wrapper *Br.* dust cover (of a book).

dusty/ Not so dusty *Br.* col. obs. Fairly well, Quite well. / usu. in an answer to How are you?

dusty answer/reply *Br.* a sharp and unpleasant response; unhelpful reply.

Dutch *Am.* col. German (language).

Dutch *Br.* sl. 1. wife. 2.. friend.

Dutch barn *Br.* a farm building without walls used for storing hay.

Dutch courage *Br., Aus.* /*Am.* **liquid courage**/ confidence that people get from drinking alcohol.

Dutch / in Dutch *Am.* a. in trouble: *I'm probably in Dutch, but so what.* - J. Kellerman. b. in disgrace.

Dutch doll *Br.* wooden doll.

Dutch door *Am., Can.* stable door.

Dutchman/ if...then I'm a Dutchman *Br.* col. that certainly isn't true.

Dutch treat *esp. Am.* occasion when you share the cost of smth.

Dutch uncle *esp. Am.* col. person who admonishes sternly and bluntly.

duty *Br.* payment for such services as the transfer of property, giving licences and the legal recognition of documents.

duty/ do (double) duty as/for smth. *Am., Aus.* have another purpose as well.

duvet *esp. Br.,* also *Br.* **continental quilt** / *Am.* **comforter,** *Aus* tdmk. **doona**/ quilt: *you still didn't take Roget's duvet* - R. Carter, M. McCarthy; **duvet cover** *esp. Br.* quilt cover.

dweeb *esp. Am.* col. a contemptible or boring person (used by young people): *Why do you have to sound like such a dweeb?* – R.L. Stine.

dyed in the grain *Br.* dyed-in-the wool, impossible to change.

dyke, dike 1. *esp. Br.* a long narrow hole cut into the ground to take water away. 2. *Aus., NZ.* col. obs. toilet.

dynamo *esp. Br.* machine converting mechanical energy into electrical.

E

E *Br.* /**Earth**/ a connection between a piece of electrical apparatus and the ground.

each to his/her own *Br.* /*esp. Am.* **to each his own**/ different people like different things.

each-way *esp. Br.* (of a bet) winning if a horse or dog one chooses comes first, second, or third.

eagle freak *Am.* sl. conservationist, environmentalist: *The eagle freaks oppose building the dam.* - R.A. Spears.

ear/ bash sb.'s **ears, earbash** *Aus.* bore sb. with talking too much.

ear/ bend sb.'s **ears** *Am.* tell to sb. insistently and at length: *Whenever I sit next to that old lady, she bends my ear until I'm ready to scream.* - H.C. Whitford., R.J. Randisi.

ear/ can do smth. **on their ear** *Aus.* col. do it very easily.

ear/ chew sb.'s **ears** *Am.* sl. scold.

ear/ give sb. **a thick ear** *Br.* col. humor. hit sb.

ear/ keep one's **ears to the ground** *esp. Br.* be aware of what people are doing or saying.

ear/ nibble sb.'s **ears** *Aus.* sl. try to get smth. out of sb.

ear/ pin back one's **ears** 1. *Br.* listen carefully to smth. 2. *Am.* tell sb. off for having done smth. wrong. 3. *Br.* (sports) run very quickly in an attempt to score and help their team win.

ear/ set smth. **on its ear** *Am.* get a lot of attention and interest.

ears/ sb.s **ears are flapping** *Br.* sb. is listening to this private conversation.

ears/ sb. **is solid/thick between the ears** *Br.* sb. is very stupid.

ears/ set sb./smth. **by the ears** *Br.* cause a split or arguments in an organisation by doing smth. new.

ear-bender *Am.* col. an overly loquacious person.

earhole *Br.* col. one's ear.

early/ take an early bath *Br., Aus.* col. stop doing smth. sooner than one intended.

early closing day *Br.* one on which shops, etc. are closed during the afternoon: *It was early closing and the store was shut.* - G. Greene.

earner, a nice little earner *Br.* col. profitable deal: *at 70 pounds a week it's a nice little earner* - T. Thorne.

earnings-related *esp. Br.* adj. (of money payments or plans) higher as one earns more.

earth 1. *Br., Aus /Am.* **ground**/ v. n. /**make**/ (an additional safety wire that makes) a connection between a piece of electrical apparatus and the ground, often in **be earthed,** also **earthed, connected (returned) to earth** *Br.,* **earth (ing) connection, earth** *Br. /Am.* **ground(ing) connection, ground**). 2. *esp. Br.* the hole where certain wild animals live, such as foxes.,

earth/ burn the earth *Am.* move very fast.

earth/ go to earth 1. also **go to the ground** *Br.* hide from sb. or smth. 2. *Br., Aus.* hide away in a secret table.

earth/ look/feel, etc. **like nothing on earth** *Br.* look or feel very strange.

earth/ pay the earth *Br.* col. pay a fortune / British also say **cost the earth.**

earth/ run sb./smth. **to earth** *Br., Aus.* find sb./ smth. after searching for a long time.

earth closet *Br.* privy.

earthen ware *esp. Am.* /*esp. Br.* **crockery**/ cups, plates, etc., made from baked clay.

earthly/ have/stand an earthly *Br.* col. (usu. in questions and negatives) have the slightest chance, hope, idea.

earthnut *esp. Br.* peanut.

earwitness *esp. Am., Can.* witness who heard smth. personally during a crime.

East *Am.* the part of the US east of the Mississippi, adj. **eastern,** adv. **back East**: *I went to school back East.* - J. Kellerman.

East/ out East *Br.* in / to Asia.

Easter egg 1. *Br.* chocolate egg usu. given as a present at Easter. 2. *Am.* egg that has been coloured and decorated usu. by a child.

Easterner *Am.* person who lives in or comes from the Eastern US.

easy as apple-pie, tea drinking *Aus.* col. very easily.

easy/ be as easy as rolling off a log *Am.* be very easy.

easy/ be on easy street *esp. Am.* col. having a lot of money.

easy/ I'm easy *esp. Br.* col. I don't mind: *But, hey, I'm easy.* - New York.

easy/ on easy terms *Br.* paying for smth. with several small payments instead of paying the whole amount at once.

easy meat *esp. Br., Aus.,* also *Br.* sl. **easy game /** *Am.* **an easy mark**/ smth. done or acquired very easily or a person easily deceived; also *Br., Aus.* col. **make easy meat of** smth/sb.

easy/ it's easy to be smart after the fact *Am.* it's easy to be wise after the fact.

easy-peasy *Br.* col. (used by children) smth. very easy.

eat/take one's **meal** *Am.* /*Br.* **have** one's **meal**/.

eat lunch, dinner, supper *Am.* /*Br.* **have lunch, dinner, supper**/.

eat it *Am.* col. (of cost or expense) accept that sb. won't profit from it.

eat out *Am.* /*Br.* **go out for dinner**/ eat outside of one's home.

eat (sb.) **out** *Am.* sl. reprimand (sb.): *Out came Loe McCarthy from the Boston dugout all set to eat me out* - R.L. Chapman.

eat crow *Am., Aus. Can.* col. be forced to admit that one was wrong: *we are ready to eat crow* - H. Truman.

eat one's **dinners** *Br.* study for the Bar.

eat your heart out *Am.* sl. humor. I can do better than this famous person in his own field: *William Shakespear, eat your heart out!* - Longman.

eat one's **heart out** *Br.* be unhappy about smth. or to want smth. very much.

eat right *Am.* eat food that keeps sb. healthy.

eat/ be eating one's **dust** *Am., Can.* col. be much less successful in a contest than other competitors.

eater *Br.* col. an eating apple.

eatery *esp. Am.* col. restaurant or other place to eat.

eat-in *Am., Can.* (of a kitchen) one in which a person can eat as well as cook.

eating club /or **hall**/ *Am.* dining club or hall, esp. university canteen.

Eats *Am.* road cafe.

eavestrough *Am., Can.* gutter.

Eccles cake *Br.* a flat cake with a filling of dried fruit, esp. currants, and spice.

echo *Am.* close follower and popularizer of another's ideas.

echo/ cheer sb. **to the echo** *Br.* obs. shout and clap in support of smth.

edge/ be drunk over the edge *Aus.* col. be very drunk.

edge/ keep sb. **on the edge of their chair** *Am.* be very exciting (of a story).

edge city *esp. Am., Can.* large urban area on the outskirts of a city, usu. close to the main road.

edge-to-edge *Br.* adj. (of floor covering) wall-to-wall.

edition *Am.* one occasion on which smth. that is done repeatedly is presented.

educational technology *Am.* /*Br.* **teaching aids**/ special equipment, pictures, maps, photographs, etc. which are used to make teaching more effective.

educator *esp. Am.* a person who educates, esp. as a profession.

-een *Irish Eng.* diminuitie suffix.

eff and blind *Br.* euph. sl. use rude words.

effing (and blinding) *Br., Aus.* col. damned.

eff off *Br.* sl. fuck off.

effectives *esp. Am.* armed men ready to serve.

efficiency (apartment) *Am.* one-room flat with a kitchen recess inside: *I even ended up describing my one-room efficiency apartment.* - A. Hitchcock Mystery Magazine.

Effie *Am.* annual award for the best advertisement.

egg/ Go lay an egg *Am., Can.* taboo col. go away.

egg/ go suck an egg *Am., Can.* col. expression of anger or resentment.

egg/ lay an egg *Am.* 1. col. obs. fail to make people enjoy or be interested in smth. 2. fail in smth.

egg beater *Am., Can.* col. helicopter.

egg cream *Am.* drink made of milk, soda and syrup.

egg-flip *Br.* /*Am.* **egg-nog**/: drink of eggs beaten up with sugar, milk or cream and often some alcohol.

eggplant *esp. Am., Can., Aus.* /*Br.* **aubergine**/: *Gianturo also brought along some munchies - eggplant sandwiches.* - G. O'Neill, D. Lehr.

egg-pop *Am.* egg-nog.

egg roll *Am., Can.* /*Br.* **pancake roll, spring roll**/ spring roll, a Chinese dish made of a thin case of egg pastry filled with bits of vegetables and often meat and usu. cooked in oil: *we could get on with the egg roll.* – P. Roth.

eggs over easy *Am.* fried eggs turned over quickly before serving.

egg whisk *esp. Br.* /*esp. Am.* **egg-beater**/ a tool used in the kitchen to mix up eggs for cooking and to make them light and full of air: *His heart was frothing hate like an eggbeater.* - C. Woolrich.

Egyptian *Am.* joc. a native of the southern part of Illinois.

eh *Br.* col. excl. (used for showing surprise or doubt, or when asking sb. to agree or repeat what they have just said): *There were three boys but only two girls, eh.* - W. Magnuson, *Well it was just something he could buy, eh Dad?* - W. Grady.

eiderdown *esp. Br.* a quilt filled with down.

eight/ behind the eight ball *Am., Can., Aus.* col. in a difficult situation.

eight/ have one over the eight *Br.* col. obs. have one drink too many.

eight ball (pool) *esp. Am., Can.* 1. a variety of pool. 2. col. one eighth of an ounce portion of illegal drug.

eighteen (18) *Br.* a category in which a cinema film is placed by the British Board of Film Classification to show that no person under the age of 18 will be admitted.

eighth note *esp. Am., Can.* /*Br.* **quaver**/ quaver.

eighty-six *Am.* sl. destroy, kill: *he eighty-sixed 007 almost two decades ago* - Time.

eilasha *Aus.* sl. young woman, girl.

either/ me either *Am.* col. it's true about me too.

eject *Am.* /*Br.* **send off**/ send off a player during a game after his doing smth. wrong.

ejector seat *esp. Br.* /*esp. Am.* **ejection seat**/ one that throws the pilot out in case of emergency.

EKG *Am.* /*Br.* **ECG**/ ECG, electrocardiograph: *An EKG ruled out an organic brain disorder.* - Guideposts.

El, L *esp. Am.* col. elevated railway: *An El train clattered raspingly* - J. Dos Passos., *a dime covered the "L" fare.* – J. O'Hara.

elasticated *esp. Br.* (of a garment) made elastic by the insertion of rubber thread or tape.

elastic band *Br.* rubber band used for fastening things together: *He pulled an elastic band from his pocket.* - W. Grady.

Elastoplast tdmk. *Br.* also **plaster** /*Am.* **Band-Aid**/ a kind of sticking plaster: *he appears in the next scene bruised and wearing Elastoplast.* - Woman's Own.

elbow *Br.* col. dismissal from a relationship, esp. one's job, etc. also v.: *OK, elbow the buskers* - T. Thorne; also **give** sb. **the elbow** *Br.* col. /*Am.* **give** sb. **the (old) heave-ho**/ dismiss sb. or end a relationship with sb.

elbow/ at one's **elbow** *esp. Br.* close by and ready when needed.

elbow/ rub elbows with sb. *esp. Am. /Br.* **rub shoulders with** sb./ associate with famous people for a while.

elders *Aus.* sl. breasts.

elective 1. *esp. Am., Can.* n. adj. also elective course /*Br.* **optional classes, optionals, subsidiary curriculum/** non-compulsory course which is studied at school or college: *Some ninth-and-tenth graders are choosing their own elective courses.* - Time., *I took an elective course in the New Testament.* - Reader's Digest. 2. *Br.* derog. **elective dictatorship** is a government which is elected but which has won so many votes that it can do what it likes.

electorate *Aus., N.Z.* area represented by one Member of Parliament.

electric cord; wire *Am. /Br.* **flex/** wire with protective covering, for connecting electrical equipment to a supply of electricity.

(electric) fire, radiator *Br. /Am., Aus.* **electric) heater/** electric incandescent or converter heater.

(electric) ice-box *Am.* fridge.

electric outlet *Am. /Br.* **power point, socket/.**

(electric) ring, gas ring *Br. /Am.***burner/.**

electrics *Br.* the electric system, esp. of a car or machine.

electroshock therapy *Am.* electric shock therapy.

element *Am.* 1. electrode in a vacuum tube. 2. flight of three air planes, section. 3. /*esp. Br.* **(electric) ring/** a circular piece of material that is heated to cook things on.

elementary school /also **grade school, grammar school/** ages 6-12 *Am., Can. /Br.* **primary school/** (**infant school**) ages 5-7; (**junior school**) ages 7-11/ a school at which elementary subjects are taught for the first six to eight years of child's education.

elephant/ see the elephant, get a look at the elephant *Am.* begin to see the light, begin to know what life is about.

elevated railway *Br. /Am.* **elevated railroad/** one which runs on a kind of continuous bridge above the streets in a town.

elevator 1. *Am., Can. /Br.* **lift,** *Aus.* either of these/ an apparatus in a building for taking people from one level to another: *I locked the door and went to the elevator.* - S. Sheldon., *Thousands of people found themselves stranded in elevators and subway cars.* - J. Riffkin, T. Howard., *Elevator, an upright coffin with a mirror to comb hair could fit two deeply in love.* - J.P. Donleavy. n. **elevator car, shaft, operator,** etc. 2. *Am., Can.* a building for storing grain.

elevator operator *Am. /Br.* **lift man/.**

elevator music *Am.* muzak, relaxing music in public places, usu. thought to be boring.

elevator/ sb.'s **elevator/** *Br.* **the lift/ doesn't go all the way to the top (floor)** *Am.* col. humor. sb. is silly or a little mad.

eleven-plus *Br.* an examination by children aged 11 in some places of Great Britain to decide what type of school they will go next.

elevenses *Br.* col. /esp. *Am.* **coffee break/** coffee, tea, or a light meal, which is taken at about eleven o'clock in the morning: *The gardener, Dobbs, was in the small potting shed having his elevenses* - A. Christie., *So it's you who entertain a friend to elevenses, I see.* - A. Christie., *two old women sat happily with ample elevenses.* - A. Burgess.

elimination tournament *Am.* one in which only the winners in each stage play in the next until the final event.

ell *Am.* an extension to building: *One big room with an ell, it was completely white* - T. Murphy.

el...o *Am.* sl. noun form, Spanish pattern applied to mean " the supreme, etc."

el primo *Am.* sl. the very best: *This stuff is el primo.* - R.A. Spears.

ELT *esp. Br.* English language teaching, the principles and practice of teaching English to speakers of other language.

Elvis/ 50 million Elvis fans can't be wrong *Am.* col. smth. must be true because so many people think so.

E.M. *Am.* Engineer of Mines.

embarcadero *Am.* wharf: *four rooms behind the chandler shop on the Embarcadero* - H. Fast.

emboss print. *Am. /Br.* **stamp, block/**

Emcee, MC *Am., Can., Aus.* col. compere: *Dellacrocce wanted to play the emcee* - J. O'Brien, A. Kurins., *Davis emceed a show* - D. Mortman; v.

emergency 1. *Am., Can.* hospital department providing immediate treatment. 2. *Aus.* a reserve, esp. a runner in horse racing.

emergency brake *Am. /esp. Br.* **handbrake,** *Am., Aus.* **parking brake/** brake pulled by hand and used to stop a car in case of emergency: *She just yanked the emergency brake.* – Reader's Digest.

emergency cord *Am. /Br.* **communication cord/**

emergency room *Am., Can. /Br.* **casualty/** the part of a hospital where you go if you've been injured in an accident: *it had taken her a while to persuade the emergency room* - R.J. Randisi., M. Wallace.

emergency services *Br.* the official organisations that deal with crimes, fires and other emergencies.
emergency stop *esp. Br.* (of a car, bus, etc.) done suddenly to avoid hitting sb. or smth.
emolument *Br.* payment in money or other form for the work done.
Empire/ Golden Empire *Am.* California.
Empire City *Am.* New York.
The Empire State *Am.* New York State / also **The Excelcior State.**
The Empire State of the South *Am.* Georgia.
employe *Am.* employee.
employee bargaining agent *Am.* agent defending the rights of the hired employees.
employment/ Are you in employment at the moment? *Br.* Do you have a job now?
empty nester *esp. Am., Can.* col. a parent whose children have grown up and left home; the family then is called **empty nest.**
emulsion *Br.* paint with emulsion paint.
emulsion paint *Br.* paint in which the colour is mixed into an emulsion and which is not shiny when it dries.
enamel paper *Am.* print. coated paper.
encamp *esp. Br. /Am.* **camp/** set up tents.
encrustation *Am., Aus.* incrustation.
end *Am.* one of the two players in American football who begins playing furthest from the ball.
end/ at the end of the day *esp. Br., Aus.* col. in the end of the day, finally.
end/ (at the) sharp end *esp. Br.* actually involved in smth.
end/ come to a sticky end *Br.* be killed violently or have smth. very unpleasant happen to sb.
end/ get/have one's **end away** *Br.* euph. sl. have sex.
end/ get the wrong end of the stick *Br.* be seriously mistaken about a situation.
end/ go off the deep end 1. *esp. Am.* go mad or strange. 2. *Br.* become very angry.
end/ hand/ the short /the dirty/ end of the stick *Am.* put sb. at a disadvantage; **get the short end (of the stick)** *Am.* be unfairly treated.
end/ it'll all end in tears *Br.* col. situation will end unpleasantly.
end/ keep/hold one's **end up** *esp. Br.* col. go on facing difficulties bravely and successfully.
end/ at loose ends *Am. /Br.* **at a loose end/**, having nothing to do.
end/ be/reach at the end of your tether *Br., Aus. /Am.* **at the end of your rope/** be extremely tired, worried, or annoyed.

end/ living end *Am.* sl. expression of strong (dis) approval.
end/ play both ends against the middle *Am.* col. try to make two people or organisations compete in order to get advantage for oneself.
end/ the (absolute) end *Br.* col. used to show disapproval of sb. or smth. in amused way.
end/ the sharp end *Br.* humor. the bow of a ship.
endgate *Am., Can.* tailboard.
endive *Am. /Br.* **chicory,** *Aus.* **witlof/** a vegetable with bitter tasting white leaves: *the aragular salad with endive* - New York.
endmatter print. *Br. /Am.* **backmatter/**
endorse (usu. pass.) *esp. Br.* (of a court) write a note on (a driving license) to say that the driver has broken the law, esp. in **be endorsed**: *A driver...will still end up with a heavy fine and have his or her license endorsed with 3 or 4 penalty points,* - Young Citizen's Passport. n. **endorsement.**
Endowment *Am.* Donation Fund.
end-run *Am., Can.* evasive tactic, v. evade smth.
endsville *Am.* sl. superb, unsurpassed: *Curtie, it'll be endsville!* - Arthur Hailey.
endwise *Am.* endways.
energy park *Am.* energy complex.
engage *esp. Br.* 1. (as) arrange to employ (sb.) or use sb.'s skills. 2. order (a room, seat, etc.) to be kept for one.
engaged (tone) 1. *Br. /Am.* **busy (signal),** *Aus.* **engaged (signal)/** (of telephone line) in use; **Please try later** *Br.* call later; **I'm afraid he is not available at the moment** *Br. /Am.* **I'm afraid he's tied up at the moment/**. 2. *Br.* (of toilet) already in use.
engine *Br., Can. /Am.* **motor/**.
engine driver, train driver *Br., Aus. /Am., Can.* **(train) engineer/** person who drives a railway engine: *Ah, we'll get the engine driver and Micko off the goods van* - J.P. Donleavy., *A locomotive engineer slept through a signal* - E. Segal.
engineer *esp. Br.* a person who works with machines in a factory.
engineering drawing *Br.* mechanical drawing.
engineer's cab *Am.* driver's cab.
England/ ...for England *Br.* col. humor. emphatic way of saying that sb. does a lot of a particular activity.
England/ The New England of the West *Am.* Minnesota.
English breakfast *Br.* large cooked breakfast of bacon, eggs, toast, etc.
English daisy *Am.* daisy.

English horn *esp. Am.* /*esp. Br.* **cor anglais**/, oboe type musical instrument.

An Englisman's home is his castle *Br.* British proverb.

English muffin *Am., Can.* /*esp. Br., Aus.* **muffin**/ a flat roll for toasting, often eaten with butter and marmalade for breakfast.

engraving *Am.* /*Br.* **blocking**/ print. making an impression on paper or board from a block.

enjoin (from) *esp. Am.* law. forbid, prohibit, give an official instruction, esp. to prevent sb. from going near a person or place: *Courts enjoined them* - E.L. Doctorow.

Enjoy! *esp. Am.* Relax! Have fun!

enjoy/ In *Br. English* enjoy is always followed by a noun or pronoun or by a verb with -ing, in *Am. English* enjoy is used sometimes in informal speech with the meaning "*Enjoy yourself*".

enlarge *Am.* set free.

enlist (in) *esp. Br.* join a course of study, a political group, etc., esp. by putting one's name on a list.

enlisted (wo)man *Am.* person in the armed forces whose rank is below that of an officer: *Some of these poor devils of enlisted men they sent up for twenty years for rape* - J. Dos Passos., *But enlisted men's names were unimportant in the Imperial Navy.* - B. Tillman.

enough/ enough is as good as a feast *Br.* obs. that's quite enough.

enough / leave/let well enough alone *Am.* /*Br.* **leave well alone**/ /let well alone.

enough/ near enough *Br.* col. nearly.

enough + that *esp. Am.* / *He's old enough that he can do it.* - Longman.

enplane *esp. Am.* emplane, (cause) to get into an airplane.

enquire *esp. Br.* inquire.

enquire smth. *Br.* ask for information, e.g. *enquire the time.*

enquire within *Br.* ask inside the building (where a notice is shown): *For sale: small black armchair. Enquire within.* - Longman.

Enquiries *Br.* Information (sign).

enquiry agent *Br.* private detective.

enroll *Am.* prepare in written or printed form a final perfect copy of (bill passed by a legislature).

ensign *esp. Am.* a badge or sign showing a person's rank.

ensuite *Br.* adj. **ensuite bathroom** is joined onto a bedroom.

ensure *esp. Br.* /*Am.* **insure**/; **assure** *Br.* insure oneself against death.

entrance/ in Britain an **entrance** is a gate or door by which one enters, an **entry** is either a. the act of entering. b. a narrow passage between houses, Americans may use **entry** for all three of these.

entrance gate *Am.* barrier / esp. in a railway station.

entree 1. *esp. Br.* a small meat dish, served after the fish and before the main dish in a formal dinner. 2. *esp. Am.* the main dish of a meal: *they furnished an excellent appetizer before the entree* - S. North.

entry 1. *esp. Am.* a door gate, or passage by which one enters a place. 2. *Am.* a staircase landing. 3. *Am.* the beginning (of a period).

entryism *Br.* derog. joining a political party with a secret intention of changing its principles and plans.

entryphone *Br.* tdmk. a special telephone installed at the main entrance to a block of flats or offices. If the visitor using this telephone is recognised or expected, the person to whom he speaks unlocks the door by remote control.

entryway *Am., Can.* 1. staircase landing: *They lit mostly entryways.* - G. O'Neill., D. Lehr. 2. a passage by which one enters a place, entrance: *his picture was hanging in the entryway.* - Reader's Digest.

E number *Br.* number representing a chemical that has been added to a food, shown on the outside of a container.

envision *esp. Am.* envisage: *How does Linder envision changing* - New York., *He envisioned himself pacing the empty halls* - T. Murphy.

Enzed *Aus.* col. New Zealand, **Enzedder** *Aus.* col. New Zealander.

enunciatory *Am.* enunciative, declaratory.

Epstein-Barr virus (EBV) *Am.* /*Br.* **ME**/ **myalgic encaphalomylitis**/ illness that makes sb. feel very tired and weak and can last for a long time.

equal opportunity employer *Am.* enterprise that employs the workers regardless of their race, sex, etc.

The Equality State *Am.* Wyoming.

equalize *esp. Br., Aus.* /*Am.* **tie**/ reach the same total of points, etc. as one's opponent in sport.

equalizer 1. *esp. Br.* a goal, point, etc., that makes one's total equal to that of one's opponents in sport. 2. *Am., Can.* col. pistol.

equals sign *Br.* /*Am.* **equal sign**/ sign =.

ER *Am., Can.* emergency room.

ERA *Am.* Equal Rights Amendment, a suggested change to American law, intended to give women the same legal rights as men.

erase *esp. Am. /Br.* **rub** smth. **out/** erase smth. using a rubber.

erase a blackboard *Am.* clean (the blackboard by rubbing out the chalk marks.

eraser *esp. Am.* 1. /*esp. Br., Aus.* (**India**) **rubber/** smth. that is issued to erase marks on paper, esp. a piece of rubber: *The businessman says that ink erasers are in short supply* - W. Strunk, E.B. White., *the secretaries had never seen a typewriter eraser.* - J. Fischer. 2. thing used for cleaning marks from a blackboard.

erasure *esp. Am.* rubbing away of smth. on a page.

erubescent *Am.* reddish.

escalope *Br.* a thin boneless piece of pork, beef, or esp. veal cooked in hot fat.

escape road *esp. Br.* sliproad, esp. one on a racing circuit to turn to in case of emergency.

escort duty *Am.* convoy.

escrow *esp. Am.* place in custody or trust to a third party until special condition has been fulfilled.

Eskimo pie *Am.* tdmk. a bar of chocolate-coated ice-cream.

esky *Aus.* tdmk. portable insulated container for keeping food and drink cool.

esplanade *esp. Br.* wide street next to the sea in a town.

Esq. /also rare **Esquire/** 1. *esp. Br.* (used as a title of politeness, usu. written after the full name of a man). 2. *Am.* used only after a full name of a lawyer.

essay *Br., Aus. /Am.* (**term**) **paper/**: *I need an extension for my assessed essay.* - D. Lodge.

establish a precedent *Br.* law. */Am.* law. **set a precedent/** make it so that other cases will be decided in the same way.

estate *Br.* 1. piece of land on which buildings (of a stated type) have all been built together in a planned way: *I know of all-women housing estate in Sunderland* - Observer. 2. estate car.

estate agent *Br. /Am., Aus., Can.* **real estate agent, realtor,** *Aus.* **real estate broker, realtor,** *esp. Br.* **house agent/** a person whose business is to buy, sell, or look after houses or land for people: *It was a two-storey little house of the kind which estate agents in Britain used to describe as a bijou residence.* - L. Van Der Post., *Many estate agents are advising their clients to cool their ambitions for top prices.* - Observer.

estate (car) *Br. /Am., Aus.* **station wagon, ranch wagon/** a private motor vehicle with a door at the back, folding or removable seats and a lot of room to put boxes, cases, etc. inside.

estate duty *Br.* obs. estate tax, replaced by **inheritance tax** since 1986.

eternal triangle *Br. /Am., Aus.* (**love**) **triangle/** a situation when two persons both love a third person, usu. of opposite sex.

the ether *Br.* 1. the air through which radio waves travel. 2. the upper part of the sky.

ethnic, ethno 1. *Aus.* sl. immigrant. 2. *Am., Can., Aus.* a person of an ethnic group different from the main group living in the country.

etouffe *Am.* spicy Cajun stew of vegetable and seafood.

eulogy *Am.* a funeral speech with praises for the person who has just died.

Europe *Br.* all of Europe except for the United Kingdom.

European *esp. Br.* (of people) white.

European plan *Am., Can.* a hotel rate for a room only, without food: *Most American hotels are on the European plan* - H.C. Whitford., R.J. Dixson., *Room in Coastown is thirty bucks for a double. European plan.* - J. Patterson.

euthanize *Am., Can.* put (an animal) to death humanly.

even *Am.* equalise.

even (on sb.) *Am.* make revenge on sb

even up on *Am.* col. return a favour to (sb.). .: *We can even up on Bill and Alice by looking after their children next week.* - Longman.

even break/ get an even break *Am., Aus.* get the same opportunity to improve one's situation.

evening meal *esp. Br.* the main meal of the day usu. eaten between about 6 and 8 o'clock in the evening.

evenings *esp. Am.* adv. during any evening.

evens *esp. Br. /esp. Am.* **even odds/** col. equal chances.

even-stephen, even-steven *esp. Am., Aus. /Br.* **level pegging** *Br.* col. **even-stevens/** col. adj. adv. fair, even, equable: *Give me the hundred and fifty and we'll call it even-stephen* - D. Hammet., *they came up even-stephen with the rigless boat* - J. Patterson.

event/ at all events *Br.* in any event, whatever happens.

event/ in the event *esp. Br.* as it happened.

eventer *Br.* a horse or rider taking part in eventing, usu. cross-country, dressage and show-jumping.

ever 1. *Am.* col. (used for threatening exclamations in the form of questions): *Was he ever mad!* (= He was very mad - Longman). 2. **ever so/such** *esp. Br.* col. very. 3. *Am.* very much; *Are you looking forward to your vacation?*

Am I ever! – Cambridge, *She is ever demure.* – E. Kazan.

Ever Yours, Yours Ever *Br.* col. obs. way of ending a letter.

The Everglade State *Am.* /also **The Gulf** or **Peninsula State**/ Florida.

The Evergreen State *Am.* Washington.

everyone and his brother *Am.* a lot of people.

everyplace *Am., Can.* adv. everywhere: *They were everyplace.* - S. Grafton.

everything in the garden is rosy/lovely *Br.* everything is satisfactory.

every which way *Am., Aus.* col. in every direction: *Michael was being pulled every which way on that tour in London* - D. Marsh., *we'd see some scared rabbits running "every which way".* - T. Thompson., *the nine or ten executive-size chairs were every which way.* - R. Stout.

evil/ **put off the evil day** *Br.* postpone doing smth. unpleasant as far away as possible.

exam *Am., Can.* 1. a medical test of specified kind. 2. /*Br.* **exam paper**/ the paper on which the questions for an exam are written.

examine/ **be examined in** smth. *Br.* have examinations in some subject.

excavator *Am.* navvy.

excavator *Br., Aus.* /*Am.* **steam shovel**/. a machine for excavating earth.

excelsior *Am.* tdmk. /*Br.* **wood wool**/ wood shavings, pieces of wood used for packing: *we crate the records with excelsior and nail the boxes of books* - C. McCullers., *The itch of packing excelsior getting in his nose* - J. Updike.

The Excelsior State *Am.* New York State.

Except for access *Br.* No through trucks.

excerpt *esp. Am.* take passages of text from some book.

excess *Br.* required as extra payment.

exclamation mark *esp. Br.* /*esp. Am.* **exclamation point**/ a mark (!) written after the actual words of an exclamation: *The point of the pencil snapped on the last exclamation point.* - P. Case, J. Migliore.

exclusion order *Br.* one forbidding a person to be involved in a specific activity to prevent crime from happening.

exclusive line *Br.* private telephone line.

excuse *esp. Br.* free (sb.) from a duty: *I was excused football practice because I had a cold.* - Longman.

excuse *Am.* /*Br.* **sick note**/ note written by one's doctor or one's parents saying that a person is ill on a particular day.

Excuse me *esp. Am.* sorry / In *British English* you say (**I'm**) **sorry, I beg your pardon, Pardon** to a person if you accidentally touch them or push against them or if you want them to repeat the words that you haven't heard properly, in *American English* you say **Excuse me, Pardon me.**

ex-directory *Br.* /*Am., Aus.* **unlisted**/ adj. (of a telephone number) not in the telephone book, esp. in the phr. **go ex-directory.**

exeat *Br.* permission to be absent for some time from classes at school or college or an occasion on which this is granted.

exec *Am., Aus.* col. executive: *They'd never heard of female execs* - New York, R.L. Chapman.

execu-cat *Am.* sl. executive: *capacity crowd of art mavens, execu-cats and socialites.* – Reader's Digest.

Executive /also **Chief Executive**/ *Am.* President of the State.

executive *Am.* adj. presidential.

executive council 1. *Am.* presidential council. 2. *Can.* provincial council.

Executive Mansion *Am.* 1. President's residence. 2. governor's residence.

executive privilege *Am.* right of a president or other government leader to keep official records and papers secret.

executive session *Am.* closed session (of Congress or other political body).

exemption *Am.* /*Br.* (**tax**) **allowance**/ the amount of money allowed to earn each year before you start to pay tax.

exercise book *Br.* composition book, booklet with blank pages for students to write school work or make notes in.

exercises *Am., Can.* a set of events including speeches, giving of prizes and various ceremonies /usu. in the phrs. **commencement, graduation exercises**/ In Britain the word is used only for religious exercises: *Graduation exercises felt more like a funeral* - Guideposts.

exercycle *Am.* tdmk. stationary bicycle for physical exercises.

exes *Br.* sl. expenses.

exhaust fan *Am.* /*Br.* **extractor fan**/ apparatus which takes out impure or smelly air from a kitchen, factory, etc.

exhaust (pipe) *Br., Aus.* /*Am.* **tailpipe**/ exhaust of a motor vehicle.

(exhaust) silencer *Br.* /*Am.* **muffler**/.

exhibit *Am.* exhibition: *aerospace shows, exhibits, and meetings around the world.* - Omni.

exhibition 1. *Am.* public examination. 2. *Br.* school or university grant to help a specially deserving student to study there.

exhibitioner, burser *esp. Br.* one who receives a grant.

exit *Am.* a way out / In America the sign **No exit** is much more common than in Britain and the common British sign **Way out** is not used.

expect/ I expect so *esp. Br.* col. used to agree with smth. that is thought to be true.

expenses/ be on expenses *Br.* with price included.

experience/ chalk smth. **up to experience** *Am., Aus.* put smth. to experience.

experience religion *Am.* be converted (into specific religion).

expert *esp. Am.* act or study as an expert.

expert *Am. /Br.* **specialist; subject teacher/** teacher of a particular object.

expert in teaching methods; instructor in methods; methodologist *Am. /Br.* **specialist (teacher) in (on) methods** or **principles of teaching/.**

expertise *esp. Br.* expert's report made after careful examination of smth.

expiry *Br. /Am.* **expiration/** the end of a period of time during which an official document can be used, or of a period of authority.

expiry date, sell-by date *Br., Aus. /Am.* **expiration date/** date on the product showing after which it should not be used

exploit *Am.* sl. advertise (a product).

explosion-proof *Am. /Br.* **flame-proof/.**

exportation *Am.* exported article.

express 1. *Br.* a. messenger sent on a special errand. b. dispatch conveyed by a special messenger. 2. *Am.* a system for the prompt and safe transportation of parcels, money, or goods at rates higher than standard freight charges; a company operating such merchandise freight service: *I sent the check to my bank express mail.* - R.J. Randisi., M. Wallace. 3. *Br.* special delivery, a service given by the post office, railways, etc., for carrying things faster than usual.

express 1. *Br.* adj. designated to be delivered without delay by special messenger. 2. *esp. Am.* carrying parcels quickly (of a company or its vehicles).

express *Br.* send a letter or package using a special post system so that it arrives very quickly.

express car *Am.* transportation company's carriage.

express delivery *Br.* special delivery, express letter / **send the letter express.**

express lane *Am.* lane on a freeway used by vehicles that travel very fast.

expressman *Am.* person working in a transportation company: *Then Doc fought with the express-man over the quality of the service* - J. Steinbeck.

express post *Br. /Am.* **express mail/.**

expressway, (divided) highway *esp. Am., Aus. /Br.* **(divided) motorway,** *Am.* **freeway/** very wide road built for fast long-distance travel: *Martin drove down a ramp and onto another expressway.* - Rolling Stone.

ex-service *esp. Br.* adj. (of people) formerly belonging to the armed services / **ex-serviceman, ex-servicewoman.**

extend 1. *esp. Br.* appraise or assess the value of (land, etc.). 2. *Br.* take possession by a writ of extent /*Br.* **extent** is a writ allowing a creditor to seize a debtor's property temporarily/.

extension *esp. Br.* permission for the sale of alcoholic drinks until later than usual, granted to licensed premises on special occasions.

extension cord *Am., Can., Aus. /esp. Br.* **flex with plugs, extension lead/** additional piece of wire to some equipment used when the existing one is not long enough: *I have to hang up now and find an extension cord* - A. Hitchcock Mystery Magazine.

extension/ University Extension *esp. Br.* teaching and examining students who cannot attend a university all the time / **university extension course lecturer.**

extern *Am., Can.* non-resident doctor in a hospital.

external *Br.* coming from outside a particular school or university; **external exams, external examiner,** etc.

external examiners, accountants or **evaluators** *esp. Br.* experts invited from the outside to check that the job is done fairly or impartially or in a proper way.

extra 1. *Br., Aus.* sundry / run in a cricket which is not made off the bat. 2. *Am.* col. temporary season worker. 3. *Br. /Aus.* **sundry/** reserve player.

extractor fan *Br. /Am.* **exhaust fan/.**

extra-mural 1. *esp. Br., Aus. /esp. Br.* **extension/** (of a student course, etc.) connected with a university but working or happening outside it. 2. *Am.* (of sports) between teams from different schools.

extraordinarily *esp. Br.* extremely.

extraordinary/ quite or **most extraordinary** *Br.* very unusual; also **How extraordinary!**

extraordinary general meeting (EGM) *Br.* emergency meeting of shareholders to consider a specific matter.

extra time *esp. Br. /Am.* **overtime/** additional time at the end of the game to decide a winner, if the game is ending in a draw, esp. 30 minutes at the end of football match.

exurb(ia) *Am., Can.* area outside city suburbs inhabited chiefly by well-to-do people: *Distant suburbs, or exhurbs, are among the fastest-growing communities in America.* - Reader's Digest, adj. **exurban**.

exurbanite *Am.* person who lives in exurb.

ex-works *Br.* direct from the factory or place of manufacture.

eye/ black eye *Am.* bad reputation.

eye/ clap eyes on sb./smth. *Br.* see for the first time.

eye/ be one in the eye for sb. *Br.* col. be a disappointment for sb.

eye/ close one's **eyes and think of England** *esp. Br.* humor. have sex because you think you should without enjoying it.

eye/ do sb. **in the eye** *Br.* col. (in cricket, etc.) get through practice the ability to see the ball and to judge its direction.

eye/ easy on the eye *Br.* smth. pleasant to look at.

eye/ get/keep one's **eye in** *Br., Aus.* become very good at smth. by practising it, esp. at sports such as golf and cricket.

eye/ give sb. **the eye** *esp. Am.* look at sb. angrily.

eye/ go eyes out *Aus.* col. move or work very fast.

eye/ have an eye for/on/to the main chance *Br., Aus.* want to get rich.

eye/ in a pig's eye *Am.* col. I don't believe you.

eye/ keep one's **eyes on the ball** *Am.* be on the alert: *But Craig couldn't keep his eye on the ball* – Reader's Digest.

eye/ keep one's **eyes skinned, keep** one's **eys open for** *Br.* col. watch carefully.

eye/ Mind your eye! *Br.* col. Look out! Be careful!

eye/ one in the eye for sb. *Br.* smth. annoying, esp. defeat or disappointment.

eye/ throw eyes at sb. *Am.* make eyes at sb.

eye/ without (even) batting an eye *esp. Am. /Br.* **not (even) batting an eyelid/eyelash/** at once.

eye-ball *Am.* sl. watch intently, look directly at: *Bill Barnes eyeballed the dark object* - B. Tillman., *eyeball the counter as you enter* - New York.

eyeball/ give sb. **the hairy eyeball** *Am.* obs. look at sb. angrily.

eye-bath *Br. /Am., Can* **eye-cup/** special cup used for applying remedies to the eyes.

eyeful/ get an eyeful of this/that! *esp. Br.* col. look at smth. interesting or unusual.

eyeglasses *Br.* obs. or *Am.* a pair of glasses.

eyehole *Am., Aus. /Br., Aus.* **spyhole/** peephole, a small hole in the door through which a person can look without being seen.

eye-opener *Am., Can.* early drink: *He fumbled for the jug and slurped an eye-opener* - R.L. Chapman.

eyes/ sb.'s **eyes are out on stalks, eyes popping out of** one's **head** *Br.* used when sb. is very shocked by what they see.

eyes/ make sheep's eyes *Br.* obs. look with loving eyes at sb.

eye-view *Br.* col. a point of view.

eyewash *Br.* obs. smth. that is not believed to be true.

eyot *Br.* a small island (in a river).

F

F *Br.* (grade of pencil lead) fine.

fab, fabby *esp. Br., Aus.* col. wonderful: *The livelier-minded Sunday Times commended the Beatles for enriching the English language with words from their private slang - like "gear" and "fab" which were now in fashionable use.* - P. Norman.

fabric conditioner *Br. /Am.* **fabric softener/** chemical put in water for washing clothes to make them softer.

face *esp. Br.* col. disrespectful attitude, "cheek".

face/ a face as long as a wet week *Aus.* col. very sad expression.

face/ be in one's **face** *Am.* col. criticize all the time.

face/ sb.'s **face doesn't fit** *Br.* a person is not suitable to work in an organisation.

face/ fall off the face of the earth *Am.* disapprove completely.

face/fade out blue *Am.* print. drop out blue/ colour, pencil or other marker used to write instructions on artwork and which does not reproduce.

face/ get out of sb.'s **face** *Am., Can.* col. (often imperative) stop bothering sb.: *Get out of my face!* – R.L. Stine.

face/ go up in one's **face** *Br.* (of a situation) suddenly get out of control.

face/ open one's **face** *Am.* speak up.

face/ put on a good face *Am.* try not to show one's disappointment about bad situation.

face/ set one's **face against** smth. *Br.* be very determined not to do smth.

face/ travel (or **run**) **on** one's **face** *Am.* use one's appearance to gain smth.

face about *Am.* mil. (cause) to turn in the opposite direction: *The officer faced his men about.* - Longman.

face sb. **down** *Am.* oppose or be brave enough to face sb.

face off *esp. Am., Can.* confront (sb. or smth.), n.

face-off. *esp. Am., Can.* confrontation: *Auguillo relished the retelling of this face-off with Quinn.* - G. O'Neill, D. Lehr., *Cop versus hippie face-offs began happening almost every night.* - W. Jack, B. Laursen.

face card *esp. Am., Can.* /*Br.* **court card**/ the king, queen or jack in a set of playing cards.

(face) flannel, face cloth *Br.* /*Am.* **washcloth,** *Aus.* **face washer**/ facecloth, a flannel used to wash, esp. the face, hands, etc.

face pack *Br.* cosmetic cream spread over the face to clean and improve the skin, and then removed.

facer *Am.* 1. mug, glass. 2. sl. a glass of whiskey, punch, etc.

facer *esp. Br.* col. 1. a blow to the face. 2. sudden difficulty.

face time *Am., Can.* col. time of direct contact with sb., esp. one's employer.

facing slip *Am.* one attached in Post Office to each bag, parcel, etc.

factor *Am.* tech. divide a number into factors.

factory/ **boiler factory** *Am.* noisy party.

factory farming *Br., Aus.* derog. keeping animals indoors in **factory farms** with very little space and using special foods to grow them more quickly and produce more meat, eggs and milk.

factory outlet *esp. Am., Can.* factory shop at which (surplus) goods are sold directly by manufacturer at a discount.

faculty 1. *Am., Can.* /*Br.* **teachers; (permanent) staff**/ all the teachers and other professional workers of a university or college: *These four proposals were voted on by the entire student body and faculty.* - D. Divoky., *he had seen the president at a Faculty meeting* - I. Shaw., *His sterling character, his scholarship, and his musical abilities had made him popular with both the students and the faculty.* - D. Carnegie. 2. *esp. Br.* college, school or department of a university / e.g. British *Law Faculty* is *School of Law* in America: *All the faculty of Medicine from Montpillier came to the funeral services.* - E. Segal.

faculty adviser *Am.* one who advises students on academic and related matters.

faculty man *Am.* a faculty member.

fad *esp. Br.* a set of very particular likes and dislikes.

faddy *Br.* having strange likes and dislikes about food.

fade-out halftone *Am.* print. vignette.

fadge *Aus., N.Z.* unpressed pack of wool less than a bale.

faff (about, around) *Br.* col. waste time.

fag 1. *Br., Aus.* col. a cigarette: *she bought her fags from the corner shops* - Streetwise. 2. *esp. Am., Can., Aus.* derog. sl. homosexual: *Many of the fags are actually junkies* - Harper's Magazine., *He didn't look like a fag.* - S. Sheldon., *I think you're a closet fag, you know.* - P. Norman. 3. *esp. Br.* col. obs. a young pupil who has to do jobs for an older pupil (in certain British Public Schools).

fag *esp. Br.* col. 1. (for) have to do jobs for an older pupil. 2. (away) work hard.

fag *esp. Br., Aus.* col. smth. tiring and boring.

fag/ **I can't be fagged** *Br.* I'm too tired or bored to do anything.

fag out *esp. Br.* tire very much: *I'm fagged out, let me rest a minute.* - Longman.

fag end 1. *Br., Aus.* col. the last bit of a smoked and usu. no longer burning cigarette. 2. *esp. Br.* col. the very end or last part of smth., usu. the least exciting one: *there would still be fag-ends of Tzarist regime.* - A. Burgess.

fagged (out) *esp. Br.* sl. extremely tired: *You're looking awfully fagged.* - W.S. Maugham., *They looked fagged.* - J. Galsworthy., *you'll be fagged to death.* - Cpt. Marryat.

fagged/ **I can't be fagged** *Br.* obs. be too tired to do anything.

faggot 1. *Br.* a ball of cut-up meat mixed with bread, which is cooked. 2. *esp. Am., Can., Aus.* derog. sl. homosexual: *It would mean I was a faggot.* - E. Hemingway., *And he's a faggot besides.* - J. O'Brien, A. Kurins. 3. *Br.* derog. col. an unpleasant or silly person, usu. a woman / esp. in the phr. **old faggot.**

fag hag *esp. Am.* sl. derog. heterosexual woman spending much time with homosexual men.

faint *Am.* adj. producing a sensation of faintness.

fair 1. *esp. Br.* a place of outdoor entertainment, with large machines to ride on and other amusements, funfair. 2. *esp. Am.* /*Br., Aus.* **fete**/ an event often held outside at which public can take part in competitions, buy food and and other small items, often organised to collect money for a particular purpose. 3. *Aus., N.Z.* col. complete, utter. 4. *Br.* market where animals and farm products are sold.

fair *Br.* adv. doing smth. quickly or a lot.

fair and square *Br.* obs. exactly where smth. should be.
fair/ be set fair *Br.* (of the weather) be fine and likely to stay so in future.
fair/ fair comment *Br.* reasonable comment.
fair/ fair size, number, amount, distance, etc. *esp. Br.* fairly large size, number, etc.
fair/ for fair *Am., Can.* col. completely, really, truly: *then we danced and started on the beer for fair.* - J. Kerouac.
fair/ no fair *Am., Can.* col. unfair.
fair cop/ it's a fair cop *Br., Aus.* col. you've caught me in the act of wrong doing.
fair crack/ give sb. **a fair crack of the whip** *Br., Aus.* col. give opportunity to do smth.
fair dinkum *Aus.* col. very good: *your chef cooks the most "fair dinkum" Thai Food in Perth.* - Bulletin.
fair dos *Br.* col. that's all right.
fair employment practices *Am.* employment of workers with no discrimination.
fair enough *esp. Br.* reasonable.
fairer/ I/you can't say fairer than that *Br., Aus.* col. it's fair; it's the best offer.
Fair go (,mate) also **fair suck of the pineapple / sauce stick** *Aus.* excl. Be sensible.
fair-haired (or **white-haired**) **boy (of the family)** *Am., Can. /esp. Br.* usu. derog. **blue-eyed boy/** someone's favourite (male) person: *one of Boss Khrushchev's fair-haired boys.* - J. Fischer.
fair hands/ with one's **own fair hands** *Br.* humor. by oneself and without any help at all.
fairing 1. *esp. Br.* present bought or given at a fair: *Then she would buy us ginger bread or a fairing.* - V. Holt. 2. *Br.* desserts.
fairly *Br.* quite.
fairly and squarely *Br., Aus. /Am.* **squarely/** completely.
fair play *Br.* fair treatment without cheating or dishonesty.
fair shake *Am.* col. fair treatment: *he can get a fair shake* - Time., *he was getting a fair shake from the Grossman office* - A. Scaduto.
fairy bread *Aus.* a slice of buttered bread covered with small sugar balls.
fairy cake *Br. /Am., Aus.* **cupcake/** a small sponge cake made with eggs, sugar and flower.
fairy floss *Aus.* candy floss.
fairy light *esp. Br., Aus.* small coloured light esp. one used to decorate Christmas tree.
fairy shake *Br.* a small spongecake, cupcake.
fairy story *Br.* fairy tale.
Yours faithfully *esp. Br., Aus. /Am.* **Sincerely yours/** usual way of ending a formal letter when addressing sb. as Sir, Madam, etc.

fake out *Am.* col. deceive sb. as by a trick: *some of them were the prettiest of all and could fake you out.* - M. Puzo.
faker *Am.* literary corrector.
fall *Am., Can. /esp. Br.* **autumn/** autumn; **in the fall** *Am. /Br.* **in autumn/**: *All summer and most of the fall Wyndham had been crowded* - S. Nichols.
fall about (laughing) *Br.* col. laugh uncontrollably.
fall/ fall afoul of *esp. Am., Can.* come into conflict.
fall/ fall between two stools *Br.* 1. fail trying to do two different things at the same time. 2. not really belong to either of two groups.
fall/ take the fall for sb./smth. *esp. Am.* col. accept the blame: *In 1973, Rizzo took the fall after a guest was beaten up at a Palm Springs hotel.* – A. Summers, R. Swan.
fall all over oneself **to do** smth. *Am. /Br., Aus.* **fall over** oneself/ be very eager to do smth.
fall foul of *Br. /Am., Can.* **fall afoul of/** col. 1. have trouble achieving smth. because of the law or other restrictions. 2. have problems with an angry opponent.
fall in with *Br.* agree with or to.
fall off (the back of) a lorry *Br., Aus.* col. euph. humor. be stolen: *I think it must have fallen off the back of a lorry.* - Longman.
fall on one's **feet** *esp. Br.* succeed at last: *Whatever risks Jim takes, he always seems to fall on his feet.* - Longman.
fall over *Am.* take fancy to.
fall to bits *Br.* fall apart.
fall/ fall between two stools *esp. Br.* be unable to decide between two courses of action and so be unsuccessful in regard of both.
fall sick *esp. Am.* become ill: *The director fell sick last week* - Greyhound.
fall guy *esp. Am., Aus.* col. 1. scapegoat: *Chebrikov and Radionov became the fall guys.* - H. Smith. 2. person who is easily cheated.
family/ the family *Aus.* sl. thieves gang.
family/ first family *Am.* 1. first colonists in America. 2. aristocracy.
family/ the President's official family *Am.* the cabinet ministers.
family allowance *Br.* an alternative name for **child benefit**: *I asked her about my Family Allowance today* – S. Townsend.
family circle *Am.* a gallery in a theatre or opera house usu. located above or behind a gallery containing more expensive seats.
family practice *Am.* part of medical practice in the US in which doctors learn to treat general

health problems and problems connected with families and people of all ages.
family room *Am.* room in which family can play games, watch TV, etc.: *They edged their way into the family room.* – R.L. Stine.
fan *Am., Can.* (of baseball and ice hockey) swing very good at the ball or puck.
fanciable *Br.* sexually attractive.
fancy *esp. Br.* 1. col. a. have a liking for, wish for, esp. in the phr. **take** sb.'s **fancy**: *At that particular conjecture, I fancied him.* - D. Lodge. b. be sexually attracted to. 2. **fancy** oneself often derog. have a very high opinion of oneself.
fancy one's **chances** *Br.* (used in negatives) expect smth. to happen or expect to succeed; adj. **fancied** *Br.* of. smth. most likely to happen.
fancy (that) *esp. Br.* col. exclamation of surprise or shock: *So, you're a bus driver now. Now, fancy that!* - R.A. Spears.
fancy dress *esp. Br., Aus.* /*Am.* **costume, masquerade**/ unusual clothes that you wear for fun or for a party.
fancy food *Am.* high quality food.
fancy goods *Br.* /*Am.* **notions**/ haberdashery, small decorative objects (store use).
fancy goods (store), haberdashery *Br.* /*Am.* **notions (counter, department)**/.
fancy pants *Am., Aus.* sl. an effete man: *Hey, fancy pants, why are you doing in your sister's slacks?* - A. Makkai.
fandango *Am.* tomfoolery.
fanlight 1. *Br.* /*Am.* **transom (window)**/ small window over a door or a larger window. 2. *Am.* window shaped like a half circle.
fanny 1. *esp. Am., Can., Aus.* sl. the part of the body on which one sits, bottom, buttocks: *it was better than shaking her fanny in the chorus all night.* - J. Dos Passos., *verbal pat on the fanny.* - J. DeFelice. 2. *Br., Aus.* taboo. sl. the outer sex organs of a woman.
fanny about *Br.* col. mess around and waste time.
Fanny Adams *Br.* col. nothing at all.
fanny pack *Am., Can.* /*Br.* **bumbag**/.
fan tail *esp. Am.* overhanging part of the stern of a boat, esp. a warship.
fantast *Am., Can.* impractical person.
fantod *Am., Can.* col. a state of irritability and tension.
far/ a…too far *Br.* journalism. smth. is not sensible and shouldn't have been done.
fare *Am.* fishing-boat catch.
(fare) stage *Br.* bus fare zone limit or stop marking the end of the zone.

far-forth *Am.* far, much more.
farmer cheese *Am.* one made from whole or partly skimmed milk.
farmstead *esp. Am.* farmhouse and its surrounding buildings: *the hillsides were prettily dotted with woodlands, farmsteads* - B. Bryson.
farm worker *Br.* farm hand.
farrow *Am.* adj. (of a cow) not in a calf, not settled.
far-sighted *esp. Am., Aus.* /*Br.* **long-sighted**/, able to see objects clearly when they are far from the eye.
fart about/around *Br.* taboo. waste time doing silly or worthless things.
farthing/ not have a brass farthing *Br.* obs. have no money at all.
fascia *esp. Br.* 1. dashboard, the instrument board in a car. 2. flat surface above the shop window, on which the name of the shop is written.
fashion plate *Am.* person who likes to wear fashionable clothes.
fashion victim *Br.* col. sb. who always wears or does what is fashionable, even if it doesn't look good on them.
fast ball *Am.* a type of high-speed throw in baseball.
fast/quick buck *Am., Aus.* col. money earned easily: *They'd rather make a fast buck in foreign markets* - D. Lodge.
fastener *Br.* smth. such as a button, pin or zip that is used to join two parts of smth. together.
fast lane *Am.* /*Br.* **outside lane**/ part of big road used by fast vehicles.
fast talker *Am., Can., Aus.* col. a quick persuader, often dishonest one; v. **fast-talk**.
fast-track *Am.* likely to be dealt quickly.
fast train *esp. Br.* express train: *It was the Challenger, a fast train.* – F. Edwards.
fat *Am.* sl. means for a (political) campaign; **fat-drying** *Am.* ways to obtain these means.
fatback 1. *Am., Can.* the strip of fat from the back of a hog carcass, usu. cured by drying and salting. 2. *Am.* col. menhaden.
fat cat *esp. Am., Aus.* col. comfortably rich person, esp. one who gives money to a political party: *sipping whiskey with fat cat lawyers and society doctors.* - T. Thompson., *professional poker players exploiting the traveling fat-cats from the plantations* - R. McRum, W. Cran, R. McNeil.
Fat City *Am.* sl. an ideal situation: *Nobody's asking for a free ride to Fat City* - McLean's.
fat city/ in fat city *Am.* col. having plenty of money.
fat farm *esp. Am., Can.* col. health centre for overweight people.

a fat lot of good/use, etc. *Br.* col. not at all useful or helpful.

father (smth. on sb.) *esp. Br.* say that sb. is responsible for inventing smth.

father/ How's your father?, a bit of how's your father *Br.* col. euph. refers to sexual intercourse or to penis.

Father Christmas *esp. Br.* Santa Clause: *English children look forward to the visit of Father Christmas.* - A. Makkai.

Father Knickerbocker *Am.* joc. New York City.

Father of chapel *Br.* shop steward of a printers trade union.

Father's Day *Am.* the third Sunday in June appointed for the honouring of the fathers: *The children gave nice presents to their father on Father's Day.* - A. Makkai.

Father of Waters *Am.* Mississippi: *Odor, sluggishness, and mud were part of the Father of Waters' moods* - Arthur Hailey.

fathom out *esp. Can.* explain: *I can't fathom out she had this idea* – J. O'Hara.

fathometer *Am.* tdmk. a type of echo sounder.

fatigues, also **fatigue uniform** *esp. Am.* army clothes worn for field duty: *US military women in Saudi Arabia must dress in full fatigues* - USA Today., *he could see some underwear and fatigues hung out to dry.* - J. Cheever., *I could see scores of Japanese infantrymen in brown fatigues* - Reader's Digest.

fat rascal *Br.* soft bun (with currants).

fatstock *Br.* livestock fattened for slaughter.

faucet *esp. Am., Can. /esp. Br., Aus.* **tap/**: *the faucets in the bathroom were plated of gold.* - T. Thompson., *There were no faucets they could control.* - K. Vonnegut, Jr.

faults and service difficulties *Br.* any telephone repair department.

Fava bean *Am. /Br.* **broad bean/**.

favor/ not do sb. **any favor** *Am.* do smth. that is likely to have bad effect on sb.

favour 1. *esp. Br.* a piece of metal (badge) or of coloured cloth (ribbon) worn to show that person belongs to a political party, supports a particular team, etc. 2. *Am.* small gift given to guests at a party. 3. *esp. Am.* look like one of one's (grand)parents.

favour/ Do me a favour *Br., Aus.* col. I can't believe it!

favorite son *Am.* person favoured by his State as a possible President of the US: *Robert S. Kerr from Oklahoma was another favorite-son candidate.* - H. Truman.

faze *esp. Am., Can., Aus.* col. dumbfound (sb.): *Nothing to faze him.* - T. Thompson., *his actions didn't faze his wife.* - J. Fraser., *I have never seen him fazed* - R. Stout.

fear/ no fear *Br., Aus.* col. often humor. absolutely not.

fearful *Br.* very bad, esp. in **be in fearful state/ condition/mess**.

feast *Br.* annual village festival.

feast/ enough is as good as a feast *Br.* obs. there is no point in getting more.

feast/ the ghost/spectre, skeleton at the feast *Br.* something spoiling enjoyment.

feather *Am.* come to the surface with flakes (about cream in tea).

feather/ rise at a feather *Am.* get angry.

the feathers fly *Am.* people fight or argue.

feature *Am.* col. comprehend, understand: *I don't feature that.* - A. Hitchcock Mystery Magazine.

featured *Am.* famed, advertised.

fed/ be/get fed up of smth. *Br.* col. be annoyed and bored by smth. a lot.

federal case/ make a federal case (out) of smth. *Am., Can.* col. exaggerate or overreact: *No need to make a federal case.* - P. Case, J. Migliore.

(the) Federal Department of Education *Am. /Br.* **(the) Department of Education and science/** ministry of education.

federal tax *Am.* (in the US) tax paid to the central government.

Feds /also *Am.* col. **feebies**/ *Am.* FBI men or other representatives of the central government: *In 1958 the Feds closed in.* - Reader's Digest., *the feds began to play catch-up* - G. O'Neill, D. Lehr.

feeb *Am., Can.* col. idiot: *Then why are you treating me like a feeb?* - Life, R.L. Chapman.

feed *Br. /Am.* **feeder/** person who supplies a stage entertainer with lines or situations about which he/she can make jokes: *he took to using Jane beside him as a combined interpreter and feed* - J. Fowles.

feed 1. *Aus.* sl. food. 2. *Br.* milk or food that you give to a baby.

feed/ put sb. **off** their **feed** *Am.* col. humor. upset sb. in a way that it makes them slightly ill.

feedbag *Am.* nosebag, a bag hung around a horse's head to hold its food: *Her pouch is an old feedbag* - Houghton Mifflin.

feeder 1. *Br.* child's bib. 2. *Am. /Br.* **feed/**. 3. *Am.* a source of supply. 4. *Am.* a trainer. 5. also **feeding bottle** *Br.* child's feeding bottle.

feel/ not be feeling too clever *Br.* col. be not feeling very well.

feel sb. **out** *Am.* col. ask sb.'s opinions or feelings.

feel-good *Am.* sl. causing contentment or euphoria: *These three surprise smashes are all feel-good films* - USA Today., *a simplistic, sappy, feel-good movie.* - Reader's Digest.

feelgood factor *esp. Br.* feeling among ordinary people that everything is going well and they needn't worry about spending money.

fee-paying *Br.* (of school, hospital, etc.) demanding pay for education, medical treatment, etc., **fee-paying student, patient,** etc.

fee splitting *Am.* payment by a specialist of a part of his fee to the referring physician.

feet/ be rushed off one's **feet, be run off** one's **feet** *Br.* be very busy, without getting any help or support in one's work.

feet/ fall on one's **feet** *Br., Aus.* be lucky or successful after a difficult situation.

feet/ have/get/put one's **feet under the desk/ table** *Br.* become familiar and confident in a new job or situation.

feet/ get one's **feet wet** *esp. Am.* experience smth. for the first time.

feet/ have clay feet *esp. Am.* have serious weaknesses or faults.

feet/ have one's **feet wet** *esp. Am.* get involved in smth. for the first time.

feet/ have/get itchy feet *Br.* want to get new experience away from a place where sb. lives and works.

feet/ walk sb. **off their feet** *Br.* make sb. very tired by making them walk a long way.

feet/ with both feet *Am.* completely, resolutely.

feist *Am.* (vicious) mongrel.

feisty *esp. Am., Aus.* col. excited and quarrelsome, combative: *He was a small, feisty man.* - H. Fast., *But a small note of contrariness was the presence of a feisty young black woman* - T. Thompson., *The stage was set however for the return to power of the feistiest politician of our age.* - J. Fraser.

feller *Br.* col. a man, boyfriend: *he's an able feller.* - M.M. Kaye.

fellow *esp. Br.* 1. col. a boyfriend. 2. a member of an important society or college, esp. incorporated senior member of a college.

fellowship 1. *Am.* join in a fellowship, esp. as a church member. 2. *Br.* job at a university which involves making a detailed study of a particular subject. 3. *Am.* money given to a student to allow them to study at an advanced level. 4. *Am.* group of officials who decide which students will receive this money.

felony *Br.* obs. or *Am.* law. (an example of) serious crime which can be punished by one or more years in prison.

felt tip (pen), fibre tip (pen) *Br.* a pen that the ink comes through.

Femidom *Br.* tdmk. a type of condom which a woman puts in her vagina before having sex.

fence/ In Britain **fence** is used for all barriers not just wood ones, in America **fence** is used for wood barriers, wall - for stone and brick ones, **railing** for the barriers made of wire, although **barbed wire fence** is also used.

fence *Br.* /esp. *Am.* **picket fence**/.

fence *Br.* declare (a forest, river, etc.) closed against hunting or fishing, hence **fence season.**

fence *Aus., N.Z.* col. decent behaviour / **over the fence** *Aus., NZ.* unreasonable or indecent.

fence/ make a Virginia fence, walk like a Virginia fence *Am.* go unsteadily.

fence/ refuse one's **fences** *Br.* avoid danger or risk.

fence row *Am., Can.* one with a line of shrubs.

fender *Am., Can.* 1. a. /(*Br.*) **wing** or **mudguard** on a bicycle/ the side part of a car that covers the wheels. b. mudguard: *rocks crunching and popping against the underside of the fender like grease in a skillet.* - R.P. Warren., *They had big swooping fenders* - W. Jack, B. Laursen. 2. *Am. / Br.* bumper/ a metal bar at either end of a car. 3. flap (of a horse).

fender *Br.* a low wall or bar around a fireplace to prevent wood or coal from falling out.

fender-bender *Am.* col. 1. also *Can.* a minor accident on the road: *We'd both been in minor fender-benders on the same road* - New Yorker. 2. reckless driver (one who causes minor accidents): *Don't give up on young fender-benders.* - R.A. Spears.

ferris wheel *esp. Am., Aus.* /*Br., Aus.* **big wheel,** *Br.* **Big Dipper**/, machine used in amusement parks, consisting of a large upright wheel carrying seats which remain horizontal as the wheel turns around: *There were merry go-rounds, ferris wheels* - J. Kerouac.

'fess up *Am.* col. confess, admit one's fault: *Hoving 'fessed up to fibbing to his trustees.* - Kansas City Star.

fest/ beer /song /food fest, etc. *Am.* an informal occasion when a lot of people drink, sit, or eat together.

fetch *Br.* go and get smth. or sb. and bring them back.

fetch/ fetch sb. **a blow/clip,** etc. *Br.* col. hit sb.

fetch up *esp. Br.* col. 1. finish by becoming smth.: *In spite of her family's opinion, she fetched up the winner.* - Longman. 2. finish by doing smth.: *Be careful, you could fetch up by getting hurt.* - Longman. 3. receive smth. in the end: *After trying so hard, the writer fetched up with a contract.* - Longman. 4. vomit.

fetch up *esp. Am.* col. arrive somewhere, esp. unintentionally or without planning: *Stoianev … fetches up in 1945 at the mouth of the Danube* – Harper's Magazine.

fetch up nowhere *esp. Br.* col. gain no success: *If you don't work hard, you'll fetch up nowhere.* - Longman.

fetcher *Am.* temptation, decoy.

fete 1. *Br., Aus. /esp. Am.* **fair/** an outdoor event with games, competitions, and things for sale to collect money for a special cause. 2. *Am.* a special occasion to celebrate smth.

fettler *Br., Aus.* person who does repair or maintenance work on a railway.

fever/be at a fever pitch *Am.* be at the peak of excitement.

fever blister *Am.* cold sore.

few/ a good few *Br.* fairly large number.

fiat money *Am.* money not convertible into gold.

fib *Br.* v. beat, pummel.

fibre tip pen *Br. /esp. Br.* **Biro** tdmk/ felt tip pen.

Fibro *Aus.* a type of building materiel made from asbestos and cement.

fictive *Am.* imaginary, not real.

fid *esp. Br.* thick peg, wedge, or supporting pin.

fiddle 1. *esp. Br.* col. prepare (accounts) dishonestly to one's own advantage: *Nice work if you could fiddle it, lucky bastard.* - D. Lodge., also n. 2. *esp. Br.* col. gain dishonestly. 3. *Am.* repair or change slightly.

fiddle *Am.* excl. obs. nosense, I disagree.

fiddle about (around) *esp. Br.* 1. get money in dishonest or illegal way. 2. waste time 3. (with sb.) change one's behaviour so that one is disapproved.

fiddle/ be as fit /*Am.* **fine/ as a fiddle** col. /*Br.* obs. **fit as a flea/** be very fit and healthy.

fiddle/ be on the fiddle *esp. Br., Aus.* col. get money dishonestly or illegally.

fiddle/ fiddle the books *Br.* col. change financial records dishonestly in order to steal money.

fiddly *Br.* col. 1. needing delicate use of fingers; n. smth. difficult of this kind **fiddle**. 2. fiddling.

fidgets/ get/have the fidgets *Br.* be unable to stop moving.

fidget pie *Br.* savoury pie of onions, apples, bacon and potatoes.

field (of play) *Am., Aus.* (in sports) /*Br.* **pitch/** special marked-out area of ground on which football, hockey, etc. are played.

field/ left field *esp. Br.* journalism. unusual or unconventional performer or piece of entertainment.

field/ out in/of left field *esp. Am.* off base, mad, unusual: *she was really out in left field and had to go to a hospital.* - A. Makkai.

field/ out of left field *esp. Am.* completely unexpected.

field/ play the field *Am.* sl. flirt with many girls.

field corn *Am.* maize grown to use as grain or to feed to animals, rather than to be eaten.

field day 1. *esp. Am., Can., Aus. /Br.* **sports day/** a special day for organised sports or other outside activities for students. 2. *Aus., N.Z.* day set aside for the display of agricultural machinery.

field hand *Am.* an outdoor farm worker: *He wore the battered clothes of a field hand.* - J. Steinbeck., *He is also cellar master, chief field hand, salesman, and janitor.* - National Geographic., *he was not a doctor at all but a field hand who hated hard work* - J.A. Michener.

field hockey *esp. Am. /esp. Br., Aus.* **hockey/** a sports game played with sticks and a ball.

fieldsman *Br.* fielder, one of the players who tries to catch the ball in a game of cricket or baseball.

field sports *Br.* the three sports which, together with horse racing, are traditionally associated with the English gentry - hunting (after foxes and hares), shooting (wild or reared animals or birds) and fishing.

fierce *Am.* col. difficult.

fierce/ something fierce *esp. Am., Can.* col. very much; more loudly, strongly than usual.

fifth *esp. Br.* fifth form of a school or college.

fifth/ I take/plead the fifth (amendment) *Am.* humor. I won't answer you!

a fifth of *Am.* col. one fifth of a gallon as a measure of alcoholic liquor.

fifth wheel/third wheel *esp. Am., Can.* 1. smth. unwanted, out of plan; unwanted person who is around. 2. coupling behind a vehicle for towing a trailer (**fifth wheel trailer**).

fifty-fifty scale *Br.* one used in selling, where all the proceeds are shared equally with the charity.

fig/ be all figged out/up *Am.* be dressed gaily, as for a party: *Where are you going, all figged out like that?* - Longman.

fig/ not care a fig about/for smth. *Br.* not to be concerned at all.

fight/ fight one's corner *Br.* fight hard for smth. or defend it.

fight/ fight shy of doing smth. *Br.* avoid or be unwilling to do smth.

fight/ finish fight *Am.* battle to the end.

fightback *Br.* a return attack.

fighting chair *Am.* one fixed to the deck of a boat to catch fish from.

fighting fit/fit as a flea *Br.* very fit and healthy.

fighting fund *Br.* money raised to finance a campaign, esp. political or social one.

fighting mad *Am., Aus.* col. very angry.

fighting trim/ be in fighting trim *esp. Am.* ready and fit to deal with a difficult situation.

fig newton *Am.* a soft biscuit with a fig centre: *package of nicotine patches, each about the size of a Fig Newton.* – Reader's Digest.

figure *esp. Am.* 1. col. consider, believe, expect or think that smth. will happen; form a particular opinion after thinking about smth.: *She figured the quiet-looking man must be a mouthpiece.* - S. Sheldon., *I figured you were mighty tired.* - Reader's Digest. 2. calculate an amount.

figure/ do things on the big figure *Am.* do smth. big.

figure/ miss a (one's) figure *Am.* make an error.

figure/ that/it figures *esp. Am.* col. used to say that smth. happens as expected but not liked.

figure eight *Am.* /*Br., Aus.* **figure of eight**/.

figure in *Am.* include (in a sum): *Have you figured in the cost of the hotel?* - Longman.

figure on 1. *esp. Am., Can.* plan on, include in one's plans: *The quickest way to the boneyard is to figure on us to help you out.* - W. Murphy. 2. *Am., Can.* col. depend on (smth. or doing smth.): *You can't figure on the results of the election.* - Longman. 3. *esp. Am., Can.* col. expect (smth. or doing smth.): *I always figure on succeeding.* - Longman.

figure out *esp. Am., Can.* col. calculate (smth.): *So then I figured out my options.* - J. Cheever., *I haven't figured it out yet.* - I. Shaw., *I couldn't figure it out.* - D. Carnegie.

figure up *Am.* col. reach or make a total (of an amount): *Can you figure up this bill?* - Longman.

filbert *esp. Am.* hazelnut.

file a suit *esp. Am.* bring a suit (against sb.).

file for *Am.* offer oneself formally for (a political position): *How many people filed for this office?* - Longman.

file-cabinet *Am., Can.* card index, filing cabinet.

file clerk *Am.* office worker.

filibuster *esp. Am.* try to delay or prevent action in a lawmaking body by making very slow speeches, n. **filibuster**: *The filibuster went on until an adjournment was called.* - L. Uris., *I filibustered past the time of our train departure* - H. Smith.

filing cabinet *Br.* piece of office furniture used for arranging files.

fill *Am.* railway embankment.

fill (an order or **prescription)** *esp. Am.* provide all the necessary things fo customer.

fill/ fill the bill *Am.* have exactly the right qualities.

fill in *Br.* col. thrash, beat up: *they were publicly threatening to "fill him in."* - P. Norman.

fill in *Am.* stand in for sb., substitute sb.

fill out 1. *esp. Am., Can.* /*esp. Br.* **fill in**/, complete (smth. such as paper): *You have to fill out this form before your interview.* - McGraw-Hill, 1990. 2. *Am.* follow (the doctor's instructions) in mixing a medicine: *Have this prescription filled out at the drugstore* - Longman. 3. *esp. Am.* complete (smth.) in time: *Mrs. Young offered to fill out her late husband's last few months as chairman.* - Longman.

fill out (the blanks) *Am.* /*Br.* **fill in (the) gaps)**/ fill the empty spaces: *they continued with auditions to fill out the band.* – C.R. Cross.

fill (smth.) up *Br.* complete (a form) by answering the questions in the space provided.

filled gold *Am.* rolled gold.

filler *esp. Am.* unimportant stories in a newspaper: *On order to provide some filler between WNYC's appeals for money, I interviewed a person who is still alive.* – K. Vonnegut, Jr..

filler cap *Br.* the lid that fits over the hole of a fuel tank of a motor vehicle.

fill-in *Br.* col. person who does sb. else's job when they are unable to do it.

filling station *esp. Am. Br.* **petrol station/**.

fillis *Br.* twisted string used for tying up plants.

film 1. *esp. Br.* /*esp. Am., Aus., Can.* **movie/** a cinema picture / **film set, script, studio,** etc. 2. *Br.* metal container with film init that you put inside a camera to take photographs.

film-goer *esp. Br.* /*esp. Am., Aus.* **movie-goer/**.

film star *esp. Br.* /*esp. Am.* **movie star/** a well-known actor or actress in a cinema picture.

(traffic) filter *Br.* (of traffic) turn left or right while traffic going straight ahead must wait until red light changes to green: *The driver of a Ford transit van, though he has priority, hangs* back respectfully to let Vic filter left. - D. Lodge; **filter in** *Br.* /*Am.* **merge**/.

(traffic) filter *Br.* /*Am., Aus.* **right/left turn lane**/ a traffic signal or lane which controls the movement of traffic wanting to turn left or right.

filter sign *Br.* green arrow of a traffic light.

filthy *Br.* col. (esp. of the weather) bad and unpleasant; angry, often in **give** sb. **a filthy look.**

fin *Am.* 1. flipper (of a swimmer): *They picked up their snorkels and fins and headed for the water.* - R.J. Randisi., M. Wallace. 2. sl. obs. a five-dollar bill: *What's a fin between pals?* - R. Chandler.

finagle *Am.* col. 1. obtain smth. that is difficult to get. 2. trick sb. into giving smth. esp. money: *I quit college and did a bit of finagling to land my job.* – S. Lawrence.

finalize *Aus.* finish smth.

finals 1. *Br.* exams that students take at the end of their last year at University. 2. also **final (exams)** *Am., Can.* the exams that students take at the end of each class in high school or college.

final selector *Br.* /*Am.* **connector (switch)**/ telephone exchange switch.

finance company *Am.* company that lends money, esp. to businesses.

financial *Aus., N.Z.* col. solvent: *He's fairly financial just at the moment.* - T. Thorne.

financial aid *Am.* money given or lent to students at colleges or universities for their education.

find out *Am.* v. search for (sb.).

findings *Am., Can.* small articles or tools, used in making garments, shoes or jewellery.

fine/ smth. **will do me/us,** etc. **fine** *Br.* col. smth. will be good enough.

fine smth. **down** *Br.* improve smth. by making it thinner, smaller, or more exact.

fine up *Aus., N.Z.* col. (of the weather) become bright and clear.

fine art/ have smth. **off to a fine art** *Br., Aus.* do smth. very professionally.

finesse (sb.) *Am.* col. outmanoeuvre sb. or do smth. with style and delicate skill.

the finest *Am.* sl. police force: *He had been caught not by the FBI but by New York City's finest, selling heroin.* - J. O'Brien, A. Kurins., *Facing him on the opposite sidewalk was a squad of New York's Finest armed with carbines.* - E.L. Doctorow.

finger sb. **for** *esp. Am., Can.* col. identify or chose sb. for a certain activity.

finger (to) *esp. Am., Can., Aus.* col. point out, often by fellow criminal, as being criminal: *the whole industry is fingered.* - J. O'Brien, A. Kurins.

finger/ be / feel all fingers and thumbs *Br., Aus.* col. /*Am.* **be all thumbs**/ use one's hands awkwardly or be unable to control them, be clumsy.

finger/ give sb. **the finger** *Am., Can., Aus.* col. /*Br.* col. **put two fingers up at** sb./ move the middle /*Aus.* index/ finger upwards in the direction of sb. with whom one is angry, in an extremely offensive way. /British move the first two fingers/: *Pinkworth gave me the finger.* - R. Crais.

finger/ hang by one's **fingertips** *Br.* continue to survive in a difficult situation being close to failure.

finger/ have a finger in the pie *Am.* be involved in smth., esp. when the others don't want you to.

finger/ keep fingers crossed *Br.* col. hope for the better result in a bad situation.

finger/ pull / take / get one's **finger out** *Br., Aus.* col. start working hard.

finger-food *Br.* cocktail party food.

finger-licking *esp. Am., Can.* tasty.

fingerprint *Am.* a mark left by a dirty or oily finger on a clean surface.

fingers *Br.* breadstrips.

fingerstall *Br.* cover for one's finger that protects it if it's injured.

fingertip/ to the (or one's) **fingertips** *esp. Br., Aus.* completely, in all ways.

finish 1. *esp. Br.* end. 2. *Br.* use up the entire supply of smth. esp. food.

finish sb. **off** *Am.* sl. kill sb.

finish up (with) *Br., Aus.* end up (with).

finished/ have finished with smth., also /*esp. Am.* **be finished with** smth./ *esp. Br.* no longer need smth. that one has been using.

finish with *Br.* end a relationship with sb.

finishing/ put the finishing touches on *Am., Aus.* make complete and perfect.

fink *Am., Aus.* col. 1. an informer: *Now he's looking for the fink that turned him up eight years ago.* - R. Chandler; v. **fink on** *Am.* sl. inform on. 2. /*Br.* **blackleg**/ strike-breaker: *Bruno used to be a fink.* - R.A. Spears. 3. worthless or unpleasant person: *All men are brothers, and if you don't give, you're kind of fink* - R.L. Chapman., *I felt a real rat fink* – S. Townsend.

fink out *Am.* sl. 1. back out, retreat: *Bob finked out on the plan.* - R.A. Spears. 2. fail completely.

fir cone *esp. Br.* dry fruit of a fir tree or other conifer.

fire *esp. Am. /Br.* **fire** sb. **for** smth./ dismiss sb. from job: *Mayor Foot would probably fire me* – E. Caldwell.

fire *Br.* a gas or electrical apparatus for warming a room with the flames or red-hot wires able to be seen: *I turned on all the electric fires* - Atlantic Monthly; **gas fire** *Br. /Am.* **gas heater/**.

fire/ draw (sb.'s) **fire** *esp. Am.* be criticised (by sb.).

fire/ full of bushfire *Aus.* very energetic.

fire/ get a fire *Am.* set on fire.

fire/ go through fire and water for sb. *Br.* do anything for the loved one.

fire/ light a fire under sb. *esp. Am., Can.* make sb. work better or harder.

fire brigade 1. *esp. Br., Aus. /Am., Can.* **fire department,** *Br.* **fire service/** an organisation for preventing and putting out fires / In Britain fire department is the department of insurance company handling fire insurance /: *he organised the first fire brigade* - R. McRum, W. Cran, R. McNeil., *Safety cabinets...must be approved for use by local fire department.* - K.F. Hird. 2. *Am.* group of people who are not paid but who work together to stop fires burning.

fire cracker *esp. Am., Can.* loud explosive fireworks.

fired/ oil/gas-fired *Br.* made to work by using oil, gas, etc.

firedog *Br.* one of a pair of iron supports for burning logs in a fireplace.

fire-flair *Br.* stingray.

fireguard *Am., Can.* firebreak in a forest.

fireguard/ be about as much use as a chocolate fireguard or **teapot** *Br.* be no use at all.

fire hall, fire house *Am., Can.* fire station: *the local firehall - scene of dinners, receptions, rallies, proms and craft shows* - USA Today.

fire hat *Am.* fireman's helmet.

fire house, fire hall *Am.* a fire station, esp. in a small town: *the firehouse resounded with cheers.* – Reader's Digest.

fire hydrant *Br. /Am.* **fireplug/** a hydrant used as a water supply for fighting fires: *Apparently he got blasted into a fireplug.* - B. Tillman., *I've got to shine my shoes on top of a fire hydrant.* - J. Kerouac.

firelighter *Br. /Am., Can.* **fire starter/** piece of flammable material used to help start a fire.

fireline 1. *Can.* front edge of prairie or forest fire. 2. *Am., Can.* firebreak in a forest.

fire marshal *Am. /Br.* **fire master/** chief of fire guard: *Use only those solvents and chemicals which the local fire marshal approves.* - K.F. Hird.

fire office *Br.* fire insurance company officer.

fire pan *Br.* brazier.

fire permit *Can.* permit for outdoor open fire in summer.

fire plug *Am., Can.* col. short stocky person, esp. an athlete.

fire practice *Br.* fire drill.

fire-raiser *Br.* arsonist.

fire-raising *Br.* arson, the crime of starting fires on purpose.

fire sale *esp. Am.* a bargain sale: *He looked for business opportunities - bankruptcies, joblots, mergers, fire sales* - S. Bellow., *the church was having a fire sale* - D. Mortman., *make a quick buck off the firesale of Siberia's assets.* - Time.

firescreen *Am., Aus. /Br.* **fireguard/** fireguard at a fireside.

fireside chat *Am.* President's address over the radio and TV.

fire starter *Am.* fire lighter, a special materiel used for helping to start wood or coal fires.

firestorm (of protest and criticism) *Am.* very strong protest or criticism.

fire trail *Am., Can., Aus.* a strip of land in a wood or forest from which the trees have been removed to prevent accidental fire from spreading and used in fighting fires.

fire truck *Am. /esp. Br.* **fire engine/**: *Harris backed his front-end loader into the firetruck!* - Kansas City Star., *Fire trucks and hoses were everywhere.* - Guideposts.

fire warden *Am., Can.* person employed to prevent fire in a town, camp or forest.

fire watcher *Br.* person who watched for the fire bombs in Britain during World War Two.

fireworks/ let off fireworks *Br. /Am.* **set off fireworks/**.

firing area *Am.* firing ground.

firing line/ be in (*Am., Aus.* **on**) **the firing line** *Br.* be the object of the attack: *Let them stand with us a while on the firing line* - Alcoholics Anonymous.

firm power *Am.* guaranteed power of an electric station.

first 1. *Br., Aus. /Am.* **first honors/** first class degree, an honours degree of the highest standard in British University; also a person with such a degree. 2. *Br.* first form in a school or college.

first/ first in, best dressed *Aus.* first person gets advantage.

firstaider *Br.* person trained to give first aid.
first base *Am., Can.* sl. kissing, necking.
first base/ get to/reach first base 1. *Am., Aus.* col. begin to do smth. successfully. 2. *Am.* col. (of lovers) begin to pet.
first class (postage) 1. *Br.* the higher of two postal rates, usu. providing delivery the next day within Britain. 2. *Am.* postage used for sending letters and postcards.
first-degree *Am., Can.* (of a crime) of the highest level of seriousness: *he confessed to the slayings and was convicted of eight counts of first degree murder.* - Reader's Digest.
first family *Am.* President's family.
first fleeter *Aus.* a person related to people who travelled in the First Fleet.
first floor 1. *Br.* the first floor of the building above ground floor. 2. *Am.* the floor of a building at ground level.
first gear, low gear *Am.* /*Br.* **bottom gear**/.
first hand *Am.* from one's direct personal experience.
first, last and all the time (or **forever**) *Am.* once and for all.
first name/ be on first name/terms (with sb.) *Br.* /*Am.* **be on a first name basis**/ know sb. well enough to call them by their first names.
first nations *Can.* the indigenous people.
first off *esp. Am., Can.* col. first of all.
first past the post *esp. Br.* a system of voting in elections by which the person who got the most votes in each area (constituency) is elected to parliament.
first refusal/ have/give sb. **first refusal on** smth. *Br.* let sb. decide whether to buy smth. before this thing is sold to other people.
The First State *Am.* Delaware.
first time buyer *Br.* a person who buys a house or a flat for the first time, esp. by borrowing money from a bank.
first up *Aus., N.Z.* at the first attempt.
fiscal *Am.* revenue stamp.
fiscal year *Am., Can.* financial year.
fish *Am.* col. dollar: *Iron men. Fish. Bucks to the number of one hundred.* - R. Chandler.
fish/ be fishing without bait *Am.* col. be slightly crazy.
fish/ fish or **cut a bait** *Am., Can.* col. /*Am.* sl. derog. **shit** or **get off the pot**/ make a choice: *The union leader warned that the city had until Feb 1 to "fish or cut bait."* - New York Times., R.L. Chapman.
fish bowl *Am.* round fish tank (aquarium).
fisheye *Am.* col. suspicious or unfriendly look.

fish finger *esp. Br., Aus.* /*esp. Am.* **fish stick**/ a small finger-shaped piece of fish covered with breadcrumbs and sold ready-cooked.
fishing expedition *esp. Am.* col. an exploratory search for compromising facts: *The lawyer was on a fishing expedition.* - R.A. Spears.
fishing pole *Am., Can.* /*Br., Aus.* **fishing rod**/: *My old man always kept his fishing pole standing in the corner of the porch.* – E. Caldwell.
fishmonger *esp. Br.* person who owns or works in a shop /*Br.* **fishmonger's**, *Am.* **fish store**/ which sells fish: *He assumed correctly that the fishmonger's boy had brought it.*, - A. Christie., *a dustbin stood outside a fishmonger's* - G. Greene.
fishnet stockings/tights *Br.* stockings with a pattern of small holes that make them look like a net.
fish pond *Am., Can.* a type of attraction at a fair.
fish slice *Br.* /*Am.* **(slotted) spatula**/ a kitchen tool, used esp. for lifting and turning food when cooking.
fishtail *Am.* (of a vehicle or aircraft) slide from side to side, usu because their tyres are sliding on water or ice.
fishwife/ behave like a fishwife *Br.* shout a lot and and behave like a very bad-tempered and unpleasant woman.
fist/ make a good fist of smth. *Br.* col. journalism. do smth. successfully; opp. **make a bad fist of** smth.
fist *Can.* grab smth.
fit *esp. Br.* 1. /*Am.* **physically fit**/ healthy and strong, esp. because a person exercises a lot. 2. healthy again after having been ill.
fit *Br.* col. sexually attractive.
fit/ If the (*Br.*) **cap,** (*Am.*) **shoe fits (wear it)** col. if it is true admit it.
fit/ Americans use fit for the Past Tense and the Past participle when it is used in the meaning to be the right size and to be suitable.
fit 1. *Am.* col. prepare (sb.) for the examinations to enter a university. 2. *Aus.* (also **fit out**) punish (sb.).
fit/ be as fit as a flea, be in a fit state/condition *Br., Aus.* be very healthy.
fit/ be fit to be tied *esp. Am.* col. be very angry or upset.
fit (sb., smth.) **up** *esp. Br.* furnish or arrange (esp. a place), equip: *a good-sized bedroom, that could be fitted up to make a workroom and den.* - I. Stone, n. **fit-up.**
fit (sb.) **up** *Br.* col. cause to seem guilty of a crime, frame: *I know a CID sergeant who had*

fitted a bloke up with an indecent exposure. - T. Thorne.

fit/ throw a fit *Am.* /*Br.* col. **have/throw a blue fit/** behave or react very angrily: *I'd throw a fit unless she wore it* - B. Holiday., W. Duffy.

fitment 1. *esp. Br.* a removable piece of furniture or equipment. 2. *Br.* piece of furniture that is made for a particular space in a room.

fitted *Br.* made or cut to a particular space.

fitted carpet *Br.* wall-to-wall carpet.

fitted kitchen *Br.* having the cupboards that all look the same fixed into a position.

fitter *Br.* person who puts together or repairs machines or electrical equipment.

fittings *Br., Aus.* /*Am.* **furnishings/** items such as cooker, washer machine and curtain poles, which are not permanently fixed in a house.

fitting school *Am.* preparatory courses before passing exams to a college or university.

five/ give sb. **five** *esp. Am.* col. greet sb. by hitting their open hand; often sounding **gimme five.**

five alarm *Am.* col. (of a fire) very large.

five and dime /also **five and ten, dime store**/ *Am.,Can.* col. the term for the big chain stores like Woolworth's: *So the ageing, heavy tired woman dragged all over Dallas, buying back rubber checks from grocers and five-and-dimes.* - T. Thompson., *Wal-Mart came out of a five-and-dime store in Newport, Ark.* - Reader's Digest.

five-finger discount *Am., Can.* shoplifting.

Five Nations *Br.* annual rugby union championship with teams from England, France, Ireland, Scotland, and Wales taking part in it.

fiver 1. *Br.* col. five-pound note. 2. *Am., Can.* col. five dollars /also **fivespot**/: *The tall brown-eyed man fished a crumpled five-spot out of his pocket.* - R. Chandler.

five star general *Am.* general who commands an army.

fix *esp. Am.* col. cook, esp. food or drink: *She fixed bacon, three eggs, and fried potatoes* - H. Fast.

fix *esp. Am.* solution to a problem.

fix 1. *Br.* fasten smth. firmly to smth. else. 2. *Am.* make one' hair and face look neat and attractive. 3. *Am.* col. do a medical operation on a cat or dog so that it cannot have babies. 4. *Am.* col. make a part of the body that is damaged completely better.

fix (also **big fix**) *Am.* sl. arrangement assuring exoneration from a police charge: *FBI soon began seeing and hearing details of fixes they had suspected for years.* - J. O'Brien, A. Kurins.

fix over *Am.* col. repair, redo smth.: *Can the garage man fix over the engine?* - Longman.

fix up *Am.* dress carefully or formally: *You wash yourself and go down to Lov's house and fix up for him.* - E. Caldwell.

fix smth. **up** *Br.* arrange a meeting, trip, event, etc.

fix up to do smth. *Br.* arrange smth.

fix sb. **up with** smth. *Br.* provide sb. with smth. they want: *I got him to agree to fix up Danny Ram with some special training.* - D. Lodge.

fix one's **face** *Am.* put up make-up on it.

fix/ in bad fix, out of fix *Am.* out of order.

fixed/ have no fixed abode/address *Br.* law. not have a permanent place to live.

fix/ well-fixed *Am.* rich, wealthy.

fixed fact *Am.* established fact.

fixer-upper *Am., Can.* col. (real estate term) house that needs repair.

fixing/ be fixing to do smth. *Am., Can.* col. plan to do smth.

fixings 1. *Am.* /*Br.* **trimmings/** the vegetables, bread, etc. that are eaten with a meal at a large meal: *He had the fixings for old-fashioned in the kitchenette* - J. Dos Passos. 2. *Br.* screws, bolts, etc. used to fix or assemble smth. like furniture, building elements or equipment.

fix-it *Am., Can.* col. adj. of or for fixing things.

fixture *esp. Br., Aus.* a sports event that has been arranged to happen at a particular date.

the fixtures and fittings *Br.* all the pieces of equipment that are normally included as part of a house or buildings.

fizgig *Aus.* col. police informer.

fizzer 1. *Br.* smth. outstanding. 2. *Aus., NZ.* failure.

fizz *Br.* col. champagne.

fizzy drink *Br.* soft drink with bubbles of gas.

(fizzy) lemonade *Br.* /*Am.* **lemon-soda/** lemonade.

flack *esp. Am., Can., Aus.* col. press agent, publicity man: *we flacks have a language all our own.* - L. Waller., *every flack, hack, and paparazzo is present.* - Vanity Fair.

flag *Am.* /*Br.* **masthead/**.

flag/ a red flag *esp. Am.* col. a warning of a bad situation.

flag/ be like waving/holding a red flag in front of a bull *Am.* be smth. that will certainly upset or get sb. angry.

flag/ keep the flag flying *Br.* achieve success for one's team playing well in a sport.

flag/ put the flags out/put out (the) flags *Br.* 1. celebrate smth. special that happened. 2. do smth. that will make people who want to do harm to sb. realize that that person has appeared again.

flag/ Put the flags out! - *Br.* humor. I'm pleased and surprised that it's happened.

flag/ wrap/drape oneself **in the flag** *esp. Am., Can.* try to do smth. for one's own advantage pretending to do it for one's country.

flag at half-staff *Am.* flag at half-mast.

flag day 1. *Br. /Am.* **tag day,** *Aus.* **button day/** a day on which money is collected for a charity by selling paper flags or small stickers in the street: *"Do you mean something like a jumble sale?" said Rupert Sutcliffe. "Or a flag day?"* - D. Lodge. 2. *Am.* June 14th, kept as a holiday in the US in memory of the day when the US flag was first officially used in 1777.

flag football *Am.* game like American football with flags.

flagged *Am.* sl. arrested, identified.

flagpole/ run smth. **up the flagpole** *esp. Am.* tell people about an idea in order to get their opinion.

flag stop *Am.* place where buses stop only if they are asked to do so.

flake *esp. Am., Can., Aus.* col. an unstable, unreliable or eccentric person: *Not only Amato was flake and a nobody, he was a lier, philanderer and bully.* - J. O'Brien, A. Kurins.

flake out *Am.* sl. behave eccentrically.

flakers, flaked out, Harry flakers *Br.* col. tired, flaked-out.

flako *Am.* sl. drunk.

flaky *esp. Am., Can.* col. strange, eccentric: *Bobby's the flakiest burglar we've got.* - T. Thompson., *the idea doesn't seem flaky at all.* - Time., *The rudder felt real flaky now* - J. DeFelice.

flambeau *Am.* a pot for boiling sugar.

flame/ be shot down in flames *Br.* be told that what sb. is saying is completely wrong.

flame-proof *Br. /Am.* **explosion-proof/**.

flamer 1. *Am.* sl. conspicuous blunder. 2. *Aus., Am.* sl. male homosexual.

flaming *esp. Br., Aus.* col. damned, bloody: *the old lady who showed us the house did give him a most flaming character!* – J. Austen.

flammable *Am. /Br.* **inflammable/** adj. smth. which can be easily set on fire and which burns quickly: *you can use it later to store gasoline and other flammable liquids.* - S. Grafton.

flan 1. *Am.* custard, sweet thick liquid made from milk and eggs with a layer of caramel on top. 2. *esp. Br.* round pie or cake that is filled with fruit, cheese, etc.

flannel 1. *esp. Am.* cotton cloth with a slightly fuzzy surface. 2. *esp. Br. /Am.* **washcloth/** a piece of cloth used for washing oneself: *He threw down the flannel.* - I. Murdoch. 3. *esp. Br.* col. meaningless though attractive words used to avoid giving a direct answer, to deceive, etc.

flannel *esp. Br., Aus.* col. deceive, etc. by using **flannel.**

flannel cake *Am.* thin pancake: *Last night I dreamed I was eating flannelcakes* - K. Vonnegut, Jr.

flannelmouth *Am., Can.* col. person who talks or boasts too much.

flannels 1. *Am.* and old use. flannel underclothes. 2. *esp. Br.* men's trousers made of flannel.

flap *Br.* col. behave in an anxious and excited way; also **be/get in a flap.**

flap one's **lips/gums** *Am., Can.* sl. derog. speak: *Don't just stand there flapping your gums. Help with supper.* - W. Magnuson.

flapjack *Br.* 1. biscuit made from oats, butter and syrup. 2. lady's flat compact.

flapjack, pancake, hot cake *Am., Can.* a pancake, made of milk, flour and eggs, usually rolled up or folded and eaten hot with a sweet or savoury filling, usu. at breakfast.

flare out at *Am.* say smth. suddenly in an angry way.

flares, flare trousers *Br., Aus. /Am.* **pants/** trousers that are wide below the knee.

flash *Br.* 1. a small object or a piece of material won on a military uniform as a sign of rank or a strip of different colour on clothing in general. 2. humor. quick look/glimpse. 3. adj. looking very new, bright and expensive.

flash on *Am.* sl. realise vividly.

flashfreeze *Am.* quickfreeze, freeze food very quickly so that it keeps all its taste.

flashlight 1. also **flash** *esp. Br.* a piece of equipment for taking flash photographs. 2. *esp. Am., Can.* small electric light carried in the hand to give light */Br. Aus.* **torch/**: *Bob got a flashlight and they went out to stroll beneath the trees.* - E. Segal., *we went to buy a flashlight* - J. Baez., *The flashlight brightened in the growing darkness.* - New Yorker. 3. *Am.* fire service blue light (warning light), flashing light.

flash pack *Am.* pack with a new reduced price shown flashily on it.

flask *Br.* a special type of bottle used for keeping liquids either hot or cold, vacuum flask.

flat *Br., Aus.* adj. /*Am.* **dead**/ (of a battery) having lost some or all of its electrical power.

flat 1. *Br. /esp. Am., Can.* **apartment**/ a set of rooms in a building esp. on one floor, including a kitchen and bathroom: *Noel's flat was modern.* - I. Murdoch. 2. *esp. Am., Can., Aus.* /*Br.* **puncture,** *Br.* **flat tyre,** *Can.* **flat tire**// flat tire: *I'm at the Brock turn-off with a flat.* - A. McLean., *Damn, boy, you're liable to get flat going that speed.* - J. Kerouac. 3. *Am.* a flat strawhat. 4. *Am., Can.* container in which seedlings are grown and sold. 5. *esp. Am.* shoe with a very low heel. 6. **the flat** *Br.* horse racing over a course with no jumps.

flat *Am., Can.* (of music) lower a note by semitone.

flat/ **railroad flat** *Am.* cheap flat with one room giving access into another: *The Londons lived in a long railroad flat in the three-story frame building* - I. Stone.

flat/ **...and that's flat** *Br.* col. I won't change my opinion or decision.

flat/ **go flat against** *Br.* col. directly disobey sb. or ignore them.

flat/ **go flatting** *Aus., NZ.* leave parents' house and start living in flats.

flat/ **on the flat** *Br.* on ground that is level and doesn't slope.

flat/ **tell** sb. **flat** *Br.*col. directly and definitely.

flatbread *Am., Can.* flat thin bread.

flat cap *Br.* cap with a peak at the front.

flatcar *esp. Am., Can.* standard flat wagon, platform car with no roof and sides: *He was also strapped to a steel lattice which was bolted to a flatcar on rails.* - K. Vonnegut, Jr.

flat-footed *Am.* col. resolute: *a good many came out flat-footed and said it was scandalous* - M. Twain.

flat-freight car *Am.* flat wagon.

flatlet *Br.* a very small flat.

flatmate *Br.* /*Am.* **roommate**/ person who shares a flat with another.

flat out *esp. Am., Can.* col. in a definite way, with no hesitation: *She was flat out mad as hell.* - R.A. Spears, *bandleader flat-out refused to play any songs* – Reader's Digest.

flat-out *Am.* sl. outright: *he is a "flat-out legaliser".* - Reader's Digest.

flatlet *Br.* /*Am.* **efficiency (apartment)**/ a small flat.

flatmate *Br.* a person sharing an apartment with another person.

flat pack (furniture) *Br.* furniture sold in ready cut pieces which is to be put together later at the customer's place.

flats *Br.* /also *Br.* **a block of flats, flat-block,** *Am.* **apartment house**/: *they reached the big block of flats* - D. Lessing., *a fresh clean city of grass and modern flat-blocks.* - A. Burgess.

flat share *Br.* arrangement in which two or more people share an apartment.

flat tire *Am.* sl. a tedious person: *Everybody at the party seemed to be enjoying himself except that flat tire Carl.* - H.C. Whitford., R.J. Dixson.

flattop *Am.* col. aircraft carrier.

flatware, also **silverware** *Am., Can.* /*esp. Br.* **cutlery**/ knives, forks and spoons: *Savoy's vintage Bakelite flatware.* - New York.

flatwoods *Am.* a level low-lying timberland.

flautist *Br.* /*Am.* **flutist**/.

flavour of the month *esp. Br.* smth. very popular currently.

a flea in one's **ear** *Br.* a rejection of sb.

fleabag 1. *esp. Am., Can., Aus.* a cheap dirty hotel: *Worse, some ended up in a fleabag where the mice got at the blueberry muffins* - Newsweek., *I'm in a fleabag near the old port* - I. Shaw. 2. *Br.* col. a dirty or disliked person or animal.

fleabite *esp. Br.* a small problem or cost.

flea-bitten *esp. Br.* col. dirty or in bad condition.

fleapit *esp. Br.* col. old and cheap dirty theatre or cinema.

flesh/ **be more than flesh and blood can stand** *Br.* (of a situation) make sb. very angry or upset.

flesh/ **press (the) flesh** *esp. Am.* col. shake hands, esp. with large numbers of people: *The Soviet General Secretary presses the flesh on a May visit to the Romanian capital.* - Time.

flesh-coloured *Br., Aus.* /*Am.* **flesh-tone**/ very similar to the colour of a white man's skin.

flex (with plugs) *esp. Br.* /*Am., Aus.* **(electric) cord, extension cord** *Br., Aus.* **lead,** *Aus.* **cord**/ (a length of) electrical wire enclosed in a protective covering used for connecting an electrical apparatus to a supply, bendable electrical cord, extension.

flexible (table) lamp *Br.* gooseneck lamp.

flextime *Am., Can.* flexitime, flexible schedule of work.

flick *esp. Br.* press a switch in order to start or stop electrical equipment.

flick/ **get/be given the flick** *esp. Aus.* col. be rejected, also **give the flick.**

flick through *Br.* look at a book, magazine, etc. quickly.

flicker *Am.* woodpecker.

Flickertail State *Am.* North Dakota.

flick knife *Br., Aus.* /*Am.* **switchblade (knife)**/ a knife with a blade inside the handle that springs into position when a button is pressed: *A pat-down produced a wad of cash, a flick knife with a black handle* - J. Kellerman.

flier, flyer 1. *Am., Can.* leaflet which is produced for advertising purposes and is given to people in the street: *out of desperation parents turn to posting fliers* - Reader's Digest., *Printed on flags, fliers and posters, the word was out and all over town.* - R.E. McConel., *the racist fliers kept coming.* - Reader's Digest. 2. *Am.* express. 3. *Aus.* adult kangaroo.

flies *Br.* the zip or row of buttons at the front of a pair of trousers; fly.

flies/ there's no flies on sb. *Br.* col. sb. is not stupid and can't be tricked.

flight *Br.* (in soccer, cricket, etc.) give a ball very good trajectory and pace.

flight/ in the first/top flight *esp. Br.* excellent, among the best, of the highest quality.

flight attendant *esp. Am.* steward(ess): *Deena, a former flight attendant, remembered her own training* – Reader's Digest.

fling *Br.* sl. an affair, usu. extramarital.

fling sb./smth. **out** *Br.* 1. suddenly make sb. leave an organisation. 2. get rid of smth. you no longer want or need.

flintware *Am.* glazed earthenware.

flip *Br.* col. pleasure trip or short tour.

flip 1. *Br.* sl. excl. used to express slight annoyance. 2. *Am.* col. feel very excited and like smth. very much: *the guests were "flipping out"* – S.Lawrence. 3. *esp. Am.* quickly start or stop electric equipment by pressing or moving a button.

flip *Am.* /*Br.* **toss** (**up**)/,

flip a nickel *Am.* cost a lot.

flip sb. **the bird** *Am.* make a rude gesture by one's middle finger.

flip-flop 1. *esp. Am., Can., Aus.* col. v. n. (make) a sudden complete change or reversal, a U-turn: *These flip-flops quickened the growth of cynicism* - J. Fowler., *one of his familiar flip-flops regarding the spirit of criticism.* - Time., *Recently that trend has seemed to flip-flop* - New York. 2. *Br. /esp. Am.* **thong/** (usu. pl.) a type of open shoe (sandal), which is usu. made of rubber and is held on by the toes and loose at the back: *I managed to slip my feet into a pair of rubber flipflops.* - R.L. Stine. 3. *Am., Can.* backward somersault or headspring.

flipping, also **fluffing** *esp. Br., Aus., Can.* euph. sl. bloody, damned: *And get off this flipping bottle* - T. Thorne.

flit/ do a (**moonlight**) **flit** *Br.* col. move away to avoid paying the rent one owes.

flitches *Am.* non-square wood bar.

flivver *Am., Can.* 1. col. obs. a small cheap car: *Ford's in his flivver.* - A. Huxley., *I looked up the road and saw the flivvers.* - R.P. Warren. 2. sl. failure. 3. sl. v. fail.

float *Br. /Am.* **delivery truck/** a small open delivery van.

float 1. *esp. Br., Aus.* a small sum of money provided for giving change, etc. at the beginning of selling in a shop or stall. 2. *Am.* soft drink with an ice-cream floating in it.

float a loan *Am.* col. borow money: *her husband spoke about a large loan, Mr. Richmond was floating.* – P. Roth.

float/ float on a cloud *Aus., Am.* be extremely happy.

floatable *esp. Am.* (of water) deep enough to float in.

floater *Am.* 1. person who votes illegally in various voting places. 2. temporary or seasonal worker: *They were night-shift floats, not regular staff.* - J. Kellerman. 3. deportation papers to leave town in 24 or 48 hours, issued to vagabonds, etc.: *Joseph and Mary were given a floater.* - J. Steinbeck.

floater 1. *Br.* sl. sausage in soup or gravy. 2. *Aus.* sl. meat pie swimming in soup. 3. *esp. Am., Can.* col. person who often changes jobs or residence. 4. *Am., Can.* jack-of-all-trades doing jobs as the need for them arises. 5. *Am.* insurance policy covering loss of articles without specifying a location.

floating voter *Br.* one who doesn't always vote for the same political party.

floaty *esp. Br.* (of a piece of clothing or fabric) light and flimsy.

flock *Am.* soft substance used to make patterns on the surface of wallpaper, curtains, etc.

flock/ fire into the wrong flock *Am.* miss the target badly.

flog esp *Br., Aus.* col. sell: *The travellers were cunningly steered towards eager merchants flogging their jewels and silks* - Bulletin., *He tried to get my address out of me to flog me a detailed horoscope.* - Woman's Own., *those that wanted to flog as much self-service petrol as possible would have lower prices.* - Economist.

flog *Br.* col. hard climb or struggle.

flog a dead horse, /*esp. Br.* col. **flog** smth. **to death/** *Br. /Am.* **beat a dead horse/** waste time and effort by returning once again to already settled subject.

flood/ in full flood *Am.* with a great deal of energy and enthusiasm.

floodgates/ open the floodgates *Br.* make sb. express all their feelings and thoughts.

flooey *Am.* sl. out of order, esp. in the phr. **go flooey**: *Then, of course, the whole thing all goes flooey* - Village Voice, R.L. Chapman.

floor 1. *Br. /Am.* **floorboard/** inside floor of a car. 2. *Br. /Am.* **pit/** area of stock exchange where shares are bought and sold.

floor 1. *Br.* tell sb. in school class to sit down (if one recites and is not prepared). 2. also **floor it** *Am.* col. make a car go very fast: *She floored the Porsche on the freeway and got caught.* - R.L. Chapman., *She started the car and floored it, and they sped off down the hill.* – R.L. Stine.

floor/ mop the floor with sb. *Am.* wipe the floor with sb.

floor cloth 1. *esp. Br.* piece of cloth used for washing or cleaning floors. 2. *Am., Can.* floor covering, esp. a canvas rug.

floor lamp *esp. Am., Can. /Br.* **standard lamp, stand lamp/** a lamp on a tall base which stands on the floor of a room: *thirties floor lamps, and retro sixties fixtures* - New York.

floor leader *Am.* the leader of a party in a legislative assembly.

floor manager, floorwalker *Am. /esp. Br.* **shop walker/** manager of a shop assistants in a big shop: *The floor manager accompanied him* - J. Steinbeck.

floor model *Am.* piece of furniture or electric equipment for the home such as washing machine that has been in store for person to look at and is often sold at a cheaper price.

floor-through *Am.* an apartment that takes an entire floor.

floor trader, room trader *Am.* a member of a stock-exchange.

floorwalker /also **floor manager/** *Am., Can. / esp. Br.* **shopwalker/** person employed in a large shop to help the customers and to watch the shop assistants to see that they are working properly.

flop *Am.* a hat with a soft brim.

flophouse, flop *esp. Am., Can.* col. a cheap hotel /*esp. Br.* sl. **dosshouse,** *Br.* **casualty ward/**: *His father had owned a flop-house on Madison street.* - S. Bellow.

floppy *Br.* col. (of a person) weak and tired.

Florida green *Am., Can.* col. the yellow light of the traffic light: *Oops! I just drove through a Florida green. Any cops around?* - W. Magnuson.

Florida room *Am., Can.* glazed room at the back of a house having a drinks bar and a tile floor.

floss *Am.* clean (one's teeth) with dental floss: *Flossing isn't just good for your gums, it may also protect your heart.* – Reader's Digest.

flossy *Am., Can.* col. fancy, frilly: *It may be highly important to know a flossy name for the boss* - R.L. Chapman.

flossy up *Br.* sl. gussy up, ornament (smth. or oneself) in the hope of improvement: *Pinn... would then spend a long time flossying herself up.* - I. Murdoch.

flour *Am.* v. grind. n. **flouring mill.**

flour corn *Am.* soft corn.

flow/ in full flow 1. *Am.* (talking) fluently and easily. 2. also **be in full flood** *Br.* talk endlessly about smth.

flower girl 1. *Br.* girl or woman who sells flowers in a street or market. 2. *Am.* a little girl who carries flowers in a wedding procession.

flower people *Br.* young people in 1960s and 1970s who were against war and wanted peace and love in society.

flowers/ sprinkle the flowers *Am.* give bribes.

The Flower State *Am.* Florida.

flow-on *Aus., NZ.* wage adjustment or improvement in working conditions based on already existing cases.

flow sheet *Am.* flow chart.

flub *Am., Can.* col. 1. an error, a blunder: *each made a major flub on the floor exercise* - Time. 2. ruin by blundering, make a stupid mistake: *The first crash was a flubbed landing* - J. DeFelice., *The Sterlings flubbed their third question* - P. Case, J. Migliore.

flubdub *Am.* col. 1. incompetence: *They would remove much of the amateur flubdub* - New York Daily News, R.L. Chapman. 2. a blunderer.

fluence *Br.* col. mysterious or magical power.

fluff *esp. Br. /Am.* **fuzz/** soft light loose waste from woollen or other materials: *Squirrels bound across the lawn like balls of fluff blown by the wind.* - D. Lodge.

fluff off *Am.* sl. avoid work or duty, shirk: *Nina made a show of fluffing off their concerns.* - D. Mortman.

fluff-stuff *Am.* sl. snow: *Fluff-stuff looks pretty, but it's no fun to shovel it.* - R.A. Spears.

fluffy esp. Am., Can. insubstantial.

fluke *Am.* 1. a barbed head (as of a harpoon). 2. failure: *Only the deLamerie teapot had thrown them, and that was a fluke.* - T. Murphy. 3. col. v. fail: *he had fluked out with 112.* - J. Cheever. 4. *Am., Can.* flat fish, esp. flounder.

flume *Am.* a ravine or gorge with a stream running through it.

flume ride *esp. Am.* a fairground amusement consisting of a water chute down which people can ride.

flummox 1. *esp. Br.* col. confuse completely: *You tried to flummox me again, didn't you?* - J.D. Carr., *Caldwell was flummoxed.* - A. Hitchcock Mystery Magazine. 2. *Am.* sl. a failure: *The solemn commmemoration was a total flummox* - R.L. Chapman.

flunk *esp. Am., Can., Aus.* col. /*esp. Br.* **fail**/ 1. fail (an examination or study course). 2. mark the examination answers of (sb.) as unsatisfactory: *If I flunk English I can't graduate next year.* - C. McCullers., *Loomis flunked me in math* - B. Kaufman.

flunk out (of) *Am., Can., Aus.* col. be dismissed from a school or college for failure: *I was flunked out last week, I was a premed.* - K. Vonnegut, Jr.

flunker *Am.* 1. a student who fails an exam. 2. a teacher who failed him/her.

flush off *Am.* wash (a surface) with a lot of water: *Father asked me to flush off the garage floor.* - Longman.

fluster *Br.* fit of nervousness.

flutist *Am.* /*Br.* **flautist**/ person who plays flute: *Flutists and trumpeters abound* - J. Fowles.

flutter *esp. Br., Aus.* col. the risking of a small amount money, a small bet, esp. in **have a flutter**: *I like a flutter myself.* - G. Greene.

fly *Am.* 1. (of plans, ideas, etc.) be good and useful. 2. (in baseball) hit a ball very high.

fly 1. *esp. Br.* col. sharp and clever, not easily tricked. 2. *Am., Can.* stylish and fashionable.

fly 1. *Am., Aus.* /also **flies** *esp. Br.*/ the front opening of a pair of trousers. 2. *esp. Am.* flysheet, an extra sheet of canvass stretched over the outside of a tent to keep the rain out.

fly/ fly a kite *Br., Aus.* say or do smth. in order to find out what the public opinion about a particular subject is: *I finally told him to go fly a kite.* - H.C. Whitford., R.J. Dixson.

fly/ be flying high *Am.* col. be very excited or happy, esp. after using drugs.

fly/ drink with the flies *Aus., NZ.* drink alone.

fly/ fly at sb. or **fly into** sb. *Am.* suddenly rush at sb. being angry with them.

fly/ fly into a temper/fury *Br.* become angry very suddenly.

fly right *Am.* col. behave correctly.

fly/ give it a fly /**have a fly**/ *Aus.* col. try smth.

fly/ Go fly a kite *esp. Am., Aus.* col. Go away and stop being annoying.

fly/ it'll never fly *Am.* the idea won't be successful.

fly/ like a blue-arsed fly *Br.* sl. very quickly.

fly/ on the fly *Am.* very quickly and without thinking.

fly/ there are no flies on sb. *Br. Aus.* col. person who is not a fool and cannot be tricked.

fly/ sb. **wouldn't harm a fly** *Br.* col. sb. is very gentle and no one should be afraid of them.

fly up *Br.* (in the Girl Guide organisation) move formally to the part of organisation for older girls: *We should like to welcome three Brownies who are flying up to Guides this week* - Longman.

flyblown *esp. Br.* 1. /*esp. Am.* **flyspecked**/ (esp. of meat) covered with the small spots that are the waste matter of flies: *its label a bit fly specked and faded* - J. Fischer. 2. old, dirty and in bad condition.

fly boy *Am., Can.* col. a pilot, esp. in the air force.

flyby *Am.* /also *Am.* **flyover,** *Br.* **flypast**/ the actions of a group of aircraft flying in a special formation on a ceremonial occasion, esp. at a low level in front of a crowd.

fly-drive *esp. Am., Can.* speculative investment.

fly-drive holiday *Br.* /*Am.* **fly-drive (vacation)**/ organised holiday which includes air ticket and the use of a car.

flier/ take a flier *esp. Am., Can.* take a chance.

flying *esp. Br.* lasting a very short time.

flying picket *Br.* person who with others travels to any place where there is an industrial dispute to take part in picketing.

flying squad *Br.* police group or other organisation capable to get to the place of incident quickly.

fly-on-the-wall documentary or **programme** *Br.* one in which people involved forget that they are being filmed.

flyover 1. *esp. Br.* /*Am., Aus., Can.* **overpass,** *Br.* **crossover**/ a place where two roads or railways cross each other at different levels: *Now Vic has reached the last traffic lights before the system of tunnels and flyovers* - D. Lodge. 2. *Am., Can.* **flyby** /*Br.* **flypast**/.

fly-post *Br.* put up notices on unauthorised walls.

flyposter *Br.* illegal flier.

flysheet *Br.* fabric cover over a tent used for protection against bad weather.

fly-tip *Br.* illegally dump waste.

flytrap *Am.* sl. mouth.

flywhisk *Br.* small brush used in former times for keeping flies away.

fnarr *Br.* col. humor. excl. used to say that smth. just said has sexual meaning.
FOB factor *Am.* ex works, ex factory.
foam gun *Am.* foam making branch (used in fire fighting).
fo'c'stle *Br.* /*Am.* **forecastle**/ front part of the ship where the sailors live.
fog/ not have the foggiest (**idea** or **notion**) *esp. Br.* col. have no idea at all.
fog (up) *Am.* /*Br.* **mist**, *Am., Aus.* **steam**/ (of a surface) be covered with condensed liquid: *My goggles must be fogging up* – Reader's Digest.
fogey/ young fogey *Br.* a young person who dresses and behaves as if he is much older and likes traditional ways of life.
fogged *Br.* sl. befuddled, bewildered.
fogger *Br.* person who places fog signals on railroad tracks.
Foggy Bottom *Am.* sl. State Department: *He responds in kind calling his Foggy Bottom critics "Wimps"* - Time.
fog lamp *Br.* /*Am.* **fog light**/ strong light on the front of a car that helps drivers to see in fog.
folder *Am.* matchbook.
folding money *Am.* bank notes.
foley *esp. Am.* related to adding sound effects after the shooting of a film.
folks *esp. Am.* /*esp. Br.* **folk**/ people: *The folks back home are ecstatic.* - J. DeFelice., *The folks around here are awful no-account.* - J. Dos Passos., *these two folk passed away by road* – M. Daly.
folks/ one's folks *esp. Am.* one's parents.
folkster *Am.* col. folk singer.
folksy *esp. Am.* col. 1. simple and friendly. 2. derog. pretending to be or trying to appear simple in ways, likes, etc.
follies *Am.* col. variety show.
follow sb. **around/about** *Br.* keep following sb. everywhere.
follow up on *Am.* follow smth. up, find more about smth.
follow-up *Am.* second advertisement sent after the first one had not been received.
follow-my-leader *Br., Aus.* /*Am.* **follow the leader**/ a children's game in which one of the players does actions which all the other players must copy: *he immediately suggested they play follow the leader down the mountain.* - D. Mortman.
font *Am.* /*Br.* **fount**/ print. a set of typed characters of the same design: *he's got the fonts he needed* - R. Carter., M. McCarthy.
foodaholic *Am.* joc. glutton.

food bank *Am.* a place that gives food to people who need it.
food court *Am., Can.* shopping mall area with fast food outlets.
food hall *Br.* section of department store where food is sold.
foodie *esp. Br., Aus.* col. person who is interested in cooking and good food.
food stamp *Am.* an official piece of paper that people can use instead of money to buy food.
food store, grocery store, provision store *Am.* /*Br.* **grocer's**/.
fool *esp. Am., Can.* col. adj. stupid, foolish.
fool about *Br.* col. 1. waste time in silly way. 2. behave in a careless or irresponsible way. 3. have sex with sb. else's wife, boyfriend, etc.
fool around *esp. Am.* col. adventure sexually, esp. adulterously: *She always fools around with the men-folks.* - E. Caldwell.
fool with sb./smth. *esp. Am.* use smth. in a dangerous or silly way.
fool/ (the) (then) more fool you/him, etc. *esp. Br.* col. derog. I think you were / he was a fool: *As it was he merely shrugged and said "More fool you."* - D. Lodge.
fool/ fool to oneself *Br.* one whose kind behaviour to others results in harm to himself.
foolscap *Br.* paper – 34x43cm in size.
a fool's errand *Br.* some stupid useless action.
foot/ get one's **feet under the table** *esp. Br.* start to feel confident in a new situation.
foot/ have a lead foot *Am.* col. drive very fast very often.
foot/ the boot is on the other foot *Br., Aus.* /*Am.* **the shoe is on the other foot**/ the situation changed drastically.
foot/ put a foot wrong /also **not put a foot right**/ *esp. Br., Aus.* say or do the wrong things; opp. **not/never put a foot wrong.**
foot/ can't put a foot wrong *Br., Aus.* do everything perfectly.
foot/ put one's **foot down** *esp. Br.* col. /*Am.* **put** one's **foot to the floor**/ drive very fast.
foot/ put one's **foot in** *esp. Br.* /*esp. Am., Aus., Can.* **put** one's **foot in** one's **mouth**/ say smth. wrong or unsuitable, causing an awkward situation: *Wouldn't he ever learn to put his foot in his mouth?* - A. Hitchcock Mystery Magazine.
foot/ put one's **foot to the floor** *Am.* suddenly increase one's speed.
footbag *Am.* footmuff.
football /also **soccer, Association football**/ 1. *esp. Br.* /*esp. Am.* **soccer,** *Br.* col. **footie, footy**/ game between two teams of 11 players

each with a round ball that is kicked and not handled. 2. *Am.* /*Br.* **American football**/ an American game rather like Rugby.
footballer *Br.* (professional) football player.
footballing *Br.* relating to British football.
football boots *Br.* /*Am.* **cleats, soccer shoes**/ special boots worn to play football.
football match *esp. Br.* /*esp. Am.* **football game**/.
football pools/ **do the football pools** *Br.* gamble on the results of football matches.
footer, footie *Br., Aus.* col. rare. the game of football, soccer.
foot-in-mouth disease *Am.* sl. the tendency to say the wrong thing at the wrong moment: *Very good, Dupre, foot in mouth as usual.* - T. Murphy.
footless *Am.* 1. worthless, useless. 2. clumsy, inexperienced.
foot-locker *Am., Can.* small flat trunk designed to be placed at the foot of a bed.
foot log *Am., Can.* a log used as a footbridge.
footpath 1. *Br., Aus.* pavement, a path for people to walk on. 2. *esp. Br.* /*Am.* **trail**/ a path in the country.
footplate *esp. Br.* the platform of a railway engine, where the driver and fireman stand.
footrule *Br.* narrow flat piece of wood or metal (usu. 12 inches long) marked in (parts of) inches and used for measuring.
footsie/ **play footsie (with** sb.) *esp. Am.* work together (with sb.) esp. in a way that is not completely honest or fair: *what about a bank that plays footsie with the Tammany tiger?* - L. Waller., *NFL politics don't mix so quit playing footsie with football.* - USA Today.
footsie *Br.* tdmk. FTSC index.
footslogging *Br.* col. a lot of walking around, which makes sb. very tired.
footway *Br.* tech. pavement.
footy, footie 1. *Br.* col. football. 2. *Aus.* sl. rugby.
foozle *Am.* sl. 1. mistake: *What a stupid foozle!* - R.A. Spears. 2. a fool.
for *Am.* prep. in honour of, after.
for/ after first, only, and negative or superlative forms Americans may use **in** where British use **for.**
for/ **be (in) for it** *esp. Br., Aus.* col. be likely to be punished, get into trouble, etc.
for/ **I'm for bed/home** *Br.* I'm going to bed/going home.
the force *Br.* col. the police.
force oneself (to do smth.) *Br.* col. used when trying to persuade sb. to do smth. that they seem unwilling to do, because one knows they will enjoy it.
forcemeat *esp. Br.* a mixture containing bread, herbs, and often meat which is cut up very small and used esp. for putting inside a chicken, joint of meat, etc. that is to be cooked.
forecourt *Br.* front yard of the service station where petrol is pumped, hence **forecourt attendant.**
Forefathers' Day *Am.* anniversary of the day (Dec. 21, 1620) when the first English colonists settled in America.
forehanded *Am.* 1. mindful of the future, prudent. 2. well-to-do, rich.
forehock *Br.* foreleg cut of pork or bacon.
forelady *Am.* woman who works as a foreman.
forelock-tugging, or **forelock-touching** *Br.* showing too much respect towards sb. who has a high position; **tug/touch** one's **forelock.**
forenoon *Am., Can.* the morning.
foreside *Am.* foreshore.
forest *Br.* area where game is or was hunted (and preserved), not necessarily wooded.
forest/ **can't see the forest for the trees** *Am., Can.* be over attentive to details and not see the obvious important things.
forester *Aus.* a type of grey kangaroo.
forestick *Am.* the front stick lying on the andirons in a wood fire.
forest ranger *Am.* forest guard.
forewoman *esp. Am., Can.* (in law court) woman who presides over a jury.
forfend *esp. Am.* defend.
fork *Am., Can.* point where river divides into two parts.
fork *Br.* /*Am.* **pitchfork**/ garden tool used for digging with handle and three or four points.
fork/ **fork left/right** *Br.* go left/right.
fork smth. **over** *Am.* /*Aus.* **fork up**/ col. spend a lot of money on smth. because you have to: *They stuck a gun in his ribs and made him fork over all his money.* - H.C. Whitford., R.J. Dixson, *you didn't fork over a fortune* – Reader's Digest.
fork supper *Br.* casserole meal, buffet lunch, dinner.
form *Br.* 1. sl. a record of having been found guilty of crimes, esp. **in have form.** 2. /*Am., Can.* **grade,** *Aus.* **class**/ a class in school: *the form-teacher would make a fuss if somebody was absent* – R. Westall. 3. long bench without a back. 4. hare's lair.
form/ **be bad form** *Br.* be rude or impolite.
form/ **be in good form** *esp. Br.* be healthy and cheerful.

form/ on great form *Br. /Am., Aus.* **be in a great/ good/top form/** in great form, in good spirits.
form/ be on form *esp. Br. /Am.* **in form/** be in good form (in sports).
form/ be out of form *esp. Br.* perform badly.
form/ on present form *Br.* judging by what has happened until now.
formal *Am., Can.* 1. social event at which sb. has to wear formal clothes. 2. col. formal dress, esp. long dress worn by women at formal occasion.
form book *Br.* annual racehorse performing book.
former *Br.* a pupil of the stated form (class): *Harold Wilson was Wirral Grammar School for Boys first sixth former.* - Cheshire Life.
form-room *Br.* classroom: *I wandered into the form-room* – R. Westall.
form teacher *Br.* teacher who is responsible for all the students in the same class at a school.
formula *Am., Aus.* liquid milk-like food for babies: *Infant formulas contain harmful lead deposits.* - J. Riffkin, T. Howard., *I warmed up his formula* - Reader's Digest., *The Iraqis said it made baby formula.* - Rolling Stone.
forrader *esp. Br.* col. further forward.
fort/ hold down the fort *Am.* hold the fort, look after the house while the owners are away.
forthputting *Am.* n. adj. obtrusive behaviour.
fortnight *esp. Br., Aus.* two weeks: *The whole thing would be over in a fortnight, they said.* - G. Orwell., *the necessary fortnight period has elapsed* - Cheshire Life., *In brief a fortnight slipped by without a sign* - T. Hardy. adj. adv. **fortnightly /Am biweekly/**.
fortune cookie *Am., Can.* one that has a slip of paper with a prediction or motto served in Chinese restaurant: *a tiny slip of paper, the kind you would find in a fortune cookie.* – S. Lawrence.
forty-niner *Am.* gold digger (of the California Gold Rush of 1849).
forty (or six) ways to Sunday *Am.* sl. in every possible manner, direction, etc.: *She had him beat forty ways to Sunday* - R.L. Chapman.
forum *esp. Am., Can.* court or tribunal.
fossick *Aus., NZ.* rummage, search.
foster *Br.* assign a child to be brought up by sb. other than its parents.
foul *esp. Br.* 1. very unpleasant. 2. (of weather) stormy and windy, with a lot of rain and snow.
foul out *Am.* col. take no further part in play, because of an action against the rules: *Two of our players have fouled out* - Longman.

found/ all found *Br.* getting wages along with food and room.
foundation *Am. /Br.* **foundations/** the solid base under the ground that supports the building.
foundation course *Br. /Am., Aus.* **introductory course/** the first year course taught in many universities covering a wide range of subjects.
foundationer *esp. Br.* person supported by foundation or endowment of a college or school.
foundation member, founder member *Br.* /also *esp. Am.* **charter member/** founder member.
foundation subjects *Br.* basic core subjects of National Curriculum.
founder *esp. Am., Can.* laminitis in horses.
four bits *Am.* col. 50 cents: *to smoke four-bits cigars* - R.L. Chapman.
four-F *Am. /Br.* **C three** or **C3/** mil. unfit for active service in the armed services: *He got his 4-F classification in the draft.* - I. Shaw., *I'm 4-F because I'm a chronic alcoholic.* - A. Burchwald., *Goddamn 4-F shirking bastard.* - J. Hyams.
four-flush *Am., Can.* 1. poker hand of small value. 2. bluff smth.
four-flusher *Am., Can.* col. deceiver: *Your thieving four-flusher* – M. Daly.
Four Hundred *Am.* the exclusive social set of a community.
four on the floor *Am.* (of a car) having four gears worked by a gear lever.
4-H club *Am., Can.* club that teaches agriculture, home economics, etc. to young people / improvement of head, heart, hands and health/: *I'd join 4-H and show it like you do with the cattle and horses.* - Reader's Digest.
four-in-hand *Am.* a long band of cloth worn around the neck: *He was wearing a white shirt and a black four-in-hand tie* - J. O'Hara.
fourpenny one *Br.* col. blow.
four star (petrol) *Br. /Am.* **high-test (gas)**, *Aus.* **super (petrol)/** the highest quality leaded fuel in a car.
four star general *Am.* general of a high rank in the US army.
fourth class *Am.* class of sending things unwrapped with a weight of less than one pound: *Bill sent away 98 cereal box tops and a dollar and got back a sheriff's badge and gun in the mail by fourth class.* - A. Makkai.
Fourth of July /also **the Glorious Fourth/** *Am.* the national Independence Day of the USA.
fowl *Am.* duck, goose or turkey.
fowl run *Br. /Am.* **chicken run, yard/** poultry yard.

fox *Br.* be difficult to do or understand; confuse or deceive sb. in a clever way.
fox *Am.* hunt foxes.
fox *Am., Can.* col. sexually attractive woman: *A couple of foxes working the street for him could really start pulling in the green.* - W. Murphy.
fox/ crazy like a fox *esp. Am.* sl. clever, not easily deceived.
fox fire *Am.* eerie phosphorescent light / as of decaying wood (*Am.* **fox wood**).
foxtrot *Am.* letter F in radio code.
foxy *esp. Am.* col. sexually attractive: *What a foxy dame!* - R.A. Spears.
foyer *Am. /Br., Aus.* **hall/** an entrance hall to a private house or flat: *They would be making love standing up in the foyer of her apartment.* - M. Puzo.
fracture *Am.* sl. cause (sb.) to laugh very hard: *Woo boy - that really fractured me.* - M. Jones, J. Chilton.
fractured *Am.* 1. col. spoken or written with disregard to conventional syntax. 2. sl. drunk.
frag *Am., Can.* sl. 1. hand grenade. 2. kill by fragmentation grenade: *I saw some creeps frag a guy once.* - R.A. Spears.
fragile *Br.* feeling ill after drinking too much alcohol.
fraidy cat *Am.* col. (used by children) too frightened to do smth.
frail *Am.* sl. (young) woman: *They wanted some drinks and a couple of frails.* - J. Dos Passos.
frame *Am., Can.* frame-up.
frame/ be in the frame (for) *Br., Aus.* 1. be likely to achieve smth. or to be chosen for a job or activity. 2. be responsible for a crime or unpleasant situation.
framer *esp. Am.* one of the writers of the constitution of the USA.
frame house *esp. Am., Can.* one having a wooden skeleton, often covered with timber boards: *African Americans, who lived in small frame houses* –Reader's Digest.
frame tent *esp. Br.* tent with a tall frame providing standing room throughout.
franchise *Am., Can.* 1. permission given by a league to own a sports team. 2. professional sports team. 3. also **franchise player** a star player in a team.
frank, hot-dog *Am.* col. frankfurter: *that churned out 295,000 pounds of turkey franks* – Reader's Digest.
Franklin Stove *Am., Can.* a metal heating stove resembling an open fireplace used indoors: *In the winter, we burn wood in our Franklin Stove.* - E. Caldwell.
frappe *Am.* a kind of thick milkshake: *What we eat is funny… Popeyes, salmon croquettes, frappes* – R. Brautigan.
frat *Am., Can.* col. fraternity.
fraud squad *Br.* police group investigating frauds.
frazzle *esp. Am.* col. v. 1. fray. 2. put in a state of extreme physical or nervous fatigue: *the power of the day's sudden events would so frazzle Ash Robinson that he would let something slip* - T. Thompson., *He just felt hungry and frazzled.* - J. Dos Passos.
frazzles/ beat to frazzles *Aus.* beat to a frazzle.
frazzle/ burn to a frazzle *Br.* col. burn completely.
frazzled *Br.* col. burned or dried out after being in the sun or cooking for too long.
freak *esp. Am.* col. become so angry and frightened so that almost lose control of oneself: *every great musician in London would freak out over Jimmi* – S.Lawrence.
freaking *Am.* euph. col. fucking.
freckie *Aus.* sl. also **date, ace** the buttocks.
freebie, -bee *esp. Am., Aus., Can.* col. smth. such as a meal, that is given or received without payment: *Here, a freebie.* - W. Murphy.
free collective bargaining *Br.* talks between trade unions and employers about increases in pay, improvement in conditions, etc., that are not controlled by legal limits.
free enterpriser *Am., Can.* capitalist.
freefone, -phone *Br.* tdmk. /*Am.* **800 number**, *Am., Aus.* **toll-free number/** an arrangement by which a company pays the cost of telephone calls made to it.
free house *Br.* a pub that is free to receive its supplies from a number of breweries: *A free house. High class. Lunches served.* - G. Greene.
free labour *esp. Br.* the labour of workers who are not members of trade union.
freeloader *Am., Aus.* derog. A person living on money, goods given by other people, without giving anything in return; **freeloading**.
free lunch *Am., Can.* col. smth. free (often negative).
freeman *Br.* an honorary citizen who has been given special rights in the city.
free-on-car *Am.* without charge for delivery and placing on board a train.
free pardon *Br.* /*Am., Aus.* **pardon/** official foregiving of a criminal for their crime and release from prison.

freepost *Br.* a special mail delivery service operated by the Post Office by which a letter may be sent by second class mail to a firm or advertiser free of postal charge, with the addressee paying the postage.

free-range *esp. Br.* being, concerning or produced by hens that are kept under natural conditions in a farmyard or field: *Next to them a woman was selling free-range eggs* - J. Harmer., R. Rossner, **free-range eggs.**

freesheet 1. *Am.* print. a /*Br.* **woodfree**/ paper made only from chemical pulp. 2. *Br.* print. a local newspaper without a cover price whose only revenue is from advertising sales.

free vote *Br.* parliamentary division in which members vote according to their own beliefs.

freeway, super highway *Am., Can., Aus.* / *Br.* **(divided) motorway,** *Am.* **expressway, (divided) highway**/ 1. very wide road built for fast long-distance travel: *he negotiated the exit ramp from the freeway.* - P. Case, J. Migliore. 2. toll-free highway.

freeway with on-ramp *Am.* /*Br.* **motorway with sliproad**/ wide road with a road for driving on or off motorway.

freeze 1. *Br.* period of extremely cold weather. 2. *Am.* short period of time, esp at night when the temperature is extremely cold.

freeze *Am.* cause to be fixed, standardised. etc. (about building, plans, etc.).

freeze (up) *Am.* (of an engine or lock) stop working because its parts have been stuck and no longer working.

freeze out *Am.* prevent because of great cold: *a new ice age is beginning which will freeze out all life.* - J.A. Michener.

freezer *Aus.* col. 1. a sheep destined for export. 2. exporter of freezed sheep.

freezer *Am.* part of the fridge in which food can be stored at very low temprature for a long time.

freezing works *Aus., NZ.* slaughterhouse where animals' carcasses are frozen for export.

freight 1. *esp. Am.* heavy articles which can be carried by road, train, etc. 2. *Br.* /*Am.* **cargo**/ the goods carried by a ship: *SS Reynole upbound with package freight for Toronto.* - W. Grady. 3. *Am.* freight train.

freight/ pay the freight *Am.* col. pay for smth. that cost a lot of money.

freight agent /also **shipper**/ *Am.* forwarding agent.

freight car /**wagon**/ *Am.* /*Br.* **goods waggon, goods truck** or **van**/ a wagon for heavy articles which can be carried by train: *they piled us into freight cars* - I. Shaw.

freight depot or **house** *Am.* railway goods station or shed.

freight engine *Am.* the locomotive of a freight train.

freightliner, also **linertrain** *esp. Br.* tdmk. a train that carries a large amounts of goods in special containers.

freight office *Am.* goods office.

freight (truck) *Am.* goods lorry.

freight train *esp. Am.* /*Br.* **goods train**/ one for carrying heavy articles: *It sounded as if dozens of rapid freight trains were roaring overhead.* - T. Caldwell., *I was a vagabond at 14, rode freight trains in my late teens.* - Life.

freight yard *Am.* goods yard: *Gone were the rail cars, freight yards and train stations.* – D.L. Barlett, J.B. Steele.

French/ Pardon my French! *Br.* humor. Excuse my rude language.

French bean *Br.* /*Am.* **string bean**/ green bean.

French doors *esp. Am., Can.* /*Br.* **French windows**/ a pair of light outer doors made of glass in a frame, usu. opening out onto the garden of a house: *there are six pairs of floor-to-ceiling French doors.* - S. Grafton.

French dressing *Am.* a thick liquid made of mayonnaise and ketchup.

(French) fries 1. *esp. Am., Can.* /also *Am., Can.* **French (fried) potatoes, fries,** *Br.* **chips**/ long thin pieces of potato cooked in deep fat: *- chips meaning French fries if you're American.* - World Monitor., *We'd buy the gas, hamburgers and french fries* - W. Jack, B. Laursen. 2. *Br.* long pieces of fried potato cut slightly thinner than chips.

French leave/ take French leave *Br.* obs. leave work without a warning for some time.

French letter, Frenchy *Br., Aus.* col. obs. a condom: *They filled a French letter with water and threw it at a bunch of girls* – S. Townsend.

French loaf *Br.* long thin white loaf of bread.

French mustard *Br.* mild mustard mixed with vinegar.

French polish *Br., Aus.* a type of varnish used on furniture; v.

French toast 1. *esp. Am.* pieces of bread dipped in beaten egg and cooked in hot oil: *She was frying French toast in one pan* - W. Grady. 2. *Br.* bread buttered on one's side and toasted on the other.

French vermouth *Br.* dry vermouth.

Frenchy *Can.* French Canadian.

fresh *Br.* col. (of water) cold and windy.
fresh/ be fresh from smth. *Br.* /*Am., Aus.* **be fresh out of** smth./ have just finished education or training.
fresh/ fresh out of *esp. Am., Can., Aus.* col. having just used up one's supplies of smth: *he was fresh out of ideas on what he could do* - T. Murphy.
fresh/ get fresh with sb. *Am., Aus.* talk to sb. rudely.
fresh butter *Br.* sweet butter.
freshen *Am., Can.* 1. (of milch animals) come into milk: *cows were not any good until they had been freshened.* - E. Caldwell. 2. top up, fill up smth. with a drink.
freshie *Aus.* fresh water crocodile.
fresh-made/cut/grated, etc. *esp. Am.* having just been made, cut, etc.
freshman 1. /also **fresher, first year undergraduate** *Br., Aus.* col. /*Am.* col. **frosh**/ student in the first year at college or university. 2. also *Am.* col. **frosh** *Am.* student in the first year at college or university or at high school.
freshwater *Am. Can.* col. provincial, not widely known, **freshwater college,** etc.
fret/ be/get in a fret *Br.* col. become worried or anxious about smth.
friction-primer *Am.* friction fuse.
friction tape *Am.* insulated tape, often also used to wrap objects such as handles: *I was back in my room putting some friction tape on my goddam hockey stick* - J.D. Salinger.
fridge *esp. Br.* /*Am.* obs. **icebox,** *esp. Am.* **refrigerator**/ a large box or cupboard, used esp. in the home, in which food and drink can be stored at a low temperature but without being frozen: *The food rots in the fridge* - E. Taylor., *there's a second bottle in the fridge.* - Sydney Calendar., *Then she got up and went to the kitchen and opened the fridge.* - I. Murdoch.
fridge-freezer *Br.* /*Am.* **refrigerator-freezer**/ a large box or cupboard divided into two parts, one of which is a fridge and the other a freezer.
fried *Am., Can.* col. exhausted or worn out.
fried cake *Am.* 1. doughnut. 2. cruller.
friend/ my honorable friend *Br.* referring to another member in the House of Commons, **my noble friend** refers to a fellow member of the House of Lords.
friendly *esp. Br.* a game that is played for pleasure or practice and not as part of a serious competition, also adj.
Friendship Town *Br.* /also *Br.* **twinned city**/ one closely linked (sister-citied) with another city in another country to encourage friendly relations.
fries *Am.* /*Br.* **chips**/.
Friesian *esp. Br., Aus.* /*esp. Am.* **Holstein**/ a black-and-white cow of a breed that gives a large quantity of milk: *All dairy bulls that's breeds like Friesian, Guernsey and Jersey are banned from fields crossed by public paths.* - Young Citizen's Passport.
frig around/about *Br.* col. euph. waste one's time aimlessly.
frig sb. **about/around** *esp. Br.* taboo. col. treat sb. badly or unfairly.
frightener *Br.* col. member of criminal gang who intimidates its victim.
frightener/ put the frighteners on sb. *Br.* col. threaten them into doing smth.
frightful *Br.* col. very bad.
frightfully *Br.* obs. very.
frill *Am.* col. delicacy.
fringe 1. *esp. Br., Aus.* /*Am.* **bang (of hairs)**/ short border of hair usu. cut in a straight line, hanging over a person's forehead. 2. *Am., Can.* fringe benefit.
fringe bank, deposit-taking intitution *Br.* small deposit taking institution.
fringe benefits *Br.* additional benefits or privileges provided with a person's regular salary, such as the use of a car, meals free or at reduced cost or free insurance.
fringe theatre *Br.* small experimental theatre.
frisk down *Am.* search sb. for hidden weapons, drugs, etc. by feeling their body with one's hands.
fritz/ be on the fritz *Am.* col. not working: *the new water heater is on the fritz* – J. Tesh.
frock *Aus.* dress.
froe *esp. Am.* a wedge-shaped tool.
Frog *Br., Aus.* col. usu. derog. a French person. **Frog restaurant** *Br.* col. one with French cuisine.
frog/ a big frog in a small pond *Am.* the most important person in a group.
frog/ Is a frog's ass watertight? *Am.* /*Br.* **Does Judith Chalmers have a passport?**/ used to mean that that the obvious answer is "yes."
frog *Aus.* sl. condom.
frog eye *Am.* print. bull's eye, hickie, printing defect caused by dust.
frog march *Br.* force sb. to walk somewhere by having two persons on either side of them who hold their arms very tightly.
frogskin *Am.* sl. a dollar bill: *I'll give you five hundred frogskins for the good will and futures* - R.L. Chapman.

(the) front 1. *Br.* col. courage, cheek, esp. in **have a lot of front for**. 2. **the front** *Br.* the esplanade or promenade running along the shore in a seaside town.

(strictly) from hunger *Am.* smth.or sb. bad, cheap, strange or unacceptable: *two months ago Joey was strictly from hunger.* – J. O'Hara.

front/ in the front esp. *Br.* in the part of a car where the driver sits.

front/ out front *esp. Am., Can.* in front.

front/ out in front *Br.* the area near the entrance to a building.

front (the organization) *Br.* be the most senior members of the organization.

Front *Am., Can.* Come here (call for the messenger in the hotel).

front (desk) *Am.* reception: *One of my friends worked the front desk.* - D. Mortman., *a message came through the front desk* - Time.

(front) desk clerk, room clerk *Am., Can. /Br.* **reception clerk/**.

frontage road *Am., Can.* service road.

front-and-center *Am.* very important and needing attention.

front fender *Am.* front wing (of a car): *Dented my girlfriend's front fender, glass all over the place.* - A. Hitchcock Mystery Magazine.

frontier *esp. Br. /Am.* **border/** a border between two countries

front matter *Am. /Br.* **prelims/** print. the pages of a book before the main text, containing the title page, contents, etc.

the front office *Am.* the managers of a company.

front-pager *Am.* col. front page news.

front room *esp. Br.* obs. */Am.* **living room/** formally decorated room facing the road where guests are entertained: *After supper they went into the front room again.* - E. Hemingway., *They could be heard talking in the front room.* - E. Caldwell.

front-running *Am., Can.* practice of giving one's support to a competitor because they are in front.

frosh *Am.* col. freshman: *Ken is just a frosh, but he looks older.* - R.A. Spears.

frost *esp. Am.* cover a cake with frosting */Br.* **ice/**.

frost *Am.* make narrow strips of person's hair paler in colour than surrounding hair.

frostie *Aus, Am.* beer: *Hey, toss me a frosty, will ya?* - R.A. Spears.

frosting *esp. Am., Can. /esp. Br.* **icing/** a covering on a cake made from fine sugar and liquid: *it started coming down like a cake frosting.* - J. O'Brien, A. Kurins., *I don't like frosting* - New York.

frost line *Am., Can.* maximum depth of ground below which the source doesn't freeze in winter.

frown down *esp. Am.* make sb. stop talking by looking at them disapprovingly.

frowst *esp. Br.* col. v. n. (remain indoors with) unpleasantly hot air.

frowsty *esp. Br.* col. derog. (of the conditions inside a room) hot and airless, stuffy.

frowzy, -sy *esp. Br.* 1. (of a house or room) having a closed-in heavy smell. 2. (of a person, clothes, etc.) not neat or clean because not well cared for, shabby: *Feeling about as frowzy and unloved as she was supposed to feel in the play.* - K. Vonnegut, Jr.

fruit 1. *Br.* obs. sl. (used for addressing a male friend). 2. *Am., Aus.* derog. sl. a male homosexual: *Who's the fruit who just came in?* - R.A. Spears.

fruit and vegetable store *Am. /Br.* **greengrocer's/**

fruitcake *Am., Aus.* sl. one who behaves strangely and foolishly.

fruit cocktail *esp. Am., Can.* mixture of small pieces of fruit served in a tall glass and eaten at the beginning or the end of a meal.

fruit cup 1. *Br.* a drink of mixture of fruit juices. 2. *Am., Can.* fruit salad.

fruiterer *esp. Br.* obs. a person who sells fruit in a shop or market.

fruit machine *Br., Aus. /Am.* **slot machine/** one-armed bandit, a machine with one long handle, into which people put money to try to win more money: *it was full of flashing fruit machines* - B. Bryson.

fruit salad 1. *esp. Br.* a dish made of several types of fruit cut up and served in a bowl at the end of a meal. 2. *esp. Am.* a dish made of pieces of fruit in a jelly. 3. *Am.* col. the coloured area on the left breast of a military uniform formed by the coloured squares of the medal ribbons.

fruit store, fruitseller *Am. /Br.* **fruiterer/**.

fruity 1. *Br.* col. sexually suggestive in content or style. 2. *esp. Am.* col. strange or eccentric. 3. *Am.* derog. relating to homosexuals.

fry 1. *Am., Can.* a picnic where food is fried / e.g. *fish fry.* 2. *Am.* sl. kill sb. or be killed as a punishment in the electric chair.

fryer *Am., Can.* a chicken for frying.

fryer/ deep fryer, deep fat frier *Am.* big deep pan for frying food.

frying pan *Br., Aus.* /*Am.* **skillet**/ a flat pan with a long handle used for frying food.
fry-up *Br.* col. (a dish cooked by) frying various foods, such as eggs, sausages, potatoes, etc. in order to make a quick meal.
FTA *Am., Can.* Free Trade Agreement between USA and Canada.
fubsy *Br.* col. fat and squat.
fuck *Br.* /*Am.* **fuckhead**/ fucker, disliked person.
fuck about / around *esp. Br., Aus.* taboo. sl. 1. / *esp. Am.* **fuck off**/ waste time, act in a useless or stupid way: *Don't fuck about with me, you little slag* - J. Higgins. 2. **fuck** sb. **about/around** *Br.* taboo. sl. make sb. angry or annoyed by wasting their time.
fuck sb. **over** *Am.* treat sb. in unfair and unhumiliating way.
fuck all *esp. Br.* taboo. sl. nothing at all: *He knows fuck-all about the case* - R.L. Chapman.
fucking A excl. *Am.* used when sb. is angry, surprised, shocked, etc. by smth.
fuddle *Br.* col. (of alcohol, drugs, etc.) make sb. unable to think clearly.
a fudge *esp. Br.* an attempt to deal with a situation that doesn't solve its problems completely, or only makes it seem better.
fudgy *Am.* slightly sticky with a strong chocolate taste.
fug *esp. Br.* col. heavy unpleasant airless condition of a room, etc. caused by heat, smoke, or presence of many people.
full 1. *esp. Aus.* col. drunk. 2. *Am.* (of the moon or tide) become full.
full / be full of smth *Am.* hate smth. /*Br.* love smth.
full/ be full of bull *Am.* col. say wrong or stupid things often.
full/ be full of piss and vinegar *Am.* col. have a lot of energy.
full/ be full of the joys of spring *Br., Aus.* humor. be very happy.
full/ be full to bursting *Br.* very full.
full (as a boot/bull/bull's bum, goog, tick) *Aus.* sl. drunk.
full beam *Br.* /*Am.* **high beam**/ lights at the front of a car that are on as brightly as possible.
full board 1. *Br.* accommodations and meals at a hotel or guest house. 2. *Aus., NZ.* full complement of shearers.
full-court press *Am.* col. a big effort to achieve smth.
full-cream *Br.* (of milk) unskimmed.
full cry/ be in full cry *Br., Aus.* criticize sb. or smth. in a noisy and eager way.

full flow/ be in full flow/spate *Br., Aus.* happening fast and with energy.
full-fashioned *Am.* /*Br.* **fully-fashioned**/ (of a knitted garment) made to the shape of the body exactly.
full-fat *Br.* adj. milk and cheese that haven't had any of the fat taken out.
full fledged *Am., Can.* /*Br.* **fully-fledged**/ 1. (of a young bird, etc.) having grown all its feathers, and now able to fly: *It was by any standards a full-fledged ball* - C. Woolrich. 2. completely trained.
full-grown *Am.* /*Br.* **fully-grown**/ adj. fully grown animal.
full lock *Br.* adv. (of a steering wheel) turned as far as it is possible.
full marks *esp. Br.* complete credit, praise, approval.
the full money *esp. Br.* humor. complete as possible.
full of beans *Am.* sl. 1. full of nonsense: *Pay no attention to John. He's full of beans.* - R.A. Spears. 2. /chronically/ mistaken, wrong.
full point *Am.* /*Br., Aus.* **full stop**/ period.
full professor *esp. Am., Can.* person of the highest grade in a university, higher than associate professor or assistant professor.
full quid/ not be the full quid *Aus.* col. be slightly crazy or stupid.
full stop 1. *esp. Br.* (used at the end of a sentence to express completeness or firmness of direction). 2. *Am.* (of a car) the state of being completely stopped.
full stretch/ at full stretch, be fully stretched *Br.* (working) as hard as possible.
full-throttle *Am.* /*Br.* **(at) full tilt**/ working) with full force or very fast.
full time *Br.* the end of the normal period of playing time of a match.
full up *Br.* col. having eaten a good meal and being unable to eat anything anymore: *I was full up.* – S. Townsend.
fully-booked *Br.* all seats reserved
fully found *Br.* all expenses paid.
fully-grown *esp. Br.* full-grown.
fumble *Am.* drop a ball after catching it.
fume at *Am.* show one's angriness by saying a lot of things to sb.
fume hood *Am.* /*Br.* **fume cupboard**/ ventilated enclosure in a chemistry laboratory.
fun *esp. Am., Aus.* adj. providing pleasure, amusement or enjoyment, e.g. **fun person/ girl/guy**, etc.
fun/ like fun *Am.* col. used to say that smth. won't happen or isn't true.

fundholder *Br.* a general practitioner who is provided with and controls his or her own budget.

funds/ in funds *Br.* having money to spend.

funeral furnisher *Br.* /*esp. Am.* **funeral director,** *Br.* **undertaker**/ undertaker.

funeral home *esp. Am.* /also **mortuary, funeral parlor**/ funeral director's place of business: *Hazel passed a funeral home* - J. Steinbeck., *funeral parlors were usually fronts for gambling operations* - G. O'Neill, D. Lehr., *she won't have any trouble selling it for a funeral home.* - J. O'Hara.

funfair, fair *esp. Br., Aus.* /*Am., Aus.* **amusement park, carnival**/ a noisy brightly-lit outdoor show at which one can ride on machines, play games of skill for small prizes and enjoy other amusements, and that usu. moves from town to town: *fun fairs...should no longer be forbidden on Sunday.* - J. Ruppeldtova.

fun house *Am.* building in amusement park with various devices designed to startle or amuse: *Like a fun house at a fairground.* - Harper's Magazine.

funk 1. *esp. Br.* col. cowardice: *The dog waa in such a funk that it was crying.* - R.A. Spears. 2. *esp. Am., Can.* state of depression: *felines fall into funks out of sheer boredom* – Reader's Digest. 3. *esp. Br.* obs. avoid smth. out of fear. 4. *Am.* col. strong smell that comes from sb.'s body.

funk/ in a funk *esp. Am., Can., Aus.* unhappy and without hope: *By the way, I was in a funk this morning.* – P. Roth.

funk-hole *Br., Aus.* col. safe place in time of danger, refuge for coward.

funk money *Br.* hot money, stolen money.

funky *esp. Am., Aus.* col. 1. (of jazz) having a simple direct style and feeling: *I like to be around funky people.* - R.A. Spears. 2. attractive and fashionable: *We found an actual pacifist minister and a funky little church* - J. Baez. 3. *Am., Can.* strongly musty.

funnel *Br.* metal chimney for letting smoke out from a steam engine or steamship.

funnel cake *Am.* cake made of batter poured into hot fat or oil and deep-fried until crisp: *running around with face paint, funnel cakes, snow cones and bee stings.* – Reader's Digest.

funnel-web *Aus.* a large poisonous spider.

funnies *esp. Am., Can.* col. the amusement pages in the newspaper which contain jokes and funny stories in pictures: *reading the funnies while listening to the radio.* - A.E. Hotchner., adj. **funny.**

funnily enough *esp. Br., Aus.* /*Am.* **funny enough**/ strangely or unexpected: *Funnily enough, I smoke them because I like the taste.* - D. Lodge.

funniosity *Br.* humor. comical person or thing.

funny/ go funny 1. *Br.* col. (of a TV, etc.) not work properly. 2. *Br.* feel slightly ill (after smoking, etc.).

funny *Br.* 1. unfriendly or seeming to be offended. 2. slightly crazy.

funny farm (or **house**) *esp. Am., Aus.* derog. or humor. a mental hospital: *he gets caught and sent to the state funny farm* - New York.

funny (**money**) *Am., Can., Aus.* sl. worthless, counterfeit, or play money: *Race track is a good place to pass funny.* - G.V. Higgins., *Soviet citizens treat it as funny money.* - Time.

funny paper, funnies *Am., Can.* section of newspaper with cartoons and humorous stories.

funny peculiar or funny ha-ha? *Br.* used when sb. has described smth. as funny and the person wants to know if they mean it is strange or amusing.

funster *Am.* col. joker.

fur up 1. *Br.* (of veins and arteries) become blocked. 2. *esp. Br.* become covered with fur (substance that forms on the inside of water pipes or containers).

furlough/give furlough *Am.* order sb. to stay away from duty because not enough work is available; **be furloughed.**

furnace *Am.* an apparatus which provides heat for the room, boiler: *in the cellar the furnace expelled a single loud houf!* - K. Davis.

furniture store *Am.* /*Br.* **furniture shop**/.

furphy *Aus., NZ.* col. gossip or false story: *Who started that furphy anyway?* - R.A. Spears, **furphy king** is one who spreads gossip.

furrow/ plough a lone/lonely furrow, also **plow a particular furrow** or **plow** one's **own furrow** *esp. Br.* do smth. alone and without any help from other people.

furry *Am.* sl. hair-raising, horrible.

further (up, away, along, etc.) *esp. Br.* used to say that a place is a long way from or more distant than another place.

further education *esp. Br., Aus.* /*esp. Am., Aus.* **adult education, continuing education**/ education after leaving school, but not at a university: *further education done properly for nothing.* - C. Handy.

fuse *Br.* /*Am., Aus.* **blow a**/one's **fuse**/ stop working because the fuse melted (about electrical equipment).

fuse/ the fuse has gone *Br., Aus.* it has blown or broken.
fuse/ sb.'s temper is on a short fuse *Br.* sb. becomes angry very easily.
fused *Br.* adj. (of electric equipment) fitted with a fuse.
fusilier *Br.* a low-ranked British soldier in infantry.
fuss/ be not fussed (about) *Br.* col. not care at all.
fuss/ make a fuss of sb. *Br.* /*Am.* **make a fuss over** sb./ pay a lot of attention to smth.
fuss/ not to be fussed (about) *Br.* col. not to care greatly about smth.: *I'm not fussed about the colour; you choose.* - Longman.
fuss up *Am.* make too much effort to dress with care or make (smth.) more attractive: *Just to fuss things up a bit.* - J.P. Donleavy.
fussbudget *Am.* col. /*Br.* **fusspot**/ a person who is always dissatisfied.
fussy *esp. Br.* col. (of a person) concerned, caring (usu. in questions and negatives).
future / in future *Br., Aus.* /*Am.* **in the future**/
futz *esp. Am.* taboo. sl. 1. the vagina. 2. repulsive man: *I'm an old futz* - K. Vonnegut, Jr.
futz around *Am., Can.* col. waste time: *electronic sampling and old-school turntable-futzing.* - Nesweek.
fuzz *Am.* /*esp. Br.* **fluff**/ soft light loose waste from woollen or other materials: *the rolls of fuzz under the radiators* - J. Updike.
fuzz *Br.* obs. police.
fuzzy-wuzzy *Br.* col. derog. black person with tightly curled hair.
fwy *Am.* abbr. freeway.
FYI *Am., Can.* for your information.
fyke *esp. Am.* a long bag net kept open by hoops.

G

G 1. *esp. Am., Can., Aus.* col. /*Br., Aus.* col. **K**/ 1,000 dollars. 2. *Br.* guinea(s). 3. *Am.* /*Br.* **U**/ (of a film) approved for people of any age.
Gabby Islander *Can.* sl. Newfoundlander.
gabby *Am.* col. talkative: *Shaw is a gabby playwright* - R.L. Chapman.
gabfest *esp. Am., Can.* col. an informal get-together for prolonged conversation: *You're not into a daily gabfest* – Reader's Digest.
gaff *Br.* 1. (usu. **penny gaff**) cheap theatre or music-hall. 2. foolish talk. 3. col. person's house or flat.
gaff/ blow the gaff *Br., Aus.* col. let the secret become known.
gaff/ stand the gaff *Am.* col. endure bravely: *Our mayor had to resign because he couldn't stand the gaff.* - H.C. Whitford., R.J. Dixson.
gaffer *esp. Br., Aus.* col. a man in charge, esp. in a factory, boss: *If I were you I'd go and fetch the gaffer* - T. Thorne.
gag/ be gagging for it *Br.* sl. want smth. very much, esp. sex.
gag/ gag me with a spoon! *Am.* col. used esp. by older children to express a strong feeling of disgust.
gag (on) *esp. Am.* be unable to swallow and start to vomit, choke: *Don't eat so fast. You'll gag.* - R.A. Spears.
gage *Am.* sl. 1. liquor. 2. tobacco, cigarettes: *You got any gage on you?* - R.A. Spears.
gagging order *Br.* an official order forbidding public discussion of a specified subject, in print or by broadcasting.
gaggle *esp. Am.* col. group of persons or things, cluster, aggregation: *the occasional gaggle of well-informed Euro-tourists.* - New York.
gagster *Am.* 1. col. humorist. 2. inventor of gags.
gait *Am.* pace, a manner of rate of movement.
gal *esp. Am., Can.* 1. (used esp. in writing to suggest an American or upper class obs. pronunciation). 2. col. woman working as a secretary or assistant in the office.
gala *esp. Br.* a sports meeting, esp. a swimming competition.
Galagher/ Let her go, Galagher *Aus.* Go at full speed forward.
galah, dill, droob, drongo, nong *Aus.* sl. fool: *I feel like a right galah* - T. Thorne.
galch *Aus.* 1. bright cockatoo. 2. a stupid man.
gale *Br.* rare. a periodical payment of rent, interest, etc.
gale/ it's blowing a gale *Br.* it's very windy.
gall *Br.* gallon.
gallah/ as mad as a gumtree full of gallahs *Aus.* very stupid.
galley-west *Am.* sl. confused: *The whole place was galley-west when we got there* - R.L. Chapman.
gallop *Br.* a track where horses are exercised at a gallop.
gallusses *Am.* col /*esp. Br.* **braces**, *Am.* **suspenders**/: *He stepped into his overalls, put one arm through a gallus and reached into his pocket* - E. Caldwell.
galoot *Am., Can.* sl. joc. an awkward unfashionable person: *So she told the big galoot to get lost* - R.L. Chapman.

galosh *Br., Can.* /*Am.* (**toe**) **rubber**/ high overshoe worn esp. in snow and slush.

galumphing *Br.* col. behaving in an awkward or graceless manner.

gam 1. *Br., Aus.* sl. an act of oral sex. 2. *Aus.* sl. sanitary towel or napkin.

gambrel (**roof**) *Am.* mansard roof.

game *esp. Am., Aus.* /*esp. Br.* **match**/ a form of play or sport, esp. an example of this.

game/ game over *esp. Am., Can.* col. situation is hopeless.

game/ Is the game worth the candle? *Br.* Is it really worth the effort?

game/ not play the game *esp. Br.* obs. not behave properly.

game/ on the game 1. *esp. Br.* col. working as a prostitute. 2. *Am.* involved in illegal activities.

game/ What's your game? *Br.* col. What's your secret plan?

game plan *Am., Aus.* a plan of action, strategy: *The best the FBI could do with it was devise a careful game plan* - G. O'Neill, D. Lehr.

games *Br.* (the playing of) team games and other forms of physical exercises out of doors at school; **games master** is a teacher who directs the games: *she was Head Girl and Captain of Games* - D. Lodge.

game show *Am.* quiz show.

gammon *esp. Br.* 1. /*Am., Aus.* **ham**/ the meat preserved by salt or smoke from the back part and leg of a pig. 2. col. obs. nonsense.

gammy/ also obs. **game** *esp. Br.* col. (esp. of a human leg or knee) damaged or painful, esp. in such a way that one cannot walk properly or comfortably.

gamp *Br.* obs. col. and humor. an umbrella, esp. a large one: *They will laugh at me carrying the ridiculous gamp.* - J. Fowles.

gander *Am.* col. grass widow.

gandy dancer *Am.* sl. 1. a railroad section hand or track labourer: *gandy dancers with greasy black hair I waved and smiled* - J. Kerouac. 2. railroad truck

gang *Br.* print. artworks mounted so that they can be reproduced together in proportion.

gang bang *esp. Am., Can.* sl. 1. take part in the activities of a street gang: *They've mostly been booking gangbangers and stuckup geeks.* - R. Crais. 2. act of violence of a criminal gang.

gangbusters *Am., Can.* col. a great and conspicuous success, esp. in the phr. (**come on**) **like gangbusters**: *She came like gangbusters.* - Esquire., *My DC show is going like gangbusters.* - W. Jack, B. Laursen., *bistros and brasseries are going gangbusters.* - Nation's Restaurant News.

gangsta *Am.* black sl. a gang member.

gangway *Br.* a clear space between two rows of seats in a cinema, theatre, bus or train, aisle: *down the gangway towards the vacant seat.* - A. Huxley., *the wind sighing through the gangways carried on it the echoes of a billion boos.* - I. Shaw., *the girl moved to the gangway* - A. Christie.

ganger *Br.* the foreman of a group of workers, esp. building workers /**a gang of navvies** *Br.* construction gang/: *there was a crowd of men with a ganger all working there* - F. O'Brien.

gannet *Br.* col. person who eats greedily: *keep that stuff away from those gannets.* - T. Thorne.

gaol *Br., Aus.* obs. jail.

garage 1. *Br.* (also **car dealer/showroom**) a place where you can buy a car. 2. *Br., Aus.* /*Am.* **gas station**/ petrol station.

garage *Br.* /*Am.* **storage garage**/ shelter or repair shop for motor vehicles., **garage a car** *Br.* /*Am.* **put a car in a storage garage**/.

garage sale *esp. Am., Can.* sale of unwanted things in the garage or front garden of sb.'s house: *I sold my house and my car, had a big garage sale* – Reader's Digest.

garbage *esp. Am., Aus.* /*esp. Br.* **rubbish, refuse**/ waste material, e.g. from a house or office to be thrown away, refuse: *I saw people living on garbage dumps* - P. Robertson.

garbage can /also **trashcan, ashcan**/ *Am., Can., Aus.* /*Br.* **dustbin**/ a container for refuse.

garbage bag *Am., Aus.* /*Br.* **dust bin bag/liner**/.

garbage can cover *Am.* /*Br.* **dust bin lid**/.

garbage collector, carrier, (sanitation) man *Am., Aus.* /*Br.* **dustman**/ person collecting refuse: *I saw the cage perched on a sidewalk ashcan waiting for the garbage collector.* - T. Capote.

garbage container *Am.* refuse container.

garbage disposal *Am.* /*Br.* **waste disposal unit**/.

garbage dump *Am.* /*Br.* **refuse tip**/.

garbage truck, wagon *Am., Aus.* /*Br.* **dustbin lorry, dustcart**/ refuse collection vehicle, esp. one equipped with a hopper for refuse.

garbo *Aus.* col. garbage man.

garbology *Am.* the scientific study of waste disposal.

garden 1. *Br.* piece of ground around or next to a house with usually a lawn and area for flowers, plants or vegetables. 2. *Am.* the part of a garden which has flowers or plants in it.

garden centre *Br.* place that sells plants, flowers and equipment for gardens or place where plants and trees are grown and sold.

garden chair *Br.* /*Am.* **lawn chair**/ a light folding chair used for sitting outdoors: *A rickety table of much scored oak was James's desk with two canvass garden chairs, one on each side.* - I. Murdoch.

garden city *esp. Br.* a town or part of it (**garden suburb**), planned and built to have grass, trees, and open spaces, rather than factories and signs of industry.

garden flat *Br.* /*Am.* **garden apartment**/ a flat in a basement or on the ground floor which has a garden.

gardening leave *Br.* euph. suspension from work on full pay which is given in an effort to try to prevent employee seeking employment elsewhere.

The Garden of the West *Am.* Illinois and Kansas.

garden party *Br.* /*Am.* **lawn party**/ party held in a large garden of sb.'s house.

garden produce *Br.* /*Am.* **garden truck**/ vegetables and fruit for selling.

garden roller *Br.* /*Am.* **lawn roller**/ tube-shaped piece of metal used for smoothing the surface of grass.

The Garden State *Am.* 1. New Jersey: *New Jersey had first pick, the Garden Stater quickly retorted.* - Reader's Digest. 2. Kansas.

garden suburb *Br.* one set in rural surroundings.

garden-variety *Am., Can., Aus.* /*Br.* **common-or-garden**/ very ordinary.

gargle *Br., Am.* sl. alcoholic drink: *I'll have some gargle, if you don't mind, sir.* - T. Thorne.

garibaldi *Br.* col. currant cookie.

garment bag *Am.* /*Br.* **suit bag**/ one for carrying suits.

garn *Br.* sl. go on. (excl. of surprise): *Garn, yer onny loves me fer me body.* - T. Murphy.

garnish *Br.* sl. beer or the like bought by a new workman for his fellow workers.

garrison cap *Am.* peakless cap, often won by military people.

garrison finish *Am.* col. unexpected or spectacular finish.

garrison house *Am.* strongly built log house with a projecting upper storey.

garter *Am., Can.* /*Br., Aus.* **suspender**/: *The girl put down her suitcase, pulled her stockings up under her garters* – E. Caldwell.

garter belt *Am., Can.* /*Br., Aus.* **suspender belt**/.

garter snake *Am.* common harmless snake with three stripes along the bottom: *It's only a garter snake.* – R.L. Stine.

garth *Br.* open place surrounded by cloisters.

gas 1. *Am., Can.* /*Br., Aus.* **petrol**/ fuel used for the engines of cars, aircraft, etc. 2. *esp. Am., Can.* col. /*esp. Br.* **wind**/ (the condition of having) air or gas in the stomach. 3. *esp. Am.* col. smth. funny, entertaining or enjoyable: *Actual transit of the Canal is a gas.* - R. Palley. 4. *esp. Br.* derog. col. unimportant talk.

gas 1. *Am., Can.* col. supply with gasoline. 2. *esp. Br.* chat, talk aimlessly for a long time: *I have been gassing too much.* - E. Hemingway.

gas/ run out of gas *Am., Can.* lose momentum.

gas/ step on the gas *esp. Am., Can.* make a car move faster by pressing the accelerator.

gas up *Am.* col. supply a vehicle with a full load of petrol: *Police officers who wanted their cars to run gassed up and made repairs themselves.* - Time.

gasateria *Am.* col. self-service filling station.

gas fire *Br.* /*Am.* **gas heater**/ a heater using gas as a fuel.

gas-fired *esp. Br.* using gas as fuel.

gas-guzzler *esp. Am., Can., Aus.* sl. large automobile that uses much gasoline: *Americans like their gas-guzzlers* - Voice of America.

gash *Br.* sl. 1. adj. superfluous, extra, worthless: *There's nothing in there but a pile of gash tapes.* - T. Thorne. 2. n. spare parts or leftovers which can serve as spares.

gas mains *Br.* main gas supply tubes.

gasman 1. *Am.* person who examines the mine for fire damp. 2. *Br.* col. one whose job is reading gas meters and repairing gas equipment.

gas mark *Br.* a position of a cooker's gas regulator marked by a number.

gasohol *Am.* petrol with alcohol.

gasoline /col. **gas**/ *Am.* /*Br.* **petrol**/: *my gasoline gauge was rapidly approaching the empty mark.* - Reader's Digest; **gasoline can, motor, pump, hose**: *the franchise on two Socony gas pumps* - J. Cheever.

gasoline inlet *Am.* fuel inlet.

gasoline tank /col. **gas tank**/ *Am.* /*Br.* **petrol tank**/ fuel tank.

gas pedal *Am.* /*Br.* **accelerator**/: *Your foot hits the gas pedal* - R.J. Randisi., M. Wallace.

gasper *esp. Br.* obs. cheap cigarette.

gasping *Br.* col. (for) very thirsty.

gas ring, (elecrtric) ring *Br.* /*Am.* **burner**/ one of a number of gas (electric) burners in a cooker.

gasser *Am.* sl. 1. smth. outstanding: *Remember old Jack Scott dragging out golden gassers like "My true love" and "Leroy"?* - J. Gabree. 2. smth. depressing: *We planned a blast, and got a gasser.* - R.L. Chapman.

gas station *Am., Can. /Br.* **petrol station, garage/**.
gassy *Br.* (of a drink) with too much of gas.
gat *Am.* sl. revolver: *Richard Conte would've pulled a big gat out of his inside pocket and blasted him full of holes* - D. Brenner.
gate *Br.* a. the number of people who go in to see a sports event, esp. a football match: *Now I was counting the gate in hundreds* - W. Grady. b. the money paid by these people: *strange percentage of the gate after expenses* - W. Grady.
gate 1. *esp. Br. /Am.* **campus/** punish (a student) by confining him to the grounds of a college. 2. *Am., Can.* dismissal / **get, give the gate:** *what a celesstial lulu he had given the gate to.* – K. Vonnegut, Jr.
gateau *Br.* a large cake often filled with cream and fruit: *offer them something genuinely tempting - a slice of gateau* - B. Bryson.
gated community *Am.* area of shops, houses, etc. with a fence or wall around it and an entrance that is guarded.
gateman *Am.* railway crossing keeper
gateman's box *Am.* railway crossing keeper's box.
gatepost/ between you/me and the gatepost *Br.* col. let it be a secret between us.
Gateway of the USA *Am.* New York City.
Gateway of the West *Am.* Saint Louis.
Gateway to the South *Am.* Atlanta.
Gateway to the West *Am.* 1. Ohio. 2. obs. Missouri.
gator *Am.* col. alligator: *the men in their stngy-brim hats and them gators on their feet* – E.James, D. Ritz.
gaudy (**day** or **night**) *esp. Br.* students festival or dinner held for old members.
gauger *esp. Br.* a revenue officer who inspects bulk goods subject to duty.
gauze (bandage) *Am. /Br.* **bandage/**: *One of them applied a gauze dressing.* - B. Tillman.
gawp (at) *Br.* col. look at smth. in a foolish way, esp. with a mouth open.
gayola *Am.* sl. secret payments by gays and students' clubs to operate without interference: *Homosexual bars...pay "gayola" to crime syndicates and to law enforcement agencies* - R.L. Chapman.
gazette 1. *Br.* official newspaper, esp. one from the government giving a list of important people who have been employed by them. 2. *Am.* newspaper.
gazillion *Am., Can.* col. a very large number.
gazump *esp. Br., Aus.* col. (of the owner of the house) refuse to sell a house to (sb.) who think they have bought it and sell it instead to sb. who has offered more money.
gazundering *Br.* col. unfair practice of demanding a reduction in the prize for a house you've already agreed to pay just before you buy it.
gazwelcher *Br.* person who undertakes to buy a house but withdraws from the transaction just before contracts are to be signed.
GBH *Br.* grievous bodily harm.
g'day *Aus., NZ.* excl. col. Good day (used when meeting sb. in the morning or afternoon).
gear *esp. Br.* sl. (fashionable) clothes: *Cavern Club slang like "gear", "fab" and "endsville".* -P. Norman., *lovely gear that doesn't show its age.* - Sydney Calendar.
gear *Br.* sl. excellent: *The opposite of "gear" is "grotty"* - Village Voice, R.L. Chapman.
gear/ bottom gear *Br. /Am.* **low** or **first gear/** one that is used to start a car; *Br.* **top gear** is **high gear** in America: *This was the guy who kicked Clint Eastwood's career into high gear* - W. Jack, B. Laursen., *the Soviet Union put their hopes for reform into high gear.* - P. Robertson.
gear/ in top gear *Br. /Am.* **in high gear/** doing smth. successfully and with a lot of energy.
gear stick, gear change, gear lever *Br., Aus. /esp. Am., Can.* **gear shift, shift stick, stick shift/** gear lever in a car or other vehicle: *she leaned across the gearshift and kissed him.* - R.L. Stine.; on bicycles Americans use **shifter** and British use **gear lever.**
GED *Am., Can.* General Educational Development, certificate attesting that the person has passed the exams equivalent to completion of high school.
geddit *Br.* col. interjection (used facetiously or ironically for drawing attention to a pun, innuendo, etc.
ge(e)dunk *Am.* sl. ice cream: *Let's go out and get some gedunk for dessert.* - R.A. Spears.
gee 1. also obs. **gee whiz** *esp. Am., Aus., Can.* col. excl. (an expression of surprise): *Gee! An American voice remarked. It's a regular cat-fight.* - A. Huxley., *Gee, that's keen.,* - Time., *Gee, but's it's a stemwinder.* - J. London. 2. *Br., Aus.* also col. **gee-gee** (used esp. by or to children or in horse-racing slang) a horse: *In "baby-talk", horses are often called "gee-gees"* - R. Carter., M. McCarthy.
gee up *Br., Aus.* 1. col. encourage forcefully into greater activity or effort. 2. (used as command to a horse) Go faster!

geek 1. *esp. Am., Can., Aus.* col. freak, insane or disgusting person; boring person wearing unfashionable clothes: *"fingering" is geek-speak for requesting all available information about another user* - New York., *himself referred to in a courtroom as a "nerd, a geek, a peckerwood and a cracker".* - Time. 2. *Aus.* col. a look.
gelatin paper *Br.* special paper for photographic use.
gelignite *esp. Br.* explosive substance
gem *Am.* muffin.
gem fish *Aus.* a type of sea fish or its flesh eaten as food.
The Gem State *Am.* Idaho.
gen (on) *Br., Aus.* col. the correct or complete information.
gen up(on) *Br., Aus.* col. (cause to) learn the facts thoroughly: *Michael is all genned up about computers.* - Longman, **de-gen** *Br.* extract information, **genned-up** *Br.* well-informed.
general delivery *Am., Can. /Br.* **poste restante/** post office department to which letters for a traveller can be sent and where they will be kept until the person collects them: *the return addres reading: B. Jones. General Delivery.* – M. Daly.
General Election Day *Am.* Election Day, first Tuesday in November.
general factotum *Br.* person who does general duties around the house.
general manager *esp. Am.* managing director.
general post *Br.* the first mail delivery in the morning.
general practitioner (GP) *esp. Br., Aus.* doctor who is trained in general medicine and whose work (**general practice**) is to treat people in a certain local area: *How many other general practitioners lived such a glamorous lifestyle?* – J. Hopkins.
general (servant) *Br. /Am.* **general housework maid/** maid of all work.
general store *Am.* shop selling a wide variety of goods, esp. in a small town.
generator *Am.* steam boiler.
generic *esp. Am., Aus.* not offering legal protection because of not having a trademark; n., e.g. **generic drug**: *Generics may work as well as brand names.* – Reader's Digest.
generic *Aus.* an item sold under the name of a particular group of shops, rather than under a well-known product name, and which is therefore cheaper.
genie/ let the genie out of the bottle *esp. Am.* allow smth. bad to happen; opp. **put the genie back in the bottle**.

gent *esp. Br.* col. or humor. a gentleman.
gentile *Am.* non-Mormon.
gentleman farmer *Br.* a man of high social class who has a farm for pleasure rather than for profit.
gentleman ranker *Br.* col. enlisted man of aristocratic birth or background.
gently/ take it gently, Gently! *Br. /Am., Aus.* **take it easy/** go slow and carefully.
gently/ gently does it *Br. /Am., Aus.* **easy does it/** be slow and careful.
gentry *esp. Br.* people of high social class.
gents *Br. /Am.* **men's room/** a public toilet for men: *He could have gone to the gents* - C.M. Fraser., *he asked for the gents.* - J. Fowles., - *reading the walls in the Gents.* - D. Francis.
geography of the house *Br.* location of the toilet.
Geordie *Br.* a person or language of Tyneside in NE England or their dialect.
German shepherd *esp. Am. /esp. Br.* **Alsatian/** large dog often used by police or to guard property: *They're as big as German shepherds* - New York., *a police-type dog - either a German shepherd or a Doberman* - Reader's Digest.
gesundheit excl. *esp. Am.* col. word spoken to sb. after they have sneezed.
get, git *Br.* sl. unpleasant person.
get *Am.* col. deal with or answer (a telephone, knock on the door, etc.) or to pay for (an expense).
get/ get a first place *Br.* take a first place.
get about *Br.* 1. be able to travel to different places. 2. (of news and information) be told to a lot of people. 3. (of people) have sex with a lot of different people.
get above oneself *Br.* think that one is better or more important than they are.
get across *esp. Br.* col. annoy (sb.), get (sb.) riled up: *Take care not to get across the director, he could have you dismissed.* - Longman.
get along 1. *esp. Br.* manage to deal with a situation successfully. 2. *esp. Am., Can.* go on doing smth. after interruption.
get along (with you) *Br.* col. expression of scepticism or disbelief.
get anyplace *Am.* 1. (cause) to reach some place. 2. col. (cause) to gain or reach some result or success.
get around *Am.* col. visit many places: *It's difficult for him to get around without a cane.* - H.C. Whitford., R.J. Dixson.
get at 1. *Br.* reach and discover: *This book is very hard to get at.* - A. Makkai. 2. *esp. Br.* col. (try) to bribe. 3. *Br., Aus. /Am.* **get on/** criticize.

Get away! *Br.* col. expression of surprise or disbelief.

get back *esp. Br.* be in power again: *Will the Labour Party get back at the next election?* - Longman.

get one's **own back on** sb., **get back on** *esp. Br.* revenge sb.: *I'd like to get my own back on the man who attacked my daughter.* - Longman.

get behind *Am.* 1. back, support: *If we all get behind Campbell we can easily elect him to that office.* - H.C. Whitford., R.J. Dixson. 2. inspect carefully: *The police are questioning many people to try and get behind the bank robbery.* - A. Makkai.

get beyond endurance *esp. Br.* become insufferable: *Your rudeness has got beyond endurance - kindly leave my house!* - Longman.

get down 1. *esp. Br.* (of children) to leave the table after a meal: *Please may I get down?* - Longman. 2. *Am.* sl. make an effort, get serious: *Why don't you get down with us, Bobby?* - T. Thompson. 3. *Am., Can.* dance energetically.

get down on (sb.) *Am.* col. develop a dislike or grudge against (sb.): *Don't get down on me. I didn't do that.* - R.A. Spears.

get down to brass tacks *Br., Can.* col. /*Am.* col. **get (right) down to it**/ talk about facts or practical matters: *let's get down to brass tacks and see if the plan will really work.* - Longman.

get (smth.) **in,** esp. **get the drinks in** *Br.* col. buy (a set of drinks) for all the people one is with in a bar.

get in bad with *esp. Am.* col. offend, make an enemy of, earn the dislike or disapproval of: *We got in bad with each other from the start.* - R.A. Spears.

get off *Am.* col. 1. make (a joke): *I got a good one off today!* - Longman. 2. publish. 3. get high on drugs: *He gets off on loud music, but I don't.* - Longman.

get sb. **off** *esp. Am.* help (sb.) to experience pleasure, esp. to have an orgasm.

get off/ tell sb. **where to get off** (or **where they can get off**) *esp. Br.* col. tell sb. how to behave, or esp. tell sb. not to misbehave: *I finally told her where to get off.* - R.A. Spears.

get off/ where does sb. **get off** (**doing** smth.) *Am.* col. used when sb. is angry by the other person's unfair action or insult.

get off with sb. *esp. Br., Aus.* col. start a (sexual) relationship with.

get on *esp. Br.* 1. succeed in smth. 2. have a friendly relationship with sb, often in **get on like a house on fire**.

get on for smth. *esp. Br.* /*Am., Aus.* **going on**/ (in progressive forms) to be almost reaching in time, age, number or distance, be nearly: *it was four o'clock and getting on for dark* - B. Bryson.

get on to *esp. Br.* get in touch with sb. about smth.

get onto *Am.* 1. succeed in understanding (usu. smth.): *The children didn't quite get onto what the teacher was saying.* - Longman. 2. start criticising severely.

get smth. **out** *Br.* succeed in solving a problem.

get out of here! *esp. Am., Can.* col. Go away! I don't believe you!

Get out of it *Br.* sl. Come on! Stop your kidding.

get outside of *Br.* col. eat and drink heartily.

get round *Br.* (of news, etc.) to spread, circulate.

get round *Br.* 1. persuade (sb.) to allow to do smth. by charming them. 2. find a way of dealing with a problem.

get through *esp. Br.* use up a lot of smth.

get through with *esp. Am.* finish.

get to *Am.* col. attempt to influence (sb.) wrongly as by paying money or performing favours so as to persuade him/her to do or not to do smth.: *The prisoners escaped after getting the guards to leave the gate open.* - Longman.

get up *Br.* 1. (of wind, fire, etc.) to start and increase. 2. obs. study or gain knowledge of.

get up/ What time do you want getting up? *Br.* col. What time do you want me to wake you?

Get up and dig *Aus.* Get down to business.

get sb. **up as** *Br.* dress sb. as sb. else.

get up one's **nose,** also **get on** one's **wick, tits** *Br.* sl. annoy, meddle.

get up to *Br.* col. be involved in smth. illicit or surprising.

get/ How did you get this way? *Am.* How could it happen to me?

get/ get bushed *Aus.* get lost.

get/ get craking, get weaving *esp. Br.* col. a. start working hard at smth. b. go or to leave, esp. quickly.

get one's **end away,** also **get** one's **legs over/ across** /*Aus.* **get** one's **end in**/ *Br.* sl. copulate.

get/ get hip *Am.* col. become knowledgeable about (a subject).

get/ get hot *Am.* col. (esp. of musician) perform in an excited lively manner.

get/ get it going on *Am.* sl. be very attractive.

get/ get it on *esp. Am., Can.* col. have sex.

get/ get it in one *Br.* col. guess right.

get/ get it together *Br.* col. /*esp. Am.* col. **get** one's **shit together**/ do smth. well, get oneself organised: *get your shit together and let's go.* - Longman., *"Getting your shit together," his suddenly contemporary-as-hell father had written in a long letter* - J. Patterson.

get/have one's **knickers in a twist** *Br.* col. /*Am.* col. **get** one's **panties in a bunch**/ become agitated.

get/ get knotted *Br.* sl. stop bugging me.

get/ get no place *Am.* 1. (cause) to reach no place. 2. col. (cause) to gain no result or success.

get/ get one's **bowler** *Br.* be demobilised.

get/ get one's **cards** *Br.* be dismissed from work.

get/ get one's **colours** *Br.* become a member of a team in sport.

get/ get one's **eye in** *Br.* familiarise oneself with, settle down.

get/ get one's **head down** *Br.* lie down to sleep.

get/ get one's **own back on, get back on** *Br.* col. be revenged (on).

get one's **oats** *Br.* sl. achieve sexual satisfaction: *If he plays his cards right, he should end up getting his oats tonight.* - T. Thorne.

get/ get religion *Am.* sl. be converted (into some religion): *When Dorothy got religion, she went first class* - T. Murphy.

get the hump *Br.* sl. become bad-tempered.

get there in the end *Br.* achieve smth. in spite of the difficulties.

get/ get the sack *Br.* /also **get the bird**/ be dismissed.

get/ get to the first base (with) *esp. Am., Can.* col. make a start on smth.: *He was hoping for a kiss, but he didn't get to first base.* - W. Magnuson.

get the wind up *esp. Br.* get frightened: *Don't get the wind up, it's only me.* - Longman.

get yours *Br.* get what you deserve for smth. bad that you have done.

get-go/ from the get-go *Am.* col. from the very beginning: *He was a character from the get-go.* – S. Lawrence.

get-out 1. *Am.* col. way-out. 2. *Br.* an excuse.

get-rich-quick *Am.* col. wanting to become rich quick, **get-rich-quick scheme**.

getter *Am.* a device for killing destructive animals.

geyser *Br.* /*Am.* **hot water tank, heater**, *esp. Br.* **immersion heater (tank)**/ apparatus which is used in kitchens, bathrooms, etc. for heating water by gas.

gherkin *esp. Br.* small green cucumber pickled in vinegar.

ghoulies *Br.* col. testicles.

ghost/ lay the ghost of *Br.* finally deal with a problem of the past.

ghost station *Br.* unused or unstaffed gas station.

giant killer *esp. Br.* person, sports team, etc. that defeats a much stronger opponent: *Let's have a spot of a giant killer.* - E. Hemingway.

gibber *Aus.* a stone or boulder in a plain.

gibbering *Br.* speaking so quickly that it's hard to understand (of a person being frightened, shocked or excited).

gibber plain *Aus.* stony plain.

Gibson girl *Am.* obs. the idealised girl (created in the 1890s by the illustrator G.D. Gibson): *She was waiting for him at the ferry looking like a Gibson girl.* - J. Dos Passos

giddy *Br.* obs. col. or *Am.* col. not serious, too interested in amusement, frivolous.

gift 1. *esp. Br.* v. n. present. 2. *Br.* col. smth. obtained easily or cheaply.

gift/ in someone's **gift** *Br.* in sb.'s power to give smth. to whoever they want.

gift/ Indian gift *Am.* gift given so that one expects an equivalent gift in return.

gift/ the gift of the gab *Br., Aus.* /*Am.* **the gift of gab**/ ability to speak easily and carefully.

gift tax *Am.* tax levied on the value of a gift and assessed to the gift's donor: *There may be gift taxes due on assets assigned to a trust for the benefit of others.* - L. Burkett.

gift token *Br.* /*Am., Can.* **gift certificate**/ a token that can be exchanged for a book, record, etc., given to sb. as a present.

gig *Am.* long light ship's boat propelled by oars, sail or motor.

giggle *esp. Br., Aus.* col. smth. that amuses, prank.

gig-lamps *Br.* col. joc. spectacles, specs.

gill *Br.* a liquid measure equal to one quarter of a pint.

gill *Br.* 1. ravine. 2. narrow stream or rivulet.

gill/ full (stewed, soused) to the gills *Am.* sl. very drunk.

gild the lily *esp. Br.* try to improve smth. that is already good enough, so spoiling the effect: *I hoped I wasn't gilding the lily.* - R.J. Randisi., M. Wallace.

gilt *esp. Am.* a young female pig.

gilt/ take the gilt off the gingerbread *Br.* col. take away the part that makes the whole attractive.

gilts *Br.* gilt-edged securities, government bonds for a fixed period of time at a fixed rate of interest; adj. **gilt-edged**.

gimlet *Am.* /*Br.* **gin and lime**/ cocktail made of gin and lime juice.

gimme cap *Am., Can.* col. baseball cap with a slogan.
gin 1. *esp. Am.* col. gin rummy, a card game. 2. also **lubra** *Aus.* derog. sl. female aborigene.
gin and dry martini /also **gin and it, gin and French**/ *Br.* /*Am.* **dry martini**/ a small drink, esp. of gin and Italian (dry) vermouth: *he'll always be there waiting for you with a gin and martini.* - I. Murdoch.
gin and Jag(uar) belt *Br.* expensive suburb.
ginger *Br.* /*Aus., Br.* **dry ginger**/ ginger ale.
ginger *Br.* bright orange-brown (of hair or fur).
ginger/ By ginger! *Am.* God damn!
ginger smth. **up** *Br.* make smth. more exciting.
ginger group *esp. Br., Aus.* active group, usu. within a political party, who try to urge leaders of the party to take stronger actions on a particular matter.
ginger nut/biscuit *esp. Br., Aus.* /*esp. Am.* **(ginger) snap**/ a hard biscuit with ginger in it: *Bob was eating ginger snaps.* - A. Scaduto.
ginger wine *Br.* one of green Jamaica ginger and sweet wines.
gin/ floating gin palace *Br.* derog. a large expensive privately owned boat.
gink *esp. Am., Can.* col. a fool.
gin-mill /**gin dive, gin palace**/ *Am.* sl. a saloon or tavern: *I been sitting in a gin mill all night* - R. Moore., *Babe went away after wrecking the gin mill* - D. Hammet.
ginormous *Br., Aus.* col. humor. very large.
ginzo *Am.* taboo. sl. 1. an Italian or person of Italian descent. 2. an apparently foreign person: *Everybody's gonna have at least eight hot ginzos out looking for me.* - G.V. Higgins.
gippy tummy *esp. Br.* col. diarrhoea.
gipsy *esp. Br.* gypsy.
girasol *Am.* Jerusalem artichoke.
girlfriend *esp. Am.* woman's female friend with whom she spends time and shares amusement.
(girl) guide, guide *Br., Can.* /*Am.* **girl scout**/ a member of an association for training girls in character and self-help.
giro *Br.* 1. also **giro cheque** one given by the government to the unemployed or ill person. 2. a system of directly transferring money from one's person bank account into another person's account.
git, get *Br.* col. /also *esp. Am.* sl. **jerk**, *esp. Br.* col. **twit,** *Br.* sl. **muggins, Juggins, jobbernowl**/ worthless person: *I hate to agree with that tedious git* - B. Bryson.
gite *Br.* a holiday house for renting in France.

give *Br.* (usu. pass.) (in certain games) to declare (a player) to be in the stated position.
Give a dog a bad name *Br.* British saying which means that it's difficult to change people's opinions of a person who has been considered bad in the past.
give/give smth. **a go** *Br.* try smth.
give/ give sb. **an inch and he/she will take a yard** *Br.* if one let sb. do one small thing that you don't like, they will try to do a lot more.
give/ give a party *esp. Br.* throw a party.
give sb. **a ride** *Am.* /*Br.* **give** sb. **a lift**/.
give sb. **a ring/bell** *Br.* telephone sb.
not give a toss *Br.* not care at all.
give smth. **away** *Aus., NZ.* stop doing smth.
give smth. **in** *Br.* /*Am.* **hand in**/ give an official paper or a piece of work to sb.
give of one's **best** *Br.* give smth. in a generous way.
give sb. **one** *Br.* sl. have sex.
give on/onto smth. *Br.* have a view of, or lead straight to.
give smth. **out** 1. *Br.* announce smth., esp. officially. 2. *esp. Am.* to end.
give smth. **out/offside,** etc. *Br.* decide that a player or a ball is playing against the rule.
give over (smth.) *Br.* col. stop (doing smth.): *You give over, young man.* - V. Holt.
give oneself **airs** *Br.* put on airs, behave as if they are more important than others.
give sb. **the (old) heave-ho** *Am.* col. dismiss sb. from work: *he could give them the heave-ho* – P. Roth.
Give way *Br.* /*Am.* **Yield**/ (Road sign).
give sb. **what for** *esp. Br.* col. punish sb.
give/ I give you the chairman/prime minister/ groom, etc. *Br.* col. used at the end of speech to invite people to cheer or applaud a special guest.
give-and-take *Am.* a discussion.
give-back 1. *Am., Can.* agreement by workers to surrender benefits in return for new concessions. 2. *Am.* amount of money or goods that a person receives from some companies if they buy a product from them.
given name *esp. Am.* first name: *But we have no given names like Tom and Bob.* - J.A. Michener., *C.J. Calloway was a big rawboned Texan without a given name.* - B. Tillman.
glace icing *Br.* type of icing used to decorate cakes.
glade *Am.* boggy lot.
glad eye *Br.* obs. or *Aus.* sl. a look of sexual invitation, esp. in **give** sb. **the glad eye**: *She gave*

me the glad eye and I wondered what she had been up to now. - R.L. Chapman.

glad hand *Br.* obs. or *Aus.* col. a warm welcome or greetings, esp. one made in order to gain personal advantage: *He didn't glad-hand or work the room.* - D. Mortman.

glad rags *esp. Br., Can., Aus.* col. (one's) finest or best clothes: *The glad rags were in the bag under his feet* - S. Bellow.

glam *esp. Br.* col. glamorous.

glam up *esp. Br.* col. dress (oneself) attractively (e.g. wear a make-up, etc.).

glamor stock *Am.* shares of stock having especial public appeal.

glandular fever *Br.* /*Am.* **mono(nucleosis)**/ infectious illness that makes you feel weak and tired for a long time afterwards.

glare *Am., Can.* (of ice) smooth, translucent and slipping, also n.

glass 1. *esp. Br.* col. looking glass. 2. *Br.* the measurement shown on a barometer. 3. *Br.* col. hit a person with a beer bottle.

glass/ straight glass *Br.* a glass with no handle.

glass cloth *Br.* special cloth used for smoothing or polishing smth.

glass fibre *Br.* fibreglass.

glasshouse *esp. Br.* 1. /*Am., Aus.* **green house**/ a building used for growing plants, greenhouse. 2. sl. military prison.

glass paper *Br.* sandpaper.

glass wool *Br.* fibreglass.

glaze *Am.* fancy coating of ice formed by rain that freezes on the ground, etc.

glebe *Br.* tech. the land held by a priest to provide part of his income.

glee club *Am.* group of people who sing together for enjoyment.

glider *Am.* porch seat suspended from an upright framework by short chains or straps: *I went over and made her move over on the glider.* - J.D. Salinger., *My mother and father were sitting on the glider on the front porch.* - D. Brenner.

glister/ all that glisters is not gold British proverb.

glitch *Am., Can., Aus.* col. 1. a small fault in the operation of smth: *There was only glitch when a single engine propeller plane took off from a small airstrip* - Reader's Digest., *then there was a glitch.* - Vanity Fair., *production glitches are worked out.* - Time. 2. a false electronic signal caused by a sudden increase in electric power: *There was, it seemed, a glitch in the video game.* - Rolling Stone.

glitter over *Can.* (cause to) become covered with ice after freezing rain: *I'd like to get home before the roads glitter over.* - Longman.

globe *Aus.* a light globe.

glogg *Am.* hot drink made with red wine and spices.

glom (onto) *Am., Can.* col. 1. steal, esp. an idea, plan, etc. 2. obtain (smth): *glomming a day's pay without putting in a day's work?* - J. O'Brien, A. Kurins., *selfishly glomming on to all the free stuff that was offered.* - W. Jack, B. Laursen.

glop /also **goop**/ *Am.* sl. an unappetising food: *Glops of hardened food on the stove and mysterious sticky goop in the middle of the floor.* - Reader's Digest.

glory box *Aus., NZ.* /*Br.* **bottom drawer**, *Am.* **hope chest**/.

glory hole 1. *Br.* obs. col. a room, cupboard, or drawer where unwanted articles are left. 2. *Am.* col. anonymous sexual activity between homosexual through a hole in the wall in a lavatory. 3. *Am., Can.* open quarry.

glossy *Am.* trying too hard to be attractive or perfect.

glossy magazine, also col. **glossy** *esp. Br.* /*Am., Can.* **slick**/ a magazine printed on good quality paper with a shiny surface, usu. having lots of colour pictures, esp. of fashionable clothes: *Monthly glossies that seldom pay attention to classical music* - New York.

glossy *Am., Aus.* a photograph printed on smooth shiny paper.

glove *Am.* put gloves on.

glove a ball *Am.* catch it when playing baseball.

glove puppet *esp. Br., Aus.* /*Am.* **hand puppet**/ a toy person or animal with a soft hollow body into which a hand may be put to manipulate it.

glowworm *esp. Br.* an insect that has special organs at the end of its tail which produce greenish light.

glue factory *Am.* flaying house.

glutch *Can.* gulp.

G-man *Am.* col. now rare. a special officer of the government police (FBI): *He's part G-man, part politician* - USA Today.

gnarly *Am.* sl. (used by young people) very good or excellent. 2. not good enough.

gnashers *Br.* col. teeth.

go 1. *esp. Br., Can.* (at) /*Am., Aus.* **try**/ an attempt to do smth. /**have a go at** smth/: *Let me have a go at it this time.* - R.A. Spears, *I had a go on Nigel's racing bike.* –S. Townsend. 2. *esp. Br.* an active lively quality or activity, vitality and energy. 3. *esp. Br.* (an awkward or strange) state of affairs. 4. *Br. /Am., Aus.* **turn/** an opportunity to play in a game or to do or use smth. 5. *esp. Br.* attack of illness.

go/ be on the go *Br.* col. be always busy and active.

go/ have a go at *esp. Br., Aus.* col. a. complain, criticize, attack. b. attempt to catch or stop a wrongdoer by force.

go/ have smth. **on the go** *Br., Aus.* be happening or be produced.

go *Am.* col. adj. in perfect order and ready to proceed: *It was a go.* - A. Hitchcock Mystery Magazine., *all his systems seem to be go* - Time.

go/ it's all go *Br., Aus.* (said when sb. is very busy).

go/ to go *esp. Am., Can.* (of cooked food or drinks sold in a shop) to be taken away and not eaten or drunk in the shop: *Nick made her a burger to go.* – R.L. Stine.

go about *Br.* (of a ship) turn to go in the opposite direction.

Go along with you! *Br.* col. I don't believe you! / also **Go on (with you)**/.

go around one's **ass to get to** one's **elbow** *Am.* taboo. sl. do smth. in the most difficult way.

go down *Am.* sl. take place, happen: *Something strange is going down around here.* - R.A. Spears.

go down (from, to) *Br.* col. 1. leave a university after a period of study, esp. Oxford and Cambridge or to go from a city to a less important place; opp. **go up**. 2. be sent to prison.

go down with *Br.* begin to suffer from a specific illness.

go in *esp. Br.* be understood.

go off *Br.* 1. col. go down from a higher level of skill, quality, interest, etc. 2. go bad (of food). 3. col. stop liking sb. or smth. 4. (of pain) stop hurting.

go on 1. *Am.* col. like (usu. smth.) /no pass./: *I don't go on his idea* - Longman. 2. *Br.* col. develop or make progress: *The others have been gone on to Scarborough, these three weeks.* – J. Austen.

go on at sb. **about** smth. *Br.* continue to complain or ask sb. to do smth.

be going on for *Br.* almost reach smth.

be going on with, to go on with *esp. Br.* col. to use for the present time.

to be going with *Br.* to start with.

go on the breeze *Can.* get drunk.

go on the dole *esp. Br. /Am.* col. **go on unemployment (welfare)/** be paid by the government when unable to work, etc.: *The number of people who have to go on the dole have risen* - Longman.

go on the parish *Br.* obs. be supported by the local church when without money.

go on with/ to be going on with *Br., Aus.* in order to continue with the present act or situation.

go out *Br.* 1. col. (of a programme) be broadcast. 2. (on strike) stop working in an effort to improve working conditions.

go out for dinner *Br. /Am.* **eat out/**.

go out to *Br.* 1. travel to. 2. col. lose a game to (an opposing team).

go round the bend *Br.* col. go mad or become very annoyed: *I've been going round the bend with those children today!* - Longman.

go (all) round the houses *Br.* talk about lots of other things instead of the subject you are supposed to be talking about.

go through 1. *Aus.* col. leave hastily to avoid responsibility. 2. (smth.) *Br.* slowly make a hole in smth.

go/run to earth *Br.* hide escaping from one's enemies.

go to the country *Br.* hold a general election: *they will have to go to the country.* - Longman.

go to the dogs *Br.* col. be ruined: *England has gone to the dogs, since she lost her Empire.* - Longman.

go to the mat (for sb.) *Am.* fight very fiercely about smth., esp. to help sb. who is weak.

go under *Am.* die.

go up 1. *Br.* col. go to a university (usu. Oxford or Cambridge), esp. to begin a course of study or to go to a more important place. 2. *Br.* be allowed to move to the next higher class: *Did all the children go up at the end of the year?* - Longman. 3. *Am.* go bankrupt. 4. *Br.* (in sport) move to a higher division in a league.

go with *esp. Am.* take (smth.) up and pursue it, esp. because it reaches a satisfactory standard.

go/ it's all go *Br.* col. 1. it's very busy.

go/ it's all the go *Br.* obs. it's fashionable.

go/ it's enough to be going with *esp. Br.* it's enough for your needs at the moment.

go/ go ape *Am.* col. become mad or very keen: *He's gone ape over that new girl in the office!* - Longman.

go/ go figure *Am., Can.* col. It's incredible!

go/ Go fly a kite, also *Aus., Can.* **go jump in the lake, go lay an egg, go buy a brick, go sit on a tack** *Am.* go away: *Sue told her to go fly a kite.* - A. Makkai.

go/ have a go *esp. Br.* col. 1. attack sb. physically. 2. try to catch sb. when seeing them doing

smth. wrong by oneself rather than wait for the police.
go/ have a go at sb. *esp. Br.* col. complain.
go/ going away *Am.* 1. (in horse racing) gaining ground rapidly. 2. col. by a wide margin, esp. in **win/lose** a competition **going away**.
go bush *Aus.* sl. become countrified.
go/ be going it (some) *esp. Br.* travel very fast.
go/ go do smth. *Am.* go and do smth.
go/ go missing *Br., Aus.* be lost.
go/ go much on *Br.* col. like
go/ go nap *Br.* sl. wager everything.
go native *Br.* col. live far from civilisation according to the laws and traditions of the native people: *others go native, wear the local clothes and eat the native foods, and generally behave like uncivilised men.* - Longman.
go places *esp. Am.* visit pleasant or interesting places.
go/ go slow *Br.* work slow deliberately: *the rest will go slow in sympathy.* - Longman.
go/ go some *esp. Am.* col. be very successful, busy, quick, etc.: *That's going some, isn't it?* - Longman.
go there/ I'm not (even) gonna go there or **Let's not (even) gonna go there** *Am.* col. I/we don't want to discuss that because I/we am/are fed up with it.
go to oil *Can.* become a worthless person.
go west *Br.* col. (of people) die, (of things) cease to operate or exist: *My new camera has gone west after only three months.* - Longman.
go/ What time does the next train go? *esp. Br.* When does the next train leave?
go-ahead/ be go-ahead *Br., Aus.* be enthusiastic about using new inventions and modern ways of doing things.
goal/ knock sb. **for a goal** *Am.* win completely.
goal/ keep goal *Br.* be a gaolkeeper.
goal/ play in goal *Br.* try to prevent the other team from scoring goals.
goalposts/ move the goalposts *Br.* col. change the rules, limits, etc. while sb. is trying to do smth. and make it more difficult for them.
goalscorer *esp. Br. /Am.* **scorer/** a player who wins points or scores goals for one's team.
goaltender *esp. Am., Can.* goalkeeper.
go-around *Am.* col. an argument.
goat/ act the goat, get/play the (giddy) goat *Br.* obs. behave in a silly way.
goat/ get on one's **goat** *Aus.* col. annoy sb.
gob 1. *Am., Can.* col. (usu. pl.) a large amount: *I need gobs of money to get through school.* - R.A. Spears. 2. *Am.* sl. a sailor in the US Navy. 3. *esp. Br., Aus.* col. also **cake-hole** mouth (rude word). 4. *Br., Aus.* col. v. spit. 5. *Br.* col. a lump of slimy or viscous substance.
gobbler *Am.* col. turkey.
gobby *Can.* crazy about smth.
gobsmack *Br., Aus.* col. take utterly back, overwhelm.
gobsmacked *Br.* col. astounded, overawed: *He had expected to pay one tenth of the price and was said to be "gobsmacked" of the final cost.* - T. Thorne.
gobstopper *esp. Br. /Am.* **jawbreaker/** a large sucking candy.
gob-struck *Br.* col. also **gobsmacked**, overwhelmed.
go-by/ give (sb., smth.) **the go-by** *Br.* col. avoid or pass by without noticing.
God willing and the creek don't rise *Am.* col. humor. I hope I won't have problems doing it.
god-box *Am.* sl. church.
goddammit *esp. Am.* excl. dammit.
goddamned *Br.* adj. adv. damn.
go-down *Am.* a slope to a river (for cattle).
gods *Br., Aus.* col. (in theatre) seats furthest from the stage and at the highest level.
God's gift *esp. Br.* the best or ideal thing.
godslot *Br.* col. time on radio or TV for religious programmes.
goer *Br.* col. a woman who often has sex with different men.
gofer *esp. Am., Can., Aus.* person whose job is to fetch or take things for other people: *he had been merely a gofer.* - Time.
goggle-box *esp. Br., Aus.* humor. col. */Am.* sl. **boob tube, idiot tube/** television.
goggle-eyed *Br.* col. derog. watching TV a lot.
go-go *Br.* col. (of a period of time) adj. good for making a lot of money and for business in general.
going/ be going spare *Br., Aus.* you can have it as no one needs it.
going/ (face) rough going *Am.* (be in) difficult conditions.
going/ while the going is good *esp. Br.* while the situation is good.
going-over/ give sb. **a going-over** *esp. Br.* hit sb. and hurt them.
go-kart *Br.* **/go-cart/** a small racing vehicle made of an open frame on four wheels with an engine: *I'm going to put in a gas pump and go-karts.* - W. Grady.
goldbrick *esp. Am.* col. v. n. 1. (be) a loafer (shirker from work): *Well, one of them...accused me of shamming, of gold-bricking.* - H. Fast. 2.

swindle: *This whole goddamn war's a gold-brick* - J. Dos Passos. 3. smth. seemingly valuable but in fact worthless.

gold bug *esp. Am.* 1. col. advocate of a single gold standard for currency. 2. person who prefers to invest money into gold.

gold-bug, /*Am., Can.* **gold beetle**/ *esp. Am.* leaf beetle with metallic gold coloration.

gold dust/ it's (like a) gold dust *esp. Br., Aus.* /*Am.* **like gold**/ difficult to get because a lot of people want it.

golden age club *Am.* any social or recreational organisation for elderly.

golden ager *Am., Can.* euph. and humor. old person.

golden anniversary *Am.* /*Br.* **golden wedding (anniversary)**/.

golden handshake *esp. Br., Aus.* large amount of money given to sb. when they leave a job at the end of their working life: *Isn't there something called a golden handshake?* - D. Lodge.

golden jubilee *esp. Br.* 50th jubilee of an event.

golden knop, ladybird *Br.* /*Am.* **ladybug**/.

golden parachute 1. *Am.* a large payment made to an important member of a company when he is forced to leave job. 2. *Br.* col. part of a contract which states that a person will be paid a large sum of money when the contract ends.

golden raisin *Am.* /*Br.* **sultana**/ small pale raisin, used in baking.

Goldenrod *Am.* print. a yellow, light-proof, paper used for mounting flats (an assembly of arranged film or photographic paper).

golden share *Br.* share that gives with the rest 51 per cent of voting rights.

The Golden State *Am.* California: *the past few years have been tough for the Golden State.* - Time.

golden syrup *esp. Br., Aus.* sweet thick liquid made from sugar that is spread on bread and used in cooking.

golden wedding *Br.* a fiftieth anniversary of the wedding.

goldfish bowl *esp. Br.* spherical container for goldfish.

gold note *Am.* banknote redeemable in gold.

gold record *Am., Can.* gold disc.

golem *Am.* col. stupid person.

golf *Am.* radio. letter G.

golf shirt *Am., Can.* short-sleeved shirt with buttons at the neck only.

golly 1. *Br.* taboo sl. black or coloured person; from **golliwog** *Br., Aus.* obs. derog. a children's toy in the form of a small man with a black face. 2. *Aus.* sl. a gob of spittle.

gondola 1. *Am.* (also **gondola-car**) /*Br.* **open goods waggon**/ flat railway goods wagon with no (or low) sides: *Forced to detrain from an empty gondola* - Alcoholics Anonymous. 2. *Can.* broadcasting booth rigged near the roof of arena for hockey games announcers.

gone *Br.* prep. later or older than, past.

gone/ be 5,6,7, etc. months gone *Br.* col. be pregnant for a particular number of months.

gone/ it's gone a particular time *Br.* col. it's later than that time.

gone goose, goose egg *Am., Can.* sl. failure.

gong 1. *Br., Aus.* col. (esp. used by journalists) medal: *leader of Kent County Council, may not be in line for the usual gong dished out to holders of his office.* - T. Thorne. 2. *Aus.* sl. opium (pipe).

gonif *Am., Can.* col. thief: *From gonef to kibitzer Yinglish is continuously enriching the language.* - P. Howard., *he got taken by a couple of gonefs* - L. Uris.

gonna *esp. Am.* col. or *Br.* nonst. going to.

gonzo *Am., Aus.* sl. adj. n. strange and unusual; mad, insane (person): *And then after, I'm gonzo.* - G.V. Higgins., *the great gonzo madman, Ted Nugent* - W. Jack, B. Laursen.

gonzo journalism *Am.* col. related to reporting intended to shock or excite the reader without giving true information.

goober *Am.* sl. 1. peanut. 2. spot or pimple: *Wow, look at that guber on my nose.* - R.A. Spears. 3. fool: *look like some goober from Lithuania.* - J. Patterson. 4. a gob of spit.

The Goober State *Am.* Georgia.

good *Am.* adv. well.

good/ a good bit larger/better, etc. *Br.* much larger, better, etc.

good/ good for sb. *esp. Am.* convenient for sb.

good/ in good with *esp. Am.* col. enjoying the favour of or good opinion of.

good/ very good *Br.* obs. polite. of course, certainly.

good/ good on you/her, etc. *Br., Aus.* (used to express approval and pleasure at sb.'s success, good luck, etc.: *"Good on you", Paul acknowledged* - J.P. Hogan.

good/ as good as pie (or **wheat**) *Am.* very nice, good.

good/ be a good laugh *Br.* be enjoyable or amusing.

good/ be good to go *Am.* col. have everything and be in the right condition to do smth.

good/ be no good/use to man nor beast *Br.* be no useful at all.

good/ for good and all *Am.* col. forever.

good/ give sb. **as good as one gets** *Br.* col. revenge sb. with the equal damage to them.

good going (or **not bad going**) *Br.* col. better than usual or expected.

good/ have a good one *Am.* have a nice day.

good/ in good time *Br.* early.

good/ it's a good job, and a good thing/job too *Br.* used to say when sb. is glad that smth. happened in a certain way.

good innings/ have had a good innings *Br., Aus.* col. live a long active and successful life.

good/ make (it) good *Am., Aus.* become successful.

good/ make good on smth. *Am., Aus.* col. give back money that you owe sb.

good/ take smth. **in good part** *Br.* be not upset by jokes and criticism.

good/ Good show 1. *Am.* obs. I'm glad.

good/ make smth. **good** *esp. Br.* repair.

good/ She gives as good as she gets *esp. Br.* She pays back.

goodby *Am.* goobye.

good day excl. 1. *esp. Aus., Am., Can.* (an expression of greeting in the morning or afternoon): *Good day, Mrs. Hardy. How do you do, Mr. Lane.* -W. Magnuson. 2. *esp. Br.* obs. hello or goodbye.

good doer *Br.* thing (esp. cultivated plant or domestic animal) that does well without any special attention.

goodfella *esp. Am., Can.* col. gangster.

goodish *Br.* col. 1. quite good (but not very good) in quality. 2. (with a) rather, to quite a high degree.

Good Humor man *Am.* an ice-cream van salesman.

good Joe *Am.* sl. good fellow: *He is a good Joe.* - H.C. Whitford., R.J. Dixson.

good oil *Aus.* col. reliable information.

goodo *Aus., NZ.* col. excl., adj., adv. (used to express that things are in satisfactory way or manner).

goods 1. *Br. /esp. Am.* **freight/** heavy articles which can be carried by train, road, etc.: *Some goods truck, led by a straining engine, filed by.* - I. Fleming. 2. *esp. Br.* col. a desirable thing or person: *You've been the goods, Mrs. Oliver.* - A. Christie., *Thought he'd got the goods with him, didn't you?* - A. Christie., *And he could do it for he had the goods.* - R.P. Warren. 3. *Am.* cloth.

goods/ have/get the goods on sb. *Am.* know some secret harmful information about sb.

goods lift *Br. /Am.* **freight elevator/**.

goods shed or **station** *Br. /Am.* **freight depot** or **station/**.

goods train *Br. /Am.* **freight train/**: *On it travelled passenger and goods trains carrying children and their parcels.* - L. Van Der Post.

goods van (or **wagon, truck**) *Br. /Am.* **box car, freight car (wagon)/**: *Ah, we'll get the engine driver and Micko off the goods van* - J.P. Donleavy.

goods yard *Br. /Am.* **freight yard/**.

good value *Br.* col. good stuff, worth having.

good word *Am.* good news.

goody *Br.* col. positive hero of a story or film.

goody two-shoes *esp. Am.* sl. an obviously innocent and virtuous person: *for a major Goody Two-shoes, you can be one devious broad* - D. Mortman.

goo(-goo) eyes *Am.* sl. eyes expressing enticement, desire, seduction, etc.

goof *esp. Am., Can.* 1. a silly mistake or person: *There was no way out for the goofs that lay gold eggs.* – F. Edwards. 2. also *Aus.* col. make a silly mistake: *The bank certainly goofed* - H.C. Whitford., R.J. Dixson. 3. spend time idly. 4. take a stupefying dose of drugs.

goof around *Am. /Br.* **mess about/** spend time doing silly things.

goof off (or **around/about**) *Am., Aus., Can.* col. /*Br.* **mess about, skive/** waste time or avoid work: *You're not gonna be around for a day or so and watch them goof off.* - G.V. Higgins., - *the band was just goofing around.* - D. Divoky.

goof (up) *Am.* col. spoil (smth.) carelessly: *If John goofs up his driving test again, I doubt if he'll ever pass it.* - Longman.

goofball *esp. Am., Can., Aus.* col. 1. eccentric or naive person: *You are such a silly goofball.* - R.A. Spears. 2. drug tranquilliser: *took over three hundred goof balls.* - R.L. Chapman.

goof-off *Am., Can.* col. lazy person.

goofproof *Am.* col. render (sb.) less likely to make blunders: *I'll try to goofproof my scheme.* - R.A. Spears.

goof-up *esp. Am., Can.* col. silly mistake.

goofus *Am., Can.* col. a fool.

goofy *esp. Am., Can.* stupid and ridiculous.

goog *Aus.* col. 1. an egg. 2. a fool.

googly/ blow sb. **a googly** *Br.* ask them a very difficult question suddenly.

goo-goo *Am.* advocate of political reforms.

goo-goo eyes *Am.* humor. silly look that shows that sb. loves another person. esp. in **make goo-goo eyes at** sb.

gook *esp. Am.* col. a foreigner, esp. an Asian: *How come you're slap bang in the middle of all them gooks, newsie?* - R. Borchgrave, R. Moss., *Used to stimulate gook planes.* - J. DeFelice., *Some gook at a 7-Eleven wasn't going to look twice at serial numbers.* - P. Case, J. Migliore.

goolie *Aus.* col. stone or pebble.

goolies *Br.* sl. testicles: *It's enough to take your goolies off* - T. Thorne., *Woke up with the pain in my goolies.* – S. Townsend.

goombah *Am., Can.* col. associate or accomplice.

goon 1. *esp. Am., Aus.* col. a violent criminal hired to frighten or attack people: *his two associates were beaten up by government goons.* - Economist., *The little goon must have waited in the garage* - R. Moore., *someone sends eight goons to kill us* - W. Murphy. 2. *esp. Br.* silly or stupid person.

goop, glop *esp. Am., Can.* col. a thick sticky substance, goo: *A person doesn't want to cover themselves with goop.* - W. Grady.

goose *Am., Can.* col. encourage or cause to be more active.

goose *esp. Am., Can., Aus.* taboo. sl. push one's finger between the buttocks of (sb.) or just touch or press sb. at their bottom as a rude joke: *Freddie tried to goose me!* - R.A. Spears.

gooseberry *esp. Br.* col. humor. a third person who stays in the company of two lovers although they want to be alone / esp. in the phr. **play gooseberry.**

goose egg *Am., Can.* col. 1. a score of zero: *Most of my doodles looked like great big goose eggs.* - S. Grafton. 2. a failure (also **gone goose**): *The outcome was a real goose egg.* - R.A. Spears.

goose pimples *Br.* /*Am., Can.* **goosebumps,** *Br.* col. **chicken flesh**/ goose flesh: *Saying that, he felt sudden goose-pimples starting.* - A. Burgess., *Polly still got goose bumps when she thought of the old widower* - T. Murphy.

goose-pimply/ go goose-pimply *Br., Aus.* /*Am.* **get goose-pimply**/ get goose flesh.

goosy *Am.* sl. touchy, jumpy: *a big goosy girl, unsure of herself.* - New York.

goosy *Am.* col. goose-pimply

GOP *esp. Am.* Grand Old Party, the Republican Party in the US, **gopster** *Am.* sl. a member of the Republican Party.

The Gopher State /also **The North Star State**/ *Am.* Minnesota.

Gorblimey *Br.* excl. of mild surprise.

gordo *Aus.* popular variety of grapes.

gormless *esp. Br., Aus.* col. stupid and thoughtless, slow in understanding: *free-style, gormless dance with a partner.* - P. Howard.

go-round *Am., Can.* repetition, turn: *the story is another go-round for A Star is Born* - New York.

gorp *Am., Can.* trail mix, mixture of nuts and dried fruit eaten as a snack by hikers or campers.

go-slow *esp. Br., Aus.* /*Am.* **slowdown (strike),** *Br.* sl. **ca-canny**/ a period of working as slowly and with as little effort as possible, as a form of a strike.

Gotham *Am.* joc. New York City: *Gotham is buzzing.* - Nation's Restaurant News.

gotten *Am., Aus.* past participle of get except where get means possess or must: *I'd gotten to her* - R.J. Randisi., M. Wallace.

gouge *esp. Am., Can.* 1. groove or cavity scooped out. 2. col. v. n. trick, cheat, swindle, intimidate: *seafood suppliers who have grown outraged by the mob-inspired price-gouging* - Nation's Restaurant News., *William is currently under indictment for rent gouging* - New York.

goujons *Br.* deep-fried strips of chicken or fish.

gourd *Am.* sl. head.

gourd/ out of one's **gourd** *Am., Can.* col. crazy.

government (or **administration**) *Am.* noun takes a sing. verb, *Br.* takes a verb in pl.

government *esp. Am.* the degree to which the government controls economic and social activities.

government/ be in government *Br., Aus.* (of a party) control the country.

government health warning *Br.* notice that by law must be put on some products, e.g. cigarettes, to warn people that they are dangerous for health.

Government House *Br.* the official residence of the Governor in a colony or Commonwealth state.

governor (**guvnor, guv'nor**) *Br.* 1. a man who is in position of control over one, such as an employer or father: *I saw your governor going in.* - J. Joyce., *To tell you the truth I'm glad my governor's a gentleman.* - W.S. Maugham. 2. (also **guv**) (used for addressing a man, esp. of higher position or social class). 3. also **prison governor** sl. a prison warden.

governor *esp. Br.* member of a committee that controls an organisation or institution.

gown *Br.* /*esp. Am.* **robe**/ dressing gown.

goyish *Am.* sl. non- Jewish: *Have you ever heard of anything so goyish?* - M. Torgov.

GP *esp. Br.* General Practitioner.

GPA *Am., Aus.* grade point average, the average student's mark over a period of time: *The grades for all a student's classes are then averaged together* to provide an overall grade point average (gpa). – Living in the USA.

GPO 1. *Am.* Government Printing Office. 2. *Br.* General Post Office: *a GPO van had to bring it to the door.* – S. Townsend.

grab bag 1. *Am., Can., Aus.* /*Br.* **lucky dip**/ a container with wrapped objects of various values, into which a person puts his/her hand and picks one out: *the grab-bag title of the Gang of Four* - J. Fraser. 2. *Aus.* any mixed collection of things.

grabby *esp. Am.* col. greedy.

grab(s)/ **By grab(s)** *Am.* God Damn.

grad *Am.* col. graduate: *I was going through grad school.* – Pasadena City College Courier.

grade 1. *Am., Aus.* class of a particular year of a school course: *She was my first grade teacher.* - T. Caldwell., *He'd have to start back in the first grade.* - K. Vonnegut, Jr., *he is in Grade Eight of the Toronto Conservatory piano course.* - M. Torgov. 2. *esp. Am., Can.* (give) a mark for the standard of a piece of schoolwork: *she got the best grades, straight "A"s!* - T. Capote., *He's a grade-A solid-gold genius* - Playboy., *He made good grades with little effort* - Reader's Digest. 3. *esp. Am., Can.* /*Br.* **gradient**/ gradient, degree of a slope of a road, railway, etc.: *twenty yoke of oxen helping it up the grade.* - S. North.

grade/ at grade *Am., Can.* at the same level.

grade/ be the same grade *Br., Aus.* /*Am.* **at the same grade/** (of the job) have the same importance and the same pay.

grade up *esp. Am.* improve the quality of (a product such as cattle or fruit): *Scientists have been trying to find methods of grading up cattle to provide better meat with less fat.* - Longman.

grade crossing, also **crossing at grade** *Am., Can.* /*Br.* **level crossing**/ a place where road and railway cross each other.

grader *Am., Can.* /*Br.* **former**/ pupil of a particular year in school.

grade school, also **grades grammar school** *Am., Can.* /*Br.* **primary school**/ elementary school, one at which elementary subjects are taught for the first six to eight years of a child's education: *He felt like a grade-school student reciting multiplication.* - B. Tillman.

graduand *Br.* person who is soon likely to get an academic degree.

graduate *Am., Can.* 1. /*Br.* **schoolleaver**/ person who has completed a course at a college, school, etc.: *a graduate of the Moscow State University for International Relations, a special college that trains diplomats and the officials for foreign assignments* - R.G. Kaiser. 2. also **graduate student** /*Br.* **post graduate**/ n. adj. postgraduate, studying for a master's degree or a PhD: *Graduate study, aspirantura, is three years* - Y. Richmond., *Jamie went on to do her graduate work at UCLA.* - Guideposts., *I was doing graduate research in the area* - National Geographic.

graduate *Br.* person who has completed a course at a university or college.

graduate *esp. Am., Can.* 1. (of college or university) issue qualified graduates. 2. give a degree or diploma to sb. who has just completed a course.

graduate from complete a course of study in American school /*Br.* **leave school; finish**/ college or university or British university: *he applied to join even before graduating from high school* - H. Smith.

graduate with *Am.* 1. (usu. pass.) obtain a university degree (with honours, marks, etc.): *She was graduated with high honours.* – Longman; **graduate with first-class honours** *Br., Aus.* obtain the highest degree. 2. finish high school, at the same time as (sb. else).

graduate center /also **school, courses, grad school**/ *Am., Can.* /*Br.* **post-graduate courses**/: *Still, he pressed on with his studies, with his digs, with graduate school and his research.* - T. Murphy.

graft *esp. Am.* the practice of obtaining money or advantages by the dishonest use of esp. political influence /note the phr. **graft and corruption**/: *Son, now don't get mixed up in any graft* - R.P. Warren. 2. *esp. Am.* money obtained this way: *money was graft to be paid to Salinas by drug traffickers* - Time.

graft *esp. Br.* col. 1. n. hard work. 2. v. work hard. 3. engage in dishonest or criminal activities. n.: *the usual charges of graft at City Hall* - R.L. Chapman. **-er**.

graft off sb. *esp. Am.* get money or advantages from sb. by dishonest use of influence.

grafter *esp. Am.* a person, esp. a politician who practices graft: *Grafters, he repeated, evidently delighted with his very public-school colloquialism.* - A. Huxley., *you put nine tin-horn grafters in the pen* - R.P. Warren.

grain *Am., Can.* feed (a horse) on grain.

grain separator *Am.* thresher.

gramma *Am., Can.* col. grandma.

grammar patterns / *Br.* I'd like to go now. = *Am.* I'd like for you to go now.; *Br.* I'll go out and get the car. = I'll go get the car.; *Br.* Come and take a look. = *Am.* Come take a look.; *Br.* I've just eaten.

= *Am. I just ate.*; *Br. I've not seen it yet.* = *Am. I didn't see it yet.*; *Br. I asked him to leave.* = *Am. I asked that he leave.*; *Br. I want to get out.* = *Am. I want out.*; *Br. Look out of the window.* = *Am. Look out the window.*; *Br. I'll go in a moment.* = *Am. I'll go momentarily.*

grammar school *Am.* becoming rare. elementary school: *Although he had never even completed grammar school, he became a very successful man.* - H.C. Whitford., R.J. Dixson.

gramps *Am. sl.* grandfather, any old man: *I call him gramps because he's my grandfather.* - H. Fast.

gran(ny), grandma *esp. Br. col.* grandmother.

granary bread *Br.* /*Am.* **wholegrain bread**/ a type of bread containing whole seeds of wheat.

The Grand Canyon State *Am.* Arizona.

granddad *Br. col.* impolite form of addressing an old man.

grand(d)addy *esp. Am. col.* 1. the prime example of smth: *Mr. Nixon dispatched New York's Governor Nelson Rockefeler on the granddaddy of all Latin American study tours.* - Newsweek. 2. grandfather.

grandfather clause *Am., Can.* clause which exempts certain people from obeying particular parts of legislation.

the grand final *Aus.* the final game of a sports competition which decides the winner.

grand jury *Am. law.* a jury of 23 jurors selected to examine the validity of an accusation before trial.

grand larceny *Am. law.* the crime of stealing very valuable goods.

grandmother/ teach your grandmother/granny to suck eggs *Br., Aus.* give advice to sb. who knows more than you.

grandstand *Am.* 1. play to the gallery, show off: *he is uncharacteristically circumspect grandstander* - New York, n. **grandstanding**. 2. adj. showy: *That's grandstand stuff.* - R. Chandler.

grandstand play *Am. col.* 1. a play made with special brilliance, esp. in order to impress spectators. 2. an act done to win applause: *Well, your candidates make a grandstand play* - D. Hammet.

grange *Am.* agricultural association.

The Granite State *Am.* New Hampshire: *Hart lately has been roving the icy expanse of the Granite State.* - Maclean's.

grannie, granny *esp. Br. col. adj.* 1. for the use of an old person. 2. of a style used by old women.

granny farm *Br.* an old people's house, esp. one which regularly overcharges for its services.

granny flat *Br.* a flat built onto a house, or made inside it, for an elderly relative.

granola *Am., Can.* /*Br.* **muesli**/ a breakfast food made from nuts, grains, and seeds: *Dennis took a bite of the granola bar* – R.L. Stine.

be grant-aided *Br.* /*Am.* **receive grant-in-aid**/ (of a person) be given part of money he/she needs for research by government or other organisation; **grant-maintained** (of a school).

grapevine/ hear/get smth. **on the grapevine** *esp. Br.* get it from rumours.

grape worm *Am.* berry moth.

grasp the nettles *esp. Br., Aus.* remain brave in spite of difficulties.

grass *Br., Aus. col.* 1. /*Am.* **stoolpigeon**/ a (criminal) informer. 2. (on) inform the police about the actions of (other) criminals: *that was the kind of face a nark might have a man who grassed to the bogies.* - G. Greene.

grass *Am. col.* feed (livestock) with grass.

grass/ be put out to grass *Br.* make sb. retire from their job because of the old age.

grass/ between (or **betwixt**) **grass and hay** *Am.* being an adolescent.

grass/ put the garden down to grass *Br.* plant a lot of grass in it.

The Grasshopper State *Am.* Kansas.

gratuity 1. *esp. Br.* a gift of money to a worker or member of the armed forces when they leave their employment. 2. *Am.* illegal bribe

grave/ turn over/spin in their grave *Am., Can.* /*Br.* **turn in** one's **grave**/ (if sb. dead were alive) be very upset or angry.

gravel 1. *Br.* bring (sb.) to a stop, confuse sb. 2. *Am. col.* make (sb.) angry or annoyed.

graveyard shift *esp. Am., Can.* regular period of working time at night: *He told graveyard shift supervisor Dave Silverman* – A. Summers, R. Swan.

gravy *esp. Am. sl.* smth. pleasing or valuable that happens or is gained easily: *"Good Gravy", said Fuller.* - K. Vonnegut, Jr.

gravy train *esp. Am., Can. col.* smth. from which many people can make money or profits without much effort: *I've been riding the gravy train all my life* - M. Puzo.

gray-collar *Am.* performing technical services.

gray flannel *Am.* belonging to organisation men.

graze *Am.* pick up and eat items of food while shopping in a supermarket.

grazier, squatter, pastoralist *Aus.* /*Br., Aus.* **stockholder**/ a sheep farmer: *This is the world of squatter, the runholder, the grazier* - P. Howard.

grease *Am.* sl. (bribe) money: *that grease for the doe was one of the best investments I ever made* - Rolling Stone.

grease the skids *Am., Can.* help matters run smoothly.

greaseball *esp. Am., Can.* sl. derog. a foreigner, esp a person of Hispanic or Mediterranean origin: *Almost everyone is familiar enough with the Elvis Presley greaseball types.* - D. Divoky.

greaser 1. *Br.* a ship's engineer. 2. *Am.* taboo. sl. (also **greaseball**) a native of Latin America, esp. Mexico: *Almost everyone is familiar enough with the Elvis Presley greaseball types.* - D. Divoky. 3. *Br.* col. rocker, motorcycle enthusiast.

grease monkey *esp. Am.* sl. obs. worker who lubricates machines, esp. automobiles: *The grease monkey was all dirty when he came out from under the car.* - A. Makkai., *A sinewy little grease monkey, the wrecker, flexed his knuckles* – P. Roth.

greaseproof paper *Br., Aus. /esp. Am., Can.* **wax(ed) paper,** *Am.* **parchment/** paper used usu. for wrapping food.

the greasy pole *Br., Aus.* the attempt to improve one's position at work.

great/ be a great one for writing, sailing, football, etc. *Br.* enjoy writing, etc. very much.

great/ huge/enormous great *Br.* col. used to emphasize how big smth. is.

the great and the good *Br.* the important people.

great mistake *esp. Br.* a big mistake.

The Great Central State *Am.* North Dacota.

The Great Wen *Br.* London.

The Great White North *Am., Can.* Canada.

Great White Way *Am.* Broadway: *We walked along the Great White Way and admired the sights.* - H.C. Whitford, R.J. Dixson.

grebo *Br.* sl. (a member of) a youth cult whose adherents adopt a deliberately scruffy appearance and boorish manner and favour aggressively crude rock music.

greedy guts *esp. Br., Aus.* col. glutton.

Greek *Am.* member of sorority or fraternity.

Greek/ be all Greek to sb. *Br.* be very difficult to understand.

green *Br.* an area of grass in the middle of a village.

green as grass *Br.* inexperienced or naïve.

greenback /also (**the long**) **green**/ *Am.* col. an American banknote, esp. a dollar bill: *Other oil-producing nations might bail out of the greenback* - Newsweek., *Let's talk green.* - D. Brenner., *A couple of foxes working the street for him could really start pulling in the green.* - W. Murphy.

green ban *Aus.* a ban by trade union to build anything in an area of land that is considred environmentally important.

green bean *Am.* sl. a naive person: *These two green beans are crossing the freeway* – Reader's Digest.

green belt *esp. Br.* a stretch of land, round a town or city, where building is not allowed, so that fields, woods, etc. remain: *It is in the double no-go area of green belt and conservation area.* - Sunday Times, 25.03. 1990.

green card 1. *Am.* permit for foreign workers to go to the US: *"We need Anna's green card",* the clerk said, finally. – Reader's Digest. 2. *Br.* insurance document covering motorists against accidents in foreign countries: *Contact your motor insurance company for both the Green Card and Bail Bond.* - Young Citizen's Passport.

Green Chamber *Can.* col. House of Commons in Canadian Parliament.

green crop *Br.* unripe crop used as fodder.

Green Cross Code *Br.* the road safety rules that children learn.

greener *Br.* sl. inexperienced workman, esp. a foreigner.

greenfeed *Aus., NZ.* fresh grown livestock forage.

green field *Br.* col. (of land) not yet built on or (of factory,etc.) built on land not yet used for industry.

(have) green fingers *esp. Br., Aus. /esp. Am. Can.* **(have a) green thumb/** have natural skill in making plants grow well: *You must have a green thumb.* - J.A. Michener., *Most green thumps prefer not to think about city gardening options at all* - New York.

green fish *Am.* fresh fish before salting.

greenfly *esp. Br.* aphid, garden plants and crops pest.

greengage *esp. Br.* a kind of sweet plum of greenish yellow colour.

green goods *Am.* col. counterfeit money; **green goods man.**

greengrocer *esp. Br.* a person who owns or works in a shop (**greengrocer's**) /*Am.* **fruit and vegetables store**/ which sells vegetables and fruit: *He beat down the extortionate charges of the greengrocer.* - A. Huxley., *Market gardeners and greengrocers trade in fruit and vegetables* - R. McRum, W. Cran, R. McNeil., *It was the greengrocer's assistant from the corner shop.* - G. Greene.

greengrocer's *Br.* /*Am.* **fruit and vegetables store**/: *he owns a greengrocer's shop.* – S. Townsend.
greenhead 1. *esp. Am.* biting horsefly. 2. *Aus.* ant with a painful sting.
greenhide *Aus.* untanned hide of an animal.
greenhorn *esp. Am., Can.* becoming rare. a recently arrived immigrant: *they never suspected that they could be overthrown by such a greenhorn immigrant.* - M. Puzo.
green lumber *Am.* freshly cut timber.
green lung *Br.* col. a park.
greenmail *Am.* sl. the buying at a premium price of the stock holdings of sb. who is threatening to take over a company, in order to induce the person to cease the attempt: *Edelman has collected some greenmail for quitting the attacks.* - Time.
The Green Mountain State *Am.* Vermont.
green onion, scallion *esp. Am.* /*esp. Br., Aus. Br.* **spring onion**/.
greens 1. *Am.* leaves and branches used for ornament, esp. at Christmas. 2. *esp. Br.* cooked green leaves of vegetables such as spinach or cabbage: *He made the best turnip greens* – E. James, D. Ritz. 3. one's **greens** *Br.* col. obs. sexual intercourse.
green stuff 1. *Am.* col. /*Br.* col. **green stuffs**/ green vegetables. 2. *Am., Can.* col. money, dollars: *In those days we had plenty of green stuff, so I bought a Lexus.* - W. Magnuson.
green thumb *esp. Am., Can.* /*esp. Br.* **green fingers**/ : *He seems to have a green thumb* – H.C. Whitford., R.J. Dixson.
greeter *esp. Am.* person whose job is to greet customers in shops, restaurants, and other businesses.
greeting *Am.* salutation, the words used at the beginning of a letter.
greeting area *Br.* unemployment geographical area, that is not poor enough to qualify for special government assistance.
greetings card *Br.* /*Am.* **greeting card**/ one sent for some special occasion like Christmas or birthday.
grey *Br.* connected with old people.
greyback *Am.* grey whale.
greyhound *Am.* tdmk. a type of long-distance bus.
greyness *Aus.* grey colour.
gricer *Br.* col. fanatical railway enthusiast.
grid *Br.* a network of electricity supply wires connecting power stations.
gridder *Am.* football player.

griddle cake, drope scone, Scotch pancake *Br.* /*Am.* **slapjack**/ a scone made by dropping a spoonful of batter on too hot cooking surface.
gridiron *Am., Cal.* field marked in white lines for American football or football itself: *Sort of modern gridiron Siege of Troy.* – M. Daly.
gridlock *esp. Am.* 1. a complete halting or breakdown of a system or organisation: *both prefer continuous conferences to a legislative gridlock* - Time., *The Bridge closing brought massive commuter gridlock this week* - USA Today. 2. big traffic jam.
grift *Am., Can.* col. (be involved in) cheating, n. **–er**.
grill *Br., Aus.* /*Am.* **broil**/ cook (smth.) under or over direct fire.
grill *Br., Aus.* /*Am.* **broiler**/ an arrangement of a metal shelf under a gas flame or electric heat, used to cook food quickly, often used in **grill rooms**; **grill pan** *Br.* /*Am.* **broiler pan,** *Aus.* **grill tray**/.
griller *esp. Am.* col. an informal restaurant.
grim *Br.* col. very bad in quality.
grim death/ **hang**/**hold on like**/**for grim death** *Br., Aus.* col. hold on tight because of being afraid of falling.
grind *Am.* /*Br.* **mince**/ cut food into very small pieces by putting it through a machine.
grind 1. *esp. Am.* col. /*Br., Aus.* **swot**/ study hard, esp. for an examination. 2. *Br.* sl. obs. have sex.
grind *Am.* col. often derog. /*Br., Aus.* **swot**/ a student who is always working: *I remembered a girl I'd known in school, a grind* - T. Capote., *I turned out to be a grind* - J. O'Hara.
grind the faces of the poor *Br.* treat poor people very badly, often getting money from them.
grinder *Am.* col. /*esp. Am., Can.* **hoagie**/ long roll with cheese, meat, and salad.
grip 1. *Aus.* col. job or occupation. 2. *Br.* hair grip.
grip-car *Am.* cable car.
gripe *Am.* chronic complainer.
gripewater *Br.* tdmk. a type of medicine commonly given to babies to help with digestion.
griskin *Br.* lean bacon.
grist for one's **mill** *Am.* /*Br., Aus.* **grist to** one's **meal**/ smth. useful.
grits *Am.* hominy grain which is roughly crushed, or uncrushed but with the outer skin removed, often eaten for breakfast in the southern states of the US: *he has all the pizzas of unbuttered grits.* - Newsweek.

gritter *Br.* /*Am.* **sander, salt truck**/ a special vehicle that spreads grit or salt on the icy roads.

grizzle *esp. Br.* col. derog. 1. (esp. of a young child) cry quietly and continually as though tired or worried, whine and cry complainingly: *he grizzled like an infant* - L. Lee. 2. complain in a self-pitying way: *It had always grizzled him that directors should ask so much money* - W.S. Maugham.

grocery cart *Am.* /*Br.* **grocery trolley**/.

grocery (store) /also **food store**/ *Am.* /*Br.* **grocer's, grocery shop**/ grocer's shop, small supermarket: *Your grocery store is packed with anti-bacterial products like hand soaps and lotions* – Reader's Digest.

groceteria *Am., Can.* grocery shop where people wait on themselves.

grockie *Br.* col. derog. holiday-maker at an English resort.

grody *Am.* col. (used by children) very unpleasant or offensive.

grog *esp. Am., Aus., NZ.* any alcoholic drink, esp. beer: *That's enough grog for me.* - R.A. Spears.

groggery, grogshop *esp. Br., Aus., NZ.* saloon: *Sam stopped at the groggery for a snort.* - R.A. Spears.

grok *Am.* sl. communicate meaningfully or sympathetically: *I can really grok what you're saying.* - R.A. Spears.

groom *Br.* official of the royal household.

groomsman *Am.* /*Br.* **usher**/ friend of a bridegroom who has special duties at a wedding.

groove 1. *Am.* col. the way things should be done, so that it seems easy and natural, esp. in the phr. **get back in the groove**. 2. *Am., Can.* kick or throw a ball successfully.

(sand)groper *Aus.* col. 1. citizen of West Australia. 2. /also **Westralia**/ West Australia.

groper *esp. Aus.* a large fish with a wide mouth.

gross *esp. Am., Aus.* col. adj. very unpleasant or offensive: *It had been a dream, a truly gross dream.* - R.L. Stine.

gross/ in gross *Br.* /*Am.* **in the gross**/ in large amounts, wholesale.

gross out *esp. Am., Can., Aus.* col. disgust: *Why risk grossing her out?* - E. Segal, n. **gross-out.**

gross up *Br.* tax law. increase the formal value: *If the donor bears the tax the value of the gift has to be grossed up to include the tax.* - Times.

grot *Br.* col. rubbish.

grotty *Br.* col. bad, nasty, unpleasant, etc.: *Let's not see another grotty movie tonight.* - R.A. Spears., *The flat is dead grotty* – S. Townsend.

ground *Br.* stadium.

ground 1. *esp. Am., Can.* /*Br., Aus.* **earth**/ v. n. (make) a connection between a piece of electrical apparatus and the ground with additional safety wire. 2. *esp. Am., Can.* col. prevent (a child) from going out as a punishment: *We both got grounded for a month.* - Reader's Digest.

ground/ The Dark and Bloody Ground *Am.* Kentucky.

ground/ be thin on the ground *Br., Aus.* have not much of smth. around /opp. **thick on the ground**.

ground/ break ground *Am., Can.* 1. begin digging or other work before building smth. 2. break new ground.

ground/ cut the ground from under sb.'s feet/ from under sb. *Br.* upset or confuse sb. so that they could deal less successfully with a situation.

ground/ fall on stony ground *Br.* be ignored.

ground/ go to ground *Br.* hide from sb. or police.

ground/ hit the ground running *esp. Am.* start working hard and successfully at once.

ground/ run sb. **to ground** *Br., Aus.* find sb. after searching for a long time.

ground/ run into the ground *Br., Aus.* fail.

ground/ suit sb. **(right) to the ground** *Br.* suit sb. completely.

ground *Am.* (of meat) minced.

groundage *esp. Br.* commerce charge levied on ships entering a port or lying offshore.

groundbait *Br.* bait thrown into water when fishing.

ground ball, grounder *Am.* a ball which moves along the ground in baseball.

ground beef, hamburger (meat), ground(ed), chopped meat *Am.* /*Br.* **mince**/ beef that has been cut into very small pieces: *they had finished their dinner, a casserole of ground beef and macaroni and cheese* – R.L. Stine.

ground cloth *Am.* /*Br.* **groundsheet**/ ground sheet waterproof material (used by campers who sleep on the ground).

ground floor 1. *esp. Br., Can.* /*Am., Aus.* **first floor,** *Can.* **main floor**/ the part of a building at or near ground level: *the furniture out of the ground floor* – S. Townsend. 2. *Am.* the most advantageous position in a venture: *Evans, who got in on the ground floor, made a fortune in the promotion of that stock.* - H.C. Whitford., R.J. Dixson.

ground frost *Br.* frost on the surface or top layer of the earth only.

groundhog *Am., Can.* woodchucker.

Groundhog Day *Am.* February 2nd, that traditionally indicates six more weeks of winter if sunny or an early spring if cloudy: *Punxutawney - well-known as the center of the universe on Groundhog Day* - Time.

grounding *Am.* preventing a child from going out used as a punishment for a child.

ground meat *Am.* /*Br., Aus.* **mince**/ minced meat; **ground round** *Am.* best minced meat.

ground nut *esp. Br.* tech. peanut.

groundout *Am.* (in baseball) the act of hitting a ball along so that it's caught by sb. on the other team who then cause the batter to be out.

ground rent *esp. Br.* rent paid to the owner of the land by the person who has his/her house or a flat on it.

ground rule *esp. Am.* sports rule changed according to the size of a field.

groundsman *esp. Br., Aus.* /*Am., Can.* **groundskeeper,** *Aus.* **curator**/ one employed to take care of a sports fields or large gardens: *university groundsmen posted "No trespassing" signs at the People's Park.* - Newsweek.

ground staff *Br.* 1. a team of people employed at a sports ground to look after the grass, the sports equipment, etc. 2. ground crew at an airport.

ground wire *Am.* /*Br.* **earth wire**/.

grouper *Am.* a patient treated with group therapy.

groupie *Br.* group captain.

group work *Br.* work done in a group in collaboration.

grouse *Aus., NZ.* very good.

grouter *Aus.* col. lucky but unfair advantage, esp. in **come in on the grouter.**

grouts *esp. Br.* sediments, lees.

grouty *Am.* col. sulky, cross.

grow *esp. Am., Can.* cause smth., esp. business to increase or expand.

grow/ grow on trees *esp. Br.* col. be very common or easy to get.

grow bag, gro bag *Br.* bag with a potting compost for growing plants.

growler *Am.* (draft beer) pail.

growly *Aus.* excellent.

growmore *Br.* a type of balanced inorganic fertilizer.

grub 1. *Am.* drudge, bookworm: *Merton is not exactly a grub. He gets good grades without trying.* - R.A. Spears. 2. *Aus.* sl. dirty, slovenly person.

grub smth. **off/from** sb. *Am.* sl. ask sb. for smth. when one is unable or unwilling to do it oneself.

grub screw *Br.* special headless screw used usu. to attach a handle.

grubstake *esp. Am., Can.* col. money provided to develop a new business in return for a share of the future profits. n. **-er**: *Hymie grubstaked the two of us.* - Arthur Hailey., *We had nearly three thousand dollars for grubstake* - J. Fischer.

gruel *esp. Br.* punishment.

mustn't grumble *Br.* col. that's quite good.

grumbling appendix *Br.* condition in which person's appendix causes pain from time to time.

Grundyism *esp. Br.* prudery.

grunge *esp. Am., Can.* col. oily dirt, grime: *Let's remove the grunge from the motor. It's really dirty.* - W. Magnuson.

grungy *esp. Am.* sl. shabby, dirty: *the basement spuds are grungy.* - A. Hitchcock Mystery Magazine.

grunt *Am.* sl. 1. also *Can.* an infantry soldier: *it was impossible to pause to get the name and rank and whatever of every miserable filthy grunt the camera rested on.* - H. Fast., *his fellow grunts hit the ground* - Time. 2. wrestler: *there didn't seem to be much of a future for a worn-out grunt artist* - J. Fischer.

grunter *Aus.* sl. sluttish woman interested only in sex: *Man, she's a grunter.* - T. Thorne.

grunt work /also **scut work**/ *Am.* sl. hard and/ or tedious toil: *perform the legal grunt work* - G. O'Neill, D. Lehr.

GS *Am.* Gulf States.

guarantee smth. **against** *Am.* provide complete protection against harm or damage.

guarantee *Am.* law. formal promise, esp. of payment.

guard *esp. Br.* /*Am.* **conductor**/ a railway official in charge of a train.

guard attendant *Br.* /*Am.* **car porter**/ attendant employed in a sleeping-carriage in a train.

guard-dog *esp. Br.* watch dog.

guardee *Br.* dressed up guardsman.

guardrail *esp. Am., Can.* /*Br., Aus.* **crash barrier**/ a protective bar or rail intended to prevent drivers from going off the road: *He went through a guardrail* - R.L. Stine.

guard's van *Br.* /*Am.* **caboose**/ the part of a train, usu. at the back, where the guard travels: *the guard's van crawled past him* - A. McLean., *when he reached the guard's van, he would lift the dirty green flag* - I. Fleming.

gubbins *Br.* col. 1. gadget, thingamajig: *I'd like it with all the gubbins.* - T. Thorne. 2. refuse, innards.

guck *Am., Can.* slimy, dirty, unpleasant substance.

guess *esp. Am., Can.* col. suppose, consider likely, often in **I guess so/not**: *I guess I've gotten into the rhythm, you might say, of sleeping alone.* - I. Shaw., *It's a little odd, I guess but I think it's neat.* - Time., *I guess you're going to take a lot of heat for this.* - J. DeFelice / **have** (*Br.*), **take** (*Am.*) **a guess at the answer.**

guest *esp. Am.* take part as a guest performer.

guest beer *Br.* a type of beer that is sold in a bar for a short time and which is made by a different company from the one that usually supplies the beer in a tied pub or beer that is available temporarily in a free house.

guesthouse 1. *esp. Br.* private house where visitors, esp. business travellers or holiday makers can stay and have meals for payments: *It was a small hotel that was really a guesthouse, indeed was really a boarding-house.* - B. Bryson. 2. *Am.* outbuilding, wing for guests: *There were three young women lying on towels in the little yard that separated the duplex from the guesthouse.* - R. Crais.

guidance counsellor *Am.* a person who gives information to sb. about the jobs and what subjects to study: *Your high school will probably assign you a counsellor or guidance teacher.* – Living in the USA.

guidedog *Br.* /*Am.* **seeing eye dog**/ a dog specially trained to guide a blind person.

the Guides *Br.* the Guides Association, which trains girls practical skills and tries to develop the character.

guillotine 1. *esp. Br.* a piece of equipment used for cutting paper. 2. *Br., Aus.* an act of fixing a time to vote on a law in Parliament, so that argument about it will not go on too long.

guillotine *Br.* limit (argument) in Parliament.

guilt/ send sb. **on a guilt trip** *Br.* col. /*Am.* col. **lay/put a guilt trip on** sb./ make sb. feel very guilty.

guinea *Am.* taboo. sl. Italian or Italian-American: *somebody called me a "dirty little Guinea."* – A. Summers, R. Swan.

gulch *Am., Can.* (esp. in the western US) narrow stony valley with steep sides formed by a rushing stream: *Pablo and Pilon...walked in comradeship into the gulch* – J. Steinbeck.

The Gulf State *Am.* Florida.

Gulla *Am.* blacks living on a coastal strip in South Carolina and Georgia and their dialect (containing words from western Africa).

gully *Aus.* deep ravine.

gum *Am.* 1. gum elastic. 2. also *Can.* (in pl.) galoshes. 3. col. hollowed log used as a trough.

gum/ by gum *Br.* dial. or humor. obs. excl. of surprise.

gum *Am.* 1. enlarge the spaces between the teeth of (a worn saw). 2. practise chewing using one's gums.

gum *Br.* special kind of glue used to stick light things such as paper together.

gum (**tree**) *esp. Aus.* eucalyptus tree.

gumbah *Am.* sl. close friend: *I'm his gumbah.* - J. O'Brien, A. Kurins.

gumball *Am.* chewing gum in the form of brightly-coloured sweet.

gumbo *Am.* / *Br.* obs. **ladies' fingers**/ okra.

gumboot *esp. Br.* obs. or *Aus.* /also *esp. Br.* **wellington** (**boot**), *Am.* **rubber boot**/ rubber boot which keeps water from the feet and lower part of the legs: *In gumboots and tweeds, with dogs...the gentlemen will rise early* - J. Ruppeldtova.

gumby *Can.* sl. dull, tedious person.

gump 1. *Br.* sl. /also *esp. Br.* col. **gumption**/ common sense: *not having "the gumption to look after a sick kitten."* – K. Chopin. 2. *Am.* col. a fool: *But I thought he had more sense than to tie himself to that little gump again* – K. Chopin.

gumshoe 1. *Am.* /also **gum**/ rubber overshoe. 2. *Am.* /*Br.* **plimsoll, gymshoe**/ light shoe with a top made of heavy cloth and a flat rubber bottom used for games and sports /also *Am.* **sneakers**, *Br.* **trainers**/. 3. *esp. Am., Aus.* col., also **dick** detective: *I'm just an old gumshoe.* - S. Sheldon., *We don't want FBI gumshoes clambering all over the place* - R. Borchgrave, R. Moss.

gumshoe *Am.* sl. 1. work as a police officer or detective: *You didn't tell him you'd quit gum-shoeing.* - D. Hammet. 2. go quickly and secretly. 3. adj. done secretly.

gumsucker *Aus.* Victoria State citizen.

gum tree/ up a gum tree *Br., Aus.* col. in a difficult situation with no means of escape: *something which has got man like you up a gum tree.* - D. Francis.

gun *Am.* col. sb. who is temporarily put in a position to do a particular job.

(**hired**) **gun** *esp. Am.* col. gunman, esp. one who protects or kills people: *Tell your guns to lay off.* - R.A. Spears.

gun/ be in the gun *Aus.* 1. be likely to be dismissed. 2. get into trouble.

gun/ be under the gun *esp. Am., Can.* col. feel anxious because one has to do smth. to a deadline, so his/her future is uncertain.

gun/ come out with one's **guns blazing** *Am.* journalism. use all one's energy and skill against an opponent.
gun/ spike sb.'s **guns** *Br.* make smth. ineffective.
gun/ stand by one's **guns** *Am.* col. refuse to change one's opinions.
gun *Am., Can., Aus.* col. also **gun it** speed up an engine or vehicle, esp. abruptly: *The driver gunned the motor and made the green light at first.* - L. Waller., *He gunned his motor at the stoplight* - S. Bellow., *Engines are gunned, then glacially, we move out.* - Esquire.
gun for/be gunning for *esp. Br., Aus.* col. try to find reasons for attacking or harming (sb.): *they are gunning for you* - M. Jones, J. Chilton.
gundy/ no good to gundy *Aus.* no good at all.
gunge *Br.* /*Am.* **gunk**/ col. an unpleasant, dirty, and/or sticky substance: *the green gunk they'd pressed into his ears* - T. de Haven.
gunge/ be gunged up with smth. *Br.* /*Am.* **be gunked up with** smth./ col. be blocked with a dirty sticky substance.
gung-ho/ be gung-ho about/for *Am.* col. very excited or interested.
gunkhole *esp. Am., Can.* col. shallow inlet or cove that is difficult to navigate.
gunny *esp. Am., Can.* coarse sacking.
gunnysack *Am.* large bag from hemp in which coal, potatoes, etc. are stored: *In the yard Pilon had a gunny sack in readiness.* - J. Steinbeck.
gunplay *esp. Am., Can.* the use of guns.
gunsel *Am.* col. an armed criminal, hoodlum / also **gunslinger**/: *those gunslingers, those manly, virile, straight-shooting cowboys* - M. Puzo.
gun shearer *Aus.* expert sheep shearer.
gunshy *Am.* very careful or frightened about doing smth. after having a bad experience with this before.
gunslinger 1. *Br.* a strong and determined man: *Eugene McCarthy had not yet been heard from as the gunslinger who would retire LBJ.* – N.Hentoff. 2. *Am.* person skilful at using guns, esp. a criminal.
gunyah, wurley *Aus.* aboriginal's hut.
gurgler *Aus.* col. 1. toilet. 2. plughole.
gurgler/ go down the gurgler *Aus.* be permanently lost.
gurn *Br.* pull a grotesque face.
gurney *esp. Am., Can.* wheeled stretcher for transporting hospital patients: *They wheel Lorilee out of the room on a gurney* – Reader's Digest.
gurry *esp. Am., Can.* fish offal.
gussy up *esp. Am., Can., Aus.* col. ornament (smth.) in the hope of improving it: *they are gussying up products in order to price them higher.* - Time., *we'd get all gussied up in outrageous satin cowgirl clothes and ride rodeos.* - T. Thompson.
gut/ bust a/one's **gut** *Am.* laugh a lot.
gut/ have one's **guts for garters** *Br.* col. humor. punish sb. very severely.
gut/ spill ones's **guts** *Am., Aus.* col. tell sb. all about one's problems.
gut/ sweat/slog one's **guts out** *Br.* work very hard.
gutbucket 1. *Am.* sl. strongly rhythmic emotionally evocative uninhibited style of jazz: *His voice was deep and solid gut-bucket Texas.* - T. Thompson. 2. *Br.* col. glutton.
gut course *Am.* sl. an easy course in college.
gutless *Br.* sl. cowardly.
gut rot *Br.* col. 1. rot gut. 2. stomach upset.
gutser/ come a gutser *Aus., NZ.* col. 1. fall while you're walking or running. 2. fail at smth.
gutted *Br.* col. 1. devastated, shattered: *After all those years - just no. I was gutted.* - T. Thorne. 2.very tired.
gutter out *Am.* become gradually weaker and then stop completely.
gutter-crawl *Br.* v. cruise for a pick-up.
guttering *esp. Br.* gutters of a building.
the gutter press *esp. Br.* popular newspapers that print shocking stories about people's personal lives.
guttersnipe *Am.* col. broker who is not registered at the stock-exchange.
gutty *Am., Can.* gutsy.
guv *Br.* 1. col. /also **guv'nor**/ governor, boss: *Sorry to ring your bell at this hour, guvnor.* - J. Herriot. 2. col. used sometimes as a form of address to a customer.
guy 1. (pl. is often **you guys**) *esp. Am., Can., Aus.* any person, male or female: *You're a good-looking guy.* - S. Sheldon., *My boss there was one of the toughest guys I ever hope to meet.* - K. Vonnegut, Jr., *This guy represents two-bit show-biz types.* - L. Waller. 2. *Br.* sl. slip (vanishing act). 3. *Br.* a figure of a man burnt in Britain on Guy Fawkes Night.
guyver *Aus., NZ.* col. flattery.
Guz *Br.* sl. Devonport, United Kingdom.
gymkhana 1. *esp. Br.* local sports meeting for horse racing, horse jumping, and competitions for horse and carriage: *gymkhana and dances were false tokens of community.* - D. Lessing. 2. *Am.* car race that involves difficult driving.
gym rat *Am.* sl. a gym or basketball enthusiast: *I see guys, gym rats, and their idea of being an athlete is so different from what it really is.* – Reader's Digest.

gym shoes *esp. Br.* /*Am.* **sneakers, gumshoes** *Br.* **plimsolls, trainers**/ light shoes for sports: *He was wearing a shirt, a pair of white trousers and gymshoes.* - G. Greene.

gymslip *Br.* sort of dress without sleeves, formerly worn by schoolgirls as part of a uniform: *only a gymslip on her sea-wet body.* - L. Lee.

gymslip mother *Br.* a girl who has a baby why she's still at school.

gym-vest *Br.* T-shirt.

gyp 1. *esp. Br., Aus.* sl. sharp pain or punishment, esp. in **give** sb. **gyp**: *it does give me gyp from time to time.* - Woman's Own. 2. (also **gippo**) *Can.* sl. small operator or constructor. 3. *Am.* col. swindle(r) or smth. a person has been tricked into buying.

gypsum board *Am., Can.* plasterboard.

gypsy cab *Am.* sl. taxicab operating illegally (without a taxi license, etc.).

H

H *Br.* 1. (on signs in the streets) hydrant. 2. (in fixed sporting events) home.

Hab *Can.* sl. farmer who lives in French Canada.

haberdasher obs. or tech. 1. *Br.* shopkeeper who sells pins, sewing thread and other small things used in dressmaking and sewing. 2. *Am., Can.* /*Br.* **tailor**/ shopkeeper who sells men's clothing, esp. hats, gloves, etc.

haberdashery obs. or tech. 1. *Br., Aus.* also **fancy goods store, haberdasher's shop** /*Am., Can.* **dry goods,** *Br.* obs. **drapery**/ (the goods sold in) a haberdasher's shop or department /*esp. Am.* **Notions counter**/ in a department store. 2. *Am., Can.* /*Br.* **men's and boys' outfitters, tailor('s)**/ men's outfitter shop or men's wear in general: *a nice little haberdashery and notions store in the new shopping center* - K. Vonnegut, Jr.

habit/ Why break the habit of a lifetime? *Br., Aus.* humor. col. (said when sb. doesn't believe in another's ability to give up a bad habit).

habituate *Am.* col. visit frequently.

hack 1. *Am.* col. hacking carriage. 2. *Am., Can.* col. /*Br.* **hacking carriage**/ taxi: *They better not lay a hand on my hack* - S. Bellow., *He must look for a hack at once.* - T. Caldwell. 3. *esp. Am.* hacking cough: *A hack like that can lead to pneumonia.* - R.A. Spears. 4. *Am.* col. taxi driver: *No hackie that took somebody there.* - R. Stout. 5. *Aus.* sl. girl. 6. *Br.* a ride on horseback taken for pleasure. 7. *esp. Br.* derog. an unimportant politician who is concerned mainly with party matters: *he fired old Brezhnev hacks and promoted their deputies.* - H. Smith.

hack 1. *Am.* drive a taxi. 2. *Br.* kick sb. deliberately in a game. 3. *Br.* ride (a horse) at an ordinary speed along roads or through the country. 4. *Am., Aus.* (usu. in negatives and questions) manage to deal successfully with smth.

hack around *Am.,Can.* col. waste time: *I was just hacking around.* - G.V. Higgins.

hackamore *Am.* a bridle without a bit.

hacked off *Br.* col. unhappy and dissatisfied; fed up.

hacking jacket *esp. Br.* a riding jacket.

hackman *Am.* the driver of a hack: *how lousy it is, and all the hackmen listening.* – J.O'Hara.

hackney carriage *Br.* 1. /*Am.* **hackney coach**/ carriage pulled by a horse used in the past like taxi. 2. also **hackney cab** a taxi.

hackstand *Am.* taxi rank: *At the hackstand he found a Puerto Rican driver* - S. Bellow.

had/ had up *Br.* col. (forced to appear in a law court because of being) accused of breaking the law.

haddock/ bring haddock to paddock *Am.* lose everything.

hair/ curl sb.'s **hair** *Am.* /*Br.* **make** sb.'s **hair curl**/ frighten or shock sb.

hair/ get/have a wild hair (up one's **ass)** *Am.* sl. have a strong wish to do smth. that seems strange to other people.

hair/ it will put hairs on your chest *Br.* col. humor. drink or eat it because it will be good for you.

hair/ not turn a hair *Br.* seem unaffected by a shocking situation.

hairgrip *Br.* /*Am., Can., Aus., NZ.* **bobby pin**/ flat hairpin with ends pressed close together.

hairpin bend *Br., Aus.* /*Am.* **hairpin turn**/ a U-shaped bend on a steep road: *blue Cougar made the hairpin turn in the middle of the road.* - J. Patterson., *nine miles and 21 hairpin turns, wraps around mountain slopes* – National Geographic.

(hair)slide *Br., Aus.* /*Am.* **barrette**/ a small and decorarive fastener which women wear to hold hair back off the face.

half 1. *esp. Br.* (pl. also **halfs**) half a pint, esp. of beer. 2. *esp. Br.* (pl. also **halfs**) a child's ticket. 3. **half after** *Am.* half past, half an hour later than the stated time.

half *esp. Br.* col. predeterminer. half past (the stated time).

half/ not half *Br., Aus., Can.* col. a. very (much), to a great degree. b. (to be) not at all: *Doesn't half give one hope for the future.* - J.P. Donleavy.

Not half! *Br., Aus.* col. strong approval.

half/ In America some people think it is better to say a half mile than half a mile, etc.: *the coach wanted the players present and suited up at least a half hour before the game started.* - F. Pascal.

half/ half a tick *Br.* col. half a minute, right away.

half as much again *Br. /Am.* **half again as much/** a half one more time.

half / half the cash goes for clothes *Am. /Br.* **half the cash goes on clothes/**.

half/ too..by half *Br.* col. having too much of a particular quality.

half-and-half 1. *Am.* a mixture of milk and cream (used in coffee). 2. *Br.* mixed drink of two ale drinks, esp. ale and porter (stout).

half board *esp. Br. /Am.* **modified American plan/** (in lodgings, hotels, etc.) the providing of a bed and either the midday meal or the evening meal as well as breakfast: *guess the 1958 rate for a week's half board at the best hotel in the Isle of Wight* - D. Lodge.

half cock/ go off at half cock *Br.* be unsuccessful.

half-cocked *Am.* col. unexperienced; unprepared: *Gees, if he'd of been singing the way he usually is when he gets about half-cocked why it mighta been all right* – J. O'Hara.

half cup *Am.* small container used to measure an amount of food when cooking.

half-cut *Br.* col. obs. derog. quite drunk.

half day *Br.* 1.00 p.m. workday closing, early closing: *a magic lost world of half day closings, second posts, people on bicycles* - B. Bryson.

half holiday *Br.* morning or afternoon when a person doesn't work.

(a) half hour *Am.* half an hour: *the coach wanted the players present and suited up at least a half hour before the game started.* – F. Pascal.

half-inch *Br.* col. v. steal.

half landing *Br.* area of floor where a flight of steps turns through 180 degrees.

half-mast/ (at) half-mast *esp. Br.* humor. (of full-length trousers) too short, so that ankles can be seen.

halfmoon spectacles *Br. /Am.* **reading glasses/**.

half note *esp. Am., Can. /Br.* **minim/** a musical note with a time value half as long as a semibreve (*Br.*), **whole note** (*Am.*); **half rest** *Am. /Br.* **minim/**.

halfpence/ (get) more kicks than halfpence *Br.* col. (get) more bad treatment than good.

halfpenny/ not have two halfpennies to rub together *Br.* col. be very poor.

halfpennyworth, also **hap'orth,** col. **half p.** *Br.* obs. the amount of smth. bought for a halfpenny.

half-pie *NZ.* col. imperfect.

half plate *Br.* photographic plate measuring 16,5x10,8 cm.

half seas over *Br.* col. obs. quite drunk.

half-shot *Am., Can.* sl. half-drunk, drunk.

half-staff *Am.* half-mast: *Flags flew at half-staff, but the events went on.* - Newsweek.

half term *Br. /Am.* **midterm/** a short holiday in the middle of a school term.

half tone /also **half step/** *esp. Am. /Br.* **semitone/** a difference in pitch equal to that between two notes which are next to each other on a piano.

a halfway house (between) *Br.* a compromise between two things.

half-yearly *Br.* semi-annual(ly).

hall 1. (in a college or university) a. *esp. Br.* the room where all the members eat together. b. also **hall of residence** /*Am.* **residence hall, dormitory**/: *just be around hall generally* - R. Carter., M. MacCarthy., *walking to and fro between their halls of residence and the Student's Union* - D. Lodge. 2. *Br.* large country house with landed estate.

hall/ hall of fame *Am.* a building which contains images of famous people and interested things connected with them.

hall/ sports hall *Br.* gym.

hall bedroom *Am.* 1. part of a hall used as a bedroom. 2. cheap furnished room: *I don't go for hall bedroom romance* - R. Chandler.

hallo, also **hullo** *Br.* a. (the usual word used when greeting sb. b. (the word used for starting a telephone conversation). 2. an expression of surprise: *Halloa! What is this.* – M. Daly. 3. a call for attention to a distant person.

hallway *esp. Am.* passage inside the entrance of a house from which the other rooms and usu. the stairs are reached: *the man moved out into the hallway.* - S. Sheldon., *It was a rooming-house hallway* - D. Hammet., *Think we can freshen up this hallway?* - W. Jack, B. Laursen.

halma *Br.* tdmk. an easy game like chess.

halogen hob *Br.* top surface of electric cooker heated by tubes containing halogen.

halt *esp. Br.* small country railway station without proper buildings.

halterneck *Br., Aus.* /*Am.* **halter(top)**/ a garment that leaves the wearer's back and arms uncovered and which is held in position by a strap that goes behind the back.

halves/ not do things by halves *esp. Br.* do smth. properly and thoughtfully.

ham and eggs *Br.* /*Am.* **once over easy, sunny side up**/.

hambone *Am., Can.* col. a bad performer.

hamburger (meat), ground beef, ground(ed), chopped meat *Am.* /*Br.* **mince**/ minced meat.

hamburger bun *Am.* /*Br.* **bap**/ hamburger.

ham-fisted *esp. Br., Aus.* /*Am.* **ham-handed**/ 1. lacking skills with the hands. 2. clumsy in dealing with people.

hammer/ be/go at it hammer and tongs *Br.* do it very energetically.

hammer/ under the hammer *Br.* /*Am.* **on the block**/ at auction.

hamper *Am.* /*Br.* **laundry basket**/: *it was in your hamper* - A. Hitchcock Mystery Magazine.

hampton, Hampton Wick *Br.* sl. penis: *we want to plaster-cast your Hampton Wick.* – C.R. Cross.

hand *Br.* forehock of pork.

hand/ (a hired) hand (on a farm) *Am.* farm labourer.

hand/ be the dead hand *esp. Br.* be the one who has a very negative influence on a situation.

hand/ be hands and glove with sb. *Am.* have close business and working relationship with sb.

hand/ be hands down (to happen) *Am.* be certainly to happen.

hand/ come/go hat in hand *esp. Am.* ask for money and help.

hand/ come (readily) to hand *Br.* near and easy to find or reach.

hand/ the hand of God *Br.* very good luck.

hand/ have games or **matches in hand** *esp. Br.* have a chance to score more points having more games to play than their opponents.

hand/ have/keep smth. **(ready) to hand** *Br.* / *Am.* **have/keep** smth. **on hand**/ be sure that smth. is near you or available to be used. **hand/ have the whip hand (over** sb.**)** *Br.* control sb. having more power over them.

hand/ have time in hand *esp. Br.* have more time than one needs.

hand/ in hand *Br., Aus.* /*Am.* **at hand**/ smth. important at the present moment.

hand/ not to do a hand's turn *Br.* col. do no work.

hand/ a safe pair of hands *esp. Br.* (esp. in politics) person good at his/her job and unlikely to make serious mistakes.

hand/ a steady/firm hand on the tiller *Br.* (of a country, business, etc.) being led in a sensible way without any sudden changes.

hand/ take a hand (in smth.**)** *Br.* become involved in smth.

hand/ throw in one's **hand** *Br.* stop doing smth.

hand/ overplay one's **hand** *esp. Am.* try to get more than you're likely to have.

hand/ tip one's **hand** *Am.* let other people know one's plans.

hand down *esp. Am.* make an official statement: *The city council will hand down the budget on Monday.* - Longman.

hand up *Am.* deliver (an indictment).

hand in glove 1. *Br.* closely involved with sb. else, esp. in an illegal activity. 2. *Am.* work together very well or be suitable to each other.

hand and glove *Am.* very close together.

handbag *esp. Br., Can.* /*Am.* **pocketbook, purse**/ a small women's bag usu. worn over the shoulder.

handbag/ it's handbags at ten paces *Br.* humor. neither side wins.

handbasin *Br.* washbasin.

handbrake 1. *Br.* /*Am.* **emergency break,** *Am., Aus.* **parking break**/ a car brake used to stop a car in case of emergency, esp. in **put on handbrake, emergency brake**. 2. *Am.* also **break** a device on a bicycle operated by hand that stops it.

h and c *Br.* hot and cold (about water supply in a hotel).

handcar, also **section car** *Am., Can.* railway trolley: *we came on the handcar.* – K. Chopin.

handcraft *Am.* /*Aus.* **handcrafts**/ handicrafts.

handgun *esp. Am.* pistol, small gun held in one hand while firing, not raised against the shoulder: *Eight members of the Emir's poured from the house and raced to them, rifles and handguns at the ready.* - I. Fleming., *silverware and handguns can be registered* - Reader's Digest.

handle *Am.* col. the amount of money bet over a certain period of time.

handle/ up to the handle *Am.* just right.

handler *Br.* person who assists in selling stolen property or drugs.

handover *esp. Br.* act of handing smth. over.

hands/ be rubbing one's **hands (with glee/ delight)** *Br.* be pleased to have an advantage (over sb.).

hands/ it's all hands to the pump *Br.* a lot of work that has to be done in a small amount of time.

hands/ make/do smth. **with** one's **own fair hands** *Br.* humor. telling people that they should be impressed by sb.'s actions.

hands /soil one's **hands** *Br.* get involved into dishonest or unpleasant activity.

han(d)sel *esp. Br.* 1. give a gift as a token of good wish or luck (esp. at the beginning of the year). 2. inaugurate with a token or gesture of luck or pleasure. 3. use or do for the first time.

handsome *Am.* clever, skilful.

handtruck *Am.* a frame with two wheels and two handles used to move large or heavy things.

handsome *Am.* clever, skilful.

the handwriting on the wall *Am.* warning about forthcoming worsening situation.

handy/ be handy for *Br.* be suitable.

hang *Am., Can.* col. 1. hang around. 2. hang out.

hang *Am.* deadlock (a jury) by refusing to join in a unanimous vote; **hang a jury.**

hang/ hang one's **hat** *Am., Can.* col. be resident.

hang/ hang sb. **out to dry** *esp. Am., Can.* col. leave sb. in a difficult situation.

hang/ hang tough, hang in there *Am., Can.* be persistent and firm in one's decisions or actions.

hang/ you can hang it/that up! *Am.* sl. I refuse to do that.

hang/ You might as well be hanged/hung for a sheep as (for) a lamb *Br.* British saying which means that because the punishment for either bad action is the same, there is no reason not to do the worse one.

hang about *Br.* col. 1. hang around. 2. delay or move slowly, dawdle: *I'd left him hanging about* - A. Summers, R. Swan.

hang at *Am.* col. wait at a place with no particular reason.

hang in (there) *esp. Am., Can., Aus.* col. keep going in spite of difficulties: *I take it you told her you'd hang in there.* - I. Shaw.

hang on/ (*esp. Br.*) wait; I'm afraid the (telephone) line is engaged, would you like to hang on?

hang one on *esp. Am.* col. 1. go out in order to get drunk: *You really hung one on last night, didn't you?* - Longman. 2. strike (sb.) with a blow: *I hung one on him and down he went like a stone.* - Longman.

hang on in there! *Br.* col. keep trying to deal with a difficult situation.

hang out *esp. Am.* stay somewhere for no particular reason.

hang up *Aus.* col. tie (a horse) to a post: *Hang up your horse and come in for a drink.* - Longman.

hang up one's **boots** *Br.* (of a sportsman) stop playing and retire.

hang a left/right *esp. Am.* col. turn left/right (about a car).

hang it (all) *Br.* obs. damn it.

hang loose *Am., Can., Aus.* col. stay relaxed: *In Hawaii, they tell the tourists to hang loose - to relax.* - W. Magnuson.

hang-ashore *Can.* tramp.

hanged/ I'm hanged if *Br.* 1. obs. I won't let it happen. 2. I don't think it's true.

hanger *esp. Br.* a small wood on steeply sloping land.

hangi *NZ.* pit in which food is cooked on heated stones.

hangover *Br.* /*Am.* **holdover**/ (from) attitude, habit, etc. from the past that's not suitable or practical anymore.

hanky-panky 1. *Br.* col. improper but not very serious sexual behaviour. 2. *Am.* /*Br.* **jiggery-pokery**/ cheating or deceit, often done in secret: *I'm not interested in hanky-panky.* – A. Summers, R. Swan.

ha'porth/ not a ha'porth of difference *Br.* obs. col. (not) any difference at all.

happen along/by/past *esp. Am.* go to a place by chance or without planning.

happen by *Am.* find a place by chance.

happen in *Am.* col. sit, drop in (accidentally).

happenstance *esp. Am., Can.* joc. a circumstance regarded as due to chance: *there is less fear of happenstance contact.* - J. Fraser.

happy camper/ not be a happy camper *Br., Am.* humor. /*Br.* **not be a happy bunny**/ be annoyed about a situation.

happy/ be as happy as Larry/a sandboy *Br., Aus.* /*Br.* col. **happy as a pig in muck**/, /*Am., Can.* **be happy as a clam**/ be very happy.

hard *Br.* 1. firm beach. 2. sloping stone jetty. 3. col. hard labour.

hard-ass *esp. Am.* sl. difficult; also tough, uncompromising.

hardbake *Br.* almond taffy.

hard ball *Am.* 1. also *Can.* baseball rather than softball. 2. **play hardball (with** sb.) *esp. Am., Aus.* col. esp. journalism. use methods that are not gentle and may even be unfair: *No jokes, just political hardball.* - Reader's Digest.

hard candy *Am.* /*Br.* **boiled sweet(s)/.**

hard case/nut *esp. Br.* col. sb. difficult to deal with.

hard case *Aus., NZ.* smth. funny and strange.

The Hard-case State *Am.* Oregon.

hard cheese *esp. Br., Aus.* col. obs. hard luck, bad luck.

hard cider *Am.* /*Br.* **cider**/ alcoholic drink made from apples: *I would drink hard cider out of a barrel* - Alcoholics Anonymous.

hard coal *Am.* anthracite: *they couldn't afford to buy hard coal.* - M. Jones, J. Chilton.

hard core *esp. Br.* 1. the most active and determined members of the group. 2. the most conservative group of people. 3. pieces of broken stone used as a base on which to build roads, paths or floors.

hard cover *esp. Am., Can., Aus.* a book with a stiff cover.

be/feel hard-done by *Br., Aus.* be treated unfairly.

hardhat *Am.* 1. helmet: *always in coveralls and hard hat.* - Atlantic Monthly. 2. construction worker: *Some hardhat was waving a flag* - R.A. Spears. 3. an outspoken conservative: *Haggard, then, had become caught in the crossfire between the hard hats and the hippies* - Atlantic Monthly., *The hardhats loved that piece.* - R. Borchgrave, R. Moss.

hard lines, hurd luck *Br., Aus.* col. /*Br.* obs. col. **hard cheese**/ excl. bad luck.

hard knocks/ the school, university, college of hard knocks *esp. Am.* harsh realities and experiences in life that a person learns from.

(hard) liquor *esp. Am.* /*esp. Br.* **spirits**/: *By the 1960s, he was openly flaunting his use of hard liquor.* – A. Summers, R. Swan.

hard money *Am.* gold, copper or aluminium coins.

hard nut *Br.* col. tough aggressive person.

hard-pan *Am.* fundamental part, bedrock.

hard pushed/ be hard pushed to do smth. *Br.* be in a difficult situation, esp. having no time and money.

hard sauce *Am.* sauce for desserts made with butter and sugar and usu. cream and flavouring.

hard-scrabble *Am.* adj. (of land) difficult to grow crops on: *in his hardscrabble years going back and forth, up and down* – S. Lawrence.

hard shell *esp. Am.* conservative, esp. in one's religious beliefs.

hard shoulder *esp. Br.* /*Am., Aus.* **shoulder,** *Irish English* **hard margin**/ an area of ground beside a road, esp. motorway, that has been given a hard surface where cars can stop if in difficulties, because stopping is not allowed on the road itself: *Coach crawls along on hard shoulder* – S. Townsend.

hard sledding *Am.* difficult task.

hardstanding *Br.* ground specifically prepared for parking motor vehicles on.

hard tack, ship's biscuit *esp. Br.* ship biscuit.

hardware *Am., Aus.* /*Br.* **ironmongery**/ tools or equipment used in house or garden.

hardware *Am.* sl. spirits, potent liquor: *This hardware is enough to knock your socks off.* - R.A. Spears.

hardware dealer *Am.* ironmonger.

hardware store *Am., Aus.* /*Br.* **ironmonger's**/: *the father, who owned a hardware store* - A.E. Hotchner.

hardwearing *Br.* /*Am.* **longwearing**/ (esp. of a material or clothes, shoes, etc.) that lasts for a long time even when used a lot.

hard word/ put the hard word on *Aus., NZ.* col. ask a favour from sb., esp. sex or money: *To put the hard word on somebody is to try and coerce somebody into doing something.* – Time.

hardy perennial *Br.* a book or song that stays popular with a lot of people for a very long time.

hare *Am.* rabbit.

hare (esp. **off, away**) *esp. Br.* col. run very fast.

hare/ start a hare *Br.* obs. introduce a new idea or topic.

hark at *Br.* col. (imperative) listen to (sb. or smth. that is disapproved of): *Hark at him.* - G. Greene.

harness *Am.* /*Br.* **loom**/ several wires fastened together.

harness/ be back in harness *esp. Br.* go back to work.

harness/ in harness *esp. Br.* 1. actually doing a job. 2. working together.

harp *Am.* sl. an Irish person or one of Irish descent: *The Harps and Sheenies have their town and I have mine.* - L. Waller.

harp on (about) *Br.* /*Am.* **harp on** smth./ endlessly talk about smth. in an annoying way: *He is always harping on the fact that people are so much less religious today* - H.C. Whitford., R.J. Dixson.

Harry flakers *Br.* sl. /or **flaked out**/ worn out.

Harry starkers *Br.* sl. stark naked.

hart *esp. Br.* male deer, esp. of the red deer family over five years old.

harvest festival *esp. Br.* religious occasion when thanks are given for the crops which have been gathered, marked by services in churches, schools, etc.

has-been/ It is better to be a has-been than a never was. American proverb.

hash *esp. Am., Can.* (make) a mixture of meat, potatoes and vegetables cut into small pieces and baked or fried; **hash browns** consist only of potatoes.

hash over *esp. Am., Can.* col. talk about (smth. such as difficulty) in detail and at length: *I have lost count of the number of evenings I spent hashing over individual accounts of the Cultural Revolution.* - J. Fraser., *They hashed these over.* - J. Kerouac.

hasher, also **hash slinger** *Am.* sl. cook, waiter or waitress: *I worked as a hash-slinger in an all-night diner.* - R.A. Spears.

hash-house *esp. Am., Can.* col. a cheap restaurant: *Joe and his friends went to a hash house around the corner after the game.* - A. Makkai.

hassle *esp. Am., Aus.* an argument or fight, esp. between two people or two groups: *the big hassle was, how should Jesus speak?* - J.A. Michener., *The budget meetings in Kuching were always a hassle* - L. Uris., *others want to escape the high rents and downtown hassles.*- Time.

hassock 1. *Am., Can.* /*Br.* **pouf(fe)**/ footstool: *her slippered feet up on a hassock.* - R.J. Randisi., M. Wallace. 2. *esp. Br.* a cushion for kneeling on in a church.

haste makes waste *Am.* /*Br.* **more haste less speed**/ if one tries to do smth. too quickly they will have problems.

hasty pudding 1. *Am.* mush made of cornmeal. 2. *Br.* mush made of flour and oatmeal.

hat/ My hat! *esp. Br.* obs. I don't believe (that)!

hat/ (go/come) hat in hand *esp. Am.* /*Br.* **(go) cap in hand**/ (go) begging for smth.

hat/ pass the hat around *Br.* /*Am., Can.* **pass the hat**/ collect money from a group of people.

hat/ tip one's **hat to** sb. *Am.* take one's hat off to sb.

hat/ throw/toss one's **hat in(to) the ring** *esp. Am., Aus.* start competing with others, usu. in a political competition.

hat/ (wear) the black hat *Am.* be disliked or blamed by people for what is wrong in a situation.

hatch *esp. Br.* opening in a wall, esp. between a kitchen and a dining-room which you can pass smth. such as food through.

hatcheck *Am.* obs. place where people can leave their coats in the theatre, etc.: *Frank might date a celebrity, or a hatcheck girl, or pay for sex with a whore.* – A. Summers, R. Swan

hatter *Aus.* col. farmer or gold-digger working alone.

haul ass *Am.* col. move quickly or do smth. fast.

haul off 1. *Am.* sl. raise one's arm (before hitting sb.), often in **haul off and hit**: *the cop had hauled off and hit the young guy* - J. Dos Passos. 2. *Am., Can.* col. leave, depart.

haulier *Br.* /*Am.* **hauler**/ person or transport company employed to carry goods.

have *Br.* col. obs. swindle.

have/ In Britain have is used of continuous states rather than of possession or experience at one particular moment, which is expressed by have got / cp. (*Br.*) **Have you got a cold now?** and (*esp. Am.*) **Do you have a cold now?**

have/ *esp. Br.* col. (used esp. before a noun that has the same form as a verb) perform the actions connected with, do (smth.) / e.g. *have a look, a read, a swim, a walk, a run, a wash, a chat, a sip of tea,* etc.

have / *esp. Br. I've a beautiful, new house in the country.*

have/ **...and have done with it** *Br.* to end an annoying situation.

have/ **have a clue** *esp. Br.* know.

have/ **Have a good day** *Am.* temporal greeting.

have/ **have a nice day** *esp. Am.* goodbye, said esp. to customers in shops or restaurants when they are leaving: *Now, you have a nice day, hear?* – Reader's Digest.

have/ **have got to do** *esp. Br.* must do.

have/ **have it good** *Am.* col. have enough money, be comfortably off: *Jim has had it good ever since his father died* - Longman.

have/ **have it made in the shade** *Am.* col. have everything for a good life.

have/ **have rats in the attic** *Br.* /*Am.* **have kangaroos in** one's **top paddock**/ be slightly mad.

have/ **not having any** sl. not accepting, e.g. *I tried to get her to help me with the cooking, but she wasn't having any* (*Br.*), *wouldn't have any of that* (*Am.*) - Longman.

have/ **Have you been served?** *Br.* Is somebody helping you?

have it away (on one's **toes)** *Br.* col. leave quickly.

have it away (with sb.) *Br.* col. /*Br., Aus.* col. **have it off**/ have sex.

have (got) in *esp. Br.* have or keep supply of (smth.), (not in progressive forms).

have a buck in at smth. *Aus.* try to do smth.

have a down on sb. *Br.* sl. behave as if angry with sb.

have smth. **off** *esp. Br.* col. 1. (not in progressive forms) obs. have learned, be ready to speak from memory. 2. also **have it away with** sb. also *Aus.* col. **have it off (with)** sl. have sex with.

have sb. **on** *Br.* /*Am.* **put on** sb.**/** col. trick or deceive sb.

have (got) smth. **on** *Br.* keep an arrangement.

have (smth.) **out** *Br.* be allowed to finish (with).

have sb. **up** *Br.* col. cause (sb.) to appear in court, bring charges against (sb.), often in **be had**.

have got *esp. Br.* 1. /*Am.* **have gotten** or **got**/ buy; receive smth. such as a letter, information or advice. 2. be with. sb., or be visited by sb. 3. /*Am.* **have**/ possess or own smth.

have got a friend /sister /uncle /etc. *Br.* know or be related to sb.

have got smth. **on** *Br.* be wearing smth.

haver *Br.* hesitate.

having/be having sb. **on** *Br.* col. cheat on sb.: *you're having me on again!* - Longman.

having/ I'm not having it *Br.* col. I will not accept it.

having/ not be having/wouldn't have (any of) it *Br.* not believe smth.

Hawaii *Br.* sl. a banknote of 5 or 50 pounds: *I got him to do it, but it cost me a Hawaii.* - T. Thorne.

hawk *Am., Can.* buzzard.

hawk *esp. Am.* person who supports warlike political ideas.

hawk around *esp. Br.* /*Am.* obs. **hawk**/ sell goods on the street or going from door to door asking people to buy them.

The Hawkeye State *Am.* joc. Iowa; **Hawkeye** *Am.* joc. a citizen of Iowa: *"Show-me's from Missouri and "Jayhawkers" from Kansas and "Hawkeyes" from Iowa* - K. Vonnegut, Jr.

hay/ That ain't hay *Am.* sl. that is quite a lot: *I'll see that you stay on the job at four thousand a week, which ain't hay* - H. Fast.

hay burner *Am.* sl. a worthless racehorse: *Send that old hay burner to the glue factory.* - R.A. Spears.

hayride *esp. Am., Can.* a ride taken by a picnic party (esp. in a wagon filled with hay).

hayseed *esp. Am., Can.* joc. /*Br.* sl. derog. **chaw-bacon**/ country bumpkin, yokel: *rebellious-looking hayseed in the undersized jacket caring about money.* - J. Baez., *The hayseed in the Marauder laughed at his own humor.* - B. Tillman.

haywire *Am., Can.* col. hastily or shoddily made: *In SCID the immune system goes haywire.* – Reader's Digest.

haywire/ go haywire *Br.* become very nervous or excited.

hazard sb. or smth. *Br.* put them at risk.

hazard pay, hazardous-duty pay *Am.* /*Br., Aus.* **danger money**/.

haze *Am.* 1. make (sb.) worried or uncomfortable by forcing them to do unpleasant work or by saying unpleasant things about them, harass. 2. play tricks on (a young college student) as part of the ceremony of joining a club or fraternity: *Griffith calls the hazing charge "ludicrous"* - USA Today., *the cellar was crowded with young men who had been hazed in previous years.* - J. O'Hara.

HB *Br.* hard black (letters printed on pencils meaning that lead in it is medium hard).

head 1. *esp. Br.* col. a headache: *I got a thick tongue but I ain't got head.* - E. Hemingway. 2. *Am.* sl. addict, fan (esp. a drug addict): *Some of the heads became very, very straight.* - R.A. Spears. 3. **have head for heights** *Br.* not to be afraid of the height.

head/ be beating one's **head against the wall** *Am.* try hard to achieve smth. but be unable to do it.

head/ be headed for *esp. Am.* expect smth. to happen, move in a certain direction.

head/ be off one's **head** *esp. Br., Aus.* col. 1. (of ideas or behaviour) be crazy. 2. be confused because of being drunk.

head/ be on a head trip *Am.* sl. boast too much.

head/ do sb.'s **head in** *esp. Br., Aus.* col. make sb. feel confused and unhappy.

head/ get/put one's **head down** *Br., Aus.* work hard at smth. that involves reading and writing, ignoring everything else.

head/ get one's **head/mind round** smth. *Br.* col. understand a situation at last.

head/ get it into one's **head to do** smth. *Am.* /*Br.* **take it into** one's **head to do** smth./ suddenly decide to do smth.

head/ knock smth. **on the head** *Br., Aus.* col. 1. stop doing smth. or prevent it from happening. 2. show that smth. is correct or true, thus stopping people thinking otherwise.

head/ need your head testing *Br.* humor. you're crazy.

head/ off one's **head** *esp. Br.* 1. strong, foolish or dangerous. 2. too much drunk.

head/ on one one's **head (be it)** *esp. Br.* one is responsible.

head/ put/stick/raise one's **head above the parapet** *Br.* say or do smth. risky; opp. **keep** one's **head below the parapet.**

head/ wet the baby's head *Br.* col. have a drink celebrating the birth of a child.

head out *Am.* col. reach a crucial moment: *the pals began to head out* - Longman.

headband *esp. Am.* a printed strip of decoration at the head of a chapter or page.

head boy/girl *esp. Br.* leader of the prefects representing schools on formal occasions.

headcase *Am.* sl. 1. mad person: *if I had spent all those years trying to please some great unknown audience, I'd be a headcase.* - E. Taylor. 2. *Br.* sl. a person whose behaviour is violent and unpredictable.

headcheese *Am., Can. /Br.* **brawn/** (pieces of) meat from the head of a pig, boiled and pressed in a pot with jelly, collared pork.

header 1. *esp. Br.* col. (in football) an act of striking the ball with the head. 2. also **header tank** /*Am.* **coolant tank/** *Br.* a tank in a car's engine into which water is put to keep up the correct water pressure in the car's radiator. 3. *Am.* trimmer (joist), header joist (in building).

the head honcho *esp. Am.* col. the big boss.

headlamp *Br.* headlight of the car.

headline *Am.* be the leading performer in.

headlong *Am., Aus.* adj., adv. headfirst.

headmaster, headmistress *esp. Br. /Am.* **principal/** a teacher in charge of the school: *Roberts became headmaster of Chatham Grammar School* - W. Grady.

heads/ knock heads *Am.* esp. journalism. force two disagreeing groups to reach an agreement.

heads/ heads up! *esp. Am., Can.* col. warning that smth. that is falling or being thrown towards them could hit them.

headscarf, also **headsquare** *Br.* a woman's scarf worn around the head.

headship *Br.* the position or period in office of a headmaster.

headstall *esp. Am., Can.* head collar or halter.

head start *Am.* a set of educational courses provided by the US central government for disadvantaged children below school age.

heads-up *Am.* adj. confident and of high quality: *You must play hard, heads-up baseball to win this game.* - A. Makkai.

(the) head(teacher), headmaster/mistress *esp. Br. /Am., Aus.* **principal/** a teacher in charge of the school.

head table *Am. /Br.* **top table/** table where important people or people making speeches sit, esp. at a formal meal.

head-to-head *Am.* man-to-man fight.

health center *Am.* 1. dispensary, esp. one where medical students can get medical help and advice: *All was confusion at the health center.* - Reader's Digest. 2. *Br.* a center for medical and administrative health welfare work, where a group practice is operated.

healthful *Am.* good for one's body.

health maintenance organization, HMO *esp. Am.* an organisation providing comprehensive health care in return for a fixed fee.

the health service *Br.* National Health Service.

health spa *Am.* health farm, a place where one goes for holiday, eats healthy food, takes exercises, etc.

health visitor *Br.* a person, esp. a trained nurse, employed to give advice esp. to the parents of young children about health care.

heap *Am.* sl. an old car or vehicle: *It's the same heap all right.* - R. Moore., *he gunned the heap to eighty* - J. Kerouac.

heap/ fall in a heap *Aus.* col. break down and cry.

heap/ heap coals of fire on sb.'s **head** *Br.* do everything to cause sb. remorse.

heaped *Br.* (of spoon or other container) filled with smth. above the brim or edge.

Hear! Hear! *esp. Br.* Yes! Yes! (used in public meetings to encourage the speaker).

hear/ I hear ya, I heard that *Am.* col. I agree and understand what you mean.

heart/ near and dear to one's **heart** *Am.* very important to sb.

heart/ their hearts were in their boots *Br.* col. obs. they felt worried and anxious.

Heart of Dixie *Am.* Alabama.

heart-cry *Br.* an emotional appeal.

hearty 1. *esp. Br.* col. (too) cheerful, esp. when noisy and trying to appear friendly. 2. *Br.* col. / *Am.* **jock/** person rather ostentatiously devoted to practice of sporting activity.

heat *Am. /Br.* **heating/** the system in the house that keep it warm.

(the) heat *Am.* sl. police: *It would be sheer madness to try operating an American city without the heat, the fuzz, the man.* - E. Cleaver.

heat/ put the heat on sb. *Am., Aus.* start to do better.

heat/ take heat *Am.* sl. be reprimanded: *he took heat for a Journal of Pediatrics paper he wrote* - New York.

heat/ on heat *Br. /Am.* **in heat/** in a state of sexual excitement (of animals).

heater *Am., Can.* col. obs. a gun.

heat haze *Br., Aus. /Am.* **haze/** an effect of very hot sun making it very difficult to see objects clearly.

heat lightning *esp. Am.* lightning without thunder or rain.

heat prostration *Am.* heat exhaustion, feeling weak because of the heat.

heath *esp. Br.* an area of open land covered mostly with rough grass or heather.

heather-mixture *Br.* a clothing material (tweed) of mixed colour.

Heath Robinson *Br.* usu. humor. /*Am.* **Rube Goldberg**/ (of a machine or system) clever and complicated.

heave gate *Br.* one opened by being lifted out of the sockets or mortises.

Heaven knows *esp. Br.* exclamation of disbelief or surprise.

heaven/ be in hog heaven *Am.* be very happy.

heaven/ in heaven's name *Br.* col. special emphasizing phrase used in questions to show that one is angry or surprised.

heaven/ nigger heaven *Am.* sl. /*Br., Aus.* col. **gods**/ seats farthest from the stage (in theatre).

heaven/ the heavens opened *esp. Br.* it began raining very hard.

heaving *Br.* col. very busy or full of people.

the heavies *Br.* large serious newspapers.

heavy *Am., Aus.* col. serious, profound, important: *This matter is too heavy.* - R.A. Spears.

heavy breather *Br., Aus.* /*Am.* **breather**/ a man who gets sexual pleasure from making telephone calls and saying nothing but only breathing noisily.

heavy cream *Am., Can.* /*Br.* **double cream**/.

heavy date *Am., Aus.* humor. a planned meeting between two persons who are not very interested in having a romantic or sexual relationship.

heavy-duty *Am., Aus.* col. complicated and very serious or involving strong emotions.

heavy/ have a heavy foot, be heavy-footed *Am.* col. drive a car too fast.

heavy goods vehicle, HGV *Br.* a large truck.

heavy hitter *Am.* 1. person who is powerful and has achieved a lot. 2. baseball player who hits the ball very hard.

heavy weather/ make heavy weather of smth./ doing smth. *Br., Aus.* take a longer time than necessary to do smth. or make smth. that a person is doing seem more difficult and complicated than it really is.

Hebe *Am.* sl. a Jew: *Ben and Abe were "the Jew boys". The Hebes, Yids, Sheenies, Kikes.* - L. Uris.

heck *Can.* go fast.

heck/ (just) for the heck of it *Am., Aus.* (said if one wants it or thinks it is funny).

hedgehog *Am., Can.* porcupine.

hedgerow *esp. Br., Aus.* a line of bushes and small trees growing along the edge of a field or road.

hee-haw *Am.* col. concerned with simple rural humour or attitudes.

heel *Am.* crust (of bread): *small boards that looked like heels of stale bread* – R. Brautigan.

heel *esp. Am., Aus.* sl. low and despicable person: *He was rather a heel* - R. Chandler.

heel/ lay (sb.) **by the heels** *Br.* obs. catch sb. and put them in prison.

heel/ kick one's **heels** *esp. Br.* col. /*Am.* **cool** one's **heels**/ be made to wait for some time unwillingly.

heel/ kick up one's **heels** *esp. Am., Aus.* do things that one enjoys.

heel/ set/rock sb. **back on their heels** *Br.* make them less hopeful or confident.

heel bar *esp. Br.* while-U-wait shoe repair shop.

heeler 1. *Am.* derog. a henchman of a local political boss. 2. *Aus.* a dog used to collect together cattle or sheep.

heft *esp. Am.* 1. weight, heaviness. 2. the bulk, the greater part. 3. heave up, hoist: *Palmer hefted his overnight bag* - L. Waller., *her other hand hefted the dryer.* - A. Hitchcock Mystery Magazine.

heifer-paddock *Aus.* a school for girls.

heifer-station *Aus.* farm for raising young cows.

height of land *Am., Can.* watershed.

height/the dizzy(ing) heights of smth. *Am.* very high level of success.

heist *esp. Am., Can.* col. v. n. steal, rob(bery): *The story has something to do with a jewel heist* - Bulletin.

hell 1. *esp. Br.* excl. of anger or annoyance. 2. *Am.* used for emphasis.

hell/ be going to hell in a hand-basket *Am., Can.* col. (of a system or organisation) quickly become worse.

hell/ be hell on wheels *Am.* col. behave angrily losing control over oneself.

hell/ catch/get hell *Am., Aus.* col. be blamed or punished for doing smth.

hell/ go to hell in a handbasket/handcart *Am.* col. be in a bad state and getting worse or stop working properly.

hell/ hell for leather *esp. Br., Aus.* col. very fast.

hell/ play (merry) hell (with) *Br.* col. cause disorder or confusion; **one thing plays merry hell with another** *Br.* first thing has a bad effect on the other.

hell/ raise hell *esp. Am.* behave in a noisy or wild way that upsets other people.

hell/ there'll be merry hell to pay *Br.* col. some people will be very angry.

hell around *Am.* col. go on a binge: *My father was known for helling around during his youth* - Longman.

hellacious *Am., Can.* col. very great.

hell-bender *Am.* sl. 1. playboy. 2. a spree, binge: *Jed is off on another of his hellbenders.* - R.A. Spears.
heller, also **hellion, hell-raiser** *Am.* col. mischievous man or child: *the young hellion had undergone conversion* - J.A. Michener., *Kentucky women are difficult to begin with, keyed-up, hellion-hearted* - T. Capote., *The beautiful young red-headed hellion made it a point to be rude* - L. Uris.
Hello *esp. Br.* an expression of surprise.
hello girl *Am.* col. telephone girl.
Hello Hello Hello *Br.* humor. (supposedly said by a policeman on finding smth. unusual).
hell's half acre *Am., Can.* a great distance.
hell's teeth *Br., Aus.* expression of anger, surprise or fear.
helluva *Am., Aus.* col. damned: *Helluva police dog, too.* - R. Crais.
help 1. *Br. /Am.* **helper/** person, esp. female who is employed to do some of sb. else's housework: *four cooks and five helpers, nine servants just in kitchen.* - H. Fast., *My girls are above being helps.* - W. Grady. 2. also **hired help** *esp. Am.* workers, esp. house servants: *the help were very elderly and polite* - J. Dos Passos., *Mr. B. does not fraternize with the help* - A. Hitchcock Mystery Magazine.
helping verb *Am.* auxiliary verb.
helter-skelter *esp. Br.* adj. adv. (done) in a great and disorderly hurry.
helter-skelter *esp. Br., Aus.* amusement park spiral glide: *Their sideshows include a helter-skelter, laser disco and break dancers* - You.
hem *esp. Am.* hum, move fast.
hem and haw *Am., Aus. /esp. Br.* **hum and haw/** hesitate.
hemidemisemiquaver *Br.* 1/64 note.
hen party or **night** *Br., Aus.* col. a party for women only: *I have a hen party every few weeks.* - R.A. Spears.
hen's teeth/ rare/scarce as hen's teeth *Br.* obs. very rare.
hen tracks *Am.* sl. illegible handwriting.
herd book *Br.* book with the pedigrees of cattle or other livestock.
herder *esp. Am.* shepherd.
Here! *Br.* used to get sb.'s attention or to show annoyance.
here/ I'm out of here! *Am.* sl. said when leaving a place if sb. is happy to be going.
hereabout *Am. /Br., Aus.* **hereabouts/** somewhere near here.
hereditary *Br.* a position, rank or title that is hereditary.
her indoors *Br.* col. humor. one's wife, any domineering woman in a position of control.
heritage-listed building *Aus. /Br.* **listed building,** *Am.* **landmarked building/** one of the great artistic or historical value.
herky-jerky *Am., Can.* col. moving in sudden jerks: *Another simply offers a herky-jerky nod of the head.* – Reader's Digest.
hero (sandwich), submarine (sandwich) *Am.* sandwich made of a long loaf of bread filled with meat, cheese, salad, etc.
Herring Chokers *Can.* joc. Maritimers, but esp. people from New Brunswick.
Hessian *Am.* a mercenary soldier.
hessian *Br. /Am.* **burlap/**.
het up *esp. Br., Aus.* col. usu. derog. nervous, excited, and confused: *Now, don't get so het up!* - R.A. Spears.
hew to *Am.* follow (a rule, principle, etc.): *Backstage atmosphere at Broadway musicals usually hews to a predictable pattern* - New York.
hex (on) *esp. Am., Can., Aus.* col. an evil curse which brings trouble: *The language picked up words like hex meaning "a spell"* - R. McRum, W. Cran, R. McNeil., *A friend of mine wants to put a hex on innuendo.* - A. Peterson.
hex *esp. Am.* put an evil curse on, esp. to cause harm or bad luck: *she was crazy and tilted her head and smiled like a hexed cat.* - J. Baez.
hey/ What the hey? *Am., Can.* col. euph. What the hell?
Hey, presto *esp. Br., Aus.* col. excl. Here is the result of my (magic) trick!
Hey up *Br.* col. way of greeting sb. or drawing attention to smth.
HGV *Br.* Heavy Goods Vehicle.
H-hour *Am.* mil. the time for the beginning of an attack.
Hi *esp. Br.* Hey, look here: *Hi, said a voice.* - V. Holt.
hick *esp. Am., Can., Aus.* col. country bumpkin, yokel: *Doors had been slamming, rudely in his hick-town face.* - T. Thompson., *McMurfee wasn't exactly a hick* - R.P. Warren., *You are a hick.* - S. Bellow.
hickory shirt *Am.* rough cotton shirt striped or checked.
hickey *Am., Can.* col. /*Br.* **love bite/**: *You should see the hickey on my neck.* – R.L. Stine.
hicksville *esp. Am.* col. derog. a small uninteresting town or village.

hide *Br., Aus. /Am.* **blind/** a place from where one may watch animals and birds without being noticed by them.

hide-and-go-seek *Am.* game of hide-and seek.

hiding/ be on a hiding to nothing *esp. Br.* col. completely waste one's time with no chance of success.

high *Am.* col. high school.

high/ pile it/them high and sell it/them cheap *esp. Br.* sell a lot cheaper.

highball 1. *esp. Am., Can.* an alcoholic drink, esp. whiskey or brandy mixed with water or soda and served with ice: *He even took three good high-balls before dinner instead of one.* - R.P. Warren., *I even smoked long black cigars and drank highballs.* - D. Carnegie., *They paused to order another round, Patsy a highball and the Frenchman brandy in snifters.* - R. Moore. 2. *Am., Can.* signal for a train to proceed: *the time to go to give the highball sign, get on going* - J. Kerouac. 3. *Am.* an express train.

highball glass *Am.* cocktail glass.

high beam *Am.* brightest lights at the front of car.

highbinder *Am.* col. 1. corrupt politician. 2. hoodlum.

highboy *Am., Can. /Br.* **tallboy/** a high chest of drawers mounted on a base with long legs: *A Philadelphian highboy had been moved out into the hall* - J.D. Salinger.

Highbrowville *Am.* joc. Boston, Massachusetts.

high cotton/ be in high cotton *Am.* live affluently: *Now, with Dad dead, I guess she'll be living in high cotton.* - R.J. Randisi., M. Wallace.

high day *Br.* the day of a religious festival.

high dependency *Br.* (of a hospital patient) requiring special treatment and supervision.

high-dollar *Am.* col. very expensive: *Now, a six-block-square area of high-dollar shopping malls* – R.J. Randisi, M. Wallace.

high-end *Am.* expensive or high-class: *as much as $20 million for a high-end module* – Reader's Digest.

high five *esp. Am., Can., Aus.* sl. a way of greeting by slapping raised palms together: *Hands were raised to give him a high five.* - D. Mortman., *They reach up and slap a celebretory high-five.* - Time.

high forest *Am.* forest of trees raised from seeds.

high gear *Am. /Br.* **top gear/**.

high-hat *Am., Can.* col. snub or treat condescendingly: *they all high-hatted him* - J. Dos Passos. /also **get the high hat/**.

high/ high off / on the hog *esp. Am., Can., Aus.* col. well and richly: *my doctor is doing well enough to feast that high on the hog.*- T. Thompson., *they'll be eating high on the hog.* - L. Waller., *He and Austin were living high on the hog* - Vanity Fair.

high jinks, hijinks *Am.* obs. noisy or excited behaviour.

high jump/ be (in) for the high jump *Br., Aus.* col. be about to be in trouble or get a serious punishment: *If we don't get there soon, Maria and Peter are for the high-jump.* - A. McLean.

highland moccasin *Am., Can.* copperhead snake.

highly-strung *esp. Br., Aus. /esp. Am., Can.* **high-strung/** anxious.

high money *Am.* big money.

high-muck(ety)-muck *Am., Can.* col. VIP, big gun: *We have to get rid of those high mucky-muck bureaucrats.* - H. Smith., *the muckety-mucks in Hollywood will want you* - A. Hitchcock Mystery Magazine.

high-pressure (into) *esp. Am.* persuade (sb.) to do or buy smth. by high-pressure methods.

high rent *Am.* expensive hire: *the North end was partly gentrified into high-rent district* - G. O'Neill, D. Lehr.

high riser, high rise apartment house *Am. /Br.* **tower block (of flats)/**: *it lay among high-rises in what was clearly a large city center.* - J.P. Hogan.

high road *esp. Br.* obs. main road: *A good cyclist does not need a high road* – M. Daly.

high road/ take a high road *esp. Am., Can.* take the most positive and careful course of action., make a good moral choice.

high roller *esp. Am., Aus.* col. big spender: *For Jerry Carpenter resembled nothing less than a flashy high roller.* - T. Thompson. v. **highroll**.

high school (junior high school /ages 12-15; seniour high school /ages 15-18) *esp. Am., Can., Aus. /Br.* **secondary shool/** a secondary school, esp. for children over the age of 14: *I sang at other high school's proms* - J. Baez.., *My high school teachers always told me I was an oddball.* - Downbeat., n. **highschooler**.

high season/ at high season *esp. Br.* in/during high season, when a lot of people visit the place.

high sign *Am., Can.* col. secret gesture giving warning or approving smth.

high-stepping *Am.* sl. looking elegant and living the life of a playboy but lacking means for luxuries: *he may take your dislike of his high-stepping friends as one of those insanely trivial excuses to drink.* - Alcoholics Anonymous.

high street *Br., Aus. /Am.* **main street/** the most important shopping and business street of a town: *Do not agonise too much for the high street giants* - Observer.

the high street *Br.* business done at shops, esp. for ordinary people.

high strung *esp. Am., Can. /esp. Br., Aus.* **highly-strung/** very nervous.

the high table *Br.* (in a school or at university) a table at which the most important teachers eat their meals.

hightail (it) *esp. Am., Can.* col. go and leave in a great hurry: *If he was hightailing it was catch him now or not at all.* - D. Hammet., *everybody hightailed it out the door* - J. Kerouac., *Anyway we're hightailing it southeast, man.* - B. Tillman., *she hightailed it to North Carolina.* - W. Jack, B. Laursen.

high tea *Br.* an early evening meal taken in some parts of Britain instead of afternoon tea and little dinner: *We usually have high tea at six* - I. Murdoch.

high-test *Am.* (of petrol) high-octane.

high-ticket *Am.* sl. high-priced: *Some are high-ticket items* - Time.

high-toned *esp. Am., Can.* stylish or superior.

high-top *esp. Am.* a soft-soiled sports shoe with a laced upper which extends above the height of the ankle: *He took off his canvas high-tops and jumped into the water* – R.L. Stine.

high-up *Br.* sb. who has a high rank in an organisation, higher-up.

highway *esp. Am., Can., Aus.* or *Br,* law. */esp. Br.* **main road, motorway/** a broad main road used esp. by traffic going in both directions, and often leading from one town to another: *he pulls off the highway onto a dirt road.* - Time.

highway/ the public highway *Br.* expression used in legal documents meaning roads.

The highway code *Br.* a set of government rules which have to be obeyed by drivers using public roads.

highway robbery *Am.* col. situation in which smth. costs a lot more than it should.

hijack *Br.* an act of hijacking a plane, vehicle, etc.

hike (up) *esp. Am.* col. increase suddenly and steeply: *they hiked our taxes as a way of encouraging us to sell.* - D. Mortman.

hike sb. or smth. **up** *esp. Am.* col. raise or pull with a sudden movement, esp. a piece of clothing: *Lisa hiked her skirt midthigh* - K. Lipper.

hike smth. *Am.* walk a long way in the mountains or countryside.

hike, also **raise** *esp. Am.* rise, boost, e.g. wage hike: *The government is not proposing a market, only a price hike.* - Newsweek., *8.2 percent wage hike is above the inflation rate.* - Newsweek.

hike/ take a hike *Am.* col. derog. go away.

hiking boots *Am., Aus.* walking boots.

hill/ on the Hill *Am.* on Capitol Hill or in the US government.

hillbilly *Am.* col. often derog. a farmer or person from a mountain area far from town: *she's a hillbilly or an Oakie or what.* - T. Capote., *He looked like an urban hillbilly* - J. Baez.

hill of beans *Am., Can.* col. nothing: *The money he lost doesn't amount to a hill of beans.* - W. Magnuson.

hind leg/ talk the hind leg(s) off a donkey (or **dog, horse**). *Am.* col. talk to a wearing extent.

hindsight is 20-20 *Am.* col. it is easy to say what one may have done to avoid a bad situation after it has happened.

hinky *Am.* col. suspicious, curious: *I started getting nervous or hinky* - B. Holiday., W. Duffy.

hinterlands *Am.* a part of the country away from the big city areas.

hiphuggers *Am. /Br., Aus.* **hipsters/** trousers that fit up to the hips, not the waist: *she saw several bodysuits, hip-hugger jeans* - R.L. Stine.

hipped on *esp. Am., Can.* col. obsessed with.

hip pocket *Am.* retain possession of smth. (as if) by putting it in one's hip pocket: *his predecessor, who was described by one Heck's executive as a hip-pocket entrepreneur* – D.L. Barlett, J.B. Steele.

hipshot *esp. Am., Can.* having a dislocated hip.

hipster *Br.* (of a piece of clothing) having waistline on the hips.

hire 1. *esp. Br. /Am.* **rent/** get the use of (smth.) for a special occasion or a limited time on payment of a sum of money. 2. *esp. Am.* employ or appoint to a job. /In Britain you hire things for just a short time and the owner hires them out, in America you rent things /*esp. Br.* **let/** and the owner rents them out, in America you hire people (employ them), but in Britain you only hire people for a particular purpose, not for a long period, otherwise they are appointed.

for hire *Br. /Am.* **to rent/.**

hire 1. *esp. Br.* the act of hiring or state of being hired, e.g. boats for hire, a car hire, etc. 2. *Am., Can.* recently recruited employee.

hire oneself out *Br.* arrange to work for sb.

hire smth. **out** *Br.* allow to use smth. for a short time in exchange for money.

hire-and-drive *Br.* rent-a-car.

hire and fire *esp. Am.* employ and dismiss people.

hire car *Br.* rented car.

hired girl *Am., Can.* farmhold, household servant.

hired gun *Am.* sl. professional killer: *They employ thousands of hired guns in private armies* - Time.

hired man *Am., Can.* worker, farmhand or male household servant: *He let the hired men do the farming.* - J. Dos Passos., *she was remembering the crushed arm of a hired man.* - S. North.

hire purchase, system *Br., Aus. /Am., Can.* **installment plan/** system of payment for goods by which one pays small sums of money regularly after receiving the goods (usu. paying more than the original price in total).

Hispanic *Am.* n. adj. Hispano, person from Latin America or Central America: *We had included male and female black*s, *whites, hispanics* - P. Robertson.

Hispanic American *Am.* a citizen or resident of Hispanic descent.

hit *esp. Am.* col. 1. attack or kill: *He hits up Islamic businessmen* - Time. 2. a murder: *I offered this hit to everyone in town.* - W. Murphy., *he'd gone into hiding immediately after the Bratsos and DePrisko hits.* - G. O'Neill, D. Lehr., *So the hit was arranged.* - J. O'Brien, A. Kurins.

hit *Am.* sl. save another drink to sb.

hit off *Br.* col. mimic, copy (sb. or smth.): *Good, you've exactly hit off the writer's style!* - Longman.

hit on *Am.* sl. 1. ask for a favor: *Nobody hit on me, not even Bill.* - R.J. Randisi., M. Wallace. 2. also *Can.* attempt to seduce: *she hit on me so early, so forcefully.* - R.J. Randisi., M. Wallace.

hit out at/against sb./smth. *Br.* say or show that you disapprove of sb. or smth.

hit it up *esp. Am.* col. work or esp. play hard: *The band was already hitting it up as the train arrived.* - Longman.

hit up (sb.) **for** smth. *Aus., Am.* col. /also *Am.* col. **hit** (sb.) **up, hit** sb. **up/** ask (sb.) for smth.: *You're not hitting me up for Dartmouth, are you?* - K. Lipper., *Liz hitting me up for half the money to repair the Jeep* - F. Pascal.

hit/ hit sb. **for six** *Br.* influence sb. very strongly.

hit/ hit it *Am.* travel fast, go man go.

hit the bricks *Am.* sl. go into the streets: *I'd better hit the bricks.* - R.A. Spears, *O'Connor stood by the men and women who had hit the bricks* – N. Hentoff.

hit the deck/dirt *Am., Aus.* col. fall to the ground.

hit the hay *Am.* col. go to bed.

hit town *esp. Am.* arrive in town.

hitch *Am., Can.* 1. col. period of time (esp. service in the army or armed forces.): *McCluskey…did his hitch in the Demilitarized Zone* – Reader's Digest. 2. device for attaching the tow bar on one motor vehicle to carry another.

hither and thither *Br. /Am.* **hither and yon/** in all directions.

hitman *esp. Am., Aus., Can.* col. a hired killer: *Like any professional "hitman" Angelo D'Ambrosio felt an inner satisfaction at having successfully completed a job.* - R. Cook., *The assassin was a professional hit man from Chile's secret police.* - J. Baez.

hit-out *Aus.* col. brisk run.

a **hive of activity/industry** *Br.* very busy place full of people.

hive off *esp. Br.* col. disappear or go away without warning.

hive off *esp. Br., Aus.* (esp. in business) separate a smaller part or parts from a larger organisation.

HM *Br.* 1. heavy metal. 2. His/Her Majesty.

HMO *Br.* **House in Multiple Occupation,** one in which poor people live who receive money from the government.

HMSO *Br.* Her Majesty's Stationary Office, equivalent to the US GPO.

HNC or HND *Br.* Higher National Certificate or Diploma, qualifications esp. in scientific or technical subjects that one can study for at a British college.

ho 1. *Am.* sl. derog. (esp. among blacks) a wife or woman. 2. *Br.* sl. prostitute.

hoagie *esp. Am., Can.* col. /*Am.* col. **grinder/** hero sandwich: *Let's call it a draw and get some hoagies.* - D. Brenner.

hoarding *Br., Aus.* 1. a high fence round a piece of land, esp. when building work is going on. 2. /*Am., Aus.* **billboard/** a high fence or board on which large advertisements are stuck.

hob *Br. /Am., Aus.* **stove (top)**, *Am.* **range/** the flat top of a cooker where you cook food in pans.

hob/ play hob with *Am.* cause confusion in, upset / also **raise hob.**

hobbyhorse/ be on one's **hobbyhorse** *Br.* talk for a long time about a subject that you think is interesting.

hobbyist *esp. Am.* a fan of smth.

hobo 1. *Am., Can., Aus.* col. /*esp. Br.* **tramp/** v. n. (be) a tramp, person who has no regular work or home: *I first saw the park in 1949, as a student hoboing through the South West*

- National Geographic. 2. *Am.* an itinerant (farm) worker.

Hobson's choice *esp. Br.* choice between two thing which are both unsatisfactory.

hock 1. *esp. Am.* a piece of meat from above the foot of an animal, esp. a pig. 2. *esp. Br.* a German white wine.

hockey 1. *esp. Br., Aus. /esp. Am.* **field hockey/** a game played with sticks and a ball. 2. *esp. Am. / Br., Aus.* **ice hockey/** hockey.

hocks *Can.* high boots.

hodge-podge *esp. Am. /esp. Br.* **hotch-potch/** a mixture of different things, mishmash.

hodman *Br.* worker carrying a hod.

hoe in *Aus., NZ.* col. eat heartily.

hoe into *Aus., NZ.* col. attack or criticize.

hoe-cake *Am.* bread made of cornmeal.

hoe-down *Am., Can.* social gathering with country dancing.

hoedown *Am.* sl. a noisy argument or fight.

hoe-hand *Am.* farmhand.

hog 1. *esp. Am.* a pig, esp. a fat one for eating: *He wants them raised for the hogs* - R. Chandler. 2. *esp. Br.* a young sheep before the first shearing. 3. *Br.* large male pig that has been castrated and is kept for its meat.

hog/ hog in togs *Am.* dressed up loafer.

The Hog and Hominy State *Am.* joc. Tennessee.

hogget 1. *Br.* yearling sheep. 2. *NZ.* lamb between weaning and first shearing.

hog products *Am.* products of pig breeding.

hog-tie *Am., Can.* 1. tie as a hog. 2. hinder in a secure hold: *rules and regulations hog-tied her* - A. Makkai.

Hogtown *Can.* sl. Toronto.

hogwash *esp. Am., Can.* stupid talk, nonsense: *they turned out to be a lot of hogwash.* - Time., *such notions are unadulterated hogwash* - P. Robertson.

hogwild *Am., Can.* col. crazy, esp. in **go hogwild**: *I don't go hog-wild and I don't feel guilty.* - E. Taylor.

ho-hum *Am.* sl. dull, boring: *Congress pressured him to increase a proposed grant to Poland from a measly $115 to a ho-hum $315 million.* - Time.

hoick *Br.* col. (up) lift or bring out, esp. with a jerk. n. a jerk: *Do you hoick out a woman's ovaries for that?* - L. Uris., *If the stook is some way off, he hoicks them up against his side* - J. Fowles.

hoist one, hoist a few *Am.* sl. have a drink: *Let's you and me hoist one.* - R.A. Spears.

hoist on one's **own petard** *Am.* hoist with one's own petard, be made to suffer by some evil plan by which one had intended to harm others.

hoistway *Am.* shaft of lift or elevator.

hoke up *Am.* col. treat (smth. or sb.) in a silly or false manner, adj. **hoked-up**: *They prove what Joan Warrel said was just a hoked-up lie.* - T. Thompson.

hokey *Am., Can.* col. phoney, banal: *hokey scenes of swimmer Amanda Beard cuddling a teddy bear* - Time., *the hokiest Hollywood script yet written* - USA Today.

hokonui *NZ.* moonshine whiskey.

hokum *esp. Am., Can.* col. foolish talk, esp. when intended to deceive or cause admiration, nonsense, cheap sentimentality: *the swinging element of jazz or "hokum" music was then sometimes defined as "attack."* - M. Jones., J. Chilton.

hol *Br.* col. a holiday.

hold *Am.* wait on the telephone to speak later.

hold smth. *Am., Can.* col. not to include it, esp. in a recipe.

hold out the hat *Br. /Aus.* **pass round the hat/** collect money for smth.

hold out on *Am.* refuse to give money.

hold over/ be held over *Am.* (of a film, play,etc.) be shown or performed more times than was originally planned because of its popularity with the people.

hold up *Am.* col. charge (sb.) too much: *Don't go to that shop, they hold you up.* - Longman.

hold/ hold the floor *Br., Aus.* speak to a group of people for a long time without letting anyone else speak.

holdall *esp. Br., Aus. /Am., Aus.* **carryall,** *Am.* **tote bag/** a large bag or small case for carrying clothes and articles necessary for travelling: *The silly damn thing is called an English holdall.* - J. Aldridge.

holddown *Am.* repression, prevention of rises.

holding *Br., Aus. /also Aus.* **(pastoral) property/** farm estate.

holding/ be left holding the (*Br.*) **baby,** (*esp. Am., Can.*) **bag** find oneself responsible for smth. one hasn't done: *I end up holding the damn bag.* - A. Hitchcock Mystery Magazine.

holding line *Am. /Br.* **key line/** print. 1. the outline on artwork that, when transferred to a printing plate, will give the register with other colours. 2. a line on artwork indicating to the reproduction department an area for tint laying.

holding tank *Am.* tank on a boat for holding sewage to be pumped away at a dockside station.

holdout *esp. Am., Can.* person opposing the actions of others thus stopping the situation from being resolved or the actions themselves.

holdover *esp. Am., Can.* 1. /*Br.* **hangover**/ smth. that has continued to exist longer than expected. 2. student who repeats a course, grade or program. 3. person who remains in office after his term: *One strategy was to fire corrupt Brezhnev holdovers.* - H. Smith.

hole smth. *Br.* make holes by guns or other weapons.

hole *Br.* /*Am.* **cup**/ (in golf) a. hollow place in the ground into which the ball must be hit. b. an area of play with such a hole at the far end.

hole/ be in a hole *esp. Br.* col. be in a difficult or embarrassing situation.

hole/ be…in the hole, be in the hole by… *Am., Can.* owe a particular amount of money.

hole/ be/go in the hole *Am., Can.* col. owe sb. a lot of money.

hole/ blow a hole in smth. *Br.* do smth. that greatly reduces the amount of money a person or company has.

hole/ dig oneself **into a hole** *Br., Aus.* col. do smth. embarrassing.

hole/ dig/get sb. **out of a hole** *Br., Aus.* col. help sb. in a difficult situation.

hole/ have holes in one's **head** *Am.* be stupid.

hole-and-corner, hole-in-the-corner *Br.* obs. secreteve and possibly dishonest.

hole card *esp. Am.* a hidden advantage.

hole-in-the wall 1. *Br.* col. a machine, usu. installed in an outside wall of a bank, which dispenses cash and gives information about a person's bank account. 2. *Am.* col. a small simple restaurant, shop or house: *we stopped at a dirty little hole in the wall* - B. Holiday, W. Duffy., *Don't be misled by the sleepy hole-in-the-wall atmosphere of this bohemian Irish cafe* - Reader's Digest.

holiday *esp. Br., Aus., Can.* 1. (usu. pl.) /*Am.* **vacation(s)**/ a day or period in which one travels to another place for enjoyment. 2. a day or period in which one does not go to work, school, etc. /*Am., Can.* **vacation**/.

holiday camp *Br.* site for holiday-makers with lodgings, entertainment and leisure facilities.

holiday home *Br.* house that sb. owns where they can go for holidays.

holiday-maker *Br., Aus.* /*Am.* **vacationer**/.

holiday resort *Am., Aus.* /*Am.* **vacation resort**/.

holiday village *Br.* large modern holiday camp.

Holland of America *Am.* Louisiana.

holler *esp. Am.* col. v. n. shout out, e.g. to attract attention or because of pain: *Joannie commenced to hollering that she wanted to ride the ponies.* -T. Thompson., *That guy is hollering in there.* - T.A. Harris.

hollow *Am.* a valley.

Hollywood kitchen *Am.* one with built-in cabinets, oven, stove and sink.

holm *esp. Br.* an island in a river.

Holstein *esp. Am.* /*esp. Br.* **Frisian**/ black-and-white cow of a breed that gives a large quantity of milk.

holus-bolus *Can.* all at once.

Holy City /also **Church City**/ *Aus.* Adelaide.

holy cow, cats, shit, mackerel, etc. *esp. Am.* col. excl. of surprise, admiration or fear: *Holy cow! Look what makes you thin.* – Reader's Digest.

Homberg(er) Heaven *Am.* city of Washington.

hombre *esp. Am.* col. fellow, wise guy: *I'm going to associate with the big hombres after this.* - J. Dos Passos.

Home *Aus.* col. England.

home *Am., Can.* denoting the administrative centre of an organisation.

home adv. / In America home is often used without preposition: *Why are you home so early?* – R.L. Stine.

home/ find a home for *Br.* find a place where smth. can be kept.

home/ in the home *Am.* at one's home.

home/ play away from home *Br., Aus.* col. have sex with sb. who is not one's usual partner.

home/ What's smth. **when it's at home?; Who's** sb. **when he's/she's at home?/** *Br., Aus.* humor. (said if one wants to know what smth. or sb. is really is).

home/ work from home *Br.* do work at home instead of a company.

home and dry *esp. Br.* /*Am., Aus.* **home and free,** *Aus., NZ.* **home and hosed**/ having safely or successfully completed something.

home base *Am.* home plate.

home bird *Br.* col. /*esp. Am., Can.* **homebody**/ stay-at-home type of person: *But she was very much a homebody* – A. Summers, R. Swan.

homeboy, homegirl *Am.* also **homey, homie** a boy or man/ girl or woman from one's town or a member of the same gang.

homeboy *Am.* sl. buddy, friend: *Marsalis has since performed with these "home boys"* - Time.

home cinema *Br.* /*Am., Can.* **home theater**/ a system of showing films in the home which is designed to simulate as closely as possible the viewing conditions in a cinema.

homecoming (weekend) *Am., Can.* an occasion when former students return to a school or college for a special event: *high school girls came into the fitting room with selections for their homecoming dance.* - Reader's Digest.

home farm *esp. Br.* residence farm, providing produce for its owner.

home free *Am., Can.* col. out of trouble or succeeding in the most difficult part of smth.: *a favored soldier of Zanino's might now be home free.* - G. O'Neill, D. Lehr.

home fries *Am., Can.* fried sliced potatoes.

home from home *Br. /Am., Can., Aus.* **home away from home/** a place as pleasant, comfortable, etc. as one's own house: *this lethal-injection facility no longer feels like a home away from home to me.* – K. Vonnegut, Jr.

home help *Br. /Am.* **homemaker/** person who is sent in by the medical and social services to do cleaning, cooking, etc. for someone who is very ill or old: *I can get Bert a home help* – S. Townsend.

homely 1. *esp. Br., Aus. /Am., Aus.* **homey/** simple, not trying to seem important or special. 2. *Am., Can., Aus.* derog. (of people, faces, etc.) not good-looking, unattractive: *The Washington Post called them "asexual and homely".* - P. Norman., *Carrie is a sullen cruelly homely girl* - B. Kaufman., *He was a homely, freckled sandy-haired young fellow* - M. Twain.

homemaker 1. *esp. Am.* euph. a housewife: *Said homemaker Usha Thomas* - Time., *traditional duties of wife, mother, and homemaker* - Y. Richmond. 2. *Am. /Br.* **home help/**.

home patch/ on sb.'s **homepatch** *Br.* in a place or situation that is familiar to you.

home port *Am.* port of registry.

homer *Am.* col. home run.

homeroom *Am.* 1. room where students meet, esp. to answer roll calls and hear announcements at the beginning of every school day. 2. the period when this takes place: *the bell for homeroom exploded in Miriam's ears* – R.L. Stine.

homeroom/ hit a home run *Am.* do smth. very successfully.

homeroom period/class *Am. /Br.* **Social Education; form period/**.

homeroom teacher *Am.* tutor, mentor.

home run, home *Am.* a point scored in baseball by hitting the ball so that one has time to run all the way round four corners of the playing field before it is returned.

home run/ hit a home run *Am.* do smth. that is very popular or successful.

home signal *Br.* railway signal controlling entry to the local line.

home site *Am., Can., Aus., NZ.* building plot.

homesitter *esp. Br.* a person who lives in or takes care of a home by agreements with the usual occupants while they are away, esp. as a commercial service.

homestead 1. *esp. Am., Can., Aus.* a piece of land given by the state (esp. in the former times) on condition that the owner farms it: *So that's the old homestead* - H. Fast.. n. **-er**. 2. *Aus., NZ.* owner's residence on a sheep or cattle station.

the home straight *Br., Aus.* home stretch, the last part of a race or any other difficult activity.

homestyle *Am., Can.* (of food) simple and unpretentious.

home time *Br.* the time at the end of the school day when a student can go home.

home town *esp. Am.* one's native town.

a home truth *Br.* a true but unpleasant fact.

home unit *Aus.* an apartment, esp. a flat in a new building for sale.

homework *esp. Am., Aus. /Br.* **prep/** schoolwork that is done at home.

homey, homy *Am.* col. pleasant, like home: *They gave a nice homey atmosphere.* - R.P. Warren., *There was something homey in his voice* - J. Dos Passos., *Alexandra filled her letters with homey details of their activities* - R.K. Mussle.

homicide 1. *esp. Am., Aus.* law. (an act of) intentially committed murder; adj. **homicidal**. 2. *esp. Am.* police force that deals with homicides.

homie, homey *Am.* col. */Am.* sl. **home boy** or **home girl/** friend.

hominy *Am.* maize from which the outer covering has been removed, esp. used to make grits.

honey *esp. Am., Can., Aus.* a. (used when speaking to sb. you love): *It was "honey" that steeled her.* - J. DeFelice. b. also *Am., Can.* **honeybun** (used informally as a friendly form of address, esp. by or to a woman).

honey 1. *esp. Am.* col. also **hon** remarkable, pleasant person or thing: *She's a honey.* - M.M. Kaye. 2. *Am.* v. flatter.

honey bucket *Am., Can.* col. toilet without water that has to be emptied manually.

honey trap *Br.* a big attraction.

honk *Br.* col. vomit.

honked, honkers *Br.* sl. drunk.

honker *esp. Am., Can.* col. wild goose.

honky-tonk *esp. Am.* col. a cheap usu. disreputable nightclub, saloon or gambling place: *There were fishstalls, drinking dives, a tiny honky-tonk for the fishermen.* - R. Chandler.

honky-tonk *Am.* cheap, brightly-coloured, and of not good quality: *We talked in honky-tonk truck stops* – E. James, D.Ritz.

honkie, honky *Am., Can., Aus.* derog. col. a white person: *it was suppressed as a honky hex.* - New York.

honor roll *Am. /Br.* **roll of honour**/ a list of the names of people who have earned praise: *I always made the honor roll, all As and Bs.* - D. Brenner., *it belongs on the honour roll of terms by which we live.* - A. Bloom.

honorary *Br.* (of an office or its holder) unpaid.

honors course/program *Am.* course(s) for students (**honor(s) students**) whose work is of very high standard.

honor system *Am.* 1. agreement between members of a group to obey rules. 2. a way of recording the fact that a student has achieved a high standard of work.

honours/ with honours *Br.* pasing university at a level that is higher than the most basic level; **First Class/Second Class Honours**.

honours are even *Br.* there is equality in a contest.

hoo(t)ch *Am., Can.* sl. strong alcoholic drink, esp. whiskey: *No hooch, no gals, no nothing.* - R. Chandler.

hood 1. *Am., Can. /Br.* **bonnet**/ metal lid covering the engine of a car: *parallel chrome stripes ran along the centre of the hood* - M. Torgov. 2. *esp. Br.* a waterproof covering on a vehicle or a piece of equipment, esp. on a car or pram, which can be removed. 3. *esp. Am.* col. neighbourhood: *the gym filled with boys from the "hood."* – Reader's Digest.

hood(lum) *esp. Am.* col. hooligan, criminal: *I played Marty Snyder, the crippled small-time hood* - A.E. Hotchner.

hoodoo 1. *esp. Am.* col. n. adj. v. (be) a person or thing that brings bad luck. 2. *Am., Can.* column of weathered rock.

hooey *Am.* col. stupid talk, nonsense: *It's all hooey to me.* - G. Greene., *It sounds like a lot of hooey.* - D. Hammet.

hoof *esp. Br.* dismiss.

hoof/ on the hoof *Br., Aus.* 1. quickly, intuitively 2. done while walking around doing other things.

hoofer *Am.* sl. professional dancer: *Jimmy was a Broadway hoofer.* - A.E. Hotchner.

hoo-ha *Br.* noisy talk or excitement about smth. unimportant.

hoo-haw *Can.* sl. penis: *Yes, I've seen a hoo-haw* - W. Magnuson.

hook *Am.* col. succeed in attracting sb.

hook *Am.* 1. make a rug, etc. with a hook. adj. **hooked.** 2. col. have sex for money.

hook/ get/give sb. **the hook** *Am., Can.* col. be dismissed from a job.

hook/ on one's **own hook** *esp. Am.* col. on one's own.

hook/ on the hook for *Am., Can.* col. (in financial context) be responsible for.

hook/ ring off the hook *Am.* col. ring a lot.

hook/ sling one's **hook** *Br.* col. obs. go away.

hook/ off / on 1. *Br.* uncouple / couple railway wagons. 2. **hook onto** *esp. Am.* col. understand and usu. like an idea: *The children quickly hooked onto the suggestion* - Longman.

hook smth. **up** *esp. Am.* connect a piece of electric equipment.

hook up with *esp. Am.* 1. meet sb. and become friendly with them. 2. agree to work with another organisation for a particular purpose.

hook and ladder *Am.* fire engine with long ladders fixed to it.

hook-and-ladder *Am.* sl. adj. fire / **hook-and-ladder company, truck, house,** etc.: *There was an engine company and a hook-and-ladder company.* - M. Twain.

hookbait *Br.* bait attached to a hook.

hooked *Am.* sl. 1. married. 2. cheated: *I was really hooked on this travel deal.* - R.A. Spears.

hooker 1. *esp. Am., Can., Aus.* col. a prostitute: *She was no longer some dumb black hooker from Harlem* - S. Sheldon., *Hell, a client in Vegas once sent me up a fancy hooker.* - E. Segal., *You look like an old hooker.* - R. Moore., *The town's so small the local hooker's still a virgin.* - R. Borchgrave, R. Moss. 2. *Am., Can.* col. a glass of straight brandy, whiskey, etc.

hook shop *Am.* sl. brothel: *Bear Flag ain't like any hook-shop on land or sea.* - J. Steinbeck.

hooky, hookey *Am., Can., Aus.* col. **play hooky** /*Br.* **play truant**/ is to stay away from school without permission, play truant: *Groups of little girs used to play hooky from school.* – A. Summers, R. Swan. n. **hookey player.**

hoon *Aus., NZ.* col. lout, hooligan.

hoop *Aus.* col. jockey.

hoop/ shoot (some) hoop *Am.* play or practise basketball informally.

hooped *esp. Br.* decorated with hoops or horizontal stripes or containing hoops as part of its structure.

hoop-la *Br., Aus.* /*Am.* **ring toss**/ a game in which a ring is tossed to fall over an object from a distance.

hoop-la *esp. Am.* 1. noisy advertising intended to attract attention, and also perhaps deceive, ballyhoo: *a week of hoopla leading to a gala premiere* - A.E. Hotchner. 2. nonsense.

hooray *Aus., NZ.* goodbye.

hooroo *Aus.* excl. col. hooray.

hoosegow, calaboose, can *Am.* col. jail: *We got carried away off to Pipersville and put in the hoosegow.* - Zacherlay., *he'd take him to the hoosegow for driving without license* - J. Dos Passos.

Hoosier *Am.* adj. n. a native of Indiana: *Are you a Hoosier?* - K. Vonnegut, Jr., *my long-ago Hoosier boyhood.* - Guideposts.

Hoosierland, also **Hoosierdom** *Am.* joc. Indiana.

The Hoosier State *Am.* Indiana: *his father, who claimed to represent the Hoosier State* - K. Vonnegut, Jr.

hoot *esp. Br., Aus., Can.* col. smth. very amusing: *Paul Newman calls the party "a hoot"* - New Idea.

hootchie-cootchie (or **hootch**) *Am.* sl. an erotic dance, **hootchie dancer.**

hootenanny *esp. Am.* a gathering at which folk singers entertain often with the audience joining in.

hooter 1. *Br., Aus.* col. nose: *I shall very likely punch him on the hooter.* - B. Bryson. 2. *Am.* sl. marihuana cigarette. 3. *Am., Can.* sl. (pl.) derog. women's breasts: *Hooters...has angered countless feminists and sympathizers with its double-entendre brand-name* - Nation's Restaurant News. 4. *Am.* sl. a drink of liquor: *we tied on many a hooter in the time of marital bliss.* - Alcoholics Anonymous. 5. *Br.* horn or siren that makes a hooting noise, used in cars, ships and factories

hoover *Br., Aus.* tdmk. 1. (a type of) a vacuum cleaner: *What is wrong with the hoover?* - C. Handy. 2. /*Am.* **vacuum**/ clean with a vacuum cleaner: *it really does hoover you up* - B. Bryson. 3. col. eat or drink up esp. greedily: *they lower their heads and hoover it up* - B. Bryson.

Hooverville *Am.* sl. shantytown.

hop *esp. Am.* col. get on (a public vehicle): *I guess I ought to hop a freight train to Odessa.* - J. Fischer.

hop/ catch/have/keep sb. **on the hop** *Br.* col. catch sb. unprepared.

hop/ keep sb. **on the hop** *Br.* keep sb. surprising by changing one's behaviours, intentions, etc.

hop/ on the hop *Br.* col. 1. unprepared. 2. busy.

hop it *Br.* col. go away: *Would it be proper for me to tell them to hop it.* - J.P. Donleavy.

hop and jump, also **hop, skip and jump** *esp. Am.* a short distance, (used in order to say that a place is very close): *Robin did a hop, skip and jump across the cluttered floor* - D. Lodge.

hop on *Am.* col. scold (sb.): *The director hopped on Jim for being late again.* - Longman.

hop to it *Am.* col. act quickly, to make haste: *We shall have to hop to it if we're to catch that plane* - Longman.

hop up *Am.* col. 1. excite (sb.) by means of a drug. 2. also *Can.* change (a car or engine) to make it perform better, go faster, etc.: *Some drivers cheat in the race by hopping up their engines.* - Longman. adj. **hopped-up**: *it could be some crazy hopped-up junkie.* - S. Sheldon.

hop the twig/stick *Br.* humor. col. a. die. b. leave without paying a debt.

hope/ I do hope (that), I should hope so (too) *Br.* polite way of saying that you hope smth. will happen.

hope/some hope/what a hope! *Br.* col. humor. there's no chance of it happening.

hopechest *Am., Can.* /*Br.* **bottom drawer**/ 1. collection of useful household things which a woman keeps in expectation of marriage: *finds its place in my music collection as something of a hope chest.* - BigO. 2. (in former times) a chest in which these things were kept.

hope(s)/ live in hope(s) of *esp. Br.* be hoping (for smth. to succeed).

hopeful/ be hopeful of doing smth. *Br.* hope that smth. will happen.

hophead col. 1. *Am., Can.* drug addict. 2. *Aus., NZ.* heavy drinker.

hopper/ in the hopper *Am.* (of a group of things) waiting for a decision to be made about them.

hopper car *Am.* a freight car with high sides, no top and mechanism for dumping.

hopping *esp. Am., Can.* col. very active or lively.

hopping John *Am.* a stew of bacon with rice and peas.

hops *Aus., NZ.* col. beer.

Horatio Alger *Am.* coming from rags to riches: *He had come up the hard way a Horatio Alger story without a shred of glamour or nobility about it* - G. O'Neill, D. Lehr., Today's Horatio

Alger heroes often come from modest backgrounds - Reader's Digest.

horizontal directive tendency (H.D.T.) radio. *Br.* /*Am.* **R-line value curvature quantity**/.

horizontal format *Am.* /*Br.* **landscape**/ rectangular page or printed sheet with its long sides at the top and bottom.

horizontal union *Am.* trade union with membership limited to workmen of the same craft.

horlics *Br.* sl. mess: *How to make a total horlics of it in five easy stages.* - T. Thorne.

horn *esp. Am., Aus.* col. /*Br.* sl. **blower**/ telephone: *Perkins got on the horn to Hayes* - Vanity Fair.

horn/ blow/toot one's **own horn** *Am., Can.* col. boast.

horn/ draw/pull in one's **horns** *Br.* start to spend less money or behave more carefully so as to avoid trouble.

horn in *Am.* interrupt or try to take part in smth. when you are not wanted.

hornswoggle *Am.* sl. v. cheat, hoax.

horny *Br.* col. sexually attractive.

(little) horror *Br.* col, a child who behaves oneself very badly.

horror film *Br.* /*Am.* **horror movie**/.

horse *esp. Br.* obs. soldiers riding on horses, cavalry.

horse/ a horse of another/different color *Am.* different situation.

horse/ it's (a case of) a question of horses for courses *Br., Aus.* British saying which means is similar to saying "Tastes differ."

horses for courses *Br., Aus.* it is important to choose suitable activities or people.

horse/ don't spare the horses *Aus.* col. hurry up.

horse/ ride two horses at the same time/at once *esp. Br.* journalism. follow two conflicting sets of ideas.

horse-and-buggy *esp. Am., Can.* col. old-fashioned: *my doctor, I discovered, was one of those horse-and-buggy types who didn't believe in medication* - A. E. Hotchner.

horseback 1. *esp. Am.* of or on the back of a horse. 2. *Am.* col. given offhand without full consideration: *heads of state should be very careful about horseback agreements* - H. Truman.. 3. *Am.* a sharp ridge of gravel, sand or rocks.

horsebox *Br.* /*Am.* **horsecar, horsetrailer,** *Aus.* **horse float**/ a closed vehicle usu. pulled by a car, used for transporting horses.

horse coper *Br.* obs. a horse dealer.

horse lifter *Am.* horse stealer.

horse opera *esp. Am., Can.* col. humor. cowboy film, western: *their specialty has been horse operas* - H. Fast.

horse player *Am., Can.* one who regularly bets on horse races.

horse riding *Br.* /*Am.* **horseback riding**/.

horseshit, horsesheet *esp. Am., Can.* sl. taboo. nonsense.

horse wrangler *Am.* a ranch hand.

hors(e)y *Br.* (esp. of a woman, often of high social class) interested in horses, fond of riding, etc.: *And the girl looks very upper-class Bryn Mawr and horsey.* – P. Roth.

horsiculture *Br.* the commercial development of farmland or open countryside such as wild flower meadows for the pasturing or exercising of horses.

hose *Am.* /*esp. Am.* **panty hose,** *esp. Br.* **tights**/: *She...changed hose and shoes, did her hair over.* - C. Woolrich.

hose *Am.* sl. cheat or deceive sb.

hose down *Br.* sl. rain heavily.

hose cart, also **hose wagon/carriage, truck carriage** *Am.* hose reel: *They shipped a state-of-the-art hose carriage to Columbia.* – Reader's Digest.

hose(pipe) *Br.* hose, long rubber or plastic tube, used esp. for watering.

hose-proof *Br.* /*Am.* **watertight, waterproof**/ impervious to water (esp. of electric machines).

hoser *Can.* sl. a Canadian, esp. a simple and durable northern type: *Hey, hoser. What're you doin' in my garden?* - W. Magnuson.

hospital *Am.* a specialised shop /esp. a repair shop, e.g. *clock hospital*/.

hospital/ In Britain hospital is uncountable noun.

in/to/from hospital *Br.* /*Am.* **in/to/from the hospital**/: *We all feel bad that she's in the hospital.* – R.L. Stine.

hospitalization (insurance) *Am.* one paid if the patient is hospitalised.

a hostage to fortune *esp. Br.* person who can't control the situation.

hostel *esp. Br.* /*Am.* **shelter**/ large house, owned by a council or other organisation where people can stay cheaply for a short period of time.

hostelry *Br.* humor. a pub or hotel.

hostess *Am.* a woman who takes people to their seats in a restaurant.

hostess-cart *Am.* table on wheels.

hostie *Aus., NZ.* col. air hostess.

hot *Am.* sl. wanted by police: *You people are hot.* - Arthur Hailey.

hot up *esp. Br., Aus.* col. become or make very hot, intensify: *my job hotted up* - C. Handy.

hot and cold/ feel/go hot and cold (all over) *Br., Aus.* col. be shocked.

hot and heavy *Am., Can.* col. intense, full of strong emotions and sexual feelings.

hot-blooded *Am.* (of horses) containing blood of the thoroughbred.

hot button *esp. Am., Can.* col. a central issue, concern, or characteristic that motivates people to make a particular choice.

hot cake, flapjack, pancake *Am.* thick pancake eaten for breakfast.

hotcakes/ sell like hot cakes *esp. Am.* sell very well /in America hotcakes are pancakes, in Britain hotcakes are cakes which have just been baked/.

hot dinner/ have (done, had, seen, etc) more smth. **than sb. has had hot dinners** *Br., Aus.* be much more experienced than others.

hot dish *Am.* hot food cooked and served in a deep covered dish.

hotdog 1. *Am.* col. dachshund, a small dog with a long body and short legs. 2. *esp. Am., Can., Aus.* col. a person who makes skilful movements in some sports, esp. skiing to make people notice them, also.v.

hot-dog, hot-diggety *Am.* 1. col. excl. used for showing approval or pleasant surprise: *Boy, a Happiness Machine - hot-diggety!* - R. Bradbury. 2. sl. an expert in smth.: *He's a real hot-dog.* - National Geographic.

hot dog *Am.* col. play very professionally in some sport or do a fast and exciting sport, esp. skiing..

hot gospeller *Br.* col. derog. religious supporter with an exciting and emotional way of speaking.

hot seat/ on the hot seat *Am.* in a very responsible position.

hotel 1. *Am.* the letter H in radio code. 2. *Can.* col. a place where alcoholic beverages are sold by the glasses. 3. *esp. Aus., NZ.* public house.

hotel car *Am.* saloon car, saloon carriage.

hotel clerk *Am.* receptionist: *she didn't see him go back to the hotel clerk* - M. Puzo.

hot flush *esp. Br. /esp. Am., Can.* **hot flash/** a sudden feeling of heat in the skin esp. as experienced by women at the menopause: *it can produce hot flashes* - Reader's Digest., *the menopause has added new items to the repertory: the hot flush, flooding* - D. Lodge.

hot foot *Am.* a savage practical joke, which consists of attaching a match to a person's toe when he's not looking and lighting it.

hothouse children *Am.* children who are protected by their parents from experiencing the more unpleasant parts of life.

hot house lamb *Am.* one born during autumn or winter and raised indoors.

hot ice *Br.* dry ice.

hot issue *Am.* glamour stock.

hot number *Am.* sl. 1. a popular hit. 2. a very sexy man or woman: *what a hot number she was.* - D. Brenner.

hotplate *esp. Br., Aus.* round flat metal on the electric cooker on which pans may be heated when preparing food: *all the beans they prepared on the hot plate* – P. Roth.

hotpot *Br.* mixture of meat, potatoes and onions, cooked slowly together.

hot rod *esp. Am.* col. an old car rebuilt for high speed rather than appearance: *we were hit broadside by a young man in a hot-rod* - A.E. Hotchner.

hot Scotch *Am.* whiskey with hot water.

hot seat *esp. Am.* electric chair.

hot shit *Am.* /*Br.* **shit hot/** sl. taboo. very good.

hot shot *esp. Am., Aus.* a skilful and successful person.

hot stove *Am., Can.* discussion about a favourite sport during the off season.

hotsy-totsy *Am.* snobbish.

the hot ticket *Am.* a very popular fashionable item or person, esp. **in be a hot ticket**.

hottie *Br.* col. hot-water bottle.

hotting *Br.* col. driving recklessly in a stolen car, usu. as a form of showing off.

hot-to-trot *Am.* col. sexually exciting or excited.

The Hot Water State *Am.* Arkansas.

hot water tank or **heater** *Am.* /*Br.* **hot water cylinder, geyser,** *esp. Br.* **immersion heater (tank)/** immersion tank, container which holds and heats the water for a house.

hound *Am.* sl. comb. word. a person addicted to what is indicated: *Her mother was married again to some booze hound.* - J.D. Salinger.

hour; session *esp. Am. /esp. Br.* **class; period/** lesson at school or college.

hour/ in *Am.* you can say before the hour or past the hour.

hour/ drink out of hours *Br.* /*Am., Aus.* **drink after hours/** drink at a bar at a time when it's not allowed by the law.

hour/ News to the hour *Am.* the latest news.

hours/ out of hours *Br.* before or after the usual working or business hours.

house/ *Br.* speakers think that one's **home** is the place to which one belongs and where one feels comfortable and that it is more than just a **house**, Americans often use **home** to mean **house**.

house *Br.* 1. also *Aus.* one of the groups into which the children in a school are divided for the purposes of competing in sports, etc. 2. all the people at a debate. 3. Stock Exchange. 4. performance in a theatre or cinema. 5. college or university. 6. body of pupils living in the same building.

house/ go (all) round the houses *Br.* beat around the bush before coming to the point.

house up *Am.* col. make (sb.) stay in the house, usu. because of illness: *I've been housed up for a week with a bad cold.* - Longman.

house/ keep/make house *Br.* secure a quorum in the House of Commons.

house/ move house *esp. Br.* move to another house.

house agent *esp. Br.* /also *Br.* **estate agent,** *Am.* **realtor**/ a person who sells or lets houses to others.

housebody *Am.* col. stay-at-home.

house breaking 1. *Br.* house wrecking. 2. *Br.* law. action of breaking into the house to commit a crime.

housebroken *esp. Am., Can.* /*esp. Br., Aus.* **house-trained**/ adj. 1. (of house pets) trained to go out of the house to empty the bladder or bowels: *A dog that is not housebroken is a nuisance.* - McGraw-Hill English, 1990, v. **housebreak**. 2. humor. (of people) taught to be tidy and useful at home: *yeomanry could be housebroken at a more leisurely pace.* - J. Fischer.

housecraft *esp. Br.* domestic science, a social subject.

house guest *esp. Am., Aus.* a person who stays at sb. else's house for one or more nights.

Household *Br.* groups of soldiers protecting Queen or King and their family.

household *Br.* all the people who live together in the same house.

household goods *Br.* /*Am.* **houseware**/.

house journal *Br., Aus.* /*Am.* **houseorgan**/ a newspaper produced by a company to tell workers what is happening in the company.

housekeeping/ light housekeeping *Am.* simple bachelor's housekeeping.

housekeeping room *Can.* bedsitting room with cooking facilities.

houseman 1. *Br.* /*Am.* **intern,** *Aus.* **resident,** *Br.* **house officer**/ a low-ranking doctor (man or woman) completing hospital training, and often esp. in Britain living in the hospital. 2. *Am., Can.* a male servant in a house.

housemaster *esp. Br.* /also **housemistress**/ a teacher who is in charge of one of the houses in a school.

house of corrections *Am.* one where people who committed not very serious crimes improve their behaviour.

house plant *Am.* /*Br., Aus.* **pot plant**/.

houseproud *esp. Br., Aus.* very anxious about one's house being clean and tidy and spending a lot of time on it.

house raising *Am.* joint work of neighbours to build a house for sb.

houseroom *esp. Br.* a space in a house for a person or thing.

house-sit *Am.* sl. live in and care for a house for sb. while the owner is away: *Bobby invited me, Mimi, and her husband Dick Farina, to house-sit Albert Grossman's.* - J. Baez.

house surgeon *esp. Br.* houseman who is a surgeon.

house-trained *Am.* /*Br.* **housebroken**/.

housewares *Am.* /*Br.* **household goods**/ household utencils.

housewrecking *Am.* housebreaking; housebreaker is a **housewrecker** in America.

housey *Br.* col. in the style of House music.

housing/ council housing *Br.* /*Am., Aus.* **public housing**/ houses built for the poor by local authorities.

housing association *esp. Br.* organisation where people join together so that they can build or buy houses or apartments at a low cost.

housing development *esp. Am* /*esp. Br.* **housing estate**/ a group of houses and/or flats built in one place by one owner, as by Town Council and let or sold: *I know of an all-women Housing Estate in Sunderland* - Observer., *What roots are in housing development of hundreds and thousands of small dwellings almost exactly alike?* - J. Steinbeck.

housing list *Br.* a list of people waiting to be given a house or flat by the local council.

housing project, also **project** *esp. Am.* a group of houses or flats usu. built with government money for low-income families: *There's a parking lot up there in the housing project.* - R. Moore., *We will design a house project* - A. Bloom.

hover (mower) *Br.* a lawnmower which is held slightly above the ground by a current of air below it.

how/ And how! *esp. Am., Aus.* col. very much: *Grace certainly can dance well. And how!* - H.C. Whitford., M. Wallace.

how/ How do you mean *Br.* (used to express annoyance or anger).

how/ How are you keeping? *Br.* How have you been?

how/ how's about…? *esp. Am.* col. What about…?

how/ How ya livin'? *Am.* sl. How are you?

Howdy *Am., Can., Aus.* col. excl. (used when meeting sb.) Hello: *Howdy, Ned.* - D. Hammet.

howler *Br.* col. silly mistake that makes people laugh.

hoy *Aus.* 1. a game like Bingo. 2. col. v. throw.

Hoyle/ according to Hoyle *Am., Can.* according to the rules.

hp *Br.* col. hire purchase.

HP sauce *Br.* tdmk a sauce made from vegetables, fruit and spices, sold in bottles and eaten with meat.

the Hub *Am.* joc. Boston.

hubba hubba *Am., Can.* col. excl. of approval and excitement.

hubby *Am.* bumpy (of a road).

huckleberry *Am.* /*Br.* **billberry**/small dark blue fruit.

huckleberry *Am.* sl. a foolish person.

huckster *Am.* 1. often. derog. a person who writes advertisements, esp. for radio and television: *shills, hucksters and impersonators peddling spray-on hair* - B.R. Barber. 2. derog. person selling worthless things in a dishonest or aggressive way.

huddle (up) *esp. Br.* arrange, do or make hastily or carelessly.

huffer *Br.* a long roll or section of French bread with a sandwich-style filling.

hug the fire *Br.* nurse the fire.

Hughie *Aus., NZ.* col. imaginary being held to be responsible for the weather.

huh *esp. Am.* excl. often used at the end of questions to ask for agreement.

hulking great *esp. Br.* extremely big or heavy.

hullo *esp. Br.* hello, hey (What's going on?).

hum 1. *Br., Aus.* /*Am.* **hem and haw**/ esp. in the phr. **hum and haw, hum and ha(h)** express uncertainty. 2. *Br.* col. smell unpleasant.

humane killer *Br.* instrument for painless slaughter of animals.

humbug *Br.* a sweet meant to be sucked, mint candy.

the hump *Br., Aus.* col. a feeling of bad temper or dislike of life in general, esp. in the phr. **get the hump**.

hump 1. *Br.* col. carry (smth. heavy), esp. with difficulty. 2. *Am.* make an effort, move rapidly: *Git up and hump yourself, Jim?* - M. Twain.

hump *Aus.* sl. 1. /**hump** one's **swag, swag (it)**/ a walk or tramp with a load on one's back. 2. suitable wave for surfing.

hump/ be over the hump *Am.* col. be past the most difficult situation.

hump/ bust one's **hump** *Am.* sl. try hard to do smth.

hump/ have/take/get the hump *Br.* col. be angry with sb.'s actions.

hump/ give sb. **the hump** *Br.* make sb. feel angry or upset.

humped bridge, humpback(ed) bridge *esp. Br.* bridge having a semi-circle shape.

humpy, aloo *Aus.* aboriginal shack.

hundred-percenter *Am.* 1. extreme nationalist. 2. regular guy.

hundreds and thousands *Br.* tiny pieces of coloured sugar, used for decorating cakes and sweets.

hundredth/ a hundredth *Br.* one hundredth (of a place).

hung Parliament *Br.* Parliament where no one political party has more elected representatives than the others added together.

hunker *Am.* a conservative.

hunker down 1. *esp. Am.* sit down on one's heels. 2. *Am., Can.* sl. get into the mood and posture for hard work: *Whining, they hunkered down* - J. O'Brien, A. Kurins. 3. *Am.* sl. take a sturdy defensive attitude: *The 85.000 Soviet troops "invited" into Afghanistan a year ago are hunkered down for a long occupation.* - Time., *US troops hunker down for Christmas in the desert.* - USA Today.

hunky *Am.* col. derog. a foreigner, esp. a Hungarian, Slavic or Baltic labourer: *there were a few hunkies in the patch* – J. O'Hara.

hunt/ In Britain to go hunting normally means to use dogs (hounds) to chase the animals (usu. a fox or deer) while riding a horse; the sport of killing animals or birds with a gun is called shooting. But in the US the word hunting is used for both these sports: *gentlemen killers who occupy themselves all day fishing, hunting and shooting?* - J. Aldridge., *In Britain the word "hunting" means primarily fox hunting on horseback* - J. Ruppeldtova.

hunt *Br.* a group of people meeting regularly to hunt foxes.
hunt/ in the hunt *Br.* sl. having a chance, **out of the hunt** having no chance.
huntaway *NZ.* dog trained to drive sheep forward.
hunting shirt *Am.* hunter's leather or suede shirt.
hunt saboteur *Br.* member of a group that tries to stop people from hunting foxes.
huntsman *esp. Br.* 1. man who hunts animals. 2. the person in charge of the dogs in fox hunting.
hunyak *Am., Can.* col. derog. person of Hungarian or Central European origin.
hurdle *esp. Br.* a portable section of fencing used chiefly for holding sheep.
hurler *Am., Can.* col. baseball pitcher.
hurra's nest *Am.* muddle, confusion.
hurricane tape *Am.* strong adheseve tape used to glue window glasses broken by strong winds.
hurry-call *Am.* a call for emergency.
hurrygraph *Am.* a sketch made in a hurry.
hurry-up *Am.* col. adj. used for, involving or requiring hurry / e.g. *hurry-up repairs*, etc.: *Calloway cast a glance at the hurry-up patch jobs* - B. Tillman.
hurt/ be hurting *Am.* col. fel very upset, unhappy, sad, etc.: *I could see he was hurtin'* – J. Hopkins
husking /bee/ *Am., Can.* gathering of farm families to husk corn.
husky *esp. Am.* a big and strong man.
hustings *Br.* the process of making speeches, attempting to win votes, etc., which goes on before an election: *the novelty surprise return to the Hustings wears off* - Maclean's., *Pat Buchanan remains on the hustings* - Time.
hustle *Am.* dishonest and illegal ways of getting money.
hustle 1. **(into)** *esp. Am., Can.* col. persuade by forceful, esp. deceitful activity, esp. selling or obtaining things: *And the principal requirements for success were two: an ability to snoop, an ability to hustle.* - T. Thompson., *His wife came to town to hustle yard goods and ribbons.* - M. Torgov., *He writes crapola mini-series and biblical epics to hustle products.* - Vanity Fair. 2. *esp. Am., Can.* col. work as prostitute: *I don't hustle when he's in town.* - J. Dos Passos. 3. *Am.* hurry in doing smth. or going somewhere. 4. *Am.* do smth. with a lot of energy and determination.
hustle one's **butt/ass** *Am., Can.* move or act quickly.

hustler *esp. Am., Can.* 1. a prostitute: *It's also the hustlers' bar* - J. Kerouac. 2. a confidence man, one who tries to obtain money by dishonest means: *The hustler conned me out of a month's pay.* - R.A. Spears.
hutch *Am. /Br.* **welsh dresser/** piece of furniture used for storing and showing dishes.
hydro *Can.* 1. hydroelectric power. 2. electricity as a utility distributed by a power company.
hydro *Br.* hotel in clinic providing hydropathic treatment.
hydroplane 1. *Am.* seaplane, one that can take off and land on water. 2. *Am., Can.* v. /esp. Br. **aquaplane/**.
hygienist *Br. /Am.* **dental hygienist/** a person who helps a dentist by preparing the tools, etc.
Hymie *Am.* col. derog. a Jew: *Jesse Jackson, in an informal discussion, described New York as "Hymietown."* – N. Hentoff.
hyper *esp. Am., Aus.* col. very excitable, manic: *This who I am, just hyper and emotional.* - Rolling Stone., *He was hyper and everything he said was a lie.* - Reader's Digest., *he was a bit hyper about his work.* - G. O'Neill, D. Lehr.
hyperactivity *esp. Br. /esp. Am.* **attention deficit disorder/**.
hypermarket *esp. Br.* a very large supermarket outside a town: *On Sunday Andy works at a hypermarket* - Award Journal.

I

I *Am.* Interstate, important road between states in the US.
ice 1. *esp. Br.* a serving of ice cream, esp. one bought in a shop: *Aunt Judith offered her an ice* - A. Huxley., *Then let's change to ices instead.* - G. Greene., *I purchased two chocolate ices* - J. Herriot; **choc ice** is a chocolate ice cream. 2. *esp. Am.* jewellery, esp. diamonds. 3. *Am.* sorbet.
ice *Am., Can.* col. 1. make smth. certain, esp. in the phr. **ice the decision.** 2. kill: *I'd love to ice these suckers.* - Esquire., *blacks threatened to "ice" him if he ever returned* - Harper's Magazine., *I iced my wife by mistake.* - J. Cheever.
ice *Br.* cover a cake with icing /*Am.* **frost/**.
ice/ ice smth. **down** *Am.* cover an injury in ice to stop it from swelling.
ice/ ice the cake *Am.* sl. insure a favourable result.
ice bag *Am.* ice pack, a bag containing ice used to make parts of the body cool.

iceberg *Aus.* "walrus", person who likes to swim in the wintertime.
iceblock *Aus., NZ.* a block of flavoured ice on a stick.
icebox 1. *esp. Am.* obs. /*esp. Br.* **fridge**/ a refrigerator: *There's been ice in the ice box* - J. O'Hara. 2. *Aus.* old-fashioned cupboard with blocks of ice to keep the food cold. 3. *Br.* compartment in a fridge for making ice.
icebreaker *esp. Am., Aus.* smth. such as a game, joke or story that makes people feel comfortable in public.
ice cream *Br.* small potion of ice cream for one person.
ice(cream) cone *esp. Am.* /*Br.* (**ice cream**) **cornet**/ a pastry container for ice-cream.
ice cream sandwich *Br.* ice cream wafer.
iced water *Br.* /*esp. Am.* **ice water**/ very cold water used for drinking.
ice fog *Am., Can.* fog formed of minute ice crystals.
ice hockey *Br., Aus.* /*Am.* **hockey**/.
ice lolly *Br.* /*Am.* tdmk. **popsicle, ice,** *Aus.* **ice block**/ a piece of sweet-tasting ice on a stick, which often tastes of fruit.
icemaker *esp. Am.* a device that makes small pieces of ice which are put in drinks, etc.
iceman *esp. Am., Can.* (esp. in former times) a man who delivers ice to the home for use in the ice box: *Down South the ice man was likely to be your father.* - M. Jones, J. Chilton.
ice milk *Am., Can.* ice cream with less butter fat than usual.
ice storm *esp. Am., Can.* storm that leaves coating of ice on the ground: *During a big ice storm in New Hampshire, two women stopped by storm-downed trees* – Reader's Digest.
icing *esp. Br., Can.* /*esp. Am., Can.* **frosting**/ a mixture of the fine powdery sugar with liquid, used to cover cakes: *childlike graphic design is the icing on the cupcake.* - Time.
icing sugar *esp. Br., Aus.* /*Am.* **powdered sugar, confectioner's sugar**/ confectioner's sugar: *A stream of orange icing sugar oozed steadily from the silver nozzle* - New Idea.
ickie, icky *Am.* sl. unpleasant, distasteful, nasty: *I'm not going to eat it. You cook icky.* - T.A. Harris., *ya got a 'plex-full of icky kids' films.* - Reader's Digest.
ideas man *Br.* idea man.
identify/ It is rather modern and American to use this verb in sentences like *"She identified with foreign workers."* rather than saying *"She identified herself with foreign workers."* - Longman.
identity kit *Br., Aus.* /*Am.* **composite sketch, identity kit portrait,** *Br.* tdmk. **Photofit (picture)**/ tdmk. a picture of a face of a person suspected in a crime.
identity parade, identification parade *Br., Aus.* /*Am.* **lineup**/ a situation where somebody who saw the crime tries to recognize a criminal in a line of people in a police station that includes him/her.
idiot box/tube, boob tube *Am., Can.* col. /*Br.* humor. **goggle-box**/ TV set.
idiot light *Am., Can.* warning indicator of a fault in a device.
idle a factory *Am.* close it down; **idle workers** *Am.* stop them working.
idler *Am.* empty railway car placed between others to carry extra long objects.
IEE *Br.* Institute of Electrical Engineering.
if/ no ifs and buts *Br., Aus.* /*Am.* **no ifs, ands or buts**/ stop arguing (said esp. to a child).
ignorant *Br.* col. rude or impolite.
ill *Br.* adj. /*esp. Am.* **sick**/ hurt, suffering in the stated way from the effects of injury or from disease and not feeling well.
illegal *Am.* col. illegal immigrant.
illegal aliens *Am.* illegal immigrants: *should authorities look at illegal alien Ana Castro's 12 years of good citizenship here* – Reader's Digest.
illuminations *esp. Br.* a show of (coloured) lights used to make a town bright and colourful.
illy *Am.* adv. ill, badly, hardly.
illywhacker *Aus.* col. petty swindler (of a man).
imagine/ you can't imagine *Br.* col. used to emphasize how good or bad smth. is.
imbed *Am.* embed, fix firmly into a substance.
imbo *Br.* sl. imbecile.
immediately *Br.* conj. as soon as.
immersion *esp. Am., Can.* method of teaching foreign language.
immersion *Br.* col. immersion heater.
immersion heater (or **tank**) *esp. Br.* /*esp. Am.* **hot water heater** is for the house, *Br.* **geyser** is for one room, usu. kitchen/ an electric water heater placed in a tank that provides hot water for use in the home: *At Imber the immersion heater was turned on twice a week* - I. Murdoch.
impact (on) *esp. Am., Aus.* have an impact (on): *the ever increasing traffic, urban sprawl, and other factors already impacting our community.* - Outdoor Life.

impaired *Am., Can.* sl. drunk: *How about all states providing mandatory detention for those convicted of driving while impaired?* - Reader's Digest.

impeach 1. *Br.* charge with a crime against the state, esp. treason. 2. *esp. Am.* charge the state official with the misconduct.

impregnable *esp. Br.* (of a person or team) powerful and not likely to be beaten.

imprint page *Br.* /*Am.* **copyright page**/ one that holds the printer's and publisher's name, an ISBN, credits and British Library/*Br.*/ or Library of Congress/*Am.*/ CIP.

improvements *Am.* 1. modern conveniences (in the house). 2. reconstruction(s) inside the house.

in/ prep. attending for the usual purpose / (*Br.*) *in hospital*, (*Am.*) *in the hospital* e.g. *with a broken leg*; *in school studying* (*Am.*) equals at school studying: *Emily could be in school, taking an exam* - R.L. Stine.

in/ adv. (*Br.*) a cup of tea with sugar **in** (= with sugar in it).

in/ *esp. Am.* (with no, not, first, only and superlative) during, for: *I haven't seen him in four years.* - A. Scaduto. /**in many years** *Am.* / *Br.* **for many years**/.

in adv. *Am.* (shows continuity of process). e.g. *He started in to talk. It sets in to rain.*

in/ **in** *Br., Aus.* /*Am.* **on**/ per (of rates), e.g. *tax is 25 cents in/on a pound.*

You're in there! *Br.* col. Look at that attractive girl passing by.

Inauguration Day *Am.* Jan. 20th. The day when the new president takes office.

inbound *Am.* 1. moving towards the speaker or the starting place, incoming. 2. (when travelling) coming home.

in-bounds *Am.* (of a ball) in the playing area.

in-built *esp. Br.* /*Am., Aus.* **built-in**/ belonging to smth. which has always been a part of it and which can not be separared from it.

Inc. *Am., Can.* Inorportated.

incandescent with rage *Br.* extremely angry.

incentive wage *Am.* one that encourages workers to greater activity.

inch/ **not trust** sb. **an inch** *Br., Aus.* not trust sb. at all.

incident room *Br.* a room used by police, while they are dealing with a serious crime or accident.

inclosure *Am.* enclosure

inclusive *esp. Br.* including all the numbers and dates / American speakers often use **through** in expressions where British speakers use **inclusive** / e.g. (*Br.*) *Monday to Friday inclusive* equals (*Am.*) *Monday through Friday.*

income statement, statement of earnings *Am.* profit and loss account.

income support *Br.* a special government payment for poor people, such as unemployed, OAPs, single parents, people too sick to work, and those working part-time.

income tax exemption *Am.* /*Br.* **personal allowance**/.

incoming freshman *Am.* a student in the first year at college.

Incorporated (Inc) *Am.* /*Br.* **Limited (Ltd.).**

indeed *esp. Br.* /*Am., Can.* **indeedy**/ (at the end of the sentences) and I realy mean it.

indeed 1. *Br.* used to emphasize the word very. 2. *esp. Br.* col. expression of disbelief, surprise or annoyance.

indefinable *Am., Aus.* undefinable.

indent (for) *esp. Br., Aus.* v. n. 1. (make) an order for goods to be sent abroad or for stores in the army. 2. (make) an official usu. written order for goods.

indentation *esp. Br.* the act of indenting.

independent broadcasting *Br.* one not owned or paid by the government.

independent school *Br.* a fee-paying school, usu. a public or preparatory school, that operates outside the state system.

index-linked *Br.* tech. /*Am., Aus.* **indexed**/ (of pays, taxes, etc.) varied to rise and fall with general level of prices.

Indian corn *esp. Am.* maize.

Indian giving *Am., Can., Aus.* col. practice of taking away the gift after having bestowed it. n. derog. **Indian giver**: *God is not an Indian giver.* - New York.

Indian ink *Br., Aus.* /*Am., Can., Aus.* **India ink**/ dark black ink made from natural substances.

India rubber *Am.* a rubber, overshoe.

Indian *Br.* col. Indian meal or restaurant.

Indian meal *Am., Can.* meal grained from maize.

Indian summer *esp. Br.* a pleasant or successful period at the end of one's life or career.

Indian wrestling *Am.* game in which a two persons stand face-to-face with their feet touching each other and trying to push each other with their hands.

India rubber *Br.* rubber eraser.

indicate *Br.* show which way you are going to turn when you are driving.

indicator *Br.* 1. /*Am., Can* **turn signal**/ one of the lights on a car which show which way it is going to turn. 2. information board or screen in a railway station, airport, etc.

indicator switch *Br.* /*Am.* **turn signal lever**/ a car switch used to show a turn.

indict/ law. accuse sb. officially of a crime in a *Br.* law court or *Am.* grand jury.

indictable *esp. Am.* law. offence for which a person can be indicted.

indictment *esp. Am.* law. formal accusation that sb. has committed a crime.

indignation meeting *Am.* mass protest meeting.

indirect discourse *Am.* tech. /*Br.* **indirect speech**/.

individualized instruction (teacher-student) *Am.* /*Br.* **individual teaching/tutoring (teacher-pupil)**/.

induct/ be inducted *Am.* be officially made to join the army.

inductee *Am.* sb. who has been inducted into the army.

induction *esp. Am.* a ceremony in which sb. is made officially a member of the armed forces: *The whole idea had been unpopular with him from the moment I announced my induction.* - M. Torgov., *he had kept out of jail to prepare himself for induction.* - J. Baez.

induction center, mobilization center *Am.* recruiting station.

induction examination *Am.* preparatory check-up before induction.

indue with *Am.* endue with.

industrial action *esp. Br.* action by workers (such as a strike or a work-to-rule) intended to put pressure on employers to agree to the workers' demands: *Is the six form college taking "industrial action" too?* - D. Lodge.

industrial art *Am.* subject taught at school about how to use tools, machinery, etc.: *You may be able to take other subjects, inclluding agriculture, business, industrial art (or "shop"), art, music and physical education.* – Living in the USA.

industrial estate *esp. Br.* /*Am., Can., Aus.* **industrial park**/ a special area of land, often on the edge of a city, where factories and sometimes offices are built.

industrial union *Am.* a labour union that admits to its membership the workmen of industry irrespective of their occupation or craft.

ineligible alien *Am.* immigrant that has no right to become a full citizen of the US.

inertia selling *esp. Br.* /*Am.* **negative marketing**/ the selling of goods by sending them to people who have not asked for them and demanding payment if they are not returned.

infant *esp. Br., Aus.* a very young schoolchild, esp. below the age of eight / **infant teacher, school, infants class, the infants**: *Only he must come some time between the Infant Class and the Mothers' Auxiliary.* - W. Grady.

infant formula *Am., Aus.* baby milk.

infant industry *Am.* new industry working on favourable terms.

infant school, the infants *Br.* kindergarten school: *Continuous assessment should be confined to infant schools.* - D. Lodge.

infeasible *Am.* unfeasible.

infill *esp. Br.* (of a hollow place or gap) fill it.

infirmary 1. *Br.* a hospital. 2. *esp. Am.* a place, esp. in a school, where you go if you are ill.

inflammable *esp. Br.* /*Am.* **flammable**/ capable of being easily ignited.

inflexion *Br.* inflection.

influence-peddler *Am.* lobbyist, also n. **influence-peddling**.

informal vote *Aus., NZ.* invalid vote or voting paper.

information, directory assistance *Am.* / *Br.* **directory enquiries**/: *He'd have to call information.* – R.L. Stine.

information (desk) *Am.* /*Br.* **inquiry office**/.

information question *Am.* /*esp. Br.* **special question**/.

informercial *esp. Am.* film promoting certain product in informative way.

infortainment *Am.* broadcasting information in entertaining way.

infract *esp. Am.* make an infraction.

infra dig *esp. Am.* col. below one's standard of social or moral behaviour.

inglenook *esp. Br.* seat by the side of a large open fireplace.

ingrowing *Br.* /*Am.* **ingrown**/ (of toenail which is growing into one's toe).

inhibition *Br.* law. prohibtion to deal with certain pieces of land or property.

in-home *Am.* provided at sb.'s home, e.g. in-home care for the disabled.

initiation fee *Am.* entrance fee.

inject/ be injected against illness *esp. Br., Aus.* be injected (a liquid) with a syringe to prevent illness.

injury/ do oneself **injury** *Br., Aus.* humor. hurt oneself.

injury time *Br., Aus.* (in soccer) time added at the end of a game because play was stopped to take away the player who was hurt.

ink *esp. Am., Can.* col. write, sign, esp. a contract: *Butler inks Old Lions for New Series.* - Downbeat.
ink/ be bleeding red ink *Am.* esp. journalism. lose a lot of money.
inkslinger *Am.* sl. professional writer or reporter.
inland, overland *Aus.* agricultural regions far from the sea coast and large towns.
inlander *Aus.* herdsman bringing cattle from one place to another.
Inland Revenue *Br.* /*Am.* **Internal Revenue Service**/ the office which collects national taxes.
inlet *Br.* the part of the machine through which liquid enters.
inn *esp. Br.* small pub or hotel, esp. one in the countryside, built in old-fashioned style: *we were the only Americans in the dining room of an inn.* – Reader's Digest.
inner-spring (mattress) *Am., Can.* /*Br.* **interior spring**/ mattress having coiled springs inside.
inner-tubing/ go inner-tubing *Am.* ride on an inner tube of a motor vehicle either on water or down a snow-covered mountain.
innings *Br., Aus.* col. a time when one is active, esp. in a public position.
innings/ have had good innings *Br.* col. 1. stop doing smth. that they have been doing for a long time. 2. die having lived long fulfilling or rewarding life.
innovatory *esp. Br.* innovative, new and original.
Innuit *Can.* Eskimo.
inquest *Br.* 1. coroner's court's inquiry into the cause of death. 2. coroner's jury.
inquire *esp. Am.* or *Br.* obs. enquire.
inquiry agent *Br.* obs. private agent.
inquiries/ be helping the police with their inquiries *Br.* be answering questions about a crime.
inscribed *Br.* having issued loan stocks shares that are only listed in the register.
inseam *Am., Can.* /*Br., Aus.* **inside leg**/.
inside adv. 1. *Br.* downstairs in a bus with two floors. 2. *esp. Br.* sl. in prison.
inside lane 1. *Br. Aus.* /*Am.* **slow lane**/ part of the road nearest the edge, used esp. by slower vehicles. 2. *Am.* part of the road nearest the vehicles going in the opposite direction.
inside leg *Br., Aus.* /*Am.* **inseam**/ measurement from the top of one's inner leg to one's ankle.

inside of *Am., Can.* prep. inside, within: *you're going to wind up owning that bar inside of two years' time* - K. Vonnegut, Jr.
inside track *esp. Am., Can.* an advantageous position in a competition: *I had an inside track for some good contracts* - Harper's Magazine., *Anguillo, having somehow acquired an inside track on the FBI movements, had ordered his soldiers to kidnap the agents.* - G. O'Neill, D. Lehr., *you are my inside track on what is currently passing for kinky.* - D. Mortman.
insolvable *esp. Am., Aus.* insoluble, impossible to solve (about a problem).
in so much that *esp. Am.* to such a degree that.
inspector *Br.* 1. a police officer higher in rank than a sergeant but lower than superintendent. 2. person who inspects bus or train passengers' tickets. 3. sb. whose job is to visit schools and judge the quality of the teaching.
inspector of taxes *Br.* government official who calculates what tax each person should pay.
inspectorate *esp. Br.* a group of inspectors who are employed to work on the same issue or area.
inst. *Br.* becoming rare. (used after a date in business letters) of this month.
install the carpet *Am., Aus.* set the carpet in its place.
installment plan *esp. Am., Can.* /*Br.* **hire purchase** or **hire (purchase) system**/ a system of payment for goods by which one pays small sums of money regularly after receiving the goods: *Jim McCartney's was one of the many local families which bought pianos from "Nems" on the instalment plan.* - P. Norman., *his country would be obliged to dole out the payments on the instalment plan* - Time., *We sold those encyclopedias on installment plan* - W. Jack, B. Laursen.
instant housing *Am.* high speed method of housing construction.
instant lottery *Am.* high speed lottery.
instant replay *Am.* /*Br.* **action replay**/ action replay.
instate *Am.* for or happening within a single state.
instillation *Am.* /*Br.* **phasing-in**/ gradual introduction of a new material; v. **instill** *Am.* /*Br.* **phase in**/.
institute *Am.* a meeting for instruction or a brief course of lectures.
instruct (a lawyer) *esp. Br., Aus.* law. employ or authorize them to represent sb. in court.
instruction *Am.* education.

instructor, academic teacherr *Am., Can. / esp. Br.* **university teacher, lecturer/** person who teaches a subject, esp. in a school, college or university, where one is below assistant professor: *A young instructor just beginning to make his way.* - J. O'Hara.

instructor in methods; methodologist; expert in teaching methods *Am. /Br.* **specialist (teacher) in (on) methods/principles of teaching/**.

insulating tape *Br., Aus. /Am.* **friction tape/** sticky tape put around a bare piece of electric wire to prevent other people from being harmed by electricity.

insurance adjuster *Am. /Br.* **loss adjuster/** person who calculates how much to pay to insured customer for their claim.

insurance carrier *Am., Can.* an insurer or insurance company.

insurance stamp *Br.* stamp certificating weekly payment towards National Insurance.

insure *Am. /esp. Br.* **ensure/** make (smth.) certain to happen / but it's possible to insure / **assure** (*Br.*) against death.

intercept/ radio intercept *Am.* wireless interception.

interchange *Br.* a junction at which smaller roads meet a larger road, esp. motorway.

intercity *Br.* (of a train) travelling fast between main cities); n.

interdict *esp. Am., Can.* 1. forbid sb. to do smth. 2. prevent the trafficking of illegal goods or the movement of a person.

interferance *esp. Am. /Br.* **obstruction/** the act of blocking another player in ice-hockey, American football, etc. by standing in front of them.

interfere *Am.* claim substantially the same invention and thus question the priority of invention between the claimants, n. **interference**.

interfere between *Br. /Am.* **interfere with/**.

interfere with sb., esp a child *Br.* touch and attack them sexually.

run interference *Am., Can.* col. (from American football) help sb. achieve smth. by dealing with the people or problems that might prevent them from doing it: *It's difficult for a star to run interference for himself* – S. Lawrence.

interim *esp. Br.* relating to less than full year of business activity.

interior spring *Br. /Am.* **innerspring (mattress)/**.

interleaving *Br. /*also in *Am.* **slip sheeting/** print. placing sheets of paper between the newly-printed sheets as they come to prevent smudging of ink.

intermediate *Am.* a car between the standard and the compact models in size.

intermediate school *Am.* one for 12-14 or 10-12 years old children. That is junior high school or middle school.

intermission 1. *esp. Am. /Br.* **interval/** period of time between the parts of a play, concert, etc.: *By intermission I was developing a terrible stomach ache* - J. Baez., *I was still musing when intermission arrived* - P. Mowatt., *It was during our intermission at this big night club.* - M. Jones, J. Chilton., *then it was an interval* – S. Townsend. 2. *Br., Aus.* brief period between two parts of a show in cinema.

intern *esp. Am., Can. /Br.* **houseman/** person who has nearly or recently finished professional training, esp. in medicine or teaching, and is gaining controlled practical experience, esp. in a hospital or classroom: *On the way there they met three interns.* - W. Grady. n. **internship**.

internal medecine *Am.* part of medical science dealing with discovering of illnesses inside the body and treating them without cutting it open.

international *esp. Br.* sportsman/woman taking part in an international match.

internist *esp. Am., Can.* therapist, doctor specializing in internal diseases: *her time in Los Angeles usually consists of going from analist to internist.* – N. Mailer.

intersection *esp. Am., Aus. /esp. Br.* **crossroads, junction** *Br.* **T-junction/**: *traffic jam we were causing by blocking a busy intersection.* - R.G. Kaiser.

interstate *Am.* very wide road for long distance travel.

interval *Br. /Am., Aus.* **intermission/** break separating two acts of theatre or music performances.

in the bag *Am.* sl. 1. drunk. 2. ruined.

in the club *Br.* sl. pregnant.

into/ be into smth. *Am.* be very interested in smth.

invalid home, invalid out *esp. Br.* send a soldier or the state official home from abroad because of the illness: *It's worth getting a small wound to be invalided home.* - Longman.

in there/ be in there *Br.* be likely to experience smth. good because of the situation they are in.

intitule *Br.* give a special title to an act of Parliament.

intraday *Am., Can.* Stock Exchange situation within a specific day.
intramural *esp. Am., Can.* (of courses) within a single educational institution.
intrastate *Am.* within one state.
in-tray *esp. Br., Aus.* /*Am.* **in-box**/ a flat open container where letters and documents which arrive are put.
invalid home, invalid out *esp. Br.* allow sb. to leave esp. a military force because of ill-health.
invalid chair *Br.* obs. wheel chair.
invalidity benefit *Br.* the state payment made to people who are unable to work after more than 28 weeks of sickness.
inventory *esp. Am.* stock of the company; all the goods in a shop: *donating your slow moving inventory can mean a generous tax write-off for your company.* - Time.
inverted commas *esp. Br.* quotation marks.
inverted commas/ in inverted commas *Br., Aus.* col. (about other people's words) not really true.
inverted snob *esp. Br.* derog. person who makes a show of disliking grand things and admiring things typical of low social class, also **inverted snobbery.**
invigilate *esp. Br., Aus.* /*Am.* **proctor**/ watch over (an examination or the people taking it) in order to prevent dishonesty; **invigilation, invigilator**: *Even to spot the culprits, let alone bring lawsuits against them meant a countrywide invigilation* - P. Norman.
Irish coffee *Br.* an alcoholic drink consisting of a mixture of Irish whiskey with coffee, sugar and cream.
iron fist/ rule (sb.) **with an iron fist/hand** *Am., Aus.* be very firm.
Irish potato *Am.* white potato.
iron out the kinks *Am.* deal with small problems so that one can succeed.
ironbark *Aus.* a type of eucalyptus tree which has deep lines on its stem.
iron man 1. *Am.* sl. a dollar: *I got a hundred iron men in my pocket.* - J. Dos Passos. 2. *Am., Aus.* a very strong man.
iron master *esp. Br.* manufacturer of iron.
iron monger's *Br.* obs. hardware store.
ironmonger *Br.* /*esp. Am., Aus.* **hardware dealer**/ person who owns or works in a shop / **ironmonger's**, *esp. Am., Aus.* **hardware store**/ which sells hardware, esp. if made of metal.
ironmongery *Br.* hardware, equipment for home and garden.
The Iron Mountain state *Am.* Missouri.

irregular 1. *Br.* slightly dishonest or illegal. 2. *Am., Aus.* col. constipated.
irregular/ be irregular *Am., Aus.* col. not empty one's bowels as frequently as one would use to.
-ish *esp. Br.* suffix to some degree, somewhat.
itch sb. *Am.* bring unpleasant feeling in the skin.
itchy feet/ have/get itchy feet *esp. Br., Aus.* col. want to move or do smth. different.
itchy fingers/ have/get itchy fingers *Br.* be eager to do smth. or try an activity.
itchy palm *Br.* obs. derog. liking to be paid for what one does for sb.
itemize *Am.* /*Br.* **specify**/ set out all the details (of each thing on a list).
itsy-bitsy *Br., Aus.* /*Am., Aus.* **itty-bitty**/ humor. extremely small.
IV *Am.* /*Br.* **drip**/ dripfeed.
ivories *Am.* humor. teeth.
Ivy League *Am.* adj. belonging to or typical of old and respected universities of the eastern US: *Harvard and Yale belong to the Ivy League.* - H.C. Whitford., R.J. Dixson.
izzatso *Am.* excl. of disbelief.

J

jab *esp. Br., Aus.* col. injection.
jabber *Aus.* chat; n. language.
jack 1. *esp. Am.* col. money: *I spent all my jack* - J. Dos Passos. 2. *Am.* /also **jacklight**/ portable light used in hunting or fishing. 3. *Br.* sl. a policeman. 4. *Br.* sl. a fifty pound note. 5. *Am.* col. jackshit. 6. *esp. Am.* /*esp. Br.* **knave**/a playing card.
Jack the Lad *Br.* col. overconfident silly person.
jack *Am., Can.* hunt or fish at night; **jackfishing, jackhunting.**
jack *Aus., NZ.* col. fed up, tired.
jack/ every man jack (of you/them) *Br.* obs. everyone.
jack/ I'm all right Jack *Br.* used to show disapproval that the person only cares for oneself without paying any attention to other people's problems.
jack/ not...jack (shit) *Am.* sl. not at all.
jack/ on one's **jack** (or **Jack Jones**) *Br.* sl. on one's own.
jack sb. **around** *Am., Can.* col. cause problems to sb. or waste their time by one's unfair or indecisive actions.
jack smth. **in** *Br.* col. stop, give up: *Ought to jack 'em in really.* - J. Fowles.

jack off, jerk off *Am.* taboo. sl. masturbate.

jack up *Am.* col. 1. scold, find fault with (sb.): *The director jacked Jim up for being late again.* - Longman. 2. encourage (sb.) to fulfil his/her responsibilities: *see what you can do to jack him up.* - Longman.

jack up/ be jacked up *Am.* col. be excited and nervous.

jack up *Aus.* col. give up or refuse to take part in smth.

Jack and Jill party *Am., Can.* party for both men and women held for a couple soon to be married.

jackaroo /Jacky Row/ *Aus.* col. 1. (work as) inexperienced worker on a large sheep or cattle farm. 2. a new colonist.

jackass 1. *Aus.* kookaburra. 2. *Br.* obs. or *Am.* col. annoying stupid person.

jack chain *Am.* endless lug chain.

Jack cheese *Am., Can.* type of cheese resembling cheddar.

jacked/ be jacked up *Am.* col. be excited and worried.

jackeen *esp. Irish Eng.* derog. city-dweller, esp. Dubliner.

(record) jacket *Am. /Br.* **sleeve/** (gramophone record envelope).

jacket potato *Br., Aus.* a potato baked with its skin on.

jackfish *Am.* col. pike.

jackhammer *esp. Am., Can., Aus. /esp. Br.* **pneumatic drill**: *jackhammers pounded away at the concrete encasement.* - G, O'Neill, D. Lehr.

jack-in-the-office *Br.* self-important minor official.

jackleg *Am.* n. adj. 1. amateur. 2. col. unscrupulous person: *won't he let me round and complete his knowledge by telling him how the jackleg does it?* - M. Twain. 3. temporary, makeshift thing: *We did have a sort of jackleg diplomatic status* - J. Fischer.

jacklight *Am., Can.* portable light often used for fishing at night.

jack-o'-lantern *Am.* a light made by putting a candle inside a hollow pumpkin with holes cut into it in the shapes of eyes and mouth.

jackplug *Br. /Am.* **jack/** a metal pin that could be pushed into a socket called jack to connect one part of electrical device to another part, esp. headphones to a walkman.

jackpot *Am., Can.* predicament.

Jack Robinson/ before you can say Jack Robinson or **before you can say knife** *esp. Br.* col. very quickly or suddenly: *I was out of the shelter before you could say Jack Robinson* – R. Westall.

jacks *esp. Am.* children's ball game.

jack shit/diddly *Am.* col. nothing at all.

jacksie, jacksy *Br.* col. person's bottom.

Jack the Lad *Br.* col. a showily confident and successful young working-class man.

jacky *Aus.* derog. aboriginal person.

jaffa *Br.* tdmk. a type of large orange.

jag *esp. Am., Can.* spree, lively party.

jagged *esp. Am.* drunk: *Let's go out and get jagged.* - R.A. Spears.

jailhouse *esp. Am., Can* col. prison.

jake *Am., Can., Aus., NZ.* sl. O.K., satisfactory: *we'll be jake.* - J. Dos Passos.

jam 1. *Br., Aus., Can. /Am.* **jelly/** food made of cooking fruit with a lot of sugar. 2. *Br.* smth. easy and pleasant.

jam/ sb. is jamming *Am.* sl. sb. is doing smth. well.

jam/ want jam on it *Br.* used to say that sb. wants more than is reasonable.

jam sandwich, Panda car, Z car *Br.* police patrol car.

jam tomorrow *esp. Br.* maniana; it will be done sometime in the future.

jam through *Am.* pull through / e.g. *jam a bill through.*

jammed *Am.* full of people or things; jam-packed.

jam jar *Br.* sl. a car.

jammy *Br.* sl. 1. easy: *its rich jammy language had been the stuff of very deep sleep.* - A. Burgess. 2 (used esp. with taboo words) lucky, esp. in a way that makes other people annoyed or jealous.

jams *Am.* brightly coloured trousers that stop above one's knees.

Jane *Am.* sl. women's toilet.

jane *esp. Am.* col. a woman.

Jane Crow *Am.* sl. discrimination against women.

Jane Doe *Am.* a woman whose name is kept in secret in a court of law.

jangle *Br.* col. v. gossip.

janitor *esp. Am., Can.* doorkeeper.

janitor, custodian *esp. Am., Can. /esp. Br.* **caretaker/** caretaker of school, large public building, etc.: *janitor no longer found enough empty bottles to make a twice daily trash-run into town.* - Time., *Dustin was the janitor at the school.* - New Idea., *This janitor was nervous but cooperative* - R. Moore. n. **janitress**.

JAP *Am.* sl. young Jewish girl, esp. a wealthy one.

jar *Br.* col. a glass of beer.

jar/ have a jar *Br.* col. have drinks with friends in a pub.

jasper *Am.* col. a fellow, man.

Java *Am., Can.* col. coffee.

jaw/ a punch on *Br., Aus.* /*Am.* **a punch in/ the jaw/**.

jawbone *Am.* sl. apply verbal pressure to sb. n. **-ing**: *But his greatest misdeed was his and other congressmen's jawboning of thrift regulators* - Economist., *But his jawboning did not seem to move the Lithuanian people.* - H. Smith.

jawbreaker 1. *esp. Am., Can., Aus.* col. a hard round piece of candy: *Miller has paired his knowledge of miniature jawbreakers with a desire to boost canine self-esteem.* - Newsweek. 2. *Aus.* a word which is difficult to pronounce.

Jaws of Life *Am., Can.* tdmk. hydraulic device used to pry apart the wreckage of crushed vehicles in order to free people trapped inside.

jaybird/ naked as a jaybird *Am.* completely naked.

Jaycee *Am., Can.* col. member of junior college of Chamber of Commerce, a civic organisation for business and community leaders.

The Jayhawker State /also **The Squatter** or **Sunflower State**/ *Am.* joc. Kansas, **Jayhawker** *Am.* joc. a citizen of Kansas: *the good senator is a "Hawkeye, and not a Jayhawk"* – Reader's Digest.

jazz *Am.* sl. derog. 1. empty meaningless talk esp. if used to confuse or deceive: *I'm not up on all the psychiatric jazz* - M. Puzo.. 2. v. n. taboo. (do) the sex act: *Come on upstairs and jazz a little.* - E. Caldwell., *Gee, I'm looking forward to jazzing a high-class dame like you* – K. Vonnegut, Jr.

jazz/ and all that jazz *Br., Aus.* and other similar things.

JCB *Br.* tdmk. a machine used for digging and moving earth.

J-cloth *Br.* tdmk. a type of cloth for household cleaning.

jeans/ blue jeans *Am.* /*Br., Can.* jeans/ jeans made of blue denim.

jeepers (creepers) *esp. Am.* obs. or humor. excl. of surprise.

jeez *Am.* col. excl. of surprise, anger, etc.

Jeffrey, also **Archer** *Br.* sl. 2,000 pounds.

jello, jell-o *Am., Can.* tdmk. /*Br., Aus.* **jelly**/ jelly, a dish made with sweetened fruit juice and gelatine.

Jell-O/ be like trying to nail Jell-O to the wall *Am.* col. be very difficult.

jelly 1. *Br., Aus.* /*Am.* **Jell-O**/ (a container of) transparent or coloured food, made from gelatine, fruit juice, and sugar that is eaten as a desert 2. *esp. Am.* /*Br., Aus.* **jam**/. 3. *Br.* a kind of thin, clear jam. 4. *Br.* col. gelignite. 5. *esp. Br.* solid substance made from meat juices and gelatine; aspic.

jelly/ beat sb. **to a jelly** *esp. Br.* hit repeatedly and with force.

jelly-baby *Br.* tdmk. a small soft fruit-flavoured sweet in the shape of a baby.

jelly bean *Am.* small coloured sweets with hard shells and jelly inside: *Lots of neat stuff – from skateboards and saxophones to candles and jellybeans – is made in America.* – Reader's Digest.

jelly roll *Am.* 1. also *Can.* /*Br.* **Swiss roll**/ a cake with a sweet substance (jam or cream) inside: *Jelly rolls, ice cream, chocolates - they're not good at all* – W. Grady. 2. sl. a woman chaser. 3. sl. vulva. 4. sex act. 5. sexually attractive woman.

jemmy *Br., Aus.* 1. /*Am.* **jimmy**/ a metal bar used esp. by thieves to break open locked doors, windows, etc.; v. 2. sheep's head for food.

jenny wren *Br.* col. wren.

jerk 1. *esp. Am., Can., Aus.* sl. derog. /*Br.* sl. **git, muggings, Juggins, jobbernowl,** *esp. Br.* col. **twit**/a stupid person: *Don't louse up your life by having to marry some jerk, you don't give a damn about.* - H. Fast., *Some jerk called senator Joe Clark a Communist.* - J.A. Michener., *I slapped some obnoxious jerk at a drunken party* - S. Sheldon. 2. *Am., Can.* col. /also **soda jerk(er)**/ an apparatus for drawing soda water; a seller of soda: *He takes a job as a soda jerk* - Time.

jerk sb. **around** *Am., Can.* col. treat unfairly.

jerk off *esp. Am., Can., Aus.* sl. taboo. masturbate: *He was just one of those kids who made model airplanes and jerked off all the time.* - K. Vonnegut, Jr.

jerk-off *Am.* sl a stupid person, esp. a man.

jerkwater *esp. Am.* col. (about a place) small and insignificant: *those jerkwater hotels over the state* - R.P. Warren.

jerky *Am.* meat that has been cut into long thin strips and dried in the sun.

jerky *Am.* sl. (of a person or his behaviour) silly, foolish, ungrateful.

jerry 1. *Br.* col. becoming rare. chamberpot. 2. **Jerry** *esp. Br.* col. now rare. derog. a name used esp. by soldiers for a German: *You think the Jerries'll have another shot at us?* - D. Lessing.

jersey *esp. Br.* a sweater: *Kerry looked down at his own jersey and frowned.* – R.L. Stine.
The Jersey Blue State *Am.* New Jersey.
jessie *Br.* sl. weak or effeminate man: *come on you big soft jessie.* - T. Thorne.
jetway *Br.* tdmk. /*Br.* **air bridge**/.
Jew York *Am.* sl. derog. New York.
jib at *esp. Br.* col. become suddenly unwilling to do or accept smth.
jibe (with) *esp. Am., Can.* gibe, be the same as, match, agree with: *The prisoner's story jibes with his companion's account of the robbery* - Longman.
jiffybag *Br.* tdmk. a padded envelope used for sending books and other articles through the post.
jig/ in jig time *Am., Can.* col. very quickly.
jig/ jig is up *Am., Can.* col. the secret or a trick has been discovered.
jigaboo *Am., Can.* sl. taboo. derog. black person: *I called Bokonon a jigabooo bastard* - K. Vonnegut, Jr.
jigger 1. *esp. Br.* /*esp. Am.* **chigger**/ any small insect that goes in under skin and causes discomfort: *Hell, we're as comfortable as a chigger in a lady's tit* - H. Fast. 2. *esp. Am.* sl. any small piece of apparatus, gadget. 3. *Can., NZ.* small vehicle used by railway workers.
jigger *Am.* change smth., esp. unfairly or illegally.
jiggered *Br.* col. 1. very surprised: *Well, I'll be jiggered.* - R.P. Warren. 2. also *Aus.* very tired. 3. damaged; broken.
jiggery-pokery *esp. Br.* col. /*Am.* **hanky-panky**/ secret dishonest behaviour: *some complicated piece of jiggery-pokery* - M.M. Kaye.
jillaroo *Aus.* col. country girl, esp. one learning to work on a sheep or cattle farm.
jillion *Am.* col. zillion, a very large number: *The film was developed along with a jillion other films* – F. Edwards.
jim-crow *Am.* adj. 1. derog. unfairly disadvantageous to blacks: *the moral of troops is strengthened where Jim Crow practices are not imposed.* - H. Truman.. 2. for blacks only, and usu. of poor quality: *they finally let him in the Jim Crow ward down there.* - B. Holiday., W. Duffy.
jim-dandy *Am.* col. obs. or humor. adj. n. excellent, wonderful (person): *Tommy's new boat is really a jim-dandy!* - A. Makkai.
jim-jams *Br.* col. pyjamas.
jimmy *Br.* col. an act of urinating.
jimmygrant *Aus.* sl. immigrant.

Jimmy Woodser *Aus.* col. a person who drinks alone or a drink on one's own.
jingle *Aus.* two-wheeled wagon.
jingle 1. *Am.* telephone call: *I got a jingle from Gert today.* - R.A. Spears. 2. *Br.* sl. cash, money: *I'm a bit short of jingle.* - T. Thorne.
jinker *Aus.* wheeled cart for moving heavy logs.
jitney *Am.* 1. five cents. 2. col. also *Can.* a cheap local taxi for short journeys. 3. cheap.
jive 1. *esp. Am.* sl. deceiving or foolish talk: *there was no place for his jive line or his hot pants* - E. Cleaver. 2. *Am., Can.* col. play a joke on sb. telling a lie; sneer at sb. 3. *Am., Can.* cheating or worthless: *You're all jive tonight.* – S. Lawrence.
Jnr. *Br., Aus.* /*esp. Am.* **Jr.**/ abbr. of junior used after a man's name to distinguish him from a member of the family with the same name.
job *Am., Can.* col. cheat; betray.
job/ a good / bad job *Br.* col. a good / bad thing, esp. in the phr. **make a good/bad job of** smth.
job/ a job at hand *Am.* job in hand, present job.
job/ a job of work *Br.* col. a piece of work, usu. well-done.
job/ big job *Br.* col. euph. faeces or defecation.
job/ do a job on sb./smth. *esp. Am.* col. hurt or damage sb. or smth., esp. cruelly.
job/ don't give up the day job *Br.* /*Am.* **don't quit your day job**/ humor. keep on trying.
job/ get a job *Am.* sl. stop being foolish and do smth. useful.
job/ give smth. **up as a bad job** *Br.* stop doing smth. thinking that it won't be successful.
job/ good job *Am.* col. well done!
job/ have a job (doing smth.) *Br.* col. have problems doing smth.
job/ it's a good job *Br.* col. you are lucky that it happened.
job/ it's more than my job's worth *Br., Aus.* col. I'll lose a job if I do it.
job/ just the job *Br., Aus.* /*Br.* obs. **just the ticket**/ col. exactly what is needed or wanted.
job/ make the best of a bad job *esp. Br.* do the best in unfavourable situation.
job/ on the job *Br.* col. engaged in sex intercourse.
job action *Am.* workers' protest action.
jobber 1. *Am., Can.* wholesaler. 2. *esp. Br.* stock exchange broker.
jobbing *Br.* doing separate small jobs for various people, e.g. **jobbing gardener, painter**, etc.: - *Jobbing printing has moved into the high street with the "instant print" shop.* - D. Bann.
job centre *Br.* government office for unemployed.

job creation schemes *Br., Aus.* ways to create new jobs.

job evaluation *Br.* examining one job in relation to others in an organisation.

jobholder *Am.* state employee.

jobless *esp. Br.* unemployed.

job lot *Br., Aus.* a bunch of bought things; mixed group of things that are sold together.

job pattern *Am.* staff register.

job placement *Am.* search for the job for sb.; **job placement outlet** *Am. /Br.* **job centre/** labour exchange agency.

jobs/ jobs for the boys/girls *Br., Aus.* derog. nepotism; jobs unfairly given to sb.'s friends, supporters or relatives.

a job's comforter *Br.* obs. a person who wants to make sb. more cheerful but makes them feel worse.

job security *Am.* provision of job for a certain period of time.

jobshare *Br.* divide the duties and pay of one job between two or more people who work at different times during the day or week n. **–ing**.

jobsworth *Br.* col. a person who is too much concerned about the rules and regulations connected to their job and unwilling to break them to do smth. kind and sensible.

jock 1. *esp. Am., Can., Aus.* col. derog. */esp. Br.* **hearty/** a sportsman, esp. a college student who is very keen on sport: *part of me is an old jock* - H. Fast., *He had started out as a fighter jock* - J. DeFelice. n. rare **jockette** a female jock. 2. *Am., Can.* enthusiast in a specific activity. 3. *Am., Can.* col. jockstrap, support for men's genitals worn esp. by sportsmen.

jock *Br.* col. a Scot.

jockey 1. *esp. Br.* a crafty bargainer. 2. *Am.* machine operator.

jock itch *Am., Can.* col. fungal infection of the groin area.

jocks *Aus.* col. a piece of men's underwear covering the area between the waist and the tops of the legs.

joe *esp. Am., Can.* col. 1. coffee: *New Yorkers' real fuel is plain filter-drip coffee - a "regular" cup of joe* - New York. 2. man, fellow: *it's some joe with a record* - Arthur Hailey.

Joe Blake *Aus.* sl. 1. snake. 2. (pl.) delirium tremens.

Joe Bloggs *Br. /Am.* col. **Joe Blow/Schmo/** ordinary average person.

joe job *Can.* col. menial or dull, boring job.

Joe Public *Br. /Am.* **John Q Public, Joe Schmoe, Joe Average,** *Am., Can., Aus.* **Joe Blow,** *Br., Aus.* **Joe Bloggs/** col. an average ordinary person.

Joe Sixpack *esp. Am.* derog. an average blue-collar man: *All Joe Six-pack wants is a good game on TV.* - R.A. Spears.

joey *Aus.* col. 1. young kangaroo. 2. young animal or baby. 3. smth. insignificant.

joey *Br.* sl. a schoolchild coerced into stealing and other criminal acts by older children, typically members of teenage gangs.

jog *Am.* projecting or retreating part of a line or surface.

john 1. *esp. Am., Can., Aus. /Br., Aus.* **loo/** col. toilet: *Who can tell me where is the john.* - T. Capote., *Imogene spent the whole time smoking cigars in one of the johns in the ladies' room.* - B. Robinson., *A guy rolls into the men's john* - Esquire. 2. *Am.* sl. a prostitute's customer.

John Bloggs *Br. /Am., Can.* **Joe Doakes, John Doe/** col. an average man: *John Doe was the name at the bottom of the check.* - R.A. Spears.

johnboat *Am., Can.* small flat-bottomed boat with square ends.

John Doe *esp. Am.* law. anonymous party, esp. plaintif in a legal action: *cremated, stored in a box for three years with other John and Jane Does* – Reader's Digest.

John Hancock /also *Am., Aus., Can.* **John Henry/** *Am.* col. a person's signature: *To give you a refund, we need your John Henry on this form.* - W. Magnuson.

johnny *Br.* col. 1. unknown man. 2. condom.

johnny *Am.* sl. penis.

johnny-cake 1. *Am.* flat corn-bread cake: *You can eat the same meal of bananas, johnnycakes and coffee* – Reader's Digest. 2. *Aus., NZ.* one of wheat.

johnny-come-lately *esp. Am.* new comer: *I'm a johnny-come-lately compared to you.* - H. Fast., *Another phenomenon is the johnny-come-lately rock critic.* - J. Gabree.

Johnny-on-the-spot *Am., Can.* col. person who is always ready to go and help sb.

John Q Public *Am., Can.* humor. the public.

John Thomas /JT/ *Br.* sl. penis, cock.

join up *Br.* become a member of the army, navy, etc.: *Did you join up or were you forced into the army?* - Longman.

join battle (with) *Br.* start a fight, argument, or competition with sb.

joiner *Br.* person who makes wooden doors, window frames, etc.

joinery *Br.* the skill and work of a joiner.

joint 1. *Br. /Am.* **roast/** large piece of meat for cooking, esp. containing a bone: *Young members of the family indeed would have done* *without a joint altogether* - J. Galsworthy., *a Sunday joint is a roast-beef - not a marijuana cigarette.* - Newsweek. 2. **the joint** *Am., Can.* prison.

joint *Am.* sl. penis: *He covered his joint and ran for the dressing room.* - R.A. Spears.

joint booking office *Br.* consolidated ticket office.

joint honours degree *Br.* /*Aus.* **double honours degree**/ degree for both subjects done at the same time.

jointly/ be jointly funded *Br.* /*Aus.* **be joint-funded**/ be given financial aid from two sources.

joint resolution *Am.* decision approved by both houses of the US congress which becomes a law when signed by the president.

joint return *Am.* husband and wife income.

joint stocker *Am.* tech. share holder.

joker *Aus.* a person.

joker *Am.* 1. hidden clause in a bill or document somehow affecting its operation. 2. sl. a hidden cost, qualification, defect, nasty result, etc.

the joker in the pack *esp. Br.* smth. different from others.

jok(e)y *Br.* not serious and tending to make people laugh.

joking apart/aside *Br.* used before you say smth. serious after you've been joking.

joking/ only joking *Br.* col. you didn't really mean it.

joking/ you must be joking *Br.* you have to be joking.

jollier *Am.* merry widow.

jollies *esp. Br., Aus., Can.* a good or festive time: *I'm up to my elbows in blood and getting jollies out of that?* - H. Fast., *It is not necessary to let the academics have their jollies* - McLeans.

jollies/ get one's **jollies** *Am.* col. get pleasure from a particular experience or activity.

jollo *Aus.* /*Br.* **jolly**/ col. spree, party.

jolly *Br.* col. adv. obs. 1. very: *From a British man, that's jolly good.* - Reader's Digest. 2. **jolly well** (used to give force to an expression) certainly, really: *They've jolly well got to be inventive and progressive.* - A. Huxley.

jolly *esp. Br.* happy and cheerful.

jolly (along, into, out of) *esp. Br.* col. persuade: *see if you can jolly her along a bit.* - Longman.

jolly smth. **up** *Br.* make a place brighter and more cheerful.

jolly hockey sticks/ be jolly hockey sticks *Br.* humor. behaving as if sb. were from high society.

jones *esp. Am.* black sl. addiction, often in **jones on/for** have fixation on: *She also had a jones for Herb Jeffries* – E. James, D. Ritz.

josh *esp. Am., Aus., Can.* col. 1. v. n. joke; good-natured banter. 2. make fun of, without wanting to hurt: *Never mind I'm joshing you.* - T. Caldwell., *all been boosted with much josh about ultimate answers.* - Economist., *her gruff husband joshed her.* - J.A. Michener.

joss *esp. Aus., NZ.* col. person of influence or importance.

josser 1. *Br.* col. an (old) fellow, geezer: *He's a queer old josser.* - J. Joyce. 2. *Aus.* priest. 3. *Br.* sl. foolish or contemptible person.

jostle *Am.* sl. pick pockets; n. **-er.**

jotter(pad) *Br., Aus.* a small book for writing brief notes in.

journalism/ sidewalk journalism *Am.* "yellow" press.

journey *esp. Br.* a trip from one place to another, esp. one over a long distance.

journo *esp. Am., Aus.* col. journalist.

Jove/ By Jove *Br.* obs. col. (an expression of surprise, also used for adding force to other expressions).

jowl *Am., Can.* cheek of pig used as meat.

joy *Br.* col. success in what you are trying to do; **wish** sb. **joy** is ironic congratulation.

joy *Br.* col. (usu. in negatives and questions **any joy?**) success or finding what sb. was searching for.

joy-house *Am.* col. brothel: *I ain't been in a joyhouse* - E. Caldwell.

joy rider *Br., Aus.* a person riding for enjoyment in a car stolen by him.

Jr. *Am.* Junior.

jube *Aus., NZ.* /*esp. Am., Can.* **jujube**/ jujube lozenge.

judder *esp. Br., Aus.* /*Am.* **shudder**/ (esp. of a vehicle) shake violently.

judgement call *Am.* using one's own ideas or opinions.

judge's rules *Br.* the rules governing the treatment of an arrested person by the police.

judy *Br.* col. a young woman: *One of them... attracted the attention of a local patron's "judy".* - P. Norman.

jug 1. *Br., Aus., Can.* /*Am.* **pitcher**/ a container for holding liquids that has a handle and a lip for pouring. b. also **jugful** the amount a jug will hold. 2. *Am., Can.* a. pot for holding liquids that has a narrow opening at the top that can usu. be closed with a cork. b. also **jugful** the amount this will hold: *She's likely to keep a jug of* *vodka tucked away* - J. Fischer., *A big jug of wine was passed over to us.* - B.E. Olson. 3. *esp. Am.* col. prosecute or imprison sb.

juggernaut *esp. Br.* col. usu. derog. /*Am.* **tractor-trailer**, esp. *Aus.* **semi(-trailer**/ a very large heavy truck that carries loads over long distances: *How can these men...drive their juggernauts at such insane speeds* - D. Lodge.

juggins *Br.* col. a fool, dupe: *O, you juggins, said Miss Trent, the games mistress crossly.* - T. Thorne.

jug-handed *Am.* one-sided.

jug kettle *Br.* electric kettle in a form of a jug with a lid.

juice *Am., Can.* col. 1. liquor: *they sold juice there.* - B. Holiday., W. Duffy. 2. influence, favourable position: *The boss has the juice with the board to make the necessary changes.* - R.A. Spears.

juice smth. **up** *esp. Am.* give more life, excitement, fun, etc.: *I'd creep out to the den where him and his juiced-up pals were waiting.* – E. James, D. Ritz

juiced *Am., Can.* col. drunk. n. **-er, juicehead**: *everyone was juiced to begin with.* - A. Scaduto.

juice road *Am.* col. electric railway.

juicer *esp. Am.* a machine for removing juice from fruit.

juke(-joint) *Am.* tavern with a jukebox.

jumble *Br.* /*Am.* **rummage**/ old and unwanted things that people give away to charity.

jumble sale, boot sale *Br.* /*Am.* **rummage sale**/ a sale of used articles as a way of collecting money for a good purpose. e.g. to help hospital or school: *At regular intervals we held jumble sales in the backcourts.* - C.M. Fraser., *And Dr. Lazurkina in deplorable jumble-sale high heels, led him* - A. Burgess.

The Jumbo State *Am.* Texas.

jumbuck *Aus.* col. a sheep.

jump 1. *esp. Am.* col. travel on (a train) without paying. 2. *Am., Can.* col. start a car using jump leads.

jump/ get/have a/the jump on sb./smth. *esp. Am., Can.* (used mostly by journalists) col. start doing smth. before others.

jump/ go take a running jump *Am.* col. go away and stop bothering me.

jump/ jump a claim *esp. Am., Aus.* try to claim valuable land which sb. else already owns.

jump leads *Br.* /*Am., Can.* **jumper cables**, *Aus.* **jumper leads**/ two thick wires used to carry electric power from one car to another which doesn't have it in order to start it: *So a guy walks into a bar with a pair of jumper cables hanging around his neck.* – Reader's Digest.

jump rope *Am., Can.* /*Br.* **skip**/ jump over rope: *Three stick-skinny, little black girls, may be eight years old, were jumping rope.* - T. Murphy.

jump sb.'s **bones** *Am., Can.* sl. have sex with sb.: *Sneaking up behind 'em and jumping their bones* - J. Kellerman.

jump the (a) queue *esp. Br., Aus., Can.* /*Am.* **cut in line**/ obtain an unfair advantage over others who have been waiting longer.

jumped-up *esp. Br.* col. derog. /*Br., Aus.* col. derog. **jumped-on**/ having too great an idea of one's own importance, esp. because of having just risen to a higher social class.

jumper 1. *Am., Aus., Can.* also **jumper dress** / *Br.* **pinafore dress**/ a dress without sleeves, usu. worn over a blouse. 2. *Am.* sledge. 3. *esp. Br.* /*esp. Am., Can.* **sweater, pullover**/ a warm knitted piece of clothing which covers the upper part of your body and arms: *Why do the British call them jumpers?* - B. Bryson.

jumpers *Br.* rare. /*Am.* **overalls**, *Br.* **dungarees**/ overalls.

jump head(line) *Am.* head line of continuation.

jumping rope (jump rope) *Am., Can.* /*Br.* **skipping rope**/ one repeatedly passed beneath one's feet, as a game or for exercise: *Jumping rope is good too.* – A. Miller.

jumping-off place *Am.* 1. very faraway place: *Columbus' sailors were afraid they would arrive at the jumping-off place* - A. Makkai. 2. deadlock.

jump jet *Br.* a jet aircraft that can take off and land vertically.

jump leads *Br.* two thick wires used to start a car whose battery doesn't have enough power.

jump seat *Am., Can.* extra seat in a car or taxi that folds back when not in use.

jump-start *esp. Am.* col. start a car by getting power from another car: *Yet his mind has been jump-started by books, especially Dante's Divine comedy.* - Time., *This kind of reflection may even jump-start our unconscious into a whole new approach* - C. Hoover.

jump-up *Aus.* col. escarpment.

junction *esp. Br.* /*Am., Aus.* **intersection**/ intersection of the roads: *there are even traffic jams on the sliproad at the junction 5.* - J. Harmer., R. Rosner.

jungle-bunny *Am.* taboo. sl. a black person.

jungle gym *Am., Can., Aus.* /*Br.* **climbing frame**/ large frame made of bars for children to climb on: *chasing one another around the jungle gym.* - Guideposts.

junior 1. *Br.* a pupil at a junior school. 2. *Am. / Br.* 3rd **year undergad(uate)/** (a student of) the third year in a four year course at high school or university. 3. *esp. Am.* one's son. 4. *esp. Br.* sb. who has a low rank in an organisation or profession. 5. *Am.* humor. a way of addressing or speaking about one's son.

Junior (Jnr. or **Jr.)** *esp. Am.* adj. the younger, esp. of two men in the same family who have exactly the same name.

junior college *Am.* one where students study for two years.

junior common room *Br.* room in a college used for social gatherings by the undergraduates or the undegraduates regarded collectively.

junior high school *Am.* incomplete secondary school.

junior school *Br.* a school for children between 7 and 11 years old (**juniors**) in England and Wales.

junior varsity *Am.* team of younger or less experienced sports players who represent school or college.

junk *esp. Am.* sl. heroin.

junker *Am.* sl. an old car.

junket *esp. Am.* col. v. n. often derog. (make) a trip or journey (esp. one made by a government official and paid for with government money): *last week's eight-day junket was good and even necessary* - Time.

junk bottle *Am.* porter bottle.

junk dealer *Am.* one who deals in old ship materials.

junkman *Am.* old-clothes man.

junkyard *Am.* dump.

jurist *Am., Can.* lawyer or judge.

jury/ be on/doing jury service *Br. /Am., Aus.* **jury duty/** act as a member of a jury.

just/ just, already, and yet were not used at one time with the simple past tense when speaking of time. But expressions like: *The bell just rang, I already saw him, Did you eat yet?* are common in informal American English.

just/ (*Br.*) It's just gone 8 o'clock.

just a minute, moment, second, etc. *Br.* used to interrupt sb. to ask them to explain smth, to calm them or to express disagreement.

just now *esp. Br.* at the moment.

just on *Br., Aus.* exactly.

just so, also **quite so** *Br.* Yes, I agree.

justice 1. *Am.* a judge in a law court: *they were married in Yonkers by a Justice of the Peace* – P. Roth. 2. *Br.* the title of officer in the High Court.

justice/ be rough justice for sb. *esp. Br.* be not treated fairly.

K

K *esp. Br., Aus. /Am.* **G/** one thousand dollars or pounds: *teachers never make over $48K (and that's with a doctorate).* – Reader's Digest.

k *Am.* print. used to indicate black in the four-colour process.

K/ get one's **K** *Br.* be knighted.

kaffee-klatch *Am.* informal social event where people drink coffee and talk.

kale *Am.* sl. money: *Oh, if we had kale we could live like kings.* - J. Dos Passos.

kangaroo dog *Aus.* hound-dog.

kangaroo a car *Aus.* drive a car in jerks.

kangaroo/ be happy as a boxing kangaroo in fogtime *Aus.* be dishonest.

kangaroo/ have (kanga)roos in one's **top paddock** *esp. Aus. /Br.* **have rats in the attic/** be slightly mad.

kangaroo's droop or **hop** *Aus.* col. a woman's gait or posture resembling that of a kangaroo.

katydid *Am.* a type of large grasshopper.

kayak *Can.* light boat: *all the journeys, on foot, by sleigh, by kayak - the goal, so to speak, of their lives.* - W. Grady.

kazoo *Am.* sl. 1. buttocks, ass: *- the pinch-faced child spoke with the timbre and conviction of a kazoo.* - K. Vonnegut, Jr.

KC *Br.* King's Counsel.

kebab *Br. /Am., Can.* **kabob/** small pieces of meat and vegetables, usu. cooked on skewer or spit on a barbecue.

kecks *Br.* col. trousers, knickers or underpants.

keen/ *Am.* use keen mostly as adj. before nouns. *Br.* use it in the meaning "eager and anxious to do" with infinitive and as a predicate: *I'm very keen, yes.* - A. Hitchcock Mystery Magazine.

keen (on) *esp. Br.* very interested in; very attracted to sb.

keen/ keen as mustard *esp. Br., Aus.* col. a. extremely eager. b. clever.

keen prices *esp. Br.* low and competitive prices; adv. **keenly.**

keep/ How are you keeping? *Br.* obs. How is your health?

keep the children *Am.* watch and care for them while their parents are away.

keep sb. **after** *Am. /Br.* **keep** sb. **back/** make a pupil stay after normal hours as punishment.

keep down *Br.* make (a child) remain in the same class for a second year instead of moving to a higher class as usual: *she would be kept down next year.* - Longman.

keep sb. **in** *Br.* force sb. to stay inside, esp. as a punishment in school.

keep in with *Br.* try to stay friendly with sb. because it helps.

keep off (a subject) *esp. Br.* avoid talking about it.

keep on about/at *Br.* col. go on talking in a boring way.

keep out of harm's way *Aus.* try not to get involved in a bad situation.

keep one's **chin/pecker up** *Br.* col. stay calm: *Keep your chin up! Things could be worse!* - Longman.

keep one's **hair on** *esp. Br., Aus.* col. /*Am.* **keep** one's **shirt on, keep** one's **pants on**/ col. remain calm.

keep-away *Am.* /*Br.* **piggy in the middle**/ children's game in which you try to catch a ball that's being thrown between two other people.

keeper 1. *esp. Br.* person responsible for exhibits in a museum or art gallery. 2. *Am., Can.* fish large enough to be kept.

keep-fit *esp. Br.* /*Am.* **(physical) fitness**/ classes or exercises to make people stay healthy.

keeps/ play for keeps *Am., Aus.* col. do smth. very seriously.

keester, keister *Am., Can.* col. the buttocks, rump: *You know what a pain in the keester in-laws can be?* - S. Sheldon.

keg (beer) *Br.* a sort of beer kept under pressure in a metal barrel.

kegger *Am.* sl. big party usu. outside at which beer is served from kegs.

Keith's mum *Br.* humor. stereotype of a well-meaning but dim middle-aged woman.

kennel 1. *Am.* /*Br.* **kennels**/ a place where dogs a. are looked after while their owners are away: *Pandora's father has put Sabre into kennels* – S. Townsend. b. are bred: *Charley had to go to a kennel to be stored, bathed, and Hollanderised.* - J. Steinbeck. 2. *Br.* /*Am.* **doghouse**/: *He… had promised to get Sabre a new kennel* – S. Townsend.

Kentish fire *Br.* prolonged rhythmic applause esp. to express disapproval.

kerb *Br., Aus.* /*Am.* **curb**/ a line of raised stones along the edge of a **pavement** (*Br.*), **sidewalk** (*Am.*).

kerb crawling *Br.* driving slowly along the road close to the path at the side trying to pick up a prostitute or female passing by.

kerb drill *Br.* precautions taken before crossing the street, esp. taught to children.

kerfuffle (about) *esp. Br., Aus.* col. (unnecessary and) noisy excitement, fuss.

kerosene, -ine *esp. Am., Can., Aus., NZ.* /*Br.* **paraffin,** *Am.* **coal oil, lamp oil** *Aus.* col. **kero**/ an oil made from petroleum, coal, etc. and used for heating and in lamps for light: *I bought a kerosene lamp with a tin reflector for Rocinante.* - J. Steinbeck., *it acts on me the way a match affects kerosene.* - L. Waller., *Ari threw the belongings into the kerosene stove.* - L. Uris.

key *Am., Can.* be crucial factor in achieving smth.

key *esp. Br.* prepare a surface for painting.

key smth. **to** *esp. Am.* slightly change a system, plan, etc. so that it works well with smth. else, also **be keyed up to the needs of.**

key actor *Am.* a leading actor.

keyhole surgery *Br.* medical operation in which a small hole is made in a person's body to reach the organ or tissue inside.

key line 1. *Am.* a headline in one line only. 2. print. /*Am.* **holding line**/.

keyman *Am.* telegraphist.

key money *Br.* /*Am.* **security deposit**/ money, additional to the rent and usual charges, sometimes demanded before a person is allowed to begin living in a flat or house: *landlords started waiving key money - a sum they would ask for used equipment* - Nation's Restaurant News.

keynoter *Am.* a chief speaker at the conference.

keypunch *Am., Aus.* cardpunch, machine that puts information onto cards in such a way that computers can read and understand it, used esp. in former times. n. **-er**: *Well, I take them inside to the key puncher, who prepares the cards for the card reader.* - R. Cook., *I was a keypunch operator.* - Guideposts.

The Keystone State *Am.* Pennsylvania, **Keystoner** *Am.* a citizen of Pennsylvania: *pole last week showed Dole behind in the Keystone State* - Time.

khakis *Am.* trousers made from khaki cloth.

khyber *Br., Aus.* col. posterior, the buttocks: *A kick up the Khyber.* - T. Thorne.

kibble 1. *esp. Am., Can.* col. food, meal, esp. pellets for pet animals: *OK I've got it, we'll chloroform her kibble!* - T. Thorne. 2. *Br.* iron hoisting bucket in the mines. 3. *esp. Br.* crush grain into small pieces.

kibitz *esp. Am., Can.* col. 1. give intrusive and unrequested advice while watching a game, performance, etc. 2. banter, comment. n. **-er:** *Making matters worse the kibitzing of some supposed allies* - Time., *This was my reward for having served, during the hours just past, as kibitzer* - M. Torgov., *From gonef to kibitzer, Yinglish is continually enriching the language.* - P. Howard.

kick *Am.* col. 1. n. a protest: *I got no kick on him.* - E. Hemingway. 2. v. (against, at) protest strongly, criticise: *To me the meals were very poor, but nobody seemed to kick about them.* - H.C. Whitford., R.J. Dixson.

kick *Am.* sl. be exciting: *That suit really kicks.* - T. Thorne.

kick/ be kicking *Am.* sl. sit relaxing and doing nothing.

kick/ give a kick up the arse/backside *Br., Aus.* col. /*esp. Am., Aus.* col. **a kick in the butt, pants, ass/** make sb. start doing smth.

kick/kick sb.'s **ass** *Am.* sl. 1. punish or defeat sb. 2. have fun in a noisy or violent way.

kick/ kick/whip (sb.'s) **(some) ass** *Am., Can.* sl. punish people for their mistakes; beat them easily in a fight or game.

kick (some) butt/ass at (doing) smth. *esp. Am., Can.* sl. have power; be very good at smth.: *All the musicians kick butt.* - Rolling Stone., *Something that'll totally kick the butt.* - Los Angeles Times.

kick against smth. *Br.* col. refuse to accept and react strongly against smth.

kick at the can (cat) *Can.* col. opportunity to achieve smth.

kick back *Am., Can.* relax: *she would go straight home and kick back.* – R.L. Stine.

kick in *Am.* 1. contribute money or help: *Frank regularly "kicked in" to Moretti.* – A. Summers, R. Swan. 2. sl. die.

kick smth. **in** *Am., Can.* col. contribute smth., esp. money.

kick smth. **into touch** *Br.* col. reject smth. firmly.

kick off *Am.* col. /*Br., Aus.* sl. **kick it/** 1. leave, go away: *Well, I really must kick off now* - Longman. 2. die: *I hear poor Charlie has kicked off!* - Longman. 3. stop working, fail (of a machine): *That washing machine has kicked off again!* - Longman.

kick over the traces *Br.* free oneself from control and behave as if there're no moral restrictions.

kick upstairs *Br.* col. get rid of sb. by giving him a more prestigious job: *I'll have to arrange for him to be kicked upstairs* - Longman.

kick-ass *esp. Am., Can.* col. forceful, aggressive.

kickback *Am., Can.* game combining elements from baseball and soccer.

kick-down *Br.* device in a car with automatic transmission that allows to change gears by full depression of accelerator.

kicked/ be kicked into touch *Br.* be moved to a later time.

kicker *Am.* col. 1. fault finder. 2. quarreller, brawler. 3. hidden cost, defect, etc., a catch. 4. outboard motor.

kicker *Am., Can.* col. 1. the "final straw", clincher: *I'd saved the kicker for the last.* - K. Vonnegut, Jr. 2. smth. exciting and often unpleasant.

kick-off/ for a kick-off *Br.* col. first of all.

kicky *Am., Can.* col. exciting or fashionable.

kid *esp. Am., Aus.* a young person.

kid *esp. Am.* col. adj. (of a brother or sister) younger: *My kid brother Mike goes to college* - M. Puzo.

kid/ be like a kid in a candy store *Am., Aus.* be very happy.

kid/ I kid you not *Br.* humor. I'm telling you the truth.

kid/ our kid *Br.* col. (often used as a form of address) one's younger brother or sister.

kid/ you're kidding (me)! *Am.* I can't believe you!

kid around *esp. Am.* col. play the fool: *He was consciously mocking his father just to kid around* - M. Puzo.

kiddie condo *Am.* /*Br.* **private hostel/** an owner-occupied flat in a block purpose-built as a student-accomodation.

kidder *Am.* joker.

kiddie, kiddy *esp. Br.* col. young child.

kiddo *esp. Am.* col. way of addressing a person one knows, esp. a young person.

kidology *esp. Br.* col. deliberate practise of cheating sb.

kids *Am.* young people.

kidspace *Am.* /*Br.* **children's corner/world/** place for children to play in.

kidstakes *Aus., NZ.* col. nonsense.

kids' stuff *Br., Aus.* /*Am.* **kid stuff/** smth. easy suitable only for childs not adults.

kidvid *Am.* children's television.

kike *Am., Can.* taboo. col. a Jew: *words like nigger, kike and spick are not good vocabulary.* - B. Kaufman., *We are throwing this kike out.* - L.

Uris., *They're always talking about kikes, these big Irishmen.* - E. Hemingway.

Kilkenny cats/ fight like Kilkenny cats *Br.* disagree very violently.

kill/ in at the kill *Br.* watching a critical moment in a contest.

kill *esp. Am.* entertain very much.

kill (off) a bottle (of wine), kill a beer *esp. Am.* col. drink all of it.

kill or cure *Br., Aus.* fail drastically or win.

kill sb. **with kindness** *Br.* spoil sb. (esp. children) with too much kindness.

(real) killer 1. *Am.* and col. *Aus.* a person, story or show that is very entertaining or skilful or the most interesting part of them: *He got up there and played a killer version of Howlin' Wolf's 'Killing Floor'* – R.C. Cross., *That show was a killer* – J. Hopkins.
2. *Aus., NZ.* col. animal selected for slaughter.

killing floor *Am.* sl. place where sexual act is performed.

kinda *Am.* non-standard kind of.

kindergarten 1. *Br., Aus.* (a part of) a school for children aged 2 to 5. 2. *Am.* a class for young children, usu. aged 5, that prepares them for school.

kinds/ it takes all kinds (to make a world) *Am. /Br.* **it takes all sorts (to make a world)** col. everybody is different.

kindy *Aus.* sl. kindergarten

kinfolk *Am.* kinsfolk: *We were all as fond of her as we were of our kinfolks* - H. Truman.

king hit *Aus.* col. 1. hit from behind. 2. knock-out blow.

king of the castle *Br. /Am.* **king of the hill/** the most successful person.

king's evidence *Br. /Am.* **state's evidence/ turn king's evidence** (of a criminal) is to give information in a court of law against other criminals in order to get less punishment.

king's ransom *Br.* very large sum of money: *this spheroid has been kicked, passed. carried… with a king's ransom in it!* – M. Daly.

kink *Am., Aus.* a sore muscle, esp. in the neck or back.

kinks/ iron out the kinks, work out the kinks *esp. Am.* get rid of the problems.

kiosk *Br.* obs. a public telephone box, indoors or outdoors.

kip 1. *Br., Aus.* col. (a period of) sleep; nap: *were you havin' a bit of kip then?* - J. Herriot. 2. *Br.* sl. a place to sleep: *Allen will give up his new York pad in favour of a kip in the kitchen* - Evening Standard., *This kip stinks.*- G. Greene. 3. *Am.* 1,000 pounds. 4. *Irish Eng.* dirty or sordid place.

kip *Br., Aus.* col. 1. v. sleep, often not at home. 2. go to bed: *Instead you kip off and I'm left to examine my own entrails.* - L. Waller.

kipper 1. *esp. Br.* a salted herring preserved by being treated with smoke. 2. *Aus.* col. derog. English person. 3. *Aus.* aboriginal man who has been initiated into manhood.

kipsie *Aus.* col. makeshift dwelling or shelter.

Kirby grip *Br.* tdmk. **hair grip** *Br. /Am.* **bobby pin/** flat hairpin with ends pressed close together.

kishkes *Am., Can.* sl. entrails: *they'll cut your kishkes out for a nickel.* - M. Torgov., *my kishkes are hanging out all over the arena?* - L. Waller.

kiss *Am., Can.* smal cake or biscuit.

kiss/ kiss sb.'s **ass** *Am., Can.* an. col. behave as a toadie, adj. **kiss-ass.**

kiss/ kiss my butt/ass *Am.* taboo. sl. stop bothering me, often showing disrespect to sb.

kiss curl *Br. /Am.* **spit curl/** a curved piece of hair that hangs flat against the face on the cheek or forehead.

kiss of life/ give sb. **the kiss of life** *esp. Br., Aus.* col. resuscitate sb.

kiss off *Am., Can.* col. dismiss, regard (smth.) as lost or gone: *we can kiss off the coming school year* – Longman, n. **kiss-off.**

kiss up to *Am., Can.* col. behave as a toady to sb.

kiss-ass *Am.* sl. toady.

kissing cousin *Am.* obs. distant relative that you don't know well.

kissing gate *Br.* small gate letting only one person through at a time.

kissy face *Am., Can.* col. puckering of the lips as if to kiss sb.

kit *esp. Br.* 1. particular equipment and clothing worn by a sports team or soldiers. 2. sl. humor. clothes. 3. large basket or box, esp. for fish.

kit/ get one's **kit off** *Br.* col. get naked.

kit sb. **out / up (with)** *esp. Br.* supply with necessary things esp. clothes: *at last I was fully kitted out* - B. Bryson.

kit bag *esp. Br.* a long narrow bag used by soldiers, sailors, etc. for carrying kit: *they may throw out the generals' decent kit-bags along with their dirty ones.* - Economist., *Geoff painfully packed his old army kit bag* - D. Francis.

kitchen garden *esp. Br.* a garden where fruit and vegetables are grown, usu. for eating at home rather than for sale: *he went to look for Toby in the kitchen garden.* - I. Murdoch.

kitchen paper /roll /towel *Br. /Am., Aus.* **paper towel/** soft thick paper on a roll used mostly for kitchen needs, esp. for drying and cleaning.

kitchen police *Am.* mil. sl. kitchen detail for enlisted men to help the cook.

kitchen scales *Br. /Am.* **scale/**.

kitchen-sink *Br., Aus.* done for ordinary people (of plays, films, or style of painting).

kitchen-sink drama *Br.* serious play or film about problems that families have at home.

kitchen tea *Aus., NZ.* party for a couple who are soon to be married for which female guests buy items of kitchen equipment as gifts.

kitchen towel *Am.* tea towel.

kite *esp. Am., Can.* col. 1. write or use a cheque, bill, or receipt fraudulently. 2. illegal cheque.

kite *Am.* col. also **kite up** raise the cost of smth.

kite/ go fly a kite *esp. Am.* col. go away.

kite/ kite-flying *esp. Br., Aus.* trying to find what other opinions are; also **fly a kite**.

kite/ knock higher than a kite *Am.* do (smth.) forcefully.

kitemark *Br.* Standards Institute label.

kitten/ have kittens *esp. Br.* col. be very nervous and anxious.

kitty corner *Am., Can.* col. on the opposite corner of a street from a particular case: *Kitty-corner from there, the big three-story fieldstone.* - R.J. Randisi., M. Wallace.

kiwi *Br., Aus.* col. derog. a New Zealander.

klansman *Am.* member of Ku Klux Klan.

klatch *Am., Can.* social gathering, esp. a coffee party.

Klieg (light) *Am.* a carbon arc lamp used in taking motion pictures: *A Klieg light had just blazed out* - C. Woolrich.

klutz *esp. Am., Can.* col. a clumsy person: *They are klutzes at sports* - Reader's Digest, *Sorry, what a klutz* - J. Kellerman.

klutzy *Am., Can.* sl. clumsy, stupid: *That was klutzy* – R.L. Stine.

knacker *Br.* 1. person who kills horses no longer fit to work and sells parts of them as animal food: *Jones will sell you to the knacker* - G. Orwell. 2. person who buys and breaks up old buildings, ships, etc. in order to sell materials in them that are still of use.

knacker one's **elbow/hand,** etc. *Br.* col. hurt them so that they can't be used anymore.

knackered *Br., Aus.* col. 1. extremely tired, exhausted: *But Saturday night I'm absolutely knackered.* - R. McRum, W. Cran, R. McNeil. 2. too old or broken to use.

knackering *Br., Aus.* sl. tiring.

knackers *Br.* sl. testicles: *I'll not cut off yer knackers* - B. Bryson.

knacker's yard *Br.* a place where old horses are killed; **ready for the knaker's yard** *Br.* too old to be useful or work properly: *You and me will both end up in the knacker's yard, gel.* – S. Townsend.

knapsack *Br.* obs. or *esp. Am.* rucksack used by walkers and climbers.

knave *esp. Br. /esp. Am.* **jack/** the card with a value between the ten and the queen.

kneel/ knelt is more common in *Br.* than kneeled except in literature, but kneeled is more common in *Am.*

knee-slapper *Am., Can.* col. very funny joke.

knees-up(s) *Br.* col. party or celebration.

knickerbocker Glory *Br.* dessert of ice cream served with fruit, cream, etc. in a tall glass.

The Knickerbocker State *Am.* New York.

knickers 1. also **knicks** *Br.* col. */Am.* **panties,** *Br.* **pants/** women's underpants: *Below she wore old-fashioned knickers of pink satin with elastic above the knees.* - I. Fleming. 2. *Am., Can.* knickerbockers, short loose trousers: *Gabe was dressed in blue wool knickers and a camel's hair coat.* - J. Baez., *Boys in the knickers ran alongside the car* - E.L. Doctorow.

knickers *Br.* humor. sl. excl. (used as an expression of featureless disrespect).

knickers/ get one's **knickers in a twist** *Br., Aus.* humor. col. */Aus.* col. **get** one's **knickers in a knot,** *Am.* **get** one's **panties in a bunch/** become angry or confused.

knife/ before you could say knife *Br.* becoming rare. very quickly.

knife/ go/cut through smth. **like a (hot) knife through butter** *Br.* overcome a difficulty very quickly.

knife/ have one's **knife into** sb. *Br., Aus.* col. cause problems to sb. you don't like.

knife/ put/stick the knife in *Br., Aus.* col. do smth. to sb. in an unkindly way.

knife and fork tea *Br.* light supper.

knife-edge/ be on a knife-edge *esp. Br.* be uncertain what will happen next.

knit up *esp. Br.* knit smth very easily.

(have) the knives are out (for) *esp. Br., Aus.* col. (be in) a climax in an argument.

knob *Am.* rounded, usu. isolated hill.

knob *Br.* sl. 1. (of a man) have sex. 2. penis.

knob of butter *esp. Br.* a small lump of butter of about the size of a walnut.

knobble *Br.* small knob.

knobbly *Br.* / *Am.* **knobby** / having round knob-like lumps.

knobs/ with (brass) knobs on *Br., Aus.* humor. obs. with stronger features.

knock 1. *Br.* sl. surprise greatly, shock. 2. *Br., Aus.* col. criticise, esp. unfairly.

(the) knock *Br.* sl. 1. credit, usu. **on the knock.** 2. loss or bad debt.

knock about *Br.* 1. /*esp. Am.* **hang out**/ knock around, stay somewhere for no particular reason. 2. play a game with a ball, but not in a serious way. 3. lie somewhere in the place.

knock about/around with sb. or **together** *Br.* have sex with them.

knock back *esp. Br., Aus.* col. 1. drink quickly or in a large quantities: *Knock back that drop of scotch, Paddy.* - P. Norman., *Hey, fella, you're knocking it back a bit.* - D. Francis., *Don't sip it! Knock it back!* - M.M. Kaye. 2. (no pass.) cost (a large amount). 3. surprise, shock: *Barbara Streisand...knocked back the White House* - New Idea. 4. reject person's request.

knock back *Am.* 1. also **knock down** earn money. 2. sl. embezzle money collected from the passengers' fares (about a conductor).

knock down 1. *Am.* col. earn money: *A clever lawyer can knock down $40,000 in a good year.* - Longman. 2. *Aus., NZ.* spend a paycheck freely. 3. *Am.* drink quickly large quantities of alcoholic drink.

knock off *Br.* col. 1. steal. 2. kill. 3. have sex with.

knock smth. **off** *Am., Can.* col. 1. also **knock** smth. **over** rob a shop, etc. 2. make an illegal copy or product.

knock it off! *Am.* col. stop bothering me with your actions.

knock sb./smth. **on the head** *Br.* col. prevent smth. from happening.

knock (on) wood *Am., Aus.* /*Br.* **touch wood**/ smth. you say when you don't want your good luck to end: *You'd better knock on wood when you say that.* - A. Makkai.

knock-down-drag-out (fight) *Am.* a serious fight or argument.

knock-off *Br.* sl. cheap, cut-price or mass-produced article.

knock out 1. *Br.* col. produce smth. that was difficult to produce. 2. *Am.* produce smth. easily and quickly, usu. of of not very good quality.

knock smth. **out** *Aus., NZ.* earn some amount of money.

knock spots off *Br., Aus.* col. defeat easily, be much better than.

knock over *Am.* col. rob, steal, esp. in the shop or bank: *the guy knocked over his own game* - G.V. Higgins.

knock up 1. *Br., Aus.* col. make in a hurry: *Paul had done the painting and decorating, even knocked up some rudimentary furniture.* - P. Norman. 2. *Br., Aus.* col. awaken by knocking: *A man used to go around my northern village in the early morning, knocking people up* - Longman. 3. *Br.* (in tennis) practice before beginning a real game. 4. *Br.* col. make (money): *Jim's father knocked up over $10,000 last year.* - Longman. 5. (in cricket) *Br.* add to the number of runs already made. 6. *Br., Aus.* col. (usu. pass.) tire (sb.). 7. *Br.* col. try to gain votes by visiting homes before election: *Our helpers have knocked up the whole of the street.* - Longman. 8. *esp. Am., Can., Aus.* taboo. col. cause (a woman) to be pregnant: *Is she knocked up?* - H. Fast., *he knocked her up and he didn't want to marry her* - S. Sheldon., *Hell, no girls get married around here till they're knocked up.* - E. Hemingway.

knock up copy *Br.* tech. prepare writing for printing.

knock/ go ahead/on, knock yourself out *Am.* col. do it but you won't succeed.

knock/ knock sb./smth. **flying** *Br.* col. hit sb./smth. so that they move a long distance.

knock/ knock/throw sb. **for a loop** *esp. Am., Can.* col. a. defeat sb. in a fight: *the old experienced fighter soon knocked him for a loop.* - Longman. b. confuse sb., make sb. helpless in agreement: *I'm gonna knock Howard for a loop, kid.* - A. Miller.

knock/ knock them dead, knock 'em dead *Am.* col. (of a performer in the theatre) be very successful with people watching: *here they are on home territory. Knocking 'em dead.* – I. Carr, D. Fairweather, B. Priestley.

knock/ knock smth. **on the head** *Br.* col. prevent sb. from doing smth. they have planned.

knock/ knock sb. **sideways /back /for six** *Br., Aus.* surprise sb. very much; confuse or upset sb.; spoil smth.

knockabout 1. *Aus.* a man living by getting odd jobs, esp. on a sheep farm. 2. *Am., Can.* sloop with a simplified rig. 3. *Am., Aus.* tramp.

knockabout *Br.* (of entertainers) making people laugh with their silly behaviour.

knock-back *Aus.* col. 1. rebuff. 2. blow, disappointment: *In the beginning of her career she faced many knockbacks* - New Idea.

knock-down-drag-out *Am.* using the most extreme methods to win.

knocked-up 1. *Am.* made pregnant: *Molly got knocked up again.* - R.A. Spears. 2. *Aus.* exhausted.

knocker 1. *Br.* a door-to-door salesman. 2. *Am.* col. a good looker. 3. *Am.* critic, detractor.

knocker/ on the knocker *Br.* (going) from door to door.

knocker/ right on the knocker *Aus., NZ.* at exactly that time, esp. of payment.

knocker-up *Br.* a person who calls the resident of a house to the door in order to prepare ground for sb. else to solicit or canvass.

knock-for-knock argument *Br.* agreement between insurance companies by which each pays its own policy-holders regardless of liability.

knocking-house *Br.* sl. whorehouse: *We thought she was running a knocking shop* - T. Thorne.

knocking shop *Br.* col. /*Aus.* col. **knock-shop/** a brothel.

knock-off *Am.* col. a cheap copy of an expensive product that has a trademark.

knock-on *esp. Br.* adj. marked by a set of events, actions, etc., each of which is caused by the one before; **knock-on effect** *Br.* side effect.

knock-out *Br.* contest in which the loser in each round is eliminated.

knock-up 1. *Br.* (in tennis) an act or period of knocking up, warm-up. 2. *Am.* taboo. sl. sexual intercourse.

knot/ at a rate of knots *Br.* col. very quickly.

knot/ Get knotted *Br., Aus.* col. (expresses great annoyance at a person).

knot/ tie oneself (up) in knots *Br., Aus.* become very confused in explaining smth.

knothead *Am.* sl. blockhead.

knotting machine *Am.* trimming machine in forestry.

know of smth. *esp. Br., Aus.* know of smth. because one heard about this.

know/ I might have known *Br.* col. I shouldn't be surprised that smth. has happened but still I'm annoyed.

know/ I've known him run ten miles before breakfast *esp. Br.* (= this is what he sometimes does surprisingly).

know/ know smth. **backwards** *Br., Aus.* know very good.

know/ know from nothing about *Am., Can.* col. have no information concerning (smth.): *He knows from nothing about music history.* - Longman., *He knows from nothin', said another man.* – J. O'Hara.

know/ not to know enough to come in out of the rain *Am.* /*Am.* taboo. sl. **not know** one's arm from a hole in the ground/, /*Br.* not know whether you are Arthur or Martha/ be confused.

know/ sb. **doesn't want to know** *Br.* col. that person is not interested at all in a situation.

know/ not know shit from shinola *Am.* col. derog. not know anything at all.

know/ you don't know when you're well off *Br.* col. you are more fortunate than you realize.

know/ (Well), what do you know *esp. Am.* col. (used as an expression of usu. pleased surprise).

know-all *esp. Br., Aus.* col. /*esp. Am., Aus.* col. **know-it-all/** an annoying person who thinks he or she knows everything: *She's another one like you - snotty know-it-all.* - R.J. Randisi., M. Wallace.

knuckle/ go the knuckle *Aus.* col. fight with fists.

knuckle/ near the knuckle *Br.* col. almost offensive because of being sexually improper: *it was too near the knuckle* - J. Fowles.

knuckle down *Am.* col. (in marbles) place one's hands with the knuckles hard on the ground in order to shoot: *You'll shoot in a truer straight line if you knuckle down.* - Longman.

knuckle-duster *Br.* /*Am.* **brass knuckles/**.

knucklehead *esp. Am.* col. a person whom one likes who has done a stupid thing.

komatic *Can.* open sledge.

konge *NZ.* farm or logging wagon.

kook *Am., Can., Aus.* col. a person whose ideas or behaviour are unusual or silly: *Gravitational research was long the playground of kooks and dreamers.* – F. Edwards.

kooky *esp. Am., Aus.* col. (esp. of a person) odd, behaving in a silly unusual way. n. **-ness**: *She's kind of kooky kid.* - J. Fowles., *He used to do all these kooky things.* - A. Scaduto.

KP *Am.* kitchen work for children or soldiers at a camp.

K-ration *Am.* army emergency ration: *Tell Americans we like K-rations very much* - A. Scaduto., *a money box made out of an old U.S. Army K-ration container.* - J. Fischer.

Kriss Kringle *Am.* Santa Claus.

kudos *esp. Br.* public admiration and glory (for smth. done), prestige: *For all the "kicks and Kudos"...the summer of 1961 ended on a note of anti-climax!* - P. Norman., *She wants to get kudos for this job.* - I. Fleming., *Mackeller won kudos from the moderates.* - Bulletin.

kumaru *NZ.* sweet potato.

kvell *Am., Can.* col. display pride and satisfaction: *she deserved to kvell from them.* - D. Mortman.

kvetch *esp. Am., Can.* sl. v. n. complain: *And we had a general kvetch about relationships with older men.* - J. Fowles., *his tirade touched off a kvetching session.* - H. Smith. 2. a habitual complainer.

kwanzaa *Am., Can.* secular festival observed by many African Americans at around Christmas time to celebrate their cultural heritage and traditional values.

L

L *esp. Am., Can.* 1. extension of the building or room made at the right angle to the main one. 2. bend or joint for connecting two pipes at right angles.

L abbr. (*Br.*) for (**L-plate**) learner-driver.

la, lala *Aus.* sl. toilet.

Lab *Br.* abbr. 1. Labrador. 2. Labour.

Labor camp *Am.* seasonal workers camp.

Labor Day *Am., Can.* a day when workers make a public show with marches, meetings, etc. / In America the first Monday in September.

labor skate *Am.* sl. trade union officer: *he has changed his position on free trade to suit Iowa's protectionist labor skates* – Harper's Magazine.

labor union *esp. Am., Can.* /*Br.* **trade union**/ trade union: *Labor unions are a dinosaur.* – Time, *He...talked about socialism at labor unions* - I. Stone.

Labour *Br.* Labour Party.

labour exchange *Br.* obs. job centre.

labour weekend *NZ.* the weekend including Labour Day.

lace/ tie up laces *Br.* tie laces.

laced-up *Br.* sl. 1. (of a person) fully occupied. 2. (of a thing) completed. 3. repressed: *She's a bit laced up isn't she?* - T. Thorne.

lace-ups *esp. Br.* shoes fastened with laces; adj. **lace-up**.

lacquer *esp. Br.* clear, sticky liquid used by women for making their hair stay in place.

the lad *Br.* col. a friend or colleague.

lad *Br.* col. a playfully rude man, playboy / also **a bit of a lad**.

ladder *Br., Aus.* /*esp. Am.* **run**/ a long thin upright fault in stockings, etc., caused by stitches coming undone: *ladder was slowly spreading down one of her stockings.* - I. Murdoch.

ladder *Br., Aus.* develop or cause (tights, etc.) to develop a ladder: *My best pair laddered this morning.* - A. Christie.

ladder proof *Br.* resistant to / **runs** (*Am.*), **ladders** (*Br.*).

ladder (tournament) *esp. Br., Aus.* a system in which all players are given a position in a list and improve it by beating a player in that list.

laddie, laddy *esp. Br.* a boy.

laddish *Br.* derog. having the quality of macho uncouthness and aggression exhibited by male groups. n. **-ness.**

la-di-da(h) *esp. Br.* col. derog. obs. adj. pretending to be in a higher social position than one actually is in, by using unnaturally delicate manners, ways of speaking, etc.: *it is known as talking "with a plum in the mouth" or "la-di-da"* - R. McRum, W. Cran, R. McNeil., *There was such a lot of loud haw-haw and la-di-da about the whole performance.* - A. Huxley.

(the) ladies' *esp. Br.* /*esp. Am., Can.* **ladies' room**/ a woman's toilet: *The woman in the ladies' room told us.* - I. Shaw., *The ladies' room was upstairs* - I. Shaw., *He saw Jenny go to the ladies'* - J. Fowles.

ladies' fingers *Br.* /*Am.* **gumbo**/ okra.

ladies who lunch *esp. Am.* humor. rich women who don't work spending much time shopping and eating in restaurants.

the lads *Br., Aus.* col. a group of men that one knows or works with and likes, esp. in **one of the lads**.

lady 1. *esp. Am., Can.* col. (used for addressing a woman, often in a brusque manner). 2. *Am.* (used approvingly) a woman, esp. one with a strong character. 3. *Br.* used in the title of women with a high official position.

lady/ First Lady (of the land) *Am.* the wife of a President.

lady/ The old Lady of Threadneedle street *Am.* joc. English bank.

ladybird /also **golden knop**/ *Br., Aus.* /*Am., Can.* **ladybug**/ small round beetle, usu. red. with black spots: *they are growing this stuff themselves with the help of some worms and lady-bugs* - New York., *A ladybird laboured mightily to climb a blade of grass* - W. Grady.

lady's companion *Br.* small case or bag with needlework items.

ladyfinger *Am.* small cake, shaped like a finger, used to make desserts.

lady('s) finger *Aus.* a short type of banana or a type of black grape.

Lady Muck *Br., Aus.* col. humor. or derog. a snob (of a woman).

ladyship *Br.* col. humor. way of talking about a woman who thinks she's very important.

Lady's waste *Aus.* a beer mug (about 5 ounces, i.e. 150 grams).

lag *esp. Br., Aus.* col. a man who has been sent to prison for breaking the law, esp. not for the first time: *an old lag might envy the young crook serving his first sentence* - G. Greene.

lag 1. *Aus.* col. send sb. to prison, or to arrest sb. 2. *Br.* cover water pipes with special material to prevent loss of heat.

lager *Br. /Am., Aus.* **beer/** (a glass of) a light kind of beer: *That's my lager?* - D. Lodge.

lager lout *Br.* col. a young person who, under the influence of drink, engages in fights and causes destruction to property.

lagging *esp. Br.* material used to cover (water pipes and containers) or the inside of a roof to prevent loss of heat.

lagniappe *Am., Can.* col. a dividend, smth. extra.

lagoon *Am.* small lake which is not very deep, near a larger lake or river.

laid out *Am.* sl. drunk: *I'm too laid out to go to work today.* - R.A. Spears.

lair, lare *Aus., NZ.* col. flashy young tough, v.

lake fever *Am.* malarial fever.

lake-lawyer *Am.* burbot, eel-pout.

The Lake or **Wolverine State** *Am.* Michigan.

laker *Am., Can.* col. 1. lake trout. 2. ship that sails on Great Lakes.

La-la land *Am., Can.* col. 1. Los Angeles or Hollywood' style or attitudes. 2. dreamworld.

lam/ on the lam *esp. Am., Can.* col. escaping; **lam** flee: *convict removed his prison jumpsuit before going on the lam.* – Reader's Digest.

lamb sb./smth. **down** *Aus.* 1. tend (ewe) at lambing time. 2. col. encourage sb. to squander their money, esp. on alcohol.

lam/ on the lam *Am.* col. escaping.

lam into *Br.* col. hit sb. or speak angrily to them.

lambrequin *Am., Can.* decorative topping hung over the top of a door or window.

lamb's fry 1. *Br.* lamb's testicles. 2. *Aus.* lamb's liver.

lamb's tails *Br.* catkins from the hazel tree.

lamebrain *Am.* col. a stupid person. adj.: *We're also lamebrained when it comes to going to the cinema.* - T. Thorne. **ed.**

lame duck *esp. Am.* col. a political official, esp. president or administration officer whose period in office will soon end: *We might not do much in the lame duck.* - Newsweek.

lamington *Aus.* a type of cake dipped in melted chocolate and grated coconut.

lamp holder *esp. Br.* lamp socket.

lamp-oil *Am.* kerosene.

lamp-post 1. *esp. Br.* a tall pole for streetlight. 2. *Am.* pole supporting an old-fashioned type of lamp.

land sb. *Br.* col. cause sb. to deal with smth. difficult.

land up *Br.* col. arrive somewhere after a long journey.

Land of Cactus *Am.* New Mexico.

The Land of Enchantment *Am.* New Mexico.

Land of Flowers *Am.* Florida.

Land of Gold *Am.* California.

Land of Lincoln *Am.* Illinois.

The Land of Opportunity *Am.* Arkansas.

Land of Plenty *Am.* South Dacota.

Land of Roger Williams *Am.* Rod-Island.

land/ the Land of the Rose *Br.* England.

land/ the Land of Steady Habits *Am.* rare. Connecticut.

Land of the Dacotas *Am.* North Dacota.

land/ the Land of the Golden Fleece *Aus.* Australia.

land/ Land of the Midnight Sun 1. *Can.* the Far North. 2. *Am.* Alaska.

Land of the Rolling Prairies *Am.* Iowa.

Land of the Shining Mountains *Am.* Montana.

Land of the Sky *Am.* 1. California. 2. North Carolina.

land/ the Land of Stars and Stripes *Am.* the USA.

Land of William Penn *Am.* Pennsylvania.

land/ The land knows *Am.* euph. God only knows / **Good land, My land** *Am.* euph. My God: *My lan'! Dat's w'at you'se studyin'* – K. Chopin.

land *Can.* enter or be permitted to enter Canada as landed immigrant.

land on *esp. Am.* col. scold, find fault with: *The newspapapers have landed on Tom's latest book* - Longman.

land agent *esp. Br.* 1. person who looks after the land, cattle, farms, etc., belonging to sb. else. 2. person who deals with the sale of land.

landfill *esp. Am.* 1. a place where rubbish is deposited: *we never ran the landfill.* - Reader's Digest. 2. the system of rubbish disposal. 3. the material used to fill in low or wet land. 4. a part of a body of water that is drained and filled with earth for use as a land.

land freeze *Am.* government restrictions on selling and buying plots of land.

land grant *Am., Can.* grant of public land, esp. to an organisation or American Indians.

landlord/landlady *esp. Br. /esp. Aus.* **publican/** operator of a pub.

land office *esp. Am., Can.* government office in which entries upon and sales of public land are recorded: *Could we get to the land-office and sign the papers?* - J.A. Michener.
land-office business *Am., Can.* col. a profitable deal: *Psycotherapists and gurus do a land-office business* - A. Toffler.
land/ plowing land *Am.* plough land.
fall-plowed land *Am.* land ploughed in autumn.
land patent *Am.* title deed to a plot of land.
land-poor *Am.* owing a lot of land but having a little of money.
Land Rover *Br.* tdmk. type of strong car made for travelling over rough ground.
landscape *Br.* /*Am.* **horizontal format**/.
landscaper *Am.* person whose job is arranging plants, paths, etc, in gardens and parks.
landshark *Am.* a land grabber.
landslip *esp. Br.* a small landslide.
landsman *Am.* sl. compatriot.
landwards *esp. Br.* /*Am.* **landward**/ towards the land, esp. from the sea.
lane/ hunger lane *Am.* unemployment.
language arts *Am.* training in reading, writing and speaking.
lanthorn *esp. Br.* lantern.
lap/ in the lap of the gods *Br.* dependent on luck and fate.
lap dance *esp. Am., Can.* erotic dance or striptease performed close to a playing performer.
lap of honour *Br.* /*Am.* **victory lap**/ celebratory journey made by a winner around a track or sports field.
lap robe *Am., Can.* travelling rug used for covering legs
larceny *Am.* law. the crime of stealing smth. without getting illegally into a building to do so.
lard/ be larded with smth. *Br.* have a lot of smth.
lardass *Am., Can.* col. derog. fat person.
larder *esp. Br.* a room or cupboard for food in a house.
lardy cake *Br.* cake made with dough, lard and currants.
large/ at large *Am.* in a general way.
large/ be larging it *Br.* sl. enjoy oneself by going to lots of parties.
lark *esp. Br.* col. smth. that you do for amusement.
lark/ be up with the lark *esp. Br.* get out of bed very early.
lark/ blow/sod this for a lark *Br.* col. I've had enough of this; it's too difficult.

lark/ this acting/dieting/ gardening/exercise, etc. **lark, the writing lark,** *Br.* humor. an amusing, silly, or unnecessary activity or job.
lark around/about *esp. Br.* play around wildly and silly.
larky *esp. Br.* col. playful.
lariat *esp. Am.* lasso: *She practically gave him a whole lariat* - C. Woolrich.
larrikin /also **bodgie**/ *esp. Aus.* col. hooligan, lout: *a "boyo" is a fellow who hangs about street corners, one of the bads, a larrikin.* - R. McRum, W. Cran, R. McNeil.
lash *Aus.* sl. 1. rampage. 2. attempt.
lash out *Br., Aus.* col. spend or waste a lot of money.
lashings *esp. Br.* col. obs. a large amount, esp. of food and drinks, lots.
lash-up *Br.* col. 1. fiasco. 2. temporary makeshift structure or improvised arrangement of some things for some purpose, e.g. one of electric wires and equipment.
the last but one *esp. Br., Aus.* /*Am.* **the next to last**/ the one before the final one; **second last** *Br., Aus.* second to last.
last/ in the last resort *Br.* as a last resort.
the last of *Am., Can.* the end of (a year, month, etc.).
last call *Am.* /*Br.* **last orders**/ announcing closing time in a pub when just one more drink can be ordered.
The Last Frontier *Am.* Alaska.
last hurrah *esp. Am.* a final action.
last name *esp. Am.* /*Br., Aus.* **second name**/ surname, family name.
last post *Br.* /*Am.* **taps**/ a tune played on a bugle at military funerals or to call soldiers back to camp at sunset.
Las Vegas night *Am.* sl. a gambling event based on games of chance: *He also siphoned proceeds from lucrative Las Vegas nights* - G. O'Neill, D. Lehr.
latch *esp. Br.* kind of lock for a door that can be opened from inside by turning a handle.
latch/ on the latch *esp. Br.* shut but not locked.
latch on(to) *Br.* col. understand or realise smth.: *It wasn't long before everyone latched onto what was happening.* - Longman.
latchkey child/kid *esp. Am.* child who is often alone at home because both parents are at work: *Despite his latchkey childhood, Jimi was a fragile boy* – C.R. Cross.
late developer *Br.* /*Am., Aus., Can.* **late bloomer**/ person who is slow to mature and suceed.
late in the game *Am., Can.* at a later stage.

late-model *esp. Am., Can.* (esp. of a car) recently made or of a recent design.
late tea *Br.* supper.
later *Am.* goodbye: *Later, Josh said.* – R.L. Stine.
lather/ in a lather *Br.* col. very anxious, because one doesn't have enough time.
Latino, Latina *esp. Am.* col. male or female person whose family came from Mexico or Latin America to live in the US: *described as a Latino wearing a blue shirt.* - New York., *But the young Latina doesn't respond.* – Reader's Digest.
laugh *esp. Br.* col. an amusing person to be with.
laugh/ have a laugh *Br.* col. enjoy oneself.
laugh/ be/have a (good) laugh *Br.* col. 1. be amusing. 2. laugh about smth. in a happy way with other people.
laugh/ be laughed out of cart *esp. Br.* (of ideas or plan) not accepted because people think it's absolutely stupid.
laugh/ do smth. **for a laugh** *Br.* col. do smth. in order to enjoy yourself or as a joke.
laugh/ be laughing *Br., Can.* be fortunate, lucky, rich, etc.
laugh/ get a laugh, raise a laugh *esp. Br.* make people laugh.
laugh/ get the last laugh *Am.* be successful finally, often in **he who laughs last laughs best.**
laugh/ raise a laugh or two *Br., Aus.* get a laugh.
laughing/ be laughing out of the other side of one's **mouth** *Am., Can., Aus.* col. /*Br.* **be laughing on the other side of** one's **mouth**/, experience disappointment after expecting success.
laughing academy *Am.* sl. an insane asylum: *he had been in the same laughing academies -* Alcoholics Anonymous.
laughing jaccass *Aus.* kookabarra.
laugh in one's **sleeve** *Am.* col. enjoy a secret joke, esp. to sb.'s disadvantage: *all the time he was laughing in his sleeve.* - Longman.
laugh like a drain *Br.* col. laugh noisily.
laugher *Am., Can.* col. easily won sports contest.
laugh lines *Am.* /*Br.* **laughter lines**/ lines on skin seen when a person laughs.
launch oneself **at** sb. *esp. Br.* jump with great force.
launch out (by) oneself *Br.* start smth. on one's own.
laundramat *esp. Am., Can., Aus.* tdmk. /*esp. Br.* **launderette, laundrette**/ a place where public wash their clothes: *my dad took our family's clothes to the laundramat* - Reader's Digest.,

Did some washing in a log cabin launderette – S. Townsend.
laundry *Am.* washroom.
laundry list *esp. Am.* a long itemised list: *laundry list of such episodes throughout history* - Kansas City Star.
lavatory, toilet also col. **lav** *esp. Br.* /*Am.* **bathroom**/ toilet: *they were proceeding to an underground cloakroom or lavatory* - F. O'Brien., *I wanted badly to go to the lav* – R. Westall.
lavatory jokes or **stories** *esp. Br.* the ones involving childish references to urine or faeces.
lavatory paper *Br.* toilet paper.
lavatory roll *Br.* a roll of toilet paper.
law enforcement agent *Am.* policeman or policewoman.
law enforcement organisations or **officials** *esp. Am.* those which ensure that laws of an area are obeyed: *He knew at least fifty law-enforcement officers by their first names* – K. Vonnegut, Jr.
law firm *esp. Am.* company providing legal services.
Lawk(s) *Br.* col. Lordy: *Oh, Lawky, it's mum.* - J. Fowles.
lawmaker *esp. Am.* a person with authority for proposing and passing new laws.
lawman *Am.* officer who makes sure that the law is obeyed: *White lawman came for her* – Reader's Digest.
lawn bowling *Am., Can.* bowls.
lawn chair *Am., Can.* /*Br.* **garden chair, sun lounger**/ folding chair for sitting outdoors: *She sat down slowly in her lawn chair.* - R.J. Randisi., M. Wallace.
lawn party *Am., Can.* /*Br.* **garden party**/ party held in a large garden of a private house: *there was a dance or a lawn party* - M. Jones, J. Chilton.
lawn roller *Am.* /*Br.* **garden roller**/ a tube-shaped piece of wood, metal, etc. used for smoothing the surface of grass or roads.
lawn sign *Am.* sign put in front of a private house before an election which says what political party or person the owner of that house supports.
law-office *Am., Can.* lawyer's office: *I was renting a spare room in the law-offices of Kingman and Ives.* - S. Graftman.
law society *Br.* solicitor's association.
lawyer/ in America lawyer is often called **counsellor** or **attorney** (if speaking in a court), in Great Britain **solicitor** or **barristor**.
lay an egg 1. *Am.* sl. fail: *Tom Jones in the second week of December might lay an egg completely.* – J. Hopkins. 2. *Aus.* sl. become excited.

layabout *Br.* col. a lazy person who avoids work, loafer: *Bloody shower of civvies and layabouts.* - D. Reeman., *Father Joe (Bob Mara) is a virtual stereotype of the lazy black layabout* - Sydney Calender., *John and his friends were "a right load of layabouts".* - P. Norman.

lay smth. **at** sb.'s **door** *esp. Br., Aus.* blame sb. for smth.

lay away *esp. Am.* save (a supply of goods) for a customer: *I asked the lady in the wool shop to lay away the rest of the red wool* - Longman.

lay by *Am.* col. 1. cultivate (a crop) for the last time: *We're laying by the corn in this field.* - Longman. 2. gather (a crop): *we shall be able to lay the wheat by next week.* - Longman.

lay by *Aus.* sl. put a deposit on an article in a shop, reserve: *She wanted to lay by the garden furniture.* - T. Thorne.

lay down *Am.* give up, submit, fail: *The general told the troops to lay down their arms.* - A. Makkai.

lay for *Am.* col. wait in hiding to attack (sb.): *Three men were laying for us* - Longman.

lay hold of *esp. Br.* understand.

lay off 1. *esp. Am.* col. stop wearing, put aside (certain clothes): *It's time we were able to lay off these winter clothes.* - Longman. 2. *Am.* col. mark or measure off the edges of (an area): *First, lay off the size of the picture.* - Longman.

lay smth. **on** 1. *Am.* tell sb. smth. new: *Chas laid on the compliments in that thick accent of his.* – S. Lawrence. 2. *esp. Br.* provide a service or amenity.

lay out *Am.* col. scold, find fault with (sb.): *The director laid Jim out for being late again.* - Longman.

lay oneself **out to do** smth. *esp. Br.* make a special effort to do smth.

lay over *Am., Can.* make an overnight stop on a journey, esp. by plane, stop over: *So we laid over in the channel at Havaiki.* - J.A. Michener.

lay/lay it on with a trowel *Br.* exaggerate.

layaway *Am., Can.* 1. /*Br.* **hire purchase,** *Am.* **installment plan,** *Aus., NZ.* **lay-by**/ buying in credit after paying a first deposit: *He tells of how proud he was to earn money and buy his own clothes "on layaway".* - Ebony. 2. method of buying goods in which goods are kept by the seller for a small amount of money till the final price is paid. 3. smth. set aside.

lay-by 1. esp. *Br.* /*Am.* **turnout, rest stop,** *Aus.* **rest area**/ a space next to a road where vehicles can park out of the way of traffic; roadside parking area, esp. for repairs, rest, etc.: *So you don't have to stop in a lay-by to let your passengers stretch their legs.* - Time., *Sigfrid steered carefully into a lay-by and stopped.* - J. Herriot. 2. *Br.* deposit on goods bought on the layaway plan. 3. *Aus.* system of selling or buying goods when customers order them in advance.

layer cake *esp. Am.* two or more soft cakes put on top of each other with icing.

lay of the land *esp. Am., Can., Aus.* /*Br., Aus.* **lie of the land, how the land lies**/: *I was just getting the lay of the land.* - P. Case., J. Migliore.

layout *Am.* a set or outfit, esp. of tools.

lay-over *esp. Am., Can.* /*Br.* **stop-over**/ short stay between parts of a journey: *Then on the overnight layover I naturally went sightseeing in downtown Washington.* - Alex Haley.

lay, front/side *Br.* /*Am.* **guide, front/side**/ print. guides, lays or gauges at the front and side of a feeder on a press.

laystall *Br.* a rubbish heap.

lazy Susan *Am.* /*Br.* **dumb waiter**/ small table that turns round on a fixed base, used for serving food.

LB *Am.* Bachelor of Letters.

lbw *Br.* (cricket term) leg before wicket.

L-driver *Br.* person who is learning to drive.

lead 1. *esp. Br., Aus.* /*esp. Am.* **leash**/ a length of rope, leather, chain, etc., tied to a dog to control it: *I never used a leash with him* - A.E. Hotchner. 2. *Am.* an introductory section of a news story. 3. *Br., Aus.* /*Am., Aus.* **cord,** *Br.* **flex,** *Am.* **wire**/ a power supply line. 4. *Br.* sheet of lead covering a roof.

lead *Am.* obs. bullets.

The Lead State *Am.* Missouri.

lead/ get the lead out *esp. Am., Can.* col. hurry up.

lead/ put/have lead in one's **pencil** *Br.* humor. obs. increase one's sex ability.

lead/ swing the lead 1. *Br., Aus.* obs. pretend illness so as to avoid work. 2. *Br.* col. malinger.

lead off *Am.* be the first player to try to hit the ball in an inning in baseball.

lead on to *esp. Br.* (of an event) make possible another event.

lead sb. **up the garden path** *Br.* col. /*Am., Can.* col. **lead** sb. **down the garden path**/ deceive sb.: *they've been flagrantly led up the garden path.* - J. Fowles.

leaded gas(oline) *Am.* /*Br.* **leaded petrol**/.

leaded lights *Br.* windows with thin narrow piece of lead separating small pieces of glass, shapedlike squares or diamonds.

leader 1. *Br.* /*Am., Aus.* **concertmaster**/ the chief violin player of an orchestra. 2. *Am., Can.*

conductor, person who directs the playing of a group of musicians. 3. *Br.* editorial: *the editor or his leader-writer is illiterate* - P. Norman., *Glover doubled as court reporter and occasional leader writer.* - Bulletin.

leaderene *Br.* humor. bossy female leader

lead(ing) article, also **leader, lead** *esp. Br.* editorial: *The language of the leading article was savagely violent.* - G. Greene., *Mrs. Quest took that remark from a leader* - D. Lessing.

lead-footed *Am., Can.* col. 1. slow, clumsy. 2. liking to drive fast.

leading *Br.* 1. lead used to cover a roof 2. also **leads** thin strips of lead which hold together the small pieces of glass in leaded lights.

leading dog *Aus., NZ.* sheepdog trained to run ahead of a flock of sheep to control its speed.

leading hand *Aus.* the most experienced person in a factory, etc.

leading light *esp. Br.* one of the most important, active and successful people.

leading strings *Br.* continuous control and guidance / **keep in leading strings**.

lead-off *Am.* adj. happening or going first or before others.

leadpipe cinch *Am., Can.* col. 1. certain thing: *Even getting Jones into the motel had been a lead-pipe cinch.* - H. Fast. 2. an easy thing to do: *infidelity would be a leadpipe cinch for me.* - L. Waller.

lead poisoning *Am.* sl. gunshot wounds: *The fourth mobster to die of lead poisoning this month was buried today* - R.A. Spears.

leads *Br.* usu. flat lead roof.

leaflet *esp. Br.* give out or post leaflets in (a certain area) esp. as part of political activity.

leaguer *esp. Am., Can.* a member of a certain league, esp. a sports player.

league table *Br.* /*Am.* **league standings**/ performance record.

leak/ have a leak *Br., Aus., Can.* take a leak, urinate.

lean/ leaned and leant are both used in Britain, but leaned is the main form in America.

lean *Am.* beat up.

lean and mean *Am.* sl. desperately ambitious: *Leanness and meanness can leave them permanently dislocated* - McLean's.

lean-to *Am., Aus.* a shelter or simple building with a sloping roof which is slept in when camping.

leap/ leapt is more common in Britain than leaped but leaped is more common in America.

leap/ in leaps and bounds *Am.* by leaps and bounds.

learn/ British use mostly learnt for the simple past tense and past participle but the usual American for them is learned.

learner's permit *Am.* /*Br.* **provisional license**/ official document that gives a person permission to learn to drive.

lease/ a new lease of /*Am., Can.* **on**/ **life** *esp. Br., Aus.* new strength or desire to be happy, successful, etc.: *Living in Florida each winter will give him a new lease on life.* - H.C. Whitford., R.J. Dixson.

leasehold *Br.* a building or land to be used for rent according to a lease, usu. in a phr. **have the leasehold;** n. **leaseholder.**

lease-land *esp. Br.* land-lease.

lease-purchase *Am.* a government program under which money is borrowed from private lenders.

leash *esp. Am.* /*Br., Aus.* **lead**/: *The woman tugged its leash and pulled it away.* – R.L. Stine.

leash *Am.* put a leash on a dog.

leash/ have sb. on a leash *esp. Am.* be able to control sb.

leash law *Am.* a law that requires that dogs must have leashes when they are away from the home.

least said, soonest mended *Br., Aus.* obs. forgotten more easily if not spoken about.

leotard *Am.* /*Br.* **pants**/ (men's) underpants.

Leather heads *Am.* col. people from Pennsylvania.

leatherneck 1. *Aus.* roustabout, farm hand. 2. *Am.* sl. a soldier in the US Marine Corps.

leave smth. **about** *esp. Br.* /*Am.* **leave** smth. **around**/ leave lying in different places.

leave off (doing smth) *Br.* stop (doing smth.).

leave out *Am.* (of a plant) to come into leaf.

leave it out *Br.* col. 1. stop being troublesome, scolding, etc.: *I've had enough of your complaining for one day - leave it out, will you?* - Longman. 2. I don't believe you.

leave sb. **far behind** *Br.* /*Am.* **leave** sb. **way behind**/ be a long way ahead.

leave go of/leave hold of *Br.* stop holding smth.

leave oneself **open** *Am.* jeorpadise oneself.

leave sb./smth. **standing** *Br.* do smth. much better than others or be much better than other things.

leave sb. **to do** smth. *Br.* let them choose for themselves.

lebkuchen *Am.* gingerbread.

lecey *Br.* col. electricity.

le(t)ch *Br.* col. lecher.
lech after/over *Br.* col. show sexual desire for a woman in a way that's unpleasant or annoying.
lecturer *Am.* sb. who makes speeches in different places on a subject they know well.
leery *Br.* sl. 1. clever. 2. bad-tempered. 3. untrustworthy: *Leery now, Frank turned down a request* - A. Summers, R. Swan.
leeway *Br.* loss of time or advance that puts sb. at a disadvantage.
left/ make/take/hang a left *Am.* turn into the next road on the left.
left-arm *Br.* adj. left-handed, **left-armed** *Br.* left-hander (in cricket).
left field/ be (way) out in left field, be/come out of left field *Am., Can.* col. (about ideas, methods, etc.) wrong, mistaken, crazy, strange.
left field/ come from out of left field *Am.* col. be very surprising or unexpected.
left field/ out of left field *Am., Can.* sl. suddenly: *It's rational and it's totally out of left field.* - Vanity Fair.
left hand/ marry with the left hand *Br.* mary morganatically.
left-handed compliment *Am.* compliment that seems to express admiration and praise but really is insulting statement.
left luggage (office) *Br.* /*Am., Aus.* **baggage room,** *Am.* **checkroom**/ a place, esp. at the station where one can leave one's bags for some time to be collected later.
left-off *Am.* n. adj. cast-off (of clothes).
left, right and centre *esp. Br.* col. /*Am.* col. **right and left, left and right**/ happening in a lot of places or to a lot of people: *I opened my eyes in time to see it swing right and left in the sky* - K. Ablow.
leftie, lefty *esp. Br.* usu. derog. 1. (in politics) supporter of the left. 2. *esp. Am., Can.* left hander.
leg *esp. Br.* obs. or *Aus.* col. walk or run fast, esp. when trying to escape.
leg 1. *esp. Br.* one of a series of sports games played to decide the final winner. 2. *Br.* one of the parts of a special football competition that's played in two parts.
leg/ get one's **leg over** *Br., Aus.* sl. succeed in sex.
leg/ give sb. **a leg up** *esp. Br., Can.* col. a. help sb. to climb or get on smth. by supporting the lower part of their leg. b. help sb. to improve their situation, esp. at work: *several factors could give them a leg up in dealing with landlords* - Nation's Restaurant News.

leg/ have a leg up on sb. *Am.* have advantage over sb.
leg/ have by the leg *Am.* get sb. into trouble.
leg/ have legs *esp. Am.* col. 1. continue to be talked about for a long time (of the news). 2. (of ideas, plans, etc.) be likely to work or be true.
leg/ have the legs of *Br.* go faster or further than one's rival.
leg/ on one's **hind legs** *Br.* col. standing up to make a speech.
leg/ show a leg *Br.* obs. get out of bed.
leg/ can talk the legs of an iron pot *Aus.* talk a lot.
leg/ show a leg *Br.* obs. col. get out of bed.
leg it! *Br.* col. run away quickly to escape from smth. or sb.
legal clinic *Am., Can.* place where a person can get a legal advice: *Joe Hyat, who co-founded a nationwide chain of storefront legal clinics* - Time.
legal eagle *Am.* sl. a lawyer, esp. a clever and aggressive one: *Join the local politicians and legal eagles wheeling and dealing over the steaming pastas!* - A. Frommer.
legal holiday *Am., Can.* /*Br.* **public holday**/ official public holiday.
legal-size *Am.* paper that is 14 inches long and 8 inches wide.
legless *esp. Br.* col. very drunk: *they're in here getting legless.* - T. Thorne.
leg-pull *Br.* joke in which you make sb. believe smth. that is not true.
leg-puller *Am.* col. a political schemer.
leg-rope *Aus., NZ.* noosed rope used to secure an animal by one hind leg.
legume *esp. Am.* bean, pea, lentil, etc., used as food.
leisure centre *Br.* a place where you can do sports, exercise classes, etc.
leisure suit *Am.* informal suit popular in 1970s of shirt-like jacket and trousers made of the same material.
lemon 1. *Br.* a drink made of lemon. 2. *Am.* smth. useless because it fails to work (properly). 3. *Br.* col. a foolish person.
lemonade 1. also **fizzy lemonade** *Br., Aus.* a. (*Am.* **lemon soda**) a yellow drink tasting of lemons, containing small balls of gas, to which water is not added before drinking. b. (*Am.* **lemon-lime**) a bitter-sweet tasting transparent drink, containing small balls of gas. 2. *Br.* lemon squash. 3. *esp. Am.* a drink made with the juice of lemons, water and sugar.

lemon curd/cheese *esp. Br. /Aus.* **lemon butter/** a cooked mixture of eggs, butter, and lemon juice, eaten on bread or put into tarts.

lemon kali *Br.* an artificially flavoured carbonated lemon drink.

lemon law *Am.* col. a law that lets persons who buy large machines, esp. cars get money from the seller if those don't work.

lemon squash *esp. Br., Aus.* a drink made from lemon juice and sugar to which water is added before it is drunk: *She subsided into a lemon squash* - E.M. Forster., *Will you have lime juice or lemon squash.* - E. Hemingway., *I'll have a lemon squash, if you don't mind.* - G. Greene.

lemony *Aus.* col. angry.

lending rate *esp. Br., Aus. /Am., Aus.* **interest rate/** amount that bank charges on money that it lends sb.

length(s)man *Br.* road maintenance man.

Lent term *Br.* the university term in which Lent falls.

leopard/ a leopard doesn't change its spots *esp. Br.* a person can't change one's character, habits, or way of life in a day.

leotard, body suit *Am. /Br.* **body/**.

lesson *Br. /Am.* **class/** period of time in a school in which students are taught a particular subject.

lesson/ in the lesson *Am. /Br.* **at the lesson/**.

let *Br.* 1. an act or time of renting a house or flat to, or from sb. 2. a house or flat that is (to be) rented.

let/ drop / fall information or **let it drop** *Br.* let it slip, tell about it unitentionally.

let (to, out) *esp. Br., Aus. /esp. Am.* **rent/** give the use of (a room), a building, land, etc. in return for rent: *let out rooms to less than seven people* - Young Citizen's Passport.

let/ Let George do it *Am., Can.* Let sb. else do it: *I don't have time to interest myself in politics. Let George do it.* - H.C. Whitford., R.J. Dixson.

let/ Let's not / In Britain and Australia **don't let's** is also possible and in America **let's don't/**: *Don't let's turn this into a wake.* - L. Waller., *don't let's have any of this sort of nonsense!* - J. Galsworthy., *Please don't let's talk about our dream anymore.* - G. Greene.

let/ to let *Br. /Am.* **for let/** sign outside a building showing that it is empty and can be rented.

let down *Am.* col. work less hard, make less effort: *Don't let down now, just when the job's nearly finished.* - Longman.

let smth. **down** *Br.* allow the air to escape from smth. so that it loses its shape and firmness, esp. deflate a tyre.

let into *Br.* col. attack (sb.) with blows or words: *The politician let into the government for its recent inaction.* - Longman.

let smth. **into a flat surface** *Br.* put smth. into a position so that it doesn't stick out.

let sb. **into a secret** *Br., Aus.* let sb. in on a secret, reveal a secret to sb.

let out 1. **let** (smth.) **out** *esp. Br.* give the use of (esp. vehicles or equipment) in return for payment: *These boats are let out by the hour.* - Longman. 2. *Am., Can.* end, so that people attending can leave: *theatre let out* - J. London., *School let out and the summer of 1960 arrived.* - J. Baez.

let/ let the side down *Br., Aus.* col. do smth. bad or embarassing for the group one belongs to.

lethal *esp. Am.* adj. (of foreign aid) in the form of, or for the purpose of buying weapons.

let-out *Br.* loophole.

letter *Am.* large cloth letter to put on clothes given as reward for playing in a school or college sports team/ **win** one's **letter** *Am. /Br.* **win** one's **cap/**, v. **letter** *Am.* earn a letter: *They were both wearing jeans and Shadyside letter jackets.* – R.L. Stine.

letter/ mail a letter *Am. /Br.* **post a letter/** send a letter by post.

letterbox *esp. Br., Aus. /Am., Aus.* **mailbox/** 1. a box in a post office, street, etc., in which letters may be posted. 2. also *Am.* **mailslot** a hole or box in the front of or by the entrance to a building for receiving letters from the post: *You want me to go down for the stuff from your letter-box, miss Barnet?* - B. Kaufman., *Next morning the invitation lay in my letter-box.* - G. Greene.

letter-card *Br.* one that can be posted without envelope.

letter carrier, mail carrier, mailman *Am., Can. / esp. Br.* **postman/** postman.

letter-opener *Am. /Br.* **paper opener/** one that is only slightly sharp, usu. used for opening envelopes: *she faced us and tapped the business: she faced us and tapped the business end of the letter-opener in her palm.* - R.J. Randisi., M. Wallace.

letter-perfect *Am. /Br.* **word-perfect/** adj. repeating or remembering every word with complete correctness or correct in every detail: *He is letter perfect.* - A.E. Hotchner.

letter post *Br.* first-class mail.

letters 1. *Br.* col. the initials of a degree or other qualification. 2. *Am.* school or college initials as a mark of proficiency, esp. in sport.
lettersize *Am.* paper that is 8.5 inches wide and 11 inches long.
letting *esp. Br.* tech. a house or flat that is (to be) let.
leucotomy *Br.* lobotomy.
levant *esp. Br.* run away from a debt, abscond.
levee 1. *esp. Br.* a bank built to stop a river overflowing. 2. *Am., Can.* formal reception of visitors or guests.
level *esp. Am.* spirit level: *He handled the level masterfully* - S. Bellow.
level/ be level *Br.* (of two sports teams, players, etc.) have the same number of points.
level/ find one's **(own) level** *Br.* find out what one is good at, what kind of people one likes to be with.
level/ level the score *Br.* make the score equal in a game or competition.
level/ on a level with *Br., Aus. /Am.* **even with/** each other having equal amounts; e.g. *keep wages level /Am.* **even/** *with inflation.*
level/ on the level *Br.* on flat ground.
level of attainment *Br.* rating of pupil's opinions on 10 marks scale.
level crossing *Br., Can., Aus. /Am.* **grade crossing, railroad crossing, crossing at grade/** a place where a road and a railway cross each other, usu. protected by gates that shut off the road while a train passes.
level pegging *esp. Br., Aus. /Am.* **even-stephen/** n. adj. keeping abreast.
leverage *Am.* the use of borrowed money in the expectation that the profits made on the money will exceed the interest. v.
leverage *Am.* tech. make money available using a particular method.
leverage-gearing *Am.* a ratio between a company's capital and money borrowed.
Levis *Am.* jeans: *Dean was wearing washed-out tight levis and a T-shirt* - J. Kerouac.
ley farming *esp. Br.* the alternate growing of crops and grass.
LGV *Br.* Large Goods Vehicle.
L hook *Am.* a square dress hook.
liability insurance *Am. /Br.* **third-party insurance/.**
liason *esp. Am.* a person who acts as a connection between people.
Lib *Br.* Liberal.
Lib Dem *Br.* Liberal Democrat.

liberal arts *esp. Am., Can.* university subjects (such as literature and history) except science, mathematics, and practical subjects that prepare one directly for a job.
liberal studies *esp. Br.* subjects that are taught in order to increase general knowledge and ability to write, speak, and study more effectively esp. when taught to older students in addition to their main subjects.
liberate *esp. Am.* sl. steal: *The privates liberated a jeep and went into town.* - R.A. Spears.
liberty boat *Br.* boat carrying sailors (**liberty men**) who have leave to go on shore.
Liberty Hall *Br.* obs. a place where person can do whatever they want.
liberty of the subject *esp. Br.* the right of a subject under constitutional rule.
library card *Am. /Br.* **library ticket/** borrower's ticket.
library pictures *Br.* pictures shown in a TV programme that were made at a previous time.
license/a license to print money *esp. Br.* a lot of money earned with a little effort.
licensed victualler, licensee *Br.* tech. a keeper of a shop or pub who is allowed to sell alcoholic drinks.
license/ off license *Br.* shop where liquor is sold and taken away, **on license** *Br.* the sale of liquor to be consumed on the premises.
license plate *Am., Can. /Br., Aus.* **number plate/** either of the signs on a vehicle (usu. at the front and back ends) showing its registered number: *yellow ford with license plates from Dallas area.* - T. Thompson., *It was said that my New York license plates would arouse interest* - J. Steinbeck.
licensing laws *Br.* the laws that limit the sale of alcoholic drinks to certain times and places.
licensure *Am.* the granting of a license, esp. to practice a profession.
lick *esp. Br.* col. (fast) speed.
lick/ (give smth.**) a lick and promise** 1. *Br., Aus.* obs. or *Can.* a quick careless wash or cleaning: *If you get married on a lick and promise, you may need a lot of good luck.* - W. Magnuson. 2. *Am., Aus.* a careless job.
lick/ at a great lick/at a hell of a lick *esp. Br.* col. very fast.
lick/ go / run for the lick of one's **life** *Aus.* run very fast.
lick 1. *Br.* col. cause (sb.) to be unable to understand smth. 2. *esp. Am.* col. defeat easily in a competition, fight, etc.
lick a problem *Am.* solve a problem.

lick smth. **into shape** *Br.* bring it to the desired standard.

lickety-split *esp. Am., Can.* col. at full speed: *For in 1848 there was suddenly a reason for every adventurous Yankee to head out to the West lickety-split.* - R. McRum, W. Cran, R. McNeil.

lick hole *Aus.* salt lick

licking/ take a licking *Am., Aus.* col. be defeated.

licking-place *Am.* lick, a place having a deposit of salt that the animals regularly lick.

licorice *esp. Am.* liquorice.

lid/ put the lid on smth. 1. *Br., Aus.* also **put the tin lid on** smth. obs. cause smth. to end (fail) being the last in a series of misfortunes. 2. *esp. Am.* stop smth.

lido *esp. Br.* 1. obs. an outdoor public swimming bath. 2. a special part of a beach or of the edge of a lake used for swimming and lying on the beach.

lie *Br.* 1. an act or instance of lying or resting. 2. be in a certain place in a competition.

lie/ nail a lie *Br.* say smth. that is definitely not true.

lie/ lie /*esp. Am., Can., Aus.* **lay**/ **of the land** *Br., Aus.* a. appearance, slope, etc., of an area of land. b. the state of affairs at a particular time: *I was just getting the lay of the land.* - P. Case, J. Migliore.

lie back and think of England *Br.* humor. have sex without wanting or enjoying it.

lie down on the job *esp. Am., Aus.* derog. not to do enough at one's work.

lie in *esp. Br.* stay in bed late in the morning.

lie over *Am.* break one's journey.

lie up *esp. Br.* stay in hiding or avoid being noticed, esp. by police or soldiers.

lie/ lie like a rug, lie like a big dog (on a rug) *Am.* sl. humor. lie a lot.

lie/ (I) tell a lie *Br.* col. used when sb. realized that smth. they've just said is not correct.

lie-by *Br.* /*Am.* **rest area** (at the side of a road)/.

lie-down *esp. Br.* col. a short rest, usu. on a bed: *You tuck up in here and have a nice lie-down.* - B. Tillman.

lie-in *esp. Br.* col. a stay in bed later than usual in the morning: *I only have a lie-in on Sundays* - Streetwise.

lieut *Am.* col. lieutenant.

life/ anything for a quiet life *Br.* col. allowing sb. to do what they want rather than arguing with them.

life/ as big as life *Am.* (used to express surprise).

life/ be big(ger) than life *Am.* attract a lot of attention; find sb. in an exciting place where they are not supposed to be.

life/ be the life of the party *Am., Aus.* /*esp. Br.* **be the life and soul (of the party)**/ be the most sociable person.

life assurance *esp. Br.* life insurance.

life belt, life buoy *esp. Br.* a life belt for keeping a person afloat in water.

life belt *Am.* special belt for person to wear to prevent them from sinking.

life boat *Br.* rescue operation for fringe banks managed by the bank.

lifer *Am., Can.* person who spends life in a particular career, esp. in the armed forces.

life imprisonmemt col. **lifer** *Am.* punishment of being put to prison until death according to a **life sentence**.

life preserver 1. *esp. Am., Can.* /*Br.* **life jacket**/ a life-saving apparatus, such as a life belt or life jacket: *Reindeer hair is used for life preservers.* - F. Mowatt. *They had relieved him of his life preserver* - B. Tillman. 2. *esp. Br.* short stick used as a weapon of defence.

life saver *Aus.* life guard.

life-support machine *esp. Br.* one that is used to keep a person alive when they are very ill and can't breathe without help.

life vest *Am.* a life jacket.

lift 1. *Br., Aus.* /*Am., Can.* **elevator**/ an apparatus in a building for taking people and goods from one floor to another; *They read in lifts, buses, parks* - L. Van Der Post., *there was no lift* - A. Christie. 2. *Br.* /*Am.* **ride**/ a ride in a car.

lift *Am.* 1. pay off: *He couldn't lift the bill, take people out, amuse them.* – A. Summers, R. Swan. 2. stop temporarily (about a train).

lift/ sb.'s lift /*Am.* **elevator**/ **doesn't go all the way to the top floor** *Br.* sb. is a fool or a little crazy.

liftman *Br.* /*Am.* **elevator operator**/ person in charge of a lift.

lift shaft *Br., Aus.* /*Am.* **elevator shaft**/.

lig *Br.* col. 1. a fashionable place to be seen at. 2. (take advantage of) free parties, travel, etc. offered by a company for publicity purposes.

light/ Have you got a light? *Br.* /*Am.* **Do you have a light?**/ Do you have a match or cigarette lighter.

light/ in the light of *Br., Aus.* /*Am., Aus.* **in light of**/ taking into account, considering smth.

light/ set light to smth. *Br.* cause it to start burning.

light into *esp. Am., Can.* col. attack (sb.) violently with blows or words: *Fearlessly, Jim lit into his attackers* - Longman.

light out *esp. Am.,Can.* col. leave (often in a hurry afraid of smth.): *He lights out for Chicago and the rest is history.* - Time., *I lit out mighty quick* - M. Twain., *he lights out for Boston* - D. Hammet.

light up *Br.* switch on the car lights in a street: *Be sure to light up as soon as the sun sets* - Longman.

light ale, also pale ale *Br.* 1. a type of rather weak pale beer, usu. kept in bottles. 2. a general term for a light-coloured beer.

lighten up *Am., Can., Aus.* col. Be calm!, Don't worry!; become less serious or angry: *Come on, Doc, lighten up* - A. Hitchcock Mystery Magazine.

light globe *Aus.* light bulb.

lighting fitting(s) *Br.* /*Am.* **lighting fixture(s)**/ standardised accessory part of lighting system: *light fixtures hold bare bulbs.* - R.G. Kaiser.

lighting-up time *esp. Br.* time to switch on the lights in a street or a car: *It was between lighting-up time and the real dark* - G. Greene.

lightning bug *Am., Can.* firefly.

lightning conductor *Br.* /*esp. Am., Can.* **lightning arrester** or **rod**/ a surge director.

lightning express *Am.* very fast train.

lightning rod *esp. Am.* scape goat.

lightning rod/ be a lightning rod for smth. *esp. Am.* attract that thing to oneself.

lightning strike *Br., Aus.* /*esp. Am.* **wildcat strike**/ a sudden strike without usual warning by the workers and often without official support of trade union.

light railway *Br.* /*Am.* **light rail**/ electric railway system that uses light trains and usu. carries only passengers.

lights/ punch sb.'s **lights out** *Am.* hit sb. very hard.

lights/ set lights to smth. *esp. Br.* /*Am.* **set fire to** smth./ make it burning.

like/ if you like *Br.* 1. used to suggest or offer smth. 2. used to agree to smth. even if it's not what you want yourself. 3. used to suggest one possible way of describing smth. or sb.

like/ I like watching /also **to watch** (*Am.*)/. television.

like/ I like that *esp. Br.* used to say that what sb. has said or done is rude and unfair.

like/ whatever, anything, etc. **you like** *esp. Br.* whatever you want.

likely *Br.* col. suitable to give (good) results: *A likely lad who's bound to succeed.* - Longman.

likely/ not likely *esp. Br.* I definitely won't do it.

Lilo *Br.* tdmk. /*Am., Aus.* **air mattress**/ a type of airbed, used for lying on esp. by the sea: *don't need to register - dinghies, sailboats, canoes, inflatables, lilos* - B. Bryson.

lily-pad *Am.* the broad flat, floating leaf of a winter lily: *Hello, fellow anthropoids and lily pads and paddle wheels* - K. Vonnegut, Jr., *He tried all of his tricks, once making a long run for the lily pads* - S. North.

lily white 1. *Am., Aus.* col. derog. excluding or seeking to exclude Negroes: *it took more than a fool to break into lily-white Hollywood.* – E. James, D. Ritz. 2. *Am., Aus.* completely honest.

lima *Am.* radio. letter L.

limescale *Br.* scale, a hard white or grey layer of material which forms on the inside of pipes and containers which heat water.

limey *esp. Am., Can., Aus.* col. humor. or derog. an Englishman or smth. connected with them: *she was viewed as the Limey broad with snooty accent.* - P. Howard., *I told those Limey bastards to take you to a hospital.* - L. Uris., *I deserted in B.A., see, and shipped out East on a Limey, on English boat* - J. Dos Passos.

limit/ be over the limit *Br.* drink more alcohol than it is allowed when driving a vehicle.

limit/ go the limit *Am.* go beyond the limit.

limit/ to the limit *Am.* to the end.

limit/ off limits (to) *esp. Am.* where one is not allowed to go out of bounds: *some territorials should be placed off limits to oil-field development.* - Time., *Chukotka is...off limits to foreigners* - F. Mowatt., *Keep locker rooms off limits.* - USA Today., *only the presidential bedroom was off limits* - Time.

limited company *Br.* a company, whose owners only have to pay a limited amount of money (**limited liability**) if the company becomes bankrupt; adj. **limited**.

limousine liberal *Am.* derog. wealthy liberal.

limpet mine *Br., Aus.* /*Am.* **limpet**/ a bomb that is fixed to an intended target with a magnet or glue.

limp-wrist *Am.* sl. n. adj. a male homosexual.

linctus *Br.* liquid medicine to cure coughing.

linden *esp. Am.* lime (tree).

line 1. *esp. Br.* /*esp. Am.* **track**/ a railway track. 2. *esp. Am., Can.* /*Br.* **queue**/: *The line isn't very long.* – R.L. Stine, (stand) **in line** *Am.* /*Br.* **in a queue**/. 3. *Br., Aus.* **line in** smth. /*Am.* **line of** smth./ a range of similar things (for sale or for offer).

line/ be not one's **line of country** *Br.* obs. not to know much about smth.

line/ county line/state line, etc. *Am.* border between two counties, states, etc.

line/ cross the line *Am., Can.* cross the border between the US and Canada.

line/ (right) down the line *esp. Am.* col. completely or fully, e.g. in support or encouragement: *One by one, all down the line* - C. Woolrich.

line/ feed sb. **a line** *Am.* tell a lie.

line/ get a line on sb./smth. *esp. Am.* get a special information that will help people to find sb./smth.

line/ be given lines *esp. Br.* be punished at school by being made to write a sentence many times in school.

line/ line of country *Br.* subject in which person is skilled and knowledeable.

line/ (project comes) on line *esp. Am. /Br.* **on steam/** begin to operate fully.

line/ (way) out of line *Am.* sl. behaving improperly; completely wrong: *You're out of line* - J. O'Brien., A. Kurins.

line/ shoot a line *Br.* say exaggerated untrue things.

line/ spin sb. **a line** *Br.* try to persuade sb. to believe in lies.

lineage *Br.* newspaper payment by space: *The projections on paying off the debt were based on a robust growth in advertising lineage among the business publications.* – D.L. Bartlett, J.B. Steele.

linebacker *Am.* a football player standing behind the front line of defenders.

line gauge *Br. /Am.* **type scale/**.

lineman *Am.* 1. a football player in the attack line. 2. */Br.* **linesman/**.

line manager *esp. Br.* one who is in charge of the department, shift, or project, a person is working on.

linen basket *Br.* container with a lid for holding soiled clothing.

(linen) duster *Am.* light coat worn to protect one's clothes from dust while cleaning the house.

liner note(s) *Am.* (on record jackets) information about the record or the musicians playing on it: *in the liner notes to the latter, Mingus heaped detailed praise on Shaw* – I. Carr, D. Fairweather, B. Pristley.

line-operated *Am. /Br.* **mains-operated/** getting electricity from the mains.

lineout *Br.* a way of continuing a game of rugby after the ball has gone off the field.

lines *Am.* (horse) reins.

linesman *Br. /esp. Am.* **lineman/** person whose job is repair and maintenance of telephone and electric power lines or taking care of railway lines.

lineside *Br.* trackside near a railway track.

linetrain, freightliner *esp. Br.* train that carries large amounts of goods in special containers.

lineup *esp. Am.* 1. */Br., Aus.* **identity parade, identification parade/** a line of people organised by the police containing a person thought to be guilty of a crime and looked at by witness who tries to recognise the criminal: *Put him in a lineup and I'll give you a beaucoup ID* - J. Kellerman. 2. (in baseball) the order in which players bat.

linguistics/ areal linguistics *Am.* dialectal linguistics.

lining *Br.* striping (in the painting of cars).

linkman *Br.* person serving as connection between different groups or one who provides continuity in radio and TV programmes.

link word *Br.* linking word, one showing connection between clauses or sentences.

lino *esp. Br.* /also **oil-cloth/** col. linoleum: *She has found some indecent magazines under the lino in the bathroom.* – S. Townsend.

lint *esp. Am. /esp. Br.* **fluff/** soft light loose waste from woolen or other materials: *I was expecting fluff, but this was lint.* - Reader's Digest., *Or did you leave enough lint and hairs* - A. Hitchcock Mystery Magazine.

linter *Am.* a machine for removing lint.

lionise *Br.* show the sights of a place to.

lip *Br.* col. an angry expression (on sb.'s face)

lipbalm *Br.* chopstick.

lip/ zip one's **lip** *Am.* button one's lip, not say secret or unpleasant things.

lippy 1. *esp. Am.* col. rude. 2. *Br.* col. not showing respect in the way that sb. speaks.

lipsalve *esp. Br.* medical preparation for sore lips.

liquid courage *Am. /Br., Aus.* **Dutch courage/**.

liquidizer *Br., Aus.* blender, electric machine used in the kitchen for (**liquidizing**) making solid foods into soups, juices, etc.

liquid paraffin *esp. Br.* oily mixture obtained from petrolatum, used as a laxative.

liquor 1. *Am., Aus. /Br.* **spirits/** strong alcoholic drink, such as whiskey, vodka, and gin: *He developed his taste for manly liquor in Montana.* - New York. 2. *esp. Br.* rare. the liquid produced from cooked food, such as the juice from meat. 3. *Br.* tech. alcoholic drink.

liquored up/out *Am., Can.* sl. drunk: *I wish Pa wouldn't get liquored up when he gets to town.* - W. Magnuson, **liquor up** *Am.* col. get drunk.

liquorice all sorts *Br.* mixture of differently shaped brightly coloured sweets containing liquorice.

liquor store *Am., Can.* /*Br.* **off-licence**/ wine and spirits shop.

list/ enter the lists *Br.* become involved in an argument, competition, etc.

listed *esp. Br.* included in a list.

listed (building) *Br.* /*Am.* **landmarked building,** *Aus.* **heritage-listed**/ protected by the law because of its historical or architectural importance.

listen *Br.* col. an act of listening.

listen out *esp. Br.* listen carefully, esp. for an unexpected sound.

listen up *esp. Am.* col. used to get person's attention so that they can hear what sb. is going to say: *listen up, we'll do it together!* – Reader's Digest.

lite *Am., Can.* 1. col. insubstantial. 2. courtesy light in a motor vehicle.

lite beer *Am.* beer that has fewer calories than normal beer.

literacy test *Am.* educational qualification.

literal *Br.* print. typo, typographical error.

litigator *Am.* a lawyer who specialises in taking legislation against people and organisations.

litterbin, litter basket *esp. Br.* /*Am.* **litterbag**/: *in my day, Christchurch Road was an open-air letter-bin.* - B. Bryson.

litter lout *Br.* derog. 1. /*Am., Aus.* **litter bug**/ a person who leaves litter in public places: *Coming back to litter lout London was depressing.* - Woman's Own. 2. v. throw refuse at the street.

little/ from little up *Am.* col. from childhood.

a little bit of *esp. Br.* small piece of smth.

Little Bear *esp. Br.* /*esp. Am.* **Little Dipper**/ a group of stars.

little finger *esp. Br.* /*Am., Aus.* **pinkie**/ the smallest finger of the human hand.

little house *Aus., NZ.* euph. outdoor toilet.

Little Italy *Am.* the section of the city where Italians live.

Littlle League *Am., Can.* baseball league where children from 8 to 12 play.

the little people/folk *esp. Irish English.* small imaginary creatures such as elves which look like small humans.

Little Rhody *Am.* joc. Rhode-Island.

liv(e)able (in/with) *Br.* reasonable, although probably not comfortable enough.

live out *Br.* (of students) live somewhere outside of college or university.

live/ be living large *Am.* sl. have a good time and enjoy life being wealthy.

live/ live fast (against) *Can.* be angry at sb.

live/ you live and learn *Br.* /*Am.* **live and learn**/.

live/ where one lives *Am., Can.* col. relating to the most vital vulnerable spot.

live one *esp. Am.* col. a likely target for a confidence trick.

live high *esp. Am.* col. live in a wealthy manner of unusual comfort: *Can you afford to live so high?* - Longman.

livelong/ all the livelong day *Am.* obs. all day long.

live parking *Am.* parking in which the parked vehicle's operator remains in attendance.

lively/ look lively *Br., Aus.* col. obs. hurry up.

liver *esp. Am.* an inhabitant, dweller.

liverish *Br., Can.* col. slightly ill, esp. after eating or drinking too much.

liver sausage *esp. Br.* /*Am., Aus.* **liverwurst**/ a type of cooked soft sausage made mainly of liver, and eaten (often spread) on bread: *He recently switched from liverwurst and Swiss to ham salad.* - Playboy.

liver salts *Br.* salts taken to relieve indigestion or nausea.

livery 1. *Br.* a special pattern or design put on company's goods and possessions to show that they belong to company. 2. *Am., Can.* livery stable.

living end/ be the living end *Am., Aus.* obs. 1. be extremely good. 2. be very annoying.

living will *Am.* document explaining what medical or legal decisions should be made if sb. becomes so ill that they can't make those decisions themselves.

The Lizard state *Am.* Alabama.

load *Aus.* sl. frame (a suspect) by planting an illegal subject on him or her.

a load/loads of smth. *esp. Br.* col. a lot of smth.

load of crap, rubbish, bull, etc. *esp. Br.* col. complete nonsense.

load/ take a load off *Am.* /*Br.* **take the weight off your feet**/ col. sit down and relax yourself.

loaded 1. *esp. Am.* sl. drunk. 2. *Am., Can.* col. (of a car) having a lot of optional extras.

loaded for bear *Am.* col. all set to deal with smth.

loading *Aus.* extra money compensation for special skills or qualifications.
loading bay *Br.* /*Am.* **loading dock/** space at the back of a shop where goods are delivered and taken away.
loadsamoney *Br.* col. extensive and conspicuous wealth: *I hate those lodsamoney thugs* - News of the World, T. Thorne.
load up *esp. Am.* fill (sb. or oneself) with information, sometimes imaginary: *There is no need to load yourself up with unnecessary facts for the examination.* - Longman.
loaf *Br.* sl. head.
loaf/ use one's loaf *Br., Aus.* col. behave (more) sensibly.
loafer *esp. Am.* tdmk. a light shoe with a flat bottom and leather top that you slip your foot into: *he changed in his covert-cloth coat and thin-soled loafers.* - S. Bellow., *gangsters wore blue suits and supple loafers.* - J. O'Brien, A. Kurins., *a man in Gucci loafers might wind up trying to walk all over you* - Ebony.
loan 1. *esp. Am., Can., Aus.* give (sb.) the use of (smth.), lend: *I loaned her a great deal at the bank.* - R.P. Warren. 2. *esp. Br.* lend smth. valuable for a long time to an organisation, esp. to a museum.
loan/ term loan *Am.* a loan for more than one or two years.
loaner *esp. Am.* smth. loaned for some time: *I got a Porsche recently, a loaner (from the dealer), a convertible, stick shift.* – Reader's Digest.
loblolly *Am.* thick mud swamp.
local 1. *Br., Aus.* col. a pub near where one lives, esp. a pub which one often drinks at. 2. *esp. Am.* a bus, train, etc., that stops at all regular stopping places: *I came home from a long Saturday afternoon local to Hollister out of San Jose* - J. Kerouac. 3. *Am.* a division within an organisation, esp. a branch of trade union: *the local had got an injunction from a judge* - E. Caldwell.
local authority *Br.* the group of people elected or paid to be the government of a particular area, such as a city.
local board *Am.* district conscription board.
(local derby) *Br.* sports competition, esp. a football match between two teams from the same area.
local government *Am.* one responsible for all the public services in a certain area.
local paper *Am.* newspaper printed in a town which contains local, national and international news.

local rag *Br.* col. local newspaper.
local room *Am.* local news department in the newspaper.
locate *Am.* come and establish oneself or itself, esp. a business.
location 1. *Aus.* a farm. 2. *Am.* a plot of land.
locator *Am.* person who marks the boundaries of land or mining claim.
locie *Am., Can., NZ.* col. locomotive.
lock *esp. Br., Aus.* the degree to which a steering wheel can be turned to change the direction of a travel; **on full lock** (of a steering wheel) turned as far as possible.
lock *Am., Can.* col. certainty.
lockaway *Br.* a long term security.
lock/ be locked in traffic *Am.* (of a vehicle) be unable to move.
lock/ have a lock on *Am., Can.* col. have a total control on sb.
lock sb. **down** *Am., Can.* confine prisoners to their cells, esp. when preventing a riot, n. **lock-down.**
lock up *esp. Am.* col. insure the results (of smth.) often dishonestly: *I'm pretty sure that it's been locked up.* - Longman.
locker *Am.* very cold room used for storing food in a restaurant or factory.
locking garage *Br.* garage that can be rented to keep cars, goods, etc. in.
lockstep *Am.* a strict procedure: *He would eventually be subjected to "lockstep" physical surveillance* – A. Summers, R. Swan.
lock-up 1. *Am.* col. prison. 2. *esp. Br.* a garage or shop that is not a part of sb.'s main premises.
loco *esp. Am.* col. adj. mad, crazy.
locomotive *Am.* a railway engine / **locomotive crew,** etc.
locoweed *Am.* col. cannabis.
locum *esp. Br., Aus.* someone, esp. a person in health care work, who does another person's job for a limited time.
lodge *Am.* 1. wigwam. 2. hotel in the mountains.
lodge a complaint, protest, appeal, etc. *Br.* make a formal or official complaint, etc.
lodger *esp. Br.* /*Am., Can.* **roomer/** person who lives in sb. else's house paying rent, often in **take in lodgers.**
lodging house *Br.* /*Am.* **rooming house/** a building where rooms can be rented for a short time.
loft *Br.* room or space under the roof of a building; attic.
loft *esp. Am.* 1. upper floor of a warehouse or business building: *His loft was in SoHo, on a*

Greene street. - D. Mortman., *area that was dotted with warehouses, offices and lofts.* - Guideposts. 2. an upper floor or room. 3. room that is on a raised level within another room or building that has this feature.

log up *Br., Aus.* travel.

log-book, registration book *Br.* registration document, esp. of a car: *The logbook and tax disc are from a write-off* - J. Higgins.

loge *Am.* the front of the dress circle at the theatre.

logger *Am. /esp. Br.* **lumberjack/** a man whose job is to cut down trees: *the undertaker dressed him in a flannel logger's shirt* – C.R. Cross.

logging *Am.* the work of cutting down trees for timber.

logic device *Br. /Am., Aus.* **logic circuit/** a type of electric switch.

logjam *esp. Am.* a difficulty that prevents one from continuing, impasse: *the Soviets were indeed ready to break the logjam.* - Newsweek., *That's like a logjam.* -Time., *Solidarity whips the Communist Party, causing a constitutional logjam.* - Time., *after 18 months, the logjam broke* - Reader's Digest.

log-man *Am.* woodchopper.

logrolling *Am., Can.* col. the practice of giving praise or help to sb.'s work in return for receiving the same.

logy *Am., Can.* col. adj. relating to dull heavy feeling that produces a lack of activity: *He had work to do tonight and he couldn't afford to be logy.* - A. Hitchcock Mystery Magazine.

loiter/ (*esp. Am.*) sign **No loitering.**

loiter with intent *Br.* law. get ready for the crime: *The man was taken to the police station on a charge of loitering with intent.* - Longman.

loitering *Am. /Br.* **loitering with intent/** law. getting ready for the crime.

loll about *esp. Br.* enjoy oneself in a relaxed way.

lollapalooza *Am.,Can.* col. smth. or sb. remarkable: *irrelevant after a season of Lollapaloozas* - BigO.

lollipop *esp. Br. /Am.* **popsicle/** frozen juice, ice cream, etc. on a stick.

lollipop man, woman/lady *Br., Aus.* col. warden supervising the children crossing the road, turning to the cars a stick with a sign on top showing that they should stop.

lolly *esp. Br.* 1. col. also *Aus.* a lollipop. 2. sl. money.

lolly *Aus., NZ.* a sweet, esp. a boiled one.

lollygag *Am., Can.* waste time aimlessly.

London broil *Am., Can.* grilled steak served cut diagonally in thin slices.

lonesome *esp. Am.* col. adj. 1. lonely: *he was sitting there all by his lonesome.* - J. Patterson. 2. smth. which makes one feel lonely.

lonesome/ on/by one's **lonesome** *esp. Am..* col. all alone.

The Lone Star State *Am.* Texas: *Since the death of Hollywood the Lone Star State has taken its place at the top for being interviewed, inspected and discussed.* - J. Steinbeck.

long/ So long *esp. Am., Can.* col. goodbye.

long/ How long is a piece of string? *Br., Aus.* used in uncertain answers to questions like *How big is smth?* or *How much time will it take?*

longcase clock *Br.* grandfather clock.

longest time/ for the longest time *Am.* col. for a very long time.

long green, greenback *Am.* sl. paper money: *the gross subject of the long green.* - R.P. Warren.

long gun *Am.* a rifle or shotgun.

longhair *esp. Am.* long-hair person usu. belonging to hippies or intelectuals.

long haul/ be in smth. **for the/a long haul** *Am.* continue doing smth. until it is finished.

long haul/ in/over/ the/a long haul *esp. Am.* for a long period of time.

Long Knife *Can.* sl. person from the USA.

long-life *Br.* (of milk, batteries, etc.) treated so that they stay fresh or continue working for a long time.

long-liner *esp. Am., Can.* fishing boat using long lines.

longneck *Am., Can.* col. beer bottle with a long neck of 330 ml.

longshoreman, stevedore *esp. Am., Can. /Br.* **docker/**: *the lawyer for a longshoremen's union* - I. Shaw.

long shot/ be a long shot *Am.* esp. journalism. be not likely to succeed, esp. get a job, win a contest, etc., adj. **long-shot.**

longsighted *esp. Br. /esp. Am.* **farsighted/** able to see objects or read things clearly only when they are far from the eyes: *visual maladies such as nearsightedness, and astigmatism.* - Omni.

longsighted view *esp. Am.* considering matters according to possible future concerns; opp. **near-sighted view.**

long-sleever *Aus.* col. large glass of beer.

longstop *Br.* a person or thing that serves to hold back or prevent smth. undesirable.

long story/ cut a long story short *Br., Aus. /Am.* **make a long story short/**.

long vacation /also *Br., Aus.* col. **long vac,** *Am.* **summer vacation/** *Br.* the period of three months in the summer when universities are closed.

longways *esp. Br.* adv. /*Am., Aus.* **longwise**/ along the length, lengthways.

longwearing *Am.* /*Br.* **hardwearing**/ adj. (esp. of materials or clothes, shoes, etc.) that lasts for a long time, even when used a lot.

loo *Br., Aus., Can.* col. /*Am.* **john**/ toilet: *we could see him from the back of the house, sitting on the loo.* - P. Norman., *Loo is now said to be unfashionable, lav is in.* - A. Peterson., *The most popular modern upper-class U excretory epithet for the jakes is the loo.* - P. Howard.

looey *Am.* mil. sl. lieutenant.

look/ get a look in *Br., Aus.* col. get a chance to do smth. that you'd like to succeed in.

look after *esp. Am.* col. kill, murder (sb.): *leave him to me, I'll look after him.* - Longman.

look after yourself *esp. Br.* col. (when saying goodbye) take care.

look smth. **out** *esp. Br.* search for and choose from one's possessions, find: *He had apparently found the effort to look out the change of clothes too much for him* - M.M. Kaye.

look/ look at him jumping / (*esp. Am.*) **look at him jump.**

look / look like a consumptive kangaroo *Aus.* look very ill.

look/ look sharp / also **look nippy, alive, lively** *esp. Br.* col. hurry up, do smth.quickly: *I had to look sharp and find something to do for her.* – R. Westall.

look sharp *esp. Am.* watch out, be careful.

look-in *Br., Aus.* col. a chance to do smth. or succeed, esp. in **not get/have a look-in.**

lookit *Am., Can.* col. look at.

lookout/ one's **own lookout** *Br.* col. an unpleasant situation when one must take care of oneself without other people's help, esp. in **be a poor, bad lookout for** sb.

look-see/ have a look-see *Am.* col. have a quick look at smth.

loom *Br.* /*Am.* **harness**/ several wires put together.

loon *Br.* col. act in a foolish way.

loonie *Can.* col. Canadian dollar: *I bought this rose for one loonie!* - W. Magnuson.

loony tune *Am.* a loony, a crazy person.

loop/ be in the loop *esp. Am., Aus.* col. have special knowledge or power that belongs to a group: *I've always kept you in the loop* - K. Ablow.

loop/ knock/throw sb. **for a loop** *Am.* col. upset or confuse sb.

loop/ in/(out) of the loop *esp. Am., Aus.* col. (not) within the inner circle of those directly concerned with a matter: *No, I'm out of the loop on Maris Pipers.* - B. Bryson., *share information and contacts just to stay in the loop.* – Reader' Digest.

loopy *Am.* sl. crazy: *his slightly loopy earnestness* - Time.

loopy/ go loopy *Br.* col. become extremely angry.

loose/ keep, hang or **stay loose** *Am.* col. keep or stay in a calm unworried state.

loose box *Br.* stable or enclosure for horse in which it doesn't need to be tied.

loose cannon *esp. Am., Can.* person not attached to any particular faction, who acts independently and disruptively: *it is intended to tie down us loose cannons in Washington* - R.N. Bellah and others.

loose cover *Br.* removable fitted cloth cover for a chair or sofa.

loose end/ at a loose end *Br.* /*Am., Can.* **at loose ends**/ having nothing to do: *She seems to have been at loose ends ever since her maid left.* - H.C. Whitford., R.J. Dixson.

loosen up *esp. Am.* 1. talk freely. 2. be generous with one's money: *Yet the Navy refused to loosen up with any of its hoard.* - H. Truman.

loosey-goosey *Am.* col. clumsy.

looseleaf notebook *Am.* /*Br.* **ring book**/.

loot *Am.* col. humor. things that sb. has bought or been given in large amounts.

lop 1. *Am., Can.* hang loosely. 2. *Can.* a wave.

loppy *Aus., NZ.* rouseabout.

lord/ drunk as a lord *Br.* obs. very drunk.

Lord Muck *Br.* col. snob.

lordship/ his lordship *Br.* col. humor. way of speaking about a man who thinks he is a very important person.

lorry, van *Br., Aus.* /*Am., Can., Aus.* **truck**/ a large motor vehicle for carrying heavy loads, truck: *In the yard a lorry backed towards the shed.* - G. Greene., **lorry fleet** *Br.* /*Am.* **truck fleet**/.

lorry/(come/fall) off the back of a lorry *Br.* (be) stolen.

lorryload *Br.* motor truckload.

lorry park *Br.* an open place where lorries can be parked.

lose the thread (of) *Br.* 1. fail to get the meaning of smth. 2. also **lose** one's **thread** become confused in what one is saying.

loss adjuster *Br.* /*Am.* **insurance adjuster**/.

lossmaker *Br.* business or industry that makes consistent losses or deficits.

lost/ lost in the shuffle *Am., Aus.* not getting the attention they deserve.

lost property *Br.* things that has been found in public places because some people have lost or forgotten them there.

lost property office *Br., Aus. /Am.* **lost-and-found (office)**/ one to which people who have lost anything can go in the hope of getting it back: *He gave me the phone number for lost and found* - Guideposts.

lot 1. *esp. Am., Can., Aus.* an area of land, esp. one for a particular purpose such as building or parking cars on: *I had to go to school on the lot.* - E. Taylor. 2. *Br., Aus.* col. a set of different things. 3. *Br.* col. a group of people, esp. one that person doesn't completely approve of.

lot/ all over the lot *Am.* col. in confusion.

lot/ have a lot on *Br. /Am.* **have a lot going on/** be very busy with a lot of things to do in a short time.

lot/ have a lot on one's **plate** *esp. Br.* col. have a lot of different things to deal with.

lot/ the (whole) lot *esp. Br.* the whole number implied.

lot on, upon *Am.* col. count on.

lot/ the best of a bad lot/bunch *Br.* (of people and things) not very satisfactory but the best in existing situation.

Lotus Land *Can.* British Columbia: *They went to Lotus Land for a holiday - to Vancouver.* - W. Magnuson.

loudhailer *esp. Br., Aus. /Am.* **bullhorn/** megaphone.

lough *Irish Eng.* lake or part of the sea surrounded by land.

Louie *Am.* col. citizen of Louisiana.

lounge 1. *esp. Br.* a living room in a private house: *Vacuumed hall, lounge, and breakfast room.* – S. Townsend. 2. *Br.* col. an act or period of lounging. 3. *Br.* lounge bar.

lounge about, around *esp. Br.* be lazy and waste your time doing nothing.

lounge bar (also **saloon bar**) *Br.* a comfortably furnished room in a pub where drinks usu. cost a little more than in the public bar: *Up at the lounge bar, Peter Macdonald talked to his girlfriend* - J. Patterson.

lounge lizard *esp. Am.* a playboy trying to meet rich people, esp. women in bars and at social occasions.

lounge room *Am. /Br.* **sitting room/** living room.

lounge suit *Br.* obs. /Am. **business suit/** a man's suit for wearing during the day / e.g. in an office: *dark-skinned Oriental in a blue lounge-suit* - M.M. Kaye.

lour *esp. Br.* 1. be dark and threatening (of sky). 2. frown.

louse up *Am.* col. make worse rather than better, mess up: *Don't louse up your life* - H. Fast., *Let's not louse it up.* - R. Cook.

louser *esp. Irish Eng.* col. mean, contemptible person.

Lousetown *Can.* sl. Klondike.

lousy with *Am.* having a lot of sb. or smth.

love (also **luv** nonst. or humor) *Br.* col. (a friendly form of address, esp. to or by a woman): *Come here to mother, love* - A. Christie.

(my) love *esp. Br.* form of addressing a person that you love.

love/ In Britain a waiter or waitress might address a customer as love, but only in an informal restaurant or cafe: *Nice to see you, love.* - J. Higgins.

love/ be a love/ there's a love *esp. Br.* col. expression used when a person asks sb. to do smth. for them, esp. said to a child or a member of a family.

love/ for the love of Mike *Br.* used to accompany excacerbated request.

love bite *esp. Br. /Am.* **hickey/**.

lovey *Br.* col. (a term of address for a person): *Lovey, don't dawdle.* - A. Moorehead., *Leave him be, lovey.* - V. Holt.

lovely 1. *esp. Br.* col. very enjoyable or pleasant. 2. *esp. Br.* col. friendly and pleasant. 3. *esp. Br.* beautiful and attractive. 4. *Br.* col. used when smth. is not at all enjoyable or good.

lovely *esp. Br.* col. (used for expressing thanks).

lovely and warm/cold, etc. *Br.* used to emphasize how good smth. is.

love seat *Am.* small sofa for two people: *a hideous couch and matching love seat.* – Reader's Digest.

lovey *Br.* col. way used to address a woman or child, that many women think offensive.

low boy *Am., Can.* a low dressing table with drawers, usu. having legs.

low boy (trailer) *Am., Can.* trailer with a low frame for transporting very tall or heavy loads.

lowball *Am., Can.* sl. lower, reduce: *any pol worth his consulting fee has tried to lowball his own candidate's prospects* - Time.

low-end *Am.* col. cheap and not of best quality (of product).

lower (up)on *esp. Am.* lower/lour at.

low gear, first gear *Am. /Br.* **bottom gear/**.

low grades *Am. /Br.* **poor marks/** bad marks at school or college.

low-heel, low-wheel *Aus. sl.* prostitute.
low life *Am. col.* sb. involved in a crime or who is bad: *All sorts of lowlifes were dropping by at odd hours* – S. Lawrence., also adj. **low-life**.
low loader *Br.* lorry with a low floor and no sides.
low man/ the low man on the totem pole *Am.* the least important person in the organization.
low-rent *Am. sl.* cheap, inferior: *This low-rent Valentine is not romantic enough* - McLean's.
low rider *Am.* customized vehicle with hydraulic jacks that allow the chassis to be lowed nearly to the road.
lowry *Am.* open goods wagon.
low season *Br.* the least popular season at a resort, tourist attraction, etc.
lox *esp. Am.* salmon preserved with smoke: *be dextrous and nab the stray blocks of cream cheese and lox* - Reader's Digest., *They're only ones left that make any sense with lox.* - New York.
Loyalist province *Can.* New Brunswick.
loyalty card *Br.* identity card issued by a retailer to its customers for future discounts after some credits are accumulated.
L-plate *Br., Aus.* plate on a car, showing that the driver is a learner: *a car had an L-plate on the back of it* - B. Bryson.
LPN *Am.* licensed practical nurse, nurse that is often supervised by registered nurse.
Lsd *Br. col.* 1. pounds, shillings, and pence. 2. money (used esp. before decimal money was introduced in Britain).
Ltd. *Br., Aus.* (of a company) limited.
luau *Am.* a sudden source of large profit / also *Am.* **bonanza**.
lube *esp. Am., Can. Aus. col.* lubricant.
lubra *Aus. derog. sl.* an Aboriginal woman.
lucerne *Br. /esp. Am.* **alfalfa/** a plant of the pea family grown for animal food.
Lucite *esp. Am. tdmk.* A type of transparent plastic used to make paints and decorative objects such as picture frames.
luck/ be bad/hard/tough luck on sb. *esp. Br.* come as unfortunate event to sb.
luck/ chance one's **luck** *Br.* take risk in doing smth.
luck/ sb.'s **luck is in** *Br.* smth. good happened to sb. by chance.
luck/ worse luck! *Br.* unfortunately.
luck/ Your luck's in! *Br. humor.* I think you would like to have sex with that person.
luck out *Am. col.* 1. also *Can.* be lucky: *I luck out with a patrol officer who knew Benny Shattles*

- R.J. Randisi., M. Wallace. 2. also *Aus.* have a bad luck: *Those poor marines sure lucked out in Saigon, didn't they?* - A. Makkai., *So they lucked out; a suicide verdict would most likely have validated the policies.* – S. Lawrence
luck penny *Br.* 1. a coin kept or given to bring good luck. 2. a small sum given back for luck by the seller to the purchaser in a business transaction.
lucky/ strike (it) lucky *Br., Aus.* suddenly have some good luck.
Lucky/ You'll be lucky *Br. col.* it's very unlikely.
lucky dip/bag *Br., Aus.* 1. /also *Am.* **grab bag/** a container filled with wrapped objects into which a person puts his/her hand and picks one out: *a lucky dip among almost any structure owned by British Telecom.* - B. Bryson. 2. *col.* smth. whose result depends on chance, lottery.
ludo *Br. /Am. tdmk.* **parcheesi/** a children's game played with small flat objects on a board.
lug *esp. Am. col. obs.* a rough and stupid person: *You're not dealing with a simple-minded lug.* - R. Chandler.
lug *Br., Aus.* a lughole.
lug(hole) *Br., Aus. col. humor.* an ear: *Poured some cold water down her lug 'ole.* - J. Herriot.
luggage *esp. Br., Can. /esp. Am.* **baggage/** the cases, bags, boxes, etc. of a traveller.
luggage label *Br., Aus. /Am.* **luggage tag/**.
luggage rack *esp. Br.* a shelf in a train, bus, etc. for putting one's bags on.
luggage ticket *Br. /Am.* **baggage ticket/**.
luggage train *Br. /Am.* **baggage train/**.
luggage van *Br., Aus. /Am.* **baggage car/** the part of a train in which only boxes, cases, are carried.
lugs/ put on lugs *Am. col.* put on airs.
Luke's little summer, St. Luke's summer, St. Martin's summer *Br. col.* Indian summer.
lulu 1. *Am., Aus. col.* unusual person or thing: *I gave away a lulu of a Picasso story* - J.D. Salinger. 2. *Am.* smth. very silly, bad, embarrassing, etc.
lumber 1. *esp. Br. col.* useless or unwanted articles such as furniture stored away somewhere: *This was loaded with lumber* - E. Hemingway. 2. *esp. Am., Can., Aus.* timber: *the lumber trucks roared past me.* - J. Steinbeck., *Arbus bought lumber to build Mariah a house* - Reader's Digest. 3. *Br. col.* sb. or smth. that causes difficulty, esp. by giving unwanted responsibility.
lumber 1. *Br., Aus. col.* (with) cause difficulty to sb. 2. *Am., Can.* cut trees or wood into timber. 3. *esp. Br.* clutter with unused articles.

lumber/ be lumbered with *Br.* col. be burdened with.
lumber-camp *Am., Can.* timber cutting camp.
lumber-carrier *Am.* a ship carrying timber.
lumber-drying *Am.* drying of wood, lumber kiln.
lumberer, lumberjack *esp. Am., Can.* a woodchopper: *dressed in a flannel lumberjack shirt* - New York.
lumbering *Am., Can.* wood, timber cutting.
lumber-jacket *Am.* warm short coat.
lumberman *Am.* man whose business is the cutting down of trees and the selling of wood: *it was said of lumbermen that they did their logging in the whorehouse and their sex in the woods.* - J. Steinbeck., *I had a grandfather, lumberman* - New Yorker., *she had married a lumberman from Oregon* - S. Sheldon.
lumberman's strawberry *Can.* sl. prunes.
lumber mill *Am.* /*Br.* **saw-mill**/: *He owned a lumbermill* - K. Vonnegut, Jr.
lumber-room, boxroom *esp. Br.* /*Am.* **storage room**/ a room in which useless or unwanted furniture, broken machines, etc. are stored: *Within was a lumber-room* - T. Hardy.
The Lumber State /also **The Pine Tree** or **The Polar Star State**/ *Am.* Maine.
lumber trade *Am.* timber trade.
lumme, -my *Br.* col. obs. excl. (an expression of surprise).
lummox *esp. Am., Can.* col. clumsy person.
lump *Br.* col. 1. the group of workers in the building industry working on a temporary business, independent contracting. 2. sb. who is stupid or clumsy.
lump/ take/get one's **lumps** *Am., Can.* col. suffer the bad results of one's actions bravely without letting them upset you: *the art of just turning the other cheek, taking our lumps and forging forward.* - Nation's Restaurant News.
lump it *Br.* col. accept without complaint a bad situation that cannot be changed: *She's out every night and father has to lump it.* - D. Lessing.
the lunatic fringe *Br.* the people in a political group or organisation who have the most extreme opinions or ideals.
lunch/ do lunch *esp. Am., Can.* col. meet for lunch.
lunch-bucket *Am.* col. adj. working-class, blue-collar: *it made me into a lunch-bucket lady.* - A.E. Hotchner.
lunch counter *Am.* a cafe or counter in a shop where people can buy and eat meals.
luncheonette *Am., Can.* 1. a light meal. 2. a small restaurant that serves simple meals: *It was called Douvry's Luncheonette* - J. Kerouac., *a dingy, smoke-filled luncheonette* - D. Mortman.
luncheon meat *Br.* /*Am.* **lunch meat**/ a mixture of meat (usu.) pork and cereal pressed together in a loaflike form.
luncheon voucher *Br.* /*Am., Aus.* **meal ticket**/ a voucher given to workers in addition to salary which can be exchanged for food in a restaurant.
lunch pail *Am.* the container in which a workman takes his lunch to work: *We picked up our lunch pail and headed toward the gate together.* - Guideposts.
lunch room *Am., Can.* /*Br.* **dining hall**/ snack room in a school or company: *they were parking the car in front of the lunchroom* - J. Kerouac., *The door of Henry's lunchroom opened and two men came in.* - E. Hemingway.
lund *Can.* calm, quiet.
lung *esp. Br.* an open space in a town or city where housing and traffic are not permitted.
lunger *Am.* col. a person with a TB disease.
lunk(head) *Am., Aus.* col. a blockhead: *And any lug of a lunkhead that don't stay in line will have me to answer to* – J. O'Hara.
lunker *Am., Can.* col. very large specimen of smth.
lurch *Am.* trend.
lurcher *esp. Br.* a mongrel dog, esp. one used by poachers.
lurg(y) *Br., Aus.* col. humor. an illness or disease.
lurk *Aus.* col. profitable dodge or scheme.
lush *esp. Am., Can., Br.* col. a drunkard: *I am not becoming a sorrowing lush.* - H. Fast., *he's quite a lush.* - J. O'Hara., *he was a lush.* - F. Mowatt.
luv(vie) 1. *esp. Br., Aus.* nonst. or humor. darling: *she called him luv.* - I. Shaw. 2. *Br.* col. actor or actress who behave to other people in a very friendly way that is not sincere.
luxury tax *Am.* tax on luxury products.
lyceum *Am.* organisation for arranging popular lectures.
lyrebird *Aus.* 1. Australian bird, symbol of Australia. 2. lier (esp. in **a bit of a lyrebird**).

M

M *Br.* abbr. motorway
ma *esp. Am.* col. 1. also *Aus.* a mother: *Ma! Don't shush! It's a comedy show.* - Reader's Digest. 2. sometimes not polite (a name for an (old) woman.

ma'am 1. *esp. Am.* (a respectful word used for addressing a woman): *Yes, ma'am. Yes, sir. - said the waiter backing away. -* I. Shaw., *Well, ma'am where do you go from here? -* L. Uris. 2. *Br.* female royalty or other woman in authority.

Ma Bell *Am.* sl. nickname of the Bell Telephone Corporation: *giving Ma Bell a big incentive to help it outmaneuver competitors. -* Fortune.

mac 1. *esp. Br.* col. also **mackitosh** raincoat 2. *esp. Am., Can.* col. (used for speaking to a man whose name is not known): *I can't turn around here, Mac. -* J.D. Salinger., *What's the matter with you, Mac, drunk? -* J. Steinbeck., *See the chaplain, mac. -* B. Tillman.

machine/ fight like a threshing machine *Aus.* fight desperately.

mackintosh/ also **mac(k)** *esp. Br.* obs. /*Am., Aus.* raincoat/ a coat made to keep out the rain: *a mackintosh was too hot to wear. -* G. Greene., *Cambridge porter, in grey suit and blue mac. -* You., *Dora took off her mackintosh. -* I. Murdoch.

macaroni and cheese *Am.* dish made from macaroni and cheese sauce.

mad *Br.* /*Am., Can.* crazy/.

mad (at) *esp. Am., Can.* col. /*Br.* **mad (with)**/ angry: *He was mad at you -* A.E. Hotchner., *You wouldn't get mad at me, would you, Will? -* E. Caldwell.

mad as hornet 1. *esp. Am.* very angry. 2. *esp. Br.* col. extremely stupid or unwise, crazy. 3. *esp. Br.* behaving in a wild uncontrolled way.

mad/ be mad about/over sb./smth. *Br.* col. like sb./smth. very much.

mad/ don't go mad *Br.* col. don't work too hard or get too excited.

mad/ drive sb. **mad** *Br.* make sb. so bored, annoyed or anxious that they feel like they are going crazy.

mad/ go mad *Br.* 1. behave in a wild way. 2. start acting crazy. 3. get very angry.

mad/ mad keen *Br., Aus.* col. extremely keen.

mad/ mad as beetle, as a (cut) snake, as a frilled lizard, as a gumtree full of galufs *Aus.* /*Am.* obs. **as mad(der) as a hornet,** *Br.* **stark staring mad,** *esp. Br.* **mad as hatter/** col. very mad.

mad/ run/work like mad *Br.* col. run or work as quickly as possible.

mad/ you must be mad (to do smth.) *Br.* col. it's very silly or stupid of you to act this way.

madam/ (proper) little madam *Br.* col. young girl who expects other people to do what she wants.

mad cow desease *Br.* col. BSE, a disease that damages the brain, causing the death of animals.

made/ I wasn't made for this *Br.* col. I'm not enjoying this job or activity.

Madeira cake *Br.* /*Am.* **pound cake/** a plain rather solid yellow spongecake.

made man *Am., Can.* person who is sure to succeed in life.

made road *Br.* tarmac or concrete road.

made to measure *esp. Br.* (of clothes) custom made.

mad money *Am.* sl. 1. money carried by a woman with which to pay her way home if her escort becomes offensive: *Whenever she goes out on a date, Hilda carries some mad money with her. -* H.C. Whitford., R.J. Dixson. 2. money to be spent in a frivolous way: *I got $100 in mad money for my birthday. -* R.A. Spears.

madness *esp. Br.* 1. insanity. 2. very stupid behaviour that could be dangerous.

Maggie's drawers *Am.* mil. sl. red flag raised to show that the target has not been hit in shooting drill.

magic *esp. Br.* sl. very good, wonderful: *Belfast is magic - local demotic for "super" or "marvelous" -* T. Thorne.

magic/ What's the magic word? *Br., Aus.* say please or thank you (to a child).

magna cum laude *esp. Am., Can.* (about university degree or diploma) second level degree with honours, the one after **cum laude**.: *Johnson graduated magna cum laude. –* Reader's Digest.

magnet school *Am.* one that has more classes in a particular subject than usual school and so attracts students from a wide area.

Magnolia City *Am.* Houston.

The Magnolia State *Am.* Mississippi / **Magnolia accent** *Am.* Southern aristocratic accent.

M. Agre. *Am.* Master of Agriculture.

magsman *Aus.* col. or *Br.* obs. sl. swindler, con man.

mag tape *Br.* col. magnetic tape.

mag wheel *Am., Can.* motor car wheel made from light-weight magnesium.

maiden speech *Br.* the first speech that sb. makes in parliament.

maid of honor 1. *esp. Am., Can.* a chief bridesmaid at a wedding. 2. *Br.* small tart filled with flavoured milk curds.

mail(s) *esp. Am., Can.* /*Br., Aus.* **post/** the collection, dispatch or delivery of a postal matter at particular time.

mail/ post is the more usual word in *Br.* except in certain combinations as airmail but **mail** is the usual word in America.

mail out *esp. Am.* send letters and leaflets or bills to a lot of people at the same time.

mail (to) *esp. Am.* v. post (a letter, parcel, etc.): *The cheque was mailed to you* - Longman.

mailbag *Am. /Br.* **postbag/** a **postman's bag** (*esp. Br.*), a **mailman's bag** (*esp. Am.*) / bag for carrying mail to be delivered.

mail bomb *Am.* letter bomb.

mailbox, mail drop *esp. Am., Can., Aus.* 1. /also *esp. Br.* **postbox, pillar box**/ a place for posting letters, etc. 2. place where one's mail is left near one's house (*esp. Br.* **letterbox**).

mail car *Am.* postal van: *But at the vestibule he was stopped by a blue-uniformed mail-car guard.* – M. Daly.

mail carrier obs., **mailman** *Am., Can.* postman.

mail catcher *Am.* special device for receiving and giving off mail from a moving train.

mail drop *Am.* 1. address where sb.'s mail is delivered, which is not where they live. 2. box on a post office where one's mail can be left.

mailer *esp. Am., Can.* 1. the sender of a letter or parcel by post or smth. send by post. 2. container or envelope used for sending smth. small by mail.

mailgram *Am.* tdmk. /*Br.* **telemessage**/.

mailman, also (**letter**) **carrier, mail carrier** *Am., Can. /esp. Br.* **postman**/ a person whose job is to collect and deliver letters, parcels, etc.: *DiGuilo told everyone in the family, plus the letter carrier, the doctor* - Guideposts., *Michael had a small part as a mailman in a movie* - Reader's Digest., *She was going to marry Hubert Willy, the substitute mail carrier.* – E. Caldwell.

mail order *Am.* postal (money) order: *mail-order growers are the best* – Reader's Digest.

mail order bride (or **wife**) *Can.* sl. a wife courted by correspondence, as through a matrimonial agency.

mailshot *esp. Br. /Am., Aus.* **mass mailing/** advertising leaflet or one appealing for money for some charity, usu. sent to a lot of people.

mailslot *Am. /esp. Br., Aus.* **letterbox/**.

mail sorter *Am.* person who puts letters and parcels into groups for delivery.

mail woman *Am.* a female postman: *a mail woman to bring it to the box in our entryway* - R.G. Kaiser.

main chance *esp. Br.* col. the possibility of making money or other personal gain: *He sold a bottle here and there and waited for his main chance.* - S. Bellow.

main crop *Br.* vegetable produced as principal crop of the season.

main deck *Am.* upper deck.

main drag, also **main stem** *esp. Am., Can., Aus.* col. /*esp. Br.* **high road,** *Br.* **high street/** chief street of the city: - *the I'm sooo-bad guise, gets shares along the main-drag.* - Time.

Maine/ from Maine to California *Am.* all across the USA.

mainlander *Aus.* (for Tasmanians) a continental citizen.

main man *Am.* sl. 1. boss: *"Gyp De Carlo was his sponsor, his main man.* – A. Summers, R. Swan. 2. boyfriend, husband or protector. 3. one's best friend.

main road, motorway *esp. Br. /esp. Am.* and law. **highway,** *Can.* **main road, main thoroughfare/**: *Now, this line is the mainroad.* – M. Daly.

mains *esp. Br.* 1. a supply of electricity and water produced centrally and brought to houses, etc., by wires and pumps and sewerage system. 2. electric outlet; **at the mains** turned on, plugged in, **mains-operated** *Br. /Am.* **line-operated/**.

main squeeze *Am.* sl. 1. sweetheart. 2. boss: *Mr. Bronchard is the main squeeze in this office.* - A. Makkai.

mainstream *Am.* integrate (handicapped children) with others usu. on part-time basis.

main street *esp. Am.* 1. /*Br., Aus.* **high street/** the most important shopping and business street of the town. 2. small-town America: *Main Street wants no part of their plan.* - P. Robertson.

maintain *Am.* col. continue in one's present state or course of action: *He maintained he was so hungry for the taste of meat* - I. Stone.

maintained *Br.* (of school) financed with public money.

maintenance *Br. /Am.* **alimony, child support/**.

maintenance order *Br., Aus.* a law by a court of law that a person must pay maintenance to support sb.

maisonette *Br.* an apartment that is on two floors, which is part of a larger house.

mai tai *esp. Am.* cocktail of rum, curacao and fruit juices.

maize *esp. Br. /esp. Am.* **Indian corn,** *esp. Am., Aus., Can.* **corn/** (the seed of) tall plant grown, esp. in America and Australia, for its ears of yellow seeds.

major *Br.* obs. adj. being the older of two boys of the same name at the same school.

major *esp. Am., Can., Aus. /Br.* **main/** (a student studying) a chief or special subject at a university: *I never thought to ask before, but what's your major? - English lit.* - H. Fast.,

Elizabeth had been a social science major. - S. Sheldon., *I'm a math major.* - E. Segal.

major in *esp. Am., Can. /Br.* **study as the chief subject(s)/** when doing a university degree: *Are you majoring in English Literature?* - Longman.

majority (of votes) 1. *Am.* absolute or clear majority. 2. *Br. /Am.* **plurality/** the largest number of votes in an election, esp. when less than a majority.

major league *Am., Can.* the highest ranking league in professional sport.

major medical *Am.* a broad form of health insurance.

make *Am.* sl. 1. an identification: *Send out a make on Don Vinton.* - S. Sheldon., *Hurriedly the detective ran a make on the man* - T. Thompson., *Hey, don't forget to get a make on that car anyway.* - R. Moore. 2. sex partner.

make *esp. Am.* sl. 1. identify: *We tried to make him down at the station* - R.A. Spears. 2. also *Aus., Can.* have sex with, often in the phr. **put the make** on sb.: *making (and not only in the double entendre of American idiom) has been understood as a masculine trait* - P.L. Berger and others., *If a girl tries to make me, I'll throw her in Horse Creek.* - E. Caldwell.

make out *esp. Am., Can., Aus.* 1. succeed or progress in a particular way. 2. col. (usu. in progressive tenses) have sex, make love: *Rainer Point was a big make-out spot.* - R.L. Stine., *I don't want you to think I'm a makeout artist* – J. Hopkins.

make out a case *Br., Aus. /Am.* **make a case/ for** smth. argue that it's the best thing to do.

make out like a bandit *Am.* col. get a lot of money or gifts, win a lot, etc.

make out of/ be made out of whole cloth *Am.* col. be false: *the prisoner's story is made out of whole cloth* - Longman.

make the numbers up to *Br.* reach a certain figure in number.

make time out *Am.* hurry up.

make over *esp. Am.* 1. remake (smth. 2. show fondness for (sb., usu. a child): *Please make over any lesbian girlfriend* - Kansas City Star.

make over print. *Br. /Am.* **remake/**.

makeover *Am. /Br.* **spoilage/** print. materials or labour lost on a printing job.

make up *Am.* take as an addition (an exam or course) often because of failure or lack of smth., such as a subject regarded as necessity: *I have three courses to make up before I can get my degree.* – Longman; n. **makeup**: *They give me a makeup test.* – R.L. Stine.

make up a fire *Br., Aus.* put more wood or coal on it.

make up to *Br., Aus.* derog. flatter sb. in order to get advantages.

make with *esp. Am.* sl. produce, bring: *When are you going to make with the music, man?* - Longman.

make/ it makes a change *esp. Br.* col. it's pleasantly different from normal.

make a deal *Am. /Br.* **do a deal/** agree on smth.

make a go of smth. *Br.* manage to be successful after working hard at it.

make a game of *Br.* make jokes on sb.

make a (good) job of *Br., Aus.* do (good) work on.

make a guess *Br.* try to guess.

make a House *Br.* secure quorum in a House of Commons.

make a play for *esp. Am.* col. try to get (smth. or sb.): *Lawford later made a play for Campbell, which she said she rebuffed.* – A. Summers, R. Swan

make a Virginia fence *Am.* go in a stumbling way.

make do and mend *Br.* obs. manage with less by repairing old things.

make fire *Can.* get into argument with sb.

make it big *Am.* be very successful.

make it 5 o'clock, etc. *Br.* col. tell that it's 5 o'clock by sb.'s watch.

make it up *Br.* become friendly again, esp. after a bad argument.

make it with sb. *Am.* col. have sex.

make like *Am., Can.* col. pretend to be; imitate.

make time *Am., Can.* make sexual advances to. sb.

make wonder *Can.* surprise sb.

maker(s) *esp. Br.* the company that produces smth.

maker up *Br.* maker of garments.

make-work *Am.* n. adj. 1. featherbedding. 2. providing of work for unemployed. 3. also *Can.* col. work that keeps sb. busy but has little value in itself.

makings *Am., Can., Aus., NZ.* col. paper and tobacco for rolling cigarettes.

makutu *NZ.* witchcraft.

Malee *Aus.* 1. rare. bush, region covered with bush / also **Maleeland** (or **area**). 2. small eucalyptus.

mall *esp. Am., Can.* a large shopping area, often enclosed, where cars are not permitted: *She reached the middle of the bricked mall* - R. Cook., *we have only to take a tour through a suburban mall* - J. Riffkin, T. Howard., *Many of* these wanderers end up on the pedestrian mall on Moscow's old Arbat street - Newsweek.

malling *Am., Can.* development of shopping malls and activity of spending time in them.

malt(ed) *Am.* a type of non-alcoholic drink with ice-cream, chocolate, etc. added to it.

maltings *Br.* malthouse where malts are made and stored by **malters**.

malt liquor *Am.* a type of beer.

mam 1. *esp. Br.* one's mother. 2. *esp. Am.* a form of address to any woman.

mama, mamma 1. *Am., Can.* col. *Br.* obs. /also **momma**/ a mother: *Mama Corleone was staying in the city with the friends of the family.* - M. Puzo., *Your mamma ain't able to afford now using her money upon ice tea for her friends.* – G. Stein. 2. *Am.* obs. often derog. a black woman who looks after white children. 3. *Am.* col. (attractive) mature woman.

mama's boy *Am.* /*Br.* **mummy's boy**/ a boy or man who appears to do whatever his mother tells him to.

mammy 1. *esp. Irish English, Am.* (used by children) mother. 2. *Am.* taboo. obs. black woman whose job was to take care of the children.

man 1. *esp. Am., Can., Aus.* excl. (used for expressing strong feelings of excitement, surprise, etc.): *Man, this chick is put togethairy.* - L. Waller., *Man, I was really excited* - D. Marsh., *Man, he's too strong.* - Reader's Digest. 2. *esp. Am.* used for adresing sb., esp. an adult male: *"You're nuts, man," insisted Garcia.* – Reader's Digest.

man/ my man, my dear man, my good man *Br.* these forms of addresses sometimes suggest superiority from the speaker to the person addressed.

man/ no more…than the man in the moon *Am.* col. (used to emphasize a negative statement).

man/ your man *Irish Eng.* a particular man.

the man *Am.* sl. man in authority, boss, esp. a white man or police officer.

the man on the street *Am.* /*Br.* **man on Clapham omnibus**/ ordinary person.

manage/ I can't manage the time *esp. Br.* I'm too busy.

managed care *Am.* system of health care where preventive medicine and home treatment are considered as the most important.

manageress *Br.* obs. a woman who is in charge of a shop, restaurant, or hotel.

managing *Br.* having executive control or authority.

managing director, MD *esp. Br., Aus.* chief executive of corporation, general director, president: *Felix had been right to make him managing director.* - T. Murphy.

Manchester (goods, wares) *Aus., NZ.* household linen.

Mancunian *Br.* a person from Manchester: *I couldn't name a single great Mancunian.* - B. Bryson.

mandarin *Br.* (journalist term) an important person in the Civil Services.

mandate smth. *Am.* make it mandatory.

mangetout *esp. Br.* /*Am., Aus.* **snowpea**, *Br.* **sugar pea**, *Am.* **snap pea**/ a sort of pea that can be eaten as well as its seeds.

mangle 1. *Br.* machine with two rolls used to remove water from washed clothes. 2. *Am.* machine for ironing sheets or other fabrics using heating rollers.

man in the car, also **the next man** *Am.* the average man.

manky *Br.* col. looking dirty and unattractive.

manner/ do smth. as (if) to the manner born *Br.* doing smth. easily and naturally.

manner/ not by any manner of means *Br.* col. not at all easily be defeated.

mano-a-mano *Am.* col. adj., adv. hand-to-hand; man-to-man.

man of straw 1. *esp. Br.* a person of weak character, esp. one who is unable to make decisions. 2. also **straw man** *esp. Am.* an imaginary opponent whose arguments can be weak.

manor *Br.* col. a. /*Br.* col. **patch**/ a police area: *I'll put the word out in every manor in London.* - J. Higgins. b. an area that one lives or works in or knows well, esp. in **on the manor**.

manse *esp. Br.* the house provided for a clergyman to live in.

manservant *Br.* obs. /*Am.* **houseman**/ a male servant in a private house.

mansion(s) *Br.* (in names of buildings) a building containing flats.

manshion house *Br.* the house of Lord Mayor or a landed proprietor.

mantel *esp. Am.* mantelpiece.

mantelshelf *Br.* the top part of a mantelpiece.

many/ be one too many for *Br.* obs. be clear that sb. can't gain advantage over a person.

Maori oven *NZ.* eathen oven in which foods are cooked on hot stones.

The Maple-sugar State *Am.* Vermont.

marbles/ pick up one's **marbles (and go home/ leave)** *Am.* suddenly leave a joint activity if you don't like it.

march to a different tune *Br.* /*Am.* **march to (the beat of) a different drummer**/ act differently.

marching orders *Br.* 1. /*Am.* **walking orders**/ col. official notice that one must leave, esp. in **be given/get marching orders**: *I have my own marching orders.* - K. Ablow. 2. a notice of breaking relations with sb.

marching orders *Am.* instructions given to carry out a plan.

march past *esp. Br.* ceremonial march by troops past a saluting point at review.

Mardi Gras *Aus., NZ.* carnival or fair held at any time.

mare *Br.* col. derog. woman.

mare's nest *Br.* smth. illusory that people try to get.

marge *Br.* col. margarine.

margin *Aus., NZ.* increment to a basic wage paid for extra skill or responsibility.

marginal *Br., Aus.* adj. (of a seat in Parliament) which may be lost or won by a small number of votes and so is quite likely to pass from the control of one political party to that of another; **marginal seat, constituency**.

Marine Corps, also **Marines** *Am.* soldiers who live and work on ships.

marines/ (go) tell it/that to the marines *Am.* I don't believe it.

Maritimes *Can.* New Brunswick, Nova Scotia and Prince Edward Island (PEI) / with Newfoundland these become Atlantic Provinces.

mark *esp. Br.* 1. /*Am.* **grade**/ a figure, letter, or sign which represents a judgement of the quality of sb.'s work, behaviour, performance in a competition, etc., v. 2. an acceptable level of quality: *And its depiction of investing banking is largely on the mark* - McLean's. 3. a measurement of a particular temperature level in a gas oven.

mark *Br., Aus.* 1. /*Am.* **cover**/ stay close to an opposing player, esp. in football, so as to prevent them from getting the ball or gaining points. 2. register (a sale of stocks) so as to put it on the official list.

mark *Am.* sb. that a criminal has decided to steal from or trick.

one's **mark** *Br.* smth. typical for sb.

mark/ be marked out as *Br.* /*Am.* **marked as**/ be noticed as likely to be.

mark/ be near the mark *Br.* be mostly true or almost exact.

mark/ be well off the mark *Br.* (about ideas, plans, etc.) be not true or correct.

mark/ full marks for effort/trying, etc. *Br.* used to praise sb. for trying hard to do smth. though they didn't succeed.

mark/ get off the mark *esp. Br., Aus.* score for the first time in a sports competition or start doing another activity very quickly.

mark/ mark you *esp. Br.* used to attract attention to smth.

mark/ off the mark *esp. Br.* (of words and behaviour) being unfair.

mark/ overstep the mark *Br.* /*Am.* **overstep the limits/bounds**/ offend sb. by doing or saying unsuitable things.

mark/ quick/first off the market *esp. Br.* quick to understand or respond to smth.

mark/ (not) up to the mark *Br.* (not) up to acceptable standard.

mark down/ be marked down *Br.* be given a lower mark.

mark out *Br.* mark off, separate from the rest.

mark/ on your marks *Br., Aus.* /*Am.* **mark/...get set...go**/ words said at the start of a running race.

mark/ score full marks in the test *Br., Aus.* get a maximum score in it.

mark 2 *Br.* col. a new version done after making changes.

marker *Am.* 1. revolving die hammer, marking hammer, marking iron. 2. memorial plaque. 3. also *Can.* col. promissory note.

marker pen *Br.* pen with a thick point made of felt.

market *Am.* do one's shopping / esp. in the phr. **go marketing**. n. -er.

market *Am.* shop that sells food and things for the home.

market day *esp. Br.* regular market day in the week.

market/ meat market *Am., Aus.* /*Br.* **cattle market**/ col. a place to find sexually attractive partners.

market garden *esp. Br., Aus.* /*Am.* **truck farm**/ an area for growing vegetables and fruit for sale, also v. / **market gardener** *Br.* /*Am.* **truck farmer**/: *And there's our market garden.* - I. Murdoch.

market letter *Am.* one issued by a stockbroker or investment advisory firm to its customers.

market town *Br.* town where there's an outdoor market, usu. once or twice a week.

marking *esp. Br.* activity of checking students' writing works.

marking-out, marking-off *Br.* /*Am.* **laying-out, layout (work)**/ marking (work) for drilling, machining, or filing.

marks/ Do you see skid marks on my forehead? *Br.* sl. Do you consider me a fool?

marmelise *Br.* humor. defeat, destroy utterly, annihilate: *I'll marmelise you!* - T. Thorne.

marquee 1. *esp. Br., Aus.* a large tent, used esp. for eating or drinking in. 2. *Am., Can.* a large sign outside a theatre or cinema showing the name of the film or play that is being shown there: *On the marquee of a Mexican restaurant in San Antonio: "In queso emergency, open 24 hours!"* – Reader's Digest. 3. *Am.* a cover over the entrance of a public building.

marquess *Br.* marquis.

marriage bureau *Br.* /*Am., Br.* **dating agency**, *Am., Aus.* **dating service**/.

marriage guidance *Br., Aus.* /*Am., Aus.* **marriage counseling**/ advice given by trained personnel to people who have problems with their marriages.

marriage license 1. *Br.* official written document saying that two persons are allowed to marry. 2. *esp. Am.* /*esp. Br.* col. obs. **marriage lines**/ marriage certificate, copy of the record of a legal marriage: *My wife-to-be and I were at the county clerk's office for our marriage license.* – Reader's Digest.

marrow *Br., Aus.* /*esp. Am., Aus.* **squash, vegetable marrow**/ a large vegetable with a hard skin, that can be eaten or cooked.

marrow/ be chilled/frozen to the marrow *Br., Aus.* very cold.

marshal 1. *esp. Br.* official in charge of an important public event or ceremony. 2. *Am.* officer in a court of law; sheriff. 3. *esp. Am.* the officer in charge of a city's police or fire fighting department: *I'll call the town marshall* – E. Caldwell.

marshalling yard *esp. Br.* a railway yard in which the parts of a train, esp. a goods train, are put together in preparation for journey: *His own alma mater...overlooking a railway marshalling yard* - D. Lodge.

mart *esp. Am., Irish English.* a small market or shopping centre.

martini 1. *Br.* a popular brand of vermouth often drunk straight as an aperitif. 2. *esp. Am.* a cocktail of gin and vermouth.

marvie, marvy *Am., Aus.* excl. it's a beauty.

mash *Br.* col. /also *Br.* **creamed potatoes**/ mashed potatoes.

mash *Br.* col. n. v. (make) tea.

mash up (a car) *esp. Am.* damage it.

masher *Am.* sl. a man who tries to force his attentions on a woman against her will: *One theory says females who fear molestation overeat to repel mashers.* – E. James, D. Ritz.

mash kettle *Am.* mash copper, mash tin for boiling the mash in brewing.

mash note *Am., Can.* col. love letter of adoration.

masses *Br.* col. a large number or amount of smth.

mass mailing *Am., Aus.* /*Br.* **mailshot**/.

Mason jar *esp. Am., Can.* wide-mouthed glass pot with a tight lid for preserving fruit and vegetables.

mass transit *Am., Can.* public transport, esp. in the city.

mast *Br.* tall metal tower that sends out radio and TV signals.

Master *esp. Br.* 1. (used before a boy's name) a polite way of addressing a boy in the past. 2. obs. also **Mistress** a school teacher.

master teacher *Am.* /*Br.* **head teacher**/ methodologist.

masthead *Br.* /*Am.* **flag**/ the name of a newspaper with some of information about it as well at the head of the first page: *its masthead boasted "printed in Daffodil City, USA.* - K. Vonnegut, Jr.

Ma State *Aus.* sl. New South Wales.

match *esp. Br.* a game or sports event.

match/ get into a pissing match (with) *Am.* col. derog. have an argument trying to find out who is the best.

matchbook *Am., Can.* cardboard folder of matches.

mate 1. *Br., Aus.* col. (a friendly way of addressing a man used esp. by working men): *You're in the team, mate, and no nonsense.* - D. Francis., *I lay it in cubes, mate.* - J. Fowles. 2. *Br.* col. a friend. 3. *esp. Am.* (often used in magazines) one's husband or wife. 4. *esp. Am.* one of a pair of objects.

mate/ builder's mate/ plumber's mate, etc. *Br.* sb. who works with and helps a skilled worker; assistant.

mate/ pen-mate *Aus.* shearer's colleague.

mate/ no-mater *Aus.* unfriendly man.

matelot *Br.* col. sailor.

mater *Br.* obs. or humor. col. a mother.

maternity pay *Br.* money paid for 18 weeks by an employer to a woman who leaves work to have a baby.

mateship *Aus.* col. friendship.

matey 1. *esp. Br., Aus.* col. friendly: *He and Alpha were very matey.* - M. Jones, J. Chilton; n. **–ness:** *Chas missed the "mateyness"* – S. Lawrence 2. *Br.* col. a way of addressing other men.
maths *Br., Aus.* /*Am., Can.* **math**/ col. mathematics: *I'm a math major.* - E. Segal.
Matilda *Aus.* sl. one's belongings / **waltz Matilda** *Aus.* sl. carry one's things.
matily *Br.* col. in a matey way, sociable.
matinee coat *Br.* baby's short coat.
matric 1. *Br.* col. quality, matriculation. 2. *Can.* col. high school graduation.
matron 1. *Br., Aus.* obs. a woman in charge of the nurses in a hospital (now officially called a **senior nursing officer**). 2. *esp. Br.* a woman in a school where children live who is in charge of medical care, repair of clothes, living arrangements, etc. 3. *esp. Am.* a woman who is in charge of women and/or children / e.g. in a prison or police station. 4. *Am.* (in a hospital or other institution) the woman in charge of domestic matters.
matte *Am.* adj. mat, of a dull, not shiny surface: *Small, squat, black matte and brushed steel, logo of a German manufacturer.* - J. Kellerman.
matter/ as a matter of interest *Br.* col. used to ask about smth. that is not really necessary.
matter/ be a different matter, be quite another matter *esp. Br.* situation is much more serious than another one.
matter/ the matter at hand *Am.* col. present situation.
matter/ first-class matter *Am.* letters sealed in envelopes.
matter/ it's no hanging matter *Br.* it is not a serious mistake.
matter/ second-class matter *Am.* periodicals sent by post.
matter/ third-class matter *Am.* printed matter sent by post as opposed to letters and periodicals.
mature student *esp. Br.* /*Aus.* **mature age student**/ a student at a university or college who began his/her course when aged over 25.
mau-mau *Am.* sl. black activist or black street gang member: *fight and think like Mau-Maus, the PLO and the Japanese army.* - J. Patterson .
maunder *esp. Br.* talk or complain about smth. for a long time in a boring way.
maven *Am., Can.* col. 1. expert: *the most demanding Eastern European herring maven.* - New York. 2. night-club host.
maverick *Am., Can.* unbranded calf.

max/ to the max *Am.* sl. totally, completely: *She is happy to the max.* - R.A. Spears.
max *Am., Can.* col (cause to) reach the limit of capacity or ability.
max out *Am.* col. 1. make the best score or as hard as possible: *Price maxes out on his incentives* - Newsweek. 2. do too much or eat too much.
mayhem *Am.* and law. crime of maiming.
mayn't *esp. Br.* short for may not.
mayo *Am.* col. mayonnaise: *cheese and mayo really add up* – Reader's Digest.
mayoress *Br.* 1. the wife of a mayor. 2. rare. a female mayor or woman who shares the work of a mayor.
May tree *esp. Br.* hawthorn tree / but the British use Hawthorn bush.
mazuma *esp. Am., Aus.* col. money: *let the old mazooma roll in.* - K. Vonnegut, Jr..
MB *Br., Aus.* /*Am.* **BM**/ Bachelor of Medicine.
MBA *esp. Am.* Master of Business Administration: *he wrote of the MBA program's influence on undergraduate education* - R.N. Bellah and others.
MC *Am.* Member of Congress.
MD 1. *esp. Br.* managing director. 2. *Am., Aus.* Doctor of Medicine.
mdse *Am.* merchandise.
ME *Br.* /*Am.* **Epstein-Bar virus**/.
meal *Am.* maize flour.
meal/ make a meal (out) of smth. *esp. Br., Aus.* derog. spend more time than necessary doing smth.
meal ticket *Am.* sl. any person, skill, part of the body, instrument, etc., that provides one's sustenance: *Why he'd want to get rid of the kind of meal ticket she was going to be.* - D. Hammet., *You're his meal ticket!* - D. Mortman.
meal ticket *Am., Aus.* /*Br.* **luncheon voucher**/.
mean 1. *esp. Am.* bad-tempered, liking to hurt: *Not that Jack Reagan was known to be a mean drunk* - Time. 2. *esp. Am.* col. very good, wonderful: *She was a mean blues singer* - L. Roxan., *She plays a mean guitar, too.* - New York. 3. *Am.* a. ashamed. b. indisposed. 4. *Br.* /*Am.* **cheap**/ not willing to spend money. 5. *Br.* (of an amount of smth.) very small.
mean/ *They didn't mean her to read the letter Br., Aus.* /*esp. Am.* *They didn't mean for her to read the letter*/.
means test *esp. Br.* an inquiry into the amount of money sb. has made esp. to find out if they have so little that they can be given money by state.
meant/ be meant to *esp. Br.* to have to, be supposed to.

measure *Am.* one of a group of notes and rests separated by vertical lines, into which a line of written music is divided.
measure/ panic measure *Br.* emergency measure.
measure/ take/get the measure of *Br.* discover what sb. or smth. is in order to deal with them later.
measuring jug *esp. Br. /esp. Am., Aus.* **measuring cup/** a transparent container with marks used for measuring liquids; **measuring cup** is also used for measuring solid food ingredients.
meat *esp. Am.* the edible part of fruit, nuts or eggs.
meat/ one's **meat** *Am.* col. one's preferred occupation, play, etc.: *contestants are not my meat at all* - R. Stout.
meat/ be the meat in the sandwich *Br., Aus.* be in a difficult situation, esp. be friendly with both of two people who are arguing.
meat/ one man's meat is another man's poison *Br.* what one person likes is greatly disliked by another.
meat/ meat and drink to sb. *esp. Br.* smth. easy to cope with, which sb. enjoys doing.
meat/ one's **meat and two veg** *Br.* humor. a man's sexual organs.
meat/ the meat and potatoes *Am.* col. basic parts of smth.
meatball *Am., Can.* dull person.
meat-chopper, meat grinder *Am. /Br.* **mincer/** mincing machine, meat mincer.
meat-loaf *Am., Can.* a large, baked piece of minced meat served in slices.
meat-packing *Am.* the preparation of dead animals so that they can be sold as meat; n. **meat-packer**.
meat-pie *Br., Can.* pastry case filled with meat.
meat tea *Br.* tea at which meat is served, high tea.
mechanical print. *Am. /Br.* **artwork/**.
mechanical paper *Am.* print. one containing a proportion of mechanical wood pulp (**groundwood** */Am./*).
mechanical pencil *Am. /Br.* **propelling pencil/**.
mechanical wood pulp *Am.* print. one produced by grinding wood mechanically and used in the cheaper papers.
M Econ *Br.* Master of Economics.
med *esp. Am., Can.* medical.
the Med *Br.* col. the area surrounding the Mediterranian Sea.
medallion *Am.* a. a license or permit to operate a taxicab in the form of medallion. b. a taxicab operator with such a permit: *Caldwell recognized his medallion number* - New York.

medallion man *Br.* humor. an older man who dresses in a way that he thinks women find attractive.
media center; book room *Am.* school library.
media event *Am.* a small event publicised by mass media.
median (strip) *Am., Can., Aus. /Br.* **central reservation, centre strip/** a thin area of land running down the middle of a large road to keep traffic apart: *At the first break in the median, I hung a U.* - J. Kellerman.
media specialist/expert *Am.* school librarian.
media studies *Br.* studies of newspapers, radio and television.
medic 1. *esp. Am.* soldier with medical duties: *At one point, a medic told Pryor that he couldn't find the medicine* – Reader's Digest. 2. *Br.* medical student.
medical *Br. /Am.* **physical/** an examination of one's body by a doctor to check that the person is healthy.
medical examiner *Am.* medical expert who investigates the deaths of people, who have died in a sudden, violent or unusual way.
medical officer *Br.* person in charge of the health services of a local authority or other organisation.
medical practitioner *Br.* col. a doctor.
medication *esp. Am.* medicine, esp. a drug: *She was in surgery for hours on pain medication for days.* - D. Mortman.
medigap *Am.* private health insurance intended to cover payments for treatment not included under government schemes.
meet 1. *esp. Am.* a meeting of people, esp. for sports event: *We'd gone in to New York that morning for this fencing meet* - J.D. Salinger., *He also joins the basketball team, takes part in track meets* - Time., *They watched some swimming meets.* - D. Mortman. 2. *Br.* a meeting of riders with their hounds at a place before they set off on a fox hunt.
meet (up) with *esp. Am., Aus.* have a meeting with: *You may meet up with the Hogbens sometime.* - Zacherlay.
meet the case *Br.* be adequate.
megabucks *Am.* sl. much money: *A stereo that size must cost megabucks.* - R.A. Spears.
megillah *Am.* sl. long and complicated story: *Do you know the most peculiar thing about this whole megillah?* - S. Sheldon.
Melba/ do a Melba *Aus.* return from retirement or make some farewell appearances.
mellow out *Am.* col. become more relaxed and less severe.

melon *Am.* col. a sum of money representing an excess of profits / **cut** (or **split, slice**) **a melon** *Am.* sl. divide extra profits.

melting pot/ in the melting pot *esp. Br.* journalism. constantly changing and not yet in a final state.

melt up *Am.* melt down.

member *Br.* Member of Parliament.

membership of *Br.* /*Am.* **membership in**/.

memoir *Am.* memoirs.

memorandum and articles of association *Br.* corporate charter.

memorial *Am.* a charitable donation in memory of a dead person.

Memorial Day *Am.* May 30, observed as a legal holiday in many states in commemoration of dead servicemen, at present the last Sunday in May.

memorial park *Am.* cemetery.

memory book *Am.* scrapbook.

men/ the men in (grey) suits *Br.* 1. the powerful and influential people in a political party having no official position in Parliament or government. 2. influential businessmen who don't care much for the interests of poor people.

menace/ demand money with menaces *Br.* law. threaten to cause sb. harm unless they're given the money.

mend/ in *esp. Am.* people **mend** things that are torn such as clothes and sheets and **repair** /*Br.* **mend**/ things that are broken, such as watches or furniture.

mender *Br.* person who ends a quarell or difficult situation.

mensch *Am., Can.* col. a decent human being: *he's just as much a mensch as any of us.* - M. Torgov., *Jewish lady seeks sincere, secure, sexy Jewish mensch* - New York.

men's and boys' outfitters *Br.* men's wear shop.

men's room *esp. Am., Can.* /*Br., Aus.* **gents**/ public toilet for men: *One of his favourite sports was going into a gay bar, coaxing an unsuspected homosexual into the men's room and beating him unconscious.* - S. Sheldon., *a pupil finds it necessary to visit the men's room* - B. Kaufman., *Upstairs, he dried Jeane-Claude with paper towels from the men's room.* - E. Segal.

mental *Br.* col. thinking or behaving in a way that seems crazy or strange.

mental/ go mental *Br.* sl. 1. get very angry. 2. start behaving in a crazy way.

mental home *Br.* obs. mental hospital.

mention/ be mentioned in dispatches *Br.* be commended for one's actions by being named in official millitary report, n. **mention in dispatches.**

meow *Am.* miaow.

mercer *esp. Br.* a dealer in textiles, esp. silks.

mercery *Br.* 1. the place of business of a mercer. 2. the wares sold by a mercer.

merchandiser *Am.* /*Br.* **retailer**/ person or company that sell goods to the public: *In the vitamin aisle of your drug, food store or mass merchandiser.* – Reader's Digest,

merchandising *esp. Am.* the way shops and businesses organise the sale of their products.

merchant *esp. Am., Can.* any retail shopkeeper.

merchant/ con merchant/, speed merchant, etc. *Br.* col. sb. who is involved in a particular activity, such as tricking person or one who likes driving very fast.

merchant bank *esp. Br.* bank dealing in commercial loan and investment.

merchant banking *Am.* the practice of banks investing their own money in the take-over of companies.

merchant marine *esp. Am.* /*esp. Br.* **mercantile marine, merchant navy**/ 1. all of a nation's ships which are used in trade, not war. 2. the people who work on these ships: *Merchant Marine type folks would return from America* - W. Jack, B. Laursen.

mercy flight *Can.* an airplane flight to an isolated community to fetch a sick or injured person to hospital for treatment.

mere *Br.* (used usu. in comb., as part of a name) a lake.

merge *Am.* /*Br.* **filter in**/.

merge into the background *Br.* col. behave very quietly in social situations, so that people don't notice sb.

meritorious *esp. Am., Can.* law. (of an action or claim) likely to suceed on the merits of the case.

merry *Br.* col. euph. rather drunk.

merry-me-got *Can.* sl. bastard.

mersh *Am.* sl. adj. commercial.

meshuga(na), meshuggener *esp. Am., Can.* col. a crazy person: *Only a hundred percent meshuganer would do such a thing!* - M. Torgov.

meshuganas *esp. Am., Can.* col. crazy ideas.

mess/ a mess of *Am.* col. a lot.

mess *esp. Br.* col. solid waste material from a baby or animal.

mess / mess about *esp. Br.* /*esp. Am.* **mess around**/ 1. col. spend time lazily, doing things lazily with no plan: *I've come here to play, not to mess around* – Reader's Digest. 2. act or speak stupidly: *So* *may be Oakland and Nagato are messing around.* - A. Hitchcock Mystery Magazine., *C'mon, Valerie. Don't mess about. Your Dad's tired* – R. Westall 3. (with) work without speed or plan, but according to one's feelings at the time: *I told the child to stop messing around with that bonfire if he didn't want to get burned.* - H.C. Whitford., R.J. Dixson.

mess about/around with *esp. Am.* have sexual relationship with sb. who is not their wife or husband.

mess sb. **about, around** *esp. Br.* col. treat sb. badly by one's actions.

mess sb. **up** *Am.* sl. hit sb. very badly: *I don't want the banks to mess you up.* – J. Hopkins.

mess with smth. *Am.* use or treat it without enough care.

mess/ you say **No messing** in *Br.* as a way of emphasizing that you want smth. to be done.

mess/ mess with sb.'s **head** *Am.* col. make sb. feel anxious or confused.

mess/ sell smth. **for a mess of potage** *Br.* make a bargain.

message *Irish Eng.* errand.

mess hall *esp. Am., Can.* mess, a place to eat up, esp. for soldiers or other members of armed forces: *they were marshaled into the messhall for a meal.* - J. Cheever., *There would be no formal mess hall or galley.* - L. Uris., *The mess halls weren't completed yet.* - J.W. Houston, J.D. Houston

mess kit 1. *Am.* eating utencils. 2. *Br.* formal military dress for dining in the officer's mess.

Messrs *esp. Br.* used before the names of two or more men as part of a name of a business.

Messrs. / Americans use full stop after such abbreviations as **Mr., Mrs., Ms.,** etc.

mess tin *Br.* rectangular metal dish with a folding handle used by soldiers for cooking and for eating or drinking out of.

metal *Br.* 1. small stones. 2. v. cover (a road) with them.

metalled road *Br.* /*Am.* **metallic road**/ paved road; **unmetal (unmade, dust) road** *Br.* unpaved road: *So down the bumpy metaled road to the public lane* - J. Fowles.

meter *Am.* /*Br.* **metre**/ 1. a unit for measuring length. 2. arrangement of words in poetry into strong and weak beats.

meter maid, parking policeman *Am.* /*Br.* **traffic warden**/.

meteorological office *Br.* /*Am.* **weather bureau**/.

method/ there's a method to sb.'s **madness** *Am.* there's a method in sb.'s madness, there's a reason for madness.

methodologist; instructor in methods; expert in teaching methods *Am.* /*Br.* **specialst (teacher) in (on) methods/principles of teaching**/.

meths *Br.* col. /*Am.* col. **meth,** *Aus., NZ.* col. **metho,** *esp. Br., Aus.* **methylated spirits**/ liquid used to remove dirty marks or as a fuel for some heaters and lights.

Metro *Am., Can.* n. adj. form of municipal government; metropolitan: *not knowing if the township or Metro's going to take over.* - W. Grady.

Metropolis *Br.* or humor. London.

Metropolitan police /also (**the**) **Mets** *Br.* the London police.

mews *esp. Br.* back street or yard in a city, where horses were once kept, now partly rebuilt so that people can live there, cars can be stored there, etc.: *All this was in a tiny mews flat* - D. Martin.

Mexicano *esp. Am.* Mexican.

Mexican standoff *Aus.* a situation in which people on opposite sides threaten each other but neither tries to come to an agreement.

Mexican wave *Br.* /*Am.* **wave**/ continuous rolling motion made by a crowd of people standing up with their arms in the air and then sitting down one after another.

mezzanine *Am., Can.* (the first few rows of seats in) the lowest balcony in a theatre or sports stadium or the front rows of a balcony in a theatre.

MFA *Am.* Master of Fine Arts.

MGR *Br.* merry-go-round (train).

MIA *Am.* missing in action.

mia-mia *Aus.* Aboriginal hut or shelter.

miaow *Br.* /*Am.* **meow**/.

mic *Am.* col. microphone.

Michaelmas term *Br.* the autumn term in some universities.

mick *Aus.* (in the game of two-up) the reverse side of a coin.

mick *Br.* insulting word for a person from Ireland.

mickery *Aus.* a waterhole, esp. in a dry river bed.

mickey *Can.* sl. a half-bottle of liquor: *See if you can get a mickey of something for a buck.* - R.A. Spears.

mickey/ take the mick(ey) (out of sb.) *esp. Br., Aus.* col. make sb. feel foolish by copying them or laughing at them: *he was delighted by such expressions as "taking the mickey," or "are you daft?" and even "bugger off!"* – S. Lawrence; n. **mickey-taking**.

microbrew *esp. Am., Can.* beer from microbrewery.

microlight *esp. Br.* small airplane for only one or two persons.

micromanage *Am., Can.* control every small part of business or other activity: *No signing in and out, no curriculum guides (other than state mandates), no micromanaging.* – Reader's Digest.

middle lane *Br.* /*Am.* **center lane**/.

middle name / in America first, middle and last name, in Britain two Christian names /*Am.* **given names/** or forenames and a surname. The use of surnames as given names is far more general in the United States than in England. It is common in the USA for a woman on marrying to use her maiden name as a middle name. It is also common for divorcees to use their maiden surnames in combination with their late husband's names. The English, especially of the upper classes, frequently give a boy three or more given names but it is most unusual in the USA. It is very uncommon in England for diminutives to be bestowed at baptism but in the USA it is common for many girls and boys to be christened Peggie, Flo, Mamie, Tom, Nat, Sam, etc. The American custom of annexing the regal II, III, etc. to the surnames of boys bearing the given names of uncles, grandfathers or other relatives is quite unknown in England and so is the custom of addressing boys named after their fathers as Junior: *she lost her name in the boarding school and was forever known by her middle name, Darien.* - K. Lipper.

middle of nowhere, back of Bourke *Aus.* /*Br., Aus.* col. **back of beyond**/.

middle school 1. *Am.* a school for children between the ages of 6 and 11: *his first position as an intern at Provo Dixon Middle school.* – Reader's Digest. 2. *Br.* a school for children between the ages of 8-9 and 12-13.

middy *Aus.* col. half pint beer mug.

Mideast *Am.* Middle East as a world region.

midget *Br.* col. person who is not very tall.

midibus *Br.* a small bus, seating about 25 passengers, that operates in some towns and cities.

midi system *Br.* a set of compact stacking hi-fi equipment components.

midnight feast *Br.* secret late night meal.

midsection *Am.* midriff.

Midsummer('s) Day *Br.* the 24th of June.

midterm *Am., Can.* exam in the middle of the term.

midtown *Am.* adj., adv. in the area of a city that's near the centre but which is not the main business area.

midway *Am., Can.* an avenue at a fair, exposition, carnival, or amusement park for concessions and light amusements.

MIEE *Br.* Member of the Institute of Electrical Engineering.

might *Br.* col. (used instead of may, for asking permission politely); *Might I have a word with you?* (formal request).

might/ might makes right *Am.* /*Br.* **might is right/** belief in the power of oneself to do anything.

mightn't *esp. Br.* col. might not.

mighty *Am.* col. very.

migrant *Aus.* immigrant, esp. from Australia.

mike *Am.* radio. letter M.

mild *Br.* col. clear, dark-coloured beer with a mild taste.

mile/ a mile a minute *Am., Aus.* very quickly.

mile/ be miles away *esp. Br.* be not aware what's happening around one because one deeply thinks about smth. else.

mile/ be miles out *Br.* col. misjudge seriously in one's calculations.

mile/ like five, ten, etc. **miles of bad road** *Am.* col. smth. not very enjoyable.

mile/ miles older/better/too difficult, etc. *Br.* very much older, etc.

mile/ run a mile *Br.* do anything to avoid a particular person or situation.

mile/ stand/stick a mile *Br.* be very easy to notice.

mile/ see/know/tell smth. **a mile off** *Br.* /*Am.* **away/** be easy identifiable although supposed to be a secret.

mileometer, milometer *Br., Aus.* /*Am.* **odometer/** device that shows and measures the distance a vehicle has travelled.

milepost *esp. Am., Can., Aus.* a post indicating the distance in miles from a given point, esp. a distance to the next town.

military *Am.* /a singular noun/: *Now the military was feeding me* - B.E. Olson.

military/ in the military *Am.* in the army, navy, etc.

the military industrial complex *Am.* armed forces and the industries that supply them.

military service *esp. Am.* military training.

milk and water *Br.* weak and sentimental suggestions or ideas.

milk/ come home with the milk *Br.* humor. come home very early in the morning after being at a party all night.

milk/ tiger milk *Am.* sl. raw whiskey, moonshine: *This tiger milk of yours must be doing her pipes a lot of good.* - D. Hammet.

milkbar 1. *esp. Aus.* one that mostly serves dairy products and milk cocktails. 2. *Br.* snack bar that sells milk drinks and other refreshments.

milkbar cowboy *Aus.* sl. Australian version of American drugstore cowboy.

milkbar economy *Aus.* disproportional development of the economy.

milk churn *Am.* /*Br.* **churn**/ a large tall container, fitted with a lid, for carrying milk.

milk float *Br.* a vehicle used by a milkman for delivering milk, now usu. driven by electricity: *Why do they call them milk floats? - They don't float at all.* - B. Bryson.

milk loaf *Br.* loaf of white bread made with the use of milk.

milkman *Am.* milker.

milko, milky *Aus.* sl. a milkman, a man who sells milk.

Milk of Magnesia *Br.* tdmk. a type of laxative.

milk pudding *Br.* pudding made mainly of milk and rice.

a milk round/ have a milk round *Br.* work as a milkman going from house to house delivering milk.

the milk round *Br.* 1. col. the annual tour of British institutions of higher learning by prospective employers. 2. regular journey of a milkman.

milk run 1. *Br.* col. familiar, easy journey that a person does regularly. 2. *Am.* col. train journey or regular plane flight that stops in many places.

milk shake 1. *Br.* drink made of milk mixed with fruit or chocolate. 2. *Am.* drink made of milk, ice-cream and fruit or chocolate: *consider a thick, creamy milk shake.* – Reader's Digest.

milktooth *Br.* babytooth.

milk train *Am.* a train carrying milk to the market.

milk truck *Am.* a vehicle used to deliver milk in the US.

mill 1. *Am.* one thousandth or one tenth of a dollar (used in setting taxes and for other financial purposes). 2. *Can.* one tenth of a dollar (used in taxing).

milliard *Br.* a thousand millions: *the word "billion" in this book will be used to mean 1000 million, i.e. the European "milliard".* - D.H. Meadows and others.

million/ gone a million *Aus.* col. (of a person) completely broke and defeated.

million / there were 6 millions *Br.* /*Am.* **there were 6 million**/.

million/ look/feel like a million bucks *esp. Am.* /*esp. Br.* **look a million dollars**/ be extremely attractive.

millwheel *esp. Br.* large wheel turned by water flowing past it that provides power to machinery in a mill.

milquetoast, milktoast *Am.* obs. mild-mannered weakling: *That milquetoast never questions any of his wife's statements.* - H.C. Whitford., R.J. Dixson.

Milwaukee goiter *Am.* beer belly.

mimeograph *Am.* 1. n. /*Br.* obs. **duplicator,** *Br.* **roneo**/ machine used to make copies of written pages. 2. v. make a copy using a duplicator: *These are often mimeographed and distributed to the press* - H. Truman.

mimosa *Am., Can.* a drink of champaigne and orange juice.

mince 1. *esp. Br., Aus.* also *esp. Br.* **mincemeat** / *Am.* **hamburger (meat), chopped meat,** *Am.* **ground meat**/ minced meat, chopped meat, esp. beef. 2. *Am.* mincemeat.

mince/ not mince matters *Br.* col. speak frankly.

minced *Am.* (of onions and other vegetables) chopped down.

mince pie 1. *esp. Br.* small round pie or tart with sweet mincemeat. 2. *Am.* large pie filled with mincemeat.

mincer *Br., Aus.* /*Am.* **meat grinder**/.

mind *Am., Can., Irish Eng.* be obedient to sb.

mind *esp. Br.* be careful (of); give attention to; **Mind!** *Br.* take care because smth. bad or dangerous might happen.

mind *Br.* a. be responsible for smth. for a short time. b. take care of a child while their parents are away.

Mind out! *Br.* a. used to warn sb. that they are in danger. b. used to ask sb. to move cause they are in danger.

mind/ be in two minds about *Br.* /*esp. Am., Can.* **be of two minds**/ hesitate in choosing between two alternatives.

mind/ the mind boggles *Br.* it's unbelievable.

mind/ I don't mind *esp. Br.* It's up to you to choose.

mind/ mind how you go *Br.* col. (when saying goodbye) take care.

mind/ mind the store *Am.* col. take care of smth., esp. business while the person responsible for it is away.

mind/ mind you *Br.* used to say that smth. is opposite of what has just been said or to emphasize smth.

mind/ never you mind *esp. Br.* used when telling sb. that smth. is private or secret.

mind/ of two minds *Am.* in two minds, very hesitant.

mind/ pay sb./smth. no mind, pay no mind to *Am.* / *Am., Can.* **not pay** sb. **any mind/** ignore sb./smth.

mind/ to my mind *Br.* col. used when sb. is giving their opinion about smth.

minder *Br.* person employed to protect another, often in the criminal world.

minder/ machine minder, child minder, etc. *Br.* person who looks after a machine, baby, etc.

mindless (of destructive action) *Br.* not sensible and done for no good reason.

mine/ work down the mines *Br.* work in the mines.

mine hunter *Br.* a ship equipped for laying underwater pipes.

mineral *Br.* col. soft drink.

mineral spirits *Am., Can.* white spirit.

mineral water /obs. **minerals**/ *Br.* a non-alcoholic sweet fizzy drink with a particular taste, sold in bottles.

miner's right *Aus., NZ.* license to prospect and dig for gold and other minerals.

minge *Br.* sl. woman's pubic hair or genitals.

mingy *Br., Aus.* col. derog. not generous, stingy.

miniature golf *Am.* /*Br.* **crazy golf**/.

minibeast *Br.* insect or spider.

minibus *esp. Br.* a small bus for about 6 - 12 people.

minicab *Br.* a taxi that can be called by telephone, but not stopped in the street.

minicam *Am.* a small video camera, used esp. by TV news reporters.

minim *esp. Br., Aus.* /*Am.* **half note**/ musical note with a time value half as long as a semi-breve: *her breasts swung in a grave rhythm, minims, say, to the fingers' quavers.* - A. Burgess.

mini-mall *Am., Can.* small shopping mall with each shop having access from the outside.

minimart *esp. Am., Can.* convenience store that stays open very late and sells food, cigarettes, etc.

minimum security prison *Am.* /*Br.* **open prison**/ prison that doesn't restrict prisoners' freedom as much as ordinary prison.

ministering angel *Br.* humor. a woman who takes care of a person who is ill.

mini roundabout *Br.* 1. one indicated on a road sign by a small island. 2. white circle printed on the road that vehicles must drive around at a place where several roads meet.

mini series *Br.* TV or radio series of 3-4 programmes on related topics.

minivan 1. *Br.* a small van or pickup truck. 2. *Am.* a large car with 6 to 8 seats.

Minnie *Am.* Minneapolis.

min-min *Aus.* will-o'-the-wisp.

minor 1. *Br.* obs. being the younger of two boys in the same school / (**minimus, maximus**). 2. *esp. Am., Can.* subsidiary subject, v. **minor in**.

minority *Am.* sb. who belongs to a group of people who are different from the rest in race or religion.

minority leader *Am.* leader of a political party that has fewer politicians in the law-making institutions than the leading party has.

minors *Am., Can.* minor leagues in professional sports.

minster *Br.* (now usu. part of a name) a large or important church, esp. one that formed part of an abbey.

minstrel *Am.* singer.

mint/ be minting it *Br., Aus.* col. /*Am., Aus.* **be minting money**/ earn a lot.

minter *Br.* col. smth. in mint condition, esp. a second-hand car.

mint julep *esp. Am.* a cocktail of whiskey, crushed ice, sugar and pieces of mint.

mint sauce *esp. Br., Aus.* /*Am.* **mint jelly**/ a sauce made of vinegar, sugar and mint, often served with lamb.

minus point/factor *Br.* quality that makes smth. or sb. seem less good.

minute *esp. Br.* an official message from one member of an organisation to another giving permission for or suggesting a particular action, memo.

minute *esp. Br.* make official note of smth. in the record of a meeting.

minute/ at the minute *Br.* col. at the present time.

minute/ Have you got a minute? *Br.* /*Am.* **Do you have a minute?**/.

minute/ this (very) minute *Br.* col. only a short while ago.

minuteman *Am.* a man who is always ready for action (from the group of people in the past who were not soldiers but were always ready to fight at any time).

Miranda (card) *Am.* law. a police card given to an arrested stating constitution rights: *the two of us bopped over right away, Mirandized him, and listened to what he had to say.* - J. Kellerman.

misadventure/ death by misadventure *Br.* law. the official name for accidental death.

miscellanist *esp. Br.* a writer of miscellanies.

mischief/ do sb. / oneself **a mischief** *esp. Br., Aus.* col. usu. humor. hurt sb. / oneself.

misery (guts) *esp. Br.* col. derog. person who is always unhappy and complaining.

mismove *Am.* a faulty move.

miss *esp. Br.* 1. (a form of address used by pupils to a woman teacher): *Miss Stringer taught English* – R. Westall. 2. obs. a rude or naughty girl or woman.

miss/ give smth. **a miss** *esp. Br., Aus.* col. not to do, take, etc. smth.

miss/ go missing *Br., Aus.* disappear or get lost.

miss/ miss the bus *Br.* miss the chance.

miss/ without missing a beat *Am.* confidently.

miss out *Br.* fail to include or be included.

missing *Am.* /*Br.* **away; out**/ absent at the lesson.

mission style *Am.* architectural style (using Roman Catholic missions in California as a pattern).

mission-tiled *Am.* Spanish-tiled roof.

Missouri/ a man from Missouri *Am.* a traditional sceptic (*Am.* **skeptic**) / **I'm from Missouri** *Am.* col. I'll believe it when I see it.

missus, missis *esp. Br.* col. used in addressing a woman, whose name person doesn't know.

misstate *esp. Am.* express smth. incorrectly; n. **-ment**.

misstep *Am.* a mistake, esp. one that offends or upsets people.

mist *Br.* /*Am.* **fog**, *Am., Aus.* **steam**/ condensed liquid on the surface of smth. which makes it difficult to see; v.

mistake one's **man** *Am.* mistake in one's man.

mistake/ no mistake *esp. Br.* it's a certainty.

Mister *esp. Am.* col. (used to address a man whose name you don't know): *Now, dammit, you better talk to me, Mister.* - J. Patterson.

Mister Big *Am.* sl. boss, VIP: *he turned out to be Mr. Big.* - S. Sheldon.

Mister Charlie *Am.* sl. white man (esp. used by black).

mistreat *Am.* maltreat.

mistress *esp. Br.* obs. a female teacher.

mistrial 1. *Am.* a trial where the jury didn't reach an unanimous decision. 2. *Br.* a legal trial that is conducted unfairly.

mite *esp. Br.* col. a young child, esp. an ill or hungry one.

mitt *esp. Br.* col. sb.'s hand.

mix *Br.* col. cause dissension as by spreading false tales.

mix it *esp. Br., Aus.* col. /*Am.* col. usu. **mix it (up) with** sb./ fight or behave in a rough threatening way.

mix it with sb. *Br.* meet with new or special people.

mixed *esp. Br.* for both males and females.

mixed drink *Am.* an alcoholic cocktail.

mixed-blooded *Am.* of mixed blood. n. **mixed blood**.

mixed grill *Br.* grilled mixture of different food, esp. bacon, sausages, tomatoes, and mushrooms.

mixer 1. *Am.* obs. informal social gathering or dance. 2. *Br.* col. trouble-maker.

mixing faucet, mixer faucet *Am.* /*Br.* **mixer tap**/ an apparatus which provides the necessary temperature of the flowing water, usu. in the bathroom or kitchen.

mixologist *Am.* col. person skilled at mixing cocktails.

the mixture as before *Br.* the same treatment repeated.

mizzle *esp. Br.* col. depart suddenly, vanish, also **do a mizzle.**

mizzle *esp. Am.* rain made of many very small drops; v.

mo 1. *esp. Br., Aus.* col. a very short space of time, moment. 2. *Am.* month.

mo 1. *esp. Am.* money order. 2. *Am., Can.* month.

MO *esp. Br.* col. medical officer, an army doctor.

moan *Br.* col. complain in an annoying way, esp. in an unhappy voice.

moan/ have a moan *Br.* col. complain about smth. and without good reason.

moaning minnie *Br.* col. an annoying, always complaining person.

mob 1. *Aus.,NZ.* a flock or herd of animals; a bunch of things, etc.; **a mob of sheep/cattle**, etc. 2. *Br.* col. group of people in one place having smth. in common.

mob/ be mobbed *Am., Can.* have a lot of people around: *we were afraid the farm would be mobbed* – J. Hopkins; **mob** *Am., Can.* crowd into some place.

the Mob *esp. Am., Can.* col. Mafia: *vaguely mob-connected nice guy* - New York.

mob-handed *Br.* col. in considerable numbers.

mobile *Br.* /*Can.* **cellular phone**, *Am.* **cellular**/.

mobile home 1. *Am.* type of house that looks like an ordinary house but can be moved to another place: *300 or so families, mostly African Americans, who lived in small frame houses or mobile homes.* – Reader's Digest. 2. *Br.* /*Am.* **trailer**/ large caravan, used esp. during summer holidays.

mobile library/ shop/ clinic, etc. *Br.* a library, shop, etc. that is in a vehicle and can be driven from one place to another.

mobile library *Br., Aus.* /*Am.* **bookmobile/**

mobile phone, cell phone *Br.* /*Am.* **cellular phone/** one that you can carry with you and use anywhere.

mobility allowance *Br.* benefit paid to disabled people to minimize their transportation expenses.

mobility unit *Br.* public housing adapted to meet the needs of handicapped persons.

mobilization center /also **induction center**/ *Am.* mobilisation station.

mobster *esp. Am.* gangster.

mocassin flower *Am.* Lady's slipper (Venus' slipper).

moccasin telegraph *Can.* /*Aus., Br., Can.* **bush telegraph**/.

mocha *Am.* combination of coffee and chocolate.

mock *Br.* /*Aus.* **trial/** school examination taken as practice shortly before an official examination.

mockers/ put the mockers on smth. *Br.* col. spoil smth., /*Aus.* **put the mock(s) on/**.

mockie, mocky *Am.* derog. col. obs. Jew.

The Mocking Bird State *Am.* Florida.

mock turtle *Am.* /*Br.* **turtle neck/**.

mocock *Am., Can.* basket made from birch bark.

Mod *Br.* a member of a young group of people who wore stylish clothes, listened to soul music and rode scooters.

(all) mod cons *Br., Aus.* col. (all) modern conveniences.

model *Br.* 1. person or thing almost exactly like others, but not always of the same size. 2. an article of clothing worn by a model or shown in a shop, usu. the only one or one of a very few of its kind. 3. euph. a prostitute.

model home *Am., Can.* show house.

Model T *Am.* 1. a machine or system that works reliably but lacks luxury appurtenances or sophistication. 2. adj. cheap, shabby, crude.

modem *esp. Br.* /*Am.* **data phone/**.

moderator 1. *Am.* a person who ensures that formal discussion follows a certain procedure, esp. one presiding over a town meeting. 2. *Br.* a person that ensures that all the examiners marking a student work use the same standards, v. **moderate**.

modern languages *Br.* modern European languages, such as Frenh and Italian studied as a subject at school or university.

modified American plan (MAP) *Am.* /*esp. Br.* **halfboard/**.

module *Br.* one of the parts that a course of study is divided into.

moggy, also **mog** *Br.* 1. also *Aus.* col. esp. humor. a cat: *Moggies (mixed breeds) are the most common.* - New Idea. 2. an untidy woman or girl.

Mohawk *esp. Am., Can.* Mohican haircut.

moil *Am., Can.* work hard, n.

mojo *esp. Am.* magic.

moke 1. *Br.* col. esp. humor. donkey. 2. *Aus., NZ.* an old broken down horse.

moko *NZ.* traditional Maori tatoo, esp. on face.

molasses *esp. Am., Can.* /*Br.* **treacle/** very thick sticky dark liquid made from sugar: *the clerk in the commissary passed out the black mollasses and the sowbelly.* - R.P. Warren.

molasses/ slower than mollasses (in January) *Am.* obs. very slowly.

mold *Am.* mould / **molt** *Am.* moult.

moldy *esp. Am.* old-fashioned.

moldy fig *Am.* sl. an old-fashioned person.

moll 1. *Aus.* sl. a female companion of a member of a group who ride motorcycles or surf; prostitute. 2. *esp. Am., Aus.* sl. obs. a female companion of a gangster. 3. *Am.* sl. woman.

molly dooker *Aus.* col. left-handed person.

molly mawk *esp. Aus., NZ.* albatros.

mom *Am., Can.* /*Br.* **mum/** col. mother: *I'm broke, mom. Dead broke.* - H. Fast.

mom-and-pop *Am.* (of business) operated by a family or husband and wife: *The kind you find at truck stops, drugstores, little mom-and-pop stores, and the like.* – S. Lawrence.

moment/ at the moment *Br.* col. or *Am.* now.

moment/ at this moment in life *esp. Br.* pomp. at this moment.

moment/ smth. **has its moments** *Br.* humor. some parts of experience were very annoying.

momentarily *Am., Can.* very soon: *Momentarily, he came to his senses* - H. Fast.

momma *Am., Can.* col. 1. /also *Am.* **mama**/ mother. 2. a woman.

mommy *Am., Can.* /*Br.* **mummy/** (used by children) mother.

Mondayish *Br.* adj. describing the feeling of facing the prospect of the week's work ahead.

Mondayitis *Aus.* col. describing the feeling after a weekend when a person doesn't want to go to work.

Monday morning quarterback *Am., Can.* person who is good at predicting things that have already happened.

mondo *esp. Am.* col. comb. word meaning "a situation of" or "a state of affairs characterised by": *they often turn into mondo-shoppers as they age.* - Reader's Digest.

money/ hard money *Am.* cash money.

money/ be (right) on the money *esp. Am., Can., Aus.* col. correct.
money/ throw money about *Br.* spend a lot of money not caring about the amount.
money box *esp. Br.* a container in which money is kept, esp. one with a long thin hole in the top through which coins can be pushed.
money crop *Am.* cash crop.
money for jam (or **for old rope**) *esp. Br.* col. smth. easily come by, easy pickings.
money-spinner *esp. Br., Aus.* col. smth. that brings in much money: *it proved to be a terrific money-spinner.* - D. Lodge; adj. **money-spinning**: *No previous World Cup say licensing executives has been such a money-spinner.* - Economist.
money talks, bullshit walks *Am.* col. derog. one can make sb. do anything for money.
money tree *Am.* source of easy unlimited money.
mong *Aus.* col. mongrel.
mongoloid *Am.* taboo. sl. obs. a person who has Down's syndrome.
monkey 1. *Br.* col. 500 pounds: *satisfied with a mere monkey for his services.* - T. Thorne. 2. *Am.* sl. $500. 3. *Br.* sl. a large lump (hump) on a person's back. 4. *Am.* (used in comb. sb. who works at smth. with his hands in the Navy). 5. *Br.* sl. an inferior or menial person: *the monkeys downstairs can take care of calculations.* - T. Thorne.
monkey *Am.* copy or mimic what sb. else does.
monkey around/about *Br.* col. behave in a stupid or careless way.
monkey/ a monkey on sb.'s **buck** *Am., Aus.* a serious problem.
grease monkey *Am.* mechanic; **powder monkey** *Am.* explosive handler.
monkey/ be a cartload of monkeys *Br.* obs. / *Br.* col. **as artful (clever) as a wagonload** (or **cartload**) **of monkeys/** be very cunning.
monkey/ get one's **monkey up, put** sb.'s **monkey up** *Br.* col. make sb. angry.
monkey/ have a monkey on one's **back** *esp. Am.* col. have a very serious problem, esp. dependency on drugs.
monkey/ I don't give a monkey's *Br.* col. I don't care at all.
monkey/ not give a monkey('s) (shit, bum, fart, etc.) *Br., Aus.* col. not care at all.
monkey bars 1. *Am.* /*Br.* **climbing frame**/ a structure for children to climb and play on: *There are a lot of first-graders over there by the monkey-bars.* – R. Brautigan. 2. *Br.* bars fixed to the wall in a gym.

monkey freezing *Br.* col. adj. biting cold.
monkey-nut *Br.* becoming rare. peanut in its shell.
monkey-shines *Am., Can.* /*Br.* **monkey tricks**/ col. monkey business, secret behaviour which causes trouble: *Ramona had not learned those erotic monkey-shines in a manual* - S. Bellow.
monkey spanner/wrench *Am., Can.* /*Br.* **adjustable spanner**/.
The Monkey State *Am.* Tennessee.
mono *Am.* col. /*Br.* **glandular fever**/ a serious infectious illness that makes you feel weak and tired for a long time afterwards.
monomark *Br.* registered identification mark.
mononucleosis *esp. Am.* /*Br.* **glandular fever**/.
monopoly on *Am.* monopoly of: *The communist Party has a monopoly on political power* - R.G. Kaiser.
monthlies *Br.* obs. women's period.
monty / the full monty/monte *Br.* col. everything which is necessary or appropriate.
monumental mason *Br.* person who makes tombstones.
The Monumental State *Am.* Maryland.
moo *Br.* col. becoming rare. a stupid or worthless person.
mooch 1. *Am., Can.* col. /*esp. Br.* col. **cadge**/ get by asking for it: *the panhandler who mooched a dime from me in the street.* - E. Cleaver, n. 2. *Br.* loiter in a bored or listless manner.
moody *esp. Am.* having moods that change often and quickly.
moola(h), mullah *esp. Am.* sl. money: *There was no mulah in that safe!* - R.A. Spears.
moon about/around *Br.* col. spend one's time lazily.
moon/ ask for the moon, cry for the moon *Br.* col. be different or impossible.
moon/ bark/howl at the moon *Am.* do smth. inefficiently.
moon/ be crying for the moon *Br.* obs. want to have the impossible.
moon/ over the moon *esp. Br.* col. very happy.
moon/ throw a moon *Br.* /*Am.* **hang a B.A**, *Am.* col. **shoot the moon**/ sl. bend over and show one's bare buttocks as a joke or to insult sb.
moonglade *Am.* moon path (on the water).
moonhead *Am.* col. mad man.
moonlight *Br.* /*Am.* **double-dip**/ hold two jobs at the same time.
moonlighter *Aus.* cattle thief, **moonlighting** *Aus.* cattle theft.
moonlight flit *Br.* col. an act of secretly escaping, esp. from sb. to whom one owes smth. / **do a**

moonlight (flit), do a bunk *Br.* col. blow town at night.

moonraker *Br.* sl. blockhead, fool.

moonshine, cane corn *esp. Am., Aus., Can.* strong alcoholic drink produced illegally: *He had also given them a package of tobacco and a bottle of moonshine vodka* - Time., *I'd discovered moonshine whiskey and girls* - Reader's Digest.

moonshiner *esp. Am.* producer of the illegal drinks: *Moonshiners are buying up all the sugar to make home brew.* - Time., *a pipe for a moonshiner's still* - National Geographic.

moor *esp. Br.* a wide, open, often high area of land, covered with rough grass or low bushes, not farmed because of its bad soil, also **moorland**.: *The moor is intersected with paths* – M. Daly.

moor fowl *Br.* red grouse.

moose *Am., Can.* elk.

moose milk *Can.* alcoholic drink of rum, milk, eggs, etc.

mooseberry *Am., Can.* cranberry.

moose pasture *Can.* sl. worthless or unproved mining claims.

moot *esp. Am.* (of a situation or action) adj. no longer likely to happen or exist: *the point was moot.* – C.R. Cross.

moot court *esp. Am., Can.* mock court in which law students practise imaginary cases.

mop the floor with *Am.* /*Br.* **wipe the floor with**/ completely defeat sb. in a game or argument.

mop smth. **up** *Br.* complete a piece of work or finish dealing with smth.

mopboard, washboard, scrub board, base, baseboard *Am.* /*Br.* **skirting board**/ a board fixed along the base of a wall where it meets the floor of a room.

mope around/about *Br.* move around a place in a sad, slow way.

moreish *Br., Aus.* col. very tasty (of food).

morgue *esp. Am., Aus.* a building or room where dead bodies are kept before being identified or examined by medical examiner.

The Mormon State *Am.* Utah.

morning coffee *Br.* /also *Br.* **elevenses**/ morning coffee.

morning dress 1. *esp. Br.* formal clothes worn by a man at a ceremony in the daytime. 2. *Am.* an informal dress worn by a woman, esp. when doing work in the home.

morning room *Br.* /*Am.* **dinette, breakfast room**/ room where breakfast is usu. taken.

mornings *esp. Am.* adv. during any morning.

morning tea *Br.* one given in British country hotels.

morphemics *esp. Am.* tech. morphology.

Morris Plan Bank *Am.* a private individual bank.

mortal *Br.* col. person of the stated kind, e.g. *a lazy mortal*.

mortician *esp. Am., Can.* /*esp. Br.* **undertaker**/ undertaker: *The mortician listened impressively* - E.L. Doctorow.

mortis lock *Br.* /*Am.* **dead bolt**, *Aus.* **dead lock**/ a lock that is enclosed within the edge of a door.

mortuary 1. *Br.* /*esp. Am., Aus.* **morgue**/. 2. *Am.* funeral parlour: *Her family in Indianapolis was best known for the mortuaries some of its members ran.* – K. Vonnegut, Jr.

MOS *Am.* military occupational speciality.

Moses basket *esp. Br.* bassinet.

mosey (around, down, etc.) 1. *esp. Am., Aus.* col. walk in an unnatural way: *No more need to mosey around the mansion* - T. Thompson., *I have been known to mosey along at four or five.* - R. Stout., *Well, I'll mosey along.* - B. Tillman. 2. *esp. Br.* walk or drive leisurely.

mosey along *Am.* col. humor. leave.

mosquito hawk *esp. Am., Can.* 1. night hawk. 2. dragonfly.

moss-back 1. *Am., Can.* col. an extreme conservative: *Walter, you are such an old mossback.* - R.A. Spears. adj. **-ed.** 2. *Am.* large fish or turtle.

mossy *Am.* col. old-fashioned or extreme conservative.

most *esp. Am., Can.* col. almost: *Most everyone laughed.* - R.L. Stine..

most secret *Br.* top secret.

mot *Irish Eng.* col. girl or young woman, esp. man's girlfriend.

moth-ball *Am.* store (smth. such as a ship, tank or machinery) protected against deterioration.

mother *esp. Am.* col. 1. any unspecified object, esp. smth. large in size: *He was a big mother, about six three and all muscle.* - S. Sheldon. 2. also *Can.* motherfucker, extremely stupid person.

mother/ Shall I be mother? *Br., Aus.* humor. Will you have some food and drinks?

mother/ Who's "she", the cat's mother? *esp. Br.* col. Don't use "she" about sb. who is here! It's rude.

Mother Goose rhyme *Am.* nursery rhyme.

Mother Hubbard *esp. Am.* loose-fitting shapeless woman's dress or nightgown.

Mothering Sunday, Mother's Sunday *Br.* obs. Sunday in Mid-Lent used to visit one's relatives.

a mother load of smth. *Am.* a large collection of particular type of things.

mother lode *Am.* 1. mine that is full of gold, silver, etc. 2. place where you can find a lot of particular type of object.

Mother of Presidents, Mother of States, Mountain state *Am.* joc. Virginia.

Mother of Rivers *Am.* New Hampshire.

mother's boy/mummy's boy *Br., Aus.* /*Am.* **mamma's boy**/ a man who allows his mother to protect him too much and is therefore considered weak.

Mother's Day (the second Sunday in May) *Am.* /*Br.* **Mothering Sunday** (the fourth Sunday in Lent)/.

mother's ruin *esp. Br.* col. humor. gin.

mother-sib /or **father-sib**/ *Am.* anthropology.

motion(s) *esp. Br., Aus.* (esp. doctors and nurses use) an act of emptying the bowels.

motion picture *esp. Am., Can.* film: *archaeological adviser to a motion picture company* - T. Wilder.

motion sickness *Am., Can.* sickness induced by motion (as in travel by car or ship) and characterised by nausea: *Prone to motion sickness, I felt myself getting a bit queasy.* - Reader's Digest.

motley/ on with the motley *Br.* obs. the show must go on despite anything.

motor 1. *Br.* col. a car: *a fast motor…would get here a good hour ahead of them* – M. Daly. 2. *Br.* becoming rare. v. travel by car, esp. for pleasure: *we motored in his Jaguar* - C. Handy. 3. *esp. Am.* a device that makes a vehicle move. 4. *Br.* adj. driven by a motor.

motor/ in *Br., Aus.* **motor** is used mainly for devices powered by electricity, in *Am.* it is commonly used for devices powered by petrol, steam, etc.

motor *Br., Aus.* connected with cars and vehicles which have engines and use roads.

motorbike 1. *esp. Br., Can.* col. /*Am., Can.* **motorcycle**/. 2. *Am.* a small light motorcycle: *I could see women in full long dresses rushing to work on motorbikes.* - J. Kerouac.

motor car, motor vehicle 1. *esp. Br.* obs. or *fml.* /*esp. Am.* **automobile**/ a car. 2. *Am.* railway carriage containing motors for propulsion.

motor caravan *Br.* /*esp. Am.* **motor home**/ a car which contains kitchen equipment, beds, etc. and used for holidays.

motor coach *Br.* intercity bus: *My friend, why this passion for the motor coach?* – M. Daly.

motor court *Am.* col. motel /also *Am.* **motor lodge**/: *roar off towards the cocktail lounges, motor courts, bowling alleys, gift shoppes and pizzerias.* - K. Vonnegut, Jr., *The new Foster Motor Lodge. We passed it on our way here.* – R.L. Stine.

motor cycle *esp. Am.* a vehicle with two wheels and an engine.

motordrome *Am.* track where people can watch car or motorcycle races.

motorhome *esp. Am., Can.* motor caravan: *organizations tailored to the needs of first-time buyers of motorhomes, travel trailers, folding camping trailers and truck campers.* – Reader's Digest.

motoring *esp. Br.* relating to cars and driving: *It's always pleasant to bring bad motoring news.* - B. Bryson.

motorist 1. *Br.* a newspaper motoring correspondent who covers the automobile industry work. 2. *esp. Br.* sb. who drives a car.

motor lodge *Am.* motel.

motor lorry *Br.* motor truck.

motormouth *esp. Am., Aus., Can.* sl. derog. very talkative person.

motor pool *Am.* also *esp. Am., Can.* **car pool**, group of cars owned by a company that its members can use.

motor-spirit *Br.* gasoline.

(divided) motorway, main road *Br.* 1. /*Am.* **interstate, expressway, (divided) highway** *Am., Aus., Can.* **freeway,** *Can.* **highway, thoroughfare**/ very wide road built for fast long-distance travel, esp. in **join motorway, freeway**: *Meanwhile in a drab motorway cafeteria, near Sheffield, George sat before a plate* - P. Norman., *the M4 Motorway from Swansea sweeps past it to London* - Economist. 2. col. wide, fast, easy ski run.

motorway with sliproad *Br.* /*Am.* **freeway with on-ramp**/

Motown *Am.* Detroit, Michigan.

motser, motza *Aus.* col. large sum of money, esp. won on gambling.

motto *esp. Br.* an amusing or clever short printed phrase put esp. inside a Christmas cracker.

mould/ in the same mould (as) *Br.* /*Am.* **from the same mold (as)**/ very similar.

mouldy *esp. Br.* 1. sl. unpleasant, of little value. 2. (used by children) a. nasty. b. stingy. 3. dull or depressing.

mouldy/ go mouldy *Br., Aus.* /*Am.* **get mouldy**/ (of cheese) become unappetizingly looking.

mount guard over sb. or smth. *esp. Br.* guard them.

mountain *Br.* a large amount of food which is kept in storage instead of being sold so that prices for it don't fall.

mountain/ a mountain to climb *esp. Br., Aus.* smth. very difficult to do.

mountain lion *Am., Can.* puma.

The Mountain State *Am.* West Virginia.

Mountie *Can.* col. member of a special Canadian police force which often works on horseback.

mouse *Am.* hunt for (smth.) by patient and careful search.

mouse mat *Br. /Am.* **mouse pad/** a flat piece of rubber or plastic that you use the mouse of computer on.

mousetrap (cheese) 1. *esp. Br.* derog. often humor. cheese that is old and hard, or of bad quality. 2. *Am., Can.* induce sb. to do smth. by means of a trick.

mouth/ be all mouth and (no) trousers *Br.* col. talk a lot.

mouth/ down in the mouth *Br.* unhappy and depressed.

mouth/ put the mouth on sb. *Br., Aus.* sl. make sb.'s actions unsuccessful by saying that he is doing very well.

mouth/ speak/talk out of both sides of one's **mouth** *Am.* be too opportunistic.

mouthful *esp. Am., Can.* col. a very important statement.

mouthful/ give sb. **a mouthful** *esp. Br.* col. speak angrily to sb.

mouthful/ say a mouthful *esp. Am., Can.* col. say a lot of true and important things about smth. in a few words.

mouthful/ that'a a bit of a mouthful *Br.* col. a difficult word or phrase to pronounce.

mouthful/ you said a mouthful *Am.* col. I completely agree with you.

mouthpiece *Am.* sl. a lawyer who defends people, charged with crimes: *She figured the quiet-looking man must be a mouthpiece.* - S. Sheldon., *But the mouthpieces and accountants had generally been privileged to begin with.* - J. O'Brien, A. Kurins.

movable feast *Br.* col. smth. that happens at different times, so that people don't know exactly when it will happen.

movant *Am.* law. applicant who petitions a court or judge to reach decision in his/her favour.

move *esp. Br.* col. go somewhere or leave a place.

move about/around *Br.* change one's position.

move along *Br.* move further towards the back or front of smth.

move (sb.) along, on *esp. Br.* officially order sb. to leave a public place.

move on to better things *Am.* get a better or more important job.

move out *Am.* col. leave.

move up *Br.* change position so that there is more space for other people or things.

move/ have all the moves *Am.* sl. be very skilful: *He's a prick but he's got all the moves.* - G.V. Higgins.

move/ make a move *Br.* col. leave a place.

move/move an amendment *Br.* propose a change.

move/ move house/home *Br., Aus.* take one's furniture and other property to a new home.

move/ move the goal *Am.* change the rules in a situation in a way that's not fair.

move/ move the goal-posts *Br., Aus.* col. change the limits within which action or talk relating to a particular matter can take place.

move/ time is moving on *Br.* col. you must do smth. because it's getting late.

movements *Br., Aus.* one's activities at present time.

mover *esp. Am., Can. /Br.* **remover,** *Aus.* **removalist/** person whose job is to help people move their houses: *fat furniture movers out of 1910 Charlie Chaplin films.* - J. Kerouac.

movers and shakers *esp. Am., Can.* people of power and influence: *movers and shakers behind the plan* - Arkansas Times.

movie *esp. Am., Can., Aus. /esp. Br.* **film/** a story, play, etc. recorded on film to be shown in the cinema, on television, etc.: *They were making this movie about Jesus Christ in Mexico City.* - J.A. Michener.

movie/ movie goers, movie audience *esp. Am., Aus. /esp. Br.* **cinema goers, film goers, cinema audience/**: *My interest in films was simply that of a movie goer.* - A.E. Hotchner.

movie land *Am.* 1. cinematography. 2. cinematographic industry.

movie house, movie theater *Am., Can., Aus. / esp. Br.* **cinema/** picture house: *And the movie houses and theatres are also doing a record business by featuring sleazy skin flicks* - Newsweek., *People were coming out of a movie theatre.* - I. Shaw.

movie projector *Am. /Br.* **film, cinema projector/** sound projector.

movie script *Am. /Br.* **film script/** shooting script.

movie set *Am. /Br.* **film set/**.

movie star *esp. Am. /esp. Br.* **film star/** a well-known actor or actress in cinema pictures: *Her clients have included movie stars and Empress Michico.* - Time.

movie studios *Am. /Br.* **film studios/** studio complex.

movies *esp. Am.* /*Br.* **cinema, pictures**/ the pictures.

moving picture *esp. Am.* obs., also *esp. Am.* **movie** /*esp. Br.* **film**/: *I look at women and men and subway excavations and moving pictures* - I. Shaw.

moving staircase *Br.* escalator.

moving van *Am.* /*Br.* **removal van**/: *I spotted the blue sedan hiding on the far side of a Rider moving van* - R. Crais.

moviola *Am.* an apparatus for taping sound in the cinema.

mow *Am., Can.* stack of hay, corn or other crop.

moxie *Am., Can.* col. 1. courage: *The senate showed enough Moxie to save fragments of the plan* - Time., *They had no character, no moxie* - J. O'Brien, A. Kurins. 2. know-how, skill: *you can't beat that pure Aryan Protestant stock for real business moxie?* - L. Waller., *All you need to make them work is moxie, grit and a sense of moral proportion.* - Esquire., *His rapid rise, based on business acumen and moxie* - G. O'Neill, D. Lehr. 3. initiative.

mozz/ put the mozz on *Aus.* col. jinx sb.

mozzer *Br.* sl. /*esp. Aus.* col. **mozzie**/ luck, good fortune: *That was a bit of mozzer* - T. Thorne.

mozzie, mossie *Br., Aus.* col. /*Am., Aus.* col. **skeeter**/ mosquito.

MP *Br.* Member of Parliament.

M Phil *Br.* Master of Philosophy.

Mr. *Br.* a form of address given to a dentist or a doctor who has attained the rank of surgeon.

Mr., Mrs. these abbreviations are usu. followed by full stop in *Am.*

MRA *esp. Am.* Moral Rearmament.

Mrs. Mop(p) *Br.* col. cleaning woman or lady.

MS, MSc *Am.* Master of science.

MTB *Br.* motor torpedo boat.

MTish language *Br.* (MT is a mother tongue)

much/ be much of a muchness *Br.* col. be very similar.

much/ not be up to much *esp. Br., Aus.* of not very high quality.

much/ there's not much/a lot in it *Br.* both things are very similar or equally good.

much oftener *Am.* /*esp. Br.* **more often**/.

muck *Br.* solid waste from animals.

muck/ be (as) common as muck *Br.* col. humor. behave like a person from a low social class.

muck/ make a muck of *esp. Br.* col. spoil or do (smth.) wrong or badly.

muck/ where there's muck, there's brass British saying *Br.* obs. a lot of money in dirty or unpleasant work.

muck about / around *esp. Br.* col. 1. behave in a silly or aimless way: *But someone's been mucking about with my private papers.* - A. Christie. 2. **muck** sb. **around** / **about** treat sb. without consideration.

muck in (with) *esp. Br.* col. join in work or activity (with others).

muck out *esp. Br.* clean out all the manure and old hay (in a stable, pigsty, etc.).

muck smth. **up** *esp. Br.* col. 1. make dirty: *they perched like eagles on top of the toilet and mucked the place up terribly* - R.G. Kaiser. 2. a. spoil (an arrangement). b. do smth. wrong: *What we have here is too large, too beautiful, and too mucked up for anyone to take it casually.* - H. Fast.

muckamuck *Am., Can.* col. very important person.

mucker *Br.* 1. col. friend, buddy. 2. a heavy fall, **go/come a mucker**.

muckered, spun out *Can.* tired.

muckheap *Br.* a pile of manure in a farmyard.

muck spreader *Br.* machine used to spread manure on fields.

muck-up *Br.* sl. foul-up.

mucky 1. *esp. Br.* (of weather) bad, stormy. 2. *Br.* col. dirty. 3. *Br.* col. pornographic. 4. *Br.* (of a joke, story, etc.) slightly rude or about sex.

mud/ Here's mud in your eye! *Br.* col. toast expressing friendly feelings: *Mud in your eye!* – J. Steinbeck.

mud/ mud sticks *esp. Br., Aus.* it's difficult to change people's opinions about sb. when smth. bad was said about them.

mud/ up to the mud *Aus.* sl. worthless.

mudbug *Am., Can.* freshwater crabfish.

The Mudcat State *Am.* Mississippi.

muddle *esp. Br.* 1. also **muddle up** put things in the wrong order. 2. **get** (smth./sb.) **muddled up** wrongly think that one person or thing is smth. or sb. else.

muddle along/on *Br.* continue doing smth. without having any clear plan.

muddle through *Br.* achieve smth. even though it was confusing or difficult.

muddy/ the Big Muddy *Am.* Mississippi.

muddy up *esp. Am.* cover (smth.) with mud: *You'll get your good boots all muddied up in the garden.* - Longman.

mudflap *Br., Aus.* /*Am.* **splash guard**/ a piece of rubber or other heavy material hanging behind the wheel of a vehicle, esp. a truck, to keep the mud from flying up., the same piece on a bicycle is **mudguard** (*Br.*), **fender** (*Am.*).

mudflat *Am.* the muddy bottom of a dry lake.

mudroom *Am.* hall of a rural house.

muesli *esp. Br.* /*Am.* **granola**/ grain, nuts, dried fruit, etc. mixed together and eaten with milk as a breakfast food: *She lights the gas stove, and makes herself a breakfast of muesli* - D. Lodge.

muff *Am.* taboo. sl. vagina.

muffin 1. *esp. Br., Aus.* /*Am.* **English muffin**/ a small spongecake served toasted: *Smither should toast him some more muffins* - J. Galsworthy., *one didn't mind asking for muffins* - G. Greene. 2. *esp. Am., Can., Aus.* /*Br.* **American muffin**/ small roll (which can be eaten with butter) or sweet cup cake (without icing): *the mice got at the blueberry muffins* - Newsweek.

muffin tin, cake pan *Am.* /*Br.* **cake tin**/.

muffle up 1. *esp. Am.* col. be quiet: *Muffle up at the back there!* - Longman. 2. *esp. Br.* col. put on warm clothes: *Better muffle up, it's cold outside.* - Longman.

muffler *Am., Can., Aus.* /*Br.* **(exhaust) silencer**/ part of a petrol engine which fits onto the exhaust pipe: *The studebaker had a split in the muffler.* - S. Bellow.

mug 1. *esp. Br., Aus.* col. a foolish person who is easily deceived: *you could always find a mug in the city to write a fat cheque for the production of a play* - W.S. Maugham., *we find some mug who's a once-a-year car racing fan.* - Bulletin., *he's been had for a mug* - J.D. Carr. 2. *Am.* col. hooligan.

mug *esp. Am.* a beer mug usu. with patterns cut into its sides.

mug *Am.* col. make silly expressions with one's face or behave in a silly way, esp. in a photograph or play.

mug(-shoot) *Am.* photograph made for the police.

mug up *esp. Br., Aus.* col. study with great effort, esp. when preparing for an exam: *there's a time to mug up on newspaper form.* - Gloucester Citizen.

muggins *Br.* col. humor. a fool, esp. when used of oneself.

mug's game *Br.* col. a course of action that is unlikely to be rewarding or profitable: *it's a mug's game.* - J. Joyce., *that make exporting a mug's game* - Economist., *I don't believe in betting. It's a mug's game.* - G. Greene.

mugwump *Am., Can.* derog. person who tries to be independent of the leaders in politics.

mukluks *Can., Am.* high snow boots, esp. sealskin boots: *She was to be seen, in a long dressing-gown lent by the hospital but shod in the mukluks* - W. Grady.

mule skinner *Am.* mule driver: *The mule skinner's name was Andy.* - J. Kerouac.

muley *esp. Am.* hornless cattle.

mulga *Aus.* a type of tree found in dry regions, or its wood.

the mulga *Aus.* col. the bush, outback, esp. in **live up the mulga.**

mulga wire *Aus.* gossip.

mull smth. *Am.* think about smth. for a long time before deciding what to do.

mullah, spondulicks *Am.* sl. money: *I supply the lineage, she supplies the mullah.* - J.P. Donleavy.

mulligan (stew) *esp. Am., Can.* a stew of meat or fish with vegetables: *the entree of fried catfish or Mulligan stew.* - S. North.

mullock *Aus., NZ.* 1. rock which contains no gold. 2. smth. worthless.

mullock/ poke mullock at *Aus., NZ.* col. ridicule sb.

Mully saw *Am.* a saw with a long stiff blade with motion directed by clamps at each end, mounted on guard rails.

multigym *Br.* a machine on which you can do several different exercises, or a room in which several different exercise machines can be found.

multiple store or **shop** /also col. **multiple**/ *esp. Br.* chain store.

multistorey *esp. Br., Aus.* /*Am.* **multistory**/ (of a building) having several levels or floors.

multi-storey *Br.* col. a multi-storey car park.

multiversity *Am.* university with a lot of faculties.

mum *Br., Aus.* /*Am.* **mom**/ col. mother.

mummy *Br., Aus.* /*Am.* **mommy, momma**/ (used esp. by or to children) mother: *It'll do you good, mummy.* - W.S. Maugham.

mumsy *Br.* col. derog. 1. a woman with an old-fashioned homely appearance. 2. humor. one's mother.

mum-to-be *Br.* col. mother-to-be.

munchies *esp. Am.* col. 1. **have the munchies** feel hungry. 2. small pieces of food: *Gianturo also brought along some munchies - eggplant sandwiches* - G. O'Neill., D. Lehr.

munchkin *Am., Can.* col. a child: *They looked like munchkins in person* – C.R. Cross.

municipalist *Br.* person who is skilled in a municipal administration.

murder/ I could murder smth. like beer, pizza, etc. *Br.* col. said if sb. wants to eat or drink smth. particular very badly.

murder/ scream/yell bloody murder *Am., Can., Aus.* col. /*Br.* **scream blue murder**/ shout or complain very loudly: *young black girls screaming bloody murder for Bull Moose* – E. James, D. Ritz.

murder one or two *Am., Can.* col. first or second degree murder.

murphy *Br.* sl. potato: *I spent half my tour of duty peeling murphies.* - R.A. Spears.

Murphey's law *esp. Am.* Sod's law, law stating that if there is a chance of smth. bad happening it will happen some time eventually.

The Muscrat State *Am.* Delaware.

museum *Am.* gallery, public building where paintings are shown.

mush 1. *Am., Can.* boiled corn (maize) in a sort of porridge: *his two children eating their breakfast - buckwheat mush* - J. Fischer. 2. *Br.* col. face. 3. *Br.* col. (angry or insulting form of address) fellow: *Are you asking for a punch up the faghole, mush?* - T. Thorne. 4. *Am., Can.* travel across snow with dog sledge: *they staked out their claims, mushed behind their dogs at a swift clip* - I. Stone.

musher 1. *Am., Can.* driver of a dog sled. 2. *Br.* col. taxi driver.

mush-mouthed *Am.* col. tongue-tied.

mushy peas *Br.* a food that is made from a type of large peas, eaten esp. in the North of England.

musical box /also *esp. Am.* **music box**/ *esp. Br.* a box containing a clockwork apparatus which plays music when the lid is lifted: *it is like putting a nickel in a music box.* - R.P. Warren.

musicale *Am., Can.* social entertainment with music as the leading feature: *Connie participated in a musicale at the University of St. Thomas.* - T. Thompson.

music centre *Br.* music system combining different equipment.

music hall *Br.* /*Am.* **vaudeville (theatre)**/ theatre entertainment with songs, jokes, acts of skill, etc.

muskeg *Am., Can.* a bog formed in a depression of land: *the bake-apples speckle the muskeg in late summer.* - K. Davis.

muslin 1. *Am.* calico: *Curtains might be of cotton muslin* - Kansas City Star. 2. *Br.* cheesecloth.

muso *Br.* col. musician, esp. one who likes to use a lot of electronics.

muss *Am.* (a state of) disorderly mess.

muss (up) *esp. Am., Can., Aus.* make a mess of (esp. the hair or clothes): *I never saw your hair mussed up before, Jon.* - T. Caldwell., *His brown hair was mussed with nervous rakings* - C. McCullers., *His hair was straight and black and girls liked to muss it.* - I. Shaw.

must *esp. Am.* adj. comb. form. (used for suggesting that smth. is absolutely necessary or highly desirable): *A must-see for English literature students* - BigO.

must/ some *esp. Am.* speakers use have to instead of must (= certainly) **You have to be joking** / You can't be cold also *esp. Am., Aus.* **You mustn't be cold** / *esp. Br.* **You can't have been cold** / also *esp. Am.* **You mustn't have been cold** - Longman.

mustache *Am.* moustache.

mustard/ all to the mustard *Am.* made good as it needs to be done.

mustard/ English mustard *Br.* one mixed with water.

mustard/ not cut mustard *Am.* sl. be unimportant.

mustard keen *Br.* adj. enthusiastic.

mustard greens *esp. Am.* the leaves of mustard used in salads.

mustard pickle *Br.* cucumbers pickled in mustard sauce.

muster *Aus., NZ.* round up livestock.

muster *Aus.* col. number of people attending a meeting.

muster sb. **in (or out)** *Am.* enrol sb. into (discharge sb. from) military service.

must-list *Am.* a list of things to be done first.

mutes *Br.* professional pall bearers.

mutt 1. *esp. Am., Aus.* col derog. a dog of no particular breed: *The dog asks an older, wiser mutt how life is different under Gorbachev.* - H. Smith. 2. *esp. Am.* col. a person who behaves in a silly or careless way.

mutt *Br.* a stupid person.

mutton/ mutton dressed (up) as lamb *Br.* col. derog. old woman dressed in a way that is more suitable for a much younger woman.

mutton cloth *Br.* cheesecloth.

Mutual fund *Am., Can.* /*Br.* **unit trust**/ a company through which one can buy shares in many different businesses.

mutuel *esp. Am.* totalizator or pari-mutuel.

muumuu *Am.* long loose dress.

muzzy *esp. Br.* col. 1. confused and unable to think clearly, esp. when drunk. 2. (of a picture) blurred and unclear.

MVP *Am., Can.* col. most valuable player.

myall *Aus.* Aboriginal living in traditional, uncivilised way.

mynah/ Indian mynah *Aus.* a bird from Asia, some types of which can copy human voice.

mystery bags *Aus.* sl. sausages: *Mystery bags... snags...sausages.* - T. Thorne.

mystery tour *Br.* pleasure excursion to unspecified place.

N

Nth *Br.* /*esp. Am.* **No**/ North(ern).
nabe *Am.* col. 1. neighbourhood 2. neighbourhood motion picture theatre: *We have entered the nabe* - Esquire.
nada *Am., Can.* col. nothing: *No music lessons. No play dates. Nada.* – Reader's Digest.
naff *Br.* col. (of things, ideas, behaviour, etc.) foolish or worthless, esp. in a way that shows a lack of good judgement or good taste: *it was naff to put on a suit and tie* - B. Bryson.
naff off *Br.* col. rude way of telling sb. to go away.
naffing *Br.* col. intensifier. damned.
nail 1. *esp. Am., Can.* (of a player) defeat or outwit an opponent. 2. *esp. Am.* sl. (of a man) have sexual intercourse.
nail smth./sb. **down** *Am.* reach a final and definite decision about smth.
nail / nail sb's **ass to the wall** *Am.* sl. esp. newspapers. severely punish sb.
nail/nail one's **colours to the mast** *Br.* say clear and publicly which ideas person supports.
nail/ on the nail 1. *Br., Aus.* /*Am.* **(cash) on the barrelhead**/ everything done at once; in cash and immediately. 2. *Am.* completely correct.
nailarium *Am.* a manicurist's salon.
nailrod *Aus.* shag tobacco used by bushmen.
nail varnish *Br., Aus.* /*Am.* **nail polish**/ coloured or transparent liquid which is painted on nails to give them a hard shiny surface: *a billowing fold overset a small bottle of nail varnish.* - M.M. Kaye., *she bought herself lipstick and nail varnish.* - D. Lessing.
naked/ buck/butt naked *Am.* completely naked.
name *esp. Am.* famous, well-known: *Of the twenty-nine name fighters I met, fifteen stayed down for the count of ten.* - Playboy.
name for *Am., Can.* /*Br.* **name after**/.
name sb. **to** smth. *Am.* officially choose sb.
name a member *Can.* make sb. leave the meeting.
name to conjure with *esp. Br.* a very important person.
name-calling *Am.* saying insulting things about sb.
namecheck *esp. Am.* col. refer to sb. specifically by name.
name part *Br.* title role.
nametape *Br.* /*Am.* **label**/ small piece of cloth with one's name on it that is sewn onto clothes.

namma *Aus.* little lake, well.
nana *Br.* col. a fool.
nance *Am.* derog. sl. /*Br.* **nancy (boy)**/ a homosexual.
nanny *esp. Br.* 1. a woman employed to take care of children in a family. 2. also col. a **nan(n)a** a grandmother: *Nana, granny, grams.* – *Pick up a title that denotes your wife's special role* – Reader's Digest.
the nanny state *Br.* derog. state with a government that tries to control their citizens' lives too much.
nap *Br.* col. 1. (esp. of a newspaper writer) say that one thinks a certain horse will win a race. 2. n. a tip (on the horse) / **go nap** stake a lot, bet one's stack; **not go nap on** *Aus.* col. not be too keen on.
nap *Aus.* col. bedroll for sleeping in in the open.
nap selection *Br.* expert's list of betting recommendation.
nap/ bring / get sb.'s **nap** *Am.* get sb. angry.
napkin *Br., Am.* /*Can.* **serviette, table napkin**/.
nappy also **napkin** 1. *Br., Aus.* /*Am., Can.* **diaper**/ baby cloth: *Wayne Sleep jumped out of nappies long ago.* - You. 2. *Am.* shallow open serving dish. 3. also **sanitary napkin** *esp. Am., Can.* sanitary towel.
napper *Br.* col. person's head.
nappy *Am.* col. (of black person's hair) tightly curled and twisted: *I got older and started cursing bad as any jet-black nappy-haired man or woman* – E.James, D. Ritz.
nappy rash *Br., Aus.* /*Am.* **diaper rash**/ a rough area of skin around baby's bottom that has become so because it has been rubbed by a wet nappy.
narc, nark 1. *esp. Am., Can.* col. narcotics detective: *Everybody is hunting around and half of them're narcs.* - G.V. Higgins. 2. *esp. Aus.* sl. troublesome person. 3. *esp. Br.* col. derog. obs. becoming rare. /*Am.* **stool pigeon**/ informer: *I regret to inform you like a copper's nark* - P. Howard. 3. *Aus., NZ.* annoying person or thing.
narco *Am.* col. 1. narcotic. 2. dealer in narcotics. 3. narcotics detective.
narcotic *esp. Am.* illegal drug, such as heroin and cocaine.
nark *Br., Aus.* col. 1. annoy, make angry: *I like narking people.* - T. Thorne. 2. complain. 3. betray, **narked** *Br.* col. sore, angry.
nark it *Br.* col. stop doing smth.: *Nark it! The police is coming!* - Longman.
narky *Br.* col. bad-tempered: *I didn't mean to get narky with you.* – R. Westall.

narrow bed *Br.* grave.
narrow boat *Br.* long narrow boat for use on canals.
narrow casting *Am.* cable casting.
narrows *Am.* narrow part of a river, lake, etc.
narrow squeeze *Br.* narrow escape or victory.
nary *Am., Can.* col. not a bit: *nary a one of the incorporeal benefits he dreamed of* - H.H. Richardson., *your characters have nary a concern* - C. Hoover.
nasty/ do the nasty *Am.* sl. have sex.
nasty/ get/turn nasty *esp. Br.* col. suddenly start behaving in a threatening way.
nasty piece (bit) of work *Br., Aus.* unpleasant person.
natch *Am.* sl. naturally.
the nation *Am.* 1. our country, USA (also **this nation**): *it was duly reported in countless other papers across the nation.* – F. Edwards. 2. Americans.
National Assistance *Br.* obs. social security, welfare payments to the needy.
National cemetery *Am.* military cemetery.
National convention *Am.* party congress.
National grid *Br., Aus.* a network of electric power supply lines or similar structure of water or gas pipes.
National Health Service *Br.* the state system for providing medical care paid for by taxes.
National holiday *Am.* legal holiday: *even the strict observance of national holidays had been a conscious noble decision* – P. Roth.
National Insurance *Br.* the state system of paying money to people who are ill, unemployed or retired.
National monument *Am.* historic sight monument.
National seashore *Am.* public beach.
National service 1. *Br. /Am.* **selective service, draft/** the system of making all persons serve in the armed forces for a limited period: *Just to look at them made Vic want to start campaigning for the restoration of National Service* - D. Lodge. 2. *Am.* a system in which young persons spend a period of time doing useful work for their country, such as repairing old houses, putting out forest fires or teaching children.
Nation of shopkeepers *Br.* England: *Neither the Spanish Armada, nor Napoleon nor Hitler could conquer the nation of shopkeepers* - Mclean's.
The Nation's State *Am.* District Columbia.
native 1. *Aus.* (about a white man) native citizen of Australia. 2. *Br.* oyster reared in British waters, esp. in artificial beds. 3. *Aus., NZ.* resembling other animals and plants familiar elsewhere; e.g. **native bear** *Aus.* koala bear
Native son *Am.* a native of one of the states of the USA: *There were two or three native-son nominations that year* - H. Truman.
natter (away, on) *esp. Br.* col. v. n. chatter: *Perhaps I'm drunk? I'm nattering.* - L. Waller., *societies have merely been nattering about it.* - Cheshire Life., *people chattering and nattering all over the house.* - M.M. Kaye.
naturalisation papers *Br.* citizenship papers.
natural-born fool, singer, etc. *Am.* col. sb.who has always had a particular quality or skill without having to try hard.
(natural) wastage *Br. /Am., Aus.* **attrition/** a reduction of people working for some organisation which is achieved by not replacing those who leave.
nature strip *Aus.* piece of public land between the front boundary of a building and the street.
naugahyde *Am.* leatherette, cheap material made to look like leather.
naught *Am., Aus. /Br.* **nought/** zero.
naughty *esp. Br.* used jokingly about adult when sb. pretends to disapprove of their behaviour.
naughty bits *Br.* col. humor. sexual scenes.
naughty jokes/ magazines/pictures, etc. *Br.* dealing with sex in a rude but not very serious way.
nauseous *esp. Am.* col. feeling nausea or great distaste, */esp. Am.* **nauseated/**: *Now I felt nauseated by the idle chatter* – Reader's Digest.
naval academy *Am.* naval college.
naval dockyrd *Br.* Navy yard.
naval establishment *Am.* naval forces.
naval officer *Am.* customs officer.
navvy *Br.* obs. col. labourer doing a heavy unskilled job in digging and building: *he could see the six-year-old face convulsed like a navvy's with labour.* - G. Greene., *I missed seeing women navvying on the job* - L. Van Der Post.
navy bean *esp. Am., Can.* haricot.
naw *Am., Can.* col. no.
naysay *esp. Am.* say no, deny, oppose.
nayword *esp. Br.* 1. watchword. 2. byword.
NC-17 *Am.* (of a film) no children under 17 admitted, because of showing scenes of sex acts and a lot of violence.
Neanderthal *esp. Am.* person who unthinkingly opposes all change, reactionary.
near/ (as) near as dammit/damn it *Br.* col. almost true; almost happened.
near/ come/be near (to) doing smth. *esp. Br.* almost do smth.

nearside 1. *esp. Br., Aus.* adj. on the left-hand side, esp. of an animal, car or road. 2. *Br.* **nearside lane** slow lane, the lane nearest the edge of the road.

near-sighted *esp. Am.* /*esp. Br.* **short-sighted**/ seeing clearly only the objects which are close to them; n. **-ness.**

neat 1. *esp. Am., Can.* col. very good, very pleasant, fine: *it would be neat to have Jeane-Claude around to help.* - E. Segal., *Preppies use favoured hurray-words such as "neat", "tremendous", "love"* - P. Howard., *It's neat to watch someone who loves what they are doing.* - Maclean's. 2. *esp. Br.* strong alcoholic drink without anything like tonic or water added to it. 3. *Am.* /*Br.* **tidy**/.

nebbish *Am.* sl. a dull person: *She was a Jewish girl from Brooklin and made no bones about it larding her conversation with words like shmur and schmuck and nebbish.* - I. Shaw.

neck *Br.* col. allow smth., esp. a drink.

neck/ (brass) neck *Br.* col. nerve (impudence).

neck/ get in the neck *Br., Aus.* col. be punished for smth.

neck/ shot in the neck *Am.* sl. drunk.

neck/ talk through (the back of) one's **neck** *esp. Br.* sl. talk nonsense.

necktie *esp. Am., Can.* tie: *I wore my guns as today I wear my necktie.* - Alex Haley.

necktie party *Am., Can.* col. lynching or hanging: *the cowboys caught them and had a necktie party.* - A. Makkai.

neddy *Aus.* (race) horse.

Ned Kelly *Aus.* sl. belly.

Ned Kelly/ game as Ned Kelly *Aus.* very brave.

need / In British English need can be both a modal verb and an ordinary verb, as a modal, it is most often used in questions and negatives, e.g. *You needn't have done that.* In American English it is not used as a modal.

need/ *She needs her hair washed* /(*Br.*) *washing*.

needful *Br.* humor. money.

needle *Am.* col. 1. strengthen a beverage with whiskey, wine, etc. 2. colour the truth.

needle *Br.* col. tease. n. irritation, resentment, hostility, provoked by rivalry.

needle cord *Br.* fine- ribbed corduroy fabric.

needle match *Br.* grudge match, (hotly contested match with some ceremony): *Granger's lads engage in a needle match of dominoes.* - D. Francis.

needletime *Br.* the airtime in radio broadcasting devoted to recorded music.

needn't, mustn't, oughtn't / The contracted forms are common in British English but rarely used in American English.

needs must (when the devil drives) *Br.* obs. a person must do smth. they don't like because they are in trouble.

neighbor with *Am.* have a friendly relationship with (sb.): *I was only trying to neighbour with her!* - Longman.

nelly *Br.* sl. foolish or feeble person.

nelly/ not on your Nelly *Br., Aus.* col. humor. certainly not: *Not on your Nelly.* – J.P. Donleavy.

(the) Nelson touch *Br.* masterly or sympathetic approach to the problem.

neocon *esp. Am.* neoconsevative.

nerd *esp. Am.* col. /*Br.* col. **nerk/** foolish boring person.

nerdish, nerdic, nerdy *Am.* sl. /*Aus.* **nurdish/** tiresomely, gormless, stupid and thoughtless: *a terminally nerdy male* - Rolling Stone., *Nerdy kids like me weren't real popular in those days.* - Reader's Digest.

nerve oneself **to do** smth. *Br.* become brave enough to do smth.

nerves/ be a bag of nerves *Br.* col. be very nervous.

nerves/ live on one's **nerves, live on** one's **nerve ends** *Br., Aus.* be always anxious.

nervous/ nervous about smth. *Am.* /*Br.* **nervous of** smth./: *she was nervous about me taking her to the airport* – Reader's Digest.

nervous Nelly *Am.* sl. any nervous person: *And do you think you have Nervous Nellies in your caucus?* - McLean's.

nervy col. 1. *esp. Br.* nervous and anxious: *I'm a little nervy about it.* - E. Hemingway., *The whole business was pretty nervy.* - A. Christie., *Suddenly he was again the nervy and despairing priest* - G. Greene. 2. *Am., Can.* disrespectfully rude, having nerve; brave and confident: *I considered myself nervy and cunning enough to live by my wits* - Alex Haley., *that was a darn nervy thing to do* - J. Dos Passos.

nest/ foul one's **own nest** *Br.* spoil one's chances of success by one's own actions.

nesting *Br.* a search for birds nests to get eggs / **to go nesting.**

nestle/ grasp the nettle *Br., Aus.* take action at once to deal with unpleasant situation.

net *esp. Am.* earn a particular amount of money as a profit after having paid taxes.

net/ cast/spread one's **net wide** *Br.* be involved in a lot of activities or have a wide choice of things to choose from.

netball *Br.* a ball game usu. played by women.

net cord judge *Br.* /*Am.* **net judge/** tennis judge who watches how the ball flies over the net.

net curtain(s) *Br.* pieces of lacy material that people hang on their windows.
nett *Br.* net (of an amount) when nothing further is to be subtracted.
nettle rash Br. condition that causes areas of red spots on one's skin.
nettlesome *esp. Am.* annoying.
network 1. *esp. Br.* broadcast (a program) over a radio or TV network. 2. *Am.* cover with a network of railways.
network announcer *Am.* radio or television announcer.
neutralist *Am.* tending not to support either side in a war, quarrel, etc.
never *Br.* col. excl. surely not: *He's never 55. It's hard to believe that he's 55.*
never/ no I never *Br.* col. used by a child when they say that they didn't do smth. bad when other people say that they did.
never-never 1. **on the never-never** *Br.* humor. col. /also *Br.* **by hire purchase,** *Am.* **by installment plan**/: *The never-never on my motorbike, Sir.* - D. Francis. 2. *Aus.* the inner part of the country (esp. remote region of north-western Queensland).
new boys/girls *esp. Br.* /*Am.* col. **the new kid on the block**/ children who have recently started going to school or new people in activity or organisation.
new broom *esp. Br., Can.* a newly appointed person who is eager to make changes: *He's still Mr New Broom, slightly feared.* - D. Lodge.
new-day *Am.* contemporary.
New Englander, New Englisher *Am.* a citizen of New England.
Newfie *Can.* sl. a Newfoundlander.
the new kid on the bloke *Am., Aus.* /*esp. Br.* humor. **new boy/girl**/ novice in a place.
a New Man *esp. Br., Aus.* person who believes in the equality of sexes and helps his/her partner with the care of the children and by sharing the work about the house.
New Mexican *Am.* a citizen of New Mexico.
the new rich *Am.* people who have become rich recently.
newsagent *Br., Aus.* /*Am.* **news dealer**/ a person who owns or works in a shop (**newsagent's**) which sells newspapers and magazines, as well as sweets, cigarettes and stationery: *Newsagents do not have to open* - Observer., *He stopped at a newsagent's to read the headline of a placard.* - J. Joyce., *popular freaks, such as old athletes, crippled newsdealers* - J. O'Hara.

news bulletin 1. *Br.* a short news program on radio or TV. 2. *Am.* /*Br.* **newsflash**/ a short news programme about smth. important that has just happened, that is broadcast suddenly in the middle of a TV or radio programme.
newscast *esp. Am.* a news programme on the radio and TV.
newsie, newsy /also *esp. Am.* **paper boy, girl, newsboy**/ *Am.* newsboy: *How come you're slap bang in the middle of all them gooks, newsie?* - R. Borchgrave, R. Moss., *A tough-talking Federal agent yelled at the newsies.* - Newsweek.
newsmaker *Am.* a newsworthy person or event: *prison life served to hone the latent communicative talents of one of America's top newsmakers.* - E. Cleaver.
New South *Aus.* /also **Ma (State)**/ New South Wales.
newspaper post *Br.* /*Am. Can.* **second class mail** /one for newspapers and magazines/.
newspaper proprietor *Br.* publisher.
newsreader *esp. Br., Aus.* /*Am.* **anchor**/ newscaster.
news release *esp. Am.* a written statement about a matter of public interest given to the press by the organisation concerned with the matter.
news stall *Br.* newsstand.
news to this hour /or **on the hour**/ *Am.* latest news (on the radio).
newsvendor *Br.* newspaper seller.
newsy 1. *esp. Am., Aus.* boy selling or delivering newspapers. 2. *esp. Am.* col. a reporter.
New Year *Br.* n. the beginning of the year.
New Year's *esp. Am., Can.* col. adj. of or related to the first day or beginning of the year; New Year's Eve or Day: *Noel Coward wrote in his diary after spending New Year's at the Palm Springs house.* – A. Summer's, R. Swan.
next door *Br.* col. people living in the house or apartment next to sb.
next door to *Br.* nearly the same as.
next to last day *esp. Am.* the day before the last day.
next turning/ beyond the next turning *Br.* in the next block.
nibbles *Br.* col. small amounts of food that are eaten between or before meals, often with alcoholic drinks.
a nice little earner *Br., Aus.* col. a profitable job or business.
nice/ make nice(-nice) *Am., Can.* col. be extremely polite to sb., esp. hypocritically.
Nice one! *Br., Aus.* col. said about clever, amusing or helpful remark, idea, etc.

nice to hear you *Br.* nice to hear your voice (on the telephone).

nice meeting you *Am.* col. /*esp. Br.* **nice/pleased/glad to meet you/** it's nice to have met you: *And then I added, "Nice meeting you."* – R.L. Stine

nice talking to you *Am.* col. it's been pleasant, good-bye (on leave-taking): *Nice talking to you, but I need to catch up on my sleep.* - J.P. Hogan.

Nice work! *Br.* col. Well done!

nick 1. *Br., Aus.* col. prison /*Am.* sl. **the slammer/** or police station, esp. in the phr. **in the nick**: *Being in the nick brought detachment to my writing.* - Bulletin. 2. *Br., Aus.* col. a stated physical condition, shape, often in phr. **in good/bad nick**: *She's gone right down t' nick over the last three days.* - J. Herriot.

nick 1. *esp. Br., Aus.* col. steal: *They started nicking his clothes.* - P. Norman., *The famous Australianism sheila is probably Irish, and so it is said, are colloquialisms like to nick, to nobble, to peg out, and to take a rise out of somebody.* - R. McRum, W. Cran, R. McNeil., *someone else had nicked the caps anyway.* - New Idea. 2. *Br., Aus.* col. arrest: *The cops nicked Paul outside his house.* R.A. Spears. 3. (for) *esp. Am., Can.* col. overcharge; cheat sb. of smth.: *He started nicking a few bucks here and there* - W. Jack, B. Laursen. 4. *Aus.* col. move quickly trying not to be noticed, often in **nick off**.

Nickel! *Am., Can.* a penny for your thoughts!

nickel-and-dime *Am.* col. 1. draining in small increments: *Cuts on that scale cannot be carried out by any nickel-and-dime process.* - Time. 2. unimportant; cheap: *that screams of nickel-and-diming.* - BigO. 3. not important or too concerned; ordinary.

nickel-and-dime *Am.* col. charge sb. small amounts of money for doing smth.; function on a small scale: *Companies, hard pressed for money are taking every possible opportunity to nickel-and-dime people to death.* – Reader's Digest.

nickelodeon *Am., Can.* 1. cheap entertainment place. 2. jukebox: *another assortment of teenage zoot-suited music-lovers who feed the nickelodeon at Capy's Grill on Saturday nights.* - M. Torgov.

nicker *Br.* col. a pound: *It was well over a thousand nicker.* - A. Burgess.

niff *Br.* col. bad smell. **niffy** adj.: *the diarrhoeal niff of liquid cheese from the kitchen.* - A. Burgess.

niggerhead *esp. Am., Can.* 1. tangled mess of the roots and decayed remains of sedges in a swamp. 2. black rounded rock stone or coral. 3. strong black tobacco.

nigger heaven *Am.* the gods (in theatre).

night/ have a bad night *Br.* not sleep much.

night/ it'll be all right on the night *Br.* col. everything will be all right in the end.

nightclub/ go nightclubbing *Br.* spend an evening at a nightclub.

night club hostess *Br.* /*Am.* **B-girl/**.

night crawler *esp. Am., Can.* a large night worm (used as a bait in fishing): *an appetizing bait of night crawlers on the hook.* - S. North.

night depositary *Am.* /*Br.* **night safe/** special hole at the outside wall of a bank into which a customer can put money or documents when the bank is closed.

nightery, nitery *Am.* col. night club.

nightgown *esp. Am.* /*esp. Br.* **nightdress/**: *She emerged a few minutes later in her nightgown and bathrobe.* - E. Segal., *she stood there at the doorway in her nightgown.* - I. Shaw.

night hawk 1. *Am., Can.* night owl. 2. *esp. Am.* col. person who enjoys staying awake all night.

night letter(gram) *Am.* one sent at night at a reduced rate: *I can say more for the same price in a night letter.* - A. Makkai.

nights *Am.* during any night.

night safe *Br.* safe with access from the outer wall of the bank for the deposit of money when the bank is closed.

nightspot *Am.* col. night restaurant: *It is the granddaddy of several other nightspots around town.* - A. Frommer.

night stand/table *Am.* a small table beside a bed: *I sat on my bed and stared at the phone beside me on the nightstand.* – RL. Stine.

nightstick *Am., Can.* /*Br., Aus.* **truncheon,** *Am.* **billy(club), baton/** policeman's truncheon: *his fingers wet on the long nightstick in his hands* - I. Shaw., *police patrolled the freshly strung fence rattling their nightsticks along it as they walked.* - Newsweek., *Brother Hinton was attacked with nightsticks.* - Alex Hailey.

night table *Am., Can.* low bedside table, often with drawers.

nig-nog *Br.* sl. taboo. obs. derog. coloured person.

nil *Br.* /*esp. Am.* **zero, nothing/** nothing, esp. the number 0 in sports results: *There is a new notice over my bed. It says "Nil by mouth!"* – S. Townsend.

nil norm, also **zero norm** *Br.* standard of minimum wage and price increases set by government.

991 candidate *Am.* sl. one who is put up for election at the last moment when another candidate or candidates from the same party seems unlikely to be successful (in Britain 999).

ninepence/ be as right as ninepence *Br.* obs. be very fit and wealthy.

ninepins/ go down/fall/drop like ninepins *Br.* be injured or fail in large numbers.

nines/ dressed up to the nines *Br.* very smartly dressed.

Nineteen Suburbs Looking for a Town / in search of a Metropolis *Am.* Los Angeles.

ninety-nine *Br.* cone of ice-cream with a stick of flaky chocolate in it.

nine yards/ go the whole nine yards *esp. Am., Can.* col. go on doing smth. dangerous or difficult: *They fly you here, put you up - the whole nine yards.* - K. Ablow.

ning-nong *Aus.* col. fool.

nip/ put (stick) the nips into sb. *Aus.* col. borrow money from sb.

nip *Am.* a strong taste. adj. **nippy.**

nip *Br.* col. a small amount of strong alcoholic drink.

nip *Br.* 1. col. also *Aus.* go quickly or for a short time: *Are you supposing her to have nipped into her bed* - A. Christie., *He nipped away in a blind rage.* - J.D. Carr., *they had meant to nip across to Biarritz* - A. Huxley. 2. suddenly and accidentally press smth. tightly between the edges or surfaces.

nip in *Br.* col. move quickly sideways in traffic or in a race.

a nip and (a) tuck 1. *Am.* col. a plastic surgery done to improve the appearance of one's face. 2. *Am.* small changes or reductions made in order to improve smth., often in **a nip here and a tuck there.**

nip and tuck/ be nip and tuck, neck-and-neck *Am.* col. be equal competitors: *neck-and-neck with the fearsome New York Yankees* – Reader's Digest.

nip and tuck *Am.* col. 1. arriving or finishing smth. just in time. 2. equally likely to happen or not happen: *So if you could nip it or tuck it, push it or pull it, she had it done.* – Reader's Digest.

nipper *esp. Br., Aus.* col. a child, esp. a small boy.

nippers *Am.* col. handcuffs, leg fetters.

nipping *Br. /Am.* **smash/** print. a pressing that takes place in book binding after the case has been applied to improve its formation.

nipple *Am. /Br.* **teat/** teat on the end of a baby's bottle.

nippy *Br.* (usu. of a car) able to move quickly.

Nisei *Am.* first-generation Japanese-American: *He didn't seem to expect I would be Nisei.* - B. Tillman.

Nissen hut *Br. /Am.* **Ouonset hut/** a shelter whose roof and side walls are made in one round piece from iron sheets: *a light went suddenly on in one of the Nissen huts* - G. Greene.

nit 1. *Br., Aus.* col. derog. nitwit, a fool: *only a raving nit would take a job there.* - D. Francis., *You thought he was an old Etonian nit.* - J. Fowles. 2. *Aus.* col. excl. of warning that sb. is approaching.

nit/ pick nits *esp. Am., Can.* look for and criticize small faults.

Nitchie *Can.* Canadian Indian.

nite *esp. Am., Can.* col. night.

nit-lamp *Can.* lamp used for fishing or hunting at night.

nitrochalk *Br.* fertiliser used to make grass grow.

nix *esp. Am.* col. 1. also *Aus.* adv. no. 2. v. (esp. in newspapers) answer no to, forbid, reject: *Columbia nixed the offer* - Time., *The Pats nixed a deal for George over money* - USA Today., *Hence even pilot studies to test the approach may get nixed* - Omni. 3. nothing.

no-account *esp. Am., Can.* col. n., adj. (a person of) of little use.

Noah('s) *Aus.* col. shark.

nob 1. *esp. Br.* col. derog. or humor. a rich person with a high social position: *It's hard to tell with the titled nobbies.* - T. Murphy. 2. *Br.* sl. the head.

nobble *Br.* col. 1. prevent (a racehorse) from winning, esp. by giving it drugs: *nobbled him with a squirt of acid* - D. Francis. 2. get the attention of (sb.), esp. in order to persuade them or ask for a favour. 3. seize: *So far oligos have been shown to nobble herpes and AIDS viruses.* - Economist. 4. also *Aus.* steal, get dishonestly. 5. bribe or threaten sb. in order to make them do smth. 6. prevent sb. from achieving what they want.

nobble *Br.* sl. 1. a trick: *the nobble is to give me some money and I'll get you some (drugs).* - T. Thorne. 2. a race horse.

nobbler *Aus., NZ.* a glass of beer or hard liquor.

No bear! *Br., Aus.* col. I don't want to do it.

nobody home *Am.* sl. this person is crazy or a fool.

no brainer *esp. Am., Can.* col. smth. that can be achieved without much intelligence: *Really, a no-brainer. Peter Kump's New York cooking school* - New York.

no can do *Am.* sl. I am unable or unwilling to do that: *It's what I told you "no can do"*. - D. Hammet.

no-claims bonus *Br., Aus.* an amount subtracted from the money paid to insurance company, esp. for the motor vehicles, because no claims have been made for a certain period of time.

nod/ a nod and wink *Br.* communication by saying smth. directly, esp. when two persons easily understand each other.

nod/ give/get the nod/ sb. **the nod** *Br., Aus.* col. permit sb. to do smth.

nod/ on the nod *esp. Br., Aus.* col. 1. obs. on credit. 2. accepted without discussion, esp. in **go through/ be approved/be passed on the nod.**

a nod's as good as a wink or **a wink's as good as a nod (to a blind man)** *Br., Aus.* col. this small thing helps to do it just as well; smth. understood quite easily, esp. smth. that concerns illegal matters.

noddle *Br.* col. obs. /*Am.* col. obs. **noodle/** the head of a person or their ability to think.

no duh *Am.* col. I've known it before.

No entry *Br.* Do not enter. (Road sign indicating one-way street).

noggin *esp. Am.* col. the head or mind of a person.

no-go area *esp. Br.* col. an area, esp. in a city controlled by one of two opposed groups and dangerous for anyone else to enter.

no good, no-gooder, no-goodnick *Am., Aus.* col. derog. worthless person or thing: *All day I work and see no-goods on Hotel Street.* - J.A. Michener., *Tommy Agro is a no good* - J. O'Brien, D. Lehr.

no-hoper *Aus., Br.* col. worthless, lazy person, a loser: *But men's surgical was the real no-hopers.* – R. Westall.

nohow *esp. Am.* non-standard. not in any way.

noise/ be a lot of noise *Am.* be a chatter box.

noise/ be noised abroad/about/around *esp. Br.* col. be much talked about.

noisemaker *Am., Can.* a device which can be used to make noise, esp. a horn or rattle for use at a party or sports match.

no-knock *Am.* relating to search made by police without permission or warning.

no-load *Am., Can.* (of shares in mutual fund) sold directly to the buyer by the firm: *the so-called no-load funds that do not charge commissions when you buy or sell shares* – Reader's Digest.

no-lose *Am.* sl. said of smth. that will certainly have a happy and successful result.

no messing *Br.* col. I've done it completely.

and no messing *Br.* col. without any difficulties.

non-affiliated/non-sectarian school *Am.* /*Br.* **non-denominational** or **secular school**/.

non-affiliated union *Am.* one not included in any trade union organisation.

no-name *esp. Am., Can.* (of a product) having no brand name.

nonconformist churches *Br.* protestant churches which are not part of the Church of England.

none *Am.* not a bit: *The doctor arrived none too soon, as Mary's high fever was very alarming.* - H.C. Whitford., R.J. Dixson.

nong *Aus.* col. (also **drongo, dill, galah**) a fool.

non-immigrant *Am.* foreign tourist.

nonism *Am.* abstention from activities and substances considered damaging to one's health and well-being.

non-lethal *esp. Am.* (of foreign aid) in the form of, or for the purpose of buying food, clothing, and medical supplies.

non-net *Br.* (of a book) not subject to a minimum selling price.

nonpareil *Am.* round concoction of chocolate covered with white sugar sprinkles.

nonpareils *Am.* very small pieces of coloured sugar used to decorate cakes.

non-profit-making *Br.* /*esp. Am.* usu. **non-profit, not-for-profit/** not run in order to make a profit: *a nonprofit think tank in Topeka, Kan.* – Reader's Digest.

non-quota immigrants *Am.* immigrants above the legal quota.

nonsense/ make (a) nonsense of smth. *Br., Aus.* make it appear ridiculous or wrong or spoil it.

nonsense/ stand no nonsense *Br.* not accept bad or foolish behaviour.

nonsked *Am.* col. non-scheduled airline or aircraft.

nonsmoker *Br.* col. a railway carriage or compartment where smoking is not allowed.

nonstarter *esp. Br., Aus.* col. a person or idea that has no chance of success: *I'm afraid it is a non-starter, Brian* - D. Lodge.

non-U *esp. Br., Aus.* humor. (esp. of words and behaviour) not typical or done by the upper class: *non-U vocabulary and idiom* - P. Howard.

noodle 1. *esp. Br.* sl. stupid person, fool: *He's nothing in the world but a pretty-faced noodle.* - H.H. Richardson. 2. *Aus.* col. search opal dump for opals.

noodle *Am.* col. play a musical instrument without giving it full or serious attention.

noodles *Am.* col. pasta.

noon basket *Am.* dinner basket.
noon recess *Am.* dinner break.
noon (it) *Am.* col. make a break / **nooning** (*Am.*) / for a meal.
nooner *Am., Can.* col. event that occurs in the middle of the day, esp. a sexual act.
No overtaking *Br.* /*Am.* **No Passing**/ highway signs.
no-place *esp. Am., Can.* col. adv. nowhere: *This is really getting us no place.* - M. Puzo.
nor/ British can use and and but before nor, Americans cannot / (*Br.*) *I don't want to go and nor will I.*
Nor can I, nor does he, etc. *esp. Br.* used to add a negative statement to the one that has just been mentioned.
No Reply *Br.* No Answer (telephone term): *Sorree, there's no reply* - D. Lodge.
nork *Aus.* col. woman's breast.
normalcy *esp. Am., Can.* normality, the quality or fact of being normal: *a return to something approaching normalcy.* - B. Tillman.
normally *esp. Br.* usually, or under normal conditions.
normal school *Am.* now rare. teacher training college / **summer school** *Am.* summer refresher course for teachers.
North East *Am.* New England.
Norther *Am.* wind blowing over Texas, the Gulf Coast, Florida and Gulf of Mexico during autumn and winter months.
The North Star State *Am.* Minnesota.
north-wester (coat) *Am.* rubberised raincoat.
nose *Br.* sl. 1. an informer. 2. act as an informer.
nose/ be given a bloody nose *Br.* be defeated unexpectedly.
nose/ blue nose *Am.* col. a Canadian, esp. one from Nova Scotia.
nose/ get (right) up sb.'s **nose** *Br., Aus.* col. annoy sb. very much.
nose/ have a nose round *Br., Aus.* col. look around a place.
nose/ hold one's **nose** *Am.* accept the necessity of doing smth. unpleasant.
nose/ on the nose 1. *esp. Am., Can.* exactly right: *he said to me to play this horse on the nose.* – J. O'Hara. 2. *esp. Aus.* unpleasant and offensive.
nose/ poke one's **nose into** smth. *Br.* be so interested in sb.'s private life that they get annoyed or angry by this.
nose/ put sb.'s **nose out of joint** *esp. Br., Can.* col. make sb. jealous, esp. by taking their places as the centre of attention: *The Queen of Motown Diana Ross put a few noses out of joint with some of her demands.* - New Idea.
nose/ right out from under sb.'s **nose** *Br.* in an obvious way without sb.'s noticing it and possibility to react.
nose around *Am.* col. /*Br.* **nose about**/ nose about, search for: *I nosed around the tourist information centre* - B. Bryson.
nose out /also **win by a nose**/ *esp. Am.* /*esp. Br.* obs. col. **pip (at the post)**/ win against (sb.) in a race, etc., esp. by a small amount: *the horse I was betting on managed to nose out the favorite.* - H.C. Whitford., R.J. Dixson.
nosebleed *Am., Can.* cheap seats located very high in a stadium, theatre or concert hall.
nose candy *Am., Can.* illegal inhaled narcotic, esp. cocaine.
no-see-um *Am., Can.* biting midge.
nosepiece *esp. Am., Can.* horse's noseband.
nose to tail *Br.* col. bumper to bumper.
nos(e)y parker *esp. Br., Aus.* derog. col. a nosy person, rubberneck: *I remember Nosy Parker as a comic strip in a Melbourne daily paper* - New Idea., *Mrs. Hemphill was a real nosy parker* - V. Holt.
nosh *Br., Aus.* sl. 1. v. eat: *two lovebirds have stopped noshing* - A. Burgess. 2. a meal. 3. food: *when you're eight they bring a posh nosh at Kenwood House* - You., *I'll give Sparking Plug his extra nosh* - D. Francis.
nosh *Am.* small amount of food eaten between meals; snack.
nosh-up *Br., Aus.* col. a big satisfying meal.
no-show *Am., Can.* person who fails to appear on a plane, etc.: *he used public money to hire no-show staffers.* - USA Today, also v.
nosy parker *Br.* col. derog. nosy person.
not at all *Br.* used to be polite when sb. has thanked you or asked you to do smth. for them.
not/ not that far *Am.* not far away.
not/ not too bad *Am.* quite well.
notch *Am., Can.* a narrow passage between mountains.
note *Br., Aus.* /*Am.* **bill**/ paper money, banknote: *I have five hundred pounds in notes on me* – M. Daly.
note/ change note *Br.* (of noise) change its note.
notecase *esp. Br.* /*Am., Can.* **billfold**/ wallet.
notelet *Br.* /*Am.* **note card**/ a small folded sheet of paper or card usu. with a picture on the front, on which a short letter can be written.
not-for-profit *Am.* non-profit making: *I was inducted into the American Academy of*

Achievement, a not-for-profit organisation- Reader's Digest.

nothing *esp. Am.* 1. sl. adj. worthless. 2. /*Br.* **nil**/ (in sports) no points.

nothing daunted *esp. Br., Aus.* col. not worrying about problems.

nothing/ here goes nothing *Am., Aus.* col. it won't succeed.

(there is) nothing (else) for it *Am.* /*esp. Br.* **no help for it**/ there's no alternative.

nothing to do / That idea is (*esp. Br.*), **has** (*esp. Am.*) **nothing to do with it**.

notice/ give sb. notice to quit/leave *Br.* tell sb. officially to leave.

notice board *esp. Br., Aus.* /*Am.* **bulletin board**/ a board on a wall which notices can be fixed to: *digging a drawing-pin out of the notice board* - D. Lodge.

notifiable *esp. Br.* tech. (esp. of certain diseases) needing by law to be reported to an office of public health.

notions (counter, department) *esp. Am., Can.* small things for sewing, such as pin or thread, sold in one part of a large shop (*Br.* **haberdashery, fancy goods**): *Quickly the Hills branched out, adding work clothing, notions, seeds, and farm equipment to their inventory.* - T. Thompson., *Her cargo consisted of what the Americans called notions, that is, in English, an assorted cargo.* - Cpt. Marryat.

nought *esp. Br.* /*esp. Am.* **zero, naught**/ (the figure 0, zero); *go from nought to 60 mph in 4 seconds.*, *figure with 5 noughts.*

noughts and crosses *esp. Br., Aus.* /*Am.* **tick-tack-toe**/ game in which two players take turns to write O and X in a pattern of nine squares, trying to win with a row of three Os or three Xs.

nous *Br.* col. practical good judgement, common sense.

Novacain *Am.* tdmk. drug used for stopping pain during a small operation, esp. on one's teeth.

now/ just now *esp. Br.* a. at the momemt. b. a moment ago.

now/ now now *esp. Br.* used when telling sb. not to behave badly.

no way *Am.* not at all, by no means: *"Hey – no way!" I shouted.* – R.L. Stine.

nr. *Br.* near (on envelopes).

NOW account *Am.* a negotiable order of withdrawal account, a bank account from which you can take money at any time and which also earns profit.

nowhere/ be/come in nowhere *Am.* get lost.

nubbin *Am.* 1. smth. small, stunted or imperfect. 2. small or imperfect ear of Indian corn: *Buttermilk skin, chubby cheeks, nubbin nose.* - J. Kellerman.

nubby *esp. Am.* (of fabric) coarse or knobbly in texture.

nuclear/ go nuclear *esp. Br.* go ballistic, go very angry and crazy.

nude contract *Br.* void contract.

nudge nudge (wink wink) *Br.* col. humor. words used to show that smth. just said has a sexual meaning.

nudnick *Am., Can.* col. a bore, a crank: *Okay, girls, the last nudnick has gone. Close up.* - M. Torgov.

Nueva York *Am.* sl. New York City.

nugget *Aus.* sl. 1. calf. 2. small but solidly-built horse.

nuggety *Aus., NZ.* 1. occuring in nuggets. 2. (of a person) stocky.

nuisance grounds *Can.* rubbish damp.

nuisance value *Br.* smth. useful because it causes problems for one's opponent.

nuke food *esp. Am., Aus.* cook it in a microwave oven: *I'll nuke some cheese and salsa, too.* – R.L. Stine.

number 1. *Am.* sl. prostitute: *what a hot number she was.* - D. Brenner. 2. *Br.* motor vehicle registration number.

number/ a recent/ an old/last month's number *Br.* a copy of magazine printed recently.

number/ back number *Am.* an old copy of a magazine.

number/ do a number on *Am., Can.* col. treat sb. bad and unfairly.

number eight *NZ.* a wire of 4mm. gauge used esp. for fences.

Number is engaged *Br.* line is busy.

number off *Br.* /*Am.* **count off**/ (in military use) call out one's number when one's term comes.

Number One *Br.* first lieutenant or First Mate of the Navy.

number plates *Br., Aus.* /*Am.* **license plates**/ either of the signs (usu. at the front and back ends) on a vehicle showing its official number.

numbers/ by the numbers *Am.* /*Br., Aus.* **by numbers**/ done as an ordered set of small sections.

number(s) runner *Am.* one who collects bets: *Another brother, Gustavo, was arrested several times for running numbers.* – A. Summers, R. Swan..

numeracy *esp. Br.* the state or condition of being numerate.

numerate *esp. Br.* adj. having a general understanding of mathematics.
Numero Uno *esp. Am.* col. smth. or sb. remarkable: *Mary is numero uno in our office.* - R.A. Spears.
nummy *Am., Can.* col. (of food) delicious.
nunky *Am.* Uncle Sam, USA.
nursery, creche *Br. /Am.* **day care center/** a place where young children are looked for during the day.
nursery nurse *Br.* nurse trained to take care of young children.
nursery slope *Br. /Am.* **beginners' slope, bunny slope/** gentle slope on a mountain used by people learning to ski.
nursery stakes *Br.* race for two-year old horses.
nursing aid *Aus. /Br.* **auxiliary nurse**, *Am.* **nurses' aid/**.
nursing home *Br. /esp. Am.* **private hospital/** a small private hospital.
nursing officer *Br.* senior nurse with administrative responsibilities.
nurturance *Am.* loving care and affection that a person gives to sb.
nut 1. *esp. Am.* taboo. sl. testicle: *I can bust my nuts with a black bitch* - E. Cleaver. 2. *Br.* usu. pl. a small lump of coal. 3. *Br.* a knob of butter. 4. *Am.* col. the cost of undertaking: *The fixed nut was $20 million.* - K. Lipper. 5. *Br.* col. v. strike with a head, headbutt. 6. *esp. Am.* col. crazy person or one who behaves strangely: *a middle-aged juvenile delinquent...a nut case.* – A. Summers, R. Swan. 7. *Br.* col. one's head or brain.
nut/ be/go off one's **nut** *Br.* col. become slightly mad.
nut/ do one's **nut** *Br., Aus.* col. be very angry or worried.
nut crackers *Br.* things used for cracking the shells of nuts.
nut cutlet *Br.* cake made of chopped nuts, breadcrumbs and other ingredients.
nutmeg *Br.* col. (in sport) deceive a player or make him look foolish by passing the ball between his legs.
The Nutmeg State *Am.* Connecticut.
nuts, nerts, nertz *esp. Am., Can.* sl. 1. excl. of annoyance and anger: *Nuts. Go as you are.* - J. Steinbeck., *Nuts, I don't know where he is.* - J. Updike. 2. a strong expression of fearless refusal.
nuts/ for nuts *Br., Aus.* col. (esp. after can't) at all: *a pack of peroxide blondes who couldn't act for nuts* - W.S. Maugham.

the nuts *Am.* sl. the best: *It will be the nuts.* - R.P. Warren.
nutso, nutsy *Am., Can.* col. crazy: *A rabidly nutso rescues a famed romance novelist* - USA Today.
nutter *esp. Br., Aus.* col. crazy person: *Hitler is a nutter* – R. Westall.
nutty/ be as nutty as a fruitcake *Br., Aus.* col. be crazy.

O

O *Am.* Ohio.
oak *Br.* sl. a door of oak or other wood.
oak/ sport the (or one's) **oak** *Br.* (in some universities) show the outer door to show that sb. doesn't want to be disturbed.
OAP *Br.* old age pensioner, a woman over 60 or a man over 65.
oar/ put/shove//stick one's **oar in** *esp. Br., Aus.* col. intrude in the situation against the wishes of the others.
oar/ rest/lean on one's **oars** *Br.* be in danger of suffering harm or defeat.
oarlock *Am.,Can. /Br.* **rowlock/** a pin or U-shaped rest on the side of a boat, for holding an oar in place.
oast house *Br.* building for drying hops.
oater /also **oat opera**/ *esp. Am.* col. n. western (film, etc.): *I don't want to see an oater.* - R.A. Spears.
oath/ My oath! *esp. Aus., NZ.* excl. of agreement or endorsement.
oath/ on oath *Br.* having sworn to tell the truth.
oatmeal *Am. /Br.* **porridge/** soft breakfast food made by boiling crushed oats: *cook up some oatmeal, using milk* – Reader's Digest.
oats/ be off one's **oats** *Br.* col. have lost the desire to eat.
oats/ feel one's **oats** *Am.* col. feel lively and energetic.
oats/ get one's **oats** *Br.* col. have sex regularly.
oatsy *Am., Can.* full of vigour and self-importance.
OB 1. *Am.* col. obstetrician. 2. *Br.* outside broadcast.
OB-GYN *esp. Am.* col. obstetrician- gynecologist.
object *Br.* col. smth. or sb. unusual or smth. that causes laughter.
obligate 1. *esp. Am.* (usu. pass.) make (sb.) feel it necessary (to do smth.), esp. because of a sense of duty, esp. in the phr. **be/feel obligated**

to sb.: *The Biomed library was filled with the inquisitive and the obligated.* - J. Kellerman. 2. *Am.* commit (assets) as security.

oblique (stroke) *Br., Aus.* also tech. **solidus** slash, sloping line often used for separating numbers or words.

obo *Am., Can.* or best offer.

observation platform, open platform *Am.* / *Br.* **open end verandah**/: *His hands caught the guardrail of the observation platform.* - E.L. Doctorow.

obsess (about) *esp. Am., Aus.* col. worry continuously and unnecessarily: *you are obsessing and talking too much about your weight.* - E. Taylor., *she didn't obsess about Martin and Althea* - D. Mortman.

obstacle course *Am.* /*Br.* **assault course**/: *from early morning marching drills to strenuous obstacle courses* – Reader's Digest.

occasional table *Br.* small light table that can be easily moved.

ocupation *Br.* adj. for the sole use of the occupier of the land.

occupier *esp. Br.* person or company residing in or using a property as its owner or tenant, or (illegally) as a squatter.

the ocean *esp. Am.* the great mass of salt water that covers most of the earth's surface.

The Ocean State *Am.* Rhode Island.

ochre, ocker, okker *Aus., NZ.* col. dull, boorish person, usu. a working class male from Australia: *It seems to be common ground that an ocher (sometimes with a capital O as befits a defined species) is an uncultivated boorish, chauvinistic and constantly disparaging Australian.* - A. Peterson.

October *Br.* ale brewed in October.

October Surprise *Am.* an unexpected but popular political act made just prior to November election in an attempt to win votes.

OD *esp. Am.* sl. an overdose.

odd/ the odd drink, game, occasion, etc. *esp. Br.* a few drinks, games, etc., but not often and not regularly: *Life would be very dull without the odd adventure now and then.* - Longman.

oddball *esp. Am.* col. eccentric person: *oddball use of the language must seem to flow naturally* - C. Hoover., *There goes that goddamned odd-ball again.* - J.A. Michener., *Tinseltown regards Greena as an odd-ball* - New Idea.

odd-job man, odd-jobber, odd man *esp. Br.* a man who is employed to do various small pieces of work (**odd jobs**) for pay, usu. in people's houses.

odd man out/odd one out *Br.* col. sb. who is not usu. included in groups of people and friends.

odd lengths *Am.* /*Br.* **off cuts**/.

odds *Br., Aus.* noticeable differences.

odds/ by all odds *Am., Can.* certainly.

odds/ it/that makes no odds, What's the odds? *Br.* col. it/that makes no difference, has no importance: *it's no odds.* - J.D. Carr.

odds/ over the odds *Br.* more than acceptable, esp. of a price.

odds/ pay/charge over the odds *Br., Aus.* col. pay more for smth. that it's really worth.

odds and sods *esp. Br., Aus.* col. odds and ends, small articles without much value.

odd sizes *Br.* broken sizes (not all sizes available).

odds/ ask/beg no odds (of) *Am.* not to ask for advantages.

odometer *esp. Am.* /*Br., Aus.* **mileometer**/: *a speedometer and trip odometer* – Outdoor Life.

odour/ be in bad/good odour (with sb.**)** *Br.* be disapproved or approved for one's actions.

of *Am., Can.* (used in telling time) before / Americans also say five thirty, British say half past five/: *two unnerving things occurred at about two minutes of seven.* - J.A. Michener.

ofay *Am.* derog. sl. a white person (Negro term): *Ofay had placed a pair of his pyjamas on the bed.* - S. Sheldon., *There are three reasons why us ofays should check out Cleaver's literary masterpiece* - D. Divoky., *The ofays were not used to seeing coloured boys making fine music for them to dance by.* - M. Jones, J. Chilton.

off 1. *esp. Br.* (with preceding number) denoting a quantity produced at one time. 2. *Br.* col. annoying or unfair. 3. *Br.* col. unwell. 4. *Br.* col. unfriendly or hostile. 5. *Br.* (of behaviour) rude and not what is expected.

off 1. *esp. Br., Can.* (of food) no longer good to eat or drink, not fresh. 2. *Am.* sl. v. kill: *Arafat offs his number two* - Vanity Fair., *You'll get offed with all that crap on your mind.* - Esquire.

off/ be off and running *Am.* start doing smth; start happening (of smth.).

off/ be off with sb. *Br.* col. be unfriendly towards sb.

the off *Br.* col. an act of leaving; the start of a race; beginning.

off/ from the off *Br.* from the beginning.

off/ go right off *Br.* be no longer interested with smth.

off/ straight off *esp. Br.* col. immediately.

offa *Am.* col. off from.

offal *esp. Br. /esp. Am.* **variety food/** the heart, head, brains, etc. of an animal used as food: *they banned the export from Britain of beef offal* - Economist.

off-board *Am.* (of stocks) dealt with elsewhere than a stock exchange.

off colour *Br.* adj. not well, ill.

off cuts *Br. /Am.* **odd lengths/** remnants (of textiles, lumber).

offence *Am., Can. /Br.* **attack/** (part of the game in which) the players in a game such as football (who) try to get points: *I was running the offense.* – Reader's Digest, adj. **offensive.**

offer/ on (special) offer *Br., Aus.* a. available to buy, use or do. b. being sold at a very cheap price.

offer/ under offer *Br.* (of a house, flat, etc. for sale) having a possible buyer who has offered money.

off hours *Am., Can.* col. leisure time.

office 1. **physician's** or **dentist's office, (doctor's) office** *Am., Can.* consulting room of a professional person, esp. surgery. 2. *Am.* v. work in the office.

office block *Br., Aus. /Am.* **office tower, office building/** a large building in which there are several offices.

office hours *Br., Aus.* hours during the day when people who work in offices are usu. at work.

office junior *Br.* a young person who has recently left school and who works in an office doing mainly unskilled work.

officer *Am.* a title for policeman or policewoman.

offices *Br.* conveniences, such as laundry and kitchen in which servants carry out household work.

officialese *Am.* language often used in government documents which is very formal and often difficult to understand.

official assignee *NZ. /Br.* **official receiver/** a receiver of a bankrupt business.

official secret *Br.* a piece of confidential information which is only for use by the government and its employees.

officiary *Am.* 1. officer, official. 2. a body of officers and officials.

offie *Br.* col. an off-licence.

offish *Br.* col. offhand, not friendly, even slightly rude.

off-island *Br.* adj. visiting or temporarily residing on an island. **off-islander** n.

off-licence *Br. /Am., Aus.* **liquor store,** *Am.* **package store/** a shop where alcohol is sold to be taken away: *You know the off-licence is just round the corner.* - I. Murdoch.

off-load *Br.* 1. (onto) get rid of (smth. unwanted): *Even a modest 25-ton marijuana shipment could bring its owners as much as $12 million when off-loaded to American importers.* - Reader's Digest., *Once the inevitable "extras" have been offloaded, the real expedition can begin* - Award Journal. 2. sl. displace an ordinary airplane passenger in favour of a VIP.

off-peak adj. *esp. Br.* 1. less busy. 2. used or in effect during less busy period, **off-peak travel, electricity,** etc. is cheaper because it is done or used at these times.

off-piste *esp. Br.* done on snow away from the areas that have been specially prepared for skiing.

off-price *Am., Can.* method of retailing in which branded goods (esp. clothing) are sold for less than usual retail price.

off-putting *esp. Br.* unpleasantly surprising and/or causing dislike, annoying: *Her expression was cold, her manner offputting.* - D. Mortman.

offramp *Am., Can.* one of the roads leading off a main highway: *Don't stop on an offramp or in a business lot at night* - Reader's Digest.

off-shears *Aus., NZ.* (of a sheep) recently shorn.

offside *esp. Br.* adj. on the right-hand side, esp. of an animal or of a car or road: *His off-side front wheel mounted the grass bank* - J. Higgins.

off-sider *Aus., NZ.* col. assistant, partner or deputy.

offtake *Br.* 1. consumption. 2. deduction. 3. a means of drawing off or away as pipe, tube or course.

off the peg *Br. /Am., Aus.* **off the hook,** *Am.* **off the rack/** buying in a standard size rather than having smth. made to order.

off-the-wall *esp. Am., Aus., Can.* col. 1. amusing, foolish, zany: *All of their songs have great off-the-wall lyrics.* - Rolling Stone. 2. (of a person) angry: *Chas was going to go totally off the wall with Jimi* – S. Lawrence.

off-track *Am., Can.* situation or place away from race track.

off-year *Am.* 1. n. adj. happening between elections. 2. a year of unfavourable conditions or lower than usual yield.

oftentimes *Am., Can.* often.

OHP *Br.* overhead projector.

oico *Br.* (used in ads) offer in excess of.

oik *Br.* sl. derog. unpleasant person from low social class.

oil *Am.* col. flattering talk.

oil/ dinkum oil *Aus.* real truth.
oil/ (be) no oil painting *Br., Aus.* humor. not attractive or ugly.
The Oil State *Am.* Pennsylvania.
oilcloth *esp. Br.* linoleum: *Mr. Kelly guided doctor Myers to an oilcloth-covered table* – J. O'Hara.
oiled/ well oiled *Br.* col. very drunk.
oiler 1. *Am., Can.* col. oil-well. 2. also **oilers** *Am., Can.* oilskin coat. 3. also **oilman** *Am.* oil industrialist: *Dad"s image for me was that of a big Irish oilman* - Alcoholics Anonymous.
oil pan *Am.* /*esp. Br.* **sump**/ part of an engine, at the bottom, which holds the supply of oil.
oink *Am.* derog. sl. a policeman: *Here come the oinks!* - R.A. Spears.
oiro *Br.* (in ads) offer in the range of.
OJ *Am.* orange juice: *I like to have a big glass of fresh O.J. every morning.* - R.A. Spears.
OK *esp. Am.* nice, helpful, honest, etc.
Okie *Am.* col. 1. a citizen of Oklahoma: *more cruel than asking hope-to-die Okie music buff to cop the sounds of John Coltrane* - E. Cleaver. 2. a migrant agricultural worker (esp. from Oklahoma): *the United States is peopled almost entirely by Babbits and Okies.* - J. Fischer.
okie-dokie *Am.* sl. O.K.: *okey-dokey, I'll be there at noon.* - R.A. Spears.
OK press *Am.* /*Br.* **pass for press**/ print. an indication that a job has had all the corrections made and is ready for printing.
old/ a good old, a right old *Br.* col. used to talk about smth. one enjoys.
old age pension *Br., Aus.* /*Am.* **social security**/ money paid by the government to old people who no longer work.
old age pensioner *Br.* /*Am.* **retiree**/ retired person: *I already had a paper round to do, an old age pensioner to look after* – S. Townsend.
old-bat *Am.* sl. an old woman, esp. a repulsive gossipy shrew: *The old bat doesn't get any wrong ideas.* - G.V. Higgins.
the Old Bill *Br.* col. the police.
old boy / old girl *esp. Br.* col. 1. a former pupil of a school: *"Old boys", or former pupils of public and grammar schools.* - J. Ruppeldtova. 2. obs. (used as a form of address to a friend, sometimes disrespectfully): *Say, Jack, old boy, could you lend me a couple of dollars until tomorrow?* - I. Stone. 3. col. an old person.
old-boy network 1. *Br.* a support system among former pupils of the same school in later life. 2. *Am.* a group of people who knew each other for a long time and are important and have influence, esp. in politics and business.

Old Dart *Aus., NZ.* col. England.
Old Dirigo State *Am.* Maine.
Old Dominion 1. *Am.* Virginia. 2. *Can.* also **Old Colony, Tenth Province** Newfoundland.
The Old Country *Am., Can., Aus.* one's country of origin.
(my) old Dutch *Br.* wife.
olde worlde *Br., Aus.* col. sometimes derog. too consciously old-fashioned, quaint.
old faithful *Am.* anything or anybody totally reliable.
old-fashioned 1. *Br.* col. obs. (of a look, expression, etc.) suggesting disapproval. 2. **old-fashioned glass** *Am.* special wine glass with a heavy base. 3. *Am.* alcoholic drink made with whiskey.
old folk *Br.* /*Am.* **old folks**/ old people.
Old Glory /also **Stars and Stripes, Star-spangled Banner**/ *Am.* the American flag: *It was Old Glory, the flag of the United States of America on Earth.* – K. Vonegut, Jr.
Old Harry *Br.* obs. the devil.
old identity *Aus., NZ.* person who lived in specific place for a long time and is well known there.
old lag *esp. Br.* col. obs. an old prisoner (in former times).
old-line *Am., Can.* 1. conservatively minded. 2. well-established.
The Old Line State *Am.* Maryland.
old man *Br.* obs. col. (used as a form of address to a friend): *Kit, old man, you're coming with us.* - J. Aldridge.
old man *Br.* col. 1. your husband. 2. your father: *I'll ask my old man if I can go.* - R.A. Spears.
Old Nick *Br., Aus.* obs. humor. the Devil.
The Old North State /also **The Turpentine State**/ *Am.* North Carolina.
Old Pals Act *Br.* col. humor. using one's position of influence to help friends.
(the) old school tie 1. *esp. Br.* a special tie that is worn by sb. who has been at a certain school, esp. a public school: *And you in your linen suit and old-school tie?* - J. Fowles. 2. also *Br., Aus.* **old-boy network** often derog. a support system among former pupils of the same school in later life, adj. **old-school-tie.**
old shoe *Am.* adj. pleasant, casual, informal: *Cab drivers told this genial old-shoe of a man their troubles* - Guideposts.
old-stager *Br.* col. person who has had long experience in a particular activity.
oldster *esp. Am., Can.* col. older person.
old thing *Aus.* meal of beef and damper.

old-timer *esp. Am., Aus.* col. an old man: *we are able to put the old-timers out to pasture.* - L. Uris., *Well, old-timer, I've got to run along* - J. Dos Passos.

old trout *Br.* sl. disagreeable woman: *two old trouts and a man should be in the army.* - T. Thorne.

old woman *Br.* sl. 1. derog. sb.'s wife or mother. 2. man who plays too much attention to unimportant details.

oleo *Am.* margarine.

olive-drab *esp. Am.* having greyish-green colour, used esp. for military uniforms: *There were several soldiers in olive-drab uniforms* - R. Borchgrave, R. Moss.

omadhaun *Am., Can., Irish Eng.* a fool.

omelet *Am.* omelette.

omnibus *esp. Br.* a book that has a lot of stories, or a single radio or TV programme that includes several separate programmes shown before.

on *Br., Aus.* prep. used to show amount of points a person or a team has in a competition; e.g. *This team is on 5 points.*

on/ They arrive on Tuesday / (*Am.* They arrive Tuesday.).

on/ in the street / (*Am.*) on the street., *Am.* on weekends equals *Br.* at weekends.

on/ be on 1. *Am.* alert, aware of surroundings and often being watched. 2. *Aus.* earn (wages or salary), e.g. *He's on $90000 a year.*

on/ be/go on about *Br., Aus.* col. be talking about smth., esp. for too long in a boring way.

on/ be on at sb.'s **case** *Br., Aus.* /*Am.* **be on** sb's **case**/ speak to them complainingly and try to persuade them do smth.

on/ be on it *Aus.* col. be drinking heavily.

on/ be really on *Am.* perform well.

on/ not (just) on *esp. Br., Aus.* col. impossible, not acceptable or reasonable.

on again, off again *esp. Am.* 1. undependable. 2. being supposed to start and then not starting.

on/ be on the go *Br.* in the process of being produced.

on/ hit the side on *Br., Aus.* hit the side of smth.

on/ turn smth. **sideways on** *Br., Aus.* turn to one side.

on/ this way on *Br., Aus.* in this position.

once over easy, sunny side up *Am.* /*Br.* **ham and eggs**/.

oncer 1. *Br.* person who does smth. only once. 2. *Aus.* Member of Parliament who is likely to serve only one term.

one/ in Britain one is usu. followed by one's and oneself / One should wash oneself, wash one's hair. One should do one's duty; in America it is also correct to say One should wash himself, wash his hair regularly, if he can. One can't be too carefully, can you? One should do his duty. One can't enjoy oneself, if one / (*Am.*) he is too tired: *Everything comes to him who waits.* - I. Shaw.

one 1. *Am.* one dollar bill. 2. *Br.* one pound coin.

one *esp. Am.* col. certainly a (an), an unusually, very, extremely, e.g. **one wonderful woman, one interesting job**, etc.: *it's one fine show.* - Reader's Digest.

one/ one of the lads *Br., Aus.* col. /*Am.* col. **one of the boys/** a member of a group of people having similar interests.

one/ one swallow doesn't make a summer *Br., Aus.* one good thing doesn't necessarily improve the situation.

one/ be one in the eyes of sb. *Br., Aus.* col. annoy sb. by being too sure of oneself.

one/ be/have had one over the eight *Br.* obs. have drunk too much alcohol.

one/ get one over on sb. *Br.* do smth. better than one's competitor.

one/ (you've) got it in one *Br.* you've guessed it correctly.

one/ there's always one *Br.* col. humor. sb. is always causing problems.

a one *esp. Br., Aus.* col. (expressing shocked admiration) an amusingly disrespectful person.

a (right) one 1. *esp. Br.* col. a fool. 2. *Br.* col. an eccentric person who amuses or annoys sb., esp. used in **you are one, he is a one** *esp. Br.* obs. used to tell about sb. who are rude, foolish, etc.

one-armed bandit *esp. Am., Aus.* old-fashioned slot machine.

one-arm (joint) *Am.* a place with slot-machines: *she went with me to this one-arm where I eat* – J. O'Hara.

one-horse town *esp. Am., Aus.* a small town where very little happens.

one-nighter *Am.* 1. one-night stand: *we went on a one-nighter tour on the Crosby bus.* - A.E. Hotchner. 2. performer doing this.

one-off, also **one of a kind** *esp. Br., Aus.* /*Am.* **one-shot/** 1. happening or done only once. 2. made as a single example; **one-off** is noun as well.

one-liner *Am.* wise crack: *other joined in with quick one-liners* - D. Brenner., *Comedians used my appearance for routines and one-liners.* - E. Taylor., *I don't want visual one-liners.* - Esquire.

one-on-one *esp. Am.* a kind of activity where one works with only one person.
one-piece *Br., Aus.* /*Am.* **one-piece swimsuit**/.
oner *Br.* col. 1. always the first or best of its kind. 2. one pound sterling.
one-reeler *Am.* a short motion picture.
one-shot *Am.* happening only once.
one-size-fits-all *esp. Am.* a piece of clothing designed to fit a person of any size.
one-stop shop/store, etc. *Am.* one where one can buy a lot of different things.
one the halves *Am.* equally.
a one-two punch *Am.* two unpleasant things which happen together.
one-way *esp. Am.* /*Br., Aus.* **single**/ (of a ticket or its cost) for a trip from one place to another but not back again: *give them a desert island and a one-way ticket to get there* - Time.
one-worlder *Am.* col. a person who favours internationalism.
onion/ know one's **onions** *Br., Aus.* humor. col. know a lot about a particular subject.
onion skin *Am.* very thin light paper, used esp. for writing letters on.
onkus *Aus.* col. 1. unpleasant. 2. disorganised.
only just *esp.Br.* a. a moment ago. b. almost not; hardly.
only that *esp. Br.* col. conj. but (before a reason): *He'd succeed only that he's rather lazy.* - Longman.
o.n.o. *Br., Aus.* or near offer (often used in real estate and used car ads).
on-ramp *Am.* /*Br.* **slip road**/ a side road leading to a main one: *I found the 118 on-ramp within the concrete pretzel* - J. Kellerman.
on time *Am.* punctual.
onto/ be/get onto *esp. Br.* col. get in touch with sb.
onward train *esp. Br., Aus.* passing train.
oof *esp. Br.* old sl. money, cash, adj. **oofy.**
oops-a-daisy *esp. Br.* col. or humor. excl. (used to encourage sb. who falls down).
op *esp. Br., Aus.* col. medical operation: *miners getting over hernia ops* – R. Westall.
op *Am.* opportunity.
op-ed (page), (opposite editorial) *Am., Can.* a page opposite the editorial page devoted to personal comment, feature articles, etc.: *Maybe she'd send it to the newspaper for the op-ed page.* - F. Pascal.
open-and-shut *Can.* (of weather) changeable.
open-cut *Am., Aus.* open cast.
open out *esp. Br.* start to say exactly what one thinks or feels; become less shy.

open bar *Am.* a bar at an occasion such as a wedding where drinks are served free.
opencast (colliery) *Br.* /*Am.* **stripping,** *Am., Aus.* **open-cut,** *Am.* **open-pit,** *Br.* **opencast mine/mining**/ open coal mine.
open classroom *Am.* completely informal, esp. at elementary level.
open date *Am.* available for future use with no specific date arranged.
open day 1. *Br., Aus.* a day when a school or company lets people come in and see the work that is being done there. 2. *Br.* /*Am., Can.* **open house**/ time when a house or apartment that is being sold can be looked at by the public
open-ended spanner, (ring) spanner *Br.* /*Am.* **(open-ended) wrench, box end spanner**/.
open end verandah *Br.* /*Am.* **observation platform,** also *Am.* **open platform**/ railway platform used for observation.
open enrollment *Am.* policy of admitting everybody so as to achieve racial balance.
open fireplace *Am.* open fire.
open go *Aus.* fair chance.
open goods waggon *Br.* /*Am.* **gondola car**/ railway carriage with no top, flat bottom and fixed sides used chiefly for hauling heavy bulk commodities.
open house 1. *esp. Br.* a time when a school or company lets people come in and see the work that is being done there: *My friend, who drives a city bus, attended an open house at her third-grader's school.* – Reader's Digest. 2. *Am., Can.* /*Br.* **open day**/ time when a house or apartment that is being sold can be looked at by the public.
open housing *Am.* sale or rental of a house, etc. without discrimination against race, religion and national origin.
opening *Am.* 1. an area without trees or with scattered usu. mature trees that occurs as a break in a forest. 2. fashions show (in the university).
opening act *Am.* supporting act, performance done before a leading band.
opening hours *Br.* (of a business such as bar, shop or bank) open for use by custom.
opening night *Am.* first night, first official performance of a play.
open mike *esp. Am., Can.* club activities, such as singing or theatre performances, in which anyone could take part.
open pit *Am., Can.* open cast.
open primary *Am.* primary elections open to all registered voters.

open prison *Br.* /*Am., Aus.* **minimum-security prison**/ one where prisoners are not locked because they are trusted not to escape.
open range *Am., Can.* tract of land without fences or barriers.
open seater *Aus., NZ. col.* a possibility to carry out one's actions without interference.
open time 1. *Am.* /*Br.* **standing time**/ print. unused production time, due to a break in a schedule. 2. *Br.* (of a bar or pub) time when they open.
opening time *Br.* the time when the public houses may be legally opened for custom.
Open University *Br.* /*Am.* **Off-campus plan**/ studying by correspondence: *And the Open University has courses you can follow without doing the examinations.* - D. Lodge.
open water *Can.* (the time of) spring melting of ice on rivers and lakes.
opera pumps *Am.* women's open high-heeled pumps.
opera slippers *Am.* men's house slippers.
operating room, OR *Am., Can.* /*Br., Aus.* **(operating) theatre**/ a part of a hospital where doctors do operations: *the ER staff prepared to take Mark Thurman into the operating room.* - R. Crais., *bled to death on the operating theatre table.* – S. Townsend.
operative *esp. Am.* secret agent, private detective: *five CIA operatives - top men in the Caribbean account - ate, slept, and read Penthouse* - J. Patterson.
operator *Am.* employer / **big operator** *Am.* VIP.
operator/ **farm operator** *Am.* farm worker.
opera window *esp. Am.* small, usu. triangular window at the back of either side of a motor car.
opinion/ **horseback opinion** *Am.* quick, unconsidered opinion.
opium joint *Am.* opium den.
oppo *Br. col.* close companion, opposite number, counterpart.
opportunity shop, col. **op-shop** *Aus.* shop run by charity organisation to help hungry and homeless people and which sells second-hand clothes.
opposite prompt *Br.* stage-right.
the Opposition *Br.* the second biggest political party in Parliament, which is not in the government.
opposum *esp. Br.* possum.
ops *esp. Br. col.* military operations: *Ops officer comin' aboard at 14.00.* - D. Brenner.
ops room *Am.* operations planning room.

optic *Br.* tdmk. measuring device fastened to the neck of liquor bottles in pubs.
optician 1. also **ophthalmic optician** *Br.* /*esp. Am., Can., Aus.* **optometrist**/ person who tests people's eyes and sells them glasses in a shop: *I go to my optometrist, who hesitates to up my prescription.-* Reader's Digest. 2. *Am.* person who makes glasses. 3. *Am.* /*Br.* **dispensing optician**/ a person who sells glasses.
option *Br.* subject that person can choose to study as part of a course at college or university.
optometry *esp. Br., Aus.* the science and activity of testing person's sight and providing people with glasses or contact lenses to correct problems with their sight.
opt out *Br.* (of a school or hospital) withdraw from local authority control, n. **opt-out**.
opt-out clause (in an agreement) *Br.* one that gives participants the chance not to be involved in one part of that agreement.
oracy *Br.* the ability to express oneself fluently and grammatically in speech.
oral 1. *Br.* spoken test, esp. in a foreign language. 2. *Am.* spoken test for a Master's Degree.
oral surgeon *Am.* dentist.
orange squash *esp. Br.* /*Am.* **orangeade**/ orange juice sweetened and mixed with plain or carbonated water.
The Orange State *Am.* Florida.
orangeade *Br.* /*Am.* **orange soda**/ fizzy sweet drink which usu. tastes of oranges.
orange badge *Br.* badge on the windscreen of a motor car indicating that the disabled driver has parking concessions.
orbital *Br.* circular road /also *Br.* **ring road,** *Am.* **beltway**/ or a bypass encircling a town.
orchestra (seats) *Am.* /*Br.* **(orchestra) stalls**/ the seats in the front part of the main level of a theatre: *the theater manager upgraded their balcony seats to the orchestra.* – Reader's Digest.
order/ **be in order** *Br., Aus.* be allowed.
order *Am.* tech. /*Br.* **queue**/ a list of jobs that a computer has to do in a particular order.
order sb. **about/around** *Br.* continuously give orders in an annoying or threatening way.
order/ **in the order of** *Br.* /*Am.* **on the order of**/ about, as much or as many as, similar to.
order/ **on order** *Br., Aus.* /*Am., Aus.* **on the order**/ from sb.
order/ **out of order** *Br. col.* behaving in a wrong or unacceptable way.
order/ **in short order** *Am.* at once.
order/ **order of the boot** *Br. sl.* dismissal.

order/ order to view *Br.* appointment to look at the house that is for sale.

order/ the lower orders *Br.* obs. people who belong to the lowest social class.

order book *Br.* 1. book for recording incoming business orders. 2. book of vouchers which are exchanged for weekly payments of a pension.

Order in Council *Br.* sovereign's order on administrative matter.

orderly bin *Br.* street litterbox.

orderly book *Br.* mil. regimental or company's book in which orders are entered.

orderly officer *Br.* mil. duty officer responsible for security and administration on specific day.

order mark *Br.* school punishment for a bad behaviour.

Order Paper, O.P. *Br., Can.* paper on which the day's business for a legislative assembly is entered; **die on the O.P.** *Can.* (of a bill) fail to be voted on before the end of a legislative session.

ordinance *esp. Am., Can.* a law in a city or town, which states that smth. is not allowed or is limited.

ordinarily *esp. Am.* usually.

ordinary *Br.* law. person, esp. a judge exercising authority by justice of office and not by deputation.

ordinary 1. *Br.* meal served to all comers at a fixed price. 2. *esp. Br.* a tavern or eating house serving regular meals.

ordinary/ in ordinary *Br.* (in titles) by permanent appointment, esp. to Royal household.

ordinary/ in the ordinary way *esp. Br.* normally.

ordinary call *Br.* station-to-station call.

ordinary level *Br.* O level.

ordinary share or **stock** *Br.* a share of common stock.

ordinary way/ in the ordinary way *Br.* as usual.

ordnance survey map *Br.* map which shows all the roads, path, hills, etc. of an area in detail.

oreo *Am.* tdmk. chocolate biscuit with a white cream filling: *most of his bands were integrated – but in no way an "Oreo."* – N. Hentoff.

organ grinder's monkey *Br.* person closely associated with a powerful person and acting on their behalf.

organise 1. *esp. Am.* unionise, (cause) to become a member of a trade union. 2. *Br.* arrange, coordinate things for an event or activity.

orient *esp. Am.* /*Br.* **orientate**/.

orientation *esp. Am.* training and preparation for a new job or activity.

orientation course *Am., Can.* course giving information to newcomers to university or other institution.

origination *Br.* print. all the preparatory stages for printing, including phototype setting, the making of halftones and colour reproduction.

ornery *esp. Am., Can.* humor. 1. bad-tempered, difficult to deal with: *it had always been such an ornery little town.* - J.A. Michener., *it's a whole lot harder to change a pit bull, bred to be ornery and protective into a loveable cocker spaniel.* - Newsweek., *How did a sweet looking kid like you get so ornery!* - L. Uris. 2. ordinary.

Oscar *Aus., NZ.* col. money.

other half *Br.* person's spouse or partner.

other place *Br.* humor. hell.

other ranks *Br.* serviceman (or women) other than commissioned officers.

other shoe/ wait for the other shoe to drop *Am.* wait for smth. to happen.

other side/ bat for the other side *Br.* humor. be a homosexual.

or otherwise *esp. Br.* or not.

OTT *Br.* col. over the top.

ottoman *Am.* soft piece of furniture shaped like a box, used to rest one's feet when sb. is sitting down.

ouster *esp. Am., Can.* an act of ousting.

out *esp. Am. and Br.* col (with verbs of movement). prep. out of: *I'd stare out the window a long time.* - C. McCullers.

out/ out *Am.* a long distance away from somewhere.

out *Br.* open or flat; e.g. *open out a map, a sofa bed,* etc. /*flowers opened* **out** *Br., Aus.*/

out *Am.* col. an item that is out of stock.

out/ be out *esp. Am.* (of a machine or piece of equipment) not work.

out/ be (way) out there *Am.* col. be very strange.

out/ be the stupidest/selfishest, etc. **person out** *Br.* be extremely stupid, etc.

out/ come out *Br.* stop working in a protest about smth.

out/ on the outs, also **at outs** *Am., Can.* in a mild dispute with sb.: *he and Mike Slattery were, in Mike's phrase on the outs with each other.* - J. O'Hara.

out/ be out of order *Br.* col. /*Am.* **be out of line**/ (of behaviour) be unacceptable.

out/ out of it 1. *Am., Can.* be too drowsy to react properly. 2. *Br.* drunk.

outage *Am.* /*Br.* **power failure**/ time when electricity supply is cut off to a building or area.

outasite *Am.* sl. 1. very advanced or unconventional. 2. wonderful.
outback *Aus.* adj. n. remote inland district, province; provincial: *I grew up in the outback wrestling alligators* - Daily News.
outbacker *Aus.* inhabitant of the central part of the country.
outbound *esp. Am.* opp. of inbound.
outdoor pursuits *Br.* open air sporting and leisure activities.
outdoors/ all outdoors *Am.* all the world, everybody.
(outdoor) tap *esp. Br. /esp. Am.* **spigot/**.
outdoorsy *esp. Am., Can.* col. relating or fond of open air life.
outer 1. *Br.* container for packaged goods for their further transportation or display later. 2. *Aus.* col. the part of a racecourse outside the enclosure.
outer/ on the outer *Aus.* col. in dire straits.
outer city *Am.* suburb.
outer garment /also **outer wear/** *Am.* outer clothes: *the mandatory checking of outergarments makes good sense.* - Y. Richmond.
outfall *Am.* rainfall or snowfall.
outfitter 1. *Am., Can.* shop that sells equipment for outdoor pursuits. 2. *Br.* obs. shop that sells men's clothes.
outfront *Am.* col. 1. open, frank, honest. 2. taking a leading position.
outgoing *Br.* an instance of going out.
outgoings *esp. Br.* money that have to be spent, usu. regularly, e.g. to pay for heat and rent.
outgrow one's **strength** *esp. Br.* grow too quickly when sb. is a child, so that they become weak or unhealthy.
outhouse 1. *Am.* an enclosed outside lavatory: *I'll bet he'd like to visit the outhouse.* - J.A. Michener., *She had relieved herself in wooden outhouses behind the tenements.* - E.L. Doctorow. 2. *Br.* outbuilding, a smaller building forming part of a group with a larger main building, guest house or other detached building: *returning to obtain food, which was generally left for him in an outhouse.* - W. Grady.
outhouse publisher *Am. /Br.* **packager/**.
outlander *esp. Am., Can.* foreigner; stranger.
outlay *esp. Am.* spend (money) for a purpose, lay out.
(convenience) outlet, wall outlet *Am. /Br., Aus.* **socket (outlet), (power) point/** an opening fixed in a wall, into which electric plug can be fitted: *What the hell had he done, stuck a fork in the outlet?* - S. Grafton.

outlet *Am.* compass point.
outline *esp. Am.* a plan for a report, story, etc. in which each new idea is separately recorded.
out-of-sight *Am.* adj. extremely large, esp. of an amount of money.
out-of-the-way *Br.* unusul or strange.
out of whack *Am., Can.* sl. inoperative, out of order: *the rouble's official rate of exchange with Western currencies was seriously out of whack.* - Time., *the DJs themselves were out of whack a lot more often than the machines.* - W. Jack, B. Laursen.
outplace *Am.* give another place of work for a discharged worker. n. **-ment**.
outport 1. *Br.* any port other than London. 2. *Can.* remote fishing village, esp. in Newfoundland.
outreach *esp. Am.* 1. services based close to people's homes to help those who cannot easily come to an office, hospital, etc. or service centre, etc. 2. the work a church does to teach or serve people who are not its members.
outrider *Am.* 1. mounted official who escorts racehorses to the starting point. 2. herdsman who prevents cattle from straying.
outs *Br.* money paid off in taxes.
outs/ on the outs *Am.* col. unfriendly.
outside of prep. col. 1. *esp. Am., Can.* outside: *He's on the highway outside of Cedar Rapids.* – P. Roth. 2. *esp. Am.* except for.
outside (lane) 1. *Br. /Am.* **fast lane/** one nearest the vehicles moving in opposite direction. 2. *Am.* one nearest the edge of the road for slow-moving vehicles.
outside broadcast *Br., Aus. /Am.* **remote broadcast/** programme that is not made within radio or TV building.
outside station *Aus.* farm in the inner part of Australia.
outsize(d) *esp. Br.* 1. of things that are much larger than usual. 2. (of clothes) used for very large people.
outsquatter *Aus.* rich farmer.
outstate *Am.* n. adj. the area away from Metro and industrial cities or another state.
outstation 1. *Br.* col. n. adj. outlying military post, trading post, etc. 2. *Aus.* Aboriginal community located far from a centre on which it depends.
out stringer *Am.* outer string (in building).
out(t)a *esp. Am.* col. out of.
out-tray *esp. Br. /esp. Am.* **outbox/** out basket: *The marble head was sitting on Felix's desk, gazing arrogantly up from the Out box.* - T. Murphy.

outwork *Br.* /*Am.* **buyout**/.
oven glove *Br.* /*Am.*, *Aus.* **oven mitt**/ pot holder.
over 1. *Am.* again; **start over, do it over**. 2. *esp. Am.* during or beyond a certain period: *they're going to ask me what I did over the summer* - J.D. Salinger., *The CBC pilot was shot in Toronto over about one week.* - W. Jack, B. Laursen. 3. *Am.* please turn over (PTO).
over (on) *Br.* on the opposite side of smth. from where sb. is.
over/ be over *Br.* be left after a meal.
overall 1. *esp. Br.* /*Am.* **work coat**/ a loose-fitting coat-like garment worn over other clothes to protect them: *drab, greasy overalls and trousers.* - D. Lodge. 2. *Am.* overalls.
overall minority *Br.* the difference between this number of votes and the number of votes gained by all the other parties.
overalls 1. *Br.* /*Am.* **overall, coveralls** *Br.* **boiler suit**/ a garment made in piece to cover the whole body, worn esp. by workers over other clothes to protect them. 2. *Am.* /*Br.* **dungarees, jumpers**/ a workman's trousers with a bib and shoulder straps: *men with lean, lanky frames and patched overalls flooded the store* - Guideposts. 3. *Br.* trousers formerly worn as part of an army uniform, now worn only on formal occasions.
overarm *esp. Br.* /*Am.* **overhand**/ adj., adv. (of a ball) thrown with one's arm high above one's shoulder.
overbalance 1. *esp. Br.* (cause to) fall over from the loss of balance. 2. *Am.* outweigh.
overdraft facility *Br.* agreement with the bank that a customer may take more money from the bank that they have in their account up to a certain amount.
over easy *Am., Can.* (of a fried egg) turned over when almost cooked and fried lightly on the other side.
overegg the pudding *Br.* col. do more than is nesessary, or add smth. that is not needed.
over garment *Am.* outer clothes.
overexposure *Am.* ballyhoo.
overhaul *Br.* overtake sb., esp. in a sporting event.
overheads *esp. Br.* /*esp. Am.* **overhead**/ money spent regularly to keep a business running: *the tour might not quite cover its gigantic overheads* - P. Norman., *they don't benefit from the huge overhead costs.* - McLean's.
overland *Aus., NZ.* drive the cattle for a great distance. n. **-er**.
overlander *Aus., NZ.* col. tramp.
overlook *Am.* /*Br.* **viewpoint**/.

overmatch *esp. Am., Can.* be stronger, better armed and more skilful.
overmighty *Br.* much more powerful.
overnighter *Am., Can.* a trip or stay for one night only.
overparted *Br.* having a very complicated role or too many roles to play.
overpass *Am., Aus.* /*esp. Br.* **flyover**, *esp. Br.* **crossover**/ place where two roads or railways cross each other: *Susan used the pedestrian overpass to cross the intersection* - R. Cook., *swarm onto overpasses - all to get a glimpse* - Newsweek., *I crossed a railroad overpass* – J. Kerouac.
overpitch *Br.* exaggerate.
overprinting *Br.* /*Am.* **surprinting**/.
overreacher *Am., Can.* swindler, fraudster.
override *esp. Am.* an attempt to cancel sb.'s decisions by using your authority over them or by gaining more votes than them in an election or contest.
overrider *Br.* either of the two projecting pieces on the bumper of a car.
overside *Am.* over the side of a ship into the water.
overskirt *Am.* one worn over another skirt.
overstay market *Am.* lose the favourable moment for selling goods and securities at the highest price.
overslaugh 1. *Am.* pass over for appointment or promotion in favour of another. 2. *Br.* a. excuse from (military duty). b. do this in order to perform some other duty. 3. *Br.* n. excusing or exemption from military duty. 4. *Am.* a sandbank or bar obstructing navigation in a river. 5. *Am.* v. hinder.
overspend *esp. Br.* /*Am.* usu. **overrun**/ (business term) spend more money than was planned or allowed in the budget of an organisation or business.
overspill *esp. Br.* people who leave a city because of overpopulation there and settle on the edges or beyond.
overstock *esp. Am.* supply or quantity in excess of demand.
overtake *Br., Aus.* /*Am.* **pass**/ come from behind and move in front of another vehicle or person, often in **pull out and overtake**.
Do not overtake *Br.* No passing.
overtaking lane *Br., Aus.* /*Am.* **passing lane**/ lane nearest the centre of the road used for overtaking.
over-the-counter (OTC) *Am.* (of business shares) not appearing on official stock exchange list.
overthrow *Am., Aus.* throw a ball beyond the target; also *Am.* n.

overtime *Am.* /*Br.* **extra time**/ time added to the end of a game when time has been lost during the game.
overtime ban *Br., Aus.* refusing to work beyond the usual time.
owing *esp. Br.* (of money) not yet being paid to the person who should receive it.
owl train *Am.* col. night train; **owl car** *Am.* col. night taxi.
own/ be on one's **own** *Br.* col. be outstanding, spectacular.
own/ get one's **own back (on** sb.) *Br.* revenge sb.
own brand/label *Br.* 1. /*Am.* **store brand/label,** *Aus.* **generic brand/label/** brand of goods in a shop with the name of it rather than a name of a producing company. 2. some specific feature of a person or a group of people.
own goal *esp. Br.* 1. (in football) a goal against one's own team scored by mistake by one of one's own players. 2. col. a mistake that makes one look foolish or harms their own interests, often in **score an own goal.**
own hook/ on one's **own hook** *Am.* without sb. else telling you or asking you to do.
own tail/ tell its own tale *Br., Aus.* show the truth about a situation.
own trumpet/ blow one's **own trumpet** *Br., Aus.* /*Am., Aus.* **blow/toot** one's **own horn/** boast about one's success.
owner-driver *esp. Br.* person who drives his/her own car.
owner-occupier *esp. Br.* a person who owns the house or flat in which he/she lives: *Now I will never be an owner-occupier.* – S. Townsend.
ownership/ be in/under ownership *Br., Aus.* have an owner.
Oxbridge *Br.* universities of Oxford and Cambridge put together.
oxford *Am.* 1. shoe, a tie shoe, laced shoe, oxford shoe: *scuffing the petalled bow of my oxfords* - W. Grady. 2. type of shirt made of thick cotton.
The Oyster State *Am.* Maryland.
oyster cocktail *Am.* oyster served with trimmings.
Oz *Br., Aus.* col. Australia.
The Ozark State *Am.* Missouri.
Ozzie, Aussie *Aus.* Australian.

P

p *Br.* col. penny, pence: *I wouldn't give you five pee for them* - D. Lodge.
PA *Br., Aus.* personal assistant or secretary.

PACE *Br.* Police and Criminal Evidence Act, Act of 1984 stating conditions on which suspects can be detained without charge.
pace/ change of pace *esp. Am., Can.* change from the usual routine.
pacer *esp. Am.* horse bred and trained to have a lateral gait.
pacesetter *Am.* pacemaker, one that sets a speed that others in a race try to equal.
pac(e)y *Br.* col. 1. fast. 2. lively.
pacifier *Am., Can.* /*Br., Aus.* **dummy/** rubber teat for sucking put in a baby's mouth to keep it quiet: *He was born with a silver pacifier in his mouth* - D. Mortman.
pack (of) 1. *esp. Am.* /*Br., Aus.* **packet/** a small parcel, a small container for cigarettes, chewing gum, etc.: *Sergeant Fourier became quiet and nervously took out a pack of cigarettes.* - I. Shaw., *I smoked another half a pack of cigarettes* - R.P. Warren., *The pack was empty.* - R. Borchgrave, R. Moss. 2. *Br.* a bag carried by soldiers or walkers on their shoulders. 3. *Br., Aus.* /*Am.* **deck/** a set of playing cards.
pack 1. *Am.* v. n. (use) the practice of rising the price of a car to offer a larger discount: *the Oldsmobile was packing over $ 360,000.* - W. Jack, B. Laursen. 2. *Am., Can.* carry in a pack. 3. *Am., Can.* carry regularly as part of one's usual equipment, esp. **pack a gun**: *He's packing plenty of gun* - D. Hammet., *he packed a pistol for self-protection.* - Time., *The Panthers began to be a threat when they started to pack gun* - E. Cleaver.
pack/ go the pack *Aus., NZ.* col. get worse, fall apart.
pack/ pack heat *Am., Can.* col. carry a gun.
pack (it) in 1. *esp. Br., Aus., Can.* col. stop doing: *Now for fuck's sake pack it in.* - J. Fowles. 2. *Br.* col. end a romantic relationship with sb.
pack smth. **out** *Am., Can.* pack smth. up and take it away.
pack up 1. *esp. Br., Aus.* col. (of a machine, etc.) stop working: *This is no ruddy time for your heart to pack up.* - J.P. Donleavy., *It seemed that the tractor had already packed up.* - A. McLean. 2. *Br.* col. stop doing smth. such as job.
package 1. *Am.* a radio or TV series offered at a lump sum. 2. *Am., Can.* /*Br., Aus.* **packet/** the box, bag, etc., that food is put in. for selling
package advertising *Am.* advertisement printed on a wrapper or package.
package freight *Am.* part-load goods, general goods in general consignments.

packager *Am.* person making a TV or radio program.

packager *Br. /Am.* **outhouse publisher/** print. a company producing books for regular trade publishers whose imprint appears on the title page and who will sell the book as if it was one of their own titles.

package goods *Am.* alcoholic drinks sold on the off-lisence.

package holiday *Br. /Aus.* **holiday package/** holiday arranged by a travel company for a fixed price that includes one's hotel and travel.

package store *Am.* obs. */Br.* **off-lisence/** a store selling alcoholic beverages in sealed containers.

pack drill/ No names, no pack drill *Br.* col. If I tell you no names then there will be no blame or punishment.

packed lunch *Br. /Am.* **box lunch, bag lunch,** *Aus.* **cut lunch/** food that you prepare at home and take to eat at work, on a trip, etc.: *7:05. Ate packed lunch.* – S. Townsend

packed-out *esp. Br.* col. (of a room, building, etc.) completely full of people: *the town is packed out.* - M.M. Kaye.

packer 1. *Am., Can., Aus.* person who transports goods by means of pack animals. 2. *Aus.* pack animal. 3. *esp. Am., Can.* a firm or official in charge of purchases (esp. of meat). 4. *Am.* a cannery worker.

packet *esp. Br., Aus. /Am.* **package,** *esp. Am.* **pack/** a small container, usu. made from paper, that contains things of the same kind, esp. food, such as biscuits, etc.

packet of crisps *Br., Aus. /Am.* **bag of chips/**.

packet *Br.* col. a lot of money.

packet *Br.* taboo. sl. a man's sex organs.

packet/ catch / cop / get / stop a packet *Br.* col. obs. get into serious trouble or receive a heavy punishment.

packet/ cost a packet *Br.* col. cost a lot.

packing cases *Br., Aus. /Am.* **packing crates/** large strong boxes for transporting goods.

packing house *Am.* cannery: *the seizing of empty packing houses would avail us nothing without the livestock.* - H. Truman.

pack rat *Am., Can.* col. a compulsory keeper of stores: *The office looked as though it had been furnished by a blind hyperthyroid pack rat.* - S. Sheldon., *Pack rat-archivist Jackie had four homes* - New York.

packsack *Am., Can.* rucksack.

packsaddle *esp. Am., Can.* horse's saddle adapted for supporting sacks.

pack trip *Am. /Br.* **pony-trekking/** trip through countryside on horses for fun or as a sport.

pad *Am.* 1. **the pad** sl. graft and bribe money taken and shared by police officers (esp. in the phr. **on the pad**). 2. automobile license plate. 3. dishonestly make bills more expensive than they really are.

paddle 1. *Am.* small bat used in table tennis. 2. *Am., Can.* col. paddle-shaped instrument for administering corporal punishment of children.

paddle *Am., Can.* col. strike with the open hand in punishing: *you paddled her and sent her home.* - K. Vonnegut, Jr.

paddle *Br., Aus. /Am.* **wade/** walk with bare feet in shallow water, n., often in **have a paddle, go on a paddle.**

paddle one's own canoe *Br.* do things the way one likes without any help or control from the other people.

paddle steamer *Br. /Am., Can.* **side-wheeler/** large boat driven by steam pushed forward by two large wheels at the sides.

paddle tennis *Am.* table tennis.

paddling pool(s) *Br.* 1. */Am.* usu. **wading pool,** *Aus.* **toddling pool/** a shallow artificial pool for children to paddle in. 2. small pool which is not very deep, for children to play in.

paddock (field) *Aus., NZ.* 1. an enclosed field, cattle pen: *They've been standing in the paddocks drying out ever since.* - New Idea. 2. a field, esp. one with grass. 3. put cattle in a pen.

paddock land *Aus.* put a fence around a plot of land.

paddy(-whack) *Br.* col. a state of bad temper, often in **be in a paddy**: *Don't get into such a paddy.* - Reader's Digest.

Paddy wagon *Am., Can., Aus.* col. Black Mariah, a patrol wagon: *the kids were at that very moment being arrested and filling Paddy wagons* - J. Baez.

padrone *esp. Am.* col. employer, esp. one who exploits immigrant workers.

page *Am.* 1. a call (for guest, etc.): *During the snack John received another page on his beeper.* - T. Thompson. 2. a student who works as a helper to a member of the US Congress.

page/ be/get on the same page *Am.* col. (of two people or groups) agree on common policy in doing smth.

page three girl *Br., Aus.* a young woman who is photographed with naked breasts for some popular newspapers.

page through *Am.* look at a book, magazine, etc.

page up *Am.* put (printed matter) into numbered page order: *someone has to page it up.* - Longman.

(beauty) pageant *Am., Can.* beauty contest.

pageboy *Br.* /*Am.* **page**/ a small boy who is one of the bride's attendants at a wedding.

page-one *Am., Can.* news worthy to be printed on the first page of the newspaper.

pail 1. *esp. Am.* or. *Br.* obs. a bucket for carrying liquids: *the crater was hotter than a pail of barbecue hash.* - E. Caldwell. 2. *Am., Can.* **dinner pail** one containing worker's midday meal: *a stack of interlocking aluminum pails* - E. Cleaver. 3. *esp. Am.* also **pailful** an amount of liquid that a pail holds.

pail and shovel *Am.* a bucket and spade taken to the beach to play with.

pain *esp. Am., Can.* (of a part of a body) hurt.

pain/ be a pain in the arse/backside/bum col. *Br., Aus.* /*Am., Aus.* **be pain in the ass/butt**/.

pain/ no pain, no gain *esp. Am., Can.* suffering is necessary to achieve smth.

pain/ on pain of death *Br.* 1. col. very strictly. 2. punishable by death.

paint *Am., Can.* piebald horse.

paint cards *Am.* sl. picture cards /*Br.* **court cards**, *Am.* **face cards**/.

paint chip *Am., Can.* card showing a range of colours available in type of paint.

paint the town *Am.* col. have a good time: *Why aren't you out painting the town?* - R.P. Warren., *honey, we're going to paint this town.* - A. Miller.

painting/ be like painting the Fourth Bridge *Br.* repairs or improvements taking so much time that it has to be started again soon.

paintwork *esp. Br.* painted surfaces in a building or vehicle.

the pair of you/them *Br.* col. used when sb. is angry or annoyed with them.

pajama(s) *esp. Am.* pyjama(s).

pakeha *Aus., NZ.* white New Zealander, as opposed to Maori.

Paki *Br.* col. derog. a Pakistani: *we'll make it a family business, like a Paki corner shop.* - D. Lodge.

pal *esp. Am.* (used in unfriendly speech to a man): *I'm saving him, pally.* - L. Waller.

pal around (with) *Am.* do things together as friends: *He had no job, palled around with mobsters* – A. Summers, R. Swan.

pal up (with) *Br., Aus.* col. become friends.

palace-car *Am.* luxury railway carriage.

palais (de danse) *Br.* dance hall.

pale ale *Br.* light ale.

paleo-conservative *Am., Can.* an extreme right-wing conservative.

palimony *esp. Am.* col. compensation paid by one member of unmarried couple to another in case of separation.

palings *Br., Aus.* paling.

palisade(s) *esp. Am.* a line of high straight cliffs, esp. along a river or beside the sea: *One can see remnants of this in the Hudson River's Palisades.* - Reader's Digest.

pall *Am.* a coffin with a body inside.

palm/ cross sb.'s **palm (with silver)** *Br.* bribe sb. with money to make them do smth.

palm court *Br.* a hotel lounge decorated with potted palms (popular in '20s and '30s).

The Palmetto State *Am.* South Carolina.

palookas, paluka *Am., Can., Aus.* col. any large and stupid person: *Get out of here, you paluka.* - R.A. Spears.

palsy-walsy *Br., Aus.* col. very friendly, esp. in a way that seems insincere: *Mike's pouring on the charm and acting super palsy-walsy.* – S. Lawrence.

pan 1. *esp. Br.* the bowl of a lavatory. 2. *Am.* col. a face: *They look at that pretty pan and try to think that you're an actress.* - F.S. Fitzgerald., *Don't you like my pan?* - E. Hemingway. 3. *Am.* sl. criticism. 4. *esp. Am.* /*Br.* **baking tin**/ a metal container for baking things: *they inspected the wreckage of a burned-out box kit with a non-inflammable pie pan tied to it.* – F. Edwards. 5. *Am.* container used to separate gold from other substances by washing them in water.

pan food *Am.* cook it in a pan.

pan/ go down the pan *Br.* sl. be wasted or become useless or ruined.

Panazonian *Am.* US citizen living in the Panama Canal Zone.

Pancake Day, also **Pancake Tuesday** *esp. Br.* col. Shrove Tuesday (on which according to custom, pancakes are eaten): *My mother had forgotten that today was pancake day.* – S. Townsend.

pancake, flapjack, hot cake *Am.* griddle cake, usu. smaller and thicker than in Britain, that is served in a pile with three or four others usu. for breakfast, often with maple syrup.

pancake *Br.* /*esp. Am.* **crepe**/ a thin soft flat cake made of butter, cooked in a flat pan, and usu. eaten hot with a sweet or savoury filling.

pancake roll *Br.* /also *Br.* **spring roll**, *Am.* **egg roll**/ a Chinese food consisting of a thin case of egg pastry filled with bits of vegetables and often meat and usu. cooked in oil.

Panda car, jam sandwich, Z car *Br.* col. a small police patrol car.

Panda crossing *Br.* a place to cross a busy town road, marked with broad white lines, where the walker can control traffic lights to stop the traffic.

pandowdy *Am.* a deep-dish apple dessert spiced, sweetened with sugar molasses or a maple syrup and covered with a rich crust.

PandP *Br.* postage and packing, wrapping and sending goods by post.

pandy *Can.* almost.

panel 1. *Br.* list of medical pratitioners registered in a district as accepting patients under the National Health Service. 2. *esp. Am.* list of available jurors or a jury.

panel *Am.* cover or decorate smth. with flat pieces of wood, glass, etc., **oak-panelled, glass-panelled**, etc.

panel beater *Br.* person who hammers metal panels into shape or does body work on a car.

panel game *Br.* broadcast quiz played by a team of people.

panel pin *Br.* light thin nail with a very small head.

panel saw *Br.* light saw with small teeth for cutting wood.

panel truck *Am., Can.* small enclosed delivery truck, used mainly for delivery services.

panel van *Aus., NZ.* small van, esp. with windows and passenger seats.

panfish *Am., Can.* fish suitable for frying whole on the pan.

panhandle *esp. Am., Can.* a thin stretch of land joined to a larger area like the handle of a pan, **panhandle town** *Am.* interstate town: *Later he became a country schoolteacher in the Oklahoma panhandle* - J. Kerouac.

panhandle *esp. Am., Can.* col. beg, esp. in the streets, n. **-er**: *I'll panhandle subway fare up to 174th street* - J. Cheever., *the panhandler who mooched a dime from me in the street* - E. Cleaver.

The Panhandler State *Am.* West Virginia.

panic *Am.* sl. 1. a very funny thing, scream: *They thought that was a panic, too.* - J.D. Salinger. 2. cause to be very amused: *I was totally panicked.* - Premiere.

panic *esp. Br.* situation in which there is a lot to do and not much time to do it in.

panic button/ press/push the panic button *Br.* do smth. quickly in a critical situation without thinking enough about it.

panic stations *Br., Aus.* col. a time when one feels very anxious and has to act very quickly.

pannage *Br.* pig food.

pannikin *Br., Aus.* obs. (the amount held by) a small drinking cup.

pannikin boss *Aus.* col. nominal manager of the farm; minor overseer or foreman.

pant cuffs *Am., Can.* /*Br.* **trousers turn-ups**/.

pantec *Aus.* col. container trailer forming the rear part of an articulated lorry.

pantechnicon *Br.* obs. a very large van, esp. a removal van.

panther *esp. Aus., Am.* /*Br.* **puma,** *esp. Am.* **cougar**/ cougar or jaguar.

panties 1. *Br.* some use /*Am.* **underpants**/ *Am.* /*Br.* **knickers**/ short close-fitting underpants, worn by women or girls: *Except for the white fox fur stole and muff and her panties, everything she wore belonged to the studio.* – N. Mailer.

panto *Br.* col. pantomime, traditional Christmas show for children.

pantomime dame *Br.* male actor playing a female character in a pantomime.

pantomime horse *Br.* two persons pretending to be a horse by dressing up in special clothes.

pants 1. *Br.* /*esp. Am., Aus.* **underpants,** *Am.* **leotard,** *Can., Am.* **shorts**/ panties or underpants: *a grinning topless model tricked out in fur boots and ermine-trimmed bikini pants* - D. Lodge. 2. *esp. Am., Can.* /*esp. Br., Aus.* **trousers**/ trousers: *He sprawls across the bed in those long corduroy pants with the suspenders* - C. McCullers., *her pants ripped on stage* - "M." 3. *Br.* also **knickers** a piece of underwear worn by women or girls which has holes for the legs and elastic around the waist to hold stockings up.

pants/ in long / short pants *esp. Am.* col. (of a person) fully / not fully-grown.

pants/ deck pants *Am.* col. women's short trousers.

pants/ downhill ski pants *Am.* mountain skier's trousers.

pants/ it's/that's pants *Br.* sl. a bad performance or nonsense.

pants/ he/she puts his/her pants on one leg at a time *Am.* col. used to say that sb. is just like everybody else.

pants man *Aus.* sl. promiscuous male.

pant suit *esp. Am., Can.* /*Br.* **trouser suit**/ a suit for women consisting of pants and jacket made of the same material: *I wore a purple Holstein pantsuit* - E. Taylor.

panty hose *esp. Am., Can.* /*esp. Br.* **tights**/: *So she bought black panty hose and stopped wearing lipstick.* - J. Baez.

panty raid *Am.* male college students practice in women's dormitory to steal their undergarment.

pantywaist *Am., Can.* 1. a child's garment consisting of short pants buttoned to a waist. 2. col. n. adj. sissy: *anybody who still had his own teeth was considered a pantywaist.* - W. Jack, B. Laursen.

pap 1. *esp. Am.* derog. reading matter which is only amusing and doesn't instruct or contain ideas of any value: *Sheer religious pap!* - D. Carnegie. 2. *Am.* col. political patronage: *a pap and propaganda sheet for tourists* - H. Smith. 3. *Am.* papa.

papa /also **poppa, pap(py)**/ *Am., Can.* col. a father /also *Br.* old use/: *Meanwhile Willie was back on Pappy's farm, helping with the chores* - R.P. Warren., *I doubt her pappy'd let her* - Arthur Hailey.

paper 1. *Br., Aus.* a set of printed questions that is used as (part of) an exam. 2. *esp. Am., Aus.* essay that is done as part of a course at school or university: *the kids turned in their papers* – Reader's Digest.

paperbark *Aus.* a type of tree.

paperboy (girl) *Br.* /*Am.* **newsie, newsy**/ a schoolboy (girl) who delivers newspapers and magazines daily to private houses and commercial premises such as offices and shops.

paper chase 1. *Am., Aus.* the activity of dealing with many different documents. 2. *esp. Br.* game in which sb. runs ahead of a group of people dropping pieces of paper which they have to follow. 3. *Am.* an attempt to gain a university degree.

paperchase *Br.* cross-country races along the trail marked by torn-up paper.

paper curtain *Am.* government red-tape that prevents a free flow of information.

paper fastener *Br.* /*Am.* **brad**/ small metal object like a button used to hold several pieces of paper together.

paper knife *Br.* /*Am.* **letter knife**/ one used for opening envelopes.

paper opener *Br.* /*Am.* **letter opener**/.

paper-pusher *esp. Am.* col. bureaucrat or manual clerk worker.

paper round *Br.* /*Am.,Can.* **paper route**/ a job of delivering newspapers to people's homes usu. done by children.

papers/ first papers *Am.* first documents of a foreigner applying for American citizenship.

papers/ send in one's **papers** *Br.* (of an officer) ask to be allowed to leave.

paper shop, newsstand *Br.* one that sells newspapers, tobacco, sweets, and stationery.

paper trail *esp. Am., Can., Aus.* documents which show what sb. has been doing: *If things come to a head, you'll have a paper trail.* – Reader's Digest.

pappy *Am.* obs. one's father.

pap smear *Am., Aus.* /*Br.* **smear test**/ test of examining thick liquid on the surface of women's cervix to discover if there is any disease.

para 1. *esp. Br.* col. paratrooper. 2. *Br.* adj. paranoid.

paracetomol *Br.* common drug used to reduce pain, which doesn't contain aspirin.

parade 1. *esp. Br.* street with a row of small shops. 2. *Br., Aus.* often used in the names of streets. 3. *Br.* public square or promenade.

paraffin 1. also **paraffin oil, liquid paraffin** *esp. Br.* /*Am., Can., Aus.* **kerosene,** *Am.* **coal oil, lamp oil**/ an oil made from petroleum coal, etc., burnt for heat and in lamps for light: *We made to light the paraffin blow torches* - A. McLean. 2. *Am.* /*Br.* **paraffin wax, white wax**/ soft white substance used for making candles.

parajournalism *Am.* slanting, expressing (facts, reports, etc.) in a way favourable to a particular group.

paralegal *esp. Am., Can.* junior lawyer: *a paralegal who doubles as a runner.* - S. Grafton.

parallel *esp. Am.* an imaginary line around the earth always at the same distance from the equator.

paralytic *esp. Br., Aus.* col. very drunk.

paramedic *esp. Am.* person, such as an ambulance driver who helps in the care of sick people but is not a doctor or nurse: *As paramedics, my partner and I were dispatched to check on a 92-year-old man* - Reader's Digest.

paranumesmatica *Br.* collecting things simillar to coins and medals, such as tokens and medallions.

parapente *Aus.* the sport of jumping off a cliff or a hill with a sheet-like parachute.

paraprofessional *esp. Am., Can.* person to whom only part of professional task is given but who is not licensed to practice as a fully qualified professional.

paras *Br.* col. paratroops.

para-university *Am.* public university with a free program.

parcel 1. *esp. Br.* /*esp. Am., Aus.* **package**/ thing(s) wrapped in paper and tied or fastened in some other way for easy carrying, posting, etc. 2. *esp. law. or Am.* a piece of land, esp. part of a larger piece that has been divided: *The land has since been divided into 670 wooded parcels* - S.

Grafton. 3. *Br.* small quantity of food that has been wrapped up, usu. in pastry.
parcel (of things or people) *esp. Br.* a quantity of them.
parcel smth. **up** *Br.* make smth. into a parcel by wrapping it up.
parcel bomb *Br.* a small bomb, usu. sent in a parcel through the post and designed so as to explode on being opened.
parched corn *Am.* fried maize.
Parcheesi *Am.* tdmk. /*Br.* **Ludo**/.
parchment *Am.* /*Br.* **greaseproof (paper)**, *esp. Am.* **waxed paper**/.
pardner *Am.* col. humor. a form of address between men.
pardon *esp. Br.* /*Am., Can.* also **pardon me**/ used to ask sb. politely to repeat smth.
pardon me *esp. Am.* obs. used to politely get sb.'s attention.
pardon me for interrupting, asking, saying *esp. Br.* used to politely ask if one can iterrupt sb. to get their attention.
parenthesis *esp. Am., Aus.* or *Br.* formal. /*Br.* **(round) bracket**/.
Pardon me, also **Excuse me** *Am.* quick apology for doing something wrong accidentally / *Br.* use **I do beg your pardon** to make the apology stronger.
parent-teacher association *Br.* local organisation for promoting closer relations between teachers and parents and improving educational facilities at aschool.
parfait *Am.* sweet food made of layers of ice-cream and fruit.
parietal *Am., Can.* having to do with or having authority over the residents in the buildings of a college.
parietals *Am., Can.* visitation rules in a dormitory for members of opposite sex.
parimutuel *Am.* /*Br.* **tote**/ machine used to calculate the amount of money person can win by risking it in horse races.
(civil) parish *Br.* small country district with its own **parish council**.
parish *esp. Br.* col. an area of knowledge or work that is the special responsibility of a particular person.
parish-pump *Br.* often derog. of local interest only.
park 1. *Br.* large enclosed stretch of land with grass, trees, etc., round a large country house. 2. *Br.* col. (journalist use) /*Am.* **ballpark-playfield**/ field on which (esp. professional) soccer is played. 3. *Br.* place to leave a car or other vehicle (**car park, caravan park**). 4. *Am.* high plateau like valley among mountains. 5. *Am., Can.* enclosed arena or stadium used. esp. in ball games. 6. *Am.* col. baseball field.
parka *esp. Am., Can.* /*esp. Br.* **anorak**/ short coat that has a hood and keeps out wind and rain: *she grabbed her parka* - D. Mortman.
parkade *Can.* multi-storey car park.
parkin *Br.* kind of cake made of dark ginger bread with oatmeal.
parking *Am.* strip of land in the middle of the road planted with grass and trees.
parking bay *Br.* /*Am.* **parking space**/ a place to leave a car for a time: *in the Bronx there were stabbings over parking spaces.* - J. O'Brien, A. Kurins.
parking brake *Am., Aus.* /*Br.* **hand brake**, *Am.* **emergency brake**/.
parking garage *Am.* /*Br.* **car park**/ multi-storey car park: *that is named after a parking garage concept.* - New York.
parking light *Am.* /*Br.* **sidelight**/ either of a pair of lamps fixed usu. on the front of a vehicle at or near the sides: *Parking light wasn't even broken.* - G. O'Neill, D. Lehr.
parking lot /or **space, garage**/ *Am., Aus.* /*Br.* **car park**/ space in which vehicles may be left: *He walked like a zombie to the parking lot.* - E. Segal., *So, well on the edge of town I drove into a parking lot.* - J. Steinbeck., *we peer out at a parking lot full of cars and vans and trailers.* - T.A. Harris.
park keeper, also col. **parky** *esp. Br.* person in charge of park or one who helps to look after a park: *The park-keeper spent a great deal of time chatting us* - C.M. Fraser.
parkland *Br.* grassy land around a large country house having trees growing in it.
park ranger *Am.* ranger, person looking after a forest or area of countryside.
parkway 1. *Am., Can., Aus.* wide road divided by or bordered with an area of grass and trees: *there was a little traffic on the Belt Parkway to Manhattan.* - M. Puzo. 2. *Br.* railway station with a lot of parking facilities.
parky *Br.* col. (of the weather, air, etc.) rather cold, chilly: *But by God, it's parky out there!* - D. Reeman.
parl *Br.* Parliament.
parlay *Am.* accumulator bet, risking anew of an original stake together with its winnings.
parlay *esp. Am.* v. 1. bet in a parlay. 2. exploit successfully, magnify: *to parlay his knowledge of fixed horse races into a quick bankroll.* - G.

O'Neill, D. Lehr., *His speciality was making extortionate loans which he then parlayed into equity shares* - J. O'Brien, A. Kurins.

parliamentarian *Am.* expert on the rules and methods used by a group that makes laws and decisions.

parlor *esp. Am.* special shop (in comb.): *There's a pizza parlor just up the road* - R. Borchgrave, R. Moss.

parlor house *Am.* brothel.

parlour boarder *Br.* pupil in a boarding school who lives with the principal's family.

parlo(u)r car *Am., Can. /Br.* **saloon-carriage/** Pullman, a specially comfortable railway carriage, esp. for sleeping in: *We had ridden to Philadelphia in reserved parlor car seats.* - Alex Haley.

parlour maid *Br.* woman who serves at the table during meals: *parlour-maid hastened into the hall.* - A. Huxley., *as parlourmaid, she has developed certain marked eccentricities* - T. Rattigan., *a woman about thirty was a parlourmaid.* - V. Holt.

parlour pew *Br.* family pew in a church.

parochiaid *Am.* government aid to parish schools.

parochial *esp. Am., Can. /Br.* **voluntary school/** supported by a religious body, e.g. **parochial school**.

parquet *Am.* the lower floor of a theatre, esp. the part from the front of the stage to the **parquet circle** /also *Am.* **partierre,** *Br.* **pit/**.

parquet circle *Am.* the part of the lower floor of a theatre beneath the galleries.

parrot-fashion *Br., Aus.* repeating smth.

parson's nose *Br. /Am.* **pope's nose/** col. humor. 1. the piece of flesh at the tail end of a cooked bird, such as chicken. 2. the part of the body that goes over the fence last.

part *Am., Can., Aus. /Br., Aus.* **parting/** the line on a person's head where the hair is parted: *The wavy locks were fairly close cut and combed without a part.* - L. Waller.

part/ look the part *Br.* be impressive and sucessful.

part/ take sb.'s **part** *Br.* support them, esp. in an argument.

part/ take smth. **in good part** *Br.* be not offended or upset by smth.

part exchange *esp. Br. /Am.* **trade-in/** (an example of) the system of paying for smth. partly in money and partly in goods esp. with a used object of the same kind as the thing one is buying, esp. in offer **in/as part exchange**: *A wife wasn't like a car; you couldn't part-exchange her when the novelty wore off* - D. Lodge.

partner 1. *esp. Am.* col. (used esp. by and of males) a male friend: *What's the matter, pardner?* - R. Chandler. 2. *Am., Can.* associate as partners.

part work *Br.* a set of magazines on one particular subject that are produced usu. once a week and can be fit together to form a book.

party *esp. Am., Aus.* col. enjoy oneself, esp. at a party: *I went to high school, hung out, partyin' out at the lake, drinking beers and listening to Aerosmith.* - BigO.

party/ fancy dress party *Br., Aus. /Am.* **costume party/** masquerade party.

party/ party piece *Br.* humor. short performance or an action done in public.

party/ piss on sb.'s **party** *Br., Aus.* col. do smth. that spoils sb.'s plans.

party down *Am.* sl. let oneself go.

party/ necktie party *Am.* sl. lynching party.

party boat *Am., Can.* boat available for hiring by people who want to go fishing as a group.

party favors *esp. Am.* small gifts such as paper hats and toys given to children at a party.

party-hearty *Am.* sl. having a great fun: *his party-hearty college antics kept him from getting past Go with Miss South Dakota* – Reader's Digest.

party house/school *Am.* col. place that often has noisy parties.

party line *Am.* border line between private properties.

sb.'s **party piece** *Br.* smth. strange or funny often done to entertain people in social situations.

party political broadcast *Br., Aus. /Am.* **paid political broadcast/** short program on TV where politicians talk about their party's ideas and plans.

party wire *Am.* party line, common telephone line for several subscribers.

pass 1. *Br.* a successful result in an exam, enough to get a university degree without honours (**pass degree**). 2. *Am.* a mark given to show that a student has successfully completed a course or an exam but won't be given a grade for them. 3. *esp. Am.* a document which allows a student to leave a class for a special reason.

pass *Am.* omit a regularly scheduled declaration and payment of a dividend.

pass/ sell the pass *Br.* betray sb.

pass degree *Br.* a degree given to students in a university or college who have passed their exams without getting an honours degree.

pass degree *Aus.* a degree for a college course done in three years instead of four.

pass-fail exam or **course** *esp. Am.* one where no mark is given for it.

pass mark *Br., Aus. /Am.* **passing mark/** number of points that must be achieved to succeed in an exam.

pass off *Br., Aus. /Am.* **come off/** happen.

pass out *esp. Br., Aus.* finish a course, esp. at a military school or police college.

pass up *Am.* pass (sb.) without recognising (him/her): *I wasn't going to pass it up* – Reader's Digest.

passbook 1. *Br.* book in which a record of the money one puts into and takes out of a building society is kept. 2. *Am.* bank book: *Imagine the wold with no ATMs, no passbook savings* – Reader's Digest.

passel *esp. Am.* col. obs. large group of things or people.

passenger *Br.* derog. a member of a team or other group who does not do his or her share of the group's work.

passing *Br.* (referring to a bill in Parliament) passage.

passing lane *Am. /Br.* **overtaking lane/**.

passion-pit *Am.* col. a drive-in movie theatre: *She wanted me to drive down to the passion-pit* - R.A. Spears.

passive bonds *Am.* bonds bearing no interest.

pass-out check *Am.* pass-out ticket.

pastille *esp. Br.* small round sweet, sometimes containing medicine for a sore throat; lozenge.

pasting/ take a pasting *esp. Br.* col. 1. be severely criticized. 2. (in sports and politics) be heavily defeated; opp. **give** sb. **a pasting.**

pastoral *Aus.* agricultural.

pastoralist, grazier, squatter *Aus. /Br., Aus.* **stockholder/** big cattle breeder.

(pastoral) property *Aus. /Br., Aus.* **holding/** farm, estate.

(leave for) pastures new *Br. /Am., Aus.* **new pastures/** leaving one's own job or home in order to go to a new one.

pasty *esp. Br.* small case of pastry, filled usu. with meat, vegetables, or cheese: *I could bake our bread and pasties* - V. Holt.

Pat *Br.* col. derog. nickname for Irishman.

pat/ know/learn/have smth. **down pat** */Br., Aus.* **off pat/** *Am.* know smth. very well.

pat/ on one's **Pat Malone, on** one's **pat** *Aus.* col. on one's own.

pat/ stand pat *esp. Am., Can.* col. */Aus.* col. **sit pat/** refuse to make any changes.

patch *Br.* col. 1. /also *Br.* sl. **manor/** area for which sb. is responsible or in which they are good, esp. police beat, small area in which sb. esp. policeman always works: *London was the Metropolitan Police's patch and noone else's.* - R. Cox. 2. special period of time.

sb.'s **patch** *Br.* col. */Am.* **turf/** an area that sb. knows very well because they work and live there.

patch/ be in / hit / strike a bad (difficult, sticky) patch *esp. Br.* experience a time of trouble or misfortune: *Ferdie and Meldy Marcos are going through a bad patch.* - Bulletin.

patch/ good, interesting, boring in patches *esp. Br.* good, etc. in some parts but not all the time, adj. **patchy.**

patch/ not a patch on *Br., Aus.* col. not nearly as good as.

patent right *Am.* n. patent.

pater *Br.* col. obs. or humor. father.

paternity suit *esp. Am.* court case held to establish formaly the identity of a child's father to make him pay compensation for the child.

path *Br.* bicycle or foot racing track.

path breaking *esp. Am.* and *Br.* journalism. doing smth. completely different; **break a new path**.

pathfinder *esp. Am.* 1. person who goes ahead of a group and finds the best way through unknown land. 2. person who discovers new ways of doing things; trailblazer.

pathmaster *Am.* road maintenance master (foreman).

patience *Br., Aus. /esp. Am.* **solitaire/** a card game for one player.

patio doors *esp. Br.* glass doors that open from a living room onto a patio.

patootie *Am., Can.* col. 1. sweetheart. 2. obs. young woman. 3. buttocks: *You bet your sweet patooties it would.* - H. Fast.

patrial *esp. Br.* tech. person who has a lawful right to settle in the UK, esp. because of his ancestors.

patrician *Am., Can.* person of long well-established wealthy family.

patrolman 1. also **patrol officer** *esp. Am., Can., Aus. /esp. Br.* **constable/** policeman who regularly patrols a particular area: *He could make out a patrolman from the truck* - R. Moore., *She rode in the police wagon with a young patrolman.* - E.L. Doctorow. 2. *Br.* person working for a car-owners association who drives along certain roads to give help to motorists who need it.

patrol wagon *Am., Aus. /Br.* **Black Maria/** a vehicle used to carry prisoners,: *patrol wagon and ambulances hauled away Schwartzes.* - K. Vonnegut, Jr.

patronage *Am.* /*Br.* **custom**/ support that a person gives to a particular shop, restaurant, etc. by buying their goods or using their services.

patsy *esp. Am., Can., Aus.* col. an easy victim: *making the protagonist a mere patsy, a strawman* – Harper's Magazine.

pattern *Am.* a length of fabric sufficient for an article (such as dress).

patty 1. *esp. Am.* a small round meat pie. 2. *Am., Can.* small round flat chocolate covered peppermint sweet. 3. *esp. Am.* small flat pieces of cooked meat or other food.

pavement 1. *Br., Can.* a paved surface or path at the side of a street for people to walk on, pedestrian path /*Am., Can.* **sidewalk**, *Br.* **footway**, *Aus.* **footpath**/. 2. *Am., Can., Aus.* / *esp. Br.* **road** (**surface**), **tarmac**/ the hard surface of a street: *girl stood on the London pavement in bewilderment* - P. Norman., *The wet tires sung off the pavement* - L. Uris.

pavement artist *Br.* /*Am.* **sidewalk artist**/ one who draws pictures on a pavement with coloured chalk, hoping that people passing will give money.

pavilion 1. *esp. Br.* building beside a sports field for the use of players and those watching the game. 2. *Am.* a large building in which sports and entertainment events take place. 3. *Am.* one of a group of related buildings.

pawky *esp. Br.* amusing in an odd clever way: *Christian's flowing lines, pawky sound and rhythmic grace* – I. Carr, D. Fairweather, B. Priestley. /**pawky humour**/; **pawk** *Br.* a trick, joke.

pawpaw *esp. Br.* papaya.

pay *Am.* adj. requiring payment: *what happened to the pay-toilet business* - K. Vonnegut, Jr.

pay out *Br.* obs. sl. pay back, return punishment: *What should anyone want to pay me out for?* - M. Daly.

pay out of pocket *Am.* pay for smth. by oneself and claim the money back later.

pay sb. at their own game *Br., Aus.* beat sb. at their own game.

pay sb. back in their own coin *Br., Aus.* obs. revenge sb. in the same bad way.

pay/ **if you pay peanuts, you get monkeys** *Br.* if employer pays his workers very low, he won't get good staff.

pay/ **pay on tick** *Aus.* buy things on credit.

pay/ **pay the piper** *Am.* suffer from one's own mistakes.

pay top dollar for smth. *Am.* pay a lot.

payback *esp. Am.* benefits from smth. you have worked on.

payback is bitch *Am.* col. smth. bad has happened as a result of smth. else.

pay bed *Br.* paid hospital bed as opposed to a free bed under National Health Service.

payboard *Am.* board responsible for setting standards for wage and salary increases, esp. to curb inflation.

pay box *Br.* a cashier's booth, box office.

pay cable *Am.* TV service available on subscription basis.

pay check *esp. Am.* /*Br., Aus.* **pay packet, pay cheque**/ the amount of wages a person earns: *your future paychecks may serve as collateral.* - Reader's Digest., *you can begin working at once and collect a paycheck come Friday.* - J. Kerouac.

pay claim *Br., Aus.* a demand for an increase in pay.

pay dirt *esp. Am., Can., Aus.* 1. earth found to contain valuable minerals, such as gold. 2. col. valuable or useful discovery, esp. in **hit/strike pay dirt**: *She had put him into political pay dirt.* - R.P. Warren., *After drilling a series of holes he struck a pay dirt* - Omni., *he hit real pay dirt in Paris* - R. Borchgrave, R. Moss.

PAYE *Br.* pay as you earn, a system by which income tax is taken away from wages before the wages are paid.

pay envelope *Am., Can.* /*Br., Aus.* **pay packet**/ an envelope containing a person's pay: *C.A.A. could push the pay envelope* - Time.

pay for the call/ the words used by the operator in putting through a **collect call** (*Am.*) or **reverse-charge call** (*Br.*) are in America: **Will you accept the charge?** and in Britain: **Will you pay for the call?**

payess *esp. Am., Can.* uncut sidelocks worn by male Orthodox Jews.

paying guests (PG) *Br.* a person who lives as a lodger in a private house, paying rent to the owner of the house.

paying-in book *Br.* book of forms used to pay money in the bank account.

paying-in slip, credit slip *Br.* /*Am.* **deposit slip**/ slip for putting money in a bank.

payola *esp. Am.* col. (the practice of) making a secret or not direct payment in return for a business favour: *I wrote "VOID" on those payola checks* - W. Jack, B. Laursen.

pay packet 1. *Br., Aus.* /*Am.* **pay envelope**/ one containing a person's pay. 2. *Br.* /*Am.* **paycheck**/ an amount of wages a person earns: *Inflation is biting into pay-packets.* - Economist., *You know*

what I got in my pay packet this morning - D. Francis.
pay pause *Br.* wage freeze.
pay-per-view *Am.* a system of cable TV in which viewers only pay for particular programs.
pay policy *Br.* wage control.
pay rise *Br., Aus.* /*Am.* **pay raise**/.
payroll/ Federal payrolls *Am.* state employees.
paysheet *Br.* payroll.
pay station *Am.* pay phone.
PC *Br.* police constable.
pcm *Br.* per calendar month.
pct *Am., Can.* per cent.
PCV *Br.* passenger carrying vehicle.
PD *Br.* Police Department.
peace/ no peace/rest for the wicked *Br.* humor. work must be done anyway.
Peace Garden State *Am.* col. North Dacota.
peacemaker *Am.* or humor. revolver.
peace officer *esp. Am., Can.* civil officer appointed to preserve law and order, such as sheriff or policeman: *there lived a local peace officer.* – N. Hentoff.
The Peach State, Peanut State *Am.* Georgia.
peacherino *Am.* col. peach, beauty.
peach fuzz *Am., Can.* col. the down on the chin of an adolescent male.
peachy-keen, also **peachy** *esp. Am., Can.* col. wonderful: *That was just peachy* - R.J. Randisi., M. Wallace.
peacock *Aus.* sl. pick out the choicest piece of land so that adjoining land loses its value to anybody else.
pea jacket *Am.* reefer, a navy-style duffel coat: *I'd bundle up in my hat and pea jacket and go out in all kinds of weather* - A.E. Hotchner.
peak *esp. Br.* /*Am.* **visor**/ the flat curved part of a cap which sticks out in front above the eyes.
peak *Br.* peak times are when the largest number of people are travelling, using a service, etc.
peak (viewing) time *Br.* prime time.
peaky *esp. Br.* col. /*Am.* **peaked**/ rather pale or ill: *I didn't like the look on my face in Dad's shaving mirror in the bathroom. All white and peaky.* – R. Westall.
peanut gallery *Am., Can.* col. humor. the top gallery in the theatre.
peanut politician *Am.* insignificant corrupt politician.
peopleless *Aus.* having very few or no people around.
pearl *Br.* picot, a special loop in embroidery.
a pearl of great price *Br.* smth. of great value.

pearl-diver *Am.* sl. a dish washer: *Ed Dunkel said he was an old pearldiver from way back and pitched his long arms into the dishes.* - J. Kerouac.
pearl bulb *Br.* electric light bulb with translucent glass.
pearly *Br.* fruit and vegetable pushcart vendor (**pearly king** or **queen**), often wearing pearl buttons (**pearlies**).
pearly whites *Br.* col. person's teeth.
pears *Aus.* sl. breasts.
pear-shaped/ go pear-shaped *Br., Aus.* col. fail (of a plan).
pease pudding *esp. Br.* dish of split peas boiled with onions and carrot and mushed to a pulp.
pea soup *Am., Aus.* /*Br.* col. obs. **pea souper**/ a very dense fog which looks slightly yellow.
pea-souper *Can.* derog. French-Canadian.
pea-time/ the last of pea-time *Am.* the last stage; **pea-time's past** *Am.* it is all over.
peavey *Am., Can.* lumberer's cant hook with a strong sharp spike at the end used esp. in handling logs.
pebble/ not the only pebble on the beach *esp. Br.* col. not the only important person in a situation.
pebbledash 1. *esp. Br.* mortar with pebbles in it, used as a coating for external walls. 2. *Br.* surface for the outside walls of the houses, made of cement with a lot of small pebbles set into it, v.
peck *esp. Br.* sl. food.
pecker 1. *Am., Can.* sl. penis: *Billy took his pecker out, there in the prison night and peed, and peed on the ground.* - K. Vonnegut, Jr., *I switched my pecker to my left hand.* - W. Jack, B. Laursen. 2. **keep** one's **pecker up** (be careful with American English speakers where pecker means penis!) *Br., Aus.* col. obs. remain cheerful even when it is difficult to do so: *Keep your pecker up, hen.* - C.M. Fraser. 3. *Br.* sl. a nose.
peckerhead *Am., Can.* sl. despicable person.
peckerwood *Am.* col. derog. white person, esp. a poor one: *I didn't know peckerwoods were Caucasians.* – E. James, D. Ritz.
peckish *esp. Br., Aus.* col. slightly hungry: *Are you feeling peckish, sir?* - A. McLean.
Peck's Bad Boy *Am., Can.* enfant terrible: *Then there was...Mencken, who has so often suggested "Peck's Bad Boy."* – V.W. Brooks.
pedal/ with the pedal to the metal *Am., Can.* col. with accelerator pressed to the floor.
pedal bin *Br.* rubbish bin with a lid opened by means of a pedal.

pedalist *Am.* bicyclist.
peddle *esp. Am.* col. sell goods that are of low quality.
peddle/ peddle one's **papers** *Am.* go about one's business.
peddler 1. *Am.* /*Br.* **pedlar**/ person who goes from place to place trying to sell small articles: *the junk peddler with its rickety old wagon and a single horse* - H. Truman. 2. *Br.* sl. blabbermouth.
peddler/ drug peddler *Br., Aus.* drug seller.
Peddler's French *Br.* obs. sl. thieves' jargon.
pedestal *Br.* toilet bowl.
pedestrian crossing *Br.* /*Am.* **crosswalk/**.
pedestal basin/table *esp. Br.* one that is supported by a single column.
pedestrian precinct, shopping precinct *esp. Br.* /*Am., Aus.* **pedestrian mall**/ an area with shops where vehicles are not allowed.
pedestrian subway *Br.* /*Am.* **pedestrian underpass**/ underground crossing.
pedlar *Br., Aus.* peddler.
pedola *Br., Aus.* pedal boat, a small boat moved or operated by pedals.
pedway *esp. Am., Can.* footway built for pedestrians in an urban area.
pee (down) *Br.* col. rain heavily.
peel off *Br.* col. take off some or all of one's clothes.
peel out *Am., Can.* col. leave quickly: *"Peel out," Winks said enthusiastically.* – R.L. Stine.
peeler 1. *Am.* col. striptease dancer. 2. *esp. Br.* obs. sl. policeman: *The "Peelers" (Police) would beat your legs off with their sticks* - M. Jones, J. Chilton.
peen *Am.* the end of the head of a hammer opposite the face: *Sounded like somebody hitting a milk bottle with ball peen hammer.* - K. Vonnegut, Jr.
peep *Br.* (used esp. by children) the sound of a car's horn.
peep-bo *Br.* children's game.
pee-pee *Am., Can.* col. act of urinating.
peeper *Am.* 1. sl. private detective: *Peeper, huh, pally?* - R. Chandler. 2. a kind of frog that peeps: *peepers that chirped unendingly near the pond* - Reader's Digest., *The peepers shrilled* - S. North.
peep toes *Br.* col. open-toed shoes.
peer group pressure *Br.* peer pressure, strong influence of a group, esp. of young people to behave as everybody else.
peer of the realm *Br.* a member of the nobility who has the right to sit in the House of Lords.

peeve *Am.* a pet peeve.
peewee 1. *Am.* col. short or small person, animal, etc. 2. *Aus.* magpie lark. 3. *Am., Can.* level of amateur sports for 8-9 years old in the US and 12-13 in Canada.
peg 1. also **clothes peg** *Br., Aus.* /*Am.* **clothes pin**/ small forked instrument used for holding wet washed clothes on a clothesline. 2. *Br.* becoming rare. a small amount of a strong alcoholic drink, esp. whiskey or brandy: *Drink it up; not a bad notion, a peg.* - E.M. Forster. 3. *esp. Br., Aus.* sl. cricket stump. 4. *Am.* col. a low fast throw in basketball; v.
peg/ off the peg *esp. Br., Aus.* /*Aus.* **off the hook,** *Am.* **off the rack**/ (of clothes) not specially made to fit a particular person's measurements.
peg 1. *Br.* (out, up) fasten (wet clothes) to a rope with a peg for drying. 2. *Am.* taper or bind a pair of trousers at the lower end / also **peg pants** n.: *I arrived in purple pegged pants.* - W. Jack, B. Laursen. 3. *Am., Can.* col. identify, classify: *You would not have pegged him as gangster.* - J. O'Brien, A. Kurins., *It's what sometimes happens to people who get sick of being pegged for worthless.* - W. Jack, B. Laursen. 4. *Am.* sl. run, hustle. 5. **peg it** *Am.* sl. die.
peg/ a peg to hang smth. **on** *Br.* controversial subject.
peg/ have sb. **pegged** *esp. Am.* know exactly what kind of person sb. is.
peg/ have pegged it *Br.* col. humor. die.
peg away at *Br.* col. work hard and with determination.
peg out 1. *esp. Br., Aus.* col. die or fall from exhaustion: *may be she'll even peg out?* - J. Herriot. 2. *Br.* hang clothes: *help me to peg out washing* - Longman.
pelf *Br.* sl. money: *She admires nought but Pelf.* - T. Thorne., *she knows her trade and can produce pleasure in exchange for pelf.* – Anonymous.
pelican crossing *Br.* a pedestrian crossing with traffic lights that can be set to stop traffic by people who wish to cross.
The Pelican State *Am.* Louisiana / **Pelican** *Am.* a citizen of Louisiana.
pellet 1. *esp. Br.* medicinal pill. 2. *Am.* sl. the ball used in a ball game.
pelmet *esp. Br.* /*esp. Am.* **valance**/ narrow piece of wood or cloth above a window that hides the rod on which curtains hang.
pelt/ (*esp. Br.*) *It's pelting with rain.* - Longman.
pelt/ at full pelt *Br.* with full force.
pen *Am., Can., Aus.* col. prison: *you put nine tin-horn grafters in the pen* - R.P. Warren.

penal *Br.* having a harmful effect.
penalty envelope *Am.* envelope for a free-of-charge sending of official correspondence.
penalty point *Br.* note made on a driver's license to show that they have done smth. wrong while they were driving.
penant *Am.* a flag that is given to the team that wins a league championship in baseball: *The Tigers won the pennant* – Reader's Digest.
pen and ink *Br.* sl. stink.
pence, p *Br.* 1. penny. 2. pl. of penny.
pencil-pusher *Am., Can.* col. derog. /*esp. Br., Aus.* col. derog. **pen pusher**/ an office worker: *City Hall is filled with a bunch of overpaid pencil-pushers.* - R.A. Spears.
pencil-sharpener *Am.* instrument for sharpening pencils: *I always liked to think of that hole as a kind of a pencil-sharpener.* R. Brautigan.
pencil whipping *Am.* the practice of falsifying certification.
pendant *Br.* pennant or tapering flag.
pen friend *esp. Br., Aus.* /*Am.* **pen pal**/ a person with whom one has made friends by writing letters, esp. a foreigner.
penitentiary *Am., Can.* prison.
pen lid *Br.* /*Am.* **pen cap**/ cover which goes over the top of a pen.
The Peninsular State *Am.* Florida.
pennies *Br.* in Britain refers only to coins.
pennies/ **look after/take care of the pennies and the pounds will look after themselves** *Br.* obs. be frugal with the money and you will finally have a large amount.
pennies/ **not have two pennies/half-pennies to rub together** *Br.* col. be very poor.
penn'orth/ **have** one's **two penn'orth** or **put in** one's **two penn'orth** *Br.* /*Am.* **put in** one's **two cents worth**/ add one's opinion.
Pennsy *Am.* sl. Pennsylvania: *My cousin lives in Pennsy.* - R.A. Spears.
penny *Am., Can.* col. one cent coin.
penny/ **be ten/two a penny** *esp. Br., Aus.* /*Am.* **a dime a dozen**/ be very common.
penny/ **in for a penny (in for a pound)** *Br., Aus.* it is said if sb. wants to be more involved in smth.
penny/ **the penny (has) dropped, the penny drops** *Br., Aus.* col. the meaning (of smth. said) was/has been at last understood: *The penny dropped and Tom shot up* - New Idea.
penny/ **spend a penny** *Br., Aus.* col. obs. go to the toilet.
penny/ **turn up like a bad penny** *Br.* keep appearing in a situation where they are not wanted.

penny ante *Am., Can.* col. trivial, cheap: *he returned a few dollars in his pocket from a penny ante burglary* - T. Thompson., *it was a shame to waste Hugo's card sense on penny-ante poker games* - I. Shaw.
penny arcade *esp. Am., Can.* amusement arcade.
penny dreadful *Br.* a book about exciting adventures or violent crime.
penny farthing *esp. Br.* an old-fashioned bicycle with a very large front wheel and a small back wheel.
penny-gaff, gaff *Br.* a cheap theatre or music hall.
penny plain *Br.* simple / opp. to **two-pence coloured.**
penny-wise and pound-foolish *esp. Br.* obs. careful in small matters but careless in more important ones.
pennyworth *Br.* obs. as much as can be bought for a penny.
pen pal *esp. Am., Can.* /*Br., Aus.* **pen friend**/: *My Canadian pen pal looked taller on his last visit.* - McGraw-Hill, 1990.
penpoint *Am.* point of a pen.
pen pusher *esp. Br.* col. derog. /*Am.* col. derog. **pencil pusher**/.
pension/ **draw a pension** *Br.* receive or collect a pension.
pension sb./smth. **off** *Br.* 1. col. make sb. leave their job, esp. because of old age or illness and pay them a pension. 2. col. get rid of smth. because it's too old or not useful anymore.
pension book *Br.* a booklet of payment slips issued by the government which the pensioners can exchange for the money each week at a Post Office.
pensioner *Br.* a retired person.
pension scheme *Br., Aus.* pension plan, a financial plan to receive money which a person or his/her employer paid earlier when this person retires.
penstock *Am., Can.* channel for conveying water to a water wheel or turbine.
Pentagonese *Am.* col. cryptical language used by high military personnel.
peon 1. *esp. Am., Can.* usu. humor. person who does menial jobs. 2. *Am.* sb. in Mexico or South America who works as a kind of slave to pay his debts.
(the) people *Am.* 1. prosecution for the state. 2. sl. a person. 3. col. used to get attention of a group of people.
people's park *Am.* park for the use of people as they see fit.

PEP *Br.* personal equity plan.
pepper *Br.* /*Am.* **bell pepper**/.
pepper box, also **pepper shaker** *Am.* /*Br., Aus.* **pepper pot, pepper caster (-or)**/ a container with small holes in the top, used for shaking powdered pepper onto food.
peppercorn rent *Br.* a very small amount of money (much less than one would expect) paid as rent.
(Philadelphia) pepperpot *Am.* thick soup of tripe, meat, dumplings, and vegetables highly seasoned esp. with crushed peppercorns.
pepper-upper *Am.* sl. a stimulant: *You need more sleep, not a pepper-upper.* - R.A. Spears.
peppy *esp. Am., Can.* col. lively and high-spirited.
pep rally *Am., Can.* col. rally intended at inspiring enthusiasm, esp. made before a sports event: *The principal might as well have taken the coach's salary to pep rallies* – Reader's Digest.
perambulator *esp. Br.* obs. pram.
percale *Am.* cotton cloth, used esp. for making sheets.
perch *esp. Br.* 1. a rod, a measure of length. 2. a square rod of land.
perch/ fall off one's **perch** *Br.* obs. humor. die.
perch/ knock sb. **off** their **perch** *Br., Aus.* make sb. fail or lose their leading position.
Percil-white *Br.* col. (of clothes) a powder or liquid for washing clothes.
percolate, also **perk** *Am.* sl. run smoothly and well (of an engine).
Percy boy (or **pants**) *Am.* sl. an effeminate male.
per diem *esp. Am.* money paid by an employer to workers who are paid by the day.
peremptory writ *Br.* law. a written order to appear in court.
perfecting press *Am.* press that prints both sides of paper at one time.
perform *Aus.* make a row, brawl.
performance *esp. Br.* col. a. smth. that needs a lot of work, effort, or preparation. b. derog. example of bad and socially unacceptable behaviour.
perfumier *Br.* /also becoming rare. or *Am.* **perfumer**/ maker or seller of perfume.
period 1. *esp. Am., Can.* /*Br., Aus.* **full stop, full point**/ mark at the end of a sentence. 2. *esp. Am.* (used at the end of a sentence to express completeness, or firmness of decision): *James Carpenter was entitled to wear the American Defense Ribbon - period.* - B. Tillman., *Bed of Roses is a tale of Boy meets Girl. Period.* - McLean's.

periodical room *Am.* newsroom (in a library).
perish *esp. Br.* (cause to) decay or lose natural qualities.
perisher *esp. Br.* col. often humor. a troublesome person, esp. a child.
perishing *esp. Br., Aus.* col. 1. (with) also **perished** (of a person) feeling very cold: *sitting half-perished in a stiff English gale.* - B. Bryson. 2. (of weather) very cold: *Let's get on with it. It's perishing in here.* - D. Lodge. 3. obs. annoying, damn.
perishing track *Aus.* one used for caravans.
periwinkle *Am.* winkle.
perk (up) *Aus.* sl. vomit.
perm *Br.* /*Am.* **permanent**/.
perm (from) *Br.* col. (in the pools) pick out and combine (the names of football teams) in a particular order; n.
permanent *Am., Can.* /*Br.* **perm**/ the putting of waves or curls into straight hair by chemical treatment so that they will last for several months: *Four things in the world that I really wanted - a permanent, a brassiere, high heels, and false teeth.* - A.E. Hotchner.
permanent secretary *Br.* government official who belongs to the Civil Service.
permanent way *Br.* /*Am.* **right of way**/ a railway track and the stones and beams on which it is laid.
permissive society *Br., Aus.* derog. the type of society that has existed in most Western countries since 1960s in which there was a lot of freedom, esp. sexual one.
perp *Am., Can.* col. the perpetrator of a crime.
perry *esp. Br.* an alcoholic drink made from pears.
persnickety *Am., Aus.* /*Br.* **pernickety**/ 1. col. often derog. worrying about small or unimportant things, fussy: *And he's a persnickety bastard to boot.* - R. Cox. 2. detailed and needing a lot of attention, fiddly.
persona *esp. Am.* an outward character a person presents to others to persuade them that he/she is a particular type of person.
personal *Br.* /*Am., Aus.* **person-to-person**/ (of a telephone call) made to one person in particular, and not needing to be paid for if they are not there and sb. else answers.
personal *Am.* a short personal advertisement placed in a newspaper or magazine by sb. who wishes to find a friend or lover.
personal allowance *Br.* /*Am.* **income tax exemption**/ an amount of money you can earn before you start to be taxed.

personal column *Br., Aus. /Am.* **the personals/** a part of newspaper that gives information, messages, etc. about particular people: *I thought I'd scan personals column* – Reader's Digest.

personalities *Br.* obs. unkind and rude remarks about sb.'s appearance, character, etc.

person-to-person/ talk to or meet sb. **person-to-person** *esp. Am.* talk to or meet them directly.

perspex *Br.* tdmk. */Am.* **plexiglass/** a strong plastic material that can be seen through and is used instead of glass: *Robin peered through a Perspex window* - D. Lodge.

perv *Aus., NZ.* (take) a lustful look at sb. or smth.

perve *Br., Aus.* col. derog. pervert.

pesky *esp. Am.* col. annoying and causing trouble: *Those pesky glaciers which gave us the Great Lakes and terrible weather will come again.* - Omni., *Pesky radicals like Yeltzin have even less of a political clout* - Newsweek.

peso *Am.* col. a cent.

pet *Br.* col. way of addressing sb. who you like or love.

pet/ be in a pet *Br.* obs. be annoyed.

peter 1. *esp. Am.* taboo. sl. penis: *He calls it a "prick", a "peter", a "pecker."* - E. Cleaver. 2. *Aus., NZ.* prison cell.

peter away *Br.* peter out, be gradually reduced to nothing.

Peter Principle *Am., Can.* joc. the law of the advancement of the mediocre persons.

pet hate *Br., Aus. /Am.* **pet peeve/** smth. that particularly annoys you.

petitioner *Br.* law. a person asking for a divorce.

petit pois *esp. Br.* small peas.

pet napping *Am.* the practice of stealing dogs and cats in order to sell them elsewhere.

petrol *Br., Aus. /Am., Can.* **gas, gasoline/** liquid obtained esp. from petroleum, used as fuel., **petrol-resistant** or **proof** *Br. /Am.* **gasoline-resistant** or **proof; petrol tank** *Br. / Am.* **gas tank/**.

petrolatum *Am., Can. /esp. Br.* **petroleum jelly/** vaseline used esp. as a medicine for the skin: *it won't remain on vaginal walls like petrolatum jelly can.* - Reader's Digest.

petrol bomb *Br.* col. Molotov cocktail.

petrol cap *Br. /Am.* **gas tank door/**.

petrol gage *Br. /Am.* **gas gage/**.

petrol pump *Br. /Am.* **gas pump/** fuel pump.

petrol station *Br. /Am.* **gas station/** filling station.

pettifogging *Br.* obs. 1. too concerned with small events. 2. too unimportant to be worth considering.

petting zoo *Am., Can.* an open area in which small or young animals are kept which children can hold, touch, and sometimes feed.

petty bourgeois *Br.* petit bourgeois.

petty coat *esp. Br.* a piece of women's underwear that is worn under a dress or skirt: *I had a good laugh telling girls that their petticoats were showing when they weren't.* – S. Townsend.

pew *Am.* col. excl. */Br.* col. **pooh/** used when there is a very unpleasant smell.

pew *Br., Aus.* humor. seat/ **Take a pew.**

pfft *Am.* excl. **phut.**

pfui *Am.* excl. phooey.

pg *Am.* abbr. **page.**

PG. *Br.* parental guidance of films unsuitable to see in parts for children under 15.

phantom pregnancy *Br., Aus. /Am.* **false pregnancy/** one that isn't true.

Phar. B. *Am.* Bachelor of Pharmacy.

pharmacist, chemist *esp. Br. /esp. Am., Can.* **druggist/**: *pharmacists brought Watson's case to Duke's senior administrators.* – Reader's Digest.

pharmacy *esp. Am.* shop or part of it where medicines are prepared and sold: *director of pharmacy at Duke University Hospital in Durham, N.C., returned an urgent beeper message* – Reader's Digest.

phase/ in phase/out of phase (with) *Br.* working together that produces the right effect., or not.

Ph.B. *Am.* Bachelor of Philosophy.

phenobarbitone *Br. /Am.* **phnobarbital/** powerful drug that helps sb. to sleep.

Ph.G. *Am.* Graduate in Pharmacy.

phial *esp. Br.* obs. */Am.* **vial/** a small glass bottle for liquid medicine.

Philadelphia bankroll, also **Michigan roll** *Am.* a roll of one-dollar bills with a larger bill wrapped around it.

Philadelphia lawyer *Am.* col. one who makes things unnecessarily complicated and obfuscates matters.

Phillie, Philly *Am.* col. Philadelphia: *We stopped off in Philly for a day.* - R.A. Spears.

phizog *esp. Br.* obs. humor. the face.

phlox *Am.* low, spreading plant with pink or white flowers.

phone/ be on the phone *esp. Br., Aus.* have a phone in one's home or at one's work; opp. **not on the phone.**

phone/ hold the phone *Am.* sl. wait a minute.

phone/ put down the phone *Br., Aus. /Am.* **hang up/** replace the part of the telephone that you hold.

phone/ put the phone down on sb. *Br., Aus. / Am.* **hang up on** sb./ replace the receiver before the conversation ends.

phone bank *Am.* battery of the telephones.

(tele)phone booth *Br. /Am.* **pay (public) phone)/** a place in a building where there s a telephone for use by public.

(tele)phone box, call box, telephone kiosk *esp. Br., Aus. /Am.* **(tele)phone booth/** a rectangular shelter in the form of booth with a public telephone: *in the phone box at your end of the village.* - D. Francis., *He went into a dark wooden phone booth* - J. Patterson.

phone card *Br., Aus.* a card having limited duration used to operate a public telephone.

phone up *Br.* col. telephone sb.: *Have you phoned up all your relatives?* - Longman.

phone-in *Br., Can. /Am.* **call-in/** a radio or TV show in which telephoned questions, statements, etc. from the public are broadcast: *Who talks the most in radio phone-ins?* - R. Carter., M. McCarthy.

phoney *Am.* col. falsify.

phoney war *Br.* a war period without fighting, when the situation appears calm.

phonograph 1. *esp. Am., Can.* obs. a record player: *Sometimes she would open the door to me and turn up the phonograph* - R.P. Warren. 2. *Br.* early form of gramophone.

phonograph record *Am., Can.* record.

photo call *Br. /esp. Am., Can.* **photo op(portunity)/** occasion on which few people pose for photographers by arrangement: *Leonard Nimoy...partied with Jimmi, leading to a strange photo op.* – R.C. Cross.

photocopier *esp. Br. /Am.* **copier/**.

Photofit (picture) *Br.* tdmk., *Am.* **composite photograph/sketch, identity kit portrait** *Br., Aus.* **identity kit/**.

photogravure *Br. /Am.* **rotagravure/** gravure printing.

phut *Br., Aus.* col. 1. */Am.* **pfft/** dull sound like smth. bursting: *The gas-fire phutted at his match.* - D. Martin. 2. **go phut** *Br., Aus. /Am.* **go pfft/** break down completely.

physical *Am. /Br.* **medical/**.

physical jerks *Br.* col. humor. obs. physical exercises such as bending and stretching done to be healthy.

physical therapy *Am.* physeotherapy.

physically challenged *esp. Am.* physically handicapped.

physician *esp. Am.* fml. or *Br.* obs. */Br., Aus.* **doctor/** medical doctor (not a surgeon): *advised by a physician to spend a month in a special sanitorium for treatment* - R.G. Kaiser.

physician's office, doctor's, dentist's office *Am. /Br.* **surgery/** general practice, consulting room.

physio *Br., Aus.* col. physiotherapy.

pi *Br.* col. pious, virtuous.

piazza 1. *esp. Br.* an exterior covered walk with columns. 2. *Am.* dial. verandah.

picayune *Am.* trifling, petty: *whatever business a customer might bring to them was pretty picayune stuff indeed.* - L. Waller.

piccaninny daylight *Aus.* breaking dawn.

pick 1. *esp. Am.* sb. or smth. that has been selected. 2. *Am.* col. plectrum, small flat object for pulling at the strings of an instrument.

pick *Am.* play (a string instrument) by quickly pulling the strings: *the ones who pick and sing for fun* – Reader's Digest.

pick up *Br., Aus.* col. stop sb. in order to correct their behaviour.

pick smth. **up** *Am., Can.* tidy a room or a building.

pick up after *esp. Am.* col. tidy up things left strewn around by sb.

pick up the threads (of) *Br.* 1. come back to normal life. 2. renew an old activity.

pick and mix *Br.* combine things that are not similar.

picker/ stock pickers *esp. Am.* people who select companies in which others should invest.

picket fence *esp. Am. /Br.* **fence/** one made of a line of pointed sticks fixed into the ground.

pickle 1. *esp. Br.* a thick sauce eaten with food esp. cold food, consisting of pieces of vegetable preserved in vinegar or salt water: *Pickles and mustard and potato crisps came too.* - I. Murdoch. 2. *Am.* vegetable, esp. a cucumber preserved in this: *To urbanites it's memories of pickle stands lining the streets* - Reader's Digest. 3. *Br.* col. a child who playfully does bad but not very harmful things.

pickled *Br.* drunk.

pick-mattock *Am.* pickaxe.

pick'n'mix *Br.* a system in shops when a person can choose a few of several different small things, esp. sweets.

pick-up *Am.* acceleration, also adj.

pick-up (truck) *esp. Am.* small open motor vehicle with low sides used for carrying goods: *My father had an old Ford pickup truck* – Reader's Digest.

pick-up truck *Br. /Am., Aus.* **tow truck/** truck used to carry other vehicles in case of emergency.

picky *esp. Am., Can., Br.* derog. choosy: *Picky, aren't you? he sneered.* - K. Davis.

picnic *Br.* the food taken to be eaten somewhere outdoors, esp. on a picnic.

picnic races *Aus., NZ.* race meeting for amateurs held in a rural area.

picture *Br.* smth. beautiful.

picture/ be in pictures *esp. Am., Can.* act in films or work for the film industry.

picture/ sb.'s **face is a picture** *Br.* they look very surprised and angry.

picture/ be/look a picture *esp. Br.* look very pretty.

picture/ put/keep sb. **in the picture** *Br.* 1. tell them about the situation what they need to know. 2. keep them aware of changes.

picture/ the big picture *Am.* col. situation considered as a whole, rather than its details.

pictures *Br. /esp. Am.* **movies/** 1. obs. the cinema: *We're going to the pictures tonight.* - W.S. Maugham., *You're taking her to the pictures, then?* - J. Herriot., *afterwards they were going to the pictures.* - D. Lessing. 2. the business of producing or acting in cinema films.

picture-perfect *Am.* perfect in appearance and quality.

picture postcard *Br.* one with a picture on the front of it.

piddle about/around *Br.* col. waste time doing unimportant things.

pie/ In Britain a pie usu. has a pastry cover, if there is no cover it is called a tart (if it is filled with fruit) or a flan, in America a pie may or may not have a cover; British **pie** is called **deep dish pie** in North America, tart in America is used only to mean a small sweet pie: *deep-dish pie with what appeared to be children hearts floating around on the top* - T. de Haven.

pie 1. *Br.* a food made of meat, fish, or vegetables with potato on top. 2. *esp. Br.* food made of meat and vegetables baked in a pastry covering.

pie *Am.* 1. the sum total of income, costs, etc. described as a pie-chart. 2. sl. an easy job or task: *Of course that was pie.* - R. Stout.

pie a la mode *Am.* pie served with ice cream.

pie and mash *Br.* a small pie served with mashed potatoes.

piece *esp. Am.* 1. a musical instrument. 2. also *Can.* col. small gun, revolver: *I bet there's not more'n fifteen heavies in that room with the pieces all set to go.* - G.V. Higgins. 3. a part or share of smth. 4. obs. short distance away.

piece/ be a piece of piss *Br.* sl. be very easy.

piece/ come to pieces *Br. /Am.* **break down/** be designed so that it can be divided into smaller parts.

piece/ of a piece *Br.* 1. being the same all the way through. 2. similar to other parts.

piece/ take to pieces *Br.* separate smth. into the parts that make it up.

piece/ want a piece of sb. *Am.* sl. want to talk to a famous person.

a piece of action *Am.* sl. a share of smth. esp. in profits, business, etc.: *they want a piece of action in Hong Kong.* - Time.

a piece of ass *esp. Am.* col. a sexually attractive woman.

a piece/slice of the pie *Am. /Br.* **a slice/share of the cake/** a share of joint profit.

a piece of piss *Br.* col. very easy thing to do.

a piece of work/ be a piece of work *Br.* (of a person) be strange or unpleasant.

piece accents *Am.* print. floating accents used where many languages have to be typeset.

pie crust 1. *Br.* pastry on the top of a pie. 2. *Am., Can., Aus.* pastry on the top and bottom of a pie, shortcrust pastry.

pie-in-the sky *Am.* (of plans and ideas) impossible to achieve.

pieplant *Am.* the common garden rhubarb.

pierced earrings *Am.* earrings.

pier *Br.* 1. a structure extending into navigable water used as promenade having entertainment facilities and places to eat. 2. long structure projecting from airport terminal along which passengers go to and from an aircraft.

piffle *Br.* obs. nonsense; adj **piffling** unimportant or useless.

pig *Br.* col. eat a lot of food, even if sb. is not very hungry.

pig/ a pig of a job, task, etc. *Br.* col. a very difficult work; be a **pig** *Br. /Am.* **bitch/** be difficult or unpleasant to do.

pig/ be sick as a pig *Br.* col. be envious and annoyed of sb.'s success, esp. if a person has tried to achieve it himself.

pig/ like a greased pig *esp. Am.* moving very fast.

pig/ on a pig's back *Can.* under good conditions.

pig/ pig between two sheets *Am.* sandwich with ham.

pig/ make a pig's ear of *esp. Br.* col. do smth. awkwardly or wrongly.

pig/ pigs might/can fly *esp. Br.* expression of disbelief.

pig out *esp. Am., Can.* sl. /*esp. Br.* **pig oneself/** eat food greedily and in large amounts, **pig-out**

n.: *you're saving your calories for another meal or atoning for a recent pig-out.* - Reader's Digest.

pigboard /also **teardrop**/ *Aus.* a kind of surfboard.

pig bucket *Br.* slop bucket or slop pail.

pigeon *esp. Am.* col. gullible person.

pigeon/ be sb.'s **pigeon** *Br., Aus.* obs. be sb.'s responsibility.

pigeon loft *Br.* a building in which pigeons are kept.

pigeon-fancier *Br., Aus.* person who keeps pigeons as pets.

piggery *Br.* 1. pig farm. 2. pig sty.

piggy in the middle 1. *esp. Br., Aus.* person who is caught between two opposing sides but is unable to influence either of them: *I wanted to live in the middle; like a pig in the middle.* – R. Westall. 2. *Br.* col. /*Am.* **keep-away**/ game in which two people throw ball to each other which the third person is trying to catch.

piggyback on(to) *Am.* col. join or be joined with smth. that is larger, more important or more effective.

Pig Island *Aus., NZ.* col. nickname for New Zealand.

pig-jump *Aus.* col. jump made by a horse from all four legs.

pigpen *Am., Can.* 1. pigsty. 2. col. very dirty or untidy place.

pig's arse! *Aus.* col. I don't believe it!

pig's ear/ make a pig's ear of smth. *Br.* col. do smth. very badly and carelessly.

pig's eye/ in a pig's eye! *esp. Am., Can.* col. it is said if there is no chance that it's true or will happen.

pigskin *Am., Can.* col. football: *When Bill picked up the pigskin and ran ninety yards for a touchdown, the crowd roared.* - H.C. Whitford., R.J. Dixson.

pigswill *Br.* 1. food that is given to pigs. 2. tasteless or unpleasant food.

pigtail *esp. Br.* /*Am.* **braid**/ hair tied into one or two bunches and then plaited.

pi-jaw *Br.* sl. moral lecture.

pike/ come down the pike *Am.* col. show up, appear: *We are doing all this for generations down the pike.* - R.N. Bellah and others.

pike on *Aus., NZ.* drop plans of doing smth. for fear of failure.

piker *esp. Am., Can., Aus.* 1. person who gambles or speculates with a small amount of money: *Americans are clearly pikers compared with the growing crowds of Arabs abroad* - Newsweek. 2. tightwad, cheapskate: *You cheap little piker!*

- R.A. Spears., *God is no piker!* – K. Vonnegut, Jr. 3. a shirker, loafer: *Come on, you lazy piker.* - R.A. Spears. 4. a person who avoids getting into dangerous situations.

pilaf *Am., Aus.* pilau.

pile *esp. Br.* large tall old building or group of buildings.

pile *Am.* col. dash, run, thrust oneself.

pile it high (and) sell it cheap *esp. Br.* col. get products in large amounts so that to sell them cheap.

pile on the agony *Br.* col. make existing problems seem much worse.

piledriver *Br.* col. smth. very powerful.

piles *Br.* col. haemorrhoids.

pilgarlic *Am.* a man looked upon with humorous contempt or mock pity.

pill 1. *Am., Can.* sl. cigarette. 2. *Am.* a drug: *You're in you're on pills I seen you, don't forget.* - G.V. Higgins. 3. *Am.* tranquilliser. 4. *Am.* col. sb. who annoys sb., often a child.

pillar/from pillar to post *Br.* and *Am.* obs. being shuffled a lot.

pillar/ from pillar to post victory *Br.* winner in the lead from the start.

pillar box *Br.* /*Am.* **mail box**/ post box: *But Asquith's letters were all in the pillar-box within half an hour.* - Observer.

pillor box red *Br.* bright red colour.

pillion *Br., Aus.* a back passenger seat in a motorcycle.

pillock *esp. Br.* col. a foolish worthless person: *Among the many terms new to me were "dirty weekend", "loo", complete pillock* - B. Bryson.

pillow *Am.* sofa cushion: *our firm received an order from a furniture dealer for 100 throw pillows* – Reader's Digest.

pillow-puncher *Am.* col. parlour maid.

(pillow) sham *Am., Can.* decorative pillow case with which it is covered when it's not used.

pill-peddler /**pill roller**/ *Am.* physician: *Older doctors had sometimes sneered at him as the "pill-roller".* - T. Capote.

pilot *Am.* (also **cowcatcher**) the cowcatcher of a train or streetcar: *I rode the blinds, the tender of the engine, the cowcatchers, the pilots of the doubleheader.* - I Stone.

pilot's biscuit *Am., Can.* ship's biscuit.

pilot scheme *Br., Aus.* /*Am.* **pilot program**/ one used to judge how good smth. is before introducing it.

pimp *Aus., NZ.* col. /*Br.* **grass**/ person who secretly tells the police about the activities of criminals; an informer.

pimpmobile *Am.* col. long flashy car.

pin 1. *Am.* /*Br.* **brooch**/ attractively shaped piece of metal, sometimes containing jewels, used on clothes as decoration: *the trading of collector's pins is still the official obsession of the summer games.* - Newsweek. 2. *Br.* short thin piece of metal with a decoration at one end, used as a jewellery.

pin *Am.* obs. give one's fiancee a piece of jewellery to show that they love each other.

pin/ on pins and needles *Am., Can.* in a state of anxious expectation.

pin/ Pin your ears back *esp. Br.* col. Listen carefully: *Pin back your years, people, this is quite a story!* - Longman.

pin sb.'s **ears back** *Am.* col. give sb. a thorough scolding or beating: *Pin his ears back, colonel.* - K. Vonnegut, Jr.

pin one's **faith on** *Br.* think that one particular person, thing or event will make a person happy, successful, etc.

pinafore *Br.* a dress that doesn't cover your arms, usu. worn over a shirt, etc.

pinafore dress *Br.* /*Am., Can., Aus.* **jumper (dress)**, *Br., Aus.* **pinafore/.**

pinch *esp. Br., Aus.* col. take without permission, steal: *a switchblade knife and a strong hand combined to pinch it off.* – M. Daly.

pinch/ at a pinch *Br., Aus.* /*Am., Can.* **in a pinch**/ if necessary: *in a pinch he may prove to be more influential than the First Secretary.* - R.G. Kaiser.

pinch/ in a pinch *Am.* in a complicated situation.

pinch-hit *Am., Can.* 1. hit for sb. else in baseball. 2. col. substitute for sb. in any job or role: *Last night at our club meeting I had to pinch hit for our chairman* - H.C. Whitford., R.J. Dixson.

pine barren *esp. Am.* sandy tract covered sparsely with pine trees.

pine kernels *Br., Aus.* pine nuts, often used for cooking.

The Pine-tree State *Am.* Maine.

ping *Am., Aus.* /*Br.* **pink**/ (of a car engine) make high knocking sounds as a result of not working properly.

pink-collar jobs, workers, industries, etc. *esp. Am.* job done by women, esp. in offices and for little money, etc.

pink-eye *Aus.* walkabout of an Aboriginal.

pink gin *esp. Br.* (a glass of) an alcoholic drink made of gin with angostura added to give it a pink colour.

pinkie, pinky 1. *esp. Am., Aus.* the smallest finger of the human hand: *those who dirtied their little pinkies with honest work.* - T. Caldwell., *they won't lift a pinkie to help one another.* - Reader's Digest., *I got more in my pinkie finger than he's got in his head.* - A. Miller. 2. *Aus.* cheap or home-made wine.

pinking shears *Br.* /*Am.* **pinking scissors**/ special type of scissors that have v-shaped teeth, used for cutting cloth.

pinko 1. *Aus., Am., Can.* col. derog. person of left-wing attitudes. 2. *Br.* left wing sympathiser.

the pink pound *Br.* /*Am.* **the pink dollar**/ money spent by homosexuals on entertainment.

pink slip *Am., Can.* col. discharge paper: *They may want lower taxes as much as anyone else, but not in exchange for a pink slip.* – Time; v. be **pink-slipped.**

Pinkster *Am.* Whitsun Day.

pinny *esp. Br., Aus.* col. pinafore.

pinole *Am.* a finely ground flour made from parched corn with sugar, etc.

pins *Br.* col. legs.

pins/ be/sit on pins and needles *esp. Am.* be very nervous.

pins/ for two pins I'd… *esp. Br.* obs. if it were only possible I would…

pint *Br.* col. a pint of beer served in pubs: *Michael tossed it off and got himself another pint.* - I. Murdoch.

pint/ go for a pint *Br.* go to the pub to drink beer.

pinta *Br.* col. obs. a pint of milk.

pintable *Br.* a machine for playing pinball.

pinto *Am.* /*Br.* **piebald**/ skewbald.

pinwheel *Am.* /*Br.* **windmill**/ children's toy.

pip 1. *Br.* obs. any of the stars on the shoulders of the coats of army officers of certain ranks: *He switched his tabs with the three pips to his clean shirt* - I. Shaw., *his pips were pinned on him by his cousin.* - L. Uris. 2. *esp. Br.* obs. col. a feeling of annoyance or lack of cheerfulness / **give** sb. **the pip**: *these English boys give me the pip, they're so stuck-up* - D. Lessing. 3. *Am.* col. remarkable person or thing: *Ain't you a pip?* - D. Hammet., *My idea was a pip.* - F.S. Fitzgerald. 4. *Br.* a small seed of a fruit such as an apple or orange: *White cheese covered in grape pips.* – S. Townsend. 5. (pl.) *esp. Br.* also **time signal** /*Am.* **beep**/ radio. a series of short high-pitched sounds used as a time signal. 6. (pl.) *Br.* a signal to put in more money when a person is making a call from a public telephone.

pip *Br.* col. 1. beat narrowly in a race, competition, etc. / esp. in **pipped at the post/to the post**

Br., Aus. col. /Am. **nose out/**. 2. (cause to) fail (an examination). 3. hit with smth. fired from the gun. 4. blackball.

pipe *Am.* sl. an easy task: *It's a pipe he knows the others are with him* - D. Hammet.

pipe-laying *Am.* political scheming.

pipeline *Am.* a direct means of receiving important news or facts.

pipe-opener *Br.* col. warm-up exercises.

pipes *Br.* col. bagpipes.

piping *Br. /Am.* **decoration top/** decoration on the top of a cake.

pippin *Am.* a highly admired person or thing.

pip-pip *Br.* good-bye.

pique one's **interest, curiosity** *esp. Am.* make sb. feel interested in sb. or smth.

piss *Br.* sl. alcoholic drink.

piss 1. *esp. Br., Aus.* taboo. sl. (of rain) fall heavily: *Always seems to be pissing down these days.* - J. Higgins. 2. also **piss** oneself **(laughing)** *Br.* col. laugh uncontrollably.

piss about/around *Br., Aus.* col. behave in a silly, childish way.

piss sb. **about/around** *Br.* col. treat sb. badly.

piss off *Br., Aus.* sl. go away.

piss/ be/go (out) on the piss *Br., Aus.* col. frequent bars drinking alcohol; go on a spree.

piss/ full of piss and vinegar *Am.* col. full of energy.

piss/ go piss up a rope *Am.* col. very rude way of saying go away.

piss/ not have a pot to piss in *Am., Can.* col. be very poor.

piss/ a piece of piss *Br.* col. very easy thing to do.

piss/ piss and moan *Am.* col. /*Br.* **whinge,** *Am.* **whine/** complain in a very annoying way.

piss/ piss or get off the can/pot *Am.* taboo. sl. make up your mind.

piss/ take the piss out of sb. *Br., Aus.* col. make fun of them or show disrespect to sb.; n. a **piss-taker**.

pissant *Am.* col. 1. insignificant or of low quality or value: *I don't have time for her little piss-ant problems.* - R.A. Spears. 2. annoying person with a weak character.

piss-artist *Br., Aus.* col. 1. a know-it-all. 2. a drunkard. 3. person who doesn't do things correctly.

pissass *Am.* worthless or unimportant.

pissed taboo. sl. 1. *Br., Aus.* drunk: *mainly he played sport and got pissed.* - T. Thorne. 2. also **pissed-off** *Am., Can. Aus.* annoyed, disappointed or unhappy: *Smithy's really pissed.*
- B. Tillman., *Emile had to field phone calls from pissed-off parents* - W. Jack, B. Laursen. 3. **pissed as a newt/fart, pissed out of** one's **head/mind** *Br. /Br., Aus.* **pissed as a fart/** very drunk.

pisser *Am.* col. smth. unusually big or bad.

pisspot *Aus.* sl. a drunkard.

piss-take *Br.* an act of making fun of sb. or smth., esp. in **do a piss-take** of sb. or smth.

piss-up *esp. Br., Aus.* taboo. sl. an occasion of drinking lots of alcohol.

piss-up/ couldn't organise a piss-up in a brewery *Br., Aus.* col. couldn't organise anything.

pissy *esp. Am.* impudent and aggressive.

pistol *Am.* sl. remarkable person: *She's a bright kid. A real pistol.* - R.A. Spears.

pistols at dawn *Br.* humor. serious confrontation between two people.

pistol-whip sb. *Am., Aus.* hit sb. with a pistol.

pit 1. *Br.* the seats at the back of the ground floor of a theatre behind the stalls: *people had already been assembling at the pit and gallery doors* - W.S. Maugham. 2. *Am. /Br.* **floor/** (usu. in comb.) commodity exchange for buying and selling particular article of trade: *brokers spotted some wrongdoing in the pits.* - Time. 3. *Br.* humor. col. a (particular person's) bed. 4. *Am., Can., Aus. /Br.* **stone/** the hard central part of certain types of fruit: *You've got all those pits to worry about.* – P. Roth. 5. *Am.* remove the pit from a fruit / **pitted** *Am., Aus.* adj. without a pit. 6. *Am. /Br.* **the pits/** the place beside a race track where a race car gets petrol, changes tyres, etc. 7. *Am.* col. armpit.

pit smth. **out** *Am.* col. sweat so much that one's clothes become wet under sb.'s arms.

pita *esp. Am., Can.* pitta bread.

pit boss *esp. Am.* col. a casino official in charge of gaming tables: *Ed Walters, a Sands pit boss* – A. Summers, R. Swan.

pitch 1. *Br., Aus. /Am., Aus.* **field/** (in sport) a special marked-out area of ground on which football, hockey, etc. are played: *It had...a cricket pitch and social club* - B. Bryson. 2. *esp. Am.* col. sell by high-pressure means. 3. *Am.* sl. a sexual approach, a pass. 4. *Am.* col. the situation, matter, point: *And what's the pitch?* - J. Kerouac. 5. *Br. /Am., Aus.* **stand/** a place in a public area where a person regularly sells goods or peforms. 6. *Br. /Am., Aus.* **site/** a piece of ground on which one can camp.

pitch/ pitch sb. **a line/yarn** *Am.* col. sell sb. a story or give them an excuse that is difficult to believe.

pitch/ queer sb.'s/**the pitch** *esp. Br., Aus.* spoil sb.'s chances of doing smth.
pitch (the) woo *Am.* sl. kiss and caress: *They were out by the barn pitching woo.* - R.A. Spears.
pitch up *Br.* col. arrive somewhere, turn up.
pitch-and-putt *Br.* game of golf played on a very small course.
pitcher, pitchman *Am.* 1. street vendor. 2. person making a sales pitch.
pitcher 1. *Br.* a large container for holding and pouring liquids usu. made of clay and having two ear-shaped handles. 2. *Am. /Br., Aus.* **jug/** a container for holding liquids that has a handle and a lip for pouring: *a pitcher of lemonade to refresh passer-by.* - Guideposts.
pitchforks/ It rains pitchforks *Am.* It rains cats and dogs.
pitchman *Am., Can.* col. person delivering sales pitch.
pitchperson *Am.* a person who promotes a product, appeal, etc. with high-pressure talk.
pithead *esp. Br., Aus.* the area and buildings at the entrance to a mine.
pit lamp *Can.* a Canadian miner's lamp.
pitman 1. *Br.* journalism. a coalminer. 2. *Am., Can.* connecting rod in machinery.
pit stop *esp. Am., Can.* col. a stop so that people may go out to the toilet, esp. in **make a pit stop**: *Returning to Toronto, Hawkins made a pit stop in Manhattan* - Vanity Fair.
pitter *Am.* machine for taking the pits from the fruit.
pix *Am.* sl. movies.
pixilated *esp. Am.* col. humor. 1. slightly mad: *That little old lady is pixilated.* - R.A. Spears. 2. drunk: *It's shot on film at 16 frames a second instead of 25 to give the characters a pixilated look.* - Bulletin.
pizza house *Br. /Am.* **pizza parlor/** pizzeria.
pizza pie *Am.* pizza.
pizzaz *Am.* sl. pep, punch, glitter and excitement: *The fastest way to stardom is to produce pizzazz early and often* - Time., *the computer business has lost some of its pizzaz.* - Time., *She had great pizzaz.* - Vanity Fair.
pizzle *esp. Aus.* the penis of an animal, esp. a bull.
pjs *Am., Aus.* col. abbr. pyjamas: *Put on those p-j's now.* - S. Bellow., *he comes to the door in his p.j.'s as usual.* - J. O'Brien, A. Kurins.
place/ Americans use place with some and any to form words meaning anywhere, somewhere.
place/ place **on** *Br., Aus. /Am.* **in/** a course of study.

place/ get a first place *Br.* take a first place.
place 1. *esp. Am.* finish second in a horse or dog race. 2. *Br.* take 2nd or 3rd place in a race.
place/ in place *Am., Can.* staying in place, not going anywhere.
place a call *Am.* order a telephone call: *why he didn't place the call* - Time.
place bet 1. *Br.* a bet on the chance that a particular horse will be 1st, 2nd or 3rd in a race. 2. *Am.* a bet on a chance that a particular horse will be 1st or 2nd in a race.
placed *esp. Br.* 1. (for) in the stated situation; **How are you placed for?** What is your situation?. 2. **be placed** (esp. of a horse) be of the first three to finish a race.
place words in inverted commas *esp. Br.* put speech marks round a certain word or words to show it is spoken or special in some other way: *In this sentence "Fred" has been placed in inverted commas.* - Longman.
placeman *Br.* derog. person appointed to a government position for personal profit or in exchange for his political support.
placement *esp. Br.* job, usu. as part of a course of study, which gives a person experience of a particular type of work.
placer *Br.* col. person who deals in stolen goods.
placet *Br.* affirmative vote in a church or university assembly.
Placido *Br.* sl. the sum of 10 pounds.
Placidyl *Am., Can.* tdmk. a type of sedative for insomnia.
plaid *Am. /Br.* **check/** material with a pattern of squares and lines or the pattern itself, tartan: *The man was dresed quietly, except for a fancy plaid cap* – J. O'Hara.
plain/ (as) plain as a pikestaff *Br.* obs. very plain.
plain chocolate 1. *Br. /Am.* **dark chocolate/** dark chocolate without added milk and with very little sugar. 2. *Am. /Br.* **cooking chocolate/** chocolate with no milk at all.
plain-coloured *Br.* of one colour only.
plain cook *Br.* one who provides simple English cooking.
plain flour *Br., Aus. /Am.* **all purpose flour/** flour with no chemicals which make cakes rise (one without baking powder).
Plain People *Am.* the Amish, the Mennonites and the Dunkers, religious sects who support a simple way of life.
plaint *Br.* law. accusation, charge.
plain time *Br.* working time paid for at normal rate as opposed to overtime.

plait *esp. Br. /esp. Am.* **braid/** v. n. form (hair, dried stems of grass, etc.) into a ropelike length by twisting three or more lengths of it over and under each other.

plan/ sb.'s **best plan** *Br.* the best course of action.

plane-maker *Am.* aircraft manufacturer.

plane-post *Br.* 1. send by plane post. 2. n. air-post.

planet/ What planet are you on? *Br.* used to express that sb. lost contact with reality.

plank 1. *Am.* cook and serve on a board usu. with an elaborate garnish, **planked** adj. 2. *esp. Am., Can. Irish Eng.* col. put or set smth. forcefully or abruptly

plank/ walk the plank *Am.* be discharged.

planning *Br.* print. imposing or film assembly.

planning permission *esp. Br. /Am., Aus.* **building permit/** official permission to put up a new building or change an existing one.

plant *Br., Aus.* a large heavy machine used for building roads, industry, etc.

plant/ heavy plant *Br.* heavy vehicle.

plant to a crop *Am.* plant with a special crop.

The Plantation State *Am.* Rod-Island.

planter *Aus.* cattle thief.

plant pot *esp. Br. /Aus.* **flower pot,** *Am.* **planter, pot/** a pot for a house plant.

plaque/ blue plaque *Br.* (on the wall) one showing that a famous person once lived there.

(sticking) plaster, Elastoplast *esp. Br. /esp. Am.* **bandage,** *Am., Aus.* tdmk. **band-aid/** (a thin band of) material that can be stuck to the skin to protect small wounds.

plaster *Am.* sl. (one dollar) bank note.

plaster/ be in a plaster *Br. /Am., Aus.* **be in a cast/** (of arm, leg, etc.) be covered with a hard white substance.

plastic bomb *esp. Am.* a small bomb made by hand.

plasticene *Br.* tdmk. /*Am.* **play dough,** *Am.* tdmk. **Play-Doh/** soft claylike substance made in many different colours, used by young children for making small models, shapes, etc.

plastic wrap *Am., Can., Aus. /esp. Br.* **clingfilm,** *Am.* **Saran wrap/**.

plat 1. *Am.* make a plan of a piece of land. 2. *Aus.* col. a fool.

plate 1. *Br.* usu. pl. one's foot: *I've been on me plates all day.* - T. Thorne. 2. *Am.* sl. attractive person. 3. *Am., Can.* main course of the meal, served on one plate. 4. *Aus., NZ.* plate of food contributed by a guest to a party. 5. *Am., Can.* radio. anode of thermionic lamp. 6. *esp. Br.* metal ring on an electric cooker that sb. puts pans on when cooking.

plate/ hand sb. smth. **on a plate** *esp. Br.* let sb. have smth. with too little effort.

plate-face *Aus.* sl. person of oriental origin.

platelayer *Br. /Am.* **tracklayer/** a workman who builds or repairs railway tracks: *Platelayers in Sierra Leone are paid sixpence a day* - G. Greene.

plate race *esp. Br.* a horse race with a plate as a prize.

plate rack *Br. /Am., Aus.* **dish rack/** a frame where plates can be put vertically to dry.

platform 1. *esp. Br.* the open part at the end of a bus, where passengers enter and leave. 2. *Am.* vestibule (of a railway passenger car). 3. *Br., Aus. /Am.* **track/** a flat raised structure from which people get on and off the train. 4. *Br.* the people who are on the raised part of a room to make speeches.

platform-car, flat-car *Am.* a railway goods vehicle with no raised sides and ends and no roof.

platform ticket *Br.* one permitting a person other than a passenger to enter upon a railway platform.

platter 1. *esp. Am., Can.* a large flat dish used for serving food, esp. meat, plate: *platters with hot cheese puffs and red fruits.* - A. Hitchcock Mystery Magazine. 2. *esp. Am., Aus.* col. a gramophone record: *Jackson family playing old Chubby Checker platters* - R. Crais. 3. *Br.* obs. large plate, usu. made of wood.

play *Am.* (in sports) a plan or a small set of actions.

play ball *Am.* a. play with a ball. b. col. agree to do what sb. else wants you to do: *It is often good business to play ball with a political machine.* - A. Makkai.

play both ends against the middle *Am.* try to get opposing groups fight or disagree so that one will get advantage from this.

play/keep one's **cards close to the vest** *Am., Can.* col. be very cautious.

play favourites *esp. Am., Can.* show favouritism towards sb. or smth.

play sb. **for a fool** *esp. Am., Aus.* take advantage of sb.: *No man plays me for that kinda fool.* - R.J. Randisi., M. Wallace.

play gooseberry *Br.* col. /*Am.* **be a third wheel/** be unwanted third party, esp. accompany romantic couple as a chaperone.

play hardball *esp. Am.* col. be firm and determined.

play house *Am. /Br.* **Wendy house/**.

play piano *Am.* play the piano.

play politics *Br., Aus.* use the relationships between people for one's own advantage.

play silly buggers *Br. sl.* behave in a foolish or annoying way.

play the field *esp. Am., Aus., Can. col.* go out socially with more than one member of opposite sex: *I realize you want to play the field.* - S. Bellow.

play the lottery *Am.* /*Br.* **do the lottery**/.

play the whale *Aus. sl.* vomit.

play to the gallery *Br.* show off trying to make oneself popular.

play away *Br.* play a sports event on an opponent's ground.

play up 1. *esp. Am., Can. col.* advertise smth.: *it gets played up in the right way.* - Longman. 2. **play sb. up** *Am.* use sb. 3. *Br., Aus.* cause (sb.) trouble or pain, esp. by working or behaving in an unexpected way. 4. *Br. col.* not to act in a proper way. 5. *Br.* make all that is possible in a sports game.

play with a straight bat *Br. obs.* be fair and honest.

play/ **what's** sb. **playing at?** *Br. col.* used when asking sb. to explain their unpleasant behaviour.

playback, action replay *esp. Br.* /*Am.* **instant replay**/.

playbill *Am., Can.* theatre programme.

play-by-play *Am., Can. adj.* being a running commentary on a sports event: *the artists themselves, who were outside by the gates giving a play-by-play commentary to foreign journalists* - J. Fraser., *LBA seems to be tossing coins and giving me a play-by-play report.* - R. Stout.

play-centre *esp. NZ.* preschool play group.

play doctor *Am.* writer employed to revise a playscript prior to production.

play dough, tdmk. **Play-Doh** *Am* /*Br.* **plasticene**/.

playdown *esp. Can.* game or match forming part of a competition.

playground 1. *Am* /*Br.* **recreation ground**/ a piece of public land set aside for games: *Another day they go to the playground.* - J. Updike., *There was a big grassy lot and a playground.* - Guideposts. 2. *Am.* one's sphere of activities.

playgroup, also **playschool** *esp. Br.* /*Am.* **preschool**/ informal school for very young children esp. of three to five years old: *looking after kids in a playgroup.* – S. Townsend.

playpit *Br.* children's playground, sandbox.

playtime *Am.* time when a theatre performance begins.

plaza *Am.* 1. the wide area on a toll highway where tollbooths are situated. 2. service area alongside an expressway. 3. also *Can.* shopping centre.

please *Br.* used by children to a teacher or other adult to get their attention.

pleased *esp. Br.* happy or satisfied.

pleased/ some American speakers consider very pleased bad English and would rather say very much pleased.

pleasure/ **during the king's pleasure** / **queen's pleasure, at his/her Majesty's pleasure** *Br. law.* with no fixed limit on the time one is kept in prison.

pleasure-ground *Am.* hippodrome.

pleats/ **put** sb. **in pleats** *Br. col.* annoy sb.

plebs *Br. col. derog.* ignorant and uncultured people.

pled *Am.* past participle and simple past tense of plead.

pledge *Am.* 1. commit oneself to join a fraternity or sorority or to be so committed. 2. a student who has accepted an invitation to join a fraternity: *she had been eager to become a pledge again.* - F. Pascal.

plenty *Am. adv.* to a large degree, very: *In fact, I thought about it plenty and it sure was news.* - E. Taylor., *You gummed thing up plenty* - D. Hammet., *this was plenty good enough circumstantial evidence* - M. Twain.

plimsoll, trainer *Br.* /*Am., Aus.* **sneaker, running shoe** *Aus.* **runner, sandshoe,** *Am.* **gumshoe**/ a light shoe with a top made of heavy cloth and a flat rubber bottom used esp. for games and sports: *Miscreants may abscond on fleet foots: what Brits call plimsolls and Americans call sneakers.* - P. Howard., *I often shop in a tracksuit and plimsolls.* - Cheshire Life.

plinth, skirting (board), skirtboard, base moulding, base-board *Br.* /*Am.* **base-shoe**/ baseboard.

(PC) plod *Br. col.* police officer.

plonk *esp. Br., Aus. col.* cheap wine: *But I'm not thinking about run-of-the-mill plonk.* - Evening Standard., *the days of plonk are over.* - New York.

plonk smth. *esp. Br. col. derog.* /*Am.* **plunk**/ put or drop smth. heavily or carelessly.

plonker *Br. col.* 1. an idiot. 2. penis: *she's game and wants your plonker* - T. Thorne.

plot 1. *Am.* ground plan of a building. 2. *esp. Am.* diagram, chart or map.

plot/ **have lost the plot** *Br. sl.* lose the grasp of the situation and become ineffective.

plot/ lose the plot *Br., Aus.* humor. become crazy.

plotz *Am., Can.* col. 1. collapse. 2. be very worried.

The Plough *esp. Br. /esp. Am., Can.* **Big Dipper/** a group of seven bright stars seen only from the northern part of the world.

plough 1. *Br.* sl. fail an exam. 2. *esp. Am., Can.* (clear a snow with) a snow plough.

plough under *Am.* col. destroy smth.: *The searched vehicle was promptly plowed under* – F. Edwards.

ploughed *Am.* sl. drunk.

ploughman's (lunch) *Br., Aus.* simple midday meal, usu. bread, cheese, pickle and onion eaten in a pub: *She glanced at the bar menu. "Ploughman's Lunch" with Stilton."* - D. Bryson.

plow *Am. /Br.* **plough/**.

pluck *Br.* col. reject (a candidate) in an exam.

plug *Am.* (at) col. shoot (sb.) with a gun: *So if I got plugged from the front you'd get it too.* - K. Vonnegut, Jr., *I don't mind plugging you Jeff* - D. Hammet., *Get away from the door or I'll plug you.*- J. Hyams.

plug 1. also **plug-hat** *Am.* col. high silk hat, tophat. 2. *Am.* counterfeit money. 3. *Am., Can.* col. inferior old horse. 4. *Can.* col. log-jam. 5. *Br.* col. electric wall socket for connecting electric equipment to power supply.

plug *Am.* jack plug.

plug-and-socket *Br. /Am.* **connector assembly/** connection using plug and socket.

plughole *Br. /esp. Am.* **drain/** a hole into which a plug is fitted.

plughole/ go down the plughole/pan *Br., Aus.* col. fail or be wasted.

plug-ugly *esp. Am., Can.* col. a rude rough man, thug: *tell his plug-ugly here not to call me a fool* - A. Burgess.

plum *Br.* sl. rare. 100,000 pounds.

plum/ speak with/have a plum in one's **mouth** *Br., Aus.* derog. pretend to be from high society.

plumb *esp. Am., Aus.* col. often humor. completely: *I'm plumb tuckered out.* - J. London.

plumb smth. **in** *esp. Br.* fix in a place and connect to a supply of water.

plumber's helper, plumber's friend *Am.* col. plunger, instrument used for unblocking pipes: *Go get the plumber's helper.* - Omni.

plum cake *esp. Br.* becoming rare. a cake with raisins and currants.

plum duff *Br.* plum pudding.

plum job *Br.* col. good, well-paid and often easy job that people wish they had: *The Irish ran the city, held the plum jobs, occupied the best housing.* – A. Summers, R. Swan..

plummy *Br.* col. choice; highly desirable.

plump for (smth.) *Br.* col. decide in favour of, choose: *Compilers of critical and reference works have plumped more or less equally for Louis Daniel* - M. Jones, J. Chilton.

plum pudding *Am.* or *Br.* obs. */Br., Aus.* **Christmas pudding/** heavy sweet pudding with a lot of dried fruit, served at Christmas: *you've filled your bottomless tummy with plum pudding* – M. Daly.

plunger *Am.* col. sb. who grumbles a lot.

plunk 1. *Am.* hit sb. abruptly. 2. *esp. Am., Can. /esp. Br.* **plank/** put smth. down heavily or abruptly. 3. *Am.* a heavy blow.

plunk down 1. (smth.) *esp. Am.* put it down carelessly. 2. (sb.) *Am.* col. sit down heavily and clumsily.

plunk for *Am.* col. be keen to vote for (one person from a wide choice): *many of us just used one vote, plunking the one man who seemed fit for the job.* - Longman.

plurality tech. *esp. Am.* the largest amount of votes in an election, esp. when less than a majority */Br.* **majority/**. (*Am.* majority is *Br.* **absolute** or **clear majority**): *Culhane always managed to be re-elected by phenomenally wide pluralities.* - L. Waller.

plus ca change (plus c'est la meme chose) *esp. Br.* everything remains the same although people or things involved in a situation changed.

plus point *Br.* positive point.

ply for hire, business or trade *Br.* (of taxis) drive around or wait for passengers.

PM *esp. Br.* col. Prime Minister.

PMS, Premenstrual Syndrome *Am. /Br.* **PMT, Premenstrual Tension/** pain, headache, bad temper, etc. before woman's period.

pneumatic drill *esp. Br. /esp. Am., Aus.* **jackhammer/** a powerful hand-held tool that is worked by air pressure and is used for breaking up hard materials, esp. road surfaces.

poacher turned gamekeeper *Br.* a person who parodoxically works against the person who is doing a job now that the former did before.

pocho *Am.* citizen of Mexican origin.

pocket/ out of pocket *Br.* losing money after a deal.

pocket/ pay out of pocket *Am.* pay for smth. and claim money back later; adj. **out-of-pocket.**

pocket/ be/live in each other's pockets *esp. Br.* spend much time together.

pocketbook 1. *Am.* obs. /*Br.* **handbag**/ woman's handbag used for carrying money, keys, etc., esp. one without a shoulder strap: *he carried her to the roof and strangled her with the strap of her pocketbook.* - Reader's Digest. 2. *Am.* a wallet for papers and paper money or purse. 3. *Am.* journalism. people's concern about the money they have or hope to earn. 4. *Br.* notebook. 5. *Am., Can.* one's financial resourses.
pocket/ in pocket *Br.* having made a profit.
pocket/ out of pocket *Br., Can.* having paid a certain amount, usu. without good results: *You are likely still to be left considerably out of pocket.* - T. Rattigan., *I can't have you out of pocket because I'm late.* - G. Greene.
pocket-handkerchief *esp. Br.* col. adj. square and very small.
pocket money 1. *esp. Br., Can.* /*esp. Am.* **allowance**/ money given weekly to a child by its parents: *And his father had given him two five shilling pieces for pocket money.* - J. Joyce., *she had a little pocket money of her own.* - I. Murdoch., *She had ransacked the local library and spent her pocket money on books* - M.M. Kaye. 2. *esp. Br.* a small amount of money that a person earns and which he/she can use for buying the things that they want.
pocket train schedule *Am.* pocket timetable.
pocket veto *Am.* presidential veto of a congressional bill.
poddy *Aus.* a young calf, lamb, etc. taken from mother and fed by hand.
podgy *Br.* col. /*Am.* **pudgy**/ a little overweight but not fat.
podiatrist *esp. Am., Aus.* /*esp. Br.* **chiropodist**/: *companies excise people with no more sentiment than a podiatrist plucking a corn* - McLean's.
podium *Am.* lectern.
podunk *Am.* col. any small town or village: *I don't want a job in Podunk.* - R.A. Spears.
p.o.ed *Am.* col. adj. very annoyed.
po-faced *Br., Aus.* col. derog. having a silly solemn expression on the face, esp. showing disapproval: *No party poopers these despite po-faces.* - You.
pogey *Can.* col. unemployment or welfare benefit.
point 1. *Am.* full stop. 2. also **power point, socket (outlet)** *esp. Br.* /*Am.* **wall outlet, convenience outlet, (electric) outlet**/ electric socket: *I could repair one of his electrical outlets.* - Alcoholics Anonymous.
point *Am.* print. used to refer to the thickness of board.

point *esp. Am., Can.* 1. the position at the head of a column of troops. 2. /*Am.* **pointman**/.
point/ labour the point *Br.* /*Am.* **belabor the point**/ discuss smth. repeatedly in an annoying way.
point/ put too fine a point on smth. *Br.* sound a bit unpleasant.
point/ take sb.'s **point** *esp. Br.* accept sb.'s ideas.
point at *Am.* suggest (smth.) in an indirect way: *The Minister's remarks seemed to be pointing at an early election.* - Longman.
point down *Am.* make (a surface) smooth: *Do you use a special tool to point the wood down?* - Longman.
point up *Am.* roughen (a surface): *This wall should be pointed up before it is covered with cement* - Longman.
point blanket *Can.* type of Hudson Bay blanket.
point duty (on) *Br.* the controlling of traffic by a policeman (**point-duty**) standing usu. at a point where two roads cross each other.
pointman *Am.* 1. cowboy moving at the head of a herd. 2. soldier who goes ahead of a group to see if there is any danger.
points 1. *Br., Aus.* /*Am.* **switches**/ a pair of short rails that can be moved to allow a train to cross over from one track to another: *the points shift and the signal goes down* - G. Greene., *the train joggled past over the points* - E.M. Forster.
pointsman 1. *Br.* /*Am.* **switchman**/ railway worker in charge of the moving of points. 2. *Br.* traffic policeman.
point spread *Am., Can.* number of points with which a sports team is expected to defeat the weaker one used in betting.
point(y) head *Am., Can.* derog. col. intellectual: *The pointy-heads seem to be living in a world of their own.* - R.A. Spears, adj. **pointy-headed**.
point-to-point *Br.* race for horses that goes across country areas.
poison *esp. Br.* infect (esp. a part of the body).
poisonous/poisoned chalice *Br.* smth. that harms the person it's given to although it seemed very nice at first.
poke *Am.* 1. slowpoke, adj. **pok(e)y**. 2. sl. obs. wallet with money.
poke around/about *Br.* col. 1. look for smth. by moving a lot of things around. 2. try to find out information about other people's lives, business, etc. in a way that annoys them.
poker machine, col. **pokie, pokey** *Aus.* slot machine.
pok(e)y 1. *Br.* col. derog. (of a place) uncomfortably small and unattractive. 2.

Am., Can. doing things too slowly, esp. in an annoying way.

pokey *esp. Am., Can.* col. a jail: *It's the pokey for him.* - J.A. Michener.

pol *esp. Am., Can.* col. politician.

Polack *esp. Am., Can.* derog. a Polish person.

pole/ be in pole position *esp. Br., Aus.* be in the best position to win a competition.

pole/ move/climb up the greasy pole *Br.* esp. journalism. succeed after working very hard.

pole/ up the pole 1. *esp. Br.* col. a. slightly mad. b. in difficulty: *a midget randy groom once got every girl in the household up the hole.* - J.P. Donleavy., *do you want to drive me up the pole?* - J.D. Carr. 2. *esp. Irish Eng.* pregnant.

pole bean *Am., Can.* climbing bean.

polecat *Am.* col. skunk.

poley *Aus.* hornless.

police constable, also **PC** *esp. Br. /Am.* **patrolman/** policeman who patrols an assigned area.

police court *Am.* court of law for small crimes.

police department *Am.* department of a division of a town or city for police purposes.

policeman's helmet *esp. Br.* protective headgear of a policeman.

poli sci *Am.* col. political science.

police station *esp. Br. /Am.* **station house/** the local office of the police in a town, part of a city, etc.: *go to the police station voluntarily* - Young Citizen's Passport.

polish off *Am.* col. kill or defeat sb.

politeness / Speakers of British English tend to say *Thank you* for small or unimportant things (often, for example, when a shop assistant is giving change to a customer both people will say *Thank you.* Speakers in American English do not usually do this. On the other hand, in some situations it is possible in British English to make no replies when somebody thanks you, but in American English, as in some other languages, it is necessary to respond, for example, by saying *You're welcome.* Speakers of British English often use indirectness or tentativeness in order to be polite in situations where other languages are more direct. The speakers of American English tend to be more direct in similar situations.

political action committee (PAC) *Am.* organisation formed by businesmen, union or interest group to help raise money so that people who support their ideas can try to be elected for congress.

political football *esp. Br.* difficult problem which opposing politicians argue about or which each side deals with in a way that usu. brings them advantage.

polka-dot *Am. /Br.* **dotted, spotted/** dress material with a number of circular spots forming a pattern.

polka dots, chocolate vermicelli, hundreds and thousands *Br. /Am.* **chocolate chips/**.

pollack *Can.* sl. look for usable or saleable items that others discarded.

polling booth *esp. Br., Aus. /Am.* **voting booth/** a partly enclosed place inside a polling station where sb. marks their voting papers secretly.

Polling Day *Br., Aus. /Am.* **Election Day/**.

polling place *Am., Can.* the place where you can go to vote in an election.

polling station *esp. Br., Aus. /Am.* **polling place/** a building or other place where people go to vote at an election /**Polling station** (*Br.*), **Vote here** (*Am.*) signs/.

polliwog *Am., Can.* tadpole.

the polls *esp. Am.* the place which you can go to vote in an election.

poll tax, community charge *Br.* tax paid to local authorities for local services.

Pollyanna *esp. Am., Aus.* derog. person characterised by sunny everlasting optimism. adj. - **ish**: *I'm under no Pollyanish illusions.* - A. Toffler., *Am I advocating an habitual Pollyana attitude toward all our problems?* - D. Carnegie.

polo neck, roll neck *esp. Br. /esp. Am.* **turtleneck/** a round rolled collar, usu. woollen.

polony *Br.* 1. sausage made of partly cooked pork; bologna. 2. a length of this.

poly *esp. Br.* col. polytechnic.

poly bag *Br.* col. */Am., Aus.* **plastic bag/** a simple bag made of polythene.

polyethilene *esp. Am. esp. Br.* **polythene/**.

polystyrene *Br. /Am.* tdmk. **styrofoam/** a light plastic substance, used esp. to make containers.

polythenal *Br.* a type of thin plastic material, used esp. for making bags.

pommel *esp. Am.* pummel.

pommel horse *Am.* side horse used in gymnastics.

pom(my) *Aus., NZ.* col. often derog. an English person, esp. one who recently came to live in Australia: *You're quite a nice Pommie, as it happens.* - D. Reeman., *In three decades he went from a penniless Pom to one of the richest people in Australia* - New Idea.

pompadour *Am. /Br.* **quiff/**.

Pompey *Br.* sl. Portsmouth.

Pompier ladder *Am.* hook ladder.

ponce *Br., Aus.* 1. derog. col. a man who acts in an effeminate way. 2. a pimp: *A ponce lives off women.* - J. Higgins. 3. parasite **-y** adj.

ponce about / around 1. *Br., Aus.* derog. sl. (of a man) act like a ponce, or in a foolish time-wasting way: *it was naff to put on a suit and tie and ponce about with paintboxes.* - B. Bryson. 2. *Br.* col. do smth. slowly or badly.

ponce off *Br.* ask sb. to give a person smth. such as cigarette or drink without offering to pay.

ponc(e)y *Br.* col. (of a man) too concerned with one's appearance.

poncho *Am.* raincoat made of one large piece of material with a cover for one's head.

the Pond *Br.* humor. the Atlantic ocean: *Some cross the pond as if taking the 79th street Transverse* - New York.

pond scum *Am., Can.* mass of algae forming a green film in the surface of stagnant water.

pone *Am.* col. corn pone.

pong 1. *Br., Aus.* col. derog. or humor. v. n. (make) an unpleasant smell: *the mildewy pong of damp plaster and peeling wallpaper.* - B. Bryson. **-y** adj. 2. *Am., Aus.* derog. Chinaman.

pontoon *Br.* 1. /*Am.* **twenty-one**/ blackjack, card game played for money. 2. combination of 21 points.

pony 1. *Br.* col. 25 pounds: *She's backed Black Boy for a pony.* - G. Greene. 2. *Am.* col. /*Br.* **study aid**/ a crib, a paper from which examinations are copied. 3. *Am.* sl. translate with the aid of a pony.

pony-trekking *Br.* /*Am.* **pack trip**/ a holiday activity or sport in which people ride across the country on ponies: *For six weeks the Princess Royal and her children go pony-trekking* - New Idea.

pony up *Am.* col. pay (money usu. owed), settle account, produce: *Gorbachev had ponied up deep cuts in Soviet conventional forces in Europe* - Time., *producer Serg Silberman (Ran) ponied up some dough* - Premiere.

pooch *Am.* col. protrude.

pooched *Am.* col. (of lips) protruding: *Her lips were pooched out like Marilin Monroe's* - J. Baez.

poodle/ be sb.'s **poodle** *Br.* humor. derog. be too ready to obey sb. or support them in whatever they do.

poof, pouf, poufter *Br., Aus.* derog. col. a male homosexual. **-y** adj.: *For instance boys who arrive at school with "Proper" speech patterns are liable to be regarded as "Cissies" or worse "poofters".* - R. McRum, W. Cran, R. McNeil., *You could pick poofters just by looking at them.* - Bulletin.

pooh *esp. Br., Aus.* /*Am.* **poop**/ col. (used by children) a piece of excrement.

pool *Aus.* col. implicate or inform on.

the Pool *Br.* sl. Liverpool.

pool/ do the (football) pools *Br.* gamble on the results of football matches.

pool hall *Am.* building where people go to practise pool.

poolroom *Am., Can.* 1. bookmaking room. 2. also **billiard parlor, billiard saloon** a room for playing pool.

poolside *esp. Am., Can.* adv. beside a swimming pool: *tips for staying safe poolside.* – Reader's Digest.

poon *Aus.* col. 1. simple or foolish. 2. dress in such a way so as to attract attention.

poon, poontang *Am., Can.* taboo sl. 1. the female pudenda. 2. women in general seen as sexual objects: *I guess this means my poon days are over.* - T. Thorne. 3. sexual activity.

poop *Am., Can.* col. 1. gossip, information: *He don't know who was giving him straight poop.* - A. Scaduto., *The poop is they know they'd been spotted.* - B. Tillman. 2. (esp. used by children) excrement. 3. stupid person. 4. /*Br.* **poo**/ the act of defecating.

poop *Am., Aus.* col. become very tired.

poop sheet *Am.* document containing information or instruction.

poop out *Am., Can.* col. (cause to) fail, become tired, worn out / **pooped (out)** adj.: *he woke late feeling pooped.* - J. Dos Passos.

poor boy (sandwich), submarine sandwich *Am.* large oval sandwich filled with simple but substantial ingredients.

poor farm *Am.* one maintained at public expense.

poorhouse *Br.* work house.

poorly *esp. Br., Aus.* col. /*Am.* **sick**/ ill: *I hope you're not feeling poorly.* - I. Shaw., *You look poorly.* - G. Greene.

poor-mouth *Am., Can.* col. 1. plead poverty, emphasize one's deficiencies, n.: *Although he earns a good salary, that poor-mouth won't even chip in to buy flowers for our hospitalized fellow employee.* - H.C. Whitford., R.J. Dixson. 2. speak ill (of sb.).

poors-house *Am.* poor-house.

pootle about/around *Br.* col. walk or travel in a leisurely manner.

pop *Am., Can.* col. costing a specific amount per item.

pop 1. *Br.* obs. col. v. n. pawn. 2. *Br.* fasten (smth.) with press studs. 3. *Am.* roast (popcorn).

pop *esp. Am.* col. also **pops** 1. a father: *Pop and I were walking home* - Guideposts. 2. any older man (also a term of address): *No trouble, pops* - H. Fast.

pop smth. **in/on/into** *Br.* col. put smth. somewhere.

pop off *esp. Am.* col. speak or write without care, in anger, etc.: *There he goes, popping off again!* - Longman.

pop out/ make sb.'s **eyes pop out** *Am.* col. greatly surprise sb.

pop one's **clogs** *Br.* humor. die.

pope's nose *Am., Can., Irish Eng. /Br.* **parson's nose/**.

pop-out *Am., Can.* designed so as to be easily removable for use.

popover *Am., Can.* a light hollow cake made with eggs, milk and flour and often filled with fruit: *The girls said he made the best popovers in the world.* - J. Steinbeck.

poppa *Am., Can.* col. a father: *You tell Poppa what he needs is lay off this here booze.* – J. O'Hara.

popper 1. *esp. Br.* col. */Am.* **snap**, *Br., Aus.* **press stud/**. 2. *Am.* basket or pan for roasting popcorn.

poppet *Br., Aus.* col. a child or animal that one loves or that pleases one.

poppethead *Br.* mineshaft's upper frame used in hoisting coal.

Poppy Day *Br.* Remembrance Day.

pops concert/orchestra *Am.* one who performs classical and popular music.

pop quiz *Am.* a short test given to students when they do not expect it.

popshop *Br.* sl. pawn shop.

popsickle *Am., Can.* tdmk. */Br.* **ice lolly/** frozen juice bar on a stick, which often tastes of fruit: *the girls in shorts stroll past with chocolate popsicles.* - J. Updike.

popskull *Am.* sl. bootleg whiskey.

popsy *esp. Br.* col. a young and attractive woman.

pop-top *Am., Can. /Br., Aus.* **ring-pull/**.

p.o.q. *Aus.* col. leave hurriedly.

porch *Am.* a. */Br.* **veranda/** b. room open to the outside air, often having no walls or walls of screen or glass: *It had a wide porch, that extended around three sides, roses and honeysuckle climbing over trelises, two stories of clapboard with paint peeling.* - H. Fast., *Porches and balconies projected well out into space* - J.A. Michener.

porch climber, also **second story man** *Am. / Br.* **cat burglar/** a thief who enters and leaves a building by climbing up walls, pipes, etc.

porcini *esp. Am., Can.* the cep, a kind of wild mushroom, esp. as an item on a menu.

pork *esp. Am.* sl. 1. (of a man) have sex. 2. government money spent in a particular area in order to gain political advantages.

pork barrel *Am., Can.* col. a government plan to spend a lot of money in an area in order to gain political advantage. **-ing** adj.: *the military regime has dipped into the pork barrel to secure additional votes* - Newsweek., *Congress's pork-barrel dam projects are creating flood dangers all over the country.* - Reader's Digest.

pork butcher *Br.* a dealer in meat who sells pork (products).

porkies/ tell porkies *Br.* col. humor. tell lies.

pork pie *Br.* small round pie with pieces of cooked pork.

pork rinds *Am. /Br.* **scratchings/** small pices of pig's skin that have been cooked in hot fat and are eaten cold.

porky (pie) *Br.* sl. a lie.

porridge *Br. /Am.* **oatmeal/**a soft breakfast food made by boiling oatmeal (=crushed grains) in water or milk.

porridge *Br.* col. a period of time spent in prison.

port *Aus.* col. a travelling bag or case.

portacrib *Am.* tdmk. also **baby basket** */esp. Br.* **carrycot/**.

Portakabin *Br.* tdmk. small portable building used as a temporary office, classroom, etc.

Portaloo *Br.* tdmk. / *esp. Am., Can.* tdmk. **Porta Potti/** small portable toilet.

porte cochere *Am., Can.* a roofed structure at the entrance of a building where vehicles stop to set down passengers.

porter 1. *esp. Br. /Am.* **doorman/** a person in charge of the entrance to a hotel, school, hospital, etc.: *Still present is the burly figure of the bowler-hatted Cambridge porter in grey suit and blue mac.* - You., *there is no porter or hall attendant* - A. Christie., *negro porter took in Bernard's card and they were admitted almost immediately.* - A. Huxley., *a concierge is a hall porter here.* - New York. 2. *Am., Can.* an attendant employed in a sleeping-carriage in a train: *the porter had pulled down the three beds from inside the wall* - E. Hemingway., *The porter was nowhere to be seen.* - J. O'Hara.

porter house *Am.* cheap restaurant.

porterhouse (steak) *Am., Aus.* a thick slice of meat containing a T-shaped bone cut from the side of a cow: *enjoy their favourite foods – porterhouse steak, ribs.* – Reader's Digest.

porter's lodge *esp. Br.* a small room for the porter at the entrance to a school, etc.

portfolio *esp. Br.* the area of responsibility of a particular government minister.

pose *Br.* v. n. behave in a way that is different from one's real character and pretending to be a different kind of person, **it's just a pose**; adj.

posey *Br.* col. derog. striking a pose.

posh *esp. Br.* col. behaving or speaking in a way that is typical of people from a high class.

posh up *Br.* col. make oneself appear well-dressed, of high class, etc.: *you should posh yourself up a bit*. - Longman.

position/ finish in 3rd position/ *esp. Am.* **place/** *Br.* be the third winner.

position/ jostle for position *Br.* struggle to obtain an advantage over other people.

positive discrimination *Br.* a practice of giving advantage to a group of society which are often treated unfairly, esp. because of their race or sex.

Positively *Am.* (of an answer) Yes, indeed.

positive vetting *Br.* detailed examination of a person's past, political beliefs, etc. in order to determine their fitness for government jobs.

poss. *Br.* col. abbr. for possible, esp. in the phr. **if poss; as poss.**

posse *Am.* sl. (in youth slang) one's gang or crowd.

possession order *Br.* a court order to give property to the owner or other claimant.

possie *Aus.* position.

possum *Am., Can.* col. opposum.

possum *Am.* electronic device for paralysed person to communicate.

possum/ happy as a possum up a gum-tree *Aus.* col. very happy.

post *esp. Br., Aus., Can. /esp. Am., Can.* **mail/** 1. the official system for carrying letters, parcels, etc., from the sender to the receiver. 2. (official single collection or delivery of) letters, parcels, sent by this means. 3. col. an official place, box, etc., where stamped letters are left for sending. 4. a job, esp. important one; position.

post *Am.* a local group in an organisation of military veterans.

post 1. *esp. Br. /Am.* **station/** send or appoint to a particular army group, a place of duty with a company, involving going to different countries and towns, etc. 2. *Am.* forbid (esp. property) for trespassers. 3. *esp. Br., Aus.* stick or pin (a notice) on a wall. 4. *Am.* pay (money) so that accused can be free until their trial.

post (off, to) *esp. Br., Aus. /esp. Am.* **mail/** send (a letter, parcel, etc.) by post: *this card was posted from Mary's holiday address*. - Longman.

post/ deaf as a post *Br.* unable to hear anything at all.

post/ take a letter to the post *Br.* col. put it in a special post box in the street.

postage and packing *Br. /Am.* **shipping and handling/** charge for packing and posting.

postage meter *Am., Can.* franking machine.

postal *esp. Br.* done by post.

postal/ go postal (on sb.) *Am.* col. become angry suddenly, esp. at the place of work.

postal ballot *Br. /Am., Can.* **absentee ballot/** voting by post because the person can't vote in person.

postal (card) *Am.* col. post-card.

postal car *Am.* a railway carriage carrying post.

postal code *Can.* code of letters and numbers for more quicker delivery of post.

post course *Br.* correspondence course.

postal note 1. *Am.* an order issued by a post office, bank or telegraph office for a small sum of up to 5 dollars. 2. *Aus., NZ. /Br.* **postal order/**.

postal order *esp. Br. /Am., Aus.* **money order,** *Aus., NZ* **postal note/** an order issued by one post to pay special amount of money to another post: *the postal order was taken by your son* - T. Rattigan, *Nova would case a bank by going in for a money order* – Reader's Digest.

postal or **post office substation** *Am.* branch post office.

postal or **post truck** *Am.* one delivering mail.

postal service *esp. Am.* the public service for carrying letters, parcels, etc. from one part of a country or the world to another.

postal or **post truck** *Am.* mail van.

postal van *Br. /Am.* **post office car/** mail van, railway carriage carrying post.

postal vote *Br. /Am.* **absentee vote/** vote sent through the post.

postbag *esp. Br.* 1. */Am., Aus.* **mailbag/** a postman's bag for carrying letters. 2. also **mail** col. all the letters received by sb. at one particular time.

post-bellum *Am.* pertaining to smth. that happened after the Civil War in the US.

postbox *esp. Br., Aus., Can. /Am., Aus., Can.* **mailbox, maildrop,** *esp. Br.* **letterbox/** an official metal box in a public place fixed to the ground or on a wall, into which people can put letters to be collected and sent by post.

post code *Br., Aus. /Am.* **zipcode,** *Can.* **postal code/** a group of letters and/or numbers written on the letters to facilitate their dispatch.

post-cost *Br.* review prices and costs (in government contracts) respectively.
post doc *esp. Am.* col. sb. who is studying after they have finished their PhD.
poster paint *Br.* brightly coloured paint that contains no oil, used esp. by children to paint pictures.
post graduate 1. *Br. /esp. Am.* **graduate/** sb. at a university who is studying to get a Master's Degree or PhD. 2. *Am.* sb. who is studying after they have finished PhD.
poste restante *esp. Br. /Am.* **general delivery/** a post office department to which letters for a traveller can be sent and where they will be kept until the person can collect them: *Answer care Poste Restante? Newcastle-on-Tyne.* - D. Francis.
post-free *esp. Br. /esp. Am.* **postpaid/** adj. adv. without any further charge to the sender for posting: *return it to sender in the post-paid envelope.* - B. Bryson.
postie *esp. Can., Aus., Br.* col. postman.
posting (to) *esp. Br. /Am., Aus.* **post/** an appointment to a post, esp. in the armed forces: *he would not have been particularly happy about the prospect of a posting to Yugoslavia.* - A. McLean., *after his posting to Moscow he felt very much at home.* - Y. Richmond.
postman's knock *Br. /Am.* **post office/** a children's game in which a player pretends to deliver a letter to another player and gets a kiss as a reward: *that was the sort of mouth some girls would offer in Postman's Knock* - A. Burgess.
postman *esp. Br. /esp. Am., Can.* **mailman, letter carrier/** person whose job is to collect and deliver letters, parcels, etc.
Post no bills *Am.* Stick no bills (sign).
the Post Office *Br.* national organisation which is responsible for collecting and delivering mail.
postroom *Br.* department of a company dealing with mail.
post season *esp. Am., Can.* (of a sporting or other events) happening after the regular season
post-teens *Am.* youth older than 19 years old.
post town *Br.* town having a main branch of Post Office.
pot 1. *Am.* all the money put together by a number of people for some common purpose (such as for their weekly food supply): *How large is the pot this month?* - R.A. Spears. 2. *Br.* any of the six bags at the edge of billiard ball. 3. *esp. Br.* col. an important person (esp. in the phr. **big pot**). 4. *Br.* a small container (**pot of honey**).

pot *Br.* hit a ball into one of the six billiard bags; n.
pot/ be potted *Br.* sit on a chamber pot.
pot/ not have a pot to piss at, not have two cents to rub together *Am. sl. derog.* be very poor.
pot/ pot smth. **on** *Br.* move a plant into a larger pot.
pot/ put sb.'s **pot on** *Aus., NZ.* col. inform on sb.
potato 1. *Am.* sl. the head: *I got a nasty bump on my potato.* - R.A. Spears. 2. *Br.* col. a hole, esp. in one's socks.
potato chip, also **chip** 1. *Am., Aus. /Br.* **potato crisp/** a thin piece of potato cooked in very hot fat, dried and usu. sold in packets: *She also began eating more fruits and vegetables and get rid of cookies and potato chips.* - Reader's Digest. 2. *Br. /esp. Am., Can.* (**French**) **fry, French (fried) potato/** a long thin piece of potato cooked in deep fat.
potatoes/ small potatoes *Am., Can.* col. something of little value: *it's small potatoes compared to Grandpa's modest way of life* - H. Fast.
potbound *Br. /Am.* **rootbound/** adj. plant that can't grow anymore because its roots have grown to fill the pot it is in.
potcheese *Am.* cottage cheese.
pot egg *Br.* China egg, nest egg.
pot(h)een *esp. Irish Eng.* illicitly made alcoholic drink, usu. made from potatoes.
pot holder *esp. Am., Can., Aus.* a protective piece of material used when removing hot dishes or pans from a cooker.
pot hole (lake) *Am., Can.* pond formed by a natural hollow.
pot holer *Br. /Br., Aus.* **caver,** *Am.* **spelunker,** *Aus.* **speleologist/** person who does cave exploring in his free time.
pot holing *esp. Br. /Br., Aus.* **caving,** *Am.* **spelunking,** *Aus.* **speleology/** leisure activity of exploring underground holes.
pot liquor *esp. Am.* liquid in which meat, fish or vegetables has been oiled; stock.
potluck (dinner/supper) *esp. Am.* one where each guest takes a different dish which is then shared with the other guests.
potman *Br.* man who collects the glasses and cleans up in a pub: *the potman called across with a laugh* - G. Greene.
pot pie *esp. Am., Can.* 1. meat pie. 2. stew with dumplings: *He mashed his fork into his chicken potpie* – R.L. Stine.
potplant *esp. Br., Aus. /Am.* **house plant, potted plant/** a plant in a flower pot which is grown

indoors: *her son had taken all of her potted plants* – P. Roth.

pots/ have pots of *Br.* col. have a lot of smth., esp. money.

potted 1. *esp. Br.* col. often derog. (of a book) produced in a shorter simpler form (about history, version, etc.). 2. *esp. Am.* sl. drunk. 3. *Br.* (of meat or fish) made into a paste for spreading on bread.

potted lecture *Br.* col. canned lecture, spiel.

potter *Br.* /*Am.* **putter**/ 1. col. go in unhurried way. 2. spend time moving about the place slowly doing small things that need little effort. n., e.g. *a potter around the shops.*

potting shed *Br.* small building, usu. made of wood where garden tools, seeds, etc. are kept.

potty *esp. Br.* col. 1. silly, slightly mad: *It sounds potty.* - New Idea., *Mildly potty, I believe* - A. Christie., *Potty communications are good for a feature.* - I. Murdoch. 2. (about) having an extremely strong interest or admiration for. 3. insignificant, feeble.

potty trained *Br.* toilet trained.

pouch *Am.* 1. mail bag: *they will have to be sent by pouch.* - H. Truman. 2. area of loose skin under sb.'s eyes.

pouf(fe) *Br.* col. /*Am., Can.* **hassock**/ round soft piece of furniture used to sit or put one's feet on.

poulterer *Br.* obs. sb. who sells poultry.

pound cake *Am.* /*Br.* **Madeira cake**/ spongecake made heavier by adding fat in to the mixture.

pouf *Br., Aus.* sl. derog. poof

pouf(fe) *Br.* /*Am.* **hassock**/.

poulterer *Br.* dealer in poultry and often game.

pound the beat *Br.* (of policeman) work regularly around his area.

pound the pavement *Am.* col. 1. work a police beat. 2. also *Can.* trudge about the streets, esp. looking for work: *John pounded the pavement looking for a job.* - A. Makkai.

poundage *Br.* amount of pounds sterling involved in a transaction.

pounding/ take a pounding *esp. Br.* col. 1. be severely injured or damaged. 2. be severely defeated (at a sports event).

pour/ (*Br.*) /*Am.* **it's pouring rain/** it's pouring with rain this morning.

pour it on *Am.* col. 1. also *Can.* overpraise sb. or smth.: *was there any need to pour it on like that?* - Longman. 2. work hard, use a lot of effort: *Pour it on, boys.* - Longman. 3. also **pour on the coal** move quickly: *Better pour it on if you're to catch your plane!* - Longman.

pourer *Br.* a spout attached to a bottle.

poverty line *Am.* lowest living standard.

poverty trap *Br.* a situation in which sb. would end up even poorer if they had a job, because they'd no longer receive money from the government.

powder/ take a powder *Am., Can.* col. vanish, get away: *I've taken a powder briefly* - S. Bellow.

powdered sugar *Am.* /*Br.* **icing sugar**/.

powder monkey *Am., Can.* col. a specialist in the use of dynamite: *How long do powder monkeys live?* - R.A. Spears.

powder room *Am.* small room with a toilet and washbasin next to the main living room in a house or apartment: *In the middle, I went to the powder room.* – A. Summers, R. Swan.

power/ all/more power to sb.'s **elbow** *esp. Br., Aus.* col. /*Am., Aus.* **more power to** sb./ good luck to sb.

power/ do sb. **a power of good** *Br.* col. make sb. feel more healthy, happy and hopeful about the future.

power/ the power behind the throne *Br.* real authority in an organisation.

power cut *Br., Aus.* /*Am.* **power outage/** a failure in the supply of electricity.

power up *esp. Am.* be prepared to do smth. that requires a lot of energy and effort.

power plant, power house *esp. Am.* power station: *the power plant was untouched* - J. Fischer., *She pictures the man at the power plant pulling the switches* - J. Updike.

(power) point, socket *Br., Aus.* /*Am.* **(electric) outlet, power outlet, wall oulet, convenience outlet**/ electric wall socket.

power-striding *Am.* vigorous walking as a form of exercise to improve fitness: *In the morning, Chalabi takes a power walk with his permanent companions* – Harper's Magazine.

poxy *Br.* col. (of sb. or smth. pathetic and insignificant) worthless.

PR *Am., Can.* Puerto Rico.

practical *Br.* a lesson or test where you do or make smth. rather than writing.

practical politics *esp. Br.* ideas, plans, etc., that may be used at once and that will show successful results.

prad *esp. Br., Aus.* col. horse.

pr(a)eposter *Br.* monitor.

prairie oysters *esp. Am., Can.* testicles of a calf cooked and served as food.

The Prairie Provinces *Can.* Manitoba, Saskatchewan and Alberta.

prairie schooner *Am., Can.* covered wagon in which the pioneers travelled westwards: *The*

term prairie schooner described many covered wagons. - McGraw-Hill English, 1990.
The Prairie State *Am.* Illinois /also **The Sucker State**/: *Nope, I'm a Prairie Stater. "Land of Lincoln" as they say.*- K. Vonnegut, Jr.
Prairie States *Am.* Illinois, Wisconsin, Iowa, Minnesota.
prairie wolf *Am., Can.* coyote.
pram /also obs. **perambulator**/ *esp. Br., Aus.* /*Am.* **baby buggy, baby carriage**/ a wheeled carriage, pushed by hand in which a baby can sleep or be taken about: *she had a big pram, with the twins in it.* - J. Baez., *a kind lady held the door open for me and the pram* - Woman's Own.
pram park *Br.* area for prams.
prang *Br.* col. v. n. /*Am.* col. **fender-bender**/ crash.
prang up 1. *Br.* col. cause (a plane, car, etc.) to crash: *He's pranged up the plane* - Longman. 2. *Br.* col. spoil (smth.): *they pranged up the whole operation.* - Longman.
prat *Br.* derog. col. 1. a worthless stupid person. 2. person's bottom.
prat about/around *Br.* col. behave stupidly.
pratfall *esp. Am.* sl. 1. a fall on the backside: *I took a pratfall right on the sidewalk.* - R.A. Spears. 2. any laughable mischance.
prawn *esp. Br.* /*esp. Am.* **shrimp**/ a small shellfish that can be eaten.
prawn/ come the raw prawn *esp. Aus.* try to cheat or trick sb.
prawn cocktail *Br.* /*Am.* **shrimp cocktail**/ dish served before the main course of a meal and consisting of prawns in mayonnaise on a bed of lettuce leaves.
pray to the porcelain god *Am.* sl. vomit.
prayer *Am.* sl. (always in the negative) a chance: *I didn't think I had a prayer of getting that done without his guidance.* - Reader's Digest.
prebuilt *Am.* (about building material) prefabricated.
precinct 1. *Br.* part of a town planned for or limited to the stated use: *I walked from the station through a concrete shopping precinct* - B. Bryson. 2. *Am., Can.* a division of a town or city for election or police purposes: *Write a letter to the precinct Captain and describe the problem to him.* - J. Updike.
preemie *Am., Can.* col. /*Aus.* **premmie**/ col. a baby born earlier than expected.
preempt *Am., Can.* settle on (land) with the right to buy it before others, **preemption** n.
prefect *esp. Br.* an older student in a school who has special powers and duties: *All but the girl prefects, who wore striped blazers* – R. Westall.

prefer *Br.* law /*Am., Aus.* **press**/ make an official accusation.
preference stock (or **shares**) *Br.* /*Am.* **preferred stock** or **shares**/ business shares that give the owners the right to be paid interest before any money is paid to owners of ordinary shares: *Their analysts don't know preffered stock from livestock.* - K. Lipper.
preferential shop *Am.* shop which prefers taking trade union members.
prefix, dialling code *Br.* /*Am.* **area code**/ dialling tone.
preggers *esp. Br.* sl pregnant.
pregnant/ fall pregnant *Br.* (of a woman) become pregnant.
prelims *esp. Br.* col. /*Am.* **front matter**/ the material (such as title, preface, etc.) which comes before the main part of the book.
premed *esp. Am., Can.* col. 1. member of preparatory courses in the medical college: *I was a premed.* - K. Vonnegut, Jr. 2. preparatory medical course: *Two years of premed in the Hebrew tongue* - H. Fast.
premenstrual tension *Br.* /*Am.* **premenstrual syndrome**/.
premie, preemie *Am., Can., Aus.* /*Aus.* **premmie**/ col. premature baby: *lung damage, mental retardation or other ill effects common to preemies.* - Reader's Digest.
premier 1. *Aus., Can.* prime minister of state or province (not of federal government). 2. *Am.* Secretary of State.
prenatal *esp. Am., Aus.* /*Br.* **antenatal**/ adj. of or for the time before a birth: *That didn't include the money he had already given her to cover the prenatal checkups.* – P. Roth.
prenup *Am., Can.* col. a prenuptial agreement, establishing the legal claims of one party on the assets of the other if the marriage fails: *you have to have a prenup.* – Reader's Digest.
preowned *esp. Am., Can.* second-hand.
prep 1. *Br.* col. /*Am., Aus.* **(home) assignment, homework**/ school work that is done at home, homework in some private schools. 2. *Am., Can.* student in preparatory school.
prep 1. *Am., Can.* prepare oneself for an event. 2. *Am.* col. prepare food for cooking in a restaurant.
prep *Am.* col. 1. attend preparatory school. 2. do school work at home. 3. prepare (sb.) for an operation or examination: *POWs shouting "Death to Khomeini" were obviously prepped on what else to say.* - McLean's.
prepackaged *Am., Aus.* wrapped or put into containers before being sent.

preparatory school 1. *Br.* private school of pupils between the ages of 7 and 13. 2. *Am., Can.* preparatory school that prepares pupils for college or university.

prepositions / Americans prefer **round** to around: *We went round the corner.*; **around** to about: *They walked about a mile.*; **aside from** to apart from, **in behalf of** to on behalf of and they also often **use atop, off of and back of**/ I get in a train and get out of it *Br.* /*Am.* I get on a train or aboard it and get off it/ ; We put coal in a grate *Br.* /*Am.* We put coal on a grate/, *armoured trucks perched atop twenty-four-inch tires.* - K. Ablow.

preppy *esp. Am., Can.* col. adj. n. (typical of) student or former student of expensive private school in the US (esp. in being neat and well-dressed): *Preppies use favoured hurray-words* - P. Howard.

preprint *Am.* 1. part of the book or article published before the finished version is issued: *days of shuffling of preoriented forms.* - R.J. Randisi., M. Waalace. 2. signal copy.

prep-time *Am.* a period at school when teachers don't teach and therefore are able to prepare for later classes.

prerogarive *Br.* law. arising from the prerogative of the Crown and based in common law rather that statutory one.

preschool *Am., Aus.* /*esp. Br.* **preschool, pregroup,** *Br.* **nursery**/ nursery school for **preschoolers**, children between 2 and 5 years of age: *he didn't have to pay for a mortgage or for preschool like the rest of us.* - R.J. Randisi., M. Wallace.

preschooler *Am.* child who doesn't yet go to school.

prescription/ have several **refills on** one **prescription** *Am.* use it several times without talking to one's doctor.

present *esp. Br., Aus.* col. introduce a TV or radio programme or a person; n. **-er.**

present/ all present and correct *Br.* /*Am.* **all present and accounted for**/ everyone who is supposed to be in a place or meeting, etc. is now here.

present company excluded *Am.* humor. present company excepted.

presenter *Br.* /*Am.* **announcer**/ news commentator.

presently *esp. Am., Can.* at present, now.

preservationist *esp. Am.* col. sb. who works to prevent historic places, buildings, etc. from being destroyed.

preservation order *esp. Br., Aus.* an official order that smth., esp. a historical building, must be preserved and not destroyed.

preservator *Am.* historical sight preserver.

preserve *esp. Am.* reserve for animals.

president *esp. Am., Can.* 1. the head of a business company, bank, etc. 2. the head of a university.

presidential year *Am.* the year when the president is elected.

presidio *Am.* garrisoned place.

press *esp. Irish Eng.* clothes cupboard, usu. placed in recess.

press/ **a free-court press on** sb. or smth. *Am.* making a lot of effort to get good results.

press/ **press (the) flesh** *esp. Am., Can.* col. shake hands: *For Hawk, that means stepping up his program of travel and pressing the flesh.* - Bulletin., *The Soviet General Secretary presses the flesh on a May visit to the Rumanian capital.* - Time.

press baron *esp. Br.* col. one who owns and controls one or more important national newspapers.

pressboard 1. *Am.* an ironing board, esp. a small one for sleeves. 2. *esp. Am., Can.* board made from wood or textile pulp or laminated waste paper and used as an electric insulator and for making light furniture.

press button *Br.* push button.

press cutting agency *Br.* /*Am.* **clipping bureau**/ newspaper cuttings bureau.

pressie, prezzie *Br., Aus.* col. present.

pressman *esp. Br.* col. a newspaper reporter: *Armstrong turned Europe's pressmen on to Jazz Power* - M. Jones, J. Chilton.

press mark *esp. Br.* (in older libraries) a mark in a library book indicating its position on a shelf.

press stud *Br., Aus.* /*Br.* **popper,** *Am.* **snap (fastener)**/ snap fastener.

press-up *esp. Br., Aus.* /*esp. Am., Aus.* **push-up**/ a form of exercise in which a person lies down on the ground and pushes his body up with his arms: *Bond went down on his hands and did 20 slow press-ups* - I. Fleming.

pressurise (into) *esp. Br.* /*esp. Am.* **pressure**/ force (sb.) to do smth.

pressurized *Br.* pressured, feeling worried because of the amount of things one has to do.

presto/ **Hey Presto** *Br.* excl. It's magic!

preteen *Am.* child who is 11-12 years old.

pretty pass/ **(if/when) things have come to a pretty pass** *Br.* if things reached such a state they are really going bad.

pretty pretty *Br.* spoilt by too much pretty decoration.

pretzel *esp. Am., Can.* glazed and salted biscuit having the form of a knot.

prevention is better than cure *Br., Aus. /Am.* **an ounce of prevention is worth a pound of cure/** it's better to stop smth. bad happening than to deal with it after it happened.

preventive detention *Br.* law. imprisonment for a long time for habitual criminals over 30 years old.

preventor *Am.* ceiling hook in firing service.

Prex(ie), Prexy, Prez *Am.* col. President: *The prexie broke the tied vote.* - R.E. Spears.

prezzie *esp. Br., Aus.* col. a present.

price/ What price...? *esp. Br.* a. derog. What's the use? b. rare. What chance...?

price commission *Am.* one regulating price and rent increases to curb inflation.

pric(e)y *esp. Br.* derog. col. expensive: *The private beaches still come pricey* - Woman's Own., *Abe, I think she's a bit pricey for the likes of us.* - L. Uris.

price ring *esp. Br.* persons acting together to set a non-competitive price on the product.

prick/ kick against the pricks *esp. Br., Aus.* fight against people in authority.

prick/ like a spare prick at a wedding *Br.* taboo. sl. having no role in a particular situation.

pride comes before a fall *Br., Aus. /Am.* **pride goes before a fall/**.

pride of place (in) *esp. Br.* the highest or best position.

primary grades *Am.* first 3-4 years in a school.

primary school 1. *Br. /Am.* **elementary school, grade school, grammar school/** one for children between 5 and 11 years old. 2. *Am., Can.* an elementary school with 3-4 grades and often kindergarten.

prime minister *Can.* Federal prime minister.

primer 1. *Am.* set of basic instructions. 2. *Br.* obs. beginner's book in a school subject.

prime rib *Am., Can.* roast or steak out of the ribs immediately before the loin.

prime time *esp. Am.* time in the evening when the greatest number of people watch TV.

primitive area *Am.* preserved forestland.

primus stove *Br.* tdmk. small portable stove that burns oil.

Prince Albert (coat) *Am.* a long double-breasted frock coat: *a schoolteacher's switch hidden in the folds of his Prince Albert.* - J. O'Hara.

principal 1. *esp. Am., Aus. /Br.* **headmaster, headmistress, head teacher/** a person in charge of a school or college for children of 11-18 years old. 2. *Can.* person in charge of a private school.

principal boy/girl *Br.* the chief male/female character in a pantomime, usu. played by a woman.

Principality *Br.* pomp. Wales.

print *esp. Am.* newspaper, publication: *sleepy village in an old Russian print.* - W. Kerr., *The print which merely falls with ordinary opinion* - E.A. Poe.

printed papers *esp. Br.* printed matters.

printed paper rates *Br.* third class rates.

printery *Am.* printing office.

priority mail *Am.* preferential rating mail.

prise *esp. Br., Aus. /esp. Am.* **pry/** move, lift, or force with a tool or metal bar,

prison van *Br. /Am.* **patrol wagon/** police wagon.

private bar *Br.* an additional bar in a pub, similar to a lounge bar.

private car *Am. /Br.* **private coach** or **saloon/** railway carriage used by an individual.

private company *Br.* one whose shares may not be offered to the public for sale and which operates under legal requirements less strict than those of a public company.

private hospital *esp. Am. /Br.* **nursing home/** small private hospital.

private means *Br.* income from investments, property, or inheritance, as opp. to earned income or state benefit.

private medicine *Br.* the system in which medical treatment and advice are provided not by the government but is paid by the **private patient** who needs it or by their insurance company.

private member *Br.* Member of Parliament who is not a minister in the government.

private practice *Am.* the business of a professional person, esp. a doctor who works alone rather than with others.

private school 1. *Br.* independent school supported wholly by the payment of fees. 2. *Am., Can.* school supported by private organisation or individuals rather than by state.

private soldier *Am.* a soldier of the lowest rank, who is not a recruit.

privatism *Am.* retreat into privacy.

prize day *Br.* occasion when prizes are given to pupils who have done well in particular subject.

prize fight *Am.* professional boxing match.

prizeman *esp. Br.* a person who wins a (particular) university prize.

prizes/ no prizes for guessing *Br., Aus.* col. it's very easy to guess it.

pro *Br.* col. prostitute.

probable cause *esp. Am.* law. reasonable grounds for supposing that a criminal charge is well-founded.

probate *Am.* law. prove (a will) to be legal: *a trust does not require probating.* - L. Burkett.

probation *Am.* fixed period of time in which sb. must improve the work or behave well so that they won't have to leave their work, **be on probation**.

problem/ No problem *esp. Am., Aus., Can.* It was no trouble: *You want to open a checking account for your under-age daughter? No problem.* - H.C. Whitford., R.J. Dixson.

processing tax *Am.* agricultural tax on processed produce.

procession *Br.* col. (in sports, esp. in cricket) a very easy defeat of one's opponent.

proctor *Am., Can. /Br.* **invigilator/** a person appointed to make sure students do not cheat in an examination.

proctor *Am. /Br.* **invigilate/** watch over (an examination) in order to prevent dishonesty.

prod/ on the prod *Am., Can.* col. looking for trouble.

produce *esp. Am.* fruit and vegetables, produced in large amounts through farming.

producer 1. *esp. Am.* person who arranges for the performance of plays or musical shows: *she has a little money in the bank from a great big mad love affair with a producer.* – J. O'Hara. 2. *esp. Br. / Am.* **director/** the man who directs the play in a theatre, theatrical manager.

professional foul *Br.* rule broken in sport done deliberately to gain some advantage.

professor 1. *Br.* a teacher of the highest rank in a university department, higher than lecturer, senior lecturer or reader. 2. *Am., Can.* any full member of the teaching staff at a university or college. 3. *Am.* sl. a piano player in a cheap saloon.

profiterole *Br.* small round pastry with a sweet filling and chocolate on the top.

program *Am., Aus. /Br.* **programme/**.

program/ get with the program *Am., Can.* col. accept new ideas and give more attention to what's happening now.

(housing) project, col. **the projects** *Am., Can.* group of houses or flats usu. built with government money for low-income families: *from the projects of New York to the musical mountaintop.* - Ebony., *I have lived in the projects* - Daily News.

prolabor *Am.* supporting the trade union.

prole *esp. Br.* col. derog. proletarian.

prom 1. *Br.* col. promenade concert, **the proms** is a series of them. 2. *Br.* col. promenade, a wide path beside a road along the coast in a holiday town: *I had a long stroll along the prom to boost my appetite* - B. Bryson. 3. *Am., Can.* a formal dance party given for students in a high school or college class: *they introduced their girls to him at their proms.* - I. Shaw., *I sang at other high school's proms* - J. Baez.

promenade *Br.* a wide path next to the sea which people walk along for pleasure.

promenade concert *Br.* one at which many of the listeners stand rather than sit.

promenader, prommer *Br.* col. person who regularly attends promenade concerts.

promise (sb.) **the earth** *Br., Aus.* promise sb. impossible.

promo *Am., Aus.* advertisement or any social event designed to give attention to a new book, film, etc., in order to increase their sales.

promote 1. *esp. Br.* put (a team) up to a higher level in a sporting competition. 2. *Am.* put up to the next higher grade at the end of a school year.

prong *Am.* sl. penis.

proof 1. *Am.* proof-read: *By morning the speech was finished and proofed* - S.B. Oates. 2. *Am., Can.* activate (yeast) by the addition of liquid.

proof/ the proof is in the pudding *Am.* finding out if smth. works by trying it and seeing the results.

prop *esp. Aus.* (of a horse) stop suddenly, n.

propelling pencil *Br., Aus. /Am.* **mechanical pencil/** pencil in which the lead can be pushed forward by turning or pressing a part of it.

proper *esp. Br.* col. adv. 1. properly. 2. **good and proper** completely.

proper *esp. Br.* col. (often of smth. unpleasant or undesirable) thorough, complete; satisfactorily. adv. **-ly**.

properly *esp. Br.* completely, thoroughly; properly speaking *esp. Br.* really.

property *Br. /Am., Aus.* **real estate/**.

prophylactic *Am.* often humor. condom.

proposal *Am.* a bid for government contract, tender.

proposition *Am.* constitutional proposal.

pro rate *Am.* 1. n. proportional rate. 2. v. distribute proportionally.

prose *Br.* a student's exercise in translating a piece of writing into a foreign language.

prosector *esp. Am., Can.* anatomist doing dissections of dead bodies.

protective *Br.* thing that protects sb. or smth.

prosecuting attorney *Am.* district attorney.
protest (smth) *Am.* make a protest against smth.
protocol *Am.* a course of medical treatment to a person who is ill or has an addiction.
proud *esp. Br.* tech. obs. sticking out above a surface or surrounding area / also in the phr. **in a proud manner.**
proud/ treat sb. **proud** *Br., Aus.* obs. treat them very well, esp. by giving them the best food and making them feel most comfortable.
prove up *Am.* 1. prove that patent can be lawfully taking place. 2. adduce the proof of right (esp. for obtaining the state land).
proven *esp. Am.* past participle of prove: *they have already proven a success.* - Sydney Calendar Magazine.
provincials *Br.* local newspapers.
provision /or **food**/ **store** *Am.* grocery store.
provisional licence *Br., Aus.* /*Am.* **learner's permit/** a licence which a person has to obtain before they can learn to drive.
provost 1. *Br.* a person in charge of a college in some universities. 2. *Am., Can.* a person of high rank who helps to run a college or university.
provost guard *Am.* police detail of soldiers under the authority of the provost marshal.
prowl *Am.* col. search by running the hands over the person.
prowl car, prowler *Am.* police patrol car: *Bobby attracted attention of a police prowl car* - T. Thompson., *He turned in time to see a prowl car tear past* - L. Waller., *he called the prowl car in town.* - J. Kerouac.
prox *Br.* becoming rare. of next month (in letters).
pruning shears *Am.* /*Br.* **secateurs**/ strong scissors for cutting bits off garden plants.
pry (**off, up, open**) *esp. Am., Can.* /*esp. Br.* **prise/** prize: *You couldn't pry him loose* - E. Caldwell.
pry bar *esp. Am., Can.* a tool for prying like a small crowbar.
PSBR *Br.* public-sector borrowing requirement.
pseud *Br.* col. derog. person who pretends to have great knowledge and good judgement in matters such as art or literature. **-y** adj.
PSV *Br.* public service vehicle.
psyche *Am.* raise oneself to a state of keen readiness and capability, **be psyched**.
psych(e) out 1. *esp. Am., Aus.* sl. frighten using only the power of one's mind: *it was just to psych you out?* - J. DeFelice. 2. *esp. Am.* sl. understand by intuition: *I'm starting to psych out an entire culture* - Time. 3. *esp. Am.* col. sympathise with (sb.): *One of the first things a teacher has to do is to psych the children out.* - Longman. 4. *esp. Am.* cause (sb.) to suffer or be uncomfortable in their feelings: *His attempt to psych out the other competitors seemed to work* - Toronto Globe and Mail., Aug. 9, 1976. 5. *Am., Can.* col. become afraid or nervous, etc.: *I psych out every time I enter an examination room.* - Longman 6. *Am.* col. pretend to be mad so as to avoid smth. unpleasant: *some men were able to get out of the army by psyching out* - Longman.
psych(e) up *esp. Am.* sl. make (esp. oneself) keen and ready: *you can get the committee members (all) psyched up before the meeting* - Longman., *We were perpetually psyched up!* – S Lawrence.
PTO 1. *esp. Am.* /*Aus.* **Parents and Citizens, PandCs/ Parent-Teacher Organisation.** 2. *Br.* Please Turn Over look at the next page.
PT *esp. Br.* physical training.
Pte *Br.* private.
P-Town *Am.* sl. Philadelphia.
Pty *Aus., NZ.* proprietary, in the names of private companies to show that owners are responsible for only a limited amount of the company's debts.
pub *Br., Aus.* /*Br.* **public house,** *Am.* **bar,** *Can.* **pub, bar**/.
pub *Aus.* a hotel.
pub-crawl *esp. Br., Can., Aus.* sl. v. n. (make) a visit to several pubs one after another usu. having a drink at each place: *a little pub-crawling in Mont Parnasse.* - A. Huxley., *I wanted to do a pub-crawl.* - G. Greene.
public *Br.* of, for, or acting for a university.
public / government agency *Am.* authority.
public/ Great British Public *Br.* col. often humor. British people.
publican, also **pubkeeper** *esp. Br., Aus.* person who (owns and) runs a pub: *It was no brain of a county publican* – M. Daly.
publican *Aus.* a hotel keeper.
public analyst *Br.* health official who analyzes food.
public bar *Br.* a plainly furnished room in a pub, hotel, etc., where cheaper prices are charged for drinks than in a saloon bar: *as if he were gazing at life itself in the public bar.* - G. Greene.
public comfort station *Am.* /*esp. Br., Aus.* euph. (**public**) **convenience**/ a public toilet provided by local government.
public company *Br.* /*Am.* **public corporation**/ company that offers its shares for sale on the stock exchange.
public corporation *esp. Br.* (**plc**) a large company that provides services to the public and is owned

by the government but supposed to be more independent than the ordinary nationalised industry.
public day *Am.* reception day for public.
public debt *Am.* country's national debt.
public defender *Am.* law. public lawyer who defends accused person unable to pay for legal assistance.
public footpath *Br.* path that everyone has the right to use.
public house *Br.* pub: *Beside this bridge is Wrenberry mill, now converted into a public house.* - Cheshire Life.
public housing *Am.* /*Br.* **council housing**/ housing operated by municipality.
public pay station *Am.* /*Br.* **public call box**/ public pay phone.
public purse/ be provided by by public purse *esp. Br., Aus.* derog. be paid by the government.
public school 1. *Br.* an expensive school that parents pay to send their children to. 2. *Am.* / *Br.* **state school**/ a free school that is controlled and paid for by the government.
public servant, also **public service corporation** *Am.* public utility.
public service *Am.* a service performed by public utility.
public service announcement *esp. Am.* special message on TV or radio, giving information about an important subject.
public toilet *esp. Br.* /*Am., Can.* **rest room,** *Can.* **bathroom**/.
public transportation *Am., Can.* /*Br.* **public transport**/.
public trough, also **pork barrel** *Am.* government project or appropriation yielding rich patronage benefits.
public warehouse *Am.* private general warehouse.
publish *Am.* begin distributing (printing matter).
publisher *esp. Am., Can.* newspaper proprietor.
pud *Br.* col. pudding.
pudding *Br.* 1. /*Am., Aus.* **dessert**/ sweet food served at the end of a meal, dessert. 2. solid hot sweet dish based on pastry, rice, bread, etc. with fat and fruit and other substances added, and usu. served hot. 3. an unsweetened dish of a mixture of flour, fat, etc., either covering or enclosing meat or vegetables and boiled with it. 4. sl. fat and stupid person.
pudding/ be in the pudding club *Br.* col. be pregnant.
pudding/ overegg the pudding *esp. Br.* spoil smth. by trying too hard to improve it.

pudding basin *Br.* 1. a deep round bowl used for making puddings. 2. hairdo in the shape of an upside down bowl.
puddle jumper *esp. Am., Can.* col. small light airplane used for short trips.
pudge *Am., Can.* col. fat on a person's body.
pudgy *esp. Am.* podgy.
puff *Br.* an ad, esp. one exaggerating the value of goods.
puff/ get one's **puff back** *Br.* col. be able to breath normally again after doing smth. that made sb. breath very hard.
puff/ in all one's **puff** *esp. Br.* col. in one's whole life.
puff/ out of puff *Br.* col. breathing very hard and feeling very tired.
(puff) paste *Am.* puff pastry, vol-au-vent.
puff/ puff at (one's pipe) *Br.* puff on (one's pipe).
puffed (out) *Br.* /*Am., Aus.* **pooped**/ breathing very hard after making a lot of physical effort.
puffer train *Br.* child's word for a steam train.
puff piece *Am., Can.* col. derog. a piece of writing or speech which praises smth.
puff-puff *Br.* children's word for steaming engine or train.
pukka *Br.* sl. authentic, genuine.
pull *Br.* obs. difficult climb up a steep road.
pull 1. *esp. Br.* get (beer) out of a barrel by pulling a handle. 2. *esp. Am.* sl. succeed in doing (a crime, smth. daring, smth. annoying or deceiving, etc.).
pull birds *Br., Aus.* col. pick up a member of the opposite sex so that to start sexual relationship with them later. 4. *Am., Can.* disqualify (a player) from a game.
pull a boner *Am., Can.* col. make a mistake.
pull a stroke *Br.* sl. succeed in a clever manoeuvre.
pull/be on the pull *Br.* col. be actively looking for sexual partners.
pull/ pull the other one (it's got bells on it) *Br.* col. I don't believe you.
pull/ pull your head (scone or **skull)** *Aus.* col. mind your own business.
pull/ take a pull (on oneself) *Aus.* get oneself together.
pull down 1. *esp. Am.* col. pull in, earn (money): *I pull down about ten thousand a year.* - K. Vonnegut, Jr. 2. *Br.* obs. make sb. feel ill and weak. 3. *Am.* make sb. less healthy or successful.
pull in *Br.* col. (of police) arrest sb. and take them to a police station.
pull round *esp. Br.* recover from illness.

pull/bring sb./oneself. **up short** *Br.* make sb./oneself stop and think.

pull up stakes *Am., Aus. Can.* col. /*Br.* col. **up stakes**/ leave a place where one has lived or worked: *every two years or so he pulls up stakes* - Longman.

pull date *Am., Aus.* /*Br.* **sell-by date**/.

pull-in, pull-on, also **pull-up** *esp. Br.* col. /*Am.* **rest stop**/ a place by the roadside where vehicles may stop and the drivers can get drinks and light meals.

Pullman (car), parlor car *Am.* /*esp. Br.* **sleeping car**/ a specially comfortable railway carriage, esp. for sleeping in.

pull-off *Am.* place by the roadside where vehicles may stop.

pullover, sweater *esp. Am., Can.* /*esp. Br.* **jumper**/: *revolting electric blue pullover.* – Alain de Botton.

pull-quote *Am.* brief catchy quotation often used as a subheading.

pull tab *Am.* /*Br.* **ring-pull**/ ring on a can used to open it.

pullthrough *esp. Br.* string used for cleaning the inside of the barrel of a gun.

pull-up *Am.* exercise in which one uses arms to pull oneself up towards a bar above one's head.

pulperia *Am.* a grocery store where hard liquor can be obtained.

pummel *Am., Can.* col. criticize severely.

pump 1. *esp. Am., Can., Aus.* /*Br.* **court shoe**/ dancing shoe, woman's formal shoe with no fastener: *You put these pumps on and you feel like walking everywhere.* - Omni. 2. *Br., Aus.* a woman's shoe with low heels and no fastenings for dancing, exercise. 3. *Am.* pump-action shotgun. 4. *Br.* col. shoe made of canvas with rubber on the bottom, used for sports, tennis shoe.

pump *Am.* sl. have sex with.

pump/ prime the pump *esp. Am.* do smth. in order to make smth. succeed.

pump/ pump gas *Am.* put petrol in one's car at a gas station.

pump up *esp. Am., Can.* col. excite, often in **get/ be pumped up about** smth.: *Roethlisberger pumped up the crowd with his intensity* - Time.

pumped *esp. Am., Can.* col. excited: *Everyone is really pumped!* – R.L. Stine.

pumper 1. *Am.* oil well. 2. *esp. Am., Can.* fire engine that carries a hose and pumps water.

pumpkin 1. also **punkin** *Am., Can.* col. affectionate form of address, esp. to a child. 2. *Br.* squash.

pumpkin /usu. **some pumpkin**/ *Am.* col. person or thing of considerable consequence.

pun *Br.* consolidate earth or rubbish by pounding it.

punch *Am.* move cattle from one place to another.

Punch/ as pleased / proud as Punch *Br.* extremely pleased / proud: *I was pleased as Punch to discover him* - New York.

punch (in, out), punch the (time) clock *Am., Can.* clock (in, out): *Guess who's been punching him in every morning?* - B. Kaufman., *I have to punch in at work.* - Daily News.

punch *esp. Am.* hit quickly and hard with one's fingers (esp. buttons on telephone or keyboard).

punch *Am., Can.* 1. work as a cowboy: *And now he's punching cows.* - J. Kerouac 2. drive (cattle) by prodding them with a stick, **puncher** *Am.* cowboy.

punch/ beat sb. **to the punch** *Am.* do smth. before others.

punch/ punch above one's **weight** *Br.* try to do smth. above one's abilities.

punch/ punch holes in an argument/idea, etc. *Br.* disagree with sb.'s ideas and show what's wrong with them.

punch/ punch sb.'s **lights out** *Am.* col. hit sb. so hard that they fall over.

punch/ punch on the nose *Br., Aus.* /*Am.* **punch in the nose**/.

punch/ roll with the punches *Am., Aus.* be able to deal with difficulties and criticism.

punch (sb.) up *Br.* col. 1. hit (sb.) repeatedly. 2. fight (sb.) with bare hands: *I will not allow anyone to punch people up in my hotel* - Longman.

punch ball, punch bag *Br.* /*Am., Can., Aus.* **punching bag**/ long leather ball fixed on spring which is punched for exercise or practice: *like a boxer working out a flabby punching bag.* - J.W. Houston, J.D. Houston.

punch ball *Am.* a rubber ball filled with air which is hit with a fist when playing a game similar to baseball.

punching bag/ use sb. **as a punching bag** *Am.* /*Br.* **use** sb. **as a punch bag**/ 1. put all the blame on some people. 2. hit sb. a lot.

punch-up, also **dust-up** *esp. Br., Can* col. a fight, esp. in **have/get into a punch-up**: *One of which spilled over into a punch-up in the car-park.* - New Idea., *They are currently enmeshed in this punch-up* - Maclean's., *a brief mime of a punch-up.* - A. Burgess.

puncture *Br.* /*esp. Am., Aus., Can.* **flat**/ a small hole made with a sharp point, esp. in a tire.

puncture/ slow puncture *Br. /Am.* **slow leak/** a tire that is a bit flat.
punctured *Br.* sl. drunk.
punk *esp. Am., Can.* derog. col. rough and unpleasant young man or boy: *the young punks who have come here for a sexual holiday* - J.A. Michener., *the other boys seemed like a silly crowd of punks.* - C. McCullers.
punk *Am.* substance that burns without a flame and is used to light fireworks, etc.
punk *Am., Can.* 1. col. worthless: *this punk cunt's listening to Mr. Straight.* - J. Kellerman. 2. rare. sl. in poor health.
punker *esp. Am., Can.* punk rocker.
punkie *Am.* biting midge.
punnet *esp. Br., Aus.* small fruit basket (used when selling fruit).
punt *Br., Aus.* col. bet on the result of a horse race. **-er** n.: *big chaps with muscles, bookies and punters.* - L. Lee., *A punter walked off with 3,100 pounds* - Evening Standard., *Punters put out thousands of pounds on hunches* - Gloucester Citizen.
punt *esp. Br.* travel along a river in a punt.
punt/ take/have a punt at *Aus., NZ.* col. attempt to do smth.
punter *esp. Br.* 1. person who moves a boat by using a pole. 2. also *Aus.* col. person who makes a bet on the result of a horse race. 3. also *Aus.* col. the user of a product or service, customer. 4. col. a prostitute's customer.
pup/ sell sb. **a pup** *Br.* col. obs. deceive sb; also **be sold a pup/buy a pup.**
pupil 1. *esp. Br.* a child in a school. 2. *Br.* trainee barrister who is in charge of (**pupil master**).
puppy fat *Br., Aus.* col. often euph. */Am.* **baby fat/** fatness in boys and girls that usu. disappears as they grow older.
pup tent *Am., Can.* small triangular tent without sidewalls.
purdonium *Br.* a coal scuttle for indoor use.
purgatory *Am.* ravine.
The Puritan State *Am.* Massachusetts.
purler *Br.* col. 1. a heavy fall, usu. head first / **come a purler.** 2. a heavy blow that knocks sb. down.
purple *Br., Aus.* a style of writing or speaking which is unneccessarily complicated and with too much details.
purple/ be born to the purple *Br.* obs. be of the highest level of society.
purple heart *Br.* col. amphetamine pill.
purpose/ of set purpose *esp. Br.* with planned intention.

purpose-built, purpose-made *esp. Br.* originally made for a particular use.
purse 1. *Br.* a small flattish bag, usu. made of leather or plastic, used, esp. by women. a. for carrying coins (*Am.* **change purse, coin purse**): *she handed him her change purse, from which he extracted coins.* - Reader's Digest. b. (esp. divided into two parts) for carrying both coins and paper money, used esp. by women (*Am.* **wallet**). 2. *Am., Can.* a woman's handbag (*esp. Br.* **handbag**): *I retrieved my purse* - Reader's Digest., *she opened her brown purse of simulated leather.* - J. Steinbeck., *she turned to pick up her purse.* - B. Tillman.
push *Aus.* obs. col. the band, gang, social group: *He joined the push, or crowd.* - I. Stone.
push along *Br.* col. go away, depart.
push in *Br.* col. jump the queue.
push off *Br.* col. (used to rudely tell sb. to go away).
push/ at a push *esp. Br.* col. if really necessary in spite of difficulties.
push a pen *Am.* work in the office.
push/ be pushed 1. *esp. Br. /Am.* **be pressed/** for smth. (esp. time and money) not have enough of it. 2. *Am., Aus.* find it difficult to do smth.
push/ give/get sb. **the push/shove** *Br., Aus.* col. end a relationship with sb. or take away their job.
push/ push all sb.'s **buttons** *Am.* annoy sb. by doing things they don't like.
push the boat out *Br.* col. make a special effort to make smth. enjoyable esp. by spending more money than usual.
push the envelope *Am.* do smth. extravagantly.
pushbike *Br., Aus.* col. obs. a bicycle.
pushchair, buggy *Br. /esp. Am., Aus.* **stroller/** a small chair on wheels for pushing a small child about: *Mam had to wheel her round in a pushchair* - C.M. Fraser.
pusher *Br.* a small tool for pushing food onto a spoon at meals used by very young children.
pusher/ pen pusher *Br., Aus. /Am.* **pencil pusher/** a person who has a boring job in an office.
pushpin, thumbtack *esp. Am., Can. /Br., Aus.* **drawing pin/** steel point for sticking into a wall or board for holding notes: *Kids even touched the pushpins on a bulletin board* – Reader's Digest.
push-up *esp. Am., Can., Aus. /Br., Aus.* **press-up/**: *Fifteen push-ups, twenty-five sit-ups.* - I. Shaw., *Jonah Cobb had advised him to try pushups.* - R. Borchgrave, R. Moss.

puss 1. *Am., Can., Irish Eng.* col. face or mouth of a person: *two party promoters...have been drawing glamor-pusses* - New York., *I owe you a smack in the puss, too.* - R. Chandler. 2. *Br.* col. also **pussy** a cat

pus(sy) *Br.* col. a cat

pussy 1. *esp. Am.* the act of having sex. 2. *Am.* col. insulting word for a man who is weak and not brave.

pussyfoot *Am.* a careful person.

put it about 1. also **put** smth. **about** *esp. Br.* col. spread the news, esp. unpleasant or untrue: *people had long been putting it about that he was a year or two younger than he was.* – A. Summers, R. Swan. 2. *Br.* col. (of a woman) also **put** oneself **about** have sex with a lot of people.

put across *esp. Br.* col. deceive (sb.) into believing or doing (smth.) esp. in the phr. **put it/that across** sb.: *I know it's too late for him to put it across in court.* - D. Hammet.

put back 1. *Am.* move (a student) to a lower class than would be expected: *Jane failed her examination and was put back a whole year.* - Longman. 2. *Br.* delay smth. 3. *esp. Br.* col. drink (a lot of ale) quickly.

put (sb.) **down** *Br.* 1. allow to leave a vehicle. 2. kill an animal from mercy: *it was kinder to have him put down* - Longman.

put down *Br.* /*Am., Br.* **bring down/** reduce (a price or charge).

put smth. **down** *Br.* write smth. on a piece of paper.

put sb. **down for** $5 *esp. Br.* write sb.'s name on a list with an amount of money that they have promised to give.

put down the phone *Br.* hang up.

put forth *Am.* state, offer (smth. such as plan): *many countries have put forth a better system for preventing world war.* - Longman.

put off 1. *esp. Br.* disconnect (electricity or other power), stop (an electric machine) working: *Please put off all the lights* - Longman. 2. *Br.* **put** sb./smth. **off** confuse sb. about what they are doing.

put sb. **off their stroke/stride** *Br., Aus.* make them fail.

put on *esp. Am., Can.* col. play a trick on, deceive.

put-on n.: *Noone has entertained so well or put on so much as Dylan.* - J. Gabree., *it could almost have been put-on.* - J. Kessel., *I think you're really putting me on.* - W. Jack, B. Laursen.

put on *esp. Br.* provide (smth., esp. for the benefit of other people).

put on a bus/train/coach *Br.* provide a bus, etc. to take a person somewhere.

put (sb. or smth.) **on the pan** *Am.* col. find fault with sb. or smth.: *he'll put you on the pan.* - Longman.

(put sb.**) on the rack** *esp. Br.* (put sb.) in a state of anxiety of distress.

put out 1. *esp. Am., Aus., Can.* sl. produce, deliver expected results as money or sex in return for what one owes: *Georgia means to persuade someone to put out without pay* – Esquire. 2. *Am.* produce smth. such as book, record, film, etc.: *a contract had indeed been put out.* – A. Summers, R. Swan. 3. (for) *esp. Am., Can.* col. make love to sb., agree to have sex: *Elenore sure is putting out.* - J. Dos Passos.

put smth. **over** *Am., Can.* postpone smth.

put to *esp. Br.* close (smth. such as door) firmly: *Please put the door to.* - Longman.

put up *esp. Br.* 1. find food and lodging: *he put up at the fashionable Hotel Baur au Lac in Zurich.* - A. Moorehead., *Have you friends in Luc to put you up?* - G. Greene., *the twain moved on towards the inn at which he had put up.* - T. Hardy. 2. increase the cost of smth.

put up (for) *esp. Br.* offer oneself for election.

put upon *esp. Br.* be a cause of inconvenience to.

put a/the whammy on, put/work a mojo on (sb.) *Am.* col. cause (sb.) to have bad luck as if by magic.

put paid to *Br., Aus.* ruin, finish completely (smth. such as an idea): *The army today put paid to the bionic fish* - Evening Standard., *"Corazzini" put paid to any ideas we might have had of taking advantage of the situation* - A. McLean.

put their **pants on one leg at a time** *Am.* (of famous person) be like everybody else.

put the arm/bite/touch on sb. *Am.* ask for or borrow money from sb.: *he had the nerve to try and put the touch on me.* - J. O'Hara.

put the law on sb. *Am.* put an action against sb.

put the low beams on *Am., Can.* dip the headlights of a car.

put the mouth on *Br., Aus.* sl. make or seem to make (sb.) fail by telling others that he/she is succeeding: *I'd have won if you hadn't put the mouth on me at the wrong moment* - Longman.

put wise *esp. Am.* col. inform correctly: *the other people put me wise* - Longman.

put one's **wits against** sb. *Br.* try to defeat sb.

put words in inverted commas *esp. Br.* place speech marks round a certain word or words to show that it is special in some way or spoken.

put work out to sb. *Br. /esp. Am., Aus.* **contract work out/** employ sb. outside one's organisation to do it.

put-off *esp. Am.* excuse.

putter *Am., Can. /Br.* **potter/** spend time in activities that demand little effort: *you can get up and putter around the house for a few days.* - Longman.

putting green *Br.* smooth area of grass with many holes in it for playing simple type of golf.

putty/ give sb. **/ deserve a putty medal** *esp. Br.* becoming rare. humor. or derog. give sb. / earn praise for some worthless action.

put-u-up, put-you-up (bed) *Br. col.* convertible sofa.

putz *Am., Can.* col. 1. detestable person: *May be her husband is a putz but he's a good provider* - L. Uris. 2. taboo. men's penis.

pvt *Am. /Br.* **pte/** private in the army.

pylon *Am.* one of a set of plastic cones placed on a road to control traffic and protect people working there.

PYO *Br.* (pick your own) used by farms that let people pick their own fruit and vegetables.

pyramid scheme *Am.* a way of deceiving investors in which money which the company receives from its new customers is not invested for the benefit of it but used instead to pay debts it owes to existing customers.

Q

Q-tip *Am.* tdmk. cotton bud.

QT/ on the QT *Br.* obs. done secretely.

quack 1. *esp. Br.* a doctor who is not qualified. 2. *Br., Aus.* col. a humorous word for doctor: *Bunch of quacks who promise to help* - J. Kellerman.

quad *esp. Br.* col. 1. a square open place with buildings around it esp. in school or college: *Instead she passed the lobby and crossed the quad.* - R. Cook. 2. quadruplet. 3. sl. a prison.

quadrillion 1. *Br.* the number 1. followed by 24 zeroes. 2. *Am.* the number followed by 15 zeroes.

quodrominium *Am., Can.* condominium consisting of four apartments.

quodroplex *Am., Can.* building divided into 4 self-contained residences.

Quaker City *Am.* Philadelphia.

The Quaker State *Am.* Pennsylvania.

quality (paper) *esp. Br.* magazine or newspaper for sophisticated reader, also **quality press, journalism.**

quango *Br.* derog. non-departmental public body, i.e. one that is funded by the government to oversee or develop activity in an area of public interest but is not itself a government department.

quant *Br.* pole for propelling a barge or punt.

quantity surveyer *Br.* a person whose job is to calculate the cost of the materials and work needed for future building work.

quantum jump *Am.* quantum leap, very large and important improvement.

quart *Am., Can.* unit of dry capacity equal to 1.1 litre.

quart/ get/put a quart into a pint pot *Br. col.* try to put too much of smth. into a small place.

quarter *esp. Am.* 1. 1/4 of a school semester, usu. 10-12 weeks: *I take one course a quarter* – P. Roth. 2. 1/4 of sports game.

quarter *Br.* grain measure equal to eight bushels (28 pounds).

quarter/ a quarter of/after *Am.* a quarter to/past (in defining time).

quarterback *Am., Can.* person who directs or controls an operation

quarterback *Am.* 1. play as a quarterback in American football. 2. col. organise or direct an activity, event, etc.

quarter day *Br.* a day which officially begins a three-month period of the year and on which payments are made /also **Q-days/**: *The rent of the flat would be falling due on quarter-day.* - W.S. Maugham.

quarter light *esp. Br.* door vent, a small window in the side of an auto, which usu. turns on a swivel.

quarter note *esp. Am., Can. /Br.* **crotchet/** a musical note a quarter as long as a semi-breve.

quarter plate *Br.* photographic plate (8.3x10.8cm.).

quarter section *Am., Can.* quarter of a squre mile of land; 160 acres (approximately 64.7 hectares).

quart-pot tea *Aus.* tea made in the open air in the billy.

quaver *esp. Br., Aus. /Am.* **eighth note/** musical note half as long as a crotchet.

Quebecois *Can.* person from Quebec province.

(the) Queen *Br.* col. (**God save the Queen**) the British anthem **/ stay at the dance through the Queen** *Br.* stay to the very end.

Queen/ toast to the Queen *Br.* loyal toast.

Queen Ann's lace *esp. Am.* cow parsley.

Queen City 1. *Am., Can.* the pre-eminent city of a region. 2. Cincinnati.

Queen of the Lakes *Am.* Chicago.
Queen of the Plains *Am.* Denver.
Queen of the Upper Lakes *Am.* Buffalo.
Queen of Vermont *Am.* Berlington.
Queen's English/ speak the Queen's English *Br.* speak very correctly and in a way that is typical of people from the highest social class.
queen's evidence, also **king's evidence** /*Am.* **state's evidence/ turn queen's evidence** *Br.* (of a criminal) give information in a court of law against other criminals, esp. in order to get less punishment oneself.
queensize *esp. Am.* (of bed, sheet, etc.) larger than the standard size for a bed of two people.
queer *Br.* ill or sick.
queer/ in queer street *Br.* col. humor. obs. in debt, in trouble over money: *You'll find yourself in Queer Street.* - J.D. Carr.
queer/ queer sb.'s **pitch** *Br.* col. spoil sb.'s plans.
queer fish *Br.* obs. a strange person.
query *esp. Am.* ask questions of (esp. sb. with power).
question master *esp. Br.* /*Am.* usu. **quizmaster/** one who asks the questions in a quiz game.
queue 1. *esp. Br., Aus.* /*Am., Aus.* **line/** a line of people, cars, etc. waiting to move, to get on a vehicle, enter a building, etc.: *There were never any queues on the road.* - Cheshire Life. 2. *Br.* tail of hair hanging down from the back of the head. 3. *Br.* /*Am.* **order/** list of jobs for computer to do.
queue/ jump the queue *Br., Aus.* move in front of people who have been waiting longer for smth. than you; v. **queue-jump;** n. a **queue-jumper.**
queue (up, for) 1. *Br.* /*Am.* **line (up)/** form or join a line while waiting: *So now you've got all the boys queuing up, eh?* - D. Lessing. 2. *esp. Br.* want to do or have smth. very much.
queue-jump *Br.* go out of turn, do or get anything unfairly.
quick and dirty *esp. Am.* col. makeshift; done in a haste.
quick buck *Am.* sl. also **fast buck,** quickly or easily earned profit: *make a quick buck off the fire sale of Siberia's assets.* - Time.
quick bread *Am.* one made with a leavening agent that permits immediate baking.
quick(set) (hedge) *esp. Br.* a line of growing bushes used as a fence **quick one/half/pint** *esp. Br.* col. drink that a person has in a hurry.
quick study *Am.* col. a person who is able to learn things quickly.
quid *Br., Aus.* col. a pound (of money): *I'd love to lend you a quid, but I'm absolutely stony* - W.S. Maugham., *Just a couple of quid that's all I need.* - A. Burgess. / **quids** *esp. Br., Aus.* sl. money, cash.
quid/ be quids in *Br.* col. be making a profit.
quid/ not for quids *Aus.* col. I wouldn't do it for quids = I'd hate to do it.
quid/ not the full quid *Aus., NZ.* col. not very intelligent.
quiet/ have a quiet word (with) *esp. Br.* talk to sb. privately when criticizing them.
quieten *esp. Br.* /*esp. Am., Can.* **quiet/** 1. (down) (cause to) become quiet: *He tried to quiet the crowd* - J. O'Hara. 2. allay: *she had quieted down* - R.P. Warren.
quietly confident, optimistic *esp. Br.* fairly confident of success, but without talking proudly about it.
quiff *esp. Br.* /*Am.* **pompadour/** forehead lock or locked hair style, esp. of a man.
quilt *esp. Am.* thin cloth cover used on a bed to make it look attractive: *cold again despite the quilt.* – R.L. Stine.
quilt *Aus.* col. punch (sb.).
(continental) quilt *Br.* duvet.
quilting bee *Am., Can.* social gathering of women at which quilts are made: *The ladies are having a quilting bee!* - Guideposts.
quim *Br.* taboo sl. the female sex organs: *this little cavern of joy we happily call pussy, cunt, twat, quim, box, hole* - "M."
quin *esp. Br., Aus.* /*Am., Can.* **quint/** col. quintuplet.
quinine water *Am.* bitter tasting drink often mixed with strong alcoholic drinks.
quirt *Am.* v. n. (use) a riding whip with a rawhide lash: *He...carried a small quirt of some kind* - J. Kerouac.
quit *esp. Am.* col. leave a job, school, etc., esp. if a person is annoyed or unhappy.
quit *esp. Am.* col. stop an action or activity, esp. in **quit doing** smth.
quit/ have a...that (just) won't quit *Am.* sl. used to mention some fine feature.
quit claim *Am.* formal renunciation of a claim.
quite 1. *esp. Br.* adj., adv. fairly. 2. *Br.* very or completely, **quite the best/worst.**
quite 1. *esp. Br.* (used as an answer) I agree, that's true, **quite right, quite so.** 2. *Am.* very, **quite good/funny.** 3. **quite a/an, quite some, quite something** *esp. Am.* an unusual, an above average: *Maybe he's quite a poet* - T. Wilder. / **Quite nice** means very nice in America, and fairly nice in Britain.
quite/ quite like *Br.* like smth. but not very much.

361

quite/ I'm quite happy to do smth. *Br.* (used to say that one is willing to do smth.).

quite/ quite enough *Br.* when annoyed with what sb. is saying or doing and wanting them to stop.

quite/ quite frankly/honestly *Br.* used when giving a very direct or honest opinion.

quitted *Br.* past tense and past participle of quit.

quitting time *esp. Am.* the time at which work is ended for the day.

qui vive/ on the qui vive *Br.* obs. on the alert, aware of the situation.

quiz 1. *esp. Am., Can.* a short examination at a class: *we'll get one of Ms. Roper's hideous pop quizzes.* - R.L. Stine. 2. *esp. Br.* col. an act of questioning of sb., esp. done during a police investigation.

quiz/ pop quiz *Am.* surprise quiz (esp. at school).

quiz kid *Am.* col. child prodigy: *In fact, Bill had been a Quiz Kid.* – P. Roth.

quiz-master, question master *Br.* person who asks questions and enforces rules in a TV or radio quiz program.

quiz night *Br.* (in a pub) a game or competition in which you answer questions.

quod *Br.* obs. sl. prison: *None o'yer bloody quod for him.* - H.H. Richardson.

Quonset hut *Am., Can.* tdmk. /*Br.* **Nissen hut/** large shelter with a round roof made of iron sheets: *Red found an old Quonset hut for lease.* - W. Jack., B. Larsen.

quorate *Br.* (of a meeting) attended by a quorum.

Quorn *Br.* tdmk. vegetable substance that can be used in cooking instead of meat.

quote, end quote, quote, unquote *Am.* (said when you want to show that you are using sb. else's phrase, esp. when you do not think that phrase is true.

qwerty *Br.* adj. (of the keyboard of a typewriter or computer) of the ordinary sort, whose top line begins with the letters Q.W.E.R.T.Y.

R

R *Am.* 1. (of films) restricted to viewers over 17 year old. 2. Repulican Party. 3. (of a film) not to be watched by children under 17.

rabbit *Am.* sl. a lettuce, salad greens.

rabbit a player *Aus.* injure a player in a game.

rabbit (on) *esp. Br., Aus.* col. derog. talk continuously, esp. in an unattractive or complaining way, n.

race/ be in the race *Aus., NZ.* succeed.

race car *Am.* /*Br.* **racing car/** car designed for car races.

racecard *Br.* programme giving the races, times, and horses at a horse-racing event.

racecourse 1. *esp. Br., Aus.* /*esp. Am.* **racetrack/** a track round which horses race. 2. *Am.* a racetrack: *career means "to rush along at high speed", as on a racecourse.* - Reader's Digest.

race meeting *Br.* sporting event consisting of a series of (horse) races.

race-way *Am., Can.* 1. a canal for a current of water, mill stream, mill race. 2. channel for loosely holding electrical wires in buildings. 3. track for horse races.

Rachmanism *Br.* unscrupulous practices by landlords, esp. in rundown properties.

racialism *Br.* obs. racism; **racialist** *Br.* obs. racist.

rack 1. *Am., Can.* col. bed. 2. *Am.* three-sided frame used for arranging the balls at the start of a game of snooker or pool.

rack/ rack of bones *Am.* sl. very lean person.

rack/ rack of lamb/pork *Br.* fairly large piece of meat from the side of an animal.

rack/ off the rack *Am., Can.* of the peg.

rack/ on the rack *Br.* in a complicated unpleasant situation.

rack off *Aus., NZ.* col. go away.

rack (out) *Am.* sl. lie down or go to sleep: *What time do you rack out?* - R.A. Spears.

rack up *esp. Am.* col. 1. also *Can., Aus.* gain (points, etc.) in a competition: *one could rack up higher scores and win more free games.* - D. Brenner., *the two leading men rack it up to a higher level altogether.* - New Yorker., *In 1982 Apple closed out its best year to that point, racking up sales of $ 750 million.* - Maclean's. 2. cause (sb.) to fall, as with a blow: *He racked up his opponent with a well-placed blow.* - Longman. 3. defeat (sb.) completely: *By clever planning, we were able to rack up the other team* - Longman. 4. damage or ruin smth.

rack car *Am.* a railway carriage for transporting motor cars.

racked-off *Aus.* sl. irritated.

racked-up *Am.* sl. tense, stressed: *I remember my first shot. You know I was really racked-up.* - T. Thorne.

racket *esp. Am., Can.* snowshoe.

racon *Am.* radar beacon.

rad *esp. Am.* col. really good or exciting: *But the really rad word is still to be had.* - T. Thorne.

raddled *Am.* 1. confused. 2. broken down: *Her youthful complexion and Elisson figure made*

Shirley look raddled and overblown in comparison. - D. Lodge.
raddled *Br.* looking old or tired.
radical *Am.* sl. very good or enjoyable.
radical chic *Am.* jet set person, associated with radicals.
radical-lib *Am.* col. liberal associated with radicals.
radio/ continuous wave radio *Am.* radiotelegraph.
radio active dating *Am. /Br.* **carbon dating/** scientific method of calculating the age of a very old object by measuring the amount of a certain substance in it.
radiogram(ophone) *Br.* a piece of furniture, popular esp. formerly, combining a radio and a record player: *The moment my Russian companion saw the radiogram he went to it.* - L. Van Der Post., *somewhere in the shadows a radiogram was softly pouring out "Body and Soul".* - J. Herriot.
radwaste *Am.* radioactive waste.
Rafferty's rules *Aus., NZ.* col. no rules at all.
a (whole)raft *esp. Am.* col. a large number or amount: *you have a raft of behaviorial indices.* - T.A. Harris., *A raft of legal opinions covered both administrations* - J. DeFelice., *Louis was playing sporadic solo dates and making rafts of records.* - M. Jones, J. Chilton.
rag 1. *esp. Br.* an amusing procession of college students through the streets on a special day (**rag day**) or during a special week (**rag week**) each year collecting money for charity. 2. *esp. Br.* col. a rough but harmless trick. 3. *Br.* coarse stone. 4. *Am.* duster. **rag** *esp. Br.* col. v. n. (play) rough tricks on (or make fun of): *I was only ragging.* - E. Hemingway., *When you were ragging my room?* - M.M. Kaye., *She thought it would be a frightful rag on poor Montgomery Jones.* - A. Christie.
rag on *Am., Can.* col. constantly criticize sb.
rag/ lose one's **rag** *Br., Aus.* col. become very angry and start shouting.
rag/ like a red rag (*Br.*), **flag** (*Am.*) **to a bull** col. /*Am.* also **be like waving/holding a red flag in front of a bull/** likely to cause uncontrollable anger.
rag/ on the rag, OTR *Am., Can.* col. (of women) having her menstrual period and so sometimes behaving herself unreasonably.
rag-and-bone man *esp. Br., Aus. /Am.* **ragman/** junkman.
rag-book *Br.* a book for very small children made of strong cloth.
rage *Aus., NZ.* col. (go on) a wild party or celebration.
rag felt *Am.* roofing paper.

ragged *esp. Am.* torn and in bad condition.
ragged edge/ be on the ragged edge *Am.* be very tired or upset to deal with a situation.
ragged out, ragged up *Am.* sl. dressed up.
raggedy *esp. Am., Can.* col. scruffy, shabby.
raggedy-ass(ed) *Am., Can.* col. miserably inadequate.
rag-head *Am., Can.* col. derog. person who wears a turban.
the rag trade *Br.* the business of making and selling clothes, esp. women's clothes.
rah *esp. Am., Can.* col. cheer of encouragement and approval.
rah-rah *Am., Can.* col. marked by the enthusiastic expression of college spirit: *It was sort of a rah-rah party.* - R.A. Spears. / **rah-rah boys:** *I lost my appetite for rah-rah* – R.L. Stine.
raid (a place or a building) *Br.* enter them by force in order to steal smth; n. **raider**.
rail/ be back on the rails *Br.* be making progress once more; also **put** sb. **back on the rails**.
rail/ (go) off the rails *esp. Br.* 1. start to behave strange. 2. go wrong.
rail/ jump the rails *esp. Br.* go wrong suddenly.
railbird *Am., Can.* col. an ardent horse-racing devotee.
rail car 1. *Am., Can.* any railway carriage or wagon: *monstrous cranes lifted into the air entire flatbed railcars* - K. Lipper. 2. *Br.* powered railway passenger vehicle designed to operate singly or as a part of multiple unit.
railcard *Br.* an identity card that allows people to buy train tickets cheaply.
rail fence *esp. Am., Can.* a fence of posts and split rails: *The woods they'd been passing suddenly gave way to rolling green meadows behind log rail fences.* – R.L. Stine.
railroad *Am., Can.* 1. send (goods) by railway. 2. get (an enemy) sent to prison on untrue charges: *McGreavy would try to railroad Dr. Stevens.* - S. Sheldon., *We can see people in other countries being railroaded* - E. Cleaver., *the dentist claimed they had been railroaded* - S.B. Oates. 3. travel or work on the railway.
railroad *Am., Aus. /Br.6 Can.* **railway/** 1. a track for trains. 2. also **railways** a system of these tracks with its engines, stations, etc.: *His father had been a brakeman on the railroad* - C. Woolrich.
railroad/ line-haul railroad *Am.* main railway.
railroad avenue, depot street *Am. /Br.* **station road/**.
railroader *Am.* 1. one who works on a railroad. 2. one who owns and operates it.

railroading *Am.* construction and operating of railroads.
railroad man *Am.* person who works on a railroad.
railroad station or **depot** *Am.* railway station.
railroad rates, track, yard *Am.* railway rates, line, track, yard: *a jumble of factories and railroad yards.* – A. Summers, R. Swan.
rail splitter *Am.* person who splits logs into fence rails.
railway car *Am.* /*Br.* **railway coach**/ railway carriage.
railway journey *Br.* train ride.
railway man *esp. Br.* /*Am.* **railroader, rail worker, railroad worker**/ a person working on a railway.
(railway) station *esp. Br.* /*Am.* **train station**/.
rain/ be (as) right as rain *Br.* col. be fit and healthy.
rain/ keep out of the rain *Aus.* avoid trouble.
rain (smth.) off *Br.* /*esp. Am., Can.* **rain (smth.) out**/ col. cause (an event or activity) to stop because of rain: *Looks like it might be rained out?* - R.L. Stine.
rain/ rain on sb.'s **parade** *esp. Am., Can.* spoil sb.'s exciting plans.
rain/ rain pitchforks / darning needles, chicken coops, hammer handles *Am.* /*Br.* **rain stair-rods, like billy-o, trams and omnibuses, pour with rain**, obs. **cats and dogs**/ col. rain very heavily: *It's raining pitchforks, so we can't go out to play right now.* - A. Makkai.
raincheck *esp. Am., Can., Aus.* col. act of not accepting smth., when it is offered with the condition that one may claim it later, esp. in **take a raincheck on** smth.: *the baseball game was called off. Everyone received a raincheck.* - H.C. Whitford., R.J. Dixson., *he would have to "take a rain check" on Saturday's flick* – S. Townsend.
raincoat *esp. Am., Aus.* /*esp. Br.* **mackintosh, mack**/.
rainfly *Am., Can.* the flysheet of a tent.
rainmaker *Am., Can.* col. powerful and successful representative: *a Christie's senior director and rainmaker in American collections* - New York.
rainout *Am., Can.* cancellation of an event because of the rain.
raise *esp. Am., Can., Aus.* /*Br.* **rise**/ an increase in amount, price, or pay, rise / *a* **rise** to an American often means a male erection, so British getting a **rise** can provide an unexpected response: *she didn't give him a raise.* - S. Grafton.
raise/ raise cattle or wheat on a farm *esp. Am.* / *esp. Br.* **rear** cattle and **grow** wheat, flowers or vegetables.

raise 1. *esp. Am., Can.* /*Br.* **bring up**/look after and help a child to grow. 2. *Br.* col. establish contact with sb. (esp. by telephone or radio).
raise a check *Am.* alter cheque to show larger amount: *I raised a cheque and was sent to prison for it.* – J. O'Hara.
raise (one's) hand *esp. Am.* put one's arm in the air to show that one wants smth.
raise hell/Cain *esp. Am.* behave in a wild, noisy way that upsets other people: *he was liable to "raise Cain" during her absence* – K. Chopin.
raised biscuit *Am.* one leavened with yeast rather than with baking powder or soda.
raisin bread *Am.* currant bread.
raising bee *Am., Can.* social affair at which neighbours pool efforts to raise the frame of a house, barn, etc.
rake *Br.* a number of railway carriages or wagons coupled together.
rake down *Am.* rake in, earn or gain (a lot of money).
rake out smth. *Br.* look for it and find it.
rake over the ashes *esp. Br.* bring to memory unpleasant events which are best forgotten.
rallycross *Br.* motor races over rough terrain and tarmac roads done in heats.
ramada *Am.* an arbour or porch.
rambler *Br.* sb. who goes on rambles.
rambunctious *esp. Am., Can.* humor. /*Br.* **rumbustious**/ col. energetic in a cheerful, noisy way: *he enjoyed the razzmatazz of the rambunctious little group they formed.* – A. Summer's, R. Swan.
rammies *Aus.* col. trousers.
ramp 1. *Am., Can.* usu. exit or entrance ramp /*Br.* **slip road**, *Am.* **access road**/ a road for driving onto or off a large main road: *he negotiated the exit ramp from the freeway.* - P. Case., J. Migliore. 2. *Br.* transverse ridge in a road to control the speed of a vehicle. 3. *Br.* a change in the level between two parts of a road when repairs are being made.
ramp *Br.* col. a dishonest trick to make people pay a high price.
rampike *Am., Can.* a broken or dead tree that still stands.
ram-raid(ing) *Br.* col. a robbery on a shop or other building in which a car is used to smash their way into the building; also v. and n. **–er**.
ranch *Am.* 1. a farm that produces a stated thing. 2. v. work as a farmer: *A year later his father remarried, retired from ranching and moved to town.* - Guideposts.
ranch/ dude ranch *Am.* one used for paying guests.

ranchero *esp. Am.* person who farms or works on a farm.

ranch (style) house, rancher *Am., Can.* 1. a house built on one level, usu. with a roof that does not slope much. 2. a house on a ranch in which the rancher and his/her family live: *Pablos turned down a lane and headed for what looked like an Arizona ranch house.* - J.A. Michener.

ranch wagon, also **station wagon** *Am.* /*Br.* **estate car**/.

Random Breath Test (RBT) *Aus.* one given by police to drivers by chance to measure how much alcohol they have in their blood.

RandR *Am.* rest and relaxation; a holiday given to people in the army, navy, etc. after a long period of hard work or during a war.

randy *esp. Br., Aus.* col. (of a person or his/her feelings) full of sexual desire: *the heat made them both continuously randy* - J. Fowles.

rangatira *NZ.* Maori chief or noble.

range *Am.* 1. two-sided shelves (in a library). 2. land for animals to feed on.

range *Br.* obs. place in a kitchen with a set of cookers burning wood or coal, or heated by fire. 2. *esp. Am., Can.* electric or gas cooker with several burners.

range *Br.* print. align (type), esp. at the end of successive lines

Ranger (Guide) *Br.* member of the senior branch of the Guides.

ranges *Aus., NZ.* mountainous or hilly country.

rangy 1. *Aus.* mountainous. 2. *Am.* leggy, lanky: *a striking, rangy brunette with a superb figure* - Arthur Hailey.

rank *Br.* stand, a place where a passenger vehicle stops or parks.

rank *Am.* (of an officer) be of higher rank than (sb.), **ranking** *Am., Can.* adj. of highest rank: *Democratic ranking members of the Senate and House* - H. Truman.

ranker *esp. Br.* soldier in the ranks, a private.

ransom/ hold to (*Am.* **for**) **ransom** *Br.* hold (a captive) and demand ransom for his release.

rap/ beat the rap *Am., Can.* col. escape punishment.

rap/ get a bum rap *Am.* sl. be punished unfairly.

rap/ take a rap *Am.* col. suffer a blow.

rap *esp. Am.* col. a. talk, chat, esp. make lengthy impromptu talk: *some loud-mouthed prick had rapped about it.* - S. Sheldon., *They noticed a guy who kept coming nightly to rap with Tibbs* - J. Gabree. b. speak the words of a song to a musical accompaniment with a steady beat.

rap *esp. Am., Can.* col. criminal charge.

(the) rap *esp. Am.* sl. reputation of sb. or smth. based on gossip or judgement: *Coffee gets a bad rap when it comes to teeth* – Reader's Digest.

raper *esp. Am.* person who raped sb.

rapid transit (system) *Am.* system for moving people quickly around a city using trains; subway.

rap sheet *esp. Am.* col. information kept by the police about sb.'s criminal activities: *a high school dropout with a growing rap sheet* – Reader's Digest.

rappel *Am.* /*Br.* **abseil**/: *they could traverse the east ridge below, rappel 150 feet down a cliff* – Reader's Digest.

rapper *Am.* door knocker.

rapt *Aus.* col. 1. wrapped. 2. very pleased and happy.

rare *Br.* obs. unusually good or extreme.

rareripe *Am.* adj. n. (of) an early ripening fruit or vegetable.

rasher *Br.* a thin piece of bacon.

raspberry/ wild raspberry *Am.* cloudberry.

raspberry/ blow a raspberry *Br., Aus.* col. /*Am.* **give a raspberry**/ make a rude noise by putting one's tongue between one's lips and blowing.

rat 1. *Am.* v. n. (provide with) a roll of hair to puff out a woman's hair. 2. *Am., Can.* a habitual visitor of some place.

rat-arsed *Br.* sl. very drunk.

ratbag *esp. Br., Aus.* derog. col. an unpleasant or worthless person: *She's a total ratbag* - T. Thorne.

rate 1. *Br.* col. think that sb. or smth. is very good. 2. *esp. Am.* col. deserve, esp. in **rate a mention** (be important enough to be in the news).

rate 1. *Br.* (at) fix a local tax (rate) on (a building), paid if one owns property or rents unfurnished property: *These local taxes are called rates.* - J. Ruppeldova. 2. *Am.* give a (school) mark.

rate/ at a rate of knots *Br.* col. very quickly.

rate up *esp. Am.* increase (usu. a payment) by an equal share: *The insurance payments have to be rated up for people with poor health.* - Longman.

rat(e)able value *Br.* a value given to a building so as to fix a tax on it.

rate-cap *Br.* (of a central government) limit the amount of rate that can be charged by (a local council).

ratepayer 1. *Br.* a person who pays local taxes. 2. *Am., Can.* a person who pays for the services offered to his/her property by electricity, water, or telephone companies.

ratface *Am.* sl. sly, underhanded person.

rat fink *Am.* col. very unpleasant person: *I felt a real rat fink* – S. Townsend.

rather 1. *esp. Br.* col. obs. (used as an answer) yes, certainly. 2. *Am.* on the contrary. 3. *Br. / esp. Am.* (esp. in written language) **pretty/** a little, fairly.

rather you than me *Br. /Am.* **better you than me/** col. said when sb. is pleased that the other person will do smth. unpleasant.

rathole *Am., Can.* col. refers to the waste of money and resourses, esp. in **down the rathole of** smth.

rat(h)skellar *Am.* basement restaurant.

rating 1. *Am.* the business responsibility that a person or firm is thought to have. 2. *Am.* (school) rating. 3. *Br.* non-commisioned sailor in the Navy.

rationalise, -ize *esp. Br.* make (system) more modern and sensible and less wasteful.

rat pack *Am.* sl. a teenage street gang.

rat run *Br.* col. a small residential street which drivers use during busy times in order to avoid traffic on the main roads.

rat's tails *Br.* col. hair hanging in lank damp or greasy strands.

ratted *Br.* col. very drunk.

rattle through *esp. Br.* finish smth. quickly.

rattler *esp. Am., Can.* col. rattlesnake.

rat trap *Am.* a dirty old building that is in very bad condition: *No way it's gonna keep us both, even in this rattrap.* - P. Case, J. Migliore.

ratty 1. *Br.* col. bad-tempered, irritable: *The ratty driver was excited.* - D. Hammet. 2. *Am., Aus.* col. untidy and in bad condition, shabby: *He'd busted into apartments and ratty hotel rooms* - G. O'Neill, D. Lehr.

raunchy *esp. Am.* (of a person or place) slovenly; grubby.

rave 1. *esp. Br.* col. (attend) a rave party where a lot of people gather. 2. *esp. Am.* col. very enthusiastic recommendation or appraisal.

raver *esp. Br., Aus.* col. person who leads an exciting life of social and sexual freedom: *They've got no room for ravers.* - T. Thorne.

rave-up, rave (party) *esp. Br.* col. a wild exciting party, often in a warehouse or in the open air.

rave-up *Am., Can.* col. fast, loud or danceable piece of popular music.

raving mad *esp. Br.* col. completely crazy.

raw *Am.* (of a language) containing a lot of sexual details.

raw *Can.* rough person.

raw/ catch/touch sb. **on the raw** *Br., Aus.* upset sb.

raw/ come the raw prawn with sb. *Aus.* col. try to deceive sb. pretending not to know what sb. is talking about.

raw/ in the raw *Am.* col. not wearing any clothes.

raw bar *Am.* bar or counter which sells raw oysters or the sea food.

rawhide *esp. Am., Can.* whip or rope made of stiff untanned leather of a cow.

Rawl plug *Br.* tdmk. */Am.* **Molby/** small plug inserted in a wall as a fixing for a screw: *never got around to buying Molby bolts.* - J. Updike., *Most of them...were counting Rawl plugs into boxes.* - B. Bryson.

rays *esp. Am., Can.* col. sunbathing sunlight.

razoo *Aus., NZ.* col. very small amount of money.

razorback 1. *Br.* a kind of large sea animal (whale). 2. *Am.* a type of partly wild pig of the southern US. 3. *Am.* labourer: *Farragut went up to the razorback who ran the controls.* - J. Cheever.

razor knife *Am. /Br.* **Stanley knife/**.

razz *esp. Am., Can., Aus.* col. ridicule or express scorn for sb.: *King would razz them back* - S.B. Oates, *I, however, got a rather good-natured razzing* - Guideposts.

razzle *esp. Br.* col. obs. **/be/go (out) on the razzle/razz** having a wild enjoyable time.

razzle-dazzle *esp. Am.* 1. confusion caused by very noisy or very colourful appearance intended to attract attention. 2. col. complicated series of actions untended to confuse one's opponent, esp. in American football.

RD *Br.* refer to drawer, (used by banks when suspending payment of a cheque).

RE *Br.* religious education, a school subject at which religion and other social matters are studied.

reach sb. **down** smth. *Br.* stretch a hand and get smth. for sb.

reach-me-down *Br.* (usu. pl.) n. hand-me-down.

read *esp. Br., Aus.* col. 1. an act or period of reading. 2. smth. of the stated kind to be read: *It's a fascinating read.* - Omni., *It's a quick read, it's scannable* - New York.

read (a subject at university) *esp. Br.* study it.

read/ read my lips *Am., Can.* col. listen carefully.

read/ take smth. **as read** *esp. Br., Aus.* accept smth. as true or right without the need to hear it, talk about it, etc.

read/ you wouldn't read about it *Aus., NZ.* col. expression of disbelief or disgust.

read for smth. *esp. Br.* study in order to gain (esp. a university degree).

read out *esp. Am.* make (sb.) leave an organisation, usu. for a fault: *they ought to be read out of the party.* - J. O'Hara.

readdress *Br.* forward.

reader *Br.* a senior lecturer at a university with a rank just below that of a professor.

reading glass *Br.* magnifying glass.

reading glasses *Am. /Br.* **halfmoon spectacles/**.

readjustee *Am.* col. person who served long time in the armed service and is going back to civilian life.

ready 1. also **readies** *esp. Br.* col. ready money: *I didn't hold them up for too much of the ready* – J. O'Hara. 2. *Br.* excl. **ready, steady, go**, also **on your mark(s), get set, go** (used when telling people to begin a race).

ready/ at the ready *esp. Br.* available to be used immediately.

ready/ be ready to roll 1. *esp. Am.* be going to start soon. 2. *Am.* be going to leave soon.

ready reckoner *Br.* a table used for most frequent actions in business housekeeping.

reafforest, reforest *esp. Br., Aus.* plant (land again) with forest trees.

real/ for real *esp. Am., Aus.* col. serious(ly), esp. in **Are you for real?**: *I couldn't believe he was for real he seemed so insane.* - D. Divoky., *Are you for real, buddy?* - R. Cook.

real/ Get real! *esp. Am., Can.* col. It's foolish.

real *esp. Am., Aus.* col. adv. very: *They want you real bad.* - T. Thompson., *this terrible war would come to an end real soon.* - J. Baez.

real *Br.* (esp. of food) product made with using traditional methods and without artificial substances.

real ale *esp. Br.* beer which is stored in a barrel and is pumped from it.

real estate *esp. Am., Can., Aus. /Br.* law. **real property/** houses to be bought: *Because real estate's a turkey.* - J. Kellerman.

real estate agent, also **realtor** *Am., Can., Aus. /Br.* **estate agent,** *Aus.* **real estate broker/** person whose business is to buy, sell, or look after houses or land for people: *To the realtor's surprise I walked five minutes later and said "I'll take it".* - E. Taylor.

real estate office or **agency, realty office** *Am. /Br.* **estate agency/** one where real estate agents work.

reality check *esp. Am., Can.* occasion on which a person is reminded of the real state of things.

really 1. *Am.* used to express agreement. 2. *esp. Br.* used to express disapproval.

real property *Am.* property in the form of land and buildings, rather than personal possessions.

real tennis *Br.* court tennis.

ream 1. *Am.* 500 pieces of paper. 2. *Br.* 480 pieces of paper.

ream *esp. Am., Can.* 1. make (a hole or opening) larger, clear out or remove (material) from smth. 2. col. treat badly, esp. by cheating: *A head nurse reamed her out.* - T. Thompson. 3. sl. have sex.

ream/ ream sb.'s **ass/butt** *Am., Can.* sl. criticize sb.

ream out *Am.* sl. express severe disapproval.

reamer 1. *esp. Am.* a tool used to make a hole or opening wider. 2. *Am., Can.* lemon-squeezer.

reap hook *esp. Am.* reaping hook, sickle.

rear/ *Br.* speakers say at the rear for smth. that is behind and in the rear for the back part of smth., *Am.* speakers generally say in the rear for both: *rent-free residence at the rear of the Navy Yard.* – I. Stone.

rearrange/ be like rearranging the deckchairs on the Titanic *Br., Aus.* humor. have absolutely no effect.

rear-end *Am.* col. hit the back of the other vehicle: *One day while stopped at a red light, his car was rear-ended.* – Reader's Digest.

rear fender *Am.* rear mudguard (on a bicycle).

rear light *esp. Br. /Am.* **tail light/**.

recall *Am., Can.* the removal of an elected government official from office by petition followed by voting.

recap *Am. /Br.* **remold/** v. n. retread, renew the rubber covering on the bare surface of (a worn tire): *by recapping and careful driving, the tires had managed somehow to survive.* - D. Carnegie.

recce *Br.* col. */esp. Am., Can.* **recon/** (do) a reconnaissance.

receive (stolen goods) *esp. Br., Aus.* law. buy or give things that have been stolen; n. **-er**.

receiver/ official receiver *Br., Aus.* law. person who deals with the companies who cannot pay their debts; n. **-ship**: *receivership in Canada, the equivalent of bankruptcy court.* – D.L. Barlett, J.B. Steele.

reception *Br.* lobby, the area around or in front of the desk or office where visitors arriving in a hotel or large organisation go first.

reception centre *Br.* one established by the local authorities for homeless families.

reception class *Br.* the first class that the children are in when they start school, usu. at the age of five.

room clerk, (front) desk clerk *Am.* /*Br.* **receptionist, reception clerk**/ desk clerk in a hotel.

reception order *Br.* order authorizing the admission and detention of a patient in a psychiatric hospital.

reception room *esp. Br.* tech. a room, esp. living room in a private house that is not a kitchen, bedroom, or bathroom: *there was nothing to do but follow him into the reception room.* – P. Roth.

recess *esp. Am., Can., Aus.* a short pause between school classes: *he was pressed on the playground at recess to protect his charge.* - M. Twain.

recess *esp. Am.* /*esp. Br.* **break**/ take a pause for rest during the working day or working year: *Castellano's trial would be recessed for the Christmas holidays* - J. O'Brien, A. Kurins., *There was an older crowd, recessing now from a duty* - J. O'Hara.

rechipping *Br.* the practice of changing electronic identification numbers of a stolen mobile phone so as to enable it to be reused.

reckon *Br.* col. rate highly.

reckon/ **not reckon much to** (*Br.*)/ *Am., Aus.* **of**/ one's **chances** have little hope of success.

reckon up *esp. Br.* col. 1. understand the nature of (sb.)., *Takes up a bit of reckoning up, doesn't it?* - J. Herriot. 2. count smth.: *Reckon up all your money and see if you have enough* - Longman.

reckon without sb./smth. *Br.* not consider a possible problem when making plans.

recommend/ (*Br.*) **Can you recommend me a good hotel?** (= Can you recommend a good hotel to me?).

recommendation *esp. Am.* a letter or statement saying that sb. is suitable for a job, a course of study, etc.

Recommended Daily Allowance (RDA) *esp. Am.* amount of substance, esp. vitamin one should eat every day.

recon *Am., Can.* col. /*Br.* col. **recce**/ reconnaissance.

recondition *Br.* overhaul or renovate (a vehicle engine or a piece of equipment).

record card *Br.* index card.

recorded delivery *Br.* /*Am.* **certified mail**/ a method of sending mail by which one can get official proof that it has been delivered.

recorder *Br.* a person chosen from experienced lawyers to work somewhere as a judge.

recovery position *Br.* position used in first aid to prevent choking in unconscious patients.

recovery program *Am.* one for rehabilitating drug addicts.

recovery van *Br.* /*Am.* **wrecker**/ tow truck.

Recreational Vehicle (RV) *Am.* camper van: *Go RVing, life's a trip.* – Reader's Digest.

rec(reation) center *Am.* a building open to the public where meetings are held, sports are played and special services are offered for youth and old people: *Meet on October 31 at the rec center to dicuss a cease-fire.* – Reader's Digest.

recreation ground *Br.* /*Am.* **playground**/ a piece of public land set aside for game.

recreation room *Am., Can.* a room in a house used for playing games in, usu. in the basement: *The den, the rec room - again they're off by themselves.* - J. O'Brien, A. Kurins.

rector *Am.* person in charge of university or college.

recuse *esp. Am., Can.* (of a judge) excuse oneself from a case because of the possible conflict of interests and lack of impartiality.

red-bait *Am., Can.* col. harrass or persecute sb. because of their left-wing views.

redbone *Am.* a hound with a red coat used for hunting racoons and boars.

red breast *esp. Br.* col. robin.

redbrick universities *Br.* universities in large cities outside London that were established at the end of 19th or early 20th centuries.

red cap 1. *Am., Can.* railway station porter: *I frequently shake hands with a redcap who has carried my grip.* - D. Carnegie., *the only person Louis found waiting for him was the red cap.* - M. Jones, J. Chilton. 2. *Br.* col. military policeman.

red cent/ **not one**/**a red cent** *esp. Am., Can.* col. not a penny, no money at all.

Red Chamber *Can.* Canadian Senate.

redd smth. **up** *Irish Eng.* tidy smth. up.

red duster *Br.* col. red ensign flown by British registered ships.

redecorate *Br.* put new paint or paper on the walls of a room.

red eye *Am.* col. 1. strong cheap whiskey: *Her eye was on the bottle of red eye on my table.* - R.P. Warren. 2. also **red eye gravy** gravy made from the grease of fried meat.

red eye (flight) *esp. Am., Can.* col. night flight or plane: *That night Hockney caught the red-eye flight to New York* - R. Borchgrave, R. Moss., *We...hopped the red-eye to Las Vegas.* - W. Jack, B. Laursen.

red hot *Am.* sl. hot dog, frankfurter: *In Chicago they eat red hots with catsup.* - R.A. Spears.

rediffusion *esp. Br.* the system of broadcasting both the sound and television from a central receiving apparatus to other receivers in public places.

red ink *esp. Am., Can.* financial deficit or debt.

redirect *Br.* send sb.'s letters to their new address.

redistrict *Am.* divide into new districts for voting purposes.

redline *Am.* col. 1. discriminate in lending, esp. because of poor financial responsibility: *housing program that produced redlining and blockbusting* – N. Hentoff. 2. drive above rated engine's speed.

redneck *esp. Am., Can.* col. derog. person who lives in a country area in Southern US, esp. one who is uneducated or poor and has strong, unreasonable opinions: *and Phil sort of looks like a redneck.* - H. Fast., *Mason county is a redneck county* - R.P. Warren.

red Ned *Aus.* sl. cheap red wine.

red osier *Am.* dogwood.

Red Power *Am., Can.* movement in support of rights and political power for American Indians.

red rag/ be like a red rag /*esp. Am.* **flag/ to a bull** *esp. Br.* be certain to make sb. very angry.

red ribbon *Am.* award for the second-place winner in a competition.

red shirt *Am.* col. college athlete withdrawn from university sporting events for a year in order to develop his skills.

redskin *Am.* obs. now taboo. American Indian.

reduce *esp. Am.* become thinner by losing weight.

redundancy *esp. Br., Aus.* /*Aus.* **retrenchment**/ (a case of) being made redundant: *I told her about his redundancy.* – S. Townsend. / **redundancy pay** *Br.* /*Am.* **severance pay**/ unemployment benefit.

redundant *esp. Br., Aus.* /*esp. Am.* **laid off**/ adj. (of a worker) no longer employed because there is not enough work; *We'll have to make you redundant. Br.* /*Am. We'll have to let you go*/.

reef knot *esp. Br.* /*Am.* usu. **square knot**/ double knot that will not come undone easily.

reel *Br.* /*Am.* **spool**/ round object on which a length of sewing thread, wire, cinema film, fishing line, recording tape, etc. can be wound.

reelman *Aus.* lifeguard.

reeve *Can.* president of a village or town council: *He phoned the reeve* - W. Grady.

ref *Br.* col. referee.

refectory *Br.* /*Am.* **cafeteria**/ a large room in a school, college, etc., in which meals are served and eaten.

refer to drawer, RD *Br.* phrase used by banks when suspending payment of a cheque.

referee *Br., Aus.* reference, a person who provides information about sb.'s capabilities to future employer.

reffo *Aus.* col. refugee.

reflectors *Am.* /*Br., Aus.* **cat's eyes**/.

reflexive(ly) *Am.* done automatically without thinking.

reformatory, also **reform school** *Am.* or obs. use. /*Br.* **community home**/ approved school: *This time in reform school...proved to be a soul breaker.* - E. Cleaver.

refresh sb.'s **drink** *Am.* col. add more of an alcoholic drink to sb.'s glass.

refrigerator car *Am.* refrigerator van, wagon.

refrigerator freezer *Am.* /*Br.* **fridge freezer**/.

refueling probe *Am.* in-flight refuelling.

refuge *Br.* tech. /*Am.* **safety island**/ place in the middle of the road where people can wait, while crossing the street.

refuse, rubbish *esp. Br.* /*esp. Am., Can.* **garbage, trash**/.

refuse can *Am.* litter bin.

refuse collector *Br.* /*Am.* **garbage man**/.

refuse tip/dump *Br.* /*Am.* **garbage dump**/ refuse dump.

L.reg, M.reg. *Br.* used to define what the age of a car is according to the year when it was registered.

the regions *Br.* parts of a country that are not the capital city and its surrounding areas.

register *Am.* 1. movable metal plate that controls the flow of air in a heating or cooling system: *I couldn't close the register.* - K. Vonnegut, Jr. 2. also *Can.* till, cash register: *they all know how much was in the register* – J. O'Hara.

register/ be on the register *Am.* be suspected.

registered nurse 1. *esp. Am., Can.* graduate fully trained nurse. 2. *Br.* State Registered Nurse.

registered post *Br.* /*Am.* **registered mail**/ a postal service which for an additional charge, protects the sender of a valuable letter or parcel against loss: *Registered mail comes by the regular mailman?* - R. Chandler.

register office, registry (office) *esp. Br.* a place where births, marriages and deaths are officially recorded and where people can get married without a religious ceremony: *they are getting married on January 16th at Pocklington Street Register Office.* - S. Townsend.

registrar *Br.* 1. also *Aus.* a hospital doctor. 2. a person who keeps official records of register office. 3. a senior administrative official in a British college or university.

registration *Br.* 1. a roll call at school. 2. also **registration number** a car's registration numbers.

registration *Am. /Br.* **registration document/** official document with details about a motor vehicle and the name of its owner.

registration number or **plate** or **mark** *Br.* also col. **reg**, *Aus., NZ.* **registration plate** */Am.* **license plate number/** the numbers and letters on a car's number plate.

rego *Aus.* col. (car) registration.

regular 1. *esp. Am., Can.* ordinary: *He used to be just a regular writer when he was home.* - J.D. Salinger. 2. *Am.* coffee with cream and sugar: *Harry, if you're going for coffee pick me up a regular and a Danish.* - R. Cook. 3. *Am.* person who stands by his party. 4. *esp. Am.* (of food or drink) of medium size. 5. *esp. Am.* of a normal or standard size. 6. *Am.* nice and friendly.

regular 1. *esp. Br.* customer who goes to the same shop, bar, etc. very often. 2. *Am.* petrol that contains lead.

regular (sort of) guy *esp. Am., Can.* ordinary honest man.

regular mail *Am.* surface mail.

regulate a voltage (a power supply) *Am. /Br.* **stabilize a voltage (a power supply)/**.

regulo *Br.* tdmk. a degree of heat in a gas cooker shown by the stated number.

rehab 1. *Am., Can.* an. rehabilitate, restore. 2. *esp. Am.* col. treatment to help sb. who takes drugs or drinks too much alcohol, **be in rehab**.

rehash *esp. Am., Can.* discuss at length smth. that has already passed.

rein (from, up) *Am.* fence off (from the cattle).

rein/ draw rein *Br.* stop one's horse.

rejig *esp. Br., Aus. /Am.* **rejigger/** change and improve the arrangement of smth.

relate *Am.* col. feel that one understands another person's problem, situation, etc.

release/ be on (*Br., Aus.*) */Am.* **in/ general release** (of films) be available and showing in cinemas.

released time *Am.* one given by schools for religious education, etc.

relegate *esp. Br.* (of football team) move down to a lower position; n. **-ion**.

relet *esp. Br.* let a property for a further period or to a new tenant.

relevancy *Am.* relevance.

relief 1. *Br. /Am.* **benefit/** a part of one's income on which one does not have to pay tax for some special reason. 2. *esp. Am., Can. /Br.* **dole/** money given by the government to help people who are poor, old, unemployed, etc.: *In 1943... only 90,000 people were on relief.* - Reader's Digest; **be on the relief/be on the dole**. 3. *Br.* extra vehicles providing supplementary transport at peak times or in emergencies.

relief bus service *Br.* special bus service.

relief road *esp. Br.* one made in order to take away heavy traffic from congested urban area.

religion/ get religion *Am.* humor. start doing smth. in a serious and careful way.

rello, rellie *Aus., NZ.* col. relative.

remake *Am. /Br.* **make over/** print. remake a printing plate or film due to an error at the first attempt.

remand/ be remanded in custody *Br.* be kept in prison or */Br.* **remand centre/** until the trial.

remand centre/home *Br., Aus. /Am.* **detention home/center/** a place where young people accused of committing a crime are sent to wait until the trial begins.

remedial teaching, lessons *Br., Aus.* special lessons for people who have difficulties in reading or writing.

Remembrance Day (or **Sunday**) the Sunday nearest to November 11th when people in Britain and Canada remember those killed in the two world wars.

remission *Br.* law. a reduction in time that a person has to stay in prison.

remit *Br.* an area of work that sb. is responsible for.

remodeler *Am., Can.* person who alters the structure of an existing building to add smth. new to it, for example new bathroom.

remould *Br. /Am.* **recap, retread/** an old tire which has been given a new surface and can be used again.

removal van *Br. /Am.* **moving van/** van used for moving furniture when moving from one house to another: *I was lifted in my chair into the removal van* - C.M. Fraser.

removalist *Aus. /Am.* **mover**, *Br.* **furniture remover/** manager of an office or other person dealing with transporting furniture.

rendering *esp. Br.* rendition.

renig on *Am.* renege on, break a promise.

rennin *Am.* rennet, substance used for thickening milk, esp. to make cheese.

rent *esp. Am.* 1. */esp. Br., Aus.* **let/** give the use of (room, building, etc.) in return for rent. 2. */Br.* **hire/** pay money for the use of (a car, boat, etc.) for a short time: *The rented limousine slipped* *quietly through the blistering August afternoon.* - T. Murphy. / **To rent** *Am.* For hire.

rent *esp. Am.* money paid regularly for the use of (a car, boat, clothes, etc.).

rent-a-car *Am.* a car rented for a day, week, etc.: *Is there a rent-a-car place in town?* – R.L. Stine.

rental *Am.* 1. also *Can.* a property or thing rented, esp. house or a car: *Oh, it's just a rental.* - K. Lipper. 2. a sum of money that rental library gets from its activity.

rental library *Am.* a commercially operated library (as in store) that lends books at a fixed charge per book per day.

rentalism *Am.* a system of renting things.

rent-a-person or **thing** *Br.* derog. seeming to have been rented to do smth. and not sincere.

rent boy, renter *Br., Aus.* col. a young male prostitute.

renter *Am.* rented car or video cassette.

rent out *esp. Am.* /*Br.* **let, hire out**/: *we could rent out rooms to boarders* - J. Baez., *A government program to rent out tractors to farmers has degenerated into a front for officials.* - Time., *I also had our property to get under control and rented out.* - New Idea.

rent party *Am.* party held to raise money to pay rent by charging guests for attendance.

rent rebate *Br.* money some people get from local government to help them pay their rent.

rep *Am., Can., Aus.* col. reputation: *What about somebody really tough who hasn't made his rep yet, a good rookie?* - M. Puzo.

Rep *Am.* Republican.

repair truck, tow truck *Am.* /*Br.* **breakdown van, lorry**/.

repartition *Am.* distribution.

repay one's **interest, attention, time** *esp. Br.* be worth the effort.

repayable *esp. Br.* /*Am.* **payable**/ (of a loan) that must be paid back within a certain time.

repeat *esp. Br.* /*Am.* **rerun**/ a TV or radio programme that has been shown before.

repeat *Am.* vote more than once in an election.

repeater *Am.* 1. one who votes more than once in an election. 2. a student who fails to pass on to the next grade.

repeat prescription *Br.* an order for medicine that sb. has had before, which one can get without seeing one's doctor.

reply-paid letter *Br.* one that is paid for by the sender.

repo *Am., Can.* a car or other item which has been repossessed, v.

repo man, repossessor *Am., Can.* col. person who repossesses cars for a living: *What kind of guy is lower than a repo man?* – R.A. Spears.

report/ on report *Br.* during the report stage of a bill in Parliament.

(school) report, record book/card *Br.* /*esp. Am., Can.* **report card**/ a written statement by teachers about a child's work at school, sent to its parents: *Your weight was supposed to be a big secret, like what you got on your report card.* - B. Robinson., *I had picked up my report card.* - J. Baez., *He got a good school report every term.* – R. Westall.

report card *Am.* journalism. a report on how well a person, organisation or a country has been doing recently.

report out *Am.* return (a matter sent for further study or decision) to people who can put it into action: *report out the full employment legislation.* - H. Truman.

reportorial *esp. Am., Can.* pertaining to reporter's work.

repossession agency *Am.* firm giving things back to the shops or rental institutions from persons in default of the payment of the instalments due.

repro house print. *Br.* /*Am.* **color separator**/.

request stop *Br.* special stop made only if sb. waiting there signals a busdriver to stop.

required (course, studies, subjects, etc.). *Am.* compulsory: *There will be required courses in world citizenship* - P. Robertson.

required (intended) track, track required *Br.* /*Am.* **course (line)**/ intended course of a plane.

rerun *Am.* /*esp. Br.* **repeat**/.

reservation 1. *esp. Am.* an area of land set apart for animals to live unharmed without being hunted. 2. *Am.* /*Can.* **reserve**/ Indian reservation. 3. *esp. Am.* /*esp. Br.* **booking, advanced registration**/.

reserve bank *Aus., NZ.* central bank.

reserved occupation *Br.* one from which a person won't be taken for military service.

reserve grade *Aus.* (in sports) a second division.

reserve price *Br.* the lowest price offered by the owner of the property being auctioned or sold.

reshuffle *Br.* change around the jobs of the people who work in an organisation, esp. in a government, n.

residence *Br.* also **hall of residence** /*Am.* **dormitory**/.

residency 1. *Am., Can.* advanced training, similar to the medical residency. 2. *Br.* musician's regular engagement at a club or other place.

resident 1. *Br.* a guest in a hotel who stays for a very short time. 2. also **resident physician** *Am., Can.* /*Br.* **registrar**/ medical graduate in special practice under supervision in a hospital.

Resident Alien *Am.* foreigner residing in the US.

residenter *Am.* one who resides in a place constantly.

residential rental *Am.* rent for a flat.

residential treatment facility *Am.* tech. a mental hospital.

residual *Am.* payment (as to an actor or writer) for each rerun after an initial showing (as of a TV tape).

resit *esp. Br.* /*Am.* **retake**/ take (an examination) again: *Failed his first-year exams and the resits.* - D. Lodge. n.

reskilling *Br.* the teaching of new work skills, esp. to unemployment people.

resort *Am.* a hotel for people on holiday.

resourced *Br.* (of an organisation) having all the things, such as money and materials needed to function properly.

responsibility *Am.* solvency.

rest *Am., Can.* conclude the case for the prosecution or defense in a law case.

rest/ and all the rest of it *Br.* col. used at the end of a short list to mean other things of a similar type.

rest/ and the rest *Br.* col. humor. used to say that real figures are much bigger or the situation is much worse.

rest/ be resting *Br.* euph. (of actors) be without work.

rest/ for the rest *Br.* used to introduce a short final remark at the end of a speech or written works.

rest/ give it a rest! *Br.* col. used to tell sb. to stop talking about smth.

rest/ no rest for the weary *Am.* /*Br.* **no peace/ rest for the wicked**/ humor. keep on working in spite of being tired.

rest area *Am.* /*Br.* **lie-by**/ place at the side of a road used for a short rest or in case of emergency repairs.

restaurant car *Br.* /*esp. Am., Aus.* **dining car**/ dining car in a railway train.

rest up *Am.* relax in order to have strength: *there's time to get rested up* – S. Lawrence.

rest home *Br.* a common term for an old people's home.

resto *Can.* sl. restaurant.

restricted area 1. *Br.* area in which there's a speed limit. 2. *Am., Can.* area where unauthorized people are not allowed to enter.

restrictive practice *Br.* (in industry or business) an action taken by a union which limits the freedom of workers or employers, esp. by slowing down output or restricting the entry of new workers.

rest room 1. *Am., Can.* euph. /*Br.* **ladies, gents** *esp. Br.* **public toilet, WC**/ a public toilet in a hotel, restaurant, etc.: *They'd walk in the rest room later, by themselves.* - A. Hailey., *The terminal had two restrooms for males* - S.B. Oates., *This is how coin locks help keep rest rooms in good condition.* - Playboy. 2. *Br.* a lounge in a public building where people can relax.

rest stop, turnout *Am.* /*Aus.* **rest area,** *esp. Br.* **lay-by**/.

result 1. *Br.* col. /*Am.* **score**/ (esp. in football) a win or score, **get a result**. 2. *esp. Br.* /*Am.* **score**/ a number or letter which shows how successful sb. has been in a test or examination.

resume, biodata *esp. Am., Can., Aus.* /*Br.* **CV, curriculum vitae**/ biographical summary: *Resume and references necessary.* - W. Murphy., *Video resumes run about 5 minutes* - Omni.

retail park *Br.* special area outside a town with many large shops and space for cars to park.

retail politics *esp. Am.* electoral campaigning of the traditional variety.

retail price index (RPI) *Br.* /*Am.* **cost of living index, consumer price index**/ a list of prices of typical goods which shows how much the cost of living changes from one month to another.

retail store *Am.* retail shop.

retainer *Br.* reduced rent paid to retain accomodation during a period of non-occupancy.

retake *Br.* exam or test that sb. takes because they failed it.

retardat *Am., Can.* derog. slightly handicapped person.

retard(ee) *Am., Aus.* col. retarded person: *What's the matter, retard?* - Reader's Digest.

retiracy *Am.* 1. solitude. 2. means that enable one to live in a solitude.

retiree *esp. Am.* a retired person: *a really unique gift for any retiree, this calender* – Reader's Digest.

retirement pension *Br.* pension given to a person above a certain age.

retirement plan *Am.* system of saving money for one's retirement, esp. if a person won't receive money from their employer.

retool *esp. Am., Can.* col. adapt or reorganise smth. to make it more efficient.

retread *Am.* col. 1. smth. that is made or done again with a few changes added. 2. sb. who has

been trained to do work which is different from what he did before.
retread 1. *Am., Aus.* veteran of the two wars. 2. *Aus.* a teacher called to school during his vacation.
retrench *esp. Aus.* make an employee redundant.
retrenchment *Aus. /Br., Aus.* **redundancy/**.
retro *Am.* col. retrospective.
return *Br.* elect sb. to a political position, esp. to represent them in Parliament.
return (ticket) *Br., Aus. /Am.* **round trip ticket/** return ticket.
return *esp. Br., Aus., Can. /Am.* **round-trip/** adj. (of a ticket or its cost) for a trip from one place to another and back again: *They gave them a return ticket from America to Britain* - J. Ruppeldtova.
return ticket *Am.* one for the returning part of a journey.
return/ by return (of post) *esp. Br., Aus. /Am., Aus.* **by return mail/** by the next post: *I waited impatiently for an answer and by return of post received one with a black seal.* - Cpt. Marryat., *She received by return of post from Paul a cold and business-like note* - I. Murdoch., *Theo answered by return mail.* – I. Stone.
return/ many happy returns (of the day) *Br.* (used to wish sb. a happy birthday).
return thanks *Br.* express thanks.
returner *Br.* sb. who goes back to work after a long time away, esp. a woman who left work to look after her children.
returning officer *Br.* the official in each town or area who arranges an election to Parliament and gives out the result.
returns *Am.* the results of voting in an election.
return trip *Br. /Am.* **round-trip/** a trip to a place and back.
rev counter *Br.* an instrument in a car or aeroplane which shows the speed of the engine.
Revd *Br.* Rev, Reverend.
reverse (a car) *esp. Br., Aus. /Am.* **back up/** drive it backwards.
reverse down (the drive) *Br. /Am.* **back down (the drive)/**.
reverse charge call *Br., Aus. /Am., Can.* **collect call/**.
reverse the charges, /Br.* **reverse charge/ *esp. Br., Can. /Am.* **call collect/**: *My father refused a reverse-charges call from Tunisia* – S. Townsend.
reversible *esp. Am. /Br.* **turnabout/** (about a coat) one that can be worn on either side.
reversing light *Br. /Am., Can.* **backup light/** white light at the rear of a vehicle indicating that the vehicle is reversing.

reversionist *Am.* a very conservative person.
review *Am. /Br., Aus.* **revise (for)/** study again (lessons or a subject already learnt), usu. before an examination. **revision, review** n.
revise upwards, downwards *Br., Aus.* increase, decrease.
revise (for) *Br., Aus. /Am.* **review/** study again (smth. learned) usu. before an examination.
revolving door *esp. Am.* the movement of people from one organisation to another, esp. from government jobs to private companies.
rewrite man *Am.* newspaper reporter skilled in rewriting.
RFP *esp. Am., Can.* request for proposal, a list of required goods and services that a company sends to potential contractors and suppliers.
rhapsody/ go into rhapsodies *Br.* express admiration.
rheumatics *esp. Br.* col. rheumatism.
rhino *Br.* sl. money: *I see you look so sharp after the rino* - Cpt. Marryat.
rhubarb 1. *Am.* sl. a noisy argument: *There's a noisy rhubarb down on the field.* - R.A. Spears. 2. *Br.* col. noise made by a group of actors to produce the illusion of a crowd.
Rialto *Am.* a theatre region on Broadway.
ribbon development *Br., Aus.* long rows of buildings along the roads leading out of towns.
rib roast *Am.* a joint taken from the forequarter.
rice burner *Am.* derog. Japanese motorcycle.
The Rice or **Swamp State** *Am.* South Carolina.
rich/ rich as Croesus *Br.* very rich.
rich/ strike it rich *Am.* col. have a sudden success.
Richest Hill on Earth *Am.* Butte, Mont.
rick *esp. Br., Aus.* twist (a joint or part of the body) slightly, wrench, sprain.
rickey *Am., Can.* drink containing (liquor), lime juice, sugar, and soda water.
rick *Am., Can.* 1. pile of firewood smaller than a cord. 2. a set of shelving for storing barrels.
rickle *Irish Eng.* loosely piled heap of smth.
ride 1. *esp. Am., Can.* a. travel in (in a car, train, on train, bicycle), esp. habitually. b. travel across, usu. on horseback: *And he always wanted me to ride up with him* - B. Holiday., W. Duffy. 2. *esp. Am., Can.* annoy: *the Negroes I knew rode me so badly I knew I had to do something.* - Alex Haley., *The fact is the Commissioner's been riding us for action* - D. Hammet. 3. *esp. Br.* ride a horse for exercise and pleasure. 4. *Am., Can.* travel up and down in a lift.
ride 1. *Am., Can.* person giving sb. a lift. 2. *Am.* col. a motor vehicle.

ride in(to), back, etc., also **ride bus** *esp. Am.* travel in a bus, car, etc.

ride/ get sb. **a free ride** *Am.* esp. journalism. be allowed to do what you want without being criticized.

ride/ hitch a ride *Am.* col. get a free ride: *I hitched a ride with that guy* – R.L. Stine.

ride/ ride a train *Am.* take a train.

ride/ ride herd on sb./smth. *Am., Can.* be responsible for controlling a group of people and their actions.

ride/ ride sb. **on the rail** *Am.* col. tie sb. to a fence post and carry him out of town for punishment: *anyone who offended against the moral standard of the village would be ridden on a rail.* - Longman.

ride/ ride the countryside/range *Am.* travel on a horse across the countryside.

ride/ ride the pine (or **bench**) *Am., Can.* col. (of an athlete) sit on the sidelines.

ride/ ride shotgun *esp. Am., Can.* col. act as a guard, esp. on a vehicle: *He was going to ride shotgun in the holdup* - G. O'Neill, D. Lehr.

ride/ ride the rods (or **rails**) *Can.* col. ride on a freight train without paying.

ride/ ride to hounds *esp. Br.* hunt small animals such as foxes on horseback for sport: *It used to be the custom for most wealthy families to ride to hounds* - Longman.

ride/ take sb. **for a ride** *esp. Am.* euph. remove sb. by force or murder him/her: *the police assume the victim had been taken for a ride by some of his enemies.* - H.C. Whitford., R.J. Dixson.

ride-off *Am., Can.* (in riding competition) round held to resolve a tie or determine qualifiers for a later stage.

ride-on *esp. Am., Can.* a toy car that a child can sit in and move by pedals, battery power, etc.

rider *Br.* 1. addition or ammendment to a bill at its third reading. 2. recommendation or comment added by the jury to a judicial verdict.

ridership *esp. Am., Can.* the number of passengers using a specific kind of public transport.

ridge/ have been around the ridges *Aus.* have a lot of experience.

riffle *esp. Am., Can.* 1. a. shallow extending across a stream bed and causing broken water. b. a stretch of water flowing over a riffle. 2. a ripple.

rig 1. *esp. Am., Can., Aus.* col. a large truck or semi-trailer, esp. when fully loaded: *I'll have to get off this rig at Cheyenne* - J. Kerouac., *Men kicked off shoes, climbing aboard while rigs were rolling.* - Arthur Hailey. 2. *Am.* col. a set of equipment for a special purpose.

right *Br.* col. (used to emphasise how bad sb. or smth. is).

right 1. *Br.* col. used to get sb.'s attention or to tell them to be ready to do smth. 2. *Aus.* used to comfort sb. and try to persuade them that there is not a problem.

right *Br.* sl. adv. very: *Right interesting to an artillery man.* - H. Truman.

right *Br.* use to say that one is ready to do smth.

right *esp. Br.* used to say yes to a suggestion or order.

right/ be on the right lines *Br.* be done in a proper way to succeed.

right/ Come right in *Am.* Please, walk in.

right/ right and left *Am.* /*Br.* **right, left and centre/** everywhere.

right/ right off *esp. Am.* right away, at once: *We're going to take a trip right off.* - E. Caldwell.

right/ right off the bat *Am., Can.* sl. immediately: *Anybody can tell. Right off the bat.* - C. McCullers.

right/ right there *Am.* /*Br.* **just there/** over there.

right/ see sb. **right** 1. *Br.* col. pay for the work done. 2. *Br., Aus.* col. help sb.

right/ she's (she'll be) right *Aus.* col. That'll be all right!

right/ take, make, col. **hang right** *Am.* turn right.

right/ Too right *esp. Am.* You are correct, I agree.

right/ we've got a right one here! *Br., Aus.* col. He/she is silly or stupid.

right-angle triangle *Br., Aus.* /*Am.* **right triangle/**.

righteous *Am.* sl. 1. good, genuine. 2. large, excessive.

rightly/ quite rightly *Br.* for a good sensible reason.

righto, right oh, righto ho, right you are *Br.* col. an exclamation of approval.

right of abode *esp. Br.* person's right to take up residence or remain resident in a country.

right of way *Am., Can.* or *Br.* law. /*Br.* **permanent way/** a public path or track across land that is otherwise private property, such as a farmer's field: *Once a right of way has been established it can be used by the public forever.* - Young Citizen's Passport.

Right on! *Am., Aus.* I agree completely.

right-on 1. *Am.* col. admirable, saying correct things. 2. *Br.* believing that people should be treated in a fair way.

a right one *Br.* col. silly or foolish person.

right people, places, schools, etc *Br.* the best or most important ones.

rights/ get/catch/have sb. **bang to rights** *Br.* / *Am., Can.* **have** sb. **dead to rights**/ col. have enough proof to show that sb. has done smth. wrong.

rightsize *esp. Am.* convert smth. to more convenient size.

right-to-work *esp. Am.* of or promoting a worker's right not to be required to join a trade union.

right triangle *Am., Can.* /*Br., Aus.* **right-angled triangle**/ a triangle with a right angle.

righty *Am., Can.* col. 1. right-hand person. 2. right-wing politician.

rigour *Br.* strictness or severity of a punishment.

rig-out *esp. Br., Aus.* col. often derog. a set of clothes of a particular, esp. unusual type.

rile *Am., Can.* make water turbulent or muddy.

rile up *Am.* col. make sb. very angry.

riley *Am.* col. 1. angry. 2. turbid.

Riley/ lead the life of Riley *Br.* col. have enough money to do what one likes.

(electric) ring *Br.* 1. /*Am., Aus.* **element**/. 2. also **gas ring** /*Am.* **burner**/.

(leg) ring *Br.* tech. /*Am.* **tag**, *Am., Can.* **band**/ (a bird) put a ring around its leg so that to trace its movements and habits in the future.

ring *Br.* draw a circle.

ring/ give sb. **a ring** *esp. Br.* col. /*Am., Aus.* **give** sb**. a call**/ telephone sb.

ring/ hold the ring *esp. Br.* hold the line.

ring (up) *esp. Br.* 1. /*esp. Am.* col. **call (up)**/ telephone sb.: *he might perhaps ring up later.* - A. Burgess 2. a telephone call.

ring back *esp. Br.* col. /*Am.* **call back**/ return a telephone call to (sb.): *I'll find out the address, and ring you back.* - Longman.

ring in 1. *Am.* mark the time of one's arrival at work: *Most of the workers had already rung in by the time I arrived.* - Longman. 2. *esp. Br.* telephone to a place.

ring off *Br.* /*Am.* **call off**, *Am., Aus.* **hang up**/ end a telephone conversation (by putting a telephone down): *Mrs. Oliver rang off.* - A. Christie.

ring off the hook *Am., Can.* (of telephone) be constantly ringing.

ring out 1. *esp. Br.* make an outgoing telephone call. 2. *Am.* mark the time of leaving work: *I'll ring out your time card later tonight.* - D. Brenner.

ring round *esp. Br.* make telephone calls to (a number of people).

ring up *esp. Br.* /*esp. Am.* **call**/ make a telephone call: *About once or twice a week my sister'll ring me up.* - R. Carter., M. McCarthy.

ring bearer *Am., Can.* a boy who ceremoniously bears the rings at a wedding.

ring book *Br.* /*Am.* **looseleaf notebook**/.

ringer 1. *Am.* person who enters a sports competition against the rules: *That college football team was disqualified because they used a ringer who was not enrolled in the college.* - H.C. Whitford., R.J. Dixson. 2. *Aus., NZ.* the shearer who sheared more sheep than any other in a certain period of time. 3. *Aus.* a stockman, esp. one employed in droving.

ring-in *Aus.* col. a person included in activity at a later stage.

ring main *Br.* 1. reliable electric supply serving several consumers and returning to the original source, providing thus an alternative path in case of a failure. 2. the same arrangement with the pipes of water supply. 3. electric circuit serving a number of power points with one fuse in the supply to the circuit.

ring-pull *Br., Aus.* /*Am.* **pull-tab**/.

ring road, orbital *esp. Br., Aus.* /*Am.* **beltway,** *Can.* **ring road**/ a road that goes round the edge of a large town so that traffic does not have to pass through the centre: *struggle against the noise and pollution of the ring road.* - D. Lodge.

ring spanner, (open-ended) spanner *Br.* /*Am.* **box end spanner, (box end) wrench**/ a type of spanner with a hollow end that fits over the nut to be screwed or unscrewed.

ringster *Am.* a member of a ring, esp. political.

ringtoss *Am.* (a game) /*Br., Aus.* **hoopla**/.

rink rat *Am., Can.* col. 1. ice-hockey enthusiast spending a lot of time at skating rinks. 2. synthetic broom used in the game of curling.

rinky-dink 1. *Br.* sl. cute, neat, smart. 2. *esp. Am., Can.* col. shoddy, cheap: *Marilyn Monroe...had a sweet little rinky-dink of a voice* – N. Mailer.

rinse hands under the tap *Br.* rinse them using a tap.

riotous behaviour *Br.* wild, excited and uncontrolled behaviour.

rip *Am., Can.* fraud, rip-off.

rip *esp. Am., Can.* col. attack verbally, criticise severely.

rip/ let it/her rip *esp. Am.* col. make it move.

rip/ let rip *Br., Aus.* col. allow gas to escape from one's bottom loudly.

ripe *Br.* col. rude but amusing.

ripper *Aus.* sl. excellent.

riprap *Am., Can.* loose stone used to form foundation for a breakwater or other structure.

rise *Br. /Am., Can., Aus.* **raise/** an increase in wages: *This year's pay rise can be next year's base line* – C. Handy.

rise/ take a rise (out of sb.) *Br.* col. annoy sb. very much.

risers *Am.* a group of steps on which people sit or stand to see or to be seen better: *he saw the stage for the first time, with individual risers, or platforms for the members of his backup band* – J. Hopkins.

rising *esp. Br.* prep. nearly (the stated age).

rising damp *Br.* condition when water comes up from the ground and gets into the walls of a building.

rising main *Br.* vertical pipe supplying mains water to a building.

rising powder *Br.* baking powder.

ritz *esp. Am., Can.* ostentatious luxury and glamour.

river / River Thames *Br. /Am.* **Hudson River/**.

river/ send sb. **up the river** *esp. Am., Can.* col. send sb. to prison: *he went up the river in 23 or 24.* - D. Hammet.

RN *Br.* Royal Navy of the UK.

roach *Am.* brush (the hair) in a roach (with the hair brushed straight back from the forehead or side of the head): *curly hairs roached down over his coat collar* - J. Fischer.

roach *esp. Am., Can.* col. cockroach.

roach *Am., Aus.* sl. 1. despicable person. 2. unattached or ugly girl.

road 1. *Am., Can.* railway. 2. *Br.* railway track, esp. clear or otherwise for a train to proceed.

road/ be on the road *Am.* work as a travelling agent: *He has always been on the road and enjoys the work very much.* - H.C. Whitford., R.J. Dixson.

road/ be on the right road *Br. /Am.* **be on the right track/** succeed.

road/ down the road *esp. Am., Can.* col. somewhere in the future.

road/ get out of the/one's **road** 1. *Am.* col. stop blocking it. 2. *Br.* col. rude way of telling sb. to move.

road/ live in road *Br., Aus. /Am.* **on road/**.

road/ one's **road to Damascus** *Br., Aus.* a very important experience which changes one's whole life.

road/ take the road *Am.* go on tour.

road/ take the high road *Am.* follow the most moral or correct course; opp. **take the low road.**

road agent *Am.* a highway man.

roadbed *Am., Can.* the part of a road on which vehicles travel.

roadblock *Am.* a problem that stops sb. from achieving smth.

road craft *Br.* driving skills.

road fund licence *Br.* disc displayed on a vehicle indicating that road tax has been paid.

road gang *Am.* a gang of prisoners assigned to work on roads: *Herridge – a former poet (published), road-gang worker, expert in nineteenth-century American literature, and dishwasher* – N. Hentoff.

roadhouse *esp. Am.* obs. a restaurant or bar on a road outside a city: *there is a roadhouse about twenty miles from here* – J. O'Hara.

road-kill *esp. Am., Can.* col. the killing of an animal by a vehicle on a road.; an animal killed in this way.

road markings *Br. /Am.* **lines/**.

road pricing *Br.* a system of making motorists pay money for driving on certain roads by electronically recording the movements of vehicles on them.

road sense *Br.* person's ability to drive safely in heavy traffic.

roadshow *Br.* group that travels around the country giving performances for entertainment or advertising.

road surface *esp. Br., Can. /Am.* **pavement,** *Can.* **asphalt/**.

road-sweeper *Br.* street cleaner.

road tax *Br.* one which the owner of a vehicle must pay to be allowed to drive it on the road.

road test *Am.* one testing driver's ability to control a vehicle so as to obtain official permission to drive.

road toll *Aus.* a number of people who died in road accidents.

road train *esp. Aus.* large lorry pulling one or more trailers.

road trip/ take a road trip *Am.* travel to a place to play sports game or on a businees trip.

Road Up *Br.* Road under repair.

roadworks *Br., Aus. /Am.* **roadwork/** work that is being done to repair a road.

roaring/ be a roaring success *Br.* be very successful.

roaring/ do a roaring trade (in) *Br., Aus.* col. / *Am.* **do a roaring business/** sell a lot of smth. very quickly.

roaring drunk *Br.* very drunk and noisy.

roast 1. *esp. Am., Can.* a meal eaten outdoors where the stated food is roasted over an open fire; **hotdog roast, oyster roast,** etc. 2. *Am.* heavy criticism. 3. *Am.* occasion at which people celebrate a special event in sb.'s life by telling funny stories or giving speeches about them. 4. *Am. /Br.* **joint/** large piece of meat for cooking, esp. containing a bone.

roast *Am.* criticise severely.

roasting/ give sb. **a roasting** *esp. Br.* col. talk angrily to sb. disapproving their actions.

roasting tin *Br. /Am.* **roasting pan/** tin used for roasting meat.

robbery/ highway robbery *Am., Aus. /Br.* **daylight robbery/** a situation when you're overcharged heavily.

robbery with violence *Br., Aus.* one where violent actions take place.

(bath)robe 1. *esp. Am. /Br.* **(dressing) gown/** a long loose garment worn informally indoors: *I was shocked to see Marty in his robe and slippers* - A.E. Hotchner. 2. *esp. Am., Can.* lap robe, a warm covering (usu. buffalo skin) used as protection against moisture and cold: *It was antique carriage robe.* - K. Davis.

the robe *esp. Br.* the legal profession.

robin/ the first robin *Am.* the beginning of spring.

rock 1. *Am., Aus.* any stone, large or small / *Br.* apply rock only to a boulder or large stone. 2. *esp. Am.* sl. diamond. 3. *Br. /Am.* **(rock) candy/** a sweet made in long hard sticks which are often sold in seaside towns in Britain or USA; **stick of rock** *Br. /Am.* **stick of candy/**.

The Rock *Can.* col. Newfoundland, Canada: *We know a girl from the Rock.* - W. Magnuson.

rock/ between a rock and a hard place *Am., Can.* sl. in a dilemma: *In this regard I find myself as Americans have taken to saying, between a rock and a hard place.* - A. Bloom., *Aimless between the rock of resurgent White House and the hard place of a G.O.P. freshman.* - Time.

rock and rye *Am.* rye whiskey flavoured with a blend of fruits.

rockaway *Am.* a four-wheeled carriage with a fixed top and open sides.

rock cake/bun *esp. Br., Aus.* a small hard cake with a rough surface: *their treats...teacakes, scones, crumpets, rock cakes* - B. Bryson.

rock candy *Am., Can.* boiled sugar crystallised in large masses on strings: *At the upper end they narrowed down to points of rock candy, brilliantly colored* - J.A. Michener.

rock dash *Am.* pebbledash cement with lots of small pebbles set in it, used for covering the outside walls of a house.

rocker *Am.* 1. a rocking chair: *I rocked Aimee in the huge rocker* - Reader's Digest., *Aunt Lillie sat in her rocker beside a small table* - S. North. 2. a rock song or a person who really likes pop music.

rockery *Br., Aus. /Am.* **rock garden/** one where plants grow between piles of stone.

rocket/ give sb. **/ get a rocket** *Br., Aus.* col. scold sb. / be scolded severely.

rocket/ go like a rocket *Aus.* work very well.

rocket/ put a rocket under sb. *Br., Aus.* do smth. to make sb. hurry.

rocket scientist *esp. Am., Can.* very intelligent person.

rocket ship *Am.* a spacecraft which is powered by a rocket.

rock-hard *Br.* humor. strong and not afraid of anybody.

rock-head *Am.* sl. stupid person.

rock-hound *esp. Am., Can.* col. geologist or amateur collector of mineral specimens.

rocking horse manure/ as scarce as rocking horse manure *Aus.* very scarce, rare.

Rockies *Am.* col. Rocky Mountains.

rock jock *Am.* col. mountaineer.

rockmelon *Aus.* cantaloupe.

rock pool *Br. /Am.* **tide pool/** small pool of water between rocks by the sea.

rock-ribbed *Am., Can.* col. 1. inflexible: *Gus is a rock-ribbed Republican.* - H. Fast. 2. rocky.

rocks *Am.* sl. money, dollars: *Don't take no brains, just the rocks.* - G.V. Higgins.

rocks/ have rocks in one's **head** *Am.* col. be very stupid.

rock salmon *Br.* euph. dogfish, sold as food.

rocky slip *Am.* landslide, landslip.

rod *Am., Can.* col. pistol: *Don't pack no rod?* - R. Chandler.

rod/ make a rod for one's **own back** *Br.* do smth. that is likely to cause problems for you in the future.

rode *Am., Can.* rope, esp. one securing an anchor or trawl.

roger *Br., Aus.* sl. v. screw, (have) a sexual intercourse with: *Little lier said it was her first time rogered.* - J.P. Donleavy.

roil *Am.* rile, annoy: *politicians dodge the whole roiling issue* - Time., *large numbers were roiled by the sudden requirement that they learn Lithuanian* - H. Smith.

roily *Am., Can.* (of water) muddy, turbulent.

roll 1. *Am.* money, esp. a pack of money: *We reformers are on a roll* - Newsweek., *He saw 49 Hudson for sale and rushed to the bank for his* *entire roll.* - J. Kerouac. 2. *esp. Br.* also **bread roll** (esp. for sandwich), small loaf for one person either long or round: - *a little basket of hot, fresh rolls.* - J. Aldridge.

roll *Am.* 1. sl. rob (a sleeping or unconscious person): *first entertaining, then rolling foreign sailors.* - T. Thompson., Say, *Mac, did they roll her?* - J. Dos Passos., *We never actually rolled any of these guys* - W. Jack, B. Laursen. 2. reduce (smth.) such as prices: *Kennedy forced the steel industry to roll back a price increase in 1962.* - Atlantic Monthly. 3. col. also *Can.* overturn (a vehicle).

roll/ ham/cheeseroll *Br., Aus. /Am.* **ham/cheese on a roll/**.

roll back *esp. Am.* reduce price, wages, etc.: *Kennedy forced the steel industry to roll back a price increase in 1962.* - Atlantic Monthly n. **rollback**.

roll on *esp. Br., Aus.* col. used to express a wish that a time or event will come quickly.

Roll up!, Roll up! *Br., Aus.* come and look at smth. unusual and interesting.

roll with the pitches *Am.* col. be able to deal with a series of difficult situations.

roll/ a roll in the hay *Am.* sl. a casual and joyous sex act: *They would no doubt have a roll in the hay.* - J. Baez., *a bar of chocolate could procure a weekly roll in the hay with a luscious German blonde* - E. Williams.

roll one's own *Br.* col. make one's own cigarettes instead of buying them.

roll/ be ready to roll *esp. Am.* col. used to say when sb. is ready to do smth.

roll/ roll the bones *Am.* sl. play dice.

roll/ strike sb. **off the roll** *Br.* debar a solicitor from practising as a penalty for dishonesty or other misconduct.

roll/ sweet roll *Am.* bun or Danish pastry.

rollaway *Am., Can.* adj., n. movable (of bed, etc.).

rolled oats *esp. Br.* kind of oats used for making porridge.

rolled gold *Br., Aus. /Am.* **gold-plated/** (of a piece of jewellery) made of cheap metal covered with a thin layer of gold.

roller *Am.* 1. rock bit (a kind of drilling bit). 2. sl. policeman.

roller *Br.* col. a Rolls-(Royce) car.

Rollerblade *Am., Aus.* also **in-line skate** tdmk. a type of shoe with a single row of small wheels on the botton used to travel along for enjoyment.

roller blind *Br., Aus. /Am.* (**window**) **shades/** blind that rolls up and down over a window:

the lids would turn up with a sudden click like a roller blind. - G. Greene.

roller derby *Am.* a race between two teams of roller-skaters around a circular track.

roller towel *Br. /Am.* **towel roll/** a cloth that has its ends joined to form a circle so that a dry part can be pulled out for drying the hands on: *He turned to wipe them on the roller-towel* – M. Daly.

rollicking *Br.* col. an act of expressing angry disapproval of sb., **give** sb. **a rollicking.**

rolling/ get smth. **rolling** 1. *Am., Aus.* start a business. 2. *Am.* leave a place.

rollmop *Br., Aus.* piece of herring that has been rolled up and pickled.

roll neck, polo neck *Br. /esp. Am.* **turtle neck/** polo neck, round rolled collar, usu. woollen: *a mop of hair falling across his forehead, and wearing a baggy, roll-neck sweater* - J.P. Hogan.

roll of honour *Br., Aus. /Am., Aus.* **honor roll/** a list of the names of people who have earned praise, e.g. passing an examination, showing bravery in battle, etc.

roll-off *Am.* a play-off between bowlers.

roll-on *Br.* light and elastic corset.

roll-on roll-off (**ship**) *esp. Br., Aus.,* col. **ro-ro** (ship) allowing vehicles to drive on and off.

Rolls Royce *Br. /Am.* **Cadillac/** smth. of best quality.

roll-up 1. *Aus.* col. a meeting. 2. *Br. /esp. Am., Can., Aus.* **roll-your-own/** col. hand-rolled cigarette(s).

Rolodex *Am., Can.* tdmk. type of desktop card index.

rollway *Am.* road for rolling logs.

roly-poly (**pudding**) *Br.* pudding made of sheet pastry covered with jam or fruit, formed into a roll and steamed or baked.

roly-poly *Aus.* bushy tumbleweed.

romaine (**lettuce**) *esp. Am., Can., Aus. /Br.* **cos lettuce/** a lettuce with long leaves: *pushing a piece of romaine around her salad plate with her fork.* - F. Pascal.

Romeo *Am.* radio. letter R.

romp *Br.* humor. sexual activity, used esp. by newspapers.

romp home/in *Br.* esp. journalism. win the race easily.

romp through *Br.* col. succeed in doing or finishing smth. quickly and easily.

roneo *Br. /Am.* **mimeograph/** v. n. (make) a copy on a Roneo machine (tdmk.) which presses ink through the holes in a stencil.

roo *Aus.* col. kangaroo.

roof/ the roof caves in/falls in *Am.* col. (said if smth very bad happens to sb. suddenly).

roof/ hit the roof *Br.* col. become very angry.

roof/ lift the roof *Br.* make a loud noise.

roofer *Br.* col. bread-and-butter letter thanking sb. for their hospitality.

roof rack *Br. /Am.* **luggage rack/** metal frame fixed on top of a car and used for carrying bags, cases, etc.

rookie 1. *esp. Am., Aus.* col. person who is new and has no experience of an activity, esp. a new soldier or policeman: *He showed his identification to the young rookie behind the wheel.* - S. Sheldon., *he has already presided at a press conference for rookie pitcher* - Reader's Digest., *Miami's Sims provides the bottom line for rookies* - USA Today. 2. *Am.* a professional sportsman who has been competing in sports events for less than a year.

room 1. *Am.* have lodgings, have a room, or rooms: *Half of Harlem roomed* - Alex Haley., *He roomed with an Italian* - J. Dos Passos. 2. *esp. Am.* share a room with sb., esp. at college.

room/ local room *Am.* department of local news in the newspaper.

room and board *Am. /Br.* **room and lodging/**: *room and board together run twenty dollars a week.* - H.C. Whitford., R.J. Dixson.

roomage *Am.* place, square.

room clerk, (front) desk clerk *Am., Can. / Br.* **reception clerk, receptionist/** hotel receptionist: *The night room clerk was an old-timer* - Arthur Hailey.

roomer *esp. Am., Can. /Br.* **lodger/** person renting a room without board: *He's the only roomer I've got now* - R. Chandler.

roomette *Am.* 1. small sleeping compartment on a train. 2. small bedroom for letting.

rooming house *Am. /Br.* **lodging house/** house where rooms can be rented for a short time: *Then I got a cheaper room at Mrs. Fisher's rooming house* - Alex Haley., *It was a rooming house for university students* - E.L. Doctorow., *managing a rooming house to put yourself through college.* - B. Tillman.

rooming-in *Am.* arrangement in some hospitals where new babies stay with their mothers.

roommate 1. *Br.* a person not a member of one's family, with whom one shares a bedroom for a period of time, for example at school or on holiday. 2. *Am., Can.* also col. **roomie** */Br.* **flatmate/** a person with whom one shares a room, apartment or house for a certain period of time.

rooms *esp. Br.* obs. a rented set of rooms in a building, lodgings, esp. in a college or university.

room trader, floor trader *Am.* stock or commodity exchange broker.

rooster *esp. Am., Aus.* cock, */Br.* **cock/** a male domestic fowl: *My mother was the hen; my father was the rooster.* - J. Baez., *A rooster tried to eat him* - Guideposts.

rooster tail *Am., Can.* col. spray of water drawn up behind a speed boat or surfboard.

root *Aus., NZ.. Irish Eng.* sl. (have) a sexual intercourse.

root/ have a (good) root round *esp. Br.* col. search for smth. by moving other things around.

root for *esp. Am., Aus., Can. /Br.* **support/** give strong support to (sb. who is competing) **rooter/supporter** n.: *he couldn't get Dolly root for any team.* - T. Capote., *You had to root for him* - Reader's Digest.

root sb. **on** *Am., Can.* col. cheer or spur sb. on.

root beer *Am., Can.* beer drawn from extract of the roots and barks of certain plants: *Our ice-cream habit morphed into a root-beer-float addiction.* – Reader's Digest.

rootbound *Am. /Br.* **potbound/** (of a plant) that can't be grown because it doesn't have enough space for its roots.

root canal *Am., Can.* procedure of replacing infected pulp of a tooth by inert material through the use of a root canal.

root cellar *Am., Can.* domestic pit used for storage of root crops or other vegetables.

rooted *Aus.* sl. ruined.

rooter 1. *Br.* sl. energetic sex partner. 2. *Am., Can.* col. fan, enthusiast.

root-faced *Aus.* sl. humourless-looking.

rootin'-tootin' *esp. Am., Can.* col. brashly enthusiastic.

rootle *Br.* (esp. of a pig) search for food by digging with the nose.

rootle around/about *Br.* col. search for smth. by moving many things around.

rope *esp. Am.* catch (an animal) with a rope, lasso.

rope *Am.* sl. cigarette: *Get that rope out of here!* - R.A. Spears.

rope/ be at the end of one's **rope** *esp. Am.* have no more patience or strength left to deal with a problem.

rope/ be on the ropes *esp. Am.* be doing badly and likely to fail.

rope/ go piss up a rope! *Am.* sl. derog. stop bothering me.

ropeable *Aus., NZ.* col. very angry.
ropeline *Am.* sl. greeting and shaking hands with a group of well-wishers or onlookers.
rope-a-dope *Am.* col. boxing tactic of pretending to be trapped against the ropes goading an opponent to tire himself out through ineffectual punches.
ropeline *Am.* sl. giving handshakes to people meeting sb.
roper *Am.* cowboy.
rop(e)y *esp. Br., Aus.* col. 1. adj. in bad condition or of bad quality. 2. slightly ill.
rort *Aus.* col. 1. cheat, manipulate: *The Federal Government is to crack down on abuse of English language courses to rort the migrant selection system* - T. Thorne; n. 2. wild party.
rorty *Aus., Br.* col. wild, usu. drunk.
roscoe *Am.* col. obs. gun.
rosebud 1. *Am.* debutante. 2. *Br.* obs. young woman.
Rose City *Am.* Portland, Oregon.
rose-coloured spectacles, rose-tinted spectacles *Br., Aus.* thinking that smth. is more pleasant than it is, esp. in **look at/see/view a situation through rose-coloured/tinted spectacles.**
rosella *Aus.* a type of brightly-coloured parrot that lives mostly in Eastern Australia.
rose-tinted *esp. Br.* rose-coloured.
roster *esp. Am., Aus.* a list of people's names often with the jobs they have been given to do.
rot *Br.* 1. obs. col. foolish remarks or ideas, nonsense: *The blasted fool, why does he talk all the rot?* - W.S. Maugham., *Don't talk rot.* - K. Blair., *And what's all this rot about mad hoses?* - J.D. Carr. 2. **the rot** decline in standard.
rot/ stop the rot *Br.* prevent the situation from getting worse.
rot/ the rot sets in *Br.* the situation has changed to much worse.
rota *esp. Br. /Am., Aus.* **roster/** a list giving details of things which are to be done in a particular order, esp. by different people taking turns.
rotary, also **traffic circle** *Am., Can. /Br., Aus.* **roundabout, circus/** a circular road at a point where roads meet: *At large traffic circles, called rotaries, vehicles also proceed to the right* – State of Maine Motorist Handbook and Study Guide.
rotary scythe *Br.* lawn mower.
rotary tiller *Am. /Br.* **disc harrow/** machine with a set of discs on a frame which is rolled over the ground to break it up so that the crops can be planted.
rote *Am.* the noise of surf on the shore.

rotovator *Br.* tdmk. */Am., Can.* **rototiller/** a tool with blades that turn round to break up soil.
rotovate *Br.* rototill.
rotten/ fancy sb. **rotten** *Br.* humor. be extremely attractive to sb. in a sexual way.
rotter *esp. Br., Can.* obs. col. humor. worthless or dishonourable person: *A damned rotter like me.* - W.S. Maugham., *Her husband was a down-and-out rotter.* - A. Christie., *he had been a rotter at college* - E. Hemingway.
rough 1. *Br.* col. hard, severe. 2. *esp. Br.* violent and rough person.
rough/ a bit of rough *Br.* humor. sb. from a lower social class than you.
rough/ cut up rough *Br.* obs. become very angry.
rough/ in rough *Br.* doing smth. without paying attention to details or tidiness.
rough/ sleep rough *Br.* sleep outdoors because a person has no home.
rough/ take the rough with the smooth *Br., Aus.* accepting the unpleasant parts of situation as well as pleasant ones.
rough diamond *esp. Br., Aus. /Am., Aus.* **diamond in the rough/** col. person who has a kind and generous nature and/or great ability, but whose outward manner is rough: *The boss looks grouchy but he is a diamond in the rough.* - A. Makkai.
the rough end of the pineapple *Aus., NZ.* col. disadvantageous position.
rough house *esp. Am.* 1. (display) rough boisterous behaviour. 2. play roughly or fight; wrestle.
roughhouse *Br.* obs. noisy fight.
roughie 1. *Aus., NZ.* hooligan. 2. *Aus.* unfair or unreasonable act. 3. *Aus.* outsider in a horse race.
roughneck 1. *esp. Am., Aus.* col. rough bad-tempered person: *everyone from church people to roughnecks, had the greatest respect for his mother* - M. Jones, J. Chilton., *uncouth one, or roughneck, or dead-end kid.* - J.W. Houston, J.D. Houston., *he did everything in his power to be a "roughneck"* - Ebony. 2. *Am.* a man who does heavy unskilled work in an oil field: *That was were the drillers and the roughnecks lived.* - Reader's Digest.
rough paper *Br.* paper used to do incomplete or additional work.
rough-rider *Am., Can.* a person who rides horses a lot.
rough road/ take over a rough road *Am.* 1. give a scolding. 2. put sb. in a difficult situation.
rough side/ give sb. **the rough side/edge of** one's **tongue** *Br., Aus.* obs. speak angrily to sb.

rough stuff *Br.* col. violence, violent behaviour: *I'd have got that pro-Red so-and-so before he started any rough stuff.* - M.M. Kaye.

rough time/ give sb. **a rough time** *Br.* harshly criticise sb.

roughy *Aus.* col. rough person.

round *esp. Br., Aus. /Am.* **route/** a set of regular visits that a person makes to a number of people or places, esp. as a part of their job.

round (of sandwiches) *esp. Br.* a. sandwich made with two whole pieces of bread. b. one whole piece of bread.

round of toast *esp. Br.* one made of two pieces of bread that have been toasted.

round *esp. Br. /esp. Am.* **around/** prep., adv. on every side of smth.

round/ all round *esp. Br.* used to emphasize that smth. affects all parts of a situation or all members of a group.

round/ do the rounds *Br., Aus. /Am., Aus.* **make the rounds/** visit or telephone people or organisations.

round/ do the rounds/go the rounds *Br.* (of illness or a piece of news) be passed from one person to another.

round/ go round to the pub *Br.* and *Aus.* non-standard. drop in the pub.

round up *esp. Am.* col. give a short account of (smth. such as news): *And now here's Jim Brown to round up the main stories in today's news.* - Longman.

round about *esp. Br.* approximately

roundabout 1. *esp. Br., Aus., Can. /Am.* **traffic circle, rotary/** a central space at a road crossing which makes cars go in a circle round it and not straight across: *At the bottom there is a roundabout* - D. Lodge. 2. *Br., Aus. /Am.* **carousel,** *Br.* **giddy-go-round,** *esp. Am.* **merry-go-round/**: *Moira stopped the car and looked about her at the crowd, at the swings, at the whirling roundabouts* - A. Haley. 3. *Am.* short close-fitting jacket worn by men and boys: *he got me a coarse shirt and a roundabout* - M. Twain. 4. *Am.* a chair with a round back. 5. *Br., Aus. /Am.* **merry-go-round, carousel/** a circular platform in a playground that children sit or stand on and which people push to make it spin round.

roundball *Am.* col. basketball.

round bracket *Br. /esp. Am., Aus.* **parenthesis/** bracket.

rounder *Am.* col. 1. dissolute person: *he had chosen to be a rounder and a roué* - J. O'Hara. 2. person doing a beat of hospitals asking for medical help.

roundheel *Am., Can.* col. 1. person who is easily swayed. 2. promiscuous woman: *Her mother's such a compulsive roundheel, jumps anything with a - in pants.* - J. Kellerman

round-house *Am.* 1. /*Br.* **running shed/** a circular building for housing and repairing locomotives: *new engines keep rushing up from the roundhouse* - J. Kerouac. 2. col. punch done with a powerful circling, sweeping motion of the arm: *Damion's girl suddenly socked Damion on the jaw with a round-house right.* - J. Kerouac.

round robin *Am.* competition in which each player plays against each of the other players.

roundsman 1. *esp. Br. /Am., Can.* **route man/** man employed by a shop to go round delivering goods to people's houses. 2. *Am.* police inspector. 3. *Aus.* journalist covering a special subject.

round-trip (ticket) *esp. Am., Can. /Br.* **(day) return (trip), day ticket/** (of a ticket or its cost) for a round trip, usu. during one day: *I had only enough money for the round-trip train ticket.* - B.E. Olson.

roundup *Am.* bringing together cattle, horses, or other animals so that they can be counted and sold.

rouse *Aus.* col. get into a fit.

rouseabout *Aus., NZ.* (sheep) ranch handyman, unskilled labourer /also *Am., Aus.* **roustabout/**.

roust 1. *Am., Can.* col. disturb, harass or arrest: *those still outside were being rousted by the police on any pretext.* - E. Cleaver. 2. *Am.* make sb. move from a place.

roustabout *esp. Am., Can.* man who does heavy unskilled work, esp. at seaport or in an oilfield or in a circus: *patron of roustabouts, tavern brawlers and reformed drunkards.* - J.A. Michener., *Canadian English lacks the roustabout adventurousness of American English* - R. McRum, W. Cran, R. McNeil.

rout/ put sb. **to rout** *Br.* defeat sb. thoroughly.

rout cake *Br.* cake for routs.

route *Am.* 1. /*Br., Aus.* **round/** a delivery round (of a milkman, newspaper, etc.). 2. used in front of a number in the main roads between major cities.

rout seat *Br.* light chair rented for use at evening parties.

Rover *Br.* 1. senior boyscout (of 18 years old or older). 2. also **Rover ticket** unlimited travel ticket, general admission to certain sports events.

roving commission *Br.* authorization given to sb. conducting an enquiry to travel if necessary.

row *esp. Br., Aus.* 1. an angry argument, v. (**have a row, make/kick up a row**). 2. (have) a noisy public debate; v.

row/ be at the end of one's **row** *Am.* do everything possible.

row/ have a hard/tough row to hoe *Am., Can.* face a difficult problem.

row/ it doesn't amount to a row of beans / pins *Am.* it isn't worth anything.

row/ row up Salt river *Am.* sl. defeat (sb.) in an election.

row boat *esp. Am., Can. /Br.* **rowing boat/** rowing boat.

rowen *Am.* stubble field left unploughed for late grazing.

row house *Am., Can. /Br.* **terraced house**, a row of such houses is called a **terrace/** a house which is part of a terrace of houses: *she pointed out a handsome five-story row house* - New Yorker., *tapes rolled five miles away on the top floor of a row house* - G. O'Neill, D. Lehr., *He followed him along streets of shabby row houses* - E.L. Doctorow.

rowlock *Br. /Am.* **oarlock/** a pin of U-shaped rest on the side of a boat for holding an oar in place: *She fitted the two oars into the rowlocks* - I. Murdoch.

royal *esp. Am.* col. thorough, definitive: *That's something else that gives me a royal pain.* - J.D. Salinger.

royal icing *esp. Br.* hard white icing made from icing sugar and egg whites, used to decorate fruit cake.

the royal we *Br.* the use of we by King or Queen.

rozzer *Br.* col. a policeman.

RR *Am., Can.* 1. railroad. 2. rural route.

RRP *Br.* recommended retail price.

RTA *Br.* road traffic accident.

rub along *Br.* col. 1. (**by, on**) survive, get by. 2. (**with, together**) get along fine but without intense relationship.

rub out 1. *Br. /esp. Am.* **erase/** remove or be removed with a rubber (esp. pencil writing): *you can rub it out if you change your mind.* - Longman. 2. *esp. Am., Can.* col. v. murder: *Any Indian that gives resistance will be rubbed out.* - B.E. Olson. **rub-out** n.

rub sb./ each other up the wrong way *esp. Br., Aus. /Am.* **rub** sb./ **each other the wrong way/** col. annoy sb. by dealing with them without proper care or thought.

rub elbows with sb. *Am., Aus.* col. */esp. Br.* **rub shoulders with/** spend time with famous people.

rub/ not have two nickels/cents to rub together *Am. /Br.* **not have two pennies to rub together/** col. be completely without money.

rub/ the rub of the green *esp. Br.* esp. journalism. good luck, esp. in sports competition.

rubber 1. *esp. Br. /esp. Am., Can.* **eraser/** smth. that is used to erase marks from paper or blackboard. 2. *Am., Can. /Br.* galosh/: *Until I was fourteen I never had any rubbers or overshoes.* - D. Carnegie., *He wore stagged trousers and lumbermen's rubbers* - E. Hemingway. 3. *Am., Can.* col. condom: *Mike doesn't believe in using rubbers* - D. Divocky.

rubber/ lay rubber *Am., Can.* burn rubber, drive very quikly.

rubber/ where the rubber meets the road *Am.* a situation in which the practical use of smth. is tested.

rubberboot *Am. /Br.* **wellington (boot), wellie,** *esp. Br.* **gumboot/** one which keeps water from the feet and lower part of the legs: *We found a lot of rubber boots - all made in '37, '38.* - H. Smith.

rubbercheck *Am.* col. humor. one that can't be cashed, because not enough money is on deposit: *buying back rubber checks from grocers and five-and-dimes.* - T. Thompson.

Rubber City *Am.* sl. Akron, Ohio.

rubberneck *esp. Am., Can., Aus.* col. 1. look about or watch smth. with too much interest: *The dinner crowd comes to rubberneck and dance.* - New York. 2. go on a pleasure trip as one of a group with a guide, n.: *I didn't want a bunch of stupid rubbernecks looking at me when I was all gory.* - J.D. Salinger.

rubberneck car, auto, bus *Am.* tourist bus.

rubbing alcohol *Am. /Br.* **surgical spirits/**: *ablaze with lumps of sugar dipped in rubbing alcohol.* - Alcoholics Anonymous.

rubbish, refuse *esp. Br.* 1. */esp. Am., Can., Aus.* **garbage,** *Am., Can.* **trash,** *Can.* **refuse/** things or material of no use or value that will be or have been thrown away: *they didn't make rubbish like the French and Japanese* – R. Westall. 2. nonsense (**a load of** (**old**) **rubbish**). 3. book, film or smth. else of bad quality, adj.

rubbish *esp. Br., Aus.* col. criticise severely.

rubbish/ be rubbish at smth. *Br.* col. be not skilful or good at smth.

rubbish bin/bag *Br. /Am., Can.* **garbage can, trash can/** 1. a dustbin. 2. a container for rubbish: *elsewhere we stick these objects in rubber bags.* - B. Bryson.

rubbish can *Am.* litter bin.

rubbishy *esp. Br., Aus.* col. worthless and silly, trashy.
rub board *Am., Can.* washboard.
rubby *Can.* col. drunkard, who often drinks rubbing alcohol.
rube *Am., Can.* col. a country bumpkin: *We call this Rube trap.* - L. Waller., *He sounded the rube.* - G. O'Neill, D. Lehr.
Rube Goldberg *Am.* col. /*Br.* **Heath Robinson**/ a very complicated and not very practical plan or equipment.
ruby type print. 1. *Br.* /*Am.* **agate type**/. 2. *Am.* /*Br.* **brilliant**/.
ruck 1. *esp. Br.* (esp. in a game of rugby) a loose disordered group of players. 2. *Br.* col. brawl involving several people.
rucksack *esp. Br., Aus.* col. **ruckie** /*Am., Aus.* **pack, backpack**/ a bag you carry on your bag.
ruckus *esp. Am.* col. a noisy argument or a noisy confused situation, rumpus: *he remembered the ruckus over the sloppy autopsy of the doctor's first wife.* - T. Thompson., *she didn't make any ruckus about it.* - T. Capote., *but what's the ruckus about* - R.P. Warren.
ruction(s) *esp. Br., Aus.* col. noisy complaints and anger.
ruddy *Br., Aus., Can.* obs. col. euph. 1. adj. (used to add force, esp. to an expression of anger). 2. adj. adv. bloody, damn: *It's a ruddy must.* - J.P. Donleavy.
rude *esp. Br.* (esp. of health) vigorous and hearty.
rufus *Am.* sl. a country man.
rug 1. *esp. Am.* humor. toupee: *His forehead became so furrowed that his rug shifted.* - J. O'Brien, A. Kurins. 2. *esp. Br.* a type of blanket that's used esp. to sit on outdoors.
rug /travelling rug *Br.* rug that can be used outside, esp. one worn around shoulders.
ruggedized *esp. Am.* strengthened for a better resistance to wear, stress and abuse.
rugger *esp. Br.* 1. rugby: *we had rugger* – E. Townsend. 2. col. Rugby Union.
rug rat *Am., Can.* col. a child.
rulable *Am.* col. according to the rules.
rule/ Liverpool rules! *Br., Aus.* Liverpool is the best team!
rule/ run the rule over *Br.* examine cursorily for correctness or adequacy.
rum *Am.* any kind of alcoholic drink.
rum *Br.* col. obs. strange.
rum do *Br.* obs. a strange situation.
rumble *Am.* 1. /also *Am., Can.* **rumble seat**, *esp. Br.* **dicky**/: *I think ignition locks would go the way the rumble seat and the running board.* - K.

Vonnegut, Jr., *They'd stuffed her into the rumble seat of Big Eddie's old coupe* - T. Capote. 2. *esp. Am.* sl. a /*Br.* sl. **bundle**/ street fight: *There's been a rumble* - T. Thompson.
rumble *Am., Aus.* take part in a street fight.
rumble *Br.* col. find out or make known the true facts about (esp. a dishonest person or activity): *I let him know I'd rumbled* - Arthur Hailey.
rumbled/ be rumbled *Br.* col. (of concealed truth) be discovered at last.
rumble on (of an argument) *Br.* journalism. continue long after it should have been settled.
rumble strip *Br.* speed bump, a narrow raised part placed across a road to force traffic to move slowly.
rumdum *Am., Can.* col. a drunkard.
rumbustious *esp. Br.* /*esp. Am.* **rambunctious**/ col. noisy, lively and cheerful: *Rumbustious young Beatles* - P. Norman.
rummage *esp. Am.* /*Br.* **jumble**/ old clothes and other things found by rummaging about: *They ran teas and bake sales, sold rummage* - M. Torgov.
rummage sale *esp. Am. Can.* /*Br.* **jumble sale, boot sale**/ a sale of used articles as a way of collecting money for charity: *The set looks like a rummage sale in a czarist attic.* - Time.
rummy *Am.* sl. drunkard: *Do you think I'm a rummy, Bill.*- J. Dos Passos.
rump *Br.* the part of a group or government that remains after most of the other members have left.
rumpot *esp. Am., Can.* col. an alcoholic.
rumpus/ kick up a rumpus *Br.* make a complaint.
rumpus room *Am., Can., Aus., NZ.* a room, usu. below ground level in a house used for active games and parties: *One critic called it "depressing rumpus room decor".* - New York.
rumpy-pumpy *Br., Aus.* humor. sexual activity.
rum-runner *Am.* col. person or ship smuggling alcoholic liquor into a country.
run 1. *Am.* stream: *There was honeysuckle and laurel blooming in the runs* - J. Dos Passos. 2. *Am., Can.* /*Br.* **ladder**/ long thin upright fault in stockings: *May-be a last minute run in her stocking* - C. Woolrich. 3. *Aus.* farm: *This is the world of squatter, the run holder, the grazier* - P. Howard.
run/ dummy run *Br., Aus.* a dry run.
run 1. *esp. Am., Can.* (for) be or become a candidate (for election): *I decided to run for this office.* - E. Hautzig. 2. *esp. Am., Can.* (of a hole in a woven cloth) /*Br.* **ladder**/ v. spread.

3. *Am., Aus.* tease sb., molest. 4. *esp. Am., Can.* navigate (rapids or waterfall) in a boat. 5. *Aus., NZ.* provide pasture for (sheep or cattle); raise livestock. 6. *Am., Can.* cost sb. (a specific amount of money).

run /across, along, down (to), in(to), out, over/ *esp. Br.* ride sb. to a place: *I'll get the car and run you across to your mother's* - Longman.

run afoul *Am., Can.* come into conflict.

run against *esp. Am.* be a contester at the election: *At least you are running against some worthy opponents* - Longman.

run back *esp. Br.* bring sb. back in a car: *Jim will run you back.* - Longman.

run down *Br.* reduce (a business, organisation, etc.) in size, importance or to become reduced.

run down (to) *esp. Br.* give a lift to sb.: *Jim will run you down to the station after dinner.* - Longman.

run in *Am.* (usu. of words) (cause to) be joined and added: *I want you to run the next sentence in.* - Longman.

run in *Am.* /*Br.* **run on**/ print. instruction that two paragraphs should be set as one without the customary break.

run in *Br., Aus.* /*Am.* **break in**/ use a new engine carefully until it works normally.

run off *esp. Can.* (of ice and snow) melt.

run off at the mouth *Am., Can.* col. talk too much: *have them hear you running off at the mouth* - K. Vonnegut, Jr.

run out *esp. Am.* force sb. to leave: *the boys will run him out.* - Longman.

run out of steam *Br.* col. /*Am., Aus.* col. **run out of gas**/ lose interest or desire to do smth. suddenly.

run sb. out of town *esp. Am., Can.* force them to leave a place.

run out the clock *esp. Am.* keep control of the ball in defensive play until the end of the game: *The Fliers, with a 3-0 lead, are simply running out the clock* - Longman.

run to *esp. Br.* be or have enough to pay for smth. (not used in progressive forms).

run up *Br., Aus.* raise (a flag).

run with it *Am.* handle or develop smth.

run with the hare and hunt with the hounds *Br.* obs. try to support both sides in an argument or quarrel.

run/ get the run of the ball *Br.* be successful in a sports match.

run/ go on a…run *Am.* col. want to eat or drink smth. immediately.

run/ run an errand *Am.* go to a shop, office, etc. to buy or get smth. that one needs: *He runs errands with his parents* – Reader's Digest.

run/ run before you can walk *Br.* do smth. not knowing enough about it.

run/ run sb./smth. close *Br.* almost beat sb. in a contest.

run/ run scared *Am.* col. behave as if expecting failure: *the other party are running scared.* - Longman.

run/ (this one will) run and run *esp. Br.* humor. (of a problem, joke, etc.) (it will) last or be popular for a long time.

runabout 1. *esp. Br.* a small car used mainly for short journeys. 2. *Am., Can.* small motor boat.

run-abouts *Aus.* stray cattle.

runaway (as in bathtub) *Br.* drain.

rundown (of an industry or organisation) *esp. Br.* reduction in size or activity.

runes/ read the runes *Br.* try to look into the future.

run-in *esp. Br.* the period of time leading to an event.

runner *Br.* col. 1. freelance antique dealer. 2. contender for a job or position. 3. practical idea or suggestion.

runner/ do a runner *Br.* run away to escape difficulties, esp. to avoid paying money to sb. or meeting sb.

runner bean *esp. Br.* /*Am., Can.* **string bean,** *esp. Br.* **scarlet runner**/ a climbing bean with long green pods which are used as food: *The tall lines of runner-beans swayed dangerously* - I. Murdoch.

running/ be running on empty *Am., Aus.* have no ideas or not to be as effective as before: *Could be your testosterone is running on empty.* – Reader's Digest.

running/ do/make (all) the running *esp. Br.* 1. be the person who causes things to happen or develop. 2. compete in a race, election, etc.

running account *Br.* /*Am.* **checking account**/ current account in the bank.

running expenses *Br.* operating costs.

running jump/ go and take a running jump *esp. Br.* col. go away and stop being annoying.

running mate *esp. Am.* a person running for the post of vice-president in an election.

running order *Br.* order stipulating how and when each item will happen.

running pine *Am., Can.* clubmoss which propagates by means of runners.

running shed *Br.* /*Am.* **round-house**/ a roundhouse for locomotives.

running shoes *Am., Aus.* /*Br.* **trainers**/.
run-off 1. *esp. Am.* /*Br.* **runway**/ drain: *The launching was on Saunder's Creek, which had risen many feet above its banks in the spring runoff.* - S. North. 2. *NZ.* a plot of land where young animals are kept.
run-on sentence *esp. Am.* a sentence that has two main clauses without connecting words or correct punctuation.
runs *Br.* diarrhoea: *That stuff we ate gave me the runs.* - R.A. Spears.
runt *esp. Br.* col. a small person.
run-up 1. *Am.* a sudden increase: *The run-up in the stock market this year also is helping brokers* - USA Today., *the rapid speculative runup in gold prices.* - L. Burkett. 2. *esp. Br.* (the activities in) the period of time leading to an event: *Americans still resent France for defying the Bush Administration in the run-up to the Iraq invasion* – Reader's Digest.
runway *Br.* /*Am.* **run-off**/ drainage.
runway *Am.* long narrow part of a stage that stretches into the area where the audience sits.
rurban *Am.* adj. of area marked by both rural and urban features: *In truth, this is rurbania* - J. Harmer., R. Rossner.
rush 1. *Am.* col. lavish attention on, court. 2. *Am.* sl. persuade a student to join a fraternity (or sorority) by giving parties, having meetings, etc. n.: *She impersonated her sister during rush* - F. Pascal. 3. *Br.* col. obs. overcharge sb.
rush *Am.* urgent / **rush meeting, telegram,** etc.: *Where to go to do some rush reading?* - R.L. Stine.
rush/ be rushed off one's **feet** *esp. Br.* be so busy so that sb. doesn't have any time to stop or rest.
rush/ give sb. **a bum's rush** *Am.* sl. throw sb. out, esp. from a bar.
rush one's **fences** *Br.* act with undue haste.
Russian salad *Br.* salad of mixed diced vegetables with mayonnaise.
Russian thistle *Am., Can.* prickly tumbleweed.
rusk *esp. Br.* a hard dry biscuit for babies often made from a piece of bread baked hard.
rusticate *Br.* send (a student) away from university for a period as a punishment.
rustle 1. *Am.* col. do or get with energy or speed, hustle. 2. *esp. Am., Aus.* steal (cattle, esp. horses, etc.): *And we wouldn't dream of rustling any of you dogies off the local range.* - L. Waller., *Two cowpokes rustle cattle, then wonder what to do with them.* - USA Today; n. **rustling**.
rustler 1. *esp. Am.* cattle thief: *We foreclose on the ranch only after Paw has been shot by rustlers.* - L. Waller. 2. *Am.* sl. energetic person.

rutabaga *esp. Am., Can.* /*Br., Aus.* **swede**/, round yellow vegetable like a large turnip.
RV, Recreational Vehicle *Am., Can.* /*Br.* **camper**/ a recreation vehicle, a van equipped with beds and cooking equipment, where people mostly live while they are on holiday.
Rx *Am., Aus.* abbr. for medical prescription.
rye *esp. Am.* 1. also *Can.* rye whiskey: *he drank off half a tumbler of rye* - J. Dos Passos. 2. also *Can.* rye bread.

S

s 1. *esp. Am.* (forms an adverb to describe period of time) e.g. nights, etc. 2. *Br.* (forms a word for a shop or sb.'s home). e.g. *baker's*.
S *Am.* satisfactory mark for an exam or course.
sab *Br.* col. saboteur.
Sth *Br., Aus.* /*Am.* **So**/ South.
sabra *esp. Am.* col. a citizen of Israel who was born there: *Just a normal Israeli sabra.* - L. Uris.
sachem *Am., Can.* boss or leader.
sachet *Br.* /*Am.* **packet**/.
sack 1. *esp. Am.* col. a bag of strong paper for shopping. 2. *Br., Aus.* col. dismissal from one's job (**get/give the sack**): *The Principal had me up and threatened to hand me the immediate sack.* - A. Huxley. 3. *esp. Am., Can., Aus.* col. a bed, esp. as a place for sex: *Hell, honey, I'd rather be in the sack with my husband* - T. Thompson., *Openheim is already in the sack.* - J.D. Salinger., *jump in the sack with some good-looking woman.* - Time.
sack *Br., Aus.* col. /*esp. Am.* **fire**/ dismiss from the job.: *He had been sacked from the "Oh, Boy" television show.* - P. Norman., *Homosexuals would continue to be sacked.* - Bulletin., *Sacked my gamekeeper, ruddy chap tried to shoot me.* - J.P. Donleavy.
sack/ hop/jump in the sack *Am.* col. have sex without thinking seriously about one's sexual partners.
sack out *esp. Am., Can.* col. sleep, esp. for the night: *Where ya going? - To sack out.* - E. Segal., *he wasn't feeling well and was going to sack out for a while.* - D. Brenner.
sack up *Am.* col. gain (a profit): *How much did we sack up this time?* - Longman.
sack lunch *Am., Can.* col. /*Br.* **packed lunch**/.
sack suit *esp. Am., Can.* a suit with a straight loose-fitting jacket.

saddle *esp. Br.* meat cut from the back of deer or sheep / esp. in the phrs. **a saddle of mutton, lamb, venison**.

saddle horse, saddler *esp. Am., Can.* horse kept for riding only.

saddle shoes *Am.* low-cut, laced white shoes with a brown or black instep.

saddo *Br.* col. contemptible or inadequate person.

sad sack *Am.* sl. pessimist or ineptitude person: *a sad-sack former t'ai chi master* - New York.

sae *Br.* stamped addressed envelope /*Am.* **self-addressed envelope**/.

safari bed *Br.* /also *Br.* **camp bed,** *Am.* **cot**/ a light narrow bed which folds and is easily carried.

Safari park *esp. Br.* one in which wild animals are kept, so that one can drive around in a car and look at them.

safe *Am., Can.* col. condom.

safe/ be (as) safe as houses *Br., Aus.* be very safe.

safe/ a safe pair of hands *Br., Aus.* a person one can trust to do important job without mistakes.

safe/ play safe *Br.* not risk.

safebreaker *Br., Aus.* /*esp. Am.* **safecracker**/ person who opens safes by force to steal: *The subject is safecracking* - C. Hoover.

safety bonnet *Am.* crush-proof bonnet (in woodcutting machine).

safe heaven *Am.* safe place with official protection for refugees or other people.

safety island *Am.* /*Br.* **refuge**/ (traffic) island, place in the middle of the street where people can wait until it is safe to cross the rest of the way.

The Sage State /also **The Sagebrush** / *Am.* 1. joc. also **Silver State** Nevada. 2. Wyoming.

Sage States *Am.* Rocky mountains states.

said/ You said it! *Am.* col. I agree and understand how you feel.

sailboat *Am., Can.* /*esp. Br.* **sailing boat**/ single-masted sailboat for racing and pleasure trips.

sailing/ plain sailing *Br.* /*Am.* **clear, smooth** or **easy sailing**/ smth. easy to achieve.

sailor's yarn *Am.* a tall story, fantastic story.

sainted/ my sainted aunt *esp. Br.* obs. col. (used for expressing surprise).

Sakes alive. *Am.* Goodness Gracious.

salad *Am.* a soft mixture mainly of small pieces of a stated food, served cold and often between two pieces of bread / e.g. *chicken, tuna, egg salad.*

salad cream *esp. Br.* thick cream-coloured liquid, similar to mayonnaise but usu. sweeter, for putting on salads.

salary sheet *Br.* payroll.

sale/ as is sale *Am.* selling of goods without any guarantee.

sale/ on sale *Am., Can.* /*Br., Aus.* **in sale**/ sold at reduced prices.

sale/ on sale *esp. Br.* (of products) which can be bought in shops.

sale of work *Br.* a sale of home-made goods (such as knitwear, ornaments, furnishings, cakes and sweets) usu. organised by a group of women or by a school in aid of a particular charity.

sale or return *Br.* a system by which goods are supplied to shops which can return them if they are not sold within a certain period of time.

saleroom *esp. Br.* /*esp. Am.* **salesroom**/ place where auction sales are held.

the sales *Br.* time of the year when all the shops have a sale.

(sales)clerk, sales girl, (store)clerk *Am., Can.* /*Br.* **shop assistant,** *Br., Aus.* **sales assistant**/ person who serves customers in a shop: *Salesclerks in Soviet stores often set aside choice goods, sell them at inflated prices and pocket the profits.* - USA Today.

sales lady *Am.* sales woman: *"How would I know, why ask me?" the sales lady snaps.* - R.G. Kaiser.

salesman *Am.* /*Br.* obs. **commercial traveller, bag man,** *Am.* **travelling salesman,** *Am.* col. **drummer**/ sales person, esp. one using door-to-door tactics: *he rejoiced in the agreeable calling of a travelling salesman* – K. Chopin.

sales promotion *Am.* wide publicity of merchandise.

sales slip *Am.* receipt given in a shop: *Mrs. Smith checked the sales slip with what she bought.* - A. Makkai.

sales tax *Am., Can.* tax on things that a person buys in shops.

The Sallies *Aus.* /*Br.* **Sally Army,** col. **Sally**/ Salvation Army.

sallow *esp. Br.* willow tree.

salmon trout 1. *Br.* sea trout. 2. *Am., Can.* lake trout. 3. *Aus.* Australian trout.

saloon *Br.* 1. also **saloon car** /*Am.* **parlor-car**/ comfortable railway carriage esp. for sleeping in. 2. also **saloon (car)** /*Am., Aus., Can.* **sedan**/ a car for four to six passengers. 3. obs. also *Aus.* **saloon bar, lounge bar** a comfortable room in a pub: *they were alone in the saloon bar.* - G. Greene.

saloon *esp. Am., Can.* humor. a place where alcoholic drinks are sold and drunk.

saloon/ (drinking in) the last chance saloon *Br.* final opportunity to succeed.

saloon keeper, man, saloonist *Am., Can.* publican, bar keeper: *prosperous saloonkeeper can afford to give his boy an education out of his own pocket* – J. O'Hara.

salt/ below the salt *Br.* (of a person) of a lower rank.

salt/ take smth. **with a pinch of salt** *Br., Aus. /Am.* **take** smth. **with a grain of salt/** not completely believe smth.

salt-and-pepper *esp. Am.* of black and white pattern.

salt beef *Br.* corned beef.

salt-box *Am., Can.* old style two-storey house: *we were in front of a tiny saltbox.* - R. Crais.

saltcellar *esp. Br. /Am.* **salt shaker/** container for salt at meals usu. with holes in the top: *with a sticky salt shaker, salting and eating* - Guideposts., *But it also explained a lot of Bo's system of arranging salt-cellars* - J. Aldridge.

salt chuck *Am., Can.* col. inlet of the sea which flows into freshwater lakes or rivers.

Salt City *Am.* Syracuse, New York.

saltine *Am., Can.* thin crisp savoury biscuit sprinkled with salt.

salting *Br.* tract of land overflowed at times by the sea.

The Salt Lake State *Am.* Utah.

salt meadow *esp. Am., Can.* salt marsh.

salt truck, sander *Am. /Br.* **gritter/** little vehicle that puts salt on the roads in winter to make them less icy: *Snowplow salt trucks: Saltshakers.* – Reader's Digest.

saltwater taffy *Am.* one sold at resorts.

salute *Am.* firecracker, banger.

salutorian *Am.* college graduate speaking a salutory address in the beginning of the new year.

salutory *Am.* adj. pertaining to graduation address.

salutotary *Am., Can.* expressing salutations or welcome.

salvage yard *Am., Can.* place where disused machinery is broken up.

Salvo *Aus.* col. member of Salvation Army.

same/ on the same time *Br.* compared with the same period.

same/ sing from the same hymnsheet, songsheet *Br.* say the same things about subject in public.

same difference *esp. Am.* col. used to say that different actions, behaviour, etc. have the same result or effect.

samey *Br., Aus.* col. dull, because lacking variety.

samp *Am.* coarsely ground corn.

sanatorium *Br.* room or building for sick children in a boarding school.

sanatarium, sanitorium *Am.* sanatorium.

sanctuary *esp. Am.* the room where the main meetings for worship are held.

sand *esp. Am., Can.* col. courage.

sandbag (into) *Am., Can.* col. force (sb.) roughly to do smth.: *He had made his several millions by sandbagging everybody that stood in his way* - D. Hammet.

sandbox *Am. /Br., Aus.* **sandpit/** low box holding sand for children to play in: *a park that had lots of swings, a sandbox and a jungle gym* - D. Mortman.

sandfly *Aus.* black fly.

Sandgroper *Aus.* col. non-Aboriginal Western Australian.

Sand Hill State *Am.* Arizona.

sandhog *Am., Can.* col. labourer who works in a caisson in driving underwater tunnels: *Sandhogs working behind a hydrolic shield excavated riverbed silt* - E.L. Doctorow.

The Sand-lapper State *Am.* South Carolina.

sandlot *Am., Can.* 1. a piece of waste ground in a city where kids play. 2. sl. a rough or improvised baseball field: *Rogers Hornsby, who was National Leaugue baseball batting champion six times, first started playing on Texas sand lots.* - A. Makkai. 3. adj. (of games) between college teams.

sandpail *Am.* children's bucket.

sandpit *esp. Br., Aus. /esp. Am.* **sandbox/** hollow place in the ground containing sand for children to play in.

sands *Br.* an area of beach.

sandshoe *Br., Aus. /Am.* **canvass shoe,** *Br.* **plimsoll/** light cloth shoe as a plimsoll.

sandtrap *Am. /Br.* **bunker/** (in golf) place dug out and filled with sand, from which it is hard to hit the ball.

sandwich/ be the meat/filling in the sandwich *Br.* in a very awkward situation.

sandwich (cake) *Br.* cake of two flat parts with jam or cream between them.

sandwich bar *Br., Aus.* a small shop where you can buy sandwiches, esp. during your working day.

sandwich course *Br.* course of study in an industrial or professional subject at a college or university which includes periods of usu. three or six months spent working for a company: *The sandwich course is the main form of advanced full-time course* - J. Ruppeldtova.

sandwich generation *esp. Am.* generation of people in their 30-40s responsible for their own children and for the care of their ageing parents.

sandy beach *Br.* one that is made of sand not stones.

sandy blight *Aus.* type of eye illness.

sanguinary *Br.* (of language) rude and marked by curses.

sanitary fittings *Br. /Am., Aus.* **bathroom fittings/** toilet, bath, etc.

sanitary landfill *Am.* controlled tip, dump.

sanitary napkin, pad *Am., Can. /Br.* **sanitary towel,** *Aus., Am.* **sanitary pad/** tampon: *there was only the sanitary napkin, which she knew was already soaked with her own blood.* - R. Cook.

sanitation worker (**man**), **garbage collector, garbage man** *Am. /Br.* **dustman/** person employed to remove waste materials: *began to feel a little like a Fairmont Park sanitation man* - J. Patterson., *his income was less than that of a sanitation worker.* – N. Hentoff.

sansei *Am., Can.* Americans or Canadians whose grandparents were immigrants from Japan.

Santa's grotto *Br.* a place where children can receive present from a person dressed like Santa Clause.

sap 1. *esp. Am., Can.* col. stupid person likely to be tricked or treated unfairly: *You damn sap, she said angrily.* - R. Chandler. 2. *Am., Can. /Br.* **cosh/** heavy object made to hit with: *He could hear the crack of saps on men's skulls.* - J. Dos Passos., *I've been sapped by a hold-up man.* - R. Chandler.

sapid *esp. Am., Can.* having a strong, pleasant taste.

sapper 1. *Br.* col. army engineer or soldier whose job involves digging and building. 2. *Am.* soldier skilled in getting secretly through the defences around the enemy camp.

sappy *esp. Am., Can.* col. /*Br.* col. **soppy/** silly, foolish, sentimental: *there's something sappy about him.* - J. Dos Passos., *Sounds sappy, but could work* - Time.

Saran Wrap *Am.* tdmk /*Br.* **clingfilm/** thin transparent plastic used for wrapping food.

Saratoga trunk *Am.* large travelling trunk with a rounded top: *packed her Saratoga trunk and departed on a steamer* - I. Stone.

sarky *Br., Aus.* col. sarcastic: *the wood-pigeon sounded a bit sarky, but amused.* – R. Westall.

sarnie *Br.* col. /*Aus.* **sanger/** sandwich: *He said he didn't know people had ham sarnies in Germany.* - P. Norman.

SASE *Am., Can.* self-addressed stamped envelope.

sashay *esp. Am., Can.* col. (of a person) move or go, esp. smoothly or easily: *Magic simply sashayed past him and laid the ball in.* - Time., *I'm going to sashay down there* - A. Hitchcock Mystery Magazine.

Saskatchewan pheasant *Can.* magpie: *Two Saskatchewan pheasants flew out of the bush.* - W. Magnuson.

sass *Am., Can., Aus.* col. v. n. sauce, (make) a rude, disrespectful talk: *It includes everything from grades to ... the sassing of parents.* – J. Tesh.

sassy adj.: *I'll have none of your sass, Annette.* - Zacherlay., *Do not sass building manager.* - Reader's Digest.

sassy *Am., Can.* 1. (esp. of a child) cheeky and disrespectful. 2. col. (of people and things) smart, trendy, and streetwise. 3. (of a woman) behaving in a way that is intended to be attractive to men.

sastrugi *Can.* ridges of hard-packed snow, formed by the wind.

SAT 1. *Am.* **Scholastic Aptitude Test,** an examination which is often taken by students who wish to enter college or university as undergraduates: *strong scores (SATs above 1400) won't automatically get you into a top college.* – Reader'sDigest. 2. *Br.* **Standard Assessment Task,** a set of tasks given to 7, 14, and 17 year old schoolchildren in order to test their abilities.

satellite *Am.* suburb.

satisfy the examiners *Br.* reach the standard required to pass an exam.

satsuma *esp. Br.* a small seedless orange-like fruit: *there is a magic spell of cooking and satsumas in the air.* – S. Townsend.

satsuma plant *Aus.* a small dark-red round fruit with a sweet soft flesh and a large hard seed inside.

Saturday/ He'll arrive Saturday (*Br.* col. or *esp. Am., Can.*).

Saturday night special /also *esp. Am.* **handgun/** *esp. Am., Can.* col. pistol: *That's the tenth shooting done with a Saturday night special this week.* - R.A. Spears.

Saturday staff *Br.* people who work in a shop on Saturday.

sauce 1. *Am., Can.* stewed fruit or the like. 2. *Am.* sl. alcoholic liquor: *How are you and the sauce?* – J. O'Hara. 3. *Am., Can.* vegetable eaten with meat as a relish. 4. *Br.* col. obs. impertinence, cheek, esp. to the person whom one should respect.

sauce-boat *Br.* gravy boat.

sauced *esp. Am., Can.* col. drunk.

saucer/ be off one's **saucer** *Aus.* sl. go crazy.

saucy col. 1. *esp. Br.* (of pictures, jokes, etc.) sexually suggestive. 2. *esp. Am., Can.* bold, lively, and full of spirits. 3. *esp. Am., Can.* (of food) covered with sauce.

sauerbraten *esp. Am., Can.* over-roasted or pot-roasted beef marinated before cooking in vinegar with peppercorns, garlic, onions, and bay leaves.

sault *Can.* waterfalls.

sausage *Br.* a form of address, esp. to a child.

sausage/ not a sausage *Br.* col. obs. nothing at all.

sausage dog *Br.* col. dachshund, small dog with short legs and a long body: *the Garden is full of dogs of every kind - terriers, Pekes, German sausage dogs* - A. Christie.

sausage machine *Br.* dealing with all as if they were the same like products in a factory.

sausage roll *esp. Br., Aus.* a small amount of sausage meat which is covered with pastry and cooked.

sausages *Am. /esp. Br.* col. **bangers**, *Aus.* **snags, snaggles/**.

savage *Br.* col. very angry.

save/ save sb.'s **butt/ass** *esp. Am.* keep oneself from harm.

save/ save it *Am., Can.* col. derog. stop talking.

saveloy *Br.* a special kind of dry cooked sausage.

(regular) saver *esp. Br.* sb. who saves money in (a particular) a bank or building society.

saving account 1. *Br.* any of various kinds of bank accounts earning higher interest than a deposit account. 2. *Am. /esp. Br.* **deposit account/** any interest earning bank account: *Setting up separate saving accounts can, however, cause conflict and guilt.* - Reader's Digest., *she kept it in a passbook savings account in her local bank.* - L. Burkett.

savings and loan association *Am. /Br.* **building society/** business organisation into which people pay money in order to save it and gain interest and which lends money to people who want to buy houses: *He'd been working for one of those Texas savings and loan companies* - R.J. Randisi., M. Wallace.

savoury *esp. Br.* adj. (of a dish) having the taste of meat, cheese, vegetables, salt, etc. without sugar.

savoury *esp. Br.* dish of stimulating flavour served usu. at the end of dinner but sometimes as an appetiser before the meal.

savvy *esp. Am., Can.* col. 1. having a good understanding and practical knowledge of smth. 2. showing a lot of practical knowledge.

saw, sawed, sawn (*esp. Br.*), **sawed** (*esp. Am., Can.*) forms of verb **saw** (cut with a saw).

sawbones *esp. Am.* humor. a doctor or surgeon: *Not a single one of this springcrop of sawbones was mediocre.* - M. Torgov., *Our sawbones had a wooden leg.* - C. Nordhoff, J.N. Hall.

sawbuck *Am., Can.* 1. sawhorse. 2. sl. obs. a ten-dollar bill: *A cop will take a sawbuck bribe and run like a thief* - L. Waller.

sawed off *Am., Can.* short of stature.

sawney *esp. Br.* col. n. adj. fool(ish).

sawn-off shotgun *Br., Aus. /Am.* **sawed-off shotgun/** a shotgun with a short barrel often carried as a weapon by criminals: *A sawed-off shotgun lay under a towel.* - R. Chandler.

saw-off *Can.* sl. swapping of concessions, compromise.

sawyer *Am.* a tree fast in the bed of a stream.

say *Am.* col. excl. (used for expressing surprise or a sudden idea and also used to attract the attention of a stranger): *Say, you can save the Nav dope, pal.* - B. Tillman.

say/ I say 1. *Br.* col. */Am., Can.* col. **say/** excl. used for calling sb.'s attention or expressing surprise. 2. *Br. /Am.* **say/** obs. or humor. (a rather weak expression of interest, anger, etc.).

say/ have the say *Am.* give orders.

say/ not to say *esp. Br.* used to show that you could have used a stronger word to descibe smth.

say/ not say a boo to a goose *Br., Aus. /Am.* **not say boo to a goose/** be very shy and nervous.

say/ You said it *esp. Am.* You're right, I agree.

say fairer (**than that**) *Br.* col. make a more generous or reasonable statement or offer.

Says I (**he, she,** etc.) *esp. Br.* col. used after direct speech.

say what you like *esp. Br.* used when giving opinion that one is sure is correct, even if the other person one talks to disagrees.

sayonara *esp. Am.* col. goodbye.

S.B. / Sc.B. *Am. /Br.* **BS./** Bachelor of Science.

SBA *Am.* Small Business Administration.

S-bend *Br. /Am.* **S-curve/** bend in a road in the shape of S that can be dangerous to drivers.

scab *Am., Aus.* derog. sl. work as a strike-breaker: *Oliver's band was out of union and was scabbing* - M. Jones, J. Chilton.

scabby 1. *esp. Irish Eng.* col. loathsome. 2. *Br.* (used by children) nasty and unpleasant.

scads (of) *esp. Am., Aus., Can.* col. large numbers or amounts: *There are scads of good restaurants within walking distance of the Empire.* - A. Frommer., *I told him I had scads of it.* - E. Hemingway.

scaf *Am.* col. self-centred-altruism fad, popular product which apart from its attractiveness purports to have beneficial effect on the user.

scaffold *Am.* /*Br.* **cradle**/ structure that can be moved up and down to help people work on high buildings.

scaffolder *Br.* person who erects scaffolding.

scalawag *esp. Am.* /*esp. esp. Br.* **scallywag**/ humor. sb. esp. a child who causes trouble but not in a serious way.

scale 1. *Br.* a schedule of professional fees laid down by statute or by professional body. 2. *esp. Am.* /*Br.* **scales**/ balance: *She handed a spring scale to Karl.* - McGraw-Hill English, 1990. 3. *Am., Can.* the amount of timber that will be produced from a log or uncut tree. 4. *Am.* hard grey chemical substance that forms on the inside of water pipes and containers. 5. *Am.* payment benefits from trade union. 6. *Am.* standard work for hour pay: *I would be willing to work for scale* – J. O'Hara.

scale back *esp. Am.* /*Br.* **scale down**/ (of an organisation, plan, etc.) make it smaller so that it operates at a lower level.

scaler *Aus.* passenger trying to get a ride without a ticket.

scallion, green onion *Am.* and old use /*Br.* **spring onion**/ one with bulb and long green stems, usu. eaten raw: *stalks of scallion fenced everything in.* - M. Puzo.

scalp *esp. Am., Can., Aus.* col. /*Br* **tout**. / buy and then resell at very high prices or profit: *We still have some savings bank to scalp.* - L. Waller.

scalper *Am., Can., Aus.* /*Br.* **tout**/ ticket agent who charges exorbitant prices: *She thereupon gave away her ticket to the fight in Madrid, paid a scalper's price for a ticket to the new fight* - J.A. Michener.

scam *Am.* sl. cheat, perpetrate a fraud: *As a kid I used to...scam my way into NBC.* - New York.

scampi *Br.* (a dish made from) large prawns (covered in batter and cooked in oil): *The menu had plunged downmarket to the scampi, chips and peas level* - B. Bryson.

scandal sheet *Am., Aus.* col. cheap tabloid: *scandal sheets teased with outrageous headlines* - D. Mortman.

scant *esp. Am., Can.* provide grudgingly or in insufficient amounts.

scar *Br.* cliff on the side of a mountain.

scarce / **scarce as a rocking-horse manure** *Aus.* /*Am., Aus.* **be as scarce as hen's teeth**/ very scarce, rare.

scare/ throw a scare (into) *Am.* frighten sb.

scare smth. **up (from)** *esp. Am., Can.* col. make from things that are hard to find or not easy to use: *hoping to scare up a word of fact that would give him a start.* - R. Stout., *I'm trying to scare up a laundryman* - J. London.

scare/ be scared shit *Am.* taboo. sl. be very frightened.

scared/ run scared *esp. Am.* be worried that you're going to be defeated.

scarf *Am.* narrow decorative cloth cover for a table or dresser top.

scarf (down, up) *Am., Can.* col. /*Br.* col. **scoff**/ eat eagerly and quickly.

scarlet runner *esp. Br.* /also *Br.* **runner bean**, *Am.* **string bean**/ a climbing plant with long green pods.

scarper *Br., Aus.* col. run away.

scatter cushions *Br., Aus.* cushions designed to be moved around.

scattergun *Am.* col. shotgun.

scattiness *esp. Br.* flightiness.

scatty *esp. Br., Aus.* col. slightly mad or scatter-brained: *She developed a soft spot for John Lennon in whom she recognised much of her own scatty humour.* - P. Norman., *Another of your scatty ideas?* - New Idea., *they're nearly all scatty.* - A. Christie.

scavenger *esp. Br.* person employed to remove dirt and refuse from streets.

scene/ bad scene *Am.* col. different or unpleasant situation.

scene/ make the scene *Am.* come on the scene, appear, arrive.

scene-of-crime *Br.* of civilian branch of the police force, concerned with the collection of forensic evidence.

scene-shifter *esp. Br.* person who moves the scenery on a stage between the scenes of a play.

scenester *esp. Am., Can.* col. person associated with a particular fashionable cultural scene.

scenic railway, also **switchback** *Br.* roller coaster.

scent *esp. Br.* perfume: *a heady waft of glamour and exceedingly expensive scent* - M.M. Kaye.

scent spray *Br.* atomiser.

sceptic *Br.* /*Am.* **skeptic**/.

schedule *esp. Am. /esp. Br., Aus.* **timetable/** a timetable of trains, buses, airlines, etc.

scheme 1. *esp. Br.* a formal, official or business plan. 2. *Can.* misfortune.

scheme of arrangement *Br.* reorganisation plan (of a corporation in financial difficulties).

s(c)hemozzle *esp. Br.* sl. 1. a mix-up. 2. a fight: *just for the fun of making a schemozzle.* - A. Christie.

schizzed-out *Am.* sl. 1. uncontrolled. 2. drunk.

schlep(p) *esp. Am., Can., Aus.* col. 1. carry or drag (esp. smth. heavy which makes one tired): *I don't want to schlep boxes* - K. Lipper. 2. (around) spend a lot of time and effort in getting from one place to another: *You're going to schlep a bag of rocks all the way to Hong Kong?* - D. Brenner., *Why should I schlepp out my guts.* - S. Bellow.

schlepper *Am., Can.* col. annoying person who always wants a bargain or a favour: *Schleppers - the Jewish word for people who lag behind, who have no sense of style, who are losers - is the designation he gave to the poor.* - M. Torgov.

schlock *esp. Am., Can.* col. derog. low quality goods.

schlong *Am.* sl. penis.

schlockmeister *Am., Can.* col. successful maker or seller of inferior products (**schlock**): *Sure, there are still shows specializing in shock, schlock, sex* - Kansas City Star.

schlub *Am.* col. talantless, unattractive, or boorish person.

schmaltzy *esp. Am.* col. (of books, films, etc.) dealing with emotions such as love and sadness in a way that seems silly and insincere: *orchestrating a succession of schmaltzy stories* – A. Summers, R. Swan.

schmatte *Am.* col. a shabby or unstylish garment: *Those whores on Spadina, I can see them now, dragging out some lousy shmater after another* - M. Torgov., *more or less unusable schmattege - granny-pants with a waist high enough to choke you* - New York.

schmear *Am.* col. 1. a bribe. 2. ingratiate oneself with sb. 3. **the whole schmear** everything.

schmeck *Am.* sl. sniff or taste.

schmendric *Am.* sl. fool: *Tell the schmendric to drop dead.* - R.A. Spears.

schmo *Am., Can.* col. a fool.

schmooze *esp. Am., Can., Aus.* sl. converse, esp. lengthily and cosily: *They don't know how to schmooze* - Esquire., *How often do I get to schmooze with the FBI?* - J. O'Brien, A. Kurins.

schmuck *Am., Can., Aus.* col. a fool: *Listen, schmuck, this mixer's free of charge.* - E. Segal., *She was a Jewish girl, from Brooklyn and made no bones about it, larding her conversation with words like schmeer and schmuck and nebbish.* - I. Shaw., *I look like a total schmuck!* - D. Brenner.

schnook *Am.* col. a sucker or ineffectual person: *Stay out in the rain, schnook.* - J. O'Brien, A. Kurins., *Not the smaller schnooks who went to Mac for political influence.* - L. Waller., *that poor, heartbroken schnook signed up for the RAF* - D. Mortman.

schnorkel *Aus.* snorkel.

schnorrer *esp. Am., Can.* col. 1. a beggar. 2. person who habitually haggles, niggard: *Did someone call me schnorrer?* - New York.

schnozz(le) *Am., Can.* col. humor. nose: *Look at that schnozz on that guy!* - R.A. Spears.

scholastic *Am.* relating to secondary school.

scholer *Br.* obs. a child in a school.

school 1. *Am., Can.* university, any educational institution; in Britain mainly primary and secondary levels institutions: *I'm going to send my husband to school and make him a CPA.* - R. Stout. / **learn at school** *esp. Am.* col. study at the university or college. 2. *Br.* group of people gambling together.

school/ at school *Br.* attending a school, rather than college or university.

school/ in school *Am.* attending a school or university as opposed to having a work: *her daughter was happy in school* – Reader's Digest.

school/ teach school *Am.* teach in a school.

(school) auditorium *Am. /Br.* **assembly hall/**.

school board *Am., Can.* local board or authority responsible for provision and maintenance of schools.

schoolbook *esp. Am.* oversimplified.

schoolboy 1. *esp. Br.* a boy who goes to school. 2. adj. (of jokes) silly and rude but not offensive.

school district *Am., Can. /Br.* **LEA (Local Education Authority/** unit for the local administration of schools.

school for academically gifted students *Am. / Br.* **specialised school/**.

schooler 1. *esp. Am.* a person attending a special school. 2. *Aus.* school teacher or pupil.

schoolfriend *esp. Br.* friend that goes to the same school as you.

schoolgirl *esp. Br.* a girl who goes to school.

schoolhouse *Am.* a small building used as a school.

schoolie *Aus.* col. teacher.

school land *Am.* land set apart for the maintenance of school.

school-leaver *Br., Aus.* student who has just left or is about to leave school after completing a course of study: *school-leavers are despairing all over the country.* – S. Townsend; adj., n. **school-leaving (age)**.

schoolman *Am.* school teacher.

schoolmarm *esp. Am.* a woman teacher in school: *a busful of baptist schoolmarms from Texas* - New York.

schoolmaster, schoolmistress *esp. Br.* 1. a teacher at public school. 2. obs. a schoolteacher: *Paid our schoolmaster to give him special coaching.* - A. Huxley., *The schoolmaster was at his door* - G. Greene., *Then restlessly he went back to schoolmastering.* - I. Murdoch.

School of the Air *Aus.* Public Radio Network catering for farmers having short wave radios.

(school) report *Br. /Am.* **report card/** written statement by teacher about a child's work.

school section *Can.* land given for the support of public schools.

school superintendent; (the) Chief State school officer *Am. /Br.* **the Chief of Education; the Director of Education/**.

schoolyard *esp. Am.* outside area next to school where children can play games or sport.

school year *Am. /Br.* **academic year/**.

schooner 1. *esp. Br.* large tall drinking glass, esp. for sherry or port. 2. *Am., Can., Aus.* a tall beer glass.

s(c)htick *Am.* sl. 1. small theatrical role: *His schtick was a trained dog-and-cat act.* - R.A. Spears. . 2. typical personal feature. 3. clever device: *When Woody is playing Jazz, he's all stick and no shtick.* - Time., *Let's act out all the shtick* - S. Bellow., *this forum is a celebration of shtick.* - Time.

science/ blind sb. **with science** *Br., Aus.* confuse sb. by using technical language.

science park *esp. Br.* an area often started by a college or university where companies involved in science work or new technology are based.

scoff *esp. Br.* col. **/Am. scarf/** eat eagerly and fast: *She scoffed three hamburgers and a large order of fries.* - R.A. Spears.

scofflaw *Am., Can.* col. person who regularly flouts the law: *scrounging through all your beat baggage for signs of the scorpion of scofflaw.* - J. Kerouac.

scoop/ get the scoop (on sb./smth.**)** *esp. Am., Can.* col. get some special information about smth., also **what's the scoop (on** sb./smth.**):** *And he was more fascinated by ideas than by scoops* – N. Hentoff.

scoop the pool *Br., Aus.* col. win all the prizes.

scoot *Am.* slide while sitting.

scope (out) *Am., Can.* col. look over, check out: *Cruise had the chance to scope out his competition.* - Time., *He scoped out the situation from the air* - W. Jack, B. Laursen

scorch (round a place) *Br.* col. move round it very quickly, either in a car or on foot.

scorcher *Br.* remarkable or extreme example of smth.

score 1. *Am.* col. berate. 2. *Br.* keep score, record the points won. 3. *Am., Aus.* obtain smth. 4. *Am.* the number of points a student has earned for correct answers in a test.

score/on the score of *Br.* because of.

score off *Br.* col. outdo or humiliate, esp. in an argument.

scorecard *Am.* a system or procedure that is used for checking or testing smth.

scorer *esp. Am.* also *Am.* **score keeper** a person who scores a point or goal in a game.

Scotch *Am.* sl. frugal.

Scotch bonnet *Am., Can.* chilli pepper of the hottest variety.

Scotch egg *Br.* boiled egg cooked inside a covering of sausage meat.

Scotch mist *Am.* sl. 1. phantom. 2. downpour.

Scotch mist/ What's that, Scotch mist? *Br.* col. Don't you see? It's right before you.

Scotch pancake, drop scone, griddle cake *Br. / Am.* **slapjack/** pancake.

Scotch tape *esp. Am., Can., Aus.* tdmk. **/Br. sellotape,** *Aus., Br.* **sticky tape,** *Aus.* **durex/** sticky thin clear material used for sticking paper, mending light objects, etc.: *Burleton also produced a roll of Scotch tape* - Reader's Digest.

Scotch whiskey *esp. Am. /Br.* **whiskey/**.

Scotch woodcock *Br.* scrambled eggs /*Br.* sometimes called **buttered eggs/** on toast first spread with anchovy paste.

Scotland Yard *Br.* col. the part of London police that deals with serious crimes, or their main office.

scouring pad *Am., Aus.* scourer, a metal or stiff plastic object used to clean dirt off the surfaces.

Scouse *Br.* sl. of or from Liverpool.

scout 1. also **girl scout** *Am.* guide. /*Br.* **girl guide/**. 2. *Am.* col. fellow, guy. 3. *Br.* col. (round) a quick search of an area.

scout *Am.* find out information about the abilities of sports players, musicians, etc.

scout car *esp. Am.* fast armoured vehicle used for military reconnaissance and liason.
scow *esp. Am.* flat-bottomed boat used to carry cargo to and from ships in harbour.
scrag 1. *esp. Br.* col. manhandle roughly. 2. *Am.* col. a. kill, destroy: *A truck almost scragged Max.* - R.A. Spears. b. have sex with.
scrag (end) *Br.* inferior end of a neck of mutton.
scraggly *esp. Am., Can., Aus.* col. (of things that grow) poor and uneven-looking, badly grown: *The distant white cottage over scraggly fields.* - J.P. Donleavy., *He had a little black scraggly beard* - I. Shaw., *The trench works ran past a few scraggly trees.* - L. Uris.
scrambler *Br.* motorcycle for riding over rough and hilly ground.
scran *Aus.* food.
scrape *esp. Am.* only just succeed in passing an exam or dealing with a difficult situation.
scrape *Br.* thinly applied layer of butter or margarine on bread.
scrape/ scrape a living *Br.* earn enough money just for food, clothing and housing.
scraperboard *Br.* board with blackened surface which can be scraped off for making white line drawings.
scrap merchant *Br.* a person who buys and sells scrap metal.
scrap paper *esp. Br. /Am.* usu. **scratch paper/** paper, esp. in single sheets already used on one side, which may be used for unimportant notes: *The room was a jumble of old books, mostly outdated PDRs (Physician's Desk Reference), scratch paper, dirty coffee cups* - R. Cook., *they have been tearing and folding scrap paper* - New York.
scrapple *Am.* seasoned mush of meat scraps and cornmeal served spiced and fried: *he went into the kitchen and cooked himself a skilletful of hog-liver scrapple.* – E. Caldwell.
scrappy *Am., Can.* col. 1. liking to fight: *He had become Little Caesar, a short scrappy satrap* - G. O'Neill, D. Lehr. 2. determined, gutsy: *But they are on occasion scrappy in an intramural sort of way* - T. Thompson., *he is impressed with the scrappy opponent* - McLean's.
scrapyard *Br.* place where scrap is collected before being discarded, reused, or recycled
scratch *esp. Am., Can.* sl. money: *Then he called up Johnny Collins, told him to get the scratch from the valet* - M. Jones, J. Chilton.
scratch *Am.* col. decide not to do smth.
scratch/ not (come) up to scratch *Br., Aus.* not be of an acceptable standard or quality; also **bring** sb./smth. **up to the scratch.**

scratch coat *Am., Can.* rough coat of plaster scratched before it's dry to ensure adherence of the next layer.
(pork) scratchings *Br. /Am.* **pork rinds/** crisp pieces of pork fat left after rendering lard, eaten as a snack.
scratch pad, also rare **scratch block** *esp. Am., Can., Aus. /Br.* **scribbling block/** small pile of loosely joined sheets: *Tageka was seating on the cobbler's bench, making neat ideographs with a brush and ink on a scratch pad.* - I. Shaw., *Dietrich scribbled hastily on a scratch pad.* - R. Cox., *the ministers covered their scratch pads with abstract doodles* - R.K. Mussle.
scratch paper *Am. /esp. Br.* **scrap paper/**.
scratch sheet *Am.* sl. daily horse-racing newsletter at the racetrack: *Even the cost of a scratch sheet is going up* - R.A. Spears.
scratchy writing *esp. Br.* uneven writing.
screamer *Am.* sensational headline: *I never read screamers.* - R.A. Spears.
screaming habdabs *Br.* sl. hysteria.
screaming meemies *Am.* sl. jitters: *They sent Max away with the screaming-meemies.* - R.A. Spears.
screen *Br. /Am.* **shield/** (use) a protective frame.
screen *esp. Am.* smth. intended to hide smth. bad going on.
screen door *Am., Aus.* door before the main one which allows air but not insects to move through.
screen washer /or **wiper/** *Br.* car washer /also **windscreen washer** (*Br.*), (*Am.*) **windshield washer/**.
screen *Br. /Am.* **shield/** protect a wire with a screen.
screw *Br.* 1. obs. small twisted paper packet: *eating prawns out of screws of paper.* - L. Lee. 2. col. obs. pay, wages. 3. col. a weak old horse: *She's the worst screw in the place now.* - J. Herriot. 4. obs. scrooge, miser. 5. sl. prison warder: *Support the screws* - Old Bill out. - T. Thorne., *Your Aunt Susan is one of the best screws in here* – S. Townsend.
screw *Am.* sl. leave hastily.
screw around *Am.* sl. waste time: *I want to screw around for a few years, Dad.* - L. Uris.
screw smth. **out of** sb. *Br.* col. obtain it by force or threats.
screw up *esp. Am., Can.* col. completely mismanage or mishandle.
screwball 1. *esp. Am., Can.* col. person whose ideas or actions seem wild or mad, usu. in a harmless way: *I didn't want to look like a screwball or something.* - J.D. Salinger., *at Princeton there*

had been professors who were just as screwball. - J. O'Hara., *he is a bluffer and a screwball, a kind of freak* - S. Bellow. 2. *Am., Can.* col. (in baseball) ball which is thrown to a batter and spins in the opposite direction to a curve: *Don't swing at the fastballs, the screwballs* - K. Lipper.

screwed *esp. Br.* sl. drunk: *She spends a lot of time screwed.* - R.A. Spears.

screw-up *Am.* sl. 1. also *Can., Aus.* foul-up, a state of confusion: *It was just a screw-up all around.* - T. Thompson., *the screw-up was the FBI's own fault.* - G. O'Neill, D. Lehr. 2. a chronic bungler: *a perpetual screwup who storms into his ex-girlfriend's wedding, begs her to take him back* - New York.

screwy *esp. Am., Can.* col. rather odd and strange.

scribbling block or **pad** *Br. /Am., Can.* **scratch pad, scratch block/**: *I bought myself a tartan scribbling pad.* – S. Townsend.

scribbly gum *Aus.* eucalyptus tree with bark marked by irregular markings by insects.

scribe *Am.* col. writer.

scrimshank *Br.* col. rare. try to avoid doing the job.

(land) scrip *Am., Can.* document entitling the holder to obtain a certain plot of public land.

script (usu. pl.) *Br., Aus.* piece of writing done by a student in an examination to be read and given mark by a teacher.

scrod *Am., Can.* young cod.

scroggin *NZ.* mixture of dried fruit, nuts and other food eaten as a snack by hikers.

scrounge/ on the scrounge *Br.* col. begging and stealing.

scrub *Am., Can.* 1. scrubby. 2. player not belonging to the first league: *They had a club and a scrub football team.* - C. McCullers. 3. domestic animal of inferior brand. 4. team game played by children in a public area.

scrub *Aus.* tech. illness caused by contact with some shrubs.

scrub/ give smth. **a scrub** *esp. Br.* clean smth. by rubbing it hard.

scrub round *Br.* col. (the rules, etc.) avoid smth. or take no notice of smth.

scrub (country), bush *Aus.* bush, inner wild part of the country.

scrub bashing *Aus.* clearing of the scrub to make a farmfield.

scrubber 1. *Br.* derog. sl. woman who has sex with many partners. 2. *Br.* derog. sl. female prostitute: *The Beatles, in their turn were flattered by the interest of this gentle, beautiful ghost-eyed girl, so different from the usual freiheit scrubber.* - P. Norman., *they can be ribald courtesans or very desperate children that English stars contemptuously call "scrubbers" or "bad molls".* - L. Roxon. 3. *Aus., NZ.* col. also **scrub cattle** cattle fed in a scrub, esp. bullock.

scrubbing brush *esp. Br. /Am.* **scrub brush/** stiff brush for heavy cleaning jobs like scrubbing floors.

scrub board, base(board, mopboard *Am. /Br.* **skirting board/**.

scrub dashing *Aus.* forced travels through scrub.

scrubland *Aus.* forest region.

scrub suit *Am., Can.* suit worn by surgeons and other theatre staff during an operation.

scrub woman *Am. /esp. Br.* obs. **charwoman** or **charlady/** woman who works as a cleaner in a house, office, etc.: *the old scrubwoman opened the door to make the bed* - J. Dos Passos.

scruff *Br.* col. dirty and untidy person: *The four still slightly sceptical and uneasy Liverpool scruffs* - P. Norman., *On a day off she's a self-confessed scruff* - New Idea.

scrum *Br.* col. disorderly crowd of people pushing each other trying to get smth. or a group of things.

scrummy *Br.* col. delicious.

scrump *Br.* col. obs. steal fruit (esp. apples) from the trees it is growing on.

scrumpy *Br.* col. a strong kind of cider.

scrunch up (one's shoulders) *esp. Am.* bring them close together, esp. trying to get through the gap.

scrutineer *Br., Aus.* an official examiner or counter of votes in an election.

scuffs *Am.* flat-soled house slippers without quarter or counter.

scug *Br.* sl. bad sport, ill-favoured, untalented and unpopular schoolboy.

sculet *Can.* large group of fish which migrated from the open sea to inshore waters.

scumbag *esp. Am., Can., Aus.* sl. derog. 1. condom. 2. despicable person: *enough anyhow to hire a scumbag lawyer to get the transfer reversed!* - K. Ablow.

scunge *Aus., NZ.* col. disagreeable person.

scungy *Aus., NZ.* col. dirty.

scupper *esp. Br.* 1. sink (one's own ship) intentionally. 2. (usu. pass.) wreck or ruin (a plan, chance, etc.): *hellium balloon floats away... scuppering an attempt to set a skydiving record.* – National Post.

S-curve *Am. /Br.* **S-bend/**.

scut (**work**) *Am*. sl. menial work such as would be given to a novice: *You'll be paged for all the blood work and other fascinating scut.* - R. Cook.

scuttle *esp. Br.* **coal scuttle**

scuttlebutt *esp. Am.* col. rumour, gossip: *the scuttlebutt may have been inspired by the imaginative Wurtzel herself.* - New York.

scutwork *esp. Am.* col. tedious, manual job.

scuzz *esp. Am., Can.* col. despicable person.

scuzzball *Am., Can.* col. unpleasant or disgusting person /also **scuzzy**/: *I feel real bad about abusing your constitutional rights, scuzzball!* - Kansas City Star., *I was starving in the scuzzy part of Hollywood* – S. Lawrence.

sea *esp. Br.* /*esp. Am.* **ocean**/.

sea/ **be all at sea** *Br., Aus.* completely confused.

seabag *esp. Am., Can.* sailor's travelling bag or trunk.

the seals *Br.* the symbols of public office.

sea puss *Am.* a swirl undertow.

sea-run *Am., Can.* (of migratory fish) having returned to the sea after spawning.

seaside *esp. Br.* the edge of the sea esp. as a holiday place: *it had been mostly summer seaside work* - J. Fowles.

season *Br., Aus.* /*Am., Aus.* **festival**/ a period of time of planned entertainment, esp. when a set of programmes, plays or musical events are broadcast or performed.

season/ in the off season *Am.* (esp. of holiday business) at the least busiest time of the year.

season (ticket) *Br., Aus.* /*Am.* **commuter's, commutation ticket**/ season ticket.

season/ the holiday season *Am.* Thanksgiving, Christmas and New Year's.

season/ tourist season *Am.* /*Br.* **holiday season**/ the season when people come to a particular place for a holiday.

seasonal norm *Br.* the average weather conditions for a particular season.

seasonally adjusted figures *Br.* figures esp. about the number of unemployed people that are changed according to what usu. happens at a particular time of the year.

season ticket (to opera house, etc.) *Br., Aus.* subscription (ticket).

seat *esp. Br.* 1. place in an elected Parliament or council. 2. parliamentary constituency.

seat/ **be in the driving seat** *Br.* /*Am., Aus.* **be in the driver's seat**/ be in control of a situation.

seat/ **on the hotseat** *Am.* making important decisions.

seat/ **put bums on seats** *Br., Aus.* col. /*Am.* col. **fannies in the seats**/ be very popular (about a public performance or sports event).

seat/ **win a seat** *Br.* be elected to parliament.

secateurs *esp. Br., Aus.* /*Am.* **pruning shears**/ strong scissors for cutting bits off garden plants.

second *esp. Br.* 1. second form of a school or college. 2. place in the second grade in an exam, esp. for a degree.

second (**from, to**) (usu. pass) *Br., Aus.* move (sb.) from their usual duties to a special duty, usu. for a limited time: *I was seconded to go back to save them.* - New Idea; n. -**ment.**

second/ come a good second *Br., Aus.* /*Am., Aus.* **be a strong second**/ take a solid second place.

second/ on second thoughts *Br., Aus.* /*Am.* **on second thought**/: *No - on second thought, better make it a thousand.* - I. Shaw., *On second thoughts perhaps it is just as well that we don't have those trains anymore.* - B. Bryson.

second breath/ get a/one's **second breath** *Am.* suddenly have new energy to continue doing smth.

second-class *Br.* second highest division in the results.

second (class degree) *Br.* almost as good as the best.

secondary subject *Br.* /*Am.* **minor**/ additional, not the main subject of studies.

second class mail *Am., Can.* /*Br.* **newspaper post**/ newspapers and magazines delivery by mail.

second-degree (crime) *esp. Am., Can.* one less serious than first degree crime: *D.A. did charge him with second-degree murder* – Reader's Digest.

second floor *Am.* second storey; **first floor** *Am.* /*Br.* **ground floor**/.

second-guess *Am.* col. 1. make a judgement about (sb. or smth.) only afterwards when an event has already taken place: *The losing team's coach is always second-guessed.* - A. Makkai. 2. also *Can.* try to say in advance what (sb.) will do, how (smth.) will happen, etc.: *in a move bitterly second-guessed at the time, Dowman traded Sheppard* - Time.

second-hand smoke *Am., Can.* smoke inhaled involuntarily from tobacco being smoked by others.

second-last *Br.* one before last.

secondment *esp. Br.* temporary transfer to another position or period of time which the person spends away from their usual job, either doing another job or studying, **be on secondment.**

second name *Br., Aus.* /*Am.* **last name**/ surname, family name.

secondary school *esp. Br.* a school for children from 11 to 18 years old.

secondary subject *Br.* /*Am.* **minor**/ auxiliary subject of study.

second floor *Am.* upper floor / in America ground floor is a first floor.

second-last *Br.* second-to-the-last.

second papers *Am.* col. the second phase in obtaining American citizenship.

second story man, porch climber *Am.* /*Br.* **cat (burglar)**/ thief who enters and leaves a building by climbing up walls, pipes, etc.

second year student *esp. Br.* /*Am.* **sophomore**, *Am.* col. **soph**/.

the Secretary of Education *Am.* /*Br.* **the Secretary of State for Education and Science; the Education secretary**/ minister of education.

secret service 1. *Br.* a government department that controls the activities of its country's spies. 2. *Am.* a government department dealing with special kinds of police work, esp. protecting high government officials.

sectarian *esp. Am.* supporting a particular religious group and its beliefs.

section 1. *Am.* a piece of land one square mile in area forming one of 36 subdivisions of a township, esp. in the western US. 2. *Am.* part of a sleeping car containing an upper and lower berth. 3. *Am.* one or more trains operating on the same schedule. 4. *esp. Am.* a small class into which a large group of students is divided.

section boss (foreman, head) *Am.* foreman of a railway section: *boss of a section of the Pensilvania-Erie Railroad, he married Ann Jane Cavett.* - I. Stone., *Gladys Baker was a foreman, a section head* – N. Mailer.

section car, hand car *Am.* small locomotive used for railway repairs.

section gang (or crew) *Am.* group of workmen keeping one section of a railway line repaired: *The section crew was called out to fix the broken bridge.* - A. Makkai.

section hand *Am.* railway section workman: *so he got a job working as a section hand.* - D. Carnegie.

sectional *Am., Can.* (of furniture) made up of parts which can be arranged in different ways, esp. as chairs.

security blanket *Br.* secret protection for a person or place threatened by a violent attack or sanction imposed on information to maintain complete secrecy about smth.

security deposit *Am.* /*Br.* **key money**/.

sedan *esp. Am., Aus., Can.* /*Br.* **saloon (car)**/ car for 4 or 6 passengers with a roof, 2 or 4 doors and a separate enclosed space for luggage: *a vintage sedan pulling a short coupled trailer like a box turtle lumbered down from the road* - J. Steinbeck., *Richard lounged in a battered old sedan* - Rolling Stone., *the sedan was not in sight* - R. Moore.

see/ **See here** *Am.* Listen.

see/ **see sb. damned first** *Br.* col. said when refusing (to do) smth. outright.

see/ **see oneself in hell before one does** smth. *Br.* be determined not to do smth.

see/ **see sb. right** *Br., Aus.* col. make certain that sb. is helped and treated well.

see/ **see the back of** smth. *Br., Aus.* see the last of, be pleased that one would no longer have to deal with smth.

see/ **see one's way (clear) to** *esp. Br.* Can. be able or willing to (esp. lend money): *he couldn't see his way clear to allowing us to rent the house.* - H.C. Whitord., R.J. Dixson.

see/ **see you in a bit** *Br.* /*Am.* **see you in a while**/ see you soon.

see after *esp. Am.* take care, look after.

see sb. off *Br.* repel an invader or intruder.

see off *Br.* sl. kill sb.

see sb. out *Br.* (of an article) last longer than the remainder of one's life.

see smth. out *Br.* come to the end of a period of time or undertaking.

see over *Br.* examine smth. large such as a house, esp. when one is considering buying it.

seed *Am.* /*Br.* **pip**/ a small fruit seed, esp. of an apple, orange, etc.

seedcorn *Br.* assets set aside for the generation for profit or other benefit in the future.

seed money *Am., Aus.* money used to start a business or other activity.

seeing eye dog *Am., Can., Aus.* tdmk. /*Br.* **guidedog**/: *he had served handicapped patrons for years, letting one customer regularly bring in his Seeing Eye dog.* – Reader's Digest.

seek dead *Br.* instruction to the retriever to go and look for game that has been shot.

seep *Am.* 1. seepage. 2. place where petroleum or water oozes slowly out of the ground.

seg *Am.* sl. segregationist: *racist cracker spewing out Johnny Reb songs for the segs* - Atlantic Monthly.

seize up *esp. Br.* /of (part of) a machine/ become stuck and fail to move or work, jam: *their minds* would begin to seize up like the overheated engines of the trucks - Rolling Stone., *the winch seized up.* - Reader's Digest.

selectee *Am.* man called up for military service.

selective buying *Am.* a boycott.

Selective Service *Am., Can.* /*Br.* **National Service**/ conscription: *a strengthening of national defense through universal military training and the restoration of Selective Service.* - H. Truman.

selector 1. *Aus.* a small farmer. 2. *Br.* a member of a committee that chooses the best people for smth. such as a sports team.

self-catering *esp. Br., Aus.* (of a holiday or holiday lodging) in which one cooks one's own meals.

self-certify *Br.* attest or confirm (one's financial standing) in a formal statement.

self-contained *Br.* (of a flat) with its own kitchen and bathroom.

self-destruct *esp. Am.* destruct oneself: *Are you trying to self-destruct or what?* - P. Case, J. Migliore.

self-drive (car) *Br.* /*Am.* **rental car**/ (of a vehicle) one that can be or has been hired to be driven by oneself.

self-raising flour *Br., Aus.* /*Am.* **self-rising flour**/ flour that contains baking powder.

sell/ sell one's **support/vote** *Am.* give them to the party which will give a person the biggest financial advantage.

sell out *esp. Am.* sell up, sell everything to pay a debt: *Many businessmen, losing everything on the Wall Street crash, had to be sold out* - Longman.

sell up *Br., Aus.* 1. make sb. sell everything to pay a debt: *Jim's father was sold up because he owed so much money.* - Longman. 2. sell up one's house and most of what one owns, as part of a big change in one's life.

sell short *Am.* col. underappreciate smth.: *Take care that you don't sell his suggestion short* - Longman.

sell-by date *esp. Br.* /*Am., Aus.* **pull date,** *Am.* **expiration date**/ the date printed on a food product after which it should not be sold, (**be past its/her/his sell-by date, pass** one's **selling date**) (about people and ideas) be no longer useful, successful or relevant.

sell-off 1. *esp. Am.* sale of shares, bonds, or commodities, that usu. causes a fall in price. 2. *Br.* the act of selling an industry, esp. one that the government owns to private buyers.

sellotape *Br.* tdmk. /*Am., Aus.* **Scotch tape,** *Aus.* and *Br.* col. **sticky tape**/ (use) sticky thin clear material used for sticking paper, mending light objects, etc.

sell-out *Am.* clearance sale.

seltzer, club soda *Am.* fizzy mineral water.

semester *esp. Am., Aus.* /*esp. Br.* **term**/ one of two periods into which the school or college year is divided: *we'll have all the fat cats from Yale and John Hopkins and Duke lining up to spend semesters with us.* - D. Lodge.

semi 1. *Br., Aus.* col. /*Am.* **duplex**/ a semidetached house: *endless grey suburbs with their wandering ranks of terraced houses and stuccoed semis.* - B. Bryson.; adj. *Br.* **semi-detached**. 2. *Am., Can., Aus.* /*Br.* **juggernaut**/ an articulated lorry, carrying goods over long distances: *I spotted the semi coming in the other direction* - Fortune.

semibreve *esp. Br., Aus.* /*Am.* **whole note**/ musical note with a time value equal to two minims.

semidemisemiquaver *esp. Br.* demidemisemiquaver.

semidetached *Br.* adj. (a house) that is one of a pair of joined houses: *I wouldn't waste thirty thousand pounds on buying a semi-detached house.* – S. Townsend.

semi-monthly *esp. Am., Can.* occuring or published twice a month.

seminary *Am.* college for training clergymen of any denomination. **-ian** adj.

semiquaver *esp. Br., Aus.* /*Am.* **sixteenth note**/ musical note with a time value half as long as quaver.

semi-skimmed *Br.* /*Am.* **two-percent milk**/ milk that has had about half the fat removed.

semitone *Br.* /*Am.* **half step,** *Am., Aus.* **half tone**/ a difference in pitch equal to that between two notes which are next to each other on a piano.

semi-trailer *esp. Am., Can.* trailer having wheels at the back but supported at the front by a towing vehicle.

sempstress *esp. Br.* seamstress.

Sen *Am., Can.* 1. Senate. 2. Senator.

send/ send sb. **crazy, mad, wild** *Br.* annoy sb. very much.

send down *Br.* 1. (usu. pass.) dismiss (a student) from a university because of a bad behaviour): *He led a wild youth and was sent down (from his university) for taking drugs.* - Longman. 2. col. / *Am.* **send up**/ send to prison: *he was caught and sent down again* - Arthur Hailey.

send in *Am.* bring on (another person to do the job).

send off *Br., Aus.* /*Am.* **eject**/ (in sport) order (a player) to leave the field because of a serious breaking of the rules.

send smth. **on** *esp. Br. /Am.* **forward/** send sb.'s letters or possessions to their new address from their old one.

send (sb.) **to Coventry** *Br.* col. refuse to speak to sb. as a punishment: *His fellow workers disapproved of his action, and sent him to Coventry for a week* - Longman.

send up 1. *Br.* col. make fun of, parody sb.: *And didn't they used to send up that other lad, Stuart?* - P. Norman. 2. *Am., Can.* col. send to prison: *Some of those poor devils of enlisted men they sent up for twenty years for rape* - J. Dos Passos.

send-up *Br.* col. parody.

senior 1. *Am., Can /Br.* **4th year undergrad(uate)/** n. adj. (a student) of the last year of four in a high school (**senior high school** is school for the last two years of high school) or university course. 2. *Am., Can.* a senior citizen, retired person: *The Internet Designed For Seniors.* – Reader's Digest.

Senior /also **Sr.** or **Snr.**, *Br.* **Snr**/ adj. (after n.) *esp. Am.* the older, esp. of two men in the same family, who have exactly the same name).

Senior Commision Room, SCR *Br.* room used for social purposes by fellows, lecturers and other senior members of a college.

senior nursing officer *Br., Aus. /Am.* **head nurse**, *Br., Aus.* obs. **matron/** one in charge of nurses in a hospital.

Senior Registrar *Br.* hospital doctor undergoing specialist training, one grade below that of consultant.

Senior Service *Br.* The Royal Navy.

sense/ have a sense of occasion *Br., Aus.* have the feeling that people have when there is a very important event or celebration.

sense/ have sense of humor *Am., Aus.* have a sense of fun.

sensible clothes/shoes *esp. Br.* practical, comfortable, and strong rather than attractive or fashionable.

sentinel *esp. Am.* used in the names of some newspapers.

sentry-go *esp. Br.* the patrol or duties of a sentry / **on sentry-go** *Br.* on duty as a guard: *This was Hale's Job to do sentry-go* - G. Greene.

separate school *Can.* school receiving pupils from a particular religious group.

septic 1. *esp. Br.* infected with disease bacteria. 2. *Am., Can.* drainage system including a sceptic tank.

sequel/ in the sequel *Br.* as things develop.

sequestration *Am.* law. keeping a jury together as a group not allowing them to discuss the case or read or hear news reports about it; v. **sequestrate**.

sergeant 1. *Br.* a police officer with the next to the lowest rank, ranking below inspector. 2. *Am.* police officer ranking below a lieutenant.

serigraph *esp. Am., Can.* printed design produced by means of a silk screen.

serious-minded *Am.* having a serious disposition or trend of thought.

serve *Aus.* col. a reprimand.

serve smth. **out** *Br.* put food onto plates.

serve out one's **time** *esp. Am.* col. hold office for the normal time.

servery *esp. Br.* the part of an informal eating place where people get food to take back to their tables.

service *esp. Br.* a particular government department.

service/ take smth., e.g. a car **for a service** *Br.* / *esp. Am.* **servicing/**.

service/ in the service *Br.* in the army, navy, etc.

service area *Br.* a place on a motorway where a number of facilities are available for drivers and travellers, usu. including a service station, restaurant or cafe and toilets.

service charge *Br.* an amount of money added to a bill to pay for additional service: *ask the landlord exactly how the service charge is calculated.* - Young Citizen's Passport.

service club *Am., Can.* club of business or professional men or women organised for their common benefit and active in community service.

service dress *Br.* military uniform worn on formal but not ceremonial occasions.

service engineer *Br.* skilled mechanic repairman (esp. of household appliances).

service flat *Br.* flat whose rent include a charge for certain services, such as cleaning, providing sheets, etc.: *The usual service flat in Hyde Park* - J. Higgins. / **block of service flats** *Br.* apartment hotel or residential hotel.

service lift *Br.* lift for moving food plates from one story to another.

services *esp. Br.* a place where you can stop to buy petrol, food, etc. on a motorway.

service station *Br.* a commercial garage supplying petrol, oil, mechanical parts, etc. and carrying out repairs: *a brightly lighted service station suddenly blacked out.* – F. Edwards.

serviette *esp. Br., Can.* col. table napkin: *The last time she ordered three linen tea-clothes and two dozen serviettes.* - W. Grady.

serving spoon *Am. /Br.* **tablespoon/** one for giving a helping of food.

sesquicentennial *Am.* 150th jubilee: *The brilliant streets flashed a sesquicentennial fireworks display* - R.J. Randisi., M. Wallace.

session *Am.* any of the parts of the year when teaching is given at a university.

set *Br.* 1. group, stream of pupils. 2. exclusive apartment suite.

set *Aus., NZ.* col. a grudge.

set *Br.* adj. (of a restaurant meal) with a single fixed dish for each course and at a fixed price / **set lunch** *Br.* table d'hote, prix fix.

set 1. *Br., Aus.* /*Am.* **assign**/ give or provide (a piece of work), esp. for a student in one's class or sb. working for a person or company, **set** sb. smth.. 2. *esp. Am., Can.* start (a fire).

set smth. **by** *Am.* save smth. for future use.

set down *Br.* (of a vehicle or its driver) stop and let (a passenger) get out / *Br.* Road signs **Pick up and set down. No parking. Setting down point.**

set on *Br.* begin employing (sb.): *Trade was so good that the firm was able to set on more workers.* - Longman.

set to *Br.* start doing smth. eagerly and with a lot of effort and determination.

set up *Br.* set a new record or set a legal precedent.

set up (for) *Br., Can.* col. (often pass.) cause to seem guilty, incriminate: *I let him take me to a house and set me up.* - B. Holiday., W. Duffy.

set/ make a dead set at *Br.* a. combine to attack sb. b. try to gain the favour (of sb. of the opp. sex).

set/ look set fair *Br.* (of weather) seem likely to be good.

set/ set (words) in inverted commas *esp. Br.* place speech marks round certain word(s) to show it's spoken or special in some way: *Why do you set up the name of the shop in inverted commas* - Longman.

set/ set out one's **stall** *Br.* col. show one's abilities, display one's credentials: *how well you can set out your stall.* - Longman.

set/ set the Thames/heather, etc. **on fire/alight/ablaze, set…alight** *Br.* col. do smth. important and unusual: *Tom's new book won't set the Thames on fire* - Longman.

setback *Am., Can.* the distance by which a building or part of it is set back from the property line.

set book/textbook *Br.* book that must be studied for an examination.

set menu/meal *Br.* meal with a fixed price that includes a comination of foods suggested by a restaurant.

set piece *Br.* any of certain football plays which takes place when the ordinary action of the game is stopped, such as corner or free kick.

setsquare *Br., Aus.* /*Am.* **triangle,** *Am., Aus.* **square,** *Am.* **Tee-square**/ plastic plate used for drawing and testing angles: *T-square, do your stuff.* – Reader's Digest.

set tea *Br.* afternoon tea.

settee 1. *Br.* comfortable seat for 2 or 3 people. 2. *Am.* a long wooden seat which has a back.

settle smth. **on** *Br.* make a formal arrangement to give money or property to sb.

settle to smth. *Br., Aus.* give one's whole attention to smth.

set-up *Am.* water, soda or some other soft drink for mixing with drinks: *Who ordered the set-ups?* - R.A. Spears.

Seven Sisters *Am.* seven prestigious women's colleges.

Seventh Avenue *Am.* col. the garment and fashion industry.

severance pay *Am.* /*Br.* **redundancy pay**/: *after fifteen years of service – received no severance pay.* – A. Summers, R. Swan.

sewage works/farm *Br.* /*Am.* **sewage plant**/ a place where sewage is treated so that it can safely be got rid of or changed into fertilizer.

sexcapade *esp. Am.* col. illicit love afair.

Seymour *Br.* sl. a six-figure salary.

shack town *Am., Can.* shanty town.

shacky *Am., Can.* col. adj. (of a building) dilapidated or rundown.

shad *Can.* little snow.

shade *Am.* reduce lightly (esp. a price).

(window) shade *Am., Can., Aus.* /*Br.* **(roller) blind**/ window blind that can be rolled up and down: *the shades were drawn.* - G. O'Neill, D. Lehr., *he locked the windows and pulled the shades.* - S. Bellow.

shade/ have it made in the shade *Am.* col. be extremely rich.

shade tree *Am., Aus.* a tree which is planted to provide darkness or coolness.

shaft *Am., Can.* 1. col. severe and unfair treatment / **give** / **get** sb. **the shaft**: *many investors would initially get the shaft* – Reader's Digest. 2. obelisk.

shaft *esp. Am., Can., Aus.* col. treat unfairly and very severely: *I was about to be shafted by the Hollywood star who played me in the film of my book.* - H. Fast., *I really shafted 'em.* - S. Sheldon., *Naturally, if anybody has to shaft Joe Loomis, I'd rather it weren't me.* - L. Waller.

shaft into *Am.* cheat on sb.: *I've been shafted into signing for something I don't want.* - Longman.

shag 1. *Am.* sl. run after, leave quickly: *four boys were shagging flies.* - I. Shaw. 2. *Br., Can., Aus.* sl. a. have sex with: *all the bedrooms are named after his chums or women he shagged there* - B. Bryson; b. sexual partner or the act of having sex.

shag/ like a shag on a rock *Aus.* col. alone.

shagged (**out**) *Br., Aus.* sl. very tired: *we were all feeling that big shagged and fagged and fashed* - A. Burgess., *I say, Jane, I'm getting hellish shagged.* - J. Fowles.

shake *Am.* col. 1. milk shake: *go nearby for a hamburger and a shake.* - A.E. Hotchner. 2. also *Can.* treatment of the stated type, esp. in **a fair shake**: *he can get a fair shake* - Time.

shake *Aus.* sl. v. steal.

shake down 1. *esp. Am., Can.* col. get money from sb. by a trick or threats: *He tried to shake Wynant down by threatening to shoot him* - D. Hammet., *It started with a couple of tips that he was shaking down some merchants.* - S. Sheldon., *You want to shake it down?* - R. Moore. 2. *Am., Can.* col. search thoroughly: *shaking down more than 9 million travelers who come through JFK every year.* - New York. 3. *Br.* col. get accustomed to smth. new: *You'll soon shake down to your new job.* - Longman. 4. *Br.* test a ship or plane under real conditions.

shake down (in, on, etc.) *Br.* col. sleep on the floor, on a seat, etc. instead of a proper bed, adj. **shakedown**.

shake/ give sb. **the shake** *Am.* sl. rid oneself of, get away from.

shake/ more than one **can shake a stick at** *Br.* col. humor. a very large number (of.): *I've been deposited for safekeeping in more saloons than you could shake a stick at* - H. Fast.

shake/ shake a leg *Br.* col. (usu. impers.) act fast, hurry: *We'd better shake a leg or we'll miss the train.* - H.C. Whitford., R.J. Dixson.

shake/ shake like a jelly *Br., Aus.* be very nervous.

shake/ shake the plum tree *Am.* col. give jobs as a reward for political support.

Shake City *Am.* sl. Los Angeles.

shakedown *esp. Am., Can.* col. 1. also *Aus.* an act of getting money dishonestly, esp. by threats: *The shakedown took nearly an hour.* - L. Uris. 2. thorough search: *There'll be a shakedown, starting at the top.* - Arthur Hailey. 3. makeshift bed. 4. radical change, esp. in a hierarchy of an organisation. 5. test of new product or model: *It was a sort of test run, a shakedown tour* - J. Hopkins.

shall / In British English first person questions expressing willingness or wish use shall (Shall we...? = Do you wish me/us to...?; Shall I give you a hand with the dishes? (offer); Shall we buy a present? (suggestion).

sham *Am., Can.* pillow sham.

shambles *esp. Br.* a meat market or butcher shop.

shambolic *esp. Br.* col. completely disordered or confused.

shamus *Am., Can.* col. police officer, private detective: *Not a real copper at that! Just a cheap shamus.* - R. Chandler.

shandy *esp. Br., Aus.* drink made from a mixture of beer and ginger beer and lemonade: *A shandy is what he wants* - F. O'Brien.

shanghai *Aus.* catapult.

shank *Am.* the end of, the last part of: *It's the shank of the night and the rain is falling.* - J. Higgins.

shank's pony (or **mare**) *Br.* obs. or *Aus.* col. humor. one's own legs as a method of going from one place to another, walking.

shan't *esp. Br.* shall not.

shanty *Aus.* pub.

shantyman *Am., Can.* lumberjack.

shape/ get/be bent out of shape *Am.* col. be very angry.

shape up (or **ship out**) *esp. Am., Can.* col. start working or leave.

shape-up *Am.* a system of hiring longshoremen when they are given work each day.

share *esp. Am.* tell a person about an idea, problem, etc.

sharecropper *esp. Am.* a tenant farmer, esp. in the Southern US who takes as his wages a part of the crop he farms. **sharecrop** v.: *To me, they were simply sharecroppers.* - H. Smith.

shared house/flat *Br.* one where people not related to each other live; such situation is called **flat/house share**.

shared line, also called **shared service** /opp. is **exclusive line/** *Br.* party line, telephone line connected to two or more telephones belonging to different people.

sharefarmer *esp. Aus., NZ.* tenant farmer who receives an agreed share of the profits from the owner.

shareholder *esp. Br.* /*esp. Am.* **stockholder/** an owner of shares in a business: *He's one of the chief shareholders in Riviera Sunbeds.* - D. Lodge.

share out *Br., Aus.* an act of dividing smth. between several people.

share pushing *Br.* stock touting.
shark *Am.* col. an expert in smth.*: I believe that Minnesota Fats, the world-famous pool shark, is really my father.* – E. James, D. Ritz.
shark bait(er) *Aus., NZ.* col. swimmer ignoring anti-shark force warnings or one well out from shore.
shark bell (siren) *Aus.* shark alarm.
shark-mesh, shark fence *Aus.* anti-shark net.
shark patrol plane *Aus.* a special plane to watch over sharks.
shark spotter *Aus.* a helicopter which flies along the beach so that it can detect a shark and warn the swimmers of the danger.
shark tower *Aus.* one for watching for sharks and giving alarm.
sharp 1. *esp. Am.* (of cheese) having a strong taste. 2. *Am.* /*Br.* **smart**/ wearing clothes that look neat and attractive.
sharp/ be as sharp as a tack *Am., Can.* be very smart.
the sharp end *esp. Br.* the most difficult part (of activity).
sharpie *Aus.* col. young person resembling skinhead.
sharpish *esp. Br.* col. adv. quickly.
shatter *esp. Br.* col. cause to be very tired and weak.
shattered *Br.* col. very tired.
shattering *Br.* col. making sb. very tired.
shave *Am.* reduce or lessen smth. (esp. prices): *They shaved the waiting time to six months.* - R.A. Spears.*, you can shave up to $960 from your taxes* – Reader's Digest.
shave hook *Br.* paint scraper.
shaver point *Br.* /*Am.* **shaver outlet**/ an opening into which the plug of a shaver can be put in to connect it to a power supply.
shavetail *Am.* mil. sl. newly commisioned officer, esp. a second lieutenant; col. any inexperienced person.
shaving bag *Am.* toilet bag.
shaw *esp. Br.* the tops and stalks of cultivated crop (potatoes, turnips).
shay *esp. Am.* chaise, a light horse-drawn carriage.
she *Aus., NZ.* col. it (about weather and other things not usually considered female).
she/ Who's she? – the cat's mother? *Br.* col. used as a mild reproof to be more specific, esp. to a child.
shear *esp. Br.* shearing (used to indicate the age of sheep).
shearer *Aus.* person whose job is to shear sheep.

sheath *Br.* condom.
shebang *esp. Am., Can., Aus.* col. affair, business, thing (esp. in the phr. **the whole shebang**): *I'll make yeh superintendent of the shebang.* - J. London., *I suppose I am a stand-in for the whole she-bang.* - J. Fowles.
shed 1. *Br.* (of a vehicle) drop (a load of goods) by accident. 2. *Aus., NZ.* open-sided building for shearing sheep or milking cattle.
shedhand *Aus., NZ.* unskilled labourer in a shearing shed.
sheenie, sheanie *Am.* derog. col. a Jew: *The Harps and Sheenies have their town and I have mine.* - L. Waller., *Ben and Abe were the Jew boys. The Hebes, Jids, Sheenies, Kikes.* - L. Uris., *Yes, indeed, you're a mean little sheenie, aren't you?* - L. Uris.
sheep/ sort (out) or **separate/tell the sheep from the goats** *Br., Aus.* choose the people or things of high quality from a group of things of mixed quality.
sheep-cote *esp. Br.* sheepfold.
sheepman *Am.* sheepowner or sheepbreeder.
sheepskin *Am.* humor. diploma: *John graduated and finally secured his sheepskin.* - H.C. Whitford., R.J. Dixson.
sheep station *Aus.* a large farm on which sheeps are kept.
sheepwalk *Br.* tract of land on which sheep are pastured.
sheers; underdrape *Am.* /*Br.* **net curtains**/.
sheet home *Am.* col. cause (smth.) to be clearly understood: *The failure of the firm's efforts at last sheeted home the need for proper preparation of business conditions.* - Longman.
sheila *esp. Aus., NZ.* col. a girl, lover: *The famous Australian sheila is probably Irish* - R. McRum, W. Cran, R. McNeil., *Still I expect you had some little sheila to keep the cold out, eh?* - D. Reeman.
shelf *Aus.* an informer.
shelf/be (left) on the shelf *Br., Aus.* obs. believed to be too old to get married.
shell 1. *esp. Am.* a bullet, esp. the case holding the part to be fired. 2. *Am.* light racing boat.
shell out *Am.* col. give out presents at the Halloween: *I'll buy fruit this year to shell out when the children come round* - Longman.
shell/ like shelling peas *Br.* very easy.
shellac(k) *Am., Aus. Can.* col. defeat severely **-ing** n.: *Thirty-five to nothing, the worst shellacking in this traditional series since 1925* - J. O'Hara.
shellback *Am., Can.* col. old or experienced sailor., esp. one who crossed the equator.

shell game *Am., Can.* thimble ring played with three walnut shells: *The recognition of a shell game still leaves the question about its purpose.* – Harper's Magazine.
shell game/ be/play a shell game *esp. Am.* esp. journalism. deliberately deceive people.
shell suit *Br.* light brightly-coloured piece of clothing consisting of trousers and a jacket, that fit together at the wrists and at the bottom of a leg.
shelter income *Am.* legally avoid paying taxes on it.
sheltered housing or **accomodation** *Br.* a form of housing for retired or elderly people in newly built blocks of flats where help is provided when they need it.
sheltered workshop *Br., Aus.* a factory specially designed for people with mental or physical disabilities to work in.
shemozzle *esp. Br., Can., Aus.* col. a fight, mix-up, row.
she-oak net *Aus.* a safety net under ship's ladders.
shepherd's pie *Br.* a dish consisting of minced meat, usu. lamb covered with a layer of mashed potatoes: *they get through the evening's shepherd's pie* – Alain de Botton.
sherbet 1. *Br., Aus.* a powder eaten as a sweet or added to water to make a cool drink, esp. for children. 2. *esp. Am., Can.* also **ice** /*Br.* obs. **water ice**/ sorbet, water ice with the addition of the white of an egg, milk, etc. 3. *Aus.* humor. beer.
shicer *Aus.* col. a swindler or worthless person.
shickered *Am., Aus., NZ.* col. drunk.
shield *Am.* 1. rare. policeman's badge: *Carella showed her his shield.* - E. McBain. 2. /*Br.* **screen**/.
shift *Br.* col. 1. move quickly. 2. eat and drink smth. hastily or in large amounts.
shift oneself *Br.* go away or rouse oneself from a state of inactivity.
shift *Br., Aus.* col. 1. get rid of smth., such as stain or dirt from a surface or a piece of clothing. 2. sell smth.
shift gear (shift up, down, into, to) *esp. Am., Can.* /*Br., Aus.* **change gear**/ change (engine's speed): *I heard her shifting gears furiously* - J. Baez., *the deployment debate shifted into high gear.* - Newsweek., *Now the system really had to shift gears.* - J. DeFelice.
shift *Am.* a gear shift.
shift bar *Am.* selector rod (in a car) / **shift stick, gear shift** *esp. Am., Can.* **shift lever** *Am.* **gear lever**, *Br.* **gear stick, gear change**/.

shifter *Am., Can.* gearbox.
shift key lock *Br.* /*Am.* **shift lock key**/ the key on a typewriter which is pressed in order to print capital letters.
shikkered *esp. Aus., Am.* drunk.
shiksa *Am.* sl. a non-Jewish woman: *You might as well marry a shiksa now and get it over with!* - M. Torgov.
shill *Am., Can.* col. accomplice of a hawker, gambler, or swindler who acts as an enthusiastic customer to entice others.
shilling/ not the full shilling *Br.* col. not intelligent or quick enough.
shilling/ take the King' (or **Queen's**) **shilling** *Br.* enlist a soldier.
shilling shocker *Br.* short sensational novel.
shilly-shally *esp. Br.* hesitate to do smth.
shimmy *Am.* (of a car) shake slightly, which is rather unusual.
shindig *esp. Br., Aus.* a noisy argument.
shindy *Br.* col. a noisy quarrel or disagreement: *You know we had that sort of shindy thing in the courtyard?* - A. Christie.
shine 1. *Aus.* rural area with its own elected council. 2. *Am.* derog. sl. Negro: *Who's that shine standing over there?* – E. Caldwell.
shine up to sb. *esp. Am.* col. try to win in the favour of sb. by insincere praise: *It won't do the student any good to shine up to the teacher* - Longman.
shined *Am.* col. past tense and past participle from shine (= polish).
shingle *Am., Can.* a small sign advertising services.
shingle/ hang up / out one's **shingle** *Am., Can.* col. establish an office (doctor's, lawyer's, etc.): *Not long after hanging out his shingle he received a summons from the largest house in the region.* - T. Thompson.
shinny *Am., Aus.* shin, climb vertically a pole or tree using hands and shins: *Shinny up these other trees* - T. Capote., *People climb onto station-house roofs, shinny up signal poles, swarm onto overpasses* - Newsweek., *To shinny up from a friend's shoulders* - J. Updike.
shinola *Am.* tdmk. brand of boot polish: *this is shinola, and that over there is shit.* – Harper's Magazine.
ship *Am., Can.* aircraft.
ship a sea *Br.* (of a boat) be flooded by a wave.
shipping forecast *Br.* radio broadcast that says what the weather will be like at sea.
shipping master *Br.* official presiding over the signing on and discharging of seamen.

ship's biscuit, also **hard tack** *esp. Br.* ship biscuit, a hard-baked bread eaten, esp. formerly by sailors at sea.

shir(r) *Am.* shirring (of material).

shiralee, also **swag** *Aus.* col. bag containing all the necessary things.

shire *Aus.* rural area with its own elected council.

shires *Br.* the country area of England away from the big cities esp. in the centre of England.

shirred eggs *Am.* eggs removed from the shells and baked until set: *They dined on half grapefruit and shirred eggs* - E.L. Doctorow., *shirred eggs with Canadian bacon and hominy grits* - Arthur Hailey, v.

shirt/ lose one's **shirt** *Am.* go bankrupt: *he lost his shirt in quick-frozen foods.* – P. Roth.

shirt/ put one's **shirt on** smth. *Br., Aus.* col. risk all one's money on smth. because one is sure to win.

shirtlifter *Br.* col. derog. a homosexual.

shirtwaister *Br. /Am., Can.* **shirtwaist/** a woman's dress in the style of a man's shirt: *Harold looked at his mother, at her...severe white-silk shirt-waist.* - T. Caldwell., *Evelin arrived looking crisp in her high-collared shirt-waist* - E.L. Doctorow.

shirty *esp. Br., Am., Can.* col. bad-tempered, angry and rude: *reporters getting shirty with the brass* - McLean's.

shit *Am.* sl. 1. something excellent. 2. used in negatives to mean anything. 3. tell a lie.

shit *esp. Br.* adj. very bad.

shit/ give sb. **the shits** *Aus.* annoy them.

shit/ have/get one's **shit together** *esp. Am.* col. become effective, organised and skilful.

shit/ have shit-earing grin *Am.* derog. sl. look very satisfied and happy about smth.

shit/ have shits for brain *esp. Am., Can.* derog. sl. be very stupid.

shit/ in the shit *Br.* in a lot of trouble.

shit/shit or **take a shit** *Am.* have a shit, defecate.

shit/ shit a brick/bricks *esp. Am.* sl. be very frightened or worried: *Sammy Davis Jr. shit a brick, when he sees this.* – J. Hopkins.

shit/ shit or get off the pot *esp. Am.* do smth. properly.

shit list/ be on sb.'s **shit list** *esp. Am.* be not liked by sb.

shit/ no shit! *esp. Am.* used for emphasis when sb agrees with sb. fully or when he is surprised by their words.

shit/ no shit (Sherlock!) *esp. Am.* col. derog. Don't tell me what I already know.

shit/ same shit, different day, SSDD *Am.* sl. business as usual.

shit/ shoot the shit *Am.* sl. shoot the breeze, talk a lot about smth. unimportant.

shit/ think as shit *Br.* col. very stupid.

shit/ think one's **shit doesn't stink** *Am.* col. derog. consider oneself better than other people.

shite *Br.* col. derog. smth. of poor quality, shit.

shitepoke *Am., Can.* col. heron.

shitheel *Am.* taboo. sl. a despicable person.

shithouse *Am.* sl. outside toilet.

shitkicker *Am., Can.* col. 1. stupid person, esp. from a rural area. 2. boots with thick soles.

shitlist *Am., Can.* sl. list of those who one dislikes or plans to harm.

shitstirrer *esp. Br.* taboo. sb. who deliberately makes trouble for other people.

shivaree *esp. Am.* v. n. (make) a noisy mock serenade (esp. to a newly married couple).

shivoo *Aus., NZ.* col. obs. party fun.

shlump, also **schloomp** *Am.* sl. a stupid person: *That doesn't mean you have to look like a shlump.* - E. Taylor.

shoal 1. *esp. Br.* col. large number of people. 2. *Am., Can.* adj. (of water) shallow.

shoat *Am.* a young hog usu. less than one year old, piglet.

shock *esp. Am., Can. /Br.* **shocker/** shock absorber.

shock/ short, sharp shock *Br.* brief but hard custodial sentence handed down to an offender.

shocking *Br.* col. very bad.

shockingly *esp. Br.* col. very.

shoe/ if the shoe/hat fits (wear it) *Am. Can. / Br.* **if the cap fits (wear it)/** col. if the cap fits wear it.

shoe/ low shoes *Am.* (Oxford) shoes.

shoe/ high shoes *Am.* (high) boots: *A transistor radio was standing on the pavement between his high shoes.* - K. Vonnegut, Jr.

shoe/ the shoe is on the other foot *Am., Can. / Br.* **the boot is on the other foot/** the situation changed.

shoe/ wait for the other shoe to drop *Am., Can.* col. wait for the next part of smth. bad to happen: *I'm still waiting for the shoe to drop, but she's been great.* – Reader's Digest.

shoe/ walk/stand in sb.'s **shoes** *Am.* know how sb. feels from one's own experience.

shoe-mender *Br.* shoe maker.

shoe-pac(k) *Am., Can.* 1. waterproof boot with laces for wear in cold weather. 2. high moccasin.

shoe-parlor *Am.* a place where shoes are polished by shoe-shine boys.

shoeshine *esp. Am., Can.* act of polishing shoes.

shoe-shine boy, also **bootblack** *Am.* a boy that shines boots.

shoeshine stand *Am.* place, usu. in the street, where a person can pay to have their shoes polished.

shoestring 1. *esp. Am., Can. /Br.* **shoelace/** shoelace. 2. *Am.* adj. long and thin (of tie, potatoes, etc.).

shoestring/ on a shoestring budget *Am.* spending very little money to do smth.

shoestring/ tie one's **own shoestrings** *Am.* 1. care for one's own business. 2. be absolutely independent.

shoestring/ walk on one's **shoestrings** *Am.* become poor.

shoestring potatoes *Am., Can.* potatoes cut into long thin strips and deep-fried.

shonky *Aus., NZ.* col. 1. of low quality. 2. dishonest, unreliable, n.

shoo-fly pie *Am., Can.* rich tart made of treacle baked in a pastry case with a crumble topping.

shoo-in *esp. Am., Aus., Can.* esp. journalism. col. 1. an easy or sure winner (esp. in an election): *that he didn't want it to look like a shoo-in for our side.* - L. Waller., *Well, I was shoo-in for best costume at the Halloween party* - D. Brenner. 2. sure thing.

shook 1. *esp. Br.* a shock of corn. 2. *esp. Am., Can.* a set of staves and headings for one's hogshead, cask or barrel. 3. *esp. Am., Can.* v. n. (pack in) a bundle of parts ready to be put together (to make a box, etc.).

shook on *Aus., NZ.* keen on.

shook up *Am.* sl. excited, disturbed, upset: *Basically, I think you're just "shooked up", as you say in America.* - E. Segal.

shoot *esp. Am.* a sending up of a space vehicle or rocket shot.

shoot *Am.* col. 1. (used to tell sb. that you are ready to listen): *Shoot. I love rumours.* - W. Magnuson. 2. also *Can.* exclamation used when you are annoyed, disappointed, or surprised: *Shoot, I'm no Engelbert Humperdinck!* – S. Lawrence.

shoot 1. *Am., Can.* col. play a game of esp. billiards, craps, pool or marbles. 2. *Br.* card used for shooting game.

shoot/ it's all over bar the shooting *Br., Aus.* it's certain to happen.

shoot for / at *esp. Am.* col. try to reach, have a goal, aim at: *There's no harm in shooting at the directorship* - Longman.

shoot off *Br.* col. leave quickly and suddenly.

shoot through *esp. Aus., NZ.* col. 1. leave esp. in a hurry. 2. die.

shoot/ have shot one's **bolt** (*Br., Aus.*) / one's **wad** (*Am., Can.*) col. have used up all one's strength, arguments, etc.: *he was through...he had shot his bolt* - I. Stone.

shoot/ shoot a line *Br.* col. overexaggerate smth. boastfully.

shoot/ shoot one's **wad** *Am.* col. (of a man or boy) ejaculate.

shoot/ shoot at the mouth, also **shoot off** one's **face** *Am.* col. talk too freely and without care: *But during the meeting I shot off my mouth a little* - M. Puzo., *right off you shoot off your face* – J. O'Hara.

shoot sb. **down (in flames)** *Br.* say that what sb. has suggested is wrong or stupid.

shoot/ shoot 'em up *Am., Aus.* 1. movie or TV show with much gunplay and violence: *I like a good shoot 'em up every now and them.* - R.A. Spears. 2. shoot-out: *Cabey who was paralyzed in...subway shoot 'em up* - New York.

shoot/ shoot from the hip *Am.* col. behave or speak carelessly or foolishly: *he's always shooting from the hip without thinking first.* - Longman.

shoot/ shoot the bull / the breeze *esp. Am., Can.* col. have an informal, not very serious conversation: *So I shot the bull for a while.* - J.D. Salinger.

shoot/ shoot the lights *Br.* col. keep driving even though the traffic lights tell sb. to stop.

shoot/ shoot the works *esp. Am.* col. a. risk all one's money in a game. b. use all one's efforts: *Shoot the works, baby.* - Reader's Digest., *What I want's some impractical son of a gun that'll shoot the works.* - D. Hammet.

shooter 1. *esp. Br.* sl. a gun: *we'll need a couple of shooters* - J. Higgins. 2. *esp. Am., Can.* col. small alcoholic drink, esp. of spirits.

shooting *Br.* hunting animals with a gun as a form of sport or recreation.

shooting box *Br.* lodge used by hunters in the shooting season.

shooting gallery *Am., Can.* col. place for using drugs, esp. injecting heroin, often a large empty building in a city.

shop 1. *Br., Can. /Am., Can.* **store/** a room or building where goods are regularly kept and sold or services are sold: *he sold up the shop lock, stock and barrel months ago* - A. Burgess. 2. also **shoppe** *Am.* small shop or one where special kinds of goods are sold. 3. *Am.* garage. 4. *Am.* a subject taught in school, in which students use tools and machinery to make things out of wood and metal. 5. *Am., Can.* window-shop.

shop/ all over the shop *Br.* col. 1. scattered in disorder; happening in many different areas: *They chased it all over the shop.* – R. Westall. 2. annoyed and disorganised.

shop/ close up shop *esp. Am. /Br., Aus.* **shut up shop/** stop doing business either temporarily or permanently.

shop/ parlor shop *Br.* trader's shop.

shop/ provision shop *Br. /Am.* **food store/** grocery shop.

shop 1. *Br.* derog. col. tell the police about (a criminal). 2. *Br.* sl. v. jail or be jailed. 3. *Am.* put a car into a repair's shop.

shop around *Am.* look for a job: *Lana was rapidly "discovered" and shopped around the studios by a talent agent.* – A. Summers, R. Swan.

shop assistant *Br., Aus. /Am.* **salesclerk, salesperson, (store)clerk/** a person who serves customers in a shop: *not a man pays the smallest attention to me except a bloody little shop-assistant.* - W.S. Maugham., *shop assistants become shop ladies* - P. Howard.

shop chairman *Am.* trade union organiser.

shop class *Am., Can.* class in which practical skills such as carpentry or engineering are taught.

shop fitter *Br.* person who installs furnishings and displays equipment in a shop.

shopfitting *Br.* the business of putting equipment in shops such as shelves.

shop floor *Br.* 1. the part of a workshop or factory where production is carried out. 2. the ordinary workers in a factory, as opposed to the managers

shopkeeper *esp. Br. /Am.* **storekeeper/** person usu. the owner in charge of a small shop.

shoplike *Am.* 1. mercenary. 2. vulgar.

shop-maid *Am. /Br.* **shop-girl/** one who serves customers in a shop.

shopman 1. *esp. Br.* a salesman in a shop. 2. *Am., Can.* factory worker.

shopper *Am.* 1. a newspaper filled with ads for local shops and businesses freely distributed to attract customers. 2. representative of a trade organisation watching over the prices and range of goods sold by the other firms.

shopper *Br.* bag for holding things bought in a shop that is attached to wheels to be pushed along or pulled.

shopping *Br.* things sb. has just bought from the shop.

shopping/ do the shopping *Br.* col. go and buy food and other things that one needs regularly.

shopping/ go shopping 1. *Br.* go to one or more shops to buy things, often for enjoyment. 2. *esp. Am.* go to shops to buy clothes.

shopping bag 1. *Am. /Br.* **carrier (bag)/** one for carrying goods bought in a shop: *practically everyone carries shopping bags or briefcases* - Y. Richmond., *shopping bags full of food to tide him over till his next meal* - New York. 2. *Br.* any bag intended to carry items bought in shops, esp. one used many times.

shopping cart *Am., Can. /Br.* **shopping trolley/** a large metal basin on wheels used by customers in a shop.

shopping centre *Br.* 1. */Am.* **(shopping) mall/** a covered area where many shops have been built and where cars are not allowed. 2. an area of land with these shops.

shopping center *Am., Aus.* a group of shops with a common area for cars to park, which usu. provides goods and services for local people.

shopping precinct *Br.* area with a lot of shops where cars are not allowed.

shopsoiled *Br., Aus. /Am.* **shopworn/** slightly damaged or dirty from being kept in a shop for a long time: *Though shopworn, the dress was still usable* -H.C. Whitford., R.J. Dixson.

shopwalker *esp. Br.* obs. */esp. Am.* **floorwalker, floor manager/** person employed in a large shop to help the customers and to watch the shop assistants to see that they are working properly.

shopwindow *Br. /Am.* **store display window/**.

shopworn story or **joke** *esp. Am.* boring or uninteresting one, esp. because it's familiar to people.

shore *Am.* the seashore as a space of vacation resort.

shore dinner *Am.* seafood dinner.

shore patrol *Am.* shore watch: *The shore patrol was ordered to search every sailor who went on board the ship.* - A. Makkai.

short *esp. Br.* col. a strong alcoholic drink such as whiskey or gin.

short *Am.* (on the Stock Exchange) sell shares which one doesn't own: *I wouldn't short IBM.* - R.A. Spears.

short/ be (a bit/rather) short *Br.* not have much money.

short/ be taken / caught short 1. *Br., Aus.* col. have a sudden and strong need, esp. to go to the toilet: *Don't get short at the Taj.* - Bulletin. 2. *Am., Aus.* find suddenly that you're not prepared to do smth. 3. *Br.* be put at disadvantage.

short-arse *Br.* sl. a short person.

short back and sides *esp. Br.* men's haircut: *England was full of words I'd never heard before - streaky bacon, short back and sides* - B. Bryson.

short/ a short sharp shock *Br., Aus.* quick and severe punishment.

short/ go short of smth. *esp. Br.* lack smth. essential.

short/ not be short of a bob or two *Br., Aus.* obs. col. or humor. have a lot of money.

short/ pull up short *Am.* stop doing smth. suddenly.

short ballot *Am.* one after which only the principal offices are filled.

shortcake 1. *Br.* thick shortbread. 2. *esp. Am., Can.* cake usu. a kind like scones over which sweetened fruit is poured: *I had prevailed on cook to make his favourite dishes strawberry shortcake.* - T. Caldwell., *she ordered filet mignon and strawberry shortcake* - M. Torgov.

shortcrust *Br.* crumbly pastry made with flour, fat and a little water.

short curlies/ (have sb.) by the short curlies *Br.* (have them) completely in their control.

short-ender *Am.* col. contestant not favoured to win, underdog.

short end of the stick *Am., Aus. Can.* sl. responsibility, burden, blame: *Here I am stuck with the short end of the stick again.* - R.A. Spears; **get the short end of the stick** *esp. Am.* end up in a worse situation than others.

shortening *Am., Aus.* butter or other fat used in cooking, esp. to make pastry soft and crumbly.

short hairs/ have sb. **by the short hairs** *esp. Am.* sl. have absolute control over sb.

shorthand *Br., Aus.* /*Am.* **stenography**/.

shorthand typist *esp. Br., Aus.* /*esp. Am., Can.* **stenographer**/.

short-hand writer *Br.* court stenographer.

shorthorn *Am.* col. an inexperienced man.

short-lifter *Br., Aus.* col. derog. a homosexual.

short-list *Br.* a list of people or things that have been chosen, for example, for a job or prize.

short-list (for) *Br.* put on a short list, usu. **be short-listed**: *We compiled a list of Demiro and Rita's known friends and short-listed half a dozen or so* - J.P. Hogan.

short notice/ at short notice *Am.* /*esp. Br.* **on short notice**/ with very little warning that smth. is going to happen: *Thanks for coming on such short notice.* - J. Kellerman.

short order *Am., Can.* easily prepared snacks: *Rajahwat was a valet, house-maid, short-order cook, and general help.* - Bulletin.

short order/ in short order *esp. Am.* quickly and with no trouble: *We dressed in short order* - C. Nordhoff, J.N. Hall., *It'll go through in short order.* - J. Dos Passos.

short-order cook *Am.* sb. in a restaurant kitchen who makes the food that can be prepared easily and quickly: *like a sleepy short-order cook cracking eggs over a grill* – R. Brautigan.

short rib *Br.* floating rib.

short ribs *Am., Can.* cut from the brisket of beef.

shorts 1. *esp. Am., Can.* /*esp. Br.* **underpants**/ men's short underpants: *Early on he created red tartan shorts* – Reader's Digest. 2. *Am.* refuse, clippings or trimmings discarded in various manufacturing processes (esp. of wood).

shorts/ eat my shorts *Am.* sl. derog. stop bothering me.

shortsheet *Am.* fold the top sheet on a bed so that no one can get into it, as a trick.

shortsighted *esp. Br.* /*esp. Am.* **nearsighted**/ unable to see objects clearly if they are not close to the eyes: *He was a small, thin, nearsighted man* - H. Fast.

short-staffed *Br., Aus.* short-handed.

short straw/ draw the short straw *esp. Br.* be chosen to do job that nobody wants to do.

short subject *esp. Am.* a film shown before screening a feature film.

short-swing *Am.* adj. covering six month or less financial transaction.

short time/ be on short time *Br.* (of a factory or office) operate for less than usual number of hours or days.

short-timer *Am.* mil. sl. person nearing the end of the military service.

shot (of) 1. *esp. Am.* col. a small alcoholic drink for swallowing at once: *He reached in, picked up a bottle of Scotch and two glasses and poured each of us a shot of drink.* - D. Brenner., *Whitman threw back several shots of whiskey.* - E.L. Doctorow. 2. *Am., Aus., NZ.* col. drunk. 3. *Am.* col. an injection of drugs.

shot/ get/be shot of sb./smth *Br.* col. get rid of sb./smth.

shot/ have a shot at sb. *Aus.* col. criticise sb.

shot/ have a/another shot(left) in one's **locker** *Br.* obs. make another attempt.

shot/ like a shot *esp. Br.* very fast and eagerly.

shot/ not a shot in one's **locker** *Br.* no money at all.

shot/ a shot across the bowls *Br.* smth. one says or does to warn sb. what might happen if they fail to do what they are told to do.

shot/ take a shot at smth. *Am. col.* try to do smth., often for the first time.

shot glass *Am., Can.* small glass used for serving drinks.

shotgun marriage *Am.* obs. one arranged very quickly because the woman is going to have a baby.

should *esp. Br.* used after I and we in conditional sentences.

should/ (*esp. Br.*) **I should have thought** (used in remarks expressing surprise or sometimes annoyance) / **I suggest that John should go** / (*Am.* also) **that John go**.

should/ I should like *esp. Br.* used to say politely that one wants smth.

shoulder *Am., Aus.* /*esp. Br.* **hard shoulder**/ an area of ground beside a road where drivers can stop their cars, if they're having trouble: *the other passed me on the shoulder of the road* - K. Ablow.

shoulder/ put one's **shoulder to the wheel** *Br.* obs. begin to work seriously.

shoulder-loop *Am.* shoulder-strap.

shout *Br., Aus., NZ. col. v. n.* (be) a particular person's turn to buy drinks for others / **shout drinks** *Br., Aus., NZ. col.* stand drinks: *It's my shout.* - T. Thorne.

shout, shout at the floor *Aus. sl.* vomit.

shout/ all over bar the shouting *Br. Can. col.* almost finished, so that the result is no longer in doubt.

shove *esp. Br. col.* move oneself.

shove down *Br.* write quickly and carelessly.

shove up/over *esp. Br. col.* move along on a seat to make place for sb. else.

show *Am.* finish in third place in a horse or dog race / an **each-way bet** in America is a bet on a horse to win, place, or show.

show 1. *esp. Br., Aus.* arrive later or when others are not expecting them. 2. *esp. Am. col.* arrive at a place where sb. is waiting for you, show up.

show *Am., Aus.* traces of smth. (e.g. gold, affection, etc.).

show/ give sb. **(a fair) show** *Am. Aus., NZ. col.* give a chance.

show/ (jolly) good show *Br.* obs. col. I am glad.

show/ show a leg! *Br. col.* get out of bed.

show/ show a clean pair of heels *Br. col.* obs. run away very fast.

show/ show one's **teeth** *Br.* use one's power in aggressive way.

show/ show/reveal (oneself **in**) one's **true colours** *Br.* /*Am.* **show** one's **true colors**/ reveal one's true feelings or opinions about a subject.

show and tell 1. *esp. Am., Can., Aus.* primary school activity when children discuss objects they have brought to schools: *One of my third-grade students brought in a snake for show and tell.* - Reader's Digest. 2. *Am. sl.* an elaborate display, usu. for selling or other persuasion: *We had only time to begin, to play enough psychic show-and-tell to know we would get along* - J. Baez., *I've been to Cabinet meeting when (they have) been a show-and-tell.* - Time., *It makes the show more show-and-tell.* - Vanity Fair.

show sb. **over** smth. *esp. Br., Aus.* guide through (esp. an interesting building or a house for sale).

show sb. **up** *esp. Br., Can.* cause to feel shame, embarrass: *Louis could show him up* - M. Jones, J. Chilton.

show bag *Aus.* bag of goods, used for promotion purposes, esp. at annual shows.

showboat *esp. Am. col.* 1. behave in a showy way: *nothing more than a bad case of showboating.* - New York. 2. also *Can.* person who shows off: *I'm not a showboat.* - USA Today.

shower 1. *Br. col.* derog. a group of unpleasant, worthless, lazy, etc. people: *this shower of scientific cabbages* – F. Edwards. 2. *esp. Am.* also **shower party** a. party given on a special occasion. b. a woman's friends' party at which they give her suitable gifts (esp. if she's going to be married or have a baby): *If I had had a bridal shower, I would have had a few decent pots and pans of my own.* - A.E. Hotchner. 3. *Am.* hold shower party for sb.

shower/ send sb. **to the showers/ earn a trip to the showers** *Am., Can. col.* 1. remove sb. from a game. 2. reject, dismiss.

shower/ take a shower *esp. Am.* /*Br.* **have a shower**/.

shower bath *Am.* act of washing oneself in a shower.

shower gel *Br.* type of liquid soap used to wash oneself with in a shower.

shower proof *Br., Aus.* /*Am.* **water repellent**/ not absorbing water when it's raining lightly (esp. of garment and fabric).

shower tea *Aus.* a party held for a woman just before she gets married, at which usu. female friends gather and give her presents for her future home.

show home/house or **flat** *Br.* /*Am.* **model house** or **apartment**/ one of a group of similar apartments or houses, decorated and filled with furniture shown to possible buyers.

show-me *Am.* adj. 1. col. demanding demonstration. 2. sceptical.

The Show Me State *Am.* joc. Missouri: *Would you like to hear from other males in Show-me State.* - K. Vonnegut, Jr.

show pony *Aus.* a person who appears to perform well, but who has no real abilities.

shrewdy *Aus.* col. shrewd person.

shrift/ receive short shrift *Br.* get little attention or sympathy.

shrimp *Am* /*Br.* **prawn**/.

shrimp cocktail *Am.* /*Br.* **prawn cocktail**/ shrimps without shells in a red sauce, eaten before the main part of a meal.

shroud *Am., Can.* a cordial made from juice and water.

shrub *Am.* a beverage made by adding acidulated fruit juice to iced water.

shtick, schtick *Am.* style of humour that a particular comedian or actor typically uses: *Elvis and Ed Parker talked karate shtick, they got up and demonstrated.* – J. Hopkins.

shtuck/ in shtuck *Br.* sl. expecting trouble, problems or difficulties.

shuck *esp. Am.* 1. (remove) the outer shell or peel: *I slit them all and shucked out the insides* - E. Hemingway. 2. undies. 3. col. take off smth. one is wearing.

shuck off *Am.* 1. shuffle off, get rid of (sb. or smth.) and pass it on to sb. else. 2. take off a piece of clothing: *I shucked off my trench coat.* – M. Daly.

shuck *esp. Am.* 1. pod or husk (esp. of corn). 2. rubbish, small matter, nothing, e.g. *not worth shucks, no great shucks.*

shucks *Am., Can.* col. excl. (an inoffensive expression of annoyance or disappointment): *but shucks, that was just 'cause folks wouldn't leave him alone.* - J. Gabree., *Calloway shifted his feet underneath in an aw-shucks gesture.* - B. Tillman.

shuffle *esp. Am., Aus.* a change in the people who are governing the country or managing an organisation.

shuffle/ get/be lost in the shuffle *esp. Am., Can.* be ignored in a confused situation.

shufti (at) *Br., Aus.* col. a quick look / **have/take a shufti.**

shunpike *Am.* col. road taken by travellers to avoid major highways (esp. to avoid paying toll on paid turnpike).

shunt 1. *esp. Br.* a railway switch. 2. *Br.* motor accident, esp. a collision of vehicles travelling close behind others.

shunter *Br.* a railway shunting engine or its driver.

shunting yard *Br.* railway switchboard.

shut *esp. Br.* stop being open to the public (of a shop, bank, etc.).

shut *Br.* /*Am.* **closed**/ not open for business.

shut sb. down, /*esp. Am., Can.* **shut out sb.** *Am.* col. prevent an opposing team or player from playing well or getting points.

shut out *esp. Am., Can.* /*Am.* col. **shut sb. down**/ (in a game) prevent (one's opponent) from gaining a point: *The Flyers shut out the Leaps 3-2 in last night's game.*- Longman; n.

shut up (the shop) *esp. Br.* /*Am.* **close up (the shop)**/ 1. get ready to go home and lock a shop. 2. close business for the day or permanently.

shut/ shut it! *Br.* col. used to tell sb. rudely and angrily to stop talking.

shut-in *Am., Can.* person confined to one's home or institution by illness or incapacity: *Our priests visit the shut-ins - people who must stay at home.* - W. Magnuson., *It's a privilege of the shut-in.* – P. Roth.

shut-in *Am.* adj. brooding, secretive.

shutout *Am.* person who is excluded or prevented from succeeding.

shutterbug *esp. Am., Can.* col. photographer, esp. an enthusiastic amateur.

shuttering, shutters, formwork *Br.* /*Am.* **forms**/ wooden form used to pour concrete in (used in building).

shutters/ put up the shutters *Br.* col. close a business for the day or permanently.

shutters/ the shutters come down *Br.* deciding not to show one's inner feelings.

shy (of) *esp. Am.* lacking, short of: *she was shy two months of nineteenth birthday.* - T. Capote., *They fought shy of numbers.* - Economist., *Mr. Marain was just shy of a Ph.D. in mathematics.* - Reader's Digest.

shy/ several cards shy of a full deck, one sandwich short of a picnic *Am.* acting very strange.

shypoo *Aus.* cheap beer.

shyster *Am., Aus.* col. a dishonest person, esp. a lawyer or politician: *Our girl's going to need fancier shysters that I can afford.* - T. Capote., *She'll go to a shyster firm!* - S. Bellow.

sic *Am.* col. tell a dog to attack sb., esp. in **sic 'em!**

sick *Br.* col. n. vomit: *Ms Fossington-Gore covers sick in sand.* – S. Townsend; **sick** smth. **up** *Br., Aus.* col. vomit: *I think I'm going to sick up.* - R.A. Spears.

sick/ be sick *esp. Br.* vomit /also *Br., Aus.* col. **sick** smth. **up**: *The only thing you can do with* *too much food is to be sick with it.* - A. Huxley., *I went to the lavatory and was sick.* - G. Greene.

sick/ be sick about *Br. /Am.* **over/** smth. be unhappy about it.

sick/ be as sick as a dog *Am., Aus.* be very sick.

sick/ be as sick as a parrot/pig *Br.* col. humor. be very disappointed or annoyed.

sick/ be on the sick *Br.* col. receiving sick benefit.

sick/ get sick *Am.* become ill.

sick/ look sick *esp. Am.* col. look worthless by comparison: *Even those Coca-Cola signs they put up around Marion look pretty sick up beside something fine like this* - E. Caldweel.

sick/ sick to one's **stomach** *Am., Aus.* feeling nausea, queasy: *After the first treatment he felt sick to his stomach.* - J. Hyams.

sick bag *esp. Br.* a bag for vomiting into.

sicken/ be sickening for smth. *Br.* be about to become ill: *You are sickening for something* – R. Westall.

sickening *Br.* col. making sb. feel jealous.

sickie *esp. Br. Aus.* col. /*Br.* **throw a sickie,** *Aus.* **chuck a sickie,** *Am.* **call in sick/** a day off work, esp. when pretending to be ill.

sick-making *Br.* col. very annoying.

sickness benefit, incapacity benefit *Br.* money paid, esp. by the government, to sb. who is too ill to work, esp. to self-employed or unemployed people when they are sick for at least four days.

sick note *Br. /Am.* **excuse/** note written by one doctor or parents saying that sb. is ill and can't go to school or work.

sicko *esp. Am.* sl. sb. who gets pleasure from things that most people find unpleasant and upsetting: *You're definitely a sicko* – R.L. Stine.

sick-out *esp. Am., Can.* col. truancy under the guise of going sick, a type of strike.

sick parade *Br. /Am.* **sick call/** the daily time or place for soldiers to report themselves as ill: *Better go on sick call!* - J. Dos Passos.

side 1. *Br.* col. television channel or station. 2. *esp. Br.* the spinning of a snooker ball caused by hitting it on the side rather than in the middle. 3. *esp. Br.* col. becoming rare. unpleasantly grand behaviour towards others (esp. in the phrs. **put on side, have no/ be without side.** 4. *esp. Am., Can.* dish served as subsidiary to the main one. 4. *Br.* page of writing or one side of a piece of paper. 5. *Br.* sports team.

side/ sb. will be laughing on the other side of their **face** *Br. /Am.* **sb. will be laughing out of the other side of** their **mouth/** obs. be miserable later because of their current actions.

side/ criticize, scold, curse sb. **up one side and down the other** *Am.* col. criticize sb. without worrying about how they feel.

side/ let the side down *Br., Aus.* embarrass or cause problems for a group of people that one is part of.

side/ on the side *Am., Can.* served separately from the main dish. **side/ on the side** 1. *esp. Am.* beside or in addition to the main thing, job, etc.: *he got greedy and was doing a little shake-down business of his own on the side.* - S. Sheldon. 2. *Br.* as a usu. cheating or dishonest additional activity.

side/ pass by on the other side *Br., Aus.* ignore a person who needs help.

side/ be speaking/talking out of both sides of one's **mouth** *Am.* always agree with different people's opinion on the same subject.

side/ prompt side *Am.* the right (from an actor/ actress) side of the stage.

side/ this (other) side of the black stump *Aus.* col. this (other) world.

side bar *esp. Am., Can.* a short news story relating to a larger magazine or newspaper story and giving details or extra information.

sideboards *Br. /esp. Am.* **sideburns/** hair grown down the sides of a man's face in front of the ears: *He still had his walrus sideburns and moustache.* - J. Baez.

sideburned *Am.* adj. wearing sideburns.

sidehill *Am., Can.* a hillside.

sidehorse *Am.* also **pommel horse** vaulting horse with handles.

side issue *esp. Br.* subject or problem that is not as important as the main one and may take person's attention away from the main one.

sidekick *esp. Am.* col. a (less important) helper or companion: *the gangster Charney has set his sidekick, Greceo, to guard his, Charney's mistress* - C. Hoover., *Mike Howard was my on-the-air sidekick* - W. Jack, B. Laursen.

side lamp *Br.* parking lamp.

sidelight *Br. /Am., Aus.* **parking light/** either of a pair of lamps fixed usu. on the front of a vehicle at or near the sides.

sideline *esp. Am., Aus. /Br.* **touchline/** a line marking the side areas of play, esp. for football: *my contributions were mostly from the sidelines* – Reader's Digest.

sideline *esp. Am.* (usu. pass.) put (a person esp. a player) out of action from the main activity: *Arthritis in her ankles sidelined her.* - Reader's Digest.

sideman *Am.* a musician in a jazz ensemble other than a leader: *I'm never going to be anything more than just a sideman in a band.* - A.E. Hotchner.

side marker lamp *Am.* sidelight in a car.

sidemeat *Am., Can.* salt pork or bacon, esp. cut from the side of the pig.

side mirror *Am. /Br.* **wing mirror/** mirror at the side of a motor vehicle.

sidesman *Br.* churchwarden assistant.

sideswipe *esp. Am., Can.* hit with a blow directed along the side: *A fellow we know was pretty shook up after sideswiping a couple in a small foreign car.* - Reader's Digest., *The government Plymouth might get sideswiped by a taxi on the way uptown.* - J. O'Brien, A. Kurins.

sidetrack *Am.* short track connected to a main one.

sidewalk, also **sideway** *esp. Am., Can. /Br.* **pavement; foot(path)/** a usu. paved surface or path at the side of a street for people to walk on: *he invited me to join him at the sidewalk cafes.* - J.A. Michener., *The sidewalks were gleaming with moisture in the dusk.* - T. Caldwell., *I saw the cage perched on a sidewalk ashcan* - T. Capote.

sidewalk artist *Am. /Br.* **pavement artist/** one who draws pictures on a pavement with coloured chalk, hoping that people passing will give money.

sidewalk superintendent *Am.* annoying person watching sb.'s work and giving advice, esp. when not qualified to do so.

sideways/ knock sb. **sideways** *Br., Aus.* surprise, confuse or upset sb. very much.

side wheeler *Am., Can. /Br.* **paddle steamer/**: *a side-wheeler, sink on him in Lake Abbitibbi.* - W. Grady.

sidewinder *Am.* heavy swinging blow from the side.

siding 1. *Am., Can.* covering planks in the outside wall of a house: *barracks siding bleached as gray as the bones of the dead* - Time. 2. *Br.* a short railway track next to a main track where trains are kept when they are not being used. 3. *Am., Can.* loop line: *the engine was backing into the siding* – E. Caldwell.

Sierra *Am.* radio code for letter S.

The Sierra State *Am.* California.

a sight for sore eyes *Br.* sb. or smth. that is very unattractive or very funny to look at.

sightly *Am.* offering a fine view.

sight/ out of sight *esp. Am.* sl. 1. very good, wonderful. 2. very large.

sightgag *Am.* col. worthless joke or prank.

sign for Liverpool, Manchester, etc. *Br. /Am.* **sign with/** sign a contract agreeing to play for a particular football team.

sign off 1. *Am.* col. stop talking: *I hope this speaker signs off soon* - Longman. 2. *Br.* (of unemployed) officially inform the authorities that they have found a job.

sign off on *Am.* col. assent or give one's approval to.

sign on *Br.* col. declare that one is available for work when unemployed by signing a paper: *Have you signed on this week?* - Longman.

signage *esp. Am., Can.* signs collectively, esp. commercial or public display signs.

signal box *esp. Br. /esp. Am.* **signal tower/** a small raised building near a railway from which the signals and points are controlled: *The Complete Encyclopaedia of Signal Boxes.* - B. Bryson.

signalman *Br. /Am.* **tower man/** person who controls railway traffic and signals.

signature *Am., Can.* the part of a medical prescription which contains the directions to the patient.

signature tune *Br.* distinctive piece of music before specific radio or TV programme.

signboard *esp. Am., Can.* board displaying a sign to direct traffic or travellers.

significant other *esp. Am.* a spouse or lover.

signify *Am.* col. (among blacks) exchage insults as a game or ritual.

signing *Br.* sb. who has just signed a contract to join a sports team.

signpost *esp. Br.* 1. provide with signposts to guide the driver, **be signposted**. -ed adj. 2. show clearly and unmistakably.

silence cloth, also **silencer** *Am., Can.* thick cloth laid under table cloth to protect table from heat and scratches.

(exhaust) silencer *Br. /Am., Aus.* **muffler/** part of a petrol engine which fits onto the exhaust pipe.

silent majority *Am.* the politically non-vocal section of a population: *Sidney Miltner is a member of the silent majority.* - A. Makkai.

silent partner *Am., Can. /Br.* **sleeping partner/** partner in a business who takes no active part in its operation: *they were basically silent partners.* - L. Burkett.

silk *Am.* (of corn) produce silk / **silk brusher** *Am.* machine for picking up silk.

silk *Br.* law. KC or QC.

silk/ take silk *Br.* tech. become a K.C. or Q.C., become a lawyer of high rank: *a patent appointing him a Queen's Counsel - a proceeding known as "taking silk."* - J. Ruppeldtova.

silk-stocking *Am., Can.* wealthy well-dressed person: *Nor did he have access to the silk stocking district through marriage or family.* - T. Thompson, adj. aristocratic; wealthy.
silly billy *esp. Br.* col. a fool.
silly buggers/ play silly buggers *Br., Aus.* col. behave in a stupid or annoying way.
the silly season *esp. Br., Aus.* col. a period of time in the summer when there's not much news, esp. political news so that newspapers write about events that are not important.
silt *Am.* scale, fur.
silver band *Br.* brass band playing silver-plated instruments.
silver foil *Br.* foil, very thin sheets of metal.
silver jubilee *esp. Br.* 25th anniversary, esp. of Queen's coronation.
silver paper *Br.* paper that is shiny like metal on one side used esp. for wrapping food.
silver print *Am.* print. blue print.
silver sand *Br.* fine, white sand used in gardening.
silverside *Br., Aus.* the top side of meat (beef) cut from the leg of cattle.
The Silver State *Am.* Nevada.
silver streak *Br.* English channel.
silverware, flatware *Am. /esp. Br.* **cutlery,** *Aus.* either of these/ metal knives, forks and spoons: *they pick up the silverware, and off they go* - E. Tailor.
simnel (cake) *esp. Br.* rich cake often coated with almond paste and baked for Mid-Lent, Easter and Christmas.
simoleon *Am.* col. a dollar.
simonize *Am.* tdmk. polish (a motor ehicle).
Simon Legree *Am.* a harsh taskmaster: *he was playing Simon Legree all the time* - B. Holiday., W. Duffy.
simp *Am., Can.* col. a fool.
simpatico, sympatico *esp. Am.* col. 1. nice, pleasant: *Kazan instantly sympatico to many her customers.* - Time., *Clark is strict but sympatico* - Time. 2. in agreement.
simulcast *esp. Am., Aus.* a broadcast by radio or TV stations of the same programme at the same time: *the show would be shown in twenty-eight European countries via a Eurovision simulcast* – J. Hopkins.
SIN *Can.* Social Insurance Number.
sin/ be more sinned against than sinning *Br.* obs. be unfairly treated by others, esp. when they don't deserve this.
sin/ for my sins *esp. Br., Aus.* humor. col. it's my punishment for being bad (esp. additional responsibilities).

sin-bin *Br., Aus.* col. an area off the field where a player who committed an act which is against the rules could be sent for some time.
Sincerely (Yours) *Am. /Br.* **Yours Sincerely/**.
Sin City *Am.* sl. Las Vegas.
the sinews of war *esp. Br.* money needed for weapons and supply.
sing *esp. Am.* sl. (out) (of a criminal) give information to the police: *The contact will sing to us* - A. McLean.
sing/ sing from the same (hymn/song) sheet *Br.* agree about smth.
sing up *esp. Br., Aus. /Am.* **sing out/** sing more loudly.
single *Br.* 1. */Am., Can.* **one-way/** (of a ticket or its cost) for a trip from one place to another but not back again. 2. a single ticket: *I asked the man in the ticket window for a single to Barnstaple.* - B. Bryson.
single *Am.* col. one-dollar note.
single cream *Br. /Am.* **coffee cream,** *Am., Aus.* **light cream/** a thin table cream as opposed to whipped cream (*Br.* **double cream,** *Am.* **heavy cream**).
single cuff, also **double cuff** *Br.* barrel cuff or French cuff.
single-decker *esp. Br.* bus with only one deck.
single-foot *Am., Can.* (of a horse) go at a rack.
single-lane road *Am. /Br.* **single-track road/** road only wide enough for one car to go along in.
singlet *esp. Br., Aus. /Am.* **sports-shirt/** man's garment without sleeves worn as a vest, or as an outer shirt when playing some sports: *She likes to run about dressed only in PE shorts and a singlet.* – S. Townsend.
single-track *Br.* adj. one-lane (about a road).
singsong *Br.* col. */Am.* **songfest, singalong/** informal gathering or party for singing songs: *They'd bring their guitars with them, and we'd have a singsong at the end of the ward.* - P. Norman., *We have to have a singsong.* - Cheshire Life.
sink, also **washbowl** *Am. /Br.* **basin/** wash basin for washing the hands and the face (at the bathroom), (dishes can also be washed in sink): *Then he scoured tub and sink with lye and soap.* - M. Puzo.
sink *Br.* kitchen sink.
sink *Br.* col. (of a number of alcoholic drinks) drink them quickly.
sink/ sink one's differences *Br.* forget one's disagreements.
sinker *Am.* col. a doughnut or biscuit: *This sinker must be four days old.* - R.A. Spears.

sinking standards *esp. Br.* falling standards.
sin tax *Am.* col. a tax on alcoholic liquor, cigarettes, sweepstakes, etc: *sin taxes on beer or cigarettes, or lotteries.* - New York.
The Sioux State *Am.* North Dacota.
sippet *Aus.* toasted bread.
Sir 1. *Br.* col. one's male teacher (used as address to male teacher by a school child). 2. *Br.* a form of address, usu. to a customer. 3. *Am.* a form of address to older people. 4. *Am.* col. used to get attention of unknown man.
Sir/ No, Sir!, No Siree *Am.* col. certainly not: *The Lord doesn't neglect his workers, no sirree, no, sir.* - T. Wilder.
siree *Am., Can.* col. used for emphasis after yes or no.
siren suit *Br.* coveralls.
sis *esp. Am.* col. (used when speaking to one's sister): *I don't like it, sis.* - Arthur Hailey.
sister 1. *Br., Aus.* (a title for) a nurse (usu. a female) in charge of a department (ward) of a hospital. 2. *Am.* (used when speaking to one's sister or obs. col. other woman): *What's on your mind, sister?* - J. Steinbeck. 3. *esp. Am., Can.* col. (used by other blacks) black woman.
sister/ be a true sister under the skin *Br.* (of a man) support women's actions to improve their rights.
sit 1. *esp. Br.* also **sit an exam** /*Am.* **take an exam**, *Aus.* **sit for** one's **exam**/ take (a written examination for): *He had not sat the 11-plus exam* - P. Norman. 2. *Br.* (for) represent (a place) in Parliament: *Members of his family have sat for the town for over a century.* - Longman. 3. *Am.* take part in a sit-in. 4. *Am., Can.* not use (a player) in a game.
sit-down *Br.* (of a meal) adj. at which people are served while seated at a table: *Nina worked five sitdown black-tie dinners.* - D. Mortman.
sit about *Br.* sit around doing nothing.
sit down *Br.* accept or put up with an unwelcome situation.
sit for smth. *Br.* 1. (prepare to) take an examination. 2. be the Member of Parliament for a specific constituency.
sit in *esp. Br.* take care of a child during the parent's absence: *Have you found anyone suitable to sit in this evening?* - Longman.
sit out *esp. Br.* sit outside.
sit under *esp. Br.* attend classes or religious services given by a teacher: *In my youth I had the great honour to sit under a very famous teacher?* - Longman.

sit/ not sit well with sb. *esp. Am.* not like or accept the situation.
sit/ sit on one's **arse** *Br.* /*Am.* **ass,** *Aus.* **bum**/ do nothing.
sit/ sit right/well with sb. *Am.* agree with sb.'s ideas, please sb.
sits vac *Br.* col. situations vacant.
sitter *esp. Am.* babysitter.
sitter-in *esp. Br.* baby-sitter (esp. one looking for a child, not a baby) in the evening (in the daytime it is usu. called /*esp. Br.* **child-minder**/).
sitting *Br.* adj. 1. that is now a member (**sitting member**) of an official body, such as Parliament for an area. 2. that now lives in a place.
sitting *Am.* in office.
sitting room *esp. Br.* /*Am.* **lounge room**/ living room: *I finally strolled into our sitting room* - A. Christie.
sitting tenant *Br.* someone who lives in a rented house or a flat, esp. when there's a change of owner.
situations vacant or **wanted** *esp. Br., Aus.* section of newspaper where vacant jobs are listed.
sit-upon *Br.* humor. euph. ass, bottom.
situs *esp. Am.* law. the place to which for purposes of legal jurisdiction or taxation a property belongs.
sitzfleisch *esp. Am.* col. the person's buttocks; stamina, staying power to endure and persevere.
Siwash sweater *Can.* thick sweater made by Siwash Indians.
six/ at sixes and sevens *Br.* col. confused.
six/ be hit/knocked for six *Br., Aus.* col. be suddenly and badly affected by smth. that happens.
six/ six of one and half a dozen of the other *Br., Can.* col. (a situation that is) good and bad to an equal degree.
six/ six of the best *Br., Aus.* col. obs. or humor. a beating, esp. six blows with a stick given to a school child as a punishment: *hauls out some kit and gives him six of the best?* – R. Westall.
six-bits *Am., Can.* sl. 75 cents: *Shave and a haircut, six-bits.* - S. North.
six-by-six *Am.* col. six-wheeled motor vehicle with six driving wheels.
sixer *Am.* a six-pack.
six-form college *Br.* college where pupils can enter at the age of 16.
sixpenny *Br.* cheap.
six-shooter, also **sixgun** *esp. Am.* a revolver holding six bullets: *I might have a six-shooter strapped to one hip.* - S. Grafton.

sixteenth note *esp. Am., Can.* /Br. **semibreve**/ note with a time value half as long as a quaver.

sixty/ **like sixty** *Am.* col. with great speed or force: *The phone's been going like sixty.* - E. McBain., *They're using 'em up...like sixty in there* - J. Dos Passos.

the sixty-four dollar question *Am.* the most important question: *Now for the sixty-four dollar question, which ex-beat is it?* - R.J. Randisi., M. Wallace.

sixty-fourth note *esp. Am., Can.* demi-semi-semi quaver.

sixty-miler *Aus.* col. small freight ship.

size/ **try** smth. **for size** *Br., Aus.* /Am., Aus. **try** smth. **on for size**/ try to decide whether smth. works.

size up (to, with) *Am.* be comparable with.

sizzling *esp. Am.* very hot.

skag *esp. Am.* col. heroin.

skank *esp. Am., Can.* col. unpleasant or ugly: *Rollins' vocals has no litheness, no skankiness to bring them across* – BigO, n.

skate *Br.* a kind of flat sea fish.

skate through *Br., Aus.* succeed in a test or an examination easily.

skates/ **get/put your skates on** *Br., Aus.* col. (used to tell sb. to hurry).

sked *esp. Am., Can.* col. schedule.

skeeter *esp. Am., Can., Aus.* col. mosquito.

skeet shooting *Am.* /Br. **clay pigeon shooting**/ sport of shooting at clay objects that have been thrown into the air.

skeleton in the cupboard *Br., Aus.* /Am., Can. **in the closet**/ col. unpleasant often shocking event or fact from the past that a person or family keeps secret: *The skeleton in the closet from the same session is a feature for Louis (For British release the Skeleton was prudishly placed in the Cupboard to avoid any suggestion of lavatorial necrophilia!).* - M. Jones, J. Chilton.

skeeve *Am.* sl. digust, repel: *she was initially skeeved out by the prospect of eating garbage* – Marie Claire

skell *Am.* a homeless person or derelict, esp. in New York.

skeptic *Am., Aus.* sceptic.

skerrick *Aus., NZ.* col. (usu. in negatives) smallest piece.

skew-whiff *esp. Br., Aus.* col. usu. humor. not straight, skewed.

skid *Am., Can.* 1. move heavy objects on skids. 2. each of a set of wooden rollers used for drawing a log or a heavy object.

skidlid *esp. Br., Aus.* col. motorcycler's protective hat: *How much did you pay for that handsome skid lid?* - A. Makkai.

skidoo *esp. Am., Can.* motorized toboggan, v.

skidpan *Br.* /Am., Can. **skidpad**/ prepared slippery surface where drivers practise controlling skidding vehicles.

skidroad *Am., Can.* road formed by skids along which logs are hauled.

skid row *esp. Am., Can.* col. poor dirty part of a town where unemployed and drunk people gather: *I look like something left after a New Year's party on skid row.* - I. Shaw.

skids *Aus.* sl. hard luck: *"Them's the skids",* as the young fry say. - T. Thorne.

skids/ **hit the skids** *Aus.* col. 1. leave a place quickly. 2. make a vehicle stop quickly. 3. get into a bad situation, esp. by losing money, home, or job.

skids/ **put the skids under** sb./smth. *Br., Aus.* /Am. **put the skids on**/ col. make smth. likely to fail.

skiffle 1. *esp. Br.* music popular in the late 1950s, based on American folk music and played partly on instruments made by the performer. 2. *Am.* style of jazz in 1920-30s developed from blues, ragtime and folk music played on conventional instruments.

skillet 1. *esp. Br.* small kettle or pot usu. having 3 or 4 often long feet and used for cooking on the hearth. 2. *Am.* /Br., Aus. **frying pan**/: *We sprayed along with the rocks crunching and popping against the underside of the fender like a grease in a skillet.* - R.P. Warren.

skilly *Br.* broth made of oatmeal and water flavoured with meat.

skim *Am.* 1. put a finishing coat of plaster. 2. take money illegally, esp. by not saying that one has made profits so that they don't have to pay tax: *Jilly Rizzo had received a share of the skim* – A. Summers, R. Swan.

skim stones/pebbles, etc. *Br.* /Am. **skip rocks/ stones,** etc./ throw smooth, flat stones into a river, lake, etc. in a way that makes them jump across the surface.

skimmed milk *Br.* /Am., Can. **skim milk**/ milk that has had most of the fat removed from it.

skimmer *Am., Can.* darter.

Skimo *Can.* Eskimo.

skin 1. *Br.* col. skinhead. 2. *Am.* card game.

skin *Am.* col. completely defeat sb.

skin/ **give** sb. **(or get) (some) skin** *Am.* sl. (used esp. by blacks) touch hands in greeting.

skin/ **it's no skin off my back/teeth** *Am.* col. / *Br.* **it's no skin off my nose**/ col. I don't care about it because it doesn't affect me; no harm done.

skin down, up *Am.* shin down, up.

skin through *Am.* 1. be only just able to pass through (smth.) narrow: *we should be able to skin through.* - Longman. 2. be only just be able to pass smth. (such as an examination: *himself only skinning through an only German measles.* – P. Roth.

skin up *Br.* sl. make a cannabis cigarette.

skin and blister *Br.* sl. a sister.

skin-dip *esp. Am., Can.* col. swim in the nude: *My best friend will go skinny dipping late at night* - Arkansas Times.

skinful/ have had a skinful *Br.* col. be very drunk.

skin game *Am., Can.* col. swindle: *they had been operating a skin game, and not a legitimate business.* - H.C. Whitford., R.J. Dixson.

skinhead *Br.* a young person whose hair is shaved or cut very short: *I found him bossing a gang of skunheads and punks about.* – S. Townsend.

skin house *Am.* sl. striptease joint: *This week Atlanta offers boxed reviews of skin houses.* - Time.

skinner *Am.* 1. mule driver. 2. a driver (of a tractor or bulldozer).

skinny *Am.* col. the truth, information, esp. in **get/give the skinny on**: *a talkfest that gave all the inside skinny on the entertainment industry.* - D. Mortman., *they like getting the skinny themselves* - Fortune.

skin-pop *esp. Am., Can.* inject drugs subcutaneously.

skint *Br.* col. completely without money, broke, esp. for a short time: *they were skint until payday* - D. Francis.

skip *Br. /Am., Can.* **jump rope, skip rope/** jump over a rope (**skipping rope** *Br. / Am., Can.* **jump rope**) passed repeatedly beneath one's feet, as a game or for exercise.

skip 1. *Am., Aus.* skim (stones). 2. **skip** smth. *Am.* not do it.

skip 1. *Br.* a builder's large metal container for carrying heavy materials, esp. old bricks, wood, etc. to be taken away. 2. *Br., Aus. /Am.* tdmk. **dumpster/** large metal garbage container, which is usu. taken away by truck.

skip out on sb. *Am.* leave sb. when they need you.

skipper *Br.* sl. boss.

skipping rope *esp. Br. /Am.* **jump rope/** skip rope.

skip tracer *Am.* sl. bounty hunter: *I pick up a few odd jobs, worked a few skip traces.* - A. Hitchcock Mystery Magazine.

skirt *Br.* cut of meat from the lower flank.

skirting (board) *Br., Aus. /Am.* **baseboard, mopboard, washboard, scrubboard/** board fixed along the base of a wall where it meets the floor of a room: *But a side of a shoe had brushed the skirting board.* - J.D. Carr.

ski scooter *Br.* skidoo.

ski stick *Br.* ski pole.

skite *Aus., NZ.* 1. v. boast. 2. a boaster.

skive (off) *Br.* col. avoid work, school or duty or leave it early without permission, **-er** n.: *It was mostly skiving.* - P. Norman.

skivvies, BVDs *Am., Can.* col. tdmk. a man's undergarments, esp. a vest and underpants: *he's gonna go right out in his skivvies and do the job now.* - G.V. Higggins., *I grabbed a flashlight and ran outside in my skivvies.* - Reader's Digest., *One was drunk and sleeping in his soiled skivvies.* - S. Bellow.

skivvy *Br.* 1. derog. col. a servant, esp. a girl, who does only the dirty unpleasant jobs in a house: *In fact I'm treated like a skivvy in this house* - C.M. Fraser. 2. col. (esp. of a woman) do the dirty unpleasant jobs in a house.

skivvy-bin *Br.* dumpster, public rubbish receptacle.

skivvy shirt *Am.* lightweight high-necked long-sleeved garment.

skol *Aus.* col. drink (smth.), esp. beer at a gulp.

skookum *Am., Can.* strong.

skookum-house *Am., Can.* col. jail.

skosh *Am.* col. a small amount.

skua *Br.* a large sea bird of Northern Atlantic which steals food from other birds.

skull *Aus.* sl. drink alcohol.

skull session *Am.* col. joc. briefing session.

skulk *esp. Br.* malinger, shirk (a job).

skunk *Am., Can.* col. defeat (an opponent) completely: *I skunked them.* - R.A. Spears.

sky *esp. Br.* throw up or toss up, flip.

skybox *Am., Can.* luxurious and enclosed seating area high up in a sports arena.

skycap *Am., Can.* person who carries passengers' cases at an airport: *resist shocks like going over the curb or the skycap's foot.* - Time., *The luggage the skycap had reached for was actually a soft-sided tackle bag* - Outdoor Life.

sky sign *Br.* an ad set up so as to be visible against the sky.

sky truck *Am.* col. big transport airplane.

skyway *esp. Am., Can.* 1. recognised route followed by an aircraft. 2. covered overhead walkway between buildings. 3. raised motorway.

slab *Br.* table used for laying a body in a mortuary.

slack/ pick/take up the slack *Am., Aus.* col. do the work which sb. stopped doing but which still needs to be done.

slacker 1. *Am.* person who evades military services. 2. *esp. Am.* a person, esp. of 1990s subculture characterized by apathy and aimlessness.

slag *Br.* derog. col. promiscuous woman or girl: *come clean on this Agnes slag* - J. Higgins.

slag *Aus.* col. spit.

slag (off) *esp. Br.* col. criticise harshly, often unfairly: *time for a cream tea and to slag off the locals* - B. Bryson.

slagheap *esp. Br.* a pile of slag at a mine, factory, etc.: *numberless slagheaps of broken, rain-shiny slate.* - B. Bryson.

slam *Am., Can., Aus.* harsh criticism: *I don't want to hear another nasty and hateful slam at my sister.* - R.A. Spears.

the slam 1. *Am., Can.* prison. 2. *esp. Am.* poetry contest.

slambang esp. *Am., Can.* col. violent, vigorous, etc.: *Slits thought his slambang style lacked style.* - W. Murphy.

slam-bam-thank-you-ma'am *Am.* sl. a quick sex act: *this was a simple slam-bam-thank-you-ma'am lay.* - D. Mortman.

slam-dancing *esp. Am., Can.* a type of dancing in which dancers (**slammers**) deliberately collide with one another.

slam dunk *Am.* (of proposals, plans, etc.). derog. force through.

slam dunk/ be a slam dunk *Am.* sl. smth. very easy to do or smth. successful, adj. **slam-dunk.**

slang *Br., Aus.* 1. col. attack with rude angry words: *The public slanging of a year and more ago has given way to euphoria* - Bulletin. 2. sl. cheat, swindle.

slanging match *esp. Br., Aus.* col. noisy quarrel: *These niggles deteriorated into a huge verbal slanging match* - New Idea., *Ivona won't be drawn into a slanging match with the media.* - New Idea.

slant *Am.* a look, glance / **take a slant.**

slant-tailed *Br.* fastback (of a car).

slantways *Am.* slantwise.

slap and tickle *Br., Aus.* col. humor. playful lovemaking: *his progress was one slap and tickle and free drink.* - G. Greene.

slap-bang *Br.* col. directly or right.

slap bang in the middle (of somewhere) *Br.* col. exactly in that place.

slapjack *Am., Can.* /*Br.* **dropscone**/ griddle cake.

slapper *Br.* col. humor. a prostitute.

slap-up (meal, dinner, etc.) *esp. Br., Aus.* col. (esp. of food) excellent and in large amounts: *They did it for nothing, but they got a slap-up meal* - P. Norman.

slap-up *Aus.* col. a fight.

slash 1. *Br., Aus.* col. not polite. an act of passing water from the body, often in **have/take a slash.** 2. *Am.* reduction, cutback (in prices, etc.). 3. *Am., Can.* low swampy area with brush. 4. *Am., Can.* debris resulting from the felling or destruction of trees.

slate 1. *Am., Can.* list of people, esp. those of the same party, who are candidates in an election. 2. *Br.* col. a record of things bought but not yet paid for. 3. *esp. Am., Can.* range of smth. to offer.

slate/ (put) on the slate *esp. Br., Aus.* col. obs. / *Am.* **on the cuff**/ to be paid later on credit.

slate *esp. Am., Can., Aus.* a. choose for a position or job: *Now I was slated for the Bridge house myself.* - D. Carnegie., *The two men were slated to sign an agreement on cultural operation* – Time. b. expect or plan to happen: *European market is slated to become a reality.* - Time.

slate/ be slated to be/to do smth. *esp. Am., Can., Aus.* be expected to succeed in getting a particular position or job.

slate *Am., Aus.* a person chosen by a political party to take part in an election.

slate *Br., Aus.* col. attack in words, criticise severely.

slate/ on the/one's **slate** *Br.* on credit.

Slate club *Br.* Mutual aid society, weekly dues there are called subscriptions.

slather(s) *Am., Can.* col. a lot, a great quantity.

slather *esp. Am.* spread thickly or wastefully on.

slaughterer *Am.* slaughterman, killer at the abattoir.

slaughterhouse *esp. Am.* abattoir.

slaw *Am., Can., Aus.* coleslaw: *I was in a back booth finishing an order of spiced slaw* - A. Hitchcock Mystery Magazine.

slay (slain) 1. *esp. Am., Can.* journalism. or *Br., Aus.* obs. kill violently, n. **slaying.** 2. *Am.* col. amuse sb. a lot.

sleave note *Br.* /*Am.* **liner note**/.

sleazeball, sleaze(bag) *esp. Am., Can.* col. despicable person: *he created two sleazeballs who can't handle women!* – Esquire, adj. **sleazoid.**

sled; sleigh *esp. Am., Can.* /*esp. Br.* **sledge, toboggan**/ sledge: *Papa pulls the sled up the tiny hill* - R.G. Kaiser.

415

sledge 1. *esp. Br.* /*esp. Am.* **sled**/ go or race down slopes on a sledge. 2. *Am.* travel or carry on a sledge. 3. *Br.* toboggan.

sledgehammer/ use a sledgehammer to crack a nut *Br., Aus.* do smth. with more force than is necessary.

sleep over *esp. Am., Can.* stay overnight at sb. else's home: *He never sleeps over with a broad.* - M. Puzo, n. **sleep-over**.

sleep/ sleep like a top *Br.* sleep very well.

sleep/ sleep the night *Br.* sleep at sb.'s else's house for the night.

sleep/ sleep rough *Br.* (about homeless person) sleep in the street.

sleeper *Br., Aus.* a train with beds for passengers to sleep on.

sleeper 1. *esp. Br., Aus.* /*Am.* usu. **tie, crosstie**/ any of the row of heavy pieces of wood, metal, etc., supporting a railway track. 2. *Br.* a small ring worn in the ear so as to keep open a hole made there for an earring. 3. *esp. Am., Can.* something such as a book, play, record, etc., that has a delayed or unexpected success: *In Hollywood they would call it a sleeper.* - Time., *Old Shawcloss had come up with another of his sleepers.* - L. Uris. 4. *Br.* railway sleeping carriage. 5. *esp. Am., Can.* sleep suit for a baby. 6. *Am., Can.* sofa or chair that converts into a bed.

sleeperette *esp. Br.* sleeping compartment on a train or boat.

sleeping car *Br.* /*Am.* **sleeper**/ a train with sleeping carriages: *the sleeping-car conductor entered the diner* – M. Daly., *the first all-black labor union, the Brotherhood of Sleeping Car Porters* – N. Hentoff.

sleeping partner *Br.* /*Am., Aus.* **silent partner**/.

sleeping policeman, (speed) humps, road bumps *esp. Br.* raised part placed across a road to force traffic to move slowly.

sleeping porch *Am.* bedroom open to the outside air.

sleeping sickness *Am.* /*Br.* **sleepy sickness**/.

sleep out *Aus.* a small building in a garden or enclosure outside part of a house used for sleeping in.

sleepover *Am.* party for children in which they stay the night at sb.'s house: *It includes everything from grades to sleepovers* – J. Tesh.

sleepsuit *Br.* one-piece garment used as a nightwear.

sleeve *esp. Br.* /*Am., Aus.* usu. **jacket**/ a stiff envelope for keeping a gramophone record in, usu. having printed information (*esp. Br.* **sleeve notes**, *Am.* **liner notes**) about the contents.

sleigh bed *esp. Am., Can.* bed resembling a sleigh in form.

sleeving *Br.* tubular covering for electric and other cables.

sleeve link *Br.* cuff link.

slenderize *Am., Can.* col. make (oneself) thinner by eating less, playing sports, etc.: *ah, slenderizing for somebody, he thought.* – P. Roth.

slew *Am.* bog.

slew(s) *esp. Am., Can.* col. **a slew of** a large number: *Niagara Falls has slews of tourist accomodations.* - A. Frommer.

slice of the pie *Am.* /*Aus.* **a slice of the cake**/ a part of the money to be shared by everyone.

slice/ any way you slice it, no matter how you slice it *esp. Am.* col. however you consider it.

slick *Am., Can.* col. 1. /*esp. Br.* **glossy magazine,** col. **glossy**/: *The slicks are all carrying ads for products and services* - R.A. Spears. 2. smart and confident person.

slick (sb./smth.) **up** *Am., Can.* make smart; tidy up.

slick-chick *Am.* attractive girl: *Who was that slick chic I saw you with last night?* - R.A. Spears.

(rain)slicker *Am.* 1. /*Br.* **oilskin**/ a coat made to keep out the rain: *A liitle kid in a yellow rainslicker waved me* – R.L. Stine, *He held up a yellow oil-skin slicker.* - S. Sheldon. 2. a silver fish, bristle-tail.

slicker *esp. Am., Can.* col. 1. convincing rogue. 2. **city slicker**.

slide *Am.* sudden fall of earth, stones, etc. down a slope.

(hair) slide *Br., Aus.* /*Am.* **barrette**/ hair slide, women's decorative hair fastener.

slide fastener *Am., Can.* zip fastener.

slim *Am.* light (about breakfast, etc.).

slime *Am.* remove slime from (esp. when preparing fish for cannery).

slim(p)sy *Am.* flimsy, frail.

slimy 1. *Am.* vile, offensive. 2. *Br.* col. friendly and pleasant in an insincere way.

sling 1. *Am.* a drink made of whiskey, brandy or esp. gin with water, sugar and sometimes bitters, lemon and nutmeg. 2. *Aus.* col. bribe or gratuity.

sling/ put sb.'s/**have ass in a sling** *esp. Am., Can.* col. put sb./be in a very difficult situation.

sling-bag *Br.* cloth bag, usu. worn over the shoulder.

sling beer *Am., Can.* col. work as a bartender.

sling hash (or **plates**) *Am., Can.* col. serve food in a café or diner.

sling one's **hook** *Br.* sl. go away.

sling off *Aus.* 1. sl. go away, leave. 2. also *NZ.* make fun, mock.
sling pump *Am.* sling-back court shoe.
slingshot *Am., Aus.* /*Br.* **catapult,** *Aus.* **catapult**/ n.: *his body seemed stretched like a slingshot.* - T. Thompson.
slinky *Can.* thin.
slip *esp. Br.* a small mistake.
slip *Am.* a long seat or narrow pew.
slip/ slip one over, slip smth. **over on** sb. *Am.* col. trick, deceive sb.: *He took great delight in slipping one over the guards.* - Longman.
slip/ slip one's **trolley** *Am.* sl. go mad.
slip cover *Am.* 1. paper cover for a book; dust jacket. 2. loose cloth for furniture: *There was an armchair in that room with a slip-cover in Delft blue.* – M. Daly.
slippery/ be on the slippery road/slope *Br.* have started a process or habit that will develop into smth. dangerous or harmful.
slip proof *Br.* galley proof.
slipperette *Am.* tdmk. soft slipper.
slippy/ look slippy *Br.* col. obs. hurry up, be quick.
slip road *Br.* /*Am.* **on-ramp, access road,** *Am., Aus.* **exit** or **entrance ramp**/ a road for driving onto or off a motorway or **A-road**: *she glimpsed a slip-road to her left and swerves down it.* - D. Lodge.
slip seat *Br.* jump seat.
slips *Br.* the sides of the uppermost level of sitting in some theatres.
slip sheeting *Am.* /*Br.* **interleaving**/.
Sloanes *Br.* rich young people from upper middle class background in London.
slob around *Br.* sl. spend time doing nothing and being lazy.
sloe-eyed *Am.* having soft dark-bluish eyes or purplish black eyes.
slog *esp. Br., Aus.* col. 1. **slog away, through, slog** one's **guts out** do hard dull work without stopping: *In the middle of the second quarter I slogged over to the field* - J. Baez., *It had been tough slogging even for two keen and slender 17-years old* - Reader's Digest. 2. (esp. in cricket) hit ball hard and wildly. **-er** n.
slog *Br., Aus.* col. 1. (a period of) hard dull work without stopping: *My story is one of slog and grind and disappointment and overcoming.* - Time. 2. (esp. in cricket) a wild hard hit.
slog it out *Br.* fight or argue about smth. until one side wins.
sloganeer *esp. Am.* employ or invent (political) slogans.

sloosh *Br.* col. rushing of water; energetic rinsing.
slop *Am.* feed slop to pigs.
slop(s) 1. *Am., Aus.* sl. bad beer: *Why do we have to drink slops like this?* - R.A. Spears. 2. *Br.* liquid waste from food or drinks. 3. *Br.* dirty water or urine.
slop about/around 1. *esp. Br.* dress in an untidy or casual way. 2. *Br.* col. spend time being lazy. 3. *Br.* col. play or move around in mud, dirty water, etc.
slop out *Br.* (esp. of prisoners) empty the containers used as toilet during the night.
slop over *esp. Am.* col. show too much love for (sb. such as child or animal): *she has to go and slop (all) over it.* - Longman.
slop basin, /*Am., Can.* **slop bowl**/ *Br.* bowl used at table for holding the leavings of tea or coffee.
slope(head) *Am., Aus.* taboo. sl. a person from South East Asia.
slope/ at the slope *Br.* held sloping on one shoulder.
slope arms *Br.* (usu. impers.) (of a soldier) hold weapon by the end with a barrel at a slope on the left shoulder.
slope off *Br., Aus.* col. go away secretly, esp. to escape or avoid work: *Poor Norma, why shouldn't she slope off on her own if she wants to?* - A. Christie.
sloppy Joe 1. *Am., Can.* hamburger with the minced beef served with tomatoes and spices. 2. *Br.* big, loose-fitting sweater.
slops *esp. Br.* ready-made or cheap clothing.
slosh *Br.* col. hit, punch.
sloshed *Br.* col. drunk.
slot car *Am., Can.* electrically driven miniature racing car which travels in a slot in a track.
slot machine 1. *Br., Aus.* /*Am.* **vending machine**/. 2. *Am.* /*Br., Aus.* **fruit machine,** *Aus.* **poker machine**/ one-armed bandit: *his mother played the pinball/slot-machine hybrid of pachinko.* - Newsweek.
(slotted) spatula *Am.* /*Br.* **fish slice**/ kitchen tool, used for lifting and turning food.
slouch hat *Am., Aus.* a hat with a soft brim worn esp. by soldiers.
slough *Am., Can.* muddy side channel or inlet.
slough over *esp. Am.* col. deal quickly with (smth. esp. wrong), so as to reduce its importance: *The chairman tried to slough over the problems in the contract* - Longman.
sloven *Am.* adj. uncultivated, undeveloped.
slovey *Can.* tender; mild.

slow burn *esp. Am., Aus.* col. steady change from calmness into greater and greater anger: *a slow burn the likes of which the monitoring agents had not heard before* - J. O'Brien, A. Kurins., *By the next morning my anger had subsided to a slow burn.* - Reader's Digest; **do a slow burn.**

slowcoach 1. *Br., Aus.* col. /*Am., Can.* col. **slowpoke**/ person who thinks, moves, or acts slowly: *I gunned around a bevy of slowpokes and crossed unto Westland.* - R.J. Randisi., M. Wallace. 2. *Aus.* a fool, dumb person.

slow-down (strike) *Am.* /*Br.* **go-slow,** *Br.* sl. **ca-canny**/ period of working as slowly and with as little effort as possible.

slow handclap *Br.* a slow regular clap used by annoyed crowd waiting for a performance to start.

slow lane *Am.* /*Br., Aus.* **inside lane**/.

slow-mo, slo-mo *esp. Am.* slow motion action that is intentionally made to appear slower than it was until it happened.

slow pitch *Am.* game like softball, played by mixed teams of men and women.

slow poke *Am., Can.* col. /*Br., Aus.* col. **slowcoach**/.

slow puncture *esp. Br.* puncture causing only gradual deflation of a tire.

slow train *Br.* local train / **fast train** *Br.* express train.

slue *Am.* /*Br., Aus.* **slew**/ turn or swing violently.

slug 1. *esp. Am., Aus.* col. a bullet: *I can still get you with slugs in me.* - D. Hammet., *even a thirty-eight slug didn't stop him.* - P. Case, J. Migliore. 2. *Am.* col. coin-shaped object illegally put into a machine instead of a coin. 3. (of) *esp. Am. Aus.* col. an amount of strong alcoholic drink taken at one swallow: *The novelist poured himself a generous slug before addressing his topic.* - R. Borchgrave, R. Moss. 4. *Am.* sl. a dollar. 5. *esp. Am.* col. a slow-moving large person.

slug 1. *esp. Am., Can.* col. hit with a heavy blow, esp. with the closed hand and so as to make unconscious: *You want I should slug him, teach?* - B. Kaufman., *I didn't slug him.*- R.P. Warren., *he slugged a detective* - G. O'Neill, D. Lehr. 2. *Aus.* charge sb. a lot of money.

slugfest *Am., Can.* col. 1. free-for-all: *she gets involved in a child-child slugfest with junior* - T.A. Harris. 2. baseball game dominated by heavy fighting.

slugger *Am.* sl. boxer more notable for hard hitting than artistic finesse: *215 pound-slugger he put fear into the heart of every opposing pitcher.* - Reader's Digest.

sluice *Am., Aus.* wash, gold-bearing sand.

slumber party *Am., Can.* gathering of young people, esp. girls to spend a night together: *she gets a slumber party or a bump in her allowance* – J. Tesh.

slumgullion *Am., Can.* cheap meat stew.

slumlord *Am., Can.* col. (profiteering) landlord of slum property.

slummock *Br.* col. dirty, untidy, or slovenly person.

slump *esp. Am.* a period of time when a player or team does not play well.

slur *esp. Am.* make damaging or insulting insinuations or allegations.

slush *Am.* a crushed-ice drink.

slush fund *esp. Am.* sum of money (**slush money**) secretly kept for dishonest use, such as by a politician in an election: *The slush fund is bankrupt.* - R.A. Spears.

sly-grog *Aus., NZ.* col. 1. bootlegged alcoholic drink. 2. home brew.

smack *Can.* short period of time.

smack smth. *esp. Am.* col. hit it forcefully.

smack sb. *Br.* col. hit sb. hard with one's closed hand; punch, n.

smack/ have a smack at smth. *Br.* col. try to do smth.

smack down *Am.* col. scold (sb.) for a fault: *That boy deserves to be thoroughly smacked down* - Longman.

smack-dab /*Br.* **smack-bang**/ *esp. Am., Can.* col. adv. directly, exactly right: *a cottage smack dab in the middle of the busy hospital.* - R. Cook., *she's smack dab in the middle of it.* - D. Mortman.

smacker *Am.* the lips or the outer part of the mouth.

smacker(oo) col. 1. *Br.* one pound sterling. 2. *Am., Can.* one dollar.

small ad *Br.* /*Am.* **want ad**/ classified ad given by sb. who wants to buy or sell smth.

small beans *Br., Aus.* col. /*Am.* **small potatoes**/ sb. or smth. unimportant.

small beer *esp. Br.* smth. unimportant in comparison with smth.

small-bore *Am., Can.* col. trivial, unimportant.

small claims (court) *Am.* small debts (court).

the smallest room *Br., Aus.* col. euph. a toilet.

small fry *Am.* humor. children: *Don't worry about the small fry.* - R.A. Spears.

smallgoods *Aus.* cooked meats and meat products.

smallholder *Br.* person who owns or rents a smallholding.

smallholding *Br.* a piece of land farmed by one person, smaller than ordinary farm: *Adamson's*

place was a smallholding on the edge of the town. - J. Herriot.
smallish *esp. Br.* fairly small.
small potatoes *Am., Aus.* col. /*Br.* **small beans**/ smth. not important.
smalls *Br.* obs. col. small articles of underclothing, handkerchiefs, etc. esp. for washing.
small stuff/ don't sweat the small stuff *Am.* col. don't worry about unimportant things.
small town 1. *Am.* village. 2. adj. *esp. Am.* not very interested in anything new or different: *I'm a seventh-generation Appalachian – a small-town girl from a blue-collar family.* – Reader's Digest.
smarm *esp. Br.* 1. smooth down (hair). 2. behave in ingratiating way in order to gain favour.
smarmy *esp. Br.* col. unpleasantly and falsely polite, unctuous: *smarmy, hypocritical version of brotherly love.*- A. Bloom.
smart 1. *esp. Br., Aus.* or *Am.* obs. /*Am.* **sharp**/ intelligent or neat and stylish in appearance: *Feeling fat and hot in the smart featureless coat and skirt* - I. Murdoch; adj. **–ey**; n. **-ness**. 2. *esp. Am.* good or quick in thinking, clever: *That's one smart girl.* - J. DeFelice. 3. *esp. Am., Can.* showing impertinence by making clever and sarcastic remarks. 4. *Br.* obs. excellent.
smart *Am., Can.* col. intelligence.
smart/ play it smart *esp. Am.* col. get wisely, do the right thing.
smart cookie *Am.* sl. a clever person: *Even a smart cookie like you.* - L. Waller., *For Sadie was a very smart cookie.* - R.P. Warren.
smart drugs *Br., Aus.* drugs which make you more intelligent and make you think more clearly.
smarten up *Br.* 1. also **smart** oneself **up** make oneself look neat and tidy. 2. **smarten** smth. **up** (of rooms, etc.) make smth look neater.
smartish *esp. Br.* col. quickly; briskly.
smart money 1. *Am.* col. a. money for betting and investing by person with special knowledge. b. informed speculators: *Most of the smart money is going into utility stocks right now.* - R.A. Spears. 2. *Br.* a. money allowed to soldiers and sailors for injuries. b. money to obtain the discharge of a recruit.
smart mouth *Am., Can.* col. person speaking too cleverly, not showing enough respect for other people; impudence, esp. in **have a smart mouth**.
smarts *esp. Am., Can.* col. brains, wit, intellect: *we look the smarts to absorb his lessons.* - Playboy.
smash *Br.* serious road or railway accident.
smash print. *Am.* /*Br.* **nipping**/.

smash-and-grab (raid) *esp. Br., Aus.* adj. (n.) (of a robbery) done by quickly breaking a shop's window, taking the valuable things behind it and running away.
smasher *Br.* col. an attractive person or thing.
smashing *esp. Br.* col. becoming obs. or *Can., Am.* /*esp. Br.* **wizard**/ very fine, excellent: *There's a smashing thing.* - K. Vonnegut, Jr., *I know some pretty smashing tall girls* - I. Shaw., *It's a smashing town and the people are so friendly.* - Cheshire Life.
smear *Am.* sl. overwhelm, defeat, outscore sb.: *We smeared them 50 to 20.* - R.A. Spears., *the Spartans left tackle...smeared the play* – M. Daly.
smear-sheet *Am.* yellow press newspaper.
smear test *Br.* /*Am., Aus.* **pap smear**/.
smell/ smelt was much more common in *Br.* than smelled which is more common in America.
smell/ come up smelling of roses (*Am.* **come out like roses**) *Br., Aus.* be good and honest after a difficult situation which could have made you seem bad or dishonest.
smell out *esp. Br.* /*Am.* **sniff out**/ discover where smth. is by smelling.
smell up *Am., Can.* fill (a place) with a smell, usu. bad: *one was all smelled up with beer* - Alcoholics Anonymous.
smidgeon *esp. Am., Can.* sl. little bit: *Lucille wore one of those little smidgeons of hats held on by interned combs.* - J. Steinbeck.
smithy *Am.* blacksmith.
smoke *Am., Can.* col. kill (sb.) by shooting or defeat overwhelmingly.
smoke/ blow smoke (in sb.'s **face, eyes**) *Am.* say untrue things in order to show the situation is better than it really is.
smoke/ blow smoke up one's **ass** *Am.* be insincere, try to cheat sb.
smoke/ smoke and mirrors *esp. Am., Aus.* smth. confusing or deceiving which makes people believe that a situation is better than it really is.
smoke/ There's no smoke without a fire saying esp. *Br., Aus.* /*esp. Am.* **Where there's smoke, there's fire**/.
smoke up 1. *Am.* col. fill (a place) with smoke: *Open the window, the committee have smoked the whole room up!* - Longman. 2. *esp. Am.* smoke drugged tobacco: *How many high school students in this city regularly smoke up?* - Longman.
the (big) smoke 1. *esp. Am., Aus., Br.* col. the big city, as opposed to the country, esp. London, Sydney or Melbourne: *Excellent freight train*

back to the smoke in twenty minutes. - J. Higgins. 2. *Br.* col. London.

smoke and mirrors *Am., Can.* deceiving sb. by distracting their attention.

smokechaser *Am.* forest fire fighter.

smoke-filled room *Am.* one where influential politicians meet in private: *This convention produced the term "smoke-filled room"' to suggest that the strings had been pulled to manipulate the convention.* - H. Truman.

smokehouse *esp. Am., Can.* shed or room for curing food by exposure to smoke.

smoke-jumper *Am., Can.* forest fire fighter who parachutes to locations otherwise difficult to reach.

smokeless zone *Br.* areas where people use smokeless fuels such as gas instead of wood and coal.

smokeless tobacco *Am.* tobacco which is chewed or placed in the mouth.

smoker *esp. Am., Can.* social gathering for men.

smokestack *Am.* the funnel of a railway steam engine: *for a headrest one had the smokestack, it was so hot.* - J. Kerouac.

smoke room *Br.* smoking room in a hotel or a bar.

smokestack industry *esp. Am.* branch of industry that produces heavy goods or industrial materials, such as cars, ships, or steel: *a predominantly urban society, still dominated by smokestack industry.* - H. Smith.

smokey *Am.* sl. state trooper, esp. a highway patrolman: *A Smokey was hiding behind a billboard!* - R.A. Spears.

smoking gun *esp. Am., Can.* journalism. 1. incontestable evidence: *In the early months of the investigation a number of smoking guns were found in this equipment.* - Time., *The radicals were on the hunt for a smoking gun* - H. Smith.

smoko *Aus., NZ.* col. short period of rest, esp. for workers (**break for a smoko**).

smolder *Am.* smoulder.

smooch *Br.* dance slowly and very close together to romantic (**smoochy**) music; n.

smoodge *Aus., NZ.* col. 1. curry favour. 2. kiss, flirt.

smoothie *esp. Am.* thick, smooth drink of fresh fruit pureed with milk, yogurt, or ice cream.

smooth sailing *Am.* course of action or situation that is free from difficulty or trouble.

smother *Am.* welter, mix-up.

smudge *esp. Am., Can.* v. n. (make) a smoke fire to drive away insects, give a signal or keep fruit trees from freezing (usu. built in a **smudge-pot**): *the Focke-Wolfe started to smoke like a crazy smudge-pot* - I. Shaw., *Or go camping together and after supper lie by a little smudge fire for the mosquitoes and never say a word.* - R.P. Warren.

smudge one's **own shoes** *Br.* damage one's reputation.

smush *Am., Can.* col. crush, smash.

snack *Aus.* col. thing that is easy to accomplish.

snack *Am.* eat a snack.

snacketeria *Am.* snack bar.

snaffle *Br., Aus.* 1. col. get, esp. by deceitful means or stealing. 2. sl. take (a catch)., catch (a ball) easily: *I snaffle an order from your introductions.* - K. Blair.

snafu *esp. Am., Can., Aus.* col. a state of having gone completely wrong: *I witnessed one amusing snafu in this business.* - J. Fraser., *So commenced the first of several snafus* - R. Cook., *There's been another snafu.* - B. Tillman, adj., v.

snag *Am., Can.* dead tree.

snag 1. *Am.* col. catch or get esp. by quick action: *I can snag two seats for tomorrow's taping* - P. Case, J. Migliore. 2. *esp. Am.* cause difficulties for sb. 3. *Am.* col. try to get sb. to notice one, esp. when they want help.

snag(s), also **snaggles** *Aus.* col. /*Br.* **bangers**, *Am.* **sausages**/ sausage.

snake *Am.* col. 1. drag, haul. 2. yank, jerk.

snake/ go kill a snake *Aus.* col. go to lavatory.

snake/ wriggle like a cut snake *Aus.* fuss (about), dodge.

snakebite *Br.* alcoholic drink that is half lager and half cider.

snakebitten *Am., Can.* col. unlucky.

snake fence, also **Virginia fence** *Am., Can.* worm fence, a zigzag fence made of horizontal rails coming together at an angle: *more kinks in it than a snake fence.* - W. Grady.

snake-headed *Aus.* angry.

snake juice *Aus.* sl. whiskey.

snake oil *esp. Am., Can.* col. 1. one formerly sold by peddlers, posing as doctors, etc. 2. useless advice or solution to problems: *In a business lubricated with snake oil, colonel Parker seemed without peer.* – J. Hopkins.

snake oil salesman *esp. Am.* col. person who tries to sell sb. worthless things.

snakes and ladders *Br.* /*Am.* **chutes and ladders**/ children's board game.

snap *Am., Can.* 1. col. n. adj. something that is very easy to do: *Buying your ticket can be a snap too.* - Newsweek., *Phase Two would be a snap.* - L. Waller. 2. snap fastener /*Br., Aus.* **press-stud**,

Br. **popper/**: *the oddest assortment of things on sale: knicker elastic and collar snaps, buttons and pinking shears* - B. Bryson.

snap *Br.* excl. 1. (said when one notices two similar things together). 2. (said in the game of snap when one notices two similar cards have been laid down).

snap *esp. Br.* col. photo taken by sb. who is not a professional photographer.

snap/ in a snap *esp. Am., Can.* col. in a moment.

snap/ snap it up *Am.* col. hurry up: *We're late. Snap it up!* - R.A. Spears.

snap/ snap sb.'s **head off** *Br.* say smth. in a very angry way.

snap-brim (hat) *Am.* hat usu. of felt with brim turned up in back and down in front and a dented crown.

snap (fastener) *Am. /Br.* **press-stud, popper/.**

snap pea *Am., Aus. /esp. Br.* **mangetout/.**

snapper *Am.* punch line, the point of climax of a story or joke: *This was the snapper.* - K. Vonnegut, Jr.

snapping bug *Am.* snapping beetle.

snappy *Br.* col. (of clothes) attractive and fashionable; a **snappy dresser**.

snappy/ look snappy *Br.* (used impers.) hurry up.

snap-tin *Br.* col. sandwich-box.

snarf *esp. Am.* col. eat or drink quickly or greedily.

snarky *Am., Can.* col. (of a person, words, or a mood) sharply critical; cutting.

snatch *Am., Can., Br.* sl. 1. kidnap, steal, esp. by shoplifting: *Somebody snatched my car.* - R.A. Spears. 2. taboo. vagina: *They put a pleasing coyote scent on the trigger(probably the smell of a coyote snatch)* – R. Brautigan.

snatch squad *Br.* squad used to quell riots.

sneak (on) *Br.* derog. col. /*Am.* **snitch**, *Aus.* **dob/** (used by schoolchildren) give information esp. to a teacher, about the wrongdoings of others.

sneak *Br.* col. /*Am.* **tattletale**, *Aus.* **dobber/** a person who sneaks.

sneak boat or **box** *Am.* one used for hunting wild fowl.

sneaker, col. **sneak** *esp. Am., Can., Aus. /Br.* **trainer** or (thick) **plimsoll, gym shoe/** a strong light soft shoe for sports with a rubber sole: *Anyone could tiptoe in a good quality pair of sneakers and get me around the neck.* - J.P. Donleavy., *Mr. McHabe came in to speak about no sneakers on cafeteria tables.* - B. Kaufman., *Miscreants may abscond on fleet foots: what Brits call plimsolls, and Americans call sneakers.* - P. Howard.

sneeze/ be nothing to sneeze/sniff at *Am., Aus.* col. smth. not very important.

snell *Am., Can.* short line from a fishhook to a longer line.

snick 1. *Br., Aus.* hit the ball off the edge of a bat, esp. in cricket. 2. *Br.* make a small cut or mark on smth., n.

snicker *esp. Am.* /*esp. Br.* **snigger/** v. n. usu. derog. laugh quietly or secretly in a disrespectful way.

snide *esp. Am.* sl. illegal, dishonest: *Are you accusing me of selling snide gear?* - R.A. Spears.

sniffy *Br.* 1. having a bad smell, esp. as a result of long disuse or spoiling. 2. col. having a disapproving attitude towards smth. or sb., esp. because one thinks they are not good enough.

snifter 1. *esp. Br.* obs. a small amount of alcoholic drink: *But I is pleased to take a light snifter in your company.* - R. Chandler. 2. *Am. /Br.* **brandy glass/** bowl-like glass that grows narrower at the top, on a short stem, for drinking brandy: *Sir Winston Churchill...closed his eyes at ninety-one, sitting in a rocker with a good cigar in one hand, a snifter of brandy in the other.* – A. Summers, R. Swan.

snig *Aus., NZ.* derog. heavy load, esp. timber, fastened with ropes or chains.

snip 1. *Br.* col. esp. journalism. an article for sale at a surprisingly cheap price, bargain, esp. **be a snip (at)**: *A snip having this spell of fine weather.* - W.S. Maugham. 2. *Am., Can.* col. small or insignificant thing.

snipe *Am.* 1. col. cigar(ette) butt: *Down on the skid row, a snipe won't be on the sidewalk for 10 seconds.* - R.A. Spears. 2. sb. who is strongly disliked.

snipe hunt *Am.* a prank of inviting sb. to a desolate place and not showing there.

snippy *Am.* col. quick to show that sb. is so angry or offended, that they won't obey: *I got snippy* – S. Lawrence.

snips *Br.* /*Am.* **tinshears/** scissors that cut metal.

snit *Am., Can., Aus.* col. an angry mood, esp. in **be in a snit**: *He was in a snit.* – A. Summers, R. Swan.

snitch 1. *Br.* col. usu. humor. nose. 2. *Aus.* dislike.

snog *Br., Aus.* col. hold and kiss each other, esp. for a period of time. n.: *Just for a quiet alfresco snog.* - J. Fowles.

snook/ cock a snook (at) *esp. Br.* col. /*Am.* **thumb** one's **nose** 1. journalism. show one's disrespect to sb. by doing smth. that insults them. 2. express contempt by a gesture of placing a thumb to the nose and spreading othr fingers out.

snooker/ be snookered *Br., Aus.* have no chance to do smth one wants to do.

snooker *Am.* deceive or trick sb.

snoopy *Am.* col. given to snooping, esp. for personal information about others.

snoot *esp. Am.* col. nose: *Don't think I'm pushing my snoot into Paul's affairs* - D. Hammet.

snootful *Am.* sl. great quantity: *he certainly had a snootful now.* - K. Vonnegut, Jr.

snooze/ you snooze, you lose *Am.* col. don't lose your chance.

snork *Aus.* sl. baby.

snorker *Aus.* sl. 1. sausage. 2. penis.

snot-nosed *Am.* col. impolite word used to describe children who are not very clean.

snotty-nosed *Br.* col. wet and dirty with mucus.

snout *Br.* col. 1. tobacco. 2. a cigarette. 3. informer to the police. 4. nose.

snow *esp. Am., Can., Aus.* col. persuade or win the respect of (sb.), esp. by making oneself sound important: *He'd start snowing his date in this very quiet sincere voice.* - J.D. Salinger., *Snowing the West has been easy for Gorbachev.* - Time., *She snowed you completely.* - S. Bellow., *Don't let them snow you, man.* - L. Graham.

snow under *Am.* col. (usu. pass.) defeat completely: *Because with us behind him he'll snow Roan under* - D. Hammet.

snowball/ not have a snowball's chance in hell *esp. Am., Aus.* not have any chance to succeed.

snow bank *esp. Am.* a large pile of snow.

snowbirds *Am., Can.* col. Canadians who go south for the winter: *It's November, and the snowbirds are leaving Alberta for Arizona.* - W. Magnuson.

snowblower *esp. Am.* machine cleaning snow from roads by blowing it away.

snow-broth *Am.* mixed snow and water.

snowjob *esp. Am., Can., Aus.* col. systematic deception, a cover-up: *they did a pseudopsychedelic snowjob for Nilsson* - J. Gabree., *Don't give me a snow job.* - Arthur Hailey.

snow machine *Am., Can.* snowmobile.

snowmelt *esp. Am., Can.* melting of fallen snow.

snowpea *esp. Am., Can., Aus. /esp. Br.* **mangetout,** *Am.* **sugar pea/.**

snow route *Am.* important road in a city that cars must be removed from when it snows so that it can be cleared of snow.

snowslide *Am.* (snow) avalanche.

snow tire *Am.* special tire used when driving on snow or ice.

Snr. *esp. Am.* abbr. for Senior.

snuck/ (*esp. Am., Can.* col.) past tense and past participle of sneak: *I guess I snuck up on you.* - J. DeFelice.

snuff/ up to snuff 1. *esp. Am.* up to the acceptable standard. 2. *Br.* obs. not good enough.

snuff it *esp. Br., Aus.* col. die: *but I didn't snuff it* - A. Burgess., *she'll snuff it tomorrow.* - J. Herriot.

snuff out *Am.* (of a person) die.

snug as a bug in a rug *Br.* obs. very comfortable.

snug(gery) *Br.* small room or enclosed place for sitting privately, esp. in a pub: *Ten yards away I walked into the snug of a public house.* - J.P. Donleavy., *and sure enough in the snug there were three or four old baboochkas* - A. Burgess.

snuggery *esp. Br.* snug position or place, one's particular hideaway at home.

sny *Am., Can.* a river channel.

so *Am.* or *Br.* dial. (used esp. by children, for answering a negative charge or statement): *I didn't do it - You did so.* - Longman.

so/ ever so *Br.* very.

so/ I do so/it is so, etc. *Am.* used esp. by children to say that smth. is true, can be done, etc., when sb. else says the opposite.

so/ just so, also **quite so** *Br.* Yes, I agree.

soak *Am.* sl. hit, strike, punish severely.

soak in (to) *esp. Am.* col. become gradually and clearly understood and accepted: *allow the facts to soak into your mind.* - Longman.

soak *Aus., NZ.* waterhole.

soak/ an old soak *Br.* humor. drunkard.

soakaway *Br.* place through which water soaks and drains away (as a cesspool).

soap *Am.* sl. money (esp. for bribery).

soap/ no soap *Am., Can.* col. no result or success: *But it was no soap.* - R.P. Warren.

soap powder *Br.* one made from soap and other chemicals, used for washing clothes.

soapy *Br.* col. so pleasant that it seems false.

s.o.b. *esp. Am.* col. son of a bitch: *Never complained that the guard was a SOB?* - R.J. Randisi., M. Wallace.

sob(by) *Am.* adj. intended to arouse pity.

sober as a judge *Br.* obs. not drunk.

sobersides *esp. Am., Can.* col. sedate and serious person.

sob sister *Am.* 1. weak woman prone to cry: *I had another sob sister in the office today.* - R.A. Spears. 2. female reporter.

soc *Am., Can.* col. sociology, as an academic subject.

soccer *esp. Am., Aus.* /also *esp. Br.* **football, Association football**/ game using a round ball that is kicked but not handled: *She...loved to ice skate and play soccer* – R.L. Stine.
soccer shoes, cleats *Am.* /*Br.* **football boots**/.
sociable 1. *Am.* obs. planned informal friendly gathering of members or esp. church. 2. *esp. Br.* an S-shaped couch for two persons who sit patiently facing each other.
social assistance *Can.* social security.
social housing *Br.* housing provided for rent or sale at a fairly low cost by organisations such as housing associations and local councils.
socialized medicine *Am.* medical care provided by a government and paid for by taxes.
Social Register *Am.* a book detailing who's who in the social elite.
social security 1. *Br., Aus.* /*Am.* **welfare**/ government money paid to people who are unemployed, old, ill, etc.: *There are long queues in the Anglesite Social Security office this morning* - D. Lodge. 2. *Am.* the system of government payments, esp. to retired people, **be on social security**.
social services *esp. Br.* the special services provided by a government or local council to help people, such as education, health care, etc.: *If the Social Services hear about it she will get down!* – S. Townsend.
social studies *Br.* a subject taught at schools and colleges which includes sociology, politics, and economics.
society *Am.* church corporation.
sock/ mismatched socks *Am.* odd socks, esp. of different colour.
sock *esp. Br.* sl. adv. (of the giving of a blow) firmly and exactly.
sock away *Am., Can.* col. save (money) by putting it aside: *we should start socking away an equal amount each month into our bank account.* - Longman.
sock in *Am., Can.* (of weather) envelop, esp. with fog.
sock it to *esp. Am.* hit hard, express forcefully: *The usual drive-in scene sockin' it to your girl in the backseats.* - D. Divocky.
sock/ pull one's **socks up** *Br.* col. make an effort to improve oneself, one's work, etc.: *Acapulco needed to pull its socks up and fast to avoid falling into real decline* - Hotel and Motel Management., *things will be set aright, if we professors would just pull up our socks.* - A. Bloom.
sock/ put a sock in it *esp. Br.* humor. keep quiet, stop talking.

socked/ be socked in *Am.* col. (of a plane) be prevented from flying; (of airfield) be closed for flying: *But Boston was socked in* - K. Vonnegut, Jr., *It was cloudy, socked in with no light from the sky.* - L. Uris., *We're socked in* - B. Tillman.
sockdolloger *Am.* sl. 1. something unusual. 2. finishing blow.
sockeroo *Am.* col. smth. that is very successful and impressive.
(mains) socket (outlet) *Br.* /*Am.* **(convenience) outlet,** *Br., Aus.* **power point, socket**/: *The plug was in the socket* - R. Crais.
socket set *Br.* /*Am.* **socket wrench**/.
sock hop *Am.* a party where everyone dances in stocking feet: *And what they like is remembering sock hops* – J. Hopkins.
socking *esp. Br.* col. adv. extremely (big).
socking great *Br.* col. very great.
socko *esp. Am.* col. (something) very successful, terrific: *It seems to have that old emotional socko.* - F.S. Fitzgerald.
socks/ knock sb.'s **socks off** *Am.* col. surprise sb. very much: *Knock their socks off. You've only got seconds to make your best impression.* – Reader's Digest.
socks/ work, laugh, dance, scream, etc. one's **socks off** *Br.* do smth. very hard; laugh a lot, etc.
sod *Br.* taboo. sl. 1. stupid or annoying person, esp. a man: *Where are you, Bagster, you sod?* - G. Greene., *Stupid sod, he thought.* - D. Reeman. 2. (used in expressions of good or kind feeling) fellow, **poor sod**. 3. something that causes a lot of trouble or difficulty, **be a sod**. 4. **not give / care a sod** not to care at all.
sod *Br.* taboo. sl. v. (usu. impers.) (used in expressing annoyance or displeasure at the stated thing or person) esp. in the phr. **Sod it/ that.**
sod off *Br.* taboo. sl. (usu. impers.) go away: *I told them to sod off and leave me alone.* - T. Thorne.
sod all *Br.* sl. nothing at all.
sod/ Sod's Law *Br.* humor. (said when bad things happen and plans fail if there's a possibility of them going that way).
soda (pop) *esp. Am., Can.* col. pop, any carbonated drink esp. with a fruit or ginger flavour: *he consumed a tub of popcorn and two giant sodas.* - A. Hitchcock Mystery Magazine., *blotting up the soda I had just spilled.* - Guideposts.
soda *Am.* ice-cream soda.
soda cracker *Am., Can.* /*Br.* **cream cracker**/ plain biscuit usu. eaten with butter.
soda fountain *esp. Am.* /*Br.* **soda bar**/ place in a shop at which fruit drinks, ice cream, etc.

are served: *Would you care to drop in at the soda fountain before we call it a night* - Reader's Digest., *The soda fountain was one of their hang-outs.* - Alex Haley., *Every town had its own ice-cream soda fountain of Belgian marble.* - E.L. Doctorow.

sodbuster *Am., Can.* col. farmer or farm worker who ploughs the land.

sodding *Br.* taboo. sl. adj. (used for giving force to an expression, esp. showing annoyance): *We'll need a sodding professor to translate.* - J. Higgins.

soddy, also **sod house** *Am.* a house built of turfs.

sofa *esp. Br. /esp. Am.* **couch**/ a long comfortable seat with a back usu. with arms, which two or three people can sit on.

soft *Br.* stupid or silly.

soft/ be soft in the head *Br.* col. be not sensible or a little crazy.

soft/ be soft on sb. *Am.* love them a lot.

soft/ soft as shit *Br.* very weak.

(soft) cider *esp. Am.* apple juice.

soft cover *Am.* (of a book) with a bendable cover.

soft fruit *esp. Br.* small eatable fruit that has no hard skin or hard inside seed.

soft furnishings *esp. Br. /Am.* **soft goods**/ (the materials used to make) curtains, mats, seat covers, cushions, lampshades, etc. used in decorating a room: *there are classes connected with their hobbies, such as soft furnishings* - J. Ruppeldtova.

soft goods *Br.* textiles.

softly-softly approach *Br., Aus.* a gradual way of solving a problem, when one deals with it patiently and carefully.

soft money *Am.* col. bank notes.

soft option *Br., Aus. /Am.* **easy option**/ one that is easier between two choices.

soft-pedal *esp. Am.* play down, make (a subject, fact, etc.) seem unimportant.

soft shoulder *esp. Am., Can.* unmetalled strip of land at the side of a road.

soft sugar *Br.* granulated or powdered sugar.

soft toys *Br. /Am.* **stuffed animals**/ toy animals made of a soft filling and which are pleasant to hold.

soggy *esp. Br.* (of weather) rainy.

SoHo *Am.* sl. the area in New York City south of Houston Street: *tourists who had come to gawk at the SoHo galleries* - J. O'Brien, A. Kurins., *Michelle plays Nikki Sheridan, a SoHo art gallery owner* - Ebony.

soil pipe *Am.* drainage pipe.

solar *Br.* upper chamber in a medieval house.

solarium *Am.* a room connected to a house in which plants are grown or kept.

sold/ be sold a pup *Br.* col. be tricked into buying smth. worthless.

(soldering) tag *Br. /Am.* **(soldering) lug/**.

soldiers *Br.* col. long narrow pieces of bread or toast, often given to small children.

soldier on *esp. Br., Can.* carry on in spite of difficulties: *Still they soldiered on* - Time., *Being brave and stoical by soldiering on is often unwise* - New Idea.

solicit *Am.* sell smth. by taking orders for a product or service, usu. by going to people's houses or businesses.

solicitor *Am., Can.* 1. /*Can.* **lawyer,** *Am.* **attorney**/ the chief law officer of a city, town, or government department. 2. a person who tries to obtain business orders.

solid *Am.* adj. completely of the stated colour without mixture of others: *a little white stone in his solid-blue tie.* – J. O'Hara.

solid/ be solid *Br.* be in a complete agreement.

solid with 1. *Am.* col. on good terms with. 2. *Aus., NZ.* col. severe; unfair (on sb.).

solid sender *Am.* sl. exciting musician.

solidus *esp. Br. /Br., Aus.* **oblique (stroke)**/ slash.

solitaire *Am. /Br., Aus.* **patience**/ a card game of patience (for one player): *just take out the candle and play solitaire.* - Reader's Digest.

solvent abuse *Br.* the dangerous activity of breathing in certain chemicals to get a feeling of pleasure and excitement.

some *esp. Am., Can.* col. adv. rather, to a small extent or degree: *Darling Jill is crazy some, Pluto.* - E. Caldwell.

some/ and then some *esp. Am., Can., Aus.* col. a lot more: *she gained all the weight back - and then some.* - R.L. Stine.

some pumpkin *Am.* col. important person.

someplace *esp. Am.* col. somewhere: *Well, you have to start someplace.* - S. Grafton.

something/ (have really got)/be quite something *Br.* be special often in a stated way but for reasons which are difficult to explain.

something else *esp. Am.* sl. something special, remarkable: *Ah, Little Richard, he was something else.* - A. Scaduto.

sometime *Am., Can.* occasional.

someway(s) *esp. Am., Can.* col. adv. somehow.

somewhat/ more than somewhat *Br.* very much.

son/ every mother's son (of you/them) *Br.* obs. everyone.

son et lumiere *esp. Br.* performance which uses recorded sounds and coloured lights to tell the story of a historical place or event.

song/ be on song *Br. col.* journalism. be playing or performing well.

a song and dance *esp. Am., Can.* col. a long and complicated statement or story.

a song and dance/ make a song and dance about smth./doing smth. *Br., Aus.* col. make smth. seem more important than it really is.

songfest *Am.* concert made with the audience: *we'd have a songfest.* - A.E. Hotchner.

sonic bang *Br.* sonic boom produced by aircraft going faster than the speed of sound.

son of a bitch *esp. Am.* col. God damn.

son of a bitch, son of a gun 1. *Am., Aus.* col. unpleasant or irritating person. 2. *Am.* col. smth. which causes difficulties. 3. *Am.* excl. of surprise.

son of a gun *Am., Aus.* 1. col. exclamation of surprise. 2. affectionate term of address. 3. smth. difficult to deal with. 4. excl. of surprise.

song/ on song *Br.* esp. journalism. doing very well in sport.

Sonny Jim *Br.* obs. or humor. the way of addressing sb., esp. a man.

sook *esp. Aus., NZ, Can.* a shy or cowardly child or person.

sooky *Aus. sl.* 1. sulky. 2. sentimental.

sool *esp. Aus., NZ.* 1. (of a dog) attack or worry (an animal). 2. urge (sb.) into doing smth.

The Sooner State *Am. joc.* Oklahoma: *Why is Oklahoma called the Sooner State?* - Houghton Mifflin English, **Sooner** *Am. joc.* a native of Oklahoma.

sooty *Br. sl.* black or coloured person: *we've only got one rule: no sooties.* - T. Thorne.

sophomore *Am., Can.* also col. **soph.** /*Br.* **2nd year student** or **undergrad(uate)**/ a student in the second year of a course in a US college or high school.

sophomoric *Am.* childish and not very sensible.

sopped *Am.* very wet.

soppy *esp. Br.* col. /*Am.* **sappy**/ 1. too full of expressions of tender feelings like sorrow, love, etc.: *Don't go soppy on me: she said.* - D. Lodge 2. (about) having a very great fondness (for). 3. foolish: *It's a soppy name.* - G. Greene.: *It's a soppy fame.* - G. Greene., *I was soppy daft about him* - J. Fowles. **ipily** adv. **-iness** n.:

sorbet *Am.* /*esp. Br.* **water ice**/ a frozen sweet made of fruit juice or water with colour and taste added.

sore *esp. Am.* col. angry, esp. from feeling unjustly treated: *Don't get sore.* - E. Hemingway., *I had wanted to make him sore* - R.P. Warren., *I would come home at night sore and grouchy* - D. Carnegie.

sorehead *Am., Can.* col. a bad-tempered person: *You're a professional sorehead.* - J. O'Hara., *I've got boys out picking up soreheads and wobblies and getting 'em to town.*- R.P. Warren.

sorority *Am., Can.* organisation for female students at some US colleges.

sorry *esp. Br., Aus.* excl. (used for asking sb. to repeat smth. one has not heard properly).

sorry/ British use **I'm really/awfully/so/ terribly sorry** to make the apology stronger.

sorry/ say sorry *esp. Br.* say sorry to your mother.

sort *esp. Br.* type, some things or people having similar features; **of this/that sort; of some sort; sort of** (of an unknown type); **of one sort or another.**

sort *Br.* sb. who has a particular type of character; **good/bad sort.**

sort/ all sorts *esp. Br.* all types, often in **it takes all sorts (to make the world)** used when some people behave or act strange.

sort/ a sort of *esp. Br.* used when describing smth. in a not exact way, also **sort of thing, sort of like.**

sort/ be sorted *Br.* 1. col. deal with a problem successfully. 2. be repaired or put in good order.

sort/ nothing of the sort *esp. Br.* it's not true and it shouldn't be done.

sort/ What sort of…? *esp. Br.* used when sb. is angry about what other people have just done.

sort of *esp. Br.* used when a person is not sure if they use the best word to describe smth.

sort of price/time/speed, etc *esp. Br.* price within a certain range, etc.

sort out *Br.* 1. deal with, make clear: *He was offering to sort out Apple - for nothing!* - P. Norman., *It will give me a chance to start my investigation as well as sort out this morning in my mind.* - R. Cook., *It's a problem we will have to sort out.* - You. 2. col. attack and punish. 3. sl. beat up: *She said he really sorted those skinheads.* - J. Higgins. 4. sl. have sex with.

sort sb. **out** *esp. Br.* make them realize that they behaved wrongly, e.g. by talking to them or by punishing them.

sorted *Br.* col. organized; arranged; fixed up.

sort-out *Br.* col. an act of putting things in order, esp. in **have, need a sort-out.**

sorts/ it takes all sorts (to make a world) *Br.* / *Am.* **it takes all kinds (to make a world)**/ all people are different.

sou *Br.* obs. (usu. in negatives) a very small amount of money.

soul *Am.* adj. of or for black people: *Walking into the tiny soul-food restaurant with him was like walking in with God.* - J. Baez., M.L...*relished soul food - fried chicken, cornbread and collared greens with ham hocks and bacon drippings.* - S.B. Oates; adj. **soulful.**

soul brother, soul sister *Am.* black person (used esp. among young black people).

soul food *Am.* food that African Americans like to eat.

soul case *Am., Can.* col. the body.

sou marker *Am.* trifling sum, little or nothing.

sound *Br.* col. excellent.

sound/ be as sound as a dollar *Am.* obs. working very well.

sound off *Am.* (of soldiers) shout out their names to show that they are present.

sound bite *esp. Am.* sl. catch phrase: *That was the sound bite in the summer of 1990* - Reader's Digest., *He knows how to give good sound-bites.* - USA Today.

soundman *Am.* sound producer.

sounds *Br.* col. music, esp. on a record, cassette, etc.

sound truck *Am.* one with loudspeakers (used for advertising, etc.): *The night before the election the streets were full of sound trucks.* - H.C. Whitford., R.J. Dixson.

soup *Am.* col. nitroglicerine or gelignite, esp. used for safe-breaking.

soup/ from soup to nuts *Am., Can.* col. from beginning to end, completely and in detail.

soup/ in the soup *Br.* obs. in trouble.

soup and fish *Am.* col. dinner jacket: *Everyone who attended the party wore soup and fish.* - H.C. Whitford., R.J. Dixson.

soup/ packet soup *Br., Aus.* /*Am.* **instant soup/**; **tinned soup** *Br., Aus. Am.* **canned soup/.**

sour *esp. Am.* drink made with lemon juice, sugar and the stated strong alcohol: *We had whiskey sours* - R. Chandler.

sour on *Am.* turn the opinion of (sb.) against (smth.): *Is the public souring on me?* - I. Stone.

source/ deduct/pay tax at source *Br., Aus.* be deducted by one's employer.

sourdough *Am., Can.* 1. a kind of slightly alcoholic flour mixture for making bread: *cowgirls in ten-gallon hats tossing out sourdough flapjacks from the chuck waggons where they are cooked.* - R.E. McConel., *he had served sourdough bread and pate and caviar to everybody* - Rolling Stone. 2. experienced prospector in the Western US or Canada; an old-timer.

soured cream *Br.* sour cream.

sour mash *Am.* 1. fermenting grain mash: *This "sour" mash provides the proper balance of nutrients* - Esquire. 2. whiskey made of this.

souse *Am., Can.* food, esp. a pig's head in a pickle.

souse *Am.* sl. 1. drunkard: *Are you one of us souses, too?* - Alcoholics Anonymous. 2. a binge: *That was one fine souse we had.* - R.A. Spears.

soutener *Br.* pimp.

south/ down South *Br.* col. to the southern part of Great Britain.

south/ go south *Am.* col. lose value or quality; not work properly: *the things go wrong, or just go south* – J. Tesh.

southerly buster *Aus.* fresh wind.

southern-fried *esp. Am.* (of food, esp. chicken) coated in flour, egg, and bred crumbs and then deep-fried.

south paw 1. *Br.* a left-handed boxer. 2. *esp. Am., Can.* col. left-handed person, esp. a left-handed pitcher (in baseball): *Our baseball team needs another pitcher - preferably a southpaw.* - W. Magnuson.

sov *Br.* col. a pound sterling.

sow belly *Am.* col. bacon: *some brokers play with sow bellies and soybeans* - T. Murphy.

sow bug *Am.* wood louse, slater.

sox col. or in tdmks. *esp. Am.* socks.

sozzled *Br., Aus.* humor. slightly drunk: *that would undoubtedly come from the sozzled gentleman* - C.M. Fraser.

SP/ the (full) SP *Br.* col. all the facts about smth.

spa 1. *esp. Am.* a place where a person goes in order to become more healthy by doing exercises, eating special food, etc.: *Quaint shops and spas abound.* – Reader's Digest. 2. *Am.* jacuzzi.

space/ be spaced out *esp. Am.* col. (esp. after using drugs) be euphoric or disoriented.

space cadet *Am.* sl. 1. eccentric person. 2. one who is always high on drugs.

space opera *esp. Am.* col. novel, film, or TV program set in outer space.

spackle *Am., Can.* tdmk. compound used to fill cracks in plaster.

spade up *esp. Am.* col. 1. dig (soil or garden) with or as with a spade: *The garden needs spading up* - Longman.

spades/ in spades *esp. Am.* col. par excellence, in large amounts or to a very great degree:

Wright had paid in spades, over Serbia. - J. DeFelice., *Frost was a son of a bitch, in spades.* - New York.

spag bol *Br.* col. spaghetti Bolognese, a dish made of spaghetti and meat sauce.

spaghetti junction *Br.* clover leaf (of roads).

spaghetti western *Am.* sl. western film, produced by Italians: *I like spaghetti westerns. Lots of action.* - R.A. Spears.

span *Am.* a pair (of animals e.g. *a span of oxen*).

spandy *esp. Am.* col. adj. very good or fine, smart.

spang *Am.* col. adv.1. with a sudden spring or impetus. 2. directly; completely.

spangler *Am.* sequin.

Spanglish *esp. Am.* mixture of Spanish and English.

Spanish State *Am.* New Mexico.

spanner, also **open-ended spanner, ring spanner** 1. *esp. Br., Aus.* /*Am., Can.* **(monkey) wrench, box wrench**/ metal tool with jaws or a hollow end, for fitting over and twisting nuts. 2. **throw/put spanner in the works** *esp. Br., Aus.* col. /*Am., Can.* **throw/put (monkey) wrench in(to) the works**/ be a cause of confusion or ruin to a plan or operation: *my uncle refused to give up his money and put a spanner in the works.* - Longman.

spar-dust *Am.* sawdust.

spare (often pl.) *Br.* new spare part for vehicles and machines.

spare *Br., Aus.* col. very angry, hopping mad / **go spare, send** sb. **spare**.

spare/ be going spare *Br.* col. be left because nobody wants it.

spare/ spare sb.'s **blushes** *Br.* avoid making sb. feel embarrassed in public.

spare ground *Br.* vacant lot.

spare-part surgery *Br.* /*Am., Aus.* **organ transplant**/ human organ transplantation.

spare prick/ be like a spare prick at a wedding *Br.* taboo. humor. feel silly because nobody needs you or no one is talking to you at an event.

spare tyre *Br.* a person having a noticeable fat waist.

spark 1. *esp. Am.* encourage, stimulate into greater activity: *it's time to spark up a partnership that's begun to feel stale.* - Reader's Digest. 2. *Am.* obs. pay special attention to sb. one is sexually attracted to.

spark out *Br.* col. completely unconscious.

spark/ some/a bright spark *Br.* col. often derog. a clever or cheerful person: *Some bright spark in the agency came up with the idea of rippling silk with a cut in it.* - D. Lodge.

spark/ strike spark off each other *Br.* react to each other in an exciting and effective way.

spark guard *Am.* fire guard.

sparking plug *Br.* obs. spark plug.

sparkling water *Am., Can.* soda water.

spark plug *Am.* col. person with a lot of energy and ideas who encourages other people in a group.

sparrow *Can.* sl. an Englishman, esp. a Cockney.

sparrowhawk *Am., Can.* American kestrel.

spasm/ go into spasm *esp. Br., Aus.* have uncontrolled tightening of a muscle.

spat *Am., Aus.* have an argument.

spate *esp. Br.* a large number or amount, esp. of events of the same kind, coming together in time: *a rare spate of fidgety phrasing* - M. Jones, J. Chilton., *a large new spate of indigents.* - J. Steinbeck., *Luckily, a spate of customers entered the store* - I. Shaw., *a spate of balloon blowing.* - Bulletin.

spate/ in (full) spate *esp. Br.* (of a river) having a lot more water than usual and flowing very fast.

spatter up *esp. Am.* spoil (smth.) with drops (of usu. liquid): *Passing traffic has spattered the wall up with mud.* - Longman.

spatula *Br.* /*Am.* **tongue depressor**/ special instrument used by doctor to hold sb.'s tongue down so that they can examine a throat.

(slotted) spatula *Am.* /*Br.* **fish slice**/: *She moved...holding a spatula* – P. Roth.

spaz(z) *esp. Am.* col. derog. spastic.

spaz out *esp. Am.* col. lose physical or emotional control.

speak / In British English it is more usual to **speak to** somebody than to speak with somebody, which suggests a long formal talk. But in American English **speak with** is used more generally.

speak volumes for *Br.* /*Am.* **about**/ smth. show clear the real nature of smth.

speak/talk to the organ grinder, not his monkey *Br.* derog. talk to a person with authority.

speak(-easy) *Am., Aus.* a night-club during prohibition years: *The "speaks" usually sold whiskey.* - Alcoholics Anonymous.

speakerphone *esp. Am., Can.* telephone with a loudspeaker and microphone.

speaking of *esp. Am.* while talking of.

spec/ on spec *Br., Aus.* col. as a risk or speculation: *Talk a group of engineers into laying it out on* *spec, and then take the specifications and raise the money.* - H. Fast.

spec builder *Aus.* a person or company that builds houses for everyone wanting to buy them rather than to particular people.

special *Am.* col. an advertised reduced price in a shop / **have** smth. **on special.**

special *esp. Am., Aus.* a meal that is available on a particular day.

special agent *Am.* sb. who works for FBI.

special delivery *Am.* express delivery: *She always got it special delivery* - R. Chandler.

Special (Education) Needs (SEN) *Br. /Am.* **Special Education/** special education for mentally and physically disabled children.

special offer/ on special offer *Br.* at reduced price.

specialist *Am.* sworn stock broker, exchange broker or inside broker.

special licence *Br.* one allowing a marriage to take place at a time or place not normally permitted.

specialty *esp. Am., Can., Aus. /Br., Aus.* **speciality/** a. an unusually good product at a certain place. b. a subject of study: *He was lucky to choose as his specialty a branch of chemistry* - R.G. Kaiser.

specialty shop *Am.* agent's garage.

specs *Br.* col. glasses to help sb. see.

spectacles *Br.* a pair of glasses.

spectator's terrace, also **waving base** *Br.* observation deck (at the airport).

spectre/ghost at the feast *Br.* person who spoils enjoyment at the event or social occasion.

speed *esp. Am.* each of the possible gear ratios of a motor vehicle.

speed bag *Am., Can.* small punchbag used by boxers for practising quick punches.

speed/ travel at speed *Br.* travel very fast.

speed humps/ rumps/ rumbles (also **humps, road humps**), **strip** or **sleeper policeman** *Br.* speed bump, a transverse ridge in the road to control the speed vehicles.

speedo 1. *Aus.* special swimsuit for lifeguards. 2. *Br.* col. a speedometer.

speedway, also **expressway** *Am., Can.* 1. */Br.* **motorway/** road for fast traffic: *the insurance investigators are blaming the speedway.* - R.L. Stine. 2. road or track used for motor-car racing.

spell v. / (*esp. Br.* **spelt,** *esp. Am.* **spelled** past tense and past participle of spell.

spell v. / **spelled** 1. *esp. Am., Aus., Can.* take the turn of, allow (sb. else) to rest by taking over their work, relieve sb.: *Sybil came over every day to spell the nurses* - D. Mortman., *he refused an offer to be spelled.* - Reader's Digest. 2. *Aus.* take a brief rest.

spell(-o) *Aus.* n. respite, rest.

spell down *esp. Am.* defeat sb. in a spelling competition: *See if you can spell all the other students down* - Longman. / **spelldown** *Am. /* also *Am., Aus.* **spelling bee/** test in spelling.

speller *Am.* a book of teaching spelling.

spelunking *Am., Can. /Br.* **caving, potholing/** speleology; also **spelunker** *Am. /Br.* **caver, potholer/** a person involved in speleology.

spend on smth. *Br.* the amount paid for smth.

spend for *Am.* use (an amount of money), pay for (smth.): *How much did you spend for that book?* - Longman.

spend a penny *esp. Br.* col. euph. obs. urinate.

spew up *Br.* col. vomit.

spic(k), spik 1. *Am., Aus.* derog. col. a Spanish-speaking American, esp. a Puerto Rican or Mexican: *You look around in New York and all you can see is spics.* - G.V. Higgins., *words like nigger, kike and spick which are not a good vocabulary.* - B. Kaufman., *He lived there above a spick restaurant* - R.P. Warren. 2. *Aus.* any European language other than English.

spice-nut *Am.* a biscuit with cinnamon, etc.

spider *Am., Can.* 1. an iron frying pan. 2. frame with three legs to support a pot or pan over the fire.

spider *Br.* set of radiating elastic ties used to hold a load in place on a vehicle.

spiderman *esp. Br.* col. construction worker who erects the steel framework of a tall building.

spiderweb *Am. /Br.* **cobweb/.**

spiel *esp. Am.* col. talk volubly and extravagantly, **-er** n.

spiel off *esp. Am.* speak (words) quickly and easily from memory: *The child can spiel off the names of all the Presidents* - Longman.

spieler 1. *Am.* TV announcer, esp. one reading an ad. 2. *Am., Aus.* sl. card sharper or professional swindler.

spiel truck *Am.* truck used for advertising and propaganda.

spiff up *Am.* col. dress up, begin wearing smth. stylish.

spiffing *Br.* col. obs. very good: *Oh, I say, jolly spiffing old boy!* - T. Thorne.

spiffy 1. *Br.* obs. col. very good. 2. *esp. Am., Can.* col. stylish, attractive: *All spiffy in his tuxedo.* – S. Lawrence.

spiflicate *Br.* col. treat (sb.) roughly.

spigot 1. *esp. Am. /Br., Aus., Can.* (**outdoor) tap/** outside tap: *We stopped at a rusty old spigot* *sticking out of the ground* - Guideposts. 2. *esp. Br.* a type of valve that controls the flow of liquid from one source to another.

spike 1. *esp. Br.* pointed metal rod standing on a board and used for filing paper items such as bills, etc. 2. *Br.* col. hostel offering temporary accommodation for the homeless.

spike sb.'s **guns** *Br.* spoil an opponent's plans.

spike-buck *Am.* a young male deer.

spike-heels *Am.* /*Br.* **stilettos**/ women's shoes with very high narrow heels.

spikes *Am.* stiletto heels.

spike-tail *Am.* col. a tail coat.

spike team *Am.* a team of three draft animals.

spiky *Br.* col. easily offended or annoyed.

spile *Am., Can.* a spout for tapping the sap from a sugar maple.

spill v. / p.p. and p.t. *esp. Br.* **spilt**, *esp. Am.* **spilled.**

spill 1. *Am.* a spout for drawing off sap. 2. *Aus.* vacating of all or several posts in a cabinet or parliamentary party to allow reorganisation after one important change of office.

spill one's **guts** *Am.* tell everything to sb. because a person is very upset.

spillover *esp. Am.* overflow.

spin 1. *esp. Am.* col. a particular interpretation or slant given to a proposal, policy, piece of information, etc.: *His skills at media manipulation or, as they say in the White House, "spin control" easily surpass any other Australian politician.* - Bulletin., *But I'd like to offer a different spin* - New York. 2. *Aus., NZ.* col. a piece of good or bad luck.

spin/ give smth. **a spin** *Br.* turn clothes very fast in a machine to remove water from them.

spin smth. **off** *esp. Am., Aus.* form (a separate partly-independent company) from parts of an existing company.

spin out *Am., Can.* (of a vehicle) leave a road by turning accidentally as on a slippery surface: *Suddenly the car spun out and crushed into the fence.* – Longman, n. **spin-out.**

spin smth. **out (over)** *esp. Br.* derog. make (smth.) last an unnecessary long time: *I spun out the meal, hoping the weather would ease off* - B. Bryson.

spin/ go/get/be in a (flat) spin *Br., Aus.* col. become or be confused and unable to do anything.

spin/ spin one's **wheels** *esp. Am., Can.* col. be idle for some time: *we could spin our wheels thinking about kamikaze mission* - K. Ablow.

spindle *Am.* 1. a newel, main column of a winding staircase. 2. also *Can.* a pin for fastening paper.

spin drier *esp. Br.* a machine that removes water from wet clothes by spinning them around very fast, v. **spin-dry.**

spinet *Am.* a low upright piano: *there had been a long procession of choice examples through that room, spinets, desks, tables, chairs* - R.P. Warren.

spin-meister or **spin-doctor** *Am., Can.* a person who provides **spin**: *spin doctors and political gurus talked of packaging Presidential candidates* - Reader's Digest.

spinney *esp. Br.* a small area full of trees and low growing plants, copse: *a beech spinney was cleared.* - G. Orwell.

spin-out *Am., Can.* col. spin-off.

spirit level *Br.* /*Am.* **level**/ level used in building.

spirit *esp. Br.* liquid such as alcohol used for cleaning.

spirit/ get into the spirit/enter into the spirit *Br.* start to feel as happy, excited, etc. as people are around sb.

spirit lamp *Br.* small lamp that burns methylated spirits.

spirits *esp. Br., Can.* /*esp. Am.* /**(hard) liquor**/ a strong alcoholic drink produced by distillation.

spit *Br.* /*Am.* **sprinkle**/ rain very hard.

spit/ be the (dead) spit of sb. *Br., Aus.* col. be the exact copy of sb.

spit/ spit and sawdust *Br.* col. pub or bar.

spit/ spit nails *Am., Aus.* col. /*Aus.* col. **spit chips/tacks**/ speak or behave in a way that shows you are very angry.

spit/ spit (out) the dummy *Aus.* col. behave in a bad-tempered way.

spit up *Am., Can.* col. (esp. of a baby) vomit food.

spit-and-sawdust *Br.* col. dirty and untidy pub which is not modern or attractive.

spitball *Am.* 1. chewed-up paper to be thrown as a missile: *Clemenza rolled the little green spitball* - M. Puzo. 2. sl. a nasty but feeble attack. 3. make weak accusations. 4. col. throw out (a suggestion) for discussion: *Elizabeth and Maia had been spitballing ideas for the last half hour* - F. Pascal.

spit curl *Am., Can.* kiss curl.

spiv *Br., Aus.* col. derog. obs. a man who lives by cheating society, making money in small rather dishonest ways: *He winked up at Dan from his book, playing the spiv* - J. Fowles.

splash (money) (out, on) *esp. Br., Aus.* col. spend (a lot of money) on nice but unnecessary things: *Led Zeppelin singer then splashed out $500,000* - New Idea., *they are happy to splash out $50 on a pair of earrings* - New Idea.

splash *esp. Br.* a small added amount of liquid, esp. to a drink: *Dallow took a splash of soda.* - G. Greene.

splashback *Br. /Am.* **splashboard/** panel behind a sink or cooker that protects the wall from splashes.

splash guard *Am. /Br.* **mudflap/** piece of material hanging behind the wheel of a vehicle to keep the mud from flying up.

splashy *esp. Am.* big, bright, and very noticeable, flashy: *I saw faint glimpses of my young child and his splashy crayon pictures* - New Yorker.

spleen/ in a fit/burst of spleen *Br., Aus.* being very angry.

splendiferous *Br.* col. humor. splendid.

splice 1. *Br.* col. (usu. pass.) join in marriage, often in **get spliced**. 2. *Br.* sl. make love to sb.: *I spliced his woman while he was away on bar duty downstairs.* - T. Thorne.

splice the mainbrace *Br.* obs. have an alcoholic drink.

splinter bar *Br.* /also *esp. Br.* **swingletree/** part of a horse harness.

split 1. *Am.* (of shares) be multiplied so that each holder gets certain number for each one held. n. 2. (on) *Br., Aus.* col. (esp. among children) tell secret information about sb.: *We'd never split on you, boys.* - A. Burgess.

split 1. *Am., Can.* drawn match or series. 2. *Am.* split level house.

split a gut *Am., Can.* col. be convulsed with laughter.

splitrail fence *Am.* a fence of rails split from logs: *a shed with a split-rail fence next to it* - A. Hitchcock Mystery Magazine., *I'd never seen Emma walk the split-rail fence* - Reader's Digest.

splits *Br. /Am.* **split/** a movement in which a person's legs are spread wide apart and touch the floor along the whole length.

split ticket *Am.* a vote for candidates from more than one party.

splodge esp. *Br. /Am., Aus.* **splotch/** col. blotch.

splosh *esp. Br.* col. splash.

spod *Br.* col. dull or socially inept person.

spoil *Am.* used list of paper.

spoil a (ballot) paper *Br.* make a special mark on it so that it can't be officially counted.

spoilage print. *Br. /Am.* **makeover/**.

spoiler (party) *Am.* 1. third party to split votes. 2. person or team that spoils another's winning record.

spoilsman *Am.* person who serves a party for a share of the spoils.

spoils system *esp. Am.* the practice of a successful political party giving public offices to its supporters (**spoilsmen**).

spoilt *Br.* spoiled.

spoilt/ be spoilt for choice *Br.* have a lot of possibilities to choose from.

spoke/ put a spoke in sb.'s **wheel** *esp. Br., Aus.* spoil sb.'s plans.

spondulicks, also **mullah** *esp. Am., Can., Aus.* sl. money: *I don't have enough spondulix to swing the deal.* - R.A. Spears.

sponge *esp. Br.* act of washing smth. with a sponge.

sponge (cake) *Br. /Am.* **layer cake/** sponge cake.

sponge/ throw up the sponge *Br.* col. accept defeat: *I don't like to see a fellow throw up the sponge that way.* - G. Greene.

sponge bag, toilet bag *Br., Aus.* a small usu. plastic bag for carrying one's soap, toothbrush, etc.: *I never lose my sponge bag* - G. Greene., *neat black-and-white check spongebag.* - I. Murdoch.

sponge bath *Am., Can.* blanket bath.

sponge fingers *Br.* lady fingers (a kind of biscuit).

sponge pudding *Br.* steamed or baked pudding of fat, flour and eggs.

sponge rubber *Am.* foam rubber.

sponsor 1. *Br.* person who agrees to pay sb. money, usu. for charity, if they complete (part of) activity, also. v. 2. *esp. Am.* business or organisation that pays for a contribution to the casts of a radio or TV program in return for advertising.

sponsored walk, swim, etc. *Br.* one in which many people take part in order to collect money for charity.

spoof *Am.* col. try to deceive sb. by making them believe in smth. that is not true.

spook *esp. Am.* col. cause (esp. an animal) to be suddenly afraid: *And now you're all spooked crazy over Mississippi* - H. Fast., *quit spooking around here in the dark?* - R.P. Warren., *Sniper fire spooked American soldiers.* - Newsweek.

spook *esp. Am., Can., Aus.* col. a CIA man, a spy: *The superspook's colleagues were concerned about his judgement.* - Time.

spook *esp. Am.* taboo. obs. Negro.

spook at *esp. Am.* col. be scared of sb.: *they will spook at a bush, and run wild for no reason.* - Longman.

spooked *Am., Can.* col. frightened or startled.

spool *Am. /Br.* **reel/** bobbin on which sewing thread, wire, cinema film, fishing line, recording tape, etc. can be wound/ **spool of thread** *Am. /*

Br. **reel of cotton/**: *I could see clouds unwinding with great rapidity...from an invisible spool.* - K. Davis.

spoonbread *Am.* soft maize bread.

spoonfed *Am.* col. (about a person) spoilt.

sport 1. *esp. Aus., NZ., Br.* col. (used as a friendly form of address, esp. when speaking to a man): *you are the sport, Madame.* - A. Christie. 2. *Am.* player. 3. *Am.* (esp. of clothes) informal in style: *the leaders donned sport jackets and slacks.* - Newsweek. 4. *Br.* sports in general.

sport/ do/play a lot of sport *Br., Aus.* be engaged in sport activities a lot.

sport car *Am.* sports car.

sport coat, jacket, shirt, etc. *Am.* sports coat,etc.

sporting *Br.* fair and generous, esp. in sports.

sports *Br.* /*Am.* **meet/** a meeting at which people compete in athletics.

sports bar *Am.* a bar where non-stop televised sport is shown.

sportscast *esp. Am., Can.* a TV programme of a sports game.

sportscaster *esp. Am.* a sports commentator on radio or TV.

sports centre *Br.* a place where you can do different sports.

sports day *esp. Br.* /*Am.* **field day/** a day in school when children compete in activities such as races, the high jump, and throwing the javelin.

sports shirt *Am.* /*Br., Aus.* **singlet/**.

sportswear *Am.* clothes that are suitable for informal wear.

sporty *esp. Br.* good at and/or fond of sport.

spot 1. (of) *esp. Br. Can.* col. a little bit, small amount,e.g. **a spot of bother**: *give him a spot of lunch.* - W.S. Maugham., *Been a spot of bother off the Cape Verde Islands.* - D. Reeman., *Have a spot of Scotch.* - G. Greene., *Quite a pretty little spot of embezzlement to his credit.* - A. Christie. 2. *esp. Am., Can.* col. a bank note of small denomination, esp. a dollar; **five/ten spot**: *I'm picking my own spots from now on.* - G.V. Higgins. 3. *Am.* sl. night-club, etc.: *The Five Spot on 5th Street and Bowery some time features Thelonious Monk.* - J. Kerouac. 4. *Br.* /*Am.* **zit/** a small red mark on sb.'s skin: *I have got five spots as well as the one on my chin.* – S. Townsend. 5. *esp. Am., Can.* a pip on a domino, playing card or dice.

spot 1. *Am., Can.* col. give or lend (money) to (sb. smth.). 2. *esp. Br.* perform an action without moving from one's original position.

spot on adj. (not before noun) *Br.* col. exactly right.

spot/ have a weak spot for smth. *Am.* like it very much.

spot/ hit the spot *Am.* sl. satisfy one's need (of a drink, food, etc.).

spot/ knock spots off *esp. Br., Aus.* col. defeat easily.

spot 1. *Br.* (of rain) fall lightly and regularly. 2. (up, out) *Am.* tech. remove (a spot) from (paper, clothes, etc.). 3. *Am.* allow as advantage in a game. 4. *Am.* identify, put on record (esp. in **spot on the records**). 5. *Br.* find smth. after a search.

spot *Br.* col. adv. exactly.

spot lamp *esp. Br.* spotlight.

spotlight/ be/steal in the spotlight *esp. Am.* get attention from the public.

spot-on *Br., Aus., Can.* col. adj. exactly right: *his captions - they are so spot-on.* - Bulletin., *Doyle's estimate was spot-on* - New York.

spots *Br.* polka dots.

spots of rain *Br.* a few drops of rain.

spotted *Br.* /*Am.* **polka-dot/**.

spotted dick (or **dog**) *Br.* a heavy sweet boiled pudding with currants: *She put my curry and rice, spotted dick and custard into the oven to keep warm.* – S. Townsend.

spotted gum *Aus.* a tree whose trunk is pale with small darker areas.

spotter *Am.* 1. detective. 2. a person who works at the dry cleaner's: *Nellie - the laundry's best spotter - would have to work hard today* - Arthur Hailey.

bird/train/, etc. **spotter** *Br.* sb. who spends time watching birds, trains, etc.

spotty derog. 1. *Br.* col. having spots on the face: *He was small, spotty, undistinguished* - G. Greene. 2. *Am., Can., Aus.* /*Br., Aus.* **patchy/** with some parts different from others, esp. in quality: *staging conditions are spotty* - Time., *The government record is spotty as well.* - Reader's Digest.

spousal rights and duties *Am.* rights and duties one gains if one is married.

spout/ up the spout *Br., Aus.* col. a. in a hopeless state, wasted or spoiled: *Takes thirteen plus one up the spout.* - J. Higgins. b. obs. pregnant. c. (of a bullet) in the barrel of a gun. d. completely wrong.

spout off *esp. Am.* col. speak in a careless irresponsible way: *he has a bad habit of spouting off about things that concern him* - Longman.

spraddle *Am., Can.* spread (one's) legs far apart.

sprat to catch mackerel *Br.* obs. some small thing that helps to gain big results.
sprawl out on the floor *esp. Am.* stretch one's body lying on the floor.
spread 1. *esp. Am., Can.* a large farm or esp. ranch: *I went to check the herd I keep on a spread just North of town.* - Guideposts. 2. *Br., Aus.* obs. a special meal, esp in **lay on/put on a spread**. 3. *Am., Can.* bedspread.
spread (on the records) *Am.* write down.
spread city *Am.* uncontrolled extension of a city into suburb.
spreadeagle *Am., Can.* stretched out with one's arms and legs extended.
spring for *Am., Can., Aus.* col. pay for, esp. as a treat for sb. else.
spring break *Am., Can.* week's holiday for school and college, esp. at Easter.
spring chicken, springer *esp. Am.* a young chicken suitable for cooking.
spring-clean *Br.* /*Am.* **spring-cleaning**/ a thorough cleaning, esp. of a house: *Is that sort of like spring-cleaning?* - F. Pascal.
spring /*Br.* **sprung**/ **floor, furniture** *esp. Am., Can.* one that is supported by springs.
spring garden *esp. Br.* public pleasure garden.
spring greens *Br.* young cabbage.
spring house *Am.* small outbuilding over a spring used as a dairy.
spring onion *esp. Br., Aus.* /*esp. Am.* **scallion, green onion**/ an onion with a bulb and long green stem usu. eaten raw.
spring roll, pancake roll *Br.* /*Am.* **egg roll**/.
spring training *Am.* the period during which a baseball team gets ready for competitions.
sprinkle *Am., Can.* /*Br.* **spit**/ rain a little; n. **it's sprinkling**.
sprinkles *esp. Am., Can.* tiny sugar shapes used to decorate cakes and desserts.
sprinkling can *Am.* watering pot, watering can.
sprint/ put on a sprint *esp. Br.* run very fast.
spritely *esp. Br.* sprightly, live.
spritz *esp. Am., Can.* 1. force liquid out of container by putting pressure on it. 2. a container itself.
spritzer *Am., Can.* a mixture of wine and soda water.
spritzig *Aus.* (of wine) slightly fizzy.
sprog *Br.* col. 1. a green recruit. 2. derog. youngster, new boy in school.
sprog *Br., Aus.* col. 1. humor. a baby or a small child. 2. give birth to a baby.
sprout 1. *esp. Br.* Brussels sprout. 2. *Am.* an alfalfa seed which has grown a stem and is eaten. 3. *Am.* bean sprout.

spruik *Aus., NZ.* col. speak in public, esp. to advertise show.
sprung *Am.* past tense of spring.
spud *esp. Am.* foolish or incompetent person.
spud-bashing *Br.* col. the action of peeling potatoes, esp. for a prolonged period.
Spud Islanders *Can.* joc. people of Prince Edward Island.
spumoni *Am., Can.* ice-cream dessert with different colours and flavours in layers.
spunk 1. *Br.* taboo. semen. 2. *Aus.* col. a devastatingly handsome young man; adj. **spunky**.
spunk (up) *Am.* col. (cause to) become more cheerful: *Perhaps you need a holiday to spunk you up.* - Longman.
spur/ earn/win one's **spurs** *Br.* be able to do smth. well.
spurt *esp. Am.* increase suddenly (of share prices, costs, etc.).
spyhole *Br., Aus.* /*Am., Aus.* **eye hole**/ peephole.
squab *Br.* back of a car seat.
squab *esp. Am.* a young pigeon eaten as food.
squab pie *Br.* pigeon pie.
squad 1. *Br.* group of people that a sports team is chosen from. 2. *Br.* obs. or *Am.* a special police force. 3. *Am.* a group of cheerleaders.
squad car *esp. Am.* /*Br.* **patrol car**/ patrol car used by police on duty: *I can see figures in squad cars parked in the distance* - Reader's Digest., *Adventurous bands of partisans stoned cops and squad cars* - Newsweek., *The police Captain had arrived in the squad car.* - F.S. Fitzgerald.
squaddie, squaddy *Br.* col. soldier.
squall *Am.* (of wind) blow in a squall.
square 1. *Am.* block of buildings bordered by four streets. 2. *Br.* mortarboard. 3. *Am., Can.* cigarette containing tobacco rather than cannabis. 4. *Am., Can.* col. square meal.
square *Am., Aus.* /*Am.* **triangle**, *Br., Aus.* **setsquare**/ a tool for drawing or testing right angles.
square *Aus.* six square metres of flat surface.
square/ be on the square *esp. Am.* be completely honest in what you say or do.
square away 1. *Am., Can.* col. (often pass.) put in order, settle correctly: *She's squared away.* - J.A. Michener., *we're as squared away as we're going to be.* - B. Tillman. 2. *esp. Am., Can.* col. /*Br., Aus.* **square up**/ also **square off** (of two people) take up a fighting stance: *The two brothers are squaring away* - Longman.
square off *Aus.* sl. settle a difference peacefully.
square off *esp. Am., Can.* /*Br., Aus.* **square up**/ prepare to fight or compete.

square up to *Br.* /*Am., Aus.* **face up to**/ deal bravely with smth.
square-bashing *Br.* col. practice, esp. in marching, by soldiers.
square brackets *Br.* a type of brackets used for enclosing information.
square dress hook *Br.* L hook.
square-eyed *Br., Aus.* col. humor. watching a lot of TV; a person who does it is a **square eyes**.
squareface *Br.* sl. gin.
squarehead *esp. Am., Can.* col. derog. a Scandinavian or German.
square knot *Am.* /*esp. Br.* **reef knot**/ double knot that will not come undone easily: *He ripped a vine from a tree and tied it in a square knot above his wound.* - Reader's Digest.
(the) Square Mile *Br.* the heart of the city of London.
square stock *Am.* square iron.
squash 1. *Br.* a sweet drink made by adding water to the juice of a citrus fruit: *She once told me over a glass of orange squash* – Alain de Botton. 2. *esp. Am., Aus.* also **vegetable marrow** /*esp. Br.* **marrow**/ any of a group of large vegetables with hard skins, including marrows, gourds, and pumpkins: *He was somehow like a summer squash* - K. Vonnegut, Jr.
squat 1. *Br.* a home that people are living in without permission and without paying rent. 2. *Am., Can.* col. diddly squat; nothing.
squatocracy *Aus.* squatters, esp. important sheep ranchers.
squatter *esp. Br.* 1. a person who lives in an empty building without permission or payment of rent. 2. a settler on unowned land who does not pay rent but has legal rights over it and may sometimes become its owner.
squatter, also **pastoralist, grazier** *Aus.* /*Br., Aus.* **stockholder**/ sheep farmer: *This is the world of squatter, the runholder, the grazier* - P. Howard. **-acy, -dom, -ting** n.
The Squatter State *Am.* Kansas.
squaw *Am., Can.* humor. a wife or elder woman.
squawk box *esp. Am.* col. loudspeaker, esp. in intercom system.
squaw-man *Am., Can.* derog. the white man married to an Indian woman.
squeak, also **squealers** *Aus.* sl. soldiers.
squeaker 1. *esp. Am., Can.* a competition or election in which. sb. wins narrowly, only just avoiding failure. 2. *esp. Br.* young person.
squeaky clean *esp. Am., Aus., Can.* col. adj. a. very clean: *She curled her hair at night in huge plastic rollers, was hygienically squeaky-clean* - J. Baez. b. morally pure: *drug smugglers can turn cocaine-tinged bills into squeaky-clean assets.* - Time., *only suckers remain squeaky-clean.* - Time.
squeaky win *Am.* one by a narrow number of points, votes, etc.
squeeze 1. *Aus.* sl. woman's waist. 2. also one's/ **main squeeze** *Am., Can.* col. sweetheart: *The boy's her main squeeze.* - J. Kellerman. 3. *Br.* sl. money, cash.
squeeze bottle *Am.* one whose contents can be forced out by pressing the sides of it together.
squelch *Am.* 1. **squelch** sb. silence them. 2. **squelch** smth. end it quickly, stop idea from developing. 3. a critical remark.
squib 1. *esp. Br.* a mean person. 2. *Aus.* coward. 3. *esp. Am.* a small explosive of a tube with powder which makes a hissing noise when it is lit. 4. *Am.* a short piece of writing used in newspapers or magazines to introduce a longer article or to fill space.
squidgy *esp. Br.* col. soft and wet, e.g. like thick mud.
squiff *Aus.* sl. 1. drunkard: *It's no fun living with a squiff.* - R.A. Spears. 2. drinking bout.
squiffing *Br.* sl. the practice of postal workers reposting mail that is ready for delivery.
squiffy *esp. Br.* col. obs. /*Am., Can.* usu. **squiffed**/ slightly drunk: *She was a little squiffed, but still entertaining.* - R.A. Spears.
squiggle *esp. Am.* write or make in a wavy or twisting lines.
squinch *esp. Am.* (of a face) squeeze it together.
squire *Br.* col. (used esp. by a man as a friendly way of speaking to another man whose name is not known, and who may be of a higher social class).
squireen *Br.* small landowner, esp. in Ireland.
squirrel away *esp. Am., Can., Aus.* col. store (smth.) such as money: *Italians are great savers squirreling away 15% of their income* - Time., *who would guess she had that kind of cash squirreled away?* - A. Hitchcock Mystery Magazine.
squirelly *Am.* col. restless.
squirt gun *Am., Can.* water pistol.
squit *Br.* col. 1. small or insignificant person. 2. **the squits** diarrhoea.
squiz *Aus., NZ.* col. a look or glance.
Sr *Br.* abbr. of Sister, used in front of the name of a nurse.
SRN *Br.* State Registered nurse.
SRO *Am., Can.* single room occupancy.
St., stone *Br.* stone, a measure of weight (6.35 kg).

stabilise a power supply or **a voltage** *Br.* /*Am.* **regulate a power supply** or **a voltage**/.

stabiliser *Br.* a method used to limit changes in prices or to limit the level of production.

stable lad *Br.* /*esp. Am.* **stableman**/ one who works in a stable or who cares for horses.

stack *esp. Am.* (an organisation) fill it with their own supporters so that the necessary decisions can be made.

stack *Aus.* col. a car accident, esp. one that causes damage; **stack-up** *Aus.* col. a road accident involving a row of cars.

(sea) stack *Br.* column of rock standing in the sea.

stack *Br.* measure for a pile of wood, equal to 3.06 cubic metres.

stack/ stack of bones *Am.* col. tired person.

stack/ stack the deck (against sb.) *Am.* /*Br.* **stack the cards**/ do smth. dishonestly.

stacks of smth. *Br.* col. a lot of smth.

stack up 1. (against) *esp. Am., Can.* col. compare, measure, match: *How do the kids in that school district stack up against the rest of the nation.* - Omni., *Marsalis "stacks up miles ahead of" such past greats as Armstrong* - Time. 2. *esp. Am.* col. be in a certain state: *This is how things stack up today.* - Longman.

stacked *Am., Aus.* sl. having large breasts.

staff 1. *Br.* members of the group of workers who carry on a job or do the work of an organisation, esp. of a teaching or business organisation: *Auditors find 300 extra printing staff at Telegraph* - B. Bryson. 2. *Am.* stave, the set of five lines on which music is written. 3. *Br.* spindle in a watch. 4. *Br.* a token in the form of a rod given to a train driver as authority to proceed over a single track line.

staff/ short-staffed *Br.* short-handed.

staff/ staff finder *Br.* help wanted.

staff bureau or **agency** *Br.* employment agency.

staffer *esp. Am.* one of the people who works for an organisation, esp. for a newspaper: *You can almost hear the Kerry staffers* – Reader's Digest.

staff nurse *Br.* nurse with a rank below that of a sister or charge nurse.

staffroom *esp. Br.* common room for teachers in a school or college.

stag 1. *esp. Am., Can.* person who goes to a social gathering unaccompanied by a partner. 2. *Br.* Stock Exchange. 3. *Am., Can.* col. roughly cut (a garment, esp. trousers) to make it shorter.

stag *Br.* 1. person who buys shares in a new company hoping to sell them quickly at a profit. 2. spy on, observe. 3. turn informer.

stag/ go stag *esp. Am.* col. go without a woman to a social event.

stag party/night 1. *esp. Br.* /*Am.* **bachelor party**, *Aus.* **bucks party**/ party for the man who is going to get married to which only males are invited. 2. *Am., Can.* any party attended by men only.

stage *Am.* a level (of water).

stage carriage *Br.* stage coach.

stage director 1. *esp. Am.* a theatre director. 2. *esp. Br.* a stage manager.

stager *esp. Br.* col. person with experience (esp. in the phr. **old stager**).

staggered juncnion *Br.* a place where several roads meet a main road at a slight distance apart.

staggerer *Br.* col. a blow.

staggering bob *Aus.* col. a very young calf.

staging *Br.* shelving unit for plants in a greenhouse.

staging post *Br.* a stop which ships usu. make on a long journey.

staircase *Br.* a set of stairs and the rooms leading off it in a large building, esp. school or college.

stairhead *esp. Br.* landing at the top of a set of stairs.

stairrod/ come down or **rain in stairrods** *Br.* rain very hard.

stairs/ below stairs *Br.* obs. the floor where servants live; **above stairs** the floor where the owners of the private house live.

stake body *Am.* open motortruck body consisting of a platform with stakes inserted along the outside edges to retain a load.

stake/ go to the stake (for) *esp. Br.* obs. risk everything to defend smth.

stake (to) *Am.* give financial or other support to sb.; treat sb. to: *She staked him for a while* - E. McBain., *He always said he'd stake me.* - A. Miller.

stake out *esp. Am.* col. (esp. of people) watch (a place) continually in secret: *The devout Catholic had been part of a team of agents staking out a church to arrest radical priest* - G. O'Neill, D. Lehr., *That would mean a police stake-out in the lobby* - Arthur Hailey.

stake driver *Am.* bittern.

staker *Can.* person who makes a mining claim.

stalk *Am.* a stem of a plant.

stalk/ eyes out on stalks *Br., Aus.* eyes wide open with surprise.

stalking horse *Am.* a candidate used as a blind: *Gorbachev used a right-winger and Russian Nationalist as a stalking horse - Ivan Polozkov.* - H. Smith.

stall 1. *esp. Br.* (often in comb.) a table or small open-fronted shop in a public place: *the lights of the stalls glimmering weakly* - D. Lessing. 2. *Br.* (usu. attr. use) in or of the stalls in a theatre: *Michael gave me a stall.* - W.S. Maugham. 3. *Am.* pretext or excuse for delaying. 4. *Am.* a small enclosed area for washing or using the toilet. 5. *Am., Can.* marked-out parking space for a veicle.

stall off *esp. Am.* prevent from catching sb.

stall/ set out one's **stall** (to do smth.) *Br., Aus.* be determined to do smth.

stallholder *esp. Br.* person who rents and keeps a market stall: *Stallholders swapped with their neighbours, or ate their own wares* - L. Lee., *the stallholders were ready to pack up.* - G. Greene.

stalls *esp. Br., Aus. /Am.* **orchestra/** the seats on the main level of a theatre or cinema: *No, I'm sitting by myself in the stalls.* - A. Christie.

stamp print. *Am. /Br.* **emboss, block/**.

stamp *Br.* a small piece of paper you can buy which then represents the value of the money it costs, e.g. *vehicle license stamp*

stamp duty *esp. Br. /Am.* **stamp tax/** tax collected by means of stamp purchased and affixed, esp. a tax on the sale of property.

stampede *Am.* entertainment event at which cowboys show their skills and there are competitions, dancing, etc.

stamp office *Br.* office for the issue of government stamps and the receipt of stamp duty.

stanch *Am.* staunch.

stampede *Am., Can.* annual cowboy festival.

(witness) stand *Am., Can. /Am.* **(witness) chair,** *Br.* **witness box/** often in **take the stand**: *Shall I put those two on the stand under oath* - S. Bellow., *cops lie on the stand* - New York.

stand 1. *Am.* a. a party member. b. a period of performance. 2. *esp. Br.* upright structure on which an organisation displays promotional material at an exhibition.

stand 1. (for) *Br., Aus. /esp. Am.* **run/** be a candidate in an election: *he may choose to stand as Independent* - Longman. 2. *Am., Aus.* (of a vehicle) park for a short time (used esp. in signs, as **No standing,** etc.).

stand sb. **down** *esp. Br.* a. (of a soldier) go off duty. b. send (a soldier) off after a period of being on duty.

stand/wait in line *Am. /Br.* **queue/**: *Anger informs your every encounter, from standing in line to reading the stock page* – Reader's Digest.

stand in with (sb.) *esp. Am.* col. have a friendly relationship with sb.: *If you stand in with Retane in this town, you're made man.* - E. Hemingway.

stand off *Br.* lay off (sb.), stop employing (sb.).

stand on/in *Br.* accidentally stop on or in smth.

stand to *esp. Br.* (of soldiers). 1. take a position ready for action. 2. cause (soldiers) to do this.

stand up (to) *Am., Can.* fulfil a promise.

stand/ I could stand smth. *Am.* col. humor. used to say that one would like smth.

stand/ stand one's **guns, stand pat** *Am.* refuse to change one's opinions, intentions or behaviour.

stand easy *Br.* (of soldiers) stand completely at ease.

stand tall *Am.* be proud and feel ready to deal with anything.

standard *Am.* pole: *It was very dark and the eerie light from lamp standards around Tienamen cast somber shadows everywhere.* - J. Fraser.

standard/ come with smth. **as standard** *esp. Br.* have the usual requirement, e.g. guarantee for some goods.

standardbred *Am., Can.* a horse of a breed able to attain a specific speed, developed esp. for trotting.

standard class *Br.* a term for the majority of seats on a railway train as distinct from first class.

standard deduction *Am.* fixed amount of money that sb. earns that they don't have to pay tax on.

standard English, spelling, pronounciation, etc. *Br.* the form of English, etc., that most people in Britain use.

standard lamp, stand lamp *Br., Aus. /Am., Can.* **floor lamp/** a lamp on a tall base: *He lit the gas fire, turned on a stand lamp.* - G. Greene., *A standard lamp in the living room was already on.* - J. Patterson.

standee *esp. Am.* col. 1. person standing in a theatre. 2. a standing passenger.

standing *Am.* parking (of a car, esp. for a short time).

standing/ leave sb./smth. **standing** *Br., Aus.* be much better than everybody.

Standing Operating Procedure (SOP) *Am.* usual way of doing smth.

standing order, also **banker's order** *Br.* an order to a bank to pay a fixed amount from an account to a named person or organisation at a regular time each month, year, etc. (for example to a newsagent).

stand of colours *Br.* battalion's flags.

standing time print *Br.* /*Am.* **open time**/.
stand-off *esp. Am.* a stalemate or deadlock between two equally matched opponents in a dispute or conflict.
standout *esp. Am., Can.* 1. an excellent or the best example of smth. 2. sb. who is better at doing smth. or more attractive than other members of a group.
stand-pat(ter) *Am.* col. a conservative.
stand-up *Am.* col. courageous and personally accountable: *And he's very stand-up.* - G.V. Higgins., *Lee Franiere turned out to be the ultimate stand-up guy.* - G. O'Neill, D. Lehr.
stand-upper, stand-up piece *Am.* a piece spoken directly into a TV camera.
Stanley knife *Br., Aus.* /*Am.* **razor knife**/ tdmk. a sharp knife with a short blade which can be pulled back into the handle.
starch *Am., Can.* col. (in boxing) defeat an opponent by a knockout.
starch/ be starched up *Am.* col. be dressed up showily: *The children were all starched up in their new dresses for the wedding ceremony.* - Longman.
starch/ take the starch out of sb. *Am.* snub. sb.
star chamber *Br.* derog. a court or other group of people who meet privately and make judgements which can be severe.
stare *esp. Br.* stand out, be conspicuous.
stare sb. **out** *Br.* /*Am.* **stare** sb. **down**/ force to look away under the power of a long steady look: *I tried to stare her down.* - R. Chandler.
stargazer *Aus.* col. a horse that turns its head when galloping.
staring *esp. Br.* unpleasantly bright and noticeable to the eye.
stairing/ be (stark) staring/raving mad *Br.* be completely crazy.
star jump *Br.* one of a series of exercise jumps that one does from a standing position with their arms and legs pointing out at each side; jumping jack.
starkers *esp. Br.* humor. col. naked: *I had been running around starkers* - C.M. Fraser.
star route *Am.* postal delivery route served by a private contractor.
Stars and Stripes, also **Star-Spangled Banner, Old Glory** *Am.* /*Am.* col. **The Stars and Bars**/ the flag of the US.
start/ Don't (you) start! *Br.* col. used to tell sb. to stop complaining, arguing or being annoying.
start/ for a start *Br.* col. at first.
start in on *Am., Can.* 1. begin to do or deal with. 2. attack verbally.

start over *esp. Am., Can.* start (all) over again: *He started over.* - S. Bellow., *I'm going to New York and I'm starting over.* - D. Mortman.
starter 1. *Br.* (nonassertive) a possibility with any chance of success. 2. *esp. Br.* col. the first part of a meal, usu. soup, fruit juice or fish; appetizer: *From a demure reserve over the starter to giggling irresponsibility by the time the dessert was served.* - D. Lodge.
starter/ be under starter's orders *Br.* be ready to start work.
starter/ your starter for ten *Br.* col. humor. used before asking a question.
starter home *Br.* small house or apartment, bought by people who are buying their first home.
starting handle *Br.* crank (to start an engine of a car).
star turn *esp. Br.* the most widely publicised person or item in a group, esp. a top performer.
starve/ (*Br.*) **I'm starving!** / (*Am.*) **I'm starved!** (= very starved).
starve/ be starved for (not of) *Am.* 1. not get enough of smth. you need very much. 2. col. be very hungry.
Starve the crows *Aus.* expression of surprise, disbelief, etc.
stash *Am.* col. moustache: *Jerry has this enormous stash* - R.A. Spears.
state *esp. Br.* col. a very nervous anxious or excited condition: *He looks a right old state, doesn't he?* - T. Thorne.
state/ the state of play *Br., Aus.* the present situation in an ongoing process.
state-house *Am.* the building which houses a state legislature.
Stately Home *Br.* a large old house which usu. has beautiful furniture, decorations and gardens and is often owned by government or by a preservation organisation now.
statement *Br.* (of education authority) give school additional money to help teach children who have special educational needs.
statement of earnings, income statement *Am.* report about all the money earned for a certain period of time.
statement of financial position *Am.* balance sheet.
state('s) attorney *Am.* a lawyer representing a state in court.
state school *Br.* a school which provides free education and is paid by the government.
State's evidence *Am.* law. /*Br.* **Queen's evidence**/ information given by a criminal in a court of

law against other criminals, esp. in order to get less punishment for oneself, esp. in **turn state's** or **Queen's evidence**: *there was even more temptation for those charged to turn state's evidence.* - J. O'Brien, A. Kurins.

stateroom *Am.* a private room in a railroad car with one or more berths and a toilet.

state school *Br.* /*Am.* **public school**/ a free local school, controlled and paid for by the state.

stateside *esp. Am.* col. adj. adv. of, in, or towards the US.

statesider *Am.* native American.

state tax *Am.* one that is paid to the state rather than to federal government.

state trooper *Am.* state policeman.

State University *Am.* one which every state has and supports, tuition being almost free to qualified residents of the state.

statewide *Am.* affecting the entire state.

static *Am., Can.* col. criticism: *We're getting a lot of static from higher up now* - T. Thorne.

station 1. *Aus., NZ.* a large sheep or cattle farm. 2. *Am., Can.* a branch post office in the US. 3. *Am.* telephone extension number. 4. *esp. Br.* also **railway station** /*Am.* **train station**/ a place where trains regularly stop.

station *Am.* /*esp. Br.* **post**/.

station/ back station *Aus.* the far side of the farm.

station/ station black *Aus.* aboriginal farm worker.

station/ head station, station home *Aus.* Central Estate.

station/ train station *esp. Am.* /*esp. Br.* **railway station**/.

station/ subway station *Am., Can.* /*Br.* **underground station**/.

station agent 1. *esp. Am.* /*Br.,* **station manager**/ station master. 2. *Aus.* a worker at the cattle farm: *the stockrider and station agent are characters in the story* - P. Howard.

station break *Am., Can., Aus.* a pause during a radio or TV broadcast for local stations to give their names.

station buffet *Br.* snack bar at the station.

station calendar *Br.* bulletin board (on the wall at major railroad stations).

stationer *Br.* sb. who is in charge of a shop that sells stationery.

stationer's *Br.* a shop that sells things for writing.

station hand *Aus.* person working on a station.

station house 1. *Aus.* main building of the farm. 2. *Am.* police /*Br.* **police station**/ or fire station: *I went back in the station house.* - J. Kerouac.

station jack *Aus.* traditional farmer's treat (usu. a meat pudding).

station mark *Aus.* brand on cattle.

station road *Br.* /*Am.* **railroad avenue, depot street**/ spur track leading to the railway station.

station super(intendent) *Aus.* manager of the farm.

station wagon, ranch wagon *esp. Am.* /*Br.* **estate car** or **wagon**/ motor-car which carries both people and goods with folding back seats and doors at the back which can be opened to put bags, cases, etc. inside: *Florio arrived in Camden in 1964 in a beat-up station wagon* - Reader's Digest.

statute book *esp. Br.* a record of all the laws made by the government.

statute of limitations *Am.* tech. a law that gives the period of time within which action may be taken on a legal question or crime.

statutes at large *esp. Am.* laws stated in their original version.

statutory offence *Am.* tech. crime that is described by a law and can be punished by a court.

statutory rape *Am.* law. sex intercourse with a girl below the age of consent.

stave *esp. Br.* five lines that music is written on.

stave up (usu. pass.) *Am.* col. be tired, worn out: *Don't ask me to move, I'm stove up.* - Longman.

stay down *Br.* stay in the same class for a second year: *she would have to stay down, repeat the work* - Longman.

stay home *esp. Am.* /*Br.* **stay at home**/.

stayer *Br.* horse or person who can keep going to the end of a long race, job, etc.

stay-in strike *Br.* sit-down strike.

(go) steady (on) *Br.* /*Am., Aus.* **(go) easy (on)**/ col. excl. be careful, watch what you're doing.

steady *Am.* col. boyfriend or girlfriend that sb. has been having a romantic relationship with.

steak *Br.* cattle meat of average quality, used esp. in small pieces in dishes with vegetables or pastry (casseroles): *I even grew to like English cooking - steak-and-kidney pie.* - D. Martin.

steal *esp. Am., Can.* col. 1. smth. for sale very cheaply: *It's a steal.* - L. Uris. 2. an act of stealing smth.

steam *Br.* humor. obs. e.g. steam radio.

steam in *Br.* col. start or join a fight.

steam/ blow off steam *esp. Am., Aus.* /*esp. Br.* **let off steam**/ try to lose one's anger.

steam/ pick up steam *Am.* start to be much more effective or successful.

steam beer *Am.* tdmk. effervescent beer, esp. one brewed in the western US.

steamed 1. *Am.* col. furious: *All those guys in front of us were getting really steamed.* - R.L. Stine. 2. *Br.* col. extremely drunk.

steamer rug *Am.* a warm covering for the lap and feet, esp. of a person sitting on a ship's deck.

steaming *Br.* col. 1. extremely drunk. 2. very angry.

steamroll *esp. Am., Can.* steamroller, force sb. to do smth. or use all one's power to do smth.

steam shovel *Am.* /*Br., Aus.* **excavator**/: *America was in the dawn of the Twentieth Century a nation of steam shovels, locomotives, airships* - E.L. Doctorow., *Modern stem shovels and bulldozers are pitifully scarce.* - J. Fischer.

steam table *Am., Can.* table having openings to hold containers of cooked food over steam or hot water circulating beneath them.

The Steel State *Am.* Pennsylvania.

steep/ that's/it's a bit steep *Br.* col. use to say that a request or action is unreasonable.

steer/ (get/give a) bum steer *esp. Am.* col. (get/give) a piece of bad advice or misleading information.

steer *Am.* col. 1. take or inveigle sb. to a place or person where gamblers or confidence men might victimise him. 2. also **steerer** one who steers victims.

steering *Am.* the practice of trying to ensure that non-white prospective tenants or house-purchasers do not move into all-white areas.

stein *Am.* /*Br.* **tankard**/ mug (for beer, etc.): *no way I could have passed up the cold overfoaming steins* - A.E. Hotchner.

stellar *Am.* done extremely well.

steller *Am.* leading, principal (about actor, role, etc.).

stem *Am.* col. pipe used for smoking crack or opium.

stem/ from stem to stern *Am.* from one end of smth. to the other.

stem, bow *Am.* /*Br.* **arm**/.

stem-winder *Am.* 1. obs. stem-winding watch. 2. col. first-rate person or thing: *Gee, but it's a stem-winder.* - J. London. 3. col. entertaining or rousing speech.

stemwork *Am., Can.* goblets and stemmed glasses regarded collectively.

steno *esp. Am., Can.* col. stenographer.

stenographer esp. old use or *Am., Can.* /*Br.* **shorthand typist** or **writer**/: *The company does not use male stenographers* - K. Vonnegut, Jr.

stenography *Am.* or *Br.* obs. a system of writing quickly.

stenopad *Am.* shorthand pad: *Did you see her fall? An officer asked, scribbling rapidly in his steno pad.* – R.L. Stine.

step *esp. Am.* /*Br.* **(a pair of) steps, tone**/ in music) a tone, a difference in the highness of a musical note equal to that between two notes which are two notes apart on a piano.

step/ mind the/one's step *Br.* /*esp. Am.* col. **watch one's step**/ be careful.

step along *Am.* col. move quickly.

step off *Am.* sl. make a mistake.

step on the gas, step on it *Am., Aus.* col. drive more quickly.

step out *esp. Am., Can.* go out with sb. for a short time or go somewhere, esp. go to a party, date, etc.: *he stepped out and returned to the group.* - New York.

step out on sb. *Am.* col. have sexual relationship with people other than that person.

step-ins *esp. Am., Can.* obs. a pair of one's briefs.

step lively! *Br.* hurry up.

steps *esp. Br.* stepladder.

sterling 1. *Aus.* col. Englishman who migrated to Australia. 2. *esp. Br.* (of a person or their work, efforts, or qualities, character, etc.) excellent or valuable.

stevedore *esp. Am.* /*esp. Br.* **docker**, *Am., Can.* **longshoreman**/ person whose job is loading and unloading ships.

stevedore barge *Am.* lighter.

stew 1. *Br.* make strong tea. 2. *Br.* pond for keeping fish in. 3. *Am., Can.* col. air steward(ess).

steward *Br.* person who helps to organise a race or other public event.

stewbum *Am.* col. drunkard.

stewed 1. *Br., Aus.* (of tea) kept too long before pouring, and so tasting too strong and bitter. 2. *esp. Am.* col. drunk.

stewing/braising steak *Br., Aus.* meat from cattle which is usu. cut into small pieces and cooked slowly in liquid.

stewpond also **stew** *esp. Br.* fish tank, one where fish are kept until needed for table.

stick 1. *Br.* col. severe treatment, esp. in the phr. **give** sb. **(some) stick** criticise severely: *What have I done to deserve all this stick?* - T. Thorne. 2. *esp. Br.* obs. col. a person of the stated type: *I know, old stick, can't women be devil?* - J. Higgins.

stick 1. *esp. Br., Aus.* col. (not in progressive forms) like or accept, bear, esp. smth. unpleasant, often in **can't stick** (dislike very much). 2. *Br.* sl. keep (smth. unwanted). 3. *Am.* col. a stick shift or car with a stick shift: *You're not used to driving a stick?* – Reader's Digest.

stick at (it) *Br.* continue to study or work hard at smth. in a very determined way.

stick at nothing *Br.* col. willing to do anything, even illegal in order to achieve smth.

stick sb./smth. **up** *esp. Am.* col. rob sb. at gunpoint, n. **stick-up**.

stick/ a stick to beat sb./smth. **with** *Br.* smth. that gives one an excuse for criticising sb. or smth. that he/she doesn't like or approve of.

stick/ be beat/hit with an ugly stick *Am.* sl. be very ugly.

stick/ get on the stick *Am.* force oneself to hurry or start working.

stick/ get/take/come in for (a lot of, some) stick also **give sb. (a lot of/some) stick, come in for/get/take stick, get a lot of/some stick** *Br.* col. be criticised or laughed at because of smth. that they do, usu. in a kind way.

stick/ in a cleft stick *esp. Br.* in a difficult situation.

stick/ stick in one's **throat** *Br.* /*Am.* **stick in** one's **craw/** a. (of a situation) be so annoying that one can't accept it. b. (of words) be unable to say what you want.

stick/ old stick *Br.* obs. used to describe sb. in a friendly way.

stick/ shake a stick at *Am.* col. take no notice of.

stick/ stick no bills *Br.* post no bills.

stick/ up sticks and… *Br., Aus.* col. /*Aus.* **pick up sticks (and…)**, *Am.* **pull up stakes (and…)**/ leave the place where one has been living and go somewhere else.

stick/ up the stick *Br.* col. pregnant.

stickball *Am., Can.* col. game resembling baseball and lacrosse.

sticker *Br.* col. sb. who is trying to do smth. even when it becomes very difficult.

sticker price *Am., Can.* official price of smth., esp. a car, given by its maker: *It's the only car that when you buy it, there is no sticker price* – Reader's Digest.

sticker shock *Am.* col. shock or dismay, esp. by the potential buyers of a particular product on discovering its high or increased price.

sticking plaster, also **plaster,** (now rare), **patch** *esp. Br.* /*Am., Aus.* tdmk. **Band-Aid/** medical plaster: *Poor chap probably thought 'e could cure a dose with stickin' plaster.* - D. Reeman.

stick-in-the-mud *esp. Br.* col. a very conservative person.

stickjaw *Br.* chewy candy.

stickle at *Am.* oppose (an idea) because of one's conscience: *One of the committee members is stickling at the plan because it offends him morally.* - Longman.

stickman *Am.* sl. 1. croupier. 2. one who handles a stick or bat in sports. 3. drummer.

stickpin *Am., Can.* /*Br.* **breastpin/** a decorative pin, esp. one worn on a tie: *The green stone in his stickpin was not quite as large as an apple* - R. Chandler. / *Am.* **breastpin** is a **brooch** in Britain.

stick shift *Am., Can.* /*Br.* **gear lever/** a way of working gears in a car by means of a gear lever or a gear lever itself: *Kavanaugh's big hand moved lightly on the stick shift.* - T. Murphy.

stick-to-itive *Am., Can.* col. persistent. **-ness** n.: *The kid has sticktoitiveness.* - R.A. Spears.

stickum *esp. Am., Can.* col. a sticky or adhesive substance; gum or paste.

stickwork *Am.* col. skill in baseball hitting.

sticky *Br.* not willing to help sb. or do what they want.

sticky beak *Aus., NZ.* a prying inquisitive person, v.

sticky end/ come to/meet a sticky end *Br., Aus.* col. humor. die in unpleasant way, esp. violently.

sticky tape *Br., Aus.* col. /*Br.* **Sellotape,** esp. *Am., Can., Aus.* tdmk. **Scotch tape,** *Aus.* **durex/** adhesive tape: *sticking extra bits on the ends of gas-masks with sticky-tape* – R. Westall.

sticky wicket *Br.* col. a situation that is or may become difficult, esp. in **be (batting) on a sticky wicket**: *There are four general rules for dealing with this sticky wicket.* - A. Frommer.

sticky wicket/ go (betting) on a sticky wicket *Br., Aus.* be in a difficult situation because one hasn't behaved in the correct way.

stiff 1. *Am.* col. a person of the type described, e.g. *a working stiff, you lucky stiff.* 2. *esp. Am., Can.* col. boring conventional person.

stiff *Am.* sl. 1. dead drunk: *and they could tell when one of them was stiff* - G.V. Higgins. 2. hobo.

stiff/ working stiff *Am.* col. ordinary person who works to earn enough money to live.

stiff 1. *esp. Am., Can.* sl. cheat, esp. out of money, fair wages, etc., or by not giving a tip in a restaurant: *Brooklyn milliner emerged as a penny-pinching tyrant who tried to stiff just about everybody.* - Time. 2. *Br.* sl. have sex with.

stiff/ be stiffed *Am., Can.* be cheated.

stiff-arm *Am.* sl. treat unfairly and harshly: *Each time he stiff-armed the legal system.* - Reader's Digest.

Stiffen the lizzards (snakes, wombats) *Aus.* God damn.

stiff upper lip *esp. Br.* keeping calm appearance in spite of feeling very upset.

stiffy *Br.* taboo. sl. an erection.

still *Br.* (of a drink) not having gas.

still alarm *Am.* fire alarm transmitted without sounding the signal apparatus (as by telephone call).

still and all *Am.* col. after all.

stilletto heels *Am.* col. spike heels.

stilettos *esp. Br. /Am.* **spike heels/** woman's shoes on thin high tapering heels.

still hunting *esp. Am., Can.* stalking, esp. deer-stalking in the game preserve: *That is still-hunting with a vengeance, thought I.* - W. Grady, v. **still-hunt**.

sting *Br., Aus. /Am.* **stinger/** a sharp often poisonous organ used as a weapon by some animals, esp. insects.

sting *esp. Am.* sl. 1. a well-planned scheme to entrap criminals, esp. by pretending to be involved in criminal activities themseles: *the kidnapping was a sting operation.* - Vanity Fair., *That was the beauty of the sting operation* - J. O'Brien, A. Kurins. 2. a confidence trick or other clever act of stealing, in which large amounts are involved: *We got stung $15 a seat to listen to his aging voice crack* – J. Hopkins.

sting sb. **for** smth. col. 1. *esp. Br.* charge sb. too much for smth. 2. *Br.* borrow money from sb.

sting/ a sting in the tail (of) *Br., Aus.* an unpleasant end to smth. that began pleasantly, esp. a story or suggestion.

stingaree *Am., Can., Aus.* stingray.

stinger 1. *Am.* col. cocktail of brandy and creme de menthe: *Hockney ordered a stinger.* - R. Borchgrave, R. Moss. 2. *Br.* whiskey and soda.

stingo *esp. Br.* (a type of) strong beer.

stink/ kick up a stink *Br.* col. */Am.* col. **make/ raise a stink/** *Am.* col. complain angrily about smth. that one is not satisfied with.

stink up *Am.* col. */Br., Aus.* **stink out/** fill (a place) with a bad smell: *you stink up the joint.* - R.L. Stine.

stink/ work/run/go like stink *Br.* work as fast as one can.

stinker *Br.* obs. or *Aus.* col. something or someone very unpleasant or bad: *this was so palpably a stinker.* - A.E. Hotchner.

stinking *esp. Br.* col. very unpleasant.

stinking letter *Br.* angry letter in which sb. complains very strongly about smth.

stinkpot *esp. Am.* col. vehicle that emits foul-smelling exhaust fumes.

stir 1. *Br., Aus.* spread malicious gossip, **stirrer** a person who does this. 2. *Am.* **stir trouble** cause trouble.

stir *Am.* sl. prison.

Stir yourself! *esp. Br.* try to do smth.!

stirabout *esp. Irish Eng.* porridge made by stiring oatmeal in boiling water and milk.

stir-crazy *esp. Am.* col. upset after being in a place too long.

stirrer *esp. Br.* col. troublemaker, one who likes to cause trouble between others: *She might have got away with it if a couple of stirrers on the cast (of EastEnders) hadn't made a fuss.* - T. Thorne.

stitch sb. **up (together)** *Br.* col. arrange or secure a deal to one's advantage.

stitch up *Br.* col. make sb. seem guilty when they are not, frame up.

stitch-up *Br.* sl. doing smth. bad or illegal and trying to hide the truth about it.

stock 1. *Am.* part of the ownership of a company which a person buys as an investment. 2. *Br.* money that people invest in the government's papers which produce a fixed rate of interest. 3. *Aus.* cattle.

stock/ summer stock *Am.* group of actors who work together on several plays during the summer; **do stock** *Am.* work as an actor in this group.

stock up *Aus.* breed livestock.

stockade *Am.* 1. enclosure made with posts and stakes. 2. also *Can.* military prison: *nine months of his stateside tour were spent in the stockade.* - Reader's Digest., *The men faced six months in the stockade* - Time.

stock and station *Aus., NZ.* denoting a firm or agent dealing in farm products and supplies.

stockbroker belt *Br.* col. a suburb where rich people live in large houses.

stockcar *Am., Can.* a railway carriage for carrying cattle.

stock certificate *Am.* official document that shows that sb. owns shares in a company.

stock-company *Am.* 1. a group of actors who perform a certain set of plays. 2. joint-stock company.

stockholder 1. *esp. Am., Can. /Br.* **shareholder/** an owner of shares in a business: *he was a major shareholder in private bus and cab fleets* - L. Waller. 2. *Aus.* also **pastoralist** livestock farmer (also used in Britain).

stock horse *Aus., NZ.* trained horse used for herding cattle.
stock house *Aus.* farm.
stock hut *Aus.* cattle yard.
stockinette *esp. Br.* soft cotton material that stretches, used esp. for bandages.
stocking *Am.* long sock worn by men.
stocking cap *Am.* /*Br.* **woolly hat, bobble hat,** *Aus.* **beanie,** *Can.* **tuque**/: *I brought ...the little blue stocking cap he wore that day.* – Reader's Digest.
stocking stuffer *Am.* stocking filler, a small cheap Christmas present.
stockist *Br., Aus.* person or firm that keeps a particular sort of goods for sale.
stockjobber 1. *Br.* jobber. 2. *Am.* derog. stockbroker.
stock-keep *Aus.* breed livestock.
stock-keeper *Aus.* farm owner.
stock list 1. *Am.* share price index. 2. *Br.* publication listing a retailer's stock of goods with current prices.
stockman 1. *Aus., NZ.* stock station owner or worker. 2. *Am.* owner of a livestock. 3. *Am.* store keeper. 4. *Am.* person who looks after a stockroom or warehouse.
stock prices *Am.* /*Br., Aus.* **share prices**/ prices of company's shares.
stock rider *Aus.* cowboy.
stock route *Aus.* a road on which traffic must stop sometimes so that the cattle or sheep can be passed through it.
stock-saddle *Am.* cowboy saddle.
stock split *Am., Can.* issue of new shares in a company to existing shareholders in proportion to their current holdings.
stock station *Aus.* cattle station.
stocktaking *Br.* /*Am.* **inventory**/ checking stock of the goods in a shop or business.
stockyard *Am., Can.* large yard containing pens and sheds in which livestock is kept and sorted.
stodge *Br.* col. smth. written that's very dull and difficult to read, adj. **stodgy**.
stodgy 1. *Br.* (of food) heavy and making one feel full very quickly: *The food was predictably stodgy - steak pie or fish fried in batter* - D. Lodge, n. stodge. 2. *esp. Am.* bulky or heavy in appearance.
stogie *Am.* col. a cigar.
stogy *Am.* 1. heavy-duty boot. 2. also *Can.* col. a cheap cigar: *He was smoking a thin black stogy* - J. Dos Passos.
stoked *Am.* col. very excited about smth. good that is happening and that sb. didn't expect.

stollen *Am.* yeast bread.
stomp (**on** sb.) *esp. Am.* col. stamp, beat sb., when he's already on the ground; defeat or treat people badly: *an agent had been stomped and beaten for taking pictures at a funeral.* - J. O'Brien, A. Kurins.
stomping ground *Am., Can.* favourite haunt.
stone *Br.* 1. a measure of weight (14 pounds or 6.35 kg): *he was half a head taller and two stone heavier than the actor.* - S. Nichols. 2. /*Am.* **pit**/ a single hard seed inside some fruits, such as cherry, plum, and peach; v. take the stone/pit out of fruit.
stone boat *Am., Can.* a sled (esp. for carrying stones).
stone-broke *Am., Can.* col. completely without money.
stone fence *Am.* stone wall.
stoner *Br.* person who weighs specific number of stone.
stone tablet/ be set in tablets of stone *Br.* (of plans, decisions, etc.) be firmly fixed.
Stone the crows!, also /*Br.* **Stone me!**/ *Br.* or *Aus.* obs. col. (used for expressing surprise, disbelief, etc.): *Stone me, I should do.* - J. Higgins.
stonewall *esp. Br., Aus., Can.* 1. obstruct discussions: *they completely stonewalled my requests.* - H. Smith., *the two Presidents have largely stonewalled the tribunal.* - Time. 2. (of a batsman in cricket) play slowly and carefully.
stonker *Br.* col. smth. that is very large or impressive of its kind.
stonkered *Br., Aus., NZ.* col. defeated or extremely tired.
stonking *Br.* col. used to emphasize how good smth. is.
stony broke *Br.* col. having no money at all: *now they are stranded, stony broke* - New York.
stooge (esp. **around, about**) *Br.* sl. 1. (of a pilot) fly to and fro over quite a small area: *we've been stooging around at 25,000 feet* - Longman. 2. walk or go to and fro without any fixed purpose, kill time: *just stooging about most of the morning.* - Longman.
stooge *Am.* stool pigeon, informer.
stook *Br.* group of sheaves of grain stood on end in a field: *the stook is some way off* – J. Fowls.
stool *Am.* derog. bird in hunting.
stoolie, stool pigeon *Am., Can.* derog. col. police informer: *This stoolie reported this sinful event to Krogh* - A.E. Hotchner.
stoop *Am., Can.* porch or small veranda (with steps in front of the house): *I sit for about an hour on the stoop of a shoemaker's shop* - J.A.

Michener., *On the little stoop behind the house he drank the cool water* - C. McCullers., *I stood up from my iron back stoop to greet him.* - J. Steinbeck.

stoop labor *Am., Can.* one requiring much stooping, esp. in agriculture: *the Mexican illegals who perform the state's stoop labor.* - Time.

stop 1. *esp. Br.* remain, stay. 2. *Br. col.* stay somewhere for a short time.

stop *esp. Br.* a dot as a mark of punctuation, esp. a full stop.

stop (a)round *esp. Am.* visit sb. briefly, esp. at their home.

stop back *Am.* go back to a place where sb. has been earlier.

stop by *esp. Am.* drop in: *Can you stop by for a moment* - Longman.

stop in *Br.* stay at home.

stop on a dime *Am., Can.* stop very quickly.

stop out 1. *Am.* interrupt one's education to pursue some other activity. 2. *Br. col.* stay out, esp. longer or later than might be expected.

stop over *Br.* /*Am.* **stay over**/ stay at a place for one night or more.

stop round *esp. Am. col.* make a short visit, esp. to sb.'s home.

stop up *Br. col.* not to go to bed; stay up.

stop payment on a check *Am.* stop a cheque, prevent money from being paid from one's bank account.

stop-and-go activity *Am.* one in which short periods of movement are regularly interupted by a lack of it.

stopbank *Aus., NZ.* embankment built to prevent a river flooding.

stopcock, also **turncock** *Br.* /*esp. Am.* **valve**/ a valve used to control the flow of water in a pipe.

stop-go *Br., Aus.* col. derog. n. adj. periods of inflation and deflation quickly following one another.

stop-go approach, policies, etc. *Br.* way of controlling the economy by restricting government spending for a period of time and then not restricting it so severely for a time.

stoplamp *Br.* brake light.

stoplight 1. *Am., Can.* /*Br.* **traffic light**/ a set of traffic light: *Sitting at a stoplight, I was puzzling over the meaning of the vanity plate on the car in front of me.* – Reader's Digest. 2. *Br.* red traffic light.

stopoff *Am. col.* stopover: *The show is a stop-off for loads of celebreties* – Reader's Digest.

stopout *Am.* a college student taking a break in one's education.

stop-out *Br. col.* person who stays out late at night.

stoppage *Br.* the act of stopping smth. from moving or happening.

stoppage(s) *esp. Br.* /*Am., Aus.* **deduction**/ amount officially subtracted from one's pay, esp. before one gets it.

stopper *Am.* bung.

stop press *Br., Aus.* a certain space on the front or back page of newspaper which contains very recent news items which are added to them after the printing process had stopped.

storage heater *Br.* electric device for heating rooms which uses electricity during the hours when it is cheapest in order to store warmth for later use.

storage room *Am.* /*esp. Br.* **lumber room, boxroom**/.

store 1. *esp. Am., Can., Aus.* /*esp. Br.* **shop**/ shop of any kind or size: *We had stopped at the only store which keeps open throughout the year* - J.A. Michener. 2. *esp. Br.* large shop selling a variety of goods.

store/ in store *Br., Aus.* being stored.

store/ mind the store *Am.* be in charge of smth. while the person responsible for it is away.

store(-bought) *Am., Can.* /*Br.* **shop-bought**/ bought in a store: *We might better spend it on some store-bought clothes.* - A. Hitchcock Mystery Magazine., *six cans of store-bought chicken soup.* - Guideposts.

store brand *esp. Am.* type of goods that are produced for a particular shop and have the shop's name on them.

store-cheese *Am.* American cheese.

(store) clerk *Am.* /*Br.* **shop assistant**/ person who serves customers in a shop.

store-clothes *Am.* ready-made clothes.

storefront *esp. Am., Can.* 1. /*Br.* **shop front**/ outside part of a shop facing the street including the doors and windows. 2. a small shop or office, etc. that opens onto the street and is part of a row of shops or offices.

storefront church *Am.* a shop that a religious group uses as a church.

storefront legal clinic, law office *Am.* law office in a shop.

store-front school *Am.* free school.

storehouse *Am.* /*Br., Aus.* **warehouse**/ a special house for storing goods before they are sold.

storekeeper 1. *Am., Can.* /*Br.* **shopkeeper**/ person in charge of a small shop: *Around the square a few store-keepers were preparing to open* - T. Capote. 2. *esp. Br.* supply keeper, esp. in the Navy.

storeman *Br.* a man responsible for stored goods.
store teeth *Am.* false teeth.
store-wide *Am.* adj. applying to an entire store.
store window *Am.* shop window.
storey *Br., Aus. /Am.* **story**/ 1. any of the levels on which a building is built. 2. **-storey**, also **-storeyed** *Br., Aus. /Am.* **storied**/ having the stated number of storeys.
storied *esp. Am.* famous.
storm/ be storming *esp. Am.* (of weather) be stormy.
storm/ storm in a teacup *Br., Aus.* col. */Am.* **a tempest in a teapot**/ a lot of worry and nervous annoyance over smth. unimportant.
storm/ up a storm *esp. Am., Can.* col. very intensively, very competently, esp. **dance, sing, party up a storm**, etc.: *someone will see the numbers on your credit card and start charging up a storm.* - Omni., *he'd been cursing up a storm about now.* - J. DeFelice.
storm cellar *Am.* a cellar with an entrance outside the house where refuge can be taken during fierce storms.
storm cone *Br.* device used as a storm signal.
storm door/window *esp. Am., Can.* extra one which is fitted to the usual door for protection in bad weather: *I jumped up as someone pulled the storm door open without knocking.* – R.L. Stine.
stormer *Br.* col. smth. particularly impressive or good of its kind, adj. **storming**.
storm lantern *esp. Br.* hurricane lamp.
storms *Am., Can.* storm windows.
storm sewer *Am.* storm drain.
story *Am., Can.* storey.
story/ cut a long story short *esp. Br. /Am., Can.* **make a long story short**/ give only the basic facts.
story/ end of story *Br.* col. there is no more to say.
stoush *Aus., NZ.* col. beating, brawl, v.
stout *Br.* a strong dark beer brewed with roasted malt: *So I...went into the King Lud pub for a sixpenny Welsh rarebit and a stout.* - J. Kerouac.
stove 1. *esp. Am., Aus. /esp. Br.* **cooker**, *Am.* **range**/ an enclosed apparatus for cooking or heating which works by burning coal, oil, gas, etc., or by electricity on its top: *The kitchen had a stove and table, but no running water.* - H. Smith. 2. *esp. Br.* green house. 3. *Br.* raise (plants) in a hothouse.
stoved *Br.* (of vegetable or meat) stewed.
stove-enamel *Br.* heatproof enamel.

stovepipe hat *esp. Am.* col. a man's tall silk hat: *ancient SP of another era with stovepipe hats and flowers in their lapels* - J. Kerouac.
stove(top) *Am., Aus. /Br.* **hob**, *Am.* **range**/: *Something was boiling in a round copper pot on the stovetop.* – R.L. Stine.
straddle *esp. Am.* derog. v. n. (take) an uncertain stand, esp. in politics.
straight *Am.* adv. by piece.
straight/ as straight as a pin *Am. /Br., Aus.* (**as**) **straight as a die**/ 1. completely straight. 2. very honest.
straight/ couldn't lie straight in bed *Aus.* col. be very dishonest.
straight/ damn straight *Am.* col. completely true or right.
straight-arm *Am.* col. ward off (an opponent) or remove an obstacle with an arm held straight.
straight arrow, straight shooter *Am., Can.* col. very conventional, reliable, honest person: *A blue-collar straight arrow who was decorated in Vietnam.* - Time.
straightaway *Am., Can.* 1. */Br.* **straight**/ straight part of a racetrack. 2. extending or moving in a straight line.
straight bat/ play a straight bat 1. *Br.* hide information from sb. 2. *Br.* obs. be honest and traditional in one's ideas and beliefs.
straight fight *Br.* contest between just two opponents, esp. in an election.
straight from the shoulder *Am.* col. directly and honestly.
straight off *esp. Br. /esp. Am.* **right off**/ right away, at once: *After school is over, you come home straight off* - A. Makkai.
straight on *Br. /esp. Am.* **straight ahead**/ forwards.
straight up 1. *Br., Aus., Can.* col. used to emphasise that sb. is saying true and honest things or when asking sb. if they are telling the truth: *She is one of the most straight up brokers in town.* - R.A. Spears. 2. *esp. Am., Can.* unmixed, unadulterated: *Martini, straight up. The classic American cocktail.* – Harper's Magazine.
straighten (up) *esp. Am.* clean a room that is untidy.
straighten up (and fly right) *Am.* clean up your act, start working seriously.
straight-faced *Am.* poker-faced: *a straight-faced, very serious attempt was made* - J. Patterson.
straight man *Am.* person who sets up jokes or gags so that sb. else can make a punch line: *I'm tired of being a straight man for a has-been comic.* - R.A. Spears.

straight-out *esp. Am.* adj. directly, not trying to deceive.
straight razor *Am., Can. /Br.* **cutthroat razor/**.
straight shooter *esp. Am., Can., Aus.* reliable and honest person.
straight ticket *Am.* ballot cast for all the candidates of one party: *My father always voted the straight Republican ticket.* - H.C. Whitford., R.J. Dixson.
straight-up *Am., Can.* col. honest.
straight waistcoat *esp. Br.* straitjacket.
strand *Br.* the bank of the river Thames.
strand *Am., Aus.* single connected row, e.g. a strand of pearls.
strange *Am.* adv. in a way that is different from what is normal.
strange to say *Br.* strangely.
strangled *Am., Aus.* strangulated, becoming tightly pressed and stopping the flow of blood or air through human organs.
strap (up) (often pass.) *Br., Aus. /Am.* **tape (up)/** tie bandages firmly round (a part of the body that has been hurt, esp. a limb): *Jerry was better at strapping a horse* - D. Francis., *I said nothing, just concentrated on finishing the job of strapping up Helen's arm* - A. McClean.
straphanger *esp. Am.* public transport passenger who commutes to work; such practice is called **straphanging**.
strapper *esp. Aus.* person who grooms racehorses.
strappy *Br.* col. belligerent.
strategize *Am., Can.* devise a strategy.
straw/ grasp at straws *esp. Am.* clutch at straws.
straw bail *Am.* unsafe guarantee.
strawberry shortcake *Am.* one topped with strawberries and whipped cream.
strawberry shrub *Am.* shrubs with fragrant brownish red flowers.
straw boater *Br.* stiff hat made of straw that is usu. worn in summer.
straw boss *esp. Am., Can.* col. assistant foreman, subordinate boss, charge hand: *Purabaev was the straw boss of the small local staff* - J. Fischer.
strawhat *Am.* adj. (of plays, etc.) performed at the countryside.
straw man *Am.* weak and easy (to defeat).
straw ride *Am.* hay ride.
a straw in the wind *Br.* a sign of how situation will develop.
streak *Br.* sl. */Am.* sl. **stretch/** tall thin person.
streaky 1. *Br.* (of bacon) from the belly, having alternate strips of fat and lean, **streaky bacon**. 2. *esp. Am., Can.* col. variable in quality; unreliable.

stream 1. *esp. Br., Aus. /Am.* **track/** (esp. in schools) a level of ability within a group of pupils of the same age: *Berry...got caned quite a lot for a top-stream kid.* – R. Westall, v. 2. *Br., Aus. /Am.* **track/** group (schoolchildren) in streams: *The bias against working-class child operates throughout the school system, through streaming selection* - J. Ruppeldtova.
stream/(come) on stream *Br. /Am.* **(come) on line/** (be) operating fully.
streamer *Am.* big newspaper headline.
street/ in a street or road *Br. /Am.* **on a street or road/** In *Am.* street or avenue are often left out in names.
the street *Am.* Wall Street: *Yahoo's stock "worked," as they say on the Street.* - Fortune.
street/ not in the same street *Br.* sl. far inferior in terms of ability.
street/ *Am.* **on the street,** *Br.* **in the street.**
street/ by a street, streets ahead *Br.* col. by a large margin.
streetcar, also **trolley (car)** *Am., Can. /Br.* **tram/** tram: *I could hear the streetcars and the blatting of automobile horns off yonder* - R.P. Warren.
streetcar *Am., Can. /esp. Br.* **tram(-car)/** pertaining to streetcars / **streetcar driver, motorman**, also **trolley man, driver; streetcar line** (or **track**), also **trolley line**: *my husband has to watch pennies like a streetcar conductor.* - I. Shaw.
street club *Am.* city block juvenile gang.
street credibility/ have street credibility (also **street-cred**) *Br., Aus.* be likely to be accepted by urban youth because of knowing or sharing their fashions, interests, style, culture and opinions.
street floor *Am.* ground floor.
streetname *Am., Can.* the name of stockbroking firm, book or dealer in which stock is held on behalf of a purchaser.
street-railway *Am.* tram or bus line.
streets ahead (of) *Br., Aus.* col. much better than sb. or smth. else.
street people *Am.* homeless.
street smart *esp. Am., Can.* col. wise in the ways of urban life: *He's got one in the works about a street-smart 10-years old* - USA Today., *I had a kind of street "smarts" about what people like.* - Reader's Digest., *street smarts and toughness had made him a favorite in New York* - G. O'Neill, D. Lehr; n. **street-smarts.**
street sweeper *Am.* road sweeper.
street worker *Am., Can.* a social worker.
the strength *esp. Aus., NZ.* the point or meaning of; the truth about.

strength/ be below strength *esp. Br., Aus.* work with fewer people than is needed.

strength/ give me strength! *esp. Br.* excl. of surprise or amused annoyance.

strep *esp. Am.* col. streptococcus.

stress *Am.* col. become stressed: *He felt fluttery, totally stressed out.* – R.L Stine.

stretch 1. *Am.* sl. /*Br.* sl. **streak/** tall thin person: *Come on, stretch, let's get it in the basket! -* R.A. Spears. 2. *esp. Am., Can.* straight part of a racetrack.

stretch/ at full stretch *Br.* a. (working) at full force; using everything that is available. b. with one's body or part of it stretched as far as possible.

stretch-out *Am.* a system of industrial operation when workers are required to do extra work with slight or no additional pay: *cut out the stretchout, or go back to the old pay.* - E. Caldwell.

stretch pants *Am.* trousers for use at home.

streusel *esp. Am.* a topping for cakes and bread made with butter, sugar, flour, spices and sometimes nuts, or a cake made with this topping.

strewth, struth *Br., Aus.* col. excl. (an expression of surprise, annoyance, etc.).

stride/ do smth. **without breaking stride** *Am.* do smth. calmly and efficiently in spite of difficulties.

stride/ hit one's **stride** *Am., Aus.* /*esp. Br., Aus.* **get/go into** one's **stride/** start to do smth. well after getting some experience.

stride/ put sb. **off** one's **stride/stroke** *esp. Br.* disturb sb. making it more difficult to do what one is doing.

stride/ take smth. **in stride** *Am.* /*Br.* **take** smth. **in** one's **stride/** deal calmly and easily with smth. difficult.

stride/ without breaking stride *esp. Am.* without allowing smth. to interrupt or annoy sb.

strides *esp. Aus.* col. trousers: *I'm not taking me strides off for anyone.* - T. Thorne.

strife/ be in strife *Aus.* be in a difficult position.

strike 1. *Am.* work as a military orderly, batman. **-er** n. 2. *Am., Can.* refuse to work as a form of organised protest against employer. 3. *Can.* form (a committee).

strike/ be on strike against company *Am.* stop working because of disagreement with the employers.

strike/strike (it) lucky *Br.* col. suddenly have good luck in some matter.

strike/ take two/three/several strikes against sb./ *esp. Am.* have two or more factors which can make smth. impossible: *You've got two strikes against you now.* – R.L. Stine.

strike down *Am., Can.* (a law or regulation) abolish them (by court): *decision striking down state capital-punishment laws because they were administered arbitrarily.* - Time.

strike (sb.) **for** *Am.* ask sb. for a job, loan of money, etc.: *she'd worry Mac about striking his boss for more pay -* J. Dos Passos.

strike off/ be struck off *Br., Aus.* (esp. of a doctor or lawyer) be prevented from continuing the job because they have done smth. seriously wrong.

strike on/ be struck on *Br.* col. think that smth. is good or well-made.

strike out *esp. Am., Can.* col. miss a chance, fail: *You really struck out that time, didn't you?* - Longman., *Having struck out with Andrew Loog Oldham... Linda Keith felt she had failed.* – C.R. Cross.

strike up *Am.* (usu. pass.) be enthralled.

strike up with sb. *Am.* meet sb. accidentally.

striker *Br.* device striking the primer in a gun.

strike force *esp. Am., Aus.* specially trained group, esp. in police.

strike-out *Am.* ex-convict forbidden to work as longshoreman because of his undesirable associations.

Strimmer *Br.* tdmk. /*Am.* tdmk. **weed whacker/** a machine for cutting grass.

strine *Br., Aus.* col. Australian English, esp. its accent.

string/ another string to one's **bow** *Br., Aus.* extra skill or qualification; **have (a lot of, a few, several,** etc) **strings to** one's **bow**.

string along *Br.* go somewhere with sb. for a short time, esp. if a person doesn't have anything else to do.

string (with) *esp. Am., Can.* deceive, fool sb.: *You're not stringin' me?* - J. London.

string bean 1. *Am., Can., Aus.* /*Br.* **runner bean, French bean,** *esp. Br.* **scarlet runner/** climbing bean with long green pods which are used as food: *Mary set a serving platter of potatoes and string beans in front of Matthew.* – R.L. Stine. 2. *Br.* vegetables similar to French beans but thicker and coarser.

stringer *Am.* string (of a staircase).

string vest *Br.* vest that keeps people warm by trapping air between their skin and clothes.

stringy bark *Aus.* eucalyptus tree with a hard fibrous outer covering.

strip/ tear sb. **off a strip** *Br.* col. /*Br., Aus.* col. **tear a strip off** sb./ speak angrily to sb. because they've done smth. wrong.

strip 1. *Am.* a long road, usu. just outside a town, where there are a lot of stores, restaurants, and hotels. 2. *esp. Am.* (in newspapers and magazines) a series of drawings which tell a story. 3. *Br., Aus.* clothing worn by football team which has the team's colours on it. 4. *Br.* programme broadcast regularly at the same time.

strip cartoon *Br.* /*Am.* **comic strip**/: *There was even a strip-cartoon in a newspaper.* - G. Greene.

strip club *Br.* a small theatre where strippers perform.

stripe *esp. Am., Can.* a type, distinct variety or sort: *you must waste no sympathy on rascals of that stripe.* - C. Nordhoff, J.N. Hall., *retired cops of every stripe* - New York.

strip mall *Am., Can.* shopping mall on a busy main road.

strip (mining), stripping mining *esp. Am.* / *Br.* **opencast colliery**/ mining using open-cast methods: *the jet dived into old strip mine and exploded.* – Reader's Digest.

stripy *Br.* striped.

strobe *Am.* electronic flash for a camera.

stroke *Am., Can.* reassure or flatter sb. in order to gain their cooperation.

stroke *Br.* used when sb. is saying a number with the mark (/) in it, e.g. 15/1.

stroker *Br.* paper folder.

stroller 1. *Br., Aus.* a light pushchair that can be folded up. 2. *esp. Am., Can., Aus.* /*Br.* **pushchair, buggy**/ a small chair on wheels for pushing a small child about: *the fat little diapered thing sitting in his stroller* - J. Baez., *She pushed Isabelle's stroller up and down the streets* - D. Mortman.

strong/ be a bit strong *esp. Br.* col. be annoyed about smth.

strong/ come on strong *esp. Am.* speak to sb. in a very angry and threatening way.

strong flour *Br.* flour made from durum or hard wheat.

strong man *Am.* hired bandit: *A correct evaluation of Joseph Walthey as a potential strongman* - J. Patterson.

strong meat *Br.* ideas or language likely to be found unacceptably forceful or extreme.

strong point *esp. Br., Aus.* /*esp. Am., Aus.* **strong suit**/ a particular skill or ability which a person has.

strop *Br., Aus.* col. a bad mood, esp. in **be in a (real) strop.**

stroppy *Br., Aus.* col. bad-tempered, unwilling to help, and tending to argue; n. **-ness**.

strung out/ be strung out *Am., Can.* be under the influence of drugs or alcohol: *Devon was increasingly strung out from snorting cocaine and heroin* – C.R. Cross., *Elvis was strung out on pills.* – J. Hopkins.

strung-up *esp. Br., Aus.* col. very nervous, worried or excited.

stub *Am.* counterfoil (of a checkbook, etc.).

stubblejumper *Can.* grain farmer, esp. from Saskatchewan: *My uncle is a stubblejumper.* - W. Magnuson.

stubby *Aus., NZ.* col. squat bottle of beer of 375 cl.

Stubtoe State *Am.* Montana.

stuck *Br.* sl. n. trouble, esp. in **be in stuck**.

stuck/ get stuck in(to) *Br., Aus.* 1. col. start work or an activity eagerly or forcefully. 2. sl. start eating.

stuck in the muck *esp. Am.* unable to move out of a difficult situation.

stud 1. *Am.* the height of a room. 2. *Br., Aus.* /*Am.* **cleat**/ a pointed or lumplike part that sticks out from the bottom of a shoe to prevent slipping. 3. *Am.* a small piece of metal many of which are fixed to special tyres used for driving in the snow. 4. *Am.* the kind of board that is used to make the frame of a house.

student *esp. Am., Can.* a person studying at school or college: *students write research reports* - McGraw-Hill English, 1990.

student/ A/B/C, etc. **student** *Am.* sb. who always earns As, etc. for their work.

student-at-law *Can.* an articling law student.

student body *Am.* all the students in high school, college or university: *the man who stood in the lobby each morning, greeting the entire student body* – Reader's Digest.

student council *Am.* elected group of students in high scool, college or university who represent the students in meetings and who organise school activities.

studentship *Br.* a grant for university study.

students union *Br.* student committee which organises leisure activities, provides welfare services, and represents students political interests.

student teaching *Am.* /*Br.* **teaching practice**/ the part of time those who are learning to be teachers practise teaching in a school.

studio couch *esp. Am., Can.* sofa bed.

studio flat *Br.* /*esp. Am., Can.* **studio apartment**/ studio, one-room flat / also *Br.* **bed-sitter**: *they all lived in one-room studio apartment.* - Daily News.

stud-muffin *Am., Can.* col. a sexually attractive person.

study up *Am.* learn intensively about smth., esp. preparing for a test.

study bedroom *Br.* room used as a bedroom and a study, esp. by a student who is a resident at a university.

study hall *Am., Can.* period of time in a school curriculum set aside for the preparation of school work at school: *He thought about Mandy through all his classes and through two study halls.* – R.L. Stine.

stuff 1. *Am.* put more votes than there are voters. 2. *esp. Br., Aus.* sl. (of a man) do the sex act. 3. *Am., Can.* (in sport) spin given to a ball to make it vary its course. 4. *Br.* col. (in sport) defeat heavily.

stuff/ get stuffed *Br.* sl. (used for expressing very strong dislike, anger, etc.).

stuff/ stuff the situation, person or thing *Br., Aus.* sl. damn it.

stuff/ not give a stuff *Br.* col. not give a damn.

stuff/ stuff and nonsense *Br.* obs. it's foolish and untrue.

stuff/ stuff it *Br.* expression of indifference or rejection.

stuff/ that's the stuff! *Br.* col. expression of approval.

stuff gown *Br.* gown worn by a barrister who's not a king's counsel.

stuffed animal *Am.* /*Br.* **soft toy**/.

stuffing/ knock the stuffing out of sb. *Br.* (of an event, news, etc.) make them lose control.

stumblebum 1. *Am.* sl. a drunken drifter: *Mandelbaum picked up a pair of stumblebums* - L. Uris., *I could live with a stumblebum in a culvert and be a good wife.* - J. Steinbeck. 2. *esp. Am.* col. clumsy or inept person.

stumer *Br.* col. 1. a forged or worthless check. 2. anything worthless. 3. failure.

stump *Am., Can.* v. n. dare, challenge: *stumping for a new phase of economic reform Gorbachev bowed to popular resistance to raising prices* - H. Smith.

stump (the country), stump for a candidate *esp. Am.* travel around making campaign speeches (**stump speeches**) before an election: *what do you call those – stump speeches.* – Reader's Digest.

stump/ on the stump *esp. Am.* travelling around making speeches (about a politician): *He expressed his enthusiasm for the event in terms he might use on the stump back home* – Washington Post.

stump/ up a stump *Am.* col. in a bad situation.

stump/ stir one's **stumps** *Br.* obs. hurry up.

stump up *esp. Br.* col. pay (money), esp. unwillingly: *How does he expect us to work for him if he won't stump up?* - J. Joyce., *Japan should continue to stump up* - Economist.

stumpage *Am., Can.* value of timber as it stands uncut.

stumper *Am.* stump orator.

stumpjump plow *Aus.* machine by which land can be ploughed without clearing it of stumps.

stumpy 1. *Am.* full of stumps. 2. *Br.* (of legs, fingers, etc.) stubby, short and thick in unattractive way.

styrofoam *Am.* tdmk. /*esp. Br.* **polystyrene**/ polystyrene: *Joe O'Brien put down his styrofoam cup of coffee* - J. O'Brien, A. Kurins., *He handed her the Styrofoam cup of coffee* - P. Case, J. Migliore.

sub 1. *Br., Aus.* col. subscription: *Would you like to buy a sub to the local newspaper?* - R.A. Spears. 2. *Br.* /*Am.* **advance**/ an amount of money paid to sb. from his/her wages before the usual day of payment; loan against expected income. 3. *Br.* give a sub (2.) to sb. 4. *Am.* subway railway. 5. *Am., Can.* col a large, long sandwich, **hoagie**. 6. *esp. Br., Aus.* a player who is brought into a match to substitute another player. 7. *Am.* substitute teacher. 8. *Br.* subeditor; v. subedit smth.

subaltern *Br.* an army officer lower in rank than a captain: *these subalterns would probably make much more a piece than any of the three matadors.* - E. Hemingway.

subaqua *Br.* related to sports that take place under water.

subchaser *Am.* submarine chaser.

sub-community, also **sub-division** *Am., Can., Aus.* suburbia.

subcompact *Am., Can.* a car that is smaller than a compact.

the subcontinent *Br.* the area that includes India, Pakistan and Bangla Dash.

subcontinental *Am.* related to a subcontinent.

subdivision *Am., Aus.* a plot of land for building houses, housing estate.

subedit *esp. Br.* /*Am.* **copyedit**/ check, correct or adjust the extent of a newspaper before printing; **subeditor**.

subject *esp. Br.* 1. a citizen of a country ruled by a monarch. 2. a special area of study.

submarine (sandwich) *Am.* col **sub** also **Hero sandwich, poor boy** a section of French loaf with a lot of filling: *He ordered a submarine* - R.A. Spears.

sub-postmaster *esp. Br.* person in charge of a subscription office.

subscribe *Br.* 1. pay money regularly to be a member of an organisation or to help its work. 2. give money regularly for a service; **subscriber.**

subscriber trunk dialling *Br. /Am.* **direct dialling/** long-distance direct dialling.

subscription *Br.* amount of money one pays regularly to be a member of an organisation or to help its work.

subsistence allowance (money) *esp. Br.* allowance or advance on sb.'s pay, esp. granted as travelling expense.

substantive rank *Br.* an actual paid position in the army.

substation *Am., Can.* a branch post office or police station: *it was a post office substation and it had a good reputation.* – J. O'Hara.

substitute (teacher) *Am. /esp. Br.* **supply teacher/.**

subtopia *esp. Br.* the suburbs of a city. **-an** adj. **-ionise** v.

suburbonite *Am., Aus.* a person who lives in the suburb of a large town or city.

subvene *Am.* help sb. when one is accidentally close by.

subway 1. *Br., Aus. /Am.* **underpass, tunnel/** a path under a road or railway by which it can be safely crossed. 2. *esp. Am., Can. /Br.* **underground/** metro.

subway *esp. Am., Can.* underground railway: *Thousands of people found themselves stranded in elevators and subway cars.* - J. Riffkin, T. Howard.

subway kiosk *Am.* ground pavilion of the subway.

succeed oneself *Am.* be reelected.

succotash *Am.* lima or shell beans and green corn cooked together.

suck *esp. Am., Can.* col. be without value or interest; be disgusting.

suck/ suck it and see *Br., Aus.* saying. col. try smth. that you haven't done before.

suck/ smth. **sucks** *esp. Am.* col. derog. smth. is very bad.

suck at *Br.* suck on (sweets, etc.).

suck up *Br., Can.* col. derog. try to make oneself liked esp. by unnaturally nice behaviour: *Sucking up like mad to Andrew.* - J. Fowles.

suck it up *Am.* col. accept hardship.

sucker *Am.* 1. also *Aus., Can.* col. lollipop. 2. trick or victimise sb., deceive: *word is out that he suckered me* - K. Lipper. 3. unpleasant thing or person or difficult task. 4. col. unspecified thing or person.

sucker *Br., Aus. /Am.* **suction cup,** *Br.* **suction cap/** a circular piece of rubber which sticks to surfaces when pressed against them.

sucker sb. **into** *Am.* persuade sb. to do smth. they don't want to do.

sucker/ play sb. **for a sucker** *Am., Aus.* col. treat sb. as if they were stupid.

sucker/ there's a sucker born every minute *Am.* col. there's another person foolish enough to believe sb. or smth.

sucker list *Am.* a list of prospective customers, victims, etc.: *The crook got hold of a sucker list and started out to sell his worthless stock.* - A. Makkai.

The Sucker State *Am.* Illinois.

sucker-punch *Am.* sl. attack from behind or without a warning: *Fruitfly sucker-punched me.* - T. Thorne.

suckhole 1. *Am.* col. whirlpool. 2. *Can., Aus.* sl. (behave like) a sycophant.

sucks! *Br.* col. phrase used to express derision and defiance.

suck-up *Am., Can.* col. sycophant.

suds *esp. Am., Can.* col. 1. a mass of small bubbles on the surface of liquid: *Mop and scrub floors and walls with a non-sudsing household ammonia* - S. Whang. 2. col. beer: *he had some kind of vintage suds* - Reader's Digest.

sudser *Am., Can.* col. soap opera.

sudserie *Am.* sl. beer pub: *we already have a first-class sudserie* - New York

sugar *esp. Am.* col. (used when speaking to sb. you like usu. by a man to a woman): *I already told you, sugar. I work here.* - Arthur Hailey.

(Oh) sugar! *esp. Br.* col. used when sb. is very annoyed about smth. stupid they have just done, or when smth. goes wrong.

sugar off *esp. Am., Can.* take sugar from the maple tree: *Which is the right season for sugaring off?* – Longman, n. **sugaring (off).**

sugar-coat smth. *Am.* make smth. bad seem less unpleasant, esp. in **sugar-coat the pill** *Am. /esp. Br.* **sugar/sweeten the pill/.**

sugar crystals, also **coffee sugar** *Br.* large crystal sugar, usu. brown.

sugar lump *esp. Br.* square piece of sugar.

sugar (snap) peas *Br. /Am., Aus.* **snow peas,** *Am.* **snap peas/.**

sugar soap *Br.* preparation containing washing soda and soap, used for cleaning and removing paint.

The Sugar State *Am.* Louisiana.

suit *Am.* sl. a serious business and professional person: *hiring high-paid suits who are sleazy enough to work for him.* - J. O'Brien, A. Kurins., *I was surrounded by corporate suits of the highest rank.* - W. Jack, B. Laursen.

suit *Am., Can.* put on clothes, esp. for sporting activity.

suit/ the men in (grey) suits *esp. Br.* men in control of an organisation or company.

suit/ sb.'s **strong suit** *esp. Am.* smth. that sb. is good at.

suit/ suit sb.'s **book** *Br.* col. be convenient or acceptable to sb.

suit/ suit sb. **to the ground** *Br.* col. be very acceptable.

suit up *esp. Am.* put on special clothing, usu. for work: *The Detroit Red Wings break off the fun to suit up for the night's work.* - Time., *off-the-rack approach to suiting up* - New York.

suit bag *Br. /Am.* **garment bag/** a long flat bag which is carried folded in half in which a suitcase is kept while travelling.

suitcase farmer *Am.* dry-land farmer who lives far from the farm most of the year.

suite *esp. Br.* a set of matching furniture in a room; **three piece suite** a large seat and two chairs.

sulfur *Am., Aus.* sulphor.

sulk/ in a sulk *Br.* angry and silent.

sultana *esp. Br. /Am.* **golden raisin/** a dry white grape, used in cooking.

sum *Br.* a simple calculation such as adding or dividing numbers.

sum/ do one's **sum** *Br.* col. calculate whether sb. has enough money to do smth.

sum/ have got one's **sum wrong** *esp. Br.* miscalculate.

summa cum laude *esp. Am., Can.* adj., adv. academic degree with highest distinctions.

summer complaint *Am.* col. diarrhoea: *Does summer heat cause the summer complaint?* - R.A. Spears.

summer holiday(s) *Br. /Am.* **summer vacations/**.

summer house *Am.* a house at the beach or in the mountains that a person lives in in summer.

summer normal *Am.* summer refresher course for aviators.

summer pudding *Br.* pudding of soft summer fruit encased in bread or sponge.

summer rental *Am.* house or apartment that one rents only during the summer.

summer sausage *Am., Can.* hard dried and smoked sausage which is similar to salami in preparation.

summer school *Am.* courses for those who missed or failed during other seasons or advanced courses for those who want to graduate or get a degree more quickly.

summer soldier *Am.* person who supports cause only when going is easy.

summer stock *esp. Am., Can.* theatrical productions by a repertory company organised for the summer season, esp. at holiday resorts.

summer time *Br. /Am.* **daylight saving time/** a period in spring and summer during which the clocks are put forward to achieve longer evening daylight.

sump *esp. Br. /Am.* **oil pan/** a part of an engine at the bottom, which holds the supply of oil.

sun/ catch the sun *Br. /Am.* **get the sun/** a. (of a person) become slightly red or brown because they have been outside in the sun. b. (of a room, etc.) become very bright when the sun shines.

sunbeam *Br., Aus. /Am., Aus.* **sunray/** a beam of light from the sun.

sunbed *Br. /Am.* **tanning bed/** a bedlike frame on which one can lie containing device for getting artificial sun tan.

sunblind *Br.* 1. awning erected over a window in sunny weather. 2. the thing pulled down over a window to keep the sun out of a room.

sunburnt, also **sunburned** 1. *Br.* having a brown skin, sun-tanned. 2. *Am.* suffering from sunburn.

sun cream *Br.* a skin cream to stop the sun from burning you.

Sunday 1. *esp. Am.* spend Sunday. 2. **Sundays** *Am., Can.* and *Br.* col. during any Sunday. 3. **the Sunday** *Br.* Sunday of the week being mentioned.

Sunday joint or **roast** *Br.* a large piece of cooked meat, eaten as part of a traditional Sunday lunch.

Sunday punch *esp. Am.* col. devastating punch or the attacking action.

Sundays *Br.* the Sunday papers.

sun deck *Am., Can.* terrace or balcony positioned to catch the sun.

sundown 1. *Am.* Lady's wide-brimmed hat. 2. *esp. Am., Can., Aus. /esp. Br.* **sunset/** time when the sun sets.

sundowner 1. *esp. Br.* col. an alcoholic drink taken in the evening: *I had not been to Jimmie's for a sun-downer* - G. Greene., *the first sundowner, gulped down hastily to give her vitality* - W. Jack, B. Laursen. 2. *Aus.* a wanderer (tramp) who often asks for a place to sleep, seasonal worker.

sundry *Aus.* /*Br.* **extra**/ a run in cricket which is not made off the bat.

The Sunflower State *Am.* Kansas: *he's from the tall corn state, not the Sunflower State* – Reader's Digest.

sunnies *Aus.* sl. breasts.

sun lounge *Br.* /*Am.* **sun porch, sun parlor**, also *Br.* **conservatory**, *esp. Am., Can., Aus.* **sun-room**/ a room with large windows which lets in a lot of bright sunlight: *He and the old lady sit on the screened sunporch with iced tea* - J. Updike., *an empty sun lounge overlooking the bay* - B. Bryson.

sunlounger *Br.* lounge used for sunbathing.

sunray *Am., Aus.* /*Br.* **sunbeam**/.

sunny-side up 1. also *Am.* /*Br.* **ham and eggs**/ adj. (of an egg) cooked in hot fat on one side only, not turned over in the pan; opp. **once over easy**: *the eggs fried sunny-side up* - H. Fast. 2. *esp. Br.* journalism. bright and cheerful.

sunset provision *Am., Can.* stipulation that an agency or programme be disbanded or terminated at the end of a fixed period unless it's formally renewed.

The Sunset or **Webfoot State** *Am.* Oregon.

The Sunset State or **Land** *Am.* Arizona.

sunshine *esp. Br.* col. sometimes threatening form of address.

Sunshine Coast *Can.* seashore area north of Vancouver.

sunshine law *Am.* law about specific records to be open to the public.

The Sunshine State *Am.* 1. Florida. 2. South Dakota. 3. New Mexico. 4. California.

sunspace *Am., Can.* room or area in a building having a glass roof and walls and intended to maximize the power of sun rays.

sunspot *Br.* col. a place with much sunshine and heat where people like to go on holiday.

suntrap *Br., Aus.* a sheltered place that receives a lot of light and heat from the sun.

sunup *esp. Am., Can.* /*Br.* **sunrise**/ time when the sun rises.

sup *esp. Br.* to drink or to eat.

super 1. *Br.* col. superintendent, esp. in the police. 2. *Am.* col. superintendent, one responsible for keeping a building in a good condition: *The super gave out water bottles.* – Reader's Digest. 3. *Am.* adv. extremely.

superannuation (plan) *esp. Br., Aus.* /*Aus.* col. **super**/ money paid as a pension, esp. from one's former place of work.

superblock *Am.* city block closed to auto traffic.

supergrass *Br.* col. a police informer.

superhighway, freeway *Am., Can.* /*Br.* **motorway**/ fast motorway with several lanes: *I had avoided the great high speed slashes of concrete and tar called "thruways" or "superhighways"* - J. Steinbeck., *There was inside information that a superhighway was being built that way by the city.* - I. Shaw.

superintendent 1. *Br.* senior police officer of the rank above an inspector. 2. *Am.* the head of a police department. 3. *Am.* /*Br.* **caretaker**/ sb. who is in charge of apartment building.

supermarket tabloid *Am.* newspaper sold in a supermarket containing reports about the life of famous people.

supersaver *Br.* any item which you buy at a specially reduced price.

superserviceable *Am.* officious.

supershopper *Am.* supermarket customer.

superstore *Br.* a very large shop that sells many different types of goods, usu. just outside a town.

supertitle *Am.* surtitle, words sung in an opera shown above the stage.

(town or **county) supervisor** *Am.* elected official who manages local government services.

supplemental *esp. Am.* supplementary.

supplementary benefit, income support *Br.* government money given to people with no income or low income.

supplies *Br.* grant of money by Parliament for the costs of government.

supply teacher *esp. Br.* /*Am.* **substitute (teacher)**/ a teacher who takes the place of regular teachers for short periods while they are away.

support *esp. Br.* /*Am.* **root for,** *Aus.* **barrack for**/ cheer a particular sports team (said of *esp. Br.* **supporters** /*Am.* **fans**).

support/ **price supports** *Am.* government subsidies to farmers.

supporting film, programme *Br.* one in advance of the main feature.

suppose/ **I suppose** *esp. Br.* used when sb. thinks smth. is true or agrees to let sb. do smth. or when guessing.

suppose/ **I don't suppose (that)…** *esp. Br.* used when asking for smth. in a very polite way or if smth. is unlikely to happen.

supremo *Br., Aus.* col. a ruler or director with unlimited powers.

sure 1. *esp. Am., Can., Aus.* col. certainly: *Sure, dumbbell, we know all that.* - C. McCullers., *you sure devastated me, bo* - D. Hammet. . 2. *Am.* col. used as a way of replying to sb. when they thank you. 3. *Am.* col. used to emphasize statement. 4. *Am.* col. used at the beginning of a statement that smth. is true, esp. before adding smth. very different.

sure/ for sure *Am.* used to agree with sb.

sure/ to be sure *Br.* col. used to admit that smth. is true, before saying smth. that is quite the opposite.

(as) sure as eggs (is /are eggs) *Br.* obs. certainly.

(as) sure as hell *esp. Am., Aus.* col. (said to emphasise that sb. is angry or very determined about smth.).

a sure bet *Am.* smth. that is certain to succeed.

surely *esp. Am., Can.* col. certainly, of course. / In British English **surely** doesn't have the same meaning as certainly. Compare He surely doesn't expect me to pay him immediately (= I hope he doesn't expect this and I don't think he ought to) and He certainly doesn't expect me to pay him immediately (= I know he doesn't expect the money now). But especially in American English, **surely** (often shortened to **sure**) can be used like certainly and of course in answer to requests to show willingness to help: Can I borrow this book? Yes, certainly, of course, surely, sure.

surely to God/goodness *Br.* obs. You must admit that!

sure thing *esp. Am., Aus., Can.* col. of course: *Could he have a clip of this story, he said, Sure thing.* - USA Today.

surf *Aus.* v. n. bathe in the ocean. **-ing** n.

surf beach *Aus.* ocean beach.

surf boat *Aus.* special life saving boat.

surf carnival *Aus.* life guards' festival.

surf club *Aus.* life guards station.

surf-flag *Aus.* life guard buoy.

surfie *esp. Aus.* col. surfing fan.

surf lifesaver *Aus.* life guard.

surf marathon *Aus.* life guard marathon.

surf patrol *Aus.* a shift of life guards.

surf race (or **racing**) *Aus.* lifeboats contest.

surface car *Am.* tram car.

surface-effect ship *Am.* cushion vehicle.

surf-board riding, also **board-surfing** *Aus.* surfing.

surfie *Aus.* a good surfboard swimmer.

surfman *Am.* surfboard crew swimmer.

surgery *Br.* 1. */Am.* **doctor's** or **dentist's office/** (*/Am.* **office hours/** the hours of opening of) a place where one or a group of doctors or dentists give people advice on their health and medicines to treat illnesses: *He expected me to stagger to his surgery* – S. Townsend. 2. period of time during which people can come and see a member of Parliament, lawyer, etc. and ask their advice: *Most MPs and some MEPs have local surgeries for which no appointment is necessary.* - Young Citizen's Passport. 3. *esp. Am. /Br.* **theatre/** place where operations are done in a hospital.

surgical spirit *Br. /Am., Aus.* **rubbing alcohol/** a type of alcohol used for cleaning wounds or skin in hospital.

surplus/ be surplus to requirements *Br.* (of goods) be no longer needed.

surprinting *Am. /Br.* **overprinting/** print. printing a second image on a previously printed sheet.

surrey *Am.* light horse-drawn carriage with four wheels and two seats: *Jonathan helped her to place the picnic baskets in the surrey.* - T. Caldwell.

surrounds *Am.* area near smth.

survey (a building) *Br. /Aus.* **inspect/** examine the building in order to discover if there is smth. wrong with it (this is done by a specially trained person often for a prospective buyer).

survey *esp. Br.* a professional examination of a house, for measurement and valuation purposes, esp. for sb. who may buy it, n. **surveyor**.

survey course *Am.* university course that gives introduction to a subject for people who have not studied before.

surveyer *Am.* obs. customs official.

surveyer *Br. /Am.* **structural engineer/** a trained person inspecting the structure of the building.

survival from *esp. Br.* smth. that has continued to exist from a much earlier period; relic.

survivors *Am.* members of a person's family who continue to live after that person dies.

susceptible of other explanation *Br.* interpreted in another way.

suspender *Br., Aus. /Am.* **garter/** a fastener hanging down from an undergarment (a **suspender belt/garter belt**) to hold a woman's stocking up.

suspenders *Am., Can. /Br.* **braces**, *Am.* col. **galluses/** a pair of elastic cloth bands worn over the shoulders by men to hold up trousers: *He sprawls across the bed in those long corduroy pants with the suspenders* - C. McCullers., *And red suspenders have been known to make many a woman's heart snap.* - Ebony.

sus(s) *Br., Aus.* col. discover the fact that, realise: *The constabulary sus should not be confused with the Rockspeak "suss" meaning nous or common sense* - P. Howard., *We adopt his word: "suss" which means to spy out something.* - New Yorker.

sus(s) 1. *Aus.* col. suspicious. 2. *Br.* col. shrewd and wary.

suss out *Br., Aus.* col. find out details about quietly or secretly: *Youth susses things out for itself.* - A. Burgess.

sussed *Br.* col. clever and knowledgeable in smth.

swab(by) *Am.* col. sailor of enlisted rank.

swacked *Am., Can.* drunk.

swag *Aus., NZ.* set of clothes and belongings wrapped in a cloth as carried by travellers and wanderers / also *Aus.* sl. (**waltzing**) **Matilda.**

swag (it), also **hump** one's **swag** *Aus.* go wandering. **-ing** n.

swagger, also **swaggy, swagman, swagsman** *Aus., NZ.* wanderer, tramp.

swale *esp. Am.* low-lying stretch of boggy land.

swallow dive *Br., Aus.* /*Am.* **swan dive**/ a dive into water, starting with the arms stretched out from the sides of the body.

swamp *Am.* open by removing underbrush and debris.

The Swamp State *Am.* South Carolina.

swamp buggy *Am.* motor vehicle used for travelling over swamp: *He had a vehicle known as a swamp buggy* – F. Edwards.

swamper *Am.* 1. an inhabitant of swampy terrain. 2. general assistant, helper: *As a swamper I cleaned mud from the heavy machinery parts* - Guideposts. 3. *Am., Can.* assistant to the captain of a riverboat or to a lorry driver. 4. *Am., Can.* worker who trims felled trees or clears a road for lumberers in a forest.

swan (off, around, about) *Br.* col. move about or do things in a casual relaxed way.

The Swan City *Aus.* joc. Pert.

swan dive *Am., Can.* swallow dive.

swank *esp. Br.* behave or speak too confidently, esp. to try and make other people admire them.

swank *esp. Br.* proud believer.

swank *Am., Can.* swanky.

swanky *esp. Br.* tending to act too confidently to get attention.

swanney *Br.* place set aside for swans to breed.

swan-upper *Br.* person who marks swans, n. **swan-upping.**

swap over/round *Br.* /*Am.* **swap seats**, *Aus., Br.* **swap places**/ exchange seats.

swap market *esp. Am., Can.* gathering of collectors trading items with each other; flea market.

swap meet *Am.* /*Br.* **car-boot sale**, *Aus.* **garage sale**/ gathering where people buy and sell or exchange used goods: *he was stealing tires off cars..and then selling them at swap meet* – Reader's Digest.

SWAT *Am.* special weapons and tactics police unit, trained to deal with violence and terrorism: *SWAT was represented on TV* - New York.

swayback *Am.* condition in which one's back curves inward too much.

sway bar *Am., Can.* (in a big vehicle or car) antiroll bar.

swear blind *Br., Aus.* col. /*Am., Can., Aus.* **swear up and down**, *Aus.* **swear black and blue**/ say that smth. is completely true.

swear for *Am.* promise that (smth. or sb.) is trustworthy: *I will swear for his appearance in court* - Longman.

swear smth. **out** *Am.* law. obtain the issue (of a warrant for arrest) by making a charge on oath.

sweat 1. *Br.* cook gently in melted fat. 2. *Am.* col. worry about smth.

sweat/ break a sweat *Am.* col. exert oneself physically.

sweat/ Don't sweat it! *Am.* col. Don't worry!

sweat/ Don't sweat the small stuff *Am.* col. Don't worry about unimportant matters.

sweat/ sweat bullets *Am., Can.* col. be very nervous.

sweat/ sweat smth. **out of** sb. *Am.* col. find out information from sb. by asking lots of questions in a threatening way.

sweat/ sweat the small stuff *Am.* col. worry about trivial things.

sweat equity *Am., Can.* col. interest in a property earned by a tenant in return for labour towards upkeep or restoration.

sweater, pullover *esp. Am.* /*esp. Br., Aus.* **jumper**/: *Daddy pulled off his sweater* - K. Davis., *jacket was unsnapped revealing an olive-green pullover.* – R.L. Stine.

sweater girl *Am., Can.* col. a girl with a shapely bust: *small-town drugstore racks were filled with sweater girls – cheesecake!* – N. Mailer.

sweatpants *Am.* /*Br.* **tracksuit trousers, tracksuit bottoms**/ part of a sweatsuit that covers person's legs: *Candice threw on sweat pants and a T-shirt* – Reader's Digest.

sweats *esp. Am., Can.* col. clothes made of thick soft cotton, usu. worn for playing sports: *A dark man in shabby gray sweats stood behind her* - R.J. Randisi., M. Wallace.

sweat sock *Am., Can.* thick, absorbent calf-length sock, often worn with trainers.

sweatsuit *Am.* /*Br.* **tracksuit**/ a loose warm stretchy suit which people wear to relax or do exercises: *We can be people wearing sweat suits in the airports of Europe!* – Reader's Digest.

swede *Br., Aus. /esp. Am., Can.* **rutabaga/** a round yellow vegetable like a large turnip.

Swede saw *esp. Can.* saw with a bowlike tubular frame and many cutting teeth.

Sweeney *Br. col.* member of a police flying squad.

sweep *Am.* room cleaner in the dormitory.

sweep *Am. col.* win all the prizes (of a contest) or win easily.

sweep/ sweep smth. **under the rug** *esp. Am. /esp. Aus.* **under the mat,** *Br.* **under the carpet/** keep a problem secret instead of dealing with it.

sweeper 1. *Br.* (in football) a player who defends from behind other defending players. 2. *Aus.* also **broomie** shearer.

sweeps *Am., Can.* 1. a period of time when measurements of the number of people watching different TV stations are made so that the cost of advertising on each station can be set. 2. an instance of winning the entire award or place in a contest, sweepstake.

sweet 1. *Br., Aus., Can.* also (children's use) *Br. col.* **sweetie /Am., Can.* **candy,** *Aus.* **lolly/** a small piece of sweet food made of sugar or chocolate (usu. toffee, chocolate, and mint): *One of the young women presented me with a boiled sweet on a tray.* - L. Van Der Post. 2. *Br. / esp. Am., Aus.* **dessert/** sweet food served at the end of a meal, dessert. 3. *Am. col.* sweet potato. 4. *Am.* any sweet with a lot of sugar in it.

sweet *esp. Br.* (of children, or small things) looking pretty and attractively cute.

sweet/ cop it sweet *Am. col.* be lucky in a way that you didn't expect.

sweet/ keep sb. **sweet** *Br.* please them.

sweet/ she's sweet *Aus. col.* all is well.

sweet/ sweet as pie *esp. Br.* very kind.

sweet butter *Am.* butter with no salt added to it.

sweet chestnut *Br. /Am.* **chestnut/** a large tree with large round nuts that are cooked and eaten hot.

sweet corn *esp. Br. /esp. Am.* **corn/** (the tender young seed of) a sweet type of maize.

sweet deal *Am., Aus. col.* a very good business agreement or arrangement.

sweetened condensed milk *esp. Am. /Br.* **condensed milk/** one that has been made thicker and sweeter and is usu. sold in cans.

sweet FA, sweet Fanny Adams *Br. sl. derog.* nothing.

sweetheart contract *Am.* one between employer and unscrupulous trade union leader.

sweetheart deal or **job** *Am. sl.* deal made between friends so that both may profit well (usu. with the use of illegal or unethical practices): *Marcia promptly landed a sweetheart job* - T. Thompson., *many members resist the temptation of sweetheart deals not available to ordinary citizens.* - Reader's Digest.

sweetie *Br. col.* 1. used as a form of address to and by children. 2. (used by children) a sweet. 3. smth. or sb. that is small, pretty and easy to love.

sweetie pie *Am. col.* way of addressing the person that one loves.

sweetmeal *Br.* sweetened wholemeal.

sweetmeat *Br. obs.* sweet or any food made of or preserved in sugar.

sweetness/ be all sweetness and light *Br. derog.* be very pleasant and friendly.

sweet roll *Am.* bun or Danish pastry.

sweetshop *esp. Br., Aus. /Am.* **candy store/** a confectioner's shop.

swell *esp. Am., Can. col. obs. adj.* very good, excellent: *You're a swell kid.* - C. McCulers., *Gosh, you look swell!* - W.S. Maugham., *She's a swell girl.* - E. Hemingway., *That's a swell town.* - D. Hammet.

swelled head *esp. Am., Can. /Br.* **swollen head/** too much pride: *The notices gave him a badly swelled head.* - J. Hyams; *adj. Am.* **swell-headed.**

swerping *Am.* sound distortion on magnetic tape.

swiftie *Am.* a type of adverbial pun.

swifty *esp. Aus. col.* 1. deceptive tricks. 2. person who acts or thinks quickly.

swill *Br.* wash or rinse out by pouring large amounts of water or other liquid.

swimming bath(s) *Br. obs.* public swimming pool, usu. indoors: *I went to the swimming baths this morning.* – S. Townsend.

swimming cap *Br. /Am.* **bathing cap/.**

swimming costume *Br., Aus. /esp. Am.* **swimsuit,** *Br., Aus.* **bathing suit,** *Br., Aus. col.* **cossie,** *Aus. col.* **swimmers,** *esp. Aus. col.* **togs/** a piece of clothing worn for swimming: *And did you take off your swimsuit?* – R.L. Stine.

swimming hole *esp. Am., Can.* bathing place in a stream or river.

swimming trunks *Br. /Am.* **bathing trunks,** *Aus.* **board shorts,** *Aus. col.* **swimmers,** *esp. Aus. col.* **togs/** men's shorts for swimming.

swindle sheet *Am. sl.* expense account.

swing 1. *Am. sl.* interval between two working periods: *it was the Sunday to Monday swing.*

- G. O'Neill, D. Lehr. 2. *Am., Can.* swift tour involving a number of stops, esp. as part of a political compaign.

swing around the clock *Am.* a political swing or tour.

swing by *Am.* col. visit a place or person for a short time, usu. for a particular purpose.

swing/ get into the swing of smth. *Br.* become fully involved in an activity or situation.

swing/ go with a swing *Br.* col. 1. be exciting and successful. 2. have a strong beat and clear tone it is easy to dance to.

swing/ swing the lead *Br.* obs. avoid doing work pretending to be ill.

swing/ what you lose on the swings you gain on the roundabouts (often shortened to **(it's) swings and roundabouts**) *esp. Br., Aus.* col. the disadvantages of a particular situation or course of action are balanced by the advantages.

swingbin *Br.* rubbish bin with a lid that swings shut after being pushed open.

swingboat *esp. Br.* boat-shaped swing with seats for several people at fairs.

swing bridge *Br.* bridge that can be pulled upwards when tall ships need to pass through.

swing door *Br., Aus. /esp. Am., Can.* **swinging door/** swinging door.

swingeing *esp. Br.* 1. (esp. of arrangements concerning money) very severe in force, degree, etc., esp. **swingeing cuts**: *Universities everywhere were in disarray, faced with swingeing cuts in their funding.* - D. Lodge. 2. col. adj. whopping, excellent, superlative.

swingletree *esp. Br.* (in a horse) a crossbar to which their traces are attached.

swingman *Am.* outrider who keeps outmoving herd in order.

swingometer *Br.* col. special machine used on TV programmes during elections to show how much support each political party is getting as results become known.

swingset *Am., Can.* frame for children to play on, often including one or more swings and a slide: *It has a big backyard and a swing set.* – Reader's Digest.

swing shift *Am.* evening shift at work: *18 men on the 3 p.m. to 11 p.m. swing shift gathered at its entry portal* – Reader's Digest.

swing-span *Am.* swing bridge.

swing vote *esp. Am.* a vote that has decisive influence on the result of a pole.

swinish *Br.* extremely unpleasant or difficult to deal with.

swipe *Am.* sl. a person who rubs down horses at a racing stable.

swipe *esp. Am.* (esp. of a car) touch smth. when moving.

swipes *Br.* sl. weak beer.

swish 1. *Br.* col. smart and fashionable. 2. *Am.* col. derog. a man who behaves like a woman and who lacks manly qualities; adj. **swishy**.

Swiss cheese/ have more holes than Swiss cheese *esp. Am.* (of an argument or theory) have so many faults that it can't be taken seriously.

Swiss roll *esp. Br. /Am.* **jelly roll,** *Aus.* **jam-roll/** a cake baked in a thin piece with jam or cream inside.

swiss steak *Am.* thick flat piece of beef covered in flour and cooked in a sauce.

switch *Am., Can.* a set of points on a railway track.

switch over *Br.* change from one TV or radio station to another.

switch/ that's a switch *Am.* used to say that sb.'s behaviour is unusual for them.

switchback, scenic railway *esp. Br.* a (rail)road which rises and falls many times.

switchblade (knife) *esp. Am., Can. /Br.* **flick knife/** one with a blade inside the handle that springs into position when a button is pressed: *he was suspended from school for two weeks for carrying a switchblade knife.* - B. Kaufman., *He ran with the hand gripping the handle of the switchblade in his pocket.* - J. Kessel., *A frisk produced three knifes, one a switchblade* - R. Moore.

switch(card) *Br.* tdmk. plastic card from a person's bank that they use to pay for things and that allows the money to be taken through one's account.

switcher *Am., Can.* railway engine used for switching, shunting locomotive.

switcheroo *Am., Can.* col. sudden reversal: *she had sneaked over to our house and pulled the old switcheroo.* - Reader's Digest.

switches *Am. /Br., Aus.* **points/** a pair of short rails that can be moved to allow a train to cross over from one track to another: *running out to throw switches in front of it* - J. Kerouac.

switched-on *Br.* alert.

switchman, switch keeper, switch tender *Am. / Br.* **pointsman/** person who attends a switch.

switch-hitter *Am., Can.* col. bisexual.

switch tower, also **signal tower** *Am. /Br.* **signal box/** a building near a railway from which the signals and points are controlled: *officials at switch towers and telephones are thinking up* - J. Kerouac.

switching yard, classification yard *Am. /esp. Br.* **marshalling yard/** shunting yard.

switchyard *esp. Am., Can.* 1. the part of a railyard taken up by points in which trains are made up. 2. enclosed area of a power system containing the switchgear.

swivet *esp. Am.* a state of extreme agitation or worry.

swiz(zie) *Br., Aus.* col. (esp. used by children) something that makes one feel cheated or disappointed, often in **What a swizz!**

swollen head, big head *Br. /Am., Aus.* **swelled head/** col. too great a sense of one's own importance; adj.**-ed**.

swop *Br.* swap.

swot *Br., Aus. /Am.* **grind**, **cram** col./ derog. person who works (too) hard at his/her studies esp. when trying to get good examination results and seems to have no other interests: *Swots put up their hands to answer every question* – R. Westall.

swot *esp. Br., Aus. /Am.* **grind/** work hard: *we saw him swotting* - J. Fowles.

swot smth. **up** (on) *Br.* col. work hard in order to learn (a subject one is studying) usu. before an examination: *I must swot up some facts about Shakespeare's life* - Longman.

swy *Aus.* (game) two-up.

sycamore *Am., Can.* buttonwood tree.

Sydneysider *Aus.* a resident of Sydney.

sympathy vote *Br., Aus.* col. a lot of popular support or votes for a certain person who suffered a lot recently.

syndicate *Am.* a highly organised crime gang.

syndicated *Am.* (of TV and radio programmes) sold to several different broadcasting organisations.

syrup *esp. Br.* a very thick sticky pale liquid made from sugar.

T

ta *Br.* col. excl. thank you: *"Ta", said Gladis and walked in.* - A. Huxley., *"Ta", I said.* - D. Francis.

TAB *Aus.* Totalisator Agency Board.

tab *esp. Am., Can., Aus.* col. */Br.* **bill/** the amount you owe for a restaurant meal or a service, esp. in the phr. **pick up the tab**: *Keep a tab. I'll make up for it after* - J.P. Hogan.

tab/ run up a tab (of) *Am.* (at a bar, shop, etc.) agree to pay later.

tab *esp. Am., Can. /Br., Aus.* **ring-pull/** a metal strip that one pulls off the top of a can of drink in order to drink it.

tab 1. *Br.* (strip worn by) staff officer. 2. *Am.* col. tablet: *A tab a day keeps reality at bay.* - T. Thorne. 3. *Am., Can.* col. tabloid newspaper.

tabby 1. *esp. Br.* spinster. 2. *Aus.* sl. a woman or girl.

table 1. *Br., Aus.* suggest (a subject, report, etc.) for consideration by a committee, parliament, etc., **table an offer, idea**, etc. 2. *esp. Am.* leave (a subject, report, etc.) until a later day for consideration, **table a bill, measure, proposal**: *he tabled his usual multi-million salary.* - Time.

table/ at table *Br.* during a meal, having a meal.

table/ falling table *Am.* folding table.

table/ keep a good table *Br. /Am.* **set a good table/** provide a lot of good food.

table/ lay smth. **on the table** *esp. Am.* set smth. remaining to be talked about at a later date.

table/ on the table *Am.* delayed for later consideration.

table/ set the table *esp. Am. /Br.* **lay the table/** *Br.* put knives, forks, dishes, etc. on a table before a meal.

table/ take from the table *Am.* renew discussions.

table/ under the table *esp. Am., Aus.* money paid secretly, esp. if it's illegal; adj. **under-the-table**.

tableboard *Am.* board without lodging.

table cream *Am.* single cream.

table licence *Br.* licence permitting restorateur or hotelier to serve alcoholic drinks only with meals.

table money *Br.* an extra allowance to higher officers of the British Army and Navy, cover charge.

tablespoon 1. *Br. /Am.* **serving spoon/** large spoon for serving food or the amount held in it. 2. *Am. /Br.* **dessert spoon/** medium-sized spoon which is used for eating. 3. *Am.* spoon that holds exactly 1/128 of a US pint of liquid.

tablet 1. *Am., Can.* writing pad. 2. *esp. Br.* medicine pill.

tablet (of soup) *Br.* a block of dried stock used to make soup.

table-top sale *Br.* occasion of selling unwanted possessions from table, esp. if some money goes to charity.

tabloid *esp. Br.* newspaper that has articles about sex, famous people, etc. and not much serious news: *The tabloids kept churning out the crud* – Reader's Digest.

tach *Am., Can.* col. */Br.* col. **tacho/** tachometer.

tachograph *esp. Br.* a device for recording the speed of a lorry or coach and the distance it has travelled.

tack, thumbtack *Am., Can. /Br.* **drawing pin/** tack with a broad flat head for presing into a board with thumb.

(wedding) tackle *Br.* sl. men's genitals.

tacky *esp. Am., Aus.* col. of poor quality, shabby, shoddy: *once the "in" spot for socialites, sailors and salesmen, is today a tacky memorial to an old dance craze* - Newsweek.

taco(**-bender**) *Am.* sl. person of Hispanic origin, esp. Mexican.

tad *esp. Am.* col. a very small boy, chap.

taffy *Am., Can.* 1. toffee: *he sucked on cannon balls or chewed taffy slabs.* - I. Stone. 2. insincere flattery.

Taff(y) *Br.* col. or derog. a Welshman.

tag *Am.* licence plate of a motor vehicle.

(soldering) tag *Br. /Am.* **(soldering) lug/** a fitting of copper or brass to which electric wires are soldered or connected.

tag out *esp. Am.* (in baseball) cause (a player) to leave the field when he fails to reach base in time: *I am tagged out a good ten feet down the line* - Longman.

tag day *Am., Can.* flag day for charity.

tag end *esp. Am.* the last remaining part of smth.

tag line *esp. Am., Can.* col. catch phrase or slogan, used in advertising, as a punchline or joke.

tag question *Am. /Br.* **disjunctive question/**.

tag sale *Am.* a sale of low-value household items held at the vendor's own home: *At age 18 I came upon tag sale one Sunday* - Guideposts.

tag team *esp. Am., Can.* col. pair of people working together.

tail *esp. Am., Can.* person's buttocks.

tail/ get off one's **tail** *Am.* col. stop being lazy and start doing smth.

tail/ have one's **tail up** *Br.* col. be sure of success.

tail/ sit/be on sb.' **tail** *Br.* col. */Am.* **tailgate/** (of another car) follow sb.'s car too closely.

tail back *esp. Br. /Am.* **back up/** form a tailback.

tailback *esp. Br. /Am.* **back-up/** a still or slow-moving line of vehicles covering a certain distance on the road from where the traffic has been stopped, e.g. by accident, road repairs, etc.: *We once spent eleven days in a tailback there* - B. Bryson.

tailcoat *Br.* men's formal morning or evening coat with tails.

tailer *Br.* a device for securing a fish by the tail.

tailgate 1. *esp. Am., Aus.* tailboard of a car or lorry: *kids ride on the roof or hung on singing and screaming from the tailgate.* - J. Kerouac. 2. *esp. Br.* the lower gate of a canal lock. 3. *Am., Can.* relating to informal meal served from the back of a parked vehicle.

tailgate *esp. Am., Can.* col. */Br.* **tailboard/** drive (too) closely behind (a vehicle): *Just one more chick he'd been tailgating and could now overtake.* - J. Fowles.

tail light *Am. /esp. Br.* **rear light/** warning lights mounted at the rear of a vehicle.

tail pipe *Am. /Br.* **exhaust (pipe)/** exhaust: *the tailpipe would scrape on the rock.* - S. Bellow., *a small van that poot-pooted thin blue smoke out the tailpipe.* - A. Hitchcock Mystery Magazine.

tailplane *Br.* horizontal aerofoil at the tail of an aircraft.

tailspin/ go into a tailspin *Am.* (of a system or organisation) go out of control and start to fail.

taint *esp. Am.* make (food) unfit for use esp. because of decay, adj. **tainted**.

take (smth.) 1. *Br.* buy or have smth. delivered to one's home regularly, esp. newspapers, magazines, etc. 2. *Br.* rent smth., esp a house. 3. *Br.* obtain (an academic degree, etc.) e.g. *take a first in college.* 4. *Br.* also *Aus.* teach (a subject) in a school or college. 5. *esp. Am.* the money received at a cinema or theatre for seats: *a world record for a single night by a single artist, beating out the Beatles' take at Shea stadium in 1964.* – J. Hopkins. 6. *esp. Am.* col. amount of money earned by a shop or business in a particular period of time.

take/ sb.'s **take on** smth. *Am.* col. sb.'s opinion about a situation or idea.

take against (sb.) *Br.* come to dislike sb. for no obvious reason.

take smth. **away** *Br. /esp. Am.* **take out/** buy food at a cafe or restaurant for eating elsewhere.

take back *esp. Am.* lend (for buying one's own house), take back mortgage: *The seller will take back the mortgage.* - Longman.

take in *Am., Can.* col. visit (a place of amusement, the sights), go and watch (a performance, etc.), **take in a movie, show,** etc.: *He decided to...take in the painting show later on.* - T. Murphy.

take off 1. *Am.* kill (sb.): *She was taken off by a rare tropical fever some years ago.* - Longman. 2. *Br., Aus.* copy, mimic sb., make a parody of them.

take on *Br.* col. be very upset, esp. needlessly.

take out in *esp. Am.* pay a debt with smth. other than money: *When the boy broke the window,* the owner let him take it out in garden work. - Longman.

take up *Am.* (of trousers, skirt, etc.) make shorter.

take a bath *Am.* 1. /*Br.* **have a bath**/ wash one's whole body at one time: *Mama, it turned out was upstairs taking a bath.* - K. Davis. 2. *esp. Am.* lose a lot of money in business or in investment operation.

take/ have an early bath *Br.* be ordered to leave the field in a football game because of breaking the rules.

take a guess *Am.* /*Br.* **make a guess**/ try to guess.

take a hike (walk) *esp. Am.* col. go away.

take a leaf out of sb.'s **book** *Br.* copy smth. successful sb. else has done.

take a leak *Am.* /*Br.* **have/go for a slash**/ sl. (used by men) urinate.

take a poor view of smth. *Br.* disapprove.

take a shine to sb. *Br.* like them a lot: *MacLaine... eventually took a shine to Martin* – A. Summers, R. Swan.

take smth. **as read** *Br.* accept smth. without considering or discussing.

take the shine off smth. *esp. Br.* make it less enjoyable.

take a walk *Am.* go for a walk: *Take a walk, beakface.* – R.L. Stine.

take care of sb. *esp. Am.* col. bribe sb. so as to keep him out of criminal's way: *Have police in this area been taken care of?* - Longman.

take it easy *Am.* col. goodbye.

if you take my meaning *Br.* /*Am., Aus.* **if you catch my drift**/ these words suggest that there is more information than can be given openly.

take sb. **out of** themseles *Br.* try to change their mood, esp. to cheer them up.

take it out of *Br.* take reprisals against.

take sick *Am.* col. become ill.

take sb. **up for** smth. *Br., Aus.* ask sb. for the latest information about smth.

take things easy *Br.* take it easy.

take the fifth *Am.* refuse to answer.

takeaway *Br., Aus.* /*esp. Am.* **carryout, takeout** also *Aus., Can.*/ n. adj. (a meal bought from) a shop from which cooked meals can be taken away to be eaten somewhere else: *Some get takeout and eat at their desks.* - J. O'Brien, A. Kurins., *I've found Chinese takeout restaurants.* - D. Brenner., *he was fed warm takeout food.* - Time., *everything was ordered by number in a newsagent's, like a Chinese takeaway.* - B. Bryson.

takedown *esp. Am., Can.* 1. the act of bringing up one's opponent in amateur wrestling under control to the mat from a standing position. 2. col. police raid or arrest. 3. firearm with detachable barrel and magazine.

take-home sale *Br.* adj. off sale (selling alcoholic drinks off the premises).

taking attendance *Am.* /*Br.* **taking register**/ making a roll call at a classroom at school.

tale/ tell tales *esp. Br.* /*Am.* **tattle**/ tell sb. in authority bad things about sb.

tale/ thereby/therein hangs a tale *Br., Aus.* humor. said when one is asked about smth. that needs a long explanation.

talent *Br., Aus.* sl. humor. sexually attractive people.

talent spotter *Br.* talent scout.

talk/ all talk and no cider *Am.* much ado about nothing.

talk/ talk on the big white telephone *Am.* sl. vomit.

talk/ walk one's **talk** *Am.* do what one recommends other people to do or what one promises.

talk down 1. *Am.* make (sb. speaking) silent by argument or loud speech: *he'd have talked him down.* - R. Cox. 2. *esp. Br.* persuade sb. to accept less money than they originally asked for.

talk out *Br.* prevent (a law) from being passed by Parliament by talking until no time is left: *It was talked out in the last meeting of the House.* - Longman.

talk sb. **round** *esp. Br.* persuade sb. to change their mind.

talk up 1. *esp. Am., Can.* praise or try to encourage support of (smth.): *Billy Black started talking up the idea in public.* - Reader's Digest., *Talk up your son's or daughter's strengths.* - Reader's Digest., *the backseater had purposely talked up that side of him* - J. DeFelice. 2. *esp. Br.* persuade sb. to pay more than they originally offered.

talk with sb. *esp. Am.* /*esp. Br.* **talk to** sb/.

talk/ don't talk rubbish/nonsense/crap etc. *esp. Br.* don't say silly or wrong things.

talk/ talk nineteen to the dozen *Br.* /*Am.* **talk a blue streak**/ talk very quickly and a lot.

talk with *esp. Am.* /*esp. Br.* **talk to**/.

talk/ talk rubbish/talk out of one's **arse** *esp. Br.* talk nonsense.

talk/ can talk the hind leg(s) off a donkey *Br.* humor. col. annoy with long conversations.

talk/ set (the neighbours, etc.) **talking** *Am.* give them smth. to discuss.

talk/ talk through one's **neck/backside** *Br.* col. talk in a way that no one understands sb.

talk/ could talk under water/under wet cement *Aus.* col. /esp. *Am.* **talk under water/** have a lot to say in any situation.

talk/ you should(n't) talk *Am.* col. smth. that one says when sb. criticises another person for doing smth. that they do themselves.

talk turkey *esp. Am., Can.* col. talk seriously and openly, esp. about business matters: *I want to talk cold turkey to you man to man!* - K. Vonnegut, Jr., *Let's talk turkey.* - L. Uris.

talkback *Aus.* a radio programe in which listeners use telephone to take part in.

talkfest, also **talkathon** *esp. Am., Can.* col. long discussion: *a talkfest that gave all the inside skinny on the entertainment industry.* - D. Mortman.

talking of *esp. Br.* while we are on the subject of.

talk(ing) shop *esp. Br.* discussions which have no practical results.

talk jockey *Am.* col. radio announcer.

talk radio *esp. Am., Can.* radio broadcast where listeners ring in to talk about topical issues.

talk show 1. *Am., Aus.* /*Br.* **chat show/** radio or TV show on which well-known people talk to each other and are asked questions: *I actually heard it on a TV talk show.* - E. Taylor., *I share Oprah Winfrey's contempt for most daytime TV talk shows* - Ebony. 2. *Br.* one on which ordinary people appear to discuss interesting, often personal matters.

tall *Am.* adj. (of a drink) having a small amount of alcoholic drink mixed with a large one of non-alcoholic drink and served in a tall glass.

tallboy *Br.* /*Am.* **highboy/** a tall piece of wooden furniture containing several drawers: *Then he went to a tallboy and opened a secret drawer* - T. Murphy.

tall poppies *Aus.* sl. persons of prominence.

tall poppy syndrome *esp. Aus.* col. tendency to discredit those who have achieved a state of wealth or prominence in public life.

a tall tale *Am.* /*Br.* **a tall story/** an extravagant story: *Only two small children believed his tall stories* - H.C. Whitford., R.J. Dixson.

tall timber *Am., Can.* col. also **boondocks** some remote well-forested uninhibited place: *so I made tracks for the tall timber* - J. Dos Passos.

tally clerk, also **teller** *esp. Am.* person employed to receive and pay out money in a bank.

tally man / woman 1. *esp. Br.* person who sells goods on instalment plan. 2. *Br.* person who calculates totals or points won.

tally plan or **system** *Br.* becoming rare /also *Br.* **hire purchase, never-never,** *Am.* **installment plan/** a system of buying goods by which one pays small amounts of money regularly after receiving the goods.

tally-room *Aus.* room in which votes are collected after an election.

tally shop *Br.* discount house or store specialising in instalment sales.

tamarack *Can.* larch.

tame *Am.* (of a plant) produced by cultivation.

Tammany *esp. Am.* adj. of or related to an organisation trying to win or keep political power in a city by dishonest and unfair methods: *a political machine that competed with Tammany Hall of New York in rapacity and mendacity.* - H. Fast.

tamper-evident *Br.* /*Am.* **tamper-resistant/** (of a container) made so that one can see if sb. has opened it before it is sold in the shop.

tan(ned) *Am.* having darker skin after spending a lot of time in the sun, tanned.

T and A *Am., Can.* sl. /*Br.* sl. **B and T/** tits and ass: *He looks a bit tired; it's too much B and T.* - T. Thorne.

tanga *Br.* a pair of briefs consisting of small panels connecting by strings at the sides.

tangent *Am.* col. a straight section of a (rail) road.

tangent/ go off at a tangent *esp. Br.* /*Am., Aus.* **on a tangent,** *Br., Aus.* **fly off at a tangent/** suddenly start talking about a different subject.

tanglefoot *Am., Can.* desinfectant applied to a tree trunk.

tank 1. *Am.* col. fail (of smth.), esp. at a great financial cost: *the oil businesses tanked.* - Forbes. 2. *Br.* sl. crush, move powerfully: *They'd all tank Tyson.* - T. Thorne. 3. *Am., Can.* (in sport) deliberately lose or fail to finish (a match).

tank 1. *Am., Can.* col. jail or cell in a police station: *bailed out of the tank by some guilty liberal.* - E.L. Doctorow. 2. *Aus., NZ.* reservoir.

tank up *esp. Am.* fill a car's fuel tank.

tank car *Am.* tank wagon.

tankard *Br.* /*Am.* **stein/** a large usu. metal drinking cup usu. with a handle and lid, used for drinking beer: *pubs with tankards on the ceiling* - A. Burgess.

tanked (up) *esp. Br., Can., Aus.* sl. drunk, esp. from drinking beer: *I got tanked up and he fired me* - Kansas City Star.

tanker *Am.* tankman.

tank locomotive *Am.* one with an engine carrying fuel and water.

tank top 1. *Br.* a piece of clothing like sweater but without sleeves. 2. *Am.* a piece of clothing like a shirt but without sleeves.
tank town *Am., Can.* a small town (esp. one where trains stop mainly to get water).
tank truck *Am.* tanker lorry for oil.
tanner *Br.* col. sixpence.
Tannoy *esp. Br.* tdmk. a system of giving out information to the public by means of loudspeakers, **over the tannoy**: *the explorer did not communicate as in Hollywood films by tannoy* - P. Norman.
tantalus *Br.* stand in which spirit decanters may be locked up though still visible.
tap *esp. Br., Aus., Can* /**faucet** *Am.*/: *the bathroom with its kidney-shaped handbasin and gold-plated taps* - D. Lodge.
tap/ on tap *Am., Can.* esp. journalism. smth. that is likely to happen soon.
tap/ be tapped *Am.* col. be designated or selected for a task or honour, esp. a membership of an organisation: *President Reagan tapped Henkel for a seat on the board.* – D.L. Barlett, J.B. Steele.
tap (for) *Br.* col. get some money from.
tape 1. *Br., Aus.* sticky tape. 2. *Am.* Scotch tape. 3. *Am. /Br.* **v.t.**/ video tape.
tape/ have/get sb. **taped** *Br., Aus.* col. know about sb. doing smth. bad beforehand; be aware of sb.'s faults.
tape (up) (often pass.) *Am.* /*Br.* **strap**/ bind with bandages.
tap parts *Am.* pair of brief lingerie shorts, usu. worn with a camisole top.
tapped out *Am.* penniless: *I'm tapped out, Mark.* - T. Thorne.
tapping *Br.* 1. electric connection made to some point between the end terminals of a transformer coil or other component. 2. taproom.
taps *Am. /Br.* **last post**/ the last signal of the day blown on a bugle to signal that light should be put out: *the bugle sang taps* – J. Steinbeck.
tapu *NZ.* forbidden; taboo.
taqueria *esp. Am.* Mexican restaurant specialiing in tacos.
tar/ beat/knock/whale the tar out of sb. *Am., Can.* col. keep hitting sb. hard or to completely defeat sb.
taradiddle *esp. Br.* col. minor lie.
target-firing *esp. Br.* target practice.
The Tar Heel State, Old North State *Am.* North Carolina.
Tarheeler *Am.* resident of North Carolina.

tariff *esp. Br.* a list of fixed prices, such as the cost of meals or rooms charged by a hotel, restaurants, etc.
tariff reform 1. *Am.* a reduction of most important duties. 2. *Br.* an increase or extension of most of them.
tarmac *Br.* /*Am., Can.* **blacktop, pavement**/: *Bill walked into a Bar with a lump of Tarmac under his arms* – Reader's Digest.
tarmac *Am.* sl. go by air in short hops from location to location when electioneering.
tarnation *esp. Am., Can.* euph. damnation.
tarp *esp. Am., Can.* col. tarpaulin sheet or cover.
tart 1. *Br.* any fruit pie, esp. open pastry case containing fruit or jam: *He ordered himself, too, the very dinner the boy had always chosen - soup, white bait, cutlet and a tart.* - J. Galsworthy. 2. *Am., Can.* a very small pastry with fruit and jam or custard without a top crust. 3. *esp. Br.* derog. a prostitute.
tart sb./smth. **up** *esp. Br.* col. usu. derog. make noticeably attractive or decorative by painting in bright colours, putting on cheap jewellery or colourful clothes, etc.: *Two of the shopping arcades had been nicely tarted up* - B. Bryson.
tarty *esp. Br.* wearing kind of clothes that people think prostitutes would wear.
tassel *Am., Can.* (of maize, etc.) form tassels.
Tassieland, also **Raspberryland, Apple Island** *Aus.* Tasmania.
taster *Br.* col. a portion of ice-cream served in shallow glass.
tasty *esp. Br.* col. (used esp. by men to a woman) attractive (usu. considered offensive by women): *Love the threads. Really tasty.* - T. Thorne.
tat *Br.* col. derog. something of very low quality: *shops, aimed at the tourist trade and full of gaudy tat* - J. Fowles.
ta-ta *esp. Br.* col. goodbye: *Ta-ta and adios.* – K. Vonnegut, Jr.
tatter *esp. Br.* junkman.
tattle-tale *Am.* /*Aus.* **dobber,** *Br.* **telltale**/ col. informer.
tatty *esp. Br.* col. derog. untidy or in bad condition, shabby: *the indelible image of all your tatty underpants.* - S. Grafton. **-ily** adv. **-ness** n.
tavern 1. *Am., Can.* an inn or public house. 2. *Br.* obs. pub where one also stays the night.
tax *Am.* col. sum levied on members of an organisation to defray expenses, dues.
tax *Am.* col. price, charge, get dues.

tax a car, motorbike *Br.* pay the sum of money charged each year for using a motor vehicle on British roads.
tax/ hidden taxes *Am.* taxes on goods and services, indirect taxation.
tax/ nuisance tax *Am.* small tax paid off in instalments.
tax break *Am.* special reduction in taxes that the government allows for a particular purpose.
tax-deductable *Am., Aus.* pertaining to smth. you don't need to pay taxes for.
tax-deferred *Am.* not-taxed until later time.
tax disc *Br.* a round piece of paper displayed on cars and motorcycles which proves the owner has paid road tax.
taxi-dance hall *Am.* dancing hall with taxi-dancers.
taxi *Br., Can.* /*Am.* **cab**/.
taxi-dancer *esp. Am., Can.* a gigolette.
taximan *esp. Br.* the operator of a taxi.
taxing master *esp. Br.* law officer involved with taxes.
taxi rank *Br.* /*Am.* **taxi-stand, cab stand**/.
taxi stand, also **cab stand** *esp. Am.* taxi rank: *I say, excuse me, is there a taxi rank near here?* - R. Carter., M. McCarthy.
taxman *esp. Br.* the person in the government department that collects taxes.
tax-paid *Am.* kept on the money of taxpayers.
taxpayer *Am.* col. any small building.
tax refund *esp. Am.* repayment of tax.
tax relief *Br.* the right to not have to pay tax on a part of what you earn.
tax therapist *Am.* tax expert who advises clients on filling in income-tax forms.
TB *Br.* /*Am.* **Tb**/ abbr. tuberculosis.
tchutchke *Am.* col. trinket.
tea 1. *esp. Br.* also **afternoon tea** a small meal served in the afternoon with a cup of tea. 2. *Br.* a light supper taken after work among working class members. 3. *Aus.* evening meal. 4. *esp. Br.* a cup of tea.
tea/ More tea, vicar? *Br.* col. humor. used after saying smth. embarrassing.
tea and symphony *Br.* humor. kind words for people in trouble.
tea ball *Am.* a small wire ball which is filled with tea leaves to make usu. a pot of tea.
tea biscuit *Br.* a shortbread or cookie cracker.
tea boy *esp. Br.* a male servant.
tea break *Br., Aus.* /*Am.* **coffee break**/ short pause during the working day.
tea caddy *esp. Br.* a small tin in which you keep tea.

tea cake or **bread** *Br.* a light bread or scone, a light flat cake usu. with dried fruit: *their treats... tea cakes, scones, crumpets, rock cakes, rich tea biscuits, fruit shrewsburys - are so cautiously flavourful.* - B. Bryson.
tea-cart, also **tea wagon** *esp. Am.* /*Br., Aus.* **tea trolley**/ a small table on wheels from which food and/or drinks are served.
tea chest *Br.* a large wooden box in which tea is packed when it's exported.
teach/ teach sb.'s **grandmother (to suck eggs)** *Br.* give sb. advice about smth. they already know.
teach school, college, etc. *Am.* be a teacher in a school, etc.: *During ten years of teaching college, I've seen how widespread the practice is.* – Reader's Digest.
teacherage *Am., Can.* house or lodgings provided for a teacher by school.
teacher-training college *Br.* /*Am.* **teacher's college,** *Aus.* **teachers college**/ one which trains teachers.
teaching background *Am.* /*Br.* **teacher's service experience**/.
teaching hospital *Br.* hospital where students can practise medicine under the guidance of experienced doctors.
teaching practice *Br.* /*Am.* **student teaching**/.
tea clam *Am.* a very small clam.
tea cloth, tea towel *Br.* 1. /*Am.* **dish towel, kitchen towel**/ a small towel for drying dishes, silverware, etc. 2. a small cloth for spreading over a small table from which tea is to be served.
tea cooper *esp. Br.* a docker who unloads tea.
teacup/ a storm in a teacup *esp. Br.* /*Am., Can.* **tempest in a teapot**/ a lot of fuss about smth. unimportant.
tea-ho *Aus.* a pause for tea.
tea-house *esp. Br.* the office of a firm that imports tea.
tea lady *Br.* a member of the staff bringing tea at 11 and 14 p.m. at the job: *uncle once lived next door to a tea lady at Broadcasting House.* – S. Townsend.
tealeaf *Br.* humor. sl. thief.
team/ a whole (or **full**) **team** *Am.* expert or champion.
team/ in a team *Br.* /*Am.* **on a team**/: *I'm on the wrestling team at school.* – R.L. Stine.
teaman *Br.* sl. prisoner allowed one pint of tea instead of gruel.
teammate *esp. Am.* sb. who plays in the same team with sb.

teamster *Am.* 1. /*Br.* **lorry driver**/ person who drives a large road vehicle. 2. a member of transportation workers union: *Trucks were donated by the French teamsters.* - L. Uris.

tea party/ be no tea party *Am.* col. be very difficult or unpleasant to do.

tear *Am.* sl. a binge, spree: *Sally is off on a tear again.* - R.A. Spears.

tear off *Br.* col. write smth. in a short time.

tear/ it'll (all) end in tears *Br.* col. it will finish badly.

tear/ tear sb. off a strip/ tear a strip off sb. *Br.* col. rebuke sb. angrily.

tearaway *Br., Aus.* col. a noisy and violent young person.

tearing *Br.* sl. 1. adj. excellent. 2. adv. very.

tearing hurry/ be in a tearing hurry *Br.* be doing smth. very quickly, because sb. is late.

tea room *Am., Can.* col. public toilet used as a meeting place by homosexuals.

tear-sheet *Am.* advertisement torn from a publication, used to make an order.

tease *Am.* /*Br.* **backcomb**/ comb hair towards the scalp with the comb: *No extreme makeup, no shorts, no slacks, no curlers, no tight sweaters, and no teased hair.* - D. Divoky.

teaser *Am.* col. anything offered as a sample and intended to increase appetite or desire.

teashop *esp. Br.* tea room, a type of restaurant serving tea and occasionally light evening meals.

teat *Br.* /*Am.* **nipple**/ the rubber cap on a nursing bottle.

teathings *esp. Br.* tea cups, etc.

teatime *esp. Br.* time when people have their tea, usu. in the late afternoon or in the early part of the evening.

tea towel, tea cloth, wash cloth, wash rag *esp. Br.* /*Am., Can.* **dish towel**/ a small towel used for drying cups, plates, etc.: *drying her hands on the tea-towel she'd been washing up with.* – R. Westall.

tea trolley *esp. Br.* /*esp. Am.* **tea wagon**/ a table on wheels for serving food and/or drinks: *Hillenketter brought in the refreshments on an old-fashioned tea-wagon.* - J. O'Hara.

tech, technological college *Br.* one where arts and technical subjects are studied.

techie *Am.* col. technician.

technic *esp. Am.* technique.

technical *esp. Am., Can.* small truck with a machine gun mounted on the back.

technical officer *esp. Br.* industrial official engaged in investigation, research and development.

technie *esp. Am.* rare. a technical detail.

Ted *Br.* Teddy boy.

teddy *Br.* (soft toy) teddy bear.

tee *esp. Am., Can.* col. T-shirt.

tee off (on) *esp. Am., Can.* col. express anger (about smth.), **teed off** *Am., Can.* col. angry, fed up: *I got really teed off when she kept on being so rude to me.* - Longman.

teem down *Br.* rain very heavily.

teen *Am.* col. /*Br.* **teenager**/ a teenager: *it's one of the hot holiday gifts for teens.* – Reader's Digest.

Tee-square, also **triangle** *Am.* /*Br.* **setsquare**/.

teeterboard, teetering board, teeter-totter *esp. Am., Can.* seesaw: *It was no more stable than a teeter-totter.* - K. Vonnegut, Jr.

teeth/ cut one's **eyeteeth** *Am.* get one's first experience at a particular job.

teeth/ fed up/sick to the back teeth *Br.* annoyed very much.

teeth/ grind one's **teeth** *Br.* be very worried but try not to show it.

teeth/ have teeth *Br.* (of an organisation or law) have enough authority to make people obey them.

teeth/ like pulling teeth *esp. Am.* very difficult.

teethgnashing *Am.* angry protests.

teething troubles/problems *Br., Aus.* /*Am.* **teething pains**/ problems with smth. new.

teetotally *Am.* adv. in the whole.

teg(g) *esp. Br.* a sheep from its weaning till its first shearing.

telco *Am.* telecommunication company.

tele *Am.* telly.

telecast *Am.* a program that is broadcast on TV, esp. a live one.

telecine *Br.* a film chain, the device which both projects and transmits TV film.

telecommuting *esp. Br.* teleworking, working from home using computer.

telecopter *Am.* a helicopter equipped with a telecamera.

telegraph boy *esp. Br.* a boy personally delivering telegrams.

telegrapher *esp. Am.* /*esp. Br.* **telegraphist**/.

telegraph pole *Br., Aus.* / *Am.* **telephone pole**/ a tall wooden pole for supporting telephone wires.

telegraph post *Br.* telegraph pole.

telemarketing *esp. Am.* telesales, sales done through using TV.

telemessage *Br.* /*Am.* **mailgram**/ tdmk. a mail sent by telephone or Telex and delivered in printed form.

telephone book *Am.* /*Br.* **directory**/.

telephone box, kiosk *esp. Br.* /*esp. Am.* **call box, (tele) phone booth, phone box**/ public telephone booth: *he dived suddenly into a telephone box and rang a number.* - G. Greene., *Then she went to a telephone box* - I. Murdoch., *I slowly made my way to a telephone booth* – S. Lawrence.

telephone/ **on the telephone** *Am.* engaged or talking on the telephone.

telephonist *Br.* /*esp. Am.* **telephone operator**/ person who makes connections at a telephone exchange.

TelePrompter *esp. Am., Can., Aus.* tdmk. / *Br.* **autocue**/: *he reads his lyrics from television TelePromTers* – A. Summers, R. Swan.

telesoftware *Br.* software transmitted or broadcast via a network or TV system.

teletypewriter *esp. Am.* /*Br.* **teleprinter**/ an apparatus for sending and receiving messages by telegraphic methods.

televangelist *esp. Am.* evangelical preacher who regularly preaches on TV.

televisual *esp. Br.* of, related to or suitable for broadcasting by TV.

tell/ **Do tell!** *Am.* It can't be true!

tell/ **I can't tell you** *Br.* col. used for emphasis before and after statements.

tell/ **I'll tell you what**... *Am.* I really mean what I say.

tell/ **tell sb. good-bye** *Am.* say good-bye to sb.

tell/ **tell it like it is** *Am.* col. tell the truth: *Joe is the leader of our commune; he tells it like it is.* - A. Makkai.

tell/ **tell me another** *Br., Aus.* /*Am., Aus.* **tell me another one**/ I don't believe what you've told me!

tell/ **tell tales** *Br.* say untrue things about sb. to cause them harm.

tell/ **tell the time** *Br.* /*Am.* **tell time**/ be able to know what time it is by looking at a clock: *Although Ernest is only four years old, he's already able to tell time.* - H.C. Whitford., R.J. Dixson.

teller, tally clerk *esp. Am., Aus.* person employed to receive and pay out money in a bank: *A customer is seen approaching a teller's window in a bank.* - R.L. Berger and others.

telling-off *esp. Br.* col. reprimand.

telltale *Br.* /*Am.* **tattletale**/.

telly *Br., Aus.* col. /*Am., Can., Br.* **TV**/ television: *This would be the telly.* - A. Burgess., *Telly was on.* - Arthur Hailey.

temblor *Am.* a tremor, earthquake.

temp *esp. Br.* col. work as a temporary worker.

tempest in a teapot *Am., Can.* /*esp. Br.* **storm in a teacup**/ a situation where people get very angry or worried about smth. unimportant.

temple *Am., Can.* synagogue.

temporary guest *Br.* /*Am.* **transient**/ temporary dweller.

ten/ **ten out of ten** *Br.* used in schools to give a perfect mark or to praise sb. humorously.

ten-cent store, also **dime store** *Am.* penny arcade.

tend (for) *esp. Am.* serve customers in (a store, bar, etc.) e.g. tend a shop: *She tends bar here now.* - J. O'Brien, A. Kurins., *For a couple of years he tended bar at a lounge* - A. Hitchcock Mystery Magazine.

tender/ **put work out for tender** *Br.* ask people to make offers to do it.

tenderfoot *esp. Am., Can.* col. inexperienced person who recently arrived in a rough place: *cowboys call people like us tenderfeet.* - Reader's Digest.

tenderloin *Am., Can.* col. a district of a city largely devoted to vice and other forms of lawbreaking that encourage political or police corruption: *case extended much farther up the Gambino family tenderloin.* - J. O'Brien, A. Kurins.

ten-foot pole/ **I wouldn't touch it**/sb. **with a ten-foot pole** *Am., Can.* /*Br.* **barge pole**/ I would never be concerned with it/sb.: *Angels wouldn't touch him with a ten-foot pole* - Zacherlay.

ten-four (also **10-4**) *esp. Am.* a message has been received.

tenner 1. *Br.* col. ten-pound note. 2. *Am., Aus.* also **tenspot** ten dollar bill.

tennies *Am., Can.* col. tennis shoes.

tennis shoes *Am.* /*Br.* **plimsolls,** *Am.* **sneakers**/ shoes for sports games: *a waiter in white coat and tennis shoes* - A. Burgess., *They wear tennis shoes in the pulpit* - B.E. Olson.

tenon saw *Br.* /*Am.* **back saw**/.

tenpin bowling *Br.* /*Am.* **tenpins, bowling**/ bowling: *One guy I know recollects a ten-pin bowling alley.* - B. Bryson.

tenstrike *Am.* 1. a strike in tenpins. 2. highly successful stroke or achievement.

tenure *esp. Am.* the right to stay in the job, esp. as a university teacher, without needing to have a new contract of employment usu. given after a fixed number of years: *youngest tenured professor in Harvard's 363-year history* - Fortune.

tenure track *esp. Am., Can.* employment structure whereby the holder of a post is guaranteed consideration for eventual tenure.

term *esp. Br.* /*esp. Am., Aus.* **semester**/ any of the three periods of time into which the teaching year is divided at schools, universities, etc.: *The term was nearly at the end.* - I. Murdoch.

terminate sb. **with extreme prejudices** *esp. Am.* euph. murder or assassinate sb.

terminus *esp. Br.* a railway or other transport route terminal; a station there.

termly *esp. Br.* happening each term.

term of years *Br.* /*Am.* **term for years**/ law. tenancy of a fixed period.

term paper *Am., Can.* /*Br.* **essay, project**/ school composition: *Like a term paper - delusions of grandeur.* - J. Kellerman.

terms of reference *Am.* ideas and experiences which people use to make decisions.

terrace 1. (usu. pl.) *esp. Br.* any of a number of wide steps on which watchers stand at a football match. 2. *Am.* parklike strip as in a centre of a road. 3. also **terracing** *Br., Aus.* a row of houses joined together. 4. *esp. Br.* /*Am.* **deck**/ roofless raised wooden entrance built out from the back or side of a house.

terraced house *Br., Aus.* /*Am.* **row house**/ a house which is part of a terrace of houses: *It was lined with Victorian terraced houses.* - J. Higgins.

terrible twins *Br.* col. two persons who behave in a way which attracts attention.

terribly *Br.* extremely.

terrycloth *Am.* /*Br.* **towelling**/ thick, usu. cotton material with uncut threads, used esp. for making towels, bath mats, etc.

territorials, Territorial Army *Br.* armed force whose members are not professional soldiers but train as soldiers in their spare time.

tertiary education *Br., Aus.* /*Am.* **higher education**/ connected with education in colleges and universities.

Terylene *Br., Aus.* tdmk. /*Am.* tdmk. **Dacron**/ a man-made cloth similar to nylon.

TESOL *esp. Am.* teaching English to speakers of other languages /*esp. Br.* **ELT**/.

test (match) *Br.* a match between two international sides, usu. at cricket, rugby union, or rugby league.

test certificate *Br.* official paper that proves that a car is legally safe enough to drive.

testify *Am.* stand up and tell people how God has helped them in their life.

testing *esp. Br.* difficult to deal with.

test paper *Am.* document used to identify a signature.

test-pattern *Am.* /*Br.* **test card**/ testing-card (on television).

tetched *Am.* col. slightly crazy.

tetchy *esp. Br.* easily offended, irritable.

tether/ be at the end of one's **tether** *Br.* /*esp. Am.* **at the end of** *one's* **rope**/ be extremely worried and tired (because a person can't solve the problem).

texas *Am.* a structure on the awning deck of a steamer containing the officers' cabin and having the pilot house in front or top.

Tex-Mex *Am.* col. connected with the music, cooking, etc. of Mexican American people.

Thames/ set the Thames on fire *Br.* col. do anything unusually successful.

Thanksgiving Day 1. *Am.* a national holiday, the fourth Thursday in November on which God is thanked for the crops that have been gathered. 2. *Can.* harvest festival holiday, celebrated on second Monday of October.

Thanksgiving Dinner *Am.* turkey and pumpkin pie.

thank-you-ma-am *Am.* col. 1. a hollow on the road. 2. a hole on the face of a hill draining water away.

that *Br.* and *Aus.* nonst. so much, e.g. *it hurts me that much.*

that/ and (all) that *Br.* col. and similar people and things.

that long/many, etc. **(that)** *Br.* col. so long, etc. that smth. happens.

thataway *esp. Am.* col. in that direction and in that way; like that.

the/ *(The) author of "Escape"(,) Mr. J. Hall(,) arrived in New York last night.* The and the commas here are more likely to be absent in American English than in British. (R.A. Close - A reference grammar for students of English. Longman. 1975); (*Br.*) *The injured were taken to hospital.*

theatre 1. *Br.* an operating theatre. 2. (**movie**) **theater** *esp. Aus., Am., Can.* /*Br.* **cinema**/ building where films are shown.

theatre goer *Am.* /*Br.* **cinema goer**/.

The Golden Heart of Alaska *Am.* Fairbanks, Alaska.

theme *Am.* short piece of writing on a particular subject usu. done for school.

theme party *Br.* party where everyone has to dress in a particular way connected with specific subject.

then/ and then some *Am.* and many other things.
theological college *Br.* /*Am.* **theological seminary**/ school for training people to become priests or church ministers.
theologue *Am.* a student of theology.
there's, there was *esp. Br. There was four of us* - R. Carter., M. McCartney.
they've *esp. Br.* used esp. in verb compounds.
thermionic valve *Br.* /*Am.* **thermionic tube**/ tech. a system of electrodes arranged in an airless glass or metal container, esp. used to control the flow of current in radios and televisions.
thermos bottle *esp. Am.* thermos flask: *take sandwiches and milk in a thermos bottle.* - J. O'Hara.
The World's Image Center *Am.* Rochester, New York.
thick 1. *esp. Br.* col. 1. also *Aus.* (of a person) stupid, slow to understand: *I'm not some blinkin' thickie* - T. Thorne. 2. (with) very friendly. 3. esp. (**it's**) **a bit thick** beyond what is reasonable or satisfactory.
thick/ give sb./**get a thick ear** *Br.* col. punish/be punished with sb. with a blow, esp. on an ear.
thick/ thick as shit/thick as two (short) planks or **as a plank** *Br.* col. very stupid.
thick/ thick on the ground *esp. Br.* col. plentiful.
thick/ the thick end of smth. *Br.* col. almost as much as (an amount); the greater part of smth.
thin/ be as thin as rail *esp. Am.* be very thin.
thin/ have a thin time *Br., Aus.* col. have a wretched or uncomfortable time, esp. because of the lack of money.
thin/ the thin end of the wedge *esp. Br., Aus.* something which seems unimportant but will open the way for more serious things of a similar kind.
thin/ thin on the ground *Br., Aus.* col. not plentiful; not common.
thing/ do one's **thing** *Am.* col. do smth. planned.
thing/ do the/that…thing *Am., Can.* col. do a particular activity as a whole.
thing/ have a good thing going *Am.* col. be in an advantageous position to succeed.
thing/ taking one thing with another *Br.* considering all the things.
the thing to do *Am.* /*Br.* **the done thing**/ the correct way to behave in a particular social situation.
things *esp. Br.* 1. the tools, equipment, clothes, etc. that a person needs for a specific job, sport, etc. 2. clothes and possessions.

things/ breakfast, dinner things, etc. *Br.* the plates, dishes, used for a particular meal.
think on *Am., Can.* think of or about.
the thinking man's/woman's crumpet *Br.* humor. a man or woman who is popular with the opposite sex because they are both intelligent and sexually attractive.
thinning shears *Am.* hairdresser's thinning scissors.
third *Br.* 1. third form of school or college. 2. place in the third grade in an exam, esp. for a degree.
third (gear) *Am.* high gear.
third age *Br.* period in life between middle age and old age (55-70).
third class *Am.* mail that is printed, other than magazines and newspapers that are published regularly, and packages that are not sealed and weigh less than a pound: *Much advertising is sent by third-class mail.* - A. Makkai.
third-degree *esp. Am., Can.* col. the least serious category of crime, esp. murder: *it was sort of like the third degree.* – J. O'Hara.
third house *Am.* a body of lobbyists.
third market *Am.* one in listed stocks not traded on a stock-exchange.
third-party insurance *Br., Can.* /*Am.* **liability insurance**/ insurance made for a person not named in a insurance agreement, but who will be protected by it if an accident happens.
third time lucky *Br.* /*Am.* **third time is the charm**/ col. said after trying to do smth. twice and hoping to succeed for the third time.
thirty-second note *esp. Am., Can.* /*esp. Br.* **demi-semi-quaver**/.
this after *Aus.* sl. this afternoon.
this, that and the other thing *Am.* col. all the mentioned things of different kinds
thong *esp. Am., Aus., Can.* /*Br.* **flip-flop**/ a sandal which is usu. made of rubber and is held on by the toes and loose at the back: *expensive thongs with Velcro ankle straps attached.* - Reader's Digest.
thorn in sb.'s **flesh** *Br.* annoying problem.
thousand/ be batting a thousand *Am.* be very successful.
thousand islands dressing *Am.* mayonnaise with chopped pimentos and gherkins added.
thread *Br.* the thicker kind of cotton used for heavier sewing such as buttons.
three-day event *Br.* horse-riding competition that takes place for three days.
threads *esp. Am., Can.* col. obs. clothes.
three-peat *Am., Can.* win three times, esp. consecutively, esp. in a sporting event, n.

three-piece suite *esp. Br.* /*Am.* **living room suite**/ sofa with two matching chairs.

three-ring circus *esp. Am., Aus.* 1. circus with three rings for simultaneous performance. 2. col. a lot of noisy or confused activity.

three-strikes *Am.* col. a law whereby a person convicted of three serious felonies is subject to mandatory life imprisonment: *with nopossibility of parole for 50 years – for stealing $153 of videotapes under California's three-strikes blow.* - Time.

thrift (institution) *Am.* savings bank.

thrift shop/store *Am., Can.* /*Br.* **charity shop**/: *Between the chairs a thrift shop end table supported a coffee maker* - J. Kellerman.

thrill/ to be thrilled to pieces *Am.* col. be extremely pleased.

thrillcraft *esp. Am.* recreational water vehicles, used in exciting or dangerous water sports, and capable of high speeds.

throatlatch *Am.* horse throat band.

throstle *Br.* worsted spinning wheel.

throttle bottom *Am.* harmless ineffective holder of public office.

through *Am., Can.* 1. prep. (esp. in expressions of time) up to and including, e.g. Friday through Sunday: *new library hours were three to five P.M., Monday through Wednesday.* - J. Kellerman. 2. col. having no prospect of any future relationship.

through/ Are you through? 1. **be/get through** *Br.* Are you connected to the other speaker?: *Presently he was through.* - A. Christie., *the operator put the call through* - A. McLean. 2. *Am.* Have you finished talking on the telephone?

No through road *Br.* /*Br., Aus.* **No through way,** *Am.* **No through traffic, No thoroughfare**/ the road the end or part of which is blocked.

throughother *Irish Eng.* mingled through one another.

throughway, thruway *Am., Can.* very wide road for high speed traffic; major road or motorway.

throw *esp. Am.* col. a single item or unit of smth.

throw/ 5 pounds a throw *Br.* col. 5 pounds each.

throw down *esp. Am.* decline, refuse: *I'd throw 'im down for you any time.* - J. London., *This is a hell of a time to be throwing me down.* - D. Hammet.

throw in with *Am.* join (sb.) in a plan or attempt, often wrong, also throw in one's lot with: *He would hardly want to throw in with them.* - P. Norman., *Do you think she meant to throw in with Peppler again when he got out.* - D. Hammet.

throw off *esp. Am.* confuse: *Any small interruption is likely to throw me off in my calculations.* - Longman.

throw up *Am., Can.* berate, criticise: *That's the third time this week you have thrown that mistake up to me.* - H.C. Whitford., R.J. Dixson., *And he never threw it up* – J. Hopkins.

throw/ throw (sb.) a curve *Am., Can.* sl. do smth. quite unexpected: *storms during winter's end threw us a curve* - Outdoor Life.

throw/ throw a monkey wrench into smth. **(in the works)** *Am.* /*Br.* **throw/put a spanner in the works**/ col. spoil smth. on purpose: *you threw a monkey wrench into the works by fussing about the rules.* - A. Makkai., *Don't you go throw a monkey wrench.* – P. Roth.

throw/ throw/knock sb. **for a loop** *esp. Am., Can.* col. a. defeat sb. in a fight: *old fighter soon threw him for a loop.* - Longman. b. confuse sb., make sb. helpless in an argument: *Walking and Talking tells of two thirtyish friends who get thrown for a loop.* - Newsweek.

throw/ throw smth. **out of gear** *Br.* prevent smth. from happening as it was planned.

throw/ throw the baby out with the bath *Am.* destroy smth. good while trying to change it and make it better.

throw/ throw the bull *Am.* sl. chat, blabber.

throw/ throw up the sponge *Am.* /*Br.* **throw in the sponge**/ admit defeat: *I don't like to see a fellow throw up the sponge that way.* - G. Greene.

throwing stick, woomera(ng) *Aus.* boomerang.

thru *esp. Am.* col. adj. adv. prep. through: *Enrique high on tea looking at you thru the smoke* - J. Kerouac.

thrush *Am.* sl. female singer: *Anyway, their attempts to remake Kim into a sexy thrush fail* - Rolling Stone.

thruway, also **throughway** *esp. Am.* very wide road for high speed traffic: *The 550 mile super-expressway is known as the N.Y. State thruway.* - A. Frommer.

thumb/ be under the thumb *Br., Aus.* col. be completely controlled by one's wife.

thumb/ be all fingers and thumbs *Br., Aus.* /*Am.* **be all thumbs**/ be clumsy.

thump/ give sb. **a thump on the back/head,** etc. *esp. Br.* hit sb.

thumb/ thumb a lift *Br.* col. /*Am.* **thumb a ride**/ persuade a driver to take one by putting one's hand out with thumb raised.

thumbsucker *Am.* col. derog. serious piece of journalism concentrating on the background and interpretation of event.

thumbtack, pushpin *esp. Am., Can., /Br., Aus.* **drawing pin/** shortpin with a broad flat head used esp. for putting up notices: *he stepped on a thumbtack.* - J. Dos Passos., *Concert tickets were pinned by thumbtacks to the bulletin boards.* - S. Bellow.

thump *esp. Br.* col. attack and hit sb. with one's fist.

thumping *esp. Br.* col. adj., adv. very (big), **thumping great/big**.

thunderbox *Br.* col. primitive or makeshift toilet.

thundergust *esp. Am.* thunderstorm with wind.

thundering *Br.* obs. col. adj. adv. very.

thus and so *Am.* so, thus.

tick *Br.* col. obs. short term credit, esp. in **on tick**.

tick 1. *esp. Br., Aus.* col. a short time, moment: *we can be there in half a tick.* - J.D. Carr., *Brando waited two or three ticks* - W. Jack, B. Laursen, often in **hold/hang on (just) a tick/two ticks**. 2. *Br.* col. an annoying and worthless person.

tick (off) 1. esp. *Br., Aus. /Am.* **check/** mark (an answer, name, etc.) with (*Br., Aus.*) **tick,** (*Am.*) **check** mark to show that it is correct: *the names ticked off by clerks for publication in the official report.* - J. Ruppeldtova. 2. *esp. Am., Can.* col. make sb. angry: *If only that girl had behaved herself so Jack hadn't got so ticked off* - P. Case, J. Migliore. 3. *Br., Aus.* col. angrily tell sb. that they shouldn't have done smth.; n. **ticking-off**.

tick over *Br.* 1. continue working at a slow steady rate without producing much. 2. run at a low speed or rate (of an engine).

ticker *Am., Can.* telegraphic or electronic machine that prints out data or a strip of print, esp. Stock Exchange information or news report.

ticker-tape parade *Am.* a ceremony in which person or people being honoured walk or drive along streets and confetti is thrown at them from windows of tall buildings.

ticker *esp. Br.* col. obs. a heart.

ticket *Br.* 1. the range of ideas and plans that people support in the time of elections. 2. certificate of discharge from the army.

ticket, also slate *esp. Am., Aus.* a list or group of people supported by one political party in an election: *Dukakis should offer Jackson the second spot on the ticket.* - Newsweek.

ticket *esp. Am.* give (a parking, etc.) ticket (printed notice of an offence against driving laws): *Motor vehicles can be ticketed for being dirty.* - Y. Richmond.

ticket/ have tickets on oneself *Aus., NZ.* col. have too high an opinion of oneself.

ticket/ punch one's **ticket** *Am.* col. deliberately take particular assignments that are likely to lead to promotion at work.

ticket/ ticket to succees/fame, etc. esp. *Am.* a way of getting success, etc.

ticket/ write one's **(own) ticket** *esp. Am., Can.* col. dictate one's own terms.

ticket agent, clerk, seller, also **ticket master** *Am. /esp. Br.* **booking clerk/** ticket clerk: *ticketing agent for the mainland's six regional lines.* - Time., *An airline ticket agent in Minneapolis confirmed this one day.* - Reader's Digest.

ticket office, ticket agent, ticket booth *esp. Am. /esp. Br.* **booking office, booking hall/** place where seats, hotel rooms, etc. can be reserved: *We spent some time trying to sleep on the beach at the railroad ticket office* - J. Kerouac., *They rushed the ticket booth and damaged it.* – A. Summers, R. Swan.

ticket-of-leave *Br.* parole.

ticket-of-leave man *Br.* a convict released on parole.

ticket pocket *Br.* change pocket (tailor's term).

ticket-tout *Br.* col. /*Am.* **ticket scalper, ticket skinner/** man speculating with theatre tickets.

ticket window *Am.* box office.

ticking-off/ give sb. **a ticking off** *Br.* col. berate sb.

tickler *Am., Can.* a memorandum (book).

tick-tack-toe *Am., Can. /Br., Aus.* **noughts and crosses/** a game in which two players take turns to write 0 or X in a pattern of nine squares trying to win with a row of three 0s or three Xs: *Oh, try mowing tic-tac-toe.* – Reader's Digest.

ticky-tack *Am.* a small house / esp. in California.

ticky-tack(y) *Am., Can.* 1. sl. a shabby material, esp. used in suburban building. 2. adj. shabbily made or done: *ticky-tacky houses and their scrawny trees.* - P. Case, J. Migliore., *suburban ticky-tacky* - Time.

tic-tac-man *Br.* a man at a race-track who (quite legitimately) keeps on-track bookmakers informed of the changing odds by hand signals (**tic-tacs**).

tidbit *Am. /esp. Br.* **titbit/** very little bit.

tiddler *Br.* col. 1. very small fish: *Beluga whales are relative tiddlers measuring about 15 feet.*

- You. 2. small child. 3. something small and unimportant. 4. penny coin.

tiddledywinks *Am.* tiddlywinks: *people could play tiiddledywinks with huge chunks of stone.* - K. Vonnegut, Jr.

tiddl(e)y *Br.* col. 1. obs. also *Aus.* slightly drunk: *You are making us quite tiddly.* - G. Greene. 2. very small.

tideland(s) *Am., Can.* land that is submerged at high tide.

tidemark *Br.* dirty mark left by water, esp. around the inside of a bath or washbasin at the level reached by water.

tide pool *Am.* /*Br.* **rock pool**/.

tidewater *Am.* low coastal land, sea shore, esp. in Eastern Virginia.

tideway *Am.* 1. narrow area of water through which the tide flows. 2. strong current flowing through a tideway.

tidy 1. *esp. Br.* /*Am.* **neat**/ a. (of things) kept neatly arranged and in the right place. b. (of people) neat and clean. 2. *Can.* quick.

tidy/ desk/car/sink tidy *Br.* container for putting small objects, etc. to keep desk, etc. tidy.

tidy/ tidy sum/profit *esp. Br.* col. large amount of money.

tidy smth. **away** *Br.* put things back in the place where they should be.

tidy up/out *Br.* make a place look tidy.

tie, crosstie *Am., Can.* /*esp. Br.* **sleeper**/ heavy piece of wood, metal, supporting a railway track: *The ties began to blur under him.* - E.L. Doctorow.

tie *Am.* lay the ties.

tie 1. *Am.* shoe tied with a lace. 2. *Br.* special match between two or more players or teams in which the winners proceed to the next round of the competition.

tie/ count the ties *Am.* walk on ties.

tie/ tie one on *esp. Am., Can.* col. get drunk: *The boys really tied one on last night* - Longman.

tie into *Am.* col. 1. also *Can.* attack (sb.) forcefully: *You should have seen how our Jim tied into that man!* - Longman. 2. deal with vigorously: *a tribute tied into the twentieth anniversary of his death.* – S Lawrence.

tie oneself **(up) in knots** *Br.* col. become very confused when sb. tries to explain smth.

tie up/ be tied up *esp. Am.* (of traffic) be so blocked that it is almost impossible to move.

tie smth. **up with** another thing *Br.* find the connection between two things.

tie break *Br.* tie breaker, extra playing time at the end of regular game which ended in a draw to decide a winner.

tied *Br.* restricted or limited in some way.

tied cottage/house *Br.* house owned by a farmer and rented to one of his workers for as long as the worker continues to be employed by the farmer.

tied house *Br.* pub that is controlled by a particular beer-making firm, and must sell the beer that the firm makes: *It's not a tied house.* - G. Greene.

tie-in sale *Am.* sale when smth. is added to things bought: *almost every program having product tie-ins of all kinds.* - World Monitor., *As ever, the Colonel was the master of the "tie-in" campaign, the guru of the market blitz.* – J. Hopkins.

tie rod *Am.* track rod.

tie-up *Am.* 1. short interruption in work because of an accident, industrial trouble, etc.: *Strikers menace complete tieup of New York City.* - J. Dos Passos. 2. telecommunication link or network. 3. traffic jam. 4. building where cattle are tied up for the night.

tie-up *Br.* close connection between two or more things, esp. when one causes another.

tiffin *Br.* obs. a light meal taken at midday or in the middle of the morning.

tig *esp. Br.* tag, small part attached to the main body.

tiger 1. *Aus.* Tasmanian wolf. 2. *Br.* a groom in livery, esp. young or small groom. 3. *Am.* extra yell at the end of cheer / esp. in the phr. **three cheers and a tiger.** 4. *Am.* sl. a game of faro.

tiger/ blind tiger *Am.* sl. speakeasy: *Then he went to a blind tiger he knew* - J. Dos Passos.

tiger milk *Am.* sl. raw whiskey, moonshine: *This tiger milk of yours must be doing her pipes a lot of good.* - D. Hammet.

tight/ in the tight *Br.* in close formation or play.

tightly/ not too/very tightly wrapped *Am.* col. be a little crazy or not very smart.

tight-knit *Am.* (of plan) very carefully arranged so that nothing can go wrong.

tights *esp. Br.* also *Am., Aus.* **panty hose** very close fitting garment made of thin material covering the legs and the body worn by acrobats, ballet dancers, etc.: *you kept your leotard and tights, your expensive new toe shoes.* - K. Davis.

tightwad *esp. Am., Aus.* col. derog. person who hates to spend or give money.

tiles/ be/go out on the tiles, have a night on the tiles *esp. Br., Aus.* col. enjoy oneself at the parties or dances.

till *esp. Br.* /*Am.* **register**/ cash register machine.
till/ have one's **hand/finger in the till** *Br.* /*Am.* **caught with** one's **hand in the cookie jar**/ be caught while actually stealing smth. or doing some other misdeed.
tiller *Am.* cultivator.
tilt *Can.* small hut in a forest.
timber *Br.* /*Am.* **lumber**/ wood for building.
timber cruise *Can.* survey of forest area.
timber-getter *Aus.* lumberjack.
timberland *Am., Can.* land covered with forest suitable or managed for timber.
timberline *esp. Am., Can.* tree line, the height above sea level or the distance South or North of the equator beyond which the trees don't grow.
timber merchant, timberyard *Br.* /*Am.* **lumberyard**/ wood store.
time/ at this time *Am.* at the present time, for now.
time/ be (all) out of time *Am., Aus.* col. have no time available.
time/ be before one's **time** *Br.* have new ideas and opinions long before others do.
time/ call time *Br.* tell the customers in a pub that it is time to stop drinking.
time/ have a high (old) time *Br.* obs. have a good time.
time/ Have you got the time? *Br.* /*Am.* **Do you have the time?**/ What time is it?
time/ in a long time *Am.* for a long time.
time/ in your own time *Br.* /*Am.* **on your own time**/ in your free time; outside working hours; without being paid.
time/ make time *Am.* go fast.
time/ not before time (after a statement) *Br., Aus.* emphatic way of saying that smth. should have been done sooner; and about time, too.
time/ on time *Am.* 1. on instalment plan. 2. *Br.* / **in time**/ early or soon enough: *The train which was due at four o'clock arrived exactly on time.* - H.C. Whitford., R.J. Dixson.
time/ sell time *Am.* sell radio or TV time.
time/ What time do you make it? *Br.* /*Am.* **What time do you have?**/ used when asking time from sb. with a watch.
time card *Am.* time sheet, on which employees record the number of hours they worked.
timely/ happen in a timely manner/fashion *esp. Br.* happen quickly.
time-out *esp. Am.* smth. said when a person wants to stop people what they are doing for a short time, esp. when they're having an argument.

times/ four-times champion *Br., Aus.* /*Am.* **four-time champion**/ one who was a champion three times before.
times/ change/keep up/move with the times *Am.* change one's life style to make it more modern.
the times *Br.* on many occasions, e.g. *the times I've told you that.*
time signal, the pips *Br.* series of high-pitched sounds that are broadcast on the radio to mark certain times.
time switch *Br., Aus.* a timer.
timetable *esp. Br., Aus.* /*esp. Am., Can.* **schedule**/ a list of times when classes in a school, collge, etc. are planned to happen, v.
timetable/ be timetabled *esp. Br.* be scheduled to do or happen at a certain time.
tin (of) 1. also **tin can** *Br., Aus., Can.* /*esp. Am., Can.* **can**/ small enclosed metal container in which food or drink is sold or its contents. 2., also **baking tin** *esp. Br.* /*esp. Am.* **pan**/ a metal container in which food is cooked, esp. baked. 3. *esp. Br.* sl. money.
tin *Br., Aus.* /*esp. Am., Can.* **can**/ preserve (esp. food) by packing it in tins, adj. **tinned/canned**.
tin can *Am.* sl. any naval warship, esp. a destroyer.
tin ear/ have a tin ear *Am.* col. be unable to hear the difference between musical notes.
tincture *Br.* col. alcoholic drink.
tin hat *esp. Br.* col. soldier's steel helmet.
tinhorn *Am.* col. a loud-mouthed boaster making fraudulent claims, often used as a tout: *You made the fur fly and you put nine tin-horn grafters in the pen.* - R.P. Warren.
tinhorn gambler *Am.* boastful gambler having no money.
tinker 1. *Br.* col. disobedient or annoying young child. 2. *Am.* a small mortar. 3. *Br.* derog. traveller or gypsy, esp. one who is Irish.
tinker/ have a tinker with smth., like TV, radio, etc. *Br.* try to repair it.
tinker/ not give a tinker's cuss *Br., Aus.* obs. / *Am.* **tinker's damn**/ not be interested at all.
tinkle *Br.* col. a telephone call, **give** sb. **a tinkle**.
tin Lizzie *Am., Can.* col. a cheap car: *we'll push your tin lizzie back on the road* - E.L. Doctorow.
tinned *esp. Br.* canned.
tinner *Br.* a canner (of food).
tinner's shears *Am.* metal shears, tinner's snips.
tinnie *Aus.* can of beer.
tinny *Aus., NZ.* col. lucky.

tin-opener *esp. Br., Aus.* /*esp. Am.* **can-opener**/ apparatus for opening tins: *Stuart dropped the tin-opener and split a plate.* - K. Blair.

tin pants *Am.* lined canvas trousers.

tinpot *esp. Br.* leader, country or government considered to be unimportant and inferior to most others.

Tinseltown *esp. Am.* sl. Hollywood: *Tinseltown regards Greena as an oddball* - New Idea.

tinshears *Am.* /*Br.* **snips**/ scissors that cut metal.

tip, also **refuse tip** 1. *esp. Br., Aus.* /*esp. Am.* **dump, garbage dump**/ large place where unwanted waste is taken and left. 2. *Br.* col. a very dirty or untidy place.

tip *Br.* 1. also *Aus.* pour (a substance) from one container to another, onto a surface, etc. 2. also *Aus.* /*Am., Aus.* **dump**/ (of rubbish) get rid of it by leaving it somewhere. 3. also *Aus.* **be tipped as/for** be thought likely to be.

tip down/ be tipping (it) down, be chucking it down *Br.* col. be raining very hard.

tip up *esp. Am.* col. pay, esp. for drinks: *He generously offered to tip up for the drinks.* - Longman.

tip/ be tipped *Br.* predict as likely to win or achieve smth.

tip/ tip one's **hands** *Am.* col. reveal one's intentions inadvertently.

tip/ tip one's **hat to** *Am.* show great respect to sb.

tip/ tip sb. **the wink** *Br.* col. give sb. private information.

Tipp-Ex *Br.* tdmk. /*esp. Am., Aus.* tdmk. **Liquid paper,** *Am., Aus.* **whiteout**/ white liquid used for painting over mistakes in a piece of writing.

tippex (out) *Br.* cover over a mistake in writing, typing, etc. by using white liquid.

tipple 1. *Am.* /*Br.* **tip**/ an apparatus by which loaded cars are emptied by tipping. 2. *Br.* col. an alcoholic drink that is usu. drunk by sb.

tipple/ favourite tipple *esp. Br.* col. one's favourite alcoholic drink.

tipple down *Br.* col. rain heavily.

tippler *esp. Br.* col. drunkard.

tippy *Am., Can.* inclined to tilt or overturn.

tipsy cake *Br.* sponge cake saturated with wine and spirits, usu. served with custard.

tiptoe/ on one's **tiptoes** *Am., Can.* on tiptoes.

tip-top *Am., Can.* line guide on a fishing rod.

tip truck *esp. Aus.* /*esp. Am.* **dump truck,** *Br.* **tip lorry, tipper (lorry/truck), dumper truck**/; **tipping** (*esp. Br.*), **dumping** (*esp. Am.*).

tip-up *Am., Can.* signalling device attached to the rod, raising a flag when a fish takes the bait.

tip-up seat *Br.* folding seat.

tire *Am.* 1. / *Br., Aus.* **tyre**/. 2. put a tyre on the wheel.

tired/ be tired and emotional *Br., Aus.* be drunk.

tit *Br.* col. a stupid worthless person: *Stuart Hall merely made a right tit of himself.* - T. Thorne.

tit/ get on sb.'s **tits/wick** *Br.* col. annoy sb. a lot.

titbit of information, gossip, news, etc. *esp. Br.* small but interesting piece of information, etc.

titch *Br.* col. humor. derog. small person.

titchy *Br.* col. often. derog. extremely small / **titchy bit** *Br.* just a drop.

titfer *Br.* obs. sl. a hat.

tits and ass *esp. Am., Can.* sl. /*esp. Br.* **tits and bums**/ crudely sexual images of women.

tizwas/ be in a tizwas *Br.* be so worried about a situation so that almost lose control over it.

tizz *esp. Br., Aus.* tizzy, a state of excited worried confusion.

T-junction *Br.* /*Am.* **intersection**/ a place where two roads meet and form the shape of the letter T.

T man *Am.* Treasury man, tax collector from Treasury Department.

tn *Am.* tons.

TO *Am., Can.* Toronto, Ontario.

to Am. col. prep. refers to being in one's place / e.g. *He is to home.*

to American There is nothing to the rumor equals there is nothing in the rumour.; *Am.* I wrote my mother yesterday /*Br.* I wrote to my mother yesterday.

toad-in-the-hole *Br.* savoury food which consists of sausages cooked in a mixture of eggs, milk and flour: *Nigel got thrown out of school diners for swearing at the toad-in-the-hole* – S. Townsend.

toast/ be toast *esp. Am., Can.* col. be (likely to) become finished or dead: *if anyone else tried, he was toast.* – A. Summers, R. Swan.

toast/ have sb. **on toast** *Br.* col. be in a position to deal with sb. as one wishes.

toasted *Am.* sl. drunk: *just enough to go out and get toasted some time* - T. Thorne.

toaster oven *Am.* electric device which can be used to toast or bake food.

toastie, toasty *esp. Br.* a toasted sandwich or snack.

toasty *esp. Am., Can.* comfortably warm.

tobacconist's (shop) *esp. Br.* /*Am.* **cigar store**/ place where tobacco, cigarettes, etc. are sold, **tobacconist** is an owner: *cigar store with a lot of telephone booths on the corner of 42nd and Seventh* - J. Kerouac.

tobacco-road *Am.* rundown rural area.

The Tobacco State *Am.* Kentucky.

toboggan *Can.* handsled.

toby *Am.* 1. col. a long cheap cigar. 2. /*esp. Br.* **toby jug**/ a drinking container shaped like a fat old man wearing a hat with three corners and a smoking pipe.

tod/ **on** one's **tod** *Br.* col. alone, by oneself: *I'd die of shame if we left the poor bastard on his tod.* - F. O'Brien.

today, (tomorrow, etc.)/ (*Br.*) **I'm starting my new job a week today/today week** (=a week from today, tomorrow, etc.).

todger *Br.* col. men's penis.

to-do *Am.* col. /*Br.* col. **do**/.

toe/ **make** sb.'s **toes curl** *Br., Aus.* make sb. feel extremely embarrassed and ashamed for sb. else; adj. col. **toe-curling.**

toe/ **make** sb.'s **toes curl, curl** sb.'s **toes** *Am.* frighten or shock sb.

toe/ **a toe in the water** *esp. Am.* doing smth. new.

toe/ **toe to toe** *esp. Am.* or *Br.* journalism. fight fiercely, openly and directly.

toe/ **tread on** sb.'s **toes** *Br.* /*Am.* **step on** sb.'s **toes**/ offend sb. by criticizing them or doing their job.

toe/ **turn up** one's **toes** *Br.* /*Am.* **go toes up**/ col. humor. die.

toerag *Br.* col. contemptible person.

toey *Aus., NZ.* col. (of a person or animal) nervous or restive.

toff *esp. Br., Aus.* obs. col. derog. a rich and/or well-dressed person of high social class: *I expect he's a proper toff, eh, Mike?* - D. Reeman, also **be toffed up** be dressed up.

toffee/ **for toffee,** also **for nuts** *Br.* col. (esp. after can't) at all.

toffee apple *Br.* apple coated with a thin layer of toffee and fixed on a stick.

toffee-nosed *esp. Br., Aus.* col. haughty: *He wasn't toffee-nosed sort like most doctors.* – R. Westall.

toft *Br.* a site for dwelling and its outbuilding homestead.

tog *Br.* official measurement showing how warm a blanket or quilt is.

(**swimming**) **togs** *Aus.* col. bathing suit or trunks.

tohubohu *esp. Am., Can.* col. state of chaos.

toilet *esp. Br.* a room containing a toilet. / In British English **toilet** is generally acceptable, but **lavatory** and **WC** (becoming old-fashioned except when talking about the plans of houses) are also used, esp. in the phr. **go to the toilet.** **Loo** is a fairly common informal word. In American English **bathroom, restroom,** and **washroom** are commonly used for toilet, and **John** is a common informal word.

toilet/ **go to the toilet** *Br.* urinate or defecate.

toilet bag, sponge bag *Br.* waterproof bag for toothbrush, soap, etc. for a traveller.

toilet roll *Br., Aus.* a long narrow length of toilet paper rolled around a small tube.

toiletry *Am.* toiletries: *Went shopping for new dressing gown, slippers, pyjamas and toiletries.* – S. Townsend.

token/ **book, record, gift,** etc. *Br., Aus.* /*Am.* **gift certificate**/ token that you can exchange for a book, record, etc. in a shop, given to sb. as a present.

told/ sb. **won't be told** *Br.* col. some people always refuse to listen to other people's advice.

toll *Am., Can.* a charge for a long distance call.

toll *Am.* allure, entice (esp. a wild game to approach).

toll booth *Am.* toll gate at the start of the road at which you pay to be allowed to drive through.

toll call *Am.* long distance call: *There were several toll calls on our last month's telephone bill.* - H.C. Whitford., R.J. Dixson.

tolled (motorway) *Br.* one which you pay to use.

toll-free *Am.* /*Br.* **freefone**/ adj. (of a telephone call) paid for by the organisation receiving it rather than the person making it.

toll house cookie *Am.* sweet biscuit made from flour, brown sugar, chocolate chips and chopped nuts.

toll line *Am.* long distance line.

tol-lol *Br.* col. so-and-so, fair-to-middling.

toll plaza *Am.* row of tollbooths on a toll road: *Winding up in the fastest-moving lane at a toll plaza may seem like serendipity* – Reader's Digest.

toll road, toll motorway *Br.* /*Can.* **toll highway,** *Am.* **turnpike**/ a road which people have to pay to drive on.

tollway *Am.* highway for the use of which a charge is made.

Tom *Am.* col. n. v. Uncle Tom; betray the interests of Negroes: *they are often reviled as Toms by some black nationalists* – N. Hentoff. **-ism** n.

tom *Br.* female prostitute.

tomahawk 1. *Aus.* cut a sheep while shearing it. 2. *Aus., NZ.* hatchet.

Tom and Jerry *Am.* a hot drink from sugar, eggs, spices and water or milk.

tombola *esp. Br., Aus.* lottery at a social function.

Tom Collins *Am.* long iced drink of gin, lemon juice, soda and sugar, popular in the summertime: *One strong Tom Collins in that desert on an empty stomach.* - A.E. Hotchner.

Tommy *esp. Br.* col. 1. loaf of bread. 2. food, provision, esp. worker's food.

tomorrow week/a week tomorrow *Br.* a week from tomorrow.

ton *esp. Br.* col. a hundred (esp. speed or score), **do a ton** *Br.* col. drive at 100mph.

ton/ hit sb. **like a ton of bricks** *Am.* col. surprise or shock sb. very much.

tone *esp. Am.* note, single musical sound of a particular length and degree of highness or lowness.

tone/ dial/busy tone *Am.* /*Br.* **dialling/engaged tone**/.

tone in *esp. Br.* tone, look nice together.

tong *Am.* secret Chinese organisation in the US, esp. a criminal one: *a tong war broke out.* – J. O'Hara.

tongue/ find one's **tongue** *Br.* begin speaking at last after a shock; opp. **have lost** one's **tongue.**

tongue/ get one's **tongue round** smth. *Br.* pronounce smth. with difficulty.

tongue/ give sb. **the rough side of** one's **tongue, give** sb. **a tongue-lashing** *Br.* obs. berate them harshly.

tongue depressor *Am.* a /*Br.* **spatula**/ doctor's spatula.

tonic *Am.* flavoured carbonated water.

ton-up *Br.* col. 1. a speed of 100 mph. 2. a score of 100.

ton-up driver/biker, etc. *Br.* obs. sb. who likes to drive very fast.

tony *Am., Can.* col. ritzy, fashionable: *But Paul Castelliano...was murdered on the tony East Side.* - J. O'Brien, A. Kurins., *an apartment in a tony West Side building.* - D. Mortman.

too *esp. Am.* col. in fact.

tool/ (lay) down tools *esp. Br., Aus.* refuse to work, esp. because you're not satisfied with your pay or working conditions.

tool along/down *Am.* col. drive along a street esp. for fun.

tool up, be tooled up *Br.* col. be or become armed, esp. for a crime.

tooling print. *Am.* /*Br.* **blocking**/.

toot 1. *esp. Am., Can.* col. a spree: *During our toots we concocted the best drink I ever tasted* - E. Taylor., *Bobby was off on a toot with some other girl.* - A. Scaduto. 2. *esp. Am.* col. snort (cocaine). 3. *esp. Br.* (of a car) horn, make a short, high sound.

toot *Aus.* sl. toilet.

toot one's **own horn** *Am., Can.* boast: *You'll never hear him toot his own horn* - J. Kellerman.

tooth/ have a tooth out *Br.* /*Am.* **have a tooth pulled**/ remove a tooth.

tooth/ nature red in tooth and claw *Br.* used to say how harsh and violent the world outside can be.

toothful *Br.* col. thimbleful, very small drink.

tootin' *Am., Can.* col. (used for emphasis) great; right: *You're damn tootin'* – R. Brautigan.

tootle (somewhere) *esp. Br.* go or drive in unhurried manner.

tootle *Br.* play musical instrument such as flute without producing any particular tune.

toots(ie) 1. *esp. Am.* darling: *It's me, tootsie.* - L. Waller. 2. *esp. Am.* col. a woman: *is some tootsie nestled beside you in her underwear?* – P. Roth.

top *Br.* 1. the best: *George was bottom of the class and I was top.* - Longman. 2. the maximum gear.

top/ *Br.* (of a street, garden, bed or table) the end of it that is furthest away from where you usu. enter it or from where you are: *there was a "summer house" at the top of the garden.* - C. Hoover.

top (oneself) *Br.* sl. kill, esp. oneself.

top/ from top to toe *esp. Br.* /*Am.* **head-to toe**/ the whole body.

top/ the top of the tree *Br., Aus.* at the highest position in their job or organisation.

top/ off one's **top** *Br.* col. derog. not reasonable.

top/ (go)/be over the top, (go) OTT *esp. Br., Aus.* col. (be) more than is reasonable, sensible or proper: *Some of it is so over the top* - New York., *the word idyllic sounds over the top.* - Guideposts.

top/ be over the top *Am.* win.

top/ not have much up top *Br.* col. be not very intelligent.

top/ push/put sb. **over the top** *Am.* make sb. succeed much better than others.

top/ sleep like a top *Br.* sleep very deeply and well.

top/ the top and bottom of *Br.* col. general result or meaning of a situation, esp. made in a few words.

top/ the top of the milk *Br.* creamy part that rises to the top of a bottle of milk.

top/ top whack *Br.* col. at most, at the highest.

top and tail *Br.* take off both ends of (plants, etc.).

top smth. **off** *esp. Am.* 1. also *Aus., Can.* complete successfully by a last action: *And to top it all off, there is an array of cosmetic services available*

- Bulletin. 2. top out, complete the building of (a large building) esp. with a special ceremony: *Has the tower been topped off yet?* - Longman. 3. supply (smth.) again, esp. fill up a fuel tank: *Does the car need topping off?* - Longman.

top it all off *Am., Aus.* top it all.

top out *esp. Am.* reach a top mark: *The rise in prices seems to have topped out* - Longman.

top up *esp. Br.* 1. also *Can.* (with). a. fill (a partly empty container) with liquid. b. col. put more drink into (a person's glass): *Let me top up your drink, it's half gone.* - Longman. 2. complete or bring to an acceptable level by adding smth.: *Does the car need topping up?* - Longman.

top banana *Am.* sl. the chief, boss: *Phil has always been the top banana in our club.* - H.C. Whitford., R.J. Dixson.

top dollar *Am., Can.* col. the highest rate or price: *firms...will pay top dollar for the names and addresses* - Time., *Top dollar paid for your used Channel* - New York.

top-down *Br.* (of plan) having a general idea with details added later.

the top drawer *esp. Br.* the best of their kind.

top drawer/ from/out of the top drawer *esp. Br.* from a privileged social background.

The Top End *Aus.* Northern Territory.

topfruit *Br.* fruit grown on trees rather than bushes.

top gear *Br.* /*Am.* **high gear**/.

top-hole *esp. Br.* obs. excellent, first-rate.

top-kick, also **top sergeant** *Am.* sl. 1. first sergeant: *He fell in his men in two ranks, haranguing them like an old army topkick.* - K. Vonnegut, Jr. 2. leader.

top liner *Am.* (movie) star.

topo *esp. Am., Can.* col. topographic map.

topper *Am.* 1. protective cover mounted on the back or bed of a pick-up truck. 2. camper van mounted on a truck bed.

topping 1. *esp. Br.* obs. col. excellent: *They are quite the topping people of the place.* - Cpt. Marryat., *Oh, Nancy, how topping!* - E.M. Forster., *He felt topping about it.* - E. Hemingway. 2. *Am.* snobbish.

tops *Br.* col. the highest possible amount (of money).

topside *Br.* /*Am.* **top round**/ joint of beef that is cut from the upper part of the leg, that is usu. cooked by roasting.

Topsider *Am.* tdmk. casual shoe of leather or canvas with a rubber sole designed to be worn on boats.

topside(s) *Am.* towards or onto the deck of a boat or ship.

top table *Br.* /*Am.* **head table**/ a table at a formal meal, e.g. at a wedding for important people.

top-up *Br.* 1. some amount added to restore smth. to a former level. 2. (loan or payment) one that is added to an amount of money in order to bring it up to a regular level.

topwater fishing *Am., Can.* (of a bait) floating on or near the top of the water.

top whack *Br.* col. at the most.

toque, tuque *Can.* knitted stocking cap: *Toques off to owner Tony May* - New York.

tor *esp. Br.* (the top of) a high rocky hill.

torch 1. *Br., Aus.* /*esp. Am., Can.* **flashlight**/ a small electric light carried in the hand: *One of the boys brought a flashlight (torch as Gill also called it)* – F. Edwards. 2. *Am.* blow lamp: *The white-hot torch cut steel.* - T. Murphy. 3. *Am.* sl. arsonist: *she hired a torch to burn your house.* - H. Fast.

torch *Am.* 1. catch (fish, etc.) at night. 2. also *Aus.* set fire to: *arsonists torched one of the large office buildings* - Nation's Restaurant News.

torch/ carry a torch for sb. *esp. Am.* feel love to people one cannot have a relationship with.

torch light *Am.* light produced by a torch.

torchy *Am.* moody, sad (about a song).

toreador pants *esp. Am.* women's tight-fitting calf-length trousers.

torn/ that's torn it *Br.* col. used when smth. prevents sb. to do their job.

torpedo *Am.* 1. explosive set off in an oil well to increase its flow. 2. sl. professional gunman or assassin: *There's yellow cops and there's yellow torpedoes* - R. Chandler. 3. sl. Hero sandwich. 4. railway fog signal. 5. firework exploding on impact with a hard surface.

torrid/ (give)/have (sb.) **torrid time** *Br., Aus.* journalism. (cause sb. to) experience a lot of difficulties.

tortoise *Aus.* freshwater turtle.

tosh *Br.* 1. sl. nonsense: *all been boosted with much tosh about ultimate answers.* - Economist. 2. col. used as a form of casual address to unknown person.

toss *Am., Can.* search (a place).

toss *Aus.* sl. v. defeat.

toss/ argue the toss *esp. Br., Aus.* col. waste time disagreeing with a decision or statement.

toss/ not care/give a toss *Br.* col. not care at all.

toss/ toss one's **cookies** *Am., Can.* col. vomit.

toss *Br.* sl. (usu. in negatives) the least amount, anything.

toss (up) *esp. Br.* /*Am.* **flip**/ throw a coin up and make it spin, then see which side it lands on as a way of deciding smth.

toss off *esp. Br., Aus.* taboo. sl. masturbate: *They had been taking turns to toss each other off.* - Longman.

toss-and-catch *Am.* pitch-and-toss.

toss/ win/lose the toss *esp. Br.* win or lose the right to make a choice at the beginning of a game or race according to the result of taking a coin.

tosser *Br.* sl. stupid person.

toss-up *Br.* an act of tossing a coin in order to decide smth.

tot *esp. Br.* a small amount of alcoholic drink.

tot up 1. *esp. Br.* reach a total. 2. *Br.* col. salvage saleable items from dust bins or rubbish heaps.

total *Am.* col. damage a car so badly that it cannot be repaired: *The car was totalled.* - R.A. Spears.

tote *esp. Am., Can.* col. 1. carry esp. with difficulty. 2. have and use (esp. a gun) habitually: *Boujedra...totes a Beretta pistol* - Time.

the Tote, totalizator *Br.* /*Am.* **parimutuel**/ a system of betting money on horses at a racetrack.

tote bag *esp. Am.* a shopping bag, esp. a large handbag /*esp. Br.* **holdall**/: *he saw an actress clutching a tote* - New York., *I pulled the Stevie Wonder album out of my tote bag* – S. Lawrence

tote box *Am.* box or container for carrying or storing materials: *her arms weighted down by shopping totes.* - D. Mortman.

totem/ low man on the totem pole *Am.* sb. of low rank in an organisation or business.

tote road *Am., Can.* driveway.

tottie *Br.* sl pretty girl: *A nice little tottie.* - T. Thorne.

totting-up *Br.* accumulation of penalty points on sb.'s driving licence.

totty *Br.* col. girls collectively regarded as sexually desirable.

touch (a certain level) *esp. Br.* reach it.

touch/ kick smth. **into touch** *esp. Br.* reject.

touch/ put the finishing touches on *Am.* do the last few things to complete smth.

touch base *Am.* talk to sb. for a short time, esp. about smth. you're both working on: *You said you needed to touch base with me* - K. Ablow.

touch paper/ light the (blue) touch paper *Br.* do smth. which makes other people angry.

touch wood *esp. Br., Can.* /*esp. Am., Can.* **knock on wood**/ (used as if to keep away bad luck, so that smth. good may happen.).

touch off *Am.* describe (usu. smth.) exactly or suitably: *The newspaper reports have really touched off the causes of the difficulty this time.* - Longman.

touch up *Am.* urge (usu. a horse) to go faster with or as with a light touch of a whip or waken (sb.) with a light blow: *You can make the men hurry by touching them up as you pass.* - Longman.

touch sb. **up** *Br.* /*Am.* **feel** sb. **up**/ touch sb. in a sexual way without their consent.

touch dancing *esp. Am.* dirty dancing.

touch football *Br., Aus.* an informal type of football in which play stops if a player puts one's hand onto the person who has the ball.

touchline *Br.* /*Am.* **sideline**/ one of two lines marking the long edges of the area in which playing games are played.

tough *esp. Am.* col. a violent person.

tough cookie *Am., Aus.* col. sb. who is very determined to do what they want and who usu. succeed even in difficult situations.

tough/ be as tough as shoe leather *Am.* difficult to cut or to eat (of food).

tough/ (be) tough as old boots *Br.* (be) very strong and independent.

tough/ hang tough *Am.* col. not change one's actions or opinions although other people try to make you do this.

tough/ that's a bit tough *Br.* tough luck.

tough guy *Am.* sl. hoodlum: *My boss there was one of the toughest guys* - K. Vonnegut, Jr.

tough love 1. *esp. Am.* a method of helping sb. to change their behaviour by treating them in a very severe way. 2. *Am., Can.* policy designed to encourage self-help by restricting state benefits.

tough luck *Br.* used when sb. feels sympathy about smth. bad that happened to sb.

tough titties *Br.* col. hard luck.

tour/ tour round smth. (such as city) *Br.* tour around smth.

tourist *Br., Aus.* a member of a sports team playing games in foreign countries.

(the) touristas *Am.* diarrhoea.

tourist court *Am.* motel.

tourist home *Am.* a house with rooms for rent to tourists.

tourney *Am.* tournament.

tour operator *Br.* company that arranges travel tours.

tout 1. also **ticket tout** *Br.* /*Am.* **scalper**/ derog. tickets speculator: *one could do better with black market touts in hotel lavatories.* - A. Burgess. 2. *esp. Br.* v. n. (be) a person who spies out information about race horses for use in betting. 3. *Am.* advertise one's candidate. 4. *Am.* offer racing tips for a share of any resulting winnings. 5. *esp. Br.* try to persuade people to buy goods and services (**tout business/custom**).

tow/ be on tow *Br. /Am.* **in tow,** *Aus.* **under tow/** being pulled along by another car.

towards *esp. Br. /Am.* **toward/**.

towaway zone *Am.* area where cars aren't allowed to park and from which they can be taken away by the police.

towel *esp. Aus., NZ.* col. thrash or beat sb.

towel (down) *Am.* dry oneself using a towel.

towelling *Br. /Am.* **terrycloth/**.

towel rail *Br., Aus. /Am.* **towel rack/** rail for towels in a bathroom, often heated one.

towel roll *Am. /Br.* **roller towel/**.

tower block (of flats) *esp. Br. /Am.* **high-riser, high rise apartment/** a tall block of flats or offices: *it built vast estates of shiny tower blocks* - B. Bryson.

tower man *Am. /Br.* **signalman/** person who controls railway traffic and signals.

towie *Aus.* the driver of a breakdown lorry.

town 1. *Am., Can.* township, a division of a county with some corporate powers. 2. *esp. Am.* the place where you live or work. 3. *Am. /Br.* **village/** several houses forming a small group around a church, shops, etc.

town and gown *Br.* situation in which people living in town and the students in a town seem to be separate and opposing groups.

town car *Am.* limousine.

town centre *Br. /Am., Can.* **downtown/** (the) town, part of the town where the main shops are.

town clerk *Am.* public official in charge of the records of a town.

town council *Br.* council responsible for public areas and services, such as roads, parks, etc.

town house *Am.* terrace-house.

town mayor *Br.* chairperson of a town council.

town meeting *Am.* gathering of the people who live or pay taxes in a town, for the purpose of governing the town.

town/ on the town *Am.* getting unemployment benefit: *the family has been on the town for years.* - A. Makkai.

town/ toy town *esp. Br.* smth. silly, childish or worthless.

townie *Br. /Aus.* **cityslicker/** person who lives in a town and has no experience or knowledge about living in the countryside.

township 1. *Am., Can.* an area of land, esp. part of a country which is organised as a unit of local government. 2. *Aus., NZ.* small town.

tow truck, repair truck *Am., Aus. /Br.* **breakdown van, truck, lorry/** emergency repairs truck: *The salesman called for a tow truck.* - Reader's Digest.

toy/ soft/cuddly toy *Br.* one that looks like an animal and is covered in fur.

toy boy *Br. /Am.* **boy toy/** col. an attractive young man who is kept as a lover boy by an older person.

toy bricks *Br. /Am.* **blocks/**.

trace *Am.* (beaten) path or small road.

traces/ kick over the traces *Br., Aus.* do what you want and not show any respect for authority.

traces/ work in traces *Am.* work according to plan, work systematically.

track *esp. Am.* 1. the sport of running on a track: *Thurman playing football and baseball and basketball and track for the Lankaster Wildcats.* - R. Crais. 2. **track (and field)** */ Br.* **athletics/** all the sports in an athletic competition such as running, jumping or throwing a javelin: *steroid scandals rock professional sports and the international track circuit.* – Reader's Digest.

track *esp. Am. /esp. Br.* **line/** railroad track.

track *Am. /Br.* **stream/**.

track/ have the inside track *esp. Am.* journalism. 1. */Br.* **be on the inside track/** have special knowledge about smth. 2. be the most likely candidate for a job.

track smth. **in** *Am., Can.* leave a trail of dirt and debris or snow from one's feet.

track up *esp. Am., Can.* col. make (usu. a floor) dirty with one's shoes: *I don't want your children tracking up my nice clean floor!* - Longman.

track with *Aus.* col. carry on a romantic or sexual relationship with.

trackage *Am., Can.* 1. lines of railway tracks: *they want some new trackage to take the place of the old siding.* - J. O'Hara. 2. a. a right to use the tracks or another road. b. the charge for using this road.

tracker/ black tracker *Aus.* Aborigine used by police to catch criminals.

tracker/ police tracker dog *Am.* dog used by police to help investigate crimes.

track event *Am.* running race.

tracking *Am. /Br.* **streaming/** a level of ability within a group of pupils of the same age (**track/ stream**).

tracklayer *Am., Can. /Br.* **platelayer/** workman who builds or repairs railway tracks.

track meet *Am.* a sports contest between teams, in which races, as well as jumping and throwing competitions are held.

Track One *Can. sl.* brothels district of a town.
Track Two *Can. sl.* the homosexual quarter of the city.
tracksuit *Br.* /*Am.* **sweatsuit**/ loose clothes, used esp. for sports.
track system, also **tracking** *Am.* /*Br.* **streaming**/ an education system of students grouped according to their ability or aptitude as shown in standardised tests.
tract *Am.* a measured area of land issued for a particular purpose, such as building houses or digging for oil.
tract house *Am.* one of a large group of houses built on a single area of land: *Kerry lived up in the hills in a modest, two-family tract house, part of a development that was never finished.* – R.L. Stine.
traction *Am.* urban transport.
tractor-trailer *Am.* /*Br.* **articulated lorry.** *Br.* col. **artic**/ truck with a trailer.
trackwalker, also **trackworker** *Am.* /*Br.* **platelayer**/ linesman: *Imagine his nerve and him a miserable trackwalker.* - J. Dos Passos.
trackway *Am.* tramway.
trad *esp. Br., Aus.* col. traditional.
trade (with) 1. *esp. Am.* give smth. to sb. in exchange for smth. else, e.g. **trade** blows, insults, jokes. 2. *Am., Can.* transfer (a player) to another club or team.
trade 1. *Am.* a change, transaction. 2. **the trade** *Br.* people licensed to sell alcoholic drink.
trade (at, with) *Am.* shop regularly.
trade down (or **up**) *esp. Am.* exchange (goods) for smth. of a lower (or higher) value: *It's unusual to trade your existing car down* - Longman.
trade up *Am. sl.* climb socially: *the bohemian moviemaker is very quietly trading up to a rumored $3 million pad in Bel-Air* - New York.
trade card *Br.* business card.
trade-in *Am.* /*Br.* **part-exchange**/; also **trade-in price/value/figure.**
trade(s) directory book *Br.* yellow pages.
trade plates *Br.* temporary number plates used by car dealers or manufacturers on unlicensed cars.
trade price *Br.* /*Am., Aus.* **wholesale**/ a price at which goods are sold to shops by the people who produce them.
trade school *Am.* /*Aus.* **technical school**/ an industrial school: *I am a high school graduate and a trade school graduate.* - H. Fast.
trade show *Am.* trade fair.
tradesman 1. *Br.* person who brings goods to people's houses, or has a shop. 2. *esp. Am.* sb. who works at a job or trade that involves skill with one's hands.
trade(s) union *Br.* /*Am.* **labor union**/ an organisation of workers, esp. in a particular trade or profession, formed to represent their interests and deal as a group with employers.
trading estate *Br.* /*Br.* **industrial estate,** *Am.* **industrial park**/ specially designated industrial and commercial area, often at the edge of a city.
trading vehicle *Br.* commercial vehicle.
traffic block *Br.* traffic jam.
traffic calmed, traffic calming *Br.* (of roads) having raised areas built across them or small roundabouts or other similar structures so that vehicles are forced to move more slowly along them.
traffic circle, also **rotary** *Am., Can.* /*Br., Aus.* **roundabout, circus**/ a central space at a road crossing, which makes cars go in a circle round it and not straight across: *Route 6 came over the river, wound around a traffic circle, and disappeared into the wilderness.* - J. Kerouac.
traffic cops *Am.* 1. traffic police officer who stands in the road and directs traffic. 2. police officer who stops drivers who drive in an illegal way.
traffic court *Am.* court in a town or city in the US which takes cases involving illegal wrongdoings made while driving.
traffic hub *Am., Can.* /*Br.* **circus**/.
traffic island *Am.* /*Br.* **central reservation**/.
traffic pattern *esp. Am., Can.* pattern in the air above an airport of permitted lanes for an aircraft to follow after taking off or prior to landing.
traffic school *Am.* class that teaches sb. about driving laws that they can go to instead of paying money for smth. they've done wrong while driving.
traffic warden *esp. Br.* /*Am.* **parking policeman, meter maid**/ official responsible for controlling the parking vehicles.
trailer 1. *Am.* /*Br.* **caravan**/ vehicle which can be pulled by a car and which contains cooking and sleeping equipment and in which people live (often in **caravan sites**) or travel usu. for holidays: *They are not trailers to be pulled by one's own car* - J. Steinbeck., *we peer out at a parking lot full of cars and vans and trailers.* - J. Baez. 2. *esp. Br.* advertisement of a new film or TV show usu. consisting of small scenes taken from it.
trailer park, court or **camp** *Am., Can.* /*Br.* **caravan site**/ mobile home camp: *I did the laundry in the trailer court's community washhouse.* - A.E. Hotchner.

trailer park *Am.* lacking refinement, taste, or quality; coarse.

trailer truck *Am.* articulated lorry.

train/ One travels in (or *esp. Am.* **on**) a train, bus, plane, boat, ship, etc.

train/ be in train, set in train (of a process) *esp. Br.* happen or start to happen.

train sb. **up** *Br.* col. teach sb. the necessary new skills.

train (with) *Am.* col. associate with.

train butcher *Am.* train peddler.

train dispatcher *Am.* /*Br.* **signalman**/ one who controls railway traffic and signals.

trainer, training shoe, gym shoe *Br.* /*Am., Aus.* **running shoe, sneaker,** *Am.* **gumshoes**/ a strong shoe for sports that gives extra support for the foot.

training college *Br.* a college, usu. for adults that gives specialised instruction.

training wheels *Am., Can.* a pair of small supporting wheels fitted on either side of the rear wheel of a child's bicycle.

trainman *Am.* a man who works on a railway train / there is **rear** and **head (front) trainman** (formerly called **brakeman**): *Fanucci's apartment house was occupied mostly by bachelor trainmen* - M. Puzo.

trainmaster *Am.* chief conductor on a train: *Immediately, she phoned Richie Mpran, PATH's train master on duty.* – Reader's Digest.

train schedule *Am.* official timetable, official railway guide.

train set *Br.* a set of trains, tracks and other things making up a child's model railway.

trainspotter *Br.* 1. person whose hobby is collecting the numbers that each railway has by writing them down when they see them. 2. sb. who one thinks is boring and only interested in unimportant details.

trainspotter *Br.* sl. derog. an obsessive follower of any minority interest or specialised hobby: *He wasn't just a train-spotter, but a train-talker* - B. Bryson.

train station *Am.* /*esp. Br.* **railway station**/: *Tanya...buys a copy of Working Commuter at the train station every morning.* - McGraw-Hill, 1990.

tram(car) *esp. Br., Aus.* /*Am.* usu. **streetcar, trolley**/ tram: *I stick to the road like a tramcar* - J. Aldridge.

tramline, also **tramway** *Br.* /*Am.* **streetcar line**/ the metal tracks set in the road along which a tram runs: *change is the only way forward for a tramlined society* - C. Handy.

tramlines *Br.* col. two parallel painted lines along the edge of the playing area used in tennis and badminton, a player loses a point if they hit the ball so that it lands between them, except if it's a game when four players are playing.

trammel *Am.* a hook in a fireplace for a kettle.

trammy *Aus.* col. ticket collector in a tram.

tramp 1. *esp. Br.* often derog. person with no home or job, who wanders from place to place and usu. begs for food or money. 2. *esp. Am.* col. derog. immoral woman: *That's the way tramps talk.* - A. Burgess.

tramway 1. *Am.* cable car system by which suspended cars carry ore. 2. *Br.* set of rails which forms the route for a tram.

tranny 1. *Br.* sl. transport cafe. 2. *Am., Can.* col. automobile transmission: *When you buy a used a car, check the condition of the tranny, eh.* - W. Magnuson. 3. *esp. Br., Aus.* col. transistor: *Now lean closer to your trannie.* - T. Thorne.

transatlantic *Br.* used to smth. that happens, exists or originates in the USA.

transceiver *Am.* combined transmitter and receiver.

transcript *Am., Can.* official record of a student's work showing courses taken and grades achieved.

transfer 1. *esp. Br.* /*esp. Am.* **decal**/ drawing pattern, etc. for sticking onto a surface. 2. *esp. Am.* ticket allowing a passenger to change from one bus, train, etc. to another without paying more money. 3. *Br.* reverse (of telephone charge).

transferred charge call *Br.* /*Am.* **collect call**/ reversed charge call.

transfer fee *Br.* amount of money a sports team plays in order to buy a new player from another team.

transfer list/ be on the transfer list *Br.* be offered to be sold to another team, v. **transfer-list.**

transient 1. *esp. Am.* /*Br.* **temporary guest**/ a guest who stays in a hotel for only a short time: *The transients drain the residue of bottles.* - J.P. Donleavy., *he has remained a transient on a refugee's passport* - Time. 2. *Am* tramp.

transit *Am., Can.* 1. urban transit: *another student of management innovation, as transit-police chief.* - New York. 2. a system of moving goods and people from one place to another, esp. by buses and trains.

transit camp *esp. Br.* camp for refugees.

transom (window) *Am.* /*Br.* **fanlight**/ small window over a door or large window: *deceptions* *that look truthful and speed across the digital transom* – Reader's Digest.

transportation 1. *esp. Am.* /*Br.* **transport**/ the act of transporting or of being transported. 2. *esp. Am.* means or system of carrying passengers or goods from one place to another, esp. by buses or trains: *the transportation system will have to be beefed up* - J. Riffkin, T. Howard. 3. *Am.* (railway, tram, etc.) ticket. 4. *Am.* cost of transportation.

transport cafe *Br.* /*Am., Aus.* **truck stop**/ cheap eating place on a main road used mainly by long-distance heavy-vehicle drivers: *There was a transport cafe opposite.* - J. Higgins.

trap *Am., Can.* basalt.

trap *Am.* place on a golf course where there is sand and from which it is difficult to hit the ball; bunker.

trapdoor spider *Aus.* funnel-web spider.

trapezium *Br., Aus.* /*Am., Can.* **trapezoid**/ tech. (in mathematics) four-sided shape in which only one pair of sides is parallel.

trapezoid *Br.* /*Am., Can.* **trapezium**/ tech. four-sided shape in which no sides are parallel: *They forced him to swallow a small trapezoid* - K. Vonnegut, Jr.

trap line *Am., Can.* series of game traps.

traps *Am.* drums.

trap shooting *Am., Can.* sport of shooting at clay pigeons released from a sporting trap.

trash 1. also **garbage,** /*esp. Br.* **(dry) rubbish, refuse**/ *esp. Am., Can.* waste material to be thrown away, rubbish: *Anguilo treated the citation as trash, he crumpled it and chew it aside.* - G. O'Neill, D. Lehr., *You don't build no fires and don't throw out no trash.* - J. Steinbeck., *janitor no longer found enough empty bottles to make a twice daily trash-run into town.* - Time. 2. *esp. Am., Aus.* col. derog. a worthless person or people: *But she's a useless piece of trash.* - K. Davis. 3. *Am.* sl. a lap-top computer. 4. *Br.* (of books, films, etc.) smth. of bad quality.

trash (people or their ideas) *esp. Am.* criticise them severely, saying that they are worthless.

trash *esp. Am., Can.* col. damage or wreck: *she was aware that Janie had "absolutely trashed" her in trial deposition* – S. Lawrence.

trash/ talk trash *Am.* col. talk nonsense.

trash bin, can, garbage can 1. *Am., Can.* /*Br.* **dust bin**/ waste bin: *her purse was found in a trash can* - Reader's Digest., *I left it in the trash can.* - New Yorker. 2. *Am., Can.* /*Br.* **litter bin**/ container for waste paper in a public place.

trash bag *Am.* /*Br.* **dustbin bag**/.

trash can liner *Am.* /*Br.* **dust bin liner**/.

trash compactor *Am.* machine that presses waste material together into a very small mass.

trashed *Am.* col. 1. very drunk. 2. completely destroyed.

trasher *Am.* sl. person who engages in vandalism.

trash talk *Am.* col. insulting or boastful speech used to demoralize an opponent.

travel (through a lot of things) *Br.* search through them looking for smth. that one needs.

travelling salesman *Am.* /*Am.* col. **drummer,** *Br.* obs. **commercial traveller, bag man**/.

traveller *esp. Br.* gypsy.

traveller/ (New Age) travellers *Br.* homeless or jobless people living in vehicles.

travelling allowance *Br.* mileage, transportation.

travelling post office *Br.* railway carriage in which mail in transit is sorted out and classified.

travelling rug, also **carriage rug** *Br.* lap robe.

travois *Can.* Indians' wagon.

trawl line *Am., Can.* trawl, also long fishing line to which many smaller fishing lines are fastened.

tray/ in-tray *Br., esp. Br.* **tray** /*Am.* **in-box**/ tray used for putting the incoming mail on in an office: *I checked his desk drawers and his "in" and "out" boxes* - S. Grafton.

tray/ baking tray *Br.* /*Am.* **cupcake tin**/ one used in baking.

treacle *esp. Br.* /*Am.* **molasses**/ very thick sticky dark liquid made from sugar: *- helpless as a fly in a treacle* - A. Christie.

tread *esp. Br.* /*Am.* **track**/ put one's foot on smth. or crush smth. by foot.

tread/ be treading on thin ice *Br.* be in a precarious situation.

treasure *esp. Br.* col. affectionate way of addressing sb., esp. a child.

The Treasure State *Am.* Montana.

treasure trove *Br.* law. valuable objects, coins, etc. that are found where they have been hidden and buried and which are not claimed by anyone.

Treasury note *Am.* a note used by the Treasury for use as currency.

treat/ go down a treat *Br., Aus.* col. enjoy smth. very much, be much liked by people.

treat/ look/work a treat *Br., Aus.* col. be very effective.

treaty Indian *Can.* North American Indian whose people have signed a treaty with the government.

treaty money *Am., Can.* annual payment to (treaty) Indians.

treble/ double and **treble** are used in giving telephone numbers and in stamps in Britain.

treble *Br.* 1. three sports victories or championships in the same season, event, etc. 2. system of betting in which the winnings and stake from the first bet are transferred to the second and then (if successful) to a third.

treble chance *Br.* form of football pool in which different numbers or points are awarded for a draw, an away win, and a home win.

tree *esp. Am.* col. force (sb.) into a difficult situation.

tree/ be up a tree *esp. Am., Ca. col. /Br., Aus.* col. **be up a gum tree/** be in a very difficult situation.

tree/ can't see the wood for the trees *Br., Aus. /Am.* **can't see the forest for the trees/** be too involved in details to realize the real purpose or importance of the thing as a whole: *so "close" that one cannot see the wood for the trees or the trees for the leaves* – V.W. Brooks.

tree/ not grow on trees *Br.* very difficult to obtain.

tree/ out of one's **tree** *esp. Am., Can.* col. completely stupid; mad.

The Tree Planting State *Am.* Nebraska.

trees/ can't see the forests for the trees *Am., Aus.* be unable to understand what's important in a situation because of giving too much attention to details.

trembler *Br.* automatic vibrator for making or breaking an electric circuit, often used as a fuse for an explosive device sensitive to physical disturbance.

trembles *Am.* 1. cattle and sheep disease. 2. milk sickness.

trencher *Aus.* mortarboard, a black hat with a square flat top worn on formal occasions by some teachers or students of college or university, formerly worn by school teachers.

trendy *Br.* person who wants other people to think they are very modern.

trestle *esp. Br.* A-shaped frame used as one of the two supports for a temporary table (**trestle table**).

trews *esp. Br.* trousers.

trey *Am.* 1. (basketball) a shot scoring 3 points. 2. card or the side of a dice with three marks on it.

trial/ offer smth. **on trial** *Br. /Am.* **on a trial basis/** offer smth on the basis that if a person doesn't like it they could always give it back.

trial balloon *esp. Am.* suggested idea.

trial court *esp. Am., Can.* court of law where cases are tried in the first place.

trial lawyer *Am., Can.* lawyer who practices in a trial court.

trials bike *Br.* type of motorcycle that one can race on very rough ground.

triangle, Tee-square *Am. /Br.* **setsquare/**.

TriBeCa *Am.* sl. Manhattan artists' and residential area (triangle below Canal street).

trice/ in a trice *Br.* very quickly.

trick *Am.* 1. col. a child, esp. a young girl: *She sure is a pretty little trick* – E. Caldwell. 2. plaything, toy. 3. sl. the customer of a prostitute or transaction with her: *a woman "walking the streets for tricks"*. - M. Jones, J. Chilton., *She used to go on the telephone and call up tricks all over the US and sweet talk 'em.* - T. Thompson.

trick *Am.* sl. sell sexual favours for money: *Whenever she runs out of dope she goes out tricking.* - T. Thorne.

trick *Am., Can.* adj. weak and likely to give way unexpectedly.

trick/ trick or treat *esp. Am., Can.* children's custom of collecting at houses at Halloween with the threat of pranks if they are not given a small gift.

trick/ turn a trick *Am.* col. have sex with sb. for money.

trick cyclist *Br.* col. euph. psychiatrist.

trick knee/ankle, etc. *Am.* joint that is weak and can suddenly cause problems.

tried and true *Am.* used by many people and proved to be effective.

trier *Br.* (usu said approvingly) a person who tries very hard at smth. although they are not very successful.

trifecta *Am., Can., Aus., NZ.* a bet in which the person betting forecasts to first three finishers in a race in the correct order.

trifle *Br.* cold dessert made of layers of spongecake, jelly, fruit, and usu. covered with cream.

trig *Am.* neat and smart in appearance.

trig out/ up *esp. Br.* col. make (smth.) neat: *Is his office all trigged out ready for the new director?* - Longman.

trigger/ easy on the trigger *Am.* quick, hot-tempered.

trig point *Br.* reference point on high ground used in surveying.

trike *Br.* col. tricycle.

trilby (hat) *esp. Br.* man's soft felt hat with a fold in the top: *He might be a "mod" with high-bottomed jacket, pin-collar shirt, small trilby hat, and Vespa* *motor scooter.* - P. Norman., *The manager had been listening at the door of his office, smirking, and playing with his trilby.* - L. Lee.

trim *Am.* 1. (of a house) woodwork (esp. the case or frame). 2. window dressing: *it's for outside trim.* - R.J. Randisi., M. Wallace.

trimester *Am. /Br.* **term/** 1. a term of three months at a school or college. 2. a period of three or about three months: *she stopped working completely early in the third trimester.* – Reader's Digest.

trim marks print. *Br. /Am.* **cut marks/**.

trimmer *Aus., NZ.* col. excellent or outstanding point or thing.

trimming *Am.* sl. defeat.

trimmings *Br. /Am.* **fixings/**.

trimmings/ all the trimmings *Br.* col. all the other types of food that are served with the main dish of a menu.

Trimount(ain) City *Am.* Boston.

trip *Am.* sl. person or experience that is amusing and very different from normal.

trip abroad *esp. Br.* a trip to a foreign country.

triplex 1. *Br.* tdmk. special safety glass made of a sheet of transparent plastic between two sheets of glass, esp. used in car windows. 2. *Am., Can.* adj. n. (a unit, esp. a flat) having rooms on three floors of a building: *He preferred to spend most of his time in his triplex above Fifth Avenue* - R. Borchgrave, R. Moss. 3. *Am., Can.* building divided into three self-contained residences.

tripper *esp. Br.* often derog. person on a pleasure trip, esp. one, lasting only one day: *Murder Burlap and come and be a tripper a la Maurice Barres.* - A. Huxley., *there were no trippers, no chattering troupes with cameras.* - J. Steinbeck.

tristate *Am.* adj. related to a group of three states.

trivet/ (as) right as a trivet *Br.* col. perfectly all right.

T-road *Br.* blind street, dead end street, etc.

trog (along) *Br.* col. go somewhere in an informal way, usu. by walking.

trog *Br.* sl. dull person.

troilism *Br.* sexual activity involving three people.

trolley 1. *esp. Br., Aus. /Am.* **(shopping) cart/** low two-wheeled or four-wheeled cart or vehicle, esp. one pushed by hand, used in shops or airport and railway stations. 2. *Br. /Am.* **wagon, cart/** a small table on very small wheels from which food and drinks are served: *He went to fetch a trolley* - J. Fowles., *I wheeled the trolley of cups and saucers into the scullery.* - J. Herriot. 3. *Am.* also **streetcar, trolley(car)** /*Br.* **tram(car)/** tram: *A trolley car was coming down the main street.* - J. Dos Passos.

trolley/ off one's **trolley** *Br.* humor. light-hearted, crazy.

trolley line *Am.* tram line.

troop *Am.* average party members during an election.

troop the colour *Br.* carry an army flag ceremonially in front of a group of soldiers.

trooper 1. *Am.* a member of a state police force: *my hostility doesn't extend to the state troopers* - J. Steinbeck., *The trooper looked stricken.* - Reader's Digest. 2. *Am., Aus.* mounted police officer. 3. *esp. Br.* ship used for transporting troops.

Trooping the colour *Br.* annual ceremony on the Horse Guards Parade in Whitehall, London: *emerging like some elaborate drill at Trooping the colour.* - G. Greene.

troppo *Aus.* col. crazy.

Trot *esp. Br.* col. Trotskyist.

trot *Am.* crib, book giving translation or answers to questions, often used dishonestly by students: *he worked up with the help of the trot.* - J. Dos Passos.

trot/ on the trot *Br., Aus.* 1. doing things one after the other. 2. doing things for a long time without stopping.

the trots *esp. Aus., NZ.* col. trotting races.

trotters *Br.* pig's feet which can be cooked and eaten.

trouble/ borrow trouble *Am.* worry about smth. unnecessarily.

trouble/ there's a trouble at mill *Br.* col. humor. there are some problems or arguments in an organisation, family, etc.

trouble and strife *Br.* sl. wife.

trouble man *Am.* trouble shooter.

troubs/ my troubs *Aus.* sl. my troubles.

trouser cuffs *Br. /Am.* **pant cuffs/**.

trousers *Br., Aus. /Am., Can.* **pants/**.

trouser suit *Br. /Am.* **pant(s) suit/** pants suit.

trout, esp. **old trout** *Br.* col. derog. unattractive or annoying old person.

truant/ play truant esp. *Br., Aus. /Am., Aus.* **play hooky/** stay away from school without permission.

truck *Am., Aus., Can. /Br., Aus.* **lorry, van/**: *a truck passed by, salting the road.* - K. Davis.

truck 1. *Am., Can.* vegetables or fruit grown for sale: *The farm is stocked with some truck.* - T. Caldwell. 2. *Br. /Am.* **car/** an open railway vehicle for carrying goods. 3. *Br.* baggage wagon or hand truck.

truck *esp. Am., Can.* carry by truck: *the reason I chose trucking, the next best thing to riding the open range.* - Guideposts.

truck along/down, etc. *esp. Am.* col. go, move or travel.

truck/ have/hold no truck with *Br.* not agree or not take part in some activity.

truck/ tow truck *Am.* breakdown lorry.

truck carriage, hose cart, hose wagon *Am.* fire engine.

truck crop *Am.* crop grown at a truck farm.

trucker, also **truckman** *Am.* 1. /*Br.* **lorry driver**, *Aus.* **truckie**/ a truck driver: *There were several truckers unloading shipping crates or clothing* - D. Brenner. 2. market gardener.

truck farm *Am.* /*Br.* **market garden**/ area for growing vegetables and fruit for sale: *The whole area was in truck farms* - L. Uris., *Large scale centralised farming will also have to give way to the kind of small-scale regional truck farming the United States had before World War Two.* - J. Riffkin, T. Howard.

truck farmer *Am., Can.* market gardener: *Mary Tanaka's family were truck farmers.* - B. Tillman.

truck fleet *Am.* /*Br.* **lorry fleet**/.

truckie *Aus.* col. trucker, lorry driver.

trucking *Am., Aus.* 1. /*Br.* (**road**) **haulage**/ the business of carrying goods on motor vehicles: *Vagner used a trucking company doing business in Russia* - Reader's Digest. 2. sl. the act of walking or marching, esp. for a cause.

trucking/ get trucking *esp. Am.* col. leave.

trucking line *Am., Can.* haulage company.

truckle bed *esp. Br.* /*esp. Am., Can.* **trundle bed**/ low bed on wheels: *I was on a truckle-bed.* - Cpt. Marryat.

truck stop *Am., Can., Aus.* /*Br.* **transport cafe**/ cheap cafe on the main road, often with fuel and repair services as well: *I dropped her at a truckstop in Tennessee* - A. Hitchcock Mystery Magazine., *having coffee at the local truck stop.* - Guideposts.

true/ be not true *esp. Br.* be extra special.

true bill *Am.* law. bill of indictment found by a grand jury to be supported by sufficient evidence to justify the hearing of a case.

true-blue 1. *Br., Aus.* completely faithful to the principles of the Conservatives. 2. *Am.* extremely loyal or orthodox: *they were true-blue friends* – S. Lawrence.

trug *Br.* rare. broad flattish basket used in gardens to carry flowers, tools, etc.

truly/ Yours truly *esp. Am.* (used at the end of a formal letter).

trump 1. *Aus., NZ.* col. person in authority. 2. *Am.* suit chosen to have a higher value than the others in a cards game.

trumps/ come up/turn up trumps *Br., Aus.* produce a good result unexpectedly or do smth. better than people expect.

truncheon *esp. Br., Aus.* /*Am.* **nightstick, baton, billy(club)**/ a short stick that police officers carry as a weapon.

trundle bed *esp. Am., Can., Aus.* /*esp. Br.* **truckle bed**/ a low bed on wheels which is stored under an ordinary bed ready for use by visitors.

trunk *Am., Can.* /*Br., Aus.* **boot**/ an enclosed space at the back of a car for bags and boxes: *parallel chrome stripes ran along the centre of the hood and continued again over the trunk lid* - M. Torgov., *Simone opened the trunk and handed the doctor her kit.* - E. Segal.

trunk call *esp. Br.* obs. long-distance telephone call: *I want to put a trunk call through, please.* - T. Rattigan., *there was a trunk call to London* - G. Greene.

trunk enquiries *Br.* long-distance information.

trunk line *Am.* main line railway.

trunk road *esp. Br.* main road for long distance travel not as fast or wide as a motorway.

trunk show *esp. Am.* private viewing of new dress fashions for wealthy prospective customers: *Karan is giving a trunk show of her spring clothes.* - New York.

truss *Br.* a tied parcel of hay or straw.

trust *esp. Am.* group of companies that illegally work together to reduce competition and control prices.

trust/ not trust sb. **an inch** *esp. Br., Aus.* not trust them at all.

trust (hospital) *Br.* public hospital that receives funding directly from the national government.

trustbuster *esp. Am.* col. person or agency employed to enforce antitrust legislation.

truth/ be economical with the truth *Br.* humor. not tell the whole truth.

truth drug *Br.* /*Am.* **truth serum**/ drug that is supposed to make people tell the truth.

try and *esp. Br., Aus.* col. (not used with the verb forms tried or trying) try to: *Just try and make me go before then* - E. Caldwell.

try for smth. *Br.* /*Am., Can., Aus.* **try out for** smth./ make an attempt to get or win, compete for or audition, esp. for a sports team, play, or to be given a post.: *A year before he had tried out for the track team at school.* - H. Fast., *he* yearned to get out of the steel plant in a year or two and try out for the Detroit Red Swings. - M. Torgov., Someone suggested that I try out for the school talent show - J. Baez;

trying for promotion Br., Aus. attempting to get it.

try/ be trying it on Br. col. 1. try to persuade sb. to let a person have smth. 2. try to persuade sb. to become sexually involved with them.

try/ try smth. **for size** Br., Aus. /Am., Aus. **try** smth. **on for size/** think for a short time if smth. would be useful or suitable.

try it on Br., Aus. col. behave in a deceiving or disobedient way, esp. to discover how much of this behaviour will be allowed, **try-on** n.

try over esp. Br. go through by way of experiment.

try-on Br., Aus. col. attempt to deceive, esp. to see if. sb. will believe smth. false: *the first drink - a try-on at four times the price he would have paid in an honest bar.* - Arthur Hailey.

tryout esp. Am. /Br. **trial**/ testing a sportsman in order to find out whether he/she is good enough to be on a sports team.

tsar Br., Aus. /Am., Aus. **czar**/.

tub 1. Am., Can., Aus. or Br. col. a bath: *And he seated himself on overturned tub* – K. Chopin. 2. Br. col. have a bath.

tub chair Br. /Am. **barrel chair**/ upholstered chair with a high solid rounded back.

tub of lard Am. col. short and fat person.

tube 1. Br. col. /Am., Can. **subway, Can. metro**/ underground: *I travel on the tube* - Woman's Own., *We were walking to the tube.* - A. Christie., *In the end I took a tube.* - L. Lee. 2. esp. Aus. col. a tin of beer. 3. esp. Am., Aus., Can. col. /Br. **the box**/ TV set: *Can't I watch the tube now?* - E. Segal., *Seems like every time he turns on the tube, he puts another TV dinner in our whirlpool oven.* - Reader's Digest., *If that doesn't get me on the tube, nothing will.* - A. Buchwald.

tube/ go down the tubes Am., Aus. col. be ruined or brought to a sudden unwanted end: *You and the airline are going down the tubes* - K. Lipper.

tub-thumping Br. speech or behaviour that is intended to force people to support an idea or plan; **tub the thump**.

tube top Am., Can. /Br. **boob tube**/.

tubing Am., Can. leisure activity of riding on water or snow on a large inflated inner tube.

tubular 1. esp. Am. (surfing) (of a wave) hollow and well-curved. 2. Am. (used by youth) very good.

tuchis Am. sl. posterior: *The poor son of a bitch froze his tuchis off* - M. Torgov.

tuck Br. col. food, esp. cakes, sweets, etc. as eaten by children at school as a snack: *I was in tucks even though I was scared.* - P. Norman.

tuck a child **up** in bed Br. tuck them in.

tuck/ take the tuck out of sb. Am. discourage sb., put sb. in his place: *it seemed to kind of take the tuck all out of me* - M. Twain.

tuck in (**to**) esp. Br. col. start eating eagerly: *They had just started tuckung into their eggs* - F. Pascal.

tuckbox Br. sl. box in which schoolchildren keep the food brought or sent from home.

tucker Aus., NZ. col. food / also **tucker bag, tucker time,** etc.

tucker (**out**) (usu. pass.) esp. Am., Can., Aus. col. tire greatly: *You're all tuckered out.* - Zacherlay., *he was all tuckered out at around the fifth inning.* - D. Carnegie. *I'm plumb tuckered out.* - J. London.

tuck-in Br. col. a big meal.

tuck shop Br. sl. /Aus. **tucker**/ shop, esp. at school where sweets and cakes are sold: *It had a snooker room, a badminton court and swimming-pool, a tuckshop and a chapel.* - B. Bryson.

'tude esp. Am., Can. col. attitude, style, swagger: *Are you pulling a tude with me?* - R.A. Spears.

tuft hunter esp. Br. person who tries to get acquainted with persons of rank and file.

tug-of-love Br. col. esp. journalism. situation in which a child's parent tries to get the child back from sb. else who is looking after him/her: *I will be a tug-of-war child* – S. Townsend.

tuition 1. esp. Am., Can. the price or payment for instruction. 2. esp. Br. teaching, esp. when given to a small group or a single person, such as in college or universities.

tuitor Am. /Br. **coach**/.

tumble (**to**) esp. Br. sl. understand suddenly, realise: *I'd tumbled onto that idea right away.* - A. Hitchcock Mystery Magazine.

tumble/ take a tumble Am. sl. understand.

tumble dryer Br. /Am. **drier**/ a machine for drying clothes, where wet clothes are dried by turning them in hot air.

tumbling/ do tumbling Am. go in for sport similar to gymnastics but with all exercises done on the floor.

tummler Am. person who makes things happen, esp. a professional entertainer.

tummy button Br. col. /Am., Aus. col. **belly button**/ navel.

tundish Br. broad open container or funnel used in plumbing or metal foundry.

tune *Br.* tune-up (of an engine).

tune in *Am., Aus.* listen or watch (radio, TV, etc.).

tune out *esp. Am., Can.* col. show no interest: *I found myself tuning out his analysis of her character.* - S. Grafton.

tune-up *esp. Am.* sporting event that serves as a practice for the subsequent event.

tunic *Br.* short coat worn by soldiers, police officers, etc. as part of their uniform.

tup *esp. Br.* 1. copulate with (a ewe), cover. 2. a ram.

tuppence *Br.* twopence.

tuppence/ not care/give tuppence *Br., Aus.* col. not care at all.

tuppenny *Br.* twopenny: *I don't give a tuppenny damn about the radio* - A. McLean.

tuque *Can. /Br.* **bobble hat,** *Am.* **stocking cap,** *Aus.* **beanie/** close-fitting knitted stocking cap.

turbery *Br.* legal right to cut turf or peat for fuel on common ground or another person's ground.

turf 1. *esp. Am.* col. an area claimed by a group as its own; the subject in which a person or a group has a lot of knowledge or influence: *She is too good for the turf.* - Vanity Fair., *Anguilo lost his during challenges on his turf* - G. O'Neill, D. Lehr. 2. *Br.* horse-racing as a sport or industry. 3. *Am., Irish Eng.* peat.

turf *Am.* sl. pass the responsibility: *the complaints get turfed* - New York.

turf out *esp. Br.* col. throw out, get rid of: *The old lady had been turfed out of her home* - Longman.

turf accountant *esp. Br.* bookmaker.

turfman *esp. Am.* devotee of horse racing.

turf war *esp. Am., Can.* a dispute over territory between rival groups or departments: *Would the God of Abraham destroy any of his chosen people in a turf battle* - K. Ablow.

turkey 1. *esp. Am., Aus.* col. a. a failure: *real estate is a turkey.* - J. Kellerman. b. also *Can., Aus.* useless or silly person: *This turkey is totally brain dead.* - K. Lipper. 2. *Am.* col. unsuccessful film or play.

turkey/ say turkey to one and buzzard to another *Am.* put sb. in more advantageous position than the other.

turkeys/ like turkeys voting for (an early) Christmas *Br., Aus.* humor. choosing to accept a situation which will have very bad results.

turkey/ talk turkey *esp. Am., Can.* col. talk seriously and frankly.

turkey buzzard *Am., Can.* turkey vulture.

turkey call *esp. Am.* instrument used by hunters to decoy the wild turkey by imitating its sound.

turkey-shoot *esp. Am.* 1. contest in marksmanship: *Ground-support turkey-shooting.* - J. DeFelice., *the One-Hundred-Hour war in the desert was a clearly predictable turkey shoot.* - P. Robertson. 2. col. situation, esp. in a war, in which aggressor has an overwhelming advantage.

turn 1. *esp. Br.* one of the performances or acts in a variety show. 2. *Br. /Am.* **turning/** road that connects with the one a person is on.

turn/ have a turn *Br.* obs. feel suddenly very unwell for a short time.

turn/not do a hand's turn *Br.* col. derog. not work at all.

turn/ on the turn *esp. Br.* (of milk, fish or other food) starting to become sour.

turn a profit *Am. /Br.* **make a profit/** earn more money than one spends.

turn/ take turns, also **take it in turns** *esp. Br. / esp. Br.* **turn and turn about/** do things one after another.

turn on a dime *Am., Can. /Br.* **turn on a sixpence/** turn sharply: *It can turn on a dime.* - W. Magnuson.

turn/ turn loose *Am.* mil. start using (guns) freely: *The general gave orders to turn loose all the big guns.* - Longman.

turn in *esp. Am.* hand in (work that one has done): *I turned in an examination paper* - D. Carnegie., *Susan then waited for the next request to be turned in to the man at the desk.* - R. Cook.

turn off *Br.* 1. stop employing (sb.): *His faithful servant was turned off without a penny* - Longman. 2. turn bad.

turn out *Br.* clean out a drawer, room, etc. by taking out and reorganising its content.

turn out/ turn out nice (of weather) *esp. Br.* become nice unexpectedly.

turn over *Br.* 1. change to a different TV channel. 2. *Br.* turn a page in a book or a sheet of paper to the opposite side.

turn smth. up *Br.* shorten a skirt, trousers, etc. by folding the bottom and sewing it.

turn/ Turn it up *Br., Aus.* Cut it out. Stop it.

turn up like a bad penny *Br.* obs. get in a place where they are not wanted.

turn/ turn/beat swords into ploughshares *Br.* turn to a peaceful life after war.

turnabout 1. *Am.* merry-go-around. 2. *Br.* adj. */Am.* **reversible/** (applied to a coat). 3. *Br.* complete change in sb.'s opinions or ideas.

turnabout/ turnabout is fair play *Am.* obs. You'll do smth. that sb. has done because this is fair.

turnaround *esp. Am. /Br.* **turnround**/ 1. (the time taken for) receiving and dealing with smth. and sending it back. 2. change to an opposite and usu. better situation: *A turnaround would be no small task.* - Time., *it was a 180-degrees turnaround.* - Nation's Restaurant News.

turnaround *Am., Can.* space for vehicles to turn round in, esp. one at the end of a driveway.

turncock, stopcock *Br. /esp. Am.* **valve**/ stopcock.

turn-down *Am.* person who is turned down, esp. unfit for military service.

turning radius *Am.* turning circle, the amount of space a vehicle needs in order to go around in a full circle.

turn-out *Am.,Can.* 1. */Br.* **lay-by**/ wide place in a narrow road where cars can pass or park: *I pulled into a turnout and crawled like a mole into my bed* - J. Steinbeck., *she finally found a little turnout.* - W. Jack, B. Laursen. 2. road turning.

turnover *Am.* 1. a turnover of staff. 2. (in a game) loss of possession of the ball to the opposite team.

turnpike (road), also col. **pike** *Am.* a main road for the use of fast travelling traffic, esp. one which drivers must pay to use: *New Jersey was another turnpike.* - J. Steinbeck., *An hour and a half he was on the Connecticut Turnpike.* - S. Sheldon.

turnplate *esp. Br.* a turn table for locomotives.

turn signal *Am., Can. /Br.* **indicator**/ a car light showing what way it is going to turn: *our passage marked by the ticking of the turn signal!* - K. Davis.

turntable ladder *Br.* power-operated extending and revolving ladder mounted on a fire engine.

turn-up *Br. /Am., Aus.* **cuff**/ narrow band of cloth turned upwards at the bottom of a trouser leg: *copious leftovers that I found in sweater folds and trouser turnups.* - B. Bryson.

a turn-up for the book(s) *Br. /Am.* **one for the book(s)**/ col. a surprise.

turn-ups *Br. /Am.* **cuffed pants**/ trousers with turn-ups.

turpentine *Am.* extract turpentine from (the pine trees).

The Turpentine State *Am.* joc. North Carolina.

turps *Br.* a strong-smelling liquid used for removing paints.

turtle 1. *Br. /Am.* **sea turtle**/. 2. *Am.* any reptile with a thick shell around its body.

turtle/ turn turtle *Br.* (of a ship, car, etc.) roll over onto its side or back in an accident.

turtleneck *Br. /Am.* **mock turtleneck**/ a piece of clothing for the upper part of the body or the tight part at the neck of such a top which doesn't fold over itself.

turtleneck *esp. Am., Can.* (a garment with) a round rolled neck that folds over itself, usu. woollen */esp. Br.* **polo neck, roll neck**, *Aus.* either of these/: *He wore knee-high rubber boots, a rust-colored turtleneck* - J.W. Houston, J.D. Houston.

tush *Am., Can.* col. person's bottom, posterior.

tushery *Br.* sham antique speech.

tutor 1. *esp. Br.* university or college teacher responsible and supervising assigned students. 2. *Am.* assistant lecturer in a college or university. 3. *Br.* book of instructions in a particular subject.

tutor *Am. /Br.* **coach**/ help to study often outside the ordinary educational system, esp. in a particular subject, n. person doing this.

tuxedo, also col. **tux** *esp. Am. /Br.* **dinner jacket**/ dinner jacket: *he dressed in his tuxedo* - T. Thompson., *Gabe will take a tuxedo.* - J. Baez.

twat *Br.* sl. 1. also *Aus.* unpleasant or foolish person: *The tense people are the twats who are interested in making money* - Observer, T. Thorne. 2. obs. or *Am.* vagina.

tweak *Am.* sl. (of a drug addict) exhibit withdrawal symptoms such as twitching when unable to get a fix.

twee *esp. Br.* col. often derog. too delicate or pretty, unpleasantly dainty: *they seemed to specialise in twee little cottages and castles* - B. Bryson.

tweedy *Br.* wearing tweed clothes in a way that seems typical of the British upper class.

tween *Am.* boy or girl, esp. between ages of 10 to 13.

tweeny, also **tween maid, between maid** *Br.* assistant maid to both cook and maid servant thus taking position between downstairs and upstairs: *stories bound to frighten and/or impress nervous "tweenies"* - S. Nichols.

twelfth man *Br., Aus.* a reserve, extra player in cricket.

twelve (12) *Br.* (of a film) suitable for childen 12 years old and over.

twenty-one *Am. /Br.* **pontoon**/ card game, blackjack, usu. played for money: *I sat down at a twenty-one table among the high-rolling Arabs.* - D. Brenner.

twerp *Br., Aus.* col. an annoying or silly person, fool: *After all, he was a twerp.* - A. Scaduto.

twig *Br., Can.* col. /*esp. Am.* **twig to/** (suddenly) understand (a situation): *Do you twig?* - J. Joyce., *women twigged that they might as well save themselves $250,000 and wear flakes.* - New Idea., *Providin' nobody twigs the car* - Arthur Hailey. 2. fashion style.

twig blight *Am.* apple and quince disease.

twig furniture *Am., Can.* rustic style of furniture in which the natural state of the wood is retained.

twin (with) *esp. Br.* join (a town) closely with another town in another country to encourage friendly relations; **twin town** *Br.* /*Am.* **sister city**/.

twin bed *Am.* a bed for one person, adj. **twin-bedded**.

twin-bedded *esp. Br.* having two single beds (in one room).

the Twin Cities *Am., Can.* Minneapolis and Saint Paul in Minnesota.

twinkie *Am.* 1. tdmk. small finger-shaped sponge cake with a white synthetic cream filling. 2. col. derog. gay or effeminate man.

twin set *esp. Br., Aus.* woman's jumper and cardigan made to be worn together: *Once Britain was famous for the "quality" of her tweeds and twinsets* - J. Ruppeldtova.

twin town *Br.* town which has established official or social links with another, esp. in a different country.

twin tub *Br.* type of washing machine with one part for washing and one for spinning and drying (spin-drier).

twirl a baton *Am.* be part of a group of girls who wear uniform and march while spinning batons in the air; n. **twirler, majorette**.

twist *Br.* 1. col. v. n. swindle, cheat. 2. paper packet with twisted ends. 3. drink consisting of two ingredients.

twist/ drive/send sb. **round the twist** *Br., Aus.* col. make sb. very angry esp. by continuing to do smth. annoying.

twist/ round the twist *Br., Aus.* col. a. mad. b. very angry.

twister 1. *Am., Can.* tornado: *Twister-in' the night away.* - Kansas City Star. 2. *Br.* col. sb. who cheats other people.

twist-tie *Am., Aus.* a short piece of wire covered in plastic or paper which is used to fasten a plastic bag.

twit 1. *esp. Br., Can.* col. a stupid fool: *workplaces filled with braying twits named Selera and Jasper* - B. Bryson. 2. *Am., Can.* state of nervous excitement.

twitcher *Br.* col. enthusiastic bird-watcher.

two/ fall between two stools *esp. Br.* fail because neither way is good.

two-bit *Am., Can.* col. 1. derog. insignificant: *Maudeen and Preacher were two-bit police characters* - T. Thompson., *This guy represents two-bit show-biz types.* - L. Waller., *We're just a little two-bit company in Adelaide* - Bulletin. 2. 25 cents, a quarter: *something that you can get in the mail order for two bits.* - E.L. Doctorow.

two-by-four *Am.* col. 1. small, esp. of a building: *I went to the little two-by-four post office* - J. Kerouac. 2. insignificant: *You would have compressed me into a two-by-four pigeonhole of life* - J. London.

twoc *Br.* col. steal (a car).

two cents (worth) *esp. Am., Aus., Can.* /*Br.* **two-penny worth/** sl. statement of opinion or point of view, often in **get/put/stick/throw in** one's **two cents' worth** /*Br.* **have** one's **(two) pennyworth/**: *next week David Hill is chipping in with two cents worth.* - Reader's Digest., *Sinatra puts his two-cents in.* - Rolling Stone., *But of course the navy had thrown its own two cents* - J. DeFelice.

two cents / feel like two cents *Am.* feel ashamed.

two cents/ for two cents *Am., Aus.* col. very willingly (used when describing angrily what sb. would like to do to change a situation).

two-dollar broker *Am.* one who does errands for others for a small fee.

two-dollar bill *Am.* sl. something queer: *I'll bet you he's as queer as a two-dollar bill.* - Life.

twofer *Am.* 1. a pair of tickets sold roughly for the price of one. 2. any item sold thus: *Everything in this store is a twofer.* - R.A. Spears.

two-fisted *Am.* strong, virile, or straightforward.

two-fisted drinker *Am.* sl. a heavy drinker: *Some of them I had known for years, good two-fisted drinkers* - Alcoholics Anonymous.

two-hander *Br.* a play written for two actors.

two minds/ be in two minds *Br.* /*Am., Aus.* **of two minds/** about smth. be uncertain what to choose between two things.

two nickels/ not have two nickels to rub together *Am., Aus.* col. be very poor.

twopence/ not care / give twopence *Br.* col. not to care at all.

twopence/ not give sb. **twopence** *Br.* col. not to be interested in having.

two-penny-halfpenny *Br.* col. almost worthless.

two-percent milk *Am.* /*Br.* **semi-skimmed**/ milk that has about half the fat removed.

two-seater *Br.* roadster, twin sports car.

two-up *Aus.* game with coins.

two-up-two-down *Br.* col. small house with two floors, each having two rooms.

two-way street *esp. Am.* both people must make an equal effort in order to achieve good results.

tyke, tike 1. *esp. Am.* a small child: *I've always wanted a tyke of my own aboard ship.* - J.A. Michener. 2. *Br.* person from Yorkshire in Northern England. 3. *Br., Aus.* col. a child who is badly-behaved in a playful way. 4. *Aus., NZ.* col. derog. Roman Catholic.

Tylenol *esp. Am.* tdmk. paracetomol.

Typhoid Mary *Am.* col. 1. a carrier of a communicable disease. 2. a carrier of anything harmful or evil.

typographer 1. *Br.* typographic designer. 2. *Am.* compositor, the individual who sets type.

tyre *Br., Aus.* /*Am.* **tire**/.

U

U 1. *Br., Aus.* obs. col. or humor. (esp. of words or behaviour) typical of the upper class, correct or socially proper. 2. *Am.* kosher food package mark. 3. *Am., Aus.* (of a film) considered suitable for children of any age. 4. *Br.* grade in exam that shows that the work is too bad to be marked at all. 5. *Am.* obs. abbr. for university.

ugly American *Am.* an American behaving oneself in an offending way to native people in a foreign country.

uh-uh *Am., Aus.* excl. made when sb. has done smth.wrong.

UHT milk *Br.* milk that has been heated to a very high temperature to preserve it.

U-ie *Aus.* col. U-turn.

uke *Can.* sl. Ukrainian.

ult. *Br.* becoming rare. (used after a date in business letter) of last month.

ump *Am.* col. umpire.

umpty-umph *Am.* adj. umpteenth: *This is the umpty-umph time I've told you to keep your dog out of my yard.* - R.A. Spears.

the unacceptable face of smth. *Br., Aus.* the bad side of smth.

unadopted *Br.* (of a road surface) not to be repaired by the town council but be the responsibility of those who live on the road.

un-American *Am.* derog. guilty of lack of loyalty to the US and its political system.

uncle 1. *Br.* col. a pawnbroker. 2. *Am.* **say** (or **cry/yell**) **uncle** *Am., Can.* col. admit defeat, give up: *its overlord - Syria - cried uncle.* - Time.

(Uncle Tom) Cobley and all *Br.* col. a long list of people: *he could hardly be called an Uncle Tom or an Oreo.* – N. Hentoff.

Uncle Sam's Attic *Am.* Alaska.

Uncle Sam's Handkerchief *Am.* Delaware.

Uncle Tom *esp. Am., Can.* derog. a subservient Negro.

uncovered *Am.* (of a class) without a teacher.

uncrossed *Br.* (of a cheque) not crossed.

undefinable *Am., Aus.* indefinable.

underbearer *Am.* pallbearer.

underbit *Am.* an earmark to show ownership of cattle.

underbrush *esp. Am., Can.* /*Br.* **undergrowth**/ thick undergrowth in a forest.

undercarriage *Br.* landing gear, a set of wheels and other parts which support a plane on landing.

underclassman, also **underclass** *Am.* a freshman or sophomore, lower classman: *Walter Lippman is too hard for most underclassmen* - Reader's Digest.

undercut 1. *esp. Br.* /*esp. Am.* **tenderloin**/ fillet of beef. 2. *Am., Can.* notch cut in a tree to guide its fall when felled.

underdrawers *Am.* underpants.

underfelt *Br.* felt laid under a carpet for extra support.

underfives *esp. Br.* less than five years, i.e. not a full-time education.

underfloor *esp. Br.* (of a heating system) under the surface of the floor.

undergraduate *esp. Br.* student which is doing university courses for a first degree.

underground *Br.* /*Am., Can.* **subway**, *Can.* **metro**/.

underground economy *Am., Can.* black economy.

underhand *Am.* underarm, (done by) moving the arm below shoulder level, esp. in bowling.

underlay *Br., Aus.* thick material placed between a carpet and the floor for extra warmth.

undermentioned *Br.* which is/are mentioned later in the same piece of writing.

under-occupancy *Br.* (with reference to holiday or hospital accommodation) the state of not being occupied to the expected advertised capacity.

underpants *Am., Aus.* /*Br.* **knickers, pants,** *Am., Can.* **shorts**/ in Britain underpants refer only to men's underwear, in America it refers to women's underwear as well: *the indelible image of all your tatty underpants.* - S. Grafton.

(pedestrian) underpass *Am.* /*Br.* **(pedestrian) subway**/: *We passed...through the underpass beneath the drive* – P. Roth.

underscore *esp. Am.* underline a word or phrase to show that it is important.

underseal *Br.* coat (the underpart of a motor vehicle) with waterproof material as a protection against rust.

undersecretary *Am.* important officer in a government department in rank below secretary.

underserved *Am.* not getting enough care and help from the government.

undershirt *esp. Am., Can.* /*Br.* **vest**, *Aus.* **singlet**/ short undergarment usu. without covering for the arms worn on the upper part of the body /*esp. Br.* **undervest**/: *visible clothes were an undershirt, blue pants and black silk stockings.* - D. Hammet.

undershorts *esp. Am., Can.* underpants.

undertaker, funeral furnisher *Br.* /*esp. Am.* **funeral director, mortician**/.

undocumented *Am., Can.* not having appropriate legal documents.

undocumented persons *Am., Can.* illegal immigrants.

unemployment (compensation), unemployment insurance, dole *Am.* /*Br., Aus.* col. **dole unemployment benefit**/.

unemployment line *Am.* /*Br.* **dole queue**/.

uneven bars *Am., Can.* asymmetric bars.

unfair list *Am.* a list of employers who refuse to hire union members.

unflappable *esp. Br.* col. never losing one's calmness, even in difficult situations: *Glenn Ridge appears unflappable in all situations.* - New Idea., *King was unflappable* - S.B. Oates., *the King appears to have been unflappable* - M. Jones, J. Chilton.

unget *Am.* destroy the beginning.

unglued/ come unglued *Am.* col. 1. /*Br., Aus.* **come unstuck**/ (of plans, etc.) fall apart, fail. 2. lose control, become very upset or angry.

ungraded school *Am.* small country elementary school, not divided into grades.

ungraded teacher *Am.* a teacher of ungraded school.

ungraduated *Am.* not having finished any educational institutions.

ungrounded *Am.* (of electric equipment) not connected to earth.

uni *Br., Aus.* university.

uniform *esp. Am., Can.* police officer wearing a uniform.

unincorporated *Am., Can.* (of territory) not designated or belonging to a particular country, town or area.

Unio *Br.* association of independent churches for cooperation.

unionalls *Am.* special worker's uniform.

union suit *Am., Can.* /*Br.* **combinations**/ long john underwear: *Ben Compton stood there trembling wearing a long unionsuit.*- J. Dos Passos., *the ballet dancers wear knit-goods tights nearly as substantial as a flannel unionsuit* - J. Fischer.

unit 1. *esp. Am.* a certain number of hours of classroom attendance and the accompanying outside work used esp. in computing credits and fees. 2. *Am., Aus.* a single apartment in a bigger building: *Jo and Glenn have settled in a unit in Melbourne.* - New Idea., *I just shot 5 people in the units over there.* - New Idea. 3. *Br.* a standard measure of alcohol. 4. *Am.* a police car. 5. *Br.* smallest measure of investment in a unit trust.

unit/ be a unit *Am.* be unanimous.

unitary *Br.* (of a school or local government in UK) in which official power is given to one organisation which deals with all the matters in a local area.

unit-linked *Br.* relating to a life assurance policy or other investment in which premiums or payments are invested in unit trust.

unit train *Am., Can.* train transporting a single commodity.

unit trust *Br.* /*Am.* **mutual fund**/ a company through which one (**unit holder**) can buy shares in many different businesses.

Universal Product Code *Am.* computerised checkout and inventory code.

university man *Br.* college graduate.

unknown *esp. Am., Aus.* smth. that can't be guessed or calculated because so little is known about it.

unlisted *Am., Aus.* /*Br.* **ex-directory**/ not in a telephone book: *My number is unlisted* - New York.

unload *esp. Am.* give expression to (oppressive thoughts or feelings).

unlocated *Am.* (of land) not surveyed or presented without a script.

unmade, also **unmetalled, dust road** *Br.* (of a road) without a finished level surface.

unmailable *Am.* not to be sent through mail.

unplaced *Br.* not one of the first three to finish in a race or competition.
unrated *Am.* (of a film) not officially classified, because regarded unsuitable for general release.
unrazored *Am.* unshaven.
unsafe *Br.* law (of a decision that sb. is guilty) able to be appealed against in court.
unsealed *esp. Aus., NZ.* (of a road) not surfaced with bitumen or similar substance.
unseen *esp. Br.* (of a passage for translation in a test or exam) not previously read or prepared.
unshaded *Am.* without shades (about a window).
unsit *Aus.* leave without a place.
unspoiled *esp. Br.* (of a place) beautiful because it hasn't changed and hasn't had roads, modern buildings, etc. built on it.
unstick *Br.* col. (of aeroplane) take off, n.
unstring one's **shoes** *Am.* unlace one's shoes.
unstuck/ come unstuck *Br.* fail or start to do smth. wrong.
unthaw *Am., Can.* melt or thaw.
untidy *esp. Br.* 1. not neat; messy. 2. not keeping house possessions in order.
the unwaged *esp. Br.* the unemployed or people doing unpaid work: *give cheap food to the unwaged* – S. Townsend.
up 1. *Br.* adv. to or in a place of importance from one of less importance. 2. *Br., Aus.* nonst. prep. to or at. 3. *Br.* col. (considered non-standard by some) to a certain place.
up/ be up against it *Br.* have to deal with a problem, esp. in sports.
up/ be up for it *Br.* sl. want to do smth.
up/ He is thorough up in (*Am.* **on**) **physics** He is an expert in physics.
up/ be up oneself *Br., Aus.* col. think that one is better and more important than others.
up/ be up to one's **chin in** smth. *Am.* have too much of smth., esp. work.
up/ not be up to much *Br.* col. not very good or effective.
up/ up stakes *Br.* col. /*Am.* **pull up stakes**/.
up/ up with *Am.* col. raise or pick up smth.
up/ up yours *Br., Can.* taboo. sl. (used for expressing great dislike or an annoyance at a person): *When she told him to get out of the house, he said, "Up yours!"* - W. Magnuson., *Up yours, monkey.* - J. Patterson.
up/ be up with the crows *Aus.* be awake and out of one's bed early in the morning.
up/ the score was six-up *Am.* col. six points each.

up-an-down *esp. Am.* straight, honest.
up-and-over type *esp. Br.* (of a door) open by being lifted and then sliding into a horizontal position.
up-and-up/ on the up(-and-up) col. a. *Br., Aus.* improving, succeeding: *Mr. Myatt was on the up and up.* - J. Herriot. b. *esp. Am., Can.* honest: *She was always on the up and up with me.* - D. Hammet., *the deal is on the up and up.* - I. Shaw., *Then as you American say - everything's on the up and up.* - L. Uris.
up a storm *Am., Can.* sl. very much, very intensively: *someone will see the numbers on your credit card and start charging up a storm.* - Omni.
up card *esp. Am.* place card turned face up on the table.
upchuck *Br.* col. vomit.
upcoming *esp. Am.* /*esp. Br.* **forthcoming**/ happening soon.
up for the cup *Br.* sl. in town for the big occasion.
up front *Am.* sl. the managerial section of a corporation or firm: *Joe Catwallender finally made it (with the) up front.* - A. Makkai.
upmarket *esp. Br.* /*esp. Am., Can.* **upscale**/ used by people who are rich or have a high social position.
ups/ in two ups *Aus.* in a moment.
upper circle *Br.* second balcony (in a theatre).
upperclassman or woman *Am.* a junior or senior in a college or high school: *Joanna tackled courses that had upperclassmen sweating.* - Reader's Digest., *a panel of upperclassmen answered questions about dorm life.* - Reader's Digest., *He was an upperclassman* - E. Hautzig.
uppers/ be (down) on one's **uppers** *Br.* obs. be in a very bad financial situation.
uppity/uppish *Br.* col. behaving as if sb. is more important than others.
upscale *esp. Am., Can.* /*esp. Br.* **upmarket**/: *Pam is a bartender at an upscale hotel* – Reader's Digest.
upside *Am.* prep. **upside the head/face**, etc. on the side of sb.'s head/face.
upstage and county *Br.* col. snobbish.
upstairs/ not have much upstairs, not have a lot (going on) up top *Br.* col. derog. be rather stupid.
upstand *Br.* upstanding thing.
upstate *Am.* 1. adj. of a part of a state remotest from large cities, esp. the Northern part: *She and their three-month-old daughter, Emerson,*

were visiting her parents in upstate New York. – Reader's Digest. 2. sl. in prison.
uptake *Br., Aus.* the rate or act of accepting smth.
uptick *Am.* small increase: *an uptick in minor crimes such as vandalism* – Reader's Digest.
up top *Br.* col. in the brain (with reference to intelligence).
uptown *esp. Am., Can.* adj. adv. to, towards, or in the areas or a city or town where mostly affluent people live, not the business centre; away from the city centre: *she had forgotten which way the man had told her to turn, uptown or downtown, for Smiley's Bar.* - I. Shaw., *He was expected uptown.* - S. Bellow.
urb *Am.* col. big modern town.
urban homestead *Am.* col. renovation and occupation through co-operative ownership by tenants of previously abandoned city apartment buildings: *Urban homesteading is on the rise in many big American cities these days.* - A. Makkai.
urger *Aus.* col. person who gives tips at a race meetings.
urgicenter *Am.* an emergency centre.
us *Br.* 1. undersecretary. 2. col. unserviceable; useless.
us *Br., Aus.* col. nonst. we.
use/ not in use *Am., Aus.* not operating.
use-by date *esp. Br.* used about the expiry date of use of mostly perishable products.
useful *Br.* col. satisfactory.
usen't, used not to *Br.* obs. usedn't.
user fee *Am.* tax on a service provided for the public.
usher 1. *Am.* groomsman, a male friend of the bride or groom: *he had the more presentable of his Fordham classmates for ushers* – J. O'Hara. 2. *esp. Br.* one who has charge of the door and admits people to a hall or chamber. 3. *Br.* an assistant teacher in English school. 4. *Br.* person employed to walk before a person of high rank on special occasions. 5. *Br.* sb. who works in a law court whose job is to make sure there is no trouble.
usherette *esp. Br.* a woman who shows people where to sit in a cinema or theatre.
usual *Br.* col. the drink one usually has.
ute *Aus., NZ.* col. utility vehicle, light truck or van.
utility *Br.* adj. simple and cheap while still performing its functions / **utility furniture, clothes,** etc.
utility pole *Am., Can.* tall wooden pole for supporting telephone and electric wires.
U-y/ do a U-y *Aus.* do a U-turn.

V

v. 1. *Am.* col. five dollars. 2. *Br., Aus.* /*Am.* **vs**/ abbr. in sports versus.
V *V. for Victory. In the United States it means "victory" or "peace", but in England if the palm faces inward it's a taunt especially if executed with an upward jerk of the fingers.* - Reader's Digest.
vac *Br.* col. a university vacation, **the long vac** *Br.* summer college vacation: *you promised not to mention that again this vac.* - T. Rattigan., *Three lively terms and two still more lively vacs* - A. Huxley.
vac *Br.* col. /*Br.* tdmk. **hoover**/ vacuum cleaner.
Vacancies, also **Situations Vacant** *Br.* Help wanted.
vacant lot *Am.* spare ground.
vacant possession *Br., Aus.* law. the right of a buyer of a house or other building to move into it, occupancy immediate on completion, **house/flat with vacant possession**.
vacate *Am.* col. go on a holiday.
vacation 1. *esp. Am., Can.* /*Br., Aus.* **holiday**/ a holiday, a time when you don't have to work or go to school or law court or a period of time that you spend in another place or country for enjoyment. 2. *esp. Br.* any of the periods of holiday when universities or law courts are closed: *home from university on vacation.* - V. Holt.
vacation (at, in) *esp. Am.* have a holiday: *Russian noblemen vacationed in Biarritz* - R.K. Mussle.
The Vacation Land *Am.* Maine.
The Vacation State *Am.* Nevada.
vacationer, vacationist *Am.* a holiday-maker.
vacation land *Am.* area providing attractions for holiday-makers.
vacation subscription *Am.* subscription of periodicals, esp. for the summertime.
vacuum *Am.* /*Br.* **hoover**/ use a vacuum cleaner.
(vacuum) flask *esp. Br.* also **thermos flask** /*Am.* **Thermos (bottle)** a container which is used to keep hot drinks hot or cold drinks cold.
vacuum tube *Am.* radio. valve.
vag *Am.* sl. vagrant, vagabond: *A couple of vags on the curb were trying to hitch a ride.* - R.A. Spears.
valance *esp. Am., Can.* /*esp. Br.* **pelmet**/ narrow piece of wood or cloth above a window that hides the rod on which curtains hang: *he found owls in his bedroom perched on the red valances* - S. Bellow., *the gold velvet drapes that hung from upholstered valances* - D. Mortman.

valedictorian *Am.* the student who delivers the so-called **valedictory** (*Am.*) oration at the graduation ceremony: *she was class valedictorian.* - M. Jones, J. Chilton., *He was brilliant academically, the valedictorian of our gymnasium.* - Reader's Digest.

valency *esp. Br. /esp. Am.* **valence/** a measure of the power of atoms to combine together to form compounds.

The Valentime or **Baby State** *Am.* Arizona.

valet (a car) *Br.* clean (esp. the inside of a car).

valet *Am., Aus.* person whose job is to park your car for you at a hotel or restaurant: *you treat maitre'd or the wait staff or the valet parker* – J. Tesh; **valet-parking.**

valuable citizen *Am.* respectable member of society.

valuate *esp. Am.* estimate.

value/ be bad/poor, etc. **value** *Br.* not good enough in quality for the money paid.

value for money *Br.* well worth the money spent on it.

valuer *esp. Br.* a person who says how much smth. might be sold for.

valve 1. *Br. /Am.* **tube/** radio electron tube., **valve-holder** *Br. /Am.* **tube-holder/.** 2. *esp. Am. /Br.* **stopcock, turncock/.**

vamoose (often impers.) *esp. Am., Can.* obs. sl. go away hastily: *Do we kill him, take what we want and vamoose* - R. Cox.

van 1. *esp. Br. /Am.* **car/** a covered railway carriage for goods and sometimes people: *Editions of a zoology primer awaiting forty railway vans.* - A. Burgess. 2. *Am.* col. vanilla (ice-cream). 3. *Br. /Am.* (**railway**) **car/** wheeled carriage running on overhead rail or track. 4. also *Br.* **lorry** /*Am., Aus.* **truck/**: *Dad had installed a CB radio in her van* - Reader's Digest. 5. *Br.* a medium-sized car with windows all around, used to carry more people than ordinary car. 6. *Br.* caravan. 7. *Br.* (in tennis) advantage.

van/ sales van *Am.* a motor vehicle used for selling goods.

vanilla pod *Br. /Am.* **vanilla bean/** seed container.

vanitory unit *Br.* a small cupboard in a bathroom which has a washbasin in the top.

vanity (table) *Am., Can.* 1. dressing table: *The bright vanity lights revealed every pore on her face.* - R.L. Stine. 2. /*Br.* **vanitory unit, vanity unit/.**

vanity plates *Am., Can.* number plates on a vehicle which have a particular numbers and letters on them that the vehicle owner has specially chosen and paid to have: *I was puzzling over the meaning of the vanity plate on the car in front of me* – Reader's Digest.

vanity table, vanity (dresser) *Am. /Br.* **dressing table/.**

van line *Am.* transport company.

variety *Br. /Am.* **vaudeville,** *Br.* obs. **music hall/.**

variety meats *Am., Can.* euph. (a type of) offal.

variety store *Am., Can.* shop selling different things, often at low prices: *I went into a variety store and bought some paint.* - A. Makkai.

varmint *esp. Am.* obs. col. or dial. troublesome worthless person or animal.

varsity *Br.* obs. university, esp. Oxford or Cambridge: *Alison Miller reports on the highspot of the varsity social whirl.* - You.

varsity *esp. Am., Can.* adj. being the chief group or team representing a university, college or school, esp. in sports: *Your brother in his varsity letter jacket, cheered you on all through that horrible baseball season* - Reader's Digest.

vatman *Br.* col. a government department which advises and checks the accounts of people who have to pay VAT (Value Added Tax) taxes in Britain.

vaudeville *Am. /Br.* **music hall/** variety.

vaulting horse *Br.* long wooden horse used for jumping over in gymnastics.

VCR *esp. Am. /Br.* **video/** video cassette recorder.

VDT *Am.* video display terminal.

vedette *esp. Am., Can.* leading star of stage, screen or TV.

Veep/VP *Am.* col. vice-president of the US: *It was "veep" at his best.* - H. Truman.

veg *esp. Br.* col. /*esp. Am., Aus.* **veggie/** vegetable, usu. when cooked: *Is it a fruit or a veg?* - D. Lodge.

veg out *esp. Aus., Am., Can.* sl. live a passive monotonous existence, vegetate: *I can't just veg out all the rest of this year.* - R.L. Stine.

vegeburger *Br.* veggiburger, burger made with vegetables, beans, not meat.

vegemite *Aus., NZ.* tdmk. type of savoury spread made from concentrated yeast extract.

vegetable marrow, squash *esp. Am., Aus. /esp. Br.* **squash/.**

vegetate *Am.* produce vegetation.

veggie 1. *Br.* col. a vegetarian. 2. *Am.* col. vegetable.

veggie(s) *Am., Can* col. vegetable(s): *No veggies for me.* - R.A. Spears.

vehicle car *Am.* vehicle for transporting cars.

velocipede *Am.* a child's 3-wheeled bicycle.

velox *Am.* print. photomechanical transfer.

Velux *Br.* tdmk. a window which is built into a roof.

vending machine *Am. /Br.* **slot machine/.**

vendue *Am.* public auction.
venture scout *Br.* /*Am.* **explorer scout**, *Aus.* **venturer**/ a young person of 15-20 years old which is a member of international youth organisation called Scouts.
venturesome *esp. Am.* 1. (of person) daring, ready to take risks: *Mandy, much given to sleep in the sun when not chasing venturesome poultry off forbidden ground* – K. Chopin. 2. (of actions) risky.
venue *Am.* a special city or county in which a trial happens.
veranda *Aus., NZ.* a roof over the pavement in front of a shop.
verbal *Br.* col. abuse; insults.
verbal diarrhea *Am.* sl. uncontrollable loquaciousness.
verbals *Br.* col. verbal statement with a damaging admission alleged to have been made to the police and offered as a evidence by the prosecutor.
verbarium *Am.* play with words.
verderer *Br.* judicial officer of a royal forest.
verdict/ **reach a majority verdict** of 10 to 2 *Br.* reach a verdict in favour of 10 to 2.
verdict/ **record an open verdict** *Br.* record a verdict that the cause was unknown.
verge *esp. Br.* /*Am.* **shoulder**/ the strip of land which borders the road or path.
verger *esp. Br.* person who looks after the inside of a church and performs small duties such as showing worshippers where they may sit: *a verger passed and issued a cheery hello.* - B. Bryson.
vermicelli *Br.* shreds of chocolate.
vernal *Am.* winter-hardy alfalfa.
Vero board *Br.* tdmk. type of board used to make electric circuits.
verruca *Br.* a kind of wart which occurs on the sole of the foot.
vertical stabilizer *Am.* (aeroplane) fin.
vertical union *Am.* industrial trade union.
vessel/ **empty vessels make the most noise/sound** *Br.* obs. foolish people speak a lot.
vest 1. *Br.* /*Am., Can.* **undershirt,** *Aus.* **singlet**/: *She is wearing vest, pants, tights.* - D. Lodge. 2. also *Am., Can.* **vester,** *Am., Aus.* /*esp. Br., Aus.* **waistcoat**/ close-fitting garment without arms, that is usu. worn under a jacket: *He removed his jacket and unbuttoned his vest.* - E.L. Doctorow.
vest (top) *Br.* a piece of sleeveless clothing, usu. made of cotton which is worn in the summer or for sport.
vestibule *Am.* 1. enclosed passage at each end of a railway carriage which connects it with another carriage /**vestibule train**/: *I was standing in the little vestibule of my car* - A.E. Hotchner. 2. a small enclosed area on the front of a house.
vest-pocket *Am., Can.* 1. very small book that fits into a pocket. 2. adj. very small in size.
vet *esp. Br.* col. examine carefully for correctness, past record, etc., esp. to find suitability of a person for work: *The scale on which these invitations of carefully selected and vetted groups are issued is tremendous and unique.* - L. Van Der Post., *We'll vet her properly.* - A. Christie., *I shall bring him to be vetted.* - J. Fowles.
veteran, also col. **vet** *Am., Can.* person who has served in the armed forces, esp. during a war: *As the years passed, however, the image of Vietnam vets worsened.* - Reader's Digest.
veteran *Br.* 1. old; **veteran car** one made before 1905. 2. an old man who served in the army.
Veterans Day *Am., Can.* November 11th, when people in the US and Canada remember the end of fighting in 1918 and 1945 /**Armistice Day** up to 1954/.
veteranise *Am.* mil. serve on reengagement.
veterinarian *Am.* /*Br., Aus.* **veterinarian surgeon**/ a vet, person trained in the medical care and treatment of sick animals: *The veterinarian could do nothing for the cat* - A. Hitchcock Mystery Magazine., *I wanted to be a veterinarian.* - Reader's Digest.
veto/ **put a veto on** smth./**have a veto over** smth. *esp. Br.* forbid to do smth.
v.g.c. *Br.* abbr. in advertisements meaning in very good condition.
vibraharp *Am.* vibraphone.
vic *Am.* sl. 1. victim: *Harry is a con artist, not a vic.* - R.A. Spears. 2. convict.
vice *esp. Br.,Aus.* /*Am.* **vise**/ a tool with metal jaws: *Daddy had his arms around her like a vise.* - R.J. Randisi., M. Wallace.
vice-chancellor *Br.* the head of academic and administrative matters in the university.
vice-president *Am.* person who is responsible for a particular part of a company.
vicious spiral *Br.* spiral, progressive rise or fall of prices, wages, etc. each responding to an upward or downward stimulus provided by a previous one.
victor *Am.* radio code letter V.
Victoria sandwich/sponge *Br.* cake consisting of two layers of sponge with a jam filling.
victor/victrix ludorum *Br.* male/female overall champion in a special competition at school or college.
victrola *Am.* obs. record player: *the loud arias emanating from Victrola.* - A.H. Hotchner.

video *Br.* col. /*Am.* **VCR**/ video cassette recorder.

video arcade *Am.* public place with a lot of video games machines.

videofit *Br.* a picture of suspected criminal produced electronically by combining pictures of different eyes, noses, etc. and based on descriptions made by witnesses.

video monitor *Am., Aus.* a device with a screen on which moving pictures can be shown.

video nasty *Br.* col. a video of a film containing extremely unpleasant scenes of violence and sex.

video shop *Br., Aus.* /*Am.* **video store**/.

vidiot *Am., Can.* col. habitual undiscriminating watcher of TV or videotapes.

vidkid *Am* a child who is a compulsive watcher of television or video.

view *Br.* /*Am.* **viewing**/ an occasion for a special look (of an exhibition, film, etc.).

viewless *Am.* having no definite opinion of one's own.

viewpoint *Br.* /*Am.* **overlook**, *Aus.* **lookout**/ a place where a person can look down or out, esp. at an area of natural beauty.

vig, vig(g)erish *Am.* col. 1. profits of a bookmaker, usurer, a criminal conspirator, a casino, etc.: *loan-shark interest payments known as "vig" for operating his strip joint and porno store on Mafia turf* - G. O'Neill, D. Lehr., *They get a guy behind in his vig payments* - J. O'Brien, A. Kurins. 2. excessive rate of interest on a loan.

viga *Am.* rough-hewn roof timber or rafter.

vigilance committee *Am.* a group of vigilantes.

villa *Br.* 1. a large house on the edge of town usu. with a garden and usu. built before 1914. 2. house in another country that one can rent for holidays.

villadom *Br.* the world constituted by villas and their occupants, suburbia.

village 1. *Aus., NZ.* select suburban shopping centre. 2. *Am.* small municipality with limited corporate powers; small village. 3. *Br.* very small town in the countryside; **village school, sports, life**.

village/ be in skint village *Br.* col. have very little money.

Village of Magnificent Distances *Am.* joc. Washington, D.C. **villain** *Br.* col. esp. humor. a criminal: *He found two villains in possesion of stolen goods.* - T. Thorne.

the villain of the peace *Br.* the cause of trouble.

-ville suffix *esp. Am.* obs. sl. (used to describe a place or thing of the stated quality).

vine/ die on the vine *Am., Aus.* be destroyed gradually, usu. because no one helps or supports it.

vintage *Br.* (of a car) made between 1919 and 1930.

violative *Am.* made in violation of smth.

virement *Br.* finance. the process of transferring items from one financial account to another.

Virginia creeper *esp. Br.* /*Am.* **woodbine**/ a climbing garden plant often grown on walls.

vision mixer *Br.* person whose job is to select and manipulate images in TV broadcasting or recording.

visit 1. (**in, on, at, with**) *Am., Can.* stay: *we visited with them in their home.* - Vanity Fair. 2. *Am.* col. friendly chat. 3. *Br.* go and see a professional person such as a doctor or solicitor to get a professional advice.

visit *Am.* col. a conversation with sb.

visit with sb. *Am., Can.* 1. stay with. 2. talk socially with.

visitation *Am.* 1. law. an act of divorced parent spending time with children he or she no longer live with at agreed times and under agreed conditions: *Norton had liberal visitation rights until Cynthia began to accuse him of molesting Kit.* – Reader's Digest. 2. gathering with the family of a deceased before the funeral.

visiting card *Br.* name and address sent or left in lieu of a formal social or business card.

visiting fireman *Am.* important or influential visitor: *For entertaining visiting firemen he has a separate guesthouse* - J. Fischer.

visitor's book *Br.* book in which vistors to a public building write their names and addresses, and sometimes remarks.

visor *Am.* /*Br.* **peak**/ curved part of a cap that sticks out in front of sb.'s eyes.

vista dome *Am., Can.* observation compartment in the roof of a railway carriage.

Vistavision *Am.* tdmk. widescreen cinematography.

visual *Br.* /*Am.* **comp**/ print. layout of type and illustration, not to the standard of a finished rough.

visual display unit, VDU *Br.* computing device for displaying input signals as characters on a screen, usu. incorporating a keyboard.

vita *Am.* col. cv.

vital statistics *Br.* col. humor. the measurements in inches of a woman's body round the chest, waist and hips: *Here are his vital statistics* - R.A. Spears.

viva *Br.* col. viva voce, spoken examination at a university: *Moris Zapp vivaed her briskly about its contents and methodology.* - D. Lodge.

viva *esp. Am.* excl. of approval or good wishes.

vo-ag *Am.* col. 1. vocational agriculture. 2. teacher of it.

vo-ed *Am.* col. vocational education.

void *esp. Am.* declare that smth. is not valid or legally binding.

volume print. *Br. /Am.* **bulk factor/**.

volunteerism *esp. Am., Can.* the use or involvement of voluntary labour, esp. in community services.

The Volunteer State *Am.* Tennessee. **Volunteer** *Am.* citizen of Tennessee.

vomitous *esp. Am., Can.* nauseating.

voodoo economics *Am.* economic ideas that seem attractive but don't work effectively over a period of time.

vote/ propose a vote of thanks *esp. Br.* make a short formal speech in which a person thanks sb., esp. at a public meeting or formal dinner.

vote/ vote to *Br. /Am.* **vote towards/** vote for sb. or smth., decide to give it to them.

vote/ get out the/(a) vote *Am.* make the voters come to an election in large numbers.

vote-getter *Am., Aus.* smth. that will win votes because it is popular with the voters.

voting booth *Am. /Br.* **polling booth/**.

voting machine *esp. Am.* one used to record and count votes in an election automatically.

voucher *Br., Aus.* 1. a kind of ticket that gives a buyer the right to receive certain goods. 2. one that may be used instead of money for a particular purpose.

voyageur *Can.* travelling salesman.

vox pop *Br., Aus.* col. an inquiry carried out in the street by a television, radio or newspaper reporter who tries to find out people's opinion on a matter of public interest.

VP col. **veep** *Am.* vice-president

V-sign 1. *Br.* sign made with the back of the hand facing forwards used for expressing great dislike or anger and considered very offensive. 2. *Br.* the same sign with the palm of your hand facing away from you is a sign of victory.

VSO *Br.* Voluntary Service Overseas organisation that sends skilled people to developing countries to work on projects to help the local communities.

v.t. *Br. /Am.* **tape/** video tape.

vroom *Am.* sl. speed in a roaring car: *Sellers did the Mikado with a character vrooming around on a motorcycle.* - Time.

vulgar fraction *Br.* fraction expressed by numerator and denominator, not decimally.

W

w *Br.* abbr. with.

wack 1. *Br.* col. term of address, esp. in Liverpool. 2. *esp. Am.* col. crazy person. 3. *esp. Am.* col. stupid ideas, rubbish.

wack *esp. Am.* bad, unhip, harmful.

w(h)acko *esp. Am.* an eccentric person.

wacky *esp. Am., Aus., Can.* col. silly, slightly mad / **wack** *Am.* sl. crazy or eccentric person: *the wacky brothers strayed from the script* - Reader's Digest., *Perhaps our list of the wackiest courses in America will change your mind.* - Omni., *He's a good guy, a little wacky, but he means well* - J. Baez.

wacky baccy *Br.* col. cannabis.

wad *Br.* esp. mil. sl. bun or slice of bread, sandwich, etc.

wad/ shoot/blow one's/(**the whole**) **wad/** *Am.* col. 1. spend or use everything that one has. 2. say everything that one wants to say about a particular subject.

wad up *Am.* press smth. such as a piece of paper or cloth into a small tight ball.

wadcutter *esp. Am.* bullet designed to cut a neat hole in a paper range target.

waddy *Aus., NZ.* truncheon, club.

wade in *Br.* col. interrupt sb. or become involved in an annoying way.

wadge *Br.* col. wodge, wad, bundle.

wading pool *Am., Can.* paddling pool: *the difference between the water in a wading pool and the vast Atlantic.* – Reader's Digest.

waffle 1. *esp. Br.* col. talk or write meaninglessly and at great length n. **-y** adj.: *I found the session waffly* - Woman's Own., *Religious help in time of trouble is in the hands of manipulating moralists or waffling weaklings.* - Reader's Digest., *There is at least no waffle about middle ways.* - Economist. 2. *Am.* col. hesitate to do smth. or express one's opinion.

waffle *Am.* wafer.

waffly *esp. Br.* equivocal.

wag (it), also **play wag** *Br., Aus., NZ.* col. play truant: *Wagging it, I suppose.* - D. Lodge.

wage/ wage ceilings *Am. /Br.* **wage levels/** maximum wages.

wage/ incentive wage *Am.* progressive wage.

wage packet *esp. Br. /Am.* **paycheck/** people's wages.

wage restraint *Br.* wage control.

wages freeze *Br.* wage freeze.

wages sheet *Br.* payroll.

wage stop *Br.* policy of not allowing unemployed person to receive more money from public funds than he would earn while working.

wagon /also *Br.* **waggon**/. 1. *Br., Aus.* /*Am.* **freight car**/ a railway goods vehicle, esp. one with an open top. 2. *esp. Am.* a trolley for food and drinks. 3. *Am.* police patrol car: *they all wound up in the police wagon.* – P. Roth. 4. *Am.* col. car. 5. *esp. Am., Can.* wheeled cart or hut used as a food stall.

wagon/ fix sb.'s (**little red**) **wagon** *Am., Can.* col. punish, injure, ruin: *she said her brother would fix my wagon, which he did; right here in the corner of my mouth* - T. Capote.

wahine *NZ.* Maori woman or wife.

wahoo *Am.* 1. also *Can.* excl. of pleasure. 2. col. Hawaii.

waifs and strays *Br., Aus.* people and animals who has no home and no one to care for them.

wail *Am.* sl. play a jazz instrument.

wainscot *Br.* a fine grade of oak imported for woodwork.

waist *Am.* a blouse or bodice.

waistcoat *esp. Br., Aus.* /*Am., Can., Aus.* usu. **vest**/ a close-fitting garment without arms that has buttons down the front and is usu. worn under a jacket, esp. by men as part of a suit: *He retrieved the cat and hunted through his waistcoat pocket.* - M.M. Kaye.

waistcoat/ wear several waistcoats or **wear more than one waistcoat** *Br.* act in a number of different capacities /*Am.* **wear several hats**/.

waistpack *Am.* bumbag.

wait at table(s) *Br., Aus.* /*Am.* **wait (on) table(s), shoppers**/ serve meals esp. as a regular job or serve shoppers: *Libby waiting on tables over in the executive dining-room of the Chevrolet plant.* – P. Roth.

wait/ No waiting *Br.* /*Am.* **No standing**/.

wait/ wait dinner/lunch, etc. (**for** sb.) *esp. Am.* col. delay a meal until sb. arrives.

wait a meal on sb. *Br.* delay serving it until they arrive.

wait about *Br.* wait around doing nothing.

wait for it *Br.* col. not act before the proper moment.

wait in *Br.* stay at home expecting sb. to arrive.

wait on smth. *Am., Aus.* col. wait for smth. to happen before doing smth.

wait up *esp. Am., Can.* hold on, stop sb. to talk to them or go with them: *Hey, Amie, wait up!* – R.L. Stine.

wait list *Am., Can.* waiting list, esp. housing or admission to a hospital or school.

wait person *esp. Am.* waiter in a restaurant: *you treat maitre'd or wait staff* – J. Tesh.

waits *esp. Br.* rare. Christmas carollers.

wake(s) *Br.* annual holiday or vacation.

wake up and smell the coffee *esp. Am., Can.* col. become aware of the situation, however unpleasant.

wake-up *Aus., NZ.* col. alert and not easily fooled person.

wake-up call *esp. Am., Can., Aus.* 1. telephone call notifying the person called that agreed time to wake him/her up has arrived. 2. an event that warns sb. that they need to deal with an urgent or dangerous problems: *a wake-up call to the 10th power. The difference between heartburn and a heart attack.* – Reader's Digest.

wakey-wakey *Br., Aus.* excl. col. humor. 1. wake up. 2. start working seriously.

Waldorf salad *Am.* one made up principally of diced apples, celery, nuts and mayonnaise.

walk 1. *Br.* a ceremonial procession. 2. *esp. Br.* a. plantation of coffee, banana and other trees going in straight rows with wide spaces between them. b. division of forest under the charge of forester, etc. 3. *esp. Br.* a. the round of a tradesman, official or postman. b. district travelled by him/her. 4. *esp. Br.* farm where a hound puppy is sent for training and to accustom to various surroundings.

walk *Am., Can.* col. 1. abandon or suddenly withdraw from a job, commitment or situation. 2. be released from suspicion or charge.

walk/ take a walk *esp. Am.* col. rude way of saying to sb. to go away or stop talking nonsense.

walk/ walk one's **talk** *esp. Am., Can.* suit one's actions to one's words.

walk/ walk sb. **off their feet** *Br.* make sb. tired by making them walk too far.

walk/ walk the plank *Am.* be dismissed from one's job.

walk/ win in a walk *Am.* win easily.

walk away from *Am.* col. run faster than or defeat without difficulty.

walk in *esp. Am.* col. obtain a job easily, often in spite of competition: *With your background, you should walk in (to that job).* - Longman.

walk it *Br.* col. succeed very easily.

walk over *Am.* cheat, swindle.

walk sb. **through** smth. *Am., Aus.* practise it or show sb. how to do it from beginning to end.

walk up! *Br.* used by showman as an invitation to a circus or other show.

walkabout 1. *esp. Br.* col. walk through crowds by an important person mixing and talking informally with the people: *He also began in Stavropol Krai the walkabouts that were later to cause a national sensation* - Time., *Some of the people trying to touch him during walkabouts were sobbing* - Economist. 2. *Aus., Br.* period spent, esp. by an Australian aboriginal away from regular work travelling about on foot through the country, esp. in the phr. **go walkabout.**

walkabout/ go walkabout *Br.* (of sb. or smth.) get lost, disappear.

walkaround *Am.* round dance.

walkathon *Am., Can.* walking marathon.

walkaway *Am., Aus.* col. /*Br.* **walkover/** an easily-won competition: *The election that followed was a walkaway.* - H. Truman.

walkdown *Am.* col. the slow approach of a hero and villain from the opposite sides of a street just before the showdown (esp. in Western movies).

walker *esp. Br.* hiker, sb. who walks for pleasure or enjoyment.

walkies *Br.* col. excl. said to a dog to tell it that it is time for walking.

walk-in *esp. Am.* adj. 1. large enough to be walked into. 2. easy (esp. in the phr. **walk-in victory**).

walk-in clinic or other center *esp. Am.* one where a person can go in without making an arrangement beforehand.

walk-in closet *Am.* /*Aus.* **walk-in cupboard/**.

walking 1. *Am.* sl. bought to be used off premises. 2. *esp. Br.* hiking, esp. in the countryside.

walking boot *Br.* hiking boot.

walking frame *Br.* Zimmer frame: *old ladies to form a guard of honour with their walking-frames.* – S. Townsend.

walking holiday/tour, etc. *esp. Br.* hiking trip holiday.

walking papers *esp. Am.* col. /*Br.* **marching orders/**; asking sb. to leave their job or end relationship: *As soon as she found someone she liked better, she gave George his walking papers.* - H.C. Whitford, R.J. Dixson.

walking stick *Am.* stick insect.

walk-on *Am.* sports player with no regular status in a team.

walk-out *Am.* a customer going out of shop without having bought a thing.

walk-up *Am., Can.* col. n. adj. 1. (a flat, office, etc.) in a tall block with no lift: *The Browns live in a six-story walk-up.* - H.C. Whitford., R.J. Dixson. 2. (a block of flats) that is tall but has no lift: *This party was held on the walk-up top floor of a cold-water flat* - C. McCullers., *Then he lived in New York - just one room, walk-up, cold water and no heat.* - J. Steinbeck.

walk-up *Am.* preparatory hype.

wall *esp. Am.* roll (eyes) in a dramatic manner.

wall/ go to the wall *Br.* 1. lose all money. 2. support (a person or principle) strongly and be ready to suffer for them.

wall/ go up the wall *Br.* col. be very angry.

wall/ read/get/have the writing on the wall *Am.* be sure to fail.

wallaby *Aus.* a small Australian animal related to kangaroos.

wallaby/ on the wallaby (track) *Aus.* col. (of a person) unemployed and having no fixed address.

wallah *Br.* sl. person.

wall bar *Br.* one of a set of parallel horizontal bars attached to the wall of a gym, on which exercises are performed.

wallboard *esp. Am., Can.* type of board made from wood pulp, plaster or other material, used for covering walls and ceilings.

walled lake *Am.* mountainous lake.

wallet *Am.* /*Br.* **purse/** purse for carrying both coins and paper money: *a wallet with photographs and money* - B. Tillman., *We found wallets, a little bit of metal money, made in thirties.* - H. Smith.

wallet *Br., Can.* /*Am.* **billfold/**.

wall-eyed *Am.* having eyes that seem to point to the side.

wallop 1. *esp. Br.* col. beer. 2. *esp. Am.* heavy blow or punch: *The bunny packed a wallop from back legs* – Reader's Digest.

walloper *Aus.* policeman.

wall outlet, also **convenience outlet, (electric) outlet** *Am.* /*Br.* **power point, socket (outlet)/** wall socket, plug point.

wallpaper music *Br.* /*Am.* **elevator music,** tdmk. **muzak/** piped or canned music, muzak.

wall tent *Am., Can.* frame tent.

wally *Br., Aus.* col. a foolish or useless person, esp. male: *You get the wimpy blokes, real wallies, playing starring roles* - Woman's own.

wampum *Am.* col. money.

wand *Am.* a slat used as a mark for shooting in archery.

wandering hands *Br., Aus.* humor. people trying to touch other people for sexual excitement.

wank (off) *Br., Aus.* taboo. sl. 1. masturbate: *He himself felt only guilt and depression, like he used to feel as a lad when he wanked off* - D. Lodge. 2. an act of wanking.

wanker *Br., Aus.* taboo. sl. a foolish or useless person: *One of the most common terms of abuse in modern Britain is "wanker"* - P. Howard.

wannabee *esp. Am., Aus.* col. derog. person who wishes to be like sb. else: *a clubhouse for the city's notables and wannabees.* - New York., *Ian C. MacMillan...has counseled innumerable startup wannabees.* - Fortune.

want (in, into or **out, away)** *esp. Am.* col. wish to come or go: *the CIA, USA, and all the other damn alphabet phonies who wanted in on the action.* - J. DeFelice.

want off (out) *Am.* wish to leave a building or vehicle: *At the first ripple of trouble in almost three years, you want out.* - R. Cook.

want up *Am.* wish to get out of bed: *The boy must be feeling better, he's been wanting up all day.* - Longman.

want/ American will say *I want this changed, Do you want a memo?*, British will say usu. *I would like this changed, Would you like a memo?*

want ad *Am.* /*Br.* **small ad/** classified ad: *we read the want ads of wild LA papers* - J. Kerouac.

the War *esp. Br.* World War II.

war/ have been in the wars, look like you've been in the wars *Br., Aus.* col. humor. 1. person, esp. a child who has been hurt. 2. have had a lot of bad experiences.

warby *Aus.* sl. smth. or sb. filthy or inferior.

ward 1. *Am.* one of the parts into which a prison is divided. 2. *Br.* one of the small areas that a city has been divided into for the purpose of local elections.

ward boss *Am.* political leader of a ward.

warden 1. *esp. Am., Can.* /*Br.* **(prison) governor/** the head of a prison, governor: *The warden came in.* - L. Uris., *the new warden decided to take a personal look at his prisoners* - R.K. Mussle. 2. *Br., Aus.* the head of some older schools and colleges.

warder *esp. Br., Aus.* /*Am.* **guard/** a prison guard, **wardress** female prison guard.

war dog *Am.* militarist.

ward heeler *esp. Am.* col. derog. minor official of a political party who performs small duties in a ward or other local area: *some wardheeler that didn't mean the community any good was running for office* – A. Summers, R. Swan..

Wardour English *Br.* sham antique diction.

wardrobe *Br.* /*Am.* **closet/**.

wardrobe/ fitted wardrobe *Br.* built-in wardrobe.

wardrobe trunk *esp. Am.* trunk fitted with rails and shelves for use as a travelling wardrobe.

wares/ small ware(s) *Am.* haberdashery.

warehouse 1. *esp. Br.* a store where goods are sold wholesale. 2. *Br.* a large retail establishment 3. *Br., Aus.* /*Am.* **storehouse/** a house for storing items before they are sold. 4. *Am.* col. place sb., esp. a prisoner or psychiatric patient in a large impersonating institution.

war-game *Am.* use the strategy of a military exercices.

(the) warm *esp. Br.* a warm place, state or condition: *My client is keeping a six-by-nine warm at Charles Street jail.* - R.J. Randisi., M. Wallace.

warm *Am.* adj. fairly angry or excited.

warm over 1. *esp. Am., Can.* /*esp. Br.* **warm up/** reheat (food): *It won't take a minute to warm the soup over for you.* - Longman. 2. *esp. Am.* usu. derog. repeat an idea, use (the same arguments) again: *they are only warmed-over accusations.* - Time., adj. **warmed-over**.

warm up to/towards *esp. Am.* begin to like.

warm body *Am.* col. 1. uninteresting or unintelligent boring person. 2. a human person as opposed to a machine.

warm fuzzy *Am.* sl. a compliment: *a warm-and-fuzzy buzzword that few understand* - New York., *voters rejected candidates as warm-fuzzy phonies.* - USA Today.

warmly *Am.* slightly crazy.

warm-ups *Am., Can.* tracksuit for warm-up.

warrant *esp. Br.* receipt, given a person who has deposited goods in a warehouse.

warrant/ execute a warrant *esp. Am.* do what the warrant allows them to do.

warrigail *Aus.* 1. wild dog Dingo or wild horse. 2. adj. wild.

wart *Am.* verruca, horny projection on the skin caused by a virus.

wash *Am.* 1. col. adj. washable: *He carried yellow wash gloves.* - J. Dos Passos. 2. the work of washing cloth(es). 3. /*Br.* **washing/** cloth(es) that need washing or have just been washed; **do the wash, hang the wash out**: *housewifes hung wash on lines strung across porches* - D. Lodge. 4. also **dry wash** canyon, old-river bed. 5. a drink to follow another, chaser: *Can I have a wash with this, bartender?* - R.A. Spears. 6. col. a situation or result that is of no benefit to either of two oppsing sides.

wash sb. out *Am.* col. be excluded (or exclude sb.) from a course or position after a failure to meet the required standards.

wash up 1. *esp. Br., Aus.* /*Am.* **do the dishes/** wash dishes, plates, knives, forks, etc. after a meal: *Imagine how much more you'd find entertaining* *if you didn't have to wash up afterward* - You., *he washed up to earn a crust.* - New Idea., *One man was washing up lunch into a basin* - G. Greene. 2. *Am.* wash one's hands and face: *How about washing up for dinner, Jeane-Claude?* - E. Segal., *Our hosts suggested that we wash up and rest, and then gather for dinner.* - J. Baez., *So let's go down and wash up for chow.* - J. Cheever.

washbag *Br.* toilet bag.

washbasin, also **basin** *Br., Aus. /Am.* **washbowl, sink/** a large fixed container for water for washing the hands and face, esp. in a bathroom: *as though something were being poured down the washbasin drain.* - K. Vonnegut, Jr., *a wash bowl with towels and soap* – I. Stone.

washboard, base(board), mopboard *Am. /Br.* **skirting board/**.

washboard 1. *esp. Am.* surface of a worn, uneven road. 2. *esp. Am., Can.* cause ridges to develop on the road.

washbowl *Am. /Br.* **washing-up, washing-up basin/** dishpan: *I saw a wash-bowl jammed into the corner of the wall* - R. Chandler.

washcloth, washrag 1. *Am., Can. /Br.* **(face) flannel, face cloth,** *Aus.* **washer/** cloth used to wash, esp. the face, hands, etc.: *he lets her hands win and lifts the washrag.* - J. Updike., *Joanie took a warm washcloth and gently began to swab him.-* Reader's Digest. 2. *Br. /Am.* **dish towel**, *Br.* **tea towel/** dishrag, dishcloth: *She picked up a washcloth and ran it over clean counter tiles* - J. Kellerman.

washer *Am. /Br.* **washing machine/** one for washing clothes: *guys dropped their clothes in the washer* - Guideposts., *It has clogged up the drain hose on the washing machine.* – S. Townsend.

washer-drier *Br.* machine that washes and dries clothes.

washer-up *Br.* person who washes dishes.

washing/ do the washing 1. *Br.* wash the clothes, towels, etc. 2. *esp. Br.* wash all the plates, dishes, etc., that had been used for a meal: *Did some washing in a log cabin launderette.* – S. Townsend.

washing/ put the washing out *Br. /Am.* **hang the wash out/**.

washing-book *Br.* account book (one between friends on a trip).

washing line *Br.* a piece of string for hanging clothes to dry on.

washing powder/liquid *Br., Aus. /Am.* **soap powder** or **laundry detergent/** powdered detergent used to wash clothes.

washing things *Br.* toilet articles.

washing-up *Br., Aus.* col. */Am.* **dishes, wash/** 1. the washing of dishes, knives, etc. after a meal: *Robin tried to take a hand in washing-up after the meal* - D. Lodge. 2. */Am.* **dishes/** the plates, knives, etc. that are waiting to be washed up.

washing-up bowl *Br. /Am.* **dishpan/**.

washing-up cloth, tea towel, wash cloth, wash rag *Br. /esp. Am.* **dish towel/** dish towel.

washing-up liquid *Br. /Am.* **dish (washing) liquid/** thick soapy liquid that you add to hot water to clean dirty dishes: *it's no joke trying to wash up in cold water without any washing-up liquid.* – S. Townsend.

washing-up machine *Br.* a dishwasher.

washroom *Am., Can.* euph. obs. */esp. Br.* euph. **cloakroom/** toilet: *A washroom faced the staircase* - R. Moore., *And in the bus stations the washrooms are exactly the same.* - J. Steinbeck.

wash-up *Br.* col. person who is a dish washer in the kitchen of a restaurant or hotel.

wash-up time *Am.* time given to a worker during a lunch break to wash up hands.

wash water *Am.* washing water.

WASP *esp. Am., Can., Aus.* White Anglo-Saxon Protestant: *I'm one quarter Italian, one quarter WASP, and one half Jewish.* - H. Fast., *WASP air of all-American boyishness.* - T. Thompson; adj. **-y.**

Wasserman test *Am.* the standard test for syphilis: *I almost went out and had a Wasserman.* – J. O'Hara.

wastage *Br., Aus. /Br.* **natural wastage**, *Am., Aus.* **attrition/**.

wastage *Br. /Am., Aus.* **attrition/** people who leave an educational or training course before it has finished.

waste *esp. Am., Can.* col. kill. **-ed.**. adj.: *They'll waste him.* - T. Thompson.

waste of space *esp. Br.* col. completely useless.

waste not want not *Br.* obs. be economical in food, clothes, etc.

wastebasket *esp. Am.* waste paper basket */esp. Br.* also **(waste) bin, waste paper basket/ bin,** *esp. Aus.* col. **WPB/** a container for trash: *I carried her around in a wastebasket* - J. Baez., *There was a copy of the Times in his wastebasket.* - D. Hammet., *She emptied his waste basket and whisked a cloth across his desk.* - E. Segal.

wasted *esp. Br.* extremely tired from drinking too much or after taking illegal drugs.

waste disposal *esp. Br.* 1. also waste disposal unit */Am.* **garbage disposal/** machine connected to a sink drainage which cuts solid waste into small pieces. 2. */Am.* **disposal/** the process or system of waste disposal in the kitchen.

waster *Br., Aus. /Am.* **bum/** no-good person.
wasteway *Am.* drain.
watch/ (be) on sb.'s **watch** *Am.* (be) responsible for smth., have authority.
watchband *Am. /Br.* **watchstrap/**.
(watch) crystal *Am. /Br.* **watch-glass/** the transparent cover over the face of a clock or watch.
watchdog *Am.* guard dog.
watching brief *Br.* law. brief held by a barrister to follow a case on behalf of a client who is not directly involved.
watchstrap *esp. Br. /Am., Aus.* **watchband/**.
water *esp. Br.* lake, pond or river.
water/ at the water's edge *Am.* on the border of the US.
water/ be water over the dam *Am., Can.* said if smth. happened a long time ago and no one is upset about it now.
water/ in low water, also **low in water** *esp. Br.* sl. lacking money.
water/ in smooth water *esp. Br.* sl. free from trouble (after difficulties).
waterage *esp. Br.* the movement of goods or merchandise by water or fee paid for it.
water back *Am.* a water heater set in the firebox of a stove.
water bomber *Can.* aircraft used for extinguishing forest fires by dropping water.
waters break *Br., Aus. /Am.* **water breaks/** the moment when a baby is almost ready to be born.
water bug *Am.* col. small insect that lives in or on water.
water butt *esp. Br., Aus. /Am.* **rain barrel**, *Aus.* **water tank/** a container for storing rain water which can then be used to water plants.
watercooler *Am.* 1. a machine that holds and dispenses cold drinking water along with paper cups: *Passing the watercooler he wished he had a pill to pop into his mouth.* – P. Roth. 2. col. socializing in such a place.
water diviner *Br.* person who searches for underground water by using a dowsing rod.
water dog *Am.* mud puppy.
watered stock *Am.* cattle given little water while being driven to the market and then given it to increase weight.
water fountain *Am. /esp. Br.* **drinking fountain**, *Am., Aus.* **bubbler/**.
water gap *Am.* a pass in a mountain ridge through which a stream runs.
water gun *Am., Can.* water pistol.
water heater *Am. /Br.* **geyser** or **immersion tank/** electric water heater.

water ice *esp. Br. /Am.* **sorbet/** a frozen sweet made of fruit juice or water with colour and taste added.
watering hole *Am.* col. 1. watering place (resort). 2. any stylish public area: *It became Frank's favourite watering hole.* – A. Summers, R. Swan.
watering pot *Am.* watering can.
water inlet *Am.* inlet pipe for water supply.
Waterloo/ (have) met one's **Waterloo** *Br.* finally (have) met sb./smth. that can defeat them.
watermelon/ swallow a watermelon seed *Am.* col. become pregnant.
waterproof *Br.* garment that keeps out water.
waterproof, watertight *Am. /Br.* **hose-proof/** (of electric engine) protected from water.
water rates *Br.* the charges made for the use of water from the public water supply system.
water-repellant *Am. /Br., Aus.* **showerproof/**.
watershed *Br.* a time before which TV broadcasters have agreed not to show programs unsuitable for children, e.g. **9 o'clock watershed**.
waterspout *esp. Am.* a tornado filled with water which forms over the sea.
water tower *Am.* one raised above the ground and that serves as a reservoir for small towns.
waterwaggon *esp. Am.* water cart, a vehicle carrying water for sale or for washing roads.
water witch *Am.* water diviner.
waterworks *esp. Br., Aus.* euph. or humor. (often used by doctors) the body's organs for removing urine from the body.
waterworks/ turn on the waterworks *Br.* obs. start crying, esp. as a way of persuasion.
water vole *Br.* water rat.
wattle/ bring wattle bloom *Aus.* court disaster.
wattle *Aus.* acacia.
wattle-and-dab hut, wattle *Aus. /Br.* **wattle and dab house/** one made of wattle and dab.
Wattle Day *Aus.* August the first, day when wattle blooms.
wave *Am.* col. woman who is a member of a US Navy Volonteer group.
wave/ catch the wave *Am., Aus.* try to get advantage for oneself becoming involved with smth. that is becoming popular or fashionable.
wave/ make waves *Am.* col. cause disturbances, difficulties: *If I don't make waves, I can have a better job.* - J. Kellerman.
waving base, also **spectators base** *Br.* observation desk for spectators at an airport.
wax *Br.* obs. sl. a sudden burst of anger, bad temper, rage, etc. **-y** adj.: *All the masters got into dreadful waxes.* - J. Joyce.

wax crayon *esp. Br.* a type of pencil.
waxed paper, also **wax paper** *esp. Am., Can.* /*Br.* greaseproof paper/: *she wrapped herself up like a salt water taffy in its waxed paper covering.* - D. Brenner.
waxhead *Aus.* col. surfer.
waxworks *Br.* /*Am.* **wax museum**/ place where people can see wax models of famous people.
way/ a long way to go *Am.* a long way ahead.
way *Am.* col. very.
way *Br.* col. dither, tizzy /**be in a way** or **in a great way** *Br.* be in a dither.
way/ be in a bad way *Br.* col. be very ill, injured, or upset.
way/ every which way 1. *Am.* or *Br.* col. in every direction, all over the place. 2. *Am.* using every possible method.
way/ get into the way of doing smth. *Br.* start to do smth. regularly.
way/ give way (to) *Br., Aus.* /*Am.* **yield**/ allow other traffic to get first.
way/ go back a long way *esp. Br.* /*esp. Am.* **go way back**/ be friends for a long time.
way/ No way! *esp. Am.* I don't believe you.
way/ over the way *Br.* across the way, nearby, esp. on the opposite side of the street.
way/ put sb. **in the way of doing** smth. *Br.* obs. give sb. a chance to do or get smth.
way/ see which way the cat jumps *Aus.* col. delay making decision on doing smth.
way/ that's the way the ball bounces *Am.* col. bad things sometimes happen.
way/ that's the way the cookie crumbles *esp. Am., Can.* col. that's the way things turn out.
way/ the Great White Way *Am.* Broadway.
way/ the other way about *Br.* in the opposite position or direction.
way/ way out, over, across, etc. *Am.* along distance out, over, etc.
wayfreight *Am.* local railway goods train.
way out *Br.* 1. door or passage to leave a building, exit (exit sign is confined to theatres and carparks). 2. way of getting away from a difficult situation.
way out *Am.* col. (popular in 1970s) good or exciting: *He's always been way out* – N. Hentoff.
way passenger *Am.* passenger going out of the vehicle when he demands a stop.
way point *Am.* a stopping place on a route during journey.
ways *Am., Can.* 1. way (a distance to go): *But these absences are strange and go back a ways.* - Time., *I got a long ways to go yet* - J. Dos Passos., *I still had a ways to go.* - W. Jack, B. Laursen. 2. adv. much.
Ways and Means Committee *Am.* group of representatives in the government of a US state or in the Congress who must find money for the government to spend.
a ways off *Am.* far from where sb. is.
way station *Am., Can.* a railway intermediate station: *This grotto had become more than a way station.* - J. Fraser., *an income policy was a way station to controls.* - Atlantic Monthly.
way to go! *Am., Can.* col. 1. well done! 2. humor. said when a person has made smth. foolish.
way train *Am.* local train.
waywarden *esp. Br.* one supervising highways.
way wise *Am.* knowing the road.
wazoo *Am.* col. buttocks.
wazoo/ have smth. **coming) out the wazoo/ kazoo, have** smth. **up the ying yang** *Am.* sl. humor. have a lot of smth.
wazzock *Br.* col. stupid or annoying person.
WC, toilet *Br.* /*Am.* **restroom**/ public toilet; wc is often used in ads for houses, flats, and hotels.
w/e *Br.* weekend (in correspondence).
weak sister *Am.* col. weakling: *It looks like Dave is the weak sister on the team.* - R.A. Spears.
weak spot/ have a weak spot for sb./smth. *Am.* feel affection for sb.
weal *Br.* a swelling made on sb.'s skin by a blow, esp. from smth. sharp or thin as sword or whip.
wear *esp. Br., Aus.* col. stand for, allow or find acceptable.
wear/ be/look the worse for wear *Br.* be drunk.
wear out *Am.* col. 1. wear (a garment) so as to get full use of it and finish its use quickly in order to change to smth. new: *I'm just wearing out this old coat* - Longman. 2. beat sb.: *Let me get at him, I'll soon wear him out!* - Longman.
wear/ not wear smth. *Br.* col. used to say that sb. won't allow or accept smth.
wear the pants *Am., Aus.* humor. /*Br.* **wear the trousers/ (in the family/house)/** be the person in the relationship who makes all the important decisions.
weasel *Br.* a dodge. v. behave in a devious way.
weasel out of *esp. Am.* col. escape from duty: *You can't just weasel out now when we need you!* - R.A. Spears.
weasel word *esp. Am.* one lacking force and exact meaning: *When the thief was being questioned by the police, he tried to fool them with weasel words.* - A. Makkai.

weather/ keep a weather eye on smth. *Br.* watch them carefully.
weather/ make heavy weather (out) of smth. *Br.* do smth. inefficiently making it seem more difficult than it really is.
weather/ under the weather *Am.* slightly drunk.
weatherboard *esp. Br. /esp. Am., Can.* **clapboard/** sloping board attached to the bottom of an outside door to keep out the rain.
weather bureau *Am. /Br.* **meteorological office, weather centre/**.
weather coat *esp. Br.* stormcoat.
weather eye/ keep a weather eye on smth./ sb. *Br., Aus.* watch sb./smth. carefully because they may cause trouble or they may need help.
weather-girl *Am.* a woman weather forecaster.
weather-proof *esp. Br.* a raincoat.
weave/ get weaving *Br. obs. col.* a. become busy. b. begin hurriedly, hurry up.
The Webfoot State *Am.* Oregon. **Webfoot** *Am.* citizen of Oregon.
web lettuce *Br.* loose iceberg lettuce.
one's **wedding tackle** *Br. humor.* a man's sexual organs.
wedding band *esp. Am., Can.* wedding ring.
wedding breakfast *Br.* breakfast eaten just after a wedding by the couple and the guests.
wee *esp. Br. col.* urinate.
the wee (small) hours *Am. /Br.* **small hours/** the early morning, between about 1 o'clock and 4 o'clock.
weed *Br., Aus. col. derog.* (used esp. by children to other children) a. person who is physically weak and usu. very thin and tall. b. person of weak character.
weed whacker *esp. Am.* strimmer, electric grass trimmer.
weedy *Br. col.* weak and not having a strong character.
weejuns *esp. Am. tdmk.* moccasin-style shoes for casual wear.
week/ Monday, Tuesday, etc. **week,** also **a week on Monday, Tuesday,** etc. *esp. Br., Aus. /Am.* **a week from** the stated day/ a week after (the stated day).
weekend / at the weekend, at weekends *Br. / Am.* **on the weekend. On weekends, over the weekend/**: *she'd never seen him on a weekend.* - R.J. Randisi., M. Wallace.
weekend/ look like a wet weekend, have a face like a wet weekend *Br. col.* look very sad.
weekender *Aus. col.* a cottage for weekend rest.

weenie *Am.* 1. frankfurter: *I spotted him in a white barbecue stand tickling weinies with a long fork.* - R. Chandler. 2. sl. a despicable person. 3. col. (used by children) weak, afraid or stupid person.
weeny *Br. /Am. col.* **weensie/** extremely small.
weigh up *esp. Br.* weigh.
weight/ throw one's **weight about** *esp. Br.* give orders to others, because one thinks they are important.
weighting *Br.* smth. additional, esp. an additional pay given to cover extra costs of living in certain areas.
weight training *Br.* weight lifting as a form of exercise.
weirdy *Am.* weirdo, eccentric person.
weisenheimer *Am. sl.* presumptuous smart aleck: *he smiled that wisenheimer smile of his* - D. Hammet.
weiss beer *Am.* light beer.
welcome/ You are welcome *esp. Am.* Don't mention it.
welcome wagon *Am., Can. tdmk.* an organisation that greets new residents by extending to them free promotion from local merchants.
welfare *Am.* 1. benefit for the poor, esp. in **be on welfare**: *welfare is for poor people.* - Reader's Digest. 2. /*Br.* **social security/**.
well *Br.* 1. col. adv. very. 2. the space in front of the judge in a law court where the clerks and ushers sit.
well/ *esp. Am., Can.* I'm not a well man (not in a good health): *His eyes were not a well man's now.* - D. Hammet.
well *Br. col. adj.* describing how sb. feels or which situation they're in.
well/ as well *esp. Br.* just as well.
well/ be well out of *Br.* be lucky to be in a situation.
well/ be well up in/on *esp. Br. col.* know a lot about smth.
well/ leave well alone *Br., Aus. /Am.* **leave well enough alone/** not try to improve smth. that is not causing any problems.
well and truly *Br.* used for adding emphasis to a description of smth.
well away 1. *esp. Br., Aus. col.* starting to be drunk. 2. *Br. col.* be completely involved in doing smth. 3. *Br., Aus. col.* be sleeping. 4. *Br. col.* having made considerable or easy progress.
well in/ be well in *col. Br., Aus. /Am.* **be in well/** have a good relationship with a person or group which gives you an advantage.

well out of it/smth. *Br., Aus.* col. lucky not to be involved.
well-built 1. *Br., Aus.* used to avoid saying fat. 2. *Am.* having an attractive body.
well-cooked *Br.* well done (of food).
well covered *Br.* col. slightly plump.
well-fixed *Am.* /*Br.* **well-to-do**/ rich.
well-heeled *Am.* sl. well armed.
wellington (boot), col. **welly, wellie** *esp. Br., Aus.* /*Am., Can.* **rubber boot**, *Aus.* **gumboot**, *Am.* **rubber**/ high rainproof boot: *There's some special transport for those without Wellington boots!* - Gloucester Citizen.
wellness *Am.* the state of being healthy.
well-wedged *Br.* sl. rich.
welly *Br.* 1. col. Wellington. 2. sl. effort, power. 3. sl. condom. 4. sl. dismissal.
welly/ give it some welly *Br.* col. make it well, put more effort into it.
wellnigh *Br.* almost, but not quite.
Welsh dresser *Br.* /*Am.* **hutch**/ a piece of furniture with drawers and cupboard in the lower part and shelves on top.
Wendy house *Br.* /*Am.* **play house**/ a playhouse for a child.
west/ go west *Br., Aus.* obs. humor. a. die or be lost. b. be damaged or ruined.
Westerner *Am.* person who lives in or comes from the West.
western sandwich *Am., Can.* sandwhich having an omelette filling containing onion, green pepper, and ham.
westie *Aus.* a suburban Sydneysider.
Westralia, also **Groperland** *Aus.* West Australia.
Western saddle *Am.* stock saddle for a horse.
wet 1. *Br.* col. derog. (of a person) lacking strength of character and unwilling to take firm or forceful action, weak: *He was an idiot, wet, he had missed his chance* - J. Fowles. 2. *Br.* col. n. a political moderate person in the British Conservative Party. 3. *Am.* n. adj. (person) favouring laws permitting alcoholic drinks sales. 4. *Br.* col. a drink n. adj. (in the phr. **have a wet**). 5. **the wet** *Aus.* rain period in Australian tropics.
wet/ be all wet *Am., Can.* col. be completely crazy or wrong.
wet/ In *Br.* English past tense and past participle of wet are usu. wetted except in phrs. like **wet the bed** or **wet** oneself.
wet the baby's head *Br.* col. celebrate a baby's birth with a drink.
wetback *Am.* col. derog. also **wady** an illegal immigrant from Southwest.

wet bar *Am., Can.* bar or counter in the home for serving alcoholic drinks: *right here gonna put me a little wet bar* – J. Hopkins.
wet bob *Br.* water sport enthusiast.
wet fish *Br.* fresh fish.
wet wash *Am.* still not dried or ironed.
whack *Br.* 1. also *Aus.* (a fair or equal) share: *bring me the full whack.* - B. Bryson. 2. also *Aus.* a try, attempt. 3. sl. prison term. 4. special sphere.
whack *Am.* col. contract killing, murder.
whack/ do one's **whack** *Br.* col. do one's fair share of work.
whack/ have a whack at smth. *Br.* /*Am.* **take a whack at** smth./ col. try to do smth.: *she was young enough to have a whack at whatever she wanted* – J. O'Hara.
whack/ in/at one whack *Br.* col. (done) all at once, all at one occasion.
whack/ out of whack *esp. Am., Can., Aus.* col. 1. not working properly. 2. confused and badly organised: *housing prices have got out of whack with reality* - Time.
whack/ top/(the) full whack *esp. Br.* the full amount that sb. can be charged.
whack up *Am., Aus.* col. share (usu. money): *Have we decided how to whack up the profits from the robbery?* - Longman.
whacked (out) also **whacked to the wide** 1. *Br., Aus.* col. very tired: *You two looked whacked!* - T. Thorne. 2. *Am.* behaving in a very strange way: *And Elvis hung in there – bloated and sometimes whacked out of his mind on prescription chemicals* – J. Hopkins.
whacking *esp. Br., Aus.* col. a beating: *they were backed up with old-fashioned stick-whackings.* - New York.
whacking *Br.* col. emphasizing word for how big smth is, esp. **whacking great**.
whacko *Br.* excl. of delight; great, jolly good.
whale (at, on, for) 1. *Br.* sl. expert, shark (at). 2. *esp. Am.* col. v. hit, thrash: *somebody whales the shit out of you* - G.V. Higgins., *If I had pinned my coat my mother would have whaled me* - J. Steinbeck., *Gosh, if pop finds it he'll give me a whalin'* - J. Dos Passos.
whale into *Am.* start attacking sb.
a whale of a bill, problem, etc *Am., Aus.* a large bill, problem, etc.
whaler *Aus.* col. a tramp, esp. one following the course of a river.
wham *Am.* sl. v. beat, strike.
whammy *Am., Aus.* col. evil eye: *Sarge, you got the whammy on me!* - T. Thorne.

whanau *NZ.* extended family living together in the same area.

whang *Br.* a large piece, chunk.

whanny *Br.* person who employs a nanny to look after his or her children.

whap *Am.* whop, beat hard.

wharfie *Aus., NZ.* col. waterside worker or labourer.

what *esp. Br.* excl. at the end of a sentence, used to express agreement, expecting an answer yes.

what/ What do you say we… *Am.* col. used when suggesting smth. to solve a problem.

whatever *esp. Am.* col. (used when replying to an offer or suggestion, esp. to show a lack of interest).

what for *esp. Br., Aus., Can.* col. punishment: *She'd have given John Wayne what-for* - A. Hitchcock Mystery Magazine

what's new? *Am.* col. Hello, how are you?

What's up?, What's happening? *esp. Am.* col. (used to say hello and ask about the news from sb. you know well): *Hello Bob, what's up?* - A. Makkai.

What's with…? *Am.* col. used to ask people why they are behaving strangely or violently.

Wheat Belt *Can.* the large tract on the Prairies mainly given over to the growing of wheat.

wheat meal *esp. Br.* brown flour made from whole grains of wheat.

The Wheat State 1. *Aus.* South Australia. 2. *Am.* Minnesota.

whee (**up**) *Am.* sl. fill with excitement, cheer up.

wheel *Am.* 1. bicycle: *They left their wheels by the roadside* - J. London. 2. a dollar. 3. transmit (power or electricity). 4. col. an executive, boss: *John was a natural wheel at the University of Texas.* - Atlantic Monthly.

wheel/ silly as a wheel *Aus.* very silly.

wheel/ the fifth/third wheel *Am.* excessive thing or person.

wheel/ the squeaky wheel (gets the grease) *Am.* person or people who get what they want by complaining.

wheel out *esp. Br.* col. produce in order to gain a desired result, esp. in a dishonest or insincere way: *Gorbachev…wheeled out the obedient conservative majority* - H. Smith.

wheel clamp *esp. Br., Aus. /Am.* **Denver boot/** a strong clamp fixed to one wheel of the car. It is unlocked with a special key only when the driver has paid the fine for illegal parking: *Agency…now have powers to wheelclamp and remove vehicles not showing a current (tax) disc* - Young Citizen's Passport.

wheel horse *esp. Am.* responsible and hardworking person, esp. a politician.

wheelie bin *Br.* col. little refuse bin set on wheels.

wheelman *esp. Am., Can.* person who draws a car or takes the wheel of a boat.

wheels/ oil the wheels *Br.* grease them; help things run smoothly.

wheels/ on wheels *Br.* col. 1. smoothly. 2. used to emphasize dislike of sb.

wheelsman *Am., Can.* person who steers a ship or boat.

wheeze *Br.* col. a clever advantageous idea or plan.

whelk/ sb. couldn't run a whelk stall *Br.* col. a person cannot organize anything.

when/ if and when *Am., Aus.* doing it when it's needed or convenient, not in a regular way.

when-issued *esp. Am.* finance. related to trading in securities which haven't been issued.

whenua *NZ.* land.

where it's at *Am.* col. popular or fashionable activity.

whiff 1. *Br.* col. unpleasant smell. 2. *Am., Can.* (in baseball or golf) unsuccessful attempt to hit the ball.

whiffet *Am.* col. worthless person.

whiffletree *esp. Am.* swingletree.

whiffy *Br., Aus.* col. having a bad smell, smelly: *It's a bit whiffy in here, isn't it?* - T. Thorne.

whilst *esp. Br.* while.

whinge *Br., Aus.* col. derog. complain in an annoying way about smth. unimportant: *You're not a whingeing Pom, Bru.* - J. Harmer., R. Rossner.

whip 1. *Br.* col. steal. 2. *esp. Am.* col. defeat sb. easily. 3. *Am., Can.* scythe for cutting special crops. 4. *Br.* party membership.

whip *Br.* a notice which tells the members of political party in Parliament how to vote on an important issue.

whip/ chocolate whip/strawberry whip, etc. *Br.* sweet dish made from the white part of an eggs, chocolate and fruit, beaten together to make a smooth light mixture.

whipbird *Aus.* bird with singing that reminds the sound of whip beating.

whipped cream, whipping cream *Am.* /*Br.* **double cream**/: *we have enough whipped cream to make this cake.* - R.L. Stine.

whipping *Am.* severe beating.

whip-round *esp. Br., Aus.* col. collection of money among a group of people for example in a place of work, to give to one member, esp. in the phr. **have a whip-round**.

whips of *Aus., NZ.* large quantities of.

whipsaw *Am.* col. a. defeat or cause to fail in two opposite ways at the same time: *victim to the petrodollar interest-rate whipsaw in 1975.* - K. Lipper. b. have or take advantage of, as by playing one against the other.

whipstitch/ at every whipstitch *Am.* every minute.

whipstick *Aus.* col. a small eucalyptus.

whipsy *Br.* milkshake.

whirlwind/ reap the whirlwind *Am.* have serious problems because sb. did smth. stupid in the past.

whirlybird *esp. Am., Can.* col. helicopter: *The whirly bird landed on the roof of the hospital.* - R.A. Spears., *We've got the good Dr. Lucas focused on his whirlybird* - K. Ablow.

whiskbroom *Am.* small stiff broom used to brush clothes.

whisker/ by a whisker *esp. Br.* col. by a very small amount.

whiskey *esp. Br., Aus. /esp. Am., Can.* **Scotch**, *Am., Irish Eng., Can.* **whisky/** a drink of whiskey.

whiskey *Am.* radio letter W.

Whisky Mac *Br.* drink consisting of Scotch and ginger wine in equal proportions.

whist drive *Br.* a social occasion at which whist is played.

whistle *Br.* a suit.

whistle/ be whistling Dixie *Am.* col. talk in a way that makes things better than they really are.

whistle/ you can whistle for it *Br.* col. derog. you won't get what you want.

whistlestop *esp. Am., Can.* 1. small railway station, where politicians stop on election tour: *a whistlestop outside of Elephant Butte.* - A. Hitchcock Mystery Magazine. 2. travel about the country on a political campaign.

Whit *esp. Br.* Whitson.

white *Br.* (of coffee) served with cream or milk.

white out *Can.* make (a road) impossible to see because of ice, mist and blowing snow: *If this winter storm gets any worse, it could white out the highway* - Longman.

white bread *Am., Can.* col. conventional, bourgeois: *Tom Cruise is a perfectly cast, a go-getting, white bread hero* - New Yorker., *It was kind of white-bread neighborhood* - W. Jack, B. Laursen., *he's a white-bread Beverly Hills boy* - Daily News.

white caps *Am. /Br.* **white horses/** waves at sea that are white at the top.

white coffee *Br.* coffee with milk and cream added.

whitefish *Br.* any of various fishes with flesh that is not oily, all sea fish other than herring, salmon and sea trout.

white flight *Am.* col. white residents flight to suburbs to escape the effects of desegregation.

white gasoline (or **gas**) *Am., Can.* Naphtha liquid fuel used in pressure stove lamps, etc., dry spirits.

white goods *Br.* (business term) fridges, washing machines and other large pieces of electric household equipment.

white-haired boy, also **fair-haired boy** *Am.* col. /*Br.* derog. **blue-eyed boy/** favourite.

white hat *Am.* sl. positive hero (esp. in a Western): *you went straight to the fleet as a white hat.* - B. Tillman.

white horses *Br. /Am.* **white caps/** waves which are white at the top.

white lightning *Am.* col. crude, fierce, home-made whiskey, moonshine: *Lester made friends with him and got him drunk on white lightning.* - C. McCullers.

white list *Am.* 1. diplomatic immunity list. 2. recommended list.

The White Mountain State *Am.* New Hampshire.

whiteout *Am., Aus. /Br.* tdmk. **Tipp-Ex,** *Am., Aus.* tdmk. **Liquid paper/**.

white pages *Am., Aus.* a book listing the names, addresses and telephone numbers of people and businesses operating in a city or area.

whiter than white *Br.* derog. very honest and morally right people.

whites *esp. Br.* white clothing, esp. as worn for sports such as tennis and cricket: *I remembered her bloody tennis whites.* – R.L. Stine.

white sale *Am.* period at which sheets, towels, etc. are sold for lower prices.

white-shoe *Am.* col. relating to a company, esp. a law firm, owned and run by members of the WASP elite.

white space *Am.* col. free time.

white spirit *esp. Br. /Am., Aus.* **turpentine/** methyl alcohol used for making paint thinner for removing marks on clothes, etc.

white stick *esp. Br. /esp. Am.* **white cane/** a stick that the blind use when working.

white stock *Br.* chicken or fish stock, as opposed to **brown stock**, one of beef.

white trash *Am., Can.* col. derog. poor white from the South of the US: *On this day she looked less than a battle scored whore and more like a frightened white trash housewife* - T. Thompson.

whitewall 1. *Am., Can.* of a haircut in which the sides of the head are shaved and the top and back are left longer. 2. *Am.* car tyre that has a wide white band on its side.

whitewash *Br. /Am.* **shut out/** col. defeat a player or a team while preventing them from scoring any points; n.

whitewater *Am.* rapids: *the men's expert division of a white water competition* - National Geographic., *we were running white water* - S. North., *I finally got up the nerve to try white-water rafting.* - Reader's Digest.

white wax *Br.* paraffin (wax) */Br.* **paraffin** in *Am.* is **kerosene/**.

white wedding *Br.* tradional wedding when a bride wears a white dress.

white wing *Am.* street sweeper.

whitey *Am.* sl. insulting word for white person used by blacks.

Whitsun *Br.* Pentecost.

whizbang *Am.* sl. beauty: *something like a whiz-bang ride on a historical loop-the-loop.* - J.A. Michener.

whizz 1. *Am., Can.* col. an act of urinating, v. 2. *Br.* col. amphetamines.

whizbang *Am.* col. very good, loud or fast.

whiz(kid) *esp. Am.* col. skilful or successful person: *he's no whiz* – P. Roth.

whole/ (*esp. Am.*) The storm caused a whole lot of (=a great deal) damage.

whole/ go the whole nine yards *Am.* col. do completely.

the whole bit *Br., Aus. /Am.* col. **the whole enchilada, the wholeball of wax, the whole nine yards/** everything related to smth.

whole cloth/ make smth. **up out of while cloth; invent** smth. **out of whole cloth, be made out of whole cloth** *Am.* be not true.

wholefood(s) *Br.* food that hasn't had any of its natural features taken away or any artificial substances added.

wholegrain *esp. Br., Aus.* containing whole seeds.

whole hog/ go whole hog *Am.* do smth. completely.

wholemeal *Br. /Am.* **whole wheat/** wholemeal flour or bread that uses all of the grain: *Whole-wheat flour contains bran and germ and thus is rich in vitamins* – Reader's Digest.

whole note *esp. Am., Can. /Br.* **semibreve/** musical note with a time value equal to two minims.

wholesale politics *esp. Am.* electoral campaigning via the media.

wholesale/ at wholesale *Am. /Br.* **by wholesale/** by wholesale.

the whole shebang *Am.* the structure or organisation of smth.

whomp it up *esp. Am., Can.* 1. excite (sb.): *The girls do this special dance to whomp up the crowd* - Longman. 2. prepare smth. hastily: *The tracks were then taken to Baker who womped up a massive drum sound* - Rolling Stone.

whomping, whompy *Am.* col. very big: *In addition to their whompy beat, both songs feature lyrics that have spurred interest* - Rolling Stone.

whoop *Am.* create or stir up excitement or enthusiasm.

whoop-de-doo *Am.* col. noisy party or election: *have us a good whoop-dee-doo.* – K. Vonnegut, Jr.

whoopie/ make whoopie 1. *Am.* obs. col. have sex. 2. *Br.* obs. have a good time.

whoopsie *Br.* col. euph. a piece of excrement.

whop, whup 1. *esp. Am.* col. beat or defeat sb. easily, esp. in a sport or fight. 2. *Am.* col. flop. 3. *Am.* sl. a blow.

whore after *esp. Am.* desire or try to obtain (smth.) immoral: *he was still whoring up after the pleasures of evil living.* - Longman.

whorehouse *esp. Am.* brothel.

whortleberry *Br.* bilberry.

why *esp. Am.* or obs. excl. (used to express surprise or slight annoyance).

wick/ get on sb.'s **wick** *Br., Aus.* col. annoy sb. esp. continuously.

wickiup *Am.* any small hut or shanty.

wide berth/ give sb./smth. **a wide berth** *esp. Br.* avoid them.

wide boy 1. *Br., Aus.* derog. col. cleverly, dishonest person, esp. a businessman. 2. *esp. Am.* (of a tennis racket) having a white head. 3. *Am.* col. large heavily-built person, esp. one who plays a team sport.

widget *Am.* sl. gadget, device: *Second wave businessmen worked hard to make every widget identical, and some still do.* - A. Toffler.

widgie *Aus.* a girlfriend of a dandy.

widow-maker *Can.* dead branch caught precariously high in a tree which may fall on a person below.

widow's walk *Am., Can.* a balcony near the ocean to watch ships: *widow's walk rising gently, like the swell in the ocean facing it.* - K. Lipper.

wiener, weener *Am., Can.* 1. frankfurter, (cocktail) sausage: *it was a Girl scout wienie bake.* – J. Steinbeck. 2. taboo sl. (used by children) penis. 3. col. stupid person.

wiener roast *Am., Can.* party at which sausages are roasted: *Bobby went to nearby Mountain Creek Lake for a wiener roast* - T. Thompson.

wifey *Br.* term of endearment for one's wife.

wig *Am.* sl. 1. person's hair. 2. one's head or brain. 3. v. (**out**) get excited: *What saved him from wigging out, right then and there was a slight pressure on his left hand.* - T. de Haven. 4. (**out**) get drugged.

wigan *Br.* prototype of small city architectural horror and cultural provinciality.

wigan/ come from wigan *Br.* /*Am.* **come from a beautiful downtown Burbank/** be a small town hick.

wigging *Br.* col. an act of talking angrily to sb. who has done smth. wrong: *If he was late, and missed the prayers offered daily in the hall chapel at that time he got a wigging.* - Cheshire Life., *I should have a confounded wigging and be sent on board* - Cpt. Marryat.

wiggle/ get a wiggle on! *Am.* col. do smth. faster.

wiggy *esp. Am., Can.* emotionally uncontrolled or weird.

wigwag *Am.* col. move to and fro; signal by waving an arm, flag, light, etc.

wigwam *Am.* obs. political convention temporary building.

wild and wooly *Am., Can.* uncouth, rough-and-tumble: *When cowboys are on the range, they become wild and wooly.* - W. Magnuson.

wild-call *Am.* shop department where salesmen give products to customers for earnest (money).

wild-card *Am.* a. (of sports team) qualifying for championship play-offs. b. winning an arbitrary play-off among second-place teams.

wild-cat *Am.* col. 1. a locomotive and its tender operating without other cars. 2. adj. not-scheduled, additional (of trains).

wild-cat *Am.* look for oil where nobody has found any yet.

wildcat strike *esp. Am.* a sudden unofficial stopping of work.

wildcatter *Am.* prospector who sinks exploring oil wells.

wild child *Br.* journalism. young girl who looks very attractive and grown-up and behaves in an undisciplined way.

wilderness/ in the wilderness *Br.* esp. journalism. (of a political party or politician) having failed in elections.

wilderness area *Am.* virgin land used in National Park.

wilding *Am.* col. violent rampage of a gang of youths in a public place with attacking or mugging people at random.

will/ with the best will in the world *Br.* col. used to say about some impossible thing.

willy, willie *Br.* col. (esp. children's use) penis.

willy-nilly *Aus., NZ.* col. cyclone Willy in North Western Australia.

Wimpy *Br.* tdmk. hamburger / **Wimpy Bars** fast food chain of hamburger joints: *the Golden Egg and Wimpy were not surprisingly, long gone* - B. Bryson.

win *esp. Br.* 1. get or extract (coal or ore) by mining. 2. sink a shaft for mining.

win one's cap (in school sports) *Br.* /*Am.* **win one's letter/** become a member of a school or college sports team.

win out *esp. Am.* /*esp. Br., Aus.* **win through/** gain a victory (over sb., or smth.) after a great effort: *But openness, nevertheless, eventually won out over natural rights* - A. Bloom.

winceyette *Br.* flanellette, light material with a soft surface, used esp. for clothes person wears in bed.

winch *Br.* the reel of a fishing rod.

winchester *Br.* large cylindrical bottle.

wind *Br., Aus.* /*Am.* **gas/** gas in the bowels.

wind *Br.* /*Am., Aus.* **burp/** rub and very gently hit a baby on its back to allow air to come up from the stomach.

wind/ be scattered to the (four) winds *Br.* be broken up or lost.

wind/ get/have/ the wind up *esp. Br., Aus.* col. feel anxious about their situation.

wind/ it's an ill wind that blows nobody any good *Br.* col. every problem one person has brings good thing for sb. else.

wind/ leave sb. to twist in the wind *Am.* be left in a difficult situation by the actions of another person.

wind/ put the wind up sb. *Br., Aus.* col. make sb. feel worried about smth.

wind/ sail close to the wind *esp. Br.* take a risk by doing smth.

wind/ take the wind out of sb.'s **sails** *Am.* make feel less confident.

wind/ twist/swing in the wind *esp. Am.* be left in a very difficult or weak position.

wind down/up *Br.* (windows, etc.) close or open.

wind on (automatically) *Br., Aus.* move forward (of a film in a camera, etc.).

wind up (a company, etc.) *Br., Aus.* close it down because it can't pay its debts.

wind sb. **up** *Br.* col. make sb. angry: *she was winding me up.* - T. Thorne.

wind sb. *Br.* col. annoy or deceive playfully.

windcheater *esp. Br. /Am.* tdmk. **windbreaker,** also *Am.* **windjammer/** obs. short coat intended to keep out the wind: *Aside from her windbreaker, she wore only a T-shirt and thin leggings.* - Reader's Digest., *In his leather windbreaker, his shoulders were powerful.* - J.D. Salinger.

winder *Br. /Am.* **stem/** a knob on a watch used for winding it.

windhover *Br.* kestrel.

windlestraw *esp. Br.* a thin, dried grass stalk.

windmill *Br. /Am.* **pinwheel/**.

windmill/ be tilting at windmills *Am.* try to achieve an impossible thing.

window/ go out of the window *Br.* disappear completely.

window shade *Am. /Br.* **blind/** (window) blind or awning: *He pulled the window shade down* - L. Uris.

window winder *Br. /Am.* **window roller/** one used to open or close side windows of a car.

windrow *Am., Can.* long line of material heaped up by the wind.

windscreen 1. *Br., Aus. /Am., Can.* **windshield/** the piece of glass across the front of a car: *5 million posters and car windscreen stickers were printed.* - P. Norman., *Rain pelted the windshield.* - E. Segal., *Hazards for the motorists in those days were imperfect windscreen wipers* - Cheshire Life. / **windscreen wipers** *Br. /Am., Can.* **windshield wipers/** etc.: *William Clifford invented the windshield wiper.* - Daily News. 2. *Am.* a piece of strong cloth fixed vertically with ground.

windstorm *esp. Am., Can.* very strong wind with little or no rain or snow.

wind-up *Br.* col. a joke or a trick made to deliberately annoy sb.

windy 1. *esp. Br.* col. frightened or nervous: *it was rather windy* - E. Hemingway. 2. *Br.* suffering from gas generated in the stomach or the intestines.

Windy City *Am.* Chicago: *I know the scenery from here to the Windy City like my local road into town.* - J.P. Hogan.

wine bar *Br.* one that serves mainly wine and also usu. provides light meals: *they had had wine-bars and cast-iron litter-bins.* - B. Bryson.

wine card *esp. Br.* wine list.

wine cooler *Am.* drink made with wine, fruit juice and water.

wine merchants, also **wine and spirits shop** *Br.* liquor store: *Friendly looking shops - chemists and butchers, a wine merchant* - B. Bryson.

winery *esp. Am. /Br.* **vineyard/** a place where wine is made.

wine waiter *Br.* waiter responsible for serving wine.

wing 1. *esp. Br. /Am.* **fender/** the side of a car that covers the wheels, mudguard: *the young man lays a restraining hand on the Renault's wing.* - D. Lodge. 2. *Am.* col. a hand.

wing/ try one's wings *Am.* try to do smth. that you've recently learned to do.

wing it *Am.* col. do smth. without planning or preparation.

wing dam *Am.* a barrier to protect a riverbank from erosion by fast current.

wingding *esp. Am.* col. 1. also *Can.* obs. noisy party: *I and the boys are throwing a little wing-ding.* - J. Steinbeck. 2. a humdinger. 3. a gadget. 4. adj. festive.

winge, whinge *esp. Aus., Br.* derog. col. complain, esp. continually and in annoying way.

wing mirror *Br. /Am.* **side mirror/** mirror at the side of a car.

wingtip *Am.* men's shoe with a pattern of small holes on the toe.

wingtip shoe *Am., Can.* shoe with a toecap having a backward extended point and curving sides, resembling the shape of a wing.

wink *Br. /Am.* **blink/** flash or cause (a light) to flash on and off.

wink/ quick as a wink *Am.* very quickly.

wink/ tip sb. **the wink, tip the wink to** sb. *Br., Aus.* betray sb. secretly.

winkers *Br.* col. */Am.* **blinkers/** small lights on a car to show left or right turns.

winkle *Am.* periwinkle, a small edible sea snail.

winkle out *esp. Br.* col. get or remove slowly and with difficulty: *Bleckner...winkled out the foot flaw instantly.* - New York.

winkler *Br.* sl. person employed to persuade tenants to vacate property.

winkle-picker *Br.* col. pointed shoe popular in 1950s.

winner/ be onto a winner *Br.* be doing smth. that is likely to succeed.

winningest *Am.* col. having achieved the most success in a campaign.

winning post *esp. Br.* (in horse racing) a post marking the place where a race finishes.

wino *esp. Am., Can., Aus.* sl. alcoholic addicted to wines: *his long legs blocking the sidewalk like those of a sleeping wino.* - J. O'Brien, A. Kurins., *Dean was the son of a wino.* - J. Kerouac.

winterise *Am., Can.* (about house, car, etc.) adapt for use in a cold weather.

winterkill *Am.* kill by exposure to cold weather.

wipe 1. *Br., Aus.* dry dishes that have just been washed. 2. *Aus., NZ.* col. reject or dismiss (a person or idea).

wipe off *esp. Am.* clean (smth.) after use, as with a cloth (smth. like dishes): *Don't forget to wipe off the sink* - Longman.

wipe out *esp. Am., Can.* 1. lose control, esp. of a vehicle and have an accident. 2. (in surfing) be thrown from one's board by a wave: *I wiped out twice.* - Longman.

wipe up *Br.* dry (dishes) after washing, dry dishes: *You wash up, and I'll wipe up.* - Longman.

wiped out *Am.* sl. suffering from hangover.

wire *Am.* piece of electronic recording equipment, usu. worn secretly on sb.'s clothes.

wire *esp. Am.* 1. v. n. (send) a telegram: *Not long before he died I had a wire from Ketchum, Idaho.* - J.A. Michener., *The wire was a cable from Bill Garton* - E. Hemingway., *I'll have to send a wire to Portland.* - A. Miller. 2. (of money) instruct a bank to send money by telegram message.

wire/come/go/get (right) down to the wire *esp. Am., Aus.* col. happen just before the very last moment, adj. **down-to-the-wire**.

wire/ get in under the wire *Am., Can.* reach smth. exactly on time: *Why did she always have to be just under wire?* - S. Bellow.

wire/ have smth. **wired** *Am.* sl. be sure that smth. is already arranged or done.

wire/ (as) tough as a fencing wire *Aus.* col. very strong.

wire (to) *esp. Am.* send a telegram to: *She said she wired home for money.* - J. Kerouac., *He could have wired for money.* - E. Hemingway.

wired *Am.* /*Br.* **wired up**/ equipped with overhearing devices.

wired up, wired *esp. Am., Can.* col. 1. eagerly excited; annoyed, angry: *The whole event had me so wired up I didn't mind flying around* - J. Baez., *the players are wired, looking for the way to spill some nervous energy.* - Time. 2. very active and excited, esp. after having taken drugs: *after having used amphetamines earlier that night, he would have been wired.* – C.R. Cross.

wireless *esp. Br.* obs. (a) radio: *The pigs had bought themselves a wireless set* - G. Orwell., *Henry Hall is on the wireless tonight.* - Cheshire Life.

wireman *esp. Am.* installer or repairer of electric wiring.

wire-puller *Am., Can.* col. politician who exerts control from behind the scenes.

wire service *esp. Am., Can.* news agency that distributes its news by teleprinter like Reuter and AP.

wire tap *esp. Am.* tap telephone lines.

wire wool *Br.* /*Am.* **steel wool**/ thin pieces of wire twisted together often in the form of small pads used to clean wooden and metal objects.

wise/ many new adverbs are formed esp. in Am. English by adding wise to nouns with the meaning "in connection with": *we lose our appeal or don't measure up performancewise* - "M."

wise/ act wise *Am.* /*esp. Am.* **get wise with** sb./ act to show that you don't respect sb.

wise/ It's easy to be wise after the event. *esp. Br., Aus.* saying.

wise up *esp. Am., Aus.* (cause to) learn the right information: *Some day these guys are gonna wise up* - R. Moore., *I sure wised up.* - J. Steinbeck.

wise up (to) *Am.* start to understand smth.

wise guy 1. also **wiseacre** *esp. Am., Aus.* col. an annoying person who thinks that they know more than other people: *He had been such a wise guy* - H.C. Whitford., R.J. Dixson. 2. *Am.* member of Mafia.

wisenheimer *Am.* col. smug and arrogant person.

wise use *Am.* environmental policy promoting a controlled use of natural resources.

wish/ In Britain it is rather formal to use were after wish but Americans would think it very bad English to use was after wish.

wishbook *Am., Can.* catalogue of a shop sending its produce by mail: *The new wish book just came in the mail.* - R.A. Spears.

wish list *esp. Am.* col. all the things you want to do in a specific situation.

wit/ be not beyond the wit of a man/sb. **to do** smth. *Br.* be not too difficult to do.

withdraw/ withdraw one's **labour** *Br.* stop working; **withdraw from the match** *Br.* stop playing (due to injury, etc.).

withhold *Am., Aus.* deduct from wages / **withholding tax**.

witness *Am.* speak publicly about one's strong Christian beliefs.

witness to *Br.* law. state that smth. is true in a law court.

witness box *Br. /esp. Am.* (**witness**) **stand, chair/** the raised area enclosed at the sides where witnesses stand in court when being questioned: *he would not call him to the witness stand* - M. Twain., *I'm going to get on that witness stand* - D. Mortman.

witter (on), also **rabbit (on)** *Br.* col. ramble on, talk nonsense at length: *Dad wittering on about the cost of living* - D. Lodge.

wizard, also **smashing** *esp. Br.* excellent.

wobble *Am.* be unsure whether to do smth.

wobble-board *Aus.* piece of fibreboard used as a musical instrument.

wobbly 1. *Br.* col. a fit of uncontrollable rage. 2. *Am.* col. a member of the IWW (International Workers of the World): *The wobblies were red.* - J. Dos Passos.

wobbly/ throw/show a wobbly, throw a wobbler *Br., Aus.* col. become very angry suddenly.

woc *Am.* without compensation (of work of an expert for federal government or businessman): *The committee had found that...those working WOC (without compensation) were continuing to receive their pay from their companies* - H. Truman.

wodge, wadge *esp. Br., Aus.* col. a lumpy protuberant object, chunk.

wog 1. *Br., Aus.* taboo. sl. a foreigner, esp. of a dark-skinned race: *we had our share of admirals, who took not shit from wog nor native.* - J.P. Donleavy. 2. *Aus.* any germ, small insect or grub. 3. *Aus.* col. immigrant, esp. one who doesn't know English.

wolds *Br.* hilly countryside, esp. used in names of places.

wolf *Am.* sl. a sexually aggressive man.

wolf cub *esp. Br.* former Cub Scout.

wolf whistle *Br., Aus.* sound made when an attractive woman passes by.

The Wolverine State *Am.* Michigan, **Wolverine** *Am.* citizen of Michigan.

wolves/ leave sb. **to the wolves** *Aus.* cause sb. to be in a situation where they are criticised strongly.

woman-chaser *Am.* col. womaniser.

women's room *esp. Am.* public toilet for women.

wombat/ stone the wombats *Aus.*, God damn.

women's refuge *Br., Aus.* /*Am.* **women's shelter/** shelter for wives who experience violence from their husbands.

womp, whomp *Am.* sl. beat (sb. or smth.): *The tracks were then taken to Baker who whomped up a massive drum sound* - Rolling Stone.

wonder *Br.* sb. who is clever at doing difficult things.

wonder/ a nine-day(s') wonder *Br.* short time popularity.

wonder/ I don't wonder *Br.* col. I am not surprised.

wonder/ I shouldn't wonder (if) *esp. Br.* col. it's obvious.

Wonderland of America *Am.* Wyoming.

wonga *Br.* sl. money.

wonk *Am., Can.* col. person focused on details, bookworm, grind: *Even policy wonks had troubles recalling all the stipulations of the bill.* - Reader's Digest.

wonky *Br., Can., Aus.* col. unsteady and likely to break, fall, or fail: *Bill Clinton inclines naturally toward the wonkish* - New York.

woo/ pitch woo *Am.* obs. sl. make love, court sb.

wood/ from the wood *Br.* (of a drink) stored in a wooden container.

wood/ out of the wood *Br.* free from danger, difficulties, etc.

wood/ take in wood *Am.* sl. have a drink.

wood/ saw woods *Am.* stay aside.

wood/ touch wood *Br. /esp. Am., Can.* **knock on wood/**.

wood/ woods are full *Am.* sl. there are lots and lots: *Christ the whole place, the woods're full of bottles.* - G.V. Higgins.

woodbine *Am. /esp. Br.* **Virginia creeper/**.

woodblock *Br.* one of a set of small pieces of wood which are used to make a floor.

woodcraft *esp. Am., Can.* 1. /*Br.* **woodwork/** skill in woodwork. 2. knowledge of woodland.

wooden house *Br.* frame house.

wooden/plug nickel *Am.* sl. worthless thing; esp. in **don't take any wooden nickels; don't give a wooden/plug nickel for** smth.

(take/get) wooden spoon *Br., Aus.* col. (receive) any imaginary prize to the last in a sports competition.

woodfree *Br. /Am.* **freesheet/** print. paper made only from chemical pulp.

wood pussy *Am.* skunk: *The dog had a nasty run-in with a wood-pussy.* - R.A. Spears.

wood ranger *Am.* col. forest keeper.

wood shavings, wood wool *Br.* /*Am.* **excelcior**/ small thin curled pieces of wood used for packing breakable things like glass.

woodscraft *Am.* woodcraft.

woodshed *Am.* col. rehearse, esp. play a musical instrument: *The Jacksons really had been woodshedding.* - D. Marsh.

woodshed/ **something nasty in the woodshed** *Br.* col. shocking or distasteful thing that has been kept secret.

woodsy *Am., Can.* pertaining to forest: *Maine smelt all woodsy* - J. Dos Passos.

woodtrim *Am.* woodwork in a house.

woodwork *esp. Br.* /*esp. Am.* **woodworking**/ the skill of making wooden objects, esp. furniture, carpentry: *I had a woodworking business then* – Reader's Digest.

woodwork/ **come out of the woodwork** *Am.* col. come out of the blue: *Entrepreneurs came out of the woodwork* - H. Smith.

woof *Am.* sl. (used by blacks) talk idly, ostentatiously or aggressively: *yell obscenities out the window before you woof up* - D. Divoky.

woofter *Br.* col. derog. effeminate or homosexual man.

wool/ **all wool and a yard wide** *Am.* col. genuine: *He's a wonderful brother - all wool and a yard wide.* - A. Makkai.

wool clip *Aus.* annual amount of shearing.

woolen *Am.* woolen.

woolhat *Am.* col. n. adj. a Southern farmer or back country rustic.

woolly 1. *Aus.* a sheep. 2. *Br.* piece of clothing made of wool.

wooloomooloo yank *Aus.* Sydney dandy.

woolshed *Aus., NZ.* place where sheep are sheared.

wooly *esp. Br.* col. a garment made of wool, esp. knitted, such as pullover: *Better bring a wooly. It will be cool in the car.* - E. Hemingway.

wooly *Am.* col. live in a simple and not very comfortable way.

wooly *Am.* col. rough like in frontier, uncivilised.

woomera(ng), also **throwing stick** *Aus.* boomerang.

woopie *Br.* col. a well-off older person.

woop-woop, Woop Woop *Aus., NZ.* col. humor. unknown land; remote outback town or district.

worcester sauce *Br.* /*Am., Aus.* **worcestershire sauce**/ dark-brown spicy liquid added to food to increase its flavour.

word/ **get a word in edgeways** *Br.* /*Am.* **get a word in edgewise**/ get a chance to speak.

word/**have**/**drop a (quiet) word in** sb.'s **ear** *Br.* speak quietly and privately.

word/ **in words of one syllable** *Br.* simple and easy to understand.

word/ **stuck for words** *Br.* unable to say anything because of surprise.

word/ **What's the good word?** *Am.* What positive news can you tell me?

wordage *Am.* volume of printed matter.

word perfect *Br., Aus.* /*Am.* **letter perfect**/ showing correctness in repeating every word: *she was word-perfect* - New Idea.

word spinning *Br.* written and verbal skill.

work 1. *Br.* study a subject by reading books, doing exercises, etc. esp. in order to pass an exam. 2. *Am.* col. calculate the answer to a math problem.

work/ **be hard work** *Br.* be difficult to talk to or have relations with.

work/**be too much like hard work** *Br.* col. be too difficult to be worth the effort.

work/ **have** one's **work cut out** *Br.* need to work hard to achieve smth.

work/ **work all the hours (that) God sends** *Br.* spend all the time working very hard.

work/ **work like a Trojan** *Br.* /*Am., Aus.* **work like a dog**/ work very hard.

work/ **work to time** *Br.* col. watch the clock.

work out *Am.* pay (a debt) with work, instead of money: *He offered to work out the debt* - Longman.

work smth. **out (for** yourself) *esp. Br.* think about smth. and manage to understand it.

work over *esp. Am.* redo (smth. such as work): *A motley factory band worked over some patriotic music.* - Newsweek.

workbox *esp. Br.* workbasket in which items for sewing, such as needles and pins are kept.

work coat *Am.* /*Br.* **overall**/.

workday *esp. Am., Aus.* working day.

work experience *Br.* period of time that a young person spends working in a particular place, as a form of training.

work gang *Am.* railway repairs team.

workhouse *Am.* jail for petty criminals.

working/ **be working it, work it** *Am.* sl. try to be sexually impressive at a social occasion.

working class *esp. Br.* people who traditionally do physical work and don't have much money or power.

working day *esp. Br.* work day.

working expenses *Br.* operating costs.

working majority *Br.* enough support in Parliament for a government to go on making laws and ruling a country.

working papers *Am.* permission to work for adults under age (under 16 years old).

working party *Br.* /*Am.* **working group**/ a committee established to investigate a particular problem and produce a report how to resolve it.

working stiff *Am.* sl. a common working man: *A mix of working stiffs and suit-and-tie semi-execs* - J. DeFelice., *I'm working stiff.* - J. O'Brien, A. Kurins.

workmate *esp. Br.* person with whom one works.

work people *esp. Br.* those who work for wages (esp. with hands or machines).

works/ in the works *esp. Am., Can.* in progress; being planned, worked on or produced.

works/ pizza with the works *esp. Am.* pizza with all available type of food.

works/ a works *Br.* a place where smth. is produced; **works** refers to more than one of these.

works/ Road works *Br.* Men working / road sign.

works/ sewage works *Br.* a sewage system.

works/ ex-works *Br.* from the factory.

works/ get the works *Am.* sl. get in trouble.

works convener *Br.* factory union official who convenes workers meetings.

works council *esp. Br.* employers group for discussing working conditions, wages, etc.

workshy *Br.* derog. disliking work and trying to avoid it by all means.

work to rule *esp. Br.* work slowly intentionally: *air traffickers are working to rule again in support of their demand for better working conditions and shorter hours.* - Longman.

worktop, work surface *Br.* /*Am., Can.* **counter,** *Aus.* **bench(top)**/ flat surface in a kitchen where food can be prepared for cooking.

workweek *Am., Can.* the total number of hours or days worked in a week.

world/ (all) the world and his wife/her husband *Br., Aus.* col. /*Am.* **everyone and his brother**/ a lot of people.

world/ move down/up in the world *Am., Aus.* /*esp. Br.* col. **go up/come down in the world**/ have less/more money and worse/better social position than you had before.

world/ put/set the world to rights *Br.* talk about improving life on earth without having any authority to make changes for the better.

world-beater *Br.* person or smth. that are better than most other people or things of their kind.

worm/ a worm's eye view *Br., Aus.* knowing or understanding part of a problem, usu. the worst or least important part.

worms/ must have had worms for breakfast *Am.* col. sb. can't sit still.

worriment *Am.* humor. worry.

worry/ Not to worry *esp. Br., Can. Aus.* Don't worry: *Where is the cocaine? I asked. - Not to worry.* - K. Ablow.

worrisome *esp. Am., Can.* causing anxiety or concern.

worrywart *esp. Am., Aus.* col. person who worries a lot about unimportant things.

worse luck *Br.* col. I don't like the situation.

Worship *esp. Br.* (used for addressing or speaking of certain officials, esp. a Mayor or a Magistrate).

worshipful *esp. Br.* adj. (used as a respectable form of address).

worst/ if worst comes to worst *Am.* if the worst happens.

worth/ not worth the candle *esp. Br.* col. not worth the effort.

wot *Br.* col. what.

wotcher, watcha excl. *Br.* col. (esp. in south-eastern England) hello.

(would) better *Am.* had better.

wowser, wowzer *Br., Aus., NZ.* col. fanatic, puritan spoilsport, teetotaller.

WPC *Br.* Woman's Police Constable.

wrack *esp. Am., Aus.* bad state, ruin, rack.

wrangle *Am., Can.* herd or tend cattle (esp. in the West).

wrangler *Am.* 1. cowboy, esp. one who looks after horses. 2. person winning a high honour in mathematics.

wrap 1. *esp. Am.* garment which is used as a covering, esp. round a woman's shoulders: *Would you like me to fetch you a wrap?* - S. Nichols. 2. *Am.* plastic used to cover food.

wrap sb. (up) in cotton wool *Br.* spoil, coddle.

wrap/ wrap oneself in Union Jack *Br.* /*Am.* **Stars and Stripes**/ be overpatriotic.

wrapped *Aus.* col. overjoyed; delightful.

wrapper *Am.* 1. loose robe or gown, esp. night-dress: *She readjusted her wrapper* - C. Woolrich. 2. /*Br.* **wraparound**/ a loose piece of clothing worn around the body. 3. tobacco leaf of superior quality enclosing a cigar.

wrap-up *Am.* 1. also *Can.* summary or resume, esp a news round-up: *he was sitting on his bed watching the wrap-up of a news broadcast.* - Guideposts.

2. sl. something easy to trade. 3. also *Can.* adj. overview of products of one company.

wreck 1. *Br.* /*Am., Can.* **crash**/ an accident in which moving vehicle hits smth. and is damaged or destroyed. 2. *esp. Am., Can.* engage in breaking up body damaged vehicles, demolishing old buildings and similar structures to obtain usable spares or scrap: *Terry Buttler worked among the metal carcasses at Staystown Auto Wreckers* – Reader's Digest.

wrecked *Br.* col. very drunk.

wrecker 1. *Am., Can.* /*Br.* **recovery van**/ vehicle used for moving other vehicles when these have stopped working or after accident. 2. *esp. Am., Can.* person employed to knock down buildings: *"Thank you" to the skilled ironworkers and wreckers.* – Reader's Digest. 3. *Am.* railway emergency repairs worker.

wrecking *Am.* emergency repairs.

wrecking bar *Am., Can.* packing case opening tool.

wrecking crane, crane truck *Am.* /*Br.* **breakdown van, lorry**/.

wrecking crew *Am.* /*Br.* **breakdown gang**/ emergency repairs crew.

Wren *Br.* col. woman of the Royal Naval Service.

wrench 1. *Am., Can.* /*esp. Br.* **spanner**/ spanner: *The mechanic shrugged and pulled a wrench from his tool belt.* - F. Pascal. 2. *Br.* spanner with jaws that can be moved so as to be close together or far apart / **monkey wrench** *Am.* /*Br.* **adjustable spanner**/.

wringer/ go through the wringer *Am.* col. have an upsetting experience.

Wrinkle City *Am.* sl. wrinkled or lined skin, as a sign of age: *Wrinkle City time.* - J. Fowles.

wrinklie, wrinkly *Br., Aus.* col. humor. or derog. an old person.

wrinkles *Br.* col. humor. older people.

wrist-slapping *Am.* (of punishment or criticism) not serious.

writ *esp. Br.* Crown document summoning a peer to Parliament or ordering the election of an MP or MPs.

write 1. *esp. Am.* /*Br., Aus.* **write to** sb./ produce and send a letter to (sb.). 2. *Can.* take (an exam or test).

write away for *Am.* write to a company for smth. that has been advertised.

write (sb. or smth.) **in** *Am.* 1. a. vote for (sb., esp. unlisted candidate) by writing their names on the voting paper. b. add (a name) to a list in an election. 2. tend a complain to a boss.

write (smth.) **off** *esp. Br.* damage (esp. a car) so badly that it cannot be repaired.

write up sb. *Am.* report them for not obeying a law or rule.

write-in *Am.* a vote given by writing the name of the person voted for.

write-off *esp. Br., Aus.* smth. which has been so badly damaged that it cannot be repaired: *His plane's a write-off though.* - B. Tillman.

writer-in-residence *Am.* writer teaching a literature in the institute: *in 1965-66 he was the University of New Brunswick's first writer-in-residence.* - W. Grady.

write-up *Am.* an increase in the book value or alleged assets of a corporation.

the writing is on the wall *esp. Br.* /*esp. Am., Can.* **handwriting is on the wall**/ a bad omen.

wrong/ on, from the wrong/other side of the tracks *esp. Am.* on / from the less respectable part of a town or society, esp. the part lived in by poor people: *He was Irish from the wrong side of the tracks.* - R.P. Warren., *All my friends were the wrong side of the tracks people* - A. Scaduto.

wrong-foot sb. *Br., Aus.* (in tennis and football) hit or kick a ball in such a way that you make the player believe the ball will go in the opposite direction to the one in which it'll really go.

wrongo *Am.* sl. villain: *A wrongo. An opposition guy. Maybe we better straighten 'im out.* – J. O'Hara.

wrong 'un *Br.* col. person of bad character.

wrong way/ rub sb. **up the wrong way** *Br., Aus.* /*Am.* **rub** sb. **the wrong way**/ annoy sb. without intending to.

wrote/ (and) that'sall she wrote *Am., Can.* col. there's nothing more to say.

wurley, also **gunyah** *Aus.* aborigine's house.

wuss *Am.* sl. weak and not effective person.

wye *Am., Can.* triangle of railway track, used for turning locomotives or trains.

X

X *Am.* col. 1. ten-dollar bill. 2. remove (from a list).

X-acto knife *Am., Can.* tdmk. utility knife with a very sharp replaceable blade.

xeriscape *esp. Am.* 1. style of landscape design requiring little or no irrigation or other maintenance, used in arid regions. 2. garden or landscape created in such a way.

X out *Am.* mark or remove a mistake in a piece of writing using an X; cross out.

XX *Am.* col. twenty-dollar bill.
XXXX, four-X *Br.* sl. a humorous euphemism for a four-letter word.
X-ray *Am.* radio code letter X.
XV *Br.* col. 15 members of a Rugby team.

Y

Y *Am., Can.* col. YMCA (hostel).
ya *Am., Can.* (colloquial pronunciation) you.
yabber *Aus.* n. v. talk, speech.
yachting *esp. Br.* sailing, travelling, or racing in a yacht.
yada yada yada *Am.* col. smth. very boring.
yah *Br.* col. yes.
yahoo *Aus.* noisy and unruly person.
yakka, yakker *Aus.* col. hard work.
Yalie *Am.* col. student or graduate of Yale university.
y'all *Am.* dial. you or all of you: *Y'all didn't have to do this* - M. Jones., J. Chilton.
yam *esp. Am., Can.* a sweet potato.
yammer *esp. Am.* col. complain in a sad voice: *they were yammering and arguing and orating.* - R.P. Warren., *Amanda kept yammering about her parents.* - A. Hitchcock Mystery Magazine.
yammer (on) *Br.* col. talk noisily and continuously.
yandy *Aus.* separate (gross seed or a mineral) from the surrounding refuse by shaking it in a special shallow dish.
yang *Am.* sl. penis: *Hanging around toilets waiting for some poor guy to reach for a cop's yang by mistake.* - T. Thorne.
Yank 1. *Br., Aus.* derog. Yankee, citizen of the USA: *The yanks had a lot of influence in Zanzibar* - M.M. Kaye., *His misssis is a Yank.* - A. Burgess. 2. *Am.* inhabitant of New England or one of the northern states.
yank/ yank out *esp. Am.* remove suddenly (from school, job, etc.).
Yankee 1. *Am.* col. person born or living in the northern or north-eastern states of the USA: *she was a Yankee newly come to Texas* - T. Thompson. 2. *esp. Br.* sb. from the USA.
Yankee corn *Am.* flint corn, flint maize.
The Yankee State *Am.* Ohio.
Yankeeism *Can.* sl. Americanism.
yap *Am.* sl. country bumpkin: *The poor yap was made a fool of.* - R.A. Spears.
yapp *Br.* form of bookbinding with a limp leather cover.

yard 1. *Am., Can., Aus. /Br.* **garden/** backyard, a piece of land around a house, usu. covered with grass (a back garden): *we were doing yard work* – Reader's Digest. 2. *esp. Am., Can.* an area in which moose and deer gather for feeding during the winter. 3. *Am.* col. $100: *I got five yards that want to grow.* - R. Chandler. 4. *Br.* col. Scotland Yard. 5. *Can.* gather logs into one place. 6. *esp. Br.* piece of uncultivated ground adjoining a building, usu. enclosed by walls or other buildings. 7. *Am., Can.* store or transport (wood) in or to a timber yard.
yard/ front yard *Am.* a small garden at the front of the house: *three women posed in the front yard among plantings of ornamental shrubbery* - K. Davis.
yardbird *Am.* sl. 1. convict: *So, Charlie was a yardbird.* - R.A. Spears. 2. recruit.
yarded timber *Am.* timber skidded to the stack.
yard engine *Am.* shunter, shunting engine.
yard goods *Am.* materials sold in yards: *his wife came to town to hustle yard goods and ribbons.* - M. Torgov., *brightly colored yard goods* - S. North.
Yardie *Br.* sl. a member of a criminal Jamaican or West Indian gangs.
yardman *Am.* person who does various outdoor jobs.
yard of ale *Br.* two or three pints of beer held by a narrow glass about a yard high or a glass of this kind.
yard sale *Am., Can. /Br.* **car boot sale, boot fair/** sale where people sell their own things they don't want from a little stall or from the back of their car: *at the next yard sale it was the first thing she put out.* – Reader's Digest.
yard-wand *esp. Br.* yardstick.
Yar Mouth bloater *Br.* a smoked herring.
yarn 1. *esp. Am.* a long cotton or wool thread used in knitting, making cloth, mats, etc. 2. *Aus., NZ.* chat, v., n.
yarra *Aus.* sl. crazy.
Yarrah *Aus.* a popular kind of eucalyptus.
Yarrah bankers *Aus.* Melbourne dandies.
yarraman *Aus.* a horse.
yatter *Am.* sl. chatter: *The freaks yattered at him.* - E.L. Doctorow.
yawp *Am., Can.* (make) a foolish or noisy talk.
yay *esp. Am., Can.* col. (with adjectives of measure) so; to this extent.
year/ from/since the year dot *Br., Aus.* col. often derog. /*Am.* **from/since the year one/** from a very long time ago.

year/ first year/ third year/ final year, etc. *Br., Aus.* (used for saying what class sb. is in a school or college according to their age or how long they have been there.

year/ roll back the years *Br.* remind oneself of the past by doing things one used to do.

yearbook *Am., Can.* book containing photos of the senior class in a school or university and details of school activities in the previous year: *I was chosen to be the model for the all-American girl in our year-book.* – Reader's Digest.

yeech, yecch *Am.* col. excl. of disgust; yuck: *All in all, more yeechs than yocks.* - Playboy.

yeehaw *Am., Can.* expression of enthusiasm or exhuberance.

yegg *Am.* col. a petty thief: *we think about old time yeggs* - R. Chandler.

yell 1. *Am.* special cheering cry for a team. 2. *esp. Am.* col. ask for help.

yell *Br.* col. a good joke or party: *We had a real yell last night.* - T. Thorne.

yellow *Am.* yoke of an egg.

yellow-back *Am.* currency note.

yellow-dog *Am., Can.* col. 1. person not joining the trade union: *goons of organisers of yellow-dog unions.* - K. Vonnegut, Jr. 2. despicable person.

yellow dog contract *Am., Can.* one forbidding employees to join a union: *Injunction and the "yellow dog" contract had been outlawed* - H. Truman.

The Yellowhammer State *Am.* Alabama.

yellow jacket *Am., Can.* col. wasp or hornet: *yellow jacket sneaking into soda cans* – Reader's Digest.

yellow journalism *Am.* sensational writing.

yellow line *Br.* a line on the side of a road that shows that you must not park there.

yellow poplar *Am., Can.* tulip tree.

yenta *Am., Can.* col. gossip or busybody.

yeoman *esp. Br.* a farmer who owns and works his own land: *he was a yeoman of apparent respectability* – M. Daly.

yeomanry *esp. Br.* country landowners.

yeoman service *Br.* long and loyal service, help and support.

yep *Am., Aus., Can.* col. yes.

yes sb. *Am.* say yes to sb. all the time.

yessir *Am., Can.* used to express emphatic affirmation.

yessum *Am.* (used by blacks) polite form of assent addressed to a woman.

yet/ (*Am.*) Did you eat yet?

Y-fronts *esp. Br.* tdmk. men's underpants with a sewn part in front in the shape of an upside down Y: *it can be coaxed back into his Y-fronts only with the greatest difficulty.* - D. Lodge.

Yidney *Aus.* sl. derog. Sydney.

yield *Am.* /*Br.* **give way**/ allow other traffic to go first: *truck coming up the feeder road too fast barreled through a yield sign into their lane.* - P. Case, J. Migliore.

yield *Am.* /*Br.* **give way**/ road sign.

yike *Aus.* a brawl.

yo *esp. Am.* sl. excl. used to greet sb. or get their attention.

yob(bo) *Br., Aus.* col. derog. a rude or troublesome young man, lout: *There were these four big yobboes in one night that I knew were out to give the Beatles a good thumping.* - P. Norman., *None of your yobs and yobos.* - J.P. Donleavy., *"Yobbo" is the Irishman's "boyo" backwards, and a "boyo" is a fellow who hangs about street corners, one of the bads, a larrikin.* - R. McRum, W. Cran, R. McNeil.

yob culture, uniform, element, etc. *Br.* behaviour, clothes, etc. connected with yobs.

yock *Am.* col. a laugh, esp. a loud hearty one.

yoke *esp. Am., Can.* control lever in an aircraft.

yomp *Br.* col. (of a soldier) march with heavy equipment over difficult terrain.

yonks *Br., Aus.* col. obs. a very long time: *God, I haven't seen you for yonks.* - T. Thorne.

you/ *Would you get me a coffee? Sure, you got it.* *Am.* I'll do it quickly.

you-all, y'all *Am.* col. (esp. used in the South) you: *Y'all didn't have to do this* - M. Jones, J. Chilton.

young fogey *Br.* middle-class person, esp. male of less than middle age who adopts or affects the dress, habits and right-wing views of an earlier generation.

young marrieds *esp. Am.* people who have recently been married.

The York State *Am.* New York.

Yours sincerely, faithfully *Br.* /*Am.* **Sincerely (yours)**/ Yours truly, common way of ending a letter.

youse *Aus.* you.

youth cottage *Aus.* hostel for homeless young people.

(go) youth hostelling *Br.* the activity of staying in youth hostels and walking or cycling between them.

Yowie *Aus.* yes.

yo-yo *esp. Am., Can.* sl. 1. jerk: *Who's the yo-yo in the plaid pants?* - R.A. Spears. 2. vacillating

person: *I was a yo-yo in my weight for the whole world to see* - E. Taylor.
yucca *esp. Am.* cassava.
yuppie flue *Br.* col. myalgic encephalomyelitis.

Z

Z *Am.* col. sleep; **catch/get some Zs.**
Z car, also **jam sandwich, Panda car** *Br.* police car.
zap 1. *esp. Am.* col. go somewhere or do smth. quickly. 2. *Am.* col. cook smth. in a microwave.
zap *esp. Am.* col. energy and enthusiasm, adj. **zappy.**
zapper 1. *Am.* col. a TV remote control. 2. *Am., Can.* electronic device used for killing insects.
zappy *Br.* col. interesting and exciting.
zebra crossing *Br., Aus.* /*Am.* **crosswalk**/ pedestrian crossing: *It's safer to cross at subways, footbridges, islands, Zebra and Pelican crossings.* - J. Harmer., R. Rossner.
zed *Br., Can.* /*Am.* **zee**/ the name of the letter Z.
zero/ *Br.* use **nought** esp. before and sometimes after a decimal point or **O**, esp. after decimal points or in telephone numbers or nil esp. in sports games; Americans can use **zero** in each of these cases.
zero grazing *Br.* zero pasture (in a barn).
zero norm, also **nil norm** *Br.* standard of minimum wage and price increases set by government.
zero rate *esp. Br.* exempt from paying a value-added tax.
zero-sum game *Am.* a situation where people compete and if one of them won smth. exactly the same must be lost by the other.
zilch *esp. Am., Can.* sl. nothing, zero: *we found zilch* - B. Tillman., *Nutritional value is zilch.* - E. Taylor.
zillionaire *Am.* sl. super-tycoon.
Zimmer (frame) *Br.* /*Br., Aus.* **walking frame,** *Am.* **walker**/ a frame that old people sometimes use to help them walk.
zing *Am.* sl. insult, attack verbally: *zinging attacks on feminists* - Time.
zinger *esp. Am., Can.* sl. a funny crack or punch line: *You used to ask a million questions. They were real zingers* - D. Mortman.
zip 1. also **zip (fastener)** *Br.* /*Am.* **zipper**/. 2 *Am.* col. zip code. 3. *Am., Can.* also **zippo** col. none, zero: *Bob pays $8, I pay zip* - Forbes.

zip (fastener) *esp. Br.* /*esp. Am., Aus., Can.* **zipper**/ fastener made of two sets of metal or plastic teeth and a sliding piece; **do up/undo** one's **zip**: *they're yanking their zippers before their dick is put away* - J. O'Brien, A. Kurins.
zip/ **zip your lip** *Am.* col. stop talking.
zip code *Am.* /*Br.* **post code**/.
zip gun *Am.* col. a home-made gun that fires a projectile by means of a spring.
zipper *Am.* col. provide with a zipper.
zipper head *Am.* derog. oriental person.
zip-up *esp. Br.* (of a garment) able to be fastened with a zipper.
zit *esp. Am., Can.* col. a spot on the skin, pimple: *their zit is not as big as they think it is.* - Reader's Digest., *I never had zits.* - A. Hichcock Mystery Magazine.
zizz *Br., Aus.* col. a short sleep.
zoftig, zaftig *Am., Can.* col. pleasing, voluptuous: *Amy Gertner had become over the summer gorgeous: tan and zaftig* - K. Davis.
zone *Am.* a postal department.
zone for *esp. Am.* give a building permission: *it had adopted big-town upscale zoning regulations.* - R.J. Randisi., M. Wallace.
zone out *Am.* col. fall asleep or lose concentration or consciousness.
zoned (out) *Am.* col. 1. under the influence of drugs or alcohol. 2. unable to think clearly and quickly, esp. because one is tired or ill.
Zonian *Am.* American living in the area of Panama Canal.
zonked *Am.* sl. excited: *I had never been so zonked in my life.* – Reader's Digest.
zoom *Am.* sl. gain an entry to smth. without paying.
zoot suit *Am.* a men's suit popular in 1930s and 1940s: *another assortment of teenage zoot-suited music lovers* - M. Torgov.
zowie *Am.* col. expression of surprise or admiration.
Zs *Am., Can.* col. sleep, esp. in the phr. **catch/cop/get/make some/a few Zs.**
zuchinni *esp. Am., Can., Aus.* /*Br.* **courgette**/ small green marrow eaten cooked as a vegetable: *rows of sweet corn, and some zuchini* - Sign of the Times.
Zulu *Am.* radio code letter Z.
zwieback *Am.* /*Br.* **rusk**/ kind of hard dry bread, often given to babies.